NOTABLE
SPORTS
FIGURES

2
NOTABLE
SPORTS
FIGURES

Dana Barnes, Editor

VOLUME 2 • F-L

GALE®

THOMSON
★
™
GALE

Detroit • New York • San Diego • San Francisco • Cleveland • New Haven, Conn. • Waterville, Maine • London • Munich

Notable Sports Figures

Project Editor
Dana R. Barnes

Editorial
Laura Avery, Luann Brennan, Frank Castronova, Leigh Ann DeRemer, Andrea Henderson, Kathy Nemeh, Angela Pilchak, Tracie Ratiner, Bridget Travers

Research
Gary J. Oudersluys, Cheryl L. Warnock, Kelly Whittle

Editorial Support Services
Charlene Lewis, Sue Petrus

Editorial Standards
Lynne Maday

Permissions
Lori Hines

Imaging and Multimedia Content
Randy Basset, Dean Dauphinais, Leitha Etheridge-Sims, Lezlie Light, Dan W. Newell, Dave G. Oblender

Product Design
Jennifer Wahi

Manufacturing
Evi Seoud, Rhonda Williams

Library of Congress Cataloging-in-Publication Data

Notable sports figures / project editor, Dana R. Barnes.
    p. cm.
Includes bibliographical references and index.
ISBN 0-7876-6628-9 (Set Hardcover) -- ISBN 0-7876-6629-7 (Volume 1) --ISBN 0-7876-6630-0 (Volume 2) -- ISBN 0-7876-6631-9 (Volume 3) -- ISBN 0-7876-7786-8 (Volume 4)
1. Sports--Biography. 2. Athletes--Biography. 3. Sports--History. I. Barnes, Dana R.
GV697.A1N68 2004
796'.092'2--dc21

2003011288

Contents

Introduction

Notable Sports Figures provides narrative biographical profiles of more than 600 individuals who have made significant contributions to their sport and to society. It covers sports figures from the nineteenth, twentieth, and twenty-first centuries who represent a wide variety of sports and countries. Lesser-known sports such as cricket, equestrian, and snowboarding are featured alongside sports like baseball, basketball, and football. *Notable Sports Figures* includes not only athletes, but also coaches, team executives, and media figures such as sportscasters and writers.

Notable Sports Figures takes a close look at the people in sports who have captured attention because of success *on* the playing field or controversy *off* the playing field. It provides biographical coverage of people from around the world and throughout history who have had an impact not only on their sport, but also on the society and culture of their times. Each biography features information on the entrant's family life, early involvement in sports, career highlights, championships, and awards. *Notable Sports Figures* also examines the impact that the subject had and continues to have on his or her sport, and the reasons why the individual is "notable." This includes consideration of the successes and failures, on the field and off, that keep the person in the public eye.

The biographies in *Notable Sports Figures* profile a broad variety of individuals. Athletes such as **Babe Ruth, Michael Jordan,** and **Martina Navratilova** are featured for their record-breaking accomplishments. **Jackie Robinson** and **Janet Guthrie** remain in the public consciousness because of their determination to cross racial and gender boundaries. Other sports figures have captured our attention by their controversial activities. Skater **Tonya Harding** continues to hold public interest not because of any medals won, but because of the scandalous attack on **Nancy Kerrigan.** Baseball player **"Shoeless" Joe Jackson** was one of the greatest players of his era, but he is remembered more for his complicity in the **"Black Sox"** scandal of 1919 than for his accomplishments on the field. Their lives, accomplishments, and reasons for the public's ongoing fascination with them are examined in *Notable Sports Figures.*

SELECTION PROCESS AND CRITERIA

A preliminary list of athletes, team executives, sportswriters, broadcasters, and other sports figures was compiled from a wide variety of sources, including Hall of Fame lists, periodical articles, and other biographical collections. The list was reviewed by an advisory board, and final selection was made by the editor. An effort was made to include athletes of varying nationalities, ethnicities, and fields of sport as well those who have contributed to the success of a sport or team in general. Selection criteria include:

- Notable "first" achievements, including those who broke racial or gender barriers and paved the way for others

- Impact made on the individual's sport and on society as a whole

- Records set and broken

- Involvement in controversial or newsworthy activities on and off the playing field

FEATURES OF THIS PRODUCT

For easy access, entries are arranged alphabetically according to the entrant's last name.

- **Timeline**—includes significant events in the world of sports, from historic times to the present.

- **Entry head**—lists basic information on each sports figure, including name, birth and death years, nationality, and occupation/sport played.

- **Biographical essay**—offers 1,000 to 2,500 words on the person's life, career highlights, and the impact that the individual had and continues to have on his or her sport and on society. Bold-faced names within entries indicate an entry on that person.

- **Photos**—provide a portrait for many of the individuals profiled. Several essays also include an action photo.

- **Sidebars**—present a chronology of key events in the entrant's life, a list of major awards and accomplishments, and, as applicable, career statistics, brief biographies of important individuals in the entrant's life, "where is s/he now" information on previously popular sports figures, and excerpts from books and periodicals of significant events in the entrant's life and career.

- **Contact Information**—offers addresses, phone numbers, and web sites for selected living entrants.

- **Selected Writings**—lists books and publications written or edited by the entrant.

- **Further Information**—provides a list of resources the reader may access to seek additional information on the sports figure.

- **Appendix**—offers a glossary of commonly used sports abbreviations.

- **Indices**—allow the reader to access the entrants by nationality or sport. A general subject index with cross-references offers additional access.

We Welcome Your Suggestions. Mail your comments and suggestions for enhancing and improving *Notable Sports Figures* to:

The Editors
Notable Sports Figures
Gale Group
27500 Drake Road
Farmington Hills, MI 48331-3535
Phone: (800) 347-4253

Advisory Board

Contributors

Don Amerman, Julia Bauder, Cynthia Becker, David Becker, Michael Belfiore, Kari Bethel, Michael Betzold, Tim Borden, Carol Brennan, Gerald Brennan, Paul Burton, Frank Caso, Gordon Churchwell, Gloria Cooksey, Andrew Cunningham, Lisa Frick, Jan Goldberg, Joyce Hart, Eve Hermann, Ian Hoffman, Syd Jones, Wendy Kagan, Aric Karpinski, Christine Kelley, Judson Knight, Eric Lagergren, Jeanne Lesinski, Carole Manny, Paulo Nunes-Ueno, Patricia Onorato, Tricia Owen, Kristin Palm, Mike Pare, Annette Petruso, Ryan Poquette, Susan Salter, Brenna Sanchez, Lorraine Savage, Paula Scott, Pam Shelton, Ken Shepherd, Ann Shurgin, Barbra Smerz, Roger Smith, Janet Stamatel, Jane Summer, Erick Trickey, Amy Unterburger, Sheila Velazquez, Bruce Walker, Dave Wilkins, Kelly Winters, Rob Winters, Ben Zackheim

Acknowledgments

Photographs and illustrations appearing in *Notable Sports Figures* have been used with the permission of the following sources:

AP/WIDE WORLD PHOTOS:
1980 U.S. Olympic hockey team, photograph. AP/Wide World Photos./ Aamodt, Kjetil Andre, photograph. AP/Wide World Photos./ Aaron, Hank, photograph. AP/Wide World Photos./ Abbott, Jim, photograph. AP/Wide World Photos./ Abdul-Jabbar, Kareem, photograph. AP/Wide World Photos./ Abdul-Jabbar, Kareem, photograph. AP/Wide World Photos./ Agassi, Andre, photograph. AP/Wide World Photos./ Aikman, Troy, photograph. AP/Wide World Photos./ Akers, Michelle, photograph. AP/Wide World Photos, Inc./ Albert, Marv, photograph by Ron Frehm. AP/Wide World Photos./ Albright, Tenley, photograph. AP/Wide World Photos./ Alexander, Grover Cleveland, photograph. AP/Wide World Photos./ Allison, Davey, photograph. AP/Wide World Photos./ Alamo, Roberto, photograph. AP/Wide World Photos./ Anderson, George "Sparky," photograph. AP/Wide World Photos./ Andretti, Mario, photograph. AP/Wide World Photos./ Anthony, Earl, photograph. AP/Wide World Photos./ Armstrong, Lance, photograph. AP/Wide World Photos./ Armstrong, Lance, photograph. AP/Wide World Photos./ Ashe, Arthur, photograph. AP/Wide World Photos./ Ashford, Evelyn, photograph. AP/Wide World Photos./ Auerbach, Red, photograph. AP/Wide World Photos./ Autissier, Isabelle, photograph. AP/Wide World Photos./ Bailey, Donovan, photograph. AP/Wide World Photos./ Banks, Ernie, photograph. AP/Wide World Photos./ Bannister, Roger, photograph. AP/Wide World Photos./ Barton, Donna, photograph. AP/Wide World Photos./ Baugh, Sammy, photograph. AP/Wide World Photos./ Baumgartner, Bruce, photograph. AP/Wide World Photos./ Baylor, Elgin, photograph. AP/Wide World Photos./ Beckenbauer, Franz, photograph. AP/Wide World Photos./ Becker, Boris, photograph. AP/Wide World Photos./ Bedard, Myriam, photograph by Roberto Borea. AP/Wide World Photos./ Bell, Bert, photograph. AP/Wide World Photos./Bell, James "Cool Papa," photograph by Leon Algee. AP/Wide World Photos./ Bench, Johnny, photograph. AP/Wide World Photos./ Berra, Yogi, photograph. AP/Wide World Photos./ Biondi, Matt, photograph. AP/Wide World Photos./ Bird, Larry, photograph. AP/Wide World Photos./Bjoerndalen, Ole Einar, photograph. AP/Wide World Photos./ Blair, Bonnie, photograph. AP Wide World Photos./ Blair, Bonnie, portrait. AP/Wide World Photos./ Blake, Sir Peter, photograph. AP/Wide World Photos./ Bogues, Tyrone, "Muggsy," photograph. AP/Wide World Photos./ Bonds, Barry, photograph. AP/Wide World Photos./ Bonds, Barry, photograph. AP/Wide World Photos./ Borders, Ila, photograph by Nick Ut. AP/Wide World Photos./ Borg, Bjorn, photograph. AP/Wide World Photos./ Bossy, Michael, photograph. AP/Wide World Photos./ Bradley, William Warren, photograph. AP/Wide World Photos./ Bradman, Don, photograph. AP/Wide World Photos./ Bradshaw, Terry, photograph. AP/Wide World Photos./ Brock, Lou, photograph. AP/Wide World Photos./ Brock, Lou, photograph. AP/Wide World Photos./ Brooks, Herb, photograph by Gene J. Puskar. AP/Wide World Photos./ Brown, Jim, photograph. AP/Wide World Photos./ Brown, Jim, photograph. AP/Wide World Photos./ Brown, Mordecai, "Three Finger," photograph. AP/Wide World Photos./ Brown, Tim, photograph. AP/Wide World Photos./ Bubka, Sergei, photograph. AP/Wide World Photos./ Budge, Don, photograph. AP/Wide World Photos./ Butcher, Susan, photograph. AP/Wide World Photos./ Button, Dick, photograph. AP/Wide World Photos./ Campanella, Roy, photograph. AP/Wide World Photos./ Campbell, Earl, photograph. AP/Wide

World Photos./ Canseco, Jose, photograph. AP/Wide World Photos./ Capriati, Jennifer, photograph. AP/Wide World Photos./ Capriati, Jennifer, photograph. AP/Wide World Photos./ Carter, Cris, photograph by Michael Conroy. AP/Wide World Photos./ Carter, Vince, photograph by Chuck Stoody. AP/Wide World Photos./ Carter, Vince, photograph. AP/Wide World Photos./ Cartwright, Alexander Joy, photograph. AP/Wide World Photos./ Caulkins, Tracy, photograph. AP/Wide World Photos./ Chamberlain, Wilt, photograph. AP/Wide World Photos./ Chelios, Chris, photograph. AP/Wide World Photos./ Chun, Lee-Kyung, photograph. AP/Wide World Photos./ Clark, Kelly, photograph. AP/Wide World Photos./ Clark, Kelly, photograph. AP/Wide World Photos./ Clemens, Roger, photograph. AP/Wide World Photos./ Clemens, Roger, photograph. AP/Wide World Photos./ Clemente, Roberto Walker, photograph. AP/Wide World Photos./ Coachman, Alice, photograph. AP/Wide World Photos./ Coleman, Derrick, photograph. AP/Wide World Photos./ Colorado Silver Bullets (Samonds, Shereen, and former major league pitcher Phil Niekro), photograph. AP/Wide World Photos./ Comaneci, Nadia, photograph. AP/Wide World Photos./ Connors, Jimmy, photograph. AP/Wide World Photos./ Conradt, Jody, photograph. AP/Wide World Photos./ Cooper, Cynthia, photograph by David J. Phillip. AP/Wide World Photos./ Cosell, Howard, photograph. AP/Wide World Photos./ Courier, Jim, photograph. AP/Wide World Photos./ Cousy, Bob, photograph. AP/Wide World Photos./ Daly, Chuck, photograph. AP/Wide World Photos./ Davis, Terrell, photograph by Ed Andrieski. AP/Wide World Photos./ Dawes, Dominique, photograph by John McConnico. AP/Wide World Photos./ Dean, Dizzy, photograph. AP/Wide World Photos./ Decker-Slaney, Mary, photograph. AP/Wide World Photos./ Deegan, Brian, photograph. AP/Wide World Photos./ DeFrantz, Anita, photograph by Douglas C. Pizac. AP/Wide World Photos./ De La Hoya, Oscar, photograph. AP/Wide World Photos./ Dickerson, Eric, photograph by Bill Janscha. AP/Wide World Photos./ Dimaggio, Joe, photograph. AP/Wide World Photos./Disl, Uschi, photograph. AP/Wide World Photos./ Ditka, Mike, photograph. AP/Wide World Photos./Doby, Larry, photograph. AP/Wide World Photos./ Dolan, Tom, photograph. AP/Wide World Photos./ Dorsett, Tony, photograph by Bruce Zake. AP/Wide World Photos./ Dravecky, Dave, photograph. AP/Wide World Photos./ Durocher, Leo, photograph. AP/Wide World Photos./ Dyroen, Becky, photograph. AP/Wide World Photos./ Earnhardt, Dale, photograph. AP/Wide World Photos./ Edwards, Teresa, photograph. AP/Wide World Photos./ Egerszegi, Krisztina, photograph. AP/Wide World Photos./ Elway, John, photograph. AP/Wide World Photos./ Erving, Julius, photograph. AP/Wide World Photos./ Esposito, Phil, photograph by Kevin Frayer. AP/Wide World./ Evans, Janet, photograph. AP/Wide World Photos./ Ewbank, Weeb, photograph. AP/Wide World./ Fangio, Juan Manuel, photograph by Eduardo DiBaia. AP/Wide World Photos./ Faulk, Marshall, photograph. AP/Wide World Photos./ Favre, Brett. AP/Wide World Photos./ Fernandez, Lisa, photograph. AP/Wide World Photos./ Figo, Luis, photograph. AP/Wide World Photos./ Fisk, Carlton, photograph. AP/Wide World Photos./ Fittipaldi, Emerson, photograph. AP/Wide World Photos./ Fleming, Peggy, photograph. AP/Wide World Photos./ Flowers, Vonetta, photograph by Darron Cummings. AP/Wide World Photos./ Foreman, George, photograph by Charles Rex Arbogast. AP/Wide World Photos./ Forsberg, Magdalena, photograph. AP/Wide World Photos./ Foyt, A.J., photograph. AP/Wide World Photos./ Foyt, A. J., photograph by Dave Parker. AP/Wide World Photos./ Freeman, Cathy, photograph. AP/Wide World Photos./ Gable, Dan, photograph. AP/Wide World Photos./ Galindo, Rudy, photograph by Craig Fujii. AP/Wide World Photos./ Garcia, Sergio, photograph by Beth A. Keiser. AP/Wide World Photos./ Garnett, Kevin, photograph. AP/Wide World Photos./ Gehrig, Lou, photograph. AP/Wide World Photos./ Gibson, Althea, photograph. AP/Wide World Photos./ Gibson, Josh, photograph. AP/Wide World Photos./ Gonzales, Richard "Pancho," photograph. AP/Wide World Photos./Goolagong, Evonne, photograph. AP/Wide World Photos./ Goosen, Retief, photograph. AP/Wide World Photos./ Gordeeva, Ekaterina, photograph. AP/Wide World Photos./ Graf, Steffi, photograph. AP/Wide World Photos./ Granato, Cammi, photograph. AP/Wide World Photos./ Grange, Harold "Red," photograph. AP/Wide World Photos./ Grange, Red, photograph. AP/Wide World Photos./ Graziano, Rocky, photograph. AP/Wide World Photos./ Greenberg, Hank, photograph. AP/Wide World Photos./ Greene, Joe, photograph. AP/Wide World Photos./ Griese, Bob, photograph. AP/Wide World Photos./ Griffey, Jr., Ken, photograph. AP/Wide World Pho-

Lewis, Lennox, photograph. AP/Wide World Photos./ Lieberman-Cline, Nancy, photograph. AP/Wide World Photos./ Lipinski, Tara, photograph. AP/Wide World Photos./ Lloyd, Earl, photograph. AP/Wide World Photos./ Lobo, Rebecca, portrait. AP/Wide World Photos./ Lopez, Nancy, photograph by Pat J. Carter. AP/Wide World Photos./ Loroupe, Tegla, photograph. AP/Wide World Photos./ Louganis, Greg, photograph. AP/Wide World Photos./ Louis, Joe, photograph. AP/Wide World Photos./ Madden, John, photograph by Aaron Rapopart. AP/Wide World Photos./ Maddux, Greg, photograph. AP/Wide World Photos./ Mahre, Phil, photograph. AP/Wide World Photos./ Maier, Hermann, photograph. AP/Wide World Photos./ Malone, Karl, photograph. AP/Wide World Photos./ Malone, Moses, photograph. AP/Wide World Photos./ Mantle, Mickey, photograph. AP/Wide World Photos, Inc./ Mantle, Mickey, photograph. AP/Wide World Photos./ Marino, Dan, photograph. AP/Wide World Photos./ Martin, Billy, photograph. AP/Wide World Photos./ Martin, Casey, photograph by John Kicker. AP/Wide World Photos./ Martin, Christy, photograph. AP/Wide World Photos./ Masterkova, Svetlana, photograph. AP/Wide World Photos./ Maynard, Don, photograph. AP/Wide World Photos./ Mays, Willie, photograph. AP/Wide World Photos./ McCray, Nikki, photograph. AP/Wide World Photos./ McEnroe, John Patrick, Jr., photograph by Richard Drew. AP/Wide World Photos./ McGwire, Mark, photograph by Tom Gannam. AP/Wide World Photos./ McKinney, Tamara, photograph. AP/Wide World Photos./ Mears, Rick, photograph. AP/Wide World Photos./ Messier, Mark, photograph. AP/Wide World Photos./ Meyers, Ann, photograph. AP/Wide World Photos./ Mikita, Stan, photograph. AP/Wide World Photos./ Mingxia, Fu, photograph. AP/Wide World Photos./ Moceanu, Dominique, photograph. AP/Wide World Photos./ Montana, Joe, photograph. AP/Wide World Photos./ Monti, Eugenio, photograph. AP/Wide World Photos./ Moore, Archie, photograph. AP/Wide World Photos./ Morgan, Joe (Leonard), photograph. AP/Wide World Photos./ Morris, Jim, photograph. AP/Wide World Photos./ Moses, Edwin Corley, photograph by Lennox McLendon. AP/Wide World Photos./ Moss, Randy, photograph by Jim Mone. AP/Wide World Photos./ Muldowney, Shirley "Cha Cha," photograph. AP/Wide World Photos./ Murden, Tori, photograph by Bob Jordan. AP/Wide World Photos./ Musial, Stan, photograph. AP/Wide World Photos./ Musial, Stan, photograph. AP/Wide World Photos./ Mutombu, Dikembe, photograph. AP/Wide World Photos./ Naismith, James, photograph. AP/Wide World Photos./ Namath, Joe, photograph. AP/Wide World Photos./ Namath, Joe, photograph. AP/Wide World Photos./ Navratilova, Martina, photograph. AP/Wide World Photos./ Navratilova, Martina, photograph. AP/Wide World Photos./ Neely, Cam, portrait. AP/Wide World Photos./ Newby-Fraser, Paula, photograph. AP/Wide World Photos./ O'Connor, David, photograph. AP/Wide World Photos./ Oerter, Al, photograph. AP/Wide World Photos./ Oh, Sadaharu, photograph. AP/Wide World Photos./ Ohno, Apolo Anton, photograph. AP/Wide World Photos./ Oldfield, Barney, photograph. AP/Wide World Photos./ Olsen, Merlin Jay, photograph. AP/Wide World Photos./ Olson, Lisa, photograph. AP/Wide World Photos./ O'Neal, Shaquille, photograph. AP/Wide World Photos./ O'Neil, Buck, photograph. AP/Wide World Photos./ O'Neill, Susan, photograph by Dennis Paquin. AP/Wide World Photos./ O'Sullivan, Sonia, photograph. AP/Wide World Photos./ Paige, Leroy Robert, "Satchel," photograph. AP/Wide World Photos./ Paige, Leroy Robert, photograph. AP/Wide World Photos./ Palmer, Shaun, photograph. AP/Wide World Photos./ Parcells, Bill, photograph by Bill Kostroun. AP/Wide World Photos./ Parra, Derek, photograph by Elaine Thompson. AP/Wide World Photos./ Paterno, Joe, photograph by Michael Conroy. AP/Wide World Photos./ Paterno, Joe, photograph. AP/Wide World Photos./ Patterson, Floyd, photograph. AP/Wide World Photos./ Payton, Gary, photograph. AP/Wide World Photos./ Payton, Walter, photograph by Fred Jewell. AP/Wide World Photos./ Pele, photograph. AP/Wide World Photos./ Perry, Gaylord, photograph. AP/Wide World Photos./ Pete Rose, photograph. AP/Wide World Photos./ Petty, Lee, photograph. AP/Wide World Photos./ Piniella, Lou, photograph. AP/Wide World Photos./ Pippen, Scottie, photograph by Tim Johnson. AP/Wide World Photos./ Podkopayeva, Lilia, photograph. AP/Wide World Photos./ Prost, Alain, photograph. AP/Wide World Photos./ Puckett, Kirby, photograph. AP/Wide World Photos./ Randle, John, photograph. AP/Wide World Photos./ Redgrave, Steve, photograph. AP/Wide World Photos./ Reece, Gabrielle, photograph. AP/Wide World Photos/Fashion Wire Daily./ Reese, Harold "Pee Wee," photograph. AP/Wide World Photos./ Retton, Mary Lou, photograph.

AP/Wide World Photos./ Rheaume, Manon, photograph. AP/Wide World Photos./ Rice, Jerry, photograph. AP/Wide World Photos./ Richard, Maurice, photograph. AP/Wide World Photos./ Richardson, Dot, photograph. AP/Wide World Photos./ Riddles, Libby, photograph. AP/Wide World Photos./ Rigby, Cathy, photograph. AP/Wide World Photos./ Riley, Pat, photograph by Mark Lennihan. AP/Wide World Photos./ Ripken, Calvin, photograph. AP/Wide World Photos./ Roba, Fatuma, photograph. AP/Wide World Photos./ Robertson, Oscar, photograph. AP/Wide World Photos./ Robinson, David, photograph. AP/Wide World Photos./ Robinson, Jackie, photograph. AP/Wide World Photos./ Rocker, John, photograph. AP/Wide World Photos./ Rodman, Dennis, photograph. AP/Wide World Photos./ Rodriguez, Alex, photograph. AP/Wide World Photos./ Roy, Patrick, portrait. AP/Wide World Photos./ Rubin, Barbara Joe, photograph. AP/Wide World Photos./ Ruud, Birger, photograph. AP/Wide World Photos./ Rudolph, Wilma, photograph. AP/Wide World Photos./ Russell, Bill, photograph. AP/Wide World Photos./ Ruth, Babe, photograph. AP/Wide World Photos./ Ryan, Lynn Nolan, photograph by Tim Sharp. AP/Wide World Photos./ Sabatini, Gabriela, photograph. AP/Wide World Photos./ St. James, Lyn, portrait. AP/Wide World Photos./ Sale, Jamie, and David Pelletier, photograph by Lionel Cironneau. AP/Wide World Photos./ Sampras, Pete, photograph. AP/Wide World Photos./ Sampras, Pete, photograph. AP/Wide World Photos./ Samuelson, Joan Benoit, photograph. AP/Wide World Photos./ Sanders, Barry, photograph by Rusty Kennedy. AP/Wide World Photos./ Sanders, Deion, photograph. AP/Wide World Photos./ Sanders, Deion, photograph by Rusty Kennedy. AP/Wide World Photos./ Sawchuk, Terry, photograph. AP/Wide World Photos./ Sayers, Gale, photograph. AP/Wide World Photos./ Schayes, Dolph, photograph. AP/Wide World Photos./ Schilling, Curtis Montague, photograph by Lenny Ignelzi. AP/Wide World Photos./ Schmeling, Max, photograph. AP/Wide World Photos./ Schmidt, Mike, photograph. AP/Wide World Photos./ Schmirler, Sandra, photograph. AP/Wide World Photos./ Schramm, Tex, photograph. AP/Wide World Photos./ Schumacher, Michael, photograph. AP/Wide World Photos./ Scott, Wendell Oliver, photograph. AP/Wide World Photos./ Scurry, Briana, photograph. AP/Wide World Photos./ Selanne, Teemu, photograph. AP/Wide World Photos./ Seau, Junior, photograph. AP/Wide World Photos./ Seaver, Tom, photograph. AP/Wide World Photos./ Secretariat, photograph. AP/Wide World Photos./ Secretariat, photograph. AP/Wide World Photos./ Seles, Monica, photograph. AP/Wide World Photos./ Selig, Bud, photograph. AP/Wide World Photos./ Sharp, Sterling, photograph. AP/Wide World Photos./ Shea, Jack, photograph. AP/Wide World Photos./ Sheffield, Gary, photograph. AP/Wide World Photos./ Shula, Don, photograph. AP/Wide World Photos./ Simpson, O. J., photograph. AP/Wide World Photos./ Smith, Tommie, photograph. AP/Wide World Photos./ Sosa, Sammy, photograph by Gary Dineen. AP/Wide World Photos./ Spinks, Michael, photograph. AP/Wide World Photos./ Spitz, Mark (Andrew), photograph. AP/Wide World Photos./ Sprewell, Latrell, photograph by John Dunn. AP/Wide World Photos./ Staley, Dawn, photograph by Rusty Kennedy. AP/Wide World Photos./ Starr, Bart, photograph. AP/Wide World Photos./ Staubach, Roger, photograph. AP/Wide World Photos./ Steinbrenner, George, photograph. AP/Wide World Photos./ Stengel, Casey, photograph. AP/Wide World Photos./ Stenmark, Ingemar, photograph. AP/Wide World Photos./ Stewart, Jackie, photograph. AP/Wide World Photos./ Stewart, Jackie, photograph. AP/Wide World Photos./ Stewart, Kordell, photograph. AP/Wide World Photos./ Stockton, John, photograph. AP/Wide World Photos./ Stojko, Elvis, photograph. AP/Wide World Photos./ Strawberry, Darryl, photograph. AP/Wide World Photos./ Strawberry, Darryl, photograph by Ron Frehm. AP/Wide World Photos./ Street, Picabo, photograph by David Longstreath. AP/Wide World Photos./ Street, Picabo, photograph. AP/Wide World Photos./ Strug, Kerri, photograph. AP/Wide World Photos./ Strug, Kerri, photograph. AP/Wide World Photos./ Suleymanoglu, Naim, photograph. AP/Wide World Photos./ Summitt, Pat, photograph. AP/Wide World Photos./ Suzuki, Ichiro, photograph by Eliane Thompson. AP/Wide World Photos./ Suzuki, Ichiro, photograph. AP/Wide World Photos./ Swoopes, Sheryl, photograph. AP/Wide World Photos./ Tarkanian, Jerry, photograph. AP/Wide World Photos./ Tarkanian, Jerry, photograph. AP/Wide World Photos./ Tarkenton, Fran, photograph. AP/Wide World Photos./ Taylor, Lawrence, photograph. AP/Wide World Photos./ Tendulkar, Sachin, photograph. AP/Wide World Photos./ Thomas, Frank, photograph. AP/Wide World Photos./ Thomas, Isiah, photograph by

Michael Conroy. AP/Wide World Photos./ Thomas, Isiah, photograph. AP/Wide World Photos./ Thomas, Thurman, photograph. AP/Wide World Photos./ Thompson, Jenny, photograph by Paul Sakuma. AP/Wide World Photos./ Thorpe, Ian, photograph by Russell McPhedran. AP/Wide World Photos./ Tomba, Alberto, photograph. AP/Wide World Photos./ Tomba, Alberto, photograph. AP/Wide World Photos, Inc./ Torrence, Gwen, photograph. AP/Wide World Photos./ Torvill, Jayne, and Christopher Dean, photograph. AP/Wide World Photos./ Trottier, Brian, photograph. AP/Wide World Photos./ Tunney, Gene, photograph. AP/Wide World./ Turner, Cathy, AP/Wide World Photos./ Tyson, Mike, photograph by Lennox McLendon. AP/Wide World Photos./ Tyus, Wyomia, photograph. AP/Wide World Photos./ Unitas, Johnny, photograph. AP/Wide World Photos./ Unitas, Johnny, photograph. AP/Wide World Photos./ Unser, Al, photograph. AP/Wide World Photos./ Vaughn, Mo, photograph. AP/Wide World Photos./ Ventura, Jesse, photograph. AP/Wide World Photos./ Vicario, Arantxa Sanchez, photograph. AP/Wide World Photos./ Vitale, Dick, photograph. AP/Wide World Photos./ Wagner, Honus, photograph. AP/Wide World Photos./ Waitz, Grete, photograph. AP/Wide World Photos./ Waitz, Grete, photograph. AP/Wide World Photos./ Walcott, Joe, photograph. AP/Wide World Photos./ Waldner, Jan Ove, photograph. AP/Wide World Photos./ Walton, Bill, photograph. AP/Wide World Photos./ Warne, Shane, photograph. AP/Wide World Photos./ Warner, Kurt, photograph by James A. Finley. AP/Wide World Photos./ Watters, Ricky, photograph. AP/Wide World Photos./ Webb, Anthony, "Spud," photograph. AP/Wide World Photos./ Webb, Karrie, photograph. AP/Wide World Photos./ Webber, Chris, photograph. AP/Wide World Photos./ Weber, Dick, photograph. AP/Wide World Photos./ Wehling, Ulrich, photograph. AP/Wide World Photos./ Weihenmayer, Erik, photograph. AP/Wide World Photos./ Weishoff, Paula, photograph. AP/Wide World Photos./ Weissmuller, Johnny, photograph. AP/Wide World Photos./ West, Jerry, photograph. AP/Wide World Photos./ West, Jerry, photograph. AP/Wide World Photos./ White, Reggie, photograph. AP/Wide World Photos./ Whitworth, Kathy, photograph. AP/Wide World Photos./ Wigger, Deena, photograph. AP/Wide World Photos./ Wilkens, Lenny, photograph. AP/Wide World Photos./ Wilkens, Lenny, photograph. AP/Wide World Photos./ Wilkins, Dominique, photograph. AP/Wide World Photos./ Wilkinson, Laura, photograph. AP/Wide World Photos./ Williams, Serena, photograph. AP/Wide World Photos./ Williams, Serena, photograph. AP/Wide World Photos./ Williams, Ted, photograph. AP/Wide World Photos./ Williams, Venus, photograph. AP/Wide World Photos./ Williams, Venus, photograph. AP/Wide World Photos./ Winfield, Dave, photograph. AP/Wide World Photos./ Witt, Katarina, photograph. AP/Wide World Photos./ Wooden, John, photograph. AP/Wide World Photos./ Wooden, John, photograph. AP/Wide World Photos./ Woods, Tiger, photograph by Dave Martin. AP/Wide World Photos./ Woods, Tiger, photograph by Diego Giudice. AP Wide World Photos./ Woodson, Charles, photograph. AP/Wide World Photos./ Woodson, Rod, photograph. AP/Wide World Photos./ Woodward, Lynette, photograph by Orlin Wagner. AP/Wide World Photos./ Wright, Mickey, photograph. AP/Wide World Photos./ Yamaguchi, Kristi, portrait. AP/Wide World Photos./ Young, Cy, photograph. AP/Wide World Photos./ Young, Sheila, photograph. AP/Wide World Photos./ Young, Steve, photograph. AP/Wide World Photos./ Zaharias, Babe (Mildred Ella) Didrikson, photograph. AP/Wide World Photos./ Zidane, Zinedine, photograph. AP/Wide World Photos./

ASSOCIATED FEATURES, INC.:
Dryden, Ken, photograph. Associated Features, Inc./ Esposito, Tony, photograph. Associated Features, Inc./ Hasek, Dominik, photograph. Associated Features./ Plante, Jacques, photograph. Associated Features./ Sakic, Joe, photograph. Associated Features.

BRUCE BENNETT STUDIOS, INC.:
Belfour, Ed, photograph. Courtesy of Bruce Bennett./ Bowman, Scotty, photograph. John Giamundo/B. Bennett./ Gretzky, Wayne, photograph. Courtesy of Bruce Bennett./ Gretzky, Wayne, photograph. Courtesy of Bruce Bennett./ Lefleur, Guy, photograph. Courtesy of Bruce Bennett./ Lemieux, Mario, photograph. Michael DiGirolamo/B. Bennett./ Lindros, Eric, photograph. Courtesy of B. Bennett./ Lindros, Eric, photograph. Courtesy of Bruce Bennett.

CORBIS:

Alexander, Grover Cleveland, photograph by George Rinhart. (c)Underwood & Underwood/Corbis./ Ali, Muhammad, photograph. UPI/Corbis-Bettmann./ Ali, Muhammad, photograph. (c) Bettmann/Corbis./ Allen, Marcus, photograph. (c)Bettmann/Corbis./ Ashe, Arthur, photograph. (c)Hulton-Deutsch Collection/Corbis./ Auerbach, Arnold, photograph. (c)Bettmann/Corbis./ Bench, Johnny Lee, photograph. (c)Bettmann/Corbis./ Benoit, Joan, photograph. Corbis-Bettmann./ Berra, Yogi, photograph. (c)Bettmann/Corbis./ Bird, Larry Joe, photograph. (c) Reuters New Media Inc./Corbis./ Blake, Hector "Toe", photograph. (c) Bettmann/Corbis./ Brisco-Hooks, Valerie, photograph. Corbis-Bettmann./ Brown, Paul, photograph. Corbis/ Bettmann./ Caray, Harry, photograph. UPI/CORBIS-Bettmann./ Carter, Don, photograph. (c) Bettmann/Corbis./ Chamberlain, Wilt, photograph. UPI/Corbis-Bettmann./ Chang, Michael, photograph. Reuters/Bettmann./ Clemente, Roberto, photograph. UPI/Bettmann./ Conner, Bart, photograph. (c)Bettmann/Corbis./ Connolly, Maureen, photograph. UPI/Corbis- Bettmann./ Corbett, James John, photograph. (c)Bettmann/Corbis./ Costas, Bob, photograph by Wally McNamee. Wally McNamee/Corbis./ Court, Margaret Smith, photograph. UPI/Corbis-Bettmann./ Court, Margaret Smith, photograph. UPI/Corbis-Bettmann./ Davis, Al, photograph. (c)AFP/Corbis./ De Varona, Donna, photograph. (c) Bettman/Corbis./ Devers, Gail, photograph. Reuters/Bettmann./ Faldo, Nick, photograph. Reuters/Bettmann./ Fleming, Peggy, photograph. Corbis./ Frazier, Joe, photograph. (c) Hulton-Deutsch Collection/Corbis./ Furtado, Julie, photograph. (c) Ales Fevzer/Corbis./ Gibson, Althea. Portrait. UPI/Bettmann./ Gifford, Frank, photograph. (c)Mitchell Gerber/Corbis./ Graf, Steffi, photograph. (c) Dimitri LundtCorbis./ Graham, Otto, photograph. Bettmann/Corbis./ Guthrie, Janet, photograph. Corbis-Bettmann./ Halas, George Stanley "Papa Bear," photograph. (c) Bettmann/Corbis./ Hamill, Dorothy, photograph. UPI/Bettmann./ Hamill, Dorothy, photograph. (c) Corbis./ Hawk, Tony, photograph by Jason Wise. (c) Duomo/Corbis./ Hayes, Robert, photograph. (c)Bettmann/Corbis./ Heisman, John, photograph. (c) Bettmann/Corbis./ Heisman, John, photograph. (c) Bettmann/Corbis./ Hill, Lynn, photograph. UPI/Corbis-Bettmann./ Hingis, Martina, photograph. (c) Torsten Blackwood/Corbis./ Hogan, Ben, photograph. (c) Bettmann/Corbis./ Holyfield, Evander, photograph. UPI/Corbis Bettmann./ Holyfield, Evander, photograph. Reuters/Bettmann./ Hornsby, Rogers, photograph. Bettmann/Corbis./ Hunter, Catfish, photograph. (c)Bettmann/Corbis./ Jagr, Jaromir, photograph. (c) Reuters NewMedia Inc./Corbis./ Jenner William Bruce, photograph Neal Preston. Corbis./ Johnson, Earvin "Magic," photograph. Bettmann Newsphotos./ Johnson, Jack, photograph. (c) Bettmann/Corbis./ Jordan, Michael, photograph. Reuters/Corbis-Bettmann./ Jordan, Michael, photograph. Reuters/Corbis-Bettmann./ Joyner-Kersee, Jackie, photograph. Reuters/Bettmann./ Kahanamoku, Duke, photograph. The Bettmann Archive./ King, Billie Jean, photograph. (c) Bettmann/Corbis./ Knight, Bobby, photograph by Gary Hershorn. NewMedia Inc./Corbis./ Korbut, Olga, photograph. Corbis./ Koufax, Sanford (Sandy), photograph. (c)Bettmann/Corbis./ Kwan, Michelle. Reuters/Corbis-Bettmann./ Landry, Thomas, photograph. (c)Bettmann/Corbis./ Laver, Rod, photograph. UPI/Corbis-Bettmann./ Lemon, Meadowlark, photograph. (c)Bettmann/Corbis./ Liston, Sonny, photograph. (c)Bettmann/Corbis./ Lombardi, Vince, photograph. Corbis/Bettmann./ Louis, Joe, photograph. Corbis-Bettmann./ Madden, John, photograph. (c) Bettmann/Corbis./ Maris, Roger (Eugene), photograph. (c)Bettmann/Corbis./ McEnroe, John, photograph. UPI/Corbis-Bettmann./ Mikan, George, photograph. (c)Bettmann/Corbis./ Miller, Shannon, photograph. (c)Mike King/Corbis./ Mirra, Dave, photograph. (c) Duomo/Corbis./ Moise, Patty, photograph. UPI/Corbis-Bettmann./ Montana, Joe, photograph. (c)Bettmann/Corbis./ Moody, Helen F., photograph by George Rinhart. (c)Underwood & Underwood/Corbis./ Moore, Archie Lee, photograph. (c)Bettmann/Corbis./ Olajuwon, Akeem, photograph. UPI/Corbis-Bettmann./ O'Neal, Shaquille, photograph. (c) Reuters NewMedia Inc./Corbis./ Orr, Bobby, photograph. (c) Bettmann/Corbis./ Owens, Jesse, photograph. UPI/Corbis-Bettmann./ Payton, Walter, photograph. (c)Bettmann/Corbis./ Piazza, Mike, photograph. (c)Reuters NewMedia Inc./Corbis./ Reeves, Dan, photograph. (c) Bettmann/Corbis./ Robinson, Brooks Calbert, Jr., photograph. (c)Bettmann/Corbis./ Robinson, Shawna, photograph. UPI/Corbis-Bettmann./ Robinson, Sugar Ray, photograph. (c) Bettmann/Corbis./ Rozelle, Pete, photograph by Sande. (c) Bettmann/Corbis./

Rose, Pete, photograph. (c) Stephen Dunn/Getty Images./ Russell, Bill, portrait. (c) Sporting News/Getty Images./ Sayers, Gale, photograph. Sporting News/Archive Photos, Inc./ Shoemaker, Willie, photograph. APA/Archive Photos, Inc./ Shriver, Eunice, photograph. Archive Photos, Inc./ Skobilikova, Lydia, photograph. (c) Hulton Archive/Getty Images./ Sorenstam, Annika, photograph by Steve Marcus. Archive Photos./ Starr, Bart, photograph. Sporting News/Archive Photos, Inc./ Sullivan, John Lawrence, photograph. (c) Hulton Archive/Getty Images./ Swann, Lynn, photograph. Sporting News/Archive Photos./ Thomas, Derrick, photograph by Susumu Takahashi. Reuters/Archive Photos, Inc./ Torre, Joe, photograph. Reuters/Ray Stubblebine/Archive Photos./ Tretiak, Vladislav, photograph. (c) Getty Images./ Trinidad, Felix Tito, photograph. (c) Gary M. Williams/Liaison Agency/Getty Images/ El Neuvo Dia./ Turner, Ted, photograph. Archive Photo/Malafronte./ Van Dyken, Amy, photograph. Reuters/Eric Gailard/Archive Photos./ Wenzel, Hanni, photograph. (c) Tony Duffy/Getty Images./ Williamson, Alison, photograph. (c) Mark Dadswell, Getty Images./

HOCKEY HALL OF FAME:
Blake, Hector, photograph. Courtesy of Hockey Hall of Fame./ Vezina, Georges, photograph. Courtesy of Hockey Hall of Fame.

THE LIBRARY OF CONGRESS:
Dempsey, Jack, photograph. The Library of Congress./ Rockne, Knute, photograph. The Library of Congress. Rudolph, Wilma, photograph. The Library of Congress./ Ruth, Babe, photograph. The Library of Congress.

BILLY MILLS:
Mills, Billy, photograph. Courtesy of Billy Mills./ Mills, Billy, photograph. Courtesy of Billy Mills.

NATIONAL ARCHIVES AND RECORDS ADMINISTRATION:
Thorpe, Jim, photograph. National Archives and Records Administration.

NATIONAL BASEBALL LIBRARY & ARCHIVE:
Chicago White Sox team, photograph. National Baseball Library & Archive, Cooperstown, NY.

NEW YORK KNICKS
Ewing, Patrick, photograph by George Kalinsky. The New York Knicks.

THE NEW YORK PUBLIC LIBRARY:
Washington, Ora, photograph by D. H. Polk. Photographs and Prints Division, Schomburg Center for Research in Black Culture, The New York Public Library, Astor, Lenox and Tilden Foundations.

PENSKE MOTORSPORTS, INC.:
Jackson, Joe, photograph. From The Image of Their Greatness: An Illustrated History of Baseball from 1900 to the Present, revised edition, by Lawrence Ritter and Donald Honig. Crown Trade Paperbacks, 1992. Copyright (c) 1992 by Lawrence S. Ritter and Donald Honig./ Penske, Roger. Photo courtesy of Penske Motorsports, Inc.

POPPERFOTO:
Patterson, Floyd, photograph. Popperfoto/Archive Photos./ Retton, Mary Lou, photograph. Popperfoto.

MITCHELL B. REIBEL:
Borg, Bjorn, photograph. Mitchell Reibel.

SPORTSPICS:
Petty, Richard, photograph. SportsPics.

UNITED PRESS INTERNATIONAL:
U. S. Olympic Hockey team, 1980, photograph. Courtesy of United Press International.

WIREIMAGE.COM:
Bryant, Kobe, photograph. Steve Granitz/WireImage.com.

Entry List

VOLUME 3

M

VOLUME 4

T

Timeline

776 B.C.
Greece's first recorded Olympic Games. Only Greeks are allowed to compete, and the games are limited to foot races of approximately 200 yards.

490 B.C.
According to Greek satirist Lucian, a courier named Pheidippides runs from the plains of Marathon to Athens, a distance of about 22 miles, with news of a Greek victory over the Persians. This becomes the inspiration for modern-day "marathon" races.

1457
Scotland's Parliament forbids "futeball and golfe" as their popularity is distracting men from practicing archery which is required for military training.

1552
Scotland's Royal Golf Club of St. Andrews begins. Its official founding comes 200 years later in 1754.

1702
Queen Anne of England gives approval for horseracing and introduces the idea of sweepstakes.

1744
First recorded cricket match in England. Rules of the game are codified in 1788.

1842
Alexander Cartwright invents baseball. Although the game has been played for many years, Cartwright writes down rules of play.

1863
The official rules for soccer are established by the Football Association in England.

1869
Princeton and Rutgers play the first college football game. Rutgers wins 6-4.

1874
British sportsman Walter Clopton Wingfield codifies the rules for lawn tennis.

1875
First running of the Kentucky Derby, won by Aristides.

1876
The National League (NL) is formed. The NL becomes the first stable baseball major league.

1877
The first Wimbledon tennis championship is won by Spencer Gore.

1891
Basketball invented by **James Naismith,** a physical education instructor at Springfield Men's Christian Association Training School. Naismith wrote the first 13 rules for the sport.

1892
"Gentleman Jim" Corbett defeats **John L. Sullivan** to win the first boxing championship fought with padded gloves and under the Marquis of Queensberry Rules.

1896
First of the "modern" Olympics are held in Athens, Greece. Competing are 311 athletes from 13 countries.

1900
The American League (AL) is formed. It soon joins the National League as a baseball major league.

Britain's Charlotte Cooper wins the first women's Olympic gold medal in women's tennis. Margaret Abbott wins the nine-hole golf competition, becoming the first American woman to win Olympic gold.

1903
The National Agreement calls an end to the war between the American and National baseball leagues. The agree-

ment calls for each league to be considered major leagues, the same alignment as today.

The first World Series is played. It features the Pittsburgh Pirates of the National League and the Boston Pilgrims of the American League. Boston wins the series 5-3.

1908

Jack Johnson defeats Tommy Burns to become the first African American to hold the world heavyweight boxing championship.

1911

First Indianapolis 500 is run.

Cy Young retires with a career record 511 wins. The trophy given annually to the best pitcher in each league is named after Young.

1912

Jim Thorpe wins three Olympic medals, one of them a gold medal in the decathlon. The medals are stripped from him in 1913 when it is discovered that he accepted a token sum of money to play baseball. The medals are restored and returned to his family in 1982.

1917

The National Hockey League (NHL) is formed. The new league contains only four teams.

1919

The **Chicago "Black Sox"** throw the World Series against the Cincinnati Reds in the biggest sports gambling incident of all-time. Eight players, including the great **"Shoeless" Joe Jackson,** are banned from baseball by commissioner Kennesaw Mountain Landis.

1920

The New York Yankees purchase the contract of **Babe Ruth** from the Boston Red Sox. "The Curse of the Bambino" prevents the Red Sox from winning a World Series since.

The National Football League (NFL) forms in Canton, Ohio. The original league has 14 teams.

1926

Gertrude Ederle becomes the first woman to swim the English Channel. Her time is nearly five hours faster than the previous five men who made the crossing.

1927

Babe Ruth of the New York Yankees hits 60 home runs in one season, breaking his own single-season record.

His total is more than 12 *teams* hit during the season. Ruth retires with 714 career home runs, also a record at the time.

1928

Ty Cobb retires from baseball with a lifetime .366 average that still stands as a record today. Cobb also retired with the career record for hits (4,189) and runs (2,246).

1930

Uruguay hosts and wins the first soccer World Cup. The event has been held every four years since.

Bobby Jones wins "Grand Slam" of golf by capturing the U.S. and British Opens and Amateurs.

1931

Knute Rockne dies in a plane crash. He finishes with a 121-12-5 record, a winning percentage of .881. Rockne led Notre Dame to five unbeaten and untied seasons.

1932

The Negro National League is formed. This is the first "major" league set up for African-American players.

Babe Didrikson Zaharias wins three gold medals at the Summer Olympics in Los Angeles, California. She sets new world records in the javelin throw and 80-meter hurdles.

1936

Sonja Henie wins the Winter Olympics gold medal for women's figure skating for the third consecutive time.

Jesse Owens wins four gold medals in track and field at the Summer Olympics in Berlin, Germany. Owens' feat comes as a shock to German dictator Adolf Hitler.

1937

Don Budge wins tennis's "Grand Slam." He is the first player to win Wimbledon and the Australian, French, and U.S. championships in the same calendar year.

1938

Helen Wills wins the final of her 19 "Grand Slam" singles tennis titles. She wins eight Wimbledons, seven U.S. Opens, and four French Opens.

The great **Joe Louis** knocks out German fighter **Max Schmeling.** The victory carries extra meaning as it also marks a win against Nazi Germany.

1939

The first baseball game is televised. The game features Cincinnati and Brooklyn.

On July 4, **Lou Gehrig** gives his famous farewell speech. He dies soon after from Amyotrophic Lateral Sclerosis (ALS), now called Lou Gehrig's Disease.

1941

Ted Williams of the Boston Red Sox hits .406. He is the last player to hit over .400 for an entire season.

Joe DiMaggio of the New York Yankees hits safely in 56 consecutive games. He breaks the record of 44 set by Wee Willie Keeler.

1943

The All American Girls Professional Baseball League is formed. At its peak in 1948 the league boasts 10 teams.

1945

Brooklyn Dodgers' executive **Branch Rickey** signs **Jackie Robinson** to a minor league contract.

1946

The color line in football is broken. Woody Strode and Kenny Washington play for the Rams and Marion Motley and Bill Willis join the Browns.

The Basketball Association of America is founded. Within three years it becomes the National Basketball Association (NBA).

1947

Jackie Robinson breaks the color barrier in baseball. This heroic ballplayer is subjected to harsh treatment from fans, fellow ballplayers, and even teammates.

1949

The Ladies' Professional Golf Association (LPGA) forms. **Babe Didrikson Zaharias** is a co-founder.

1957

Althea Gibson becomes the first African American to win Wimbledon and U.S. tennis championships. She repeats her feat the next year.

1958

Baseball's Brooklyn Dodgers move to Los Angeles and New York Giants move to San Francisco. The moves devastate long-time fans of each team.

What is now called the "greatest game ever played" is won by the Baltimore Colts in sudden-death overtime over the New York Giants 23-17. The game is widely televised and has much to do with the growth in popularity of football.

1959

Daytona 500 is run for the first time. It now is one of the most watched sporting events in the United States.

The American Football League (AFL) is founded. The league brings professional football to many new markets.

1960

Sugar Ray Robinson retires from boxing. During his career he wins the welterweight title once and holds the middleweight title five times. His lifetime record is 182-19.

Cassius Clay wins a gold medal in the light-heavyweight class at the Summer Olympics in Rome, Italy. Later, Clay throws his medal into the Ohio River as a reaction against the racial prejudice with which he is forced to contend.

Wilma Rudolph becomes the first American woman to win three gold medals in one Summer Olympics in Rome, Italy. She wins the 100- and 200-meter dashes and is a part of the winning 4 x 100 relay team.

1961

Roger Maris of the New York Yankees hits a single-season record 61 home runs. His record is tarnished by some observers because Maris plays a 162 game schedule while **Babe Ruth,** whose record he broke, played only 154 games in 1927.

1962

Wilt Chamberlain of the Philadelphia Warriors scores 100 points in a single game. He accomplishes this feat on March 2 against the New York Knicks. Chamberlain goes on to set another record when he averages 50.4 points per game during the same season and also leads the NBA in rebounding with 25.7 boards per game.

Oscar Robertson averages a triple double for an entire NBA season. He averages 30.8 points, 12.5 rebounds, and 11.4 assists per game.

1964

Cassius Clay scores a technical knockout of **Sonny Liston** to win the heavyweight championship. The victory is seen as a gigantic upset at the time. The day after his victory over Liston, Clay announces that he is a member of the Nation of Islam. He also announces that he is changing his name to **Muhammad Ali.**

1965

Star running back of the Cleveland Browns, **Jim Brown,** retires to pursue an acting career. He leaves the game holding the record for most career rushing yards, 12,312, in only eight seasons.

1966

The Boston Celtics win their eighth consecutive championship. No other major sports franchise has won this many consecutive titles.

Texas Western beats Kentucky 72-65 for the NCAA basketball championship. The champions feature an all-African American starting five while Kentucky starts five white players.

1967

First Iditarod dog sledding race held. The race begins as a 56 mile race, but by 1973 it evolves into a 1,152 mile trek between Anchorage and Nome, Alaska.

Charlie Sifford becomes the first African American to win on the PGA golf tour when he captures the Greater Hartford Open.

The first Super Bowl is played between the Green Bay Packers and Kansas City Chiefs. It is originally called the AFL-NFL World Championship Game.

1968

Bill Russell becomes the first African-American coach in any major sport. He leads the Boston Celtics to two championships as player-coach.

Americans **Tommie Smith** and John Carlos protest racism in the U.S. by raising black glove-clad fists on the medal stand after finishing first and third in the 200-meters at the Mexico City Olympics. The two are suspended from competition.

Eunice Kennedy Shriver begins the Special Olympics. The program grows into an international showcase for mentally challenged athletes.

The "Heidi" game becomes a piece of sports history as fans in the East miss the Oakland Raiders's thrilling comeback against the New York Jets. NBC decides to leave the game with 50 seconds left to start the movie *Heidi* on time at 7:00 p.m. ET. The network is barraged with calls complaining about the decision.

The American Football League (AFL) and National Football League (NFL) merge. The league retains the NFL name and splits teams into American and National conferences.

1969

Rod Laver of Australia wins the tennis "Grand Slam" for the second time in his career. He also won the Slam in 1962 as an amateur.

1970

Pele plays in fourth World Cup for his home country of Brazil.

On September 21, ABC's Monday Night Football debuts. The game features a contest between the Cleveland Browns and New York Jets. **Howard Cosell** and Don Meredith are the commentators.

1971

Gordie Howe, "Mister Hockey," retires from the NHL. At the time he holds career records for goals (801), assists (1,049), and points (1,850). Howe goes on to play seven more seasons in the World Hockey Association (WHA).

1972

Congress passes the Education Amendment Act, which includes Title IX. Title IX bans sex discrimination in federally funded schools in academics and athletics. The new law changes the landscape of college athletics, as more playing opportunities and scholarships are open to women.

Secretariat wins horse racing's Triple Crown, setting records for every race. He is the only horse to run under two minutes in the Kentucky Derby and wins the Belmont Stakes by a record 31 lengths.

Mark Spitz wins seven Olympic swimming gold medals. He sets the record for most medals won at a single Olympic Games.

Black September, an Arab terrorist group, kills eleven Israeli athletes held captive in the Olympic Village. The Games are suspended the following morning for a memorial service, after which, with the approval of the Israelis, they reconvene.

Out of respect to the Native American population, Stanford University changes its nickname from Indians to Cardinals. Other schools do the same, but professional teams do not.

1973

UCLA wins its seventh consecutive NCAA basketball championship. Coached by the legendary **John Wooden,** the Bruins during one stretch win 88 games in a row. UCLA goes on to win three more titles under Wooden.

Billie Jean King defeats Bobby Riggs in a "Battle of the Sexes" tennis match. Riggs, a self-proclaimed "male chauvinist," is 25 years older than King.

Running back **O.J. Simpson** of the Buffalo Bills becomes the first NFL player to ever rush for over 2,000 yards in a season. Simpson is the only player to accomplish this feat in 14 games.

The Miami Dolphins finish the NFL season with a perfect 17-0 record. The Dolphins close out their season with a 14-7 victory over the Washington Redskins in

Super Bowl VII. No NFL team before or since has finished a season with a perfect record.

1974

Hank Aaron breaks **Babe Ruth**'s career home run record. Aaron has to overcome not only history but racist attacks as he hits number 715 in Atlanta.

Muhammad Ali stuns the world with his eighth round knockout of **George Foreman** in "The Rumble in the Jungle." Ali uses the "rope-a-dope" strategy to wear out the much more powerful Foreman.

1975

Muhammad Ali defeats **Joe Frazier** in the "Thrilla in Manila." The victory was Ali's second in three fights with Frazier.

Pitchers Dave McNally and Andy Messersmith win their challenge to baseball's "reserve clause." Arbitrator Peter Seitz rules that once a player completes one season without a contract he can become a free agent. This is a landmark decision that opens the door to free agency in professional sports.

1976

Romanian **Nadia Comaneci** scores perfect 10s seven times in gymnastics competition at the Summer Olympics in Montreal, Quebec, Canada. This marks the first time that a 10 has ever been awarded.

Kornelia Ender of East Germany wins four Olympic gold medals in swimming. Her time in every one of her races breaks a world record.

1977

Janet Guthrie qualifies on the final day for a starting spot in the Indianapolis 500. She becomes the first woman to compete in the Memorial Day classic.

A.J. Foyt wins the Indianapolis 500 for a record-setting fourth time.

1978

Nancy Lopez wins a record-breaking five LPGA tournaments in a row during her rookie season. She goes on to win nine tournaments for the year.

1979

ESPN launches the first all-sports television network. The network now carries all the major professional and college sports.

1980

The **U.S. men's Olympic ice hockey team** defeats the heavily favored team from the Soviet Union, 4-3, in what becomes known as the "Miracle on Ice." The Americans go on to win the gold medal.

Eric Heiden of the U.S. wins five individual gold medals in speed skating at the Winter Olympics in Lake Placid, New York. No one before or since has won five individual events in a single Olympic Games. No other skater has ever swept the men's speed skating events.

The U.S. and its allies boycott the Summer Olympics in Moscow, USSR. The Americans cite the Soviet invasion of Afghanistan as the reason for their action.

1981

Richard Petty wins the Daytona 500. His win is his record-setting seventh victory in the big race.

1982

Louisiana State defeats Cheney State for the title in the first NCAA women's basketball championship.

Wayne Gretzky, the "Great One," scores 92 goals in a season. He adds 120 assists to end the season with 212 points, the first time anyone has scored over 200 points in one season.

Shirley Muldowney wins last of three National Hot Rod Association (NHRA) top fuel championships. Muldowney won 17 NHRA titles during her career.

1983

Australia II defies the odds and wins the America's Cup after 132 years of domination by the U.S. defenders. The New York Yacht Club had won 24 straight competitions.

1984

The Soviet Union and its allies (except Romania) boycott the Summer Olympics held in Los Angeles, California. Many believe this is in response to the U.S. boycott of Moscow Games in 1980.

Carl Lewis repeats **Jesse Owens**'s feat of winning four gold medals in track and field at the Summer Olympics in Los Angeles, California. Lewis wins the same events as Owens: the 100- and 200-meters, the long jump, and the 4 x 100m relay.

Joan Benoit Samuelson wins the first ever Olympic marathon for women. Her winning time over the 26.2 mile course is 2:24.52.

Dan Marino of the Miami Dolphins throws for 5,084 yards and 48 touchdowns, both NFL single-season records.

1985

On September 11, **Pete Rose** breaks **Ty Cobb**'s record for career hits when he gets his 4,192nd hit. Rose finishes his career with 4,256 hits. Unfortunately, Rose is banned from baseball after allegations of his gambling on the sport come to light.

1986

Nancy Lieberman is the first woman to play in a men's professional league - the United States Basketball League.

Jack Nicklaus wins his record 18th and final major championship at the Masters. During his illustrious career he wins 6 Masters, 4 U.S. Opens, 3 British Opens, and 5 PGA Championships.

1988

Greg Louganis wins gold medals in both platform and springboard diving. He is the first person to win both diving medals in two consecutive Olympics. Louganis wins despite hitting his head on the board during the springboard competition.

Florence Griffith-Joyner sets world records in both the 100- and 200-meter dashes.

Steffi Graf of Germany wins the "Golden Slam" of tennis by winning each of the "Grand Slam" events in addition to the Olympic gold medal. Graf retires with a record 22 victories in "Grand Slam" events.

1992

Jackie Joyner-Kersee establishes herself as the most dominant athlete in the five-event heptathlon, winning her second consecutive Summer Olympics gold medal in the event. Joyner-Kersee had set the world record at 7,291 points and held the next five highest scores.

Cito Gaston becomes the first African-American manager to take his team to the World Series. He is also the first to manage the world champions as his Blue Jays win the title the same year.

1993

Michael Jordan retires from basketball after leading the Bulls to three consecutive NBA championships. He says he is retiring to try to play professional baseball.

Julie Krone becomes the first woman jockey to win a Triple Crown horse race. She rides Colonial Affair to victory in the Belmont Stakes.

The Miami Dolphins defeat the Philadelphia Eagles 19-14, giving Dolphins coach **Don Shula** his 325th win. The victory moved Shula into first place on the all-time list, beating the record held by **George Halas** of the Chicago Bears.

1994

The husband of figure skater **Tonya Harding** hires two men to attack Harding's rival, **Nancy Kerrigan.** The men strike at the U.S. Figure Skating Championships in Detroit, Michigan. Kerrigan is knocked out of the competition, but still qualifies for the Olympic team.

Speedskater **Bonnie Blair** wins her fifth Winter Olympic gold medal, the most by any American woman. She won the 500-meters in 1988 then won both the 500- and 1000-meters in 1992 and 1994. Blair won a total of seven Olympic medals.

Pole-vaulter **Sergei Bubka** of the Ukraine sets the world record in the pole vault with a jump of 6.14 meters. Bubka holds the top 14 jumps of all-time in the event.

A baseball player's strike wipes out the end of the regular season and, for the first time since 1904, the World Series. The strike hurts baseball's popularity for years to come.

1995

Michael Jordan returns to the Chicago Bulls. He leads Chicago to three consecutive championships then retires again in 1998. Jordan retires as a five-time winner of the NBA Most Valuable Player Award and six-time winner of the NBA Finals MVP.

Extreme Games (X Games) are held for first time in Rhode Island and Vermont. The X Games and Winter X Games have been held every year since.

1996

Sprinter **Michael Johnson** wins a rare double at the Summer Olympics in Atlanta, Georgia. He wins both the 200- and 400-meter races, the first man ever to accomplish this feat at the Olympics.

Carl Lewis wins the long jump gold medal at the Summer Olympics in Atlanta, Georgia. It is the athlete's ninth gold medal, tying him for the most all-time with Finnish track legend Paavo Nurmi and Soviet gymnast **Larisa Latynina.**

Jackie Joyner-Kersee wins a bronze medal in the long jump at the Summer Olympics in Atlanta, Georgia. This brings her medal total for three Olympic Games to six, making her the most decorated female track and field athlete in U.S. history.

U.S. women capture the first-ever women's soccer Olympic gold medal.

Dan Marino retires. He leaves the game holding the NFL career record for yards (51,636) and touchdown passes (369).

1997

The Women's National Basketball Association (WNBA) is formed.

Tiger Woods is only 21 when he wins the Masters by a record-shattering 12 strokes. He also sets a record by shooting 18 under par.

1998

Team USA captures the first women's ice hockey gold medal at the Winter Olympics in Nagano, Japan.

Cal Ripken, Jr. breaks **Lou Gehrig**'s iron man record when he plays in his 2,632nd game on September 19.

1999

Vote-buying scandal rips the International Olympic Committee (IOC). Several IOC members are forced to quit because they took bribes from cities hoping to host the Olympics.

Wayne Gretzky retires with NHL records that may never be broken. He holds or shares 61 single-season and career records including the career records for most goals (894), most assists (1,963) and points (2,857). Gretzky also holds the single-season records for goals (92), assists (163), and points (215).

2000

New York Yankees win their 26th World Series. The win makes the Yankees the winningest organization in sports history.

2001

Tiger Woods becomes the first golfer to hold the championship for all four professional "Grand Slam" events when he wins the Masters. His accomplishment is not called a "Grand Slam" because all his victories do not occur in the same calendar year.

Roman Sebrle of the Czech Republic earns the title of "world's greatest athlete" by setting a world record in the 10-event decathlon. His final score is 9,026 points, making him the first man to surpass the 9,000 barrier.

Barry Bonds of the San Francisco Giants hits 73 home runs, a new major league single-season record. The next season he becomes only the fourth major leaguer to hit over 600 career home runs.

Michael Jordan returns to the NBA, this time playing for the Washington Wizards, a team in which he holds partial ownership. His 30.4 career scoring average is the highest of all-time.

2002

Brazil wins record fifth World Cup championship.

Coach **Phil Jackson** of the Los Angeles Lakers sets a record by coaching his ninth NBA champion. He won six titles as coach of the Chicago Bulls and three with Los Angeles. Jackson also tied **Scotty Bowman** of the NHL for most professional titles won as coach.

Hockey coach **Scotty Bowman** retires. He holds career records for most regular season (1,244) and playoff (223) wins.

Lance Armstrong wins the Tour de France cycling race for the fourth straight year. His victory comes only six years after doctors gave him little chance of surviving testicular cancer that had spread to his lymph nodes and brain.

Pete Sampras breaks his own record by winning his 14th Grand Slam tournament, the U.S. Open. He defeats rival **Andre Agassi** in the final.

Emmitt Smith of the Dallas Cowboys sets a new NFL career rushing record with 17,162 yards. Smith passes the great **Walter Payton** of the Chicago Bears.

Jerry Rice scores the 200th NFL touchdown of his remarkable career, the only man to reach this plateau. He ends the 2002 season holding the records for receptions (1,456), yards receiving (21,597), and touchdowns (202).

2003

Serena Williams wins four "Grand Slam" tennis championships in a row. She defeats her sister, **Venus Williams,** in the final of every event.

Nick Faldo
1957-

British golfer

Britsh golfer Nick Faldo has won six major golf events and more than 30 titles on the European Professional Golf Association tour, primarily from the mid-1980s to the mid-1990s. Though Faldo is a great golfer, he has not been a popular nor particularly high profile figure in the United States, in part because of his personality. Faldo only achieved success when he changed his golf swing in the mid-1980s, and was known for his straight driver.

Faldo was born July 18, 1957, in Welwyn Garden City, England, the only child of George Arthur and Joyce (née Smalley) Faldo. His father worked as an accountant at a chemical company. Faldo's mother encouraged her son's interests in all sports. As a young child, he was an enthusiastic swimmer and cyclist. When Faldo was 10 years old, he won the Hertfordshire county medal in the 100-meter breaststroke. He also played soccer, rugby, basketball, cricket, and tennis, and ran track and threw the discus, while receiving his education at Sir Frederic Osborne School.

Nick Faldo

Discovered Golf

When Faldo was only 13 years old, he was watching the Masters tournament on television one year when **Jack Nicklaus** won and decided he would like to try golf. His mother arranged for Faldo to have six golf lessons, and he was hooked. He played his first round of golf when he was 14 years old.

Faldo soon became a good golfer, despite his late start. The sport so captured his attention that it made him lose interest in school. Faldo recalled to Sarah Ballard of *Sports Illustrated,* "I love school, until golf came along. Then the only thing I was interested in was getting out of the gates as quick as possible and going to the golf course."

When he was 16 years old, Faldo convinced his parents to let him quit school to work on his golf game and become a professional. He played every day all day for

two years. The work paid off when in 1974 he was part of an All-England boys golf team. In 1975, Faldo won two amateur championships, the British Youths Open and the English Championship.

Turned Professional

Faldo's golf prowess was soon noticed in the United States, where he was given a golf scholarship to the University of Houston. He attended for ten weeks, but he felt the distraction of going to school hurt his golf game. After leaving the school, Faldo then turned professional in 1976 and joined the European Professional Golfers Association.

In the late 1970s and early 1980s, Faldo did decently as a professional. He won his first tournament in 1977, the Skol Lager, and was named rookie of the year for

Chronology

1957	Born July 18 in Welwyn Garden City, England
1971	Took first golf lessons
1976	Attended the University of Houston for ten weeks; turned professional and joined the European Professional Golfers Association
1978	Member of Hennessy Cup team
1979	Member of Ryder Cup Team
1980	Member of Hennessy Cup team
1981	Member of Ryder Cup Team
1982	Member of Hennessy Cup team
1983	Member of Ryder Cup Team
1984	Member and captain of Hennessy Cup team; divorced first wife Melanie Rockall
1985	Member of Ryder Cup team
1985-86	Member of England's Dunhill Cup team
1986	Marries second wife Gill Bennett in January; daughter Natalie Lauren born on September 18
1988	Member of England's Dunhill Cup team
1989	Son Matthew Alexander born on March 17
1990	Hired Fanny Sunesson as his full-time caddy
1991	Member of England's Dunhill Cup team
1991	Member of Ryder Cup team
1993	Member of England's Dunhill Cup team
1993	Daughter Georgia Kate born on March 20
1993	Member of Ryder Cup Team
1996	Divorced from second wife
1999	Split with Sunesson as caddie
2001	Rehired Sunesson as caddie; signs a ten-year deal with Bally Golf; marries third wife, Valerie

Awards and Accomplishments

1975	Wins the British Youths Open and the English Championship
1977	Wins the Skol Lager; named Rookie of the Year on the European PGA Tour
1978, 1980-81, 1989	Wins the British PGA Championship
1983	Finishes on top of the Order of Merit
1987	Wins the British Open
1998	Awarded MBE (Member of the Order of the British Empire) by the Queen of England
1989	Wins the Masters; named BBC Sports Personality of the Year
1990	Wins the British Open and the Masters; wins PGA's Player of the Year Award
1992	Wins the British Open; finished on the top of Order of Merit
1996	Wins the Masters

ready practiced obsessively. This action also improved Faldo's putting game.

The hard work paid off when Faldo came into his own in the late 1980s and early 1990s, winning several majors and becoming the pride of Great Britain. Faldo led a high profile life on the European PGA Tour, but also had a number of run-ins with the press. In 1987, Faldo won his first major, the British Open. He won it at Muirfield in Scotland, shooting a 279 on the tournament and making 18 pars in the final round. He repeated in 1990, when he won by five strokes and shot a 270, and in 1992, with a total of 272. Faldo was also the runner-up in 1993.

Winning the majors in the United States proved harder. Though Faldo won the Volvo Masters in 1988 and was in contention to win the U.S. Open that year as well, he lost in a playoff to Curtis Strange. But in 1989, he won his second major tournament, the Masters, in a sudden death playoff against Scott Hoch. Faldo repeated as Masters champion in 1990 (again in a playoff, this time over Ray Floyd) and in 1996. Faldo won a number of other tournaments in 1989, including the Volvo PGA Championship and the Dunhill British Masters.

In 1990, Faldo was at the top of his game, winning the two majors, as well as the Johnnie Walker Classic. He also finished very high at the U.S. Open. All of his success proved that he could win with the lead as well as from far behind, in both Britain and the United States, and on any kind of surface condition. He also proved himself to be a trailblazer on the greens as well, when he hired a woman, Fanny Sunesson, to be his caddie.

Faldo did not rest on his laurels. Because of the rigors of the golf tour and the possibilities of injury, he began to exercise intensely to increase the muscle mass on his 6'3" body. Though Faldo was playing well, he was never really embraced by Americans—not fans, journalists, nor other players. Despite a problematic image, Faldo supported youth golf initiatives in his country. He built Nick

the European PGA Tour. That year also began his association with the Ryder Cup, a tournament that pitted Americans against Europeans and was played every two years. Faldo was a member of every team from 1977-97, amassing more points in the competition than anyone in history.

Faldo won a number of tournaments in the early 1980s, including the British PGA Championships in 1978, 1980, and 1981, the Haig Tournament Players Championship in 1982, and the French Open and the Martini Invitational in 1983. In 1983 and 1984, he won the Car Care Plan Invitational. While Faldo did well at these tournaments, he failed to win any of the majors (the U.S. Open, the British Open, PGA Championship, and Masters). In 1984, Faldo was leading in the final round of the Masters, but lost on the front nine in the final round. These kind of losses led the British press to dub him "Nicky Fold-0."

Changed His Game to Achieve Success

In the mid-1980s, Faldo decided to take drastic action to make himself a better player. He decided to change his swing, which many observers had considered a pretty, long swing. Faldo believed it was unreliable, and used too much wrist. With the help of coach David Leadbetter, Faldos's swing became more efficient, compact, and tight. To accomplish his goal, he hit 1,500 practice balls a day, a large number for a player who al-

Faldo Golf Centers where children could learn golf for little or no cost, and later funded the Faldo Junior Series to nurture young British golf talent.

Faldo faltered in 1991, winning only the Irish Open that year. He tied for 12th at the Masters, and tied for 16th at U.S. Open, British Open, and PGA Championship. The frustrating year led Faldo to again change. He dropped the physical training, and stopped practicing so much. Faldo also modified his style of play, making his full swing different, reading greens less analytically, and becoming more creative in his shots. He told Jaime Diaz of the *New York Times,* "I had to learn to cope with my game being off. At first it was tremendously frustrating. The breakthrough came when I finally realized that you can't hit the ball as well as you'd like all the time. There is a human element."

The changes worked in the short term. Faldo had what many considered the best year of his career in 1992, winning the British Open, the Scandinavian Masters, Euro Open, and Johnnie Walker World Championship. That year, he became the first player to win more than £1,000,000 in a season, and finished atop the Order of Merit.

Career in Decline

After 1992, however, Faldo's career was in decline. He won two tournaments and was the runner-up at the British Open in 1993, then only won the Alfred Dunhill Open in 1994. In 1995, he decided to leave the European PGA Tour behind, and join the PGA Tour in the States full time. Though Faldo wanted new challenges, the only bright spot of the mid- to late 1990s was a victory at the Masters in 1996. Even this major win was somewhat tainted. Faldo won in part because leader **Greg Norman** played himself out of contention.

Faldo's last PGA win came at the Nissan Open in 1997, the same year he won the WA Open. In 1998, he won the World Cup of Golf, partnered with David Carter. This was the first time England had won. Faldo returned to the European Tour in 1999, with a more restricted swing and an inability to putt or chip well. Though Faldo continued to play on the European Tour and in majors, he began preparing for his life after golf in the late 1990s and early 2000s. He became a commentator with columns in newspapers and magazines and an analyst for television, including The Golf Channel. He also founded a company, Faldo Golf, which was planned to build a course in Moscow, Russia.

Summarizing Faldo's approach to golf, Rick Reilly wrote in *Sports Illustrated,* "That's golf to Faldo—a bicycle to be taken apart, a game to be broken down past wins, past majors, past greatness, past everything, down to the very cogs. Perfect to the tiniest screw, that's Faldo."

CONTACT INFORMATION

Address: Woodcock House, Gibbard Mews, High St. Wimbledon Village, London SW19 5BY England. Email: nfdo@faldodesign.com. Online: www.faldo-golf.com.

SELECTED WRITINGS BY FALDO:

(With Mitchell Platts) *The Rough with the Smooth: Breaking Into Professional Golf,* S. Paul, 1980.

(With Vivien Sanders) *Golf: The Winning Formula,* Lyons & Burford, 1989.

(With Bruce Critchley) *Faldo: In Search of Perfection,* Weindenfeld & Nicholson, 1994.

(With Richard Simmons) *A Swing for Life,* Viking, 1995.

FURTHER INFORMATION

Books

Hickok, Ralph. *A Who's Who of Sports Champions.* Boston: Houghton Mifflin Company, 1995.

Periodicals

Anderson, Dave. "A Mystery: Just Where Is Nick Faldo?" *New York Times,* (June 14, 1998): section 8, p. 6.

Anderson, Dave. "Why Faldo Deserves the Title." *New York Times,* (July 24, 1990): B9.

Ballard, Sarah. "Britannia Rules Again." *Sports Illustrated,* (July 10, 1989): 60.

Blauvelt, Harry. "Faldo in Fine Fettle." *USA Today,* (July 12, 2002): 1C.

Callahan, Tom. "Golf." Think Golf. *Golf Digest,* (February 1999).

Diaz, Jaime. "Faldo Is Doing Things Naturally." *New York Times,* (July 21, 1992): B13.

Diaz, Jaime. "Faldo Uses Dedication To Reach Higher Levels." *New York Times,* (July 24, 1990): B11.

Diaz, Jaime. "Faldo's Revised Style Is Fitting Him to a Tee." *New York Times,* (June 12, 1992): B15.

Diaz, Jaime. "A Methodical Faldo Develops a Plan for Higher Achievement." *New York Times,* (March 15, 1991): A28.

Diaz, Jaime. "Quest for '91 Grand Slam Left Faldo Out in Cold." *New York Times,* (March 12, 1992): B16.

Diaz, Jaime. "Swingtime Hits Jamaica and Faldo Is the Impressio." *New York Times,* (December 17, 1992): B23.

Dorman, Larry. "Faldo Is Back on Tour, Aiming to Reclaim No. 1." *New York Times,* (January 19, 1995): B15.

Dorman, Larry. "A Relaxed Approach by Faldo." *New York Times,* (February 29, 1996): B11.

Farrell, Andy. "Faldo Drives Down Memory Lane to See Reflection of Woods." *The Independent,* (July 16, 2002): 24.

Garrity, John. "The Devil Made Him Do It." *Sports Illustrated,* (April 19, 1999): G44.

Huggan, John. "All New Nick?" *Golf Digest,* (June 2002): 116.

McDonnell, David. "Faldo: It's Fanny-Tastic to Have You Back." *The Mirror,* (July 18, 2001): 42.

Reilly, Rick. "Do You Know Me?" *Sports Illustrated,* (April 8, 1991): 77.

Reilly, Rick. "Very British Open." *Sports Illustrated,* (July 27, 1987): 18.

Shapiro, Leonard. "Faldo Battles Spotlight's Glare." *Washington Post,* (July 21, 1981): D10.

Smith, Shelley. "His Girl Fanny." *Sports Illustrated,* (August 20, 1990): 24.

Swift, E.M. "Jolly Good Show." *Sports Illustrated,* (April 17, 1989): 18.

Swift, E.M. "King of Clubs." *Sports Illustrated,* (July 30, 1990): 34.

Other

"Nick Faldo." PGA European Tour. http://www.european tour.com/players/bio.sps?iPlayerNo=53 (January 13, 2003).

"Nick Faldo—Biographical Information." PGATOUR. com.http://www.golfweb.com/players/00/13/26/bio. html (January 13, 2003).

The Nick Faldo Website. http://members.aol.com/ chrisdicks/faldo.html (January 13, 2003).

Sketch by A. Petruso

Juan Manuel Fangio
1911-1995

Argentine race car driver

Race car enthusiasts around the globe consider Juan Manuel Fangio to be the all-time grand master of the racing world. From 1957 until 2002, Fangio sat alone atop Formula One racing's pedestal as the only driver with five world championships. In 2002, Germany's **Michael Schumacher** tied that record, and while he was likened to Fangio, even Schumacher said no comparison could be drawn.

Undoubtedly, Fangio competed in a different era—an era where a driver's finesse mattered more than the car. Fangio didn't have access to a carefully calculated super machine like today's racers. Instead, Fangio raced primitive machines that moved along about as gracefully as garbage trucks. There were no safety standards—drivers wore polo shirts instead of flameproof overalls, and they weren't secured inside a crash cage. Fangio saw 30 fellow racers die during his ten years in Europe. In Fangio's day, survival was as notable as performance. But Fangio didn't just survive; he won. Over his career, Fangio's technical artistry brought him 78 wins in the 147 races he finished. He also had 24 grand prix victories in 51 starts. Fangio was held in such deep regard that the people in his hometown of Balcarce, Argentina, pooled their money to buy him a car. Later, his races were broadcast throughout the country. For Argentineans, Fangio was a hero whose feats earned their nation international respect.

Developed Childhood Interest in Cars

Juan Manuel Fangio (FAHN-jee-oh) was born June 24, 1911, in Balcarce, Argentina, a town about 220 miles south of Buenos Aires. Fangio was the fourth of six children born to Loreto and Herminia Fangio, both of Italian descent.

As a child, Fangio excelled at boxing and soccer. Because he was bowlegged, Fangio's teammates called him "el chueco" or "bandy legs." The moniker was used affectionately throughout his racing career. By age ten, Fangio was so fascinated with cars that he spent his free time at a local garage volunteering to fetch tools for the mechanics.

At the age of 11, Fangio started up a car on his own for the first time and considered taking it for a spin. He described the moment in a book titled *Fangio,* noting "with my foot on the accelerator, I could call as much as forty horsepower into play. Had I dared I could have driven off and made two tons of metal answer my will."

By 13, Fangio had dropped out of school and was an assistant mechanic at Miguel Viggiano's Studebaker shop. In this way, Fangio learned racing from the inside out—he made friends with the internal combustion engine, learned what made it tick. At the shop, one of Fangio's duties was to deliver customers' cars from Buenos Aires to Balcarce. Driving Argentina's dirt roads, which were particularly treacherous in the rain, Fangio perfected his driving skills. Thus, the teenage Fangio was already learning the intricacy of driving in slippery conditions, a skill he would later become famous for.

Juan Manuel Fangio

Pieced Together Own Race Car

At 16, Fangio took part in his first race, riding as a mechanic in a Plymouth driven by one of Viggiano's customers. Fangio didn't get to the racetrack the following year because he was sick with persistent pneumonia and spent much of the year in bed. He left Balcarce in 1932 to serve his mandatory military duty.

When Fangio returned, he and his brother, Toto, opened their own garage. During the day, Fangio repaired other people's cars. At night, he worked on his own. Finally, in 1936, Fangio made his racing debut driving a modified taxi, basically a six-cylinder Ford engine fastened to a rusty chassis. Fangio's first races took place on Argentina's infamous dirt-road tracks.

"My mother disapproved of my racing at first, but not my father, though he did not encourage me," Fangio recalled in the book about him.

There's no doubt why Fangio's vocation scared his mother. Argentina's primitive dirt tracks-known as killing fields—offered crowds a spine-tingling spectacle at the cost of many lives. The main problem was the dust, so heavy at times the drivers couldn't see.

Excelled in Long-Distance Races

Fangio loved competing in South America's infamous long-distance races. These grueling events were some of the wildest and most dangerous races of all time. Drivers spent days on the course, hoping to avoid Andes Mountain drop-offs and herds of cattle. Fangio first made a name for himself by placing seventh in the 1938 Gran Premio Argentino de Carreteras, a grueling 4,590-mile race.

After this race, the proud people of Balcarce pooled their money to buy Fangio a better car: a six-cylinder Chevy coupe. In 1940, Fangio drove the car to his first noteworthy victory, winning the Gran Premio Internacional del Norte. Fangio spent 109 hours completing the 6,000-mile road race from Buenos Aires, Argentina, to Lima, Peru, and back.

The race lasted nearly two weeks and tested drivers more than their cars, as passing through the Andes Mountains caused many to suffer from altitude sickness. At those altitudes, changing a flat tire could be a life or death situation. As Fangio noted in the book about him: "In the mountains of Peru it is also difficult for the man, for the driver. We ate garlic tablets and chewed coco leaves," because of the high altitude. "You get very tired easily in the thin atmosphere and if you are not careful you get agitated, and you lose your breath."

Fangio drove his way to the Argentine National Championship in both 1940 and 1941. Just as Fangio came into his own, racing ceased in 1942 because World War II caused a fuel shortage.

When racing resumed in 1947, Fangio was ready. In 1948, he made his first trip to Europe to compete, then returned home for the 6,000-mile Gran Premio de la America del Sur. The course was basically a one-lap of South America. Fatigued and plowing through considerable fog, Fangio crashed, killing his faithful friend and co-driver Daniel Urrutia. It was the first of many times Fangio would narrowly escape death, but the experience was not enough to make him quit.

Became Five-Time World Champion

In 1949, Fangio went back to Europe and strengthened his skills. By 1951, he was the world champion. Just as Fangio was making a name for himself, his ca-

Awards and Accomplishments

1940	Placed first at the Gran Premio Internacional del Norte
1940-41	Earned Argentine National Champion title
1941	Won both races he entered, including the Argentine One Thousand Miles
1942	Won four of five races completed
1947	Won three of ten races he completed
1948	Won three of seven races completed
1949	Won nine of fourteen races completed
1950	Won the French, Belgian, and Monaco grand prix, along with the Argentine 500 Miles
1951	Won the French, Swiss, and Spanish grand prix
1951, 1954-57	Won World Championship
1952	Won six of seven races completed before season cut short in crash at Monza, Italy
1953	Won the Italian grand prix
1954	Won the Argentinean, Belgian, German, Italian, French, and Swiss grand prix
1955	Won the Argentinean, Belgian, Italian, and Dutch grand prix
1956	Won the Argentinean, German, and British grand prix, along with the Sebring 12 Hours Race
1957	Won the Argentinean, French, German, and Monaco grand prix, along with the Sebring 12 Hours Race
1958	Won one race in five starts before quitting
1980s	Had a race car museum and racetrack in his hometown named for him

reer almost ended again. In June 1952, Fangio pulled an all-nighter driving from Paris to Monza, Italy, for a race. He arrived not long before the start and had no time for a practice run. Miscalculating a curve while trying to pass, Fangio crunched his car and broke a neck bone, shutting him out for the rest of the season.

Fangio was back in full form in 1954, winning six grand prix races. Once again, he was the world champion, repeating through 1957.

Throughout the 1950s, Fangio dominated the sport. Clearly, he possessed the greatest innate driving ability of his time—perhaps of all time. Fangio could sustain a four-wheel, controlled slide around a curve without breaking a sweat. Friends used to joke that he had distilled water instead of blood in his veins. Because of his ability, Fangio was courted by many teams and throughout the 1950s drove for Alfa Romeo, Mercedes-Benz, Ferrari, and Maserati.

Fangio was 46 when the 1958 season began. From the start, nothing seemed to go right. On February 23, 1958, while Fangio was waiting to race in Havana, Cuba, he was kidnapped by Fidel Castro rebels. The kidnapping was mostly a publicity stunt meant to humiliate the Batista regime then in power. In the end, Fangio was released unharmed. The kidnapping, however, illustrates the notoriety Fangio had achieved.

Fangio also had trouble with his car. Deciding too many things were going wrong, Fangio retired in the middle of the season. He returned home to Balcarce and opened a Mercedes dealership.

Fangio

In 1971, more than ten years after he retired from motor racing—and when he was into his 60s—Fangio got behind the wheel again to shoot segments for a feature length film biography titled simply, *Fangio.*

The film contains original footage of Fangio's racing career, giving those who never saw the master race a firsthand view of his innate and unmatched driving ability. Clips for some of Fangio's races, however, could not be located. To fill in the blanks, re-enactments were filmed with Fangio driving his original cars at such circuits as Monaco; Italy's Monza; France's Reims; and England's Silverstone.

Fangio, himself, narrates the film, which is directed by Hugh Hudson, who is best known for his 2000 feature film *I Dreamed of Africa,* starring Kim Basinger.

Still shots from the movie were made into a book, also titled *Fangio* and published in 1973. In the book, Fangio's narration accompanies the pictures, giving the reader a true glimpse of the man behind the wheel as he tells his story in his own words.

Soon after ending his racing career, Fangio also ended his relationship. Throughout his race life, he'd had a companion, Andreina "Bebe" Espinosa, who waited in the pits while he raced. They parted in 1960, after 20 years together. They had no children.

Remains Legend in Own Right

Fangio spent his remaining years as an ambassador for the sport. He also coached young drivers. He died of kidney failure on July 17, 1995, at a Buenos Aires hospital. Fangio is so vividly remembered because he did what no driver had ever done before—he elevated motor racing to an art form. Much as a painter caresses a paintbrush, Fangio caressed his cars—and the outcome was beautiful.

The mystique surrounding Fangio continues today. What make him all the more legendary is the fact that he can't be compared to today's drivers because the equipment and tracks are so incomparable. All that is left is to dream about what the calm, collected Fangio could have done with today's machines.

SELECTED WRITINGS BY FANGIO:

Jenkinson, Denis, ed. *Fangio.* New York: W. W. Norton Inc., 1973.

FURTHER INFORMATION

Books

Jenkinson, Denis, ed. *Fangio.* New York: W. W. Norton Inc., 1973.

Periodicals

"Fangio: Greatest Driver of Them All." (Glasgow) *Herald* (July 18, 1995): 30.

"Juan Manuel Fangio." *Times* (July 18, 1995).

Levine, Leo. "Juan Manuel Fangio 1911-1995." *Road & Track* (October 1995): 143-46.

McCluggage, Denise. "Juan Manuel Fangio 1911-1995." *Autoweek* (July 24, 1995): 51.

Siano, Joseph. "Juan Manuel Fangio, 84, Racer Who Captured 5 World Titles." *New York Times* (July 18, 1995): B6.

Williams, Richard. "Best and Bravest Racer of Them All." *(London) Guardian* (July 18, 1995): 12.

Other

"Fangio Incomparable, Says Champion." BBC Sport. http://news.bbc.co.uk/sport1/hi/motorsports/formula_one/2142672.stm (November 19, 2002).

"Juan Manuel Fangio Statistic Page." Yardley-McLaren Grand Prix Formula 1 Team. http://www.pinasx.com/drivers/fangio/statistic/html (November 18, 2002).

Sketch by Lisa Frick

Marshall Faulk

Marshall Faulk
1973-

American football player

St. Louis Rams running back Marshall Faulk is speedy, powerful, and elusive, making him a nearly unstoppable scoring machine. Faulk can catch passes, rush for yardage, block, and evade tackles. He's a complete package—and, as *Football Digest* noted, the most complete all-around player in the NFL today. When Faulk has the ball, he flattens opponents like a bulldozer, or dashes past defenders like a bullet train. With his skills, Faulk pours on the points. In 2000, he set a new NFL record for most touchdowns in a season (26). He's also the only player in NFL history to produce four straight 2,000-yard seasons (1998-2001). There's just no telling what he'll be able to accomplish over the long haul. As **O.J. Simpson** told *Sports Illustrated,* "You don't exaggerate when you say a guy like that comes along once in a lifetime."

Raised in New Orleans

Born February 26, 1973, in New Orleans, Marshall William Faulk grew up in one of the city's rough-and-tumble housing projects, where sirens and broken windows prevailed. His mother, Cecile, stayed busy raising six sons and working odd jobs, while his father, Roosevelt, owned a restaurant and bar. He also worked part-time for a trucking company.

Faulk's childhood was filled with struggles. He moved through a number of elementary schools, his parents divorced, and he spent part of high school living on his own because his mother was sick. Yet Faulk never complained about the hardships—and he doesn't like it when people treat his success like a rags to riches story.

Faulk expressed his thoughts this way in an issue of *USA Today,* "This whole upbringing thing that people want to make my story, I don't want it. At least not the story that they want to make it. . . . I don't want my story to be something that it's not. Sure, I grew up rough, but my upbringing was like millions of other kids from the projects."

At New Orleans's George Washington Carver High, Faulk unleashed his smorgasbord of talents, helping the offense by playing quarterback, running back, tight end, wide receiver, and flanker. He was also a solid defensive back.

Despite his success, Faulk almost quit the sport. Early on in high school, Faulk told coach Wayne Reese that he needed to quit the football team so he could work at his brother's barbecue stand because the family needed money. Reese, however, had already pegged Faulk as a potential NFL star. He counseled Faulk about his future, persuading him to work through the current tough times and look toward the future. To help Faulk earn money, Reese secured a janitorial job for him at the school. Faulk's teenage years were marked by long school days—he arrived early in the morning to work, then stayed afterward for football practice.

<table>
<tr><td colspan="2">

Chronology

</td></tr>
<tr><td>1973</td><td>Born February 26 in New Orleans</td></tr>
<tr><td>1991</td><td>Joins San Diego State Aztecs</td></tr>
<tr><td>1994</td><td>Chosen by Indianapolis Colts as second overall draft pick</td></tr>
<tr><td>1995</td><td>Becomes father to Marshall William Faulk, Jr.</td></tr>
<tr><td>1999</td><td>Traded to St. Louis Rams</td></tr>
<tr><td>2000</td><td>Helps deliver Rams a Super Bowl victory</td></tr>
</table>

Energized San Diego State Football Program

During his final two years at Carver High, Faulk rushed 1,800 yards and scored thirty-two touchdowns. Because Faulk played for a mediocre high school team, his talents weren't widely recognized. Some college powerhouses, nonetheless, came knocking. The only problem was, the colleges wanted to recruit Faulk to play defensive back. After all, during his senior year at Carver, while playing cornerback, Faulk snagged eleven interceptions, returning six for touchdowns. Faulk, however, yearned to play offense.

"I didn't love playing cornerback, so I knew I wouldn't be as successful in that position," Faulk told *Sports Illustrated for Kids*. "You have to really love what you do to be a star."

Finally, San Diego State offered Faulk the chance to play running back, and he jumped at the opportunity. Faulk joined the San Diego State Aztecs during the fall of 1991. During the second game of the season, the starting running back left the game after an injury. Faulk took over. He rushed for 386 yards on thirty-seven carries—an NCAA Division I-A single game rushing record—to score seven touchdowns. The record, however, was broken before the end of the season.

Faulk got off to a tremendous start, but things went downhill. In the sixth game of the season, he collapsed a lung and fractured two ribs. The injuries forced Faulk out of the next three games. Despite his shortened season, Faulk still ended up with 1,429 rushing yards for the year. He averaged 158.8 yards per game, an NCAA freshman-record average. He was named an Associated Press first-team All-American—only the third freshman to receive the honor.

Faulk's energizing presence on the field helped boost the status of the San Diego State football program. The number of season ticket holders skyrocketed, and networks began broadcasting their games, boosting the athletic department's funds.

His sophomore year, Faulk won his second NCAA rushing title, becoming only the fifth player to win back-to-back NCAA rushing titles. That season, he also came out of his shell as a skilled receiver, catching eighteen passes for 128 yards.

Riding a huge wave of success, Faulk decided to forgo his senior season and enter the NFL draft. Though

<table>
<tr><td>

Related Biography: Football Player Darnay Scott

Just as Marshall Faulk's career bloomed at San Diego State, so did his friendship with the team's wide receiver, Darnay Scott. Scott, born July 7, 1972, in St. Louis, grew up in a St. Louis housing project, then moved to San Diego in 1988 to live with his aunt and uncle.

Since Faulk and Scott grew up under similar conditions, they just clicked—and brought out the best in each of them both on the field and off. When the two offensive players weren't out on the field, they were standing on the sideline squirting water on each other.

San Diego coach Curtis Johnson noted their friendship in a *Washington Post* article, saying, "It's always something with those two kids. They're from similar backgrounds and this is the first time they've gotten a taste of being a child. They went to see the movie 'Candyman,' and they talked about how scared they were. I've seen them get in a big argument—I mean crying mad—over Nintendo."

After college, the 6-foot-1-inch, 204-pound Scott was selected by the Cincinnati Bengals in the 1994 draft. In 2002, he joined the Dallas Cowboys.

</td></tr>
</table>

he had only played three seasons with the Aztecs, he owned the school's records for rushing touchdowns (57) and rushing yards (4,589).

Drafted by Indianapolis Colts

During the 1994 NFL draft, the Indianapolis Colts snagged Faulk as the draft's second overall pick. His contract, worth about $17 million, including a $5.1 million signing bonus was the largest ever earned by a rookie up to that point.

The Colts got their money's worth. His rookie season, 1994, Faulk rushed for 1,282 yards and scored twelve touchdowns to be named the Associated Press Offensive Rookie of the Year. He also played in the Pro Bowl (the only rookie) and rushed for 180 yards in the game, breaking Simpson's 22-year-old Pro Bowl record. Naturally, Faulk was named the game's MVP. Faulk achieved those numbers despite having wrecked his car on a slick street prior to the game. He hitched a ride to the stadium and arrived ten minutes before kickoff, completely unnerved.

During 1994, Faulk provided the spark that propelled the Colts to a winning record of 8-8. The team had gone 4-12 the previous year. Injuries slowed Faulk the next few seasons, particularly a broken big toe. In 1998, however, Faulk was dazzlingly successful as he gained a total of 2,227 yards (1,319 rushing, and 908 receiving), the sixth-best total in NFL history.

Delivered Rams to the Super Bowl

Before the start of the next season, the Colts traded Faulk to the St. Louis Rams, then the laughingstock of the NFL. But with Faulk in the lineup, the Rams' offense came alive. That season, Faulk gained more than 1,000 yards rushing and more than 1,000 yards receiving, making him the second player in NFL history to complete that feat. The 2,429 yards (1,381 rushing and 1,048 receiving) set a new NFL single-season record for

Career Statistics

Yr	Team	Rushing				Receiving				Fumbles	
		ATT	YDS	AVG	TD	REC	YDS	AVG	TD	FUM	LST
1994	IND	314	1282	4.1	11	52	522	10.0	1	5	3
1995	IND	289	1078	3.7	11	56	475	8.5	3	8	5
1996	IND	198	587	3.0	7	56	428	7.6	0	2	2
1997	IND	264	1054	4.0	7	47	471	10.0	1	5	3
1998	IND	324	1319	4.1	6	86	908	10.6	4	3	2
1999	STL	253	1381	5.5	7	87	1048	12.0	5	2	2
2000	STL	253	1359	5.4	18	81	830	10.2	8	0	0
2001	STL	260	1382	5.3	12	83	765	9.2	9	3	3
2002	STL	212	953	4.5	8	80	537	6.7	2	4	3
TOTAL		2367	10395	4.4	87	628	5984	9.5	33	32	23

IND: Indianapolis Colts; STL: St. Louis Rams.

most yards from scrimmage. More important, Faulk delivered the Rams to the Super Bowl. In the game, Faulk pulled down five passes to gain ninety yards as the Rams defeated the Tennessee Titans 23-16.

During the 2000 season, Faulk continued his torrid pace. He scored twenty-six touchdowns to set a new NFL record for most touchdowns in a season, bettering **Emmitt Smith**'s 1995 mark by one. He also led the NFC with most yards combined (1,359 rushing and 830 passing).

Faulk continues to wrack up the stats because he is so fast. "What sets him apart from everybody else is that he can go from a standing start to full speed faster than anybody I've ever seen," Colts coach Ted Marchibroda told *Sports Illustrated*. "When he runs the ball and is forced to hesitate, his next step is full speed."

While Faulk's future abilities remain uncertain, it is pretty certain he will remain a Ram for the rest of his pro career. In July 2002, Faulk signed a seven-year, $44 million deal with the club.

Faulk spends the off-season in Fort Lauderdale, Florida, and his free time with his son, Marshall William Faulk, Jr., born in 1995, to Faulk and his girlfriend Candace Patton. He calls the boy Deucie.

Over the years, Faulk hasn't forgotten the people he left behind. He purchased uniforms for Carver High's sports teams and also has given money for the school's training equipment. Faulk also donated a quarter-million dollars so San Diego State could upgrade its football offices. In addition, the Marshall Faulk Foundation raises money for inner-city children in New Orleans and St. Louis.

Called 'Best Weapon' in NFL

Faulk remains an engaging player because his skills run across the board. In his first nine seasons in the NFL, he rushed for more than 1,000 yards all but two seasons. Besides rushing, Faulk has made a mark catching passes. During his first nine seasons, he pulled down 628 passes for 5,984 yards, or an average of 9.5 per catch. Moreover, Faulk has sticky hands—when he has the ball, he's unlikely to drop it. In his first nine seasons, Faulk handled the ball 2,995 times rushing and receiving passes, yet fumbled it only thirty-two times.

Because he is a threat as both a rusher and a receiver, the 5-foot-10, 211-pound Faulk keeps his opponents on guard. "It's just a guessing game of where he's going," the Atlanta Falcons' Patrick Kerney told *Sports Illustrated for Kids*. "He's the best weapon in the NFL right now."

The NFL's best weapon will be on the gridiron for years to come, and there's just no telling what kind of legacy he'll leave behind.

CONTACT INFORMATION

Address: c/o St. Louis Rams, Dome at America's Center, St. Louis, Mo., 63101. Phone: (314) 425-8830. Online: www.stlouisrams.com.

FURTHER INFORMATION

Periodicals

Berkowitz, Steve. "Carrying the Pressure, Faulk Rushes On." *Washington Post* (October 28, 1992).

Bradley, John Ed. "Babying Himself." *Sports Illustrated* (July 24, 1995): 106.

Cosgrove, Ellen. "Marshall's Man." *Sports Illustrated for Kids* (February 2001): 25.

"Faulk First to Four Straight." *Jet* (January 21, 2002): 52.

Saraceno, Jon. "Sorry, Mom, Marshall's Busy." *USA Today* (February 1, 2002).

Silver, Michael. "Star of Stars." *Sports Illustrated* (September 3, 2001): 106.

Thomas, Jim. "Faulk Signs 7-Year Contract; New Deal Means he Could Finish Career With Rams." *St. Louis Post-Dispatch* (July 30, 2002).

Wilner, Barry. "The Perfect Man." *Football Digest* (April 2001): 30.

Awards and Accomplishments

1991	United Press International Freshman of the Year
1991-93	Associated Press first-team All-America at San Diego State; named to *Sporting News* first-team All-America
1994	Associated Press Offensive Rookie of the Year, *Football Digest*'s Rookie of the Year, and *Sporting News* NFL Rookie of the Year; also named Outstanding Player of the Pro Bowl for the 1994 season
1995	Set new Pro Bowl rushing record at 180 yards and was named Pro Bowl Most Valuable Player
1999-2001	Associated Press NFL Offensive Player of the Year three consecutive seasons
2000	Won Super Bowl ring as member of St. Louis Rams
2000	Ran for 26 touchdowns to set a new NFL single-season record; led NFC with 2,189 combined yards (1,359 rushing and 830 passing)
2000	Named *Football Digest*'s Player of the Year, *Sporting News* Sportsman of the Year (shared with Kurt Warner); and the league's Most Valuable Player
2000-01	Named NFL Player of the Year by *Sporting News*

Other

"Darnay Scott." ESPN.com. http://sports.espn.go.com/ nfl/players/profile?statsId=2761 (January 8, 2003).

"Marshall Faulk." ESPN.com. http://sports.espn.go. com/nfl/players/stats?statsID=2728 (January 6, 2003).

Sketch by Lisa Frick

Brett Favre
1969-

American football player

Quarterback Brett Favre, whose name rhymes with "carve," is a three-time winner of the NFL Most Valuable Player Award (1995, 1996, and 1997). Twice he led the Green Packers to the Super Bowl, winning the big game in 1997. Favre came from nowhere to become one of the game's greatest quarterbacks.

"Rawboned Brute Strength"

Favre grew up in Kiln, Mississippi, where his father Irvin was the local high school football and baseball coach and his mother was a special education teacher. He had two brothers and a sister, and his aunt, grandmothers, and other relatives lived nearby. Favre and both his brothers took turns quarterbacking their high school football team, but Brett was the best. Irvin Favre told William Plummer in *People,* "He was rawboned brute strength, plus he was smart." In an article in *Sports Illustrated,* Favre told Leigh Montville that most people as-

Brett Favre

sume he inherited his throwing ability from his father, but joked, "Now I think I got it from my mother. She got mad at me last summer and threw a pastrami sandwich and hit me in the head. Hard. She really had something on that sandwich."

Kiln is a small town in a rural area, and Favre was completely unnoticed by college recruiters. In 1987, after being rejected from many other schools, he finally got a scholarship to the University of Southern Mississippi as a defensive back only because another player decided not to take it. Favre initially played both that position and quarterback, but he was the seventh quarterback on the depth chart for the team. By the time his freshman year started, he had worked his way up to number three. By the second half of the second game, Favre threw two touchdown passes, helping Southern Mississippi beat Tulane. Shortly after that he was the starter. Favre noted that like him, most of his teammates had been rejected by bigger, better-known schools with stronger football teams. "We thrived on that," he explained to Montville. "We'd play Alabama, Auburn, and there'd be stories in the papers about how we'd been rejected by them. We'd come out and win the game."

Favre's longtime girlfriend, Deanna Tynes, became pregnant during his sophomore year, but they did not marry. Favre recalls that he was not ready. However, the couple remained together, and raised their daughter, Brittany.

Chronology

1969	Born in Gulfport, Mississippi
1987-90	Played football at University of Southern Mississippi
1988	Favre's girlfriend Deanna Tynes gives birth to their first child, Brittany
1991	Drafted by Atlanta Falcons
1992	Traded to Green Bay Packers
1995	Packers lose NFC Championship Game
1995	Spends 45 days in rehabilitation for drug addiction
1995	Marries Tynes
1997	Packers win Super Bowl
1998	Packers are defeated in Super Bowl by Denver Broncos
1999	Second daughter, Breleigh, is born

Awards and Accomplishments

1992-93, 1995-97	Pro Bowl player
1995-97	NFL MVP
1997	Packers win Super Bowl against New England Patriots

By the end of Favre's junior year, the team had altered its offense to make the best use of his abilities. Pro scouts began to take notice. During the summer before his senior year, he was injured in a car accident that required him to have 30 inches of his intestine removed. But five weeks after that surgery, he led his team to a 27-24 win over Alabama; the team finished the 1990 season at 8-4. Favre played in the Senior Bowl and the East-West Shrine game. At the Shrine game, Jets scout Ron Wolf noticed him, but the Atlanta Falcons drafted Favre before New York could. The Falcons gave Favre a three-year contract worth $1.2 million in 1991.

"I Just Really Liked Him"

Wolf, however, did not forget Favre, and on February 10 of 1992, when he had a new job as the Green Bay Packers' general manager, he acquired Favre for the Packers. The young quarterback had thrown only five passes all season, and was on the Falcons' third string signal caller, so Wolf's decision seemed questionable, but he recalled to Montville, "I just really liked him. He has that unexplainable something about him."

Favre's ascent with the Packers was aided by the fact that their starting quarterback, Don Majkowski, was benched with sprained ankle ligaments. Favre stepped in, won two games, and never stepped out. He finished the 1992 season with 302 completions for 3,227 yards and 18 touchdowns. The Packers missed the playoffs only in the final week of the season. That year, Favre was selected for the Pro Bowl, and the Packers redesigned the team around him. In 1993, Montville wrote, "The Packers have virtually handed their team to Favre." The team got rid of Majkowski, who was considered a hot prospect before Favre's arrival, and paid a large amount of money to bring in free agent **Reggie White**. Montville commented, "They are making a run for a division title, making it with a kid quarterback."

Despite his talent, Favre sometimes clashed with Green Bay coach **Mike Holmgren**, who insisted that Favre study plays and run them as they were planned. Favre, on the other hand, was used to a more intuitive

style of play. In *Sports Illustrated,* Peter King commented, "Favre is an act-first, think-later gunslinger who, until he reached the NFL in 1991, hadn't run something as elementary as the seven-on-seven passing drill." Favre, on the other hand, did not like memorizing complicated plays because in real life, the opposing players seldom did what they were expected to do. Favre gave King an example: "We'd call Red Right, 22 Z In. I didn't care what the defense did, I was going to the Z [the flanker] and if he was covered, boom, I was gone. I was running, trying to make something happen." Eventually, however, the two men were able to learn from each other and by 1995 Holmgren was seeking Favre's opinion on plays. Favre memorized Holmgren's advice: "Relax. Play smart."

In 1995, Favre was named NFL MVP, largely because he led the Packers to an 11-5 record and a spot in the NFC Championship Game. The Packers lost that game to the Dallas Cowboys, 38-27, but Favre swore he would do his best to bring the team back to the Super Bowl in the following season—and win it.

"Is My Daddy Going to Die?"

However, during the 1995 season he had become addicted to the painkiller Vicodin, a narcotic. Tynes told Ken Fuson in *Esquire* that in late 1995 she was cleaning out the closet and "found a bunch of little packs kind of rolled up in there. A week later, they'd be gone. I'd think, Jeez, that's a lot of pain pills." She asked Favre about it, and "he got real defensive." The drug let Favre keep playing through numerous injuries, but it changed his personality, making him anxious, angry, and unable to sleep. Tynes started throwing out the drugs when she found them, but Favre always had more, and she eventually threatened to leave him if he didn't stop. "Everybody thinks Brett's so tough," she revealed to Fuson, "but they haven't met me yet."

In February of 1996, Favre suffered a seizure, brought on by the drugs. His seven-year-old daughter Brittany, seeing this, asked, "Is my daddy going to die?" Three months later Favre admitted he had a problem and entered an inpatient rehabilitation clinic for 45 days. As part of his treatment plan, NFL doctors told him he couldn't drink alcohol for two years after he was released. On July 14, 16 days after he left the rehab clinic, he married Tynes in Green Bay.

In the 1996 season, the Packers went 13-3 and, true to Favre's 1995 prophecy, won the 1997 Super Bowl

Career Statistics

		Passing								Rushing		
Yr	Team	ATT	COM	YDS	COM%	TD	INT	SK	RAT	ATT	YDS	TD
1991	ATL	5	0	0	0.0	0	2	1	0.0	0	0	0
1992	GB	471	302	3227	64.1	18	13	34	85.3	47	198	1
1993	GB	522	318	3303	60.9	19	24	30	72.2	58	216	1
1994	GB	582	363	3882	62.4	33	14	31	90.7	42	202	2
1995	GB	570	359	4413	63.0	38	13	33	99.5	39	181	3
1996	GB	543	325	3899	59.9	39	13	40	95.8	49	136	2
1997	GB	613	304	3867	59.3	35	16	25	92.6	58	187	1
1998	GB	551	347	4212	63.0	31	23	38	87.8	40	133	1
1999	GB	595	341	4091	57.3	22	23	35	74.7	28	142	0
2000	GB	580	338	3812	58.3	20	16	33	78.0	27	108	0
2001	GB	510	314	3921	61.6	32	15	22	94.1	38	56	1
2002	GB	551	341	3658	61.9	27	16	26	85.6	25	73	0
TOTAL		5993	3652	42285	60.9	314	188	348	86.7	451	1632	12

ATL: Atlanta Falcons; GB: Green Bay Packers.

against the New England Patriots. In 1997, they again went 13-3 and made it to the 1998 Super Bowl, but lost to the Denver Broncos, 31-24. In January of 1999, the Packers, having had another excellent season, tried for another Super Bowl appearance, but lost to the San Francisco 49ers in a wildcard game in the playoffs.

After the Super Bowl years, Favre seemed to slow down. Paul Attner wrote in the *Sporting News,* "The more he altered his personal habits by shedding an addiction to painkillers, swearing off beer, dropping out of the fast lane, marrying his longtime girlfriend, fathering a second child, the less impressive he has been as a quarterback." In 1999, Green Bay had only an 8-8 record, which led the team to fire its new coach, Ray Rhodes. That year, Favre had 22 touchdowns and 23 interceptions, showing a decline in his performance. Part of this was due to a thumb injury that prevented him from throwing well. "And," Attner wrote, "the losses piled up until the Packers became average, and their quarterback didn't play well enough to make the Pro Bowl, one of the most astonishing developments of the 1999 season."

"The Most Important Thing"

Favre, however, was busy off the field. His second daughter, Breleigh, had been born in July of 1999, after in-vitro fertilization and a very difficult pregnancy for Deanna. He told Attner, "I want to be there, I want to be the first person she sees when she wakes up and the last person she sees when she goes to sleep. I think it happens to a lot of men. No matter how tough you are or how big you are, when you have a little girl it tames you." He said that he regretted not being a better father when Brittany was young. "I realize that my family is the most important thing."

Perhaps because of this change in focus, or because he suffered from tendinitis of his right elbow, in the 2000 season, Favre had only 20 touchdown passes and had 16 interceptions. As Devid Elfin pointed out in the *Washington Times,* "He didn't get an MVP vote, let alone win the award."

In 2001, Favre returned to his former level of play with his best season since 1997. In the regular season, he threw 32 touchdowns, more than in any season since he won the 1997 MVP award; and had only 15 interceptions, his fewest since 1997. He was rated the fourth-best passer in the NFL with a rating of 94.1.

In 2002, Favre continued to play well, but began considering retirement. "I miss home [in Hattiesburg, Mississippi]," he told Peter King in *Sports Illustrated.* However, if he continued playing, King noted, he could break every quarterback record on the books. Favre told King, "Shoot, if I thought like that, I'd be playing for the wrong reason."

CONTACT INFORMATION

Address: c/o Green Bay Packers, P.O. Box 10628, Green Bay, WI 54307-0628. Phone: 920-496-5700. Online: www.packers.com.

SELECTED WRITINGS BY FAVRE:

(With Marc Serota) *Favre: Most Valuable Player,* Triumph Books, 1999.

FURTHER INFORMATION

Periodicals

Attner, Paul. "A Wiser Brett Favre-Really." *Sporting News,* July 24, 2000: 10.

"Barry Sanders and Brett Favre Tie for NFL's MVP Award." *Jet.* January 19, 1998: 46.

Der, Bob. "Guts and Glory," *Sports Illustrated for Kids.* September, 1997: 46.

Elfin, David. "Favre-Ite Son." *Washington Times,* August 15, 2000: 1.

Fuson, Ken. "Guts and Glory." *Esquire,* October, 1996: 92.

"Grading the 2001 Packers: The Offense." *Green Bay Press-Gazette,* January 27, 2002: C6.

King, Peter. "Inside the NFL." *Sports Illustrated,* September 9, 2002: 70.

King, Peter. "Warmed Up." *Sports Illustrated,* January 27, 1997: 70.

Montville, Leigh. "Leader of the Pack." *Sports Illustrated,* August 23, 1993: 20.

Plummer, William. "Beating the Blitz." *People,* October 28, 1996: 129.

Other

"Brett Favre," ESPN.com. http://sports.espn.go.com/ (January 2, 2003).

"Mike Holmgren," Packers.com. http://www.packers.com (January 5, 2003).

Sketch by Kelly Winters

Sergei Fedorov
1969-

Russian hockey player

The first Russian player to win the National Hockey League's (NHL) Hart Trophy as Most Valuable Player in 1994, Sergei Fedorov exemplifies the growing presence of European players in one of North America's favorite sports. In doing so he helped the Detroit Red Wings shake off a decades-long slump to return to Stanley Cup championship viability. The team won back-to-back victories in 1997 and 1998 in significant part due to Fedorov's efforts. After prolonged contract talks

Sergei Fedorov

sparked a bidding war for his services in 1998, Fedorov renewed his contract with the Red Wings, who won another Stanley Cup in 2002. A popular figure off the ice for his extensive philanthropic efforts, Fedorov has also attracted considerable tabloid attention for his relationship with professional tennis player **Anna Kournikova**.

Plays for Soviet Army Team

Sergei Fedorov was born on December 13, 1969, in the city of Pskov in the western Soviet Union near the border with Estonia, which was under Soviet occupation at that time. His father, Viktor Alexandrovich Fedorov, worked as a hockey and soccer coach and moved the family to Apatity, a city in the extreme northwest of the Soviet Union near the border with Finland, when his son was nine years old. In the near-Arctic climate, Fedorov could practice his hockey skills under his father's guidance for most of the year. The youngster became an excellent skater with speed and agility and also learned how to handle the puck well. By the time he reached his teens, Fedorov was asked to join the elite squad of the Central Red Army hockey team.

Joining the team meant that Fedorov had to move to Moscow, but his love of hockey outweighed any hesitation to leave home. A standout player from the start, Fedorov helped the Soviet national team win the Silver Medal at the World Junior Hockey Championships in 1988 and take the Gold Medal at the senior-level World

```
Chronology

1969      Born December 13 in Pskov, Soviet Union
1985      Plays for Soviet Central Red Army hockey team
1990      Defects from Soviet Union to the United States; begins playing
          for Detroit Red Wings
1994      Wins Hart Trophy as most valuable player in NHL and Frank J.
          Selke Trophy as Best Defensive Forward in NHL
1995      Wins Frank J. Selke Trophy as Best Defensive Forward in NHL
1997-98   Detroit Red Wings win two consecutive Stanley Cup
          championships
2002      Detroit Red Wings win Stanley Cup
```

```
Awards and Accomplishments

1988       Silver Medal, World Junior Hockey Championships (Russia)
1989-90    Gold Medal, World Hockey Championships (Russia)
1994       Hart Trophy as most valuable player in NHL
1994       Lester B. Pearson Award as player of the year, National Hockey
           League Players Association
1994-95    Frank J. Selke Trophy as Best Defensive Forward in NHL
1997-98,   Stanley Cup as NHL champion (Detroit Red Wings)
2002
1998       Olympic Silver Medal in hockey (Russia)
2002       Olympic Bronze Medal in hockey(Russia)
```

Hockey Championships the following year. In 1989 and 1990 the Soviet Red Army team played a series of exhibition games in North America coordinated by the NHL. The series brought Fedorov to the attention of many NHL scouts and players and the Detroit Red Wings selected the young Soviet player in the fourth round of the 1989 draft. Unfortunately, Soviet officials refused to allow Fedorov or any other player to leave the country freely. At that time NHL players were ineligible to play on Olympic teams; thus, if top-level players left the Soviet Union to play in the NHL, the country's future medal-winning chances would be dimmed.

Intriguing Start to NHL Career

The Soviet national team repeated as world champions in 1990 and traveled to Portland, Oregon for the international Goodwill Games in July of that year. Just before a team dinner on July 22, 1990, Fedorov slipped away from the hotel where the Soviets were staying and jumped on an airplane headed to Detroit. The Red Wings immediately announced on his behalf that Fedorov had defected; the event touched off a storm of protests by Soviet officials, who threatened to boycott an upcoming series of exhibition games unless a large payment were delivered to them by the Red Wings. The team complied and Fedorov was free to begin his NHL career.

Only a handful of European players had made a significant impact on the NHL's ranks, in part because of the more physical style of play practiced on the smaller ice rinks of North America. Fedorov adapted immediately to the new style and he worked to overcome language and cultural barriers by taking intensive English lessons. At the end of the 1990-91 season Fedorov had the most points of any rookie player with thirty-one goals and forty-eight assists. He narrowly missed being named NHL Rookie of the Year, an honor that went to goaltender **Ed Belfour.**

Fedorov slowly improved on his numbers the following two seasons; the 1993-94 season, in contrast, represented a major step forward for the six-foot, one-inch, two-hundred-pound center. Finishing the season with fifty-six goals and sixty-four assists, Fedorov won the Hart Trophy as Most Valuable Player and the Frank J. Selke Trophy as Best Defensive Forward. He also re-

ceived the Lester B. Pearson Award as Player of the Year from the NHL Players Association.

Renews Contract with Red Wings in 1998

Although the Red Wings had drafted Fedorov and a few other Russians in the hope that they would immediately lead the team to its first Stanley Cup victory since 1955, it was several years before the team achieved that goal. Under Coach **Scotty Bowman,** who sometimes clashed with Fedorov over his erratic playing, the Red Wings finally returned to championship status with a sweep in the 1997 Stanley Cup finals over the Philadelphia Flyers. Just months later, however, Fedorov refused to report to the team's training camp in a salary dispute. Both sides dug their heels in and contract talks dragged out for several months, causing Fedorov to miss most of the 1997-98 season. After the Carolina Hurricanes weighed in with a $38 million offer, the Red Wings finally caved in to Fedorov's demands and met that figure with a six-year contract. After rejoining the team, Fedorov helped the Red Wings win another Stanley Cup victory, this time over the Washington Capitals.

Some Red Wings fans were angered by Fedorov's stubborn negotiating stance; others were titallated by rumors of his romance with teenage tennis star Anna Kournikova. Widely reported to be dating in 1997, when she was sixteen years old, the two were reported to be engaged in 2001. Both Fedorov and Kournikova refused to discuss the matter in public. He received more positive attention for his announcement in 1999 that he would donate his entire salary that year to establish the Sergei Fedorov Foundation, an organization devoted to helping disadvantaged children in the Detroit area and in Russia. The first Fedorov Scholarships were awarded in December 1999. Fedorov also helped to transport medical and sports supplies to Moscow-area children.

Now settled into a multi-year contract with the Red Wings, Fedorov helped the team return to another Stanley Cup victory over the Carolina Hurricanes in 2002. With three championships in six years, the success of the Red Wings dispelled once and for all the notion that European players could not adapt successfully to the

Career Statistics

Yr	Team	GP	G	AST	PTS	PIM
1990-91	Red Wings	77	31	48	79	66
1991-92	Red Wings	80	32	54	86	72
1992-93	Red Wings	73	34	53	87	72
1993-94	Red Wings	82	56	64	120	34
1994-95	Red Wings	42	20	30	50	24
1995-96	Red Wings	78	39	68	107	48
1996-97	Red Wings	74	30	33	63	30
1997-98	Red Wings	21	6	11	17	25
1998-99	Red Wings	77	26	37	63	66
1999-00	Red Wings	68	27	35	62	22
2000-01	Red Wings	75	32	37	69	40
2001-02	Red Wings	53	15	25	40	20
TOTAL		800	348	495	843	519

Red Wings: Detroit Red Wings (NHL).

ranks of the NHL. Although he brought his father to live in the United States, Fedorov retained many ties to his homeland. After the eligibility rules were changed, he played on two medal-winning Russian hockey teams in the 1998 and 2002 Olympic Games. After the controversy over his 1998 contract dispute, Fedorov regained his status as one of the sport's most popular players, in part because of his thoughtfulness off the ice. As he described his career to David Brennan in an interview for the *Institute for International Sport* in 2001, "You've got to have fun. It's part of the way I've been brought up. I think it's fun. I never thought I'd be a professional hockey player. I didn't even care. Because I did not know, first of all, anything about that. Second of all, I just love the sport. I have been fortunate and lucky enough to work with good coaches, great teammates, and I've been fortunate enough to have muscles and bones that can provide me with that particular physical force."

FURTHER INFORMATION

Books

"Anna Kournikova." *Newsmakers*. Volume 3. Detroit: Gale Group, 2000.

Diamond, Dan, ed. *Total Hockey: The Official Encyclopedia of the National Hockey League*. Kansas City: Andrews McMeel Publishing, 1998.

McFarlane, Brian. *The Red Wings*. Toronto: Stoddart Publishing, 1998.

Schabner, Dean. *Sergei Fedorov*. Philadelphia: Chelsea House Publishers, 1999.

Periodicals

Barkholz, David. "Fight Over Fedorov Renews Rivalry." *Crain's Detroit Business* (March 2, 1998).

Farber, Michael. "Wing Leader." *Sports Illustrated* (April 23, 2001).

Henning, Lynn. "Vlady Remains a Part of Wings." *Detroit News* (June 13, 2002).

Other

"Sergei Fedorov Foundation." Sergei Federov Official Web site. http://www.sergeifedorov.com/foundation/indexfoundation.htm (November 4, 2002).

"Sergei Fedorov." CNN-Sports Illustrated Web site. http://sportsillustrated.cnn.com/hockey/nhl/players/33/ (November 5, 2002).

"Sportsmanship Interview." Institute for International Sport Web site. http://www.internationalsport.com/nsd/sergei.cfm (November 4, 2002).

"Vladimir Konstantinov." Internet Hockey Database Web site. http://www.hockeydb.com/ihdb/stats/pdisplay.php3?pid=2780 (November 13, 2002).

Sketch by Timothy Borden

Lisa Fernández
1971-

American softball player

Pitcher Lisa Fernández is widely thought to be the best softball player in the world. Besides throwing countless strikeouts in international play since joining the national team in 1990, Fernández is also a solid third baseman and a powerful hitter. She is best known to most Americans for her role in winning the first Olympic gold medal in softball in 1996 and for pitching the team to a successful defense of its Olympic title in 2000.

A Rough Start in the Sport

Softball is a family sport for Fernández. Her father played semiprofessional baseball in Cuba until he fled the country as a political refugee after the Bay of Pigs invasion in 1962. After he married Fernández's mother, the two played together in slow-pitch leagues. Fernández started to play softball very young, and when she was eight she became the pitcher for a local girls' team.

Fernández's first outing as a pitcher was not very successful. She threw three balls in a row to the first batter, and then hit the child in the head with her fourth pitch. By the end of the game, her team had lost 25-0. But Fernández stuck with the sport. She and her mother practiced pitching in their backyard, and the more Fernández worked the more her team's scores improved.

Fernández turned another excuse to give up into a reason to work harder when she was 12 years old and a noted pitching coach told her that her arms were too

Lisa Fernández

short. She would never be a competitive pitcher past the age of 16, he told her. As Fernández has told the story numerous times, she left his office and started to bawl, thinking that her career was over. Her mother turned around and yelled, "Stop crying! . . . If you ever let someone in life tell you what you can or cannot do, you'll never make it," she told Larry O'Rourke of the Allentown, Pennsylvania, *Morning Call.*

Bigger Opportunities

Fernández worked hard to prove that she could be a good pitcher, and her work paid off with a spot on the University of California-Los Angeles (UCLA) Bruins softball team. With the Bruins, Fernández won numerous national awards for her playing, as well as the National Collegiate Athletic Association (NCAA) championships in 1990 and 1992. Fernández's pitching was a major contribution to those wins: She pitched five shut-outs during UCLA's 1992 postseason, setting a record for consecutive scoreless innings for the Women's College World Series. The Bruins came within one game of winning the NCAA title Fernández's senior year, too, but they lost the championship game to the University of Arizona 1-0.

World Champions

Even before she left UCLA, Fernández had already played in and won numerous international tournaments

Chronology	
1971	Born February 22
1989	Begins attending the University of California-Los Angeles (UCLA)
1990	First plays in international softball competition
1995	Is graduated from UCLA with a degree in psychology
1996	Plays in the first ever Olympic softball tournament
2002	Marries Michael Lujan, a special education teacher, in August

with the official USA softball team. She continued to do so after she was graduated, acquiring a 14-0 pitching record in international play by the time the first Olympic softball tournament ever was held in 1996, in Atlanta, Georgia. The American team as a whole had a record of 115-1 in the decade before those Olympics and was heavily favored to win the gold medal.

Fernández came within one out and a missed step of pitching the first perfect game in Olympic softball. Team USA was 5-0, the only undefeated team in round-robin play, and the United States was playing Australia in their sixth game. The game was scoreless in the first four innings. Then, in the fifth, American player Dani Tyler hit a ball over the fence. It should have been a home run, but the Australian team claimed that Tyler had failed to step on home plate and the umpire agreed. After nine scoreless innings (regulation is seven in Olympic softball), the tiebreaker rule, which allows each team to place a runner on second base at the beginning of their half of the inning, went into effect. In the top of the tenth the United States went up 1-0 on an unearned run. All Fernández had to do was strike out three Australian players to win. She struck out two and had two strikes on the last batter, Joanne Brown, when Brown hit the last pitch out of the park for a two-run homer and the win.

The United States went on to win the gold as expected, but the loss to Australia still rankled for Fernández, especially after someone (she suspects an Australian player) sent Fernández an anonymous postcard, which showed Brown celebrating her victory on the shoulders of her teammates and the message "See you in Japan," four months after the loss. Japan was where the 1998 world softball championships would be held. Fernández exorcised her demons there by beating Australia: She pitched a shutout and hit a home run herself in the first inning.

Another Olympics

The U.S. team was heavily favored again going into the 2000 Sydney (Australia) Olympics-they had a 110-game winning streak going into those games-but victory did not come as easily to them in Sydney as it had in Atlanta. The team lost three games in a row, to Japan, China, and their nemesis Australia, during the round-robin portion of the tournament. The game against Australia was an eerie replay of their 1996 round-robin matchup: In the first 12 and two-thirds innings Fernández allowed only one hit and no runners to score, and she set an Olympic record of 25 strikeouts. Then in the bottom of the thirteenth inning an Australian batter hit a home run off of her to win the game. After that, Fernández ordered her team into the showers, uniforms and all, to wash off the "voodoo." Apparently it worked, because the United States won all of their games after that. They beat China, Australia, and Japan, in that order, in the playoffs to win the gold.

Looking to the Future

Fernández is keeping her game sharp in hopes of winning a third Olympic medal in Athens, Greece, in 2004, and she continues to play professional softball with the National Pro Fastpitch league (formerly the Women's Pro Softball League), as she has for several years. Even after she retires, "I definitely want to be able to stay in the sport," she told Kevin Tran. She is currently an assistant coach of her old team, the UCLA Bruins, "And if coaching is my calling, then I will do it-[w]hether it's UCLA or internationally. Softball is in my blood and it's something I love to do, and I plan on making a contribution in the sport once my playing career is done."

FURTHER INFORMATION

Books

Lessa, Christina. *Stories of Triumph: Women Who Win in Sport and in Life*. New York: Universe Publishing, 1998.

"Lisa Fernández." *Notable Hispanic American Women*, Book 2. Detroit: Gale Research, 1998.

Periodicals

Adams, Mark. "Lisa Fernandez: The Two-Time Olympic Gold Medalist on Superstitions, Cheese-burgers and Her Next Professional Sport." *Sports Illustrated Women* (May 1, 2002): 128.

Anderson, Kelli. "Relieved Pitcher: Against a Tough Field, U.S. Ace Lisa Fernandez Kept Her Cool and Delivered When It Counted Most." *Sports Illustrated* (October 9, 2000): 54+.

Armstrong, Jim. "USA's Fernandez Preparing Special Delivery: Payback Time at Hand for Ace." *Denver Post* (September 20, 2000): D-09.

Burnett, Lisa. "Fernandez Shows Her Student Why She's the Teacher." *Fresno Bee* (June 12, 1999): D5.

Connor, Shannon. "Fernandez Fans All 21 Batters as National Team Downs All-Stars." *St. Louis Post-Dispatch* (August 12, 2000): 17.

"Gone with the Win: U.S. Women Lose Solo Home Run, Then Perfect Game, Finally the Game." *Seattle Post-Intelligencer* (July 27, 1996): D1.

Groller, Keith. "Brakettes No Longer Bulls of Women's Game, But Not Nets Either." *Morning Call* (Allentown, PA; July 22, 1997): C03.

King, Kelley. "Question 9: Will Anyone Get a Hit Off U.S. Softball Ace Lisa Fernandez?" *Sports Illustrated* (September 11, 2000): 98.

Knott, Tom. "Women Athletes Came, Saw and Conquered." *Washington Times* (August 5, 1996): 1.

Krikorian, Doug. "Title Game Is Lisa's Show." *Daily News* (Los Angeles, CA; September 27, 2000): S8.

O'Rourke, Larry. "How the Girl with the 'Too Short' Arms Learned to Pitch: Softball Devotees Gather to Hear Tales of Olympic Spirit at Lehigh U." *Morning Call* (Allentown, PA; January 24, 2000): C03.

Orozco, Ron. "Greatest of All?" *Fresno Bee* (June 13, 1999): D1.

———. "Pitching Remains Story at Festival as Fernandez Fires Championship Shutout: Red Rides a First-Inning Run to a 1-0 Title Decision over Navy." *Fresno Bee* (June 14, 1999): D5.

"Out-of-Step U.S. Stunned: Missing Plate Proves Costly." *Seattle Times* (July 27, 1996): B3.

Parker, Wendy. "Pitcher Strives for Perfection." *Atlanta Journal-Constitution* (September 16, 2000): C3.

Plaschke, Bill. "She Has Ruthless Outlook on Game." *Los Angeles Times* (September 20, 2000): U-3.

Reinhard, Paul. "Fernandez Has Always Been Able to Survive." *Morning Call* (Allentown, PA; June 10, 2001): C11.

Smith, Shelley. "Lisa Fernandez." *Sports Illustrated* (May 24, 1993): 52.

Surprenant, Tamira. "Pro Softball Set to Deliver City Its Sales Pitch." *Capital Times* (Madison, WI; July 20, 2001): 1C.

———. "Solid Gold: Fernandez Just Misses Perfect Game." *Capital Times* (Madison, WI; July 23, 2001): 2D.

"U.S. Suffers Perfectly Awful Loss: Australia's Only Hit Wins Game in 10th Inning." *San Francisco Chronicle* (July 27, 1996): D12.

"U.S. Team Captures Softball World Title: Lisa Fernandez Atones for Her Crucial Mistake by Hitting and Pitching the Americans to the World Championship." *Fresno Bee* (July 31, 1998): D1.

Other

"Lisa Fernandez." Bruin Softball. http://uclabruins.ocsn. com/sports/w-softbl/mtt/fernandez_lisa00.html (January 20, 2003).

"Lisa Fernandez." USA Softball. http://www.usasoftball. com/Women/Worlds/2002Worlds/bios/fernandez.htm l (January 9, 2003).

Tran, Kevin. "10 Questions for . . . Lisa Fernandez." U.S. Olympic Committee. http://www.olympic-usa. org/10_questions/080502softball.html (August 5, 2002).

Sketch by Julia Bauder

Luis Figo
1972-

Portuguese soccer player

Luis Figo, a World Footballer of the Year, was in such demand that he was sold from FC Barcelona to Real Madrid of Spain's elite soccer league for $56 million in 2000. In his native Portugal, Figo has been compared to the great Eusebio.

Raised in Lisbon

Figo was born in the blue-collar Almada section of Lisbon, Portugal, and after competing for the youth team Uniao Futebol Clube Os Pastilhas, joined the club Sporting Lisbon at age 11. He made his debut for Lisbon's parent soccer club at age 16 and played for world champion national teams in the under-16 and under-20 age categories He made the national squad in 1991, thus earning his first international cap.

He became Lisbon's captain for the 1994-95 season, then signed provisional contracts with Italian Serie A teams Juventis and Parma. But FIFA (Federation Internationale de Football Association), the world soccer governing body, banned Figo from playing in Italy for two years, so the rising star signed with Barcelona of the Spanish league. Barcelona coach Johan Cruyff, himself a former World Cup star for the Dutch, converted Figo from a midfielder to a right wing. Figo and Barcelona prospered together. Between 1997 and 1999, Barcelona won the Cup Winners' Cup and the European Super Cup, consecutive Spanish league titles and

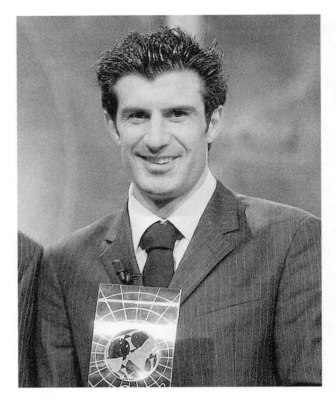

Luis Figo

the Spanish Cup. Figo scored 30 goals in 172 games for Barcelona.

Though Portugal missed the 1998 World Cup, Figo's stock rose. He earned the Ballon D'Or (Golden Ball) Award from France Football in 2000 and a year later received the FIFA World Player award. His spectacular goal during Portugal's 3-2 comeback victory over England in the Euro 2000 tournament drew special notice. "Figo's run and long-range rocket into the top corner of the net was both spectacular and match-turning. Portugal appeared out of the match at 2-0 down when he struck," CNN-Sports Illustrated wrote on its Web site.

"A wide-ranging player who is happiest on the flanks, Figo has pace, stamina, strength, excellent close control and a deadly shot," wrote Mike Penner and Grahame Jones of the *Los Angeles Times*. "Add to that exceptional dribbling skills and a crossing ability that puts him on a par with England's **David Beckham**, and you have the complete player, one equally at home as a forward, playmaker or winger."

Controversy over Transfer Fees

By 2001, however, Figo was playing not for Barcelona, but for Spanish league rival Real Madrid. In late 2000, Figo signed a six-year contract with Madrid, which agreed to pay Figo $4 million a year, and Madrid agreed to buy out his contract by paying Barcelona a

Chronology

1972	Born November 4 in Almada, Portugal
1989	First played for Sporting Lisbon, at age 16
1991-92	Made Lisbon's starting lineup
1995	Signs provisional contracts with Italian teams Juventus and Parma, but FIFA bans him from playing in Italy for two years; signs instead with FC Barcelona
1995	Barcelona coach Johan Cruyff converts him from midfielder to right wing
2000	Registers only one assist in three games as Portugal drops two, including 3-2 defeat to United States, and fails to advance in World Cup
2001	Marries model Helen Swedin

Awards and Accomplishments

1989	Plays for Portuguese world champion under-16 team
1991	Plays for Portuguese world champion under-20 team
1996	Helps Portugal reach quarterfinals of European championships
2000	Helps lead Portugal to semifinals of European championships
2000	Wins Ballon D'Or (Golden Ball) Award
2001	World Footballer of the Year
2002	Real Madrid wins European Champions Cup

world record $56 million. In joining Madrid, Figo broke a promise that he would never leave Barcelona.

"The battle was as bitter and passionate as any Cup final," Jennie James wrote in *Time Europe*. "But if the accusation of treason and the veiled threats of revenge that followed Figo's defection seemed excessive, they were trifling compared to the price Real Madrid paid for him." The size of the fees, and their degree of legality have sparked political and legal debate around Europe. "In one of the most politically and emotionally charged debates ranging in Brussels, the European Commission and the soccer establishment are fighting over how much European antitrust and labor laws should apply to this sport," Philip Shishkin wrote in the *Wall Street Journal*. The record lasted but briefly. Real Madrid executive Florentino Perez, one year later, lured former French 1998 World Cup hero **Zinedine Zidane** from Juventus for $64.45 million.

World Cup Frustration

Portugal qualified for the World Cup in 2002, having advanced past the preliminaries for the first time in 16 years. The Portuguese were considered a serious contender, despite having to play the early round in Group D with host nation South Korea. The United States and Poland, each considered decided underdogs, were also in the group.

"Take a poll of the United States players and ask them which single player they are most worried about facing in the World Cup and the answer is unanimous: Luis Figo," said *Los Angeles Times* writers Mike Penner and Grahame Jones. "As reigning FIFA world player of the year and soccer's second-most expensive player of all time behind Zindedine Zidane, Figo is to Portugal what Zidane is to France. In a word, indispensable. If anyone can lead the Portuguese to the world championship they so desperately desire, it's the 29-year-old millionaire from a working-class suburb of Lisbon." Figo had helped real Madrid win the European Champions Cup in May, 2002.

Portugal, however, ran into a roadblock in its opening game when the U.S. bolted to a stunning 3-0 lead and held on for a 3-2 upset win. The Americans, wrote the Associated Press, "held under intense pressure from Portugal in the final 10 minutes of the first half and the first 40 minutes of the second, withstanding Luis Figo, the world's top player, and his talented teammates. The result was among the five greatest wins in U.S. soccer history." By contrast, the AP added, "the Portuguese looked as if they were playing with the weight of their shoulders." Portugal never recovered from the loss. It defeated Poland 4-0 but lost to South Korea 1-0 and went home.

National Treasure

Figo, who is married to model Helen Swedin and has one child, is revered in his native Portugal. FIFA President Joseph Blatter, presenting the Footballer of the Year award in 2001, called him "the most unbelievable player from Portugal ever since the legendary Eusebio; he has the touch of an artist and the skills to be the most complete player ever." Still, Figo is past 30. In Real Madrid's 2-1 victory over Bayer Leverkusen of Germany for the 2002 European Champions Cup, he was substituted in the 61st minute (a regulation soccer game is 90 minutes) while Zidane and Spaniard Raul Gonzalez (generally known by first-name only) carried Madrid. Figo has learned to adjust, as have other aging stars. And, Phil Ball writes in ESPN's Soccernet Web site that he is prone to taking dives, in an attempt to draw foul calls from officials. "Great player though he is," Ball writes, "(He) continues to perfect the art of the balletic fall as if it were going out of fashion."

FURTHER INFORMATION

Periodicals

Shishkin, Philip. "Europe Faces Soccer Shootout over Transfer Fees." *Wall Street Journal* (January 3, 2001): B.8A

Other

2002 FIFA World Cup KoreaJapan, Luis Figo Profile, RealMadrid.com, http:/fifaworldcup.yahoo.com (May 31, 2002).

"American Dream: U.S. Holds on to Upset Portugal 3-2 at World Cup." CNN-Sports Illustrated, http://sportsillustrated.cnn.com/soccer/world/2002/world_cup/news/2002/06/04/us_portugal_ga mer/ (June 5, 2002).

Ball, Phil. "Red Card to a Bull." ESPN Soccernet, http://soccernet.espn.go.com/ (January 22, 2003).

"Bests and Worsts from Euro 2000." CNN-Sports Illustrated, http://sportsillustrated.cnn.com/soccer/world/2000/euro2000/news/2000/07/02/bests_worsts/ (July 2, 2000).

"Figo, 2001 FIFA World Player." RealMadrid.com http://www.realmadrid.es/web_realmadrid (January 16, 2003).

James, Jennie. "More Money Than Sense." Time Europe, http:///.time.com/time/europe/magazine/2000/0807/football.html (August 7, 2000).

Penner, Mike and Grahame Jones. "Profiles of Key Players." South Florida Sun-Sentinel, http://www.sun-sentinel.com/sports/soccer (January 28, 2003).

Wallace, Sam. "Fatigue Blamed for Giggs' Loss of Form." Daily Telegraph (U.K.), http://www.daily telegraph.co.uk/sport (January 11, 2003).

Whiteside, Kelly. "USA Notches Upset in World Cup Opener." USA Today, http://www.usatoday.com/sports/soccer/cup2002/games.2002-06-05-usa-portugal.htm (June 6, 2002).

Sketch by Paul Burton

Carlton Fisk
1947-

American baseball player

The New England-born baseball player Carlton Fisk is one of the sport's most legendary catchers, having caught more games (2,226) than any other player in history. In his 11 seasons with the Boston Red Sox and 13 seasons with the Chicago White Sox, Fisk set a major league record for the most home runs by a catcher (351). Fans remember one home run in particular: a 12th-inning, save-the-day homer that let the Red Sox win Game Six of the 1975 World Series. The 11-time All-Star player overcame several injuries during his lengthy career, including a knee injury that threatened to keep him on the sidelines permanently. Popular with fans and fellow teammates, Fisk won respect as a hard-working and devoted player and an extraordinarily well-conditioned athlete. In 2000, at age 52, he was inducted into the Baseball Hall of Fame, becoming the 12th catcher enshrined in the famed Cooperstown, New York, museum.

Carlton Fisk

Born in Vermont and raised in rural Charlestown, New Hampshire, Carlton Ernest Fisk was one of six children born to Cecil, a farmer and a machinist, and Leona, a homemaker. Both of his parents were athletes—Cecil was an all-around athlete and a powerhouse on the tennis court, while Leona held her own on men's softball teams—and all of his siblings played sports avidly. Fisk's first love was basketball, and he and his brothers often played pickup games in the hayloft of their grandfather's barn.

At Charlestown High School, Fisk—nicknamed "Pudge"—was a tall, rugged athlete who dominated every sport, including basketball and baseball. When he graduated, major league baseball teams took notice, including the Baltimore Orioles, who made Fisk an offer to join the club in the 1965 draft. But the young athlete chose instead to attend the University of New Hampshire, which had awarded him a basketball scholarship.

Made Strong Red Sox Debut

Yet it was not basketball but baseball that beckoned Fisk in January 1967, when the Boston Red Sox, New England's beloved team, chose to draft him. Spending his first year in basic training in Fort Dix, New Jersey, Fisk did not receive his uniform until 1968. However, a second drafting, this time by the U.S. Army, which called Fisk to prepare for action in the Vietnam War,

Chronology

1947	Born on December 26, 1947, in Bellows Falls, VT
1962-65	Dominates sports at Charlestown High School, in Charlestown, NH
1967	Drafted by Boston Red Sox
1968-71	Serves in army reserves in Chester, VT
1972	Debuts with Red Sox
1975	Hits famed 12th inning home run, letting Red Sox win Game Six of the World Series
1981	Signs five-year, $3 million contract with Chicago White Sox
1994	Retires after 24-year playing career

Awards and Accomplishments

1972	Won Golden Glove Award
1972	Named American League Rookie of the Year
1972-74, 1976-82, 1985, 1991	Named to the All-Star team
2000	Inducted into the Baseball Hall of Fame

Fisk Extends the Series to Seven Games

Tuesday, October 21, 1975, Fenway Park

This World Series had it all—good pitching, terrific fielding plays, explosive offense and plenty of drama. Veteran writers proclaimed it one of the more exciting Series in memory. After five games Cincinnati's Big Red Machine held the edge over the Boston Red Sox three games to two, and their manager, Sparky Anderson, had every intention of ending the Fall Classic this night....

The Red Sox needed this game to stay alive, and in the opening frame they drew first blood. After two outs Carl Yastrzemski and Carlton Fisk singled. Rookie Fred Lynn then smashed a towering drive into right-center field that cleared the Boston bullpen and landed ten rows deep in the bleachers....

In the Cincinnati seventh, with two on and two out, George Foster doubled home a pair, giving the Reds their first lead at 5-3. Crowd noise was non-existent, especially after Cesar Geronimo led off the visitor's eighth with a home run. The round-tripper spelled the end for Tiant, who left to a standing ovation, but trailing 6-3....

Pat Darcy, who had taken the mound for Cincinnati in the 10th, had retired six straight Red Sox. But leading off the home 12th was Fisk. On a 1-0 pitch the catcher lofted a towering drive deep to left as more than 35,000 pairs of eyes strained to see if it would stay fair. Amid a deafening roar Fisk waved the ball fair as it slammed high off the foul pole and gave Boston one of the most dramatic victories in World Series history.

Source: Dittmar, Joseph J. *The 100 Greatest Baseball Games.* Jefferson, North Carolina: McFarland & Co., 2000.

delayed his career another three years. During his time with a reserve unit in Chester, Vermont, Fisk was never called to combat. He later was grateful to the reserves for instilling in him the values of a team player. "I don't know if [the army] changed my attitude, my discipline, but it might have helped a little bit on the coachability end of it," Fisk told Phil Rogers of the *Chicago Tribune.* "Because of my talents, I was like a loose cannon on deck. I had all the firepower but no direction."

Making his first full-season debut in 1972, Fisk was off to a strong start, ending the season with 22 home runs and batting .293. He won both a Gold Glove and a Rookie of the Year award. Unfortunately, however, Fisk was prone to injuries. During spring training in 1974, he sustained a groin injury. And later that season, colliding with a runner at the plate, he faced a more serious, potentially career-ending knee injury. The surgeon who reconstructed his torn knee ligaments told Fisk that he might never be able play baseball again. Yet after nine weeks in a cast, through hard work and perseverance, Fisk recovered. To regain his strength, he lifted weights and ran in the mornings with the pastor from his family's New Hampshire church.

Rejoining the Red Sox in June of 1975, after one year on the sidelines, Fisk made a remarkable comeback. After helping his team take the American League pennant, Fisk performed phenomenally in the World Series games against the Cincinnati Reds. The powerful slugger hit a now-legendary 12th inning home run that allowed the Red Sox to clinch Game Six of the World Series, with a final score of 7-6. "The celebration of that moment has made me realize how popular baseball is and how it affects people's lives," Fisk told Larry Whiteside of the *Boston Globe.* "It's still the greatest moment in my career." (The team lost Game Seven, however, losing the title to the Reds.)

Fisk had another good year in 1977, ending the season with a .315 average and 26 home runs. Vying with the New York Yankees' Thurman Munson for recognition as the American League's best catcher, Fisk allowed only four passed balls that season. Yet that year and the

following, the Yankees kept Boston from a pennant title. Some fans attributed the Red Sox's 1978 loss to a rib injury sustained by Fisk. The same injury left Fisk on the sidelines for several games during the 1979 season.

Left the Red Sox

Meanwhile, the relationship between Fisk's agent, Jerry Kapstein, and the Red Sox's owners, Haywood Sullivan and John Harrington, grew contentious. Their troubles came to a head when the owners failed to meet a December deadline to renew Fisk's contract for the 1981 season. Fisk, at 33, was declared a free agent. Jumping at the chance to recruit the star player, the Chicago White Sox lured Fisk away from Boston with a five-year, $3 million contract. Red Sox fans mourned his departure, and Fisk, too, struggled with the decision. "It broke my heart to leave New England," Fisk told Rogers of the *Chicago Tribune.* "I grew up as a New England guy. All the kids I knew fantasized about wearing a Red Sox's uniform or a Celtics' uniform. To be able to do that, it was a dream come true."

Career Statistics

Yr	Team	AVG	GP	AB	R	H	HR	RBI	BB	SO	SB
1969	BRS	.000	2	5	0	0	0	0	0	2	0
1971	BRS	.312	14	48	7	15	2	6	1	10	0
1972	BRS	.293	131	457	74	134	22	61	52	83	5
1973	BRS	.246	135	508	65	125	26	71	37	99	7
1974	BRS	.299	52	187	36	56	11	26	24	23	5
1975	BRS	.331	79	263	47	87	10	52	27	32	4
1976	BRS	.255	134	487	76	124	17	58	56	71	12
1977	BRS	.315	152	536	106	169	26	102	75	85	7
1978	BRS	.284	157	571	94	162	20	88	71	83	7
1979	BRS	.272	91	320	49	87	10	42	10	38	3
1980	BRS	.289	131	478	73	138	18	62	36	62	11
1981	CWS	.263	96	338	44	89	7	45	38	37	3
1982	CWS	.267	135	476	66	127	14	65	46	60	17
1983	CWS	.289	138	488	85	141	26	86	46	88	9
1984	CWS	.231	102	359	54	83	21	43	26	60	6
1985	CWS	.238	153	543	85	129	37	107	52	81	17
1986	CWS	.221	125	457	42	101	14	63	22	92	2
1987	CWS	.256	135	454	68	116	23	71	39	72	1
1988	CWS	.277	76	253	37	70	19	50	37	40	0
1989	CWS	.293	103	375	47	110	13	68	36	60	1
1990	CWS	.285	137	452	65	129	18	61	61	73	7
1991	CWS	.241	134	460	42	111	18	74	32	86	1
1992	CWS	.229	62	188	12	43	3	21	23	38	3
1993	CWS	.189	25	53	2	10	1	4	2	11	0

BRS: Boston Red Sox; CWS: Chicago White Sox.

Moving with his family to Lockport, Illinois, Fisk played some of his best baseball with the White Sox. His performance was particularly strong whenever he returned to Boston's Fenway Park. In his first game against Boston, he hit a three-run, eighth-inning home run to clinch the game for Chicago. Throughout his White Sox career, Fisk rattled his former team with a .310 batting average in 105 games against them, and with 27 home runs and 67 runs batted in (RBI).

Yet Fisk's relationship with the Chicago team's management was nearly as contentious as his relationship with the Red Sox's management. Relations were particularly strained between Fisk and White Sox owner Jerry Reinsdorf. Nevertheless, Fisk went on to play out 13 seasons with the White Sox. Many believed his longevity as a player was the result of his tireless weight training and stretching sessions. When a conditioning director, Steve Odgers, joined the White Sox staff in 1990, Odgers found that he had more to learn from Fisk than to teach him.

As a catcher, Fisk was known for his notoriously slow walks to the pitcher's mound, known jokingly as "Pudge Trudges." Rumor had it that games caught by Fisk ran about 20 minutes longer than an average American League game. Fisk remained proud of his catching capabilities, however, and resisted the White Sox's attempts to move him to the outfield later in his career.

After a poor start to the 1993 season, the 44-year-old player finally conceded that his age had caught up with him. He retired just after breaking Bob Boone's record for most games caught.

In January 2000, the Baseball Writers Association of America elected Fisk to the National Baseball Hall of Fame in Cooperstown, New York. Inducted that summer, Fisk chose to wear a Boston Red Sox cap on his Hall of Fame plaque—though he had played longer with the Chicago team. "New England is still where my roots are," he explained to Whiteside of the *Boston Globe*. "And I'm a New England person even though I don't live there." As the first New Hampshire player to be inducted, Fisk remains one of New England's finest athletes. He leaves behind a legacy as one of the greatest catchers in baseball history.

FURTHER INFORMATION

Books

Dittmar, Joseph J. *The 100 Greatest Baseball Games*. Jefferson, North Carolina: McFarland & Co., 2000.

Periodicals

Lessels, Allen. "All Along the Way, Fisk Was Memorable." *Boston Globe* (July 23, 2000): 16.

Rogers, Phil. "Fisk's Body of Work." *Chicago Tribune* (July 21, 2000).

Whiteside, Larry. "Pride of New England Will Take Rightful Place." *Boston Globe* (July 21, 2000): E1.

Other

"Carlton Fisk." BaseballLibrary.com. http://www.pubdim.net/baseballlibrary/ballplayers/F/Fisk_Carlton.stm (November 5, 2002).

"Carlton Fisk." National Baseball Hall of Fame. http://
www.baseballhalloffame.org/hofers_and_honorees/
hofer_bios/fisk_carlton.htm (November 5, 2002).

"Carlton Fisk Statistics." *Baseball Almanac.* http://
www.baseball-almanac.com/players/player.php?
p=fiskca01 (November 5, 2002).

Sketch by Wendy Kagan

Emerson Fittipaldi

Emerson Fittipaldi
1946-

Brazilian race car driver

Brazilian racing car driver Emerson Fittipaldi survived the deadliest period of auto racing history to emerge as the most successful driver of both the European Formula One (F1) and American Indy leagues. After he almost single-handedly unraveled his promising career in F1, he switched his focus to American racing, and managed to pull off an entire second career there.

Fittipaldi was born December 12, 1946 in Sao Paulo, Brazil. His father, Wilson, was a motor racing journalist and commentator. He started racing in his older brother Wilson's go-kart. Fittipaldi's brother also was an F1 driver. Wilson Sr. was commentating the first time his sons competed together, and made no effort to conceal his pride when they were racing in the first and second positions.

Fittipaldi stepped off the plane from Sao Paulo to London in the spring of 1969, to race in the Formula Ford and F3 series. Within weeks, he was winning British Formula Ford races. He graduated to F1 in 1970, racing for the Lotus team. Fittipaldi was forced to assume Lotus team leadership in his rookie season when former leader Jochen Rindt died in a crash. Fittipaldi remained with Lotus through the 1973 season. He fell into a slump during the 1971 season after he crashed in his road car on his way home and broke several ribs, and finished in sixth place over all. After just one F1 win to his name, he came back strong in 1972, becoming the youngest driver ever to win the F1 world championship. He won the F1 title again in 1974 after switching to the McLaren team. By 1975, Fittipaldi looked as if he would become a legendary F1 driver. But his F1 career began to unravel, after he made a few questionable decisions.

Fittipaldi, nicknamed "Emmo," is known for his meticulously precise driving style. He also is a runner and used to train with the Brazilian soccer team to keep fit, and monitored his high-carbohydrate diet carefully. He also was a leader in the campaign to improve notoriously dangerous F1 track and car safety. He stopped his car after one lap in the 1975 Spanish Grand Prix to protest what he felt were dangerous track conditions. The race continued until another driver's car flew off the road, killing four onlookers.

Fittipaldi made the first of his questionable career choices at the end of the 1975 season, after finishing second behind Niki Lauda in the championship. He chose to leave the McLaren team in favor of the startup Copersucar team, which was founded by his brother, Wilson Fittipaldi, and backed by the Brazilian state-run sugar cartel. The move would mark the premature end of his glory days on the F1 circuit. His Copersucar car proved uncompetitive and unreliable, and he finished the season a miserable 16th in the championship in 1976, 12th in 1977, ninth in 1978, and 21st in 1979. A strong second place finish behind Ferrari's Carlos Reutemann in 1978 at the Brazilian Grand Prix was one of the few highlights of Fittipaldi's career from this point on. Fittipaldi retired from the European circuit in 1980, intending to manage the family team, but the Fittipaldi Automotive team, lacking credibility and capital, folded in 1982. All told, Fittipaldi ran in 144 Grands Prix, winning fourteen.

Feeling that he had more good racing in him, Fittipaldi set his sights on racing in America. He still longed to do "what I do best in life—making a racing car go very fast," he is quoted as saying in *Sports Illustrated.* He joined the American Championship Auto Racing Teams (CART) Indy-Car series in 1984. He finished fifth in his debut Indy-Car race, the Long Beach Grand Prix, and knew he had made the right choice, even if American race fans

Chronology

1969	Born December 12 in Sao Paulo, Brazil
1970	Debuts in F1, drives five races, wins in Watkins Glen Grand Prix
1972	Becomes youngest world champion in F1 history
1980	Leaves F1 to compete in America
1985	Joins CART series with Patrick Racing
1986	First CART road course win at Elkhart Lake
1990	Joins Team Penske
1996	Crashes at Michigan International Speedway, retires

Awards and Accomplishments

1967	First place, Brazilian Formula-Vee Championship
1967	First place, F3 Lombank Championship
1972, 1974	First place, F1 World Championship
1975, 1980	Second place, F1 World Championship
1985	First place, Marlboro 500
1989, 1993	First place, Indianapolis 500
1989	First place, CART Championship
1990	Fifth place, CART Championship
1992	First place, Marlboro Challenge
1992	Fourth place, CART Championship
1993-94	Second place, CART Championship
2000	Honored, Legend of the Indianapolis Motor Speedway

may not have agreed. He was greeted with snickers when he showed up in 1984 at America's most prestigious race, the Indianapolis 500, in a pink car. "There was laughter at this supposedly over-the-hill foreigner in his flashy machine," Ed Hinton wrote in *Sports Illustrated*.

Fittipaldi resurrected his racing career and returned to racing full time in 1985 on the Patrick Racing team. He went on to take the CART championship in 1989, and won the Indy 500 in 1989 and 1993. His 1989 Indy 500 win will go down as one of the most dramatic finishes in history. He and Al Unser Jr. were battling each other at 220 mph for the top spot in the final moments of the race when Unser hit the wall, leaving Fittipaldi to take the checkered flag. In 1990, the reinvigorated driver joined Team Penske, becoming successful enough to remain a permanent member of the team until 1995, when he joined the reformed Penske Hogan Racing team.

When he started in F1 in 1970, the odds were that, of the top twenty-one drivers, three would not live to see the end of a season. He watched many of his friends and colleagues die on the track. Since then, track and car safety has improved radically, in great part because of Fittipaldi, who campaigned for safety. But he defied the odds for ten years in F1, and then managed to live through another sixteen years racing in America.

In 1996, Fittipaldi walked out of a hospital after surviving a crash that almost left him completely paralyzed. It took a team of neurosurgeons to repair the crushed vertebra and destabilized spinal cord he suffered in a fiery crash at Michigan International Speedway. "It was incredible," he recalled in and interview with *Runner's World*. "It sounded like a bomb going off."

Fittipaldi took the accident as his cue to quit. He retired in 1996, but has remained very much involved with auto racing with his business ventures. He owns Fittipaldi Motoring Accessories, and has owned the lucrative Brazilian TV rights to the CART FedEx Championship Series since 1985. As a consultant for Chrysler and Wellcraft, he designed a high-performance boat called the Fittipaldi Scarab. He is a spokesman for British Airways, Ericsson, Hugo Boss, Mercedes-Benz, and Michelin, among others. He also owns hundreds of thousands of orange trees on a plantation in Brazil. Fittipaldi was seri-

ously injured in 1997 when he crashed a small plane near his farm, but regained movement in his legs. He and his wife, Teresa, have homes in Sao Paulo, Brazil and Key Biscayne, Florida. In 13 seasons as a CART driver, Fittipaldi earned more than $14 million in prize winnings.

FURTHER INFORMATION

Books

Henry, Alan. *Grand Prix Champions: From Jackie Stewart to Emerson Fittipaldi*. Motorbooks International, 1996.

Periodicals

Hanc, John. "Speed demon." *Runner's World* (July 1993): 48.

Hinton, Ed. "Miracle man." *Sports Illustrated* (August 12, 1996): 18.

Other

"Emerson Fittipaldi." Grand Prix Hall of Fame. http://www.ddavid.com/formula1/fitti_bio.html (January 15, 2003).

"Grand Prix drivers: Emerson Fittipaldi." GrandPrix. com.http://www.grandprix.com/gpe/drv-fiteme.html (January 15, 2003).

The Official Emerson Fittipaldi Web site. http://www.emersonfittipaldi.com (January 15, 2003).

Sketch by Brenna Sanchez

Peggy Fleming
1948-

American figure skater

Peggy Fleming

Chronology

1948	Born on July 27 to Albert and Doris (Deal) Fleming in San Jose, California
1958	Begins taking figure skating lessons
1965	Begins working with coach Carlo Fassi
1968	Retires from amateur ranks
1970	Marries Greg Jenkins on June 13
1980	Begins working as commentator for ABC Sports
1998	Recovers from breast cancer

One of the most influential female athletes of the past century, Peggy Fleming combined grace and power to create some of the most memorable figure-skating programs of her era. After winning a surprising victory at the 1964 United States Figure Skating Association (USFSA) National Championship as a fifteen-year-old, Fleming went on to capture four more consecutive national titles. She also added three International Skating Union (ISU) World Championship titles from 1965 to 1968 to her list of accomplishments. At the 1968 Winter Olympics in Grenoble, France, Fleming became the only American athlete to win a gold medal at the games. Retiring from the amateur ranks after winning her third World Championship later that year, Fleming went on to star in a number of figure skating television specials and appeared with various touring ice shows in the 1970s. Her work as a skating analyst for the ABC network kept her in the public eye in the 1980s and 1990s. After a diagnosis of breast cancer in 1998, Fleming also campaigned to raise awareness of the importance of early detection and treatment for the disease. Married to dermatologist Greg Jenkins since 1970 and the mother two sons, Fleming remains one of the most admired figures in the world of sports.

Showed Early Promise

Peggy Gale Jenkins was born on July 27, 1948 in San Jose, California. She was the second of Albert and Doris (Deal) Fleming's four daughters. For the first several years of her life the Flemings lived in the San Jose area, where Al Fleming had a job as a newspaper press operator for the *San Jose Mercury News.* Fleming started skating at age nine and found it to be a good outlet for her naturally competitive spirit. Just a year after starting skating lessons, Fleming took home the gold medal in the Bay Area Juvenile Championship.

In 1960 the Flemings moved to Pasadena in southern California. Fleming's figure skating activities increasingly became the center of her family's life. Her father got up early to resurface the ice at a local rink so that his daughter could have extra practice time in the morning, and her mother sewed her costumes, found suitable coaches, and cleared away any distractions that might take her daughter's focus away from her skating. As Fleming recalled in her 1999 autobiography, *The Long Program: Skating Toward Life's Victories,* "I wouldn't have started skating if it weren't for my Dad, but I became a *skater* because of my mom. It is not stretching the point to say, 'We became a skater,' two people, one pair of skates. We each had a job to do to make me a champion skater, and I certainly didn't do it on my own."

With her family's support, Fleming rose quickly through the USFSA's ranks. She won the gold medal in the Pacific Coast Juvenile Championship in 1960, followed by another gold in the Pacific Coast Novice Championship in 1961. In 1962 she continued her winning streak with a gold at the Pacific Coast Championship and added a silver medal in the National Novice Championship. A bronze medal at the 1963 National Junior Championship earned Fleming a berth at the following year's National Championship as a senior-level skater. Astounding everyone at the event, Fleming won the title, which meant that she also qualified to go to the 1964 Winter Olympic Games in Innsbruck, Austria. Fleming placed sixth at the Games and then attended her first ISU World Championship, where she placed seventh.

Thrown into Spotlight

Under her mother's watchful eye, Fleming had made a spectacular rise in the figure-skating world and was ranked as the best American skater by the time she was fifteen years old. Part of her rapid rise in the sport was due to the 1961 airplane crash in Brussels, Belgium, that had claimed the lives of almost the entire U.S. figure skating delega-

Awards and Accomplishments

1959	Won gold medal, United Figure Skating Association (USFSA) Bay Area Juvenile Championship
1960	Won gold medal, USFSA Pacific Coast Juvenile Championship
1961	Won gold medal, USFSA Pacific Coast Novice Championship
1962	Won gold medal, USFSA Pacific Coast Championship
1962	Won silver medal, USFSA National Novice Championship
1963	Won bronze medal, USFSA National Junior Championship
1964	Placed sixth at the Innsbruck Winter Olympic Games
1964	Placed seventh at the International Skating Union (ISU) World Championship
1964-68	Won gold medals, USFSA National Championship
1965	Won bronze medal, ISU World Championship
1966-68	Won gold medals, ISU World Championship
1967	Named ABC Athlete of the Year
1968	Received Babe Didrickson Zaharias Award
1968	Won gold medal, women's figure skating, Grenoble Winter Olympic Games
1974	Inducted into U.S. Olympic Hall of Fame
1976	Inducted into USFSA Hall of Fame
1976	Inducted into World Figure Skating Hall of Fame
1981	Inducted into International Women's Sports Hall of Fame
1997	Received U.S. Olympic Committee Olympic Spirit Award

The Long Program: Skating Toward Life's Victories

I was proud to be on the [1964 Winter Olympic] team, but I hated the Olympic uniforms. Even then, fashion was becoming an important part of the total package. How you looked said a lot about your style, and your style was what made your skating different and special. Those tight ski pants and geeky wool jackets with red and blue stripes on the collar were not my style. Still, when all the American team walked into the arena with all the thousands of other athletes, all of us in our uniforms and all of us marching behind our flags—it was breathtaking: a hundred thousand people roaring and applauding, under the snow-capped Alps and the bluest blue sky in the world. Everybody should have a first Olympics—it moves you, takes over your emotions and overwhelms you until you can hardly think. And everyone should be fortunate enough to go on to have a second Olympics, so that you have time to take it all in.

Source: Peggy Fleming, with Peter Kaminsky, *The Long Program: Skating Toward Life's Victories,* New York: Pocket Books, 1999, p. 40.

tion, which was on its way to that year's World Championship. With America's best skaters suddenly gone, the USFSA looked to younger skaters, such as Fleming, to build up a program that was previously the best in the world. Americans **Tenley Albright** and Carol Heiss Jenkins had claimed the Olympic Gold Medals in women's figure skating in 1956 and 1960, and now Fleming was the leading contender to bring home another gold medal in 1968.

In order to help her daughter live up to her initial promise, Doris Fleming often made coaching changes; one such change, after her daughter's victory at the 1965 National Championship and third-place showing at that year's World Championship, took the Flemings to Colorado Springs, Colorado, where coach Carlo Fassi was teaching. The change was a crucial one in Fleming's career, as Fassi worked with her intensively on practicing her compulsory (or school) figures, which were a major portion in the scoring of USFSA and ISU events. Fassi's demand that Fleming treat every practice session as an actual competition paid off. She repeated as National Champion in 1966 and then took the gold medal at the World Championship in Davos, Switzerland later that year. In addition to helping her skating career, the move to Colorado Springs was also significant in Fleming's personal life as it occurred shortly after her father died of a heart attack in 1966. It was during this time that she also met Greg Jenkins, a former pairs skater who would eventually attend medical school and become a dermatologist. The two started dating in 1966 and were married four years later, on June 13, 1970.

Although she continued to work with coach Bob Paul on her choreography, Fassi's technical input and insights helped Fleming to become almost unbeatable after 1966. Often described as having nerves of steel in competition,

Fleming credited her mother for helping her get ready for events by taking the pressure off of her daughter. Doris Fleming indeed earned a reputation as a formidable force on the skating circuit and went out of her way to help her daughter keep her focus on skating. On the ice, Fleming developed into a skater who combined athleticism with grace and power. Her style contrasted significantly with many European skaters, who often demonstrated significant technical ability but only rudimentary choreography. The best example of Fleming's unique style was shown in her spread eagle move into a double axel jump followed by another spread eagle. Although the combination was extremely difficult to execute, it created a breathtaking and impressive moment on the ice.

Olympic Champion

Having won consecutive World Championships in 1966 and 1967 and U.S. National Championships from 1964 to 1967, Fleming entered the 1968 season as the favorite for the Olympic gold medal. Her competitive season got off to a remarkable start at the 1968 U.S. Nationals in Philadelphia, where Fleming's free skate ranked among the best-ever performances in women's figure skating up to that time. At the 1968 Winter Olympic Games in Grenoble, France, Fleming once again led the field after the first two segments of the competition going into the final free skate. Although she had trouble with some of her jumps and the performance was not her best, Fleming skated well enough to win the event. She was the only gold medal winner among the American athletes at the Games, a feat that made her accomplishment even more notable back home. Two weeks later Fleming delivered a much better performance of her free skate at the 1968 World Championships in Geneva, Switzerland, and announced her retirement from amateur ranks.

Peggy Fleming

On Television as Performer and Broadcaster

Most Olympic champion figure skaters had previously encountered few career opportunities beyond skating in ice show reviews such as the Ice Capades. Fleming changed that pattern by forging into the realm of network television, beginning with her 1968 special on NBC, *Here's Peggy Fleming,* which included a guest appearance by Gene Kelley. It was the first of five successful specials that Fleming made for NBC. The series included a 1973 show filmed in St. Petersburg (then Leningrad), U.S.S.R., which made it the first American-Soviet joint television production. Fleming also made selected appearances with the touring companies of the Ice Follies and Holiday on Ice programs throughout the 1970s. In 1973 she appeared in her own review, "Peggy's Dinner Theater on Ice," in Lake Tahoe, California; it later toured the country as "Peggy Fleming's Concert on Ice." On January 30, 1977, Fleming gave birth to her first son, Andy. Her second son, Todd, arrived in September 1988.

In 1980 Fleming began appearing as a skating analyst on the ABC network, often teamed with two-time Olympic gold medalist **Dick Button**. Although the two had different approaches—Fleming's gentle critiques contrasted greatly with Button's sharp on-air personality—the appreciation they both had for skating was obvious. More than twenty years later, both still appear together in ABC's telecasts of national and international skating events. In 1997, while covering the World Championships in Lausanne, Switzerland, Fleming was saddened by the death of her former coach, Carlo Fassi, who was attending the event to supervise his student, American skater Nicole Bobek.

Raised Breast Cancer Awareness

At the U.S. Nationals in Philadelphia in January 1998, Fleming discovered a lump in her left breast. Although she continued to work through the next few weeks, a biopsy showed that the lump was malignant. Undergoing surgery to remove the cancer on February 10—exactly thirty years after she had won her gold medal in Grenoble—Fleming later underwent radiation therapy and made a speedy recovery.

Inducted into the U.S. Olympic Hall of Fame in 1974, Fleming was also honored with an induction into the USFSA Hall of Fame and World Figure Skating Hall of Fame in 1976. In 1981 she was inducted into the International Women's Sports Hall of Fame and in 1997 was the recipient of the U.S. Olympic Committee's Olympic Spirit Award. Each of these honors has highlighted Fleming's contribution to figure skating and to athletic endeavors in general. In combining sheer athletic power with aesthetic grace, Fleming was one of the first figure skaters to be able to integrate impressive jump sequences with choreographed ballet. As a National, World, and Olympic champion, she also has helped to popularize the

---

Where Is She Now?

The mother of two sons, Andy and Todd, Fleming makes her home in the San Jose suburb of Los Gatos with her husband, Dr. Greg Jenkins. In early 1998, after noticing a lump in her left breast, Fleming confronted a diagnosis of breast cancer that required surgery. The procedure was performed in February 1998; after undergoing radiation therapy, Fleming made a full recovery. "I have no explanation for it," Fleming told Karen S. Schneider of *People* about her speedy return to health. "Something must be lining up right. Whatever the case, I am very grateful." Fleming subsequently made numerous personal appearances to heighten awareness of breast cancer, particularly the importance of frequent self-examinations and prompt medical treatment.

After more than twenty years as a skating analyst for the ABC network, Fleming also remains a fixture on television. In addition to her duties as a broadcaster, Fleming appears frequently in advertisements for Os-Cal, a calcium dietary supplement. The recipient of numerous awards during her career, Fleming was honored in 1997 by the U.S. Olympic Committee with its Olympic Spirit Award.

---

sport of figure skating and expand the range of professional opportunities available to skaters after they had left the amateur ranks. More than thirty years after her last competition, Fleming remains a popular and admired personality, not only in the sports world but for her contributions to publicizing women's health issues as well.

SELECTED WRITINGS BY FLEMING:

(With Peter Kaminsky) *The Long Program: Skating Toward Life's Victories.* New York: Pocket Books, 1999.

FURTHER INFORMATION

Books

Brennan, Christine. *Edge of Glory: The Inside Story of the Quest for Figure Skating's Olympic Gold Medals.* New York: Scribner, 1998.

Brennan, Christine. *Inside Edge: A Revealing Journey into the Secret World of Figure Skating.* New York: Scribner, 1996.

Fleming, Peggy with Peter Kaminsky. *The Long Program: Skating Toward Life's Victories.* New York: Pocket Books, 1999.

Smith, Beverley. *Talking Figure Skating: Behind the Scenes in the World's Most Glamorous Sport.* Toronto: McClelland and Stewart, 1997.

U.S. Figure Skating Association. *The Official Book of Figure Skating.* New York: Simon & Schuster Editions, 1998.

Periodicals

Ottum, Bob. "The Perils of Peggy and a Great Silver Raid." *Sports Illustrated* (February 19, 1968): 18, 21.

Schneider, Karen S. "Gold Mettle: A Month after Being Diagnosed with Breast Cancer, Olympic Skating

Champion Peggy Fleming Is on Her Way to Recovery." *People* (March 2, 1998): 88.

Sketch by Timothy Borden

Vonetta Flowers
1973-

American bobsledder

Bobsledder Vonetta Flowers was the first African American to earn a gold medal in the Winter Olympics, and did so in her sport's first women's Olympic event. After a lifetime spent chasing the gold in track and field events, Flowers switched her focus to achieve it on the first-ever women's Olympic bobsled team.

Flowers was born October 29, 1973, in Birmingham, Alabama, and raised with three brothers by her single mother, Bobbie Jeffries. It's safe to say that children growing up in the South are not inclined to bobsledding; the sport is more popular in colder climes. Football is Alabama's sport. She took to track and field events as a child and never missed a practice. At age nine, she ran a 50-yard-dash that was so fast, her coach thought her time belonged to a thirteen-year-old boy. She was a natural, and she was dedicated. Her coach told her she could be the next great female track star, like **Jackie Joyner-Kersee**, the legendary heptathlete medallist. She was an all-state star in high school, and a seven-time NCAA All-American at the University of Alabama at Birmingham. In college, she competed in long jump, triple jump, 100 meters, 200 meters and relay teams. She failed to make the 1994 Olympic team after ankle surgery, and considered retiring, and finished 12th in the 2000 Olympic long-jump trials, still plagued by injuries. She had two knee operations and ankle surgery. Flowers is an assistant track coach at the University of Alabama at Birmingham. Her husband and coach, Johnny Flowers, is also an accomplished track and field athlete.

At the 2000 Olympic trials, Flowers saw a flyer advertising the U.S. bobsled team tryout. Veteran bobsledder Bonny Warner felt she could find raw talent in a track-and-field athlete. On a lark, Flowers and her husband decided to try out. The six-event competition included sprinting, jumping, and throwing a shot, all strong suits for Flowers. She earned a trial at the Olympic bobsled track in Park City, Utah. The only time she had even seen a bobsled was in the movie *Cool Runnings,* and didn't know what to expect. "No one told me about the G-force," she told the *New York Times* about her first 80mph ride down the icy track. "I

Vonetta Flowers

thought it was going to be a nice, comfortable ride. I was dizzy."

When Flowers sought sponsorship in her hometown to finance her training, no one could understand why someone in Alabama would want to bobsled. But with just two weeks of training Flowers, as the brakeman, with teammate and driver Warner, broke the world start record in 2000, and went on to win four World Cup medals, finishing in the top ten in all seven World Cup races. They finished the season ranked third in the world. Flowers stepped aside when Warner asked her to compete for her spot with another brakeman. Soon after, driver Jill Bakken asked her to join her team.

Competitive bobsledding started in upstate New York, where lumberjacks used to race the sleds they used to haul wood, and really took off in Switzerland. It's the brakeman's job to get the sled out of the gate fast and slow it down at the finish, and the driver guides it down the mountain. Bobsled competition was co-ed until an all-women's team took the U.S. national title. Women returned in 1992, as an exhibition at men's competitions in Europe. Women earned their own World Cup circuit in 1997, and female bobsledders campaigned the International Olympic Committee until they were granted their sport in the 2002 Olympics.

Jean Racine, the world's top driver, and Gea Johnson were the favorites coming into the Olympics. To many, Bakken and Flowers were not even a threat. But

Chronology	
1973	Born October 29 in Birmingham, Alabama
c. 1980	Begins competing in track and field
1982	Runs an astonishing 50-yard dash
c. 1987-91	Maintains all-state status in high school
c. 1991-94	Seven-time NCAA All-American while at University of Alabama at Birmingham
1994	Fails to make Olympic team
2000	Finishes 12th in Olympic long-jump trials
2000	Tries out for Bonny Warner's bobsled team
2000	Breaks the world start record
2000	Finishes the season ranked third in the world
2001	Joins driver Jill Bakken's team
2001	Places second in the Olympic trials
2002	First African-American to win gold in a Winter Olympics

Awards and Accomplishments	
2000	Four medals, World Cup championships
2000	Third place, World Cup championships
2002	Gold medal, women's bobsled, Salt Lake City Olympics
2002	Olympic Spirit Award

the number-one team was not a solid one. The world of bobsledding is surprisingly cutthroat. Racine had dropped her best friend and brakeman before the Olympic trials. When her replacement, Johnson, suffered an injury two days before the Olympics, Racine tried to lure Flowers away from Bakken. Flowers turned down the top-ranked driver to remain a part of the underdog team.

Flowers tuned out the 15,000 screaming fans, clanging cowbells and waving American flags, at the first-ever Olympic women's bobsled competition. "The crowd was tremendous," German bobsledder Nicole Herschmann told the *Atlanta Journal-Constitution*. "It was the loudest crowed I've ever heard. The noise went right through my helmet." Bakken and Flowers's first run was a course record at 48.81 seconds. The combined time for their two runs, 1:37, earned them the gold, with German teams finishing second and third. Racine and Johnson finished fifth. Some attributed the poor finish to karma.

Flowers was greeted at the finish by her mother, husband, and childhood coach. No American had won a medal in bobsledding in forty-six years. It wasn't until after her win, in a tearful celebration, that Flowers was told she was the first African American to win gold at the Winter Olympic Games. "I didn't know I was the first African-American to win a gold medal," she said, according to the *Atlanta Journal-Constitution*. "Hopefully, this won't be the end of it. I hope it gives other African-American boys and girls an opportunity to give winter sports a try."

Flowers and Bakken were chosen to carry the American flag in the closing ceremonies of the Olympics. She appeared on front page of the nation's biggest newspapers, and was a guest with Katie Couric on the *Today* show. "This was a leap of faith," she said, according to the *Milwaukee Journal Sentinel*. "The way I see it, God put me in this sport for a reason. All those years in track and field paid off. God had a plan for me in a bobsled. If God sees fit, I will be back."

FURTHER INFORMATION

Periodicals

"Flowers victory breaks ground." *Detroit News* (February 21, 2002): 8.

Hannigan, Glenn. "Salt Lake City 2002: Historic U.S. upset in bobsled—women make breakthrough in first attempt." *Atlanta Journal-Constitution* (February 20, 2002): C1.

Hiske, Michelle. "Flowers finds gold in cold." *Milwaukee Journal Sentinel*. (February 24, 2002): 1.

Plaschke, Bill. "Flowers shows what happens when someone takes a flier." *Los Angeles Times*. (February 21, 2002): U1.

Wise, Mike. "Changing sports, keeping a teammate." *New York Times*. (February 21, 2002): D5.

Other

"Athlete profile: Vonetta Flowers." U.S. Olympic Team Home Page. http://www.usolympicteam.com/ athlete_profiles/v_flowers.html (January 15, 2003).

"Red, white, and blue debut." CNNSI.com. http://sports illustrated.cnn.com/olympics/2002/bobsled/news/ 2002/02/19/women_bobsled_ap/ (January 15, 2003).

"U.S. women grab first bobsleigh gold." BBC Online. http://news.bbc.co.uk/winterolympics2002/hi/english/ bobsleigh/newsid_1830000/1830688.stm (January 15, 2003).

"Vonetta Flowers." U.S. Bobled and Skeleton Federation Home Page. http://www.usbsf.com/vonetta flowers.htm (January 15, 2003).

Sketch by Brenna Sanchez

Doug Flutie
1962-

American football player

By all accounts Doug Flutie was a great college quarterback, putting his Boston College Eagles back on the map in the 1980s. His 63-yard pass, thrown with no time remaining on the clock, sealed a win over the de-

Doug Flutie

Chronology

1962	Born October 23 in Baltimore, Maryland
1977-81	Plays basketball, baseball, and football for Natick High School in Natick, Massachusetts
1982-84	Starting quarterback for Boston University Eagles
1984	Launches "Hail Mary" pass to win Orange Bowl against University of Miami
1984-85	Plays for United States Football League's (USFL) New Jersey Generals, owned by Donald Trump
1986	Drafted by Los Angles Rams, then traded to the Chicago Bears
1987	Traded to the New England Patriots
1989	Released by the Patriots, joins Canadian Football League's British Columbia Lions
1992	Signs contract with Calgary Stampede
1996	Signs with the Toronto Argonauts
1997	Publishes autobiography, *Flutie.*
1998	Signs with National Football League's Buffalo Bills; establishes the Doug Flutie, Jr. Foundation for Autism
2001	Traded to the San Diego Chargers

fending national champions, the University of Miami, in the 1984 Orange Bowl, and made him a media darling. A scrambling, think-on-your-feet, pass-on-the-run quarterback, Flutie's play was exciting to watch, but at just under five-feet-ten-inches, much too small by most National Football League (NFL) standards, he wouldn't get a real shot at proving himself in the NFL until his fourteenth season as a professional quarterback.

Small Stature, Big Heart

Doug Flutie was born on October 23, 1962, in Baltimore, Maryland and lived for a time as a young child with his grandparents in Manchester, Maryland. When he was six years old, Flutie moved with his parents, Richard and Joan Flutie, and his three siblings to Melbourne, Florida, where he became involved in youth football and baseball. He began playing tackle football at the age of nine, and when he turned twelve years old, he joined the Pop Warner football league. When he was thirteen the family moved to Natick, Massachusetts, where Flutie attended Natick High School.

During his years in high school Flutie, an excellent student, participated in numerous sports. Basketball was his favorite, but by the time he was a senior, it was clear that football was his best. Although his high school football stats garnered the attention of numerous smaller colleges, Flutie wanted to compete at the Division 1-A level, but major universities were hesitant to take him because of his size. At just under five-feet-ten-inches

and 175 pounds, Flutie was considered too small to play Division 1-A football. At the last minute, Boston College (BC) offered Flutie its last available scholarship. Even then, the offer was made only after two other prospects chose other schools, and BC found that a slot still needed filling.

As a freshman at Boston in 1981, Flutie, listed as the team's fourth-string quarterback, sat on the sidelines of his first three games. However, in the fourth game of the season, down 38-0 against Penn State and the first string quarterback hurt, the coach called Flutie's number. It was the only opportunity Flutie needed. By the middle of the season, he was team's starting quarterback. During the 1982 season Flutie led the Eagles to their first post-season bowl game in forty years. Although BC lost the Tangerine Bowl to the Auburn Tigers, Flutie was selected as the game's Most Valuable Player. On the season he completed 184 of 386 passing attempts, with fifteen touchdowns. By 1983, Flutie's junior year, BC was gaining national attention, and two BC games were nationally televised.

The Pass

Flutie played in the biggest college game of his career in the 1984 Orange Bowl against the defending national champions University of Miami Hurricanes and their star sophomore quarterback Bernie Kosar. Despite wet and rainy conditions, Flutie threw for 472 yards and three touchdowns and ran nine yards for another touchdown, making him the first quarterback in major college history to eclipse the mark of 10,000 passing yards. But the most spectacular play of the day occurred with just seconds left in the game. Down 45-41 with six seconds on the clock and the Eagles on their own 37 yard line, Flutie had one play left. In one of the most exciting moments in college football, Flutie flung the ball sixty-three yards into the wind, where it was miraculously

Awards and Accomplishments

1984	Awarded Heisman Trophy; named First Team All American
1991	Completes 466 passes for 6,619 yards, a Canadian Football League (CFL) single-season record
1991-94, **1996-97**	Named Most Outstanding Player CFL
1992, **1996-97**	Awarded CFL Grey Cup as most valuable player
1999	Invited to play in NFL Pro Bowl

pulled down by Flutie's roommate, wide receiver Gerard Phelan, who was waiting in the end zone. With no time left on the clock, BC won the game, 47-45. It would forever be known as simply "the Pass."

The Good, the Bad, and the Outstanding

Despite winning the 1984 Heisman Trophy, the NFL had doubts about Flutie's chances of making it at the professional level, pointing again to his small stature. The Buffalo Bills had first shot at drafting Flutie but had made no commitment to do so. Disappointed in the NFL's response, Flutie opted for the United States Football League (USFL) and a five-year, $7 million contract with the New Jersey Generals, owned by Donald Trump. He suspended his studies and played in his first game as a New Jersey General just a month after hanging up his college uniform. Despite posting a winning record, Flutie's experience in New Jersey was frustrating, and he was booed by the crowds more than once. Returning home after the season's end, 22-year-old Flutie married his high school sweetheart and finished his degree in speech communication at BC.

When the USFL folded before the opening of the 1986 season, Flutie ended up with the Chicago Bears in October 1986. He appeared in just four games, and during one of those, television cameras caught him getting verbally berated by coach **Mike Ditka**. Flutie also had trouble with the team's starting quarterback, Jim McMahon, who publicly referred to him as "America's midget." In October 1987 the Bears traded Flutie to the New England Patriots, but on the year he played in just two games. During the 1988 season Flutie started nine games, passing for 1,150 yards, but he still did not gain the confidence of his coaches. After starting three games early in the 1989 season, he was benched, making only two more appearances the remainder of the year. When Rod Rust became the Patriots' new coach in February 1990, he cut Flutie from the team before spring training camp.

With no immediate takers in the NFL, Flutie turned to the Canadian Football League (CFL), where he found a welcoming home with the British Columbia Lions. Flutie quickly discovered the CFL much to his liking. The league tends toward quicker players, and its rules cater to the passing game. For the first time since he'd left BC, Flutie was again enjoying the game of football.

Playing eight seasons in British Columbia, Calgary, and Toronto, Flutie won the league's most outstanding player honors six times, led the league in passing five times, and took his teams to four Grey Cups, winning three. By 1998 he was really to give the NFL another shot.

Gives the NFL another Shot

In 1998 35-year-old Flutie signed with the Buffalo Bills, who promised him a $50,000 signing bonus and the NFL minimum pay of $275,000 (compared to his $1 million annual paycheck in the CFL), but did not promise a starting spot as quarterback. Nonetheless, Flutie wanted to give the NFL one more try. When the starting quarterback, Rob Johnson, got hurt early in the season, Flutie took over the team and quickly became a fan favorite. During the 1998 season the *Sporting News* noted his resurrection in popularity: "What a story. Left for football dead by NFL geniuses in 1989, Flutie is now America's sweetheart. Still not Robo-QB, still a little guy in a Tall & Big Man's game, he plays with an intuition in motion that can't be taught, can't be measured and will thrill you bone-deep." After the 1999 season Flutie was awarded a four-year, $22 million extension, including a $6 million signing bonus and earned his first trip to the Pro Bowl.

Despite Flutie's popularity and success in Buffalo, he became locked in a battle for the starting position with Johnson, now healthy and who the Bills were paying $5 million a year. By the end of the 1999 season, during which Flutie shared playing time with Johnson, it was clear that there was one quarterback too many on the team, and Flutie was traded to the San Diego Chargers. As the starting quarterback on a struggling team that ended the 2000 season with nine straight losses, Flutie found himself again in competition for the starting spot, this time with the Chargers' talented rookie quarterback Drew Brees. However, unlike his acrid relationship with Johnson, Flutie and Brees became friends, making it easier for Flutie to accept the team's decision to name Brees as the starting quarterback for the 2002 season. Flutie saw action in just one game.

During his time as a professional football player, Flutie has proved a number of adages attached to his career, including "it's not the size of the dog in the fight but the size of fight in the dog." Flutie, who remains close to his family and is a drummer in a band with his brother, is

Career Statistics

Yr	Team	GP	Passing						Rushing			
			ATT	COM	YDS	COM%	TD	INT	RAT	ATT	YDS	TD
1985	NJ (US)	15	281	134	2109	47.7	13	14	—	65	465	6
1986	Chi	4	46	23	361	50.0	3	2	80.1	9	36	1
1987	Chi/NE	2	25	15	199	60.0	1	0	98.6	6	43	0
1988	NE	11	179	92	1150	51.4	8	10	63.3	38	179	1
1989	NE	5	91	36	493	39.6	2	4	46.6	16	87	0
1990	BC (C)	16	392	207	2960	52.8	16	19	—	79	662	3
1991	BC (C)	18	730	466	6619	63.8	38	24	—	120	610	14
1992	Cal (C)	18	688	396	5945	57.6	32	30	—	96	669	11
1993	Cal (C)	18	703	416	6092	59.2	44	17	—	74	373	11
1994	Cal (C)	18	659	403	5726	61.2	48	19	—	96	760	8
1995	Cal (C)	11	332	223	2788	67.2	16	5	—	46	288	5
1996	Tor (C)	18	677	434	5720	64.1	29	17	—	101	756	9
1997	Tor (C)	18	673	430	5505	67.5	47	24	—	55	358	2
1998	Buf	13	354	202	2711	57.1	20	11	87.4	48	248	1
1999	Buf	15	478	264	3171	55.2	19	16	75.1	88	476	1
2000	Buf	11	231	132	1700	57.1	8	3	86.5	36	161	1
2001	SD	16	521	294	3464	56.4	15	18	72.0	53	192	1
2002	SD	1	11	3	64	27.2	0	0	51.3	1	6	0
TOTAL		229	7082	4173	56841	52.2	359	233	—	1092	6269	78

BC: British Columbia Lions; Buf: Buffalo Bills; C: Canadian Football League; Cal: Calgary Stampeders; Chi: Chicago Bears; NE: New England Patriots; NJ: New Jersey Generals; SD: San Diego Chargers; Tor: Toronto Argonauts; US: United States Football League.

content that he no longer has to wonder if he could have made it in the NFL. He has.

CONTACT INFORMATION

Address: San Diego Chargers, 9449 Friars Rd., San Diego, California. Phone: (858)874-4500.

SELECTED WRITINGS BY FLUTIE:

(With Perry Lefko) *Flutie,* Warwick Publishing, 1998.

FURTHER INFORMATION

Books

Newsmakers 1999, Issue 2. Detroit: Gale Group, 1999.

Periodicals

Ballard, Sarah. "Portrait of a Hero in Limbo." *Sports Illustrated* (December 2, 1985): 52.

Deacon, James. "The Flutie Phenomenon." *Maclean's* (November 16, 1998): 81.

Hutchings, David. "Flutie's Patootie, Laurie Fortier, Thinks He Made His Best Pass Six Years Ago: At Her." *People* (May 6, 1985): 69-70.

Kindred, Dave. "Flutie Finally Fits into the NFL." *Sporting News* (November 16, 1998): 71.

King, Peter. "Inside the NFL." *Sports Illustrated* (December 27, 1999): 138.

Lambert, Pam, Cynthia Wang, and Michelle York. "Football's Doug Flutie Proves He's Got What It Takes." *People* (December 7, 1998): 181.

Layden, Tim. "Fight to the Finnish." *Sports Illustrated* (August 12, 2002): 40.

Looney, Douglas S. "A Little Man on Campus." *Sports Illustrated* (September 26, 1983): 38+.

Looney, Douglas S. "Flutie's B.C. Connection." *Sports Illustrated* (August 20, 1990): 52.

Maloney, Rick. "Marketers Choc Full of Flutie Ideas." *Business First of Buffalo* (December 21, 1998): 1-2.

Montville, Leigh. "Passing Time." *Sports Illustrated* (June 22, 1998): 58.

Pompei, Dan. "Bills Gamble Little by Taking a Flier on Flutie." *Sporting News* (February 2, 1998): 25.

Pompei, Dan. "Flutie Fits the Bills Better, but Johnson is Coach's Pick." *Sporting News* (November 20, 2000): 14.

Silver, Michael. "Re-Charged." *Sports Illustrated* (October 8, 2001): 50.

Underwood, John. "It Wasn't a Fluke. It was a Flutie." *Sports Illustrated* (December 3, 1984): 22.

Wiley, Ralph. "A Pocketful of Dreams." *Sports Illustrated* (February 25, 1985): 24.

Wulf, Steve. "Mr. Touchdown Scores Again." *Sports Illustrated* (February 4, 1985): 20.

Zimmerman, Paul. "Magic Flutie." *Sports Illustrated,* (December 7, 1992): 44-45.

Other

"Doug Flutie." National Football League. http://www.nfl.com/ (December 28, 2002)

Sketch by Kari Bethel

George Foreman

George Foreman
1949-

American boxer

The George Foreman of today, genial, gentlemanly, and widely popular, bears little resemblance to his early thuggish person. Indeed, some have called him a "Dr. Jekyll and Mr. Hyde" in reverse, who transformed himself from the monster into the good and pleasant fellow. He captured the hearts of boxing fans when he re-entered heavyweight competitions after ten years away, and managed to recapture the title at the age of 45, twenty years after losing it to **Muhammad Ali**. Today, a successful entrepreneur, actor, founder of his own church, and a "grand old man" of boxing, George Foreman can smile out at the world. It was not always so.

More Than Enough Fury

George Foreman was born on January 10, 1949, to J.D. and Nancy Foreman, in Marshall, Texas, the fifth of seven children. Shortly after his birth, the family moved to Houston, where his mother hoped to find better work. His largely absentee father was a railroad worker, but he usually drank away his salary, so the family generally depended on his mother's earnings at various jobs. As Foreman recalled in his autobiography *By George,* "There was always more than enough fury in my house, and never enough food." Young George grew up poor and angry, but big. His size and aggression soon earned him respect on the streets of Houston's Fifth Ward, nicknamed "The Bloody Fifth," for the number of knife

fights that took place there. After dropping out of junior high, he began a life of petty crime.

By age 16 George Foreman was 6'1" and 185 pounds, and he had already gotten a taste of strong-arm robbery and work as an "enforcer." Then he spotted an ad for the Job Corps on television. He joined up and was sent to Grant's Pass, Oregon, and later to Parks Center, California. All meals were provided, so for once Foreman had enough to eat, and he got a monthly allowance of $30, plus $50 a month held in escrow until he had finished his two-year stint. Still, he could not stop fighting. He got into fights in his dormitory, and in the nearby town of Pleasanton, California. One day, while counselors were trying to pull him off one of his victims, Doc Broadus, a supervisor, stepped in to end the fight. Broadus, a boxing enthusiast, spotted Foreman's obvious potential and decided to channel it into boxing. With help from Broadus, Foreman developed his skills and within two years, he had qualified for the Olympic boxing team.

So in 1968, George Foreman headed for Mexico City. This was a difficult time in the U.S., with rioting in the streets in many American cities over civil rights and Vietnam, and there were divisions within the African American community over whether to support U.S. policy. These divisions were on display when two African American track winners, John Carlos and **Tommie Smith**, stood with clenched fists upraised during the playing of the "Star Spangled Banner." Carlos and Smith were ejected from the Olympic Village. Foreman was tempted to join their protest, but Carlos encouraged him to keep on. Foreman did, and he won the gold medal in heavyweight boxing. At the victory ceremony, Foreman waved a small American flag. For some back home, this was seen as a betrayal of Carlos and Smith, and maybe even the civil rights struggle. Feeling that he did not belong in the Fifth Ward anymore, Foreman eagerly snapped up a job offer by Doc Broadus to teach boxing at the Job Corps in Parks Center. He undertook a serious training regimen, avoiding alcohol and smoking.

Turning Pro

George Foreman turned pro in 1969, going up against Don Walheim on June 23, in his first professional boxing match. He won, and by the end of the year he was 13-0, with 11 knockouts to his credit. The following year, he knocked out 11 men, and won his twelfth match by a decision. Foreman was moving up fast, and in 1970, the respected *Ring* magazine ranked him second among heavyweight contenders. In the next couple of years, he continued his unbroken winning streak, earning twelve straight knockouts. Some grumbled that he had been fighting has-beens and never-wases, but now he had earned his shot to go up against an undisputed champion.

In January 22, 1973, in Kingston, Jamaica, he met the much-feared **Joe Frazier**. As usual, Frazier came out swinging against his opponent, but he was met by a long left and a hard right that sent him to the mat twice in the first round. The crowd was stunned, but the second round was even worse for Frazier, who hit the mat three times. Foreman actually lifted Frazier off the mat with one of his punches, and he signaled to Frazier's corner to call the fight, fearing he might kill the champ. Fortunately, the referee stepped in shortly afterwards, calling the fight for Foreman. The world had a new heavyweight champion.

Champion

At 6'3" and 220 pounds, George Foreman was certainly a powerful champ, but there was more. He seemed to give off an air of menace that reminded some observers of **Sonny Liston**. It may have been calculated, but there was no doubting that Foreman had a lot of pent-up rage. As he admitted in his autobiography: "I became the stereotypical heavyweight champ—surly and angry. If someone asked for an autograph in a restauarant, I'd say, 'What do you think, that I'm going to stop eating and sign my name?' Then my eyes would sweep the room in a mean glare."

That anger did serve him well in the ring. He easily beat his first challenger, Jose "King" Roman on September 1, 1973, with a first-round knockout in Tokyo. Ken Norton was a little harder. That knockout took two rounds, on March 26, 1974, in Caracas, Venezuela. So Foreman was looking secure when he went up against Muhammad Ali, in Kinshasha, Zaire, for the legendary "Rumble in the Jungle." It was not a good setting for

Foreman, who missed American food and living space. And there was an element of feeling rejected. As he wrote, "This was clearly Muhammad Ali country. Sentiment in his favor colored how everyone looked at me—and they did so incessantly, their eyes following me everywhere." By the time of the match, on October 30, 1974, Foreman was restless and feeling aggressive. He came at Ali with a rapid flurry of punches, but this time Foreman had met his match. Ali absorbed the blows, continually taunting his rival, and then knocked Foreman out in the 8th round. For the first time, Foreman had lost—and this time it cost him the heavyweight championship.

Difficult Years

The loss was a severe blow to Foreman's pride. He was devastated. "Now that he had lost for the first time, he lived with a quiet terror. He could not stop spending money or conquering women. Every day for the next 30 days he went to bed with a different woman—some days, two," wrote *Sports Illustrated* reporter Gary Smith. Foreman himself told Smith, "After I'd lost to Ali, I'd decided I needed more hate. I'd hit you in the kidneys or on the back of the head. I'd beat women as hard as I beat men. You psych yourself to become an animal to box, and that's what you become."

When he lost a big match to Jimmy Young, on March 17, 1977, Foreman went into a strange cathartic state in the dressing room. He tried to look past the fight, toward other opportunities in his life. "But no matter how hard I focused on positives, my thinking was dominated by death," he wrote in his autobiography. "My pacing back and forth was no longer about cooling down; it was about staying alive.... As I fell to the floor of my dressing room, my leg crumpling beneath me, my nostrils filled with the stink of infection. I recognized it instantly as the smell of absolute despair and hopelessness." At that point, he underwent a real religious conversion, embracing Christianity for the first time in his life. He even saw the signs of crucifixion on his own body.

The Road Back

George Foreman returned to Houston, where he began preaching on street corners, in prisons, and in hospitals. He gave up boxing to focus on this new career and even founded his own church, the Church of the Lord Jesus Christ, in a mobile home. He had never felt more at peace with what he was doing. Not that everything went smoothly. Between 1981 and 1983, he was married and divorced three times. One wife fled to Barbados with their children, but Foreman flew there and literally stole them back. Again, he was forced to take a hard look at his life, to try to figure out what he wanted from women, and what they expected from him.

Between 1983 and 1986, he finally achieved some inner peace, preaching at his church. He married again, and had a son named George (like all his other sons). He had also managed to build a small gym next to the church, where neighborhood kids could find alternatives to hanging out on the streets where he had gotten into so much trouble as a youngster. But the money from his boxing days was beginning to run out, and his kids (eight by now, from various wives), were approaching college age. At the age of 40, George Foreman decided to return to the ring.

It was a momentous decision, but one greeted with a lot of skepticism in the sporting world. The boxing world saw a flabby, middle-aged man with a legendary fondness for junk food. The comeback seemed like more of a joke than a serious attempt, but Foreman was serious— and successful. As Gerald Suster wrote in *Champions of the Ring,* "Big George carried right on eating vast quantities of junk food hamburgers, joking about the fact—and knocking out everyone they put in front of him, clocking up 19 straight wins by KO from 1987 to 1990."

By April 1991, Big George could not be ignored, and heavyweight champ **Evander Holyfield** agreed to fight him. The match ended with a Holyfield victory, but by going the distance, Foreman proved that he was no joke. In November 1994, he got another shot at the title, this time against Michael Moorer, who was nearly 20 years his junior. Two minutes in the tenth round, with one walloping punch, George Foreman regained the World Boxing Association and International Boxing Federation heavyweight titles at age 45. It was a remarkable achievement, and forever enshrined him in boxing legend.

In addition to his age, commentators also noted the change in George Foreman from his previous reign. Gone were the snarl and the menacing stance. Instead, a genial and even cheerful man occupied the championship. This newfound popularity was a nice change for Foreman. Due mainly to boxing politics, his title did not last long. In April of 1995, he was stripped of his WBA title when he decided to fight Alex Schultz instead of number-one-ranked Tony Tucker. That fall, he refused to fight Schultz a second time, and for that he was stripped of his IBF title. But nobody could take away that triumph of November 1994 and his new popularity.

CONTACT INFORMATION

Address: George Foreman Community Center, 2202 Lone Oak Road, Houston, TX 77093-3336.

SELECTED WRITINGS BY FOREMAN:

(With Joel Engel) *By George,* New York: Touchstone Books, 1995, 2000.
George Foreman's Guide to Life: How to Get Up Off the Canvas When Life Knocks You Down. New York: Simon and Schuster, 2003.

FURTHER INFORMATION

Books

Foreman, George, and Joel Engel. *By George.* New York: Touchstone Books, 1995, 2000.
Foreman, George. *George Foreman's Guide to Life: How to Get Up Off the Canvas When Life Knocks You Down.* New York: Simon and Schuster, 2003.

Periodicals

Hoffer, Richard. "Fat chance." *Sports Illustrated* (May 1, 1995): 40.
Hoffer, Richard. "Ko'd." *Sports Illustrated* (November 14, 1994): 18.
"Judgement call." *Sports Illustrated* (December 22, 1997): 24.
Putnam, Pat. "No joke: Evander Holyfield discovered that George Foreman was to be taken seriously." *Sports Illustrated* (April 29, 1991): 22.
Putnam, Pat. "Ungorgeous George." *Sports Illustrated* (April 20, 1992): 38.
Smith, Gary. "After the fall." *Sports Illustrated* (October 8, 1984): 62.
Zinczenko, David. "Never count him out." *Men's Health* (April 1995): 120.

Sketch by Robert Winters

Magdalena Forsberg
1967-

Swedish biathlete

Madgalena Forsberg was one of the most successful biathletes in history. She was also one of the most popular: fully one-eighth of the population of her native country, Sweden, used to tune in on television to watch her compete, even though before she won the first of her

Magdalena Forsberg

<table>
<tr><td colspan="2">Chronology</td></tr>
<tr><td>1967</td><td>Born July 25 in Oernskdelosvik, Sweden</td></tr>
<tr><td>1992</td><td>Competes in Olympics in cross-country skiing</td></tr>
<tr><td>1994</td><td>Has surgery to repair a torn Achilles tendon</td></tr>
<tr><td>1994</td><td>Takes up biathlon</td></tr>
<tr><td>1995</td><td>Wins first World Cup biathlon event</td></tr>
<tr><td>1996</td><td>Marries Henrik Forsberg</td></tr>
<tr><td>1998</td><td>Competes in Olympics in biathlon</td></tr>
<tr><td>2002</td><td>Wins first Olympic medal, a bronze</td></tr>
<tr><td>2002</td><td>Retires from competition</td></tr>
</table>

six overall World Cup titles biathlon was rarely televised at all. Forsberg achieved all of this despite not taking up biathlon until the age of twenty-seven and retiring, at the height of her success, at age thirty-four.

A Career Change

Forsberg started her athletic career as a cross-country skier. She skied for the Swedish national team for several years, and as part of that country s relay team she won a bronze medal at the 1987 World Cross-Country Skiing Championships. Forsberg missed her chance to compete in cross-country skiing in the 1988 Olympics because of an illness, and when she did compete in 1992 she fared poorly, finishing no higher than twenty-sixth in any individual event. After an injury and subsequent surgery to her Achilles tendon kept her out of the 1994 Olympics, Forsberg gave up competitive cross-country skiing.

Around the same time Forsberg took up biathlon, a sport which combines cross-country skiing and shooting. She already knew how to handle a gun; she had learned the skill from her father, Jan, who used to take Forsberg along when he went hunting for moose when she was a child. Forsberg claims that she was only interested in trying biathlon for fun, not for prizes, but she started competing on the biathlon World Cup circuit in 1994. By the end of her rookie 1994-95 season, Forsberg had finished first in one 7.5 kilometer sprint event and was fifth in the overall World Cup points

standings, much to her own amazement. "I had to ask, Who is this person?", she later recalled. "This cannot be me."

The Other Skiing Forsberg

Part of Forsberg's motivation for trying biathlon was her fiancee, Henrik Forsberg, who also began as a cross-country skier and then moved to biathlon. (The two were married in 1996; prior to her marriage to Henrik, Forsberg competed as Magdalena Wallin.) Henrik's sole win in his career came in a thirty kilometer cross-country race in 1991, but Forsberg plays down the difference in their records, attributing it to Henrik's many injuries. Because of that, he hasn t shown what he can do, she explained to CNN/SI before the 1998 Winter Olympics. Henrik missed two world championships, 1989 and 1993, because of illness, he broke his leg in 1996, and in 1997 he had surgery on one arm. Despite all of this missed time, Henrik has collected one second place finish and five third place finishes in World Cup events in his career in addition to his one win. He continues to compete, and finished forty-seventh in the twenty kilometer biathlon at the 2002 Salt Lake City Olympics.

World Cup Victories and International Defeats

Forsberg won her first World Cup titles in 1997, when she finished on top of the points standings in the overall and the pursuit categories. Her Swedish fans had strong hopes that she would win a medal at the 1998 Nagano Olympics, but it was not to be. The pressure affected Forsberg's nerves and she shot poorly. The Swedish team finished tenth in the relay, and Forsberg's individual results were fourteenth place in the individual-start event and seventeenth in the sprint. However, Forsberg did well on the World Cup circuit again that year. She successfully defended her title in the pursuit category, and she was the runner-up in two other specialties and in the overall.

In the next three seasons, Forsberg won a total of eleven World Cup titles, including the Grand Slam the overall, sprint, individual-start, mass-start, and pursuit titles, all in one year in 2000-01. Again, going into the 2002 Salt Lake City Olympics Forsberg was favored to

Awards and Accomplishments

1996	World Cup, overall and pursuit
1997	World Cup, pursuit
1998, 2000	World championships, pursuit
1998-2000	World Cup, overall, sprint, and pursuit
1999-2001	Voted most popular athlete in Sweden
2001	World championships, mass-start and individual
2001	World Cup, overall, mass-start, individual, sprint, and pursuit
2002	Bronze medal, Salt Lake City Olympics, 15 km individual and 7.5 km sprint

Forty-two career victories in World Cup races.

medal in several events, and again she faltered under the weight of expectations. She could have won the gold in the fifteen kilometer individual event if she had made at least two her final three shots, but her legs were shaking and she missed twice. Instead, she won the bronze, her first Olympic medal. A few days later Forsberg added another medal to her collection by finishing third in the 7.5 kilometer sprint.

Going Out at the Top

Forsberg, who was thirty-four in Salt Lake City, announced before the Olympics that she would retire at the end of the season that year. She did, but not before sweeping all of the World Cup titles for the second year in a row and winning eight of the twenty-two World Cup races held that season. After clinching her final World Cup, the mass-start, in the last World Cup race she would ever compete in, Forsberg reflected, "You have to stop one day. It was a perfect place to end my career. But I felt sad in the morning and tears came into my eyes when I dressed before the race."

CONTACT INFORMATION

Online: www.magdalenaforsberg.com (Swedish only).

FURTHER INFORMATION

Periodicals

Cazeneuve, Brian. "Sweden's Big Gun." *Sports Illustrated,* (February 4, 2002): 142.

"Forsberg Clinches 6th Biathlon Title." *New York Times,* (March 22, 2002): D7.

"Forsberg's Long Quest Nets Bronze." *Houston Chronicle,* (February 12, 2002): 4.

Hillenbrand, Barry. "Have Gun, Will Triumph." *Time International,* (February 25, 2002): 48.

"Swede Ends Career in Grand Style." *New York Times,* (March 25, 2002): D9.

"Who to Watch." *Newsweek International,* (February 11, 2002): 46.

Other

"Athlete of the Day: Henrik and Magdalena Forsberg." CNN/SI. http://sportsillustrated.cnn.com/olympics/events/1998/nagano/athlete_of_day/forsberg.html (January 22, 2003).

"Biathlon: Magdalena Forsberg." Washingtonpost.com. http://www.washingtonpost.com/wp-srv/sports/longterm/olympics1998/sport/profiles/forsberg.htm (January 15, 2003).

Crossen, Judith. "Four-Gold Bjoerndalen Makes it Ole-Olympics." Yahoo! Sports. http://ca.sports.yahoo.com/020221/5/kwc0.html (February 21, 2002).

"Magdalena Forsberg." International Biathlon Union. http://www.ibu.at/biographies/btswe22507196701.html (January 15, 2003).

"Magdalena Forsberg." Wintersport. http://www.wintersport.as/mforsberg/merits.php (January 15, 2003).

"Magdalena Forsberg's Home Page." http://www.magdalenaforsberg.com (January 22, 2003).

"Sweden's Forsberg Completes Biathlon's Grand Slam in Final Race." Slam! Sports. http://www.canoe.ca/SlamResults020324/ski_biathlon-ap.html (January 22, 2003).

Sketch by Julia Bauder

Rube Foster
1879-1930

American baseball player

Andrew "Rube" Foster, founder and first president of the Negro National League, is known as the Father of Black Baseball. An outstanding pitcher who began his own career as a player at age 17, Foster supported black teams throughout his life and worked for the legitimization, respect, and financial success of African-American baseball. A creative and intelligent businessman, Foster also helped to form the Chicago American Giants, a powerhouse team that some say would have rivaled the New York Yankees had they been allowed to play in the same league. Foster began his career as a team manager with the Leland Giants in 1907, urging them to a 110-10 record. His Chicago American Giants took home the Negro National League's first three pennants, in 1920, 1921, and 1922. Although his career came to an end in 1926 after he suffered a mental breakdown, Foster had firmly established the Negro leagues as an important institution in American baseball. Even though the leagues began to decline after 1945, when **Jackie Robinson** became the first African American to play in the major leagues, they had brought well-deserved recognition to

African-American athletes in the United States. Foster was inducted into the Baseball Hall of Fame in 1981 for his contribution to the sport.

Boyhood and Early Barnstorming Career

Andrew Foster was born September 17, 1879, in Calvert, Texas, the son of Andrew Foster, Sr., presiding elder at the Calvert Methodist Episcopal Church, and Sarah Foster. He suffered from asthma as a boy but became as enthusiastic about baseball as he was about attending church. He was soon organizing a neighborhood team, and his interest grew as he did. After his mother died, his father remarried and moved to southwest Texas. Andrew completed the eighth grade and left home to pursue his love of baseball. At age 17 he joined the traveling Fort Worth, Texas, Yellow Jackets and began a barnstorming career that was typical of African-American teams of his time. Ironically, the traveling ball players were looked down on by fellow blacks, who considered them "low and ungentlemanly," according to Foster, as quoted in Robert Peterson's *Only the Ball Was White*.

In addition to traveling with the Yellow Jackets, Foster pitched to white major league teams that came to Texas for spring training. Legend has it that during a 1901 batting practice with **Connie Mack**'s Philadelphia Athletics, baseball manager John McGraw recognized Foster's pitching ability and wanted him for his New York Giants. However, blacks were barred from playing in the major leagues.

Moves North, Earns Nickname

In 1902, Foster moved to Chicago, where he joined the Chicago Union Giants, better known as the Leland Giants for owner Frank Leland, a veteran of black baseball. The same year, he moved to Philadelphia and switched to E. B. Lamar's Union Giants, or Cuban Giants. Around this time he outpitched the Philadelphia Athletics's star pitcher Rube Waddell in an exhibition game, earning himself the nickname "Rube" as a trophy. It would stick with him for the rest of his life.

In 1903 he switched to a rival Philadelphia team, the Cuban X-Giants, pitching that fall in black baseball's first World Series, which the X-Giants won five games to two. Legend has it that the same year McGraw asked Foster to teach his "fadeaway" screwball pitch to his New York Giants pitchers **Christy Mathewson**, Iron Man McGinnity, and Red Ames. Soon afterward, the Giants rose from last place in the league to second.

In 1904, Foster and most of the X-Giants team switched back to the Union Giants and won the three-game World Series over their former team. Statistics on Foster are often missing or sketchy and the truth is hard to determine, but for 1905 he is noted to have won 51 out of 56 games. Unhappy with his pay by 1906, Foster left Philadelphia to rejoin the Leland Giants in Chicago, where he offered to both play for and manage the team. Bringing seven of his best players with him, including power hitters John Henry Lloyd, Grant "Home Run" Johnson, and Pete Hill, Foster persuaded Frank Leland to fire his team members and hire Foster's. The new team won the Chicago semipro title in 1907, winning 110 out of 120 games, with 48 consecutive wins. In a postseason series against the Chicago City All-Stars, a white team that hired major and minor league players, Foster pitched four winning games, and his team finished first.

Foster's pitching skills were by this time so finely tuned that Hall of Famer **Honus Wagner** once called him "one of the greatest pitchers of all time . . . smartest pitcher I've ever seen." Chicago Cubs manager Frank Chance called him "the most finished product I've ever seen in the pitcher's box." Foster was a big man, standing six feet four inches tall and weighing between 224 and 260 pounds. Although the fans loved him, many players were said to dislike or even fear him because he "engaged in personalities" when he pitched and often carried his Texas six-guns. He unnerved players by smiling and appearing jovial and unconcerned on the field. He often distracted batters and tricked them into striking out. His searing fastball and powerful underhand screwball made him a star pitching attraction of black baseball and the envy of many white pitchers.

Chicago American Giants

The facts are unclear on the year in which Foster first formed his great team the Chicago American Giants. Some sources say he changed the Leland Giants's name to American Giants as early as 1908, but most say he first formed the team in 1911, after entering into a partnership with John M. Schorling, a white tavern owner who was also baseball manager Charles Comiskey's son-in-law. This partnership allowed the American Giants to make use of the Chicago White Sox's former home at South Side Park after the white team moved into the new Comiskey Park.

Whether the Leland Giants or the American Giants, however, Foster's team in 1910 won 123 out of 129 games. No major league ball club stepped forward to respond to Foster's challenge of a series game that year. His team had narrowly lost to the Chicago Cubs in such a challenge in 1909. By 1911, the Chicago American Giants dominated semipro baseball in Chicago as well as national black baseball. They played about half of their games barnstorming and half in the Chicago City League, which included one other black team and a dozen white semipro teams.

The American Giants's popularity grew with each season. They won the Chicago semipro crown in 1911 and 1912. They enlisted **Jack Johnson**, heavyweight boxing champion, to give souvenirs to women fans and heavily advertised their games. While barnstorming, they traveled by private Pullman railroad car. The team wore a different set of uniforms each day and played with a variety of bats and balls. Foster was not above using certain tricks to ensure the success of his team. He reportedly froze baseballs to make them harder to hit and built slight ridges along the foul lines so bunted balls would stay within the playing field. Emulating such powerful white baseball executives as Ban Johnson and John McGraw, Foster paid his players well, demanded top performance from them, and enticed new players with the promise of prestige and the best in travel amenities. But for the color of his skin, Foster would likely have equaled his two colleagues in professional stature.

Some of the Chicago American Giants players who have since become baseball legends themselves were **James "Cool Papa" Bell**, Willie Wells, and Oscar Charleston. Many of the American Giants were known as "racehorses" because they could sprint a hundred yards in less than ten seconds. Foster continued to pitch for the team and developed a technique of bunt-and-run for his batters that nearly always led to successful plays. The fans, both black and white, loved the Giants. According to Michael L. Cooper in *Playing America's Game: The Story of Negro League Baseball*, one Sunday in 1911 when all three Chicago teams played at home, the Giants drew some 11,000 fans, the White Sox 9,000, and the Cubs 6,000. The American Giants won black baseball championships in 1914 and 1917 and shared the 1915 championship with the New York Lincoln Stars. They also won the California Winter League crown in 1915, competing with white major leaguers following the regular season. In 1916, with Foster still pitching for them at age 35, the Giants won the Colored World Series against the Brooklyn Royal Giants. By 1918, Foster was paying his players $1,700 a month, yet some Eastern teams enticed them away for more money.

The Negro National League

The atmosphere at the time Foster formed a separate league for black baseball players was one of growth and change, even violent unrest, in Chicago. The African-American population of the city had doubled between 1910 and 1920, as blacks fled ill treatment in the South and moved north for jobs in factories and stockyards. In 1919, Chicago and other cities were torn by race riots. National Guardsmen moved in after thirty-eight people were killed in the city. Although opportunities were plentiful for black entrepreneurs, many of the profits were retained by whites. African-American intellectual John Hope had said, "The white man has converted and reconverted the Negro's labor and the Negro's money

Awards and Accomplishments

1906	Pitched Philadelphia Giants to 3-2 win over Cuban X-Giants for Negro Championship Cup
1907	Managed and played for Leland Giants, to 110-10 finish and pennant win in Chicago's otherwise all-white City League
1911-12	Managed American Giants to win Chicago semipro crown
1914	Managed American Giants to win Chicago City League pennant
1915	Managed American Giants to tie for pennant with New York Lincoln Stars
1915	Managed American Giants to win California Winter League Crown in competition with white major leaguers after end of season
1916	Managed American Giants to win colored World Series
1917	Managed American Giants to win Chicago City League pennant
1920-22	Managed American Giants to three Negro National League pennant wins
1981	Inducted into Baseball Hall of Fame

into capital until we find an immense section of the developed country owned by whites and worked by colored. . . . We must take in some, if not all, of the wages, turn it into capital, hold it, increase it."

What was true in the general economy for blacks was also true in black baseball. White interests controlled the stadiums where black teams played and took large percentages of the gate. Teams that objected were not allowed to play. White booking agents had already begun to do away with black team owners and control the teams themselves. Foster wanted to create an all-black baseball enterprise that would keep money earned from games in black pockets. He wanted to form a league for black players that would mirror the major leagues and would eventually play the white leagues in World Series games. He also foresaw the integration of baseball and wanted to be ready to accept white teams into black leagues and vice versa.

Launching a public relations campaign through the *Chicago Defender,* in 1919 Foster called a meeting of the Midwest's best black ball clubs and proposed the formation of a Negro National League, to be governed by the National Association of Colored Professional Base Ball Clubs. After a year-long struggle, on February 13 and 14, 1920, Foster met with owners of the black clubs at the Kansas City, Missouri, Young Men's Christian Association and presented to them a constitution forming the league, with complete incorporation papers. The constitution laid down rules of conduct during games and prohibited team-jumping and raiding other teams for players, among other restrictions. Foster said his goal in forming the league was "to create a profession that would equal the earning capacity of any other profession . . . keep Colored baseball from the control of whites [and] do something concrete for the loyalty of the Race." The owners accepted the agreement, and within the year the Negro National League (NNL), whose motto was "We are the ship, all else the sea," played its first contest.

The original NNL consisted of the Chicago American Giants, Chicago Giants, St. Louis Giants, Dayton Marcos, Detroit Stars, Indianapolis ABCs, Cincinnati Cuban Stars, and the Kansas City Monarchs. It provided for black ownership of all Negro National League teams, but one white owner, J. L. Wilkinson of the Kansas City Monarchs, was retained. A highly popular owner who proved to have the players' best interests at heart, Wilkinson managed the Monarchs to become one of the most successful black teams in history. By the mid-1940s, the Monarchs would include such players as **Buck O'Neil** and Jackie Robinson. In his mid-eighties, O'Neil was considered a national spokesman for Negro league baseball and was featured prominently in the nine-part film by Ken Burns, *Baseball,* which covers the Negro leagues and deals with the subject of race in baseball as an underlying theme.

The club owners elected Foster as first NNL commissioner, and he worked wholeheartedly to make the league and its teams a success. He sent his former player Pete Hill to coach the Detroit Stars and gave up Oscar Charleston to the Indianapolis ABCs in order to strengthen those teams. To ensure that payrolls were met on time, Foster sometimes took out loans or paid salaries out of his own pocket. He called everyone "Darlin'" and smoked a big pipe, and he is said to have had total control over his players on the field. He constantly shifted players within the league to bring equality to teams and avoid criticism from some owners who claimed he had too much power and could hire umpires favorable to his own team, the American Giants. Some even called him the Godfather of Black Baseball, because he had a majority interest in the Detroit Stars and the Dayton Marcos as well. A successful businessman, Foster also owned a barbershop and an automobile service shop.

Foster's Chicago American Giants continued to play as well as ever under the new league, winning the pennant in 1920, 1921, and 1922. Inspired by the NNL, Southern teams formed the Southern Negro League in the spring of 1920. It was made up of teams from Atlanta, New Orleans, Memphis, Birmingham, and Nashville. Although not as prosperous as the NNL, these teams supplied northern teams with some players who would become famous in their day, such as George "Mule" Suttles, Norman "Turkey" Stearnes, and the great pitcher **Satchel Paige**.

In 1923, East Coast teams formed the Eastern Colored League (ECL), including teams from Philadelphia, Brooklyn, Atlantic City, Baltimore, and two New York teams. According to Cooper, in 1922 the American Giants had faced off against the Atlantic City Bacharachs and played for nineteen innings with neither team scoring. Finally, the Bacharachs placed a right fielder with a weak arm, and Foster signaled his batter to hit to right field. The fielder's throw fell short of home plate, and the Giants won the game 1-0.

Foster continued to manage his Giants and the NNL in 1923, and he made efforts to merge the NNL and the ECL in 1924 but was unsuccessful. The Kansas City Monarchs met the Philadelphia Hilldale Club in the first Negro World Series in 1924. After a tie of four wins apiece in games played in four different cities, the Monarchs won the World Series title in the last game, 5-0. In 1925, the Hilldale Club beat the Monarchs in the Series; the American Giants won the Negro World Series in 1926 and 1927, although Foster was too ill to see them play.

Decline into Mental Illness and Death

Some historians have said that Foster's tireless work in establishing and managing the NNL and his own team had ruined his health by the mid-1920s. In 1925 he was exposed to a gas leak in a room in Indianapolis and was pulled from the room unconscious. Although he recovered, his health was never the same. In 1926 his behavior became so erratic that he was placed in the Illinois State Hospital in Kankakee, where he lived out the rest of his life. Although he talked constantly of baseball and wanted desperately to win another pennant, Foster never saw his Giants play in the Negro World Series for which he had worked so hard. He died of a heart attack on December 9, 1930. More than 3,000 mourners attended his funeral in Chicago, standing in icy rain and wind to witness the procession and pay their respects. He was eulogized as the "father of Negro baseball." His widow, Sarah Watts Foster, was unfamiliar with his business arrangements and realized no benefits from his ventures. His partner, John Schorling, had sold the American Giants to a white florist, William E. Trimble, in 1928. Although black businessmen bought it in 1930, the team never reached its former level.

The NNL dissolved in 1931, during the Great Depression, after several years of declining financial success and the absence of Foster's guiding hand. It was revived, however, in the mid-1930s, and black teams went on to play in the Negro leagues until about 1960, some fifteen years after Jackie Robinson became the first African-American player of the twentieth century to sign with a white major league team. The integration of African-American players into the major leagues caused fans to follow those teams with greater interest, and the Negro leagues declined and finally folded.

Foster's Legacy

Although it meant the end of the Negro leagues, integration was the ultimate goal of Rube Foster and his colleagues, and it was achieved. Nearly forty more black players had followed Robinson into the major leagues by 1949, among them, **Roy Campanella**, **Willie Mays**, **Hank Aaron**, and Paige. Foster had devoted his energy and his life to black baseball and to the uplifting of the sport and of his fellow African-American athletes, whom he helped to gain a high level of respect. He served as a star

pitcher until his late thirties, served for some fifteen years as a baseball manager, and served as commissioner of the NNL for five years. He has often been called the greatest baseball manager of any race. Foster was also a great teacher, who taught not only his pitching skills to some of the game's greatest pitchers but his managing skills to a second generation of black managers, including Oscar Charleston, Dave Malarcher, and Biz Mackey. His induction into the Baseball Hall of Fame in 1981 and the establishment of the Negro Leagues Baseball Museum in Kansas City during the mid-1990s leave no doubt that Foster and the ideals for which he stood have achieved a national appreciation.

FURTHER INFORMATION

Books

Cooper, Michael L. *Playing America's Game: The Story of Negro League Baseball*. New York: Dutton, 1993.

Lester, Larry, Sammy J. Miller, and Dick Clark. *Black Baseball in Detroit*. Arcadia Publishing, 2000.

Notable Black American Men. Detroit: Gale, 1998.

Peterson, Robert. *Only the Ball Was White*. Englewood Cliffs, NJ: Prentice-Hall, 1970.

Periodicals

Keisser, Bob. "When Only the Ball Was White History: Former Negro League Players Spread the Word about Their Innovative Game." *Long Beach Press-Telegram* (February 24, 1997): C1.

Story, Rosalyn. "A Museum of Their Own: Kansas City Preserves the Legacy of Negro Leagues Players." *Pittsburgh Post-Gazette* (July 10, 1997): C-1.

Whiteside, Larry. "Long before Jackie Robinson's Historic Debut with the Brooklyn Dodgers, Negro League Players Thrived in Anonymity—and Made His Signing Possible, Paving the Way." *Boston Globe* (July 9, 1999): F5.

Other

"Ban Johnson: AL President 1901-1927." SportsEcyclopedia.com. http://www.sportsecyclopedia.com/mlb/al/bjohnson.html. (October 5, 2002).

Goldman, Steve. "The Genius: Foster Made Negro League Baseball Successful." MajorLeagueBaseball.com. http://mlb.com (October 5, 2002).

Kleinknect, Merl F. "Rube Foster." BaseballLibrary.com.http://www.pubdim.net/baseballlibrary/ballplayers/ (September 17, 2002).

Kleinman, Jeremy. "Baseball: A Film by Ken Burns Pt. 1." DVD Talk.com. http://www.dvdtalk.com/reviews (October 5, 2002).

Rogosin, W. Donn. "Foster, Andrew [Rube]." The Handbook of Texas Online. http://www.tsha.utexas.edu/

handbook/online/articles/view/FF/ (September 19, 2002).

Suehsdorf, A. D. "Ban Johnson." BaseballLibrary.com. http://www.pubdim.net/baseballlibrary/ (October 4, 2002).

"The 20th Century's Greatest Sports Losers." ESPN. com. http://espn.go.com/ (October 5, 2002).

Sketch by Ann H. Shurgin

A. J. Foyt
1935-

American race car driver

A.J. Foyt

A. J. Foyt Jr., is unique in the world of auto racing. While others have matched some of his most impressive records, such as his four Indianapolis 500 victories, nobody can compete with the astonishing longevity and variety of his racing career. Foyt's professional career spanned four decades, from the 1950s to the 1990s, which is an accomplishment in of itself in auto racing. However, the fact that he remained competitive during this entire time, despite a number of debilitating injuries, has made Foyt's career even more outstanding. In addition, while most auto racers specialize in driving a certain type of car or racing on a certain type of terrain, Foyt has raced in—and won—premier auto-racing events in radically different cars on a variety of road and track courses around the world. For these reasons, in 1999, Supertex, as he is known to his legions of fans, was named by the Associated Press, along with **Mario Andretti**, as the Driver of the Century.

Born to Drive

Anthony Joseph Foyt Jr. was born January 16, 1935, in Houston, Texas. Foyt's father, Tony, a mechanic and auto racer himself, owned Burt and Foyt Garage, which specialized in race cars. Foyt quickly became interested in the sport. When he was three years old, Tony built him a small open-wheel racecar to drive around their backyard. When he was five, Tony built him a midget-type racer and arranged a three-lap duel between Foyt and Doc Cossey, a local adult racer, at the Houston Speed Bowl. Foyt won the duel, and decided that he wanted to race cars for the rest of his life.

Foyt adored his father and strove to earn his approval. Yet, no matter how hard Foyt tried or how good he became in a race car, Tony never praised his son, which made Foyt work even harder. While Foyt adored his father, he also feared him. Tony was a tough man with a wild temper, which Foyt experienced on several occasions, such as when he was eleven, and he and some friends stole his father's midget racecar off of its trailer. They drove it around the yard until the engine burst into flames. While this was bad, the highest offense in Tony's eyes was lying. When Foyt was sixteen, he and some friends went hot-rodding through Houston in his 1950 Ford, until the police saw them and chased them. Foyt and his friends ditched the car, then Foyt lied to his father, saying that it had been stolen. When Tony found out the truth from the police, he imposed the strongest punishment he could think of by taking away Foyt's car for a year. Lessons like these helped Foyt to become an honest, loyal person, both on and off the track.

However, it was his tough-as-nails attitude and flat-out driving style that quickly distinguished Foyt in his races. After leaving high school during his junior year to pursue racing full-time, he quickly became the best-known driver in Texas. This was as much for his dressing style as his racing prowess. For every race, Foyt would wear silk shirts and fancy white pants, which earned him the nickname, "Fancy Pants." When he was twenty, Foyt married Lucy Zarr, and the two began attending the Indianapolis 500 as spectators. In 1957, Foyt joined the United States Auto Club (USAC) racing circuit.

The Move to Indy Cars

The same year, Foyt qualified for his first Indy car race. In 1958, he made his debut at the Indianapolis 500, where he finished 16th. The 1958 Indianapolis 500 was

Chronology

1935	Born January 16 in Houston, Texas
1938	Father builds him a small race car to drive around the backyard
1955	Marries Lucy Zarr
1957	Wins first USAC (United States Auto Club) midget race
1958	Finishes 16th in his first Indianapolis 500
1959	Wins first USAC sprint car race
1960	Wins first Indy car race at the Duquoin 100
1962	Wins first USAC stock car race
1964	Wins first NASCAR (National Association for Stock Car Auto Racing) race
1965	Breaks his back and foot during the Riverside *Motor Trend* 500 NASCAR race and is presumed dead by medics who arrive on the scene
1965	Ten weeks later, he wins the pole at a Phoenix Indy car event
1966	Sustains severe burns in an Indy car during practice
1972	Sustains burns and a broken leg in a dirt car race in Duquoin, Illinois
1981	Fractures right arm at Michigan 500
1981	Mother dies of heart failure on the night that Foyt qualifies for Indianapolis 500
1983	Father dies of cancer on the night that Foyt qualifies for Indianapolis 500
1983	Breaks two vertebrae during practice; nevertheless, he wins the Paul Revere 250 sports car race the same night
1988	Fined $5,000 and suspended from the NASCAR circuit for six months after he nearly hits several race officials with his car at the Winston 500
1990	Sustains serious leg injuries in Indy car race in Elkhart Lake, Wisconsin
1992	Races in last Indy car race at the Indianapolis 500
1993	Announces his retirement from Indy car racing shortly before he is scheduled to qualify for the Indianapolis 500
1994	Competes in his last NASCAR Winston Cup race at the Brickyard 400
1996	As a team owner, wins first Indy Racing League title with driver Scott Sharp
1998	As a team owner, wins second Indy Racing League title with driver Kenny Brack
1999	As a team owner, wins Indianapolis 500 with driver Kenny Brack

a dangerous event, which started out with a fourteen-car pileup and ended with a death and eight cars knocked out of commission. Foyt barely escaped injury himself, sliding backwards almost a thousand feet on an oil slick and avoiding a near crash. For Foyt, racing Indy cars, especially at Indianapolis—the premier auto-racing venue at the time—was a dream come true.

The next two decades intensified that dream, and not just in Indy cars. Success came quickly for Foyt, who dominated the Indy car circuit. In 1960, Foyt won his first Indy car race, then went on to win three more races that season as well as the national Indy car championship. In 1961, at twenty-six, Foyt won his first Indianapolis 500, setting a new average-speed record for the race in the process. He also won his second national Indy car championship and won a record twenty United States Auto Club (USAC) races during the year. As a testament to his versatility, these races included midget cars, sprint cars, and Indy cars. The next year, he won his first USAC stock car race, proving that he could drive all of the major varieties of racecars. In 1963 and 1964, he won his

third and fourth national Indy car championships. In the latter year, he also won his second Indianapolis 500, once again breaking the race record for average speed. In addition, in the 1964 season, he won a record ten races, out of only thirteen starts.

In 1965, Foyt won a record ten pole positions, including the pole at the Indianapolis 500. In 1967, he repeated his impressive performance from 1964, once again winning the Indianapolis with a record average speed, and once again winning the national Indy car championship. By this point, Foyt had won countless races and championships in Indy cars, stock cars, midget cars, and sprint cars. Foyt seemed truly unstoppable when it came to racing, and it was at this point that he extended his dominance outside of America. In 1967, Foyt and fellow American racer Dan Gurney teamed up to race in France's 24 Hours of Le Mans, an endurance road race that is widely considered by Europeans to be their version of the Indianapolis 500. Foyt and Gurney won the event, becoming the first Americans to do so, and in the process they beat the track record by the largest margin in Le Mans history.

The next year, Foyt continued his pattern of scoring championship victories in radically different racing events, by winning his first USAC stock car championship. In 1972, he won the crown jewel of stock car racing, the Daytona 500. The same year, he also won the USAC dirt car championship. In the late 1970s, now in his early forties, Foyt continued to score victories. In 1975, he won his sixth national Indy car championship. In 1977, he won his record fourth Indianapolis 500. In 1978, he won the USAC stock car championship. In 1979, he won his record seventh national Indy car championship. He also became the first driver to win USAC's national Indy car and stock car championships in the same season.

While many men in their mid-forties start slowing down, Foyt sped up. In 1981, Foyt won the Pocono 500. This victory was his record ninth victory in 500-mile Indy car races. While Foyt continued to race Indy cars for another twelve years, the 1981 Pocono 500 was the last Indy car victory in his career. However, the same was not true in other areas of his racing. In 1983, Foyt won the 24 Hours of Daytona, a tough endurance race for anybody, but especially for a man pushing fifty. As if to prove that this wasn't a fluke, Foyt won the 12 Hours of Sebring in 1985, two years later. From this point on, Foyt did not win any more races, although he participated in several, and remained competitive against racers half his age. In 1992, he set his last record when he qualified for his 35th consecutive Indianapolis 500. This was also his last Indy car race before he announced his retirement shortly before the 1993 Indianapolis 500. Foyt's retirement did not spell the end of racing for the Foyts, however. Foyt gained a passion for the sport through his father, Tony. Likewise, Foyt has passed the

Awards and Accomplishments

1960-61, 1963-64, 1967, 1975, 1979	National Indy car championship
1961	Wins Indianapolis 500 race at an average speed of 139.130 mph, a new race record
1961	Wins record twenty USAC (United States Auto Club) races in one year
1964	Wins Indianapolis 500 at an average speed of 147.350, a new race record
1964	Wins a record ten Indy car season victories (out of thirteen starts)
1965	Wins a record ten pole positions in Indy cars this season, including the Indianapolis 500
1967	Wins Indianapolis 500 at an average speed of 151.207 mph, a new race record
1967	Foyt and teammate, Dan Gurney, become the first Americans to win France's 24 Hours of Le Mans race
1968, 1978	USAC stock car championship
1972	Daytona 500
1972	USAC dirt car championship
1977	Wins record fourth Indianapolis 500
1979	Becomes first driver to win USAC's national Indy car and stock car championships in the same season
1981	Wins record ninth victory in 500-mile Indy car races at the Pocono 500
1983, 1985	24 Hours of Daytona
1985	12 Hours of Sebring
1989	Inaugural inductee into the Motorsports Hall of Fame
1991	USAC and Championship Auto Racing Teams (CART) reserve the number fourteen for the exclusive use of Foyt as either a driver or team owner, to be retired upon Foyt's retirement from the sport; this is the first time either of the two organizations have retired a racing number
1992	Qualifies for record thirty-five consecutive Indianapolis 500 races
1993	Wins the American Sportscasters Association Sports Legend Award
1999	Foyt named Driver of the Century by the Associated Press (along with Mario Andretti)

Foyt won a career record seven Indy car national championships (1960-61, 1963-64, 1967, 1975, and 1979).

Foyt won a career record sixty-seven Indy car races.

Foyt won a career record nine 500-mile races (the Indianapolis 500 in 1961, 1964, 1967, and 1977; the Pocono 500 in 1973, 1975, 1979, and 1981; and the California 500 in 1975).

Foyt is the only driver who has won the Indianapolis 500, the Daytona 500, and the 24 Hours of Le Mans.

Foyt is the only driver who has won the Indianapolis 500 in both a front-engine and a rear-engine race car.

Foyt's USAC career record for total victories is 158. He is the only driver who has won twenty or more victories in USAC's four major categories: Indy cars, stock cars, sprint cars, and midget cars.

auto-racing bug down to other members of his family, including his grandson, A. J. Foyt IV, who is one of the new sensations in auto racing.

No Pain, No Gain

While Foyt racked up impressive records and statistics in his long racing career, he also racked up several injuries, some of which were life-threatening. In a sport as dangerous as auto racing, injuries are common. What is uncommon is the fact that Foyt repeatedly bounced back from injuries that might convince other racers to pack it in. His first serious injury came in 1965 during a NASCAR race in Riverside, California. His brakes failed, and he tried to avoid crashing into **Junior Johnson** and Marvin Panch, two racers who were in front of him. In the process of avoiding this crash, Foyt flipped his car down an embankment, breaking his back and fracturing his heel in the process. By the time the medics, a fellow racer, and a team owner descended the 25-foot embankment and reached Foyt's car, Foyt was not breathing, his skin was blue, and they assumed he was dead. However after noticing some slight movement, and scooping the mud out of Foyt's mouth, he was able to breathe again and they took him to the hospital.

Foyt has been severely burned on several occasions, as in 1972, during a dirt-car race in DuQuoin, Illinois, when he was set on fire. During a pit stop, the fuel hose broke lose and sprayed two gallons of alcohol-nitro mixture onto Foyt's head. Assuming that it would evaporate, Foyt started to drive out of the pits. Unfortunately, one of his car's side-mounted exhaust pipes backfired, setting Foyt's head ablaze. In his panic, he jumped out of the car, intending to jump into a lake in the infield. However, the car was still moving, and the left rear tire rolled over his leg, breaking his leg and ankle. Still on fire, Foyt attempted to hobble to the infield, while his father chased after him, eventually catching up to him and spraying him with a fire extinguisher.

Foyt experienced his most painful injury during an Indy car race in 1990, at the Road America course in Elkhart Lake, Wisconsin. Once again, as in the 1965 NASCAR race, Foyt's brakes failed. Since he was going 190 mph and was coming up on a 90-degree turn, Foyt did the only thing he could to avoid a fatal roll—he plowed straight through the wooden wall, sending his car airborne into a dirt embankment. In the process, Foyt broke his left knee, dislocated his left tibia (which shot up his leg, through his knee, and into his thigh muscle), crushed his left heel, dislocated his right heel, and suffered compartment syndrome in both feet. Foyt remained awake as the rescuers tried to unearth him, and he pleaded with them to hit him in the head with a hammer and knock him out so he would not have to feel the excruciating pain. Following these massive injuries, Foyt's peers assumed that he would announce his retirement. However, Foyt surprised everybody by undergoing a grueling physical therapy regimen with the Houston Oilers's strength-and-rehabilitation coach, Steve Watterson, in an attempt to come back and win a fifth Indianapolis 500 race. Although he did not win the Indianapolis 500 in

Related Biography: Auto Racer A. J. Foyt IV

Anthony Joseph Foyt IV was born on May 25, 1984, in Hockley, Texas. Like his namesake, Foyt IV started driving race cars at an early age. When he was nine, his uncle Jerry (Foyt's son) asked Foyt IV to race a junior dragster. From this first driving experience, Foyt IV moved on to go-karts, where he quickly demonstrated his driving prowess. On the karting circuit, he won races and championships in both the International Karting Federation (IKF) and the World Karting Association (WKA). In 2001, he moved from karting to the Formula Continental Series, where he won the 2001 southwest regional championship and was named Rookie of the Year. Foyt IV also finished third in the point standings of this series, despite the fact that he had to miss three events to fulfill his commitment to working on his grandfather's Indy pit crew.

Foyt IV's pit-crew experiences exposed him to Indy Racing League cars, and also gave him the opportunity to test the cars out at the track. However, it was not long before he was driving his own. Although Foyt initially did not encourage Foyt IV to follow in his footsteps, once he saw his grandson's talent, he expressed his faith in his grandson the best way he knew how—by giving him an Indy car for his 18th birthday. The gift did not go to waste, as Foyt IV used it in 2002 to win the inaugural Infiniti Pro Series championship. The Infiniti Pro Series is an IRL-sanctioned series designed to groom young drivers to race in regular IRL competition. In October 2002, shortly after the conclusion of the series, Foyt IV passed his rookie test for his Indy Racing League license. In 2003, Foyt IV will enter regular IRL competition driving for his grandfather.

Where Is He Now?

Foyt lives in Hockley, Texas. Although he is retired from racing as a driver, Foyt remains active in the sport as a team owner, through A. J. Foyt Enterprises and Team Conseco. While team ownership initially meant Indy cars, in 2000 Foyt formed a NASCAR Winston Cup team, which is based in Mooresville, North Carolina. Foyt's youngest son, Larry, is in charge of this team. Foyt continues to promote the Indy Racing League (IRL), which is attracting an increasing number of drivers away from the rival Championship Auto Racing Teams (CART). One of the newest IRL drivers is Foyt's grandson, A. J. Foyt IV. Foyt is also on the board of directors of Riverway Bank and Service Corporation International, the nation's largest funeral service business.

1991, he did compete in it that year and in 1992, the latter at the seasoned age of fifty-seven.

Foyt's Legacy

In this age of slick, specialized auto racers with multimillion-dollar sponsorship deals, Foyt is a throwback to the old days of grit-tough racing. An expert auto mechanic, Foyt knew how far to push a car to its limits, and on some occasions finished the race right before the car was about to break down or blow a tire. During one race, a radius rod—a piece of Foyt's suspension—snapped and started to fall off. Instead of taking himself out of the race as most drivers would do, Foyt grabbed the piece of metal and held it in place with one hand, while using his other hand to finish, and win, the race.

While driving, Foyt's technique was nearly flawless. Fellow racers noted on several occasions that Foyt was cool as ice while he drove. Foyt almost never made mistakes, and would never let his emotions affect his driving as some other racers did and still do. Out of the car, however, it was a different story. While Foyt's racing prowess was legendary, so was his hot temper. When he was angry, he berated his pit crew, officials, reporters, or whoever else got in his way. Sometimes, he would beat on his race car with a hammer if it didn't run the way he wanted it to, regardless of who was watching. During the 1985 Indianapolis 500, Foyt's pit crew misunderstood what needed to be fixed on the car, so Foyt jumped out, irate, and tried to fix the problem himself. Unfortunately, he accidentally set the car on fire and knocked himself out of the race in the process.

Despite his short fuse, Foyt's loyalty to his fellow racers is also legendary. On several occasions, he has gone out of his way to help other racers' careers, such as when he let **Al Unser Sr.**, a rookie, drive Foyt's backup car in the 1965 Indianapolis 500. Foyt was also famous for helping keep racers safe. His knowledge of what cars could do, coupled with his driving talent and instinct, saved himself and others on many occasions, as he helped to avert potentially fatal accidents during a race. He also helped out during bad accidents, such as in 1968 when he pulled fellow racer, Johnny Rutherford, from Rutherford's burning Indy car.

Most importantly, Foyt was totally committed to his racing throughout his career. Enamored of the sport since he was five years old, Foyt's passion never flagged for more than fifty years, despite the fact that he sustained injuries that could—and have—crippled others. In the end, Foyt's amazing drive helped him to become one of history's most amazing drivers.

CONTACT INFORMATION

Address: A. J. Foyt Enterprises, 6415 Toledo St., Houston, TX, 77008-6226.

SELECTED WRITINGS BY FOYT:

(With Bill Neely) *A. J.: My Life As America's Greatest Race Car Driver,* Times Books, 1983.
Crash Course in Racing, Videocassette. Hallmark Entertainment, 1989.
A. J. Foyt: Champion for Life, Videocassette. Cabin Fever Entertainment, 1992.

FURTHER INFORMATION

Books

Engle, Lyle Kenyon. *The Incredible A. J. Foyt.* New York: Arco, 1977.
Foyt. New York: Hawthorn Books, 1974.
Kupper, Mike. *Driven to Win: A. J. Foyt.* New York: Raintree/Steck Vaughn, 1975.
Libby, Bill. *A. J. Foyt: Racing Champion.* New York: Putnam, 1978.

A.J. Foyt, sitting in car

Lincoln Library of Sports Champions. Columbus: Frontier Press Company, 1989.

May, Julian. *A. J. Foyt: Championship Auto Racer.* New York: Crestwood House, 1975.

St. James Encyclopedia of Popular Culture, five volumes. Detroit: St. James Press, 2000.

Wilker, Josh. *A. J. Foyt (Race Car Legends).* New York: Chelsea House Publishers, 1996.

(With Bill Neely). *A. J.: My Life As America's Greatest Race Car Driver* New York: Times Books, 1983.

Periodicals

Handzel, Will. "For a Winner." *Hot Rod* (October 1994): 104.

Moses, Sam. "Day and Night, A.J. Was Just Right." *Sports Illustrated* (April 1, 1985): 24.

Nack, William. "Twilight of a Titan." *Sports Illustrated* (September 30, 1991): 64.

Neely, Bill. "A.J. The Racer As National Institution." *Motor Trend* (June 1985): 162.

Plummer, William. "A.J.'s Back on Track: Returning from a Crippling Crash, 'the Master' Gears Up for One Last Indy 500." *People Weekly* (May 13, 1991): 77.

Other

A. J. Foyt: Champion for Life, Videocassette. Greenwich, CT: Cabin Fever Entertainment, 1992.

Crash Course in Racing, Videocassette. New York: Hallmark Entertainment, 1989.

Foyt Racing. http://www.foytracing.com (November 22, 2002).

Motor Sports Hall of Fame. http://www.mshf.com (November 25, 2002).

Schwartz, Larry. "A.J. Foyt: King of the Indy 500." ESPN.com. http://espn.go.com/sportscentury/features/00014199.html (November 22, 2002).

Sketch by Ryan Poquette

Joe Frazier
1944-

American boxer

Joe Frazier

H older of the unified World Heavyweight Champion title from 1970 to 1973, Joe Frazier is best remembered for the title fight that he lost to **Muhammad Ali** in the "Thrilla in Manila" in 1975. Yet his matches with Ali were only part of the rags-to-riches story of Frazier's life. Growing up in the rural community of Laurel Bay, South Carolina, Frazier endured poverty as his parents struggled to support a family of twelve children. After dropping out of school and working as a farm laborer at the age of fourteen, Frazier left South Carolina after his boss threatened to give him a beating. Moving to Philadelphia, the teenager worked at a meat packing plant and began training as a boxer while he raised his own family. He found early success with a Gold Medal in heavyweight boxing at the Tokyo Olympic Games in 1964, but it was another four years before he got a shot at the world title in a match sponsored by the New York State Athletic Commission. Unifying the title with another victory in a World Boxing Association bout in 1970, Frazier reigned as the undisputed heavyweight champion. He kept the title for three years before losing it to **George Foreman** in 1973. Although his attempt to reclaim the championship against Ali in 1975 failed, it became the most famous fight of his career.

South Carolina Childhood

Joseph William Frazier, or "Billy Boy" as he was called during his childhood, was born on January 12, 1944 in Beaufort, South Carolina. His parents, Rubin and Dolly Frazier, worked as farm laborers and raised their twelve

Chronology

1944	Born January 12 in Beaufort, South Carolina, to Rubin and Dolly Frazier
1961	Begins training as a boxer
1962	Wins Philadelphia Golden Gloves novice heavyweight championship
1962	Wins first of three Middle Atlantic Golden Gloves heavyweight championship bouts
1963	Marries Florence Smith
1964	Wins Gold Medal in heavyweight boxing at Olympic Games in Tokyo, Japan
1965	Begins professional boxing career
1968	Wins New York State heavyweight boxing title
1970	Wins World Boxing Association heavyweight boxing title
1971	Defends heavyweight title against Muhammad Ali
1973	Loses heavyweight title to George Foreman
1975	Fails to regain heavyweight title against Muhammad Ali
1976	Retires from professional boxing
1990	Inducted into the International Boxing Hall of Fame
1996	Publishes autobiography, *Smokin' Joe*

surviving children in the rural hamlet of Laurel Bay. Part of the Gullah community of South Carolina, Frazier's family was part of extended kinship network of the descendants of former slaves. The mutual support of the community's residents helped Frazier build his self-esteem despite the poverty and racism that he experienced in the rural South. His status as his father's favorite in the family also helped Frazier to have a happy childhood. Frazier was often at his father's side helping him manufacture and distribute illegal moonshine; the elder Frazier had lost one of his arms in a lover's quarrel some years before.

Frazier dropped out of school in the tenth grade and began to work on a nearby farm as a laborer. After he spoke out against the beating of a fellow worker by the farm's owner, Frazier came under threat himself. He was fired from his job and felt compelled to leave the region altogether. After saving enough money for a Greyhound Bus ticket, Frazier joined his older brother, Tommy, in New York City in 1959. Unable to find steady work, Frazier sometimes resorted to stealing cars to make some money. He subsequently moved to Philadelphia, where some of his relatives lived, and found employment at the Cross Brothers kosher slaughterhouse. Although he was regularly cheated out of his wages by the company, Frazier worked in the meat packing plant from 1961 to 1963. He sent part of his wages back home to support the children he had with two of his girlfriends, Florence Smith and a woman he later identified only as "Rosetta." He had two children with Rosetta in the early 1960s, but married Smith in September 1963. The couple divorced in 1985 after raising seven children together.

Olympic Gold Medalist

Inspired by watching boxing matches on his family's television set in the early 1950s, Frazier had created his own training regimen as a child, which included punch-

Awards and Accomplishments

1962	Philadelphia Golden Gloves novice heavyweight championship
1962-64	Middle Atlantic Golden Gloves heavyweight championship
1964	Olympic Gold Medal in heavyweight boxing
1968	New York State heavyweight boxing title
1970	World Boxing Association heavyweight boxing title
1990	Induction into the International Boxing Hall of Fame

Ghosts of Manila

In the thirteenth, Frazier began to flinch and wince from Ali's one-note slugging. Joe's punches seemed to have a gravity drag, and when they did land they brushed lazily against Ali. The champ sent Frazier's bloody mouthpiece flying seven rows into the audience, and nearly pulled the light switch on him with one chopping shot. . . .

The fourteenth was the most savage round of the forty-one Ali and Frazier fought. . . . Nine straight right hands smashed into Joe's left eye, thirty or so in all during the round. When Joe's left side capsized to the right from the barrage, Ali moved it back into range for his eviscerating right with crisp left hooks, and at the round's end the referee guided Joe back to his corner. . . .

"Sit down, son," Eddie [Futch, Frazier's coach] said. "It's over. No one will forget what you did here today."

With the only strength they had left, both fighters stumbled toward their dressing rooms to a continuous roar.

Source: Mark Kram, *Ghosts of Manila: The Fateful Blood Feud Between Muhammad Ali and Joe Frazier,* HarperCollins, 2001.

ing a burlap bag filled with rags, corncobs, and Spanish moss surrounding a brick in the middle. He resumed training in 1961 when he visited a local gym and trainer Yancey "Yank" Durham noticed his impressive left hook. Durham coached Frazier to a victory as the novice champion of the Philadelphia Golden Gloves tournament in 1962. That same year Frazier began a three-year run as the heavyweight champion of the Middle Atlantic Golden Gloves league. As an alternate delegate in the heavyweight squad of the U.S. boxing team, Frazier was chosen to compete in the 1964 Tokyo Olympic Games when Buster Mathis broke his thumb. Frazier returned from the games with a Gold Medal in heavyweight boxing. Despite the celebrity status that he earned from the victory, it would be another four years before he earned his first championship title as a professional fighter.

Monumental Fights Against Ali and Foreman

After turning pro in 1965, Frazier earned the nickname "Smokin' Joe" for his rapid-fire delivery of punches and seeming ability to absorb the most ferocious blows of his opponents. With then-heavyweight champion Muhammad Ali suspended for refusing to report for the military draft in 1967, a number of fighters scrambled to claim the title. Frazier won the New York State Heavyweight title against Buster Mathis on March 4, 1968 with a knockout punch in the eleventh round. He went on to defend his New York title six times before earning the chance to spar for the title sponsored by the World Boxing Association (WBA) two years later. After winning the WBA bout with a technical knockout against Jimmy Ellis in the fifth round on February 16, 1970, Frazier could claim the undisputed title of World Heavyweight Champion.

After Ali was reinstated to the sport, fans clamored for a match between the former and current title holders. The match took place on March 8, 1971 in Madison Square Garden in New York; both fighters were guaranteed a payout of $2.5 million. The bout went the entire fifteen rounds, with Frazier winning a unanimous decision by the judges at its conclusion. Although Frazier's victory was clear, Ali immediately claimed to have been robbed of the title and demanded a rematch. In addition to his poor sportsmanship, Ali made a number of humiliating remarks at Frazier's expense, including his infamous labeling of his opponent as an "Uncle Tom." Adding to Frazier's bitterness over the remark, media coverage of Ali often glamorized him as a principled rebel while Frazier was criticized as the establishment's boxer. The fact that Frazier had outboxed Ali in their first match was a secondary issue to many critics.

Frazier retained his title through two fights in 1972 before encountering George Foreman in a Kingston, Jamaica ring on January 22, 1973. Foreman battered Frazier so brutally that the bout had to be declared a technical knockout in the challenger's favor in just the second round. Frazier also encountered a setback in his second meeting with Ali in a non-title match in New York on January 28, 1974, where he lost in a twelve-round decision. After Ali took the world title from Foreman, he met Frazier in their third match for another title bout. Publicized as "The Thrilla in Manila," the match took place in the Philippines on September 30, 1975. The action continued over fourteen rounds with Frazier appearing to lead; after sustaining serious damage to his eyes, however, his coach, Eddie Futch, asked for the fight to be stopped. Ali retained his title in a technical knockout.

Retirement

In 1976 Frazier fought against George Foreman; after suffering a knockout in the fifth round, he announced his retirement. He returned to the ring for a 1981 match against Floyd Cummings, which led to a ten-round defeat by decision. Disabled by hepatitis and problems with his vision, it was Frazier's last match. His professional record stood at thirty-two wins, four losses, and one draw. Frazier won twenty-seven of his fights by knockouts. A careful manager of his finances, Frazier avoided the fate of many of his colleagues and enjoyed a successful post-boxing career as the manager of Smokin' Joe's Gym in Philadelphia and as a singer with his own band, the Knockouts. He also helped steer his son, Marvis Frazier, to a successful boxing career with over $1 million in winnings in the 1980s.

Inducted into the International Boxing Hall of Fame in 1990, Frazier's reputation as a boxer has grown since his professional career ended. Ali finally offered an apology for his earlier criticism of Frazier, explaining in a 2001 interview with the *New York Times*, "I said a lot of things in the heat of the moment that I shouldn't have said. Called him names I shouldn't have called him. I apologize for that. I'm sorry. It was all meant to promote the fight." Frazier, forever linked with Ali for their Manila fight—which many observers ranked as one of the sport's greatest matches—accepted the apology. "We have to embrace each other," Frazier told the *New York Times,* "It's time to talk and get together. Life's too short."

SELECTED WRITINGS BY FRAZIER:

(With Phil Berger) *Smokin' Joe: The Autobiography of a Heavyweight Champion of the World,* Macmillan, 1996.

FURTHER INFORMATION

Books

Frazier, Joe, with Phil Berger. *Smokin' Joe: The Autobiography of a Heavyweight Champion of the World.* New York: Macmillan, 1996.

Kram, Mark. *Ghosts of Manila: The Fateful Blood Feud Between Muhammad Ali and Joe Frazier.* New York: HarperCollins, 2001.

Roberts, James B., and Alexander G. Skutt. *The Boxing Register: International Boxing Hall of Fame Official Record Book, 2nd Edition.* Ithaca, NY: McBooks Press, 1999.

Periodicals

Sandomir, Richard. "No Floating, No Stinging: Ali Extends Hand to Frazier." *New York Times* (March 15, 2001).

Sketch by Timothy Borden

Cathy Freeman
1973-

Australian track and field athlete

Australian runner Cathy Freeman is the first Aborigine ever to compete in the Olympics, and the first to wave the Aboriginal flag at a sporting event. Freeman lit the Olympic flame at the 2000 Olympics in Sydney, and won a gold medal in the 400 meters at those Games.

Cathy Freeman

A Difficult Childhood

Freeman's grandmother was part of the "stolen generation" of Aboriginal people in Australia—from the early 20th century until the 1970s, many Aboriginal children were taken from their parents to be raised in state-run institutions. This practice was intended to remove the children from the poverty, disease, and addiction that plagued many aboriginal people, but it also resulted in tragically broken family ties and loss of ancient cultural traditions.

Although Freeman was not taken from her family, she had a difficult childhood. She was molested as a child, and both her younger sister and her father died.

When Freeman was still a girl, her talent in running was obvious. Her mother, Cecilia, encouraged her to pursue her interest in athletics, and when she was ten, her stepfather, Bruce Barber, told her she could win a gold medal at the Olympics if she trained properly. However, although she had the talent, she was also a member of a minority group that historically had not had access to the same resources that other athletes had. Freeman was one of only a few Aborigines who won a scholarship to a boarding school where she could learn and train.

At the age of 15, she competed at the National School Championships, and did well enough to be encouraged to try out for the 1990 Commonwealth Games team. She made the team as a sprinter, and was a member of the 4 x 100-meter relay team, which won gold at the Commonwealth Games.

In 1990, she competed in the Australian National Championships, winning the 200 meters, and then ran in the 100, 200, and 4 x 100-meter races at the World Junior Games in Bulgaria. During this time, she met Nick Bideau, an Australian track official who would later become her coach, manager, and boyfriend.

Competes in Barcelona Olympics

In 1992, she competed in the 400-meter relay at the Barcelona Olympics, making it to the second qualifying round. She also was a member of the 4 x 100 meter team, which ran in the final but did not win a medal.

At the World Junior Championships in 1992, she won a silver medal in the 200 meters. In 1993, she made it to the semifinals in the 200 meters in the World Championships.

In 1994, Freeman won the 200 meters and the 400 meters at the Commonwealth Games in Victoria, British Columbia, Canada. After winning the 400 meters, Freeman ran her victory lap, carrying not the Australian national flag, but the red, black, and yellow Aboriginal flag. She was chastised in the press, and Australian team leader Arthur Tunstall told her she should not display the flag again. Freeman used the publicity she got to publicly discuss what the flag meant to Aboriginal people, explaining its symbolism: red for earth, yellow for sun, and black for skin.

Defying Tunstall's orders, she ran with the flag again after winning the 200 meters.

Wins Olympic Silver

At the 1996 Olympic Games in Atlanta, Freeman won a silver medal in the 400 meters. After those Games, she broke off her romantic relationship with Bideau, although he continued as her manager. Freeman won the World Championships in the 400 meters in 1997 and 1998, even though she suffered a heel injury in 1998.

In 1999, Freeman met Alexander "Sandy" Bodecker, an American executive for the Nike shoe company, and

the two fell in love. As a result, her relationship with Bideau became strained, and she eventually fired him. Freeman and Bodecker were married on September 19, 1999, in San Francisco. Bideau subsequently claimed that she owed him over $2 million in assets from deals he negotiated while he represented her, leading to a long court battle.

Wins Gold at the Sydney Olympics

Freeman was, of course, Australia's favorite to win a gold medal in the 400 meters at the 2000 Olympics, held in Sydney. Like any athlete, Freeman wanted to win in order to meet her own goals, but she also knew that she was viewed as a representative of the Aboriginal people, and she wanted to win for them. "I could feel the crowd all over me," she told Mark Shimabukuro in the *Sporting News.* "I felt the emotion being absorbed into every pore of my body." When she won, with a time of 49.11 seconds, she was so relieved that she dropped to her knees on the track after completing the race.

Freeman's shoes were yellow, black, and red, traditional Aboriginal colors, but after she won, she took them off and ran her victory lap barefoot, in traditional Aboriginal style, carrying both the Australian and Aboriginal flags around the track as the crowd cheered. According to Andrew Phillips in *Maclean's,* an Aboriginal observer said, "Cath's done it for all of us." This time, instead of being chastised for carrying the Aboriginal flag around the track, she was widely celebrated.

"All That Pain, It's Very Strong"

Freeman's win was hailed as an achievement for Australians and Aborigines, and was celebrated by a song, "Cos I'm Free," which became an Australian hit. The words are taken from a tattoo Freeman has on her right shoulder, signifying her pride in her Aboriginal heritage.

Freeman, like many of her country's 360,000 Aborigines, would like the Australian government to apologize for the abuses inflicted on her grandmother and others who were taken from their families as children. According to Phillips, she said of the government's refusal to do so, "All that pain, it's very strong, and generations have felt it. There's a sense of sadness and anger."

After her Olympic win, Freeman endured harassment by tabloid newspapers, a continuing court fight with Bideau regarding the disputed assets, and her husband's diagnosis with throat cancer. Regarding the constant scrutiny by tabloids and the often inaccurate stories they published about her, she told Brian Cazaneuve in *Sports Illustrated*, "I get so bloody tired of [hearing about] myself. Can't people focus on others who need [publicity] more than I?" She also said, "Public approval isn't important to me. Caring for my husband is."

In 2001, Freeman was voted Sportswoman of the Year by the Laureus Sports Foundation. Because of her husband's illness, Freeman announced that she would not compete during the 2002 season, and observers speculated that she might retire from her sport. She did carry the Olympic flag into the stadium at the 2002 Salt Lake City Olympic Games. However, when Bodecker began undergoing radiation and chemotherapy treatment, her friends encouraged her to keep herself busy by training. Bodecker also encouraged her, saying it would help him to see her compete.

Thus encouraged, Freeman returned to competition at the 2002 Commonwealth Games, held in Manchester, England, as a member of the 4 400-meter relay team. Although Freeman's lack of training meant that she was not running at her fastest, her team won by 1.1 seconds. In an article in the Melbourne, Australia *Sunday Herald Sun,* Freeman told a reporter that she planned to continue competing in 2003.

CONTACT INFORMATION

Address: c/o Athletics Australia, Suite 22, Fawkner Tower, 431 St. Kilda Road, Melbourne 30004, Victoria, Australia.

FURTHER INFORMATION

Books

"Cathy Freeman," *Contemporary Black Biography,* Volume 29, edited by Ashyia Henderson, Gale Group, 2001.
"Cathy Freeman," *Newsmakers,* Issue 3, Gale Group, 2001.

Periodicals

"Cathy's Glad to Be Back on Track," *Sunday Herald Sun* (Melbourne, Australia), (January 5, 2003): 52.
Cazeneuve, Brian, "Stress Therapy," *Sports Illustrated,* (August 12, 2002): R8.
Dimmier, Eleni, and Rachel Nowak, "Cathy Freeman," *U.S. News and World Report,* (August 20, 2001): 7.
Hurst, Mike, "How Getting to Know One of the Greats of Athletics Has Changed Freeman's Life," *Daily Telegraph* (Surry Hills, Australia), (November 14, 2002).
"Laureus World Sports Awards in Monte Carlo Honors Year's Best Athletes," *Jet,* (June 18, 2001): 52.
Phillips, Andrew, "A Race for All Australia," *Maclean's,* (October 9, 2000): 51.
Shimabukuro, Mark, "Her Flame Lingers," *Sporting News,* (October 9, 2000): 60.

Sketch by Kenneth R. Shepherd

Lane Frost
1963-1989

American bull rider

Lane Frost was a rising star in bull riding who won championships at rodeos across the West during the 1980s. He was the sixteenth ranked cowboy in the nation in his first year as a professional bull rider, at age nineteen, and in the top fifteen every year after that. He became the world champion of bull riding at the age of twenty-four, but his promising career was cut short two years later when he was gored by a bull at one of the most famous rodeos of all, the Cheyenne Frontier Days, in 1989.

Early Years

Bull riding was in Frost's blood. His father, Clyde, was a bull rider, and was, in fact, away on the rodeo circuit when Frost was born. Frost's mother, Elsie, recalls that even as a baby, Frost was fascinated by bull riding. As the story is told on the Lane Frost home page, starting when Frost was about five months old he would wake up just as the bull riding competition, always the last event of a rodeo, was beginning. If the Frosts tried to leave early to beat the crowds, Frost would start to fuss, but as soon as they sat down and let him watch the bull riding he would be happy.

The Frosts owned a dairy farm in Utah, and it was here that Lane got his first riding experience, on the family's calves. At the age of ten he competed in his first rodeo, placing first in the bareback riding competition on a Shetland pony, second in calf roping, and third in calf riding. At the age of fifteen, Frost graduated to riding bulls instead of calves, and he started taking lessons from the famous bull rider Freckles Brown. In a very short period of time, Frost had become a major

Chronology

1956	Born July 13, 1956, in LaJunta, Colorado, to Clyde and Elsie Frost
1974	Wins first rodeo awards, at the Little Buckaroos Rodeo in Uintah Basin, Utah
1977	Frost family moves to Lane, Oklahoma
1982	Graduates from Atoka High School
1983	Becomes a full member of the Professional Rodeo Cowboys Association
1984	Qualifies for the National Rodeo Finals for the first time
1985	Marries Kellie in Quanah, Texas, January 5
1985	Teaches his first bull-riding class
1988	Competes in the only rodeo exhibition ever held as part of the Winter Olympics
1988	Briefly separates from Kellie
1988	Becomes a born-again Christian, March 8
1989	Dies after being gored by a bull at the Cheyenne Frontier Days, July 30
1994	*8 Seconds* is released

Awards and Accomplishments

1978	Small Fry Rodeo
1980-82	Oklahoma Youth Rodeo
1980	Runner-up, National High School Rodeo
1981	National High School Rodeo
1982	American Junior Rodeo
1982	First Annual Youth Nationals
1983	Prairie Circuit Bull Riding Champion
1983	Received "Tough Luck" award at the Super Bull
1983	Named runner-up for Bull Rider Rookie of the Year
1985	Super Bull
1986	National Bull Riding Finals, Average Winner
1986	Runner-up, Winston Tour
1987	Pendleton Round-Up
1987	Texas Circuit Bull Riding Champion
1987	National Bull Riding Finals
1988	Olympic gold (team) and bronze (individual)
1988	Dodge National Circuit Finals
1989	Received Coors Favorite Cowboy award (posthumously)
1990	Inducted into the Pro Rodeo Hall of Fame
1990	Became first recipient of the Lane Frost Memorial Award

figure on the rodeo circuit in Oklahoma, where his family had moved when he was fourteen. He was the bull riding champion of the Oklahoma Youth Rodeo Association from his sophomore year in high school, 1980, until he graduated in 1982. By his senior year he was also the bull riding champion of the American Junior Rodeo Association.

Professional Career

Frost became a professional cowboy in 1983. He placed sixteenth in the Professional Rodeo Cowboys Association standings that year, only one place short of qualifying for the National Rodeo Finals. This would be the only year of his professional career that he did not qualify. Still, he had some consolations: he was the PRCA's Prairie Circuit bull riding champion, and he was runner-up for Rookie of the Year.

In 1985 Frost married Kellie Kyle, a Texan whom he had met while competing in National High School Rodeo finals in 1980. Their marriage was sometimes strained, since Frost spent so much time on the road. The couple moved from Frost's town of Lane, Oklahoma, to Kellie's hometown of Quanah, Texas, in 1987, but by 1988 they had decided to separate for a time. They reconciled a few months later, shortly after Frost became a born-again Christian, and started making plans to build a ranch in Oklahoma, midway between Lane and Quanah. Frost was planning to spend less time on the rodeo circuit and more time at home raising his own bulls, helping his parents with their ranch, running a bull-riding school, and starting a family. Frost left for a time to compete at the Cheyenne Frontier Days in 1989, but he and Kellie already had a project lined up for when he returned: they had been hired to work together as stunt doubles in the movie *My Heroes Have Always Been Cowboys,* which was being filmed in Oklahoma. They were also awaiting

approval of their loan to buy the land where they planned to build their ranch.

Last Ride

The Cheyenne Frontier Days, a nine-day-long event attended by tens of thousands of rodeo fans, is one of the biggest, best-known, oldest (begun in 1897), and most prestigious rodeos in the country. The bull riding championships are held on the last day of the rodeo, which was Sunday, July 30, in 1989. Frost had already completed two rides earlier in the week, and he was in second place coming into the last day. He completed his ride on a tough bull, Takin' Care of Business, on which he had failed to complete a ride at another rodeo about a month prior. At the end of the eight seconds, Frost did his trademark dismount, rolling off of the animal's left hindquarters. Normally, when this was done with the bull was charging forward, it gave Frost plenty of time to get up and away before the bull could change directions and threaten him. However, on this day the bull turned and charged almost immediately. It had rained a great deal that week, and Frost, still on his knees, could get no traction in the thick mud. The bull struck him twice. The first blow knocked him flat on the ground; the second, with one of the bull's horns, fractured several ribs and severed a major artery, although the horn did not break his skin. Frost managed to get up and run for the gate, but he collapsed and died before he reached it.

Frost's Legacy

Lane's tragic death sparked a plethora of tributes, including the creation of a Cowboy Crisis Fund that provides assistance to the families of cowboys and cowgirls who are injured or killed in competitions. *My Heroes Have Always Been Cowboys* was dedicated to Frost, and several years after his death the movie *8 Seconds,* based on Frost's life and starring Luke Perry (of *Beverly Hills 90210* fame), was released in 1994. Promoted with the tag line, "The sport made him a Legend. His heart made him a Hero," *8 Seconds* focused primarily on Frost's familial and romantic relationships. As with most dramatic adaptations, the facts of Frost's life were altered somewhat to create a better story. Frost's family protested some of these changes, particularly the film's assertions that Frost cheated on Kellie during their 1988 separation and that Frost was driven to succeed in bull riding in an attempt to satisfy his hard-to-please father. The family was also disappointed that the film made no mention of Frost's embrace of Christianity.

His family's home church, the Lane Baptist Church, distributes cowboy Bibles, created in Frost's honor, which include his picture on the front and his story inside the front cover. Also, a fifteen-foot-tall statue of Frost riding a bucking bull was erected in front of the Frontier Days Park in Cheyenne. A more practical tribute was the invention of protective vests which cowboys now wear in competitions to help prevent the sort of injury which killed Frost.

FURTHER INFORMATION

Other

"Lane Frost: Gone But Not Forgotten." About.com. http://rodeo.about.com/library/weekly/aa092899.htm (October 7, 2002).

Lane Frost Home Page. http://www.lanefrost.com/ (October 7, 2002).

Savlov, Marc. Review of *8 Seconds. Austin Chronicle.* http://www.austinchronicle.com/film/pages/movies/1610.html (February 25, 1994).

Summary of *8 Seconds.* Internet Movie Database. http://www.imbd.com/Title?0109021 (October 21, 2002).

Texas Cowboy Hall of Fame. http://www.texascowboyhalloffame.com/ (October 7, 2002).

Weisfeld, Robert. Review of *8 Seconds. TV Guide.* http://www.tvguide.com/movies/database/ShowMovie.asp?MI=36043 (October 21, 2002).

Sketch by Julia Bauder

Juli Furtado

Juli Furtado
1967-

American mountain biker

In her prime, Juli Furtado had more endurance and a higher peak heart rate than any of her competitors.

Combined with her drive and determination, these physical attributes made her a standout in the world of professional mountain biking. Furtado made her foray into the world of professional mountain bike racing after nearly a decade on the U.S. junior ski team. When injury forced her to stay off the slopes, she gravitated toward cycling, first to road racing, where she earned a national championship, and then to the hills and trails of mountain biking where she won the National Off-Road Bike Association (NORBA) overall titles four years in a row. The 1993 *Velo News* Cyclist of the Year dominated her sport from 1991 to 1996.

Growing Up

Juli Furtado was born on March 4, 1967, in New York City. When she was a girl her parents divorced and her mother moved the kids to Vermont. There Furtado attended the Stratton Mountain School ski academy. She joined the U.S. junior ski team in 1980 and was well on the way to fulfilling her dream of skiing in the Winter Olympics. When offered a skiing scholarship to the University of Boulder, Juli took it and, at 18 years old, moved west to train in the Rockies.

In 1987, a series of knee operations left Furtado unable to compete on the slopes. She left competitive downhill skiing. As part of her physical therapy regimen at the University of Colorado, however, she was told to ride a bike. She immediately fell in love with the sport

Chronology

1967	Born March 4 in New York City
1974	Parents divorce and mother moves kids to Vermont
1979	Attends the Atratton Mountain School Ski Academy
1980	Joins the U.S. National Junior ski team
1987	Knee injury forces her out of skiing
1989	Prescribed bike riding as part of physical therapy for her knee injury. Falls in love with riding
1989	Wins championships in road racing, but soon finds her true passion is for mountain biking
1990	Takes the World Cross Country Championships
1991	Spends her first full season as a professional mountain biker
1991	Earns her degree in marketing from the University of Colorado
1996	For the first time in four years she fails to win World Cup title
1996	Earns spot on the U.S. Olympic team, but fatigued, she finishes only tenth.
1997	Consistently tired and finishing lower and lower in results, Furtado sees a doctor and is diagnosed with Lyme disease in the spring. In November the diagnosis will be changed to Lupus
1997	Announces her retirement from competitive mountain biking, and spends more time at her home in California

Awards and Accomplishments

1989	Wins U.S. National Road Racing Championships
1990	World Cross Country Championship
1991-94	National Off-Road Biking Association (NORBA) Overall Title winner
1991-95	National Series Overall Champion
1992	World Downhill Championship
1993	Named *Velo News* Cyclist of the Year
1993-95	Wins the World Cup
2000	Voted to *Sports Illustrated*'s Top 100 Women Athletes of the Century

and began to train as a cyclist. Soon she was back in winning form as a road racer.

Realizing that she would rather be back on the slopes, however (although this time on a bike rather than skis), Furtado made the transition to from road racing to mountain biking. Her first full season in the sport was in 1991. She took first in most of the events in which she participated, and by 1993 Furtado had become a force to be reckoned with. She won each of the six NORBA nationals she raced, and nine out of ten Grundig World Cup races. In a little under eight months, Furtado collected 17 first-place finishes in 18 events.

Forced Out Before Her Time

In 1994 Furtado won her fourth consecutive NORBA national championship. But by 1995 she felt that something was going wrong. She could not understand what was sapping her motivation and desire out on the course. "My training has been lackadaisical," she told *Velo News*. "I've lacked motivation for it." Yet, in spite of her "off" season (a season which many still considered fantastic), Furtado continued to train in hopes of competing on the 1996 Olympic squad. She qualified for the games in Atlanta that next summer, but finished a disappointing tenth overall.

The fatigue and poor finishes convinced Furtado to see a physician. The initial diagnosis, in February of 1997, was for Lyme disease, but with medication and patience, Furtado was certain that she would be able to return to the sport at full strength. Yet that season she consistently finished lower and lower in the rankings. As she became more exhausted, Furtado realized that something had gone seriously wrong.

In late 1997 she was diagnosed with systemic lupus, a chronic autoimmune disease. According to the Lupus

Foundation of America, the disease "causes inflammation of various parts of the body, especially the skin, joints, blood and kidneys." Unable to rid herself of the disease (she can only take medications to relieve some of the symptoms), and unable to remain competitive with lupus, Furtado announced in November of 1997 that she was retiring from professional mountain biking.

Critics believed that Furtado was pushed too early from the sport she controlled for the first half of the 1990s. Many believed that, were it not for her illness, she could have been a dominant star for many years to come.

After retiring, Juli Furtado moved from her home in Durango, Colorado, to Santa Cruz, California. Though she has left the competition, she still attends many mountain biking events, often as a commentator out on the trails or as a fundraiser for any of the various philanthropic organizations with which she is associated.

In her prime, Juli Furtado had more endurance and a higher peak heart rate than any of her competitors. Combine that with her drive and determination, and these physical attributes made this naturally talented and truly gifted athlete a standout in the world of professional mountain biking.

FURTHER INFORMATION

Books

"Juli Furtado." *Great Women in Sports,* Detroit: Visible Ink Press, 1996.

Periodicals

Drake, Geoff. "The Reluctant Hero." *Bicycling* (May 1994).

Giesin, Dan. "Ex-Mountain Biker Has Had Uphill Climb." *The San Francisco Chronicle* (March 26, 1998).

Kane, Michael. "Putting on the Brakes." *The Denver Post* (March 3, 1998).

Martin, Scott. "Cycling Sisters: Meet 4 women who shape the sport." *Bicycling* (May 1996).

Martin, Scott. "First Lance, then Juli." *Bicycling* (November/December, 1997).

Walters, John. "The Caffeine Queen." *Sports Illustrated* (August 7, 1995).

Other

Corbett, Sara. "The Marvelous, Manic Drive of Juli Furtado." *Outside Online* http://web.outsideonline.com/magazine/0895/8f_marv.html (January 29, 2003).

"Illness Forces Mountain Bike Champ Furtado to Quit for Good." http://classic.mountainzone.com (January 29, 2003).

"Juli Furtado." *Sports Illustrated* Top 100 Women Athletes of the Century. http://sportsillustrated.cnn.com/siforwomen/top_100/88/ (January 29, 2003).

Sketch by Eric Lagergren

G

Dan Gable
1948-

American wrestler

Dan Gable

America's greatest wrestler, Dan Gable was an Olympic medallist, an outstanding college wrestler and a tremendously successful college coach. He is an incredible example of determination and drive. A tireless proponent of wrestling, it's hard to measure just where Gable's impact in the sport of wrestling ends. It's everywhere—whether it's what he accomplished as a player or as a coach, or, currently, as a tireless proponent of the sport.

Growing Up

Danny Mack Gable was born in Waterloo, Iowa, on October 25, 1948, to Mack Gable, a real estate salesman, and Katie Gable. The small town of Waterloo was predominately a farming community, but among the cornstalks in the quiet places of Iowa lingers some of the best wrestling in America.

He didn't discover wrestling early, like most kids today, who enter the sport at four or five, competing on the weekends in highly charged meets. For Gable, swimming was the first arena in which he found success. At the age of twelve he was the state YMCA backstroke champion. When he entered junior high, however, the school had no swimming program, so Gable played football and baseball—and, he wrestled.

The night of his first loss on the mat was preceded by a day of heavy snow in Waterloo. Gable was so upset by the loss that he locked himself in his room, emerging later without speaking. He went out and shoveled the driveway until it was clean (faster, it's been said, than a snowblower could have done it). When he came back inside, he vowed never to lose another match in high school. He went on to win sixty-four straight matches.

The College Tradition

When Gable graduated from high school, Bob Buzzard, one of the older wrestlers Gable admired, was in town for the weekend from Iowa State University. Gable invited Buzzard over to work out on a mat he had set up in his basement. Gable, with no reason to think he could lose after such superb high school career, was beaten very badly. Gable never conceived that he could be defeated that easily, and realized that being a three-time state champion was not going to be enough to cut it in big time wrestling.

Gable chose Iowa State University for several reasons. Among them: it was close to home and it had a big-time program. The school suited his needs, and Iowa was the land where wrestling stars were made. Upon entering college, Gable already had a reputation—even among wrestlers—as someone who pushed well beyond the norm. In a sport where a fanatical and religious devotion is the norm, where jogging when it's hot out while wearing trashbags under your sweatsuit, or eating ice chips for dinner in order to make weight

Chronology

1948	Born October 25 in Waterloo, Iowa, to Mack and Katie Gable
1960	Wins YMCA backstroke championship
1962	Suffers first loss in wrestling
1964	Shattered when learns his sister was raped and murdered. Uses it as motivating force in his life
1968	Enters into college career, one of most successful ever, at Waterloo West and Iowa State
1972	Wins Gold Medal for the United States in the Olympics
1974	Marries Kathy Carpenter
1974	Asked by Gary Kurdelmeier at Iowa to be assistant coach
1977	Leads Iowa Hawkeyes to Big Ten Championship in first season as head coach
1979	Coaches Hawkeyes to first ever undefeated and untied season (19-0-0)
1980	Asked to coach Olympic team
1980	Honored with induction into the USA Wrestling Hall of Fame
1984	Coaches the 1984 U.S. wrestling team at Olympic games in Los Angeles. His wrestlers win seven gold and two silver medals
1985	Coaches second perfect season at Iowa (18-0-0)
1985	Enters U.S. Olympic Hall of Fame
1986	Leads U.S. team to bronze medal at 1986 Goodwill Games
1992	Coaches third perfect season
1997	Announces retirement from coaching
1997	Undergoes hip replacement surgery
1999	Airing of Dan Gable documentary on HBO, *Freestyle: The Victories of Dan Gable*
2001	Considers running for Governor of Iowa, but decides not to

Awards and Accomplishments

1960-71	U.S. freestyle champion
1964-66	Iowa State High School Champion
1968-70	NCAA Champion
1971	U.S. Pan-American Games gold medallist
1971	World Championships gold medallist
1972	U.S. Olympic gold medallist
1977-97	Big Ten Championship Team coach
1978-86, 1991-93, 1995-97	NCAA Championship Team coach
1980	Inducted into National Wrestling Hall of Fame
1980	Amateur Athletic Union Wrestling Coach of the Year
1984	U.S. Olympic Team coach
1985	Inducted into U.S. Olympic Hall of Fame

can be routine, Gable would often push even further, training for six to seven hours a day. It was said that he showed up in his class with ankle weights on, squeezing hand trainers so he could get in as much of a workout as possible.

The Worst Sort of Motivation

In 1964 a neighbor raped and killed Gable's 19-year old sister, Diane. Gable was fifteen, and his parents wanted to sell the house and move. Gable, however, didn't want to relocate. He claimed that the murderer wasn't going to take their house. He was already a young man with an almost complete focus on wrestling, and the death of his sister and the emotional turmoil it caused pushed him to work even harder. He submerged himself in his sport.

Gable spent his sophomore year at an Olympic tryout camp with Rick Sanders of Portland State. Here is where the strongest weapon of Gable's wrestling career showed up. Sanders introduced Gable to arm bars to pin his opponents. After that, Gable pinned sixty of the last sixty-five opponents he faced in college, and he would not lose a match until he faced Larry Owings of the University of Washington in the NCAA finals his senior year. As a college wrestler, Gable amassed an outstanding record of 138-1, which included three NCAA championship titles. Gable would get another chance to wrestle Owings during the 1972 Olympic trials. Gable beat him handily, 7-1.

Olympic Gold and Coaching

At the 1972 Olympic games in Munich, Gable won gold in the lightweight class (149 1/2 pound) wrestling division. It was a dominating performance that has passed into legend. In a match with six opponents, and in a much publicized event wherein the Russian team vowed to find a challenger who would take Gable down, Gable ended up beating all six opponents, not once allowing them to score even one point off of him.

When he left the Olympic arena, Gable took an assistant coaching position under Gary Kurdelmeier at the University of Iowa. Together, these teams produced national championships in 1975 and 1976. Gable eventually took over the program from Kurdelmeier, and after finishing third in the country in his first year, Iowa went on to win nine consecutive national titles.

Numbers Speak for Themselves

Gable, as both wrestler and coach, has amassed some of the most amazing numbers in the sport, unparalleled in terms of athletic competition today. He was known in his time as the **Babe Ruth** of Wrestling, and today his utter dominance might be more closely allied with other athletes who compete individually, such as **Tiger Woods**. During his prep and college careers, Gable compiled the outstanding record of 182-1, winning 99 straight matches at Iowa State. He also won six Midlands Open Championships, and he was that meet's outstanding wrestler five times (he set NCAA records in winning and pin streaks).

As a coach he may be even more impressive, becoming the University of Iowa's all-time winningest coach during his tenure from 1977 to 1997. He compiled a career record of 355-21-5 while at the school, coaching 152 All-Americans, 45 national champions, 106 Big Ten Champions, and 10 Olympians (including four gold medallists). There is no getting around his almost unequivocal influence in the modern era. And, his wrestlers loved him. As a coach, Gable kept in shape with his students. He told *American Health* that, "I need to be able to teach [my team] new techniques, and there's nothing like being able to demonstrate to them hands-on. Staying in shape is a real good example of the dedication wrestlers need, too."

Gable's approach to wrestling, to coaching, and to life was brought to the small screen in a 1999 HBO documentary, *Freestyle: The Victories of Dan Gable*. Dan's desire to have the film made was due in part because he feels wrestling needs more publicity, especially since in the wake of Title IX, many colleges let their wrestling programs fold rather than adding another sport (Title IX is the legislation passed in 1972 that prohibits discrimination in sports due to gender).

Gable has said that, "To coach someone to be the best is a much higher honor than being the best." Dan Gable knew what both were like, and he passed his legacy on to more people than can possibly be imagined.

CONTACT INFORMATION

Phone: 319-631-3429. Email: staff@dangable.com. Online: www.dangable.com.

SELECTED WRITINGS BY GABLE:

(With James A. Peterson, Ph.D.) *Conditioning for Wrestling: The Iowa Way,* Leisure Press, 1980.
Coaching Wrestling Successfully, Human Kinetics, 1999.

FURTHER INFORMATION

Books

Chapman, Mike. *A History of Wrestling in Iowa: From Gotch to Gable*. Iowa City, IA: University of Iowa Press, 1981.
"Dan Gable." *Great Athletes,* vol. 3, Farrell-Holdsclaw. Hackensack, N.J.: Salem Press, Inc. 899-901.
Gable, Dan. *Coaching Wrestling Successfully*. Champaign, IL: Human Kinetics, 1999.
Gable, Dan (with James A. Peterson, Ph.D.). *Conditioning for Wrestling: The Iowa Way*. West Point, NY: Leisure Press, 1980.
Holland, Steve. *Talkin' Dan Gable*. Limerick Publications, 1983.
Smith, R.L. *The Legend of Dan Gable: "The" Wrestler*. Milwaukee: Medalist Industries, 1974.
Zavoral, Nolan. *A Season on the Mat*. New York: Simon & Schuster, 1998.

Periodicals

Gustkey, Earl. "Iowa Legend Could Be Candidate for a Fall." *Los Angeles Times* (July 18, 2001): D2.
McKee, Steve. "Solid Gold (lives of Olympic athletes after retiring from competition)." *American Health* 11 (June, 1992): 48.
Newsweek (November 8, 1999): 83.
Raab, Scott. "Nasty Dan and his wrestling empire." *Sport* 79 (April, 1988): 38.
St. Louis Post-Dispatch (March 12, 2000): D8.
Sports Illustrated (March 31, 1997): 32.
USA Today (November 11, 1999): 3C.

Other

"Dan Gable." http://www.wrestlinghalloffame.org/champions/?name&wrestler=433/ (November 8, 2002).
"The Official Dan Gable Web site." http://www.dangable.com/ (November 8, 2002).

Sketch by Eric Lagergren

Rudy Galindo
1969-

American figure skater

Rudy Galindo's story is in many ways the classic American rags-to-riches tale of overcoming adversity to triumph in the end. Again and again, Galindo has overcome personal tragedies and professional setbacks that would have defeated many other athletes. When the departure of **Kristi Yamaguchi** from their hugely successful skating partnership left him high-and-dry, he struggled with limited success to make up for lost time in men's singles competitions. Just when almost everyone had counted him out, he returned to win the 1996 U.S. Figure Skating National Championship, right in his own hometown.

But in addition to his grit and perseverance, there is an integrity at the heart of Galindo's story, a rare

Rudy Galindo

courage that allowed him to come out of the closet as one of the very few openly gay athletes. That same courage came through when he announced that he had been diagnosed HIV-positive in 2000, and it has continued to shine through in this greatest battle of his life.

A Trailer Park Childhood

Rudy Galindo was born in 1969 to Mexican-American parents Jess and Margaret Galindo in San Jose, California. Jess was a long-distance trucker who was often away from home. Margaret suffered from manic-depression (undiagnosed until 1983) that led to hospitalizations. Even when she lived at home, she was often not able to take care of the children. Galindo had an older brother, George, but much of the parenting responsibilities fell to his older sister Laura. She became a sort of mother to him and has remained in many ways his best friend throughout his life. It was also Laura who introduced him to the sport that would make him a star.

At the age of ten, Laura attended a skating party and immediately fell in love with it. She began to take skating lessons at the nearby Eastridge Ice Arena, and six-year-old Rudy often tagged along. For Jess, the skating lessons were a great way to keep the kids out of trouble. The family lived in a trailer park in East San Jose. As Galindo put it in *Icebreaker: The Autobiography of Rudy Galindo,* "I thought our trailer was just fine. There wasn't any reason for me to think otherwise. The whole neighborhood was a trailer park, so that's how all my neighbors lived." But the fact remained that it was also a dangerous place, a haven for gangs and drug dealers, and Jess Galindo was glad that his children had found a safe place to play. It would of course prove to be much more than that for Rudy.

A Prodigy and a Partnership

Galindo began to devote virtually all his free time to skating. He and Laura would get up at 4:45 in the morning to practice skating before school. Even with that, Galindo was often late, and he actually had to change schools to find a principal willing to accommodate this chronic lateness. The money for lessons also began to put a crimp in the family budget, and when it became too expensive Laura dropped out of serious skating, taking a job at Taco Bell to help pay for Rudy's skating and ballet lessons. The financial struggle prevented the Galindos from moving out of their trailer, but according to Rudy, his father never asked him to stop skating.

The family's sacrifices and Galindo's hard work soon started to pay off. He quickly rose to prominence in the sport, taking third place in the World Junior Figure Skating Championships at age 15, and first place two years later, in 1987. But it was in pairs skating that Galindo really caught the attention of the skating world.

In 1983, Galindo met Kristi Yamaguchi, and the two began skating together. While both continued to skate separately, often winning competitions, they began to be seen more and more as a team, a special combination that transcended their separate talents. In 1989 and again in 1990 they won the U.S. Figure Skating national pairs competition, and sportswriters began to speak of them as likely medal winners in the 1992 Olympics. At the same time, Galindo grew closer to the Yamaguchi family, even moving in with them for a few years and changing the spelling of his name to "Rudi" to better match Kristi.

But on April 26, 1990, Yamaguchi told Galindo she wanted to break up the partnership. She had continued to focus on singles competitions, and her exhausting training schedule was taking its toll. Yamaguchi and Galindo took fifth place at the 1990 World Figure Skating Pairs Championships, and to the surprise of many in the skating world, Yamaguchi failed to secure a medal in the Women's Singles. Something had to give, and she decided to focus exclusively on the singles. While he understood her reasons, Galindo was clearly hurt. As he told a *Sports Illustrated* reporter, "I guess I knew it would happen. You hear comments from other skaters. But Kristi had never said anything. We were like brother and sister, then we just went our separate ways."

Difficult Times

Reluctantly, Galindo returned to the men's singles competitions. He won the Pacific Coast regionals, but the results at the Nationals were disappointing. He placed 11th in 1991, climbed to 8th place in 1992, and

Chronology

1969	Born September 7 in San Jose, California
1975	Begins skating
1983	Begins pairs skating with Kristi Yamaguchi
1985	Finishes third in World Junior Figure Skating Championships
1987	Finishes first in World Junior Figure Skating Championships
1989	Wins pairs title (with Yamaguchi) in U.S. Figure Skating Championships
1989	Former coach, Jim Hulick, dies of complications related to AIDS
1990	Wins pairs title (with Yamaguchi) in U.S. Figure Skating Championships; they take fifth at World Championships
1990	In April, Yamaguchi withdraws from pairs skating with Galindo to focus on women's singles
1991	Finishes a disappointing eleventh in U.S. Figure Skating Championships, men's singles; from 1992-1995, finishes fifth place or lower in USFSA national championships
1993	Father dies of heart attack
1994	Brother, George, dies of complications related to AIDS
1995	Former coach, Rick Inglesi, dies of complications related to AIDS
1996	Wins USFSA national championship for men's singles
1996	Places third in USFSA world championship for men's singles
1996	Begins skating with Tom Collins Campbell's Soup of World Figure Skating Champions
2000	Diagnosed HIV-positive, goes public with the news

then peaked at 5th place in 1993. In the 1994 Nationals, he placed 7th, and in 1995 was back at 8th place. At this point Galindo considered dropping out of competition altogether.

His personal life wasn't going any better. His mother continued to struggle with her depression, sometimes lashing out in uncontrollable rages. His father suffered from diabetes and in 1988 he suffered a stroke. Indeed, illness and death seemed to haunt Galindo in these years. The coach he shared with Yamaguchi, Jim Hulick, had died from AIDS in December of 1989. In 1993, his father died of a heart attack. By that time, his brother George had been diagnosed with AIDS, and shortly afterwards he began to visibly decline. Galindo took care of George in his last year, changing him, bathing him, and often waking up at night to sounds of screaming as George slipped into AIDS dementia. George died in 1994, while Galindo was taking first place in the Vienna Cup. As he told *Sports Illustrated,* "He died the same time I was doing my long program. I came right home. That was hard. I went from the ice to the funeral." The next year, another coach, Rick Inglesias, died from the same terrible illness.

Galindo himself was not doing much better. Disappointed in his skating results, shell-shocked from all the suffering around him, he began drinking heavily, experimenting with drugs, and (perhaps most dangerously) engaging in unsafe sex. While Galindo had realized he was gay at a young age, and accepted it, it was not always easy for him. His father had reacted badly when his brother George came out to the family, and Yamaguchi's mother simply refused to believe him when he confided to her that he was gay. Not that Galindo lived a life of closeted isolation. He had close gay friends, who took him in when life

in the family trailer became overwhelming, and he had occasionally gone to gay bars with George, but in 1993 a recklessness seemed to take hold of Galindo. He took up with a man, identified as "Kurt" in his autobiography, who got him onto drugs, cleaned out his bank account, and even threatened him physically before dropping him. Galindo seemed to be spiraling out of control.

Turnaround and Triumph

Then in the fall of 1995, something seemed to happen inside Galindo. For one thing he began to help out his sister in teaching young skaters. This rekindled his original love of the sport. When he found out that the 1996 Nationals would be held in San Jose, his hometown, he decided to give it one last try—a farewell performance if need be, but one to be proud of. He began to train more seriously, dropping 25 pounds and practicing his skating routines over and over to eliminate mistakes. At his sister's suggestion, he even toned down his flamboyant costumes, which had often irritated judges in the past.

Galindo hoped just to finish in the top six, mentally conceding the top spots to previous national champions Todd Eldredge and **Scott Hamilton**. Indeed, after the short program, Eldredge and Hamilton took top honors, with Galindo in third place. Then came the long program, which counted for two-thirds of the final score, on January 20, 1996. Galindo went all out, landing eight triple jumps and two triple jump combinations flawlessly. Even before he finished, the sellout crowd of 10,869 were on their feet, cheering him on. When the judges announced the final results, including two perfect marks for artistic merit, the crowd went wild. And when seven of the nine judges put Galindo in first place, guaranteeing him the championship, the chant of "Rudy, Rudy, Rudy" filled the stadium.

The media guide for the event hadn't even included Galindo's name, but suddenly he was the national champion. He was the first openly gay man, the first Hispanic, and at 26, the oldest man in 70 years to hold that title. It was an amazing comeback, and Galindo became a hometown hero. And for the first time since the breakup with Yamaguchi, Galindo was on his way to the World Championships, in Edmonton, Canada. Yamaguchi herself called to congratulate him, and for the first time in years the two had a long, warm conversation. Despite a sprained ankle, a bad case of nerves, and the competition of Olympic medallists, Galindo took the bronze medal at the World Championships. It was a result that left him and Laura, by now his coach, ecstatic.

A New Life and a New Challenge

Already, Galindo had signed on with the Tom Collins Campbell's Soup Tour of World Figure Skating Champions, for $200,000—more money than he'd ever seen. He also signed deals for his autobiography, a made-for-TV movie, and exhibitions, including the Champions on Ice. For the first time in his life, money

Awards and Accomplishments

Year	Accomplishment
1982	First place, National Novice competition
1985	Third place, World Junior Championship, men's singles
1985	Fifth place, National Championship, junior pairs (with Yamaguchi)
1986	Second place, World Junior Championship, men's singles
1986	First place, National Championship, junior pairs (with Yamaguchi)
1987	First place, World Junior Championship, men's singles
1987	Third place, World Junior Championship, pairs (with Yamaguchi)
1987	Second place, U.S. Olympic Festival, men's singles
1988	First place, World Junior Championship, pairs (with Yamaguchi)
1989-90	First place, World Championship, pairs (with Yamaguchi)
1992	First place, Pacific Coast regionals, men's singles; places eighth at nationals
1993	First place, Pacific Coast regionals, men's singles; places fifth at nationals
1994	First place, Vienna Cup
1994	First place, Pacific Coast regionals, men's singles; places seventh at nationals
1995	First place, Pacific Coast regionals, men's singles; places eighth at nationals
1996	First place, National Championship, men's singles
1996	Third place, World Championship, men's singles
2000	Second place, World Professional Men's Figure Skating Championship

was not an issue. Wisely, he let Laura handle much of the finances. From a young age family members and friends, even Mrs. Yamaguchi for a while, had handled Galindo's practical affairs while he focused on skating. Now that he was making money, he was determined not to blow it all, although he did buy presents for friends and family, including a new set of furniture for his mother—who declined his offer to buy her a house.

For the next few years, Galindo was able to concentrate on writing his autobiography, skating professionally, and enjoying his newfound fame and fortune. Then in early 2000 came news that would once again challenge his faith in the future. Skating a warm-up routine, he suddenly found himself so short of breath that he had to leave the ice. In his heart, he knew that something serious was happening, but he put off going to the doctor. When his "bronchitis" failed to clear up, he finally sought medical treatment, and found out that he was HIV-positive.

After the initial shock, as memories of George's final days came flooding into his mind, Galindo once again rose to meet the crisis. He went public with the news of his diagnosis, and with his invaluable sister's encouragement, he began to treat the disease aggressively, through antiretroviral therapy. He seems to be doing well and continues to skate for the Tom Collins Champions on Ice, while doing his best to raise public awareness of AIDS, particularly for those at greatest risk. One thing is certain: Galindo is not giving up. As his agent, Michael Rosenberg, once described his entire career in *USA Today,* "Rudy Galindo is the [best example] of never, ever, ever quit."

CONTACT INFORMATION

Address: Rudy Galindo, U.S. Figure Skating Association, 20 First St., Colorado Springs, CO 80906-3624.

SELECTED WRITINGS BY GALINDO:

(With Eric Marcus) *Icebreaker: The Autobiography of Rudy Galindo,* New York: Pocket Books, 1997.

FURTHER INFORMATION

Books

Rudy Galindo and Eric Marcus. *Icebreaker: The Autobiography of Rudy Galindo.* New York. Pocket Books, 1997.

Periodicals

Croft, T.S. "Rudy Galindo"*Advocate* (August 18, 1998): 69.

Duffy, Martha. "Edge of a dream: having overcome tragedy, Rudy Galindo is poised to win figure skating's world title." *Time* (March 18, 1996): 84.

"The fall most feared." *People Weekly* (April 17, 2000): 62.

Leonard, Amy. "Faces in the crowd." *Sports Illustrated* (January 19, 1987): 77.

Paulk, J. Sara. Review of *Icebreaker. Library Journal* (April 15, 1997): 87.

Plummer, William. "Redemption song: skating for the living and the dead, hard-luck Rudy Galindo is a champion once more." *People Weekly* (February 5, 1996): 126.

Prose, Francine. Review of *Icebreaker. People Weekly* (April 28, 1997): 38.

Review of *Icebreaker. Lambda Book Report.* (May 1997): 23.

Review of *Icebreaker. Publishers Weekly.* (March 3, 1997): 57.

Swift, E.M. "On a roll." *Sports Illustrated* (March 11, 1996): 52.

Swift, E.M. "A real gem dandy." *Sports Illustrated* (January 29, 1996): 36.

Sketch by Robert Winters

Sergio Garcia
1980-

Spanish golfer

Noticeably fun-loving and light-hearted among other more dignified golfers, Sergio "El Nino" Garcia shed his amateur status at age nineteen after accumulating twenty-one amateur victories. In 1999 as he claimed six tournament wins and picked up his first endorsement contract, he was regarded as the most promising professional golfer the year. Dubbed a wunderkind by some, Garcia easily piqued the interest of observers like no golfer since **Tiger Woods**.

Garcia was born on January 9, 1980 in Castellon, Spain. Golf was a way of life for his father, golf pro Victor Garcia, and mother Consuelo Fernandez, who was a pro shop employee. Both were employed at Club Del Campo del Mediterranean. Victor Garcia, who later joined the Professional Golf Association (PGA) European senior tour, personally taught his three children— Victor Jr., Sergio, and Mar—to play. Sergio, the middle child, took to the sport with the most flair.

Given his background, it was perhaps unremarkable when Garcia first won a junior tournament at age ten. When at age twelve he took the club championship at Del Campo, however, the significance of his victory was evident. It became clear that Garcia possessed a natural bent for the sport, and by age fourteen he had claimed a spot on the professional tour.

Garcia took the Topolino World Junior Championship in 1994, and the European Young Masters and European Amateur Championship in 1995. He went on to claim a total of twenty-one such victories over the next four years. In 1996, at age sixteen and still an amateur, he ranked third in scoring on the PGA tour. In his native Spain, he claimed four national amateur titles by that time: under sixteen, under eighteen, under twenty-one, and the Spanish Amateur. More impressive still was his win at the Catalonian Open Championship, a PGA (professional) event at age seventeen. Two years later he won the British Amateur of 1998 and was hailed as the best amateur worldwide.

Garcia turned pro on April 21, 1999. Simultaneously he picked up a five-year endorsement deal from Adidas. At the PGA Championship in Medinah, Illinois, in August of the year, he attracted international attention with a near upset of Woods. Garcia—the youngest participant in that event since 1921—lost by a single stroke.

After a professional debut at the Byron Nelson Classic in May, Garcia played his first major as a professional, at the British Open in June. One month later he snagged a tour win at the Murphy's Irish Open, to become the fourth youngest winner ever on the European tour. Garcia won six tournaments altogether during his first year as a pro. He finished second in the PGA that season, and by year's end his ranking had soared, from number 399, into the top twenty worldwide. He was hailed as the most promising professional of the year. On the PGA European tour that season he competed in twelve events, winning two.

Garcia was named to the 1999 European Ryder Cup team and to the Alfred Dunhill Cup Spanish team. After

Sergio Garcia

ranking third on the PGA European tour of 1999, he was awarded the Sir Henry Cotton Rookie of the Year award.

El Nino

As a promising new professional and in part because of his youth, Garcia came under intense media scrutiny. Nicknamed El Nino (the child), he took criticism for the volatility of his standings and for the wrist action in his swing. Ironically comparisons between Garcia and **Ben Hogan** were drawn over the same topic of the wrist action in the swing. By June of 2000 he was ranked at number fifteen. With his stroke average up from 70.3 in 1999 to 70.9 in 2000, he finished his second year as a pro without winning a tournament. He finished out the season in the top thirty-six and ranked at twenty-one on the PGA European tour. The performance caused critics to question the volatility of his skill.

With his stroke average down to 69.5 by the end of 2001, he finished the season with two USA PGA tour wins. His victory at the Colonial tournament in Fort Worth on May 21 was his first on the U.S. tour. He added $750,000 to his winnings, bringing his purse for the year to $1.1 million at that point—barely four months after his twenty-first birthday. With a second U.S. win at the Buick Classic in June, his ranking climbed to number six worldwide. Going into the British Open that year, he was top-ranked for the tournament and ranked at number five worldwide. In September 2001 he took the Trophée Lancôme.

Chronology

1980	Born January 9 in Spain
1996	Achieves third place in scoring on PGA tour while still a 16-year-old amateur
1999	Turns pro on April 21; signs with Adidas in April; becomes fourth youngest tour winner in history in July; wins two events of 12 played on European PGA tour; named to European Ryder Cup team (youngest participant ever)
2000	Ranks forty-second on earnings list; holds a ranking of fifteen in June; finishes the year ranked in top thirty-six worldwide
2001	Ranks at fifth worldwide; ranks at number one going into the 2001 British Open; is fined 5,000 pounds-sterling for an outburst at the Greg Norman Holden International Tour on February 10
2002	Earns $1,465,323 by May, to rank as the tenth-highest money-maker on PGA tour; finishes in top ten of the four major tournaments; purchases a home in Orlando, Florida

Awards and Accomplishments

1994	Topolino World Junior Championship
1995	European Young Masters Championship, European Amateur Championship
1996	Spanish Amateur Championship under-16, under-18, under-21
1997	Catalonian Open Championship (PGA event), European Masters Amateur Championship, French Amateur Championship, Spanish Amateur Championship, British Boys Championship, Grand Prix de Lendes, David Leadbetter Championship
1998	Spanish Amateur Championship, King of Spain Cup, Jacksonville Junior, European Amateur Masters, Puerta de Hierro Cup, British Amateur Championship
1999	Named Sir Henry Cotton Rookie of the Year; won the Irish Open
2001	MasterCard Colonial, Buick Classic; Trophée Lancôme
2002	Mercedes Championship; Canarias Open de Espana (Spanish Open)

At age twenty-three, Garcia stands 5-feet-10-inches tall and weighs 159 pounds. He travels with an entourage that has come to be known as La Familia (the family). Members of the so-called family include a manager, assistant manager, caddie, strength coach, and an all-important English teacher as Garcia makes professional strides in the United States and in the British Commonwealth. Following his losing year in 2000 Garcia replaced his caddie, bringing Glenn Murray of South Africa into the family.

Garcia's steadily rising driving accuracy percentage went from 69.5 in 2000 to 72.6 in 2001. Likewise his average driving distance rose from 287.9 yards to 291.4 at the same time. When he arrived at the majors of 2002, he realized top ten finishes in each of the four tournaments. In recognition of his PGA tour win at the Mercedes Championship in January, he learned to drive in order to enjoy the spoils of his victory. Other wins of 2002 included the Canarias Open de Espana at Gran Canaria in April of that year .

Garcia, who maintains his residence in Borriol, purchased a home in Orlando, Florida, in 2002. His avocations include watching cartoons, and playing tennis and computer games. Although he is admired for his boyish charm and effervescence, his shenanigans have been known to annoy those more dignified denizens of the links. The most disastrous of his offenses occurred at the **Greg Norman** Holden International Tour in Australia on February 10, 2001. In the end he took home a fine of 5,000 pounds-sterling for what was initially described as an outburst and later as a flagrant disrespect for the rules. Regardless, *Golf World* maintained that "[r]aw energy," and "cocksure exuberance," are what Garcia is all about.

CONTACT INFORMATION

Address: c/o PGA European Tour, Wentworth Drive, Virginia Water, Surrey GU25 4LX England. Fax: +44 (0)1344 840500. Phone: +44 (0)1344 840400. Online: www.europeantour.com.

FURTHER INFORMATION

Periodicals

Golf World (May 17, 2002): 42.
Golf World (October 4, 2002): 39.
Newsweek (September 27, 1999): 58.
Sports Illustrated (August 23, 1999): 32.
Sports Illustrated (May 25, 2001): 48.
Sports Illustrated (June 24, 2002): G6.

Other

"PGA European Tour - Players - Biographies." european tour.com. http://www.europeantour.com/players/bio.sps?iPlayerNo=487&sOption=other (January 21, 2003).

Sketch by G. Cooksey

Kevin Garnett
1976-

American basketball player

In 1995, Kevin Garnett became famous as one of the first high school basketball players to be drafted directly into the National Basketball Association (NBA). Despite many people's concerns about how a teenager would fare in that setting, Garnett did extremely well in his first few years. In 1997, when at the age of twenty-two he re-signed with the Minnesota Timberwolves for $126 million over six years, and became the highest-paid athlete in any team sport.

Kevin Garnett

NBA Draft, 1995

Garnett was a senior at Farragut Academy in Chicago in the spring of 1995. He had already earned a great deal of national attention as a basketball player, but his SAT scores were not high enough to play college basketball in the NCAA, so he decided to take his chances with the NBA draft. He was a hot prospect, and even before the draft happened he appeared on the cover of *Sports Illustrated* under the headline *Ready or Not....* Only hours before the draft started he learned that he had passed the SATs the last time he took them, but by then it was too late. In the first round of the draft, he was selected fifth overall by the Minnesota Timberwolves.

The Timberwolves were still a young team then, and in 1995 they had a new vice president, general manager, and owner. "I think we figured if [signing a high school kid] went bad, we'd just say, 'Hey, it was our first draft. We didn't know what we were doing,'" Timberwolves vice president Kevin McHale told *Sports Illustrated* reporter Leigh Montville in 1999. But the Timberwolves never needed any excuses.

From his first season, Garnett was an excellent player, scoring an average of 10.4 points per game and achieving a 49.1 percent shooting average. He started the season as the second-string small forward, behind veteran NBA player Sam Mitchell, but that did not last long. Several weeks into the season, Mitchell recalled to Montville, "I went to the coach and told him Kevin

Chronology

1976	Born May 19 in Maudlin, South Carolina
1995	Graduates from Chicago's Farragut Academy
1995	Drafted by the Minnesota Timberwolves in the first round of the NBA draft
1996	Records his first NBA start January 9
1996	Plays Wilt Chamberlain in "Rebound: The Story of Earl 'The Goat' Manigault," a video by HBO
1998	Becomes the first Timberwolf to start in an All-Star game
2002	Launches "4XL-For Excellence in Leadership," a program to teach minority students about careers in business

should be starting. The reason was simple: He was better. I was playing against him every day in practice, and I knew how good he was." But as good as his skills were, perhaps more impressive was the fact that Garnett quickly became the team's moral leader, calming down teammates who were angry and energizing those who felt tired or defeated.

From his first day in the NBA, Garnett was fighting a battle for respect. "Money comes and goes. Respect lasts a lifetime," McHale told Frank Clancy of *Sporting News* near the end of Garnett's first season. "He's got the right attitude." It didn't take long for Garnett to earn this respect, as he explained to *Esquire*'s Mike Lupica early in 1997. "I think the way I've played, the way I've conducted myself, has done that. . . . All I ever heard from the first day was 'This is a man's league, kid.' The only way you can get them to treat you like a man is to play like a man."

Bank-Breaking Contract

In Garnett's second season, he was paired on the court with his old friend, point guard Stephon Marbury. With this combination, the Timberwolves had their best year in franchise history, making the playoffs for the first time ever. Garnett, the unquestioned star of the team, played in the All-Star game. So when he had the opportunity to sign a contract extension with the Timberwolves at the end of the season, the Timberwolves offered him $102 million over six years to stay. He refused, believing that in another year, when he would be a free agent, he would be able to make more. After weeks of negotiations, he finally re-signed for $126 million over six years.

This contract, the most lucrative ever, led to a fight between the NBA management and the players' union over the terms of player contracts, which led to a lockout that precluded a large portion of the 1998-99 season. Under the terms of the new agreement, contracts as large as Garnett's are now banned. However, Garnett and others who were grandfathered into the agreement will be able to sign contract renewals for 105 percent of their previous contract. This means that when Garnett's current contract expires, when he will

Career Statistics

Yr	Team	GP	PTS	FG%	3P%	FT%	RPG	APG	SPG	BPG	TO	PF
1995-96	MIN	80	835	.491	.286	.705	6.3	1.8	1.08	1.64	110	189
1996-97	MIN	77	1309	.499	.286	.754	8.0	3.1	1.36	2.12	175	199
1997-98	MIN	82	1518	.491	.188	.738	9.6	4.2	1.70	1.83	192	224
1998-99	MIN	47	977	.460	.286	.704	10.4	4.3	1.66	1.77	135	152
1999-00	MIN	81	1857	.497	.370	.765	11.8	5.0	1.48	1.56	268	205
2000-01	MIN	81	1784	.477	.288	.764	11.4	5.0	1.37	1.79	230	204
2001-02	MIN	81	1714	.470	.319	.891	12.1	5.2	1.19	1.56	229	184

MIN: Minnesota Timberwolves.

Awards and Accomplishments

1994	Named South Carolina's "Mr. Basketball"
1995	USA Today's Player of the Year
1995	Named to Parade Magazine's All-America First Team
1995	Named Illinois's "Mr. Basketball"
1995	Most Outstanding Player of the McDonald's All-America high school basketball game
1995	First Annual Nike Hoop Summit (with USA Basketball's Junior Select National Team)
1996	NBA All-Rookie Second Team All-Star
1997-98, 2000	Selected for the NBA All-Star Game
1999	All-NBA Third Team All-Star
1999	Tournament of the Americas (with USA Basketball's Pre-Olympic Qualifying Team)
2000	All-NBA First Team All-Star
2000-01	NBA All-Defense First Team All-Star
2001	All-NBA Second Team All-Star
2001	Became only the seventh player in NBA history to average over twenty points per game, ten rebounds per game, and five assists per game in more than one season

be twenty-eight and presumably at the peak of his athletic prowess, he will be eligible to receive $28 million a season.

But "I don't play basketball for the money," Garnett told *Sports Illustrated*'s Michael Farber before the contract dispute. "I don't play it for the crowd. When I didn't have a friend, when I was lonely, I always knew I could grab that orange pill and go hoop. I could go and dunk on somebody. If things weren't going right, I could make a basket and feel better."

"I'm a battery"

Garnett has long been known for his enthusiasm for the game. Even when he was working out for a group of NBA coaches before the 1995 draft, he shouted as he demonstrated to them how high he could jump. By the end of the 1999-00 season, not only did he throw back his head and howl, he had his rookie teammate Wally Szczerbiak shouting as he ran down the court after making his shots. "Last summer, I couldn't get Wally to throw his fist in the air. Now this kid is going down, shaking his head like he's crazy," Garnett explained to

Darryl Howerton of *Sport*. "I'm spreading." That's fine with Garnett, as he told Howerton. "I go crazy trying to energize people 'cause that's what I am. I'm a battery, you know? if you're down, you can plug into me and get charged up." Although Garnett, Szczerbiak, and the other energized Timberwolves have yet to win an NBA championship, fans remain hopeful that this still-young team will soon be able to go all the way.

CONTACT INFORMATION

Address: c/o Minnesota Timberwolves, 600 First Avenue North, Minneapolis, MN 55403.

FURTHER INFORMATION

Periodicals

Ballantini, Brett. "'The Kid' Grows Up." *Basketball Digest* (March, 2002): 20-27.

Brauer, David. "A Season on the Brink." *MPLS-St. Paul Magazine* (November, 2000): 78.

Clancy, Frank. "The Kid's All Right." *Sporting News* (March 4, 1996): 26-29.

Farber, Michael. "Feel the Warmth." *Sports Illustrated* (January 20, 1997): 70-79.

Guss, Greg. "Hungry like the Wolf." *Sport* (November, 1996): 50-53.

Howerton, Darryl. "Energizer Buddy." *Sport* (March, 2000): 32.

Lupica, Mike. "The Go-to Guy." *Esquire* (March, 1997): 54-56.

McCallum, Jack. "Hoop Dreams." *Sports Illustrated* (June 26, 1995): 64-68.

Millea, John. "Lonewolf." *Sporting News* (November 27, 2000): 10.

Montville, Leigh. "Howlin' Wolf." *Sports Illustrated* (May 3, 1999): 38.

"NBA Star Launches Program to Introduce Students to Business." *Black Issues in Higher Education* (March 28, 2002): 16.

Young, Bob. "Marbury, Garnett Trade Barbs." *Arizona Republic* (Phoenix, AZ) (December 31, 2002).

Other

"#10-Kevin Garnett." USA Basketball. http://www. usabasketball.com/biosmen/kevin_garnett_bio.html (November 27, 2002).

"Kevin Garnett Player Info." NBA.com. http://www. nba.com/playerfile/kevin_garnett/ (November 27, 2002).

"Olympic Bio: Kevin Garnett." CNN/SI.com. http:// sportsillustrated.cnn.com/olympics/news/2000/05/25/ garnett_bio/ (November 27, 2002).

Sketch by Julia Bauder

Lou Gehrig

Lou Gehrig
1903-1941

American baseball player

L ou Gehrig, dubbed the "Iron Man" of baseball, is best known for his record for most consecutive games played, 2,130, which he held from his retirement in 1939 until Baltimore Orioles player **Cal Ripken, Jr.** surpassed him in 1995. Gehrig also had an impressive bat: he holds the Major League record for career grand slams (23), and, until St. Louis Cardinals first baseman **Mark McGwire**'s phenomenal slugging streak, Gehrig held the record for most career home runs by a first baseman (493). He stole home plate fifteen times in his career, and his lifetime batting average, .340, is the fifteenth highest ever. However, to many Gehrig is remembered primarily for the disease which took his life and his name.

Growing Up

Gehrig was born in Manhattan in 1903 to Christina and Heinrich Gehrig, both recent immigrants from Germany. He was the only one of their children to survive past infancy. Because of this, Gehrig and his mother developed an extremely close relationship. Although the Gehrig family was lower-middle class, Christina Gehrig worked hard as a maid, cook, and washerwoman to make sure that Gehrig had every opportunity to succeed. From a young age Gehrig helped his mother, delivering the washing that she took in, but he still found plenty of time to play.

Gehrig excelled at all of the sports which could be played on the streets of New York, including his favorite, baseball. In the summer, he and his friends often dove into the Hudson River, off of the cliffs at 181st Street where the George Washington Bridge would later be built. When he was eleven Gehrig swam the whole way to New Jersey and back from this point, which reportedly earned him a boxing on the ears from his father. Danger-

ous stunts aside, the elder Gehrig encouraged Lou's physical development, often taking Gehrig along when he went to the *turnvereins,* gymnasiums where German-American men gathered. Heinrich Gehrig also bought Lou his first baseball glove.

Taste of Fame

Christina Gehrig dreamed of Gehrig going to college and becoming an engineer, even though at that time it was rare for working class children to continue their education beyond the eighth grade. After Gehrig graduated from grammar school, she arranged for him to attend the High School of Commerce, where he learned useful clerking skills like typing and bookkeeping. He also gained some fame as a player on Commerce's football, soccer, and baseball teams. Commerce won three straight soccer championships in his years there, and in 1920 Gehrig was even invited to play in a national high-school baseball championship game in Chicago with the Commerce team.

Christina Gehrig was dismayed at her son's continued interest in baseball, a sport which was only for "bummers" as far as she was concerned, and it took a great deal of pleading for Gehrig to convince her to let him take the trip to Chicago. The Commerce team traveled to Chicago on an elegant train, where former president William Howard Taft and other dignitaries stopped by to wish them well. In the ninth inning of the game, which was played in Wrigley Field, Gehrig hit a grand

Chronology	
1903	Born June 19 in New York, New York
1921	Enters Columbia University
1923	Debuts in the Major Leagues
1925	Consecutive games played streak begins June 1
1933	Marries Eleanor Twitchell September 29
1938	Stars in the Western film *Rawhide*
1939	Consecutive game streak ends at 2,130 on May 2
1939	Retires from baseball
1941	Dies of amyotrophic lateral sclerosis June 2 in Riverdale, New York
1942	*The Pride of the Yankees* is released

Awards and Accomplishments	
1927, 1936	Named the American League's Most Valuable Player (MVP)
1931	Sets the American League record for most runs batted in in one season (184)
1932	Becomes the first and only player to bat in more than 500 runs in three years
1934	Wins the American League Triple Crown
1939	Elected to the Baseball Hall of Fame
1939	Becomes the first athlete ever to have his number retired

slam home run—a rare feat, for in the entire Major League season the previous year, only eighteen home runs had been hit at Wrigley Field.

Gehrig did not only play baseball with his school's team. The summer Gehrig was sixteen, he pitched in a Yonkers city league on the Otis Elevator Company team, since he had gotten an office job with that company for the summer. He also earned $5 a game playing semi-professional ball with the Minqua Baseball Club, which was sponsored by one of the many Democratic clubs which covered New York in those days. The fact that Gehrig was now making money from baseball went a long way to reconciling Christina Gehrig to the sport.

In Gehrig's senior year at Commerce, Christina took a job as a maid and cook at one of Columbia University's fraternity houses, where she made a connection with Columbia's graduate manager of athletics, Bobby Watt. Watt came to a Commerce game and watched Gehrig play football one day, and he was impressed enough to give Gehrig a football scholarship to the university.

College Ball

Although it was against the rules for college players to earn any money from their sport, this was a widely violated rule. Scores of college-age men played in the minor leagues over the summer under assumed names, and in 1921, months after graduating from high school, Gehrig was one of them. He signed a contract with the Hartford Senators, a Class A team affiliated with the New York Giants. For two weeks he played under the name "Lou Lewis," but then Columbia found out and forced him to quit. Gehrig lost his eligibility to play for Columbia for one year as a result, but for the next two summers he played semi-professional baseball on Sunday afternoons with a Morristown, New Jersey team as Lou Long. This was widely known, but no one is sure whether Columbia never found out this time, or whether they knew and decided to ignore it.

Gehrig played his one and only season of baseball for Columbia, as a pitcher, in 1923. He was almost instantly heralded as a star. In one game, he set a record for number of strikeouts—seventeen—which would stand at Co-

lumbia for almost fifty years. In another, he hit the longest home run ever at Columbia's South Field: it bounced off the steps of the library across 116th street, nearly beaning the dean of the college. Through such feats, Gehrig caught the eye of New York Yankees scout Paul Krichell, who offered him $3,500 to sign with the Yankees. Gehrig did. Although it disappointed his mother to see him drop out of school, both of Gehrig's parents were ill at the time and the family desperately needed the money.

The Beginning of a Legend

Gehrig started playing for the Yankees in June of 1923. As the story goes, his first meeting with the team was stunning. At the beginning of that first practice, before most of the team was on the field, several of the Yankees best hitters, including **Babe Ruth**, were taking some extra batting practice. Manager Miller Huggins escorted Gehrig onto the field and encouraged him to take a few swings. Gehrig grabbed a bat at random. It happened to be Ruth's favorite, a forty-eight ounce monster that was too heavy for most players to handle. Gehrig's nervousness showed as he missed a few pitches, then hit a few weak ground balls. Then some of his friends from Columbia, who were sitting in the bleachers providing moral support, started to shout encouragement to him. "Show that big guy, Lou. He's not the only one that can hit it out of the park," one said, referring to Ruth. Gehrig proceeded to hit some half-dozen balls into "Ruthsville," the section of the right-field bleachers where many of Ruth's hits wound up. The veteran Yankees were stunned, while Gehrig's friends only got louder in their cheers. Embarrassed, Gehrig walked away from the plate.

Gehrig made his major league debut only weeks later, on June 16. He spent much of the 1923 and 1924 seasons in the minor leagues, playing for the Hartford Senators, but he was learning the confidence he needed to play big-league baseball. He was called back to the Yankees in late August of 1924 and became an invaluable pinch-hitter, and in 1925 he joined the starting line-up.

Gehrig began his consecutive games streak on June 1, 1925, when he pinch-hit for shortstop Peewee Wanninger. The next day, June 2, Gehrig started at first base. The Yankees already had a good first baseman, the

---

Gehrig, 'Iron Man' of Baseball, Dies at the Age of 37

. . . When Gehrig stepped into the batter's box as a pinch hitter for the Yankees on June 1, 1925, he started a record that many believe will never be equaled in baseball. From that day on he never missed a championship game until April 30, 1939—fifteen seasons of Yankee box scores with the name of Gehrig always in the line-up. . . .

But as brilliant as was his career, Lou will be remembered for more than his endurance record. He was a superb batter in his heyday and a prodigious clouter of home runs. The record book is literally strewn with his feats at the plate. . . .

But baseball has had other great hitters before, and other great all-around players. It was the durability of Gehrig combined with his other qualities that lifted him above the ordinary players and in a class all his own.

Source: *New York Times* (June 3, 1941): 1, 26.

Lou Gehrig, catching ball

crowd-pleasing Wally Pipp, but that morning Pipp had been struck in the head with a pitch during batting practice. He spent two weeks in the hospital recovering from his injuries, and by the time he returned Gehrig was well established at first base. Pipp was eventually traded, and from June 2 on, Gehrig would play in every single game the Yankees played until 1939.

Glory Days

The Yankees of the late 1920s and the 1930s were legendary. With Gehrig and Ruth, they had the two most powerful hitters in their league; it was not uncommon for each of them individually to have more home runs in a year than many entire teams. Although the Yankees lost a close series in 1926, by 1927 they seemed invincible. Ruth set a record that year with sixty home runs, while Gehrig, the cleanup hitter, set his own record with 175 runs batted in. The Yankees became the first American League team ever to sweep the World Series, and then in 1928 they did it again. Although they did not play in a series again until 1932, the team still had an amazing record in the intervening years. In the 1931 season they set a record with 1,067 runs batted in; Gehrig's contribution to that total, 184 (including three grand slams in four days), is still an American League record.

In 1933, Gehrig became engaged to Eleanor Twitchell, a high-spirited socialite from Chicago. They were married that September in a quiet, private wedding one morning in their new apartment, close to the house which Gehrig had bought for his parents a few years before. Immediately after the wedding, a phalanx of motorcycle-riding police from their town, New Rochelle, escorted the couple to Yankee Stadium: not even getting married could make Gehrig miss a game.

In 1935, Ruth finally left the Yankees and, for one season, Gehrig was the team's uncontested star. Then **Joe DiMaggio** joined the team, and once again Gehrig was relegated to second place, batting clean-up behind a star. However, Gehrig, always a team player, did not re-

sent DiMaggio. Later in life, DiMaggio told the following tale: early in his first season with the Yankees, DiMaggio turned around and gave a look to the umpire, George Moriarty, after Moriarty had called two borderline balls as strikes. Moriarty, a long-time umpire who was not cowed by young stars, harshly told DiMaggio to turn back around. Gehrig, who was standing in the on-deck circle, shouted, "Leave the kid alone, George. If you call 'em right, he won't have to turn around."

With DiMaggio and Gehrig, the "Bronx Bombers," as the Yankees were dubbed, won two straight World Series over the New York Giants in 1936 and 1937. Gehrig still played on, going to work every day through broken fingers (at one point or another in his career, he broke every single finger at least once) and through the attacks of back pain which had recently started to plague him. Although occasionally stunts were employed to keep the streak alive, such as having Gehrig bat first and then immediately replacing him with a pinch-runner on days when his back pain was most excruciating, Gehrig was still one of the best, most reliable players in the game.

During the off season after the 1937 World Series, Gehrig went to Hollywood and starred in a Western film called *Rawhide*. This wasn't his first attempt at Hollywood stardom—there had been some talk of Gehrig replacing **Johnny Weissmuller** as Tarzan, and some amusing photographs of Gehrig posing in a loincloth even appeared—but it was by far his most successful, even if the reviews were mixed.

Career Statistics

Yr	Team	AVG	GP	AB	R	H	HR	RBI	BB	SO	SB
1923	NYY	.423	13	26	6	11	1	9	2	5	0
1924	NYY	.500	10	12	2	6	0	5	1	3	0
1925	NYY	.295	126	437	73	129	20	68	46	49	6
1926	NYY	.313	155	572	135	179	16	112	105	73	6
1927	NYY	.373	155	584	149	218	47	175	109	84	10
1928	NYY	.374	154	562	139	210	27	142	95	69	4
1929	NYY	.300	154	553	127	166	35	126	122	68	4
1930	NYY	.379	154	581	143	220	41	174	101	63	12
1931	NYY	.341	155	619	163	211	46	184	117	56	17
1932	NYY	.349	156	596	138	208	34	151	108	38	4
1933	NYY	.334	152	593	138	198	32	139	92	42	9
1934	NYY	.363	154	579	128	210	49	165	109	31	9
1935	NYY	.329	149	535	125	176	30	119	132	38	8
1936	NYY	.354	155	579	167	205	49	152	130	46	3
1937	NYY	.351	157	569	138	200	37	159	127	49	4
1938	NYY	.295	157	576	115	170	29	114	107	75	6
1939	NYY	.143	8	28	2	4	0	1	5	1	0
TOTAL		.340	2164	8001	1888	2721	493	1995	1508	790	102

NYY: New York Yankees.

The Pride of the Yankees

Lou Gehrig's life story was brought to the big screen in the 1942 film *The Pride of the Yankees*. Written by renowned Hollywood screenwriters Jo Swerling (of *It's a Wonderful Life*) and Herman J. Mankiewicz (of *Citizen Kane*) and nominated for eleven Academy Awards, including Best Picture, *The Pride of the Yankees* was a major success. Gehrig was played by Gary Cooper, a well-regarded actor, but not one with a natural affinity for baseball. This led to some difficulties filming the baseball scenes. Most notably, since Cooper was right-handed and Gehrig batted with his left, the batting scenes were filmed in reverse, with the players wearing mirror-image uniforms and Cooper batting right-handed and running to third. Although *The Pride of the Yankees* showcases Gehrig's famous hard work and dedication to the game, its most affecting moments are about Gehrig's tender and supportive relationship with his wife, Eleanor, who was played by Teresa Wright. Many actual Yankees, including Babe Ruth, played themselves in the film.

The End of the Streak

Gehrig hit the 2,000 consecutive games played mark on May 31, 1938, but shortly thereafter problems started surfacing. Gehrig was no longer hitting like he used to. His batting average that season fell below .300. The rest of the Yankees made up for it, winning the pennant and sweeping the Chicago Cubs in the World Series, but it was clear that something was wrong. Gehrig came back in 1939, but he soon realized that his poor playing was hurting the whole team. On May 2, 1939, after 2,130 consecutive games, Gehrig voluntarily benched himself. In June, the Mayo Clinic diagnosed Gehrig with amyotrophic lateral sclerosis, which would soon become known as Lou Gehrig's disease.

Gehrig formally retired from baseball on July 4, 1939, in Yankee Stadium, where he gave one of the most memorable speeches in the history of sports, declaring himself to be "the luckiest man on the face of the earth." He spent 1940 working as a parole commissioner for New York City, interviewing various convicted criminals, but by the beginning of 1941 he was too weak to work anymore, even on crutches. He died on June 2, 1941.

Immortality

Gehrig passed into the pantheon of baseball immortals almost immediately upon his retirement. The Baseball Hall of Fame inducted him in the summer of 1939, ignoring their usual five-year waiting period. His #4 was retired, making him the first player ever to be so honored. Baseball diamonds across the country were named for him, as was a Liberty ship during World War II. His life story was dramatized in the 1942 film *The Pride of the Yankees*. By facing death with the same courageousness with which he had faced life every day, Gehrig finally achieved the fame that he deserved.

FURTHER INFORMATION

Books

Bak, Richard. *Lou Gehrig: An American Classic.* Dallas: Taylor, 1995.

Gehrig, Eleanor, and Duran, Joseph. *My Luke and I.* New York: Crowell, 1976.

Robinson, Ray. *Iron Horse: Lou Gehrig in His Time.* New York: Norton, 1990.

Periodicals

"Eleanor Gehrig." *Time* (March 19, 1984): 92.

"Gehrig, 'Iron Man' of Baseball, Dies at the Age of 37." *New York Times* (June 3, 1941): 1, 26.

Neff, Craig. "A Stamp of Greatness." *Sports Illustrated* (June 19, 1989): 16.

Noonan, David. "Double Legacy of the Iron Horse." *Sports Illustrated* (April 4, 1988): 112-120.

Robinson, Ray. "A Two-Horse Race." *Sporting News* (September 11, 1995): S8.

Other

Baseball-Reference.com. http://www.baseball-reference.com/ (October 8, 2002).

Lou Gehrig Home Page. http://www.lougehrig.com/ (October 8, 2002).

National Baseball Hall of Fame. http://www.baseballhalloffame.org/ (October 8, 2002).

Sketch by Julia Bauder

Bobbi Gibb
1942-

American marathon runner

On April 19, 1966, Roberta "Bobbi" Gibb became the first woman to run and finish the Boston Marathon. In a field of 500 male runners, she was the 125th to cross the finish line, shattering the long-held belief that women could not compete in endurance sports. Her accomplishments paved the way for the passage of Title IX and the inclusion of a women's marathon as part of the Olympic games.

Good Girls Don't Run . . .

Raised in a suburb of Boston, Massachusetts, Gibb loved running even as a girl, when she would pretend to be a horse and gallop through fields like the wind. In school she played on the volleyball, field hockey, and basketball teams, training by taking her dog on runs through the woods but never considering herself a competitive distance runner. Because Title IX—the 1972 legislation opening school-sponsored sports programs equally to boys and girls—was not even envisioned, high school cross-country was off limits to Gibb—it was for boys only—and the world of long-distance road racing was unknown to her. The reason most often cited for the exclusion: long-distance running was hazardous to women's reproductive health.

After graduating from high school in 1962, Gibb spent three years at the Tufts University School of Special Studies in Boston, taking courses in sculpture at the city's Museum of Fine Arts. Her boyfriend, a member of Tufts' cross-country team, inspired Gibb to begin running distance. At first, his five-mile runs stretched her endurance, but soon she was able to master longer distances. It wasn't long before she made her eight-mile commute from her home in the city's suburbs on foot and at a run. Gibb's growing enthusiasm for running caused friends to suggest that she watch the next Boston Marathon, the oldest marathon in the country and run continuously from Hopkinton, Massachusetts into Boston since 1897. Watching the April 1965 running of the race from the sidelines, Gibb was inspired to master the marathon distance of 26.2 miles.

With no real idea how to go about training for the marathon distance, Gibb daily put on a pair of nurse's shoes and ran, no matter what the weather. Steadily she increased her distance from her base of eight miles. In the fall of 1965 she ran 65 miles of a three-day, 100-mile equestrian trail ride in Woodstock, Vermont, leaving the course on the second day only after her knees had given out from the continued strain. Marrying and moving to California with her husband, a Navy man, she continued to train for Boston.

Despite the fact that British runner Violet Piercy had officially run the distance in a competitive marathon in 1923 with no negative medical consequences, the U.S. Amateur Athletic Union (AAU), which since 1888 has established standards and overseen amateur sporting events throughout the United States, steadfastly refused to sanction women's distance running. Because the U.S. Olympic committee, the President's Council on Physical Fitness, and Boston Marathon sponsor the Boston Athletic Association (BAA) fell under AAU guidelines, women were prohibited from participating in events these organizations sponsored. Gibb only learned of this when she received notification from the BAA that she would not be granted an application for the marathon because she was a woman. Her anger quickly changed to determination; as she later wrote in her *To Boston with Love:* "I'd heard that the Marathon was open to every person in the world. It had never crossed my mind to consider myself different from the other runners. My outrage turned to humor as I thought how many preconceived prejudices would crumble when I trotted right along for twenty-six miles … I believed that once people knew women could run marathon distances, the field would naturally open up."

Gibb decided to run as a "bandit." Because the Boston Marathon requires that runners "qualify" with a finish time from a previous marathon, hosts of unregistered runners have traditionally run the prestigious course as bandits. On Patriots Day 1966, Gibb planned to jump from a clump of bushes just beyond the starting line and join her fellow bandits and the 500 registered runners on their way to the finish line. After a four-day bus ride from San Diego she was dropped off at the race start in Hopkinton. She jogged around town to warm up, inconspicuous amidst her fellow runners because her blue hooded sweatshirt hid the fact that she was a woman. Hiding as planned, she jumped into the pack at the gun. Her fellow runners, realizing

Chronology

1942	Born in Cambridge, Massachusetts
1966	First woman to run and finish the Boston Marathon
1967-68	Unofficial first-place female finisher of the Boston Marathon
1969	Earns B.S. at University of California, Los Angeles.
1978	Earns law degree at New England School of Law
1979	Joins Massachusetts Bar
1980	Publishes 28-pg. booklet *To Boston with Love*
1983	Runs Boston Marathon at age 40
1984	Designs trophies for first Women's Olympics Marathon trials
1996	Runs Boston Marathon at age 53 with a time of 6:02:24
2001	Runs 6th Boston Marathon as part of The Run for ALS Team 2001

Awards and Accomplishments

1966	First woman to run Boston Marathon, finishing in 3:21:40
1967	Finishes Boston Marathon in 3:27:17
1968	Finishes Boston Marathon in 3:30:00
1990s	Named to Road Runner's Hall of Fame
1996	Recognized by YWCA's American Academy of Women Achievers
1996	Honored at ceremony marking 30th anniversary of Boston win

Gibb was a woman, were enthusiastic about her endeavor, many wishing that the women in their lives would share their enthusiasm of the sport. Although Gibb soon warmed up due to exertion she was afraid of removing her sweatshirt; when the men running with her assured her they would not let her be ejected from the race she removed the sweatshirt to reveal her long blonde pony-tail, black bathing suit, and baggy bermuda shorts. The crowds lining the streets enthusiastically cheered her on.

Gibb continued her steady pace until the last few miles, when "Heartbreak Hill," dehydration, and fatigue began to take their toll on the un-coached runner. She also ran in new shoes—sized for boys since women's running shoes were not available—and the blisters they created began to affect her stride. "Each step sent a searing jolt of pain to my brain. . . . ," she recalled in *To Boston with Love.* "My pace dropped off. I set each foot down as if on tacks." Determined to reach the finish, Gibb ran through the pain for the last three miles, finishing the race in three hours 21 minutes and ranking in the top third. Although she was greeted by cheering crowds, a burst of media attention, and a congratulatory handshake from Massachusetts Governor John Volpe, the doors to the post-race dinner provided for exhausted marathoners were closed and locked to her. While her accomplishment made newspaper headlines around the world, BAA race director Will Cloney denied Gibb's participation in the Boston Marathon proper, acknowledging only that she had "run the same route."

Gibb returned to Boston for the next two years, ranking as the unofficial women's winner in 1967 and 1968 but never besting her first time. In 1967 her finish as first woman was overshadowed by Kathrine Switzer, who, although officially registered under the genderless name K. Switzer, was almost physically removed from the course during a tussle with race director Cloney and race official Jock Semple that was captured on film for posterity (Switzer finished in 4:20 compared with Gibb's unofficial win time of 3:27:17). Cambridge, Massachusetts runner Sara Mae Berman took up the gauntlet for the next three years, running in 1969, 1970, and 1971 and posting a record time of three hours eight minutes in her final year. Finally in 1972 the AAU changed its rules about women and the BAA allowed them to register. The first official woman winner of the race was Nina Kucsik, who bested Berman's time by only seconds in 1972.

After her milestone runs in Boston, Gibb went on to get divorced and remarried, raise a son as a single mother, and establish herself professionally. Supporting her family as a legislative aide during the day, she earned a law degree and in 1979 opened her own patent law practice in Rockport, Massachusetts. Relocating to the West Coast in the late 1990s, she now lives in Delmar, California, where she works as a sculptor. Many of Gibb's bronze sculptures focus on running; her bronze work titled "The Marathoners" is on permanent exhibit at the National Art Museum of Sport. In 1984 she created the trophies given to the top three finishers of the first-ever women's Olympic marathon trials, held in Olympia, Washington.

The April 1996 running of the Boston Marathon was celebrated for more than just the 100th anniversary of the historic race. Crowds up and down the course cheered the hundreds of women runners facing the Boston marathon challenge, women now sporting official race numbers thanks to Gibb's tenacity 30 years before. Gibb returned to Boston to join their ranks as well as to receive a long overdue winner's medal. Running the course for the fifth time, she noted to an interviewer that the 1996 Boston Marathon would not be her last. She continues to run at least an hour a day and in 2001 completed her sixth Boston Marathon in memory of a friend and fellow marathoner diagnosed with **Lou Gehrig**'s disease.

SELECTED WRITINGS BY GIBB:

The Art of Inflation, 1978.
To Boston with Love, 1980.

FURTHER INFORMATION

Books

Derderian, Tom, Joan Benoit Samuelson, and Bill Rodgers, *Boston Marathon: The First Century of the World's Premiere Running Event,* 2nd edition, Human Kinetics, 1996.

Periodicals

Runner's World, April, 1990: 30; April, 1996: 72; May,
    2001: 66.
Sports Illustrated, May 28, 1984: 26; July 15, 2002: 116.
Women's Sports and Fitness, April, 1994: 48.

Other

*To Boston with Love: The Passionate Story of Bobbi
    Gibb, the First Woman to Run the Boston Marathon,*
    http://www.angelfire.com/nd.bobbigibb/ (January 15,
    2003).
National Art Museum of Sport Web site,
    http://namos.iupui/edu/ (January 15, 2003).

Sketch by Pamela L. Shelton

Althea Gibson

Althea Gibson
1927-

American tennis player

Althea Gibson once characterized herself as a "Harlem street rebel," referring to her adolescence in New York City, when she was often without direction and—more often—in various trouble. Yet the world's first African-American tennis champion remained a gadfly all her life. In the late 1950s her scrappiness and athleticism enabled her to not only shatter the segregated, insular world of tennis but also to become the sport's dominant female player. Black tennis players such as **Arthur Ashe**, Zina Garrison and sisters **Venus Williams** and **Serena Williams** have frequently acknowledged their debt to Gibson. (Garrison in 1990 became the first black woman since Gibson to reach the final of a Grand Slam event.) After leaving the amateur tennis circuit in 1958, Gibson met the challenge of integrating women's professional golf. She has since retired from sports, having suffered a number of strokes and additional health problems, yet athletes and activists alike continue to honor Gibson's legacy. In 1971, Gibson was elected to the International Tennis Hall of Fame in Newport, Rhode Island, and in 2002 was inducted into the National Women's Hall of Fame in Seneca Falls, New York.

Lost in Harlem

Gibson's parents, Daniel and Anna Washington Gibson, worked as sharecroppers on a cotton farm in South Carolina. Sharecropping, in which farmers work someone else's land and receive a small part of their crop as pay, dates from the Civil War. Even in the best of circumstances, sharecropping rarely offered a decent living. When the cotton crop failed three years in a row due to poor weather, Gibson's family moved north to New York City.

After staying with Gibson's aunt, Sally, the family settled in an apartment on West 143rd Street in Harlem. Gibson's father found work as a handyman and car mechanic, but with the birth of three more girls (Millie, Annie and Lillian) and a boy (Daniel), the family's lot was little improved, especially as the Great Depression loomed. Gibson, however, remained irrepressible. She preferred shooting pool with the local sharks to doing schoolwork. She also bowled, boxed and played basketball and stickball with the neighborhood boys. Another favorite pastime was sneaking off to the movies. "I just wanted to play, play, play," she told a *Time* magazine reporter. More than once she ran away from home.

By 1941 she pretty much began ignoring high school completely, as the school board wouldn't transfer her to the school her friends attended. The Society for the Prevention of Cruelty to Children's staff, while providing gentle guidance, emphasized that if her delinquency were to continue, they would have to put Gibson in a reform school. She struck a bargain: She would attend school at night if the agency would help her get working papers, despite her age.

But Gibson had energy to burn. She never made good on going to night school, and was fired repeatedly from menial jobs for skipping work to do things like go to

Chronology

1927	Born August 25 in Silver, South Carolina
1930	Moves to New York City
1941	Begins lessons at Harlem's Cosmopolitan Club
1942	Enters and wins her first tournament, sponsored by the all-black American Tennis Association (ATA)
1946	Moves to Wilmington, North Carolina, to work on her tennis game and enroll in high school
1949	Finishes tenth in her high school class; accepts tennis scholarship to Florida A&M University in Tallahassee
1950	Enters her first outdoor United States Lawn Tennis Association (USLTA) tournaments; plays in the U.S. National Tennis Championships at Forest Hills
1951	Competes in the All-England Tennis Championships at Wimbledon
1953	Graduates from Florida A&M moves to Jefferson City, Missouri
1954	Works with coach Sydney Llewellyn
1955-56	Travels throughout Southeast Asia on a U.S. State Department-sponsored goodwill tour
1959	Releases soloist album; appears in the film *The Horse Soldiers*
1960	Tours with the Harlem Globetrotters playing exhibition tennis
1964	Launches her professional golf career
1965	Marries businessman Will A. Darben
1971	Retires from professional golf
1975	Becomes manager of the East Orange, New Jersey, Department of Recreation
1977	Runs for New Jersey State Senate; loses three-way Democratic primary in Essex County

Awards and Accomplishments

1944-45	American Tennis Association (ATA) junior champion
1947-56	ATA singles champion
1948-50, 1952-55	ATA mixed doubles champion
1949	Eastern Indoor Championships quarter-finalist and first black to play in a USLTA-sanctioned event
1956	French Open singles and doubles champion; Wimbledon doubles champion
1957	U.S. Clay Court singles and doubles champion; Australian doubles champion; Wimbledon singles and doubles champion; U.S. singles and mixed doubles champion; U.S. Wightman Cup team member
1957-58	Associated Press Female Athlete of the Year
1958	Wimbledon singles and doubles champion; U.S. singles champion; U.S. Wightman Cup member
1959	Pan American Games singles gold medalist
1964	First black to earn a Ladies Professional Golf Association card
1971	Inducted into International Tennis Hall of Fame
1980	Inducted into International Women's Sports Hall of Fame
1991	First female recipient of NCAA Theodore Roosevelt Award
2002	Inducted into National Women's Hall of Fame

concerts at the Apollo Theater. By age 14, New York City's welfare department helped Gibson find more suitable living arrangements and a better job. And then she discovered tennis.

Until her formal involvement in sports, Gibson always struggled to "be somebody." The Police Athletic League sponsored various recreational programs, including paddle tennis, at which she excelled. Musician Buddy Walker, who at the time coached for the PAL's recreation department, noticed Gibson playing paddleball (a popular urban sport played with a wooden paddle and ball against a wall). Suggesting she might enjoy tennis, he gave her a used racquet and taught her the basics. Convinced of her raw talent, Walker introduced her to the upscale Harlem Cosmopolitan Club, where she played a few sets with the pro there, Fred Johnson. The club members, impressed, bought Gibson a junior membership and lessons with Johnson. One member, Rhoda Smith, who had lost her own daughter a decade earlier, took Gibson under her wing, buying her tennis clothes and teaching the chronic rule breaker some new rules, those of social etiquette.

"Why Not Now?"

Tennis had changed Gibson, giving her an outlet for her energy. When she was just starting out, Gibson didn't know how to channel her feistiness. Nana Davis, who beat Gibson in the all-black American Tennis Association (ATA) national girls final, recalled in an interview with

Time magazine that Gibson was "a very crude creature," seemingly more interested in a fight than a win. But every loss made her work even more intently on her game.

In 1946, while playing a women's singles competition at Wilberforce College in Ohio, Gibson caught the eye of two surgeons active in the ATA. Hubert Eaton of Wilmington, North Carolina, and Robert W. Johnson of Lynchburg, Virginia offered to provide her with room, board, and an education at no charge. She would spend the school months in Wilmington, and the summer with Johnson for more intensive tennis lessons. But Gibson balked. She never liked school and saw little appeal in returning to high school at age 19. If not for a man she had met during her job at the New School, she might have bypassed this opportunity. **Sugar Ray Robinson**, a rising boxing star en route to world championship status, and his wife Edna, who had befriended young Gibson during her Harlem days, urged the young champion to jump at the chance to better herself. And jump she did.

In 1947 Gibson won the first of ten consecutive ATA national championships. Two years later she graduated among the top ten in her class at Williston Industrial High School in Wilmington and accepted a scholarship from Florida Agricultural and Mechanical College in Tallahassee. Between 1944 and 1950, Gibson took the New York state championship six times. There was no question of Gibson's ATA dominance. There was nowhere else for Gibson to go but crash through the formidable wall of racism.

When The United States Lawn Tennis Association (USLTA, now the USTA) was founded in 1881, it formally barred blacks from competing in its tournaments. Some Washington, D.C.-area clubs created the ATA in 1916, in response. The ATA today is the oldest African-

American sports organization in the country. When Gibson began playing tennis in the 1940s, racial segregation was legal, even institutionalized, in the U.S. and would remain so until 1954. The lanky 5-foot 10½-inch player had often tried to enter the USLTA national tournaments but to no avail. In 1950 she took the Eastern Grass Court Championships, second place in the National Indoor Championship, and made the quarterfinals in the National Clay Court Championships in Chicago. But the USLTA national championships continued to refuse her application. Finally, Alice Marble, a four-time U.S. Open winner, published an historical editorial in the July 1950 issue of *American Lawn Tennis* magazine: "If tennis is a game for ladies and gentlemen," Marble wrote, "it's also time we acted a little more like gentlepeople and less like sanctimonious hypocrites....If Althea Gibson represents a challenge to the present crop of women players, it's only fair that they should meet that challenge on the courts."

Attains World Dominance

That August, the USLTA accepted Gibson's application. She entered court 14 at Forest Hills and defeated Barbara Knapp in straight sets, 6-2, 6-2. Gibson led Denise Brough 7-6 in a tiebreaker in the next round, but a thunderstorm interceded. She dropped the tiebreaker 9-7, but made history as the first black to play at the U.S. Open. Gibson was ranked seventh in 1952, but fell to 70th the following year. Meanwhile, having graduated from college with a physical education degree, she worked in the athletic department at Lincoln University in Jefferson City, Missouri. In 1955, tennis coach Sydney Llewellyn convinced her to return to the sport.

Llewellyn rebuilt her confidence and her game. She honed her serve-and-volley game and learned how to be patient at the baseline. She had an overpowering second serve. And she began to refine her court behavior. Simply having competed at Forest Hills opened many doors for Gibson, as it would later for other blacks, and she toured Southeast Asia on a goodwill mission for the U.S. State Department. While touring Europe and Africa, she won 16 of 18 tournaments. As a result, she was invited in 1956 to Wimbledon, where she lost to Ohio-born Shirley Fry, in the final Wimbledon attempt for Fry in her long career. Fry also defeated her at the U.S. Open that year.

Unshaken, Gibson returned to the grass court in 1957. It was to be a noteworthy year for the athlete and elsewhere. Gibson had won the French Open, her first major title, in 1956, and the Italian singles championships the previous year. In January 1957 she was Australian Open runner-up. Then, funded by a consortium of Harlem businessmen, Gibson returned to England. Back home, America was simmering with racial tension. Only two months earlier National Guardsmen had kept nine black students from entering the all-white Central High School in Little Rock, Arkansas. But in July, playing "with an

Althea Gibson

athleticism never before seen in women's tennis," according to *Sports Illustrated*'s Michael Bamberger, Gibson became the first black woman to win the Wimbledon singles title, defeating fellow American Darlene Hart, 6-3, 6-2, in less than an hour. The crowd "raised only an apathetic cheer" when Queen Elizabeth II presented the singles trophy to Gibson, Bamberger quoted his magazine's report at the time. In the States, however, the champion drew a cheering crowd at the airport in New York and received a Broadway ticker-tape parade.

"I didn't give a darn who was on the other side of the net," the *Houston Chronicle* quoted Gibson. "I'd knock you down if you got in the way. I just wanted to play my best." When she faced Brough at the U. S. Open that year, Gibson beat the 1947 champion for her first U.S. Open title, 6-3, 6-2, making Gibson the world's top-ranked female player. She repeated the feat the following year, winning both Wimbledon and U.S. Open singles titles, and women's doubles titles. The Associated Press named her Female Athlete of the Year in 1957 and 1958 and she became the first African American woman to appear on the cover of *Sports Illustrated*. Unable to make enough money on the circuit, Gibson surprised fans and sportswriters and retired from pro tennis at age 30.

Life After Tennis

In 1958, Gibson published her autobiography *I Always Wanted to Be Somebody*. She began a career in music and theater. Sugar Ray Robinson had bought her a

Related Biography: Tennis Player Alice Marble

California-born Alice Marble (1913-1990) was the first woman to capture both Wimbledon and U.S. Open singles, doubles, and mixed doubles titles in the same year.

She learned her sport on the public courts of Golden Gate Park in San Francisco. Unable to afford a tennis racquet, she played with borrowed equipment until coach Eleanor Tennant discovered her. In exchange for lessons, Marble performed secretarial work for Tennant, who remained Marble's lifelong coach.

In 1934, while representing the United States in France, Marble collapsed on the court and was sent to a sanatorium to recover. Eight months later and against the advice of her physician, a bored Marble left the sanatorium and began to build up her strength and recover her game. The National Tennis Association officials, fearing her frailty, were reluctant to allow Marble to compete, but when in 1936 she won the national singles and mixed doubles championships, the world took notice of this serious challenger. Two years later she won Wimbledon, and in 1939 broke world records when she won the singles, doubles, and mixed doubles titles at both Wimbledon and the U.S. Open.

Marble's style of rushing the net evolved from lack of confidence in her ground strokes, but led to a playing style many women, such as Althea Gibson and Martina Navratilova, would emulate.

Marble confronted many difficulties. Going against the grain, she became a football reporter for WNEW radio in New York in 1940 and developed an avid following. Four years later, during World War II, she lost a baby during pregnancy and soon after learned her husband, Captain Joseph Norman Crowley, had been killed in Germany. Early in 1945 she risked her life in several missions as an Allied spy. She was an early feminist and tirelessly fought on behalf of women, homosexuals, and African Americans. In July 1950, Marble wrote her historic editorial in *American Lawn Tennis* magazine, denouncing the U.S. Lawn Tennis Association's policy of excluding blacks from competition. If Marble hadn't had such courage and stature among her peers, Althea Gibson might never have been allowed to compete. "Alice Marble was a great, kind, and gracious lady," Gibson recently said in *ABC Sports Online* forum, "and the one person that stood up for me in the tennis world, really the world at large."

Where Is She Now?

Living in seclusion at her home in East Orange, New Jersey, Gibson, who is well into her 70s and suffers from crippling arthritis, said in a recent online forum, "I want the public to remember me as they knew me: athletic, smart, and healthy.... Remember me strong and tough and quick, fleet of foot and tenacious." While avoiding the spotlight, Gibson has not disappeared altogether. As a co-founder of the Althea Gibson Foundation, she works to help inner-city youths gain an education. Of all her accomplishments, Gibson says helping children is "probably the best thing that I will ever do." The National First Ladies Library recently honored her in absentia for her leadership role in creating opportunities for minority athletes and children.

which netted $25,000 for the woman who had broken the tennis color barrier.

Gibson's Impact

Gibson had to be more than a tennis champion. She had to battle segregation, angering whites and also of some blacks who disdained Gibson for playing in what they considered a sport of privileged people. She also faced gender barriers. Fellow player Tony Trabert, who won the French Open, Wimbledon, and the U.S. Open in 1955, said, "She hits the ball and plays like a man," Neil Amdur wrote in the *New York Times*.

But the sharecropper's daughter dispensed with expectations and comparisons. As the first African American to win a Grand Slam tennis tournament, Gibson paved the way for other minority players. And as an outstanding competitor, she paved the way for other women who wanted to play aggressive, serve-and-volley games. But she stood out mostly for her unfettered courage.

saxophone when she was a youngster, and she had a sultry singing voice, with which she enchanted the crowd at the 1957 Wimbledon ball. (She sang the romantic "I Can't Give You Anything but Love.") In 1959 she cut an album, *Althea Gibson Sings,* and she made a John Ford movie, *The Horse Soldiers,* co-starring John Wayne and William Holden. In 1959 Gibson turned professional and played a couple of exhibition basketball games touring with the Harlem Globetrotters. Making another incursion into a formerly elite sport, she became the first black member of the Ladies Professional Golf Association and played tournaments until 1967. The following year she published a second autobiography, *So Much to Live For.*

In the 1970s she coached women's and girls' sports, and from 1975 to 1977 became New Jersey athletic commissioner for boxing and wrestling. In 1977 she ran unsuccessfully in a three-way Democratic primary for the New Jersey Senate. She also served on the Governor's Council on Physical Fitness. A series of strokes limited her mobility and she retired in 1992. While mentally agile, Gibson suffers from arthritis and is confined to a wheelchair. When in the late 1990s friends, fans, and colleagues realized that the former champion was nearly destitute, they began a series of fundraisers,

CONTACT INFORMATION

Address: P.O. Box 768, East Orange, NJ 07019. Email: altheagibson@newyork.com. Online: www.altheagibson.com/.

SELECTED WRITINGS BY GIBSON:

I Always Wanted to Be Somebody, New York: Harper, 1958.
Gibson, Althea and Richard Curtis. *So Much to Live For.* New York: Putnam, 1968.

FURTHER INFORMATION

Books

Contemporary Black Biography. Detroit: Gale Research, 1994.
Contemporary Heroes and Heroines, III. Detroit: Gale Research, 1998.
Encyclopedia of World Biography. Detroit: Gale Research, 1998.

Encyclopedia of World Biography Supplement. Detroit: Gale Group, 2001.

Gates, Henry Louis Jr., and Cornel West. *The African American Century,* New York: Free Press, 2000.

Johnson, Anne Janette. *Great Women in Sports.* Detroit: Visible Ink Press, 1996.

Notable Black American Women. Detroit: Gale Research, 1992.

St. James Encyclopedia of Popular Culture. Detroit: St. James Press, 2000.

Scribner Encyclopedia of American Lives. Charles Scribner's Sons, 1999.

Periodicals

"10 Greatest Women Athletes."*Ebony* (March 2002): 74.

Amdur, Neil. "After 50 Years, Gibson Hasn't Lost Her Luster." *New York Times* (April 26, 2002).

Bamberber, Michael. "Inside the White Lines: July 6, 1957: Althea Gibson Wins Wimbledon." *Sports Illustrated* (November 29, 1999): 114.

Janoff, Murray. "Tennis' Greatest Trailblazer." *Sporting News* (June 24, 1972).

Other

"Althea Gibson Answers Your Questions." ABC Sports Online. www.espn.go.com/ (December 20, 2002).

Althea Gibson Official Web site. http://www.althea gibson.com/ (December 16, 2002).

Biography Resource Center. http://galenet.galegroup. com/ (December 16, 2002; December 20, 2002).

History of Jim Crow. http://www.jimcrowhistory.org (December 17, 2002).

Houston Chronicle. http://www.chron.com (December 16, 2002).

Intercollegiate Tennis Association. http://www.wm.edu/ (December 20, 2002).

International Movie Database. http://www.imdb.com/ (December 16, 2002).

International Tennis Hall of Fame. http://www.tennisfame. org/ (December 16, 2002; December 19, 2002; December 20, 2002).

National First Ladies' Library. http://www.firstladies. org/ (December 20, 2002).

Sports Illustrated for Women. http://www.sportsillustrated. cnn.com/ (December 18, 2002).

Women's History. www.womenshistory.about.com/ (December 16, 2002).

Sketch by Jane Summer

Josh Gibson
1911-1947

American baseball player

Josh Gibson

Josh Gibson has been called the greatest hitter in the history of baseball, better in the eyes of some than **Babe Ruth**, **Ty Cobb**, **Ted Williams**, **Joe DiMaggio**, or **Mickey Mantle**. Sketchy record-keeping in the Negro leagues makes it impossible to quantify Josh Gibson's career definitively. However, historians of black baseball estimate that, in 16 years of Negro league games, post-season barnstorming and winter ball, he hit close to 900 home runs while averaging over .350. He hit .483 in nine Negro National League All-Star games. In post-season games against white all-star teams, Gibson hit .426 in 60 at bats. He clubbed some of the most monstrous home runs ever seen. The longest homers ever hit in three major league parks, New York's Yankee Stadium, Pittsburgh's Forbes Field and Washington DC's Griffith Stadium belonged to Josh Gibson. As an African American in the 1930s and early 1940s, Josh Gibson was barred from playing in the major leagues. Ironically, only three months after Gibson's tragically early death—after finishing one of the best years of his career—**Jackie Robinson** became the first black to play with a white team.

Born on December 21, 1911 in the rural Georgia town of Buena Vista, nothing in Joshua Gibson's origins seemed to point to the greatness that lay in store for him. He was the first of three children born to Mark and Nancy Gibson, poor black sharecroppers. In 1923, his father moved to Pittsburgh, Pennsylvania, where he soon found work in a steel mill; after he had saved enough money, he sent for his family and found a home

Chronology

1911	Born in Buena Vista, Georgia
1924	Moves to Pittsburgh, Pennsylvania
1927	Joins Gimbels A.C. baseball team
1928	Marries Helen Mackie
1929	Joins Crawford Colored Giants
1930	Signed by Homestead Grays
1930	Helen Gibson dies in childbirth leaving Gibson the father of twins
1931	Hits an estimated 75 home runs
1932	Hits an estimated 72 home runs
1932	Signs with Gus Greenlee's Pittsburgh Crawfords
1934	Hits an estimated 69 home runs
1937	Is traded by Crawfords back to Homestead Grays
1938	Leads Negro National League (NNL) in batting for first time with .440 average
1940	Runs out on Grays contract to play with Vera Cruz in Mexican League, and is sued by Homestead Grays
1940	Marries Hattie Jones after living together six years
1941	Wins batting title and Most Valuable Player award in Puerto Rican League
1942	Returns to Homestead Grays
1942	Washington Senators owner Clark Griffith expresses interest in signing Gibson and teammate Buck Leonard to a major league contract
1942	Gibson's health problems intensify
1942-43	Wins NNL home run title
1943	Spends ten days in hospital after blacking out and spending a full day in a coma
1946	Bats .379 and leads NNL in home runs
1947	Dies of a cerebral hemorrhage

for them in Pleasant Valley, one of Pittsburgh's black neighborhoods. The difference between the urban North and the rural South for a young black man in the 1920s was enormous. "The greatest gift Dad gave me," Robert Peterson, the author of *Only the Ball Was White*, quoted Gibson as saying, "was to get me out of the South." In Pittsburgh Gibson learned the electrician's trade at Allegheny Pre-Vocational School. He left after the ninth grade and found an apprentice's position at a local factory that manufactured air brakes. When he was seventeen he married Helen Mason.

Gibson was an athletic child who loved roller-skating and was a good enough swimmer to win several medals in local competitions. He started playing baseball as a young boy and was so captivated by the game that he would roller-skate six miles to a ball field in Bellevue, Pennsylvania to watch games. As a teen, Gibson was developing the classic hitter's physique: tall, broad shoulders, well-muscled arms, a powerful chest. At sixteen he joined his first organized team, Gimbels A.C., a black amateur club in Pittsburgh. It was there that Gibson started catching, although he occasionally played other positions as well. Around 1929, with the semipro Crawford Colored Giants, Gibson began displaying his prowess as a slugger. His rocketing line drive home runs soon won him an enthusiastic following among Pittsburgh's black citizens, and it wasn't unusual for thousands to come to see him play.

By 1930, word of Gibson's exploits reached Judy Johnson, the third baseman-manager of the Homestead Grays, at the time one of the best teams in Negro ball. Homestead's fans were urging the Grays' owner Cumberland "Cum" Posey to sign the young phenom. Unfortunately for Gibson and Grays' fans, the team already had two catchers on their roster, including Buck Ewing, one of the finest in black baseball. Circumstances conspired, however, in a fashion worthy of the movies, to bring Gibson and the Grays together. In the middle of the 1930 season, at the first night game to be played in baseball, the Grays' pitcher crossed up catcher Ewing with an unexpected fastball and split his hand open. Gibson, who was in the stands, was asked by Judy Johnson to finish the game behind the plate.

Although he didn't get any hits in the game, Gibson stayed on with the Grays, playing whatever positions were open to get his bat into the line-up. There were early moments of glory for the 18-year-old rookie, like the homer he slugged in Philadelphia's Bigler Field, the longest anyone had ever seen hit there. He came into his own in a series at Yankee Stadium for the eastern championship between the Grays and the Lincoln Giants. Gibson's tape measure homers and a .368 average for the series won him the catcher's job with the Grays. Just at the moment Gibson should have been able to savor his good fortune, however, tragedy struck. His young wife died in childbirth leaving him the father of twins, Helen and Joshua.

Gibson's contemporaries agree that he was a natural hitter, one of the purest who ever lived. He had to work hard to become a catcher however, overcoming problems handling the catcher's mitt and blocking errant pitches. His biggest handicap was his difficulty with foul pop-ups. He was often unable to get oriented after he had thrown off his mask and frequently got dizzy running as he searched the sky for the ball. His pitchers sometimes derided him for it, but the problem was probably an early sign of the mysterious condition that would eventually lead Gibson to an early grave. Gibson dedicated himself to learning the catcher's trade, frequently catching both batting practice and games to gain experience. Some maintained Gibson only managed to become an adequate catcher. Others disagreed. According to Peterson, **Roy Campanella**, a black Hall of Fame catcher in the big leagues, called Gibson "[not] only the greatest catcher but the greatest ballplayer I ever saw." Walter Johnson, who played against Gibson in off-season barnstorming games, is quoted by Patrick Butters in an *Insight on the News* article, said of Gibson, "he catches so easy, he might be in a rocking chair. Throws like a rifle. Bill Dickey's not as good a catcher."

No one doubts that Gibson could hit. He had a short, compact stroke, much like Hank Aaron's, and strong wrists that enabled him to wait on a pitch until the last possible moment. His hits, even the tape measure jobs, were line drive shots that could tear open the hand of an

Career Statistics

Yr	Team	AVG	GP	AB	H	HR	SB
1930	Grays	.242	10	33	8	1	1
1931	Grays	.372	32	129	48	6	0
1932	Pitt	.286	46	147	42	7	1
1933	Grays	.362	34	116	42	6	1
1934	Pitt	.315	41	146	46	11	1
1935	Pitt	.333	37	129	43	11	3
1936	Pitt	.360	23	75	27	11	0
1937	Grays	.500	12	42	21	7	0
1938	Grays	.311	19	74	23	4	1
1939	WAS	.330	29	88	29	17	0
1940	Grays	.167	2	6	1	1	0
1942	WAS	.335	51	158	53	15	3
1943	Grays	.517	57	209	108	16	0
1944	Grays	.361	28	97	35	6	0
1945	Grays	.316	31	98	31	11	0
1946	Grays	.379	49	132	50	16	0
Totals		.362	501	1679	607	146	11

Grays: Homestead Grays; Pitt: Pittsburgh Crawfords; WAS: WAS Homestead.

infielder unlucky to get in front of one. Gibson's performance was phenomenal. His homers were the stuff of legend. Many of his home runs were blows of 500 feet or more. He is supposed to have hit the longest home run ever in old Yankee Stadium, a 580 foot blast that missed going out of the park by only two feet. The most apocryphal story tells of Gibson hitting a ball out of sight one day for a home run. The next day, at a game in the next town, a ball appeared out of the clouds, was caught by the centerfielder, and the umpire pointed at Gibson, yelling "You're out! Yesterday, in Pittsburgh!" Records for the old Negro leagues are sketchy at best, and black leagues, after a shorter season than the majors, played clubs of widely varying skill, from local semi-pro teams up to major league All-Stars. At a time when Babe Ruth held the season home run record with 60, Gibson is thought to have hit 75 homers in 1931 and 72 in 1932. In all he is believed to have slugged well over 800 home runs, leading Judy Johnson to say, as quoted by Peterson, "If Josh Gibson had been in the big leagues in his prime, Babe Ruth and Hank Aaron would still be chasing him for the home run record." He hit for average as well as power, frequently ending seasons with an average in the high .300s. In over 60 at bats against major league pitchers, Gibson hit .426.

By his second season, Gibson was an established star on the Homestead Grays. In 1932, Gus Greenlee lured Gibson and a number of other Grays players to the Pittsburgh Crawfords. On Greenlee's new team, Gibson joined **Satchel Paige**, the remarkable pitcher who for decades dominated the Negro leagues—and later added to his legend in the big leagues. Gibson and Paige formed what has been called the greatest battery in the history of baseball. Gibson continued his epic performance with the new team in the Negro National League (NNL), as well as with barnstorming teams that saw

black and white All-Star teams squaring off against each other. In 1934 Gibson hit 69 homers, and in 1936 hit for a .457 average. In 1937 Gibson's contract with the Crawfords was up. Aware of the enormous sums Babe Ruth had earned during his heyday, Gibson held out for more money. The two were unable to come to terms and the cash-strapped Greenlee eventually traded his two biggest stars, Gibson and Judy Johnson, back to the Homestead Grays for two minor players.

Before spring training was over, however, Gibson left for the Dominican Republic, drawn by reports of the good money Satchel Paige was getting from Dominican dictator Rafael Trujillo. Despite the country's dangerous political climate, Gibson played in the Caribbean until July. He rejoined the Grays in mid-season, hitting three home runs in his first game and leading the team to an NNL championship. He had hit .360 for the Crawfords in 1936. He led the NNL in homers in both 1938 and 1939, and won his first league batting title in 1938. By then, even white baseball began to take notice. White writers like Jimmy Powers and Shirley Povich wondered in print why a talent of Gibson's magnitude hadn't been signed to play on a team in white organized ball.

By the early 1940s, Gibson had reached the peak of his abilities as a baseball player. After hitting 17 homers in 1939—more than half of his hits in league play—Gibson skipped out on his Homestead Grays contract again in 1940. Accepting an offer of $6000 from Vera Cruz—$2000 more than Homestead was paying him—Gibson played the season in Mexico. Homestead's Cum Posey had had enough. He went to court and got a $10,000 judgment against Gibson, who by 1941 was playing in Puerto Rico, where he won the batting title and was named the most valuable player, a dual honor he would later call the greatest thrill of his career. He returned to Pittsburgh for

Related Biography: Manager Judy Johnson

Besides being Josh Gibson's first manager in the Negro Leagues, Judy Johnson was one of the finest third basemen—black or white—in the history of baseball. An ardent student of the game, his greatest joy later in life was passing down his knowledge to young players. He was also an astute judge of talent who, as a major league scout, discovered the likes of Hank Aaron, Larry Doby, Minnie Minoso, and Ritchie Allen.

Born William Julius Johnson on October 26, 1899, in Snow Hill, Maryland, he would not acquire the nickname "Judy" until after he had broken into the Negro leagues and someone noticed his physical resemblance to another player, outfielder Judy Gans. Johnson got his start in 1918 playing for the Hilldale club in Philadelphia, one of the dominant clubs of the day. Johnson's skills were still shaky. However, John Henry "Pop" Lloyd, a giant of early black ball, took the young Johnson under his wing. The elder's influence was decisive. Judy Johnson would later remark that he had learned more from Lloyd than he had in 16 years playing ball.

During the 1920s with Hilldale, Johnson established himself as a wizard on the field and a solid .300 hitter. He also developed into one of the most intelligent analysts of the "inside game." He hit .364 in the first Negro World Series in 1924, leading Hilldale to a Series victory over the mighty Kansas City Monarchs. In 1929, he hit a career high .416, leading the *Pittsburgh Courier* to name him the Most Valuable Player of the Negro National League.

In 1930, when the Great Depression drove the Hilldale club out of business, Johnson signed with the Homestead Grays. He was managing the club when catcher Buck Ewing injured his hand. Johnson asked a young catcher he knew, who was tearing up Pittsburgh's black semipro circuit with his hitting, to come down from the stands and take Ewing's place. Josh Gibson was eager, willing and more than able. After the game, Gibson stuck with the team—it was plain to Johnson that he was too good a hitter to give up.

Gibson's work behind the plate left much to be desired though. So Johnson began teaching the youngster as Pop Lloyd had taught him, concentrating in particular on the foul pop-ups that caused Gibson such trouble. It was a subject which third baseman Johnson had studied long and hard. Under the veteran's patient tutelage, Gibson slowly came into his own as a catcher.

Johnson returned to Hilldale in 1931, before signing with the Pittsburgh Crawfords, where he rejoined Gibson from 1932 to 1935 and finished his playing career. After Jackie Robinson broke the color barrier in 1947, Judy Johnson became a major league scout, first for the Philadelphia Athletics, and later for the Philadelphia Phillies. He was inducted into the Hall of Fame at Cooperstown in 1975. Judy Johnson passed away in Wilmington, Delaware on June 15, 1989.

the 1942 season just as his house was about to be repossessed by the court. Once he donned the Grays flannels again, however, Posey dropped all charges against his star.

Gibson was one of the highest paid players in Negro ball, his $1000 a month salary second only to Satchel Paige. Gibson, however, was not the showman Paige was on the field, he was just a terrific ballplayer. He was a friendly, outgoing, gregarious man, quick with a smile, who would banter with opposing batters to rattle them. His friendly nature extended to young players as well, whom he frequently encouraged. He so loved playing baseball that he would often join in games with kids on his walk home from the ballpark.

In the early 1940s Gibson began a variety of problems. He had begun to drink heavily. According to some rumors, he had begun using marijuana while playing in Mexico, and estranged from his second wife, he became involved with a woman who was said to be using harder

drugs. More seriously, he was experiencing recurring headaches—that may have been related to his attacks of dizziness chasing foul pop-ups. His personality underwent a change during the 1942 season. "He wouldn't have nothing to do with you. He'd just sit. He wouldn't talk much, wouldn't joke around, he's just lost that spark," Frazier "Slow" Robinson later wrote in *Catching Dreams: My Life in the Negro Baseball Leagues*. "Josh was jolly all the time, but starting in 1942 he didn't say nothing to nobody, and he was never quite the same after playing winter ball south of the border." That season the headaches grew worse. On New Years Day 1943, Gibson collapsed and was taken to the hospital where he lay in a coma for an entire day. Doctors diagnosed a brain tumor, but Gibson refused to allow doctors to operate, feeling it would render him a vegetable.

Gibson did not reveal his condition to the Homestead Grays and continued to play for the team for four more seasons. They were among the most productive of his career. He won Negro league home run titles in 1942 and 1943, won the batting title in 1943 with an astounding average of .517. Playing part of the 1943 season in Washington D.C.'s Griffith Stadium, Gibson hit ten home runs in the spacious park—more than the entire American League hit there that year. His fine batting in 1943 led the Grays to a pennant and victory over the Birmingham Barons in the Negro World Series, and Pittsburgh celebrated a "Josh Gibson Night" that year. Despite his sterling performance on the field, his behavior was becoming more bizarre and unpredictable. He would abruptly take off all his clothes at ball games or friends' houses; he sometimes arrived at games too drunk to play. The team frequently had him put in a hospital, sometimes for more than a week at a time. Nonetheless, in 1946, his last season, Gibson batted .379 and led the league with 16 home runs. Once the season ended, his health declined rapidly. He suffered from bronchitis, a diseased liver, and nervous exhaustion, and continued to drink heavily. On January 20, 1947, at the age of 35, Josh Gibson died of a cerebral hemorrhage.

Some observers have speculated that Gibson's final decline was due in part to his disappointment at not being selected to break the big league color barrier. He had had come close at times to the majors at his peak. In 1939, according to the *Pittsburgh Courier*, there was an agreement between Bill Benswanger, the president of the white Pittsburgh Pirates, and the Homestead Grays to buy the contracts of Gibson and Buck Leonard. It fell through, Benswanger later said, because Cum Posey asked him not to sign the two players—it would have meant the death of the Negro leagues. A couple years later, Clark Griffith, the owner of the white Washington Senators, met with Gibson and Leonard and discussed the possibility of signing them. That too ultimately came to naught.

Despite the gross injustice that for so long kept black stars from competing in the major leagues, for anyone who saw him play, Gibson was a living refutation of the canard that African Americans were inherently less capable on the diamond than whites. Organized baseball belatedly recognized this fact itself in 1972 when it inducted Josh Gibson into the National Baseball Hall of Fame in 1972. He was the second player so honored.

FURTHER INFORMATION

Books

Blackball Stars: Negro League Pioneers. Westport, CT: Meckler Books, 1988.

Brashler, William.*Josh Gibson: A Life in the Negro Leagues.* New York: Harper & Row, 1978.

Clark, Dick, and Larry Lester (eds.) *The Negro Leagues Book.* Cleveland: The Society for American Baseball Research, 1994.

Contemporary Black Biography. Volume 22. Detroit: Gale Group, 1999.

Gardner, Robert and Dennis Shortelle. *The Forgotten Players: The Story of Black Baseball in America.* New York: Walker and Company, 1993.

Holway, John B. *Black Diamonds.* Westport, CT: Meckler Books, 1989.

Josh and Satch: The Life and Times of Josh Gibson and Satchel Paige Westport, CT: Meckler, 1991.

Logan, Rayford W. and Michael R. Winston. *Dictionary of American Negro Biography.* New York: W.W. Norton.

Peterson, Robert. *Only The Ball Was White.* Englewood Cliffs, NJ: Prentice-Hall, 1970.

Robinson, Frazier "Slow," with Paul Bauer. *Catching Dreams: My Life in the Negro Baseball Leagues.* Syracuse, NY: Syracuse University Press, 1999.

Rogosin, Donn. *Invisible Men: Life in Baseball's Negro Leagues.*New York: Atheneum, 1983.

Voices From the Great Black Baseball Leagues. New York: Dodd, Mead, 1975.

Periodicals

Brashler, William. "Looking for Josh Gibson." *Esquire.* (February, 1978): 104.

Butters, Patrick. "Meet the unknown slugger." *Insight on the News,* (September 21, 1998): 43.

"Josh Gibson: Greatest Slugger of 'em All." *Ebony,* (May 1972): 45.

Sketch by Gerald E. Brennan

Frank Gifford
1930-

American football player

In the national spotlight for over half a century, Pro Football Hall of Famer and Emmy-winning broadcaster Frank Gifford enjoyed a successful transition from professional athlete to respected television journalist. His fame as an anchor of ABC's *Monday Night Football* from 1971 to 1998 even transcended his reputation as one of the biggest stars of the National Football League (NFL) in its early days as a nationally televised sport in the 1950s. After two failed marriages, Gifford also seemed to find personal satisfaction with his relationship with television talk show host Kathie Lee Gifford, whom he married in 1986. Yet his image as a loving husband suffered in 1997 when his extramarital affair with Suzen Johnson was exposed in the *Globe,* a tabloid that had paid Johnson $75,000 to document one of their trysts. The Giffords publicly proclaimed their intention to remain married, but the incident tarnished his reputation. The year after the scandal, Gifford's *Monday Night Football* role was reduced to delivering pre-game commentaries and in 1998 he left the show for good.

Unsettled Childhood

Frank Newton Gifford was born to Weldon Wayne and Lola Mae (Hawkins) Gifford on August 16, 1930 in Santa Monica, California. He was the younger brother of Winona and Waine Gifford. Because of the unsteady work that Weldon Gifford found as an itinerant laborer in the oil fields of the Southwest, the Giffords and their three children were constantly relocating. In his autobiography *The Whole Ten Yards,* Gifford recalled that his mother once counted forty-seven different places that the family had lived during her youngest son's childhood.

The uncertain nature of his father's work meant that Gifford grew up in near-poverty and the constant moves never allowed him to stay in one school for an entire year until he was in high school. Frustrated by his poor

Frank Gifford

academic performance, Gifford became a habitual truant after enrolling at Bakersfield High School in Bakersfield, California. After joining the school's football team as a quarterback, however, Gifford paid more attention to his studies, an accomplishment he credited to the guidance of his coach, Homer Beatty. After completing his secondary education in 1948, Gifford spent a year at Bakersfield Junior College to muster enough academic credits to enter the University of Southern California (USC) in Los Angeles, where he had been offered a football scholarship. Still on academic probation during his first year at USC, Gifford violated the Pacific Coast Conference rules against practicing with the team, a violation that resulted in a $2,500 fine against USC.

Outstanding Player at USC

Gifford finally joined the USC football team's roster as a legitimate player in 1949. He made a sensational debut with two interceptions in a game against the U.S. Naval Academy that year, and went on to become an accomplished player in both offensive and defensive positions. In the 1950-51 season at USC, Gifford was named to the *Collier's* All-American collegiate team, one of the most prestigious honors of the day. The recognition was followed by a ream of publicity that highlighted Gifford's matinee-idol looks and six-foot, one-inch, two-hundred-pound frame. Gifford later retained an acting agent and appeared in several small movie and television roles throughout the 1950s. He also appeared in numerous com-

mercials for products ranging from Jantzen swim wear to Mennen after-shave lotion to Lucky Strike cigarettes.

Drafted by Giants

After learning that his girlfriend, Maxine Avis Ewart, had become pregnant, Gifford eloped with her to Las Vegas, Nevada on January 13, 1952. In deference to the morals of the day, the Giffords stated publicly that they had secretly married a year earlier. Gifford then signed a contract to play for the NFL's New York Giants and dropped out of college. He later completed his degree at USC in 1956 during his off-seasons from the Giants.

Although he was unhappy playing for the Giants at first, the arrival of **Vince Lombardi** as the team's defensive coach in 1954 transformed Gifford's NFL career. Under Lombardi's guidance, Gifford became one of the best running backs of the era. Named the NFL's Most Valuable Player in 1956 by United Press International, Gifford set Giants team records for average yards per carry (4.3) and total touchdowns (ninety-two) that still stood in 2002. In 1956 the Giants won the NFL Championship over the Philadelphia Eagles; it was the only championship title the team took during Gifford's football career, which lasted until 1964.

A photogenic presence on and off the field, Gifford was instrumental in popularizing football as a televised sport in the 1950s. One of the first nationally televised NFL championship games, a December 28, 1958 match between the Giants and the Baltimore Colts, came to be known as the "Greatest Game Ever Played." Gifford had fumbled twice in the early stages of the game but recovered to rush for a touchdown and bring the team close to another scoring opportunity. After a referee marked one play just short of a first down, however, the Giants were forced to punt. The Colts went on to win the game by a 23-17 margin, but many viewers were furious over the referee's call.

Career Statistics

Yr	Team	Rushing				Receiving				Fumbles	
		ATT	YDS	AVG	TD	REC	YDS	AVG	TD	FUM	LST
1952	NYG	38	116	3.1	0	5	36	7.2	0	1	0
1953	NYG	50	157	3.1	2	18	292	16.2	4	3	0
1954	NYG	66	368	5.6	2	14	154	11.0	1	1	0
1955	NYG	86	351	4.1	3	33	437	13.2	4	0	0
1956	NYG	159	819	5.2	5	51	603	11.8	4	1	0
1957	NYG	136	528	3.9	5	41	588	14.3	4	1	0
1958	NYG	115	468	4.1	8	29	330	11.4	2	5	0
1959	NYG	106	540	5.1	3	42	768	18.3	4	2	0
1960	NYG	77	232	3.0	4	24	344	14.3	3	3	0
1961	NYG	Inactive									
1962	NYG	2	18	9.0	1	39	796	20.4	7	0	0
1963	NYG	4	10	2.5	0	42	657	15.6	7	0	0
1964	NYG	1	2	2.0	1	29	429	14.8	3	0	0
TOTAL		840	3609	4.3	34	367	5434	14.8	43	17	0

NYG: New York Giants.

Success as Broadcaster

Knocked unconscious by Chuck Bednarik in a game against the Philadelphia Eagles on November 20, 1960, Gifford spent ten days in the hospital and announced his retirement. After making a surprising recovery, he returned to the Giants' lineup as a flanker. He played for three more seasons and retired as a professional athlete a second time in 1964. By that date Gifford had worked for several years as a broadcast journalist, a role he took on full-time with CBS in 1965. In 1971 he joined the team of **Howard Cosell** and Don Meredith on ABC's *Monday Night Football,* a position he retained through 1998. Inducted in to the College Football Hall of Fame in 1976 and the Pro Football Hall of Fame in 1977, Gifford nonetheless became better known to a younger generation for his work on *Monday Night Football* and other sports programs, including several Summer and Winter Olympic Games. In 1977 Gifford received an Emmy Award as Outstanding Sports Personality from the National Academy of Television Arts and Sciences.

Checkered Personal Life

Gifford had three children—Jeff, Victoria, and Kyle—with Maxine Ewart Gifford before the couple divorced. In 1978 Gifford married a second time, to Astrid Narss; that marriage ended in divorce in 1986. On October 18, 1986, Gifford married for a third time, to outspoken talk show host Kathie Lee Epstein Johnson. Despite the twenty-three-year age difference between them, the couple had two children—a son, Cody, and a daughter, Cassidy. Kathie Lee Gifford often discussed her marriage in glowing terms on television and in print, a habit that kept the couple in the media spotlight. As she wrote in her 1992 memoir, *I Can't Believe I Said That!,* "Frank is my husband, my confidant, lover, therapist, parenting partner, and best friend. We depend on each other for security, for emotional, sexual, and spiritual fulfillment, and for companionship. . . . Cheating is out of the question. Sure, Frank sees sexy flight attendants and businesswomen when he flies around the country. But the only come-on line he gets anymore is 'C'mon, Frank, show me a picture of Cody.'" The picture of domestic happiness was shattered in 1997, however, when the *Globe* published photos and a transcript of a tryst between Gifford and his lover, Suzen Johnson, who claimed to have been seeing him for four years. Kathie Lee Gifford went on a media offensive and declared that their marriage would endure. Seeking a lower profile, Gifford reduced his role on *Monday Night Football* and retired from network broadcasting in 1998.

Despite the personal scandals, Gifford was remembered by one generation as a college and professional football standout and by later generations as the familiar face of *Monday Night Football.* Helping to popularize football as a national pasttime during its introduction as a televised, mass-spectator sport, Gifford's contribution to football indeed was crucial in fostering its popularity throughout North America in the 1950s. In subsequent decades his work as a broadcast journalist helped the sport's fan base to grow. For these achievements, Gifford remains one of the most important figures in the NFL's modern era.

SELECTED WRITINGS BY GIFFORD:

(With Harry Waters) *The Whole Ten Yards,* Random House, 1993.

FURTHER INFORMATION

Books

Gifford, Frank, and Harry Waters. *The Whole Ten Yards.* New York: Random House, 1993.

Gifford, Kathie Lee, with Jim Jerome. *I Can't Believe I Said That!* New York: Pocket Books, 1992.

Periodicals

Fineman, Dana. "She Weathered the Storm of Her Husband's Betrayal with a Steely Resolve." *People* (December 29, 1997-Jauary 5, 1998).

Greenhouse, Steven. "A Crusader Makes Celebrities Tremble." *New York Times* (June 18, 1996).

Hanover, Donna. "Something Deep Inside Me Died." *Good Housekeeping* (August 1997).

Jones, Stacy. "Rival Tabloids Trade Barbs." *Editor and Publisher* (June 21, 1997).

Other

"Frank Gifford." Football Database Web site. http://www.bballsports.com (December 5, 2002).

"Frank Gifford." Pro Football Hall of Fame Web site. http://www.profootballhof.com/players/enshrinees/fgifford.cfm (December 3, 2002).

"Frank Gifford: Pro Football Hall of Famer." Sports Stars USA Web site. http://www.sportsstarsusa.com/football/gifford_frank.html (December 3, 2002).

"Frank N. Gifford." Hickok Sports Web site. http://www.hickoksports.com/biograph/giffordfrank.shtml (December 3, 2002).

"Gifford Was Star in Backfield, Booth." ESPN Web site. http://espn.go.com/classic/biography/s/gifford_frank.html (December 3, 2002).

Sketch by Timothy Borden

Diana Golden
1963-2001

American skier

Diana Golden lost her right leg to cancer at age 12 and then went on to become a world champion disabled skier. During her career, she won ten world champion titles and 19 national titles. She also won the gold medal for disabled skiing at the 1988 Winter Olympics in Calgary, Alberta. More than any other disabled athlete, she helped to popularize disabled sporting events. She retired from competitive skiing in 1990, becoming a motivational speaker and a spokeswoman for the right of disabled athletes to be recognized as athletes first. She died of cancer in 2001 at age 38.

Golden grew up in Lincoln, Massachusetts. She began skiing at age five, and the sport quickly became her passion. However, when she was 12, bone cancer in her right leg forced the amputation of the leg above the knee. She asked immediately after the surgery: "Will I still be able to ski?" Golden discovered that she could still ski, and only six months after the operation that saved her life but took her leg, she was back on the slopes.

She retrained at a school run by the New England Handicapped Sports Association for disabled skiers in Mount Sunapee, New Hampshire, where her instructors and fellow students were Vietnam veterans who had lost limbs, blind people, and paraplegics. One of her instructors later remembered Golden as "the most precocious kid I'd ever met," Scott S. Greenberger wrote in the *Boston Globe.*

A keen sense of humor carried Golden through the challenges of relearning to ski. Once, while practicing, a group of boys cut her off on the slope, causing her to lose her balance and tumble down the hill. She pulled off her artificial leg and threw it at the boys, according to Michael O'Connor of the *Boston Herald,* saying: "Look what you guys did! You knocked my leg off!"

After graduating from Lincoln-Sudbury High School, she attended Dartmouth College, continuing her training with the school's ski team. She graduated from Dartmouth in 1984. She then went on to international competition, earning gold medals at the World Disabled Ski Championships; she won ten gold medals lifetime at this event. In addition, she won 19 gold medals at the U.S. Disabled Alpine Championships, in the giant slalom, the slalom, the downhill, and the combined events.

Sense of Humor

Uncomfortable with suggestions that she was especially brave for having an international skiing career despite having only one leg, Golden preferred that people respect her for her skiing skills. She successfully fought for the right to compete with fully abled athletes, discarding ski equipment designed for use by disabled people, in favor of ordinary equipment, which could give her faster times.

The victory for which Golden became best known was her gold medal at the first Olympic games that included disabled skiing—the 1988 Winter Olympics at Calgary. The International Olympic Committee named Golden Female Skier of the Year.

Golden took about two and a half years off from skiing, from 1982 through 1985, saying it helped her per-

<table>
<tr><td colspan="2">Chronology</td></tr>
<tr><td>1963</td><td>Born in Lincoln, Massachusetts</td></tr>
<tr><td>1975</td><td>Loses right leg to cancer</td></tr>
<tr><td>1984</td><td>Graduates from Dartmouth College</td></tr>
<tr><td>1990</td><td>Retires from skiing, becomes motivational speaker</td></tr>
<tr><td>1997</td><td>Inducted into the Women's Sports Foundation Hall of Fame</td></tr>
<tr><td>1997</td><td>Marries Steve Brosnihan</td></tr>
<tr><td>2001</td><td>Dies of cancer in Providence, Rhode Island</td></tr>
</table>

<table>
<tr><td colspan="2">Awards and Accomplishments</td></tr>
<tr><td>1985</td><td>Successfully lobbies United States Ski Association (USSA) to allow disabled skiers to compete in USSA-sanctioned events</td></tr>
<tr><td>1986</td><td>Wins three gold medals at the World Disabled Ski Championships</td></tr>
<tr><td>1988</td><td>Wins two gold medals at the World Disabled Ski Championships</td></tr>
<tr><td>1988</td><td>Wins gold medal for disabled skiing at the Olympics</td></tr>
<tr><td>1988</td><td>Named Female Skier of the Year by the International Olympic Committee</td></tr>
<tr><td>1990</td><td>Wins three gold medals at the World Disabled Ski Championships</td></tr>
<tr><td>1997</td><td>Inducted into the Women's Sports Foundation Hall of Fame</td></tr>
<tr><td>1997</td><td>Inducted into the International Women's Sports Hall of Fame</td></tr>
<tr><td>1997</td><td>Inducted into U.S. National Ski Hall of Fame</td></tr>
</table>

spective both on and off the slopes. "It gave me time to find my identity apart from my skiing so that when I came back to skiing it was something I wanted to do for me and not because I needed that image from other people," she said.

After she retired from competitive skiing, Golden became a motivational speaker, exhibiting the same passion. "I loved the speaking," she told the *Boston Globe*. "There was no gold medal at the end, but to succeed you had to touch someone's heart."

Golden's illness, however, took an emotional as well as physical toll; she made at least one suicide attempt. But she rebounded, while battling the cancer. She took up mountain climbing, once climbing the more than 14,000 foot summit of Mount Rainier in Washington state.

Golden compared her fight for the rights of disabled athletes to the women's movement. "Think about women," she told *Sports Illustrated*'s Kostya Kennedy. "People used to pat us on the back and say, 'Isn't that sweet? She's competing.' Now they don't do that anymore. It's the same with the disabled. People treat us with dignity."

"To me it has to do with the dignity of each person. Each person is worthy of respect, so it's a matter of if I choose to live with that dignity myself."

In 1997, Golden married Steve Brosnihan. Brosnihan had noticed Golden years before, while they were both students at Dartmouth. He was on the school's baseball team, and he noticed her running on the baseball fields on crutches. "I remember watching her," Brosnihan said. "I admired her so much, she was always so vivacious. Sometimes I'd see her crossing the college green on crutches, and I'd speed up just to get ahead of her, so I could see her smile. She doesn't remember any of that." The two didn't get to know each other until years later, in Bristol, Rhode Island, where by then, Brosnihan was a freelance cartoonist.

Golden's cancer, in check throughout her skiing career, returned full force. In 1993, she was diagnosed with breast cancer. Then, after undergoing a double mastectomy, she learned she had cancer of the uterus and underwent a hysterectomy, destroying her ability to have children. The cancer still spread, again attacking her bones in 1996, as it had in her childhood. By 1999, the cancer had spread to her liver, and she was not ex-

pected to survive more than a few years. She died at Women's and Infant's Hospital in Providence, Rhode Island, in 2001. She was survived by her husband, her mother, Sylvia Finlay Golden, her sister, Meryl Lim, and her brother, Mark.

Golden's Legacy

While many admired Golden for overcoming obstacles, she insisted on being an athlete, period. In an interview shortly before her death, Golden described herself as a Type A personality and said, "It wasn't about wanting to overcome cancer; it was about wanting to kick butt."

She frequently scoffed at suggestions about her courage. "Sometimes, stereotypes make me laugh," she said. "Often, I've heard it on television, 'We're talking with a girl today who had cancer when she was 12, beat the odds and now she skis.' I say: 'Now wait a minute. I don't just ski. I'm the best in the world and I train my heart and soul out for this and I ski 150 days and I work out in the weight room, and to me courageous doesn't imply any of that.'"

"Athletes don't want to be courageous. They want to be good."

Among her biggest fans was filmmaker Warren Miller. Golden skied for three minutes in Miller's film, "Escape to Ski." Said Miller: "After you're with her for a few minutes, you totally forget her handicap. She has her act together, and it's not an act."

FURTHER INFORMATION

Periodicals

Araton, Harvey. "Sports of the Times; A Champion Slips Away Unnoticed." *New York Times* (August 30, 2001): D1.

Greenberger, Scott S. "Diana Golden Brosnihan, 38, Champion Skier, Motivator." *Boston Globe* (August 27, 2001): C11.

Kennedy, Kostya. "Inside Out; News and Notes from the World of Adventure Sports." *Sports Illustrated* (September 17, 2001): A17.

Litsky, Frank. "Diana Golden Brosnihan, Skier, Dies at 38." *New York Times* (August 28, 2001): B7.

Sullivan, Robert and Lynn Johnson. "Love is a Reason to Live." *Life* (October 1997): 44.

Other

Hirschfield, Cindy. "In Memoriam: Diana Golden Brosnihan." SkiingMag.com, http://www.skiingmag.com/skiing/skiing_scene/article/0,12910,328545,00.html (February 9, 2003).

Sketch by Michael Belfiore

Pancho Gonzales

Richard "Pancho" Gonzales
1928-1995

American tennis player

The Mexican American tennis player Richard "Pancho" Alonzo Gonzales had only two major singles titles to his credit, yet he was considered by many to be one of the most influential players of the late 1940s and the 1950s. After winning consecutive singles titles at the U.S. Championships (later known as the U.S. Open), Gonzales joined the professional touring circuit—a move than banned him from the major tournaments but that proved him to be one of the most formidable players in the country. During his career, Gonzales often faced racism and discrimination in the predominantly white world of his chosen sport. Developing a tough skin and a defiant, lone-wolf attitude, he became infamous among his peers, but won over tennis fans with his deft game and larger-than-life charisma.

Taught Himself to Play

Richard Alonso "Pancho" Gonzales, born in Los Angeles in 1928, was the son of Mexican immigrants Manuel and Carmen Gonzales. When Manuel was a child, he walked with his father 900 miles, from Chihuahua, Mexico, to Arizona. He later settled in South Central Los Angeles, where he met and married Carmen, and worked as a housepainter. Despite his father's strictness, Gonzales, one of seven children, was often a wild and unruly child.

When Gonzales was twelve years old, he asked for a bicycle for Christmas, but his mother gave him a 50-cent tennis racquet instead. Gonzales instantly took to tennis, teaching himself how to play on the public courts of Los Angeles. He played as often as he could, and by the time he was fourteen he was winning tournaments in his age group.

After two years of high school, Gonzales dropped out so that he could devote himself to tennis full time. The decision would hurt him, though, because as a dropout he was banned from many junior tournaments. Turned away from tennis, Gonzales became a troublemaker. At fifteen he was caught burglarizing houses. "You don't know the thrill of going out the back window when someone's coming in the front door," he once told his brother Ralph, as quoted by S.L. Price in *Sports Illustrated.*

Gonzales spent a year in juvenile detention, then joined the U.S. Navy in 1945. After two years of swabbing decks in the Pacific, Gonzales—who had been AWOL (absent without leave) and had returned late from leave a few times too many—received a discharge for bad conduct. Returning to Southern California, he resumed playing tennis, making astonishingly quick progress in the sport. Within a year he was playing the major national men's tournaments. In March 1948 he married Henrietta Pedrin, learning soon afterward that she was pregnant with their first child. Together they would have three sons.

Gonzales shocked tennis fans around the world when, at age twenty and ranked only 17th in the country, he won the 1948 U.S. Championships. His opponents took note of Gonzales's deft, powerful serve, strong volleying skills, and fierce competitiveness. Yet Gonzales was in many ways a fish out of water in the predominantly white, Anglo-Saxon world of tennis; he was sensitive to any slights against him, and resented Anglos' habit of calling every Mexican male Pancho. Nevertheless, he thrived, defending his title at the 1949 U.S. Championships, where he prevailed in a five-set match against tennis great Ted Schroeder. Also that year, Gonzales took two doubles titles—the French Open and Wimbledon—with his partner Frank Parker. After these triumphs, Gonzales joined U.S. tennis's touring circuit, accepting a contract of $75,000 under tennis pro Bobby Riggs. As a professional player in the touring circuit, however, Gonzales was no longer eligible to play in the major tournaments.

At first, the career move nearly proved to be his undoing. The touring circuit paired Gonzales against 28-year-old champion Jack Kramer, considered to be the best player in the world. Gonzales, as the challenger, faced Kramer in 123 matches, of which he won a mere twenty-seven. His reputation tarnished by the losses, Gonzales took a four-year break from tennis, but by late 1954 he got a second chance. Kramer invited him to join another round-robin tour, and Gonzales was back playing tennis, and often winning. Among those he beat was Tony Trabert, winner of three Grand Slam titles in 1955; Gonzales took 74 out of 101 games. Yet "[Gonzales's] nature had changed completely," Kramer recalled to Price of *Sports Illustrated*. The once happy-go-lucky player became "difficult and arrogant. Losing had changed him. When he got his next chance, he understood that you either win or you're out of a job."

Prevailed in the Touring Circuit

Irascible and prone to raging against his opponents and umpires, Gonzales was nonetheless popular among tennis audiences, and he always drew a crowd. As the reigning champion, he trounced Ken Rosewall, Lew Hoad, and many others. Yet he was unhappy with his touring contracts, which always offered more money to the challenging player than to him, the reigning champion. Gonzales also faced marital troubles; he and Henrietta divorced in 1958. Soon after, he married Madelyn Darrow, with whom he had three daughters.

Gonzales prevailed in the round-robin tours until his contract expired in 1961. After briefly retiring, he returned to lose a humiliating first-round match at the U.S. Professional Grass Court Championships. For the next several years he turned his attention to coaching tennis, leading the U.S. Davis Cup team to the finals against Australia in 1963, and tutoring young American players, including **Arthur Ashe**.

When tennis "opened" in 1968, allowing amateurs to compete with professional players, 40-year-old

Chronology	
1928	Born May 9 in Los Angeles, California
1940	Receives first tennis racquet as a Christmas present
1942	Wins first junior tournaments
1943	Drops out of high school; caught burglarizing houses
1945	Joins U.S. Navy
1947	Leaves Navy on a discharge; begins playing in men's tennis tournaments
1948	Wins men's singles title, U.S. Championships at Forest Hills
1948	Marries Henrietta Pedrin
1949	Wins men's singles title, U.S. Championships at Forest Hills
1949	Wins men's doubles title, Wimbledon, with partner Frank Parker
1949	Wins men's doubles title, French Open, with partner Frank Parker
1949-50	Loses to Jack Kramer in round-robin tour, 27-96
1953-59	Wins U.S. Professional Championships
1954-60	Dominates the round-robin tours, beating Frank Sedgman, Tony Trabert, Ken Rosewall, Lew Hoad, and others
1958	Divorces Henrietta
1960	Marries Madelyn Darrow
1961	Wins U.S. Professional Championships
1963	Coaches U.S. Davis Cup team to final in Australia
1968	Returns to play major tournaments after tennis "opens" to allow amateurs to compete with professionals
1968	Divorces Madelyn
1969	Plays longest Wimbledon match ever (five hours, 12 minutes), beating Charles Pasarell in the tournament's first round
1970	Remarries Madelyn Gonzales
1972	Becomes oldest man to win a tournament, in Iowa, at age 44
1974	Joins Caesars Palace in Las Vegas as a professional coach
1975	Divorces Madelyn for second time
1984	Marries Rita Agassi
1995	Dies of cancer, July 3, in Las Vegas

Gonzales, no longer in the peak of his career, returned to play the major championships. A presence at all the major tournaments that year, he made a good showing but did not win a title. In what was perhaps his last moment in the spotlight, Gonzales won a grueling 112-game match against a player half his age, Charles Pasarell, in the first round of the 1969 Wimbledon tournament. The score stood at 22-24, 1-6, 16-14, 6-3, 11-9 after the five-hour and twelve-minute match—the longest in Wimbledon history. Gonzales continued playing well into his forties, becoming the oldest man to win a tournament, in Iowa, in 1972. He retired two years later, at age 46, and played senior events until the mid-1980s.

After he retired Gonzales joined Ceasers Palace in Las Vegas as a professional coach—a job that he loved, and would keep for nearly two decades. He and Madelyn had married and divorced twice, ending the relationship for good in 1980; between his two marriages to her, he had three others. His sixth and final marriage was to Rita Agassi, sister of the U.S. tennis star **Andre Agassi**; the couple had a son, Skylar.

Gonzales died of stomach cancer on July 3, 1995. He is survived by eight children—and by his legacy as one of the finest (albeit one of the most difficult) players of mid-twentieth-century tennis.

FURTHER INFORMATION

Periodicals

Flink, Steve. "Obituary: Pancho Gonzales." *Independent* (London, England) (July 5, 1995): 18.

Irvine, David. "The Tough Guy of Tennis." *Guardian* (London, England) (July 5, 1995): 15.

Price, S. L. "The Lone Wolf." *Sports Illustrated* (June 24, 1995): 68.

Other

"Gonzales, 'Pancho' (Richard A.)." Hickok Sports.com. http://www.hickoksports.com/biograph/gonzalezp. shtml (October 15, 2002).

"Ricardo 'Pancho' Gonzales." Latino Legends in Sports. http://www.latinosportslegends.com/pancho_gonzales_ bio.htm (October 15, 2002).

Sketch by Wendy Kagan

Evonne Goolagong

Evonne Goolagong
1951-

Australian tennis player

Evonne Goolagong's 1993 memoir, *Home! The Evonne Goolagong Story,* released just a few years after she returned to her native Australia, became a bestseller in her home country. The book's ability to capture the attention of so many people indicates just how popular this Aboriginal Australian was to her fellow citizens. As a tennis champion, Evonne Goolagong captured the Australian Open four times and won Wimbledon twice (with victories coming almost a decade apart) and, by the time she retired from professional tennis, had amassed a record of a record of 285 victories, with 19 career singles titles. Coming from a background in which this type of success was unheard of, Evonne Goolagong has used her star status to fight for other causes, advocating for Aboriginal rights as well as spending time establishing tennis development programs for Australian children.

Growing Up

Evonne Fay Goolagong was born on July 31, 1951, in the town of Barellan, in New South Wales, Australia. She was the third of Kenneth and Linda Goolagong's eight children. Though they were not fully Aboriginal, each parent had native Aborigine ancesters. Evonne grew up in a poor but happy family. Her father was a farm laborer, performing tasks such as sheep shearing and fixing farm machinery, while her mother stayed home and took care of Evonne and her seven brothers and sisters (Evonne was the third of the eight children).

Evonne's mother instilled in her children a fear of being taken away from home. At this time in Australia (the fifties) there were crusades undertaken by some Australians who wanted to take Aboriginal children away from their families and raise them elsewhere so they could give the children a life free from poverty and what many in white Australian culture assumed to be a better education. "I remember when I was little," Evonne told Stephen Lamble in the Adelaide, Australia *Sunday Mail,* "... whenever a car would come down the road, my aunty and my mother would say, 'You kids better go away and hide. The welfare man will take you away.'"

Goolagong invested her early energies into tennis and never gave up. Her introduction to the sport came early, and at the age of five she had become a ball girl at the

Barellan War Memorial Tennis Club, where she earned some change retrieving balls, a task that no doubt helped contribute to her quick reflexes and helped develop her agility and create her court speed. By the time she was six, Evonne had acquired her first tennis racquet—a gift from her aunt—and left behind the bat and rubber ball that she'd been using to practice with.

Though the tennis club was not the best in Australia, it did attract people who knew the game. By the time Goolagong was ten, she had caught the eye of Vic Edwards, who was then one of Australia's best known tennis coaches. According to Edwards in *Contemporary Authors,* the young Goolagong's "most impressive quality was her grace around the court. And she could hit that ball really hard, right in the center of the bat. She had a homemade shot, a backhand volley, and it was a beauty."

But Edwards did not live in Barellan, so Goolagong and her family had a tough decision to make. Evonne could work with Edwards, and he would exercise her natural abilities and help develop her into a fantastic player. Yet in order to do so Evonne would have to sacrifice her home life and Aboriginal culture. So, at age 11, Evonne Goolagong moved into a Sydney suburb with Edwards and his family. Her family in Barellan and the people of the town realized this was a great opportunity for the young Evonne—and that there was no way she would achieve tennis fame by staying in her hometown—so together they raised enough money to help her buy the new tennis equipment she would need to fit in and compete at Edwards's tennis school. Edwards in turn became her legal guardian.

Moving into the new lifestyle was not easy for the young Goolagong, however. "I cried nearly every night," she told an Australian newspaper decades later. "I remember being very shy and scared when I first started." But she remained and trained hard, rising to become one of Australia's top tennis players.

Becoming a Tennis Star

Pulled out of one culture and thrust into another, Goolagong had some major adjustments to make. Edwards was from a relatively affluent suburb of Sydney, and he encouraged Evonne to attend finishing school so that she could, according to *Contemporary Authors,* "learn elocution and poise." After finishing school, it was on to business college, where she learned secretarial skills in the event that her pro career did not pan out. Of course, her career in tennis did take off, and after winning several of the important Australian amateur championships, Goolagong left Australia at the age of nineteen to begin her first international tour in 1970, winning seven of the 21 tournaments she played in that year. She played Wimbledon as well, but was eliminated in the first round. The exposure to a venue such as Wimbledon, however, prepared her for the future.

Chronology

1951	Born July 31 in Barellan, New South Wales to Kenneth and Linda Goolagong
1959	Begins playing tennis when she's eight years old
1961	"Decides" she's going to win Wimbledon. Vic Edwards, well-known Australian tennis coach, becomes her coach and mentor
1965	Moves to Sydney permanently to concentrate on her tennis career and live with the Edwards family
1968	Enters New South Wales Championship at fifteen and plays in the Australian women's singles championship. She's ranked as the top junior in New South Wales
1968	Completes her schooling at Willoughby Girls High School and receives her certificate; enters "secretarial studies" at Metropolitan Business College
1970	Starts playing tennis on the international tour
1971	Turns professional and wins Wimbledon; also wins French Open
1972	Wins French Open Mixed Doubles with Kim Warwick
1973	Wins Italian Open; also wins U.S. Indoor Championship (repeats in 1979)
1974	Begins string of four consecutive Australian Open championship victories
1974	Wins Virginia Slims Championship (will repeat in 1976)
1975	Marries Roger Cawley on June 19
1975	Severs relationship with coach Vic Edwards and moves to United States
1977	Gives birth to daughter, Kelly, born on May 12
1979	After time away from competition, she returns to competition and surpasses $1 million in earnings
1980	Wins 2nd Wimbledon—the first mother since 1914 to win a Wimbledon singles victory
1981	Gives birth to a son, Morgan, on May 28
1982	Makes a brief comeback attempt but abandons it after little success
1983	Announces official retirement from professional tennis
1991	Returns to home country and takes up residence in Noosa, Australia
1993	Publishes her biography, *Home*
1995	Becomes board member of Australian Sporting Commission
1997	Appointed Sporting Ambassador for the Australian Sporting Commission
2002	Announces that—in addition to the work she does for the organization—she's including The Salvation Army of Australia in her own will and testament

---

A Professional Tennis Player

Goolagong turned professional in 1971, wasting no time after gaining her pro status. She beat Helen Gourlay in that year's French Open. Then, just one year after that first round upset at her first Wimbledon, she returned to center court and defeated fellow Australian **Margaret Smith Court** in the finals, the first of her two Wimbledon victories.

In her home country Goolagong became a dominant force in the Australian Open, winning the Grand Slam event four consecutive times between 1974 and 1977. She also took home the Australian Open doubles title four times during that decade (1971, 1974-76). Goolagong also became an important part of Australia's Federation Cup team, helping her fellow Australians to victories in 1971, 1973 and 1974 (they also reached the finals in 1975 and 1976).

Awards and Accomplishments

1971	Associated Press Female Athlete of the Year
1971	Wins French Open singles; Wimbledon singles; Australian Open doubles
1971-76	Member of Australian Federation Cup Team
1972	Named "Australian of the Year"
1972	Appointed Member of the British Empire (MBE) for services to tennis
1972	Wins French Open mixed doubles
1972-73	Wins Canadian Open singles and Canadian Open doubles
1974	Wins Wimbledon Open doubles
1975-76	Wins Australian Open singles and Australian Open doubles
1977	Wins Australian Open singles
1979	Wins U.S. Indoor Championship singles
1980	Wins Wimbledon singles
1980	Wins Karen Krantzcke Sportsmanship Award
1982	Receives the honor of the *Order of Australia*
1988	Elected to International Tennis Hall of Fame
1989	Inducted into Sudafed International Women's Sports Hall of Fame

Member of Winning Australian Cup team: 1971, 73-74. When Goolagong retired she had a record of 285 victories, 72 losses and 19 career singles titles

Though she flirted with a second Wimbledon title several times throughout the decade, Goolagong just could not seem to win the final match. She made the Wimbledon finals three times in the 1970s, but it proved elusive, because she lost to **Billie Jean King** in 1972 and 1975, and then to **Chris Evert** in 1976.

Not Done Yet

As the 1970s wound to a close, Evonne's major victories seemed to be disappearing. Many critics of her game cited her two weakest aspects—a poor forehand volley and her "walkabouts" (the Aboriginal term Goolagong herself used to describe her wandering on the court)—as reasons she was losing her control of the game. In spite of her tenacious play, some people simply thought that her desire to achieve another Grand Slam victory had dissipated.

But in 1980, Goolagong returned to Wimbledon, this time as a wife and mother (she had married Roger Cawley of Britian a few years earlier), and stunned the crowd, picking off great player after great player as she climbed her way into the finals against Chris Evert to win the only Wimbledon singles finals round to end in a tie-breaker. Goolagong was also the first mother to win the title in 66 years. When she chose to retire from the world of professional tennis in 1983, Goolagong had 285 victories and only 72 losses, along with 19 career singles titles. She also left with nearly $1.5 million in prize money.

The Goolagong Impact

The International Tennis Hall of Fame elected Evonne Goolagong into its organization in 1988. Her greatness on the court, in spite of some dry years, was indisputable. But Goolagong used her tennis career as a springboard to go on and work at making the world she knows a better place. Ever since she turned pro, Goolagong had been in the spotlight. As a black woman in a sport that then consisted mostly of the white upper-class, Goolagong stood out. When she was a young star—like many young athletes of color often do—she chose to let her work on the court speak for itself and remain mostly silent when the microphones where in her face. At the time, Goolagong was not interested in the political implications of being an aboriginal black in a predominately white game.

She stirred controversy more than a few times, however, such as in 1972 when, after being invited to play in a segregated South African tournament, she agreed to participate. Goolagong had been given the classification of "honorary white," for the event, and many people were irritated that, in addition to the tournament being segregated, Goolagong agreed to play in the first place. When asked why she chose to participate, she simply replied, "Of course I'm proud of my race, but I don't want to be thinking about it all the time."

In the years since her retirement, however, Goolagong—who for some time has gone by the name Evonne Goolagong-Cawley, adding her husband Roger's surname to her own—has returned to her origins and, in an attempt to know herself better, has become a student of her people and her native culture. Looking at the world differently now than she did at twenty, Goolagong has a different take on her background. "I would like more people to come out and say they are not racist," she told the Adelaide, Australia *Sunday Mail*. She worries about the silence of people and how it gets overpowered by those who are racist. "I can feel the tension in the wider community," she said.

After moving to the United States in the 1970s and living in America for almost two decades (first on Hilton Head Island, then in Naples, Florida), Goolagong, along with husband Roger Cawley and their two children, daughter Kelly and son Morgan, returned to Australia in 1991. They bought a house in Noosa, Queensland. "I realized that I had spent too much time away," she told *Sports Illustrated*'s Jeff Pearlman. "I wanted to know who my parents were, who I was… I never knew what it really meant to be an Aborigine. Then two Aborigine elders invited me to particpate in a ceremony, one where you looked deep into yourself. It was the first time I felt truly home."

Goolagong's influence on the budding tennis stars of her home country is strong. "Tennis brought me out of myself and that's why it's been a great education for me," she told the Adelaide, Australia newspaper *The Advertiser*. This once shy girl now helps other young girls gain ground in a great sport. Goolagong runs the Evonne Goolagong Getting Started program with Tennis Australia.

Great for Game and Country

Evonne Goolagong is creating quite a legacy in her homeland of Australia. As a tennis champion, she has

Evonne Goolagong

Where Is She Now?

Since her retirement from the professional tour in 1983, Goolagong has remained in the public eye as an ambassador for the game of tennis, as well as being an advocate for her native people's rights. She works hard to bring the issues of race to the forefront. She has also been a consultant to the Australian Sports Commission's indigenous sports program, serving as an ambassador, and since 1997 has competed on the Virginia Slims Legends tennis tour.

Goolagong also works with Australia's Salvation Army as their spokesperson, recently signing over her Will to the organization as a way of urging others to do so as well (the money goes to help fight poverty, homelessness and hunger). Additionally, she consults with the company Herbal Creations in their development of an herbal tablet to help women through menopause. "I've always had an interest in natural herbs," she told the Melbourne *Sunday Herald Sun*, "and when I came back to Australia I wanted to learn more about my people and part of that was learning about natural herbs." Her mother suffered terribly through menopause, and due to the hormone heplacement therapy drugs, Goolagong's mother is now battling breast cancer, as well. It's something that Evonne Goolagong's determined to fight, just like she fought on the court.

---

instilled the love of the game for generations of young girls who look up to her as the model for what they want to become. For Australia's poor she is working to make their lives better through her work with the Salvation Army; and, as an advocate for herbal remedies for menopausal women she strives to ease the suffering and help prevent cancer in thousands of women.

Goolagong captured the Australian Open four times and won Wimbledon twice (with victories coming almost a decade apart), and by the time she retired from professional tennis, had amassed a record of a record of 285 victories, with 19 career singles titles. She has truly risen higher than most people would have expected of a girl coming out of Barellan, New South Wales. Her kind of success was, in her native culture, unheard of before Evonne Goolagong made it so.

CONTACT INFORMATION

Address: c/o IMC, 1 Erieview Plaza, Cleveland, OH 44114.

SELECTED WRITINGS BY GOOLAGONG:

(With Bud Collins) *Evonne! On the Move.* Dutton, 1975.
(With Phil Jarrett) *Home! The Evonne Goolagong Story.* Simon & Schuster, Australia, 1993.

FURTHER INFORMATION

Books

"Evonne Goolagong." *Great Women in Sports.* Visible Ink Press, 1996.
Frayne, Trent. "Evonne Goolagong." *Famous Women Tennis Players.* New York: Dodd, 1979.

Goolagong, Eve and Bud Collins. *Evonne! On the Move.* New York: Dutton, 1975.
Goolagong, Eve and Phil Jarrett. *Home! The Evonne Goolagong Story.* East Roseville, Australia: Simon & Schuster, Australia, 1993.
Herda, D. J. *Free Spirit: Evonne Goolagong.* Milwaukee: Raintree Editions, 1976.
Lichtenstein, G. *A Long Way Baby: Behind the Scenes in Women's Pro Tennis.* New York: William Morrow & Co., 1974.
Sullivan, George. *Queens of the Court.* New York: Dodd, 1974.

Periodicals

The Advertiser (Adelaide, Australia) (September 11, 1996; August 10, 1997; December 14, 1998; August 22, 2001).
Hansen, Jennicer. "Tales of a Modern Woman." *Sunday Herald Sun* (Melbourne, Australia) (August 11, 2002): 106.

Leavy, J. "Evonne Goolagong: playing winning tennis again." *Ms.* 7(1) (July 1978): 49-51.

Life (July 16, 1971).

Newsweek (July 5, 1971; July 17, 1972; March 19, 1973; June 30, 1975; April 26, 1976).

New York Times Biographical Edition (July 8, 1971; August 31, 1971).

New York Times Magazine (August 29, 1971).

Pearlman, Jeff. "Evonne Goolagong, tennis champion: April 26, 1976." *Sports Illustrated* (May 25, 1998): 17.

Sports Illustrated (February 15, 1971; July 12, 1971; March 20, 1972; August 7, 1972; October 28, 1974; April 26, 1976; October 17, 1977; March 27, 1978).

Time (March 1, 1971; July 17, 1972; June 30, 1975).

Other

"Evonne Goolagong Cawley." Tennis Corner. http://www.tenniscorner.net/player.php?playerid=GOE002&tour=WTA (January 21, 2003).

Hannan, Liz. "The Latest Goolagong Chapter." *theage. com* http://www.theage.com.au/articles/2002/04/28/1019441322609.html (January 21, 2003).

Sketch by Eric Lagergren

Retief Goosen

Retief Goosen
1969-

South African golfer

Golfer Retief Goosen's self-doubt would keep him in the shadows of fellow South African and friendly rival Ernie Els for many years. Playing primarily on the European Tour, Goosen enjoyed a quiet and mildly successful career while his friend Els competed with golf's superstars on the U.S. Tour. That would all change when Goosen, without much fanfare, won the 2001 U.S. Open and then proceeded to win five international titles in the following ten months. Although he continues in relative anonymity, his recent success allows him to do so without a doubt of his ability to compete with golf's giants.

Born February 2, 1969, in Pietersburg, South Africa, Goosen's father, a real estate agent, was an amateur golfer who introduced his son to the game at an early age. Goosen soon inherited his father's passion for the game. Beyond the realm of normal encouragement, his father pushed his son towards excellence—even going as far as to create a wooden contraption to ensure that his son kept his head still while swinging the club. By the time he was seventeen, Goosen was considered one of the top prospects in South African Golf, but not before suffering through a life changing event.

Lightning Strikes

At fifteen, Goosen was struck by lightning while golfing with a friend at Pietersburg Golf Club. On January 30, 1985, Goosen and his friend Henri Potgieter were playing through a light drizzle when lightening struck the top of a tree and traveled to the ground and across the wet grass. Potgieter who was playing ahead of Goosen was knocked off his feet. Goosen, on the other hand, suffered a fate much worse than his friend. "When I stood up I was looking for him, and I couldn't find him," Potgieter remembered in *Golf World*. "I wanted to know his reaction. What I did see was his golf clubs and his golf bag. Then I saw him lying on his back. His tongue was down his throat and his eyes were backward, and he was breathing weird. He had no clothes on; they'd been burned from his body. I remember picking up his spectacles. I didn't know what to do. It looked like he was dead. I was screaming for help. Fortunately, there were guys teeing off on the 12th hole. They came running toward us. From then on, I can't remember much. They picked him up and put him in a car." Goosen's shoes had disintegrated from his feet, his underwear and watch band had melted to his body. Relieved that their son had survived the accident, Goosen's father took it as an act of God and a hint of things to come.

The European Tour

So taken with the game, Goosen returned to the links within a few weeks of the life changing event. In 1990,

Chronology

1969	Born February 2 in Pietersburg, South Africa
1985	Struck by lightning while golfing
1990	Wins South African Amateur tournament
1990	Turns professional
1991	Wins his first tournament on South African tour
1992	Qualifies for European PGA Tour
1996	Wins first European tournament
2000	Finishes tied for twelfth in first U.S. Open
2001	Wins U.S. Open Championship

Awards and Accomplishments

1991	Won Lacor Newcastle Classic
1991	Named South African Rookie of the Year
1992	Won Spoomet, Bushveld, and Witbank Classics
1993	Won Mount Edgecombe Trophy
1995	Won Phillips South African Open
1996	Won Staley Hall Northumberland Challenge
1997	Won Peugeot Open de France
1999	Won Novotgel Perrier Open de France
2000	Won the Trophee Lancome
2001	Won U.S. Open Championship
2001	Won Scottish Open

Goosen won the South African Amateur tournament and quickly turned professional. He spent his early professional career on the South African tour. He won the Newcastle Classic in 1991 and three tournaments the following year. He won the Mount Edgecombe Trophy in 1993 and the Phillips South African Open in 1995. While still on the South African tour he qualified for the European PGA Tour in 1992 but did not win his first tournament until 1996. He had several top ten finishes in 1997, including a win in the Peugeot Open in France. In 2000, after a successful year in 1999, Goosen finished tied for 12th in the U.S. Open Championship.

The U.S. Open

In 2001, Goosen would again play in the U.S. Open, entering the tournament as the 44th ranked golfer in the world. Unknown to the American golf audience, Goosen would have to overcome conventional wisdom and defeat **Tiger Woods**, who was on a quest for his fifth consecutive major tournament. Woods, however, essentially eliminated himself from the running with an uncharacteristically poor performance. Goosen's victory was nearly foiled by a three putt performance on the final hole of the tournament. Luckily for him, he wasn't the only one having trouble on the green and a similarly poor performance by Stewart Cink left Goosen tied with Mark Brooks. After the 18-hole playoff, held the following day, Goosen had defeated Brooks and his self-doubt to become the winner of the 101st U.S. Open.

Better suited for the slower paced European Tour, Goosen shied from the spotlight and the endorsements that were offered following his win. With a win in the Scottish Open, however, Goosen entered the British Open that season with a chance to become the first golfer since **Lee Trevino** to win three National Championships in such a short period of time. Although he was unsuccessful in his bid to match Trevino's achievement, Goosen enjoyed a breakout year in 2001 with five international titles in ten months which propelled him from 44th to fourth in the World Ranking.

Although Goosen's career had been overshadowed by fellow South African Ernie Els's success and his own self-doubt, his breakout year in 2001 has allowed him to overcome his lack of confidence and afforded him the opportunity to continue without the nagging need to prove himself on the world's stage. Goosen also began designing his first golf course in 2001 for a new resort planned for Plettenburg Bay, South Africa.

FURTHER INFORMATION

Periodicals

Hawkins, John. "Beware of Rookie Mistake." *Golf World* (October 19, 2001): 48.

Hawkins, John. "The Agony and the Ecstasy." *Golf World* (June 22, 2001): 20.

Huggan, John. "Lark by the Loch." *Golf World* (July 20, 2001): 22.

Huggan, John. "French Toast." *Golf World*(September 22, 2000): 34.

Huggan, John. "Hitting the Trifecta." *Golf World* (Novemeber 2, 2001): 44.

Huggan, John. "Perth Perfect." *Golf World* (February 1, 2002): 22.

Jenkins, Dan. "Major Surprise." *Golf Digest* (August, 2001): 154.

Kindred, Dave. "Support Group." *Golf Digest* (Novemeber, 2001): 57.

Rosaforte, Tim. "Finishing Touch." *Golf World* (April 12, 2002): 26.

Rosaforte, Tim. "One Grounded Goose." *Golf World* (July 13, 2001): 34.

Other

Biography Resource Center. Detroit: Gale Group, 2002.

Sketch by Aric Karpinski

Ekaterina Gordeeva
1971-

Russian figure skater

Ekaterina Gordeeva

Figure skater Ekaterina Gordeeva, who skated with partner Sergei Grinkov, won four World Championships and two Olympic gold medals in pairs skating. Although her career was temporarily halted by Grinkov's tragic death in 1995, she has continued to skate as a solo professional.

An Early Start

Gordeeva was born in 1971 in the Soviet capital of Moscow. Her mother was a teletype operator for the Soviet news agency, Tass, and her father was a dancer for the Alexandrov Song and Dance Ensemble of the Soviet Army. From her father, Gordeeva inherited a talent for graceful movement. She began skating when she was four years old.

In 1982, when Gordeeva was eleven years old, she began skating with Sergei Grinkov, who was four years her senior, at the Central Army Club in Moscow. They developed a close relationship, much like that of a brother and sister; according to E. M. Swift in *Sports Illustrated,* they skated "lyrically, harmoniously, but without emotional tension."

In 1984, they competed in the junior world championships, coming in fifth; in the year after that, they won a gold medal. In 1986, they won the first of four world championships. They would take the world title again in 1987, 1989, and 1990.

First Olympic Gold

The pair won an Olympic gold medal in 1998, in Calgary. Gordeeva was sixteen, and Grinkov was twenty. In *Sports Illustrated,* E.M. Swift quoted skating champion and choreographer Sandra Bezic, who said, "He presented her so beautifully, like a cherished little sister. They are everything pairs skating should be."

After winning their fourth world championship, in 1990, the pair quit amateur competition, and joined Tom Collins's Tour of World Champions, planning to skate for four or five years, make some money, and then move on to separate careers. However, their plans changed when they fell in love during the Collins tour. Collins told Leigh Montville in *Sports Illustrated,* "You could see it happen. It was all very sweet. They were with each other all the time."

Gordeeva told Joanna Powell in *Good Housekeeping,* "There was something special about us. We never changed partners. I never skated with anyone else. I never touched anyone else, only Sergei. After we became lovers, our skating started to become more sensitive and more beautiful."

The two skaters were married in April of 1991, in Moscow; in 1992 they had a daughter, Daria.

Second Gold Medal

Historically, professional athletes were not allowed to compete in the Olympics, but in 1992, these rules were changed, making Gordeeva and Grinkov eligible to compete in the 1994 Olympic Games in Lillehammer, Norway. Skating to Beethoven's Moonlight Sonata, the pair, now married and parents, won another gold medal.

After winning their second Olympic gold medal, Gordeeva and Grinkov moved to Simsbury, Connecticut in 1994, and skated in the Stars on Ice tour.

A Tragic Loss

On November 20, 1995, tragedy struck when the 28-year-old Grinkov died unexpectedly while he and Gordeeva were rehearsing for a Stars on Ice show at a rink in Lake Placid, New York. Gordeeva later wrote in her memoir, *My Sergei,* "Sergei was gliding on the ice, but he didn't do the crossovers. His hands didn't go around my waist for the lift. . . . He couldn't control himself. He tried to stop, but he kept gliding into the boards. He tried to hold onto the boards. . . . Then he bent his knees and lay down on the ice very carefully. I kept asking what was happening. . . . But he didn't speak at all."

Grinkov, who had appeared to be completely healthy except for a problem with high blood pressure, had suffered a massive heart attack. After his death, doctors determined that two of the arteries in his heart had been completely blocked. Heart disease ran in his family; his father had died from a heart attack in his fifties.

Chronology

1971	Born May 28 in Moscow, Soviet Union (now Russia)
1975	Begins skating at the Central Army Club in Moscow
1982	Begins partnership with Sergei Grinkov
1984	Competes in junior world championships
1985	Competes in junior world championships
1986	Wins first of four world championships
1988	Competes in Calgary Olympics
1990	Quits amateur competition to become professional skater
1991	Marries Grinkov
1992	Gives birth to daughter Daria
1994	Competes in Lillehammer Olympic Games
1994	Begins skating for Stars on Ice
1995	Grinkov dies from a heart attack
1996	Begins solo skating career
1998	Meets skater Ilia Kulik, becomes romantically involved
2001	Gives birth to daughter, Elizaveta
2002	Marries Kulik; considers a career in coaching

Awards and Accomplishments

1985	Gold medal, junior world championships
1986-87, 1989-90	Gold medal, world championships
1988	Gold medal, Calgary Olympics
1994	Gold medal, Lillehammer Olympics

Gordeeva took Grinkov's body home to Moscow for the funeral and spent three months in Russia. Although she considered giving up skating forever, she realized that she was not trained to do anything else. In addition, she missed the feel and flow of skating, and she decided to return to the ice.

In early 1996, three months after Grinkov's death, she skated again, solo, at a tribute to Grinkov in Hartford, Connecticut. The transition from pairs skating to solo skating was difficult, but Gordeeva told Lopez, "You can't lock yourself inside yourself or you'll die. My mother told me you have to get up now. You have a daughter to live for." When Gordeeva returned as a single skater, observers were impressed by what Powell called her "elegant fusion of raw emotion and gentle, ballerina-style grace." Fellow skater **Brian Boitano** told Lopez, "People are mesmerized by her."

According to Mark Starr in *Newsweek,* Gordeeva said after that performance, "I want you to know I skated tonight not alone. I skated with Sergei. That's why it was so good."

However, she also said, "My life of great skating, and skating with him, is over," according to Steve Lopez in *Time.* "I don't try to go now for Olympics. I take skating for a job."

In 1996, Gordeeva published *My Sergei,* a tribute to her late husband and partner. By 1998, the book had sold more than one million copies in both hardcover and paperback, testifying both to Gordeeva's popularity and to the public's fascination with the intensely romantic relationship between the two skaters. For Gordeeva, writing the book helped her express her love and her grief, but it also reminded her of his death; she quit her book tour early because she found it too difficult to be constantly reminded of the tragedy. The book was later adapted for television; "My Sergei" aired on CBS in winter of 1998.

Later in 1996, she began skating in the Stars on Ice show, joining other former Olympians for the 57-city tour.

In 1997, Gordeeva moved out of the condominium she had shared with Grinkov and into a five-bedroom house in Simsbury. She told Powell that she felt weighted down by memories in the condo: "I felt I couldn't start anything new while I was there. It reminded me too much of [Grinkov]."

Gordeeva also appeared in "Snowden on Ice" in 1997. The hour-long CBS special featured Gordeeva as a young woman who, with the help of a magical snowman, rediscovers her love for skating. Her daughter Daria also appeared in the special.

In 1998, Gordeeva published *A Letter for Daria,* a children's book of reminiscences and advice for her daughter.

A New Life

In that same year, Gordeeva met Ilia Kulik, who had won a gold medal in men's figure skating at the 1998 Olympic Games in Nagano, Japan. Eventually, they became romantically involved.

Gordeeva and Kulik had a daughter, Elizaveta, born in June of 2001, and Gordeeva cut back her skating in order to spend more time with Elizaveta and Daria. Of Gordeeva's relationship with Kulik, a *People* reporter noted that Gordeeva's manager, Deb Nast, said, "She's found love again."

On June 10, 2002, Gordeeva and Kulik were married in San Francisco. Gordeeva, who was considering moving from skating into coaching other skaters, said she wanted to stay close to home. "I'm trying to live more for the kids," she told Jason Lynch and Susan Horsburgh in *People.*

CONTACT INFORMATION

Address: c/o IMG, 22 East 71st Street, New York, NY 10021-4911.

SELECTED WRITINGS BY GORDEEVA:

(With E.M. Swift) *My Sergei: A Love Story,* Warner, 1996.
A Letter for Daria, Little, Brown, 1998.

Born in Moscow on February 4, 1967, Sergei Grinkov was the son of Anna and Mikhail Grinkov, both officers in the Soviet Interior Ministry police. When he was five years old, his parents saw an advertisement in the paper saying that the Soviet Union was looking for its next group of Olympic champions, and they brought him to the Central Army skating rink for a free lesson. Grinkov was not an immediate sensation; his performance was uneven. However, he loved skating and preferred physical training to academic studies.

When he was fourteen, his coach, Stanislav Zhuk, suggested that he become a pairs skater. Grinkov was matched with the eleven-year-old Ekaterina Gordeeva, and initially told his coach, according to William Plummer in *People,* "I could never lift this girl!"

However, in time the two skaters developed a deep rapport, and won their first world title in 1986. In 1988 they won a gold medal at the Calgary Olympics, and won another gold at the Lillehammer Olympics in 1994. They had been married in 1991 and had a daughter, Daria, and their new maturity gave depth and passion to their performance. Audiences were mesmerized both by their artistic and technical skill and by the obvious passion and romance between the two.

Their partnership ended tragically when Grinkov died suddenly on November 20, 1995, while training for a Stars on Ice show in Lake Placid, New York. Gordeeva took his body back to Russia, and he was buried in Moscow's Vaganskovskoye Cemetery.

FURTHER INFORMATION

Periodicals

Ehrenpreis, Yael. "Death of a Skater." *Science World* (February 23, 1996): 7.

"Ekaterina Gordeeva." *People* (March 15, 1999): 274.

Gordeeva, Ekaterina. "Oh Why Did You Pick Me?" Excerpt from *My Sergei: A Love Story,* in *Newsweek* (December 23, 1996): 58.

Kantrowitz, Barbara. "Beyond the Tears." *People* (March 25, 1996): 78.

Kelleher, Terry. "Dramatic Turns." *People* (November 24, 1997): 17.

Lodge, Sally. "Skating Star Shines Again as Author." *Publishers Weekly* (May 4, 1998): 27.

Lopez, Steve. "Life After the Glory." *Time* (January 26, 1998): 64.

Lynch, Jason, and Susan Horsburgh. "Melting the Ice." *People* (January 13, 2003): 125.

Montville, Leigh. "Love Story." *Sports Illustrated* (December 4, 1995): 34.

"My Sergei: A Love Story." *Chatelaine* (March 1997): 137.

Plummer, William. "Soulmates on Ice." *People* (December 11, 1995): 124.

Powell, Joanna. "Everything Reminds Me of Sergei." *Good Housekeeping* (November 1997): 104.

Starr, Mark. "Solo But Not Alone." *Newsweek* (December 23, 1996): 56.

Swift, E.M. "Gordeeva and Grinkov." *Sports Illustrated* (February 28, 1994): 48.

Swift, E.M. "A Magical Twosome." *Sports Illustrated* (February 29, 1988): 36.

Swift, E.M. "She Was Not Alone." *Sports Illustrated* (December 30, 1996): 74.

"Twice Blessed." *People* (April 30, 2001): 58.

Sketch by Kelly Winters

Tom Gorman
1902-

Australian rugby player

Tom Gorman was an Australian rugby player known for his skill, passion for the game, and unselfish play. With his Kangaroos touring team, he played ten consecutive Test matches with Great Britain and was the first player from Queensland to captain the Kangaroos team. After retiring from rugby, Gorman was named a Rugby League administrator. He was listed on Rugby League Week's top 100 players, and in 2002 was included in an exhibit of memorable Queensland athletes at the State Library of Queensland.

Outstanding Player

Tom Gorman played professional rugby for the Toowoomba team in Queensland, Australia in the 1920s. Holding the center three-quarter position, he was recognized for his teamwork and unselfish play. He formed a partnership with teammate E.S. Brown that was known as "the finest center pair the game has seen."

Since 1908 when the New South Wales (NSW) rugby team first played Queensland, NSW had always won. But Queensland was able to rebound between 1922 and 1928, when Tom Gorman and fellow player Duncan Thompson led a group of outstanding players for the team. During that time, Queensland won seventeen out of twenty-four games against NSW.

In another spectacular series of games, Gorman played for the Australian team in ten successive rugby Test matches against Great Britain from 1924 to 1930. Starting in 1928 and for the last seven of the ten games, Gorman was the first Queenslander to captain the Australian team. The Ashes series that played in 1929-30 pitched Gorman's Kangaroos team against England. The series went into a 4th Test to break a tie, following a draw in the 3rd Test. Although Gorman's team eventually lost 3-0, he was regarded as being one of the best players on the Australian team during the Ashes series.

In 1926, Gorman was signed by Brisbane Brothers club for 400 pounds, becoming the club's first paid player. Gorman has held representative honors in the Past Brothers Rugby League Club, also known as the Brethren

Chronology

1902	Born in Queensland, Australia
1924	Starting this year, plays 10 consecutive Test matches against Great Britain
1926	First paid player on Brisbane Brothers team
1929	First Queenslander to captain the Kangaroos team

Awards and Accomplishments

1996	Named to Rugby League Week's top 100 Rugby League players
2002	Included in State Library of Queensland's 100 Not Out exhibition of memorable Queensland athletes

or Leprechauns. He also held representative honors in the Toowoomba Clydesdales Rugby League Inc.

Still Active

Gorman continued his passion for rugby, becoming active in Rugby League affairs and signing on as administrator following his retirement as a player. He is still active in the Old Boys' organization at the St. Mary's College boys' academy.

Rugby League Week published a list of the top 100 Rugby League players in 1992 and each year thereafter adds new players. Tom Gorman was one of three new players inducted in 1996. The State Library of Queensland in 2002 erected an exhibit called 100 Not Out, celebrating a century of Queensland sporting moments and athletes. Tom Gorman is mentioned in the exhibit.

Tom Gorman, the first Queenslander to captain an Australian rugby team, has been known as a genuine sportsman, as well as a role model for youth. The *Oxford Companion to World Sports & Games* said of Gorman, "His positional sense made him an outstanding defender, and he had inspiring qualities as a leader, especially in tight situations."

FURTHER INFORMATION

Books

Arlott, John, ed. *Oxford Companion to World Sports & Games*. London: Oxford University Press, 1975.

Other

International Sports Hall of Fame. http://www.internationalsports.com/sa_hof/hof_inductees.html (September 27, 2002).

Queensland Rugby League. http://www.queensland.rleague.com/clubs (November 15, 2002).

Rugby League Hall of Fame. http://rl1908.com/Kangaroos/1929.html (November 15, 2002).

St. Mary's College. www.stmarystmba.qld.edu.au/houses_2002.htm (November 15, 2002).

Sketch by Lorraine Savage

Steffi Graf
1969-

German tennis player

When she attained the number one ranking with the Women's International Tennis Association (WITA) in 1987 and effectively moved past tennis superstars **Chris Evert** and **Martina Navratilova**, Steffi Graf never looked back. One of the dominant forces in the game of tennis, Graf possessed a blazing forehand and an unrivaled winning attitude. She dominated women's tennis for over a decade. When she chose to retire in 1999 following a series of injuries that made playing the game more of a burden than an enjoyment, Graf had compiled an incredible record of 902 wins and 115 losses on the professional tour, with an astonishing 107 career singles titles and 22 Grand Slam singles titles (only two shy of the record held by **Margaret Court Smith**). Graf also became one of only five players in the history of the game to win tennis' Grand Slam, which she accomplished in 1988 by winning the four major tournaments—the Australian and French Opens, Wimbledon, and the U.S. Open—all in one calendar year.

Growing Up

Steffi Graf was born Stephanie Maria Graf on June 14, 1969 in Mannheim, West Germany, to Peter and Heidi Graf. Steffi grew up in Brühl, a small West German town, and with parents who were tennis players, it was inevitable that before long Steffi would have a racquet in her hands. Her father was a nationally-ranked player in Germany when Graf was little, operating a tennis facility and gaving lessons when he was not playing. Thus, when his three-year old daughter expressed an interest in the game, Peter did not pay much attention to her. But eventually she wore him down and he sawed off an old racquet and let her play with it, and, according to the 1987 edition of *Contemporary Newsmakers*, Graf had soon "broken all the lamps in the house."

Graf learned to play tennis in the family's basement on a makeshift court concocted from two chairs and some string to serve as a net. When she was five, her father realized his little girl was not going to give up and he began coaching her. "For a long time, I believed that Steffi only wanted to play because she loved me and

Steffi Graf

Awards and Accomplishments

1986	Women's Tennis Association (WTA) Newcomer of the Year
1986	West Germany's Sportswoman of the Year
1987-88	International Tennis Federation's Player of the Year
1987-90, 1993-95	WTA Player of the Year
1989	Associated Press Female Athlete of the Year
1994, 1996-97	Wins ESPY for Outstanding Women's Tennis Performer of the Year
1995-96	*Tennis* magazine's Player of the Year
1998	Voted WTA "Most Interesting Player of the Year"
1999	Receives Prince of Asturias Award (one of most important awards from Spain)
1999	Receives German Television Award
1999	Wins "Athlete of the Century" honors in Germany
1999	Awarded "Female Sports Award of Past Decade" at the ESPYs
1999	Awarded Olympic Medal of Honor
2002	Receives Medal of Honor, decorated by Prime Minister of Federal German State Baden-Wuerhemborg, in Stuttgart, Germany

When Graf retired she had 902 wins, 115 losses, and 107 career singles titles. She amassed 22 Grand Slam singles titles

wanted to be with me," he told *Tennis* magazine. "But the evidence of her talent became very strong… She was always watching the ball until it was not in play anymore."

Peter Graf helped turn his daughter into one of the toughest junior tennis players in Germany. He soon quit his other jobs and devoted his life to coaching her. He had good reason to think he was making a wise choice, because in little more than a year after he had started working with her, Graf had won her first tournament (she was six). By the time she was 13, she had won the German junior championship.

Growing up, Graf was not one to be consumed by leisure activities. Graf's parents withdrew her from the eighth grade in 1982, when she was 13, after she became the second-youngest player in the history of tennis to achieve an international ranking (no. 214 in WITA rankings). She began competing in more tournaments and then, in 1984, traveled to Los Angeles to compete in the Summer Olympics. She walked away from that competition with the gold.

The Young Professional

Graf's first year as a professional was tough. She did not win any tournaments, though she did make it to the semifinals of the U.S. Open, losing to Martina Navratilova. But then in 1986 she won 24 straight matches, quickly moving up to the number three ranking in the world.

But Graf was not satisfied. She wanted a Grand Slam, and therefore began a rigorous training program that included running, weightlifting, jumping rope, and more and more tennis. She made her hard work pay off, and in 1987 won the French open against Navratilova (6-4, 4-6, 8-6). At that time, in French Open history, she was the youngest winner ever, and with her victory moved her ranking up to number two in the world.

Soon she moved up to number one, following her many other victories that year. By the season's end, Graf had lost only two of seventy-two matches, winning an amazing 11 of the 13 tournaments she played in.

The Big Year

Winning all four Grand Slam events in one year (which is also called winning the Grand Slam) is an amazing feat in tennis. The difficulty of winning the Grand Slam is legend. Graf achieved this feat in 1988, becoming only the third woman ever to complete the honor. She started her run with a victory over Evert in the Australian Open (6-1, 7-6), and then beat Natalia Zvereva 6-0, 6-0 in the finals of the French Open. This was the first time that a player had completely shut out an opponent in a Grand Slam final. In fact, Graf lost only 20 games throughout the tournament, and, at its conclusion, actually apologized to the crowd for winning so easily.

The next tournament in Graf's Grand Slam tour was Wimbledon, where she looked to a showdown with Navratilova, who had won the previous eight Wimbledon championships. The grass at Wimbledon was Navratilova's preferred surface, and many people, in spite of Graf's amazing run, were expecting Navratilova to come out on top.

And indeed, it looked that way at first, as Graf lost the first set 7-5. But she persevered and ended up winning 12 of the last 13 games of the match, defeating Navratilova

Chronology

1969	Born June 14 in Mannheim, West Germany, to Peter and Heidi Graf
1972	At age of three gets out father's tennis racquets and wants to learn game
1974	Convinces her father to take her interest in tennis seriously
1975	Wins her first junior tournament (she's six years old)
1979	Trains under Boris Breskvar, German Tennis Federation Coach
1982	Quits school and becomes second youngest player to receive an international ranking
1982	Wins German Junior 18s Championship and European Junior 18s Championship
1982	Turns professional on October 18
1983	Playing in qualifying rounds of French open at age 13, she is mistaken for a ballgirl
1984	Wins Gold at 1984 Summer Olympic Games
1985	Breaks into the top ten of WTA Tour Rankings for the first time
1986	Wins her first title, defeating Chris Evert at the Family Circle Cup
1986	Wins U.S. Clay Court Championship; begins first of three consecutive German Open victories
1987	Wins French Open, her first Grand Slam title event (defeats Martina Navratilova)
1987	On August 17 becomes the #1 player in the world. Holds spot for 186 weeks until October 3, 1991
1988	Completes Grand Slam (only third woman in history to do so)
1988	Wins second Olympic Gold Medal
1989	Plays her first match against Monica Seles in semis of French Open
1989	Wins Wimbledon, Australian Open and U.S. Open
1989	Finishes year with 14 titles and an 86-2 record
1990	Wins Australian Open
1990	Wins first tournament ever played in Leipzig and donates her prize money ($70,000) to aid tennis development in East Germany; in October the Steffi Graf Youth Tennis Center is founded in Leipzig
1991	Wins Wimbledon
1991	Gives up no. 1 ranking to Monica Seles, and, following 1990, a mediocre year, considers quitting tennis
1992	Wins Wimbledon
1993	Wins French Open, Wimbledon and U.S. Open
1993	A "fan" of Graf's stabs Monica Seles at a tournament in Hambourg. The incident greatly upsets Graf
1994	Wins Australian Open
1994	Ranking hits 441.1746, the highest ranking average ever achieved by a player
1995	Wins French Open, Wimbledon and U.S. Open
1995	Wins her 750th match on July 6th at the Wimbledon semi-finals
1996	Wins French Open, Wimbledon and U.S. Open, her 20th and 21st Grand Slam titles
1996	Becomes the player, male or female, to be ranked no. 1 in the world the longest (total of 332 weeks over 6 years)
1997	Suffers injury to the patella tendon in her knee in February; undergoes operation in June
1998	Becomes highest-grossing female athlete ever, surpassing Navratilova
1998	Drops from singles rankings because she had not played the required number of tournaments
1999	Wins French Open
1999	Wins her 900th career match; on August 13 she announces her retirement from Tennis
2001	Marries Andre Agassi on October 22; gives birth to Jaden Gil Agassi a few days later

in the final two sets, 6-2, 6-1. It was almost anti-climactic later that season when she won her fourth Grand Slam victory in the U.S. Open, and then followed that phenomenal feat with a second gold medal only days later at the 1988 Summer Olympics in Seoul, South Korea.

Dominant Throughout the 90s

On the court, Graf compiled Grand Slam title after Grand Slam title. In between the major championships she amassed singles tournament victories as if they were just another stop on her way to becoming one of the greatest tennis players in history. In 1991, however, she fell to number two in the world rankings after an amazing 188 weeks at the top. She lost her ranking to **Monica Seles**, which meant more to her than having the record stopped. She did not like losing, and she was frustrated at having not won a Grand Slam event in over a year and a half.

Graf soon ended her dry spell with a 1991 Wimbledon victory, defeating **Gabriela Sabatini** 6-4, 3-6, 8-6. In 1992, Graf lost to Seles in the finals of the French Open, but regained her composure and defeated Seles handily at Wimbledon (6-2, 6-1).

Seles again defeated Graf in the finals of the 1993 Australian Open, and it appeared that Graf would remain at number two for a while. Then, in a bizarre and tragic occurrence, Seles, seated courtside at a German tennis match, was stabbed in the back. The authorities learned that the perpetrator was one of Graf's fans, and he claimed later that he had done so in order to restore Graf to her number one ranking.

The news of Seles's attack shocked Graf, as well as the tennis world. Graf was the first person to see Seles in the hospital. Seles remained away from tennis for over two years, and—though it was an unfortunate incident that put her back on top—Graf in fact did regain the number one ranking by dominating the last half of 1993, winning the French Open, Wimbledon, and the U.S. Open. But she was distraught over Seles's stabbing. Graf went on in 1994 to win the Australian open, and then—suffering from allergies—lost a major upset to **Mary Pierce** in the semifinals of the French Open.

The Injuries Begin, Slowly

As the 1994 season wound down, Graf found injuries to her back and leg slowing her down, and after defeats in several major tournaments, decided to take some time off, losing her number one ranking to **Arantxa Sanchez Vicario**. But she returned to form in 1995, winning the Lipton Championships, then winning the French Open against Sanchez Vicario 7-5, 4-6, 6-0 (her twenty-fifth win in a row). She took another win over Sanchez Vicario at Wimbledon in1995, in a match that saw a grueling 20-minute, 32-point game, after which Graf finally broke serve and won four quick points.

The Trials of Steffi Graf

Their bond was unbreakable, and as Steffi became a force in tennis, Peter was right beside her—controlling her life and business off the court while she controlled the rhythms on it. He picked and fired her coaches, mapped her schedule, traveled with her.... By the time Steffi, at 17, won her first Grand Slam event, beating Martina Navratilova in the French Open final in 1987, she was well on her way to her first million-dollar year in earnings. Together she and Peter were on an inexorable climb to the tennis summit. A perfectionist driven by her father and by her own relentless will, Steffi would don her stoical mask and use her cannon of a forehand, the most powerful weapon in the women's game, to overwhelm her opponents. As true as that forehand was, the mask was no less a lie. Highly emotional and sensitive, with a temperament more suited to a poet than to a professional athlete, Steffi had a poignant sadness about her. There were days when defeat would plunge her into despair. "She never appreciated a win as much as she was devastated by a loss," says Jim Fuhse, the WTA's publicity director and a longtime friend of Steffi's.

Source: Nack, William. *Sports Illustrated* 21 (November 18, 1996): 74.

Where Is She Now?

When Steffi Graf retired from tennis in 1999, she told *Tennis* magazine that "I feel I have nothing left to accomplish... I'm not having fun anymore. After Wimbledon, for the first time in my career, I didn't feel like going to a tournament." In spite of her private past, Graf has now become more outspoken and is involved with marketing her own line of handbags in her native Germany, as well as represeting a mobile phone company. She also does work with the World Wildlife Foundation.

After spending much of the 1990s in a relationship with race car driver Michael Bartels, Graf eventually found that she had more in common with tennis superstar Andre Agassi, whom she married in 2001. Together they have many homes, but prefer to spend much of their time in Las Vegas. Steffi gave birth to their first son, Jaden Gil Agassi, in October of 2001.

Drama Off Court

For years Graf remained rather reclusive and hard to talk to on the pro tour. Tennis had always been her focus; everything else came second. This caused problems with some critics and fans, who wanted her to be more accessible. As she matured, she became more open to interviews and to her public, but as she grew into a notable figure on the court, the soap opera that surrounded her professional career—in the form of her father, Peter Graf—began to unfold.

Graf had been given the means by which to become a phenomenal tennis player—tennis-loving parents, a father who took her on as a coach and who supported her no matter what—but with these gifts came burdens, and Peter Graf had no doubt caused his daughter many headaches. During her career, Peter Graf was cited many times for illegal coaching, which according to *Contemporary Newsmakers,* ranged from "talking to Steffi in German during the matches" to "using hand signals." In order to avoid getting caught, the elder Graf moved around in the crowd so that the officials could not spot him. At certain times, his actions caused Graf to be assessed penalty points for being coached while on the court, as television replays showed him clearly disobeying the rules.

Peter Graf also brought intense pressure on his daughter when he became, as *Tennis* magazine reporter Cindy Shmerler writes, "a walking tabloid headline." Indeed, in the nineties he was called out because of an extramarital affair with a German model. Then he had trouble dealing with his alcoholism. And then, in what became a major media circus, Peter Graf's income tax evasion, and his failure to pay taxes on millions of his daughter's earnings, brought her private life under intense scrutiny.

By the end of 1995, however, Graf pushed the media hype aside, winning the U.S. Open, and then going on to win Wimbledon the next season for her twentieth Grand Slam title. Injuries to her back and left knee soon forced her to take more unwanted time off. In a span of only a few years, the injuries mounted. She was hampered by knee surgery (causing her to miss much of 1997), and then an ankle injury in 1998 dropped her to number 9 in the world rankings.

In her last year on tour, however, Graf came back with a great victory, perhaps her sweetest, when she defeated **Martina Hingis** in the French Open. Hingis had been claiming that Graf was no longer a viable threat in the Grand Slams.

Overpowering

Graf's dominance might be considered one of her many contributions to tennis. She unseated some of the best players, and then consistently returned to top form throughout her professional career, scaring opponents with her forehand storke. "[It] puts fear in everybody," tennis professional Zina Garrison said of her forehand in *Sports Illustrated.* Tennis commentator Bud Collins even went so far as to dub her "Fraulein Forehand." When she retired following a series of injuries that made playing the game more burden than fun, Graf compiled an incredible record of 902 wins and 115 losses on the professional tour, with astonishing 107 career singles titles and 22 Grand Slam singles titles. She is one of only five players in the history of the game to win tennis' Grand Slam.

CONTACT INFORMATION

Address: c/o Stefanie Graf Marketing, GmbH & Co.KG, Mallaustrasse 75, 68215 Mannheim, Germany; email: contact@stefanie-graf.com.

FURTHER INFORMATION

Books

Collins, Bud and Zander Hollander, eds., *Bud Collins' Modern Encyclopedia of Tennis,* 2nd ed. Detroit: Visible Ink Press, 1994.

Heady, Sue. *Steffi: Public Power, Private Pain.* London: Virgin, 1995.

Hilders, Laura. *Steffi Graf.* New York: Time, 1990.

Steffi Graf

Rutlege, Rachel. *The Best of the Best in Tennis*. Brook-field, CT: Millbrook Press, 1998.
Shwabacher, Martin. "Steffi Graf" in *Superstars of Women's Tennis*. Philadelphia: Chelsea House, 1997.
"Steffi Graf." *Contemporary Newsmakers 1987*. Farm-ington Hills, MI: Gale Research.
"Steffi Graf." *Sports Stars*. Series 1-4. U•X•L, 1994-98.

Periodicals

Atlanta Journal and Constitution (May 6, 1998).
Cook, Kevin and Mark Mravic. "Fire and ice." *Sports Illustrated* (August 23, 1999): 23.
Los Angeles Times (June 9, 1996; July 7, 1996; September 9, 1996; September 29, 1996; November 25, 1996).
Nack, William. "The trials of Steffi Graf." *Sports Illustrated* (November 18, 1996): 74.
New York Times (March 26, 1995; June 11, 1995; July 9, 1995).
Newsday (September 9, 1995; September9, 1996).
Reilly, Rick. "Good comes to those who serve." *Sports Illustrated* (January 7, 2002): 84.
Sports Illustrated (March 16, 1987; June 15, 1987; July 11, 1988; March 27, 1989; June 19, 1989; July 17, 1989; September 18, 1989; February 5, 1990; July 15, 1991; September 16, 1991; June 15, 1992; July 13, 1992; June 14, 1993; July 12, 1993; September 20, 1993; September 18, 1995; June 17, 1996; July 7, 1996; January 20, 1997).

Tennis (October 1984; July 1986; May 4, 1998; May 29, 1998).
Thomsen, Ian. "Lioness in Winter." *Sports Illustrated* (November 30, 1998): 88-90.
Time (July 1, 1996).
USA Today (June 4, 1997; May 4, 1998; May 29, 1998).

Other

Atkinson, Rick. "Steffi's Racket?" *The Washington Post* (online). http://www.geocities.com/steffiarticles/96-01.htm (January 15, 2003).
Shmerler, Cindy. "Profile: Remembering Steffi Graf." tennis.com http://www.tennis.com/Progame/full story.sps?iNewsID=17251&itype=1296&icategory ID (January 15, 2003).
"Steffi Articles." online collection of articles on Steffi Graf. http://www.geocities.com/steffiarticles/, (January 15, 2003).
Steffi Graf official website. http://www.steffi-graf.com/ (January 15, 2003).
Steffi Graf International Supporters Club. http://www.sgisc.com/ (January 15, 2003).

Sketch by Eric Lagergren

Otto Graham
1921-

American football player

Otto Graham was one of the great quarterbacks in National Football League (NFL) history. Possessed of a powerful arm and pinpoint accuracy, Graham almost single-handedly transformed pro football from a running game of the 1940s to the passing game of the 1950s and later. In every one of the ten years Graham played, his team, the Cleveland Browns, reached the championships—first in four seasons in the All America Football Conference (AAFC) and then in six seasons after the Browns joined the NFL. In 1946 he was the first and only athlete to play in the championship game in two pro sports—basketball and football—in the same year. He was elected to the National Professional Football Hall of Fame in 1965.

Early Life

Otto Everett Graham, Jr. was born December 6, 1921 in Waukegan, Illinois (some sources say Evanston, Illinois). One of four brothers, he grew up in a world of sports and music. Both Graham's parents were music teachers and by the time he left high school he could play piano, cornet, violin and French horn. When he was six-

Otto Graham

teen years old, Graham was named the Illinois French horn champion; the Waukegan High School brass sextet he played on as a high school senior also won a national championship. Graham majored in music at Northwestern University but stopped playing altogether when he entered professional sports. After he retired he said that giving up music was his one great regret.

Graham excelled in sports in high school too. As a senior, he was named to the All-State squads in both basketball and football. His prowess on the basketball court won him an athletic scholarship to Northwestern University in Evanston, Illinois. The six-foot, 200-pound Graham proved a versatile athlete at Northwestern. While captain of the school's basketball team, he was the second-highest scorer in the Big Ten conference. He was named the most valuable player on a team of college basketball all-stars that beat the Washington Bears, then the champions of the National Basketball League (NBL). Graham racked up the third-highest batting average in the school's history as a member of the Northwestern baseball team. Graham was given a chance to join the university varsity football team, when coach Lynn "Pappy" Waldorf saw his performance in an intramural football championship. Knee surgery interrupted Graham's college career briefly, but he was back in the line-up to lead Northwestern to two victories over Ohio State, then the national champions. Ohio State's coach **Paul Brown** would remember the young man's talent and poise on the field.

Becomes Pro Athlete

After the outbreak of World War II Graham joined the Navy, marrying Beverly Collinge after his training was completed. Transferred to Chapel Hill, North Carolina, Graham worked briefly with Paul "Bear" Bryant, who later won fame as the coach of the University of Alabama's "Crimson Tide." After the conclusion of the war, Graham began playing pro basketball with the Rochester Royals of the NBL. The team, whose roster included Red Holtzman, Chuck Connors, and Del Rice, went on to win the NBL championship in 1946.

Although Graham had been drafted in the first round by the NFL's Detroit Lions, he accepted a $7,500 contract and a $1,000 bonus to play with the Cleveland Browns, a team being organizing for the upstart All America Football Conference (AAFC) by Brown—whose powerful Ohio State team Graham had helped defeat as a college player. Graham later told Fred Goodall of the Associated Press "I wasn't that smart, but I made the best move of my life to go there and work with Paul. I didn't always love him, but he ran the show and taught us the basics of everything." Brown thought just as highly of Graham. "Otto was my greatest player," Brown is quoted in *Encyclopedia of World Biography Supplement.* "He had the finest peripheral vision I had ever seen, and that is a big factor in a quarterback. He was a tremendous playmaker. He had unusual eye-and-hand coordination, and he was bigger and faster than you thought."

"Automatic Otto"'s powerful and accurate arm, his coolness under pressure and his ability to execute Paul Brown's playbook transformed pro football from a running game to the passing game of the contemporary sport. "I could throw hard if I had to, I could lay it up soft, I could drill the sideline pass. God-given ability. The rest was practice, practice, practice," Graham told Paul Zimmerman of *Sports Illustrated* in 1998. "I had the luxury of having the same receivers for almost my entire career. We developed the timed sideline attack, the comeback route where the receiver goes to the sideline, stops and comes back to the ball, with everything thrown on rhythm." Graham became one of the leading passers of the late 1940s and early 1950s. He led the NFL in passing twice, and in 1952 passed for 401 yards in a single victory against Pittsburgh, completing twenty-one of forty-nine.

Paul Brown's System

Graham ushered in another revolutionary change. Paul Brown inaugurated a system in which the coach decided all plays from the sidelines and used substitutes as messengers to shuttle plays into the huddle before each scrimmage. More ego-driven quarterbacks would have rebelled. Graham was reportedly unhappy with the system, but he never challenged Paul Brown's leadership. Graham sometimes changed Brown's plays, but he recognized Brown's right to determine a game plan. "He was the admiral, the general, the CEO," Graham said of

Chronology

1921	Born December 6 in Waukegan, Illinois (some sources say Evanston, IL)
1938	Named high school conference scoring champion
1939	Selected for All-State basketball, and All-State football squads
1941	Enters Northwestern University on basketball scholarship, invited by Northwestern football coach Lynn "Pappy" Waldorf to try out for varsity team
1942	Throws for 1,092 yards
1943	Finishes third in Heisman Trophy balloting
1943	Drafted in first round by NFL's Detroit Lions
1945	Marries Beverly Collinge; enters Navy
1945	Joins Rochester Royals of National Basketball League
1946	Appears with Rochester Royals in NBL title game and with Cleveland Browns in NFL title game
1946	Joins Cleveland Browns of All America Football Conference
1946-49	Cleveland Browns AAFC champions
1946-55	Leads Browns to ten league finals
1949	Cleveland joins National Football League (NFL)
1950, 1954-55	Cleveland Browns NFL Champions
1955	Becomes highest paid player in pro football
1955	Elected to College Football Hall of Fame
1958, 1963	Coast Guard team beats NFL champion teams
1958-65	Coaches College All-Stars team in games against NFL champs
1959-66, 1969-85	Head coach at United States Coast Guard Academy
1965	Inducted into Pro Football Hall of Fame
1966-68	Head coach and general manager of Washington Redskins
1968	Coaches East team in NFL Pro Bowl
1977	Diagnosed with colorectal cancer, becomes national spokesperson for National Cancer Society

Awards and Accomplishments

1943	Third in Heisman Trophy voting
1943	College Basketball All-Star Most Valuable Player; Big Ten football and basketball Most Valuable Player
1946-49	AAFC All-League Quarterback
1947-49	Most Valuable Player, All American Football Conference
1950, 1954-55	Most Valuable Player, National Football League
1951, 1953-55	NFL All-Pro
1952	NFL Leader, Touchdown Passes
1952, 1953	NFL Leader, Total Yardage
1953, 1955	NFL Player of the Year
1953-55	NFL Leader, Pass Completion
1955	Hickok Belt
1955	College Football Hall of Fame
1965	Pro Football Hall of Fame
1994	Elected to NFL 75th Anniversary Team
1996	Lifetime Achievement Award, Northwestern University
1999	100 Top Athletes of the Millennium, ESPN
1999	Six All-Time Top Football Players, *Sports Illustrated*
1999	#6 Top Football Player of All-Time, *Sport Magazine*
1999	#5 Top Football Player of All-Time, NFL Films

Brown in *Sports Illustrated*. The sideline pass and draw play were among the many innovations introduced by Graham and the Browns.

Whatever Graham's reservations, the proof was in the pudding—Paul Brown's system worked. With it, Graham and the Browns compiled one of the most remarkable string of winning seasons in professional sports history. Beginning in 1946, the same year the Royals were pro basketball champions, Graham led the Browns to ten championship games—every year of Graham's career. During the AAFC's brief four-year history, the Browns dominated the league with a remarkable record of 52 wins, four losses and three ties, and won the league championship every year. Graham led the league with seventeen touchdown passes in 1946 and twenty-five in 1947; he had a league-leading passing percentage of 60.6 in 1947, and led the AAFC in total yardage in 1947, 1948 and 1949. In 1948 Graham led the Browns to a 15-0 season, finishing up with four road games. Those wins were part of an unbroken string of twenty-nine wins that stretched over three seasons. Graham was named the AAFC Most Valuable Player (MVP) in 1947, 1948, and 1949.

Plays In the NFL

In 1950 the AAFC folded and the Browns, along with the Baltimore Colts and the San Francisco 49ers, joined the National Football League. Intent on putting the upstart AAFC champs in their place, the NFL scheduled the Browns to play their first game against the two-time world champion Philadelphia Eagles. Graham's first pass of the game went for a touchdown. By the time the clock had run out, the Browns had handed the Eagles a 35-10 upset defeat. Graham later called that game the highlight of his entire career. When the 1950 season ended, the upstart Browns were NFL champions, having defeated the Los Angeles Rams 30-28. That same season Graham was named the NFL MVP.

Cleveland unfortunately lost the NFL championship games the three subsequent years, 1951 through 1953. Although he was named the NFL's MVP in 1953, Graham held himself personally responsible for the championship defeats. "Emotionally, I was so far down in the dumps those three years," he told Larry Schwartz of ESPN.com. "I was the quarterback. I was the leader. It was all my fault." After losing the 1953 title game 17-16 to the Detroit Lions, he led the Browns to a crushing victory over Detroit the following year, winning the championship game 56-10. Wanting to leave the game at the top of his form, Graham planned to retire after the 1954 season. The Browns lured him back for one last year with a $25,000 contract in 1955, making him the highest paid player in the game. Far from resting on his laurels in 1955, Graham turned in one of his finest years on the gridiron. He completed 98 of 185 passes for a total of 1,721 total yards and fifteen touchdowns. Cleveland led the NFL with a 9-2-1 record and beat the Rams for the championship. Graham won his second NFL MVP in 1955 too, capping off a fine season and an extraordinary career in pro football. He retired at the close of the 1955 season at the age of thirty-three.

Where Is He Now?

In 2002 Otto Graham lived with Beverly, his wife of fifty-six years, on a golf course in Sarasota, Florida. Forced by arthritis to give up golf and recently diagnosed in the early stages of Alzheimer's disease, Graham nonetheless continues to speak his mind about pro football to sports reporters. He and his wife have three children, two foster daughters, sixteen grandchildren, and two great grandchildren.

Career Statistics

Season	Team	ATT	COM	YDS	COM%	TD	INT
1946	CLE	174	95	1834	.546	17	5
1947	CLE	269	163	2553	.606	25	11
1948	CLE	333	173	2713	.520	25	15
1949	CLE	285	161	2785	.560	19	10
1950	CLE	253	137	1943	.542	14	20
1951	CLE	253	147	2205	.555	17	16
1952	CLE	364	181	2816	.497	20	24
1953	CLE	258	167	2722	.647	11	9
1954	CLE	240	142	2092	.592	11	17
1955	CLE	185	98	1721	.529	15	8
TOTAL		2626	1464	23584	.560	174	135

CLE: Cleveland Browns.

With the Browns, Graham passed for a total 23,584 yards and 174 touchdowns. One of his most remarkable achievements is that in his ten years with the team, Graham did not miss a single game. Injury rarely saw him leave games. In one 1954 contest, he was elbowed so hard it opened a cut that required thirteen stitches, administered on the sidelines. During halftime, a Graham's helmet was rigged with a clear plastic bar to protect his face. "That's my real claim to fame right there," Graham told the Associated Press's Fred Goodall. "I was the first guy who ever wore a face mask—college, high school or pro." The injury didn't interfere with Graham's performance. He came back and played one of the best second halves of his career, hitting around ten of twelve passes.

Coaches College Football

Despite his retirement from pro football, Graham remained active in the college game. From 1958 until 1965 he coached the College All-Stars in their annual game against the NFL champion team. His teams won in 1958 and 1963. In 1959, on the recommendation of **George Steinbrenner**—who later became the controversial owner of the New York Yankees baseball franchise— Graham became Athletic Director and football coach at the United States Coast Guard Academy in New London, Connecticut. Except for the years 1966-68, Graham remained with the Academy until 1985. The high point of his years as a college coach came in 1963 when he led the Academy to a season without a defeat and an appearance in the Tangerine Bowl.

Graham was not nearly as successful as a pro football coach. In 1966—a year after he was inducted into the Pro Football Hall of Fame—he was hired as head coach and general manager of the Washington Redskins. After three seasons and a 17-22-3 record with Washington, Graham was replaced, but he took it goodheartedly. "My best claim to fame—and nobody else in the world can say this—is it took **Vince Lombardi** to replace me as coach of the Washington Redskins," he told Jason Butler of the *Austin American-Statesman.*

Graham was diagnosed with colorectal cancer in 1977 and underwent a colostomy. As a result he became an outspoken advocate of early cancer check-ups. He was later named honorary national chairman of the National Cancer Society.

By the end of the century, although Graham had been out of football for nearly fifty years, his football achievements lived on in memory. In 1994 he was named to the NFL's 75th Anniversary Team. Five years later in 1999, ESPN recognized him as one of the 100 Top Athletes of the Millennium. The same year he was number six on *Sports Illustrated*'s All-Time Top Ten Football Players list. And pro football is still a passing game.

CONTACT INFORMATION

Email: duey@gwi.net. Online: www.ottograham.net.

FURTHER INFORMATION

Books

"Otto Graham." *Encyclopedia of World Biography Supplement,* Volume 21. Detroit: Gale Group, 2001.

Periodicals

Affleck, John. "Older Browns Remember '50." *Commercial Appeal* (Memphis, TN) (August 8, 1999): D8.

Butler, Jason. "Maestro of the Browns; Multitalented Otto Graham, 77, has one regret." *Austin American-Statesman* (July 21, 1999): C7.

Daly, Dan. "'48 Browns: Perfectly fine." *Washington Times* (November 22, 1991): D1.

Elliott, Helene. "He Otto Be Happy." *Los Angeles Times* (December 22, 1995): C1.

Goodall, Fred. "Graham: It's impossible to say who's best QB ever." *Associated Press Sports News* (October 19, 2002).

Oates, Bob. "He's Calling New Signals—This Time Against Particularly Threatening Foe." *Los Angeles Times* (April 10, 1985): C1.

Zimmerman, Paul. "Revolutionaries." *Sports Illustrated* (August 17, 1998): 78.

Other

"'Otto' Biography." http://www.ottograham.net (January 4, 2003).

Schwartz, Larry. "'Automatic Otto' Defined Versatility."
http://espn.go.com/classic/biography/s/graham_otto.
html (January 4, 2003).

Sketch by Gerald E. Brennan

Cammi Granato
1971-

American hockey player

Cammi Granato

Cammi Granato was one of the best young women hockey players ever produced in the United States, and one of the most recognized. She was captain of Team USA's hockey team which won Olympic Gold in 1998. Playing center, Granato used her head on the ice and had great scoring ability.

Granato was born on March 24, 1971, in Maywood, Illinois, to Don and Natalie Granato. Her father was a beer distributor who played amateur hockey. Granato had four brothers and one sister. One brother, Tony, played on several teams in the National Hockey League, and went on to coach the Colorado Avalanche. Another brother, Don, played in the minor leagues. As a child, the second youngest of six, all four of her brothers played hockey. While her parents tried to get her interested in figure skating, she wanted to play hockey. Her brothers tried to make her play goal, but she was determined to become a skater.

Granato began playing hockey when she was five, but her parents did not become supportive until they saw how serious she was. Granato played club hockey from ages five to sixteen on a boys' team, the Downers Grove Huskies. Granato encountered some problems with other teams targeting her for injury and parents not wanting their sons to play against her, especially as she got older. She was once deliberately concussed by a player in a game, and suffered a shoulder injury another time. By the time, she reached her full height, she was only 5'7" and 141 lbs. Granato stopped playing for the team during her junior and senior years in high school because of social pressures and fear of injury as the boys became bigger than her.

While hockey was her favorite sport, Granato also played many others. She played on a boys' baseball team, and at the high school level she had success on the girls' basketball and soccer teams. Granato was also a gifted handball player, who received the national recognition, but hockey was her focus.

Played College Hockey

In 1989, Granato entered Providence College on a hockey scholarship, one of the few schools in the country with an elite women's hockey program. It was the first time she had played against other girls. Granato immediately succeeded. A four-year starter, she was also co-captain. She was freshman player of the year, and later was named Women's Hockey Player of the Year in the Eastern College Athletic Conference.

Granato's team won league titles in 1992 and 1993. Her coach, John Marchetti, told Harry Blauvelt and Carl M. Blumberg of *USA Today,* "She can score from anywhere. She's not exceptionally quick, but she's very powerful and her shot is extremely accurate." In ninety-three college games with Providence, she scored 135 and 110 assists. Granato graduated from Providence in 1993 with a degree in social sciences.

While still in college, Granato also had her eye on international play. She was one of the founding members of the U.S. Women's National Hockey Team, which finished second to the Canadians in its inaugural tournament in 1990. Granato also played on the team in 1992, 1994-97, and at other times. At the world championships in 1992, 1994 and 1997, the women won silver.

Though the women's national team provided one outlet for Granato's hockey career, they had a limited schedule and not enough time to work on skills. So, in fall 1993, Granato began working as an assistant coach for a Junior A team, the Wisconsin Capitols (United States Hockey League). It was the first time she coached.

Still wanting to play, but with no remaining NCAA eligibility, Granato decided to move to Canada to continue her education in January 1994. She attended graduate school at Concordia University in Montreal and played on their women's hockey team. The team was already powerful, but became more so with the addition of Granato. Concordia went on to win three Quebec Intercollegiate Women's Hockey League championships during her tenure. In 123 games with Concordia, she had 178 goals and 148 assists. Granato earned her master's degree in sports administration.

Played in Olympics

In 1998, Granato got to live a dream when the first women's hockey tournament was included in the Winter Olympics. Her brother Tony had played for the men's team in 1988. Granato served as captain of her team, and scored the first ever goal in a 5-0 victory over China. She went on to lead the women to a gold medal victory over Canada. When she won, Granato told Thom Loverro of the *Washington Times,* "For so many years, people told me that you weren't supposed to be on the ice. Whey are you doing this? You're not going to go anywhere with this. And now I have this gold medal around my neck, and it feels pretty good."

The success of the American women led to much exposure for all the players including Granato. She was offered a tryout with the New York Islanders. She turned it down because she did not need the attention, and did not think she had the muscle mass to compete with men. Instead, Granato tried to get other girls and women interested in the sport by conducting clinics. Granato also got endorsement deals from Nike, CBS SportsLine, and AT&T, among others.

After the 1998 Olympics, Granato tried another hockey related career when she became a radio broadcaster for the Los Angeles Kings, the second such woman in league history. This position allowed her time to continue to train for the U.S. women's team, though she only did it only for one season. In 1999, Granato devoted herself to hockey full time by playing for USA's select program for several years.

In 2002, Granato was again a member of the U.S. women's Olympic hockey team. Again named captain, Team USA won the silver medal by losing to Canada, 3-2. After the Olympics, she planned on playing for the Vancouver Griffins of the National Women's Hockey League in 2002-03, and hoped to play in the 2006 Winter games.

In describing what makes Granato a great hockey player, her 1998 Olympic coach, Ben Smith, told Thom Loverro of the *Washington Times,* "Cammi … is a player whose total is better than the sum of their parts. She is not the strongest skater or shooter, but in tight circumstances, she comes through. Her teammates look up to her as a leader."

CONTACT INFORMATION

Address: c/o USA Hockey, Inc., 1715 Bob Johnson Rd., Colorado Springs, CO 80906.

FURTHER INFORMATION

Books

Athletes and Coaches of Winter. New York: Macmillan Reference USA, 2000.

Periodicals

Associated Press (October 28, 1990).

Blauvelt, Harry, and Carl M. Blumberg. "Providence star got her start against antagonistic brothers." *USA Today* (January 8, 1993): 10C.

Career Statistics

Yr	Event	GP	G	A	Pts
1990	World Championships	5	9	5	14
1992	World Championships	5	8	2	10
1994	World Championships	5	5	7	12
1995	Pacific Women's Championships	5	4	7	11
1996	Three Nations Cup	5	5	1	6
1996	Pacific Women's Championships	5	6	3	9
1997	World Championships	5	5	3	8
1997	Three Nations Cup	4	2	2	4
1998	Pre-Olympic Tour	29	14	17	31
1998	Olympics	6	4	4	8
1998	Thee Nations Cup	4	0	2	2
1999	World Championships	5	3	5	8
2000	Select Team	20	17	25	42
2000	World Championships	5	6	1	7
2001	National Team	38	36	32	68
2001	World Championships	5	7	6	13
TOTAL		147	129	120	249

Dater, Adrian. "Granato finds voice doing radio work." *Denver Post* (January 3, 1999): C8.

Delany, Maureen. "Check out the 'other' Granato." *Press-Enterprise* (February 5, 1998): C1.

Dupont, Kevin Paul. "Back to the Future for the Golden Girls." *Boston Globe* (February 12, 2002): D13.

Hickling, Dan. "Granato's star continues to shine." *Providence Journal-Bulletin* (February 4, 1996): 17C.

Huebner, Barbara. "Granato front and center." *Boston Globe* (February 7, 1998): G7.

Huebner, Barbara. "Granato still game." *Boston Globe* (December 9, 1998): F1.

La Canfora, Jason. "Clash of the Titans Is All Set." *Washington Post* (February 20, 2002): D9.

Loverro, Thom. "Skating boundaries." *Washington Times* (February 2, 1998): B7.

Lucas, Mike. "She's Accepted, She's a Granato." *Capital Times* (September 21, 1993): 1B.

Loverro, Thom. "Cammi's old dream comes true." *Washington Times* (February 18, 1998): B1.

Michaelis, Vicki. "Granato still giving it her best shot at 30." *USA Today* (February 7, 2002): 5C.

Olson, Lisa. "One Historic Triumph for Cammi, U.S." *Daily News* (February 9, 1998): 49.

Phillips, Randy. "Granato gears up for Games." *The Gazette* (January 24, 1997): F4.

Phillips, Randy. "Granato leads Stingers to Quebec title in swan song." *Gazette* (March 3, 1997): C6.

Phillips, Randy. "That Granato." *Gazette* (February 10, 1994): C3.

Raboin, Sharon. "Granato has everything in check." *USA Today* (January 26, 1998): 19C.

Raboin, Sharon. "Worlds veteran Granato now scores by leading." *USA Today* (April 7, 200): 11C.

Robbins, Liz. "Aggressive Canadians Win Gold Over U.S." *New York Times* (February 22, 2002): D1.

Rubin, Roger. "For Cammi Granato, Hockey's Her Life." *Daily News* (April 10, 1997): 106.

Schuyler, Ed. "Cammi Granato." Associated Press (February 25, 1998).

Tuchinsky, Evan. "Cammi Granato blazes trail at Kings' microphone." *Press-Enterprise* (October 9, 1998): C7.

Woodley, Kevin. "Olympic loss keeps vet Granato on ice." *USA Today* (July 1, 2002): 3C.

Woodward, Steve. "Granato wouldn't be cowed into quitting." *USA Today* (July 30, 1993): 10C.

Other

Colorado Avalanche Web Site. http://www.colorado avalanche.com/team/granato.html (December 16, 2002).

Sketch by A. Petruso

Harold "Red" Grange
1903-1991

American football player

Harold "Red" Grange's legacy has truly stood the test of time. More than three quarters of a century after his famous four touchdowns in twelve minutes against the University of Michigan in 1925, he is remembered as one of the greatest college football players in the history of the sport. He is remembered equally for his contributions to professional football, not just for his skills on the field, but for his single-handed ability to bring previously unparalleled popularity and respect to the game. After Grange signed on with the Chicago Bears one day after his last college game, crowds at National Football League (NFL) games swelled. Grange became one of the first professional athletes to enter into endorsement deals and even starred in motion pictures, setting the stage for the cult of personality that surrounds sports stars today. For his contributions to the game, Grange was named as a charter member to both the college and professional football halls of fame.

All-Around Athlete

Grange spent his youth in Wheaton, Illinois, just outside Chicago. His mother died when he was five, and he was raised by his father, Lyle, a foreman for a lumber company who later switched professions and eventually became Wheaton's chief of police. Grange demonstrated a natural athletic ability, and at Wheaton High School he earned 16 varsity letters, in football, baseball, basketball and track. In addition to making his mark on the gridiron—he scored seventy-five touchdowns and 532

Harold "Red" Grange

points during his high-school career—he was a four-time sprint champion.

Grange built up strength and endurance during his summer job working for an icehouse, where he delivered blocks of ice door-to-door for $37.50 a week. Despite other job offers, Grange returned to this job even during his college years. Photographs of Grange at work published nationally earned him the nickname "The Wheaton Iceman."

Coaxed to the Gridiron

When Grange entered the University of Illinois in 1922, he considered participating in basketball and track, rather than football. When, on the first day of practice for the freshman team, he saw that more than 200 young men were competing for spots, he became even more reluctant to try out. His fraternity brothers convinced him to stick with the game, however, and he made the seventh team. His teammates caught a glimpse of the talent entered into their midst when Grange scored two touchdowns during a scrimmage with the varsity team, one of them a sixty-yard punt return.

By the following year Grange had made such an impression that he started at halfback for the varsity squad. He kicked off the opening game against Nebraska on October 6, 1923, by returning a punt for a touchdown from the Illinois 34-yard-line and went on to score three touchdowns and gain 208 yards in thirty-nine minutes of play. Even in this pre-television age, Grange gained national attention for his performance and went on to lead the Western Conference (now the Big Ten) in scoring and was named an All-American. His auburn hair earned him the nickname "Red."

Fateful Michigan Game

On October 18, 1924, Illinois faced the powerhouse University of Michigan Wolverines in a game that followed a dedication ceremony for Illinois' new Memorial Stadium. The Wolverines had not suffered a defeat in two years. Michigan athletic director and former coach Fielding Yost assured the press before the game that his team could handle Grange. "Mr. Grange will be carefully watched every time he takes the ball," Yost stated. "There will be eleven clean, hard Michigan tacklers headed for him."

Whether headed for Grange or not, the Michigan tacklers could not catch him. Grange scored four touchdowns—a 95-yard kickoff return and runs of sixty-seven, fifty-six and forty-five yards from scrimmage—all within the first twelve minutes of the game. Exhausted, he then sat out until the third quarter, during which he scored on a twelve-yard run. Grange followed his five touchdowns with a 23-yard touchdown pass. Illinois beat the Wolverines 39-14 and Grange's name was entered into the annals of football history where it remains to this day. The game also earned him the nickname "The Galloping Ghost of the Gridiron," bestowed upon him by sportswriter Grantland Rice.

A subsequent game against the University of Chicago, a team considered one of the nation's best, had the

Awards and Accomplishments

1923-25	All-American Team
1924	First *Chicago Tribune* Silver Football Award for Big Ten MVP
1925	Number 77 Illinois jersey retired
1931-32	All-Pro Team
1951	Charter member, College Football Hall of Fame
1963	Charter member, Professional Football Hall of Fame

Related Biography: Sports Agent Charles C. Pyle

While Red Grange's announcement that he would turn pro surprised many in the sports world, the move was actually some time in the making. The man behind Grange's deal with the fledgling National Football League's Chicago Bears was Charles C. "Cash and Carry" Pyle, a Champaign, Illinois theater owner and promoter. While Grange did not break any collegiate rules, Pyle began negotiating with the Chicago Bears while Grange continued to make headlines at the University of Illinois. By the day of his fateful announcement, the deal was ready to be inked.

Grange's entry into the NFL moved Pyle into the big time, too. Pyle was instrumental in scheduling the Bears' numerous exhibition games and, as Grange's agent, he secured his client several endorsement deals and even two movie roles. After Grange's debut season in the NFL, Pyle and his client defected, forming their own, short-lived American Football League.

While working with Grange, Pyle also brought other unsigned athletes into the professional ranks, including tennis star Suzanne Lenglen. Pyle also launched a 3,485-mile race across the United States which came to be called the Bunion Derby. Peopled by both professionals such as English hundred-miler Arthur Newton and Estonian marathoner Juri Lossman, and eccentrics like a Hindu philosopher who chanted as he jogged and an Italian runner who raced singing arias, the 1928 event ended up a virtual bust, despite Grange's promotional assistance. The second, and last, race in 1929, left Pyle temporarily bankrupt.

When Grange's contract with Pyle expired in 1928 the football star elected not to renew. The split appeared to be amicable, with Grange later remarking that Pyle was "the greatest sports impressario the world has ever known." Grange went on to promote Chicago's Century of Progress Fair and start a radio transcription company. Pyle died in Los Angeles in 1939 at the age of 56. His exploits were documented in a play, *C.C. Pyle and the Bunion Derby*, written by Tony Award-winner Michael Cristofer and directed by Paul Newman.

University of Illinois Illini down 21-0. Grange brought the team from behind by scoring three touchdowns in the game, which ended in a tie. He played for the entire sixty minutes, rushing for 300 yards and passing for 177. Grange was then injured during a game against Minnesota, which Illinois lost. He missed the season's final game, a victory over Ohio State, but was again named an All-American.

As his accomplishments on the field mounted, Grange rose to national stardom. Many factors contributed to his extreme popularity, including an increased interest in athletics developed during World War I, when members of the military often engaged in league sports themselves; a growing interest in leisure-time activities and the growth of the middle class, with their disposable incomes, following the war; and the increased use of newspaper wire services, which enabled local events to be publicized nationally.

Goes Out in Style

Recovered from his injury, Grange was named captain of the Illini for his senior year in 1925. The team got off to a shaky start, losing three of its first four games. Coach Bob Zuppke moved Grange to quarterback and the Illini won their final four games of the season. Grange's most talked-about performance occurred against the unbeaten University of Pennsylvania, regarded by many as "the champions of the East." In fifty-seven minutes of play, Grange scored three touchdowns and set up a fourth, rushed for 363 yards and passed for thirteen, all in ankle-deep mud, as Illinois beat Pennsylvania 24-2. Grange then led Illinois to a 14-9 victory over Ohio State in the last game of the season. He finished his twenty-game career at Illinois with thirty-one touchdowns, sixteen of those from at least twenty yards and nine from more than fifty. He ran 388 times in all, for 2,071 yards, caught fourteen passes for 253 yards and completed forty of eighty-two passes for 575 yards.

The Pennsylvania game, especially, sealed Grange's star status, as many influential East Coast sportswriters took notice of his unparalleled performance. Sports writer Damon Runyon wrote of him, "This man Red Grange of Illinois is three or four men rolled into one for football purposes. He is **Jack Dempsey**, **Babe Ruth**, Al Jolson, Paavo Nurmi and **Man o' War**. Put together, they

spell Grange." On October 5, 1925, the three-time All-American (he received the honor again for his senior season) was featured on the cover of *Time*.

Turns Heads by Turning Pro

Grange shocked many supporters and fans, including Zuppke, when, following the conclusion of the Ohio State game, he announced he would be leaving the University of Illinois and turning pro. The next day he signed a contract with the National Football League's Chicago Bears. While such announcements are commonplace in sports today, in Grange's day they were anything but and his decision generated widespread controversy. The following year, in response to the negative publicity accompanying Grange's move, NFL officials passed a rule prohibiting the signing of a college player until after he had graduated. "In 1925 Grange's decision touched off a national debate," wrote Benjamin Rader in *American Sports*. "By abandoning his studies for a blatantly commercial career, he openly flaunted the myth of the college athlete as a gentleman-amateur who played merely for the fun of the game and the glory of his school." Grange himself put it more succinctly. "I'd have been more popular with the colleges if I had joined Capone's mob in Chicago rather than the Bears," he said.

Grange was one of the first professional athletes playing a team sport to have an agent. Charles C. "Cash

Harold "Red" Grange

and Carry" Pyle, a Champaign, Illinois, theater owner and promoter, negotiated Grange's deal with the Bears, which landed him $100,000 and a percentage of the revenue from the gate.

Whirlwind Schedule

Capitalizing on Grange's popularity, the Bears, with the assistance of Pyle, quickly devised a whirlwind hybrid schedule of exhibition and regular season games, during which they played nineteen games in sixty-seven days. The first ten games took place over just eighteen days in the East and Midwest. After a two week break, they played nine more games in the South and on the West Coast.

Fans proved Pyle and the Bears management good businessmen. While only 7,500 attended the last Bears game before the team acquired Grange, a standing-room-only crowd of 36,000 showed up at Cubs Park (now Wrigley Field) on Thanksgiving Day 1925 to see the Galloping Ghost debut against the Chicago Cardinals. The game itself was nothing to write home about; it ended in a 0-0 tie.

Still, Grange continued to draw record crowds. More than 65,000 came out to see him in both New York and Los Angeles. Pyle used his client's overwhelming popularity to score him several lucrative endorsement deals. In the off-season, Pyle committed Grange to numerous

exhibition games and landed him two movie roles as well, in *One Minute to Play* and *The Racing Romeo*. (Grange later went on to star in his own movie serial, *The Galloping Ghost*.)

With an extra $125,000 in endorsements and acting fees on top of his money from the Bears, Grange returned to Wheaton a bona fide celebrity, with all the trappings. By this time, he was driving a $5,500 Lincoln and wearing a $500 raccoon coat. But Grange did not only bring material wealth home with him to Wheaton. He also arrived with numerous bruises and the exhaustion that accompanies such a rigorous schedule.

A League of Their Own

When Bears owner and coach **George Halas** rejected a bid by Grange and Pyle to buy into his team, the pair formed their own league. Grange played for the New York Yankees but found he could not carry a league on his own. The American Football League folded after one year, and Grange and his Yankees joined the NFL.

The following year, Grange seriously injured his right knee in the third game of the season when he collided with former Bears teammate George Trafton while reaching for a pass. Since Trafton was known for rough play, some speculated he may have intended to injure Grange. Grange attempted to quell such rumors before they started, however, stating in the locker room that the

Career Statistics

Yr	Team	GP	Passing					Receiving			Rushing		
			Att	Com	Yds	TD	Int	Rec	Yds	TD	Att	Yds	TD
1925	CHI	5	13	4	92	1	2	4	54	0	55	203	2
1927	NYY	13	21	11	206	0	4	5	77	0	29	127	1
1929	CHI	14	9	4	64	2	2	8	119	0	130	552	2
1930	CHI	14	16	8	164	3	1	7	101	2	77	470	6
1931	CHI	13	17	9	158	1	3	7	106	2	111	599	5
1932	CHI	12	13	5	96	0	0	11	168	4	57	136	3
1933	CHI	13	33	13	169	2	3	3	74	0	81	277	1
1934	CHI	12	25	6	81	1	7	2	46	2	32	156	1
TOTAL		96	147	60	1030	10	22	47	745	10	572	2520	21

CHI: Chicago Bears; NYY: New York Yankees.

game "was one of the cleanest football games I ever played in." The injury kept him out of the lineup for the rest of the 1927 season, save for an ill-fated comeback attempt, and all of the 1928 season as well.

Glory Days Come to an End

In 1929 Grange returned to the Bears, but he was no longer in his prime. His injured knee hampered his running and cutting ability so severely that he considered retirement, but Halas convinced him to carry on. Grange's own financial concerns—he lost a significant amount of money when he invested in the AFL—may have motivated him as well. Grange supplemented his income with numerous public appearances and performances on the vaudeville circuit.

Grange stayed with the Bears for another five seasons, although he was eventually moved to the defensive line. He served the team well as a defensive back, however. In the first-ever NFL championship game, he made a touchdown-saving tackle late in the fourth quarter, securing the Bears' 23-21 victory over the New York Giants. Later, Grange was reduced to a utility player.

Active Retirement

After he retired from play in 1935, Grange stayed on with the Bears as an assistant coach and he also became a successful sports commentator. Again, he served as a pioneer in a relatively new venture. In the 1930s, most sports fans relied on the daily newspapers for their pre- and post-game coverage. Grange apparently won some converts. In 1937, his show's sponsors received forty-two million requests for the 'Red Grange Score Sheet,' which accompanied the show. Grange also became one of the first television sports announcers, launching that career in 1947.

While Grange received bags full of fan mail from female admirers throughout his career and had been linked to a number of Hollywood stars, his romantic life was largely subject to speculation until 1941 when he married Margaret Hazelberg in Crown Point, Indiana. The pair met on a flight to Omaha, where Margaret was working as a stewardess. The following year, Grange opened his own insurance practice, which he maintained until he and Margaret retired to Lake Wales, Florida. Grange died of complications from Parkinson's Disease in Lake Wales on January 28, 1991 at the age of 87.

Continues to be Recognized

Grange is still widely recognized for his contributions to both college and professional football, continually showing up on "greatest athletes" lists. In 1951 he was named a charter member of the College Football Hall of Fame and in 1963 he received the same honor for the Professional Football Hall of Fame. *College Football News* named him the best player of all time, and in its century-end retrospective, ESPN named him the 28th best athlete of the 20th century.

For all his accomplishments—the astounding college career, the legendary Michigan game, the popularity and respect he brought to professional football—Grange remained profoundly modest. "If you have the football and 11 guys are after you, if you're smart, you'll run," he once remarked. "They built my accomplishment way out of proportion," he also said. "I never got the idea that I was a tremendous big shot. I could carry a football well, but there are a lot of doctors and teachers and engineers who could do their thing better than I."

Grange's old coach, Bob Zuppke, who made no secret of his opposition to Grange's decision to turn pro, begged to differ, however. "They can argue all they like about the greatest football player who ever lived," he remarked after Grange left Illinois. "But I was satisfied I had him when I had Red Grange."

SELECTED WRITINGS BY GRANGE:

(As told to Ira Morton) *The Red Grange Story: An Autobiography,* University of Illinois Press, 1993.

FURTHER INFORMATION

Books

Carroll, John M. *Red Grange and the Rise of Modern Football*. Urbana: University of Illinois Press, 1999.
"Harold 'Red' Grange." *American Decades CD-ROM*, Detroit: Gale Group, 1998.

Other

Schwartz, Larry. "Galloping Ghost Scared Opponents." http://espn.go.com/sportscentury/features/00014213.html
Sports-Trivia.net. http://www.sports-trivia.net/redgrange
College Football News http://www.collegefootballnews.com/Top_100_Players/Top_100_Players_1_Red_Grange.htm.

Sketch by Kristin Palm

Rocky Graziano

Rocky Graziano
1922-1990

American boxer

In his ten years as a professional boxer, Rocky Graziano held the title of World Middleweight Champion for less than a year; yet he remained one of the most famous athletes in the sport through the time of his death in 1990. Indeed, the 1955 film adaptation of his autobiography, *Somebody Up There Likes Me,* a series of appearances on comedy shows and television advertisements, and his work as a Republican Party spokesman kept him in the public eye far beyond his athletic career. Even those who were not boxing fans immediately recognized Graziano's New York City attitude and accent—not to mention his battle-scarred face—and enjoyed his pronouncements on fame, fortune, and just about any other topic under the sun. His down-to-earth sensibility also helped him maintain a proper perspective on the ups and downs of his various careers. As he concluded in his 1981 autobiography *Somebody Down Here Likes Me Too,* "Do me two favors. First, if your kid needs a friend, buy the kid a dog. And second, in the years to come, if you see me making my way down First or Second Avenue in New York City, please don't kick the cane out from unner me. I never really hoit nobody."

Rough-and-Tumble Childhood

Born in New York City on June 6, 1922, Thomas Rocco Barbella grew up as the fifth child of Nick and Ida (Scinto) Barbella. Nick Barbella had pursued a ca-reer as a welterweight boxer in his youth under the name Fighting Nick Bob, but retired from the sport after about seventy bouts. He encouraged his sons to take up the sport, but his youngest son felt that the elder Barbella favored his older brother, Joe, in their matches. Their relationship was further strained by his father's alcoholism, which often produced violent outbursts directed at everyone in the family. Adding to the tension, Ida Barbella was often hospitalized for mental problems. All of this occurred in the unrelenting poverty of the Barbella family's Lower East Side neighborhood, where many children pursued a life of crime on the streets in order to help their families survive.

Dropping out of school in the sixth grade, young Barbella began running with a juvenile gang that specialized in petty theft and street fighting with rival gangs. By his own estimate, he spent at least half of his time before his twenty-first birthday in reform schools or jail cells. After three terms in reform schools as a teenager, Barbella started to find a more stable influence in his life when he began visiting Stillman's Gym around 1939. Although he had hated boxing under his father's direction, he now enjoyed the discipline and physical outlet of the sport. He began fighting some bouts as an amateur and adopted a new name, Rocky Graziano, which he took from a boyfriend of his sister. As he had on the streets, Graziano quickly gained a reputation in the ring as a boxer who lacked finesse but made up for it with the raw brutality of his punches.

Professional Debut in 1942

Although he made a promising start in the amateur ranks, a parole violation sent Graziano back to reform school and then a stint in the New York City jail on Riker's Island in 1940. After being drafted into the U.S. Army, Graziano courted trouble again when he got into a fight with an officer and fled the camp. His decision to go AWOL (Absent Without Leave) caused him to serve nine months in the Federal Penitentiary in Leavenworth, Kansas. After his release on a dishonorable discharge, Graziano returned to New York and began fighting as a professional. He married Norma Unger on August 10, 1943; the couple subsequently had two daughters, Audrey and Roxie.

Classic Series with Tony Zale

Graziano immediately began compiling an impressive record in his professional career with a string of knock-out wins against his opponents. Overall Graziano racked up sixty-seven wins—fifty-two by knockout—ten losses, and six draws over the next ten years. The high point of his career came in a three-match duel for the title of World Middleweight Champion with Tony Zale between 1946 and 1948. Zale, the son of Polish immigrants known as "The Man of Steel," had served in the military during World War II. In addition to his status as a war veteran, Zale was regarded as a much more skilled boxer than Graziano. The popular favorite going into their first match in Yankee Stadium on September 27, 1946, Zale knocked out Graziano to take the fight in the sixth round. Graziano immediately demanded a rematch, but the bout was delayed when the boxer had his license suspended by the New York State Boxing Commission for failing to report an attempted bribery to the board.

Undaunted by the bad publicity, Graziano capitalized on his underdog status to fuel his rage against Zale in their second match on July 16, 1947 in Chicago. This time Graziano knocked Zale out in the sixth round to take the title. He declared at the end of the bout, "Hey, Ma, your bad boy done it. . . . I told you somebody up there likes me." The utterance later inspired the title of Graziano's colorful, if somewhat fictional, 1955 autobiography, *Somebody Up There Likes Me*. After publishing his autobiography in 1955, Graziano agreed to serve as a consultant for the film version of his life, which appeared on movie screens in 1956. He spent several weeks helping star Paul Newman learn his boxing technique, speech patterns, and physical movements in preparation for the film. Although *Somebody Up There Likes Me* took some dramatic licenses with the facts of Graziano's life and career—most notably, his second (and winning) title fight with Zale is the film's climax, but his defeat in their third match is not included—the film's realism won praise from critics. Indeed, it is still cited as one of the best dramas of the 1950s, ranked alongside *On the Waterfront, Marty,* and *Rebel Without a Cause*. It also remains one of the best films about boxing ever made.

The third Graziano-Zale match took place on June 10, 1948 in Jersey City. In their final match, Zale took back the title after knocking out Graziano in the third round. After Zale retired, Graziano made one more attempt to regain the middleweight crown in an April 1952 bout against Ray Robinson, which he lost in a third-round knockout. Graziano's last professional fight occurred in September 1952.

Career as Entertainer

In addition to his autobiography, Graziano's recurring role as comedienne Martha Raye's boyfriend on her self-titled television show kept him in the public eye throughout the 1950s. Graziano eventually turned into an all-around entertainer, appearing in television shows, movies, plays, and advertisements, almost always in a comic role that played up his Lower East Side persona and accent. Graziano published a second memoir, *Somebody Down Here Likes Me Too,* in 1981 and often campaigned for Republican Party candidates, including Ronald Reagan. In declining health throughout the 1980s, Graziano died from cardiopulmonary failure on May 22, 1990 in New York City.

Despite his rather crude technique as a boxer, Graziano was remembered at the time of his death for one of the most exciting boxing rivalries in history against Zale. Yet he was also celebrated for his accomplishments outside the boxing ring. For many professional boxers, their post-athletic careers are filled with disappointment

Somebody Up There Likes Me

After publishing his autobiography in 1955, Graziano agreed to serve as a consultant for the film version of his life, which appeared on movie screens in 1956. He spent several weeks helping star Paul Newman learn his boxing technique, speech patterns, and physical movements in preparation for the film. Although *Somebody Up There Likes Me* took some dramatic licenses with the facts of Graziano's life and career—most notably, his second (and winning) title fight with Tony Zale is the film's climax, but his defeat in their third match is not included—the film's realism won praise from critics. Indeed, it is still cited as one of the best dramas of the 1950s, ranked alongside *On the Waterfront, Marty,* and *Rebel Without a Cause.* It also remains one of the best films about boxing ever made.

and frustration. Graziano was one of the few to become even more successful after his days in the ring ended. The grade-school dropout became a published author; the reform-school inmate befriended some of the most powerful Republican politicians in the country; the quintessential New Yorker became a beloved national celebrity. Although the tales he told about his life were somewhat fanciful, Graziano's candor and commonsense outlook earned him respect far beyond the boxing ring.

SELECTED WRITINGS BY GRAZIANO:

Somebody Up There Likes Me, 1955.
(With Ralph Corsel) *Somebody Down Here Likes Me Too,* Stein & Day, 1981.

FURTHER INFORMATION

Books

Graziano, Rocky, with Ralph Corsel. *Somebody Down Here Like Me Too.* New York: Stein and Day Publishers, 1981.

Periodicals

Berger, Phil. "Rocky Graziano, Ex-Ring Champion, Dead at 71." *New York Times* (May 23, 1990): B7.
Povich, Shirley. "Graziano, He Knew the Ropes." *Washington Post* (May 25, 1990): B01.
Povich, Shirley. "Zale Was No Ordinary Boxer." *Washington Post* (March 3, 1997).

Other

"Cyber Boxing Champ Rocky Graziano." The Cyber Boxing Zone. http://www.cyberboxingzone.com/boxing/graz.htm (October 19, 2002).
"Rocky Graziano." International Boxing Hall of Fame. http://www.ibhof.com/graziano.htm (October 19, 2002).
"Rocky Graziano." National Italian American Hall of Fame. http://www.niashf.org/inductees/graziano_rocky.html (October 19, 2002).

"Somebody Up There Likes Me." American Film Institute. http://www.afionline.org/wise/films/somebody_up_there_likes_me/sutlm.html (August 23, 2001).

Sketch by Timothy Borden

Hank Greenberg
1911-1986

American baseball player

The American baseball star Hank Greenberg, celebrated in the 1930s and 1940s for his powerful batting and multiple homeruns, was baseball's first legendary Jewish player. With the Detroit Tigers from 1933 to 1947, and with the Pittsburgh Pirates for the last year of his playing career, Greenberg led the American League four times in home runs. The peak year for the Depression Era player was 1938, when he hit fifty-eight home runs—only two fewer than record-breaking slugger **Babe Ruth**. The 6-foot-4, 215-pound player held a career batting average of .313, and won his league's Most Valuable Player (MVP) Award in 1935 and 1940. While he encountered anti-Semitism throughout his career, Greenberg won over many fans and was particularly beloved among Jewish baseball aficionados.

Preferred Baseball to Schoolwork

Born on January 1, 1911, in New York City's Greenwich Village neighborhood, Greenberg was one of four children of Romanian immigrants David and Sarah Greenberg. His father owned a successful cloth-shrinking plant; his homemaker mother kept a kosher house. When their son was six, the family moved to a Jewish neighborhood in the Bronx; here young Greenberg attended Hebrew school. Hoping their son would pursue a higher education and a professional vocation in medicine or law, Greenberg's parents disapproved of the boy's early passion for baseball, and his preference for sports over academics.

"Jewish women on my block ... would point me out as a good-for-nothing, a loafer, and a bum who always wanted to play baseball rather than go to school," Greenberg recalled to the *Detroit Jewish Chronicle,* as quoted by Laurie Marzejka of the Detroit News Online. "Friends and relatives sympathized with my mother because she was the parent of a big gawk who cared more for baseball ... than school books. I was Mrs. Greenberg's disgrace."

A top athlete at James Monroe High School in the Bronx, Greenberg played both baseball and basketball. Bigger and stronger than his peers, he had a natural advantage over other athletes his age, yet he had to work

Hank Greenberg

1911	Born January 1 in New York, NY
1929	Signs with the Detroit Tigers; attends New York University one year
1930	Plays one game with the Tigers
1930-33	Plays in the minor leagues
1933	Becomes a starter with the Tigers
1934	Leads the American League with 63 doubles
1935	Leads the American League with 36 home runs and 170 RBI
1935, 1940	Wins American League's Most Valuable Player award
1937	Hits 58 home runs for a career record
1941	Enlists as an officer candidate in the Army Air Corps
1945	Returns to baseball, hitting a pennant-winning home run for the Tigers
1946	Marries department store heiress Carol Gimbel
1946	Becomes highest-paid baseball player of his day, with a $100,000 contract from the Pittsburgh Pirates
1947	Retires from baseball; becomes a baseball executive
1950	Becomes general manager of the Cleveland Indians
1956	Inducted into the Baseball Hall of Fame
1959	Divorces Gimbel
1986	Dies of cancer at age 75

hard to gain the grace and skill that athletics demanded. "Hank was so big for his age and so awkward that he became painfully self-conscious," his high school coach remembered. "The fear of being made to look foolish drove him to practice constantly and, as a result, to overcome his handicaps."

Fresh out of high school, Greenberg impressed the major-league baseball coaches with his talent and potential. Signing with a major-league team meant that Greenberg would not advance directly to the majors, but would play in the minor leagues first until he was ready. The New York Giants were looking for a Jewish player to attract fans from New York's large Jewish population, yet they passed over Greenberg, fearing that he was too clumsy to become a star player. Willing to take a chance on Greenberg, the New York Yankees made him a lucrative offer; but Greenberg, a first-baseman, turned it down, because the Yankees already had star player **Lou Gehrig** on first base. Similarly, Greenberg turned down an offer from the Washington Senators, who boasted Joe Judge on first.

Ultimately, 19-year-old Greenberg signed with the Detroit Tigers, who offered a contract that allowed him to attend New York University on an athletic scholarship. Yet after attending college for only one year, Greenberg dropped out to pursue baseball exclusively. He played one game with the Tigers in 1930, and then spent the next three years in the minor-league "farm system." Here the young player worked to overcome any lingering awkwardness, and to hone his skills as a batter and fielder.

First Jewish Baseball Star

Called back to the major leagues, Greenberg became a starter and first-baseman with the Tigers in June of 1933. The rookie made his debut with thirty-three doubles, twelve home runs, and a .301 batting average in his first season. The following year found him playing a stronger game, with sixty-three doubles (the most in his league), twenty-six home runs, 139 RBI (runs batted in), and an impressive .339 average. That year, "Hammerin' Hank," as he became known, helped lift the Tigers to their American League pennant win. The team lost the World Series to the "Gashouse Gang" St. Louis Cardinals, however, with Greenberg hitting .321, but striking out nine times.

Greenberg impressed fans and fellow players not only with his solid performance in 1934, but also with his decision not to play baseball on the Jewish high holiday of Yom Kippur. Sports writers took note of his integrity, including Bud Shaver of the *Detroit Times:* "[Greenberg's] fine intelligence, independence of thought, courage and his driving ambition have won him the respect and admiration of teammates, baseball writers, and the fans at large. He feels and acknowledges his responsibility as a representative of the Jews in the field of a great national sport and the Jewish people could have no finer representative."

Yet the budding baseball star often faced bigotry in the predominantly Gentile world of baseball. While it was rampant in pre-World War II Germany, anti-Semitism was not uncommon in the United States in the 1930s. Greenberg was often heckled by baseball spectators and by opposing players—some of whom joked that pitchers should try throwing a pork chop at him to strike him out. Throughout these trials, Greenberg maintained his dignity, and became more beloved among his fans for his fortitude and perseverance.

Career Statistics

Yr	Team	AVG	GP	AB	R	H	HR	RBI	BB	SO	SB
1930	DET	.000	1	1	0	0	0	0	0	0	0
1933	DET	.301	117	449	59	135	12	87	46	78	6
1934	DET	.338	153	593	118	201	26	139	63	93	9
1935	DET	.328	152	619	121	203	36	170	87	91	4
1936	DET	.348	12	46	10	16	1	16	9	6	1
1937	DET	.337	154	594	137	200	40	183	102	101	8
1938	DET	.315	155	556	144	175	58	146	119	92	7
1939	DET	.312	138	500	112	156	33	112	91	95	8
1940	DET	.340	148	573	129	195	41	150	93	75	6
1941	DET	.269	19	67	12	18	2	12	16	12	1
1945	DET	.311	78	270	47	84	13	60	42	40	3
1946	DET	.277	142	523	91	145	44	127	80	88	5
1947	PIT	.249	125	402	71	100	25	74	104	73	0
TOTAL		.313	1394	5193	1051	1628	331	1276	852	844	58

DET: Detroit Tigers; PIT: Pittsburgh Pirates.

Helping the Tigers take a consecutive American League pennant in 1935, Greenberg led the league with thirty-six home runs and 170 RBI. A broken wrist kept him on the sidelines after the second game of the World Series, but the Tigers prevailed nonetheless. He wrapped up the year winning the league's Most Valuable Player Award. But after a strong start to the 1936 season, he broke his barely healed wrist once again, and sat out the remainder of the season. Fans worried that his career might be over, but Greenberg proved them wrong the following year, when he performed better than ever.

Hitting forty home runs and batting .337 in 1937, Greenberg netted 183 RBI, the third-highest total on record, one short of Gehrig's American League record. The following year, at the peak of his career, Greenberg took a shot at breaking Ruth's record-setting sixty home runs—only to fall two homers short. Many fans believed his rivals deliberately foiled Greenberg by walking him instead of letting him hit the ball—and some even cited this plot as anti-Semitic. Greenberg himself, fully aware of the bigotry that surrounded him, never believed this particular myth.

Slipping a little after his banner year, Greenberg hit thirty-three home runs and 112 RBI in 1939. The following year he relinquished his seven-year position at first base, switching places with outfielder Rudy York. The move proved successful, as Greenberg quickly mastered the new position, helping the Tigers take the American League pennant from the Yankees. Earning his second Most Valuable Player Award, he ended the 1940 season with league-leading fifty doubles, forty-one home runs, 150 RBI, and a .340 average.

In a hiatus from baseball, just before American involvement in World War II, Greenberg became the first baseball player to enlist in the U.S. Army. He was discharged two days before the Japanese attack on Pearl Harbor, after which he re-enlisted as an officer candidate in the Army Air Corps. Rising to captain in the corps, he commanded a B-29 bomber squadron in the Far East until his discharge in 1945. Returning home a war hero, Greenberg, who had missed four seasons, hit a home run in his first game, thrilling fans. The Tigers went on to win another pennant, with Greenberg hitting a winning home run in the last game's final inning. He later said he believed the 1945 season was his greatest—despite his stronger 1938 record.

Highest-Paid Player

In the wake of disagreements with the Tigers' owners, Greenberg was traded to the Pittsburgh Pirates in 1946. Pleased to have Greenberg, the National League team offered the star a contract worth more than any other baseball player had ever received: $100,000. Three days after signing his contract, he married department store heiress Carol Gimbel, with whom he would have two sons and a daughter. Greenberg and Gimbel divorced in 1959.

Yet the baseball star had passed the peak of his career. Bothered by injuries, Greenberg played only one season with the Pirates, slipping to an average of .249 and hitting only twenty-five home runs. He retired in 1947.

Turning to the business end of the sport, Greenberg became vice president and farm director for the Cleveland Indians; in 1950 he became the Indians' general manager. He later moved to the Chicago White Sox, as part owner and vice president. On July 23, 1956, he was inducted into the Baseball Hall of Fame, in Cooperstown, New York. He retired from the baseball business seven years later, becoming an investment banker. After retiring, Greenberg took up a new sport—tennis—becoming a regular player on the senior circuit, where he won several celebrity tournaments.

Awards and Accomplishments

1935, 1937, 1940, 1946	American League leader in RBI
1935, 1938, 1940, 1946	American League leader in home runs
1935, 1940	Most Valuable Player Award, American League
1937	Hits 58 home runs for a career record
1937-40	American League All-Star team
1956	Elected to the Baseball Hall of Fame

When Greenberg died of cancer in 1986, at age 75, baseball fans around the country remembered a player of remarkable power, dignity, and humbleness. As the first Jewish baseball superstar, he had achieved folk hero status among Jewish youth and immigrants in his day. Of more lasting import, Greenberg helped to break the barrier of religion in America's most popular sport.

SELECTED WRITINGS BY GREENBERG:

(With Ira Berkow) *Hank Greenberg: The Story of My Life,* Triumph Books, 2001.

FURTHER INFORMATION
Books

Greenberg, Hank, with Ira Berkow. *Hank Greenberg: The Story of My Life.* Chicago: Triumph Books, 2001

Periodicals

Bates, James. "For Determined Filmmaker, Tale of Jewish Baseball Hero Became a Quest." *Los Angeles Times* (May 18, 2000).

"Hank Greenberg, First $100,000 Player, Dies." *Los Angeles Times* (September 5, 1986).

"Hank Greenberg, Top Hitter and Member of Hall of Fame." *New York Times* (September 5, 1986): A20.

Other

Frommer, Harvey. "Celebrating Hank Greenberg." BaseballLibrary.com. http://www.pubdim.net/baseballlibrary/submit/Frommer_Harvey5.stm (October 15, 2002).

"Greenberg, 'Hank' (Henry B.)." Hickok Sports.com. http://www.hickoksports/com/biograph/greenberg hank.shtml (October 15, 2002).

"Hank Greenberg." BaseballLibrary.com. http://www.pubdim.net/baseballlibrary/ballplayers/G/Greenberg_Hank.stm (October 15, 2002).

"Hank Greenberg." National Baseball Hall of Fame. http://www.baseballhalloffame.org/hofers_and_honorees/hofer_bios/greenberg_hank.htm (October 15, 2002).

Hank Greenberg: The Story of My Life

Every day I'd play ball in Corona Park, across the street from our house in the Bronx. Anytime there was less than a foot of snow, I was playing baseball. The neighbors shook their heads and warned my mother.

Baseball wasn't looked upon as a business, and most of the guys in the game were pretty rowdy. So my parents didn't think much of me pursuing it. They thought I ought to be studying instead of playing baseball. I grew up with typical Jewish parents whose objective was to send their children to college to become doctors or lawyers. As a matter of fact, my two brothers and my sister all graduated from college and went into professional work. But I loved baseball and stuck with it.

In my early days, I was completely engrossed by baseball. On weekdays after school, I'd rush to the park with my glove, bat, and ball, and come home only after it got dark. Weekends were completely devoted to the old field. And instead of coming home for lunch, I'd fill my pockets with fruit and candy and stay down at the ballpark all day. We were just in love with playing baseball and the days weren't long enough.

Source: Greenberg, Hank, with Ira Berkow. *Hank Greenberg: The Story of My Life.* Chicago: Triumph Books, 2001.

"The Tigers' 'Hammerin' Hank' Greenberg." Detroit News Online. http://www.detnews.com/history/greenberg/greenberg.htm (October 15, 2002).

Sketch by Wendy Kagan

Joe Greene
1946-

American football player

At six-feet-four-inches and 260 pounds, Mean Joe Greene was the backbone of the famed "Steel Curtain" defense for the Pittsburgh Steelers in the National Football League (NFL), during the team's dynasty of the 1970s. In 1975 sportswriter Roy Blount, Jr. profiled Greene in *Sports Illustrated,* writing, "He plays—or, sometimes, refuses to play—the conservative, regimented, technology-ridden game of football as if it were a combat poem he is writing, and gets away with it." Inducted into the Pro Football Hall of Fame in 1987, Greene was the most respected and feared defensive back of his time, or it could be argued, of all time.

Biggest in the Class

Joe Greene was born Charles Edward Greene on September 24, 1946 in Temple, Texas. He was the oldest of three children, and after his father walked out on the family when Greene was ten years old, he helped his mother, Cleo Thomas, by taking care of his younger siblings after school. Later, Greene picked cotton to supplement his mother's modest earnings as a domestic.

Always the biggest kid in his class, Greene, who early in his life was nicknamed Joe by an aunt, assumed

Joe Greene

the reputation as a bully even though he was quite shy and reserved, but his size coupled with his quiet, serious personality proved intimidating. Determined to make a better life for himself and his family, Greene dreamed of a college education; however, football soon came calling. In junior high coaches began urging the youngster to try sports. Greene quickly discovered he had little natural talent for catching baseballs and decided basketball involved too much running. As an eighth-grader he played on the junior varsity football team and fell in love with the game. Later, he also threw the discus and shotput in track, winning a state championship.

As a sophomore at Dunbar, an all-black high school in Temple, Greene became the starting middle linebacker. In eighth grade, Greene had weighed 158 pounds; by his senior year, he weighed 250 pounds. Although he was considered big for a linebacker, Greene loved the position. As he improved, his confidence both on and off the field blossomed. His sometimes overly aggressive personality earned him a reputation as a dirty player, and he was ejected from numerous games. But, to Greene, football was war, and he was determined to fight to the death.

"Mean Joe" Greene

Despite Greene's individual talents on the field, the Dunbar Panthers had only a mediocre record, and he was not heavily recruited by colleges. His options were further limited because the Southwest Conference was still segregated. Greene contacted North Texas State

(now the University of North Texas) and was eventually offered a football scholarship.

During his first year at North Texas, Greene played middle linebacker, offensive guard, and defensive tackle on the freshman team before settling permanently into the defensive tackle position. In 1966, as a sophomore, in the first game as a starting tackle on the varsity squad, Greene and the North Texas defense held Texas Western University (now University of Texas at El Paso), a team that had tromped the Eagles the previous year, to minus-forty yards rushing. Sidney Sue Graham, the wife of the North Texas sports information director, thought her husband should come up with a catchy name for the overpowering defense. Given that the school colors were bright green and white, she suggested "mean green." The next week the name began appearing in North Texas press releases and it stuck, soon replacing Eagles as the team's official nickname. It was a natural step to apply the label to the team's All-American, and Joe Greene became "Mean Joe" Greene.

Greene, who remained a gentle giant off the field, insisted the nickname didn't fit him, but those who watched his hard-hitting, no-holds-barred play on the field couldn't agree. During his junior year Greene married Agnes Craft. Also a student at North Texas, she was the daughter of a Dallas businessman, and together they had three children. For the three years that Greene played varsity football at North Texas, the team record stood at 23-5-1. As a senior, he was the unanimous choice as the top defensive lineman in the nation and was attracting the attention of nearly every team in the NFL.

Football is War

In the 1969 NFL draft, the Pittsburgh Steelers took Greene as the fourth overall pick by the team's new coach, Chuck Knoll. Steelers fans, already soured by years of losing, bemoaned the selection of an unheard-of player from an unheard-of school. The local newspaper headline read: "Joe Who?" For his part, Greene was about as excited to go to Pittsburgh as Pittsburgh was to have him, and Greene didn't endear himself to the Steelers organization immediately, either. He held out for a larger contract, and when he finally showed up at training camp, he was out of shape and overweight.

It wasn't long, however, before Greene had proved his worth on the field and became a favorite of Steelers fans, who loved his passionate, aggressive play. On the field Greene's emotions often got out of control, and he was ejected from two games during his rookie year. Stories of Greene's antics became legend. Once he threw his helmet at the goalpost so hard it broke into pieces. During one game he came off the sidelines to spit full in the face of hall of fame linebacker **Dick Butkus**, because the Chicago Bears' defense was humiliating the Steelers' offense. Greene got particularly upset if he felt he was being held by offensive linemen and would explode

Chronology

1946	Born September 24 in Temple, Texas
1965	Enrolls at North Texas State University; plays on freshman football team
1966-68	Plays defensive tackle for North Texas; acquires "Mean Joe" Greene as his nickname
1967	Marries Agnes Craft
1969	Selected as the fourth overall pick of the National Football League (NFL) draft by the Pittsburgh Steelers
1969-80	Plays defensive tackle for the Steelers
1981	Retires
1987	Defensive line coach for the Steelers
1992	Defensive line coach for the Miami Dolphins
1995	Hired as defensive line coach for the Arizona Cardinals

Awards and Accomplishments

1968	Selected as the nation's top college defensive lineman
1969	Named National Football League (NFL) Defensive Rookie of the Year
1970-77, 1979-80	Pro Bowl
1972, 1974	Named NFL Defensive Player of the Year
1977	Received Dapper Dan Award as Pittsburgh's Outstanding Sports Figure
1980	Received advertising industry's Clio award for Coca-Cola commercial
1981	Received Vince Lombardi award for dedication
1987	Inducted into the Pro Football Hall of Fame
1994	Named to the NFL All-Time Team

Greene earned four Super Bowl rings (1975, 1976, 1979, 1980).

with punches, kicks, and late hits. In a game against the Philadelphia Eagles, Greene became so frustrated that the officials weren't calling any holding penalties against the Eagles that he grabbed the ball before the Eagles' center could snap it, threw it into the stands, and stomped off the field. After a moment the stunned crowd erupted into cheers.

The Steel Curtain

Greene became one of the most dominating defensive players in the history of the NFL. Despite the Steelers' abysmal 1-13 record, he was named the NFL Defensive Rookie of the Year. He was voted the league's Most Valuable Player in 1972 and again in 1974, the year he began lining up at an angle between the center and the guard. He earned All-Pro recognition from 1970 to 1977 and received invitations to play in ten Pro Bowls. Lining up alongside Greene were teammates Dwight White, Ernie Holmes, and L. C. Greenwood. The four became known as the Steel Curtain. After Knoll added talent to the offensive squad that included **Terry Bradshaw**, Franco Harris, and **Lynn Swann**, the Steelers were well on their way to creating a football dynasty. The Steelers won Super Bowls IX, X, XIII, and XIV, a record four wins in a six-year span.

A serious shoulder injury caused Greene to miss part of the 1975 season, and chronic back pain led him to retire after the 1981 season. After taking several stabs at business ventures, he became the defensive line coach for the Steelers in 1987. Greene hoped to replace Knoll as head coach in 1992, but when the Steelers bypassed him to hire Bill Cowher, Greene left Pittsburgh to become an assistant coach for the Miami Dolphins. In 1995 Greene became the defensive line coach for the Arizona Cardinals, where he currently remains.

As a player Greene combined strength, speed, and sheer determination to become one of the most celebrated, if sometimes controversial, defensive players in the game. He simply refused to be denied. Respected and feared by his opponents, he became the building block that created the Steel Curtain defense of the Pittsburgh Steelers during the 1970s.

CONTACT INFORMATION

Address: Arizona Cardinals, 8701 S. Hardy Dr., Tempe, Arizona 85284. Phone: (602)379-0101.

FURTHER INFORMATION

Books

Contemporary Black Biography, Vol. 10. Detroit: Gale, 1995.

Fox, Larry. *Mean Joe Greene and the Steelers' Front Four.* New York: Dodd, Mead, & Company, 1975.

Harrington, Denis J. *The Pro Football Hall of Fame: Players, Coaches, Team Owners and League Officials, 1963-1991.* Jefferson, NC: McFarland & Company, Inc. Publishers, 1991.

Markoe, Arnold, ed. *The Scribner Encyclopedia of American Lives: Sports Figures.* Vol. 1. New York: Charles Scribner's Sons, 2002.

Who's Who Among African Americans, 14th ed. Detroit: Gale Group, 2001.

Periodicals

Blount, Roy, Jr. "He Does What He Wants Out There." Reprint, 1975. *Sports Illustrated* (September 5, 1994): 138-48.

"Fizz Kid: Joe Greene Mean? Not When 9-Year-Old Tommy Okon Offered Him a Coke on TV." *People* (January 15, 2001): 121.

"Hired: Hall of Fame Tackle Joe Greene, As Defensive Line Coach of the Miami Dolphins." *Sports Illustrated* (February 17, 1992): 97.

Urban, Darren. "Cardinals' Defensive Line Remains Green." Knight Ridder/Tribune News Service (August 2, 2002).

Other

"All-Time Steelers: Joe Greene." Steelers Reference. com. http://www.steelref.com (December 30, 2002)
"Joe Greene." The Pittsburgh Steelers. http://www. steelers.com (December 30, 2002)

Sketch by Kari Bethel

Bud Greenspan
1927-

American documentarian

As official filmmaker of the Olympic games, Bud Greenspan has produced International Olympic Committee (IOC)-sanctioned records of several meets—the 1984 games in Los Angeles, the 1988 games in Calgary, the 1992 Barcelona games, the 1996 games in Atlanta, the 1998 games in Nagano, the 2000 Sydney games, and the 2002 Salt Lake City games. At the same time, he has created many other independent documentaries on the games and their athletes, leading Frederick Klein in a 1988 *Wall Street Journal* article to say that Greenspan "has become to the Olympics a combination of what Degas was to ballet dancers and 'The Cosby Show' is to American family life."

From Radio to Film

A native of New York City, Greenspan began his career in 1940s radio. By the age of twenty-one, he was sports director at WMGM, then the nation's largest sports station, producing pregame and postgame shows, interview shows, and live play-by-play. Turning his attention to writing, Greenspan wrote hundreds of articles sold to major U.S. publications, including *Parade*. Greenspan was also drawn to the emerging medium of television, beginning as a producer in 1959. He worked his way up to the post of creative television supervisor in 1968, after which Greenspan founded his own production company.

Greenspan attended the 1952 Olympic summer games in Helsinki, Finland, as a sportswriter; impulsively, he hired a Finnish film crew to shoot some footage. "He brought it home, edited it down to 15 minutes, and sold it as a short," according to Klein. He has been to virtually every Olympics since then, and has filmed most of them.

By the 1960s Greenspan was marketing feature-length sports films. One early effort, *Jesse Owens Returns to Berlin,* chronicled the famed African-American track-and-field star who showed up German chancellor Adolf Hitler's "master race" theory by sweeping the 1936 summer games in Munich. Though filmed in 1964,

Bud Greenspan

Jesse Owens was not screened on American television until 1972—typical of Greenspan productions, which are often considered too slowly paced for mass audiences. Another documentary of that era, *The Glory of Their Times,* was likewise rejected by networks as "too low-key." Rather than submit to the networks' request to edit the film, Greenspan repurchased the rights to his production and waited another eight years until the Public Broadcasting System (PBS) ran the film uncut in 1977.

Documenting Terror and Triumph

In 1972, Greenspan was working the summer games in Munich as a radio reporter for the National Broadcasting Corp. (NBC). He was thus a witness to one of the most shocking terrorist attacks of the twentieth century—the kidnapping and murder of the entire nine-member Israeli Olympic team (and their two coaches) by a faction of the Palestinian Liberation Organization known as Black September. A memorial service was held the day after the event, which was dubbed the "Munich Massacre." After that, the games went on as scheduled. The decision to continue was controversial, but it was intended to demonstrate that terrorism had no place in the peaceful realm of athletic competition. Years later, Greenspan produced a ninety-minute documentary, *The 1972 Munich Olympic Games: Bud Greenspan Remembers,* which included archival footage and the producer's on-the-spot radio reports. While focusing on the tragedy of Munich, however, the film also highlighted some of the remarkable performances of those games, including **Mark Spitz**'s domination of the swimming events, and the debut of gymnastics gamine **Olga Korbut**. The film was broadcast on the Showtime network on September 5, 2002, thirty years to the day after the Munich Massacre. "I talked to a lot of the relatives and friends of the athletes and that made it seem even more like yesterday," Greenspan said in a CBS television interview.

Many of Greenspan's early films were produced by both him and his wife, the late Constance Anne ("Cappy") Petrash; the filmmaker's Cappy Productions is named in her honor. The couple notably created a documentary following the Ethiopian runners who swept the Olympic marathon in 1960, 1964, and 1968. The resulting film was expanded into *The Olympiad,* a 1980 series that aired in more than eighty countries.

In 1984, the year after Cappy's death, Greenspan was named to his first official post as documentarian of the Olympic summer games in Los Angeles. The distinction between his work and that of independent producers, he explained in a *SportsTravel* article, is that he submitted to "a bidding process within the host country for the rights to document the Games." The host country "makes the decision" who and what gets filmed. The IOC, he added, asked that Greenspan portray the games in a positive sense. "If something happens contrary to that it won't be ignored, but it won't be exploited," he elaborated.

An Olympian Effort

The official films, which are sometimes marketed under the title *16 Days of Glory,* can run up to three-and-a-half hours. With his wide access to the Olympic venues, the competitors, and their associates, Greenspan seeks to go the broadcast networks one better in the "up close and personal" stakes. The producer initially chooses twelve to fifteen possible story subjects, narrowing the field to seven or eight for the final film. "We have basic ideas," he told *SportsTravel,* "but if an idea doesn't pan out, we change gears." Greenspan used as an example a speed skater whose mother had also competed twenty years earlier. The mother was filmed in the stands as the daughter raced—and finished out of the medals. Still, the mother was thrilled; telling her daughter, "You're the sixth best in the world." "We're more interested in the humanity of the sport as opposed to chronicling the winners," said Greenspan. David Hiltbrand, reviewing *Lillehammer '94: 16 Days of Glory* for *People,* declared that Greenspan is "magisterial at presenting sports as modern mythology." A Greenspan production is characterized by sharp visuals, seldom-seen angles, and stories that are told, according to *New York Times* contributor Richard Sandomir, "straightforwardly but emotionally, with a tersely written, stentorian narration. There are no production tricks, special effects or gauzy, amber-lighted backgrounds. Just 16-millimeter footage of stirring action and emotional recollections."

Chronology	
1927	Born September 18, in New York, NY
1947	Graduated New York University
1948	Began broadcasting career in radio
1952	Produced first Olympic-themed film
1965	Married Constance Anne Petrash
1968	Founded Cappy Productions
1973	Published first of at least seven books
1983	Named official filmmaker of the Olympic Games
2002	Produced promotional film for Beijing, China
2002	Named contributing editor, *Parade*
2002	Marked fiftieth year of Olympic coverage

For his *16 Days* film on Los Angeles, Greenspan faced the challenge of offering new images and insights in a city already swarming with filmmakers, television producers, and other creative types. The producer "had to trust that his knowledge of people and of sports, filtered through a perspective of hindsight, leavened with some good old-fashioned cinematic beauty—18 crews shooting almost a million feet of film—could make even the most familiar, oft-told tales fresh," noted *Sports Illustrated* writer Frank Deford.

Widening his circle of interest, he also produced several films on non-Olympic subjects, including *Ageless Heroes, Kings of the Ring,* and *Discover Utah!* Greenspan also took the director's helm in 1977 for a made-for-television docudrama on the life of track phenom **Wilma Rudolph**.

Though virtually every other Bud Greenspan film is a documentary, the director branched out into drama with his 1977 two-hour made-for-television movie, *Wilma.* This film told the life story of the great American track athlete Rudolph, portrayed by Shirley Jo Finney, focusing on her relationship with her mother (played by Cicely Tyson) and her boyfriend. Though the movie earned mixed notices, *Wilma* became notable years later as the television debut of the young actor playing Wilma's boyfriend—future Academy Award winner Denzel Washington.

While widely acclaimed, with honors including the prestigious Peabody Award, the filmmaker did face some controversy when he agreed to produce a promotional video on behalf of Beijing, China's, bid to host the 2008 summer games. Greenspan focused on the city and its people, but the issue of human rights violation in China "wasn't touched at all and we didn't think it was necessary," as he explained to a CNN.com interviewer.

In 1996 Greenspan produced *100 Years of Olympic Glory,* a three-hour film celebrating the centennial of the modern games. As with his other films, this documentary focused on the human stories behind the medals. There is, for instance, the story of two Japanese pole vaulters who competed in 1936. They "cleared the same height and should have tied for second place," as *Star-Ledger*

Hiltbrand, David. "Lillehammer '94: Sixteen Days of Glory."*People.* (November 28, 1994).

Klein, Frederick. "On Sports: The Olympics' Cheer-leader."*Wall Street Journal.* (July 29, 1988).

Krupnick, Jerry. "A Gold for Human Drama."*Star-Ledger.* (April 15, 1996).

Sandomir, Richard. "The Official Keeper of the Olympic Flame."*New York Times.* (August 4, 1996).

Taafe, William. "The Candle Still Burns."*Sports Illustrated.* (December 12, 1983).

Other

"Bud Greenspan on China's History, Future in Olympic Movement." CNN.com. http://www.cnn.com/2001/WORLD/asiapcf/east/07/14/bud.greenspan.cnna/ (July 14, 2001).

"Ten Burning Questions for Bud Greenspan." ESPN.com.http://espn.go.com/page2/s/questions/budgreenspan.html./ (December 16, 20002).

"Witnessing the 1972 Olympic Games." CBSNews.com.http://www.cbsnews.com/stories/2002/09/04/earlyshow/leisure/celebspot/printable52084/ (September 5, 2002).

Sketch by Susan Salter

Awards and Accomplishments

1976	First of seven Emmy awards, 1976-1997
1985	Olympic Order, International Olympic Committee
1988	Ace Award
1992	Graham McNamee Award, American Sportscasters Association
1994	Ronald Reagan Media Award, U.S. Sports Academy
1994	Billie Jean King Award, Women's Sports Foundation
1995	Lifetime Achievement Award, Directors Guild of America
1996	George Foster Peabody Award
1996	Foundation Award, International Radio and Television Society
1998	New York Festivals award for best TV documentary
2000	Silver Circle inductee, National Academy of Television Arts & Sciences
2002	Lifetime Achievement Award, USA Track & Field
2002	Bernard Nath Award, Anti-Defamation League

writer Jerry Krupnick related. "When the silver was awarded to just one of them, the other vaulter getting the bronze, they cut the medals in half and had them fused together to create 'the Medal of Eternal Friendship.'"

Hype and scandal have seemed to plague many contemporary Olympics, but Greenspan set his gaze on the positive aspects of both win and loss. "They're two weeks of love," he told an ESPN.com reporter. "It's a privilege to be associated with the best in the world." Indeed, Greenspan's "approach to the Olympics would not be appropriate for the mainstream media," said Randy Harvey of the *Los Angeles Times.* "But although he is no journalist, and proud of it, he is one of the best reporters I know."

Asked by ESPN.com to recall his most memorable Olympic moment, Greenspan pointed to the 1968 summer games in Mexico City. A Tanzanian marathon runner, John Stephen Ahkwari, injured himself in the race. He struggled in last, bloodied and bandaged. "I asked him, 'Why did you keep going?'" Greenspan recounted. "He said, 'You don't understand. My country did not send me 5,000 miles to start a race, they sent me to finish it.' That sent chills down my spine and I've always remembered it."

FURTHER INFORMATION

Periodicals

Austin, Al. "Bud Greenspan." *SportsTravel.* (June, 1998).

Deford, Frank. "Sixteen Days of Glory."*Sports Illustrated.* (December 16, 1985).

Deitsch, Richard. "TV Talk." *Sports Illustrated.* (February 25, 2002).

Harvey, Randy. "He Uses Rose-Colored Filter to Catch Olympics on Film."*Los Angeles Times.* (December 17, 1999).

Hiltbrand, David. "Barcelona '92: Sixteen Days of Glory."*People.* (August 16, 1993).

Wayne Gretzky
1961-

Canadian hockey player

The dominant figure in the National Hockey League (NHL) during his twenty-year career in the majors, Wayne Gretzky more than lived up to his nickname, "The Great One." After making his debut in the NHL with the Edmonton Oilers in 1979, Gretzky earned the league's Most Valuable Player honors nine times over the next ten seasons. The top scorer in the NHL every season between 1981 and 1987, Gretzky also won top scoring honors three more times between 1990 and 1994. From 1984 to 1988 the Oilers dominated the NHL, winning four Stanley Cup championships; on the way to two of those victories, Gretzky picked up the Conn Smythe Trophy as the playoffs' Most Valuable Player. In addition to these achievements, Gretzky also helped to expand the popularity of hockey into America's growing Sunbelt cities after he was traded to the Los Angeles Kings in 1988. Although the Kings never reached the heights that the Oilers had attained, Gretzky remained, by consensus opinion, the top player in the NHL as well as one of its most popular personalities in the 1990s. In his retirement as a professional athlete, Gretzky has retained the respect

Wayne Gretzky

of his peers and the public by directing Canada's men's hockey team to its first Gold Medal in fifty years in the Salt Lake City Winter Olympic Games in 2002. His other challenges included managing the NHL's Phoenix Coyotes, a team that he partly owned, and raising a family with wife Janet Jones, whom he married in 1988.

Early Success in Hockey

Born on January 26, 1961, Wayne Donald Gretzky was the second child and eldest son of Walter and Phyllis (Hockin) Gretzky. The Gretzkys raised their five children—one daughter and three other sons in addition to Wayne—in a small, three-bedroom home on Varadi Avenue in Brantford, Ontario, Canada. The elder Gretzky had played junior-league hockey in his youth and started to give his sons informal lessons in the sport as soon as they started skating. The Gretzkys even transformed their backyard into a hockey rink every winter and opened it up to the neighborhood's kids. The Gretzkys enjoyed having their sons play hockey where they could keep an eye on them, even if it meant having the kitchen floor marred by the constant exposure to skate blades.

Gretzky also played hockey on the frozen surface of the River Nith, which ran through his grandparents' farm in nearby Canning, Ontario. He even practiced some of his shots with his grandmother with a rubber ball and toy hockey stick. From his parents and grandparents, who were hard-working immigrants of Belarusian and Polish heritage, Gretzky also learned self-discipline, perseverance,

and humility. As Walter Gretzky explained in his 1984 memoir *Gretzky: From the Back Yard Rink to the Stanley Cup,* "We've made it clear that once you started something, you finished it. School project, sport, hobby, it made no difference. You finished what you started, like it or not, because if you do it early in life you'll do it later, too. We wanted them to learn early: in everything you do, you follow through." This ingrained attitude would eventually prove crucial to Gretzky's long-term success in the NHL.

Joining his first hockey team at age six—a full four years before the minimum age requirement for the league—Gretzky scored just one goal in the first season. His improvement in subsequent years was astounding, particularly because he remained one of the youngest and smallest players in the league. In his fifth year of league play Gretzky racked up 378 goals in a sixty-nine-game season, a feat that made him a local, and increasingly national, celebrity. With the success also came criticism from some of the parents of other players, who accused Gretzky's father of pushing his son's career at the expense of their sons. Walter Gretzky, who worked at Bell Canada, was indeed active in guiding his son through the junior ranks, but the charges seemed motivated by simple jealously. As he later wrote in his memoir, "There was just this small minority of parents trying to chop Wayne down to their size. They razzed him, they insulted him, they complained to coaches that he was getting too much ice time. Some of them would sit there at games with pencil and paper, marking the times Wayne came on and off the ice and when their own kids did, and taking the lists over to the coaches as soon as the game ended." It also seemed incomprehensible that a player of such small stature—even in his NHL days Gretzky, at six feet tall, weighed in at just 185 pounds—could outplay opponents much larger than himself.

Rapid Ascent Through the Ranks

Dismayed by the negative reaction of some of the parents of other Brantford players, the Gretzkys arranged to

Awards and Accomplishments

1980-87, 1989	Hart Trophy as NHL's Most Valuable Player
1980, 1992, 1994, 1999	Lady Byng Trophy as Most Gentlemanly Player in NHL
1981-85, 1987	Lester B. Pearson Award as Player of the Year, National Hockey League Players Association
1981-87, 1990-91, 1994	Art Ross Trophy as NHL's top scorer
1984-85, 1987-88	Stanley Cup as NHL champion (Edmonton Oilers)
1985, 1988	Conn Smythe Trophy as Most Valuable Player in Playoffs
1999	Induction into Hockey Hall of Fame

The Great One

A role model on and off the ice, Gretzky transcended the sport. He was a magician who conjured virtually anything he pleased—and Canadians love him for it.

Hollywood will no doubt make a movie about Wayne Gretzky some day, and it will have to include the scene where he plays his last game in Canada, in Ottawa against the Senators. It happened like this last week: Gretzky and his New York Rangers, who had already been eliminated from playoff contention, were playing the home team to a draw, thus denying the Senators a chance to boost their own playoff position. Yet with 4:45 left in the third period, during one of Gretzky's shifts, the crowd began to chant 'One more year! One more year!' Then, minutes later during a stoppage in play, the big-screen scoreboard above centre ice replayed highlights from Gretzky's career, and the PA system played Carly Simon's 'Nobody Does It Better.' The crowd rose in tribute, and players on both benches stood, too, banging their sticks against the boards and on the ice in the quintessential hockey salute.

Source: James Deacon, *Maclean's,* April 26, 1999.

have their son move to Toronto, about sixty miles away, to play in the junior league's Toronto Young Nationals team when he was fourteen. The move proved controversial when the Ontario Minor Hockey Association attempted to block the transfer, citing Gretzky's plan to live with the family of the team's manager and not his own family. Eventually he got clearance to play for the Nationals in the junior division against players who were as much as six years older. Even though the challenge was a greater one than he had anticipated when he left Brantford, Gretzky stayed in Toronto for two years and continued to make headlines for his outstanding accomplishments.

Gretzky's next move was also controversial. Although his parents had a gentleman's agreement with the teams in the Ontario Hockey Association (OHA) that Gretzky would not be drafted by any team further than 100 miles away from Brantford, the Sault Sainte Marie Greyhounds drafted the sixteen-year-old anyway. The Gretzkys were outraged, but the team's managers arranged for their son to live with a family that they had previously known in Brantford, which allayed some of their fears. With seventy goals and 112 assists in sixty-four games, Gretzky earned Rookie-of-the-Year honors in the OHA. He also took on the number that would remain on his jersey for the rest of his career: ninety-nine. Although Gretzky wanted to adopt the number nine in honor of his hero, the Detroit Red Wings' **Gordie Howe**, the number was already taken, so his coach suggested that he take on two number nines.

Makes NHL Debut in 1979

Gretzky spent just one year with the Greyhounds; as a seventeen-year-old, he jumped to the World Hockey Association's (WHA) Indianapolis Racers in 1978. The WHA had been stared in 1972 as a competitor to the NHL and, unlike the older league, did not exempt players younger than eighteen years of age from playing. Like the other teams in the WHA, the Racers were on the brink of bankruptcy and were forced to trade Gretzky to the WHA's Edmonton Oilers after just eight games. He finished the 1978-79 season with a total of

104 scoring points to again take the Rookie-of-the-Year title, this time for the WHA. The following year Gretzky became an NHL player when the WHA disbanded and the Oilers were one of the few teams to be absorbed into its rival.

Because he had played in the WHA, Gretzky was ineligible for the NHL's Calder Trophy as Rookie of the Year in his first season. If he had been eligible, he almost certainly would have won the honor. Instead, with fifty-one goals and eighty-six assists, Gretzky had to be satisfied with the Hart Trophy as NHL's Most Valuable Player and the Lady Byng Trophy as Most Gentlemanly Player. He would go on to win the Hart Trophy every year through 1987. In 1981 he started a five-year string of Lester B. Pearson Awards as Player of the Year, given by the National Hockey League Players Association, and a seven-year run as the as NHL's top scorer, symbolized by the Art Ross Trophy. In terms of his string of successes in the 1980s, Gretzky had no rival in the NHL.

First Stanley Cup Victory in 1984

Along with center **Mark Messier**, Gretzky transformed the Oilers into one of the best-ever teams in the history of hockey. Although the team was disappointed in a four-game sweep by the New York Islanders in the 1983 Stanley Cup finals, the Oilers returned the favor in a five-game series the following year. The Oilers emerged as champions again in 1985, 1987, and 1988, with Gretzky gaining honors as the playoffs' Most Valuable Player in 1985 and 1988.

The Stanley Cup victories, along with Gretzky's seemingly endless series of individual awards, made him into the best-known player in hockey by the mid-1980s. In a country that favored hockey as its national sport, Gretzky became a uniquely Canadian hero: despite his awesome accomplishments, he remained resolutely down-to-earth, without a hint of scandal to

Career Statistic

Yr	Team	GP	G	AST	PTS	+/−	PIM	SOG	SPCT	PPG	SHG
1979-80	Oilers	79	51	86	137	+15	21	284	18.0	13	1
1980-81	Oilers	80	55	109	164	+41	28	261	21.1	15	4
1981-82	Oilers	80	92	120	212	+81	26	369	24.9	18	6
1982-83	Oilers	80	71	125	196	+60	59	348	20.4	18	6
1983-84	Oilers	74	87	118	295	+76	39	324	26.9	20	12
1984-85	Oilers	80	73	135	208	+98	52	358	20.4	8	11
1985-86	Oilers	80	52	163	215	+71	46	350	14.9	11	3
1986-87	Oilers	79	62	121	183	+70	28	288	21.5	13	7
1987-88	Oilers	64	40	109	149	+39	24	211	19.0	9	5
1988-89	Kings	78	54	114	168	+15	26	303	17.8	11	5
1989-90	Kings	73	40	102	142	+8	42	236	16.9	10	4
1990-91	Kings	78	41	122	163	+30	16	212	19.3	8	0
1991-92	Kings	74	31	90	121	−12	34	215	14.4	12	2
1992-93	Kings	45	16	49	65	+6	6	141	11.3	0	2
1993-94	Kings	81	38	92	130	−25	20	233	16.3	14	4
1994-95	Kings	48	11	37	48	−20	6	142	7.7	3	0
1995-96	Kings	62	15	66	81	−7	32	144	10.4	5	0
	Blues	18	8	13	21	−6	2	51	15.7	1	1
1996-97	Rangers	82	25	72	97	+12	28	286	8.7	6	0
1997-98	Rangers	82	23	67	90	−11	28	201	11.4	6	0
1998-99	Rangers	70	9	53	62	—	14	—	—	—	—
TOTAL		1487	894	1963	2857	—	577	—	—	—	—

Blues: St. Louis Blues (NHL); Kings: Los Angeles Kings (NHL); Oilers: Edmonton Oilers (NHL); Rangers: New York Rangers (NHL).

tarnish his wholesome image. This humility and approachability made him into a favorite of fans and players alike. From 1981 to 1985 and again in 1987, Gretzky won the Lester B. Pearson Award as Player of the Year, given by the NHL Players Association.

Marries and Moves to Los Angeles in 1988

On July 16, 1988, Gretzky married actress Janet Jones in Edmonton, an event that the media dubbed "Canada's Royal Wedding." The media soon heaped scorn on Jones in the months after the wedding when the Oilers announced that they had traded Gretzky to the Los Angeles Kings. Oilers owner Peter Pockington insinuated that Jones had pushed for the trade because she wanted to be closer to her acting jobs; the couple countered with the fact that the Oilers were in financial trouble and that Pockington had come up with the possibility of trading Gretzky on his own, pocketing $15 million and other considerations for the deal. As the controversy died down, Gretzky prepared to join the Kings and revive a team that rarely enjoyed sold-out games. With his star power as the draw, sports fans in southern California indeed began following the team's fortunes.

It was with the Kings that Gretzky attained one of his most significant records on October 15, 1989: the all-time points record of 1,850 held by Gordie Howe. Gretzky eventually racked up 2,857 points in the course of his career, yet he never claimed another Stanley Cup. The closest he came was in 1993, when the Kings lost in the finals to the Montreal Canadiens in a five-game series. His level of play remained superior throughout the 1990s, however, and he claimed his tenth Art Ross Trophy as the league's leading scorer in 1994.

Retires in 1999

Gretzky was traded late in the 1995-96 season to the St. Louis Blues and jumped to the New York Rangers the following year. He stayed with the Rangers for the final three seasons of his twenty-year NHL career and surprised many fans by announcing his retirement in 1999. When he concluded his career, Gretzky was the holder or co-holder of sixty NHL records. He was inducted into the Hockey Hall of Fame in 1999.

Although his achievements as an athlete were legendary, Gretzky made a smooth transition into a career as a business owner in the years after his retirement as a player. As part-owner of the Phoenix Coyotes, he took an active role in rebuilding the team and popularizing hockey in another Sunbelt city. He also remained a national hero in Canada by helping the men's Olympic hockey team win a Gold Medal at the 2002 Salt Lake City Winter Games.

A dynamic competitor on the ice, Gretzky's self-effacing attitude in public made him into one of the most respected and even beloved figures in the sport's history. Without peers in terms of his achievements, he nevertheless retained an almost personal connection with hockey fans. The dominant player of his generation, Gretzky also helped to expand the NHL's popularity into markets that had not previously supported winter sports. It was this accomplishment that Gretzky focused on in his retirement, as he told Ashley Jude Collie of *Hockey Digest* in January

2002. "From my point of view, hockey's on the upsurge. It's heading in the right direction and I expect big things. It's always going to be extremely strong in the traditional U.S. cities and Canada. But our popularity is also extremely strong in Europe. . . . Over the next ten years, I think you'll find more and more kids in the U.S. will become hockey players. It's a wonderful sport and I just see more kids wanting to participate in the NHL."

FURTHER INFORMATION

Books

Diamond, Dan, ed. *Total Hockey: The Official Encyclopedia of the National Hockey League.* Kansas City: Andrews McMeel Publishing, 1998.

Gretzky, Walter and Jim Taylor. *Gretzky: From the Back Yard Rink to the Stanley Cup.* Toronto: McClelland and Stewart, 1984.

Sadowski, Rick. *Los Angeles Kings: Hockeywood.* Champaign, IL: Sagamore Publishing, 1993.

Taylor, Jim. *Wayne Gretzky: The Authorized Pictorial Biography.* Buffalo: Firefly Books, 1994.

Periodicals

Collie, Ashley Jude. "He's Not Like Mike—Or Mario." *Hockey Digest* (January 2002): 18.

Deacon, James. "The Great One." *Maclean's* (April 26, 1999): 16.

Deacon, James. "How Sweet It Is!" *Maclean's* (March 11, 2002).

Deacon, James and Susan McClelland. "Wayne's New World" *Maclean's* (November 22, 1999): 62.

Farber, Michael. "The Great Ones." *Sports Illustrated* (March 4, 2002): 42.

Jones, Terry. "Telling It Like It Is." *Edmonton Sun* (August 12, 1988).

Other

"Biography for Janet Jones." Internet Movie Database Web site. http://us.imdb.com/Bio?Jones,+Janet (November 7, 2002).

"October-November 1997." BBS Hockey Quotes Web site. http://www.bbshockey.com/quotes/quote17.htm (November 9, 2002).

"Wayne Gretzky." Internet Hockey Database Web site. http://www.hockeydb.com/ihdb/stats/pdisplay.php3?pid=2035 (November 9, 2002).

Sketch by Timothy Borden

Wayne Gretzky

Bob Griese
1945-

American football player

Hall of fame quarterback Bob Griese, six-feet-one-inch and 190 pounds, did not possess exceptional speed or a necessarily spectacular throwing arm, but his ability to read defenses, deliver passes with pin-point precision, and lead his team methodically down the field is legendary. Often referred to as a field general, Griese thrived as the quarterback of the Miami Dolphins during the 1970s under the direction of hall of fame coach **Don Shula**. Griese appeared in three consecutive Super Bowls, winning two (1973-1974).

Baseball or Football?

Bob Griese was born on February 3, 1945 in Evansville, Indiana, where he grew up with two siblings and his parents, Sylverious, a plumber, and Ida (Ulrich), a secretary. Griese was involved in sports from a young age, competing regularly with his older brother Bill. When Griese was ten his father died, and the traumatic event seemed to solidify the boy's already quiet, serious personality. He played basketball and baseball as a youth. He did not play organized football until he was a freshman at Rex Mundi High School. During his last two years in school he was named as the best quarterback in Indiana. He also excelled as a baseball pitcher, posting a 17-1 record, with his only loss coming in the 1963 American Legion World Series.

Bob Griese

Not heavily recruited out of high school, Griese, who wanted to get his education, passed up an offer from the Baltimore Orioles to sign him as a pitcher to attend nearby Purdue University. Under the tutelage of the Boilermakers' coach Bob DeMoss, Griese developed his fundamental skills as a passer. DeMoss corrected Griese's three-quarter side-armed throw (the same form he used to pitch baseballs) and got the young quarterback throwing straight overhand from behind the ear, giving him a quicker and straighter release. He earned the starting position as a sophomore, and by 1965, his junior year, he was becoming nationally recognized for his passing accuracy and his intelligent play. In that year he led his team to an upset victory over top-ranked University of Notre Dame, 25-21. On the day, Griese completed nineteen of twenty-two passes, with a streak of thirteen in a row.

Named a consensus All-American during his final two years, Griese's tenure at Purdue ended by winning the Rose Bowl, 15-14, over the University of Southern California. During his career as a Boilermaker, Griese completed 348 passes on 609 attempts. He was second in the bid for the 1966 Heisman Trophy, won by Steve Spurrier. Having also lettered in basketball, he graduated in 1967 with a degree in industrial management. On June 10, 1967, he married Judi Lassus, who would become a registered nurse. The couple had three sons.

Difficult Start in Miami

Griese was drafted in the first round by the Miami Dolphins, then a struggling team in the now-defunct

American Football League (AFL). As expected, Griese suited up for his first pro game to stand on the sidelines and watch his teammates compete against the Denver Broncos. However, when starting quarterback John Stofa broke his ankle in the first quarter of play, Griese was called in. The rookie stepped up to the challenge, connecting on twelve of nineteen passing attempts, and the Dolphins won the game. After that day, Griese never relinquished his spot as the team's starting quarterback.

Griese's first few years were a struggle. The Dolphins won only four games during his rookie season, five games in 1968, and just three in 1969. With little protection from a porous front line, Griese was often required to scramble away from defensive onslaughts, but he still managed to post consistently impressive numbers. In his sophomore season, he threw twenty-one touchdown passes and only sixteen interceptions. He was invited to play in the AFC All-Star Game two years.

Shula and Griese: A Perfect Combination

In 1970 the Dolphins joined the National Football League (NFL) and hired future hall-of-famer Don Shula to coach the team. Shula used his first year to rebuild the team and teach his offensive system that focused on consistent, short-yardage gains. During the 1970 season Griese had an impressive completion rate of fifty-eight percent, but his twelve touchdown passes stood against seventeen interceptions. By 1971 Griese and the Dolphins had hit their stride, making it all the way to Super Bowl VI, before being defeated by the Dallas Cowboys, 24-3. For his performance on the field Griese was named as an All-Pro Player and *The Sporting News* American Football Conference (AFC) Player of the Year. He made his second trip to the Pro Bowl.

Although he was hampered by injury during the 1972 season, sitting out all but six regular season games, the Dolphins rolled on undefeated. Griese returned for the playoffs, taking his team to Super Bowl

Career Statistics

Yr	Team	Passing						Rushing			
		GP	ATT	COM	YDS	COM%	TD	INT	ATT	YDS	TD
1967	Miami	12	331	166	2005	50.2	15	18	37	157	1
1968	Miami	13	355	186	2473	52.4	21	16	42	230	1
1969	Miami	9	252	121	1695	48.0	10	16	21	102	0
1970	Miami	14	245	142	2019	58.0	12	17	26	89	2
1971	Miami	14	263	145	2089	55.1	19	9	26	82	0
1972	Miami	6	97	53	638	54.6	4	4	3	11	1
1973	Miami	13	218	116	1422	53.2	17	8	13	20	0
1974	Miami	13	253	152	1968	60.1	16	15	16	66	1
1975	Miami	10	191	118	1693	61.8	14	13	17	59	1
1976	Miami	13	272	162	2097	59.6	11	12	23	108	0
1977	Miami	14	307	180	2252	58.6	22	13	16	30	0
1978	Miami	11	235	148	1791	63.0	11	11	9	10	0
1979	Miami	14	310	176	2160	56.8	14	16	11	30	0
1980	Miami	5	100	61	790	61.0	6	4	1	0	0
TOTAL		161	3429	1926	25092	56.2	192	172	261	994	7

Miami: Miami Dolphins.

Awards and Accomplishments

1961-62	Twice named the best high school quarterback in Indiana
1965-66	Twice named consensus All-American
1966	Runner-up for the Heisman Trophy
1970-71, 1973-74, 1977-78	Played in Pro Bowl
1971	Named *Sporting News* American Football Conference Player of the Year; selected as an All-Pro.
1973	Won Super Bowl VII
1974	Won Super Bowl VIII
1977	Named National Football League (NFL) Player of the Year; selected to the All-Pro team; led the NFL with 22 touchdown passes
1979	Inducted into the Florida Sports Hall of Fame
1985	Inducted into the College Football Hall of Fame
1990	Inducted into the Pro Football Hall of Fame

VII, where they triumphed over the Washington Redskins. The 1972 Dolphins became the only NFL team to post a 17-game win streak in a single season. During the 1973 season Griese threw for seventeen touchdowns and only eight interceptions, and the Dolphins won once again won the Super Bowl, beating the Minnesota Vikings, 24-7.

In 1976 problems with double vision and dizziness caused by 20-200 vision in his right eye forced Griese to wear glasses, which did little to slow the quarterback down. In fact he was awarded the Maxwell Club's **Bert Bell** Memorial Trophy as NFL Player of the Year in 1977, a season he threw a career-high twenty-two touchdown passes. Following the 1980 season Griese, suffering from a painful and nagging shoulder injury, announced his retirement. During his fourteen years as a Miami Dolphin, he completed 1,926 of 3,429 passes for 25,092 yards. To his 192 passing touchdowns, he added seven more rushing touchdowns.

Griese was a perfect match for Shula's ball control offense, in which grinding away yards on the ground emphasized over a flashy passing game. Because Griese bought into his coach's system, he was just as happy to hand the ball off to his running backs as he was to throw it. It was a match made in heaven. A match made in heaven for the fans of the Miami Dolphins, as well.

Following his retirement, Griese worked as a sports analyst for NBC's coverage of the NFL from 1982 to 1986. In 1986 ABC invited Griese to join sportscaster Keith Jackson to cover college football. Since then Griese has developed a reputation as a skilled, thoughtful commentator. He has covered more than twenty seasons of college football and numerous college bowl and NFL games.

Griese's wife died in 1988 from breast cancer, leaving Griese at home with his youngest son, Brian, then 13-years-old. The two developed a special bond, and when Brian became a quarterback at the University of Michigan, Griese covered several of his son's games. Brian has since followed his father into professional football as the quarterback of the Denver Broncos. Griese remarried in 1994 to Shay Whitney; they reside in Jupiter, Florida.

CONTACT INFORMATION

Address: ABC Sports, 47 W. 56th Street, New York, New York 10023.

SELECTED WRITINGS BY GRIESE:

(With Jim Denney) *Undefeated: How Father and Son Triumphed Over Unbelievable Odds Both On and Off the Field,* T. Nelson Publishers, 2000.

FURTHER INFORMATION

Books

Harrington, Denis J. *The Pro Football Hall of Fame: Players, Coaches, Team Owners and League Officials, 1963-1991*. Jefferson, NC: McFarland and Company, Inc. Publishers, 1991.

Hickok, Ralph. *A Who's Who of Sports Champions: Their Stories and Records*. Boston: Houghton Mifflin Company, 1995.

Perkins, Steve, and Bill Braucher. *Miami Dolphins: Winning Them All*. New York: Grosset and Dunlap Publishers, 1973.

Periodicals

Masin, Herman L. "Griese Kid Stuff." *Coach and Athletic Director* (March 1998): 14.

Montville, Leigh. "His Father's Son." *Sports Illustrated* (October 13, 1997): 76.

Tresniowski, Alex. "Top Gun and Son." *People Weekly* (December 1, 1997): 175-177.

Weber, Bruce. "Always on Sunday: Bob Griese Tells It Like It Is." *Coach and Athletic Director* (October 2000): 46-60.

Other

"Bob Griese: Analyst." ABC Sports/ESPN. http://espn.go.com/abcsports/columns/griese_bob/bio.html (December 30, 2002)

"Dolphins Hall of Famers: Bob Griese." Miami Dolphins. http://www.miamidolphins.com/history/halloffamers/halloffamers_griese_b.asp (December 30, 2002)

Sketch by Kari Bethel

Ken Griffey, Jr.

lieve he would shatter **Hank Aaron**'s all-time career home run record of 755. However, Griffey's weakness has been in being human, and injuries have kept him off pace. Another interesting facet of Griffey's career is that he and his father, Ken Griffey, Sr., played together for the Seattle Mariners in 1990-1991, making them the first father-and-son duo to play on the same team together. Over the years, Griffey has touched many lives off the field through his involvement with the Make-A-Wish Foundation. When children wish to meet Griffey, he willingly goes to say hello.

Ken Griffey, Jr.
1969-

American baseball player

With his leaping-over-the-wall catches and power-packed home run swing, Ken Griffey, Jr., is one of the best all-around players major league baseball has ever seen. His mastery of both the offensive and defensive aspects of the game, coupled with his childish enthusiasm and glittery smile, made him one of the game's most popular heroes. In 1994, Griffey received a record 6,079,688 votes for the All-Star Game, surpassing the old record of most votes by nearly two million. In four of his first eleven seasons, Griffey led the American League in home runs, leading many to be-

Spent Childhood at Ballpark Watching Father

George Kenneth Griffey, Jr., better known as Ken Griffey, Jr., or simply "Junior," was born November 21, 1969, in Donora, Pennsylvania, to Alberta and Ken Griffey, Sr. At the time, Griffey's father had just completed his first minor league season in the Cincinnati Reds farm system. Early on, Griffey began imitating his father. By the time he could walk, he was swinging a chunky, plastic baseball bat.

To say baseball was in Griffey's blood is an understatement. His grandfather, Buddy Griffey, played ball at Donora High School alongside **Stan Musial**. In 1973, Ken Griffey, Sr., was called up to play for the Reds, and the family relocated to Cincinnati. Griffey and his little brother, Craig, spent their childhoods at Riverfront Stadium in pint-sized Cincinnati Reds uniforms. As chil-

Chronology

1969	Born November 21 in Donora, Pennsylvania
1979	Begins playing Little League baseball
1983	Enters Cincinnati's Moeller High School
1987	Drafted on June 2 as first-round, first pick by Seattle Mariners
1987	Plays in the minors in the Northwest League on a team based in Bellingham, Washington
1988	Swallows aspirin overdose in apparent suicide attempt in January
1988	Plays in the California League for the San Bernardino Spirit
1989	Attends Mariners training camp; plays so well he earns position on roster
1989	Makes major league debut on April 3
1990	Makes baseball history in August when his father, Ken Griffey, Sr., joins the Mariners and the Griffeys become the first father-son teammates in baseball history
1994	Becomes father on January 19 when Trey Kenneth Griffey is born
1995	Becomes father again on October 21 as Taryn Kennedy Griffey is born
1995	Fractures wrist on May 26; misses 73 games
2000	Traded from Seattle Mariners to Cincinnati Reds on February 10
2000	Plagued with sore knee and partially torn hamstring throughout season
2001	Partially tears hamstring during spring training on March 26

Awards and Accomplishments

1987	Named best major-league prospect in the Northwest League by *Baseball America* magazine
1988	Named best major-league prospect in the California League by *Baseball America* magazine
1990-99	Earned American League Gold Glove Award
1990-2000	Named to the All-Star Team
1991, 1993-94, 1996-99	Earned Silver Slugger Award
1992	Named All-Star Game MVP
1993	Became fifth player in history to hit 100 home runs before 24th birthday
1993	Set American League outfielder record for most consecutive chances (573) without an error
1993	Tied major league record for hitting homers in eight consecutive games
1993	Led league in total bases (359) and extra base hits (86)
1994	Led American League in home runs (40)
1994	Won Make-A-Wish Foundation's Celebrity Wish-Granter of the Year Award
1996	Smacked three homers in one game
1997	Set major league record for most home runs in April with 13
1997	Led American League in runs scored (125), home runs (56), and runs batted in (147); led entire major league in runs batted in (147)
1997	Named American League Most Valuable Player
1997	Named *Sporting News* Player of the Year
1998	Smacked 300th career home run
1998	Led American League in home runs (56)
1999	Led league in home runs (48)
2000	Became youngest player (30 years, 141 days) to hit 400 homers
2001	Became youngest player (31 years, 261 days) to hit 450th homer

dren, the Griffey boys hung out with stars like **Pete Rose**, **Johnny Bench**, and Tony Perez.

The elder Griffey quickly established himself as a baseball star. He was part of Cincinnati's famed "Big Red Machine," which won the 1975 and 1976 World Series. It became apparent that Griffey was a chip off the old block as soon as he began playing organized baseball. Because Griffey was so much better than the other players, parents on the opposing teams thought he was too old to play in the league. His mother had to carry his birth certificate to games to prove he belonged.

Though Griffey's father traveled during the baseball season, he remained close to his sons and taught them valuable lessons. Once, when Griffey was a teen, he smacked a crowd-awing homer and rounded the bases pumping his fists. His father caught him at home plate—with a lecture about sportsmanship. Griffey never flaunted his talent again.

At Moeller High School, the 6-foot-3, 195-pound teen starred on both the football and baseball teams. By his senior year, Griffey was pegged as a future major leaguer and baseball scouts came out in full force, sometimes outnumbering fans in the stands.

Picked No. 1 in Baseball Draft

Because of his promising future, Griffey was the first player picked in the June 2, 1987, draft. He received a $160,000 signing bonus from the Seattle Mariners, a 1977 expansion team that had yet to have a winning sea-

son. Two days after the draft, Griffey graduated from high school. Four days later, on June 8, he took batting practice with the Mariners in Seattle. By June 11, he was in Bellingham, Washington, on the roster for one of the Mariners' farm teams, and on June 16, he played his first minor league game.

For Griffey, the transition of going straight from high school to work proved tough. At seventeen, he was on his own for the first time, traveling the country in an aging bus. Nonetheless, Griffey made his mark in the Northwest League. By the end of the fifty-four-game season, he'd batted .313. He led his team with homers (14), Runs Batted In (RBIs) (40), and steals (13). *Baseball America* magazine named him the league's top major league prospect.

Griffey had had a whirlwind year of change, and living in Washington he had experienced racial slurs. He struggled to come to terms with all the changes and pressures he had endured and in January 1988, Griffey swallowed more than 250 aspirin. He didn't talk about the suicide attempt until 1992, when he recounted the event to a reporter in hopes of discouraging others from doing the same.

Ken Griffey, Sr., was born April 10, 1950, in Donora, Pennsylvania, the same city Stan Musial hailed from. Like other Donora children of that time, Griffey grew up playing baseball and dreamed of following in Musial's footsteps.

In 1969, the Cincinnati Reds drafted Griffey in the 29th round. He spent four years in the minors and in 1973 was called up to play in the Reds outfield. As Griffey heated up, so did the Reds, and he became a part of the legendary "Big Red Machine," which won the 1975 and 1976 World Series.

Griffey Sr. made the All-Star team in 1976, 1977, and 1980, and was named All-Star MVP in 1980. In 1982, he was traded to the New York Yankees. The trade was hard on the family, which stayed behind in Cincinnati. Junior Griffey was just coming into his own as a baseball star when his father left. When he needed help-or was in big trouble-he flew to New York for a consultation with his dad. Under Yankee stadium, the elder Griffey spent many hours coaching-and lecturing-his son.

By 1990, Griffey Sr. had spent eighteen years in the majors when he was released by the Cincinnati Reds partway through the season. He signed with the Seattle Mariners and hit .377 for the remainder of the season, proving the move was more than a publicity stunt to unite the father and son.

Though the two are often compared, they know they are different people. As Griffey Sr. wrote in *Sports Illustrated,* "I don't feel overshadowed by him. He had shortcuts-like my teaching him how to hit, how to turn on the ball, how to stay out of slumps-and while my career may not get me into the Hall of Fame, how many guys can say they hit .296 over 19 years and played on two World Series winners?"

After retiring in 1991, Griffey Sr. became a Reds coach. When Junior Griffey was traded to the Reds in 2000, he got to coach his son. By 2002, the elder Griffey was working as a scouting consultant for the team.

Made Major Leagues at 19

In spring 1989, Griffey joined the Mariners at training camp and ended the pre-season with a fifteen-game hitting streak and a .359 average. Though he was young, his inexperience never showed. Instead of sending Griffey back to the minors, the Mariners decided to add him to their major league roster as a center fielder. At 19, Griffey was the youngest player in the league.

It didn't take long for Griffey to establish himself. He made spectacular defensive plays, digging his spikes into the padded outfield wall and reaching up over the top, turning home runs into outs. He made diving catches other players wouldn't attempt, then gunned down runners on base. Suddenly, Seattle was interested in baseball.

By mid-July 1989, Griffey's .287 batting average topped all American League rookies. He slipped in the shower July 24 and fractured a hand bone, putting him out for a month. When Griffey returned, he struggled at the plate trying to make up for lost time and put himself back in the running for the Rookie of the Year Award.

Though Griffey ended the season without capturing the rookie award, he did capture the hearts of millions of baseball fans. Former Seattle Mariners manager Jim Lefebvre recalled Griffey's magic in an issue of the *Seattle Times,* "Here it was my first time managing, and I've got a budding superstar with me, learning every day, captivating all the fans throughout the country.... Each day,

he'd go out and do something where you'd say, 'God, that's unbelievable. I've never seen that.' Next day, he'd so something else. It was just such a thrill to watch him play with that zest, that enthusiasm, that great talent."

Turned Baseball into a Family Affair

Griffey's second season, 1990, was just as thrilling. The highlight of the season, however, occurred in August when his father, recently released by the Cincinnati Reds, joined the Mariners. On August 31, 1990, they became the first father-son duo to play on a major league team together. The Griffeys comprised two-thirds of the Mariner outfield, with Junior Griffey playing center and Griffey Sr. playing left. They also followed each other in the lineup. On September 14, 1990, the duo hit back-to-back homers. It's a record that will likely never be broken.

For father and son, the chance to play together was the dream of a lifetime. Griffey's words in the *St. Louis Post-Dispatch* speak about the experience. "I got to play with my dad. I got to go to work with him. That's the biggest thing that ever happened to me other than the days my kids were born. That's bigger than any record I'll ever set.... To play alongside him was the best."

Became Home Run Champ

Griffey continued to wow fans and in 1992 made his third All-Star appearance. He belted three hits, including a homer off **Greg Maddux**, to win the game's MVP award. In 1993, Griffey proved himself a productive hitter. That season, he clobbered forty-five home runs, batted .309, drove in 109 runs, and led the league with 359 total bases. In addition, his fielding was superb. He set an American League outfielder record for handling 573 consecutive chances without an error. He also hit eight home runs in eight consecutive games, tying a major-league record set by Pittsburgh Pirate Dale Long in 1956 and New York Yankee Don Mattingly in 1987.

Griffey's streak continued into 1994. On May 20, he became the third-youngest player to reach 150 career homers. He'd smacked thirty-two homers through June to break **Babe Ruth**'s mark of most homers (30) through June. As Griffey's streak continued, he seemed on pace to break **Roger Maris**'s single-season home run record of 61. For the fifth-straight year, Griffey was voted to the All-Star team, this time receiving a phenomenal 6,079,688 votes, surpassing the old record of most votes received by Rod Carew in 1977, when he brought in 4,292,740 votes. However, in early August, a labor dispute between players and owners closed the season early, canceling the Mariners' last fifty games. Griffey ended the season with forty home runs, twenty-two shy of beating the single-season record. Had he played the last fifty games, it's conceivable that Griffey would have broken the record four years before slugger **Mark McGwire** did.

Griffey's 1995 and 1996 seasons were marred by injuries. Though he sat out twenty games in 1996, Griffey still orchestrated his best season ever. He hit .303, belted 49 home runs, and batted in 140 runs in just 140 games.

Griffey was hot again in 1997. On September 7, he smacked his fiftieth homer of the year, making him the fifteenth major leaguer of all time to reach fifty homers in one season. He led the American League in home runs (56) and runs scored (125). His 147 RBI led both the American and National leagues. For his offensive prowess, Griffey received the 1997 American League MVP award. The Mariners finished with a 90-72 record and faced the Baltimore Orioles in a best-of-five playoff series, which they lost.

Returned to Cincinnati, Struggled

Though Griffey continued to put up the numbers into the late 1990s, the Mariners did not, and Griffey grew frustrated about his lack of a championship. With a shaky bullpen, the team couldn't win. Unhappy, Griffey forced a trade after the 1999 season. Much to his delight, he landed with the Cincinnati Reds.

Cincinnati went wild with the news that Griffey was "coming home." In the announcement, Reds General Manager Jim Bowden declared, according to *The Seattle Times* "February 10, 2000, will go down in Reds' history, major-league history, as the day the **Michael Jordan** of baseball came home to Cincinnati."

Griffey signed a nine-year, $116.5 million deal. His yearly salary stood at $12.5 million, with the rest of the money deferred. The pressure mounted. Cincinnati was counting on Griffey to return the team to the World Series. With such high hopes, Griffey bombed. His time in Cincinnati was marred by injury and ill feelings with teammates who thought he got special treatment. Leg injuries in both the 2001 and 2002 seasons restricted him to 181 games total, and he smacked just 30 homers.

Frustrated with his injuries and slump, Griffey developed an edge. Teammates and media began to characterize him as a whiner and a spoiled brat. By 2002, Griffey's wife, Melissa, quit attending games because fans were abusing her, telling her to return to Seattle and take her husband with her. By December 2002, there was talk he would be traded.

When he's not busy with baseball, Griffey resides with his family in Orlando, Florida. He and his wife met at an alcohol-free dance club. They married after Griffey's 1992 season. They have three children, Trey and Taryn, along with Tevin, whom they adopted in 2002.

Griffey is also active in the Make-A-Wish Foundation and several times a year joins with children whose dream is to meet him. In addition, since 1994, he has sponsored a yearly Christmas dinner for youngsters from a local Boys and Girls Club. He also flies in to

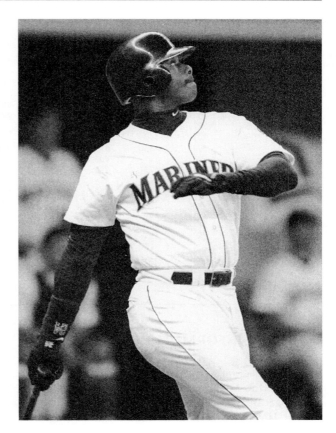

Ken Griffey, Jr.

Cincinnati children from the Seattle and Orlando Boys and Girls Clubs. He takes them to the amusement park, then brings them to the ballpark to watch him play.

Even if Griffey isn't able to get healthy and reclaim his position among the game's elite, he will still be remembered. After all, he made the All-Century Team in 1999. That puts him in the company of Hank Aaron and **Ted Williams**. Griffey may have faded from the spotlight after the turn of the century, but he has far from faded in the eyes of those who have seen him work his magic, leaping over walls to catch would-be home runs, or smacking picture-perfect homers. Those snapshots won't be forgotten.

CONTACT INFORMATION

Address: 100 Cinergy Field, Cincinnati, Ohio, 45202. Fax: (513) 421-7342. Phone: (513) 421-4510. Email: commintern@cincyreds.com. Online: http://cincinnati. reds.mlb.com/NASApp/mlb/cin/homepage/cin_home-page.jsp.

SELECTED WRITINGS BY GRIFFEY:

(Edited by Mark Vancil) *Junior: Griffey on Griffey,* HarperCollins, 1997.

Career Statistics

Yr	Team	Avg	GP	AB	R	H	HR	RBI	BB	SO	SB	E
1989	SEA	.264	127	455	61	120	16	61	44	83	16	10
1990	SEA	.300	155	597	91	179	22	80	63	81	16	7
1991	SEA	.327	154	548	76	179	22	100	71	82	18	4
1992	SEA	.308	142	565	83	174	27	103	44	67	10	1
1993	SEA	.309	156	582	113	180	45	109	96	91	17	3
1994	SEA	.323	111	433	94	140	40	90	56	73	11	4
1995	SEA	.258	72	260	52	67	17	42	52	53	4	2
1996	SEA	.303	140	545	125	165	49	140	78	104	16	4
1997	SEA	.304	157	608	125	185	56	147	76	121	15	6
1998	SEA	.284	161	633	120	180	56	146	76	121	20	5
1999	SEA	.285	160	606	123	173	48	134	91	108	24	9
2000	CIN	.271	145	520	100	141	40	118	94	117	6	5
2001	CIN	.286	111	364	57	104	22	65	44	72	2	3
2002	CIN	.264	70	197	17	52	8	23	28	39	1	3
TOTAL		.295	1,861	6,913	1,237	2,039	468	1,358	913	1,212	176	66

CIN: Cincinnati Reds; SEA: Seattle Mariners.

FURTHER INFORMATION

Books

Gutman, Bill. *Ken Griffey Jr.: A Biography*. New York: Pocket Books, 1998.

Reiser, Howard. *Ken Griffey, Jr. (The Kid)*. Chicago: Children's Press, 1994.

Stewart, Mark. *Ken Griffey, Jr., All-American Slugger*. New York: Children's Press, 1998.

Periodicals

Cannella, Stephen. "Great Pains: Another Injury Could Cost Ken Griffey Jr. Another Year-and a Chance to Restore his Rep." *Sports Illustrated* (April 15, 2002): 79.

Cannella, Stephen. "Junior Achievement." *Sports Illustrated* (May 20, 2002): 46.

Eisenbath, Mike. "5 Questions." *St. Louis Post-Dispatch* (July 1, 2001).

Griffey, Ken. "My Son, The Ballplayer." *Sports Illustrated* (June 21, 1999): 29.

"Griffey Inks $116.5 Million Deal With Cincinnati Reds." *Jet* (February 28, 2000): 48.

Massie, Jim. "Junior Finds His Return Taxing." *Columbus Dispatch* (September 22, 2000).

Stone, Larry. "Ken Griffey Jr. Down & Out at Home." *Seattle Times* (June 16, 2002).

"The Griffeys: Major-League Baseball's First Father-and-Son Pair." *Ebony* (September 1989): 78.

Other

"Junior Keeps Griffey Sr. in Cincinnati." ESPN.com. http://espn.go.com/mlb/news/2002/0224/1340065.html (December 13, 2002).

"Ken Griffey Jr." ESPN.com. http://sports.espn.go.com/mlb/players/profile?statsId=4305 (December 11, 2002).

Ken Griffey Jr. Adventures in Baseball. Stamford, Connecticut: Capital Cities/ABC Video Publishers, Inc., 1996.

"Ken Griffey Jr. Statistics." Baseball-Reference.com. http://www.baseball-reference.com/g/griffke02.shtml (December 6, 2002).

"Ken Griffey Sr. Statistics." Baseball-Reference.com. http://www.baseball-reference.com/g/griffke01.shtml (December 12, 2002).

Sketch by Lisa Frick

Archie Griffin
1954-

American football player

Archie Griffin's name will forever be linked to his improbable winning of two Heisman Trophies during the 1975 and 1976 seasons. To capture one of these honors is itself enough to etch a college football player's name into the book of legends. In a sports climate where most winners of the Heisman immediately go on to lucrative careers in the National Football League (NFL), Griffin returned for a final season, graduated a quarter early, and then went on to the NFL.

Growing Up

Archie Griffin was born on August 21, 1954, to James Griffin and Margaret Monroe Griffin in Columbus, Ohio. The middle brother in a family of seven boys,

Archie Griffin

Archie was surrounded by natural athletes—each of his brothers would play college football, and three would play in the NFL.

Griffin's father worked long and hard to support his family, knowing that the best he could do for his children was to give them a chance at a good education. At one point, he worked three jobs, balancing his days between driving a sanitation truck, cleaning a school and then working in a steel foundry at night.

Growing up, Archie Griffin was short and somewhat overweight, thus earning him the nicknames "Tank" and "Butterball" among his peers. When he began Eastmoor High in Columbus, his football coach didn't see him as the fullback he would eventually become, and he rarely touched the ball until the regular Eastmoor fullback didn't show up. Archie, a freshman, took over for the missing player, and after an impressive performance, never played another game as a lineman.

Realizing he would need to change physically to be a success at fullback, Archie hit the weight room to strengthen his upper body—the constant pulling and pounding a running back took demanded a stronger upper body than Archie had.

Though he would run track and wrestle, the football field was where his hard work and natural talent combined to propel him to greatness. Griffin remained the starting halfback at Eastmoor High School for the next three years, earning all-district honors as a junior, and being honored as a member of the All-State Team after leading them to the City Championship in 1972 (his senior year). Archie duplicated his on-field successes in the classroom, as well. He was an outstanding student.

College Success Follows High School Success

Because he was such an ambitious student, Griffin wanted to attend Northwestern University. The coach of Ohio State at the time, however—Woody Hayes—kept the young phenom in his hometown, charming Archie into playing for Ohio State.

Hayes put the 5'8" tall, 180 pound freshman into the team's starting lineup in only the second game of the season—as a running back. In a game against North Carolina, Archie broke the all-time Ohio State rushing record, gaining 239 yards and scoring a touchdown.

In his sophomore year—one filled with many outstanding achievements—Griffin began what was and still is a remarkable record of consecutive 100-yard performances, as well as leading his team to a lopsided victory over the eighth ranked University of Southern California Trojans. During the 1973 season, Griffin broke his own single game rushing record, amassing an awesome 246 yards in a performance against Iowa in a late-season contest. The Buckeyes finished the season 10-0-1, in second place in the final rankings.

When Griffin entered his junior year at Ohio State, many fans wondered what more they could possibly see out of their star. In his junior season, Griffin gained

Career Statistics

Yr	Team	GP	Rushing					Receiving				
			Att	Yds	Avg	TD		Rec	Yds	Avg	TD	Fum
1976	CIN	14	138	625	4.5	3		16	138	8.6	0	2
1977	CIN	12	137	549	4.0	0		28	240	8.6	0	3
1978	CIN	16	132	484	3.7	0		35	284	8.1	3	6
1979	CIN	16	140	688	4.9	0		43	417	9.7	2	3
1980	CIN	15	85	260	3.1	0		28	196	7.0	0	1
1981	CIN	16	47	163	3.5	3		20	160	8.0	1	0
1982	CIN	9	12	39	3.3	1		22	172	7.8	0	0
TOTAL		98	691	2808	4.1	7		192	1607	8.4	6	15

CIN: Cincinnati Bengals.

1620 yards and earned the most votes in the 1974 Heisman Trophy competition. The very next year, he came back and gained 1357 yards, again winning the Heisman and becoming the first (and most likely only) player to ever win two Heisman Trophy Awards.

The Pros

Griffin was taken as the second pick of the Cincinnati Bengals in the first round of the 1976 NFL draft. He played with the Bengals for eight seasons, and in what would become another makeover for the once-lineman turned exceptional running back, Griffin honed his pass-receiving skills, adding another weapon to his arsenal. When he retired from the Bengals in 1983, Griffin left the team ranked fourth on the team's all-time leading rusher list, gaining 2808 yards (averaging four per carry), and fifth on the all-time leading receiver list, with 192 receptions.

College Was Where It Was At

Archie Griffin was named a member of almost every major collegiate sports hall of fame for his football dominance from 1972-1976. At Ohio State, he broke nearly all standing rushing records, and in the process set national marks and Big Ten marks for single season rushing and for his college career. He had been named captain of his 1974 Buckeye team, and, in a move mostly unheard of, voted to captain a second time by his teammates in 1975.

At the conclusion of his collegiate career, Griffin received the NCAA's Top Five Award, an honor that says more about Griffin than his on-field accomplishments. This is the top honor an undergraduate can receive, and is given based on a combination of athletic skill, academic accomplishment, leadership and character. Griffin actually graduated a quarter early with a degree in industrial relations.

The Griffin Legacy

When he moved on to the NFL, his size kept him from dominating quite so handily. Though he would have a successful NFL career, his triumphs on the collegiate football fields will cement him as a standout figure in college lore forever. His name will always find a way into sports trivia as "the only man to win two Heismans."

When he retired from the Cincinnati Bengals in 1983, Griffin had a short stint playing football with the Jacksonville Bulls of the United States Football League. He also tried his business skills by opening a shoe store chain with his brother, but both of these endeavors ultimately proved unsuccessful, and unfulfilling, for Griffin.

Soon after he left Ohio State University, Griffin wrote an inspirational autobiography, *Archie: The Archie Griffin Story,* that gave readers an inside look into Archie Griffin the man. In the book, he answers the question of, "Where did his tremendous inner-strength and determination come from?" He felt he owed the course of his character and personal discipline to Christ. Griffin had long been a member of the Fellowship of Christian Athletes, and his place in the public eye and his articulate nature made him a sought-after motivational speaker both during and after his years with the Bengals.

His name is now forever linked to two Heisman Trophies, an accomplishment that will likely never be duplicated. Archie Griffin has proven his amazing skills on the football field, at both the collegiate and professional levels. But it is in his life after sports where he has made some of his greatest contributions. In his roles as goodwill ambassador for Ohio and in his responsibilities with Ohio State's athletic program-where he helps shape the lives of thousands of young people-Archie is leaving a legacy. Playing football gave Griffin fame, but his heart and courage allowed him to succeed in life.

CONTACT INFORMATION

Address: Archie Griffin, Administration, 224 St. John Arena, 410 Woody Hayes Dr., Columbus, OH 43210.

Awards and Accomplishments

1973	Came in fifth in Heisman Trophy Voting
1973	NCAA All-American; named Big Ten Player of the Year
1973-74	Silver Football Trophy
1974-75	Won Heisman Trophy
1974	UPI College Football Player of the Year
1974	Big Ten Player of the Year
1974	Walter Camp Player of the Year
1975	Maxwell Award
1975	*Sporting News* "Man of the Year" award
1981	Inducted into Ohio State Athletics Hall of Fame
1986	Inducted into National High School Sports Hall of Fame
1986	Inducted into National Football Foundation and College Hall of Fame
1987	Inducted into Columbus Urban League's Hall of Fame
1990	Inducted into Rose Bowl Hall of Fame
1990	Receives Branch Rickey Award
1993	Inducted into The Columbus Public Schools Hall of Fame
1994	Winner of Walter Camp Alumni Award
1999	Receives Price Waterhouse Coopers Doak Walker Legends Award
2001	Receives NCAA Silver Anniversary Award

Where Is He Now?

Archie Griffin returned to Ohio State University almost immediately after retiring from the Bengals. In 1985 he was named the Special Assistant to the Director of Athletics. Then, in 1987, he became the Assistant Director of Athletics. By 1994 he had been promoted to the Senior Associate Athletic Director at Ohio State University, where he still works today.

At Ohio State, Griffin is directly responsible for the football program, as well as seventeen other sports. He is known as one of Ohio's ambassadors of goodwill, and he's a legend in the lore of a state where football is its unofficial religion. Archie Griffin is married to Bonita, and they have three sons: Anthony, Andre and Adam.

Other

"Archie Griffin." http://www.buckeyeclassics.com/archiegriffin.asp/ (October 29, 2002).
"Archie Griffin." http://www.football-reference.com/ (October 29, 2002).

Sketch by Eric Lagergren

SELECTED WRITINGS BY GRIFFIN:

(With Dave Diles) *Archie: The Archie Griffin Story*, Doubleday, 1977.

FURTHER INFORMATION

Books

"Archie Griffin." *Great Athletes,* volume 3, Farrell-Holdsclaw. Hackensack, N.J.: Salem Press, Inc. 1045-1047.
"Archie Griffin, Mr." *Who's Who Among African Americans,* 14th ed. Detroit: Gale Group, 2001.
"Archie Mason Griffin." *Almanac of Famous People,* 6th ed. Detroit: Gale, 1998.
Dolan, Edward F., Jr. and Richard B. Lyttle. *Archie Griffin.* Garden City, NY: Doubleday, 1977.
Griffin, Archie, and Dave Diles. *Archie: The Archie Griffin Story.* Garden City, NY: Doubleday, 1977.
Mendell, Ronald L., and Timothy B. Phares. "Archie Griffin." *Who's Who in Football.* New Rochelle, NY: Arlington House, 1974.

Periodicals

"Griffin hangs up his cleats-again." *Sporting News* (April 1, 1985): 6.
"Griffin prepared for backup job." *Sporting News* (October 3, 1981): 50.
"Heisman hero still hoping for solid shot with Bengals." *Jet* (September 20, 1982): 50.
Ladson, William. "Didn't you used to be... Archie Griffin?" *Sport* (January 1989): 82.
Wessling, Jack, and Sandra Kobrin. "Griffins file for bankruptcy." *Footwear News* (January 4, 1982): 25.

Florence Griffith Joyner
1959-1998

American sprinter

Florence Griffith Joyner, known as "FloJo," was the fastest woman alive. She won three gold medals at the Summer Olympic Games in Seoul, South Korea in 1988-in the 100- and 200-meter runs, and the 4x100 meter relay. Her world records for the 100 and 200 meters remain unbroken. The vibrant Griffith Joyner often wore flashy running outfits and long, brightly painted fingernails while competing. She died in her sleep at her home in Mission Viejo, California in 1998, after a seizure, at age 38.

Born to Run

Griffith Joyner was born Delorez Florence Griffith, the seventh of 11 children. Her father worked as an electrical contractor, and her mother was a teacher. At age 4, her mother, also named Florence Griffith, left her husband and the house in California's Mojave Desert, taking the kids to live in a public housing project in the impoverished Watts neighborhood of Los Angeles.

Griffith Joyner's mother later told Pete Axthelm and Pamela Abramson in *Newsweek,* "We had nothing. But I explained to the children that life was like a baby. A baby comes into the world without anything. Then it starts crawling, then it stands up. Then it takes its first step and starts walking. When we moved into the project I told them, 'Start walking.'"

Florence Griffith Joyner

Chronology

1959	Born in Los Angeles, California
1978	Graduates from Jordan High School in Los Angeles
1983	Graduates from college at UCLA
1984	Left off an Olympic relay team because officials said her fingernails were too long to pass the baton
1987	Marries Al Joyner
1989	Retires from competitive running
1993	Appointed co-chair of President's Council on Physical Fitness.
1998	Dies in her Mission Viejo, California home after a seizure

Griffith Joyner began racing competitively at age seven. She also developed an interest in fashion that would become her trademark. Once her unusual style got her into trouble; she was kicked out of a shopping mall for wearing her boa constrictor pet as an accessory.

On visits to the desert, where her father still lived, she kept in shape for running by chasing jackrabbits. She actually managed to catch one or two, she recalled.

The elder Florence Griffith kept her family together with strict rules and weekly family meetings she called "powwows." At these gatherings, the mother and her children would reflect on the events of the week and use stories from the Bible as examples for how they could improve themselves. Griffith Joyner studied the Bible and prayed through adulthood. She credited her mother for keeping all her children away from the drugs and violence that ruined the lives of many of their neighbors. "We didn't know how poor we were," Griffith Joyner told *Newsweek*. "We were rich as a family."

Olympic Dreams

After graduating from Jordan High School in Los Angeles in 1978, Griffith Joyner enrolled at California State University, Northridge (CSUN), but dropped out in 1979 to help support her struggling family financially. She also had to drop running as a sport. She took a job as a bank teller, and there she would have remained if not for the efforts of her coach at CSUN, Bob

Kersee. Kersee helped her find financial aid so she could return to school. When Kersee took the coaching job at the University of California, Los Angeles (UCLA), in 1980, Griffith Joyner went with him. There she continued to build a reputation as an outstanding sprinter. She graduated from UCLA in 1983 with a degree in psychology.

With Kersee still her coach, Griffith Joyner competed in her first Olympics in 1984; Los Angeles hosted the Summer Games. Running in her hometown, she won the silver medal in the 200-meter run. After the 1984 Olympics, Griffith Joyner retired from running, again taking a bank job, and also working as a beautician. But starting in 1987, she began again to train, this time for the 1988 Olympics in Seoul, South Korea.

In 1987, Griffith Joyner married Al Joyner, who won the gold for the triple jump in the 1984 Games. Al's sister, Jackie Joyner-Kersee (married to Bob Kersee, who also coached her) was an Olympic medalist, and a world record holder in the heptathlon. When Griffith Joyner dropped Kersee as her coach, citing his controlling tendencies, and replaced him with her husband, it created a rift between the Joyners and the Kersees.

World's Fastest Woman

On July 16, 1988, while trying out in Indianapolis for the Olympics, Griffith Joyner broke the world record for the fastest time for a woman in the 100-meter run. She did it wearing a purple body suit that had one leg cut off and a pair of colorful bikini bottoms over it. Her time was 10.49 seconds, beating **Evelyn Ashford**'s record by 27-hundredths of a second. Ashford, who had set her record in 1984, went on to finish second after Griffith Joyner in the 100 meters at the 1988 Olympics.

Some accused Griffith Joyner of illegally taking human growth hormone or steroids to boost her speed, pointing to her rapid muscle development. Griffith Joyner vehemently denied these allegations, saying, according to Jere Longman in the *New York Times*, "I have never taken any drugs. I don't believe in them. It's a false accusation." She cited weight training and her renewed commitment to her sport after marrying Al Joyner.

Awards and Accomplishments

1973	Wins Jesse Owens National Youth Games
1981	Breaks American college record in World Cup 4x100-meter relay
1982	Wins NCAA championship in 200-meter run
1983	Wins NCAA championship in 400-meter run
1984	Wins silver medal for 200-meter run at Olympics
1988	Breaks women's world record time for 100 meters
1988	Becomes first American woman to win four medals in one Olympics
1988	Named U.S. Olympic Committee's Sportswoman of the Year
1988	Named Associated Press Female Athlete of the Year
1988	Named UPI Sportswoman of the Year
1988	Named *Track and Field* magazine's Athlete of the Year
1988	Named Jesse Owens Outstanding Track and Field Athlete
1988	Wins Sullivan Award for top amateur athlete
1995	Inducted into the U.S. Track and Field Hall of Fame

Shared Passion for Fitness

Recognized for her intricately painted fingernails and brightly colored, often one-legged outfits, Olympic champion runner Florence Griffith Joyner ("Flo-Jo") captured the affection of the world with a combination of speed, grace and beauty. In the 1980s, when women athletes were given much less regard than their male counterparts, Flo-Jo helped female athletes gain respect. In fact, Flo-Jo's victories may have opened people's eyes to the talented female athletes in all sports and laid the groundwork for the public's embrace of this year's FIFA Women's World Cup soccer teams.

Source: Durrett, April. *IDEA Health & Fitness Source,* October 1999, p. 47.

In 1989, Darrell Robinson, a former national 400-meter champion, said he had sold a human growth hormone to Griffith Joyner a year earlier. An angry Griffith Joyner, denying the accusation, called Robinson "a compulsive, crazy, lying lunatic."

Although the drug charges were never proven, they continued to haunt Griffith Joyner. Rumors even spread linking her death to drug use. "I think for Florence, the drug issue will always come up, whether she did it or not," Ashford told Longman.

Griffith Joyner went on to win the gold medal for the 100 meters at the 1988 Olympics. She also broke the record for the 200 meters, winning another gold with 21.34. Griffith Joyner added a third gold at that Olympiad, in the 4x100-meter relay, and took home a silver in the 4x400-meter relay.

A Life Ended too Soon

Griffith Joyner delighted crowds by dressing like no other runner before her or after. Her running suits typically left one leg bare and were colorful and brightly-patterned. She also wore her nails six inches long and had them elaborately painted. When she retired from competitive running in 1989, she took a job designing uniforms for the National Basketball Association's Indiana Pacers. Griffith Joyner's post-Olympic activities also included pursuing acting and writing careers, designing fingernail fashions, recording a series of fitness videos, and starting a family—she gave birth to her daughter, Mary, soon after retiring from racing. In 1993, she became co-chair of the President's Council on Physical Fitness.

In 1996, Griffith Joyner had a seizure while on an airplane. She was hospitalized when the plane landed, and released after a day under medical observation. She died during the night of September 20, 1998. Her husband awoke beside her the next day and discovered she was not breathing. He immediately called an ambulance, but by then it was too late.

After learning of her death, President Clinton eulogized Griffith Joyner for her athletic achievements and personal style. He praised her for never forgetting her origins in a poor Los Angeles neighborhood, and for reaching out to help children in need even after she became famous.

Not just her astonishing accomplishments on the track made Griffith Joyner beloved around the world. Her unique style and charisma inspired a generation of girls. Besides her husband, Griffith Joyner is survived by their daughter, Mary, who was age seven when Griffith Joyner died.

Griffith Joyner's Legacy

Griffith Joyner had both style and substance. She overcame poverty to be the best in her sport, all while adding a touch of style. "In sum, Griffith Joyner... is as complex and fascinating as Olympic athletes come," Axthelm and Abramson wrote, shortly before her death. "Her life and career have had been filled with steep rises and falls, and she has persevered with strength and flair. She plays up her good looks as few Olympians have. But she also reads the Bible daily, prays before every meal and calls her mother at least twice a day."

Griffith Joyner admitted to having a small circle of friends, but added: "That doesn't bother me because with or without friends I have a million and one things to do. I don't frighten people away. They frighten themselves away."

FURTHER INFORMATION

Periodicals

Axthelm, Pete with Abramson, Pamela. "A Star Blazes in the Fast Lane." *Newsweek* (September 19, 1998): 54.

Durrett, April. "Sharing a Passion for Fitness." *IDEA Health & Fitness Source* (October 1999): 47.

Huebner, Barbara. "Griffith Joyner Dead at 38; Sprinter's Heart May Have Failed." *Boston Globe* (September 22, 1998): E7.

Longman, Jere. "Florence Griffith Joyner, 38 Champion Sprinter, Is Dead." *New York Times* (September 22, 1998): C23.

Other

"FloJo: World's Fastest Woman." CNN-SI. http://www.sportsillustrated.cnn.com/olympics/features/joyner/gallery/. (January 24, 2003).
"Forence Griffith Joyner." Infoplease.com. http://www.infoplease.com/ipa/A0766184.html. (January 24, 2003).

Sketch by Michael Belfiore

Janet Guthrie

Janet Guthrie
1938-

American race car driver

In 1977, the famous words traditionally spoken at the beginning of motorsport's best known race were changed to "In company with the first lady ever to qualify at Indianapolis—gentlemen, start your engines." The change acknowledged the presence of thirty-nine-year-old Janet Guthrie. Before this historic moment, Guthrie had thirteen years of trailblazing experience in the male-dominated world of sports car racing. With her last major race, a career-best fifth place finish at the Milwaukee 200 in 1979, her career began to wind down. By then, she had earned a distinguished position in women's sports history.

A Thirst for Adventure

Janet Guthrie was born in Iowa City, Iowa, on March 7, 1938, the oldest of five children. At the age of three, she moved with her family to Miami, Florida, when her father accepted a job as an Eastern Airlines pilot. Her love of adventure, and fast machinery in particular, started early.

Guthrie earned a pilot's license at the age of seventeen, and even before she graduated from the University of Michigan in 1960 with a bachelor's degree in physics, she worked as a commercial pilot and a flight instructor. After graduation, she began a career as an aerospace engineer, working on forerunners to the Apollo rockets. She also applied for the National Aeronautics and Space Administration's (NASA) first Scientist-Astronaut program. She passed the first round of eliminations but lacked the Ph.D. necessary to advance. Meanwhile, the tug of competition, something that flying did not provide, led her to buy a Jaguar XK 120. She disassembled then reassembled the engine, with the goal of turning it

into a race car. She started competing soon after, and in 1964 won two Sports Car Club of America races and finished sixth in the Watkins Glen 500 in New York. Her work in the aerospace industry began to give way to sports car racing.

She explained the lure of competitive racing to Margie Boule of the *Oregonian*, "All these wonderful machines developed in the 20th century . . . made the difference for a woman who had the same sense of adventure as a man but didn't have the broad shoulders and the big muscles.... The good old boys weren't happy to see me coming."

A Pioneering Racing Career

By 1971, Guthrie had completed nine consecutive endurance races. But her star really started to rise in 1976, when she became the first woman to compete in a National Association for Stock Car Auto Racing (NASCAR) Winston Cup superspeedway event, finishing fifteenth out of forty starters. She did not qualify for the Indianapolis 500 that year, but racing team owner and car builder Rolla Vollstedt was impressed enough to offer her a test drive in one of his Indy cars. Pleased with her performance, she became Vollstedt's second driver at the 1977 Indianapolis 500 qualifying trials. Guthrie qualified and competed, but engine trouble forced her out of the race early. The next year, she returned to the Indianapolis 500 and finished ninth out of 33 starters. She remains the only woman to finish in the top ten.

Chronology

1938	Born March 7 in Iowa City, Iowa
1955	Earns pilot license at age seventeen
1960	Graduates from University of Michigan with B.Sc. in physics
1960	Joins Republic Aviation in New York as aerospace engineer
1960	Buys her first sports car, a used Jaguar XK 120
1963	Begins competing in high-speed car races
1964	Passes first round of eliminations of NASA's first Scientist-Astronaut Program
1967	Resigns position with Republic Aviation
1976	Granted a United States Auto Club license
1976	Becomes first woman to compete in NASCAR Winston Cup event
1976	Becomes first woman to enter Indianapolis 500 and pass the rookie test
1977	Becomes first woman to qualify and race in Daytona 500
1977	Becomes first woman to qualify and race in Indianapolis 500
1979	Finishes fifth in the Milwaukee 200, her last major race
1989	Marries Warren Levine

Awards and Accomplishments

1967	First in class, Sebring 12-Hour (GT-6)
1970	First in class, Sebring 12-Hour (Under 2 Liter Prototype)
1971	First overall, New York 400, Bridgehampton
1973	North Atlantic Road Racing Champion
1976	Finished 15th, Charlotte World 600 (NASCAR superspeedway race)
1977	Finished 12th, Daytona 500 (Top Rookie)
1977	Set fastest time of day on opening day of practice, Indianapolis 500
1978	Finished ninth, Indianapolis 500
1979	Finished 34th, Indianapolis 500
1979	Finished fifth, Milwaukee 200
1980	Finished 11th, Daytona 500
1980	Inducted into the International Women's Sports Hall of Fame
1997	Honored at "Specialty Equipment Market Association's (SEMA) Salute to Women in Motorsports", Washington, DC
2002	Received Lifetime Achievement Award in motorsports at Boy Scouts Breakfast, Portland, Oregon

Displaying racing talent and persistence, Guthrie continued to post impressive finishes. In 1977 alone, she was top rookie at Rockingham, Charlotte, Richmond, and Bristol. She competed in nineteen NASCAR Winston Cup races that year, finishing in the top twelve ten times. She also was the first woman and Top Rookie at the Daytona 500, finishing twelfth.

She also began winning over critics. Fellow driver **Mario Andretti** told *The Washington Star* in 1977, "Anyone who says she doesn't belong, just feels threatened." Driver **Bobby Unser** echoed the sentiment, telling *Philadelphia Inquirer Magazine* in 1979, "She's done a good job. I gotta admit that I had my doubts about her. But she's proven her point … she can be up there in the top 10. There are a lotta guys who can't say that."

Still, Guthrie was dogged by the allegation that she was not competitive; that her racing career amounted to an experiment. In typical fashion, she proved herself unflappable in handling the close scrutiny and frustrations she faced. In an interview with Tracy Dodds of the *Los Angeles Times,* she said, "I know that that is not true. I stand on my record … but it's hard to have your reputation kicked around again and again." The criticism ignored the fact, her supporters countered, that she was poorly funded and usually raced in cars that were entered just to complete the field.

Few Women Followed Her Lead

Guthrie's racing career did not end the way she wanted. Without adequate sponsorship, she did not have the money to continue. "I didn't quit willingly, and I didn't accomplish what I felt I could," she told Boule of the *Oregonian.*

Few women have replicated Guthrie's racing success. She points to several reasons for this—the big money corporate sponsorship the sport requires, a male network that discourages women's participation, and a persistent attitude that women don't have what it takes to race.

Guthrie argues that corporate sponsorship is still not as available to women as it is to men and remains the biggest reason women have made little progress in the sport. As for the idea that women lack the ability, in 1987 she told Dodds of the *Los Angeles Times,* "Women just can't do it? Horsefeathers. I find that highly offensive." She is armed with examples from different sports to illustrate her contention that women possess the skills, stamina, and courage to compete with men.

Attitudes among drivers, however, have shifted over the years, partly because Guthrie's success in breaking the gender barrier has made women racers more acceptable. For example, four-time Indianapolis 500 winner **Al Unser, Sr.**, who spoke out against Guthrie's 1977 appearance at Indy, is mentoring twenty-two-year-old driver Sarah Fisher. In 1999, Fisher became the youngest woman to compete in an Indy event.

Guthrie now lives in Colorado, with her husband of thirteen years. She completed the manuscript chronicling her racing days, *Lady and Gentlemen,* and is seeking a publisher. Guthrie still loves the sport and follows the progress of up and coming drivers, especially the women. She travels and gives speeches extensively. She's also active in the arts.

Guthrie's helmet and driver's suit are in the Smithsonian Institution, and she was one of the first inductees into the International Women's Sports Hall of Fame. Even though her last major race was more than twenty years ago, her pioneering influence remains. When Guthrie got Sarah Fisher's autograph during a 2002 visit to the Indianapolis Motor Speedway, Fisher wrote, "To Janet, my idol."

CONTACT INFORMATION

Online: www.janetguthrie.com.

FURTHER INFORMATION

Books

Woolum, Janet. *Outstanding Women Athletes: Who They Are and How They Influenced Sports in America.* Phoenix, AZ: Oryx Press, 1998, 2nd ed.

Periodicals

Boule, Margie. "For Racing Pioneer, Women Still Have a Long Way to Go." *Oregonian* (June 13, 2002): E01.

Dodds, Tracy. "Why Aren't Women Racing at Indy? Ask Guthrie." *Los Angeles Times* (May 24, 1987): 3.

"Pioneer Reflects on History; Guthrie Made Her Mark in '77." *Commercial Appeal* (May 24, 2002): D4.

Other

"History of Women at Indy." http://cbs.sportsline.com/ u/ce/feature/0,1518,2392629_6,00.html (October 22, 2002).

"Janet Guthrie." International Women's Sports Hall of Fame. www.hickoksports.com/biography/guthriejan. shtml (October 18, 2002).

"Janet Guthrie." www.nascar.com/2002/kyn/women/ 02/02/Guthrie/ (October 18, 2002).

"Janet Guthrie—Auto Racing Legend." www.janet guthrie.com/indexold.htm (October 16, 2002).

"Janet Guthrie Biography." www.janetguthrie.com/ Biography.htm (October 16, 2002).

"Janet Guthrie Career Statistics." www.janetguthrie. com/careerstats.htm (October 16, 2002).

"Janet Guthrie, The First Female Indianapolis 500 Driver, to be Honored On Capitol Hill May 7 at the 'SEMA Salute to Women in Motorsports.'" www. classiccarbuyersguide.com/news/press/date/19970506/ press00203.html (October 22, 2002).

"Quotes From Her Peers." www.janetguthrie.com/ quotes.htm (October 16, 2002).

Sketch by Carole Manny

Tony Gwynn
1960-

American baseball player

Tony Gwynn is one of the greatest players and most prolific hitters in major league baseball history, ranking with **Ted Williams** and **Stan Musial** for batting average. Finishing his twenty-year career with the San Diego Padres at age forty-one in 2001, he recorded a .338 overall average, with 3,141 career hits, putting him in sixteenth place for the most hits in major league history. He also

Tony Gwynn

won five Gold Glove Awards for his outfield skills—the most in San Diego Padres history—was voted a starter in the All-Star Game eleven times, and won eight National League batting championships and seven Silver Slugger Awards. Gwynn is known for videotaping his hits and studying them to improve his technique. Gwynn is expected to be inducted into the Baseball Hall of Fame in 2007.

Young Athlete

Anthony Keith "Tony" Gwynn was born May 9, 1960, in Los Angeles, California, the son of Charles (a warehouse manager) and Vendella (a postal worker) Gwynn. He grew up with his two brothers in Long Beach, California, where his dad played baseball with the boys in the backyard, using cut-up socks as balls. Young Tony also had a best friend in elementary school, Alicia Cureton, who became his sweetheart in high school and his wife in 1981.

Gwynn graduated from Long Beach Poly High School in 1977. His success in basketball and baseball won him a sports scholarship to San Diego State University (SDSU) in 1978. There he played only basketball in his freshman year but went on to play baseball with the SDSU Aztecs as well. During his sophomore year, he began using the 32-inch, 31-ounce bat that was his favorite throughout his professional career. Gwynn was named third-team All-American by *Baseball News* in 1980. In 1981 he batted .416 and was named National Collegiate Athletic Association (NCAA) All-American. On June 10, 1981, Gwynn

Chronology

1960	Born May 9 in Los Angeles, California
1977-81	Plays point guard for San Diego State University basketball team
1979-81	Plays baseball with San Diego State University Aztecs
1980	As Aztec, bats .423, with six home runs
1981	As Aztec, bats .416, with 11 home runs; is drafted by San Diego Padres pro baseball team and San Diego Clippers pro basketball team on same day (June 10); marries Alicia Cureton (they will have two children, Anthony II and Anisha Nicole); begins career with Padres with Walla Walla team in Rookie Northwest League, where he is named Most Valuable Player
1982	Plays first major league game, on July 19; breaks wrist and misses three weeks' play
1983	A second wrist injury stalls season, but Gwynn finishes batting .309, with team-record 25-game hitting streak
1984	Leads team to National League Championship Series against Chicago Cubs
1985	Injures wrist again, but makes All-Star team for second time
1986	Wins first of five Gold Glove Awards; ties a major-league record with five stolen bases on September 20
1987	Hits .370, with Padres record 218 hits, highest batting average since Stan Musial's .376 in 1948
1988	In spite of two injuries, has 18-game hitting streak and finishes with .318 average
1989	Has another All-Star, Gold Glove season, in spite of wrist and Achilles tendon injuries; files for bankruptcy, citing problems caused by his accountant
1990	Fractures index finger and misses 19 games but still bats above .300; tensions develop between him and some Padres team members, and a Gwynn figurine is found in the dugout with its arms and legs torn off; negotiates a five-year, $16.25 million contract with Padres
1991	Loses 21 games to arthroscopic surgery on left knee, bats above .300
1992-93	Has two more knee surgeries but records 2,000th hit in 1993; father dies in winter of 1993
1994	Has difficult year after loss of his father; stops training after fourth knee surgery; friend Eric Show dies of drug overdose; Major League Players Association strike halts season on August 12, as Gwynn is near to hitting .400 for season
1995	Bats .368 and has award-winning season; receiving honors for both baseball and charitable work
1996	Injures right heel and misses 56 games but bats .353 and hits a two-out, two-run eighth-inning single that he calls biggest hit of his career
1997	At age 37, has finest season of his career, batting .372; Padres extend his contract through 2000; Tony Gwynn Stadium opens as new home of the San Diego State University baseball program
2001	At age 41, announces retirement from professional baseball on June 28, effective at the end of the season; is named head baseball coach at San Diego State University (SDSU) on September 20, effective June 1, 2003—he will work as a volunteer coach during the 2002 school year; begins building Church's Chicken franchise restaurants through his company Gwynn Sports

Awards and Accomplishments

1980	Named third team All-American by *Baseball News*
1981	Named College All-American and first team All-Western Athletic Conference outfielder; named Most Valuable Player in Rookie Northwest League
1984, 1986-87, 1989, 1994	Named to *Sporting News* National League All-Star Team
1984, 1987-89, 1994-97	National League Batting Champion
1984-87, 1989-96	Voted to All-Star Game
1984, 1986-87, 1989, 1994-95, 1997	Given *Sporting News* Silver Slugger Award
1984, 1986-88, 1994-95, 1997	Voted San Diego Padres' Most Valuable Player
1984-99	Named to National League All-Star Team
1986-87, 1989-91	Gold Glove Award for outfield
1995	Branch Rickey Award for most community service in major league baseball; San Diego Padres' Chairman's Award for community service
1997	San Diego State University dedicated new baseball stadium in Gwynn's name
1997-99	San Diego State University recipient of Roberto Clemente Award for combining excellence in playing with community service and sportsmanship
1999	Recipient of Phi Delta Theta's Lou Gehrig Memorial Award
1999	Inducted into World Sports Humanitarian Hall of Fame
1999	Recorded 3,000th career hit on August 6

The Lou Gehrig Memorial Award is presented annually to the major league player who best exemplifies the leadership and character of the late Lou Gehrig, Hall of Fame first baseman

hitting that he said, "What are you trying to do, catch me after one night?"

During the 1982 and 1983 seasons, Gwynn suffered the first of several injuries that would cause him to miss games during his career. In August 1982 he broke his left wrist while catching a fly ball and then broke his right wrist playing winter baseball in Puerto Rico. By mid-1983, however, he was back with the Padres and finished the season with a .309 average.

In 1984, Gwynn took the first of his National League batting championship titles, with a .351 average and 213 hits. He came in third in voting for the league's Most Valuable Player (MVP), even though the Padres lost the 1984 World Series to the Detroit Tigers.

Tony on Tape

From very early in his career, Gwynn videotaped all of his at-bats and then studied them religiously to improve his nearly perfect technique. This practice began in 1983 when he asked his wife to tape a game during a time he felt his hitting was off. After watching the tape, he saw the error he was making. He quickly corrected it

was drafted by both the San Diego Padres and the San Diego Clippers basketball team. He chose the Padres.

"Mr. Padre"

Gwynn started his professional career in the Padres' farm system in Washington, Texas, Hawaii, and Nevada before being brought up to San Diego on July 19, 1982. He debuted against the Philadelphia Phillies' champion hitter **Pete Rose**, who was so impressed with Gwynn's

Career Statistics

Yr	Team	Avg	GP	AB	R	H	HR	RBI	BB	SO	SB
1982	SD	.289	54	190	33	55	1	17	14	16	8
1983	SD	.309	86	304	34	94	1	37	23	21	7
1984	SD	.351	158	606	88	213	5	71	59	23	33
1985	SD	.317	154	622	90	197	6	46	45	33	14
1986	SD	.329	160	642	107	211	14	59	52	35	37
1987	SD	.370	157	589	119	218	7	54	82	35	56
1988	SD	.313	133	521	64	163	7	70	51	40	26
1989	SD	.336	158	604	82	203	4	62	56	30	40
1990	SD	.309	141	573	79	177	4	72	44	23	17
1991	SD	.317	134	530	69	168	4	62	34	19	8
1992	SD	.317	128	520	77	165	6	41	46	16	3
1993	SD	.358	122	489	70	175	7	59	36	19	14
1994	SD	.394	110	419	79	165	12	64	48	19	5
1995	SD	.368	135	535	82	197	9	90	35	15	17
1996	SD	.353	116	451	67	159	3	50	39	17	11
1997	SD	.372	149	592	97	220	17	119	43	28	12
1998	SD	.321	127	461	65	148	16	69	35	18	3
1999	SD	.338	111	411	59	139	10	62	29	14	7
2000	SD	.323	36	127	17	41	1	17	9	4	0
2001	SD	.324	71	102	5	33	1	17	10	9	1
TOTAL		.338	2440	9288	1383	3141	135	1138	790	434	319

SD: San Diego Padres.

and relied on the tapes for the rest of his career, accumulating a library of them. This earned him the nickname "Captain Video." He once told *Ebony* magazine, "I do all of my preparation before I get into the batter's box—and then it's just about seeing the ball and hitting it." Gwynn favored hitting the ball in what he calls the 5.5 Hole, the gap between the shortstop and third base.

During the early 1990s, Gwynn became close friends with the great hitter Ted Williams, who became a mentor to him and spoke of Gwynn as the finest pure hitter of his generation. Williams suggested that Gwynn, a left-handed hitter, like himself and the great Stan Musial, should be the successor to his own title as the greatest living hitter. Some sportswriters argued that Musial should inherit the title, but Williams, who died in July 2002, favored Gwynn.

Winning through the Pain

Gwynn kept up his award-winning playing after the 1984 season—his batting average never dropped below .300 between 1984 and 1994, and he continued to win batting titles—along with the love of the San Diego fans. He also won his first Gold Glove Award for defense in 1986. He had an exceptional .370 batting average in 1987, with a Padres record of 218 hits.

Gwynn enjoyed eating and developed a bit of a rotund physique, but the weight gain did not slow him up on the diamond. What did continue to plague him, however, were injuries. In 1988 he had surgery on his left hand and was injured in a fall. After getting off to a slow start, however, he finished the season batting .313 and won an-

other National League batting title. In the 1989 season he injured his Achilles tendon and had another wrist injury but still managed to take home the Gold Glove and be named All-Star. That year was difficult in another way as well: in spite of his high salary, he had to file for bankruptcy because of what he called improper practices by his accountant. In 1990 he fractured an index finger, and in 1991 he had a conflict with some team members, who hung a figure of him in the dugout with arms and legs removed. He also had the first of four knee surgeries that would cause him to miss games through 1994. In spite of the lost time, he continued to play brilliantly and achieved his 2,000th career hit in 1993.

The year 1994 was perhaps the most painful of all for Gwynn, however. He had lost his father in the winter of 1993, and it was difficult for him to go on without the man on whom he had so depended for advice and support. Another knee surgery and the loss of a former teammate, Eric Show, to a drug overdose, brought Gwynn down even further. He stopped training and canceled public appearances. He soon pulled himself together, though, and concentrated on his game. In August, as Gwynn was hitting .475, the Players Association went on strike and called a halt to the games.

Back on the playing field in 1995, Gwynn had another great year, winning the league batting title and his eleventh All-Star Game designation, as well as being named Padres MVP for the sixth time. He played most of the 1996 season with a torn Achilles tendon but still batted .353, logged his 2,500th hit, and made the play that put the Padres into the playoffs. After the season ended, he had surgery to repair the torn tendon.

Fully recovered in 1997, at age 37, with a little gray in his beard, Gwynn had probably his best season with the Padres. He hit his personal best in home runs, seventeen, had 119 RBIs, batted .372, and won his eighth league batting title. The Padres renewed his contract through 2000.

In 1998 the Padres went to the World Series for the second time in Gwynn's career. They lost to the New York Yankees even though Gwynn had eight hits and a home run in sixteen times at bat. On August 6, 1999, he collected his 3,000th hit. Only **Ty Cobb** and Nap Lajoie achieved the milestone in fewer games than Gwynn had.

Retirement from Professional Baseball

Although he became a free agent in 2001, Gwynn stayed on with the Padres to finish out his career. After 3,141 hits and finishing with a batting average of .338, he retired from the Padres at the end of the 2001 season. His teammates presented him with a motorcycle during a ceremony at Qualcomm Stadium in San Diego, as some 60,000 fans cheered him goodbye. After his twenty years with the Padres, he said, "I feel I've done all I can do as a baseball player."

Tony Gwynn is a student of baseball, a hitter who never stopped trying to perfect his swing, to know his pitchers, and to help his team win. He holds five of the top eleven batting averages for a single season compiled since the end of World War II and tied with **Honus Wagner** for the most National League batting titles (eight). He is also an affable, easygoing person, always attentive to the media and the fans. Tony and Alicia Gwynn are famous for their charitable work with young people. Tim Kurkijan of *Sports Illustrated* once called Gwynn "probably the most popular and successful player in San Diego sports history" and "one of baseball's most good-natured people."

CONTACT INFORMATION

Address: c/o San Diego State University Department of Athletics, 5500 Campanile Drive, San Diego, California 92182-4313. Online: http://www.goaztecs.ocsn.com.

SELECTED WRITINGS BY GWYNN:

(With Jim Geschke) *Tony!*, Contemporary Books, 1986.
(With Jim Rosenthal) *Tony Gwynn's Total Baseball Player*, St. Martin's Press, 1992.
(With Roger Vaughan; foreword by Ted Williams) *The Art of Hitting*, GT Pub., 1998.

FURTHER INFORMATION

Books

Contemporary Black Biography, Volume 18. "Tony Gwynn." Detroit: Gale Group, 1998.

Where Is He Now?

Upon retirement in October 2001, Tony Gwynn was selected head baseball coach at San Diego State University (SDSU), his alma mater, which in 1997 named its new baseball stadium in his honor. He chose to serve one year as a volunteer coach before beginning a three-year contract term with the university. Gwynn called the coaching position "the dream gig for me."

During 2002, Gwynn moonlighted as a sports analyst for the ESPN television network. Tony and his wife, Alicia, also own Tony Gwynn Sports, and in 2000 the company bought 100 Church's Chicken restaurant franchises. They planned to build about seven stores per year, from San Diego to Bakersfield, California.

Tony and Alicia—who owns AG Sports, a company specializing in merchandising and graphic design—have continued their charity work. They routinely take disadvantaged children into their home, providing teens with job skills through Alicia's business. Their TAG Foundation supports a number of San Diego charities, including one that provides shelter for abused and abandoned children. Alicia told the *Sporting News,* "We both feel like we are blessed people and fortunate to be in the position we are in. We just try to do the right thing."

Newsmakers, Issue 4. "Tony Gwynn." Detroit: Gale Group, 1995.

Who's Who Among African Americans, 14th edition. "Tony Gwynn." Detroit: Gale Group, 2001.

Periodicals

"Coaching at His Alma Mater." *Jet* (October 15, 2001): 50.

"Community Champions." *Sporting News* (August 2, 1999): 17.

Elfin, David. "Hometown Hero." *Insight on the News* (October 1, 2001): 28.

"A Final Goodbye." *Jet* (October 22, 2001): 55.

Hocker, Cliff. "Gwynn up to Bat at Church's Plate." *Black Enterprise* (November 2000): 30.

Other

Baseball-Reference.com "Tony Gwynn." http://www. baseball-reference.com/ (November 27, 2002).

Dutton, Bob. "Who Takes Position as Greatest Living Hitter after Williams?" Knight Ridder/Tribune News Service. (July 7, 2002).

Eckhouse, Morris A., and James G. Robinson. "Tony Gwynn." BaseballLibrary.com. http://www.pubdim. net/baseballlibrary/ (November 27, 2002).

Kawakami, Tim. "Ten Good Minutes with Tony Gwynn." Knight Ridder/Tribune News Service. (July 28, 2002.)

San Diego State University Athletic Department. "Aztecs Name Tony Gwynn Head Baseball Coach: Former SDSU Baseball and Basketball Star Returning to The Mesa." http://goaztecs.ocsn.com/ (September 20, 2001.)

The SportsCoach.com. "Tony Gwynn." http://www. baseballinstruction.com/ (December 12, 2002).

World Sports Humanitarian Hall of Fame. "Tony Gwynn." http://www.sportshumanitarian.com/ (December 12, 2002).

Sketch by Ann H. Shurgin

Georg Hackl
1966-

German luger

Georg Hackl is regarded as the best ever to compete at luge, the Olympic sport in which participants lie on their backs on tiny sleds and speed feet-first down icy channels at 90 mph, their runs timed in thousandths of a second. Hackl, who is German, is good-naturedly called the "Flying Sausage" for his love of bratwurst and speed and, perhaps, his unathletic build. What he lacks in physique, however, Hackl more than makes up for in unshakable nerve and technical prowess. He dominated luge in the 1990s, becoming the first luger—and one of only five Winter Olympians from any sport—to win gold at three consecutive Olympic Games.

Mental focus

Hackl won the individual event at the Albertville Olympics in 1992, Lillehammer in 1994, and Nagano in 1998. And he book-ended these gold medals with silver medals in Calgary in 1988 and Salt Lake City in 2002. Hackl is the first Winter Olympian to win a medal in five consecutive Olympic Games and the first Olympian, summer or winter, to win a medal in the same individual event at five consecutive games. "His mental strength is phenomenal," German coach Thomas Schwab told Tim Layden in *Sports Illustrated*. "It really borders on virtuosity. Before he gets on the sled at the top of the run, he has gone through every situation that could possibly happen. As he slides, it seems to him that it has already happened before. He has this mystical air about him."

Fearless and technically savvy

Hackl was raised in Berchtesgarden, Germany, a haven for winter sports in the Bavarian Alps. He tried luge for the first time in grammar school; he was neither a natural athlete nor an immediate success. He was, however, mechanically adept. Hackl loved to design and build lightweight luge sleds and was constantly tweaking them to increase their speed. At age sixteen, he became an apprentice to a metal worker so he could make

Georg Hackl

better sleds. *USA Today* recounted the story of Hackl setting a track record in his opening run of the 2001 World Cup season in Calgary, then quickly stuffing his sled into a bag. "The move was typical for the luge legend, who guards his equipment innovations like a chef's secret sauce," the paper said. Hackl elevated the stakes in his quest for a fifth Olympic medal. Before the 2002 games, he enlisted engineers at Porsche to help him create a faster sled. "To be part of developing a sport is something that is very satisfying. If you took a sled from 10 years ago, it would be more than half a second slower," Hackl, a beer-loving sergeant in the German Army, told the *New York Times*. "I was the best, and then the others tried to beat me. They succeeded. Then I try to beat them. This pushes the process, and that is what has kept my interest for 20 years. I design my sleds. I design the start technique, the driving, the aerodynamic position and the equipment."

Chronology

1966	Born September 9 in Berchtesgarden, Germany
1982	At age 16, apprentices as a metal worker to make better luge sleds
1988	Silver medal in the individual event, Winter Olympics, Calgary, Alberta
1992	Gold medal in the individual event, Winter Olympics, Albertville, France
1994	Gold medal in individual event, Winter Olympics, Lillehammer, Norway
1998	Gold medal in the individual event, Winter Olympics, Nagano, Japan
1998	Becomes first luger - and one of only five Winter Olympians from any sport - to win gold at three consecutive Olympic Games (Albertville in 1992, Lillehammer in 1994, and Nagano in 1998)
2002	Silver medal in the individual event, Winter Olympics, Salt Lake City, Utah
2002	Becomes the first Winter Olympian to win a medal in five consecutive Olympic Games and the first Olympian, summer or winter, to win a medal in the same individual event at five consecutive games

Awards and Accomplishments

1989-90	Overall World champion and world champion in singles luge
1991, 1993, 1995	Member of world champion team
1991, 1999	Second in World Cup standings
1992	Gold medal in the individual event, Winter Olympics, Albertville, France
1992, 1994, 1996	Third in World Cup standings
1994	Gold medal in individual event, Winter Olympics, Lillehammer, Norway
1997	World champion in singles luge
1998	Gold medal in the individual event, Winter Olympics, Nagano, Japan
2000	Gold medal in team competition and bronze in individual competition, world championship; gold medal in team competition and silver medal in individual competition, European championship
2001	Gold medal in team competition and silver in individual competition, world championship
2002	Silver medal in the individual event, Winter Olympics, Salt Lake City, Utah

The other critical factor in Hackl's winning repertoire is his fearless nature. Lugers hurtle down the side of a mountain, unprotected, at astonishing speeds—but they must remain relaxed to minimize unnecessary movements that can be the difference between winning and losing. This is where Hackl excels. "The object is to steer while moving as little as possible because even the smallest of motions is transferred immediately to the runners, throwing a sled off-line. In a sport timed in thousandths of a second, any error is lethal to success," Layden wrote in *Sports Illustrated*. "Hackl rides as still as a corpse, his movements are more subtle than a whisper, his driving line a work of art. His skill and focus are no less impressive than that of the quarterback who doesn't hear the crowd."

Decade of domination

At age twenty-one, Hackl slid to a silver medal at the 1988 Winter Olympics in Calgary, and he was the world champion in 1989 and 1990. It was the beginning of a remarkable string of success. Hackl went on to win at least 20 World Cup competitions and numerous world championship medals in both individual and team events. He finished in the top three in the overall World Cup standings eight times. In 1997, he added another world championship. It was at the Olympics, however, that Hackl's performance became legendary. In 1992, he won the gold medal in the Albertville games, adding to the German-speaking nations' dominance in winter sports. Two years later, he won gold in Lillehammer, outpacing the silver medalist by 13-thousandths of a second. At the 1998 games in Nagano, Hackl joined an elite group of Winter Olympians—including U.S. speed skater **Bonnie Blair**—to have won the same event three times in a row. "Hackl is the most decorated luge racer in history," Mike Dodd wrote in *USA Today*. "He brings a reputation as a driver who saves his best for the biggest events."

Deprived of fourth gold

Hackl had a chance to make history at the 2002 Olympics in Salt Lake City—to become the first winter Olympian ever to win gold in the same event at four consecutive Olympiads. Six weeks before the games, Hackl's father watched him win a Super-Cup race in Germany, gave his son a congratulatory hug and, a few minutes later, suffered a heart attack. He died in the ambulance that came to his aid. Hackl would carry his grief to Salt Lake City, where Italy's Armin Zoeggeller prevented him from claiming his fourth Olympic gold medal. Hackl demonstrated grace despite his disappointment. Still in the finishing zone when Zoeggeller completed his winning run, Hackl spontaneously led the applause for his rival. Afterward, he told reporters: "This second place is where I belong. Armin is the right champion." When someone asked Hackl whether he was dedicating his medal to anyone, however, he thought of his father and broke down and sobbed. "I want to dedicate it to my father," he said haltingly. "Who died. A few weeks ago."

With Hackl's second-place finish behind Zoeggeller, he became the first athlete to win a medal in five consecutive Winter Olympics. He is more than the most successful luger in history, however. He is an endearing man and a fan favorite who brought unprecedented attention to his sport. "Georg has made us . . . more famous in Europe," Adam Heidt, a luger from Long Island, told the *New York Times,* "and hopefully a little more famous now in America."

After the 2002 Olympic Games, Hackl returned to the World Cup circuit. He said he would compete for at least another year, but was uncertain whether he would still be in the game in 2006, his next opportunity to extend his Olympic streak. "I feel great to have this awesome career, especially in the Olympic Games," Hackl was quoted in the *New York Times,* "and maybe I am very lucky because you also need to have good luck to win medals."

CONTACT INFORMATION

Address: Deutscher Bob-Rodelschlihen, Ander Shiesstrasse 6, Berchtesgarden, D-83471, Germany.

FURTHER INFORMATION

Periodicals

"'88 Winter Olympics; Mueller Glides to Gold in Luge." *New York Times* (February 16, 1988).

Baker, Andrew. "Hackl's Rise Ends with Silver." *Daily Telegraph* (London, England) (February 12, 2002).

Clarey, Christopher. "Nagano '98: Luge; Gold and Silver Divided by Split Seconds." *New York Times* (February 1, 1998).

Dodd, Mike. "Hackl Will be a Hard Man to Catch." *USA Today* (February 10, 2002).

Fawlty, Matt. "Iceman Suffers Rare Meltdown." *Australian* (February 13, 2002).

"Germany's 'Flying Sausage' Makes History." Agence France Presse (February 12, 2002).

"Hackl Closes Gap on Kleinheinz." *New York Times* (January 26, 2003).

Layden, Tim. "Born to Luge." *Sports Illustrated* (February 9, 1998).

Layden, Tim. "Going Four Gold at 35, Germany's Georg Hackl is Sliding for Olympic History." *Sports Illustrated* (February 10, 2002).

Litsky, Frank. "U.S. Settles for Moral Victories, not Medals, in Luge." *New York Times* (February 11, 1992).

"Record Run by Italian Threatens German Dominance in the Luge." *New York Times* (February 11, 2002).

Robbins, Liz. "A German Legend Loses to an Italian, Then Loses his Composure." *New York Times* (February 12, 2002).

Sketch by David Wilkins

Marvin Hagler
1954-

American boxer

Marvelous Marvin Hagler was a hard-hitting lefty who could switch his stance and also box right-

Chronology

1954	Born in Newark, New Jersey
1967	Moves with family to Brockton, Massachusetts
1973	Turns pro
1973-75	Wins first 26 professional fights
1976	Loses first fight on January 13 to Bobby Watts
1977-86	Doesn't lose a fight in 10 years
1980	Marries Joann Dixon
1982	Legally adds "Marvelous" to his name
1986	World Boxing Association (WBA) withdraws recognition of Hagler as world middleweight champion
1987	Loses World Boxing Council (WBC) middle weight to Sugar Ray Leonard
1988	Retires
1989	Divorces; moves to Italy; stars in action-adventure movie *Indio*
1992	Stars in *Indio 2: The Revolt*

handed. The world middleweight champion from 1980 to 1987, Hagler was a gutsy, aggressive fighter. Over the course of his 14 years as a professional boxer, he posted a record of 62-3-2 and successfully defended his title 12 times before losing to Sugar Ray Leonard in an controversial split decision in 1987.

Road to the Title

Marvelous Marvin Hagler was born on May 23, 1954, in Newark, New Jersey. He was the oldest of six children. His father, Robert Sims, left the family when Hagler was young, and he was raised along with his siblings by his mother, Ida Mae Hagler. In 1969, wanting to escape the race riots that plagued Newark at the time, Hagler's mother moved the family children to Brockton, Massachusetts, the hometown of hall of fame boxer **Rocky Marciano**. When he was 15 years old, Hagler began working out at a boxing gym in Brockton, where he met brothers Guareno ("Goody") and Pat Petronelli, who trained and managed Hagler throughout his career.

Hagler won 57 bouts as an amateur. In May 1973, a week after winning the Amateur Athletic Union (AAU) middleweight championship, he turned professional. On May 18, 1973, he won his first professional fight, with a technical knockout (TKO) of Terry Ryan in the second round. Hagler walked through his first 14 bouts with little trouble. He scored a total of three knockouts (KO; one in the first round, two in the second) and nine TKOs. He faced his first serious challenge on August 30, 1974, when he fought former Olympic champion, Sugar Ray Seales. Going 10 rounds, Hagler earned the decision in a closely matched bout. In a rematch on November 26, the two fought 10 rounds to a draw.

On January 13, 1976, with a record of 26-0-1, Hagler experienced the first loss of his career, failing to earn the decision in a 10-round bout with Bobby "Boogaloo" Watts. He lost a second time two fights later, again by decision after 10 rounds, to Willie "The Worm" Monroe.

Awards and Accomplishments

1973	Wins National Amateur Middleweight Championship; wins Amateur Athletic Union (AAU) Middleweight Championship; receives Outstanding Fighter Award
1980-87	Undisputed middleweight champion
1984	Named Boxer of the Year by the World Boxing Council
1985	Receives The Jackie Robinson Award for Athletes for simultaneously holding the middleweight title for the World Boxing Association, World Boxing Council, and the International Boxing Federation
1993	Inducted into the International Boxing Hall of Fame

Hagler later avenged both losses by beating Monroe twice in 1977 and knocking out Watts in two rounds in 1980. He would not lose again until the final bout of his career ten years later.

Finally, on November 30, 1979, Hagler entered the ring with a record of 46-2-1 to face Vito Antuofermo for his first shot at the world middleweight title. The fight went 15 rounds, and, much to Hagler's consternation, the bout was called a draw, thus Antuofermo retained his title. Eleven months later, after four more wins, Hagler got his second shot at the title, facing England's Alan Minter, who had taken the title from Antuofermo. Hagler pounded Minter during the first round, opening cuts around the boxer's left eye. By the third round Minter was bleeding profusely, forcing the referee to call the fight. Hagler had his first world middleweight title.

In his next seven bouts, Hagler defended his title via three TKOs and four KOs. Despite his dominating presence in the ring, Hagler, who legally added "Marvelous" to his name in 1982, felt as though he wasn't getting the respect, or the big prize fights, he deserved. That changed in November of 1983 when former lightweight and welterweight champion Roberto Duran resurrected his boxing career to challenge Hagler for the middleweight title. The fight itself, much hyped by the media, was itself anticlimactic. Duran, known as an aggressive boxer, worked conservatively against Hagler, throwing the champion off his game plan. Only by forcing the action in the final rounds was Hagler able to retain his title by a narrow margin on points after the full 15 rounds.

Hagler defended his title twice in 1984, knocking out both opponents. His next big fight came on April 15, 1985, when he took on challenger Thomas Hearns, a big name fighter with big-fight experience. Known for his powerful right hand, boxing analysts touted this as the bout that would prove Hagler's worth. The fight, thought by many to be one of the greatest bouts in boxing history, went three rounds. At the bell Hagler attacked with vengeance. Disregarding any boxing technique and defensive strategy, the two pummeled each other throughout the first round. Hearns had a longer reach, but Hagler was stronger. Because Hagler was willing to trade punches, he forced Hearns in close where he could reach him.

By the third round, Hagler was ahead on points but he had multiple cuts that were bleeding, opening the door for Hearns to win on a TKO. When the referee called time out to have a doctor examine him, Hagler knew his time was limited before the referee called the fight. Within a minute after the round resumed, Hagler chased Hearns across the ring and nailed him with three powerful rights. Hearns went down, and although he managed to stagger to his feet, he could not regain his balance, and Hagler was awarded the win on a TKO. It was the champion's defining moment and the highlight of his career.

Hagler vs. Leonard

In March of 1986 he defended his title for the eleventh time, knocking out the undefeated junior middleweight champion John Mugabi in the eleventh round. On April 7, 1987, Hagler slipped on his gloves and entered the ring for the last time. After a five-year absence from boxing, **Sugar Ray Leonard** announced that he was coming out of retirement to challenge Hagler. For his part, Hagler was so excited about the opportunity to prove himself against one of the best in the world, he conceded numerous advantages to Leonard, including glove size, ring size, and number of rounds (12 rather than 15).

The purse for the fight, which took place at Cesar's Palace in Los Vegas, was $20 million ($19 million for Hagler, $11 million for Leonard), the largest for a fight up to that time. Hagler surprised many by working conservatively against Leonard in the first rounds. Perhaps realizing that he was playing into Leonard's strength of dancing and circling, Hagler stepped up in the middle rounds to move in on Leonard. The fight was very close, and after 12 rounds, the title was awarded to Leonard in a controversial split decision that is still debated today.

Hagler, who was convinced he won the bout, wanted a rematch and waited a year for Leonard to agree to fight him again. Frustrated when Leonard continued to avoid a rematch, Hagler retired in 1989. He later told CBS Sportsline, "I felt as though I had accomplished everything in my career and the only thing left for me to do was to have a rematch with [Leonard]."

Like many professional athletes, Hagler struggled after he retired from the ring. He told London's *The Times,* "When I stopped boxing it drove me nuts.... I started to feel like there weren't nothing else because boxing had been everything for too long." He divorced soon after his retirement and moved to Milan, Italy, to pursue a new career in acting. He starred in two action-adventure films, *Indio* and *Indio 2,* as well as several Italian-made movies and a television series. Hagler travels to the United States often and continues to pursue new opportunities in acting. He also has increasingly appeared ringside as a boxing commentator, receiving high marks from critics for his articulate, insightful remarks. However, after so many years out of the ring, Hagler still feels the pull in his heart. He admitted to *The*

Boston Globe, "I don't go back to the gyms. I don't want to smell that smell and get that feeling again. I was born to be a fighter, I believe. Boxing was always my love, but that love is over. I moved on with my life...."

FURTHER INFORMATION

Books

Contemporary Newsmakers 1985. Issue Cumulation. Detroit: Gale Research, 1986.

Porter, David L., ed. *African-American Sports Greats.* Westport, CT: Greenwood Press, 1995.

Porter, David L., ed. *Biographical Dictionary of American Sports: Basketball and Other Indoor Sports.* Westport, CT: Greenwood Press, 1989.

Roberts, James B., and Alexander G. Skutt. *The Boxing Register: International Boxing Hall of Fame Official Record Book.* Ithaca, New York: McBooks Press, 1999.

Who's Who Among African Americans, 14th ed. Detroit: Gale Group, 2001.

Periodicals

Borges, Ron. "World Apart in South Africa: Divergent Paths of Ex-champions Hagler and Duran Intersect Again." *The Boston Globe,* (December 31, 1997): E1.

"Brains, Not Brawn, the Secret Says Marvelous Marvin Hagler." *United Press International,* (May 2, 1983).

"Hagler: Marvelous Pugilist with Bitter Sweet Memories." *Agence France Presse,* (December 5, 1999).

Kervin, Alison. "Fighting Talk Puts Hagler Ahead on Points." *The Times,* (May 21, 2002).

Vega, Michael. "New England's Top 100. No. 19, Marvin Hagler." *The Boston Globe,* (December 13, 1999): D2.

Other

"Marvelous Marvin Hagler." International Boxing Hall of Fame. http://www.ibhof.com/hagler.htm (January 30, 2003).

Turner, Allyson. "Now and Then: Marvin Hagler." CBS Sportsline.com. http://cbs.sportsline.com/u/thennow/marvinhagler.html (January 30, 2003).

Sketch by Kari Bethel

George Halas
1895-1983

American football coach

George Halas

Among the winningest coaches in the history of the National Football League (NFL), George "Papa Bear" Halas amassed 324 career victories. As owner of the Chicago Bears for over sixty years, he coached for more than forty of those years and played with the team for a decade. Prominent at the organization of the American Professional Football Association (APFA, later the National Football League—NFL) in 1920, Halas throughout his lifetime played a visible role in the history of professional football in the United States. During the 1930s he lobbied successfully for league rules that enhanced scoring capabilities and thereby contributed to the growth in the popularity of the game. By his avocation to the game he helped to bring respectability to the young sport and contributed to its evolution into a major sporting industry.

George Halas was born on February 2, 1895, in Chicago, Illinois. His parents, Frank Sr., a tailor, and Barbara, a grocer, immigrated from Pilsen, Bohemia, in the 1880s. Halas, one of four siblings, was the youngest of the three boys in a family that encouraged sports. He developed a plucky, competitive spirit as a result. After his father died in 1910, Halas and his brothers and sister helped with the grocery store and with the upkeep of their apartment building, which was owned by the family. Professional football was a young sport during Halas's formative years. History records the first professional football game in history in 1895, the same year that Halas was born.

Chronology

1895	Born February 2 in Chicago, Illinois
1919	Plays baseball with the New York Yankees
1920	Organizes the Decatur Staley's and takes the team to 13-1; formation of the American Professional Football Association in Canton, Ohio
1921	Receives $5,000 from Staley's Starch to start a franchise team in Chicago; reorganization of the APFA into the National Football League (NFL)
1922	Renames the Staley's team officially to Chicago Bears; marries Minnie Bushing on February 18
1925	Signs University of Illinois gridiron sensation Harold "Red" Grange to play with the Bears
1930	Retires permanently as a player and temporarily as a coach
1932	Buys out Bear's partner, Dutch Sternaman, for $38,000; serves as chairman of the NFL rules committee
1933	Emerges from retirement to coach the Bears
1943-45	Serves in the Pacific with the U.S. Navy
1955	Retires temporarily from coaching
1958	Returns as coach
1968	Retires altogether from coaching
1983	Dies in Chicago, Illinois

As a youth Halas played indoor baseball, a popular league sport, now known as softball. Later, at Chicago's Crane Technical High School he played baseball, basketball, and—although he was slight of build—football. After graduation in 1913, he entered the University of Illinois, having developed into a modest athlete.

As an outfielder at Illinois, Halas batted .350. During the summer of his sophomore year he played baseball with the Western Electric company team in Chicago. Additionally he captained the varsity basketball team during his senior year, but his football skills remained marginal. At six feet tall, he was slim at 170 pounds. Despite his enthusiasm Halas was often overpowered by larger players; he broke his jaw during sophomore year and broke one of his legs as a junior. Illinois head coach Bob Zuppke, keenly aware of Halas's physical shortcomings, admired the young man's spirit nonetheless and played him regularly, positioning Halas at the end and away from the center of the fray.

Halas graduated from Illinois in 1918 with a degree in civil engineering, only to be caught up in World War I. While serving as an ensign at the Great Lakes Naval Training Station he played football with the Great Lakes team. The football in those days was much larger and more awkward, and the game as a result focused on rushing more than passing. He nonetheless caught two touchdown passes during the Rose Bowl game on New Year's Day in 1919. He also returned an interception for seventy-seven yards that day, earning a taste of minor celebrity as a football star, as Great Lakes defeated the Mare Island Marines by a score of 17-9.

Fate Intervened

Halas was discharged soon after the Rose Bowl and reverted to baseball pursuits. He signed with the New York Yankees in March of 1919. Although he made a professional debut with that team on May 19, 1919, he played only eleven games and left a career record of meager statistics. As a right-handed batter he was extremely weak. With a batting average of .091, he never scored, nor did he bat in a single run. The lasting effects of a hip injury caused by a mishap during training camp in Jacksonville, Florida, in March 1919 further hastened his retirement from baseball.

He played briefly with a minor league team in St. Paul, until a contract dispute put an end to his career. Halas returned to Chicago for the duration of 1919 and worked as an engineer for the Chicago, Burlington, and Quincy Railroad. Turning elsewhere from professional baseball to satisfy his sporting interests, he joined a semi-professional football team called the Hammond Pros.

In 1920 he accepted an offer of full-time employment at the Staley Starch Works in Decatur, Illinois, where he served as athletic director and part-time coach of the company football team in addition to his full-time duties as a starchmaker. Despite his bad hip he spent summers on the company's baseball team and played right end on the football squad. His employer, A. E. Staley, provided generous support for the company football program, offering players a share of the gate receipts. Halas as a result met with success in recruiting a number of promising athletes from colleges nationwide. Among those early team members, the former Illinois halfback Ed (Dutch) Sternaman and Notre Dame center George Trafton hired into Staley's and played for the Staley Starchmakers.

The 1920s: New League, New Team

To expedite scheduling of games with other teams, Halas contacted the managers of other football organizations in support of forming a league. Halas and the Starchmakers, along with Ralph Hay and the Canton Bulldogs and ten other teams, collaborated under Hay's guidance to organize the APFA in 1920. As a formality, participating teams were required to ante $100 as a franchise fee, but history holds that no money actually changed hands.

Halas and the Staley team, with a record of 13-1 in 1921, were undisputed APFA champions that year. By 1922 the APFA had evolved into the NFL. Halas and Sternaman meanwhile moved the Starchmakers to Chicago where they arranged to lease Wrigley Field as a home stadium. The move to Chicago was funded by a $5,000 donation from Staley who could no longer support the team on a permanent basis. In Chicago, Halas sold cars while Sternaman pumped gas to subsidize the team. Although the rental of the field was based on a percentage of the gate profits, the Starchmakers operated at a loss of $71.63 in 1921. Halas took a job as a night watchman at a refrigeration plant to help make ends meet. Renamed the Bears in 1922, the team finished in second place for the next two seasons, upstaged by the

Canton Bulldogs both times. Halas and Sternaman watched their profits mushroom from $1,476.92 in 1922, to $20,000 in 1923. Despite the impressive figures, finances were fragile. The surplus was not enough to guarantee solvency in an as yet untested professional sport.

After posting finishes of 9-3 in 1922 and 9-2-1 in 1923, the Bears, with a less-impressive season record of 6-1-4 in 1924, played runner-up to Canton for a third consecutive season. Undaunted, Halas refused a buyout offer of $35,000 and continued his strategy of recruiting the most promising young players from the colleges. The dynamic new football league had grown to support eighteen teams by that year, even after the loss of two teams over the previous season.

Finances and championships aside, Halas—playing at right end for the Bears—gave the early NFL one of its more memorable moments during a contest with the Oolong Indians of Marion, Ohio, on November 23, 1923. Playing for the Indians at that time was **Jim Thorpe**, a runner of unusual speed. The stadium at Wrigley Field was drenched in rain that day when Halas and Bears' tackle Hugh Blacklock brought Thorpe to the ground, just as he was on the verge of scoring. As Thorpe hit the soggy field, he lost his grip on the ball. Halas intercepted the fumble at the two-yard line and returned the ball the entire length of the gridiron, scoring a 98-yard touchdown run, with Thorpe in hot pursuit.

In late November 1925, a dubious but shrewd business move by Halas attracted widespread interest for the Bears and for football in general. In the week before Thanksgiving, a young back—known as **Harold Red Grange** from the University of Illinois—signed to play with the Bears. A public controversy brewed over the legitimacy of signing a recruit while the player was still in college. Regardless, with Grange on the roster the Bears drew their first sellout crowd to Wrigley field. Beginning with a season opener against their hometown rivals, the Chicago Cardinals, the Bears attracted a total of 360,000 spectators in nineteen games that year.

At the end of the season—after settling with Grange and his manager for $250,000—Halas had profited $100,000 for the team. More importantly the strategic use of Grange as a nationwide box-office draw boosted professional football to unanticipated popularity. Grange and his manager abandoned the Bears in 1926 and established a rival football league, called the American Football League (AFL). Grange played that year for an AFL franchise, the New York Yankees. The AFL folded quickly, and the Yankees joined the NFL in 1927. A knee injury that same year put Grange on the bench for much of 1927 and for the entire 1928 season. Without Grange on the field, the New York team went out of business, and Grange returned to play with the Bears in 1929.

George Halas that year retired as a player and abandoned coaching for other business interests including a laundry, two retail establishments, and part ownership in

a professional basketball team called the Chicago Bruins. His interest in football remained keen.

With support from Halas, the NFL saw dynamic changes in the 1930s. In 1932 he assumed the chairmanship of the league's rules committee and has been credited with a number of policy changes that contributed to make the game more exciting. To minimize ties and scoreless games he sponsored a rule to allow forward passing from anywhere behind the line of scrimmage. Before this rule, yardage gains were usually small because players had to be five yards behind the line of scrimmage in order to throw a legal forward pass, making it easier to run the ball than to pass. To encourage field goal scores, Halas repositioned the goal posts to sit on the goal line instead of ten yards back in the end zone. Also at his urging, the college draft system for recruiting players went into place in 1936, breathing new life into professional football. Later in the decade he embraced a new practice of spotting plays from the bleachers. Critics regard these innovations as Halas's legacy to professional football.

The first NFL championship playoff game was called in 1932, to break a tie between Chicago and the Portsmouth, Ohio, Spartans for the league championship. The Bears won by a score of 9-0, and the game inspired NFL executives with a scheme to extend future NFL seasons by splitting the league into two regional divisions: Eastern and Western. Division champions would then meet in a playoff for the league championship. When Halas returned to coach the Bears in 1933, the team posted a season record of 10-2-1, securing the first-ever Western Division championship. The Bears went on to conquer the Eastern Division champions, the Giants, in the first annual NFL championship game. Attendance at Bears games swelled to 280,000 for the season.

In 1934 Halas spearheaded a move to sponsor an annual college All-Star game between the reigning NFL champions and the strongest college players in the country. For the first All-Star game the spotlight landed on the 1933 NFL Champions, the Bears, to play against the collegiate standouts. To the shock of Halas and his so-called Miracle Bears, the contest ended in a scoreless tie.

Awards and Accomplishments

1919	Named Most Valuable Player, Rose Bowl
1921	Wins American Professional Football Association Championship
1933	Wins the first National Football League title game
1940-41, **1943, 1946**	National Football League Championship
1963	Named National Football League Coach of the Year; inducted into Pro Football Hall of Fame, charter member; National Football League Championship
1965	Named National Football League Coach of the Year
1997	Stamp issued by the U.S. Postal Service to honor Halas

Halas retired in 1963 with a career coaching record of 324 wins.

The NFL Championship of 1934 was also disappointing for Halas, who went into the playoffs on the surge of an unbroken string of thirty-three games without a loss. The game was played at the New York Polo Grounds, where the field that day was a sheet of ice, so frozen that the Giants abandoned their cleats for sneakers during halftime. With Halas watching helplessly from the sidelines, the Bears suffered a 13-0 loss to the Giants. The unusual shoe-switching strategy had provided the New York team with a unique advantage in what came to be called the Great Sneaker Game.

In 1935 the Bears went 6-4-2. They finished 9-3 in 1936. In 1937 the Bears secured the Western Division title with a 9-1-1 record but lost the championship to the Redskins by a score of 28-21.

The following year Halas replaced the single wing formation with a man-in-motion T formation devised by coach Ralph Jones in the early 1930s, but the Bears dominated in only six of eleven games for the season. In 1939 Halas signed Columbia University tailback Sid Luckman and repositioned the future Hall of Famer to quarterback. The team finished second that year.

Glory Days

Beginning in 1940, after intensive coaching from Halas, Luckman led the Bears through a decade of glory days. Most memorable among these victories was the championship game in December of 1940, between the Bears and the Washington Redskins. The Bears, after posting eight wins and three losses that year, played the Redskins for the NFL Championship on December 8, 1940. Included among the Bears' three losses during the regular season was a bitterly disputed loss to the Redskins. At the subsequent meeting between the two teams for the championship, the Bears held the Redskins to a paltry three yards rushing, to win the NFL title by a score of 73-0. Remarkably, the Bears had scored eleven touchdowns in one of the classic revenge games of all time.

The Bears won the title in 1941 and again in 1943. In 1942, despite an 11-0 season, the team lost the championship in a 14-6 upset to their nemesis, the Redskins. It was their only loss between mid season 1941 and mid season 1943. During that time Halas brought the Bears to twenty-four consecutive regular season wins.

After the bombing of Pearl Harbor on December 7, 1941, many of the dominant NFL players joined the military, and the sport of professional football took a back seat to United States involvement in World War II. In mid 1942 Halas re-enlisted in the Navy as a lieutenant commander. He served in the South Pacific and was promoted to full commander; he returned on Thanksgiving Day 1945. The team failed to make the playoffs during his absence.

From 1946-49 professional football took a new turn, which marred the joys of homecoming for Halas. A new professional league in direct competition with the NFL cropped up, called the All-American Football Conference (AAFC). In addition to the league, a third professional team, called the Rockets, sprang up in Chicago. With Halas's encouragement, the NFL franchises refused to recognize the new league in the hope of bringing about its demise. The strategy proved successful, and by the end of that decade the AAFC was a thing of the past.

Increased competition for good players during the AAFC years caused player salaries to nearly double. Despite the hardship, Halas continued to rely on Luckman at quarterback and held on to other players good enough to take the NFL Championship in 1946. In 1947, after taking a 30-21 trouncing from the Cardinals in the final game of the regular season, the Bears emerged second in the Western Division with a record of 8-4. Four successive second place finishes followed from 1948-51. Luckman retired in 1950, and his replacement, John Lujack, retired in 1951 after an injury to his arm.

Halas suffered two more demoralizing losing seasons: in 1952 and again in 1953. He regrouped and recorded back-to-back seasons of 8-4, from 1954-55. At the end of the 1955 season, Halas retired for a second time, naming his long-time aide, Paddy Driscoll, as a successor. The Bears won the Western Division title in 1956, followed by a dismally deficient season in 1957. The downturn prompted Halas—at age 63—to remove Driscoll and resume the reins as coach in 1958.

Halas tried for five years to resurrect the glory that was the Chicago Bears of earlier decades, but the team was 8-4 for the next two years, in 1958-59. According to some critics, Halas's failing was his refusal to update from the T formation of the early years to the finesse of the modern slot offense that ruled the postwar NFL. A mediocre showing early in the 1960 season was fueled by a mid season upset loss to the Baltimore Colts; the Bears ended that year at 5-6-1. Despite the acquisition of veteran Rams quarterback Bill Wade after the 1960 season, the Bears were 8-6 the next year and slightly better at 9-5 in 1962.

By 1963 Halas had manned an updated offense, with **Mike Ditka** at tight end and John Farrington at wide re-

FURTHER INFORMATION

Books

Sullivan, George. *Pro Football's All-time Greats.* New York: G. P. Putnam's Sons, 1968.
Vass, George. *George Halas and the Chicago Bears.* Chicago: Henry Regnery Company, 1971.

Periodicals

Gietschier, Steve. "The Most Powerful People In Sports For The 20th Century." *Sporting News* (December 20, 1999).

Other

"George S. 'Papa Bear' Halas Sr." http://www.geocities. com/dibears201.geo/halas.html (September 17, 2002).
"No. 26—Bob Zuppke," *The Pigskin Post.* http://www. pigskinpost.com/no__26_-_bob_zuppke.htm (October 2, 2002).

Sketch by Gloria Cooksey

George Halas, in foreground

ceiver. Halas further assumed responsibility for coaching the defense and successfully brought the Bears to reign as the NFL Western Division champions. The 1963 NFL championship game, held at Wrigley field on December 29, pitted the Bears and Wade against the New York Giants with quarterback Y. A. Tittle. When the shouting stopped, Halas and the Bears had taken their first NFL Championship since 1946. Halas bowed out of his coaching responsibilities officially in 1968, although, as owner of the team, he never left the sidelines nor ceased to keep a tight grip on the workings of the team.

Halas, who married Minnie Bushing on February 18, 1922, during the infancy of the NFL, was left widowed after forty-four years of marriage with the death of Bushing on February 14, 1966. The couple had two children, George S. Halas Jr., and Virginia Marion McCaskey, both of whom became involved with the league in adulthood.

Halas died in Chicago on October 31, 1983. His remains lie at St. Adalbert's Cemetery in Niles, Illinois. In tribute to Halas, the Pro Football Hall of Fame is situated on George Halas Drive W. in Canton, Ohio. The National Football Conference championship trophy is named for Halas. In 1999 the *Sporting News* listed Halas among the "The Most Powerful People In Sports For The 20th Century." To the team that he nurtured for sixty-three years, Halas is remembered affectionately as "Papa Bear."

Glenn Hall
1931-

Canadian hockey player

Hockey Hall of Famer Glenn Hall's streak of 502 consecutive games (552, including playoffs) pales in raw number to the baseball streaks of **Cal Ripken Jr.** (2,632) and **Lou Gehrig** (2,130). It's not even the longevity mark in his own sport. But Hall's streak, from 1955 to 1962, is extraordinary because, as a goaltender, he played one of the most harrowing positions in sports and for all but his last three seasons, without a facemask. Further, Hall felt nauseous and threw up before most games, and even during intermissions. "You wouldn't think after all this time that I'd still be so afraid of a bad game I'd get sick about it," Hall told William Barry Furlong in *Sports Illustrated* in 1962.

Hall played for the Detroit Red Wings, Chicago Blackhawks and St. Louis Blues over eighteen National Hockey League (NHL) seasons. He played for one Stanley Cup champion, won or shared the Vezina Award for best goaltender three times, won the Calder Memorial Trophy as rookie of the year and the Conn Smythe Trophy as most valuable player of the playoffs. He was an eleven-time all-star and he ranks third in lifetime shutouts with eighty-four. In 1997, *The Hockey News* rated Hall 16th on its list of hockey's greatest 100 players. Goaltender historians credit Hall with popularizing the "butterfly" style of positioning, which mostly involves a goaltender dropping to his knees and spreading his skates out in a wide "V."

Glenn Hall

Chronology

1931	Born October 3 in Humboldt, Saskatchewan, Canada
1949	Marries Pauline Patrick
1952-53	Makes NHL debut with Detroit Red Wings; registers first shutout
1957	Is traded with Ted Lindsay from Detroit Red Wings to Chicago Blackhawks for John Wilson, Forbes Kennedy, William Preston and Hank Bassen
1961	Backstops Chicago Blackhawks to first Stanley Cup since 1938
1962	Streak of 502 consecutive regular-season games ends
1967	Selected by St. Louis Blues in expansion draft
1971	Retires at age 40 with 2.78 career goals-against average

Pauline Patrick, who was impressed that Hall had a car. "We girls knew that a young fellow with his own car was someone substantial," she told Kahn.

Signs with Red Wings

After signing with the Detroit organization, Hall played goal in the minor leagues for Indianapolis and Edmonton. He played six games in 1952-53 and two more in 1954-55 for the parent Red Wings. Detroit in 1955 won its fourth Stanley Cup in six years (the Red Wings and Montreal won all but one of the Stanley Cups in the 1950s), but Hall did not play enough to have his name engraved on the Stanley Cup

But Detroit General Manager Jack Adams, feeling Hall was ready, traded star goalie **Terry Sawchuk** to the Boston Bruins. Hall played all seventy Detroit games that season, sporting a 2.11 goals-against average with twelve shutouts. Montreal, however, reclaimed the Stanley Cup, winning four of five games against the Red Wings in the final.

The following season, Hall's regular season goals-against was a solid 2.24, but Boston upset Detroit in the Stanley Cup semifinals, marking only the third time in ten years the Red Wings did not play for the championship.

In addition, Hall fell into disfavor with Adams, first for reporting late to training camp, then talking back to the general manager in front of the team in the dressing room. Adams, already upset at Detroit's failure to even reach the Cup finals while Montreal won its second straight title en route to five in a row, doled out what he thought was the quintessential punishment: banishment to Chicago, which had finished in last place the four previous years. It was "then known as hockey's Siberia," wrote Brian McFarlane, author of the "Original Six" series and a longtime regular on the Canadian Broadcasting Corporation's *Hockey Night in Canada* telecasts. Adams accepted Chicago's offer of Johnny Wilson, Forbes Kennedy, Hank Bassen and William Preston for Ted Lindsay and Hall.

Years later, Lindsay said union activism triggered the deal. "I was traded because I was behind the formation of the Players Association and the trade happened right after I had my best year as a Red Wings," Lindsay told McFar-

Even in defeat, Hall was sometimes part of history. He allowed the 500th career goal of Montreal Canadiens' great **Maurice Richard**. He earned his Smythe Trophy when the Blues lost the 1968 finals and two years later, he allowed the picturesque Cup-winning goal by Boston's **Bobby Orr**, immortalized by television and newspapers capturing Orr celebrating flying through the air, Superman-syle.

Yet, Hall admits he played because he had no other way to make a living. As *Boys of Summer* author Roger Kahn wrote in the *Saturday Evening Post* in 1968, "His distaste for play is overwhelming." A former teammate, according to Kahn, said, "Hall's bucket belongs in the Hockey Hall of Fame."

Simple Upbringing

Hall was born and raised in Humboldt, Saskatchewan. In his *Sports Illustrated* article, Furlong described him as "a stoic family man whose major dream is to settle down and raise cattle." His father was a railroad worker who died on Christmas Day, 1967. Life in the Western Canadian prairies was simple for Hall. He was grateful there was food to eat. "Maybe there wasn't much beyond that, but Dad always made sure we had groceries," he said.

Hall, who played pickup hockey—Canadians called it "shinny"—on local ponds, worked his way through youth and amateur hockey leagues. He married nurse

Career Statistics

Yr	Team	GP	Min	W	L	T	GAA	TGA	SHO
1952-53	DET	6	360	4	1	1	1.67	10	1
1954-55	DET	2	120	2	0	0	1.00	2	0
1955-56	DET	70	4200	30	24	16	2.10	148	12
1956-57	DET	70	4200	38	20	12	2.24	157	4
1957-58	CHI	70	4200	24	39	7	2.89	202	7
1958-59	CHI	70	4200	28	29	13	2.97	208	1
1959-60	CHI	70	4200	28	29	13	2.57	180	6
1960-61	CHI	70	4200	29	24	17	2.57	180	6
1961-62	CHI	70	4200	31	26	13	2.66	186	9
1962-63	CHI	66	3910	30	20	15	2.55	166	5
1963-64	CHI	65	3860	34	19	11	2.30	148	7
1964-65	CHI	41	2440	18	17	5	2.43	99	4
1965-66	CHI	64	3747	34	21	7	2.63	164	4
1966-67	CHI	32	1664	19	5	5	2.38	66	2
1967-68	STL	49	2858	19	21	9	2.48	118	5
1968-69	STL	41	2354	19	12	8	2.17	85	8
1969-70	STL	18	1010	7	8	3	2.91	49	1
1970-71	STL	32	1761	13	11	8	2.42	71	2
TOTAL		906	53484	407	326	163	2.51	2239	84

CHI: Chicago Blackhawks; DET: Detroit Red Wings; STL: St. Louis Blues.

lane years later. "As for Glenn Hall, I think he was thrown into the deal because he was a Ted Lindsay fan. For the next fifteen years, Hall was the best in the league."

Streaking to a Cup

Though the Blackhawks struggled throughout the 1950s and, in fact, the league had a special draft to stock it with players, Hall and some of the "banished" quality players arrived in Chicago at the right time. The Hawks were building around such up-and-coming stars as forwards **Bobby Hull** and **Stan Mikita**, and defenseman Pierre Pilote.

Hall's consecutive-game streak, which started in Detroit, gathered steam in Chicago. "During those years, Glenn Hall was a durable superstar for the Hawks," McFarlane wrote. "Season after season, he never missed a game ... He did miss a few preseason games, however; every fall, he'd report to camp as late as possible. 'I'm painting my barn,' was his excuse when the (general) manager called, pleading for him to report. 'Glenn's either got the best-painted barn in Saskatchewan or he's the slowest painter on earth,' the manager would tell reporters."

Hall's streak finally ended on November 7, 1962, when his back tightened up while he allowed a goal to Boston's Murray Oliver at Chicago Stadium. Out he came, and a string of more than 30,000 consecutive minutes in the net ended. (Doug Jarvis, who played center for the Canadiens, Washington Capitals and Hartford Whalers, owns hockey's longevity mark at 964. It ended only when the Whalers—now the Carolina Hurricanes—sent him to the minors in 1987).

In 1961, the Hawks finished third in the regular season, and drew in the opening round of the playoffs the first-place Canadiens, who were going for their sixth straight Stanley Cup championship. Montreal's five in a row is still pro hockey's benchmark. The series turned in the third game, when Murray Balfour's goal gave host Chicago a 2-1 victory in triple overtime and a 2-1 series lead. Hall had lost his shutout when Henri Richard tied the game in the dying seconds of regulation play, but the goalie got his revenge against Richard in overtime, stopping the "Pocket Rocket" on a breakaway. Hall recorded 3-0 shutouts in games five and six as Chicago advanced. "The Habs' dynasty was over," McFarlane wrote. "It was one of hockey's greatest upsets."

Chicago also broke a 2-2 series tie in the final against Hall's old team, the Red Wings, capturing its first championship since 1938 with a 5-1 win in game six in Detroit's Olympia. "What a sweet feeling!" Hall wrote in his foreword to McFarlane's book. "There is no sense of accomplishment quite like it."

To this day, it is the Blackhawks' last championship, though Hall backstopped Chicago to appearances in the 1962 and 1965 finals. In 1967, as hockey teams began alternating goalies, Hall and teammate Denis DeJordy shared the Vezina Trophy, as Chicago's goals-against was the best in the league.

League Expands

The NHL doubled its size from six to 12 teams for the 1967-68 season, and Hall, unprotected by Chicago at age thirty-six, found a new home. Rather than develop young players for the long term, the St. Louis Blues, looking for instant success, opted for older players who had won elsewhere. Hall split the net-tending in St. Louis with **Jacques Plante**, who backstopped Montreal's championship teams

---

Awards and Accomplishments

1956	Calder Memorial Trophy for NHL Rookie of the Year
1956, 1961-62, 1967	NHL second-team all-star
1957-58, 1960, 1963-64, 1966, 1969	NHL first-team all-star
1963	Wins Vezina Trophy as top NHL goaltender
1967	Shares Vezina Trophy with Chicago teammate Denis DeJordy
1968	Wins Conn Smythe Trophy as Stanley Cup playoffs MVP
1969	Shares Vezina Trophy with St. Louis teammate Jacques Plante
1975	Inducted into Hockey Hall of Fame

---

in the 1950s and was lured out of retirement. The likes of Dickey Moore and Doug Harvey, both former Montreal mainstays, and others came to St. Louis. The expansion teams comprised a six-team Western Division and were assured a spot in the Stanley Cup final.

The Blues reached the final in their first season and lost four straight, as expected, to Montreal, but all four games were by one goal. Hall is one of only four playoff MVPs from a non-champion since the Conn Smythe Trophy's inception in 1965.

St. Louis also lost four straight in the 1969 and 1970 finals to Montreal and Boston, respectively, and Hall, who finally donned a mask for his last three seasons, retired in 1971 at age 40.

Hall's Legacy

Hall, who in his retirement years has worked part-time as a goalie consultant for the Edmonton Oilers and later the Calgary Flames, both in the Alberta province where he lives, is a throwback to a fondly remembered hockey era, long before the NHL expanded into such places as Anaheim, San Jose and Nashville. "Modern NHL teams, with four and five goaltenders under contract and a full-time reserve on the bench, dressed and ready, couldn't comprehend a time when a single goaltender went to work every night," Wayne Scanlan wrote in the *Ottawa Citizen* in November, 2002.

Could a goalie play that many games in a row today? "No," said Hall in 1999, his answer as point blank as many of the shots he faced. "In those days, a goalie had to go the whole nine innings. If one goalkeeper had a bad night, he had to play through. Today, if you're not playing well, another guy who's reasonably good can come in and play half the game."

In conjunction with the 2000 NHL All-Star game, held in Toronto, the *National Post* of Canada asked several former stars and hockey personalities to name their greatest starting six. Orr, Hull and goalies **Ken Dryden** and Lorne "Gump" Worsley voted for Hall in goal.

FURTHER INFORMATION

Books

Adrahtas, Ted. *Glenn Hall: The Man They Call Mr. Goalie.* Vancouver: Greystone, 2002.

McFarlane, Brian. *The Blackhawks: Brian McFarlane's Original Six.* With a foreword by Glenn Hall. Toronto: Stoddart, 2000.

Other

"A Sick Goalie Saves Chicago." Geocities.com. http://www.geocities.com/Colosseum (November 7, 2002).

"Break from Aches in Snowy Toronto a Feel-Good Schtick." National Post Online. http://www.nationalpost.com/ (February 5, 2000).

"Down Memory Lane." Canada's Digital Collections. http://collections.ic.gc.ca/humboldt (November 5, 2002).

"The Greatest Goalie in Hockey." True Blues. http://www.jcs-group.com/trueblues/twenty/hall.html (November 7, 2002).

"The Pre-Backup Backup Plan." Ottawa Citizen. http://www.canada.com/ottawa/sports (November 7, 2002).

Sketch by Paul Burton

Dorothy Hamill
1956-

American figure skater

In the mid-1970s, American figure skater Dorothy Hamill was the leader in her field, capping her success with a gold medal at the 1976 Winter Olympics. She was known for her signature "Hamill camel" and wedge/bob haircut which started a fashion craze. After the Olympics, Hamill turned professional, skating in shows and professional events, and later owning the Ice Capades. As a skater, her style balanced athleticism and grace, and she was a dominant freestyle specialist.

Hamill was born on July 26, 1956, in Chicago, Illinois (some sources say Riverside, Colorado, or Riverside, Connecticut), the youngest of three children born to Chambers and Carol Hamill. Hamill was raised in Greenwich, Connecticut, where her father was an executive at Pitney Bowes Company.

Begins Skating

Both Hamill's father and brother skated but were not serious about it. Hamill herself began skating when she was about eight years old. She used her brother's hockey

Dorothy Hamill

skates that were too big for her until she received a pair of inexpensive skates for Christmas. Hamill taught herself to skate forwards on a local pond, but could not teach herself to skate backwards. She also saw someone spinning on television, and thought it looked cool.

This led Hamill to convince her parents to take group lessons at a local rink. She soon became obsessed with skating and was very good. Hamill skated under USFSA (United States Figure Skating Association), moving straight from juvenile to novice, skipping intermediate. Her mother drove her to New York City and other locales to train. One of her first coaches was Sonya Dunfield (née Klopfer), who won the U.S. ladies singles championship in 1951.

Develops the Hamill Camel

By the time Hamill was 12, she was winning major championships. When she was 12, she was the national ladies novice singles championship. Among the highlights of Hamill's program at the championship was her innovation in skating, the so-called "Hamill camel." It was a flying camel that went into a sit-spin. It was developed in 1969, while she was training with Gustave Lussi in Lake Placid, New York.

In 1970, Hamill moved up to juniors and won the Eastern junior singles title. She then competed in the U.S. ladies singles competition, and finished second. Her desire to train intensely (skating seven hours a day,

six days a week) led her to drop out of school and receive her education from a tutor. Hamill later earned her high school equivalency degree. While her parents supported her skating and these kind of decisions, it was a financial burden and resulted in her mother traveling with her daughter, away from her husband. Though Hamill did well in competitions, she often suffered from stage fright.

Hamill won the Eastern sectional ladies singles title and finished seventh at the world championships in 1971. This led to another important coaching change. She met Carlo Fassi at the Pre-Olympic Invitational. He had also coached champion **Peggy Fleming** who won the gold medal at the 1968 Winter Olympics. Fassi invited her to begin training with him in Colorado.

Hamill's experiences in Colorado were positive. The high altitude improved her stamina. She also studied ballet and worked on her fitness. Fassi himself helped Hamill with compulsory figures—the aspect of competition that she struggled with the most. Hamill also began working with choreographer Bob Paul. Paul choreographed routines that highlighted her athletic abilities, especially her jumps, and her Hamill camel.

The results were positive. In 1973, Hamill finished fourth in the world ladies singles championships. In 1974 and 1975, Hamill won the U.S. championship for ladies senior singles. Her second victory was impressive, in part because she had an injured foot but still pulled out the win. Hamill still had problems with sensitivity, however. At the 1974 World Championships, she heard boos from the crowd as she was warming up for her free skate. Hamill left the ice crying, believing the booing was directed at her. However, the crowd was actually booing the judges for the previous competitors

Awards and Accomplishments

1969	Wins the U.S. national ladies novice singles championship
1970	Wins Eastern U.S. junior ladies singles title; is second at U.S. ladies singles championship; finishes seventh in world championships
1971	Wins Eastern sectional ladies singles title; wins silver at USFSA compulsory competition; finishes fifth at U.S. championships
1972	Finishes fourth at the U.S. championships
1973	Finishes fourth at the world championships in ladies senior singles figure skating; finishes second in U.S. championships
1974	Wins U.S. championship in ladies single figure skating; finishes second in world ladies singles championships
1975	Wins U.S. championship in ladies single figure skating; finishes second at world championships
1976	Wins gold medal in ladies singles figure skating at Olympics; wins World Championship; wins U.S. championship in ladies single figure skating
1984-85	Wins World Professional Skating Championship
1986-87	Wins the Women's NutraSweet Pro World Title
1991	Inducted into the U.S. Olympic Hall of Fame and U.S. Figure Skating Hall of Fame
1998	Wins Headliner of the Year Award for Enter the Night performance at Stardust Resort and Casino in Las Vegas, Nevada
2000	Skated in the first Winter Goodwill Games, placing fifth; inducted into the World Figure Skating Hall of Fame

scores. After she was reassured about the situation, she skated well. She won the silver medal.

Wins Olympic Gold

In 1976, Hamill began the year by winning her third consecutive U.S. championships. There was some controversy as some believed the judges scored her generously. Hamill received scores of 5.8 and 5.9 out of 6.0 though she took out the loop and flip jumps of her program. She followed this up with a gold medal performance at the Winter Olympics in Innsbruck, Austria. She won despite a big scare. She was walking with coach Fassi when a car carrying another skater and coach approached them. Fassi pushed her out of the way, but the car accelerated and would have hit her had she not been moved by him.

Despite Hamill's victory at the U.S. championships, she had not been favored to win the gold medal at the Olympics because she had finished second at the world championships two years in a row. She had the lead after the compulsory figures, but had an emotional moment after seeing a sign that read "Dorothy, Wicked Witch of the West." But Hamill pulled it together. She scored a perfect 6.0 in the short program, and kept her lead after the freeskate to win the gold medal. Hamill later said it was her best competition as an amateur.

After the Olympics, Hamill went on to win the World Championships in 1976, at the competition at Göteborg, Germany. She won both the compulsories and the free skate. By this time, Hamill was considered the best freestyle skater in the world and considered "America's

Sweetheart." However, her skating style would be considered somewhat dated now. Hamill's most difficult jump was the double axel, and she could not land a triple salchow consistently.

Hamill's jumps got higher later and she learned to better blend artistry and athleticism. But she explained to Vicki Michaelis of the *Denver Post* that jumps should not be valued over artistry, or vice versa. "I don't think skating should be limited to one or the other. I think it should be absolutely both. I guess I've been sort of frustrated over the years where people say it has to be one or it has to be the other . . . I think that's part of the appeal of skating, that some people like the grace and beauty, some people like the athleticism and some people just like the entertainment value of it."

Turns Professional as a Skater

After her Olympic win, Hamill became a phenomenon in the United States. Her short bob/wedge hairstyle became extremely popular. To take advantage of her commercial opportunities and pay back her parents for the cost of training (they were in debt because of it), she turned professional. Though she was shy, Hamill appeared in a number of commercials and television specials.

One of Hamill's first contracts was a two-year deal with the Ice Capades worth $1,000,000. She told Kenneth Denlinger of the *Washington Post*, that she did Ice Capades "because it was a chance to pay people for their help (literally, because that gold medal cost an estimated $75,000 in training-related expenses over the years)... I also knew that I wanted to skate, not teach, and this was the only I could see to do it."

A featured skater on the Ice Capades tour, Hamill found the demands of the professional life very different from her days as an amateur. The travel and performances were more physically demanding, and there was a very different, grinding schedule. Hamill became stressed out, especially by the weigh-ins. She had to worry about her weight. Skating with the Ice Capades led to her developing a bleeding ulcer.

In the 1980s, Hamill continued to skate professionally, and had two significant television specials. In 1983, she appeared in an ice version of *Romeo and Juliet* that aired on CBS and was very successful. The production won an Emmy Award for Hamill. Later in the decade, she appeared in *Nutcracker on Ice,* a show produced by Hamill and her second husband, sports medicine doctor/former Olympic skier Kenneth Forsythe. (Hamill's first husband was Dean Martin, Jr., the son of entertainer Dean Martin, who was a tennis player, actor, and musician. They were married from 1982-84.)

Despite her negative experience with the Ice Capades, Hamill continued to appear in touring ice shows. In 1984, she appeared with John Curry and his Ice Dancing company. In the middle of the decade, Hamill also appeared in the Stars on Ice show. She also competed in professional skating championships, winning a number of titles. In 1984 and 1985, she won the World Professional Figure Skating Championship. In 1986 and 1987, she won the Women's NutraSweet Pro World Title.

After the birth of her daughter, Alexandra, Hamill stopped skating professionally for about six years. However, she still appeared in commercials and maintained endorsement deals with companies such as NurtraSweet, Healthy Choice, Casio, and Bausch & Lomb.

Buys Ice Capades

In 1993, the Ice Capades was in serious financial trouble. The company had filed for bankruptcy in 1991. Hamill, her husband, and businessman Ben C. Tinsdale, bought the company in 1993. She put it under her own company, Dorothy Hamill International, of which she was president. She told Steve Wulf of *Sports Illustrated,* "It was breaking my heart to think there would be no more Ice Capades. It wasn't just that I once skated for the company, it was also the thought of all those skaters out of work."

When Hamill took over, she changed Ice Capades to suit her tastes as a skater. The shows had become dated using a variety format, but Hamill made it into a show on ice. She hired better quality skaters, choreographers, and costumers. She also did away with weigh-ins. One of her greatest successes was with the Ice Capades show she executive produced, 1994's *Cinderella Frozen in Time.* Praised by critics and aired as a special on ABC, Hamill herself skated the lead in many stops on the tour. Hamill also created other ice shows, including *Hansel & Gretel—Frozen in Time.*

In 1995, Hamill and her partners sold Ice Capades to International Entertainment, Inc. Though she intended to retire again from professional skating, divorce and bankruptcy problems contributed to her return to the ice. In 1995, she skated in the Legends of Figure Skating, replacing an ill **Katarina Witt**. In 1996, Hamill skated in the Hershey's Kisses Figure Skating Challenge, a team competition between three teams of four skaters. Her team included **Michelle Kwan**, Todd Eldredge, and Dan Hollander.

Hamill was asked to compete in the 2000 Winter Goodwill Games, against other professional skaters and the leading amateurs of the day. Though she had not competed in over a decade, she did well, placing fifth. As Sharon Raboin wrote in *USA Today,* "Hamill delighted with her tight, fast spins, where she looks like a blur; her tremendous edge control, mastered years ago with compulsory figures training; and her desire to make the most of every moment in her program."

Hamill believed she aged well as a skater. She told Wulf from *Sports Illustrated,* "I don't think people realize that skaters get better as they get older. Olympic skating is all about jumping, how many triples you hit

Dorothy Hamill

cleanly. Watch professional skaters, and you'll see a more fluid, more disciplined style. Some of it comes with practice, some of it comes with maturity. . ."

Though Hamill was diagnosed with osteoarthritis in 2000, she continued to skate in professional tours such as Champions on Ice. Her name was still a draw. Hamill also continued to appear in commercials and work as a skating commentator for various broadcasts. Of her life, she explained to Tim Reynolds of *The Times Union,* "There have been good times, there have been bad times, there have been hectic times. But I've always had skating. When things were, or are, going badly in my personal life, I always have my therapy. I always have my skating."

CONTACT INFORMATION

Address: PO Box 16286, Baltimore, MD 21210; 75490 Fairway Dr., Indian Wells, CA 92210-8423.

SELECTED WRITINGS BY HAMILL:

(With Elva Clairmont) *Dorothy Hamill On and Off the Ice,* A. A. Knopf, 1983.

FURTHER INFORMATION

Books

Hickok, Ralph. *A Who's Who of Sports Champions: Their Stories and Records.* Boston: Houghton Mifflin Company, 1995.

Johnson, Anne Janette. *Great Women in Sports.* Detroit: Visible Ink Press, 1996.

Layden, Joe. *Women in Sports: The Compete Book on the World's Greatest Female Athletes.* General Publishing Group, 1997.

Malone, John. *The Encyclopedia of Figure Skating.* Facts on File, Inc., 1998.

Porter, David L., editor. *Biographical Dictionary of American Sports: Basketball and Other Indoor Sports.* New York: Greenwood Press, 1989.

Sherrow, Victoria. *Encyclopedia of Women and Sports.* ABC-CLIO, 1996.

Woolum, Janet. *Outstanding Women Athletes: Who They Are and How they Influenced Sports in America.* Oryx Press, 1998.

Periodicals

Bird, Dennis. "Obituary: Gustave Lussi." *The Independent,* (July 7, 1993): 22.

Brown, Ben et al. "Hamill Revamps Ice Capades." *USA Today,* (September 24, 1993): 2C.

Denlinger, Kenneth. "Loner Hamill Now Has Many New Friends ; A Chance to Pay People Back." *Washington Post,* (February 2, 1977): F1.

"Figure Skating; Hamill Still Skating for Titles." *New York Times,* (December 27, 1987): section 5, p. 6.

Ginsburg, David. "Former Gold Medalist Hamill Copes With Painful Disease." Associated Press State & Local Wire, (September 11, 2000).

"Good skate: Dorothy Hamill Chips in to Buy the Ice Capades." *People Weekly,* (March 22, 1993): 32.

"Gustave Lussi." *The Times,* (July 2, 1993).

Harvin, Al. "Gustave Lussi." *New York Times,* (July 27, 1993): section 1, p. 34.

Little, Lyndon. "Dorothy Hamill Doesn't Miss the Pressures of Competition." *Vancouver Sun,* (January 8, 1993): E3.

Michaelis, Vicki. "Hamill Still Riding Her Camel." *Denver Post,* (February 15, 2000): D12.

"On Sister Act." *People Weekly,* (April 11, 1994): 112.

"On Very Thin Ice." *People Weekly,* (April 22, 1996): 75.

Raboin, Sharon. "Hamill, 43, Continues to Enchant Crowds." *USA Today,* (February 21, 2000): 10C.

Reynolds, Tim. "Princess of the Ice." *Time Union,* (February 16, 2000): CC1.

Schuster, Rachel. "Hamill Recalls Own Incident." *USA Today,* (January 28, 1994): 3C.

Ulman, Howard. "Hamill Has Fun in Nerve-Wrecking Return." Associated Press, (March 26, 1996).

Wilner, Barry. "25 Years Later, Hamill Still Golden." *The Record,* (February 13, 2001): S5.

Wulf, Steve. "Cinderella Story." *Sports Illustrated,* (March 7, 1994): 48.

Other

"Athlete Profile: Dorothy Hamill." US Olympic Team. http://www.usolympicteam.com/athlete_profile/d_hamill.html (January 13, 2003).

Sketch by A. Petruso

Scott Hamilton
1958-

American figure skater

Scott Hamilton has experienced the highs and lows of life—from a debilitating childhood disease, to the glory of an Olympic gold medal, to the devastating diagnosis of cancer. Through it all, he has remained a beloved fixture on the figure-skating circuit, an ambassador for his sport, and an inspiration to people facing health crises.

Born in Toledo, Ohio, Scott Scovell Hamilton was adopted at age six weeks by Ernie and Dorothy Hamilton of Bowling Green, Ohio. The little boy completed the family that included one older daughter and another adopted son, but over time the Hamiltons, both college instructors, began to notice that their toddler was not thriving. A series of tests showed that the child was not absorbing food nutrients, stunting his growth. He was prescribed different diets and treatments, none of which improved his condition. When Scott was eight, doctors handed the Hamiltons the frightening news that the boy had cystic fibrosis; that, like other diagnoses over the years, was incorrect.

Scott Hamilton

Finding His Place in the Rink

Hamilton was finally correctly diagnosed with Schwachmann's Syndrome, a rare condition that paralyzes the intestinal tract and restricts breathing. There was no medical treatment for Schwachmann's apart from a regimen of protein-rich foods and regular exercise. The latter issue was decided when the boy followed his sister, Susan, to an ice rink one day and found his calling. "This frail little kid with the tube running across his cheek turned and said, 'You know, I think I'd like to try skating,'" Ernest Hamilton related to *Sports Illustrated* reporter Bob Ottum.

Skating seemed to be the catalyst for Hamilton's recovery. Despite his small size, the boy grew in strength and endurance. He played some hockey, but his passion was figure skating. By age thirteen, Hamilton had become a competitive skater, leaving home to train with Olympian Pierre Brunet in Illinois. High-level training and competition, however, was an expensive endeavor; in 1976 Hamilton left the ice, citing the financial burden to his parents. But a year later, Dorothy Hamilton died of cancer; seemingly propelled by her memory, Scott Hamilton returned to figure skating with a drive to succeed. An anonymous couple had staked the young competitor to a sponsorship, and Hamilton trained with Carlo Fassi and Don Laws.

Hamilton's first wide exposure came at the National Figure Skating Championships, where he rose from ninth place in 1977 to third a year later. Hamilton then dominated the Norton Skate Championships (known today as

Chronology

1958	Born August 28, in Toledo, Ohio
1958	Adopted by Ernest and Dorothy Hamilton
1966	Diagnosed with Schwachmann's Syndrome
1966	Begins figure skating
1971	Leaves home to train with Olympic medalist Pierre Brunet
1976	Temporarily stops competitive skating
1980	Represents U.S. at Olympic winter games, Lake Placid, NY
1984	Represents U.S. at Olympic winter games, Sarajevo, Yugoslavia
1985	Begins career as professional figure skater and commentator
1996	Co-founder, Discover Cards Stars on Ice
1997	Diagnosed with testicular cancer
1998	Returns to professional skating
2002	Launches Chemocare.com
2002	Marries Tracie Robinson

Skate America), wining four years running. Five consecutive Eastern Figure Skating Championships also added to his credentials. After making the 1980 U.S. Olympic team, Hamilton found himself bestowed an unusual honor: "The team had a meeting about who to pick" to bear the U.S. flag in the opening ceremonies, Hamilton told Ottum. "And someone made this emotional pitch for me, pointing out that I had overcome terrible obstacles, sickness and all, and that my mom had died at a crucial point in my career, and that I was the smallest male Olympian there." He was named the flag-bearer that year.

Leaping to Gold

The winter games in Lake Placid saw Hamilton finishing a respectable fifth in the men's individual division. Apparently the skater was just beginning to hit his stride, for following the Olympics Hamilton took fifteen consecutive titles. Though never the biggest man on the ice, Hamilton distinguished himself as one of the boldest, eschewing sequins and spins for utilitarian attire and athletic triple-jumps. "My size is perfect for skating," he said in a *New York Times* interview with Frank Litsky. "I have a lower center of balance. I don't have as much body to adjust when I make a mistake, and not as much body to get tired."

By 1984, Hamilton was considered the man to beat at the Olympic winter games in Sarajevo, Yugoslavia: he had not lost a competition since September 1980, and his credits included four U.S. and world titles. He performed to expectation in the now-abandoned school-figures competition, but Hamilton's uncharacteristic shaky performance in the short program landed the skater in second place, behind Canada's Brian Orser, going into the freestyle long program. Quoted by *Time* reporter B. J. Phillips as saying he "wasn't into the ice" that day, Hamilton doubled two of his planned triple jumps. Despite the disappointing free skate, however, Hamilton had collected enough points in the school-figures and short programs to secure the gold medal and his place in

---

Awards and Accomplishments

1977	Finished ninth, National Figure Skating Championship
1978	Finished third, National Figure Skating Championship
1979	First of four Norton Skate Championships (Skate America), 1979-82
1980	Carried American flag, winter Olympics opening ceremony, Lake Placid, New York
1980	Finished fifth, winter Olympic games
1980	Wins first of fifteen consecutive championships, 1980-84
1984	Gold medalist, winter Olympic games, Sarajevo, Yugoslavia
1984	March of Dimes Achievement Award
1986	Professional Skater of the Year, *American Skating World*
1988	Jacques Favart Award, International Skating Union
1990	Inducted into U.S. Olympic Hall of Fame and World Figure Skating Hall of Fame
1993	Spirit of Giving Award, U.S. Ice Skating Association

---

sports history. As the *Time* article noted, Hamilton come to Sarajevo with a cold and an ear infection. "Though he refused to blame his curtailed performance on the illness, close observers noticed its effect." But, Phillips added, "nothing was wrong with his theatrical instincts." Hamilton provided an encore to the medals ceremony by skating a victory lap with the American flag held high.

Following Sarajevo Hamilton turned competitive professional, winning such contests as the Nutrasweet/NBC World Professional Figures Skating Championship. He also toured with the Ice Capades and formed the Scott Hamilton Amateur Tour before co-founding the Discover Stars on Ice touring company in 1986. For several years it seemed that no TV figure-skating show was complete without a turn by the gold medalist: *A Very Special Christmas, An Olympic Calgary Christmas, Scott Hamilton's Celebration on Ice, A Salute to* **Dorothy Hamill**, *Vail Skating Special, A Disney Christmas on Ice,* and **Nancy Kerrigan** *& Friends* are just a sample of his appearances. And when he wasn't skating, Hamilton was in the announcer's booth, providing expert analysis during televised competition.

Overcoming Another Obstacle

But Hamilton's life would change in 1997. Coming off a performance with his Discover Stars on Ice company, the athlete experienced severe shooting pain in his lower back and abdomen, which he attributed to an ulcer. Doctors discovered a malignant tumor—but even in the face of this diagnosis, Hamilton went on to perform that night. Later it was determined that Hamilton had contracted testicular cancer, a disease that strikes thousands of American men each year. "In the tightly knit world of skaters," wrote a contributor to *People,* "the news was devastating."

His peers rallied in support of Hamilton through the skater's chemotherapy treatment. "He's always been our big brother, someone to turn to," skating champion **Kristi Yamaguchi** explained in the *People* piece. The chemo-

therapy reduced the tumor to manageable size; in June 1997 surgery removed it along with Hamilton's right testicle. Then, characteristically, he returned to the ice with his typical showmanship plus a new direction in life. Hamilton became an advocate for cancer awareness, particularly among men. "It's all about awareness," he said in a January 2001 online chat transcribed by ABCNews.com. "The more it is discussed, the more you feel like [testicular] cancer is prevalent .The earlier you detect a problem, the better off you are. In any form of cancer—not just this kind."

After pronouncing himself "not 100 [percent] yet, but I will be" in 2001, Hamilton devoted 2002 to personal and professional causes. He had already founded the Scott Hamilton Cancer Alliance for Research, Education and Survivorship (CARES) at the Cleveland [Ohio] Clinic Taussig Cancer Center, where he was treated. In 2002, the skater then launched the web site chemocare.com to help cancer patients understand chemotherapy treatment and its side effects. In December 2002, Hamilton married Tracie Robinson in Malibu, California.

In a 1983 *Sports Illustrated* article, Bob Ottum summed up Hamilton's appeal. "Where other male and female skaters specialize," he wrote, "Hamilton is the sport's only all-around performer, equally good at athleticism and artistry. Even better, he doesn't look the part.... He looks as if you could hold him up to a strong light and see right through him. But that, too, is pure deception. Somewhere inside him are several miles of tightly drawn sinew and a startling sense of dedication."

FURTHER INFORMATION

Books

Newsmakers 1998. Detroit: Gale, 1999.

Periodicals

Litsky, Frank. *New York Times* (March 7, 1983).
Nolt, Laura Simmons. "Olympic Skaters: Taking Turns for the Better."*Saturday Evening Post* (March, 1984).
Ottum, Bob. "Great Scott! What A Doubleheader." *Sports Illustrated* (March 21, 1983).
Phillips, B. J. "A Little Touch of Heaven." *Time* (February 27, 1984).
Sports Illustrated (March 16, 1981).
Sports Illustrated (February 6, 1984).
Tresniowski, Alex. "Full of Fight." *People* (April 7, 1997).

Other

"Scott Hamilton" ABCNews.com. http://abcnews.go.com/sections/us/DailyNews/hamiltonchat_990128.html (January 21, 2001).

Sketch by Susan Salter

Mia Hamm
1972-

American soccer player

The world's most famous female soccer player, Mia Hamm, embodied the rise of American soccer, a sport played by millions of girls and boys that lacked a celebrity focus and a role model until she emerged as the leading all-time goal scorer in international soccer competition. Hamm became the biggest soccer name in the United States while playing on the U.S. national team in three World Cups and two Olympics.

Catching the Bug

Mariel Margaret Hamm was the fourth of six children born into a military family. Her father, Will Hamm, was a colonel in the U.S. army, and the family frequently moved as he was reassigned – to California, Alabama, Virginia, Texas and elsewhere. Hamm's mother, Stephanie, was a dancer, and she nicknamed her daughter Mia after prima ballerina Mia Slavenska. But Mia rejected her mother's attempts to make her into a dancer. Hamm refused to continue after just two ballet lessons when she was about six years old.

Hamm was already more interested in sports, especially soccer. When she was a toddler, her father was stationed in Florence, Italy. He bought season tickets to see the Fiorentina soccer club, and he often took Hamm to the games, where they both were mesmerized with the passion and athleticism of the players. "I believe it was in Italy that I really fell in love with the game," Hamm recalled to Greg Mazzola of *Coach and Athletic Director* magazine. When the family moved to Wichita Falls, Texas, her father started refereeing soccer games and coaching her older brother, Garrett, and older sister, Tiffany. Hamm started playing when she was five, and her father was often her coach.

Young Mia Hamm especially admired her brother's Garrett's soccer skills. "When Garrett was in high school, he was the athlete Mia wanted to be," her future husband Christian Corey revealed to Rosemary Feitelberg of *WWD* magazine. Garrett often chose Hamm to play with him in pick-up games against older boys. She also played Little League baseball, softball, tennis, basketball, and even football as a young girl, and later took up golf. There were few or no girls' teams in any sports, including soccer, so Hamm often played with the boys. At Notre Dame Middle School, she was the split end and kicker on the football team. "I was just one of the guys," Hamm later told Mike Spence of the *Colorado Springs Gazette Telegraph*.

Record Breaker

Hamm played high school soccer as a freshman and sophomore at Notre Dame High School in Wichita Falls.

Mia Hamm

When she was 15, she was invited to play for the North Texas State team in a tournament in Metairie, Louisiana. Legendary women's soccer coach Anson Dorrance of the University of North Carolina came to see Hamm; she was playing with and against college-age stars. After the opening kickoff, Dorrance recalled for *Newsweek*'s Mark Starr, "this little girl took off like she was shot out of a cannon . . . I couldn't believe the athleticism." Despite her age, Dorrance wanted her for the U.S. women's national team that he was coaching.

At 15, Hamm became the youngest player ever selected to the women's national team. She played forward and filled in as a goalie for one international game. Hamm graduated from Lake Braddock Secondary School in Burke, Virginia. Dorrance recruited her to play for his team at the University of North Carolina. His influence on Hamm was crucial to her development, especially since she lacked confidence. Dorrance once pulled her aside and told her that she could become the best player in the world. "Without his guidance, support, and teaching, I'd never have become the player I turned out to be," Hamm revealed to Mazzola.

At North Carolina, Hamm majored in political science and broke collegiate records as a soccer star. She played on four straight NCAA championship teams from 1989 through 1993, was a three-time National Player of the Year, and became the NCAA's all-time leading scorer. Hamm's 103 goals, 72 assists and 278 points were all collegiate records, as were her tourna-

Chronology

1987	Joins U.S. Women's National Team as youngest member
1989-93	Leads University of North Carolina to four national championships
1989-93	Sets all-time collegiate scoring records
1991, 1995, 1999	Plays in Women's World Cup
1996, 2000	Plays on U.S. Olympic teams
1999	Establishes Mia Hamm Foundation
2000	Founds WUSA, Women's United Soccer Association
2001-02	Plays for Washington Freedom in WUSA

ment career records of 16 goals, nine assists and 41 points. Dorrance continued to urge her to work harder and develop her skills.

In 1991, Hamm took a sabbatical from college and spent a year training with the U.S. National team and playing in the first-ever Women's World Cup, held in China. Coached by Dorrance, the U.S. women won the world championship.

Barely 5 foot 5 and 125 pounds, Hamm was quick, an excellent passer, and a devastating shooter. She also earned a reputation as an excellent dribbler and header and could score with either foot. Aggressive and determined, Hamm had an uncanny knack for penetrating defenses. "Mia has this amazing ability to go right through defenders, as if by molecular displacement," said Dorrance.

Celebrity Treatment

After graduating from the University of North Carolina, Hamm married Christian Corey, a career Marine, and played exclusively for the women's national team. In the 1995 Women's World Cup, she played forward and midfielder. One game, she even filled in at goalkeeper when the U.S. keeper was red-carded and had to leave the game. She led the team to a third-place bronze medal finish

The 1996 Summer Olympics in Atlanta, Georgia, was the first in which women's soccer was a gold-medal sport. After many years of American girls playing the sport, it was time for soccer to take center stage, and Hamm was in the spotlight. Before the largest crowd in the history of women's soccer, 76,481, at the University of Georgia's Seaford Stadium, plus a huge television audience, the U.S. team took on China for the gold medal. Sportswriter Dan Weber wrote: "...in **Pele**-like fashion, Hamm was both the difference – and the focus of everything that happened. ... Hamm had a hand – or a hamstring – in every U.S. strike." Hamm, who was playing on a badly sprained ankle, was all over the field. In the 19th minute, she took a cross from Christine Lilly and shot it past the goalie. It hit the upright, and teammate Shannon MacMillan scored on the rebound. After China tied the score, Hamm took the ball into the right corner in the 68th minute, stopped

and crossed the ball to Joy Fawcett, who fed Tiffeny Milbrett for the game-winning goal.

Olympic gold medals bring attention, and almost overnight Hamm, the biggest star on the U.S. team, became a celebrity. Advertisers hoped to connect her notoriety to the market of eight million female soccer players under the age of 18 in the United States. Hamm started doing commercials for Nike, a sponsor of the U.S. women's soccer team. Nike designed a women's sports shoe in her honor that featured her number 9. Hamm also did endorsements for Sportmart, Power Bar, Pert Plus shampoo and Pepsi. *People* named her one of the "50 Most Beautiful People in the World."

According to a 1998 *Sports Business Daily* survey, Hamm was America's most marketable female endorser. She even promoted a new Soccer Barbie doll. Hamm's most famous commercial epitomized the impact that she had on the male-dominated world of American athletics. In a widely played Gatorade spot, Hamm challenged fellow University of North Carolina superstar **Michael Jordan** to a series of sports contests, including tennis, basketball, soccer, track, and fencing, and as the song "Anything You Can Do, I Can Do Better" played, the commercial ended with Hamm flipping Jordan over her hip in a judo maneuver. "You have the greatest icon of American sports put alongside this woman who's saying, 'I can beat you,'" said Rick Burton, a professor at the University of Oregon's Warsaw Marketing Center, in a *Newsweek interview*. "That's incredibly important to the women's sports movement."

In a later commercial for Gatorade Ice, Hamm was shown executing a header and a bicycle kick as "ice" flows through her veins in a computerized rendering of her endoskeleton. All her endorsement deals gave her an estimated $1 million in annual earnings in a sport where most women players could not yet earn a full-time living by playing professionally.

Hamm had come to symbolize not only the ascendancy of soccer as an American sport, but the rise of women's athletics. She became a top role model and a much-in-demand speaker. Hamm participated widely in clinics for girls and exhibition games to promote soccer. She told audiences of young girls how soccer had transformed her from shy and uncertain to confident and strong. Hamm wrote an inspirational book, *Go for the Goal: A Champion's Guide to Winning in Soccer and Life,* which was part autobiography but primarily a soccer instructional manual filled with inspirational advice. In the book, she emphasized teamwork and practice as well as heart and attitude, insisting there was no place on a soccer team for an egotistical player with the aphorism "There is no me in Mia."

As Hamm grew increasingly comfortable as a role model for girls, she gradually shed the shyness and inhibition that were part of her personality. But she was reluctant to hog the spotlight and quick to credit others for her success. As for being labeled the world's greatest player, Hamm said it was mostly a matter of more attention being paid to goal scoring. In 1999 she told Mazzola: "I'm just another player trying to fill my role on this talented team. Since I score goals, I get more attention." Even when she described her own abilities, she downplayed them. Hamm explained to Starr: "A great finisher can analyze in a split second what the goalie is doing, what surface of the foot to use, and then put the ball in exactly the right spot. It's an ability to slow down time. You don't actually shoot any faster than other players do, but you process a lot more information in the same time . . . I'm still working on that." During the 1999 World Cup, she admitted to *Newsweek* that she wouldn't take penalty kicks because "I lack confidence."

Hamm always promoted the sport above herself. She appeared at clinics and freely gave autographs at every opportunity, but often refused photo shoots for high-profile publications. "This isn't all about me," said Hamm to *Newsweek* during the build-up to the 1999 Women's World Cup. "I won't bear the entire responsibility for my gender and my sport. I can't carry that much weight. I'm not that strong a person." Her national team coach, Tony DiCicco, told Jere Longman of the *New York Times:* "She's not only a soccer icon. She's an icon for women's athletics. That's a huge responsibility."

Hamm became a leader in other aspects of life as well. Her brother Garrett contracted a rare blood disease, aplastic anemia. Hamm joined the board of the Marrow Foundation and raised $50,000 for his bone marrow transplant with a charity soccer match. After his death, she established the Mia Hamm Foundation to raise money for bone-marrow research and to set up clinics and camps for young girls in soccer and other sports. The foundation held an annual golf tournament, the Mia Hamm Foundation Golf Classic, to raise money to help families of bone marrow transplant patients.

On a Winning Team

In 1997, Hamm participated in Nike's Victory Tour, an international competition played in six U.S. cities. Later that same year, Hamm was a top goal-scorer in the U.S. Women's Cup, scoring three goals against Canada and two against Australia.

In 1998, Hamm led the U.S. team with 20 goals and 20 assists in international play. In May 1999, Hamm set a new international scoring record with her 108th career goal. That spring, she also had a research and development building at Nike world headquarters in Beaverton, Oregon, named after her. The goal-scoring record brought her more notoriety. "When I was playing, they said soccer was a man's world and that women should remain on the sidelines," said soccer legend Pele, in an endorsement on the *Go for the Goal* book jacket. "All I can say is I'm glad I never had to go up against Mia Hamm."

Mia Hamm

In 1999, Hamm went through a drought during World Cup qualifying rounds, going eight games without scoring. Defenses double- and even triple-teamed her. The World Cup, held in U.S. cities, was no disappointment, as Hamm and her teammates pushed women's soccer to new heights of popularity in the host country. More than 90,000 fans packed the Rose Bowl in Pasadena, California, for the championship game between the U.S. team and China, the most people ever to see a women's sporting event in history. Many of the U.S. fans were wearing replica Hamm jerseys with her number 9 on them. The U.S. won on a penalty kick by **Brandi Chastain** during a tie-breaker shootout after an exciting scoreless duel.

In the 2000 Olympics in Sydney, Australia, Hamm scored a goal and the U.S. women earned a 2-0 victory in the opening game against Norway. The U.S. and China played to a 1-1 draw, and then the U.S. beat Nigeria to advance to the semifinals against Brazil. Hamm scored the only goal in the semifinal game to give her a career total of 127 goals. In the championship game against arch-rival Norway, in front of a capacity crowd in Sydney and a global TV audience, the U.S. was trailing 2-1 with time running out. Hamm had an assist on the sole U.S. goal, by Tiffeny Milbrett. Ninety seconds into stoppage time, Hamm was in the right corner and lofted a high pass to Milbrett, who headed it into the goal for the equalizer. But Norway won the game in overtime.

Hamm was heading into a new phase in her career, no longer a top goal-scorer. "Her best gift may be her

Awards and Accomplishments

1987	Youngest-ever member of U.S. Women's National team
1989-90	NCAA All-Tournament team
1989-90, 1992-93	Member of NCAA championship team
1991	Member of Women's World Cup champions
1992	Women's College Player of the Year
1992	Sets NCAA record for season scoring and assists
1992-93	Most valuable offensive player, NCAA Tournament
1993	NCAA Player of the Year
1993	Sets NCAA tournament career scoring record
1993	Sets NCAA career record for goals, assists, points
1993-94	Women's College Athlete of the Year
1993-94	Atlantic Coast Conference Female Athlete of the Year
1993-94	Mary Garber Award
1994-99	Female Athlete of the Year, U.S. Soccer Association
1996	Olympic Gold Medal
1998	Goodwill Games Gold Medal
1999	Breaks international career goals record
1999	Sportswoman of the Year, Women's Sports Foundation
1999	Member of Women's World Cup champions
2001	Women's Player of the Year, FIFA

competitive force," noted Jay Papasan of *Texas Monthly*. "If scoring eludes her, she intensifies other areas of her game, doling out assists, hounding loose balls, and stretching the defense with her long, slashing runs."

WUSA Pioneer

In 2000, Hamm was a founder of the first women's professional soccer league, the Women's United Soccer Association (WUSA), and she was counted on to provide the star power to make the league financially viable. She joined the Washington Freedom and appeared frequently at civic events to promote the new league and the Freedom team. Overcoming her quiet demeanor, Hamm often spoke of the need to support the league. DiCicco, who was the league's commissioner, referred to Hamm as "our Michael Jordan" in an article by Grant Wahl for *Sports Illustrated for Women*.

The Freedom drew a crowd of 34,148 for the league's inaugural game in 2001 and defeated the Bay Area CyberRays 1-0. Hamm, though battling injuries, dribbled past Chastain and drew a foul which set up the game-winning goal on a penalty kick. She started the first three games of the 2001 season as a midfielder, partly because she was recovering from a shoulder injury, then coach Jim Gabbara moved her back to forward.

Every place Washington played, attendance soared as young girls and their families came out to see Hamm. "Hamm has been the pied piper of the Women's United Soccer Association, attracting hoards of fans wherever she goes," noted Jennifer Starks of the *Contra Costa Times*. "Hamm's presence has been critical in the attempts to promote and sell the new soccer league to the masses." Attendance at games averaged 14,000 when Hamm appeared; without her, it averaged about 8,000.

She would spend up to 20 minutes after each game signing autographs. For the season, Hamm played six positions and scored only six goals. In September, however, she scored two goals in the U.S. national team's 4-1 win over Germany to extend her career record to 129.

Hamm was still piling up honors. At the end of 2001, FIFA – soccer's international governing body — named Hamm its first Women's Player of the Year. Also that year, she divorced Corey and later began dating Boston Red Sox shortstop Nomar Garciaparra, whom she first met in 1998 while beating him in a penalty-kick contest.

In the off-season, Hamm underwent knee surgery. In 2002, she did not play until the Freedom's tenth game, when she entered wearing a knee brace in the 65th minute of play and seven minutes later scored a goal that gave Washington a 2-1 victory. Athough Hamm started only one game, she was the key player in Washington's playoff run. The team went 10-1-2 after she rejoined the squad, and she had eight goals and six assists, including three game-winning goals. Coming in fresh in the second half, Hamm would attack defenses in her old style. Even after turning 30, she was still a force to be reckoned with.

Mia Hamm was a pioneer to a degree that few other athletes have ever been in any sport. She scored more goals in international competition than any man or woman who ever played the world's most popular game, and in doing so brought women's soccer to global notoriety. In the United States, Hamm represented the ascendancy of women's athletics, being the foremost name in the most popular sport played by girls and becoming an icon representing women's ability to compete on the playing field. As the key to the success of the first women's professional soccer league, Hamm carried a heavy weight on her shoulders, but did so with consistent grace, poise and humility. Her philosophy of team play above individual achievement set a tone that helped instruct countless young athletes, girls and boys.

SELECTED WRITINGS BY HAMM:

(With Aaron Heifetz) *Go for the Goal: A Champion's Guide to Winning in Soccer and Life.* HarperCollins, 1999.

FURTHER INFORMATION

Books

Christopher, Matt and Glenn Stout. *On the Field with ... Mia Hamm.* Little, Brown, 1998.
Rutledge, Rachel. *Mia Hamm: Striking Superstar.* Millbrook Press, 2000.

Periodicals

Collie, Ashley Jude. "Hamm It Up! Mia Hamm is Shy and Quiet, Except on the Soccer Field." *Sports Illustrated for Kids,* 11 (June 1, 1999): 22.

Diedrick, Brian. "Gatorade Scores With Ice-Cold Superstar." *SHOOT,* 43 (April 19, 2002): 10.

Feitelberg, Rosemary. "Mia Hamm: Kicking Back." *WWD,*173 (April 3, 1997): 64.

"The 50 Most Beautiful People in the World 1997." *People,* 47 (May 12, 1997): 90.

Haydon, John. "Mia Hamm Relishes Her Role as Big Cheese in Women's Game." *Washington Times,* (June 7, 1997): 7.

Hobgood, Cynthia. "Golf Tourney Boosts Hamm's Foundation." *Washington Business Journal.*19 (May 4, 2001): 10.

Hobgood, Cynthia. "Mia and Michael." *Washington Business Journal.* 19 (December 29, 2000): 8.

"It Went Down to the Wire." *Newsweek.*134 (July 19, 1999): 46.

Killion, Ann. "Mia Hamm is providing a connection." *Knight Ridder/Tribune News Service.* (May 8, 1997): 508 K5953.

Longman, Jere. "A Superstar's Burden." *New York Times Upfront.* 132 (September 6, 1999): 32.

"Match Play: The Dating Trend of the Moment?" *People.* 58 (August 19, 2002): 58.

Mazzola, Gregg. "Goals." *Coach and Athletic Director.* 68 (December 1998): 44.

"Mia Hamm: Top Scorer in the Soccer World." *U.S. News & World Report.* 126 (June 21, 1999): 13.

Papasan, Jay. "Mia Hamm." *Texas Monthly.* 28 (September 2000): 156.

"Scorecard (Mia Hamm Will Have a Building Named After Her)." *Sports Illustrated.* 90 (May 31, 1999): 23.

Spence, Mike. "Mia Hamm Emerging as Best Female Soccer Player of the Year." *Knight Ridder/Tribune News Service.* (May 16, 1996): 516 K3237.

Starks, Jennifer. "Women's Soccer Banks on the Mia Factor."*Knight Ridder/Tribune News Service.*(July 25, 2001): K4979.

Starr, Mark. "Keeping Her Own Score." *Newsweek.* 133 (June 21, 1999): 60.

Stein, Marc. "Hamm, Teammates One Win Away From Repeating for Soccer Gold." *Knight Ridder/Tribune News Service.* (September 27, 2000): K3635.

Wahl, Grant. "Mia's Excellent Adventure."*Sports Illustrated for Women.* 3 (March 1, 2001): 64.

Weber, Dan. "Mia Hamm Makes All the Difference. "*Knight Ridder/Tribune News Service.* (August 1, 1996): 80 K2154.

Wright, Ken. "Freedom to Keep Hamm in Sub Role." *Washington Times.* (August 21, 2002): C03.

Wright, Ken. "Hamm Scores Winner in Return to Freedom."*Washington Times.* (June 13, 2002): C09.

Other

"Head Coach U.S. Women's National Team." *Soccer-Times.com.* http://www.soccertimes.com/usteams/roster/women/dorrance.htm (December 30, 2002).

"Mia Hamm." *Women in Sports.* http://www.makeit happen.com/wis/bios/hammm.html(December 28, 2002).

"Mia Hamm." *WUSA.* http://www.wusa.com/players_coaches/players/mia_hamm/(December 28, 2002).

"Mia Hamm Awards." *Elaine's Mia Hamm webpage.* http://www.geocities.com/Colosseum/Pressbox/6343/awards.html (December 28, 2002).

Sketch by Michael Betzold

Anfernee "Penny" Hardaway 1971-

American basketball player

Anfernee "Penny" Hardaway, point guard for the Phoenix Suns, made a name for himself in the NBA while paired with center **Shaquille O'Neal** in Orlando in the mid-1990s. After O'Neal's departure for the Los Angeles Lakers in 1996 and several injuries, Hardaway decided to try to restart his career with the Phoenix Suns in 1999.

Childhood Experiences

Hardaway was born in Memphis in 1971. When he was very young, his mother, Fae Hardaway, moved to California and left him in the care of his grandmother, Louise Hardaway. Louise had started life as a sharecropper in Arkansas, but she, her husband, and her children moved to Memphis as soon as they had saved up enough money to buy a house there. Throughout her life, Louise, a cook in Memphis elementary schools, worked hard to do the best she could for her family, including Hardaway. Although the neighborhood in which they lived in Memphis, in the same house into which Louise and her husband had moved in 1950, was becoming more impoverished and dangerous, Louise did her best to prevent Hardaway from becoming involved in crime. The two went to the Early Grove Baptist Church together for many years, and when Louise couldn't go anymore, Hardaway went by himself.

When Hardaway was fourteen, his mother returned to Memphis and he moved back in with her. Although he became an All-American player, he was not concentrating on his schoolwork, and as a result when it came time for him to go to college he could not pass the American College Test (ACT) and had to sit out his freshman year under the rules of National Collegiate Athletic Association (NCAA) Bylaw 5-1-(j), more commonly known as Proposition 48.

Despite offers from schools across the country, Hardaway had chosen to remain close to home and attend

Penny Hardaway

Memphis State (now the University of Memphis). "Imagine walking around your hometown and everybody thinks you're a dummy," Hardaway told *Sport* magazine's Darryl Howerton. Even when he went back to his old high school to watch their games, students from the schools they played would sometimes derisively chant "A-C-T! A-C-T!" at him from across the gym.

An Epiphany

Then, the next summer, Hardaway was the victim of an armed robbery that left him with a bullet lodged in his right foot. He was with one of his cousins, in front of his cousin's house in Memphis, when four men jumped out of a car and forced them to lay face-down on the pavement, and then, while one held a pistol to the back of Hardaway's neck, the others took their money, jewelry, and shoes. Hardaway was sure that he was going to die, but instead the robbers just took their loot and ran back to their car. As they ran, one fired indiscriminately behind him. This bullet ricocheted off of the pavement and into Hardaway's foot, where it broke three bones.

As Hardaway lay in the hospital recovering, he ruminated about how fragile life was and how close he had come to losing his future in basketball. Although his foot healed well enough to allow him to play again, Hardaway returned to his classes at Memphis State that fall with a new zeal. By the end of the year, he was on the dean's list.

Onto the NBA

When Hardaway left Memphis State in 1993, he was drafted by the Golden State Warriors but immediately traded to the Orlando Magic for their first-round draft choice, future Washington Wizards and Sacramento Kings star **Chris Webber**. Magic fans were gathered in the Orlando Arena to watch a telecast of the draft, and some of them booed Hardaway when they heard of this trade. According to Hardaway, this was the worst day of his life. "How can you feel at home when your hometown fans boo you?" Hardaway said to *Sports Illustrated*'s Phil Taylor.

The Magic's O'Neal had a great deal to do with Hardaway's acquisition by that team. The two had played together in the Olympic Festival in 1990 and later worked together on the basketball-themed film *Blue Chips,* where O'Neal developed a great deal of respect for Hardaway's game. The O'Neal-Hardaway pairing was indeed magical: O'Neal, the flamboyant center, was the major attention-getter and scorer, but the less flashy, six-foot-seven-inch point guard Hardaway did an excellent job of feeding him the ball and was a serious scoring threat himself. By the end of his second season, sportswriters were confidently declaring Hardaway one of the greatest basketball players of our time.

Li'l Penny

Hardaway's fame was increased by a series of advertisements run by Nike that featured Hardaway and a loud-mouthed puppet, voiced by comedian Chris Rock, called Li'l Penny. Li'l Penny was supposedly Hardaway's little brother—little being the operative word, since Li'l Penny only stood three feet tall. Li'l Penny, who was also a basketball player, lived the sort of stereotypical professional athlete life that Hardaway himself has usually avoided: parties, women (especially supermodel Tyra Banks), and shameless self-promotion were always at the center of Lil' Penny's persona. Li'l Penny even published a book, *Knee High and Livin' Large: The World According to Me.* Although these commercials have not run for several years, they are still remembered, particularly for the role that they played in launching Chris Rock's career.

Career Statistics

Yr	Team	GP	PTS	FG%	3P%	FT%	RPG	APG	SPG	BPG	TO	PF
1993-94	ORL	82	1313	.466	.267	.742	5.4	6.6	2.32	.62	292	205
1994-95	ORL	77	1613	.512	.349	.769	4.4	7.2	1.69	.34	258	158
1995-96	ORL	82	1780	.513	.314	.767	4.3	7.1	2.02	.50	229	160
1996-97	ORL	59	1210	.447	.318	.820	4.5	5.6	1.58	.59	145	23
1997-98	ORL	19	311	.377	.300	.763	4.0	3.6	1.47	.79	46	45
1998-99	ORL	50	791	.420	.286	.706	5.7	5.3	2.22	.46	150	111
1999-00	PHO	60	1015	.474	.324	.790	5.8	5.3	1.57	.63	153	164
2000-01	PHO	4	39	.417	.250	.636	4.5	3.8	1.50	.25	3	6
2001-02	PHO	80	959	.418	.277	.810	4.4	4.1	1.53	.40	189	184
2002-03	PHO	13	140	.431	.444	.789	5.8	4.7	.92	.23	41	40
TOTAL		513	9171	.465	.311	.772	4.8	5.8	1.81	.50	1506	1196

ORL: Orlando Magic; PHO: Phoenix Suns.

Awards and Accomplishments

1990	*Parade* magazine's Player of the Year
1990	Named a First-Team All-American by *Basketball Times*
1990	Olympic Festival (with South team)
1992	Great Midwest Conference's "Newcomer of the Year"
1992	Great Midwest Conference's "Player of the Year"
1993	Finalist for the Naismith award
1993	Finalist for the Wooden award
1994	Hardaway's #25 jersey retired by Memphis State
1994	NBA All-Rookie First All-Star Team
1994	Runner-up for Rookie of the Year Award
1994	Most Valuable Player of the Schick Rookie Game
1994	Orlando Magic's Fans' Choice award
1995	NBA Player of the Month for November
1995-96	All-NBA First All-Star Team
1995-98	Selected for the All-Star game
1996	Olympics (with Team USA)
1997	All-NBA Third All-Star Team

Part II—Heaven Cent

Things began to fall apart for Hardaway after a few years. Orlando fans were still not always kind to him, he had a rocky relationship with the Magic coaches, and in 1996 O'Neal left Orlando for the Los Angeles Lakers. Knee and hamstring injuries limited his playing time in the next few seasons, and by 1999 Hardaway and the Magic were ready to part ways: he was traded to the Phoenix Suns in 1999.

Hardaway vowed to make a fresh start in Phoenix, even declaring his commitment in ink on his left bicep, where he added the words "Part II" above a previous tattoo that reads "Heaven Cent." Although the Suns have yet to make it to the NBA finals, Hardaway and such talented young players as Stephon Marbury and Shawn Marion are working hard to build a strong team, and fans remain hopeful that Hardaway will remain healthy (he had his fourth knee surgery during the 2000-01 season) and lead the team to a championship.

CONTACT INFORMATION

Address: c/o Phoenix Suns, 201 E. Jefferson St., Phoenix, AZ 85004. Online: www.pennyhardaway.net.

FURTHER INFORMATION

Periodicals

Geffner, Michael P. "Penny and His Thoughts." *Sporting News* (November 10, 1997): 29-31.

Howerton, Darryl. "After Being Swept by Houston in the NBA Finals, Orlando Guard Anfernee Hardaway Reflects on Yet Another . . . Summer of Discontent." *Sport* (October, 1995): 59-62.

"One on One with . . . Penny Hardaway." *Sporting News* (January 7, 2002): 50.

Pierce, Charles P. "The Disappearance of Anfernee Hardaway." *Esquire* (February, 2000): 56.

Plummer, William, and Grant, Meg. "Penny from Heaven." *People* (March 28, 1994): 97-99.

Powell, Shaun. "Move Over, Michael: It's Penny's League Now." *Sporting News* (November 27, 1995): 36.

Taylor, Phil. "A Monumental Beginning." *Sports Illustrated* (December 1, 1991): 101-102.

Taylor, Phil. "No More Magic." *Sports Illustrated* (May 15, 2000): 65.

Taylor, Phil. "A Penny Spent." *Sports Illustrated* (February 13, 1995): 54-57.

Taylor, Phil. "A Touch of Magic." *Sports Illustrated* (February 13, 1995): 36-38.

Weinberg, Rick. "Penny Well Spent." *Sport* (June, 1995): 74.

Other

"Anfernee Hardaway Player Info." NBA.com. http://www.nba.com/playerfile/anfernee_hardaway (November 28, 2002).

The Official Penny Hardaway Web Site. http://www.
    pennyhardaway.net (November 29, 2002).

"One-on-One with Penny Hardaway." NBA.com http://
    www.nba.com/suns/interactive/hardaway_transcript_
    021001.html (January 3, 2002).

Sketch by Julia Bauder

Tim Hardaway

Tim Hardaway
1966-

American basketball player

Although knee injuries, a broken foot, and a salary cap that made signing established veterans difficult seem to have brought Tim Hardaway's NBA career to a premature end, when he was playing he was one of the best point guards in the National Basketball Association (NBA). He was shuffled from team to team several times in his career, playing five and a half seasons each for the Golden State Warriors and the Miami Heat before a series of trades in 2001 and 2002 landed him with his final team, the Denver Nuggets. He was in a Nuggets uniform for a mere fourteen games when he broke his left foot during what appears to have been his last NBA game on March 23, 2002.

Childhood Influences

Hardaway grew up on the South Side of Chicago, playing schoolyard ball with kids who called him "Bug" because of his small size. (Even today Hardaway, at a broad, muscular six feet, is short for an NBA player.) Wanting to win respect from them helped to propel him into the NBA. As he explained to Jeff Weinstock of *Sport* magazine, "I just wanted to prove to them that I could. . . . I wasn't going to be one of the guys who go off on drugs or drinking or doing some stupid stuff in school where I wouldn't be able to get myself in this position, playing in the NBA."

Basketball has been Hardaway's love for as long as he can remember. As one family story goes, his parents put two toys in his crib for him when he was six months old: a toy car and a basketball. He tossed the car out of the crib and curled up with the basketball, put there by his father.

A shared love for basketball has been one of the few things that have kept Hardaway and his father close over the years. His parents had a rocky relationship, in large part because of his father's struggle with alcoholism, and they divorced when Hardaway was twelve. During those times, "[basketball] was always my release," Hardaway

told *Sports Illustrated* interviewer S. L. Price in 1997. "When I was going through stuff with my dad, I could get my frustrations worked out just by playing hard."

NBA Career

Hardaway went to college at the University of Texas—El Paso, where as a senior he perfected a crossover dribble maneuver that came to be known as the "UTEP two-step." Then, in 1989 he moved on to the NBA, where his career started out strong. He led the Golden State Warriors, the highest-scoring team in the league, in assists in his rookie season, becoming only the second player in NBA history to do so as a rookie. This feat earned him a unanimous selection to the 1989-90 NBA All-Rookie First Team. He also reached the 5,000 points, 2,500 assists mark faster than any other player but one (**Oscar Robertson**, a star NBA player of the 1960s and 1970s who is widely regarded as one of the best all-around players of all time), achieving this in a mere 262 games.

However, after the 1991-92 season, the Golden State team began to fall apart. Injuries sidelined several of their star players in the 1992-93 season, including Hardaway, who sat out sixteen games with an injured knee but still finished second in the league in assists. Then, in 1993, disaster struck: Hardaway tore the anterior cruciate ligament in his left knee, forcing him to miss the entire 1993-94 NBA season and to forfeit his spot on the 1994 U.S. National Team for the World Championships

Career Statistics

Yr	Team	GP	PTS	FG%	3P%	FT%	RPG	APG	SPG	BPG	TO	PF
1989-90	GSW	79	1162	.471	.274	.764	3.9	8.7	2.09	.15	260	232
1990-91	GSW	82	1881	.476	.385	.803	4.0	9.7	2.61	.15	270	228
1991-92	GSW	81	1893	.461	.338	.766	3.8	10.0	2.02	.16	267	208
1992-93	GSW	66	1419	.447	.330	.744	4.0	10.6	1.76	.18	220	152
1994-95	GSW	62	1247	.427	.378	.760	3.1	9.3	1.42	.19	214	155
1995-96	GSW	28	482	.425	.361	.821	3.5	10.0	2.07	.21	110	70
1995-96	MIA	52	735	.421	.366	.769	2.5	6.9	1.42	.21	125	131
1996-97	MIA	81	1644	.415	.344	.799	3.4	8.6	1.86	.11	230	165
1997-98	MIA	81	1528	.431	.351	.781	3.7	8.3	1.68	.20	224	200
1998-99	MIA	48	835	.400	.360	.812	3.2	7.3	1.19	.13	131	102
1999-00	MIA	52	696	.386	.367	.827	2.9	7.4	.94	.08	112	112
2000-01	MIA	77	1150	.392	.366	.801	2.6	6.3	1.17	.08	189	155
2001-02	DAL	54	518	.341	.341	.833	1.8	3.7	.74	.15	73	84
2001-02	DEN	14	134	.373	.373	.632	1.9	5.5	1.21	.14	38	25
TOTAL		857	15324	.432	.355	.782	3.3	8.3	1.66	.15	2470	2019

DAL: Dallas Mavericks; DEN: Denver Nuggets; GSW: Golden State Warriors; MIA: Miami Heat.

that year. He came back in 1994, but turmoil in the Warriors lineup and coaching staff, including an ongoing feud between Hardaway and fellow player **Latrell Sprewell**, as well as continued injury problems, resulted in the team finishing last in the league that season.

Move to Miami

Hardaway, frustrated with the team's losing record and unhappy with coach Rick Adelman, campaigned to be traded. In the middle of the 1995-96 season he was, to the Miami Heat, where he had two twenty-point games in his first week. The following season, Hardaway led the Heat in scoring and in assists, propelling the team to a 61-21 record and the Eastern Conference Finals, where they were defeated by the Chicago Bulls. Hardaway was a solid player on the still-solid team for the next two seasons as well, but by 1999 knee problems were beginning to slow his play. Hardaway also developed issues with the Heat's coach, **Pat Riley**, and these factors both contributed to Hardaway's being traded to the Dallas Mavericks for the 2001-02 season.

Hardaway did not remain in Dallas long; in February 2002 he was traded to the Denver Nuggets. He was in his fourteenth game in a Nuggets uniform on March 23, 2002, when Seattle SuperSonics player Randy Livingston stepped on his left foot and broke it during the first quarter of the game. This caused Hardaway to miss the remainder of the season. That June, only days before the 2002 draft, the Nuggets decided to buy out last two seasons of Hardaway's contract, worth $7.9 million. Although Hardaway attempted to find a place on another team, tough salary caps made teams more interested in promising, cheaper rookies than in established but more expensive veterans, and he could not find a new playing position by the start of the 2002-2003 season.

Chronology

1966	Born September 1 in Chicago, Illinois
1989	Drafted by the Golden State Warriors in the first round of the NBA draft
1993	Misses 1993-94 NBA season and the 1994 World Championships after suffering a torn anterior cruciate ligament in his left knee
1995	Misses end of 1994-95 season after injuring his hand
1996	Traded to Miami Heat February 22
1999	Selected for the USA Basketball Men's Senior National Team
1999-2000	Misses thirty games during the NBA season after injuries to his right knee and foot
2001	Traded to the Dallas Mavericks August 22
2002	Traded to the Denver Nuggets February 21
2002	Suffers broken foot during a game March 23

After he was unable to find a playing position with an NBA team in time for the 2002-03 season, Hardaway became a basketball analyst for the cable sports network ESPN. He appears on the *ESPN Shootaround* show, which airs on Friday nights before the featured NBA games. Hardaway is married, and he and his wife Yolanda have two children, Tim Jr. and Nia.

Legacy

Although Hardaway's career was marred by his frequent, acrimonious disagreements with his coaches and fellow players, he will certainly be remembered for his record-breaking early seasons and for his role in the successes of the Miami Heat in the mid to late 1990s. He may also be remembered for his many charitable activities, which include acting as an anti-drug spokesperson with the Miami Coalition while playing for the Heat, running his own summer camps for children in Chicago, Illinois and El Paso, Texas, and co-founding "The Support Group," which helps disadvantaged children in Chicago with their education.

FURTHER INFORMATION

Periodicals

Burns, Marty. "1 Miami Heat." *Sports Illustrated* (November 1, 1999): 144+.

Howerton, Darryl. "Head Games." *Sport* (June, 1998): 48-50.

Jackson, Barry. "Hardaway Gets Heated Against Orlando, Might Miss Game Against Miami." *Knight Ridder/Tribune News Service* (March 15, 2002): K1654.

McGraw, Mike. "Bulls' Search for Point Guard Continues." *Daily Herald* (Arlington Heights, IL) (September 14, 2002): 5.

"Nuggets Waive Hardaway, Say Hello to Hole at Point Guard." *Gazette* (Colorado Springs, CO) (June 26, 2002): SP7.

Perkins, Chris. "Not a Natural on TV — Yet." *Palm Beach Post* (West Palm Beach, FL) (November 10, 2002): 11B.

Powell, Shaun. "Hardaway, Laettner Start Anew as Strickland Stews." *Sporting News* (March 11, 1996): 20.

Price, S. L. "Hot Hand." *Sports Illustrated* (May 5, 1997): 28-31.

Taylor, Phil. "Tim Hardaway." *Sports Illustrated* (November 7, 1994): 142.

Winderman, Ira. "Hardaway Gets His Chance to Play on the World Stage." *Sporting News* (July 19, 1999): 38.

Winderman, Ira. "Tax, Salary Cap Leave Vets Out in Cold." *Knight Ridder/Tribune News Service* (October 5, 2002): K6748.

Weinstock, Jeff. "Steppin' Out." *Sport* (May, 1992): 44-47.

Other

"Golden State Warriors History." NBA.com. http://www.nba.com/warriors/history/00401109.html (January 5, 2003).

"Heat History Test." NBA.com. http://www.nba.com/heat/history/history.html (January 5, 2003).

"Howard's Late Bucket Lifts Nuggets Past Sonics." CBS SportsLine.com. http://cbs.sportsline.com/u/ce/recap/0,2405,NBA_20020323_SEA@DEN,00.htm (January 2, 2003).

Tim Hardaway Web site. http://www.timhardaway.com (November 28, 2002).

"Tim Hardaway Player Info." NBA.com. http://www.nba.com/playerfile/tim_hardaway/index.html (November 28, 2002).

"USA Basketball Bio: Tim Hardaway." USA Basketball http://www.usabasketball.com/biosmen/tim_hardaway_bio.html (November 28, 2002).

Sketch by Julia Bauder

Tonya Harding
1970-

American figure skater

The pre-Olympic hype prior to the 1994 Winter Olympic Games intensified considerably when American figure skater Tonya Harding was implicated in a bizarre attack on her ice rival, **Nancy Kerrigan**. The now infamous incident occurred some six weeks before the Lillehammer Games were to begin as Harding and Kerrigan vied for top position on the women's team at the U.S. Figure Skating Championships in Detroit, Michigan. As Kerrigan came off the ice one day, a mysterious man whacked her knee with a police baton, and then fled. Days later, Harding's ex-husband and three other men were linked to the attack. Kerrigan recovered and skated for a silver medal-win at Lillehammer, but Harding became the object of derision and ridicule. Her skating career effectively ended after Lillehammer, where she finished in eighth place.

Some of the intense media scrutiny surrounding the Harding-Kerrigan story seemed to be heightened because of the women's seemingly pitch-perfect storybook roles: Harding was an athletic, daring skater who came from an impoverished, somewhat rough family background. She struggled for years to pay for her skating lessons, costumes, and travel costs, and had emerged as a kind of folk-hero success story by the time she arrived in Detroit. Kerrigan, on the other hand, embodied what made figure skating such a popular spectator event: possessing classic New England cheekbones and flawless skin, she was elegant and poised both on and off the ice.

Began on Used Skates

Harding was born in 1970 and grew up in Portland, Oregon. Her mother, LaVona, had been married five times by the time Harding was born, and the family

Tonya Harding

moved often due to their reduced financial circumstances. "I changed schools just about every year, so I didn't have friends hardly at all," Harding told E. M. Swift in *Sports Illustrated.* "I was basically a loner." Harding was close to her father, Al, who taught her how to fish, shoot a rifle, and even rebuild a car engine. She began skating at the age of three, when her parents took her to a mall and she was fascinated by the skaters on the indoor rink. Enrolled in group lessons with a pair of secondhand skates, Harding proved such a natural talent that her teacher soon suggested private lessons. At the time, these were $25 a week, and her mother struggled to make enough tips at her waitressing job to pay for them.

Considered the sport of affluent youths, figure skating drains a family's time and resources immensely: costs for serious competition training can run as high as $30,000 a year. Harding's longtime coach, Diane Rawlinson, was supportive and empathized with the family's dedication to their daughter's love of skating. Rawlinson donated her lessons when money was tight, bought Tonya skates, and even found friends and business owners willing to sponsor her travel costs.

Rose in Sport Despite Hardships

Harding began dating Jeff Gillooly, two years her senior, when she was 15, partly to escape a troubled home life. Her parents' marriage was disintegrating,

and her alcoholic half-brother expressed interest in her. She dropped out of high school during her sophomore year, and was living with Gillooly by the time she was 18. By then, Harding was already making a name for herself in U.S. Figure Skating Association (USFSA)-sanctioned events: she placed sixth in 1986 at her first senior national competition, and made a strong showing at the 1989 championship event in Baltimore. The next year, she defied doctors' orders and skated in the Salt Lake City nationals despite a case of pneumonia, and placed seventh.

Harding did far better in 1991 and earned her first mention in *Sports Illustrated* when she emerged the surprise first-place finisher at nationals. She stunned spectators, sportswriters, and figure-skating fans at the Minneapolis event when she became the first American woman ever to land a triple axel in competition. "Forty-five seconds into her routine, Harding stroked the length of the ice, coiled and sprang to an improbable height," wrote Swift. "Her pony tail became a blur as she spun. Upon landing, she cried out, 'Yes!' The crowd, recognizing history in this 5 ft. 1 in., 105-pound package of fist-clenching grit, roared." Only Midori Ito of Japan had ever landed the 3½-revolution jump under the duress of competition. Moreover,

Awards and Accomplishments

1986	Sixth place, U.S. Figure Skating Association (USFSA) women's championships
1989	Bronze medal, USFSA women's championships
1990	Seventh place, USFSA women's championships
1991	Gold medal, USFSA women's championships
1991	Silver medal, World Figure Skating championships
1992	Bronze medal, USFSA women's championships
1992	Fourth place, Albertville Winter Olympics
1992	Sixth place, World Figure Skating championships
1994	Gold medal, USFSA women's championships (stripped of title later that year)
1994	Eighth place, Lillehammer Winter Olympics
1999	Second place, ESPN Professional Skating Championships

Harding's transcendence of her background into the rarified world of skating made her an interesting subject. "Harding shatters all stereotypes of the pampered and sheltered figure skater who has spent his or her youth bottled in an ice rink, training," the same *Sports Illustrated* article noted.

Back home, however, Harding endured personal problems over the next two years that seemed to keep her from skating in top form. Her relationship with Gillooly was problematic; the two divorced August of 1993, but moved in together two months later. Kerrigan, from the Boston area, had emerged as a formidable rival to Harding after a third-place finish in 1991. At the following year's nationals, Kerrigan took the silver medal, with Harding in third place this time. Kerrigan won the U.S. title outright in 1993. The next year, skating fans anticipated a showdown between the two at the Detroit championships, which would finalize their place on the Olympic team.

The Infamous Footage

On January 6, 1994, Kerrigan was attacked by an unknown figure as she came off the ice at Cobo Arena and headed backstage. When word spread, television crews rushed to capture a sobbing, hysterical Kerrigan on the ground, surrounded by people, clutching her jumping leg, and crying "Why, why?" Within days, two people contacted authorities and said they had listened to a tape of four people planning the attack. A friend of Gillooly's whom Harding had employed as a personal bodyguard, Shawn Eckardt, was immediately implicated.

On January 11, both Harding and Gillooly proclaimed their innocence. That same day, however, Eckardt—owner of World Bodyguard Service, whose only client was Harding—confessed and said that he had hired two others to carry out the attack; he also implicated Harding and Gillooly in the planning and details, noting that Harding had provided information about Kerrigan's schedule. Eckardt, the baton hit-man Shane Stant, and getaway-car driver Derrick Smith were charged, as was Gillooly. Harding denied any involvement at first and at a press conference read a prepared statement in which she asserted that upon hearing about Kerrigan's attack, "My first reaction was one of disbelief ... followed by shock and fear," according to Shannon Brownlee in *U.S. News & World Report*. Harding also claimed that her first-place finish in Detroit had been an "unfulfilling" one due to Kerrigan's absence.

Linked to Odd Phone Query

On January 18, Harding was questioned by agents from the Federal Bureau of Investigation (FBI) for more than ten hours. She claimed that her ex-husband was innocent. Meanwhile, Gillooly was implicating her in the attack, and four days later a part-time sports journalist from Pennsylvania who was friendly with Harding said that the skater had called her in December and asked questions about Kerrigan and where she trained in Cape Cod, Massachusetts. Further investigation found that Stant had traveled to the area, but did not carry out the attack. Finally, on January 24, Harding admitted that she knew of the plot before her competition, but was too fearful to take action to stop it. On February 1, Gillooly pled guilty in a deal that involved a two-year prison sentence and a $100,000 fine. He claimed the plot against Kerrigan originated in December, when Harding returned from a Japan competition dismayed over what she believed had been the judges' bias toward Kerrigan. "In the end, Shane and Smith attacked Kerrigan for less than $5,000, in the grandiose hope that if Harding won a gold medal at the Olympics, they would become 'World Bodyguard Service' to the stars," wrote Brownlee in *U.S. News & World Report*. "Eckardt exulted, 'We're going to make a lot of money.'"

The February, 1994 Lillehammer Olympic Games were imminent by this point, and a major debate raged in the media over whether or not Harding should be allowed to compete. The *New York Times* editorial page and even President Bill Clinton pointed out that Harding was, essentially, innocent until proven guilty, and she had not yet been fully implicated in a court of law. Others argued that Olympic athletes should be held to a higher standard of ethics. Other pundits decried the overblown media attention surrounding the Harding-Kerrigan story, claiming it was, in the end, unnewsworthy and salacious. Some corners threw their support to Harding simply as the underdog in a sport that seemed to be less about athletic ability than telegenic good looks and a demure demeanor. Pat Jordan, writing in *The Sporting News,* claimed that Harding epitomized the "Dirty White Girl." Such women, Jordan explained, "wake in the morning to apply new make-up over the old, have a Mountain Dew and a Clark's bar for breakfast, then go to work as a waitress. They talk tough, smoke cigarettes, have tattoos, and usually spend their weekends drinking with their boyfriends in a country-and-western bar before drag racing on the street." The sportswriter recalled the time when Harding placed sixth in her first national competition, and phoned home with the news. "Her mother told Harding she had choked and was a loser," wrote Jordan. "Harding tried to explain, but her mother wouldn't listen. When she hung up the phone, Harding turned and said, 'What a bitch! Let's order some food.' Like a proper DWG, she did not cry."

Jordan noted that such "DWG" skaters are usually far more daring on the ice than their nice-girl counterparts, taking risky jumps and skating with a great deal of verve. Kerrigan seemed to hold back in competition, but had nevertheless earned several lucrative endorsement contracts already. Just before the Detroit attack, she appeared in her first commercial for Campbell's Soups. Harding, of course, had no endorsement contracts. "Harding has been burdened all her life by the Nancy Kerrigans of the world, and if guilty, finally she must have snapped," Jordan concluded.

Banned for Life

In the end, Harding was allowed to skate at Lillehammer by the U.S. Olympic Committee and the Lillehammer Games Administrative Board, but the media frenzy seemed to finally unnerve her. Banks of television cameras lined up for her practice sessions, and she skated poorly in the events themselves. At one point, she botched a jump, and skated over to the judges to show them the broken lace on her skate, which she claimed caused her misstep; they allowed her to do it over. Harding finished in eighth place overall, with the Ukraine's Oksana Baiul taking the gold medal and Kerrigan earning a second-place silver.

Harding and her personal life continued to be the source of tabloid fodder and water-cooler jokes. Gillooly sold a private videotape of their wedding night, in which Harding appeared topless in her wedding dress, to the television show *A Current Affair*. On March 16, 1994, she entered a guilty plea in a Multnomah County, Oregon court—the jurisdiction in which the Kerrigan attack had been planned—and admitted to lying to police

and hindering prosecution efforts. She was saddled with a $100,000 fine and equally onerous court costs in addition to her own legal bills. A $50,000 donation to the Special Olympics as well as 500 hours of community service were also part of her sentence. Her community service sentence was the largest ever meted out in Oregon, and at one point Harding petitioned the court to have it reduced, but the judge refused. Her obligations included serving meals to the elderly.

In June of 1994, a USFSA disciplinary panel stripped Harding of her 1994 national championship, and banned her from skating competitively for life. She worked thereafter as a landscaper and enjoyed a brief career as a celebrity manager for professional wrestlers. She remarried and divorced once again, attempted without success to skate for another country's Olympic team—both Norway and Austria declined—and skated in a Fox television event with Kerrigan in February of 1998. They did not appear on the ice together, but made a brief joint studio appearance. One of its producers, David Krieff, told *People* writer Michael Neill that Harding seemed to want to make amends with Kerrigan. "She had nothing to lose," Krieff said. "She'd lost it all already."

Attempted Comeback

Harding moved to a town in Washington, just across the river from Portland, after her probation ended in 1997, and attempted to return to skating—this time as a professional, which skirted the USFSA ban—in October of 1999. She competed in the ESPN Professional Skating Championships in Huntington, West Virginia, but fell twice in her program. She finished in second place overall, earning polite applause from the crowd each time. Yet even on the professional circuit, Harding was cold-shouldered by other skaters, and claimed to have been blackballed entirely in the sport.

Harding's troubles with the law had not ended. In February of 2000 she was arrested on assault charges filed by her then-boyfriend, who claimed she hit him with a hubcap. There were two witnesses to the incident, and Harding entered a not-guilty plea, claiming she meant to hit his motorcycle. She served three days in jail and ten days on a work crew.

In March of 2002 Harding appeared on another Fox special, *Celebrity Boxing,* sparring with Paula Jones, the Arkansas woman who accused a then-Governor Bill Clinton of sexual harassment on the job. Again, she re-entered the public consciousness as the butt of jokes, a figure who seemed to cling to her notorious celebrity for lack of any other viable career plan. Harding remains the sole skater ever to be implicated in a physical attack on a competitor, and though the incident seems tragic-comic in retrospect, it did serve to unmask a more vicious side of women's figure skating—less a sport, some pundits note, than a telegenically-driven competition for endorsement dollars.

CONTACT INFORMATION

Address: Tonya Harding, U.S. Figure Skating Association, 20 First St., Colorado Springs, CO 80906-3624.

FURTHER INFORMATION

Periodicals

Brownlee, Shannon. "Tonya's nightmare." *U.S. News & World Report* 116 (February 14, 1994): 44.

"But it started so well....." *Time* 147 (April 22, 1996): 99.

Davis, Alisha. "Old Habits Die Hard." *Newsweek* (March 6, 2000): 75.

Duffy, Martha. "End of the winter's tale." *Time* 143 (March 7, 1994): 62.

Duryee, Tricia. "Tonya takes on Tukwila — and doesn't disappoint." *Seattle Times* (February 22, 2002): E2.

"Figure Skating: Norway Tells Harding to Try Austria." *Seattle Post-Intelligencer* (January 30, 1997): D5.

Frey, Jennifer. "The return of Tonya Harding." *Austin American-Statesman* (Texas) (October 23, 1999): D1.

"Harding concedes she drove drunk, admits problem." *Seattle Times* (August 6, 2002): C8 .

"Jail gives Tonya time to 'relax.'" *Sunday Mail* (Brisbane, Australia) (August 25, 2002): 30.

James, Caryn. "And Now The 16th Minute Of Fame." *New York Times* (March 13, 2002): E1.

Jordan, Pat. "It's not ladylike to be a DWG." *The Sporting News* 217 (February 21, 1994): 12.

Kaufman, Michelle. "What ever happened to Tonya Harding?" Knight-Ridder/Tribune News Service (February 23, 1995).

Lopez, Steve. "Life after the glory." *Time* 151 (January 26, 1998): 64.

Luscombe, Belinda. "Tonya Harding in an affair to remember." *Time* 147 (January 8, 1996): 77.

Neill, Michael. "Melting the ice." *People* 49 (February 2, 1998): 117.

Nelson, Kathleen. "Figure skating is in enough of a mess without Tonya Harding's adventures." *St Louis Post-Dispatch* (August 10, 2002): 4.

Parvaz, D. "Skater Harding Making Breast of Bad Situation." *Seattle Post-Intelligencer* (June 11, 2001): E2.

Pollitt, Katha. "Subject to debate." *Nation* 258 (March 7, 1994): 297.

Reed, Susan. "On the ropes." *People* 42 (July 18, 1994): 36.

Roberts, Selena. "Possible Mob Link Stuns Skating." *New York Times* (August 2, 2002): D1.

Sandomir, Richard. "No Knee-Whacking, but It's a Ratings Spike." *New York Times* (February 15, 2002): D7.

Smolowe, Jill. "The slippery saga of Tonya Harding." *Time* 143 (February 14, 1994): 60.

"Stage fright." *People* 44 (September 18, 1995): 233.

———. "Springtime for Tonya." *Time* 143 (March 28, 1994): 73.

Swift, E.M. "Not your average ice queen." *Sports Illustrated* 76 (January 13, 1992): 54.

———. "On thin ice." *Sports Illustrated* 80 (January 24, 1994): 16.

———. "Triple threat." *Sports Illustrated* 74 (February 25, 1991): 184.

"Tonya's fall earns her a 10—days, that is." *Star-Ledger* (Newark, NJ) (August 10, 2002): 16.

Sketch by Carol Brennan

John Harkes
1967-

American soccer player

American soccer player John Harkes was one of the first to play professional soccer in Europe, primarily in the English League. He was also a member of the U.S. national team for many years, and when professional soccer came to the United States in 1996, he played in Major League Soccer (MLS). Harkes was a midfielder, but played other positions when needed.

Harkes was born on March 8, 1967, in Kearny, New Jersey, the son of two Scottish immigrants. His father, James Harkes, had been a soccer player himself with the Dundee Juniors in Scotland. Harkes was an enthusiastic soccer player from his youth. In the 1970s, he was a ball boy for the New York Cosmos of the professional North American Soccer League, and aspired to play for them someday.

Plays College Soccer

As a teenager, Harkes played club soccer for Thistle in Kearny, a soccer power. He stood out as a creative midfielder with both offensive and defensive skills. Just as Harkes was graduating from Kearney High School, the North American Soccer League folded, and Harkes had to reconsider his plans. He decided to play college soccer at the University of Virginia, coached by Bruce Arena.

Though he did not finish his degree at Virginia, Harkes's play garnered him notice and improved his skills. In 1987, he made the U.S. national team for the first time, and appeared in international games. In 1988, Harkes played for the U.S. team at the Summer Olympics in Seoul, South Korea. Harkes had his first World Cup play in 1990.

Joins English League

After his impressive showing for the U.S. in World Cup play, Harkes was loaned to the English Second Di-

John Harkes

vision team, Sheffield Wednesday, by the U.S. Soccer Federation in 1990. The team had been in the First Division the previous year, but had dropped to Second Division that season and was looking to move back up. Though he began his stint with Sheffield as a reserve, an injury moved Harkes up to first team. He did have to play right back, a position he had not played before.

Impressive play led Sheffield to buy out Harkes's contract with the U.S. Soccer Federation and sign him to a three-year deal. Harkes was the only American to be competing at the top level of European soccer in the early 1990s. The kind of tough competition he faced and the faster game improved Harkes's skills. He made an impact by scoring an unbelievable goal in the semi-finals of the English League Cup in 1991. By 1992, Sheffield was back in the First Division again, and Harkes was the first American to play for a First Division team.

It took time, but Harkes earned the respect of the Brits. He recalled to William E. Schmidt of the *New York Times,* "At first the attitude among a lot of the reporters and other players here was, 'This guy's a Yank; he can't play here.' But I think I have their respect. They come up to me after games and they tell me I've done well and wish me luck. It's brilliant to hear that." Harkes helped Sheffield win the English League Cup, becoming the first American to score in the League Cup Final. In 1992, he became the first American to play in a UEFA Cup match.

Harkes went on to play for two more English League teams, Derby County, a First Division team, from 1993-95, and then for West Ham United in 1996. While his professional career was ongoing, Harkes continued to play for the United States in international competition. He played for the United States in the World Cup in 1994.

Played in the MLS

When MLS began playing in 1996, Harkes was released by West Ham so he could return to the United States. He played for D.C. United, coached by Arena, and was named captain of both United and the U.S. national team. The amount of games Harkes had been playing began to catch up him. In 1996, he had some injury problems, primarily with his right ankle, which led to him to take a two-month hiatus from soccer in the MLS off-season in 1997. When Harkes returned, he had a great season in 1997, and D.C. United repeated as MLS champions. Harkes had a similar experience in 1998, though D.C. lost in the finals to the Chicago Fire.

Booted from U.S. Team

In the spring of 1998, Harkes was dismissed from the U.S. national team as it was preparing for the World Cup. Coach Steve Sampson and Harkes had a personality conflict and differing opinions of the role he should play on the field. The U.S. team flopped in World Cup play in France.

Awards and Accomplishments	
1984	Named Parade Soccer Player of the Year
1987	Named ACC player of the year; won Missouri Athletic Club Player of the Year Award
1990	Scores England's Goal of the Year
1992	Named Most Valuable Player for U.S. Cup
1995	Named co-Most Valuable Player for Copa America tournament
1996	Named U.S. representative to the FIFAWorld All-Star Team; selected to play for Eastern Conference in the MLS All-Star game; named captain of U.S. national team; part of D.C. United team that wins MLS Cup and the Open Cup title
1997	Wins MLS Cup with D.C. United
1999	Named to MLS All-Star team; member of U.S. team that won bronze at FIFA Confederations Cup
2002	Wins Lamar Hunt U.S. Open Cup with Columbus

Harkes also had changes in his professional soccer life. In 1999, he was still a member of D.C. United, but the team could not afford to keep Harkes expensive contract under the MLS salary cap. He was loaned to English Premier League's Nottingham Forest, a struggling team, for part of their season.

Traded to New England

In the summer of 1999, Harkes returned to the States to play for the New England Revolution, who had acquired his rights in a trade with United. While Harkes was again captain of the team, it was also a struggling franchise. However, the team had its best season ever with a 13-13-6 record. Also in 1999, he was asked to be on the U.S. national team again by its new coach, Arena. Harkes played for them in the Confederations Cup.

Harkes was again traded within the MLS in May 2001 to the Columbus Crew. Though he had issues with how the trade was handled, his new team made the playoffs. After re-signing with the Crew in the off-season, the team won the Lamar Hunt U.S. Open Cup in 2002.

CONTACT INFORMATION

Address: 1265 El Camino Real, Santa Clara, CA 95050-4257.

SELECTED WRITINGS BY HARKES:

(With Denise Kiernan) *Captain For Life and Other Temporary Assignments,* 1999.

FURTHER INFORMATION

Periodicals

Acee, Kevin. "United's Harkes Keeps Going and Going and Going." *Daily News,* (October 19, 1996): S1.

"Forest Look to their Cyberman." *The Independent,* (February 27, 1999): 29.

Gammon, Clive. "Wednesday Wonder." *Sports Illustrated,* (April 22, 1991): 72.

Giesin, Dan. "Soccer Spotlight Again on Harkes." *San Francisco Chronicle,* (April 5, 1996): C3.

Goff, Steven. "Harkes Is Headed to England." *Washington Post,* (January 26, 1999): D1.

Goff, Steven. "Harkes to Join U.S. Team." *Washington Post,* (July 17, 1999): D10.

Haydon, John. "A Pioneer, for Kicks." *Washington Times,* (April 1, 1996): 1.

Haydon, John. "Happier Harkes has Come to Grips with MLS Ways." *Washington Times,* (April 15, 2000): 6.

Haydon, John. "Harkes Feels Fit After Taking a Rare Vacation." *Washington Times,* (February 15, 1997): 7.

Haydon, John. "Trade to Columbus Brings Renewal for Former D.C. Midfielder." *Washington Times,* (August 25, 2001): 6.

"John Harkes." *People Weekly,* (May 9, 1994): 106.

Kurland, Bob. "Harkes Is in Demand at Home and Abroad." *The Record,* (June 14, 1992).

Leonard, Tim. "Harkes Still Kicking Mad After U.S. Team Dismissal." *The Record,* (May 12, 1998): S8.

Longman, Jere. "Harkes Is Dropped from U.S. Cup Team." *New York Times,* (April 15, 1998): C2.

Longman, Jere. "Johnny Comes Marching Home." *New York Times,* (June 17, 1994): B16.

Murphy, Mark. "Harkes Hurt by Trade." *Boston Herald,* (May 17, 2000): 80.

Murphy, Mark. "Harkes Out to Write Wrong." *Boston Herald,* (June 6, 1999): B14.

Schmidt, William E. "An American with a Jolly Good Toe." *New York Times,* (April 5, 1992): section 8, p. 13.

Timmermann, Tom. "Coach Drops Harkes from U.S. Squad." *St. Louis Post-Dispatch,* (April 15, 1998): D2.

Trecker, Jamie. "Harkes Relishes Second Chance." *Washington Post,* (July 24, 1999): D5.

Tunstall, Brooke. D.C. "United Trades Harkes to New England." *Washington Times,* (February 3, 1999): 5.

Yannis, Alex. "Cosmos Spirit Infuses 2 at Tournament Debut." *New York Times,* (June 2, 1989): B11.

Yannis, Alex. "U.S. Players in Europe Learn More than Game." *Washington Post,* (November 23, 1990): D13.

Other

"John Harkes." United States National Soccer Players Association. http://www.ussoccerplayers.com/players/john_harkes/ (January 13, 2003).

"MLS-John Harkes Player Profile." Yahoo! Sports. http://sports.yahoo.com/mls/players/3/36 (January 13, 2003).

"Player Bio—John Harkes." MLSnet.com. http://www.mlsnete.com/bios/john_harkes.html (January 13, 2003).

Sketch by A. Petruso

Ernie Harwell
1918-

American sportscaster

Ernie Harwell

E rnie Harwell was known for decades as the "Voice of the Detroit Tigers." The play-by-play radio announcer broadcast his first game for the Tigers in 1960, and except for a single season with the California Angels in the early 1990s, he remained with the Tigers until his retirement in 2002 at the age of 84. Known for his perceptive and colorful narrations of baseball games, Harwell is beloved by his fans, many who grew up listening to him. Highlights of Harwell's long career include broadcasting the first American League Championship game, broadcasting the first major sporting event heard from coast to coast, and broadcasting three World Series games. In 1981, he became the first active radio announcer to be inducted into the Baseball Hall of Fame.

"I think I've done more games than anybody," Harwell told the *Pittsburgh Post-Gazette*'s Chuck Finder around the time of his retirement. "Seven decades and 55 years. Even the old-timers came a little bit after I did."

A Life in Baseball

Ernie Harwell was born in Washington, Georgia, on January 25, 1918. He fell in love with baseball at an early age, and he dreamed of becoming a sports reporter. He landed his first job as a sports reporter in the middle of the 1930s, while still a teenager. That first job was as a reporter for the *Sporting News,* and his beat was the minor league team the Atlanta Crackers. This was the start of a newspaper career that continued even after his retirement from broadcasting in 2002; he later had a regular column in the *Detroit Free Press.*

Harwell attended college at Emory University, and while in his final year there, in 1940, he landed his first job as a radio broadcaster. "I got into radio by mistake, he later told the *Detroit Free Press*'s John Lowe. This first job was as the sports director, and indeed the entire sports department, at station WSB in Atlanta, Georgia. Included in his duties were broadcasting games for the Atlanta Crackers. Getting this job was a major accomplishment for Harwell, who had initially been handicapped by a speech impediment.

At that time, radio sportscasters would broadcast in studios separate from the baseball field. This meant that, instead of calling the game as they saw it unfold, they had to recreate the game based on written descriptions from wire reports. Consequently, Harwell, and his colleagues at the time learned to fill in a lot of details to bring the game to life for listeners. Details that, according to present-day ESPN announcer Jon Miller, are often lacking in current radio broadcasts. "The actual

description," Miller told the *Pittsburgh Post-Gazette*'s Chuck Finder, "giving the count, if the guy is left-handed or right-handed, where did he go to field the ball—did he go right, did he go back—those are things lacking in radio broadcasts now. And those are the fundamentals. People need to see what's going on, not just a rough outline of it."

To these "fundamentals," Harwell himself added "wearability," as he said on the Web site of the National Baseball Hall of Fame. "You're visiting so many homes for three hours every day or night that you have to be yourself." Harwell also decided early on that he would not use his broadcast booth to cheer for his team, something many other sportscasters did. "I don't denigrate people who do it," he explained on the Detroit Tigers Web site, "I think you just have to fit whatever kind of personality you have, and I think my nature was to be more down the middle and that's the way I conducted the broadcasts."

Harwell married his wife, Lulu, in 1941. Then, after the United States entered World War II in 1942, Harwell joined the Marines. He served in the Marines for four years before returning to civilian life as a radio broadcaster.

Moves Up to the Majors

In 1948, Harwell moved up to the major leagues, broadcasting games for the Brooklyn Dodgers. This appointment came after he was traded for a player. This

Chronology

1918	Born on January 25 in Washington, Georgia
1930s	Lands first job as a sports reporter and writer for *Sporting News*
1940	Lands first job as a sports radio announcer, at WSB in Atlanta, Georgia
1941	Marries wife Lulu
1940s	Serves four years in the United States Marines
1948	Broadcasts for the baseball major leagues for the first time, for the Brooklyn Dodgers
1950	Becomes a radio broadcaster for the New York Giants
1951	Broadcasts the first U.S. coast to coast broadcast of a major sporting event
1954	Becomes radio sportscaster for the Baltimore Orioles
1960	Becomes radio sportscaster for the Detroit Tigers
1992	Tigers fire Harwell, begins broadcasting games for the California Angels
1992	Tigers rehire Harwell as broadcaster
1993	Resumes broadcasting for Tigers
2002	Broadcasts final home game on September 22
2002	Retires after season's last game

Awards and Accomplishments

1948	Became first sportscaster to be traded for a player when the Brooklyn Dodgers hire him in exchange for catcher Cliff Dapper
1981	Inducted into the National Baseball Hall of Fame
1991	Inducted into the Sportscasters Hall of Fame
1998	Inducted into the Radio Hall of Fame
2002	Honored with a statue at Detroit's Comerica Park

was the first time, and, as of the date of Harwell's retirement in 2002, the only time, a player was traded for a sportscaster. The president of the Atlanta Crackers, Earl Mann, let Harwell go to the Brooklyn Dodgers only after Dodger president **Wesley Branch Rickey** agreed to send Dapper to manage the Atlanta Crackers. (Harwell and Dapper met for the first time only in 2002, at a ceremony honoring Harwell at Detroit's Comerica Park, when Dapper took part in the ceremony.) The season Harwell joined the Dodgers was the second season with the Dodgers for **Jackie Robinson**, the first African American to player to play in the major leagues.

In 1950, Harwell moved to the New York Giants. He stayed with that team until 1953, and it was there, in 1951, that Harwell took part in broadcasting history. This was when he broadcast the first telecast of a major sporting event heard from one coast of the United States to the other. The occasion was the final game of the 1951 playoffs, and the competing teams were the New York Giants and the Brooklyn Dodgers. The highlight of that game was the game-winning home run by Giant Bobby Thomson that was later remembered by baseball fans as "the shot heard round the world." It was a big year for Harwell; also that year, he introduced the great **Willie Mays** to Giants fans, an event he remembered with much fondness in later years. "Mays was simply the best," he later told Mike Brudenell of the *Detroit Free Press*. "He could throw, hit and run."

In 1954, Harwell moved to the Baltimore Orioles. He remained with that team until 1959. Then, in 1960, he moved to the team that he would stay with for every year but one for the rest of his broadcasting career, the Detroit Tigers.

Before the 1992 season, Harwell was fired from the Tigers by Tigers president Bo Schembechler. Some

speculated that Tigers owner Tom Monaghan prompted this action. The action was later called by John Lowe of the *Detroit Free Press* "the most unpopular move the club has ever made."

Harwell then went to work for the California Angels, broadcasting games for that team for the 1992 season. However, also in 1992, the Tigers were bought by Mike Ilitch, who promptly rehired Harwell. Harwell was back as the Tigers' announcer beginning with the 1993 season. "One of the highlights of my career," Harwell said in a speech in a pregame ceremony to honor him at Comercia Park in 2002, according to John Lowe, "one of the things I'm most grateful for, is that when Mike Ilitch bought the Tigers, he brought me back to be the announcer."

"Thank you," not "Goodbye"

Harwell announced his retirement from broadcasting in 2002. To honor him and his many years of broadcasting Detroit Tigers games, the ball club honored him at a pregame ceremony at Comerica Park on September 15, 2002. The ceremony lasted an hour, and culminated in the unveiling of a statue of Harwell standing with a microphone at the stadium's entrance. The statue was created by Lou Cella, who also helped sculpt the statues of other Tigers baseball players erected at the stadium. Harwell, in a speech that lasted five minutes, thanked the Tigers for erecting a statue of him, and according to Lowe said, "When I see a statue, I think of history. Of Washington and Lincoln, generals Grant and Lee. I don't deserve a statue or part of history. But let me tell you, from my heart, I'm proud this statue is me."

Harwell finished the day by broadcasting the Tigers game that followed. At one point in his broadcast Harwell said, wrote Lowe, "Our game got started late because they had some old guy out there."

Before his final game, Harwell summed up his 55-year career in the major leagues this way, according to Mike Brudenell of the *Detroit Free Press,* "I consider myself a worker. I love what I do. If I had my time over again, I'd probably do it for nothing." And, "I had a job to do, and I did it all these years to the best of my ability. That's what I'd like to leave behind as I finish my final game in Toronto."

Harwell broadcast his last game in Detroit on September 22, when the Tigers played the New York Yankees. His final broadcast came on September 29, 2002 in Toronto. After the Tigers lost to the Toronto Blue Jays by 1-0, Harwell delivered to his listeners a farewell address that lasted less than a minute and a half. "Rather than goodbye," the *Seattle Times* reported him as saying, "please allow me to say thank you.... I might have been a small part of your life, but you have been a large part of mine. It's a privilege and an honor to share with you the greatest game of all. Now God has a new adventure for me. I'm ready to move on, so I leave you with a deep sense of appreciation for your longtime loyalty and support."

FURTHER INFORMATION

Periodicals

Finder, Chuck. "Summer's Fading Soundtrack; Baseball's Rich Radio Broadcasting Tradition Eroded by Death, Retirement and Technology." *Pittsburgh Post-Gazette* (June 30, 2002): D3.

"Harwell Calls His Last Game." *Seattle Times* (September 30, 2002): D6.

Other

Beck, Jason. "Harwell: Doing More with Less." Detroit Tigers Web site. http://detroit.tigers.mlb.com/ NASApp/mlb/det/news/det_news.jsp?ymd=2002091 5&content_id=129194&vkey=news_det&fext=.jsp (September 15, 2002).

Brudenell, Mike. "Signing Off: Harwell Modestly Reflects on His Legend, Legacy and Life after 55 Years of Big League Broadcasting." *Detroit Free Press*. http://www.freep.com/sports/tigers/booth13_200209 13.htm. (September 13, 2002).

"Ernie Harwell: Signing Off." *Detroit Free Press*. http://www.freep.com/photos/harwell2002/top.htm (September 13, 2002).

"Ernie Harwell, Sportscaster." Radio Hall of Fame. http://www.radiohof.org/sportscasters/ernieharwell. html (November 21, 2002).

Lowe, John. "Ernie Harwell: Signing Off: Emotional Farewell Address Focuses on Fans' Affection." *Detroit Free Press*. http://www.freep.com/sports/tigers/ ernie30_20020930.htm (September 30, 2002).

Lowe, John. "Waves of Joy on Ernie's Day." *Detroit Free Press*. http://www.freep.com/sports/tigers/ ernie16_20020916.htm (September 16, 2002).

"1981 Ford C. Frick Award Winner Ernie Harwell." Baseball Hall of Fame. http://www.baseballhall offame.org/hofers_and_honorees/frick_bios/harwell_ ernie.htm (November 13, 2002).

"1991 Hall of Fame Inducts Ernie Harwell." American Sportscasters Hall of Fame.com. http://www.american sportscasters.com/harwell.html (November 13, 2002).

Sketch by Michael Belfiore

Dominik Hasek
1965-

Czech hockey player

Dominik Hasek is routinely ranked by sports writers as one of the half-dozen greatest goalies in hockey's history. Although his style of goaltending seemed unconventional—with his arms and legs splayed outward to stop his opponents from scoring—Hasek racked up an impressive string of awards during his twelve seasons in the National Hockey League (NHL). A five-time winner of the Vezina Trophy as Best Goaltender in the NHL, Hasek also picked up two Hart Trophies as the league's Most Valuable Player. The sport's most prestigious award, the Stanley Cup, eluded Hasek until his final season in the NHL, when he helped the Detroit Red Wings become NHL champions in 2002. Outside the NHL, Hasek also claimed an Olympic Gold Medal as part of the Czech Republic's hockey team at the 1998 Nagano Games. Each of these accomplishments helped to maintain Hasek's image as "The Dominator," a nickname he earned for his commanding presence on the ice.

Top Goaltender in Europe

Born on January 29, 1965, Dominik Hasek grew up in the city of Pardubice, Czechoslovakia, as the Czech Republic was then known. His father, Jan, worked as a miner, a job that usually kept him away from home during the week. A fan of his town's hockey team, Tesla, Hasek always sought out the goaltender's position when he played with his friends. Even when he played soccer, Hasek insisted on being the goalie. At the age of six he tried out for a local hockey team and made the cut, in part because he was so tall for his age. Eventually,

Dominik Hasek

Chronology

1965	Born January 29 in Pardubice, Czechoslovakia
1981	Begins playing for Tesla senior hockey team
1983	Selected by Chicago Blackhawks in player draft
1989	Plays for Czechoslovakian Army's hockey team
1990	Signs with Chicago Blackhawks
1992	First of nine seasons with the Buffalo Sabres
1998	Leads Czech Republic hockey team to Gold Medal in Nagano Olympic Games
2001	Signs with Detroit Red Wings
2002	Detroit Red Wings win Stanley Cup
2002	Announces retirement as professional athlete

Hasek grew to five feet, eleven inches; weighing less than one-hundred-seventy pounds, Hasek was a relatively slight as a hockey player, but his enormous flexibility and quick reflexes more than made up for his size.

Largely self-taught as a goalie, Hasek studied other goaltenders to learn defensive plays and strategies. Part of the junior champion Tesla team in 1981, Hasek was good enough to earn a spot on the Tesla senior team that same year. He ended up playing for the team for eight years, two of which ended in national championships for Tesla. Hasek's playing was so good that he was even selected in the 1983 draft by the Chicago Blackhawks. Given the Communist Party's control over Czechoslovakia at that time, Hasek did not even learn about his draft until months later. The teenager decided not to try to leave Czechoslovakia, even though he had already begun thinking about playing in the NHL. Named the Czechoslovakian goaltender of the year for five consecutive years after 1986 and Czechoslovakian player of the year in 1987, 1989, and 1990, Hasek was widely considered to be the best European goaltender of the day.

Begins NHL Career with Blackhawks

The Blackhawks approached Hasek again in 1987 with a contract offer; with a mandatory year to serve in the Czechoslovakian military, however, Hasek again turned down the offer and instead played for the Army's hockey team, Dukla Jihlava, in the 1989-90 season. He also finished his university education with a degree in history. Ironically, just as Hasek was fulfilling his military obligation, the Communist regime that had ruled since 1948 finally fell. With the demise of the Berlin Wall and pro-democracy demonstrations arising all around eastern and central Europe in late 1989, Czechoslovakia finally withdrew from the Soviet Bloc. The changes also meant that Hasek and other athletes were able to pursue careers in North America without fear of reprisals against their families.

In 1990 Hasek finally joined the Blackhawks. With standout goalie **Ed Belfour**—who would win NHL Rookie of the Year and Vezina Trophy honors that season—already on the roster, Hasek played just five games for the Blackhawks that season. Instead, he was sent to the Indianapolis Ice for most of the 1990-91 and 1991-92 seasons. The experience helped Hasek adapt his goaltending style to the smaller rinks of North America and also helped Hasek's family—wife Alena, son Michael, and later on, daughter Dominika—adjust to life in the United States.

After the Blackhawks traded him to the Buffalo Sabres in August 1992, Hasek hoped to get more time on the ice. An injury soon sent him out of commission and when the team signed goaltender Grant Fuhr, it seemed that Hasek's career faced insurmountable setbacks. When Fuhr was injured in November 1993, however, Hasek became the Sabres' main goaltender. He did not disappoint the team: finishing the season with thirty victories and twenty losses, Hasek led the league with a save average of .930. His goals-against average of 1.95 for the season was the lowest in the NHL since 1974. Although the Sabres did not make the finals, Hasek's contribution was recognized with the Vezina Trophy as best goaltender at the end of the season. He repeated the honor in 1995, from 1997-99, and again in 2001.

Stanley Cup Quest

Although Hasek won the Hart Trophy as the Most Valuable Player in the NHL in 1997 and 1998, his talent alone was not enough to take the Sabres past the play-

Career Statistics

Yr	Team	GP	W	L	T	GAA	TGA	SV	SV%	SO
1990-91	CHI	5	3	0	1	2.20	8	93	.914	0
1991-92	CHI	20	10	4	1	2.30	44	413	.893	1
1992-93	BUF	28	11	10	4	2.68	75	720	.896	0
1993-94	BUF	58	30	20	6	1.84	109	1552	.930	7
1994-95	BUF	41	19	14	7	2.16	85	1221	.930	5
1995-96	BUF	59	22	30	6	2.77	161	2011	.920	2
1996-97	BUF	67	37	20	10	2.39	153	2177	.930	5
1997-98	BUF	72	33	23	13	2.43	147	2149	.932	13
1998-99	BUF	64	30	18	14	1.87	119	1759	.937	9
1999-00	BUF	35	15	11	6	2.21	76	937	.919	3
2000-01	BUF	67	37	24	4	2.11	137	1726	.921	11
2001-02	DET	65	41	15	8	2.17	140	1654	.915	5
TOTAL		581	288	189	60	2.26	1254	16412	.912	61

CHI: Chicago Blackhawks (NHL); DET: Detroit Red Wings (NHL); BUF: Buffalo Sabres (NHL).

offs to the Stanley Cup finals. Tensions between Hasek and the team's management fueled intense media speculation about his future with the Sabres, particularly after he was sidelined with an injury during the 1997 playoffs and then criticized for spending time with a Czech friend who played for an opposing team. Hasek found it ridiculous that he would be accused of sharing his team's secrets or faking an injury, as *Buffalo News* writer Jim Kelley alleged. After Hasek assaulted Kelley at the Buffalo Auditorium over the article, he was suspended by the NHL; the suspension coincided with his recovery period.

Despite his problems with the Sabres, Hasek was widely admired for his leadership of the Czech national hockey team at the 1998 Nagano Olympic Games. After making its way through a hard-fought semi-final match with Canada, the Czechs defeated the Russians in the final by one goal and took the Gold Medal. The win confirmed Hasek's status as a national hero in the Czech Republic and enhanced his reputation as a pressure player in the NHL. When he suffered another injury in the 1999-2000 season, however, there was further speculation that Hasek might retire from the NHL.

Hasek returned to the Sabres for a ninth season but surprised many observers by signing a one-year contract with the Detroit Red Wings for the 2001-02 season. It was clear that Hasek's decision was motivated by one factor: the desire to win the Stanley Cup. Since the mid-1990s the Red Wings had been perpetual contenders for the championship, and Coach **Scotty Bowman** was convinced that the addition of the Dominator to the lineup would ensure another win in 2002. Bowman was right; after compiling the best record in the league, the Red Wings took the Stanley Cup over the Carolina Hurricanes in the finals.

Already one of the most award-winning players in NHL history, Hasek could finally retire with a Stanley Cup victory added to his list of accomplishments. Although he was offered an estimated $8-$10 million to play for the Detroit Red Wings for the 2002-03 season, Hasek declined the offer. "Money wasn't an issue," Hasek said in a *USA Today* profile in June 2002 shortly after making the decision, "I worked so hard last year, and I'm just not sure I can compete at the level I expect from myself." Hasek did not announce any plans to remain active in the sport as a player, although coaching remained a possibility.

After Hasek declined to renew his contract with the Red Wings, he moved back to the Czech Republic with his wife and two children. Hasek's post-athletic career focused on his Dominator Clothing line of sportswear, which he had established a couple of years before. Hasek also used his celebrity for philanthropic ends. On a tour of the Czech Republic with the Stanley Cup in August 2002, Hasek raised money to assist victims who were devastated by major floods.

A hero in his homeland for his gold-medal performance in the 1998 Olympics, Hasek could also take satisfaction in the respect he had earned from his NHL colleagues as one of the best goaltenders in the history of the sport. Part of the first great wave of NHL players from Europe to make a significant impact on the sport in the 1990s, Hasek also helped to broaden the appeal of the league beyond North America.

FURTHER INFORMATION

Books

Burgan, Michael. *Dominik Hasek.* Philadelphia: Chelsea House Publishers, 1999.

Diamond, Dan, ed. *Total Hockey: The Official Encyclopedia of the National Hockey League.* Kansas City: Andrews McMeel Publishing, 1998.

Awards and Accomplishments

1986-90	Named Czechoslovakian Goaltender of the Year
1987, 1989-90	Named Czechoslovakian Player of the Year
1994	William M. Jennings Trophy for lowest goals-against average in NHL
1994-95, 1997-99, 2001	Vezina Trophy as Best Goaltender in NHL
1997-98	Hart Trophy as Most Valuable Player in NHL
1997-98	Lester B. Pearson Award as Player of the Year, National Hockey League Players Association
1998	Olympic Gold Medal in hockey (Czech Republic)
2001	William M. Jennings Trophy for lowest goals-against average in NHL
2002	Stanley Cup as NHL champion (Detroit Red Wings)

Dowbiggin, Bruce. *Of Ice and Men: The Craft of Hockey.* Toronto: Macfarlane, Walter, and Ross, 1998.

Periodicals

Allen, Kevin. "Goaltender Hasek's Persence Looms Large in Hockey World." *USA Today* (February 18, 2002).

Allen, Kevin. "Hasek Resists Wings' Pleas, Retires." *USA Today* (June 26, 2002).

Kennedy, Kostya. "Man of Mystery." *Sports Illustrated* (February 7, 2000).

St. James, Helene. "Wings Share the Cup Amid Czech Flooding." *Detroit Free Press* (August 15, 2002).

Stein, Joel. "Hockey's Flopper Stopper." *Time* (May 17, 1999).

Other

"Dominik Hasek." Internet Hockey Database Web site. http://www.hockeydb.com/ihdb/stats/pdisplay.php3?pid=2187 (November 5, 2002).

"The NHL Dominator, Dominik Hasek, Retires." PRWeb Web site. http://www.prweb.com/releases/2002/7/prweb41280.php (July 1, 2002).

Sketch by Timothy Borden

John Havlicek
1940-

American basketball player

John "Hondo" Havlicek is considered by some observers to have been the most well-rounded player in the history of professional basketball. Havlicek was never a flashy player. However, his remarkable physical

John Havlicek

conditioning, his careful study of the game of basketball and of opposing players, and his skills at both forward and a guard made him an irreplaceable part of the Boston Celtic dynasty of the 1960s. By the time he retired after sixteen years with the Celtics, he had amassed an impressive body of statistics: 1,270 regular-season games played, 26,395 points scored, 6,114 assists, 13 consecutive National Basketball Association (NBA) All-Star Games, eight NBA championships. In recognition of his contribution to basketball, Havlicek was elected to the Naismith Memorial Basketball Hall of Fame in 1983. He was named to the NBA's 50th Anniversary Team in 1996.

The Young Ohio Athlete

John Havlicek was born in 1940 in Martins Ferry, Ohio. The third child of a Czechoslovakian father and a Croatian mother, Havlicek grew up in Lansing Ohio, a mining and steel mill town near the West Virginia border. Denied a bicycle by his parents—the family house was situated on a dangerous curve in the road—when he was around five-years-old Havlicek took to running, not only to keep up with his friends on their bikes, but also because he found he loved the activity. Before long he was running everywhere. Without being aware of it, Havlicek was laying the foundation for the remarkable physical stamina which would enable him for more than a decade to play an average forty minutes in NBA games and to run opponents into the ground.

Havlicek first demonstrated his athletic versatility as a student at Bridgeport High School. He excelled at three sports there, basketball, football and baseball, and was selected for the All-State team in each one. He was a talented quarterback. He could throw eighty-yard passes and he was so skilled at faking handoffs that referees whistled plays dead thinking the ball lay at the bottom of a tackle, although Havlicek still had it looking for a receiver. On the basketball court he was such a dogged runner and scorer that opposing teams tried to stop him by setting up a two man zone under the basket and triple-teaming him man-to-man. Nonetheless Havlicek was not a natural scorer. He worked hard for his points by out-running and out-rebounding opponents. It was in high school when Havlicek received his nickname "Hondo"—a classmate saw a resemblance to John Wayne who had just played a character by the same name.

By the time he graduated from high school, Havlicek received scholarship offers from thirty-five different colleges, in football as well as basketball. He chose Ohio State, where he would play only basketball and baseball, thinking that any more would distract him from his studies. In four years on the baseball team, he played every infield position except catcher. Ohio State's basketball team at the time possessed a number of excellent shooters, most notably Havlicek's college roommate, Jerry Lucas, who went on to be the top NBA draft pick. As a result, Havlicek made up his mind early in his basketball career at the school to make defense the focus of his game. Ohio State's basketball coach Fred Taylor, already an outspoken advocate of defense, came to value Havlicek's defensive play to such a degree that he routinely assigned him to guard the best player on opposing teams. With players of Havlicek's and Lucas's caliber, Ohio State won the National Collegiate Athletic Association (NCAA) championship in 1960, and made it to the finals in both 1961 and 1962. Havlicek was named an All-Conference player in 1961 and 1962, an All-America and All-Big 10 player in 1962, and Ohio State's 1961 Most Valuable Player (MVP) and its 1962 co-MVP. As a senior, he was the captain of Ohio State's basketball team.

Wooed by Three Sports

After he graduated, Havlicek was selected as the first round draft pick of the Boston Celtics. There was high interest from other sports as well. Several baseball organizations, including the New York Yankees, Detroit Tigers, and Pittsburgh Pirates, attempted to sign him. Although Havlicek had chosen not to play college football—despite repeated entreaties of Ohio State's football coach Woody Hayes—he was also drafted by the Cleveland Browns. Thinking he might like to play two professional sports, Havlicek reported to the Browns training camp in the summer of 1962 where he was groomed as a wide receiver. It was, unfortunately, a position that the

Chronology	
1940	Born April 8 in Martins Ferry, Ohio
1958	All-State player at Bridgeport High School
1958-62	Attends Ohio State University
1960	Ohio State team wins NCAA championship
1962	Drafted by Boston Celtics of the NBA and Cleveland Browns of the NFL
1962	Attends Cleveland Browns training camp
1962	Joins Boston Celtics
1965	Steals inbound pass in conference finals game with Philadelphia 76ers in closing seconds and sends Boston to NBA finals
1967	Marries Beth Evans
1970-71	Averages 28.9 points per game
1976	Surpasses Hal Greer in total NBA games played
1978	Retires from Celtics
1983	Elected to Naismith Memorial Basketball Hall of Fame

Browns already had well-covered and Havlicek was cut just before the season began. Havlicek later called it one of the two big disappointments of his athletic career. The other was not being chosen for the 1960 U.S. Olympic basketball team.

Havlicek had accepted a $15,000 contract to play with the Celtics. He joined them as they prepared for their 1962-63 season. The Celtics, masterminded by coach **Arnold "Red" Auerbach**, were a team that put a high premium on speed, team play, versatility, and intelligent basketball. Led by **Bill Russell** and **Bob Cousy**, Auerbach's formula had proved to be potent. In the spring of 1962, the team won the fourth of what would become eight consecutive NBA titles. Havlicek, with his speed, endurance, ability to play both defense and offense, and sheer desire to win, was tailor made for Auerbach's style of basketball. Not all observers recognized Havlicek's impressive talents immediately. He was considered to big to play guard yet too small to play forward. Curry Kirkpatrick in an article for *Sports Illustrated*, quoted Cousy's initial assessment of Havlicek: a "non-shooter who would probably burn himself out."

Despite any early misgivings, Havlicek later said he was accepted right away by the Celtics. He undoubtedly helped himself arriving in August at Celtics training camp in better physical condition than players who had been working out since the beginning of the summer. Auerbach later told the *New Yorker*'s Herbert Warren Wind of the first reaction he and another coach had to seeing Havlicek play. "We were . . . flabbergasted at what Havlicek was showing us. Here he was, not having touched a basketball for months and he was far and away the best man on the court." From then on Havlicek had Auerbach's full confidence. His first year he split court time with Frank Ramsey, the Celtics veteran sixth man—a player who did not start, but rather came off the bench to spell others as they tired. Auerbach's system placed great importance on having a

Career Statistics

Yr	Team	GP	PTS	FG%	RPG	FT%	APG	PF	SPG	BPG
1962-63	BOS	80	1140	.445	6.7	.728	2.2	189	—	—
1963-64	BOS	80	1595	.417	5.4	.746	3.0	227	—	—
1964-65	BOS	75	1375	.401	4.9	.744	2.7	200	—	—
1965-66	BOS	71	1334	.399	6.0	.785	3.0	158	—	—
1966-67	BOS	81	1733	.444	6.6	.828	3.4	210	—	—
1967-68	BOS	82	1700	.429	6.7	.812	4.7	237	—	—
1968-69	BOS	82	1771	.405	7.0	.780	5.4	247	—	—
1969-70	BOS	81	1960	.464	7.8	.844	6.8	211	—	—
1970-71	BOS	81	2338	.450	9.0	.818	7.5	200	—	—
1971-72	BOS	82	2252	.458	8.2	.834	7.5	183	—	—
1972-73	BOS	80	1902	.450	7.1	.858	6.6	195	—	—
1973-74	BOS	76	1716	.456	6.4	.832	5.9	196	1.25	0.42
1974-75	BOS	82	1573	.455	5.9	.870	5.3	231	1.34	0.20
1975-76	BOS	76	1289	.450	4.1	.844	3.7	204	1.28	0.38
1976-77	BOS	79	1395	.452	4.8	.816	5.1	208	1.06	0.23
1977-78	BOS	82	1322	.449	4.0	.855	4.0	185	1.10	0.27
TOTAL		1270	23,395	.439	6.3	.815	4.9	3281	1.21	0.30

BOS: Boston Celtics.

sixth man who was capable and versatile. Havlicek was that in spades. Auerbach used him at both forward and guard. Havlicek's success was due more to determination and practice than to whatever innate physical gifts he possessed. He worked hard to develop his ball-handling and shooting. In 1963, his second season, he led the team in scoring. The following year, when Ramsey retired, Havlicek took over the sixth-man role full-time.

Clutch Player

Havlicek also displayed coolness under pressure and the ability to come through in the clutch. Nothing illustrates this better than a play that has entered the mythology of the NBA. In the last game of the divisional finals in the playoffs in 1965, the Celtics were leading the Philadelphia 76ers by one point. With five seconds left on the clock, the 76ers were bringing the ball inbounds. A basket would most likely win the game for them. Havlicek grabbed the inbounds pass and threw it to a teammate who ran the clock out. Johnny Most, the Boston announcer, went into hysterics: "Havlicek stole the ball! Havlicek stole the ball!" The Celtics went on to win the title that year.

In 1966, the Celtic management was shaken up when Red Auerbach became the team's general manager and Bill Russell was named player-coach. Faced with a team whose offensive punch was suffering from the loss of important stars like Cousy and K.C. Jones, Boston's on-court leadership was put in Havlicek's hands. Although he remained the sixth man, he was named team captain and told to run the offense. He boosted his own offensive play too, pushing his point average above twenty a game for the first time in his career, where it stayed until the mid-1970s. From 1967 through 1973, Havlicek led the Celtics in assists. With such enhanced performance, Havlicek was as responsible as anyone for the will that drove the Celtics to two more NBA titles under Russell, in 1968 and 1969.

Havlicek's role on the Celtics changed again when veterans Bill Russell and Sam Jones both left the team before the 1969-70 season. He was one of the last links to the already legendary Celtics teams of the early 1960s. "All of a sudden, in one year, I was the old man," Havlicek told the *New Yorker*'s Wind. For the first time in his career as a pro, Havlicek was starting games. He boosted his scoring even more in the early 1970s, reaching an average of 27.5 points per game in the 1971-72 season. He was the team's clutch performer too, frequently being called upon to make the critical play in the last seconds of a close game. Although he was in his thirties, he maintained his remarkable stamina, regularly playing forty plus minutes a game under new coach Tom Heinsohn. Most importantly, Havlicek was expected transmit the style and philosophy of Celtics basketball to new players as the team rebuilt.

Havlicek and his example sometimes seemed to be the only thing left of the Celtics' glory years during the often difficult period of rebuilding during the first half of the 1970s and he was outspokenly critical of new players who did not care as much about winning as he did. The frustrations of this period undoubtedly contributed to his decision not to go into coaching after retiring. He realized his own standards were far higher than those of most players; a difference that could only lead to conflict and dissatisfaction. Despite the lows of the 1970s, however, Havlicek remained true to the Celtic organization and its fans. He turned down a multimillion dollar offer to sign with the American Basketball Association, the rival league to the NBA. By 1974,

Awards and Accomplishments

1958	Chosen to All-State High School Basketball Team
1961-62	Ohio State Basketball team MVP
1962	Chosen to All America and All-Big 10 teams
1962-78	First player to score 1,000 points in sixteen consecutive seasons
1964, 1966, 1968-70, 1975-76	All-NBA Second Team
1966-78	NBA All-Star team
1969-71	NBA All-Defensive Second Team
1971-74	All-NBA First Team
1972-76	NBA All-Defensive First Team
1974	Most Valuable Player NBA Finals
1978	Havlicek's number 17 retired by Celtics
1980	NBA 35th Anniversary Team
1996	NBA 50th Anniversary Team

Boston's rebuilding effort was paying off. Under Havlicek's leadership, the Celtics were NBA champions that year, a title that justly came to be known as the "Havlicek's championship." Players and fans alike recognized that he was the player who regularly made things happen. "A team must have a catalyst, who has the ability to change the pace of a game," center Dave Cowens told Wind of the *New Yorker*. "John does that for us. He creates confidence because of the way he plays, and you pick it up yourself." Two years later Boston won the championship again.

Havlicek remained remarkably healthy and relatively free of serious injury throughout his career. In 1977, he became, for a time, the all-time leader in NBA games played. Still, he played through injury when he had to. He played the 1969 NBA finals against the Los Angeles Lakers with one eye swollen shut and part of the 1973 semi-finals with a nearly useless right arm, the result of a partial shoulder separation. By 1974, Havlicek was already in his middle thirties. Knowing he would begin losing a step here, a fraction of a second of reaction time there, Havlicek started considering retirement, a step he finally took at the close of the 1978 season.

Havlicek was well-prepared for the day he left the game. He had started working in private business in the off-season in 1964 when he joined the Columbus Ohio firm, International Manufacturing and Marketing Corporation, as a sales representative. By the mid-1970s he had become a vice president there. That same year, he launched John Havlicek All Sports Products, a line of games and sporting goods for camping, baseball, badminton and other sports. In the 1970s he endorsed products ranging from socks, to shaving gear, footwear and prepared foods. Once out of basketball, he and his wife Beth, whom he had married in 1967, settled down in Columbus with their two children. In addition to his business interests, Havlicek worked on occasion as a color commentator for basketball broadcasts.

Life After Basketball

John Havlicek lives with his wife in Columbus, Ohio. He owns three Wendy's Hamburger franchises and is the co-owner of an Ohio-based food company. In his spare time he enjoys hunting, fishing, and golf.

When John Havlicek retired he had established himself as one of basketball's all-time greats. **Bobby Knight**, who played with Havlicek at Ohio State, told *Sports Illustrated*'s John Underwood, "In my opinion John Havlicek is the greatest basketball player who ever lived, bar none.... because he can beat you so many ways." His former coach and Celtics teammate Bill Russell called Havlicek "the best all-around player I ever saw." Six months after his retirement in April 1978, the Celtics retired his number 17. In 1983 Havlicek was elected to the Naismith Memorial Basketball Hall of Fame. He was named to the NBA's 50th Anniversary All-Time Team in 1996.

SELECTED WRITINGS BY HAVLICEK:

(With Bob Ryan) *Hondo: Celtic Man in Motion,* Prentice Hall, 1977.

FURTHER INFORMATION

Books

Fitzgerald, Joe. *That Championship Feeling: The Story of the Boston Celtics.* New York: Charles Scribner's Sons, 1975.

Havlicek, John, with Bob Ryan. *Hondo: Celtic Man in Motion.* Englewood Cliffs, NJ: Prentice Hall, 1977.

Ryan, Bob. *The Boston Celtics: The History, Legends, and Images of America's Most Celebrated Team.* Reading, MA: Addison-Wesley Publishing Company, 1989.

Periodicals

Goldaper, Sam. "Retirement of Havlicek to Remove Another Link to Celtic Glory Years." *New York Times* (January 29, 1978): V6.

Masin, Herman L. "Here Comes Hondo!" *Senior Scholastic* (March 14, 1969): 19.

Tuite, James. "Havlicek in Last Farewell." *New York Times* (April 10, 1978): C3.

Underwood, John. "The Green Running Machine." *Sports Illustrated* (October 28, 1974): 46.

Wind, Herbert Warren. "The Complete Basketball Player." *New Yorker* (March 28, 1977).

Other

John Havlicek biography. http://global.nba.com/history/players/havlicek_bio.html (January 4, 2003).

Sketch by Gerald E. Brennan

Tony Hawk
1968-

American skateboarder

Tony Hawk is considered one of the greatest skateboarders in the history of the sport. From his first turns on a board at age nine, Hawk has consistently challenged physics, gravity, and his own body by accomplishing astonishing acts on a piece of wood attached to four wheels. The California native was instrumental in the evolution of skateboarding from the preppy recreation of the 1960s to the daring and extreme test of physical limits and mental creativity it has become. In seventeen years as a professional skateboarder, Hawk has invented more than eighty tricks and competed in an estimated 103 contests, winning seventy-three and placing second in nineteen. He quit competing in 1999 after landing the first-ever "900"—which is two-and-a-half mid-air spins on the board.

Hawk was an accident; his parents were both in their mid-forties when he came into the world on May 12, 1968, in San Diego, California. Hawk's two sisters were already in college when he was born and his brother was a teenager. Frank Hawk was a veteran of World War II and the Korean War, and Nancy Hawk took classes at night, eventually earning her doctorate. While Hawk's parents had aged into a relaxed style of childrearing, their youngest child was a self-described, high-strung "demon boy." He also was a gifted child who was pathologically determined and hard on himself when he could not achieve what he set out to do. He once had to be coaxed out of a forest by his father after striking out in baseball.

Skateboard Calmed Him Down

Hawk found an outlet for his hyperactivity in a skateboard that his brother gave him when he was nine years old. He became obsessed with his narrow Bahne board, and quickly became proficient riding it. Finding something he was good at calmed him down, which his mother appreciated. Still, his perfectionist nature plagued him once he started competing in 1980. Even if he won, he would banish himself to his room with his cat, Zorro, if he felt he had not skated his best. He was sponsored by the Dogtown skateboard company at age twelve, placing second overall in his first contest, and continuing to compete respectably.

Both of Hawk's parents were supportive of their son's athletic passion. His father was a regular part of Hawk's skateboarding life, driving Tony all over California to various skateboard competitions, and building countless skate ramps over the years. Frank Hawk founded the California Amateur Skateboard League in 1980 and the National Skateboarding Association (NSA) in 1983. The NSA organized many high-profile

Tony Hawk

skateboarding competitions and was a key factor in the resurgence of skate culture that took place in the 1980s.

Before his thirteenth birthday, Hawk was approached by skateboarding legend Stacy Peralta to ride for his Powell & Peralta skateboarding company. His Bones Brigade team dominated the sport for a decade, and Hawk skated for Powell until 1994. Peralta handpicked Hawk, as he had numerous other skaters who went on to superstardom, including Steve Caballero, Rodney Mullen, Colin McKay, and Bucky Lasek, among others. Hawk turned pro in 1982, at age fourteen, and placed third in his first professional contest. At the time, there were only about thirty-five professional skaters, compared to the hundreds of pros today. Hawk went pro years before skateboarders started making any serious money. Skaters earned money from boards, stickers, and T-shirts sold with their names on them. Hawk's first royalty check was for eighty-five cents.

An Outsider in Both Worlds

Small and underweight and dressed in worn, skate-punk clothes, Hawk was not popular in school and did what he could to remain unnoticed there. The fact that he was a professional skateboarder meant nothing to the bullies and jocks who harassed him. He got good grades, but school was just what he had to do when he wasn't riding his skateboard. His parents often excused him from class to travel to contests and demos.

Chronology

1968	Born May 12 in San Diego, California
1980	Father, Frank Hawk, forms California Amateur Skateboard League
1980	Is sponsored by Dogtown skateboards
1980	Joins Bones Brigade team
1982	Turns pro
1983	Frank Hawk forms National Skateboarding Association
1983	Appears in *Bones Brigade Video Show* video
1984	Is considered best skateboarder in the world
1985	Appears in *Future Primitive* video
1986	Buys first home, appears in Mountain Dew commercial, and graduates high school
1987	Appears in *The Search for Animal Chin* video
1987	Plays a pizza boy in *Gleaming the Cube*
1988	Retires from skateboarding but returns to competition
1988	Appears in *Public Domain* video
1989	Appears in *Ban This* video
1990	Marries Cindy Dunbar
1992	First son, Hudson, is born; starts Birdhouse Projects
1994	Divorces Cindy Dunbar
1995	Skates in first X Games
1996	Marries second wife, Erin
1997	Is honored with his own *Sports Illustrated for Kids* trading card
1998	Produces first video, *The End*
1998	Launches Hawk Clothing
1999	*Tony Hawk's Pro Skater* video game debuts
1999	Second son, Spencer, is born
1999	Stops competing after landing the first-ever "900" at the X Games
2000	Autobiography, *Hawk-Occupation: Skateboarder* is published, becomes a *New York Times* bestseller
2001	Third son, Keegan, is born

Awards and Accomplishments

1980	Second place overall, ASPO Series (Amateur, 12 and under)
1982	Third place, World Challenge (Professional)
1983-95	Vert champion, National Skateboarding Association
1995	First place, vert competition, second place, street competition, X Games
1996	Second place, vert competition, X Games
1997	First place, vert and doubles vert competitions, X Games
1998	Third place, vert competition, first place, doubles vert competition, X Games
1999	Third place, vert competition, first place, best trick and doubles vert competitions, X Games

Hawk appeared on the cover of *Thrasher* magazine shortly after turning pro, but was something of an outsider in the pro-skating world, as well. He was smaller, younger, and skated differently from other skaters, and invented so many "flippy tricks" that he was called the "Circus Skater." He could win contests at his home skatepark, Del Mar, but had trouble adapting to unfamiliar terrain. A string of miserable competition finishes after turning pro left Hawk frustrated.

Hawk spent the summer after ninth grade skating demos in Australia, Europe, Canada, and the United States. A change of graphics to his signature skateboard model at Powell translated into increased sales and bigger royalty checks for Hawk. After the release of the *Bones Brigade Video Show,* Hawk, aged fifteen, was making $3,000 a month.

Masters the McTwist

The McTwist is one-and-a-half rotations on a skateboard with a flip in the middle. A skater rides up a vert ramp, grabs his board, launches into the air, spins and flips around until he is headed facing back down the ramp. Hawk admitted it was one of the toughest to learn, but mastered the McTwist in 1983. He used the stunt to take first place at the St. Petersburg Pro Am that year. At the end of 1983, when all the contest results were calcu-

lated, Hawk turned up as the NSA's first world champion. He was the NSA's vert champion for each of its twelve years in existence.

Hawk mastered "720s," two full mid-air spins, while training in Sweden in 1985. The second Bones Brigade video, *Future Primitive,* captured Hawk at his best, landing tricks—with names like Airwalk, Switcheroo, and Saran Wrap—that he had yet to try in competition. Still a teen, he was one of the most popular skaters in the world, and became famous after starring in a Mountain Dew commercial. The video was a huge seller and Hawk began earning about $7,000 a month. He bought his first house before graduating high school.

By 1987, skateboarding's popularity had skyrocketed, and Hawk was making large sums of money. But he was also beginning to feel pressured to maintain his winning streak. Burned out at age nineteen, Hawk retired from skateboarding. He soon missed competition, and returned before the year was through. He married Cindy Dunbar in April 1990. They had their first child, Hudson Riley, in 1992, and divorced in 1994.

Rough Times and the Year of the "9"

The skateboard industry plummeted in the early 1990s. Sponsors faded, prize money dried up, and Hawk's own income dwindled. Facing bankruptcy, Hawk raised enough money to start his own skate company, Birdhouse, with fellow Powell pro Per Welinder. The business was draining, and Hawk budgeted his meager contest winnings obsessively to support his family. The industry got a shot in the arm in 1995, with ESPN's first Extreme Games, which included bungee jumping, BMX riding, inline skating, and skateboarding. ESPN made Hawk the star of the games. Because of the X Game's mainstream success, Birdhouse sales shot up, and sponsorship money began to flow again. He married his second wife, Erin, in 1996. They had two sons: Spencer in 1999, and Keegan in 2001. By 1998, Birdhouse was one of the biggest companies in skateboarding, and Hawk was the sport's unofficial ambassador. Mainstream media latched onto Hawk and made him the most recognizable skateboarder in the world. He still

---

Dogtown and Z-Boys

The 2001 documentary *Dogtown and Z-Boys* captures the development of skateboarding from surfing and rogue street culture in California in the 1970s to its pervasive presence in American pop culture. The legendary Z-Boys skateboarding team hailed from a run-down beachside section of Los Angeles, and was made up of ten boys and one girl, most from broken homes. The crew ignored the traditional upright stance and came up with low-to-the-ground movements and the high-flying stunts that gave way to the extreme skateboarding, snowboarding, and trick biking styles of today. *Dogtown* revisits the skaters today, some of whom parlayed their talents into lucrative careers, like Tony Alva, who started his own skate gear company. Others were not so lucky, like the scene's golden boy, Jay Adams, who is serving a prison term for drug-related charges. The film is full of vintage photos and film footage—journalists Craig Stecyk and Glen E. Friedman were part of the scene—and was directed by Stacy Peralta, one of the most commercially successful skateboarders and an original Z-Boy.

---

was a leader in competition, and enjoyed skating demos around the world.

Hawk had been flirting with a "900" or "9"—an unheard-of two-and-a-half mid-air spins on the board—since about 1986. He tried it in practice and in competition many, many times, but never could land it. As he tired of winning contests and was facing a crossroads in his career, Hawk became obsessed with the notion of landing the world's first-ever 9. After finally landing one at the 1999 X Games, Hawk announced his retirement from competition.

Retirement meant nothing for Hawk; he was more in demand than ever. He retained his superstar status in the skateboarding world, and starred in one of the most popular video game series ever, *Tony Hawk's Pro Skater*. He appears at countless demos and signed a contract with ESPN to commentate skate contests for the network. In addition to Birdhouse, he also launched the popular Hawk Shoes and Clothing lines. "I'm pretty happy with the way things turned out," Hawk is quoted as saying online at Club Tony Hawk. "I mean, I never thought I could make a career out of skateboarding."

CONTACT INFORMATION

Address: Tony Hawk, c/o Tony Hawk Inc., 132 31878 Del Obispo, Ste. 118-602, San Juan Capistrano, CA 92675. Email: tony@clubtonyhawk.com.

SELECTED WRITINGS BY HAWK:

(With Sean Mortimer) *Hawk—Occupation: Skateboarder,* HarperCollins, 2000.

FURTHER INFORMATION

Books

Hawk, Tony, with Sean Mortimer. *Hawk—Occupation: Skateboarder.* New York: HarperCollins, 2000.

Stewart, Mark. *One Wild Ride: The Life of Skateboarding Superstar Tony Hawk*. Brookfield, CT: Twenty-First Century Books, 2002.
Wingate, Brian. *Tony Hawk: Skateboarding Champion*. New York: Rosen Publishing, 2003.

Other

Club Tony Hawk Fan Club Web site. http://www.clubtonyhawk.com (January 15, 2003).
"Tony Hawk," EXPN.com. http://expn.go.com/athletes/bios/HAWK_TONY.html (January 15, 2003).
Tony Hawk Foundation Web site. http://www.tonyhawkfoundation.org (January 15, 2003).

Sketch by Brenna Sanchez

Bob Hayes
1942-2002

American track and field athlete

Bob Hayes broke records on the athletics track and the football field, and is the only person ever to win both an Olympic gold medal and a Super Bowl ring. In his prime, he was considered the world's fastest human. His speed on the football field led coaches to adopt and refine complicated zone defense strategies, since no other player could catch him in man-to-man defense.

"To Better the Conditions of My Family"

Hayes was born on December 20, 1942 in Jacksonville, Florida, the youngest of three children in a poor family. His father, who struggled to make a living in the days of legal segregation and limited opportunity for African Americans, fought in World War II and returned in a wheelchair. The family's poverty increased, as their only source of income was his disability pension. Hayes spent much of his childhood skipping school, roaming the streets with friends, and avoiding his father's military-style discipline.

Although Hayes was interested in sports, his father warned him to forget about an athletic career. He encouraged Hayes to learn to shine shoes, stay in the neighborhood, and make connections. Although Hayes was interested in football, he was a very fast runner, and he was soon recruited by his high school track coach. Even in street shoes, he outran everyone. At Hayes's first high school meet, he entered seven events—the 100, 220, 440, and 880 yards, sprint relay, high jump, and long jump—and won them all. His friends began making money by lining up races between Hayes and

Bob Hayes

older boys, and taking bets on the results. They, and Hayes, always won.

Hayes also played football through high school, and scouts for Florida A&M in Tallahassee, saw him play and offered him a scholarship. When Hayes filled out the college application in 1960, he wrote, "I want to be a professional football player and better the conditions of my family," according to Dave Kindred in the *Sporting News.* And he did play football at school, under coach Jake Gaither. He was a starter at wide receiver in the 1965 College All-Star Game.

Despite his running speed, Hayes never intended to become a world-class sprinter, and knew nothing about track and field until Robert "Pete" Griffin, who coached with Gaither on the football team and who also coached track and field, encouraged him to enter the sport. According to Kindred, Hayes later said, "I went to [Florida A&M] to play football, nothing else. But after practice every day, we'd run wind sprints and I'd be beating everybody, even the upperclassmen." Coach Griffin, seeing talent, asked Hayes to run track, and Hayes initially refused because if he joined the team he would have to stay in Tallahassee on weekends, and he wanted to go home with his friends. However, Griffin kept after him and ultimately convinced him to join the track team.

Under Griffin's direction, Hayes went from competitions in Tallahassee to Los Angeles, Des Moines, Philadelphia, and San Francisco, moving up to qualify for the 1964 Olympic Games in Tokyo, Japan.

Hayes was an unlikely sprinter. Although he was powerfully built, with small feet, long legs, and short, muscular thighs, he had such a pigeon-toed stride that he often spiked one leg with the other foot while running, and he surged heavily from side to side instead of running straight forward. However, he had phenomenal acceleration and finishing strength. Sprinters who followed him, including Britain's Linford Christie and Dwain Chambers, emulated his power and finishing kick.

Wins Gold at 1964 Olympics

At the 1964 Tokyo Olympics, Hayes's performance in the 100 meters was amazing. His time equaled the current world record of ten seconds, but he achieved it while running on a wet cinder track that had been chewed up by a previous event. In addition, one of Hayes's shoes had been misplaced, so he won the event while wearing one borrowed shoe—and he beat the other runners by more than two meters. In *Sports Illustrated,* Paul Zimmerman described Hayes's response to winning the gold medal: "He did a little hop-step across the room, stopped, put his hands on his temples, looked upward and let out a big surge of emotion: 'Ooooh! Ooooh! He did this for five minutes or so before being called out to get his medal. I can't remember ever seeing such pure joy in a human being."

In the 4 x 100-meter relay, Hayes ran the anchor leg, taking his team from fifth place, three meters behind the leader, to the gold medal, winning by three meters. His split was clocked at 8.6 seconds. The team as a whole set a world record of 39.06 seconds. When Hayes re-

Career Statistics

Yr	Team	Rushing				Receiving			
		ATT	YDS	AVG	TD	REC	YDS	AVG	TD
1965	DAL	4	−8	−2.0	1	46	1003	21.8	12
1966	DAL	1	−1	−1.0	0	64	1232	19.2	13
1967	DAL	0	0	0.0	0	49	998	20.4	10
1968	DAL	4	2	0.5	0	53	909	17.2	10
1969	DAL	4	17	4.2	0	40	746	18.6	4
1970	DAL	4	34	8.5	1	34	889	26.1	10
1971	DAL	3	18	6.0	0	35	940	26.9	8
1972	DAL	2	8	4.0	0	15	200	13.3	0
1973	DAL	0	0	0.0	0	22	360	16.4	3
1974	DAL	0	0	0.0	0	7	118	16.9	1
1975	SFO	2	−2	−1.0	0	6	119	19.8	0
TOTAL		24	68	2.8	2	371	7514	20.3	71

DAL: Dallas Cowboys; SF: San Francisco 49ers.

turned home, he went to Griffin's house, and thanked Griffin for his coaching. Then he put his gold medal around Griffin's neck. Hayes told Kindred, "In good times and bad times, Coach Pete was there for me. . . . When I was down, he was up for me."

Plays with Dallas Cowboys

After his Olympic performance, Hayes returned to Florida A&M, but was soon drafted by the Dallas Cowboys of the National Football League (NFL) as a wide receiver, and left school before finishing his degree. Although some observers scoffed at Dallas's choice because Hayes was a runner, not a football player, Dallas scouts believed that Hayes's speed was a valuable asset, and that a player either had speed or did not have it. Hayes had it, and the scouts believed he could learn football techniques from coaches.

The scouts were right. In Hayes's first two seasons, he caught 110 passes for twenty-five touchdowns, averaging twenty-two yards per catch. He made the Pro Bowl his first three seasons, and played ten seasons in all with the Cowboys, scoring seventy-one touchdowns and averaging twenty yards per catch; he helped the team win its first Super Bowl in 1972.

Other teams took notice, and the New York Giants actually signed another Olympic champion, 200-meter runner Henry Carr, to cover Hayes when the teams played each other. What the Giants didn't realize was that Hayes had beaten Carr in the 200-meter Olympic trials, and that Carr could never catch Hayes man-to-man. Other teams drafted other sprinters, such as Willie Gault, Ron Brown, and Renaldo Nehemiah. None ever duplicated Hayes's feats on the football field.

Hayes's speed was so great that opposing teams began devising improved zone defenses in order to catch him. Zone defense had existed before Hayes, but it was simple and easy for Hayes to destroy. Coaches had to come up with double zone defenses, involving more than one player, to try and catch him. No other player has single-handedly caused this kind of strategic change in the defensive game.

Hayes retired from football in 1975, after playing a season with the San Francisco 49ers.

Hayes ran into trouble in 1979, when he sold cocaine and speed to an undercover officer. He pleaded guilty and was sentenced to five years in prison, but was paroled after 10 months in jail. When he was released, he was eligible to be inducted into the Pro Football Hall of Fame, but because of his conviction, he was passed over.

The Cowboys' former president and general manager **Tex Schramm** told Zimmerman, "The situation with Bob Hayes and the Hall of Fame is one of the most tragic stories I've ever been associated with during my time in professional football." However, Schramm's comment seemed somewhat hollow, since he was the selector for the Cowboys' Ring of Honor, and he did not admit Hayes to the Ring.

Earns His Degree at Age Fifty-One

For the next decade, Hayes fought his addiction to drugs and alcohol, entering rehab three times before moving back to Jacksonville, Florida, where he lived with his parents and finally earned his degree in elementary education from Florida A&M, at the age of fifty-one. Hayes told a reporter for *Jet,* "It's a thrill at fifty-one years of age to finally be graduating from college. I think so many people give up and take the attitude that it's not worth it—but they're wrong." He also said, "I take great pride in this accomplishment. I challenge all athletes to get their diploma."

In addition to his difficulties with drugs and alcohol, Hayes also suffered from liver disease and prostate can-

Awards and Accomplishments

1964	Olympic gold medals in 100 meters and 4 X 100-meter relay
1965-67	Member of Pro Bowl team
1972	Dallas Cowboys win Super Bowl
1976	U.S. Track and Field Hall of Fame, Florida A&M University Hall of Fame
2001	Dallas Cowboys Ring of Honor
2002	Texas Black Sport Hall of Fame

cer. Hayes's old friend, fellow track athlete Ralph Boston, told Dwight Lewis in the Nashville *Tennessean* that he saw Hayes in 2001, "He was in a wheelchair and couldn't walk. He showed me his swollen feet and said, 'Cancer is something.'"

In 2001, Hayes was finally honored by being inducted into the Dallas Cowboys Ring of Honor, after being selected by team owner Jerry Jones. A track meet named after him, the Bob Hayes Invitational, hosts more than 25,000 high school athletes each year, and he is a member of the U.S. Track and Field Hall of Fame. In 2002, he was elected to the Texas Black Sports Hall of Fame.

Hayes died of kidney failure on September 18, 2002, in Jacksonville, Florida. Former Cowboys running back Calvin Hill told Teneshia L. Wright in the *Florida Times Union,* that he believed Hayes's most memorable characteristics, apart from his athletic abilities, were his kindness and humor. "Here was a guy who talked to emperors and kings," Hill said. "Yet he could meet a janitor and make that janitor feel like he's the most important person in the world."

FURTHER INFORMATION

Books

"Jake Gaither." *Contemporary Black Biography, Volume 14.* Detroit: Gale Group, 1997.

Winters, Kelly. "Hayes, Robert ('Bob'; 'Bullet')." *Scribner Encyclopedia of American Lives,* edited by Arnold Markoe. New York: Charles Scribner's Sons, 2002.

Periodicals

Carlson, Michael. "Obituaries: Bob Hayes, America's Fastest Footballer on the Athletics Track." *Guardian* (London, England) (September 27, 2002): 22.

"Football Star, Sprinter 'Bullet' Bob Hayes Earns Education Degree at FAMU." *Jet* (August 29, 1994): 48.

Kindred, Dave. "Giving the Gift of Gold." *Sporting News* (June 8, 1998): 63.

Lewis, Dwight. "'Bullet' Bob Hayes Could Not Outrun His Own Weaknesses." *Tennessean* (Nashville, TN) (September 22, 2002): A25.

Wright, Teneshia. "Hometown Tribute: 'Bullet Bob' Hayes Remembered for His Talent and His Struggles." *Florida Times Union* (September 26, 2002): A1.

Yeager, Melanie. "Tallahassee Remembers Bob Hayes." *Knight Ridder/Tribune News Service* (September 24, 2002): K0250.

Zimmerman, Paul. "Bob Hayes (1942-2002)." *Sports Illustrated* (September 30, 2002): 66.

Other

"Bob Hayes, Wide Receiver." *Football Reference.* http://www.football-reference.com/ (November 11, 2002).

Sketch by Kelly Winters

Eric Heiden
1958-

American speed skater

Speed skater Eric Heiden won five gold medals in the 1980 Winter Olympic Games in Lake Placid, New York. There, he set Olympic records in the 500-, 1,000-, 1,500-, 5,000-, and 10,000-meter races, as well as a world record in the 10,000-meter race. After winning more gold medals than any other athlete in a single Winter Olympics and becoming an international celebrity, Heiden retired from skating.

Eric Heiden

First Love Was Hockey

Eric Arthur Heiden was born June 14, 1958, in Madison, Wisconsin into an athletic and competitive family. His father, Jack, was an orthopedic surgeon who specialized in sports medicine, as well as a cyclist and former fencing champion. His mother, Nancy, was Madison, Wisconsin's senior tennis champion, as well as a swimmer and cyclist. His sister, Beth, is fifteen months Heiden's junior and followed her brother onto the ice to win a bronze at the 1980 Olympics.

Skating is a popular sport in Wisconsin, where winters are long and frozen lakes are plentiful. Heiden's grandfather took him out on skates onto a frozen pond when he was just two years old. Skating was nothing more than family fun on Lake Mendota for the Heiden family when Eric was very young.

The children soon began racing their parents and, after a time, winning. Hockey is virtually the state pastime in Wisconsin, and Heiden joined a Pee Wee team. He made up for his small stature by being aggressive and alert. He was a strong shooter and dreamed of being a professional hockey player. His parents enrolled him and his sister in the Madison Figure Skating Club, which taught them skill and control on the ice, but also frustrated the young skaters, who wanted nothing more than to go fast and race around the rink. They found their niche when they switched to the local speed-skating club.

Chronology

1958	Born June 14 in Madison, Wisconsin
1961	Begins to skate on his grandfather's pond
1972	Chooses speed skating over hockey, begins training with Dianne Holum
1975	Makes his first junior world championship team
1976	Wins 1,500-meter event at junior world championship
1976	Competes at Olympic Games in Innsbruck, Austria
1976	Competes in his first Senior world championship
1977	Becomes first American to win world championship
1977	Becomes first to sweep junior world, world, and world sprint championships
1978	Sweeps junior world, world, and world sprint championships
1979	Sweeps world and world sprint championships
1980	Wins five Olympic gold medals and retires

Found His Niche in the Oval

Both Heidens were leaders in their respective speed-skating divisions, and kept up a demanding training schedule for competitions, which are held weekends from December to February. Heiden's parents put a priority on schoolwork, and he was an honor student. He played soccer in the summer, and trained with the high-school cross-country running team. Dr. Heiden put his children on touring bikes when they were young to help them train their legs for speed skating. When Heiden was fourteen, he decided to leave hockey behind and concentrate on speed skating. He and his sister, who both skated in the American "millpond" or pack racing style, set out to learn the head-to-head racing system used in international competition.

The Heidens were fortunate to live seventy-five miles from one of the nation's two 400-meter oval rinks like those used in the Olympics and world championships. Every day, they attended high school in the morning, did their homework in the car, and skated. It was little more than chance that brought gold-medal-winning speed skater Dianne Holum to the University of Wisconsin just when Heiden was looking for a coach. She increased his already rigorous training, adding weight lifting, more running, and exercises to perfect his aerodynamic skater's crouch.

After a string of race wins, Heiden's break came in 1975, when he made the junior world Speed Skating team, which put him up against the best skaters in the world. Heiden's first European racing season was an eye-opener; speed skating is as popular in Europe as football is in America. Both he and sister Beth made the 1976 junior world team, and Heiden found himself intimidated that, at seventeen, he was often the youngest skater in his division, and much less experienced. He made his mark early on though, winning the 1,500-meter race in an impressive 2:02.82.

Both Heidens qualified for the 1976 Olympic Games in Innsbruck, Austria. Eric Heiden's best finish was sev-

Where Is He Now?

After his retirement from skating, Heiden took up competitive cycling until 1986. He won the U.S. Professional cycling championship in 1985 and rode in the 1986 Tour de France. He was a commentator for four Winter Olympics for CBS Sports, from 1984 to 1994. Heiden graduated from Stanford Medical School and followed in his father's footsteps to become an orthopedic surgeon and sports team physician. He now lives in Sacramento, California, with his wife, Karen Drews. He practices at the University of California at Davis and is an assistant professor there. He was chosen to serve as the official U.S. Speed-skating team doctor for the 2002 Olympic Games in Salt Lake City, Utah. "I feel that I'm giving back to the sport of speed skating, which in the long run has been pretty good to me," he is quoted as saying on the UC Davis Web site.

enth, but it was a good showing for a young and relatively inexperienced skater. At eighteen, he entered his sport's top competition, the Senior world Speed Skating championships at Heerenveen, the Netherlands. There, he broke the track record and won his weakest event, the 500-meter. After finishing third in the 1,500 and ninth in the 5,000, Heiden was surprised to find his name at the top of the points list for the All-Around title. Breaking his own record for the 10,000-meter race, Heiden became the first American to win the world All-Around Men's championship. He went on to take the all-around championship at the next junior worlds in Inzell, West Germany, and the world sprint championship in Alkmaar, Netherlands. Heiden repeated the unprecedented world, junior world, and world sprint championship sweep in 1978, and won both the world and world sprint championships in 1979.

Wowed the World, Modestly

Heiden was one of the first American skaters invited to the Russian Cup competition at the Medeo Sports Center at Alma Ata, one of the world's fastest rinks. Though it was not documented, Heiden set a new record for the 1,000-meter event. The world speed-skating community was shocked that an American speed skater could perform so well. Heiden credited his success to the fact that European skaters are driven hard and expected to perform well. Heiden skated because he loved it, and had only to please himself. His success inspired American interest in the sport. Despite the international accolades he was raking in, Heiden remained modest.

Both Heidens easily made the 1980 Olympic Speed Skating team to compete in Lake Placid, New York. With his championships behind him, there was much more expected of Heiden than at his first Olympics; now, he was a star. Heiden's longtime friends and neighbors in Wisconsin, Mary and Sarah Doctor, also made the 1980 Olympic speed-skating team.

Heiden started the Olympics with the 500-meter race, his weakest event. He was paired to skate against Soviet world-record holder and gold medallist Yevgeny Kulikov. After a close race, Heiden pulled ahead to beat both Kulikov and his record to win the 500-meter gold. For his next event, the 5,000-meter race, Heiden was

paired against Dutch skater Hilbert Van Der Dium. After trailing at the start of the race, Heiden again pulled in front to finish first, earning his second gold medal of the 1980 Games, and breaking another Olympic record.

It would have been unthinkable for Heiden to come away with anything less than a gold medal for the 1,000-meter event, and he did not disappoint. He never gave up the lead to Canadian Gaetan Boucher, and broke yet another Olympic record. Skaters were beginning to express their feelings of futility when skating against Heiden, and were not shy about their hopes that he would retire and give someone else a chance to win.

With two races to go, Heiden was not about to give any skater that chance. A slip during the 1,500-meter race against Norway's Kai Arne Stenshjemmet caused the crowd to gasp, as they watched Heiden break his rhythm and nearly fall. At the end of a race, when most skaters tire, Heiden mustered a burst of strength for the final push. He broke the standing Olympic record by four seconds and took his fourth gold. Heiden was just relieved that his most challenging event was over.

The night before Heiden's final event, the 10,000-meter race, the underdog U.S. hockey team was playing its final game, against the Soviet Union. Heiden was an avid hockey fan, and two of his former Pee Wee league mates were playing on the team that night. In a history making upset, the U.S. team beat the Soviets in the final moments of play. Heiden could not resist celebrating the triumph—termed the "Miracle on Ice"—with the rest of America and his friends in Lake Placid. Heiden awoke the next morning to find he had overslept. He dressed in minutes, grabbed some bread for breakfast, and rushed off to the rink.

Retired on Top

Heiden was paired with the 10,000-meter world-record holder, Viktor Leskin of the Soviet Union. The ice was particularly fast that morning, and Heiden knew he would have to outdo himself to compete. Both skaters left the starting block strong, and kept a steady and graceful rhythm, with Heiden setting a blistering pace. Coach Dianne Holum was on the sidelines encouraging Heiden to slow down, for fear he'd tire too soon. With two miles left to race, Heiden's left arm began to droop, a telltale sign of fatigue.

Yet, despite his fatigue, Heiden's final time was 14:28.13, shattering Liskin's record and earning Heiden his fifth gold. In fifty-six years of Olympic speed skating, the United States had only earned nine gold medals. Heiden earned his five in just ten days. Between the previous night's hockey win and Heiden's wins, all of America was celebrating. President Jimmy Carter called the U.S. hockey coach, and may have tried to phone Heiden. But in a move characteristic of the skater, who treasured his privacy, Heiden had disconnected his phone.

Heiden carried the American flag in the closing ceremonies of the Games, and was received at the White House soon after. He then rushed off to compete in another world championship in the Netherlands, where he relinquished his four-year reign, finishing second. While still basking in his golden glow, Heiden announced his retirement from skating. Uncomfortable with the celebrity that came with his gold medals, he eschewed most endorsement opportunities—including the coveted Wheaties cereal box. "I really liked it best when I was a nobody," he said when he retired.

CONTACT INFORMATION

Address: Eric Heiden, University of California Davis Medical Center, 2805 J Street, Suite #300, Sacramento, CA 95817. Email: eric.heiden@ucdmc.ucdavis.edu.

FURTHER INFORMATION

Books

Fox, Mary Virginia. *The Skating Heidens.* Enslow Publishers, 1981.

Munshower, Suzanne. *Eric Heiden: America's Olympic Golden Boy.* Tempo Books, 1980.

Other

"Eric Heiden." U.S. Olympic Team Web site. http://www.usolympicteam.com/athlete_profiles/e_heiden.html (January 15, 2003.)

"Heiden wins fifth gold, most for an individual." *Washington Post* online. http://www.washingtonpost.com/wp-srv/sports/longterm/olympics1998/history/memories/80-heiden.htm (January 15, 2003.)

"Profile: Dr. Eric Heiden." University of California at Davis Web site. http://pulse.ucdavis.edu/scripsts/01_02/dr%20_eric_heiden.pdf (January 15, 2003.)

"Whatever happened to… Speed skater Eric Heiden." *Christian Science Monitor* online. http://csmweb2.ecmweb.com/durable/2000/11/16/text/p23s3.html (January 15, 2003.)

Sketch by Brenna Sanchez

John Heisman
1869-1936

American college football coach

John William Heisman was immortalized in 1936, the year of his death, when the New York Downtown Athletic Club changed the name of its annual trophy awarded to the best college football player in the nation to the Heisman Memorial Award to honor the club's former director. Best known today for his name on that trophy, Heisman is also recognized for his innovative coaching during the developing years of American college football. Walking the sidelines for thirty-six years as the coach for eight different schools, Heisman was at the pinnacle of his career during his fifteen years at Georgia Institute of Technology (Georgia Tech). His often dictatorial style with his players and his habit of running up the score on his opponents sometimes hurt his popularity, but no one denied his ability to extend the game of collegiate football into new areas of strategy and style. One of the earliest and strongest supporters of legalizing the forward pass, he is credited with inventing or first implementing such modern-day offensive formations as the center snap on the signal of "hike" or "hep" from the quarterback, the double pass and fake pass, the later-outlawed hidden ball trick, and what became known as the Heisman shift.

Football Mad

Heisman was born October 23, 1869, in Cleveland, Ohio, just two weeks before Princeton played Rutgers in what is considered the first college football game. Heisman's father, a cooper, and his mother, a homemaker, were both immigrants from Germany. During the 1870s, the Heisman family moved from Cleveland to Titusville, Pennsylvania, following the oil boom in the region, and Heisman graduated from Titusville High School in 1887. During his high school years, Heisman was a motivated student and participated in baseball, football, and gymnastics. Despite his small stature, Heisman fell in love with the developing game of football. Having played soccer-style football in his youth, as a young man, he was particularly enthralled with the concept of being allowed to carry the ball, a new innovation that was spreading among East Coast colleges.

Although Heisman's father considered football to be a brutal and barbaric sport, which in the early days of the game was not far from the truth, his disapproval could not squelch his son's overflowing enthusiasm for the game. He matriculated at Brown University as a 17-year-old freshman in 1887, unfortunately the same year that the school discontinued its intercollegiate football program. Nonetheless Heisman, weighing just 144 pounds, played with unabated enthusiasm and in-

John Heisman

Chronology

1869	Born in Cleveland, Ohio
1887-88	Plays football for Brown University
1889-91	Plays football for University of Pennsylvania
1892	Coaches at Oberlin College
1892	Earns law degree from University of Pennsylvania
1893	Coaches at Buchtel College (now Akron University)
1894	Returns to coach at Oberlin College
1895-99	Coaches at Alabama A & M University (now Auburn University)
1900-03	Coaches at Clemson University
1903	Marries Evelyn Cox
1904-19	Coaches at Georgia Institute of Technology (Georgia Tech)
1919	Heisman and wife agree to divorce
1920-22	Coaches at University of Pennsylvania
1922	Authors *The Principles of Football*
1923	Coaches one year at Washington & Jefferson University
1924	Marries Edith Maora Cole
1924-27	Coaches at Rice University
1927	Retires from coaching
1929	Becomes director of the New York Downtown Athletic Club
1936	Dies in New York City
1936	The Downtown Athletic Club trophy, awarded annually to the best college football player, is renamed the Heisman Memorial Trophy

tensity in intramural games. After two years at Brown, Heisman, working toward a law degree, transferred to the University of Pennsylvania (Penn), perhaps influenced by both the school's strong football program and the national reputation of its law department. He stayed at Penn for four years, playing football and studying law.

Heisman quickly turned Oberlin's fledgling program into a winning football team, and it was during these early days of coaching that he developed many of his innovative strategies. Approaching the game in an analytical and methodical manner, Heisman deduced from his own playing experience that if a lineman came out of his position to block on the outside, it would open a path for the running back. Thus, Heisman became one of the first to consistently and successfully move the ball by pulling a guard off the line to run lead blocks. He also built on the popular wedge, or V-style, offense by introducing a smaller, secondary wedge that also wrecked havoc on opponents' defenses. Creating another new offensive formation, Heisman developed the double pass play, the precursor to the reverse play, in which a tackle pulled out of the line and handed the ball to the halfback.

In 1893 he left Oberlin to accept his first paid position at Buchtel College (now the University of Akron), receiving an annual salary of $750. During the one year Heisman spent at Buchtel, he faced numerous challenges, the first being a male student enrollment that

barely reached one hundred, which made even fielding a full team a difficult feat. He also encountered criticism from Buchtel's faculty who joined the growing protest against the violent nature of the game that commonly led to injuries. Heisman was well aware of the physical toll football could take on the body and continually sought offenses that would reduce the danger and impact on his players. As a result, Heisman erased the tradition of mirroring the offensive and defensive positions. Typically, if a player was a halfback on offense, he played halfback on defense. What Heisman reasonably felt was that this put some of his smaller players, such as his quarterback, right in the thick of the fray while some of his bigger players, such as the fullback, were often left out of the action. Thus, Heisman stopped matching offensive and defensive positions, instead placing his strongest players up front and his quicker, lighter men back in what became known as safety positions. While at Buchtel he also developed the center snap, a maneuver that quickly caught on at other schools and soon replaced the former method of rolling the ball to the quarterback.

Heisman's football team at Buchtel took five of seven games in 1893, outscoring their opponents for the season 276-82. Heisman also coached the baseball team to a state championship. However, the next year he returned to coach again at Oberlin. Although he could be hardnosed with his players, Heisman learned early in his career to carefully cultivate his public image and actively sought out relationships with the local media. His natural affinity for publicity resulted in high praise by the media, and he quickly built a reputation for his coaching

Related Biography: Coach Glenn "Pop" Warner

Glenn S. Warner earned the nickname "Pop" as captain of the Cornell University football team because he was older than most of his teammates. After graduating from Cornell with a law degree in 1894, Warner became the football coach at the University of Georgia. During the 1895 season Georgia played Auburn, and Heisman successfully used the hidden ball trick against Warner's team. Warner later copied the trick play and is subsequently sometimes credited with inventing it. After two seasons at Georgia, in which Warner's team went undefeated with a 4-0 record, Warner coached two years at his alma mater, Cornell. In 1899 he became the coach at the Carlisle Indian School in Pennsylvania. Five years later he returned to Cornell to coach three seasons. Again in 1907 Warner left Cornell to resume his job at the Carlisle Indian School, the same year that the All American halfback Jim Thorpe joined the Carlisle team.

Warner's greatest coaching success came after becoming the football coach at the University of Pittsburgh in 1914, where his team recorded a 33-game winning streak and earned two national championships. In 1924 Warner moved to California to coach at Stanford for the next nine years. During that time, his teams won three Rose Bowl championships. He spent his final years of coaching at Temple University before retiring in 1933. Best remembered for founding the Pop Warner Youth Football League in 1929, Warner is also credited with numerous innovations in college football, including the screen play, the three-point stance, the use of shoulder pads, and putting players' numbers on their jerseys. Warner and Heisman were two of college football's most influential coaches during the sport's infancy.

Awards and Accomplishments

1900-03	Establishes school record for winning percentage during three years at Clemson (19-3-2, .833)
1904-19	Goes 102-29-7 during his tenure at Georgia Tech
1915-17	Georgia Tech football team goes undefeated for three consecutive years, adding up to a 31-game streak with no losses.
1916	Georgia Tech beats Cumberland College 220-0, the most lopsided game in the history of college football
1917	Wins a national championship
1936	New York Downtown Athletic Club trophy is renamed the Heisman Memorial Trophy in his honor
1954	Inducted into the College Football Hall of Fame

Heisman retired from coaching in 1927 with a career record of 186 wins, 70 losses, and 16 ties.

abilities. In the process of developing its football program, the Agricultural and Mechanical College of Alabama (now Auburn University) caught wind of Heisman's success and offered him a coaching job. Twenty-five-year-old Heisman accepted.

Growing Reputation: Auburn and Clemson

Although Heisman's first year at Auburn was fairly unspectacular, winning two of three games, it was during the first game of the 1895 season that he first employed his innovative trick hidden-ball play. Down 9-0 to Vanderbilt University in the second half, Auburn's quarterback, under the protection of the offensive wedge, discreetly tucked the ball under his shirt. As the other Auburn players dispersed widely on the field, successfully spreading out the defense, the quarterback pretended to be out of the play, crouching down to tie his shoe. He then nonchalantly sauntered in for a touchdown. Before being deemed illegal, the play worked once again that season in a game against Georgia.

From 1895 to 1899, Heisman led Auburn to a record of 12-4-2. Considering that his teams were often outmatched in size and talent, the record earned Heisman increasing respect, with many regarding him as one of the best coaches in the country. Enticed perhaps by an increase in salary, in 1900 Heisman accepted a coaching position at Clemson University near Greenville, South Carolina, where he quickly turned the football program into a notable success. During his first year of coaching there, Clemson went undefeated, without even a tie to blemish their perfect record. The team's win over league-dominating Georgia was icing on the cake for Clemson fans.

The Glory Years: Georgia Tech

Heisman coached Clemson football, as well as baseball, through 1903. His football record of 19-3-2 and .833 winning percentage established a yet-to-be-broken school record. In 1903 Heisman married Evelyn Cox, a widow with a twelve-year-old son. The following year Georgia Institute of Technology (Georgia Tech) lured Heisman away from Clemson, offering a salary of $2,000 and 30 percent of gate receipts. Heisman was at the peak of his coaching career at Georgia Tech, compiling a record of 102-29-6 during his sixteen-year stay. As with his previous teams, Heisman began to develop the Tech program through tough workouts, strict discipline, and the highest standards of commitment from his players.

On a national level, football was under fire for the ever-increasing number of football-related deaths and injuries; twenty-one players were reported to have died in 1904 alone. Consequently, for a period of time numerous schools, including Columbia, Northwestern, California, and Stanford Universities, discontinued their football programs altogether. To create a safer game, Heisman joined those who advocated the legalization of the forward pass. By allowing the ball to be thrown beyond the line of scrimmage (up to that time, only laterals were allowed), the crushing pile of players that led to so many injuries would be neutralized by spreading play across the entire field. Heisman became one of the strongest voices in support of the forward pass, which was finally legalized in 1906.

With the forward pass now at his disposal, Heisman regularly added its use to his game plan. He also developed what became known as the jump shift, or Heisman shift, in 1906. Prior to Heisman's invention of jump shift, players lined up and stayed put until the ball was snapped. Once again breaking with traditional play, Heisman's team would line up in one formation, then one or more men would quickly shift to new positions with the snap coming as soon as they were reset. This put the opponent at a disadvantage as the defensive players had little time to assess the new formation or communicate with teammates regarding necessary changes in defensive coverage.

During his first ten years at Georgia Tech, Heisman fielded good teams that sometimes struggled against chief rivals Auburn, Georgia, and Sewanee. Rules were changing rapidly as the prototype for modern college football began to take shape. By 1912 the game had evolved into what can be recognized as American football. Gifted at forming a winning team from players who were outmatched in size and talent, Heisman's recruiting efforts eventually paid off, and in 1915 he found himself with a truly talented team. For three consecutive seasons, from 1915 to 1917, Heisman's team went unbeaten, outscoring opponents during the 31-game streak 1,599 to 99. The crowning moment came in 1917 when Georgia Tech earned its first national championship.

On October 7, 1916, Georgia Tech participated in the most lopsided game in the history of college football. According to the nearly legendary story, Tech's baseball team (coached by Heisman) had been trounced the previous spring by Cumberland University, a small school in Tennessee. Reportedly, Cumberland had loaded its baseball team with professional players out of Nashville, hoping to salvage its struggling athletic program. Heisman, in need of revenge for the humiliating defeat, offered Cumberland $500 to come to Atlanta for a football game. At halftime the score stood at 126-0, and Heisman told his team, "You're doing all right, but we can't tell what those Cumberland players have up their sleeve. They may spring a surprise." For his part, the Cumberland coach reminded his players to hang on and remember that $500 guarantee.

Legends surrounding the game include reports of several Cumberland players who jumped the fence and deserted and one player who found his way to the Tech bench. When informed he was on the wrong side, the Cumberland player refused to join his own team for fear he'd be put back in the game. The third and fourth quarters were mercifully shortened to 10 minutes, and at the end of the day Tech had racked up 528 rushing yards and an additional 450 yards in punt returns. Cumberland posted a total of 20 yards rushing, 12 yards passing, and 10 fumbles. Georgia Tech's record of 32 touchdowns and 18 consecutive extra points still stands.

The Later Years

In 1919 Heisman announced that he and his wife were divorcing and, although the split was amicable, he had agreed to live in another place as his wife wished to remain in Atlanta. Much to the dismay of Georgia Tech fans, Heisman tendered his resignation and accepted a coaching position at his alma mater, the University of Pennsylvania. Penn fans were hoping for a return to the university's glory days of football experienced under the great coach George Woodruff in the 1890s. However

John Heisman, right

during the next three seasons Heisman's Quakers posted a mediocre record of 16-10-2. In 1922, the same year he published his book *The Principles of Football,* Heisman announced his resignation to accept a coaching job at Washington and Jefferson, a small private school located south of Pittsburgh. However, Heisman's demanding and dictatorial coaching style that in the past had motivated his players was no longer achieving positive results. He had encountered problems with discipline and drive with some of his Penn players, and his difficulties forming bonds with his players increased at his new post. Consequently, Heisman stayed at Washington and Jefferson just one year before moving on to Rice University in Houston, Texas, after the end of the 1923 season. In the same year he married Edith Maora Cole, a former girlfriend from his early coaching days in Pennsylvania.

As testament to his national coaching reputation, Heisman asked for and was granted a five-year, $9,000 contract at Rice, an incredible amount considering the university's highest paid faculty received $7,500. But Heisman's glory days in football had clearly ended. Rice posted marginal records over the next couple of years, and in 1927 Heisman coached the first losing season of his entire 36-year career. After compiling a record of 1-6-1 and being outscored over the season 148 to 52, Heisman tendered his resignation.

Once relieved of the pressures that run concurrent with consistently fielding winning teams, Heisman's demeanor mellowed. In a series of eleven articles published in *Collier's,* he recounted amusing and memorable moments of his long career. Over the next two years he operated a successful sporting goods business in New York City. Then, in 1929 he was appointed the inaugural director for the newly built Downtown Athletic Club, where he served until his unexpected death on March 10, 1936, of bronchial pneumonia. The DAC trophy given to the most outstanding college football player in the nation, first awarded in 1935, was renamed the Heisman Memorial Trophy to honor Heisman's contributions to the development of college football. Popularly known as the Heisman, the trophy has become the most prestigious honor in collegiate football.

SELECTED WRITINGS BY HEISMAN:

The Principles of Football, Hill Street Press, 1922.

FURTHER INFORMATION

Books

Campbell, Jim. "John Heisman." *The Scribner Encyclopedia of American Lives, Sport Figures,* Volume 1, edited by Arnold Markoe. New York: Charles Scribner's Sons, 2002.

Hickok, Ralph. *A Who's Who of Sports Champions: Their Stories and Records.* Boston: Houghton Mifflin, 1995.

Gems, Gerald R. "John William Heisman." *American National Biography* Volume 10, edited by John A. Garraty and Mark C. Carnes. New York: Oxford University Press, 1999.

Mendell, Ronald L., and Timothy B. Phares. *Who's Who in Football.* New Rochelle, NY: Arlington House, 1974

Pope, Edwin. *Football's Greatest Coaches.* Atlanta: Tupper and Love, 1955.

Periodicals

Culley, Jennings. "Heisman's Insight Raised College Game." *Richmond Times Dispatch* (November 15, 1998): C7.

Harig, Bob. "Ward Brushes Up on Heisman History." *St. Petersburg Times* (December 11, 1993): C1.

Heller, Dick. "Georgia Tech Authored the Rout to End All Routs in '16." *Washington Times* (October 7, 2002): C15.

Huey, Anthony, and Jonathan Knight. "The Man Behind the Trophy." *Ohio Magazine* (December 1998-January 1999): 57-58.

Mulhern, Tom. "Namesake Rests in Rhineland." *Wisconsin State Journal* (December 12, 1999): D2.

Mushnick, Phil. "Legendary Coaches, Dubious Means." *New York Post* (November 30, 2001): 112.

Sapakoff, Gene. "Heisman, the Man and the Trophy." *Post and Courier* (Charleston, SC) (December 8, 1999): C1.

"Tech Wins 222-0." *Sports Illustrated* (fall, 1991): 7.

Other

"John Heisman." *1996 Clemson Football Media Guide.* http://www.hubcap.Clemson.edu/~tcrumpt/history/heisman.html/ (October 31, 2002).

Sketch by Kari Bethel

Rickey Henderson
1958-

American baseball player

One of baseball history's most prolific and long-careered players, Rickey Henderson is the sport's all-time leader in stolen bases, runs, and walks. With his powerful batting and speed, he has been deemed one of baseball's greatest leadoff hitters, and holds the record for most home runs at the start of a game (75). Since his 1979 major-league debut, the Golden Glove-winning outfielder and eleven-time All-Star has played on numerous teams, including the Oakland A's, New York Yankees, New York Mets, Seattle Mariners, Toronto Blue Jays, San Diego Padres, and Boston Red Sox. Yet the Chicago-born athlete's stellar career has often been overshadowed by his image as a boastful and egotistical player—despite his claims of being misunderstood. Still playing baseball and breaking records in the early 2000s, Henderson is regarded as a virtual shoo-in to the National Baseball Hall of Fame in Cooperstown, New York.

Richard Henley Henderson was born in the backseat of a car in Chicago, Illinois, on Christmas Day 1958. His parents separated two years later, and his mother, Bobbie, took Henderson and his siblings to live in Oakland, California. Here, Henderson attended elementary school and played baseball at local Bushrod Park. A star athlete at Oakland Technical High School, he played numerous sports; as a senior he rushed for 1,100 yards as a football player. He also distinguished himself in baseball, and was named to the All-Oakland Athletic League for three of his high school years. Upon graduating, the 5-foot-10 athlete received several football scholarship offers. Instead, he chose to forgo college and pursue a career in professional baseball. In 1976 the eighteen-year-old player was drafted in round four by the Oakland A's. He played as an outfielder in the minor-league farm system for the next three years, and was called up on June 23, 1979, for his first major-league game.

Rickey Henderson

Known as Stolen Base King

In his first half-season as a rookie, Henderson demonstrated his speed and skill for stealing bases, logging thirty-three steals in only eighty-nine games. By the middle of his second full season—before the 1981 baseball strike cut the season short—Henderson was leading not only in stolen bases (56) but also in runs scored (89), hits (135), and outfield putouts (327). The latter honor led to a 1981 Golden Glove Award. Henderson's peak as "Stolen Base King" came in 1982, when he stole a record-setting 130 bases. The following season he logged 108 steals, breaking the 100-mark for the third and last time of his career.

Henderson perfected the art of stealing bases at a time when fans tended to champion power hitters. Speed demon **Lou Brock**, Henderson's predecessor in record-setting stolen bases, was on the verge of retirement when Henderson's career was beginning. Henderson took it upon himself to keep up the tradition, and the Chicago-born player was soon on the road to eclipsing Brock's career record.

In 1984 Henderson was traded to the New York Yankees, where he was reunited with former A's manager **Billy Martin**. In one of his best seasons to date, he hit twenty-four home runs and ended with a .314 batting average. Although he did not top his personal best in 1984, he led the league that year in stolen bases (80). His value on the Yankees was second only to champion slugger Don Mattingly.

Unusual for having a left-handed throw and a right-handed batting stance, Henderson excelled as both an outfielder and a hitter. In 1986 he hit a career high of twenty-eight home runs; he also scored 146 runs—more than any other player since **Ted Williams**. He averaged more than one run per game, a percentage comparable to that of legendary Yankee **Lou Gehrig**. As an outfielder he proved himself to be versatile, moving from left to center field in 1985 (he later returned to his preferred left field). For his deft-looking catches, Henderson earned the nickname "Style Dog." As a Yankee he continued to prove his base-stealing prowess, logging ninety-three steals in 1988.

Broke Records in Steals, Runs, and Walks

After a brief slump in 1989, Henderson was traded back to the Oakland A's in June, signing a four-year, $12 million contract, one of the most lucrative deals in baseball. The move seemed to rejuvenate Henderson, who batted .325 and scored 119 runs and twenty-eight homers in 1990. For these achievements he earned his first and only Most Valuable Player award. The following year, he broke Brock's career stolen-base record, logging his 939th steal on May 1. In a ceremony to honor his achievement, he told the crowd, "Today I am the greatest of all time" (BaseballLibrary.com). Statements such as these earned Henderson his reputation as a braggart; many fans were put off by his tendency to sing his own praises. "Those words [about being the greatest] haunt me to this day," he told Dennis Manoloff of the *Plain Dealer*. "They overshadow what I've accomplished in this game."

In the 1990s Henderson was traded several times, playing for the Toronto Blue Jays, San Diego Padres, and Anaheim Angels. In 1998 he joined the New York Mets as a free agent. The aging player continued to prove himself valuable, batting a .315 average. Yet his personality clashed with the team's management. Henderson's reputation soured after the 1999 National League Championship Series, when it was rumored that he and teammate Bobby Bonilla were playing cards in the club-

Career Statistics

Yr	Team	AVG	GP	AB	R	H	HR	RBI	BB	SO	SB
1979	OAK	.274	89	351	49	96	1	26	34	39	33
1980	OAK	.303	158	591	111	179	9	53	117	54	100
1981	OAK	.319	108	423	89	135	6	35	64	68	56
1982	OAK	.267	149	536	119	143	10	51	116	94	130
1983	OAK	.292	145	513	105	150	9	48	103	80	108
1984	OAK	.293	142	502	113	147	16	58	86	81	66
1985	NY	.314	143	547	146	172	24	72	99	65	80
1986	NY	.263	153	608	130	160	28	74	89	81	87
1987	NY	.291	95	358	79	104	17	37	80	52	41
1988	NY	.305	140	554	118	169	6	50	82	54	93
1989	NY	.247	65	235	41	58	3	22	56	29	25
1989	OAK	.294	85	306	72	90	9	35	70	39	52
1990	OAK	.325	136	489	119	159	28	61	97	60	65
1991	OAK	.268	134	470	105	126	18	57	98	73	58
1992	OAK	.283	117	396	77	112	15	46	95	56	48
1993	OAK	.327	90	318	77	104	17	47	85	46	31
1993	TOR	.215	44	163	37	35	4	12	35	19	22
1994	OAK	.260	87	296	66	77	6	20	72	45	22
1995	OAK	.300	112	407	67	122	9	54	72	66	32
1996	SD	.241	148	465	110	112	9	29	125	90	37
1997	ANA	.183	32	115	21	21	2	7	26	23	16
1997	SD	.274	88	288	63	79	6	27	71	62	29
1998	OAK	.236	152	542	101	128	14	57	118	114	66
1999	NYM	.315	121	438	89	138	12	42	82	82	37
2000	NYM	.219	31	96	17	21	0	2	25	20	5
2000	SEA	.238	92	324	58	77	4	30	63	55	31
2001	SD	.227	123	379	70	86	8	42	81	84	25
2002	BOS	.223	72	179	40	40	5	16	38	47	8
TOTAL		.279	3051	10889	2288	3040	295	1110	2179	1678	1403

ANA: Anaheim Angels; BOS: Boston Red Sox; NY: New York Mets; OAK: Oakland A's; SD: San Diego Padres; SEA: Seattle Mariners; TOR: Toronto Blue Jays.

Awards and Accomplishments

1980, 1982-89	All-Star
1981	Golden Glove Award
1982	Most home runs leading off a game; most steals in a season
1990	American League Most Valuable Player
1991	All-time stolen-base champion
2001	All-time leader in runs
2001	All-time leader in walks

house while their team suffered a crushing loss to the Atlanta Braves. Henderson denied the rumor, but some say it led to his release from the team in May 2000.

Henderson joined his seventh team, the Seattle Mariners, in 2000. By the following season he was without a contract, however, as the Mariners chose not to re-sign the 42-year-old player. After a brief period without a team, Henderson signed with the San Diego Padres. His batting average had dipped to .227, but he continued scoring runs, becoming baseball's all-time leader in that category in 2001. The same year, he surpassed **Babe Ruth** in career walks with 2,063. In his final swing of the season, he logged the 3,000th hit of his career. Signing with the Boston Red Sox, his ninth team, in 2002, Henderson

proved his staying power by demonstrating one of the highest on-base percentages on the team.

The key to Henderson's longevity as a player? "[P]ush-ups, sit-ups, push-ups, sit-ups—and a lot of running," he told Manoloff of the *Plain Dealer*. "I'm not going to give [baseball] up if I can still perform, compete and enjoy the game." When he does retire, Henderson will be remembered for his base-stealing and lead-off hitting prowess, and for his many other record-breaking moments.

SELECTED WRITINGS BY HENDERSON:

(With John Shea) *Off Base: Confessions of a Thief,* HarperCollins, 1992.

FURTHER INFORMATION

Books

"Rickey Henderson." *Contemporary Black Biography,* Volume 28. Edited by Ashyia Henderson. Detroit: Gale Group, 2001.

Periodicals

Center, Bill. "Henderson's Raring to Go." *San Diego Union-Tribune* (March 20, 2001): D3.

Krasner, Steven. "Seldom-Used Henderson Provides the Spark for Sox." *Providence Journal-Bulletin* (August 18, 2002): D3.

Kroichick, Ron. "Well-Traveled Rickey Henderson Still Chasing Down Cobb, Ruth." *San Francisco Chronicle* (June 9, 2000): E1.

Manoloff, Dennis. "Catching Up with Rickey Henderson." *Plain Dealer* (September 29, 2002): D6.

Other

"Bobby Bonilla." BaseballLibrary.com. http://www.pubdim.net/baseballlibrary/ballplayers/B/Bonilla_Bobby.stm (December 8, 2002).

"Henderson, Rickey H." HickokSports. http://www.hickoksports.com/biograph/hendersonrickey.shtml (December 4, 2002).

"Rickey Henderson." BaseballLibrary.com. http://www.pubdim.net/baseballlibrary/ballplayers/H/Henderson_Rickey.stm (December 4, 2002).

Sketch by Wendy Kagan

Sonja Henie

Sonja Henie
1912-1969

Norwegian figure skater

During her lifetime Sonja Henie reigned as the "queen of ice," and today she remains the most influential individual to have been part of figure skating. During a career that spanned the 1920s, '30s, '40s, and '50s, the Norwegian skater made major contributions to women's figure skating, which would help propel the sport into the prominence it now enjoys as a dazzling, physically-challenging, personality-filled field. Henie is credited with many "firsts," including being the first international sports star, the first superstar among figure skaters, and the first—and still only—woman to win three Olympic gold medals in figure skating. Among her many victories as a competitive skater, she also won ten consecutive world championships. These honors were the result of talent, intensive training, and an interest in doing something different from other skaters. Henie is credited with transforming an originally demure, predictable activity by infusing it with her feminine charms and passion for the ballet. Short skirts and choreography were unknown in figure skating before Henie introduced them in the late 1920s. But Henie did not stop there. When she became a professional skater in 1936, she set her sights on movie stardom and quickly turned herself into a top box office draw. While also working as an ice show star and producer, she became a multi-millionaire and easily eclipsed the earnings of any other star athlete, male or female.

Early Advantages

As a child, Henie enjoyed advantages that greatly contributed to her success as a skater. Born on April 8, 1912 in Oslo, Norway, her father, Hans Wilhelm Henie, was a successful fur trader and her mother, Selma Lochman Nielsen, had a fortune of her own. When their daughter showed a special passion for skating at about age six, which she began under the instruction of her brother Leif, they provided her with whatever training she required. The family also fully appreciated Henie's interest in sports. Hans was himself very athletic; among his diverse pursuits, he was a former world champion in bicycling. His daughter began studying ballet at age five and would be active in skiing, swimming, and horseback riding. She later competed successfully in tennis and auto racing in the midst of her skating career. After taking informal lessons at a local skating club, Henie won her first figure skating competition at age nine. The next year, she began training for the national championship of Norway. To allow for a rigorous training schedule, Henie's parents took her out of school, hired a private tutor, and gave her ballet lessons in London during the summer. In 1923 she became the senior national champion of Norway. Both Hans and Selma became deeply involved in Sonja's skating career. Her mother accompanied her on all of her travels and her father would even-

Chronology

1912	Born April 8, outside of Oslo, Norway, to Hans Wilhelm Henie and Selma Lochman Nielsen
1918	Receives first pair of ice skates
1921	Wins Norway's junior-level national competition
1922	Studies with private tutor to allow for longer practice sessions
1923	Wins Norwegian National Championship
1927	Sees Anna Pavlova dance in London
1927	Wins first of ten Women's World Figure Skating Championship titles
1928	Awarded Olympic gold medal in figure skating at St. Moritz
1930	Performs in New York City's Madison Square Garden in amateur exhibition
1932	Awarded Olympic gold medal in figure skating at Lake Placid
1936	Awarded Olympic gold medal in figure skating at Garmisch-Partenkirchen
1936	Wins tenth World Championship title
1936	Signs contract to skate in U.S. tour, *Sonja Henie's Night,*
1936	Rents Hollywood arena to woo filmmakers
1936	Signs five-year contract with Twentieth-Century Fox
1936	Appears in first film, *One in a Million*
1937	Begins touring in *Hollywood Ice Review*
1938	Rated third-most-popular film star in poll
1940	Marries Daniel Reid Topping
1941	Becomes U.S. citizen
1946	Divorces Daniel Reid Topping
1948	Makes last film in Hollywood
1949	Marries Winthrop Gardiner, Jr.
1952	Ends long relationship with promoter Arthur Wirtz and tours independently
1952	Stops appearing in arena-style shows after bleacher accident injures 250 spectators
1956	Divorced by Winthrop Gardiner, Jr.
1956	Marries Niels Onstad
1956	Retires from professional skating
1958	Appears in British film *Hello London*
1968	Donates modern art collection to Norway; builds Henie-Onstad Museum near Oslo
1968	Diagnosed with leukemia
1969	Dies on ambulance plane flying from Paris to Oslo

tually leave his fur business responsibilities to his son in order to manage Henie's career.

Youthful Champion

The intensity of Henie's commitment to skating was further intensified after competing in the first winter Olympics, in Chamonix, France, in 1924. After placing last in a field of eight, she increased her practice time to some seven hours a day. Because Norway did not yet have indoor ice rinks, she traveled around Europe to train throughout the year and benefit from the best instructors. Her new goal was the 1927 world figure skating championship. Her performance, skating "at home" in Norway's Frogner Stadium, earned her the first of ten consecutive world figure skating titles (and the distinction of being the youngest world champion until **Tara Lipinski** edged her out in 1997 by a margin of thirty-two days). The pretty, blond skater stood out among the competitors in a white silk and ermine skating dress that had a short skirt. Long, black skirts were the norm,

being both modest and warm. But the fourteen-year-old Henie was too small to wear such heavy garb; it tended to act like a sail and tangle in her legs. Selma had designed her daughter's above-the-knee skirt with heavy fur trim to give it fullness. Beyond the garment's visual impact, it gave her the freedom to do jumps and other movements that had only been done by men. When Henie began her program, her ballet training was evident in the flourishes she made with her head and legs. She managed to tie together the elements in her routine in way that had not been done before. She also lit the entire performance with a dazzling, dimpled smile. The hallmarks of Henie's future successes were in place.

Later in 1927 Henie saw the Russian ballerina Anna Pavlova dance in London. The experience inspired her to introduce choreographic design in her free skating program, an innovation that helped her win an Olympic gold medal in 1928 at St. Moritz, Switzerland. Her program also included double axels, spins, twirls, and jumps. Her innovations and unparalleled determination would fuel another ten years of amateur successes, including a still unmatched Olympic record. Henie went on to win a total of three Olympic figure skating championships: she also won gold medals at Lake Placid, New York in 1932 and at Garmisch-Partenkirchen, Bavaria in 1936. The skater turned professional later that same year, after having won her tenth world championship.

Turning Professional

Henie had turned down contract offers following the 1932 Olympics, but now set about in earnest to make a career as an exhibition skater and film star. In the effort, she exercised the same mental intensity and financial resources that were the foundation of her earlier work. She already had considerable experience as an exhibition skater, having been a soloist for the New York Skating Club's production *Land of the Midnight Sun* at Madison Square Garden in 1930. She had also performed for European royalty and presented a skating version of Pavlova's "Dying Swan" that was first seen in Milan, Italy in 1933. Within a month of her last amateur victory, Henie signed with promoter Arthur Wirtz to appear in a U.S. tour. She made seventeen performances in nine cities and earned phenomenal box office returns. The tour did not, however, result in the film contract Henie desired. Henie famously asserted that she wanted to do for skating what Fred Astaire had done for dancing on film. To get the attention of film executives, Henie's father leased Hollywood's Polar Palace for two performances in May 1936. The highly-publicized shows were well attended by film stars and filmmakers, including Darryl F. Zanuck of Twentieth Century-Fox. He soon signed Henie to a five-year contract.

Sonja Henie

Awards and Accomplishments

1921	Norwegian junior-level national championship
1923	Norwegian National Championship
1927	Women's World Figure Skating Championship
1928	Olympic figure skating championship
1928-36	Women's World Figure Skating Championship
1932	Olympic figure skating championship
1936	Olympic figure skating championship
1937	Made Knight First Class of the Order of St. Olaf

Gee-Whizzer

Second Fiddle displays Sonja [Henie] as Trudi Hovland, a schoolmarm of Bergen, Minn. who is called to Hollywood because her local swain has sent her photograph to Consolidated Pictures Corp., which has been looking high & low for just such a heroine. Jimmy Sutton (Tyrone Power), the press agent sent to Bergen to fetch her, at first treats her merely as Entry No. 436. He agrees that she has no chance for the part but talks her into flying to Hollywood for the trip, with her Aunt Phoebe (Edna May Oliver). After a twirl on the ice with her pupils, Trudi consents. Although Trudi does no skating in her screen test, she makes the grade. Jimmy believes that, as the new star, she can be used to bolster the publicity value of Roger Maxwell (Rudy Vallee), a crooner on the studio pay roll whose self-esteem is more impressive than his newsworthiness. Touched by Roger's mash notes, which are really written by Jimmy, Trudi moons over him all during production of *Girl of the North*. Only when she learns the real author of the notes does Trudi realize that her heart has been bent, not broken.

Source: *Time,* 34 (July 17, 1939): 51-54.

The one obstacle that remained in Henie's way proved to be of small concern: the fact that she wasn't much of an actress. She nevertheless had negotiated an impressive contract and was an immediate hit with audiences. Zanuck first cast Henie in *One in a Million* (1936), which also starred Don Ameche, Adolphe Menjou, and the Ritz Brothers. It set the pattern for the films to follow as a light musical comedy that included songs and skating. It made the most of Henie's smiling, energetic persona and her dimpled beauty in a story about an Olympic hopeful. Moreover, her skating numbers were fantastic. Critic Roy Hemming enthused about the film when it was among seven video releases made at the time of the 1994 Olympics. "Henie skates with speed, grace, and eye-boggling abandon through four big numbers," he noted in *Entertainment Weekly.* Of the films in general, he decided, "The best of them hold up as unmatched combinations of romantic comedy, catchy songs, and dazzling skating routines." Theatergoers of the era certainly were thrilled with Henie and their introduction to figure skating. The film soon grossed $2 million and made Henie a household name.

Film Stardom

The year 1937 held some of Henie's greatest accomplishments and one of her greatest losses. Hans Henie died that year, at a time when his daughter's career had reached amazing heights. She was made a Knight First Class of the Order of St. Olaf by King Haakon of Norway, becoming the youngest person to receive this honor. She appeared in the film *Thin Ice* and was rated in a *Motion Picture Herald* poll as the eighth most popular film star of the year. As the first and only ice-skating film star, Henie is a show business phenomenon comparable only to the swimmer **Esther Williams**, who appeared in romantic comedies in the late 1940s. Following the success of *Thin Ice,* Henie showed her growing business savvy by getting Twentieth Century-Fox to renegotiate her contract. Surely she exceeded nearly everyone's expectations when she was rated as the third most popular film star of 1938, surpassed by only Shirley Temple and Clark Gable. As a result, her 1939 salary was more than $250,000. Another measure of her worth is that in 1940 her legs were insured by Lloyds of London for $5,000 per week.

Henie would make eleven films in Hollywood, with the first six being the most successful. The best paired her with some of the biggest male stars of the time, including Tyrone Power in *Thin Ice* and *Second Fiddle* (1939), Don Ameche (for the second time) and Cesar Romero in *Happy Landing* (1938), and Ray Milland and Robert Cummings in *Everything Happens at Night* (1939). *Sun Valley Serenade* (1941), in which Henie appeared with John Payne and Glenn Miller and His Orchestra, is memorable for its Academy Award nominations for best cinematography, best music, and best song. During the 1940s, Henie's popularity with movie audiences began to falter and her contract with Twentieth Century-Fox was not renewed. She made one film each with RKO and Universal in the following years, and in 1958 appeared in *Hello London,* which was only released in England.

Hollywood Ice Revue

Troubles in Henie's film career were not mirrored in her popularity as a live performer. She was showcased in the *Hollywood Ice Revue,* which began in 1938 and continued for twelve years in cities across the United States. A 2002 article in the (Cleveland) *Plain Dealer* reflected Henie's impact in these shows, an accomplishment undimmed by the passing of sixty-four years. It recounted that her appearance had been a front-page story in which Roelif Loveland had written "there is no simile to express adequately the grace and loveliness of this glamorous young woman." Loveland continued, "she seems to float, like something in gossamer wings, but anyone tempted to drift off into an ethereal realm is brought back by a pair of very shapely limbs, which move with the smoothness of running water and the strength of youth." Members of the audience paid up to $4.40 for the chance to see Henie. This was more than a day's pay for Steve Turocy, who at age eighty-two remembered having to settle for a $3.30 seat because the others were sold out. During a week in Cleveland, she would skate for more than 62,000 fans.

The *Hollywood Ice Review* was polished by Henie's unwavering pursuit of perfection. A *New York Times* obituary noted that she once summoned Eddie Pec, who was said to be the only person she trusted to sharpen her skates, from New York to Chicago by train to do a job that took only a few minutes. She also forbade the skaters in her chorus from wearing hairpins, after having fallen and broken ribs because of a pin on the ice. Henie characterized her skating as very dangerous, but others said that because she almost never fell she did not know how to do it without hurting herself. And most importantly, she hired the best skaters and choreographers and paid them handsomely.

In cooperation with promoter Wirtz, Henie honed her skills as a producer of ice shows as well as maintained her prowess as a skater. In 1940 the pair offered the ballet-on-ice *Les Sylphides,* which was so successful that they began to produce reviews throughout the year at the Center Theatre in New York City. Henie did not appear in these shows, but rather was an advisor and financial partner. In 1951 Wirtz and Henie were unable to agree on a contract and parted ways. So the skating star created her own ice show, *Sonja Henie with Her 1952 Ice Revue.* It featured spectacular costumes and included waltz and hula dances. Reviewers marveled that Henie was still in top form. According to a quote in the *New York Times,* Henie felt that she was working harder than ever: "When I was in championship competition I was on the ice for exactly four minutes. Now I arrive at the Garden at 6:45 and I never stop until 11:10. Besides, I can't quite imagine my doing the hula in the Olympics." But Henie stopped producing shows after an accident in 1952 prior to a performance. A stand of bleacher seats collapsed at a Baltimore armory, injuring more than 250 people. Henie was not judged to be responsible for the incident, but she decided not to hold any more arena-style shows. Subsequently, she appeared on television several times, including her own one-hour special.

Ends Long Career

Henie retired from skating in 1956, the same year that she married her third husband, following two earlier marriages that ended in divorce. Her union with American sports investor (and later owner of the New York Yankees) Daniel Reid Topping lasted from 1940 to 1946, likely a victim to her grueling film production and touring schedules. The year after they were married she became a U.S. citizen. Henie wed American business executive Winthrop Gardiner Jr. in 1949; he divorced her in 1956 for "desertion and mental cruelty." Less than a month later, she was married to a childhood friend, Niels Onstad, who had become a shipping magnate and art collector. Henie did not have any children and became an active collector with her new husband. Her wealth al-

lowed her to maintain a home in Hollywood, a villa in Norway, and an apartment in Lausanne, Switzerland, and to invest in impressionist and expressionist paintings. The couple decided to build a museum for their collection, and in 1968 donated 250 works to the Sonja Henie-Niels Onstad Art Center outside of Oslo. It would later house all of Henie's skating memorabilia. Not long after the center's lavish opening celebration, Henie was diagnosed with leukemia. She died a year later at age fifty-seven. The international star had managed to keep her illness a secret and was seen with her husband at an Oslo theater less than two weeks before her death. Henie died in her sleep on an ambulance plane that was taking her from Paris to Oslo to see a specialist.

Temper Remembered

Public interest in Henie has fueled continued debate about her off-ice and off-screen behavior. A bubbly, smiling figure in her performances, she was in fact a fierce competitor who wanted nothing to do with her rivals. Her brother, Leif Henie, coauthored *Queen of Ice, Queen of Shadows: The Unsuspected Life of Sonja Henie* (1985), in which he discussed her violent temper. At the time of the 1994 **Tonya Harding-Nancy Kerrigan** rivalry, their altercations were compared in the press with the sparring that went on between Henie and Swedish skater Vivi-Anne Hulten many years earlier. At the age of eighty-two, Hulten still had plenty of venom for Henie. She remembered in the *Sporting News* how Henie had screamed at her after the 1933 World Championship competition, saying she was an unworthy opponent. "She went after me in every which way from that point on," said Hulten. "Nobody hit me in the leg or tried to shoot me, but there were some likenesses to what's happening now." Hulten charged that Henie was responsible for having her strip searched and detained on suspicion of smuggling jewels while traveling across the German border in 1935. After she complained to Nazi propaganda minister Joseph Goebbels, the guard was summoned to apologize for the incident. He named Henie as the instigator. Moreover, Hulten believed that Henie's father influenced competition organizers by playing poker for "appearance fees" and, in one case, the agreement to place Hulten third in the 1936 Olympics.

Other stories echo these allegations, although in a milder fashion. During the years that Henie won her world championships, the five-member judging panel was dominated by three Norwegians. Complaints by Austrian skaters would result in new rules allowing only one judge per country for each event. In a 1999 account for *Newsweek,* silver-medal holder Cecilia Colledge also remembered competing against Henie in the 1936 Olympic games. She recalled the champion's marvelous clothes and icy disdain. "To her, there were no other skaters," wrote Colledge. "Even on the podium after the Olympics, there were no kisses, no handshakes, not even a word." A male cast member from the *Hollywood Ice*

Review had warmer memories of Henie in a 1996 interview in *Films in Review*. Bill Griffin described Henie as a perfectionist with a short fuse. It was Selma Henie, he said, who ended her daughter's squabbles and made sure that things ran smoothly. Griffin saw Henie as person intent on reaching her professional goals and little else. "You could laugh with Sonja, but she had other things on her mind. I don't think she ever really learned to enjoy life. She had to concentrate on her profession, and fulfill contracts, really from the age of nine on," he explained.

Another accusation that hurt Henie's image was the perception that she was a Nazi sympathizer. This was particularly true in Norway after World War II, where her status as one of the most admired Norwegians of all time was threatened by criticisms that she had not contributed to war relief efforts. It was also noted in *Queen of Ice, Queen of Shadows* that before the war started the Henies had visited with Adolf Hitler and that during a 1936 show in Berlin she had given him the Nazi salute and said "Heil, Hitler."

But Henie will be best remembered for putting skating above the personal and political. Her passion for performing turned her into a huge financial and popular success among athletes. During sixteen years of touring she earned something in the range of $10 million and her movies probably netted her more than $25 million. However, these are not Henie's most enduring achievements. Likewise, her films are still enjoyable, but their style and that of her skating is dated. Her jumps and spins seem ridiculously easy compared to the athletic feats of contemporary figure skaters. It is her effect on the sport of figure skating that is unrivaled. She took a largely unnoticed, technically-oriented sport and turned it into a dynamic art form that, along with its star performers, is avidly followed by fans around the world.

SELECTED WRITINGS BY HENIE:

Mitt livs eventyr, Oslo, Norway: Gyldendal Norsk Forlag, 1938.
Wings On My Feet, Englewood Cliffs, NJ: Prentice-Hall, 1940.

FURTHER INFORMATION

Periodicals

Colledge, Cecilia. "The World's First Ice Queen." *Newsweek* (October 25, 1999): 53.
Dolgan, Bob. "When Cleveland fell under Sonja's spell 64 years ago, Henie's visit enchanted the city." *Plain Dealer* (January 16, 2002).
"Gee-Whizzer." *Time* (July 17, 1939): 51-54.
Hemming, Roy. "Tonya-no! Sonja-yes!" *Entertainment Weekly* (February 11, 1994): 62.
Knisley, Michael. "Tormented by a rival who was cold as ice." *Sporting News* (February 14, 1994): S21.
O'Brien, Richard and Jack McCallum. "Ice Wars: The Prequel." *Sports Illustrated* (February 14, 1994): 18.
"Remembering Sonja Henie." *Films in Review* (July-August 1996): 60.
"Sonja Henie, Skating Star, Dies." *New York Times* (October 13, 1969).

Sketch by Paula Pyzik Scott

Luis Hernandez
1968-

Mexican soccer player

Luis Hernandez is Mexico's top all-time scorer in international soccer with 35 goals (having passed Carlos Hermosillo in that category in 2000). He led the Mexicans to one of their best World Cup showings ever in 1998 when he scored four goals in four games, winning for them a berth in the round of 16 and leading them to a near upset of powerhouse Germany. While less successful with professional teams in Argentina and the United States, "El Matador," he of the flowing blond hair, remains, even in the twilight of his career, one of his country's most revered athletes.

"Hernandez has a burst of speed second to none in the (penalty) area and also has the ability to beat players one on one," the FIFA World Cup Web site said of Hernandez during the 2002 World Cup in South Korea and Japan. "He has a temper and has been known to lose it and has been struggling with injuries the last two years."

Soccer Roots in Family

Hernandez's father and two uncles played first division soccer in Mexico. At age 18, Hernandez turned pro and joined the club team Necaxa. He led it to national championships in 1995 and 1996. Meanwhile, he had led the Monterrey Tigres to the CONCACAF Champions Cup title in 1993. (CONCACAF is the Confederation of North, Central American and Caribbean Association Football). Hernandez scored 38 goals in 64 games for Monterrey from 1996-2000; he also competed for Cruz Azul and Santos Laguna.

1997 was Hernandez's breakthrough year internationally. He scored six goals in six games at the Copa America tournament in Bolivia, and was named the event's most valuable player while propelling Mexico to a third-place finish. Now sought by teams from several countries, Hernandez signed with the Boca Juniors of Argentina, who won out over Borussia Moenchengladbach of the German elite league, the Bundesliga, and several teams from Major League Soccer of the United States.

Luis Hernandez

World Cup Standout

Hernandez was at his best in 1998, when France hosted the World Cup and the Mexicans, who had never before won a World Cup game in Europe, advanced past the opening round. Mexico became a media darling, living on the edge in its tournament games. There was even turmoil before the quadrennial event began. Mexico fired Coach Bora Milutinovic after the qualifying games and replaced him with Manuel Lapuente, who had won four national titles with Necaxa and Puebla. (Milutinovic had coached the United States to the round of 16 in the previous World Cup, which the U.S. hosted). In addition, Hermosillo, who had scored 11 goals during qualifying, was omitted from the squad.

Playing at the striker position, Hernandez, who scored only one goal throughout the qualifying, connected twice in the last 15 minutes of regulation as Mexico came from behind to beat South Korea 3-1 in its first game, at Lyon. The Koreans had to play one man short the final 60 minutes.

Mexico looked beaten in the following game, down 2-0 to Belgium and short a man with about 35 minutes remaining, but rebounded for a 2-2 draw at Bordeaux. Thanks to Hernandez, Mexico earned another 2-2 draw in its next game, against the Netherlands at Saint-Etienne. Hernandez, five minutes into injury time (added to the end of soccer games), scored against Dutch goalkeeper Edwin van der Saar off a goalmouth scramble.

Having proven its comeback ability in its opening games, Mexico faced a different challenge against the Germans. Hernandez gave his country a 1-0 lead in the 47th minute, scoring against keeper Andreas Koepke, but Mexico found that protecting a lead was tougher than coming back. Veterans Jurgen Klinsmann and Oliver Bierhoff connected late in the game, Bierhoff with less than four minutes left in regulation, and the Germans ended Mexico's run.

North of the Border

In May, 2000, Hernandez signed a three-year agreement with the Los Angeles Galaxy. To remain under the salary cap, the Galaxy had to give up several starting players and pay Monterrey several million dollars. Hernandez was also allowed to play for a Mexican team during the season.

Still, Galaxy and league officials thought the move was a boon to soccer in Southern California, with its large Mexican fan base. (U.S.-Mexico games played there usually involve a mostly pro-Mexican crowd, and American players have likened it to playing an away game.) Ticket sales spiked, though Hernandez drew fire from the Mexican media for going to the U.S. Hernandez, who joined the league midseason, found the physical play in the MLS an adjustment. "I know that there is more passion, more passion in other leagues," he told *SoccerTimes* through an interpreter. "There are leagues that let you play and enjoy soccer. Here it is very hard and strong and you need to be up to it." "I have to work and put myself in the groove of this type of soccer," he added. "I don't have time to feel sorry for myself, nor should I feel sorry for myself. [MLS] is another type of soccer, and I have to enjoy it."

Hernandez, however, contributed little in his two years with the Galaxy. Robert Wagman, in *SoccerTimes,* assailed Hernandez for lack of commitment and urged the Galaxy to sever ties after the star striker failed to show for the CONCACAF Champions Cup in January, 2001, in which the Galaxy and Washington's D.C. United competed. "Hernandez is being paid a small fortune, an amount vastly out of proportion to the minimal contribution he has made to the Galaxy, either on the field or by drawing fans to games from the team's large Hispanic fan base," Wagman wrote. "MLS strongly believes it must have a big-name Mexican player on the Galaxy to keep faith with the fans, and have thrown handsome sums to the likes of Herndandez, Carlos Hermosillo and Jorge Campos, only to turn a blind eye to the liberties that these players have taken at the expense of the Galaxy and the league." The Galaxy and Hernandez parted company after the 2001 season.

One More World Cup

Hernandez appeared as a substitute for Mexico in three games in the 2002 World Cup. The Mexicans reached the round of 16 before losing 2-0 to the United States. Hernandez had lost his spot on the national team, as Coach Javier Aguirre opted for younger, hungrier players; Aguirre, however, recalled Hernandez in April. "With so much talk of Aguirre wanting players willing to work hard and sacrifice personal objectives for the good of the team, the implication was that Hernandez had become too old and self-satisfied to earn a place in Aguirre's program," Mike Penner wrote in the *Los Angeles Times*. "His recall to Mexico's World Cup team in April was considered a surprise, even if the inclusion of a 33-year-old World Cup veteran with a knack for finding the back of the net made practical sense."

Hernandez's Impact

Hernandez, who signed with his hometown Veracruz for the Mexican League's 2002-03 closing session, satisfied soccer-hungry Mexican fans. Especially noteworthy was his play in the 1998 World Cup in France. His four goals, often amid high drama, propelled his nation to an undefeated opening round in its group, then a near-upset of mainstay Germany. He also pleased fans in such places as Monterrey and Necaxa. That Los Angeles signed him, and paid dearly in cash and players, reflect his popularity in the Hispanic sports market, even though his tenure in the MLS was marked by controversy.

He bonded with Mexican fans during the 1998 World Cup. "I think this is a message to the Mexican people," Hernandez said after its 2-1 defeat to the Germans. "You should trust us. For those who do not trust us, please under-

stand. We have done the utmost. We are extremely proud of what we have done today against the German team."

FURTHER INFORMATION
Periodicals

Penner, Mike. "Hernandez Says the Sub Way Is OK." *Los Angeles Times* (June 7, 2002): D9.

Other

2002 FIFA World Cup Korea Japan, Luis Hernandez Profile, http://fifaworldcup.yahoo.com, (January 29, 2003).
Biography Resource Center, Luis Hernandez Profile, http://galenet.galegroup.com, (January 29, 2003).
"Luis Hernandez Is out of LA and Looking for a Home." SoccerAge.com, http://www.soccerage.com, (November 30, 2001).
"Luis Hernandez Returns to Verzcruz." SoccerAge.com, http://www.soccerage.com, (December 29, 2002).
Rodriguez, Robert. "Hernandez: I Have to Work to Put Myself in the Groove." SoccerAge.com, http://www. soccerage.com, (June 30, 2000).
Wagman, Robert. "MLS Should Write off Hernandez as a Bad Investment and Send Him Packing." SoccerTimes, http://www.soccertimes.com/wagman/2001/jan22.htm, (January 22, 2001).
World Cup 1998 Online, http://www.worldcup.fr/uk/medias, (January 29, 2003).

Sketch by Paul Burton

Grant Hill
1972-

American basketball player

Grant Hill has a rare combination of size, speed, and ball-handling skills that set him apart. Able to create his own shots, Hill averaged more than twenty points per game during five of his first six seasons in the National Basketball Association (NBA); he averaged 19.9 points per game his rookie year. After four years as a star player at Duke University, Hill spent his first six seasons in the NBA with the Detroit Pistons. In 2000 he accepted an offer to join the Orlando Magic, but an ankle injury kept him off the floor for all but a handful of games during the next two seasons.

Privileged Life

Grant Hill was born on October 5, 1972, in Dallas, Texas. His father, Calvin, played football at Yale Univer-

Grant Hill

Chronology

1972	Born October 5 in Dallas, Texas
1990-94	Star forward for the Duke University Blue Devils
1994	Drafted by the Detroit Pistons
1999	Marries Grammy-nominated singer Tamia
1999-2000	Averages career-high 25.8 points, 6.6 rebounds, and 5.2 assists per game
2000	Joins Orlando Magic; injures ankle, requiring three surgeries
2002	Attempts to return to regular play with limited success due to nagging injuries

sity and was an All-Pro player for the Dallas Cowboys. His mother, Janet, a successful attorney and consultant, attended Wellesley College where she shared a suite of rooms with Hillary Rodham Clinton. The family moved to Washington, D.C. when Hill's father was traded to the Redskins, and Hill grew up in Reston, Virginia, an upper-middle-class suburb. An only child, Hill grew up amidst fame, wealth, and privilege. A Porsche and a Mercedes were parked in the driveway, and well-known entertainers, athletes, and politicians were frequent house guests.

Hill was never comfortable with his privileged position in life. "I've always just wanted to blend in and be like everybody else," he told *Sporting News*. "I didn't want anybody, especially my friends, thinking I was better than them. I just wanted to be a down-to-earth guy and have my own identity." So Hill seldom mentioned that he was Calvin Hill's son and preferred to be picked up from school in the family's third car, an old Volkswagen. When Hill's father came to his school to talk to the student body, Hill, an eighth-grader at the time, feigned illness and retreated to the nurse's office rather than endure the extra attention. At home, Hill was under strict rules set out by his parents, including no phone calls until the weekend, and then only one a day.

Naturally inclined to sports, Hill played soccer and basketball. His father refused to allow him to play football until high school, but by then, Hill was dedicated to basketball. At the age of thirteen his summer league team upset a Detroit team, whose players included fu-

ture NBA players **Chris Webber** and Jalen Rose. As a freshman at South Lakes High School in Reston, Hill was asked to skip junior varsity and join the varsity team. Hill balked; he didn't want to leave his friends behind, but his father insisted and Hill reluctantly consented. During his high school years Hill lived for basketball. When he wasn't playing, he would spend hours reviewing tapes of NBA and college games. As a senior he averaged thirty points per game. His father hoped Hill would go to the University of North Carolina, and his mother was counting on nearby Georgetown University. Hill decided on Duke University.

The Duke Years

As a freshman at Duke, Hill joined an already talented team that included Christian Laettner and Bobby Hurley. The team rumbled through the regular season and captured the 1991 National Collegiate Athletic Association (NCAA) championship by beating the University of Kansas in the final game, with Hill delivering a highlight-film, one-handed slam to clinch the win. The following year, with Laettner and Hurley both returning, the Blue Devils were able to repeat the success of the previous year and once again won the NCAA title. Hill's outstanding moment came in the final seconds of the East Regional final against Kentucky. The lead changed several times during the final minutes of the game, and with 1.4 seconds left and down by one, Hill made a perfect pass from under the Kentucky basket to hit Laettner at the free throw line at the other end. Laettner's buzzer-beater ensured the team's advancement to the 1992 finals.

During his freshman and sophomore years, Hill averaged 11.2 and 14.0 points per game, respectively. After Laettner and Hurley both graduated in 1992, Hill became the team's leader. During his junior year, he averaged 18.0 points, 6.4 rebounds, and 2.8 assists per game. Although as a senior Hill led his team back to his third NCAA championship game in 1994, the Blue Devils fell to Arkansas. Averaging 17.4 points, 6.9 rebounds, and 5.2 assists per game, Hill was named the Atlantic Coast Conference Player of the Year and First Team All-American.

Popular NBA Star

Hill was selected by the Detroit Pistons as the third overall pick of the 1994 NBA draft, signing an eight-

Career Statistics

Yr	Team	GP	PTS	P/G	FG%	3P%	FT%	RPG	APG	SPG	TO
1995	DET	70	1394	19.9	.477	.148	.732	6.4	5.0	1.8	202
1996	DET	80	1618	20.2	.462	.192	.751	9.8	6.9	1.3	263
1997	DET	80	1710	21.4	.496	.303	.711	9.0	7.3	1.8	259
1998	DET	81	1712	21.1	.452	.143	.740	7.7	6.8	1.8	285
1999	DET	50	1053	21.1	.479	.000	.752	7.1	6.0	1.6	184
2000	DET	74	1906	25.8	.489	.347	.795	6.6	5.2	1.4	240
2001	ORL	4	55	13.8	.442	1.000	.615	6.3	6.3	1.3	11
2002	ORL	14	235	16.8	.426	.000	.863	8.9	4.6	0.6	37
TOTAL		453	9683	21.4	.474	.257	.748	7.9	6.2	1.6	1481

DET: Detroit Pistons; ORL: Orlando Magic.

year contract worth $45 million. He also signed a lucrative endorsement deal with Fila. Originally contracting with Fila for $6 million a year, in 1997 Hill resigned with the athletic wear company for $80 million over seven years. During his rookie season Hill averaged 19.9 points and 5.0 assists per game. Always a crowd favorite, he became the first rookie ever to lead the league in voting for All-Star Game, and he was named the 1995 co-Rookie of the Year, with **Jason Kidd**, and to the NBA All-Rookie First Team. During the 1995-96 season Hill continued to post excellent numbers and once again led all players in votes for the All-Star Game.

Over the next several seasons, Hill continued to lead the Pistons. Although the team was not competitive in the postseason, Hill earned a reputation as one of the most athletically gifted players in the NBA. Because he didn't drink, smoke, party, use excessive foul language, or cause trouble on or off the court, he was also living up to his reputation as the ultimate NBA "good guy." During a time when the media was raving against the numerous incidents of bad behavior by players in and out of uniform, Hill's good manners and self-effacing attitude was a breath of fresh air for the NBA's image.

The 1997-98 season proved challenging for Hill, who struggled with the team's poor record, 37-45, and the controversial firing of Piston coach Doug Collins. During the 1999 player lockout Hill was criticized by other players for not taking a strong enough stand in favor of the NBA players' union. Despite the feeling the pressure of his position as leader of a losing team, Hill continued to play well, scoring more 21 points per game in both the 1997-98 and 1998-1999 seasons. During the 1999-2000 season the Pistons made it into the playoffs, with Hill averaging a career-high 25.8 points, 6.6 rebounds, and 5.2 assists per game.

Sidelined by Injury

Injury struck Hill at the end of the 1999-2000 season. He missed the last three games of the season due to a bruised bone in his left foot. Although he returned for the playoffs against the Miami Heat, in the second game of the series he broke his left ankle. As a free agency in 2000, Hill accepted an offer to join the Orlando Magic, but only played in four regular season games during the 2000-01 season. He was voted to start the NBA All-Star Game but sat out due to his injury. Hill continued to struggle with injury during the 2001-02 season, sitting out all but fourteen regular season games. By the beginning of the 2002-03 season Hill was making his third comeback attempt after undergoing three surgeries on his left ankle, but he is not pain-free and uncertainty lingers whether he can ever return to the spectacular player that he once was.

Hill married Grammy-nominated singer Tamia on July 24, 1999. Their first child, daughter Myla Grace, was born on February 11, 2002. Hill has often made good on his "good guy" reputation, including serving as the vice-chairperson of the 1999 Special Olympic World Games, donating $1 million to Duke University, and $50,000 to benefit Child Abuse Prevention. If Hill's injuries keep him from returning to prime form, he has nonetheless graced the NBA with his fluid, athletic play and his demeanor as an all-round nice guy, making him one of the most popular players in the league.

CONTACT INFORMATION

Address: Orlando Magic, PO Box 76, Orlando, Florida 32801.

FURTHER INFORMATION

Books

Contemporary Black Biography. Volume 13. Detroit: Gale, 1996.
Contemporary Heroes and Heroines. Book III. Detroit: Gale, 1998.
Newsmakers 1995, Issue 4. Detroit: Gale, 1995.
Sports Stars, Series 1-4. Detroit: U·X·L, 1994-98.

Awards and Accomplishments

1991-92	Won back-to-back National Collegiate Athletic Association (NCAA) tournament championships as a member of the Duke Blue Devils
1993	Named NCAA National Defensive Player of the Year
1994	Named Atlantic Coast Conference (ACC) Player of the Year, First Team All ACC, and NCAA First Team All American; selected third overall in the National Basketball Association (NBA) draft by the Detroit Pistons.
1995	Named NBA co-Rookie of the Year and First Team All Rookie
1995-98, 2000-02	Named NBA All Star
1997	Received the IBM Award; named First Team All NBA

Who's Who Among African Americans, 14th ed. Detroit: Gale Group, 2001.

Periodicals

Addy, Steve. "A Changed Man." *Sporting News* (April 12, 1999): 18.

Albom, Mitch. "Yes, Grant Hill Has Found Rejection Before as We Found Out in this Q & A." Knight Ridder/Tribune News Service (February 5, 1999).

Brewer, Jerry. "Grant Hill Appears to be His Old Self Again." Knight Ridder/Tribune News Service (September 16, 2002).

Chandler, Charles. "Ex-Duke Star Grant Hill, Shoe Company Will Aid Detroit Youth." Knight Ridder/Tribune News Service (August 17, 1994).

Deveney, Sean. "Better? You Bet." *Sporting News* (March 6, 2000): 12.

Farley, Christopher John. "Gentleman Slam Dunker." *Time* (February 13, 1995): 78.

Geffner, Michael P. "The Name of the Father." *Sporting News* (January 16, 1995): 24.

Gutierrez, Israel. "Bad Ankle Has Grant Hill in Regressive State." Knight Ridder/Tribune News Service (November 23, 2002).

McCallum, Jack. "The Man." *Sports Illustrated* (November 25, 1996): 40.

"NBA Star Grant Hill and Wife, Singer Tamia, Tell How They Balance Married Life and Busy Careers." *Jet* (October 30, 2000): 14.

Samuels, Allison, and Mark Starr. "Grant's Hill to Climb." *Newsweek* (October 21, 2002): 58.

Sharp, Drew. "Grant Hill Begins to Appear as Villain." Knight Ridder/Tribune News Service (July 6, 2000).

Singleton, John. "Grant Hill: Basketball's New Big Thing." *Interview* (April 1995): 96.

Stoda, Greg. "Duke's Grant Hill: Everybody's All-American." Knight Ridder/Tribune News Service (December 10, 1993).

Vincent, Charlie. "Hill's Record 1,289,585 Votes Will Go Down in All-Star History." Knight Ridder/Tribune News Service (January 26, 1995).

Zinser, Lynn. "Grant Hill's Gifts: It's Dad's Talent, Mom's Demeanor." Knight Ridder/Tribune News Service (March 16, 1994).

Other

"Grant Hill." National Basketball Association. http://www.nba.com/ (December 11, 2002)

"Grant Hill." Sports Stats.com. http://www.sportsstats.com/bball/national/players/1990/Grant_Hill/ (December 10, 2002).

Sketch by Kari Bethel

Lynn Hill
1961-

American rock climber

World Cup champion Lynn Hill is the best female rock climber in the world, and in the top five overall. In a sport dominated by men, Hill has accomplished feats in climbing that climbers of both genders marvel at. After winning dozens of competitions—against both women and men—Hill retired from competition to pursue climbs in some of the world's most exotic locales.

Hill was born in 1961 in Detroit, Michigan and grew up in Orange County, in southern California. She was the fifth of seven children of James Alan Hill, an aeronautical engineer, and Suzanne Biddy Hill, a dental hygienist. A natural athlete who excelled in swimming and gymnastics, she began climbing with her older sister at age fourteen in California's Big Rock and Joshua Tree National Park. "Early in my climbing career, a guy once said to me after a climb at Joshua Tree, 'Gee, I can't even do that,'" Hill recalled on MountainZone.com. "That statement was the start of a whole process for me in pursuing my own dreams ...." Sexist attitudes in climbing frustrated Hill, whose accomplishments speak for her, regardless of her gender.

Though she is a self-admitted tomboy, Hill is far from strapping or mannish. At five feet tall and about 100 pounds, she is petite. Her arms and shoulders are powerful, and her hands are small, which gives her an advantage slipping her fingers into tiny nooks and crannies to get up a wall. Her size made some climbs more challenging, but was an asset to her on others. She counts Chuck Bludworth, her sister's fiancée, as her first climbing mentor. He encouraged and tested her while climbing at Big Rock, and she was soon leading climbs. At age fifteen, Hill was climbing the "mini-mountains" of the Sierra

Lynn Hill

Nevada range, and had her first experience climbing in ice and snow. She decided icy climbs were not for her.

What really interested Hill was "bouldering," which she discovered at Joshua Tree and still loves to do. Bouldering is like mini-climbing, literally on boulders, usually just a few feet off the ground, but extremely difficult. In bouldering, Hill wrote in *Climbing Free,* "I discovered the heart of free climbing movement in its purest form.... Climbing was beautifully free-form and spontaneous, each movement being different from any other." Hill was obsessed with climbing; she climbed on weekends, and trained and dreamed about climbing during the week.

After twenty years together, Hill's parents divorced, and she immersed herself in climbing. In the early 1980s, Hill was one of a number of climbers from America and abroad who congregated in the Yosemite Valley, living in tents and climbing day in and day out. "I felt an urge to climb that was insistent and compelling," she wrote in *Climbing Free.* Hill became a regular on a route called The Nose up the roughly 3,000-foot face of El Capitan there. At age nineteen, she became the first woman to scale a wall called Ophir Broke in Telluride, Colorado. The accomplishment proved to Hill and everyone else that she was more than just a good climber—she had the potential to be great.

To finance her roving, climbing lifestyle, Hill competed in a TV sports competition, called *Survival of the Fittest.* The contest was a test of athletic prowess over a

series of physical challenges and obstacle courses. The grand-prize money she won four years in a row financed her lifestyle, and she began traveling and competing in Europe, winning cash prizes. She also is sponsored by the adventure gear company, The North Face. All told, Hill has won over thirty international titles.

In 1989, climbing in Buoux, France, Hill made an elementary mistake that almost cost her her life. While climbing with her new husband, Russ Raffa, Hill reached the top of the 72-foot Styx Wall, and called to him to belay her down. When she let go of the wall for him to lower her, Hill kept falling. She crashed through a tree and landed between two boulders. Miraculously, she was alive and had to be helicoptered off the mountain. She suffered only a broken ankle, dislocated arm and a host of bumps, cuts, and bruises. Her mistake? She had forgotten to safety-knot the rope to her harness.

After four months of rehabilitation, Hill was back on the competition circuit, and finished 1989 with more wins than any other female climber. At a World Cup competition in Lyon, France, Hill finally silenced sexists by scaling the same difficult course as her male competitors. In 1990, in Cimai, France, she became the first woman to complete a grade 5.14 climb, the toughest in the sport. She lived and climbed in France in the early 1990s.

Hill gave up competition rock climbing in 1992 to concentrate on often-remote climbs in exotic places like Kyrgyzstan, Vietnam, Thailand, Scotland, Australia, Japan, South America, Italy, and Morocco. In 1993, she became the first person to complete a "free" ascent of The Nose on El Capitan. A free climb is one the climber completes climbing only on rock, using only the hands and feet. Hill was allowed to rest at belay stations, and had a climbing partner to catch her when she fell, but she led all the way and managed to climb sections that had never before been completed without the aid of equipment. Hill returned to The Nose in 1994 and climbed it in less than one day. A free ascent of The Nose has not been accomplished by any other climber.

Though no longer competing, Lynn Hill continues to climb extensively. In 1995, Hill traveled to Kyrgyzstan and made the first free ascents of two 5.12 walls: The 4,000-foot west face of Peak 4810 and the Peak 4240. She established Tete De Chou, rated 5.13b, the hardest climb pioneered by a woman in Morocco. In 1999, she lead an all-woman climbing team to Madagascar to accomplish a first ascent of the 17,500 foot granite wall of the Tsaranoro Massiff. Rated 5.13, this route was the most difficult multi-pitch rock climb ever established by a team of women. She is a member of the elite North Face Climbing Team. Her global climbing expeditions are the subject of many a film crew. After ten years of recording anecdotes about her life, Hill published her autobiography, *Climbing Free: My Life in the Vertical World,* in 2002. She lives in Boulder, Colorado.

After twenty-six years of climbing, Hill seriously considered the question, "What do we conquer in a mountain?" "Certainly, we do not 'conquer' anything by climbing to the top of a rock or peak," she wrote in *Climbing Free.* "For me, climbing is a form of exploration that inspires me to confront my own inner nature within nature. No matter where I am in the world or what summit I've attained, the greatest sense of fulfillment in my life is connected to people."

SELECTED WRITINGS BY HILL:

(With Greg Child) *Climbing Free: My Life in the Vertical World,* W.W. Norton & Company, 2002.

FURTHER INFORMATION

Books

Hill, Lynn, with Greg Child. *Climbing Free: My Life in the Vertical World.* New York: W.W. Norton & Company, 2002.

Johnson, Anne Jeanette. *Great Women in Sports.* Detroit: Visible Ink Press, 1996.

Other

"Lynn Hill: Climbing Free." PlanetMountain.com. http://www.planetmountain.com/english/special/people/hill/ (January 15, 2003.)

"Lynn Hill: Climbing through the glass ceiling." MountainZone.com. http://classic.mountainzone.com/climbing/99/interviews/Hill/ (January 15, 2003.)

"Profile: Lynn Hill." *Outside* online. http://web.outsideonline.com/disc/guest/hill/profile.html (January 15, 2003.)

"Welcome to the Lynn Hill Foundation." Lynn Hill Foundation Web site. http://www.djfoundation.org (January 15, 2003.)

Sketch by Brenna Sanchez

Martina Hingis
1980-

Swiss tennis player

Martina Hingis, who has won five Grand Slam singles titles and over $17 million in prize money, was at the top of her game and the top of the world in 1997, the year she won the Australian Open, Wimbledon, and the U.S. Open, and fell just one match short of also taking the French Open title. She was a brash, self-confident, fun-loving teenager who could dissect an opponent by playing tennis with the innate strategy of a chess master. But, at just five-feet-seven-inches and 130 pounds, Hingis's game of ball movement and finesse has been overcome by a new game of women's tennis that thrives on power.

Born to Play

Martina Hingis was born September 30, 1980 in Kosice, Slovakia (then part of Czechoslovakia). Her father, Karol Hingis, was a mechanic and a tennis enthusiast. Her mother, Monica Molitor, was an eighteen-year-old ranked tennis player from Roznov when she married Hingis; Martina was their only child. Even before her daughter's birth, Molitor was convinced that Hingis was destined for tennis. Hingis first picked up a racket at the age of two, using a full-sized wooden racket with the grip cut away so she could get her small hand around it. At the age of three, the family moved to Roznov, and Hingis began playing on tennis courts. She entered her first tournament when she was four, which she lost handily, 12-0, to an older player.

Hingis's parents divorced when she was three, and her father returned to Kosice. Coached by her mother,

Martina Hingis

Hingis, who is named after Czech tennis legend **Martina Navratilova**, began to compete regularly. By the age of six she had won 80 official matches. At the age of seven, she won a tournament for nine-year-olds playing left-handed due to a broken finger on her right hand. When Hingis was eight years old, her mother married Andreas Zogg, a Swiss computer salesman, and the family moved to Trubbach, Switzerland, near the Swiss border with Liechtenstein. (Molitor and Zogg divorced in 1996.)

As a nine-year-old, Hingis began playing in international tournaments for fourteen-year-olds. Within a year, she was winning some of them. Taking the title at the European Championships in 1991, Hingis began a winning streak that would propel to the top of the professional ranks. The following year, at the age of twelve, she became the youngest player ever to win the Junior French Open, which is open to players up to eighteen years old. When she was thirteen, she won the Junior U.S. Open and the Junior Wimbledon, setting records for both as the tournament's youngest winner.

Turns Professional

Hingis turned professional in 1994, just four days after her fourteenth birthday. For Hingis, tennis was fun, as was traveling the world with her mother, receiving unending attention from the press, and earning millions in endorsement contracts. Winning, Hingis would often unabashedly admit, was easy. She didn't like to practice and traded traditional workouts for horseback riding, hitting a punching

Chronology

1980	Born in Kosice, Slovakia
1994	Turns professional; ends year ranked No. 87
1996	Becomes youngest player to ever win Wimbledon; ends year ranked No. 4
1997	Becomes youngest player in the twentieth century win a Grand Slam title; becomes youngest player to attain No. 1 ranking
1998	Becomes youngest player to defend a Grand Slam title; ends season ranked No. 2; attains No. 1 doubles ranking
1999-2000	Ends seasons ranked No. 1
2001	Ends season ranked No. 4
2002	Ends season ranked No. 11
2003	Does not play in the Australian Open, the season's first Grand Slam, due to nagging injury

bag, and rollerblading. Her ability did not lie in a dominating forehand or a killer serve; rather, Hingis's primary talent was an innate sense of how to play out points—how to manipulate each volley to set up the winning shot.

At a time when women's tennis was reeling from problems caused overzealous parents (**Steffi Graf**'s father went to jail for tax evasion, and **Mary Pierce**'s abusive father was banned from attending tournaments), Molitor received high marks for allowing Hingis to balance tennis with other interests. At most Hingis practiced a couple hours a day and filled her time with movies, dates, horseback riding, and other teenage activities. Hingis signed a five-year contract with U.S. based-agency International Management Group in 1993. Her endorsement deals included Yonex rackets and Opel automobiles, and she inked a contract with the sportswear company Sergio Tacchini for $10 million.

Hingis made her debut on the Women's Tennis Association (WTA) Tour in Zurich as a wild card, ranked No. 378. She won her first professional match, but then lost to fifth-ranked Pierce, 6-4, 6-0. During the 1995 season she won her first match at a Grand Slam event by beating **Lindsay Davenport**, ranked No. 7 at the time, in the Australian Open. She reached her first singles finals that year in Hamburg. In 1996 Hingis continued to gain ground in the rankings after finishing 1995 with a year-end ranking at No. 16. She managed to reach the quarterfinals of the Australian Open, and she defeated Graf, ranked No. 1, in the Italian Open quarterfinals before losing to Conchita Martinez in the finals. At Wimbledon she became the youngest player (15 years, 282 days) to win by taking the doubles title with Helena Sukova. She also became the youngest player to reach the semifinals of the U.S. Open. Before she turned sixteen, Hingis had become the youngest player, male or female, to earn $1 million on the court. She finished the 1996 season ranked No. 4.

Dominates Women's Tennis

In 1997 Hingis dominated the tour. She became the first player since Graf in 1993 to reach the finals of all

Awards and Accomplishments

1991	Wins European Championships
1993	Wins Junior French Open
1994	Wins Junior U.S. Open; wins Wimbledon Juniors
1996	Wins Wimbledon doubles (with Helena Sukova)
1997	Wins Lipton Championship; wins Wimbledon; wins U.S. Open; wins Australian Open singles and doubles (with Natasha Zvereva); named *Tennis* Magazine Player of the Year
1998	Wins Australian Open singles and doubles (with Mirjana Lucic); wins French Open doubles (with Jana Novotna); wins U.S. Open doubles (with Novotna); Wimbledon doubles (with Novotna); wins Chase Championships
1999	Wins Australian Open singles and doubles (with Kournikova)
2000	Wins French Open doubles (with Pierce)
2002	Wins Australian Open doubles (with Kournikova)

The Seven Year Itch

Ahead 6-4, 2-0 in the [1999] French Open final against [Steffi] Graf ... Hingis protested a poor line call, failed to get an overrule and simply couldn't let the matter go. Hingis threw an epic tantrum.... [she] walked around the net to Graf's side and pointed out the spot where her disputed shot had fallen. The French fans pounced; boos and hisses filled the air. Hingis plopped into her chair and refused to play. She was docked a point. She resumed play, held on to her lead and then, serving for the match at 5-4, blew the game. Now Graf pounced. Cheered on by the crowd, she won the second set and took a commanding lead in the third, and still Hingis couldn't stop sulking. Facing two match points, she insulted Graf and the game by serving underhand. The crowd howled, and Graf closed out the match. Hingis stormed off the court and refused to return for the awards ceremony until Molitor dragged her back, her face contorted and teary. When a WTA official tried to guide her toward the podium, Hingis smacked her on the arm.

Source: S. L. Price, *Sports Illustrated,* (June 3, 2002): 70.

four Grand Slam singles events, winning three of the four. Hingis went undefeated through her first 37 matches, tying Navratilova's 1978 second-best record (Graf went 45-0 in 1987). On March 31, 1996, after defeating **Monica Seles** in the Lipton Championships, 6-2, 6-1, Hingis attained the No. 1 ranking, the youngest player to do so since computer rankings were instituted in 1975. She walked through the Australian Open without losing a single set and won her first Grand Slam singles title by defeating Pierce in the finals, becoming the youngest player (16 years, 3 months, 26 days) in the twentieth century to win a Grand Slam title. In April 1997 Hingis took a fall from her horse, suffering a slight tear of the posterior cruciate ligament in her left knee. Undergoing surgery to repair the knee, she sat out several tournaments but returned in time to reach the finals of the French Open, but lost to surprise finalist Iva Majoli. Once again at full strength, Hingis won Wimbledon and the U.S. Open, defeating Jana Novotna (2-6, 6-3, 6-3) and **Venus Williams** (6-0, 6-4), respectively.

Named the Female Athlete of the Year for 1997 by the Associated Press, Hingis became only the fourth player in history to sweep the Grand Slam doubles, winning all four in 1998. She managed to defend her Australian Open title by defeating Martinez, 6-3, 6-3, but failed to win another Grand Slam the remainder of the year and went on a six-month, nine-tournament winless drought before claiming the season-ending Chase Championships. She was eliminated from the French Open and Wimbledon in the semifinals and reached the finals of the U.S. Open, which she lost to Davenport, who took over the No. 1 ranking in September.

Power Overcomes Finesse

During 1999, the supremely confident Hingis began to show cracks in her armor. Prone to speak bluntly and with small regard for tact, Hingis found herself in hot water at the 1999 Australian Open when she reportedly made derisive comments about her openly gay opponent in the finals, Amelie Mauresmo. Hingis was roundly criticized for her remark, which she refused to acknowledge or apologize for. Hingis defeated Mauresmo in the finals to win the Australian Open for the third consecutive year. She followed at the French Open by throwing a tantrum in the finals, which she lost to Graf, that she later called the only moment she regrets in her career.

Hingis reached the Australian Open finals once again in 2000 and 2001, but failed to retake the title either year. Although she went on to win nine tournaments in 2000 and ended the year once again ranked No. 1, something about her self-perceived invincibility had vanished. At Wimbledon in 2001 she won just two games in her first-round loss to unseeded Jelena Dokic. The media began to question whether Hingis's finesse game could stand up to the sheer power of players like Lindsay Davenport, Venus and **Serena Williams**. Questions also began to raised regarding Hingis's drive to win.

In 2002 Hingis played in the finals of the Australian Open for the sixth consecutive year, but lost to **Jennifer Capriati**, 4-6, 7-6(7), 6-2, despite having four match points during the second set. In May 2002 Hingis began to experience nagging injuries. She had surgery on her left ankle and withdrew from the French Open and Wimbledon. She returned for the U.S. Open but lost in the fourth round to Seles. Hingis made several attempts to return to the game, but ended up withdrawing from the Chase Championships and the 2003 Australian Open.

Whether Hingis has the determination and physical ability to return to the game is open for debate. Clearly, however, she came into her career at a perfect time, when women's tennis, rattled by scandalous behavior, was looking for someone gregarious, lively, and confident. Hingis, simply by being a teenager who glowed in the attention from the media and dazzled her opponents on the court, provided a much-needed breath of fresh air to game of tennis.

CONTACT INFORMATION

Address: c/o WTA Tour, 133 1st Street NE, Saint Petersburg, Florida 33701.

FURTHER INFORMATION

Books

The Complete Marquis Who's Who. New York: Marquis Who's Who, 2001.
Newsmakers, Issue 1. Detroit: The Gale Group, 1999.
Sports Stars. Series 1-4. Detroit: U•X•L, 1994-98.

Periodicals

Heilpern, John. "Born to Serve." *Vogue,* (July 1997): 159-61.
"Hingis Pulls Out of Aussie Open." *Asia Africa Intelligence Wire,* (December 11, 2002).
Jenkins, Sally. "Martina Hingis." *Sports Illustrated,* (July 12, 1993): 52-3.
Jones, Chris. "Is It the End for Hingis?" *Europe Intelligence Wire,* (October 15, 2002).
Leand, Andrea. "Second to None." *Tennis,* (April 1999): 34-7.
"New York Court Dismisses Hingis' Suit." *Swiss News,* (November 2002): 4.
Price, S. L. "Inside Tennis." *Sports Illustrated,* (July 5, 1999): 84+.
Price, S. L. "Over the Top." *Sports Illustrated,* (April 7, 1997): 64.
Price, S. L. "The Seven-Year Itch." *Sports Illustrated,* (June 3, 2002): 70+.
Roberts, John. "Tennis: Hingis Left in Wilderness as Power Game Rules World." *Europe Intelligence Wire,* (October 19, 2002).
Starr, Mark. "Martina Redux." *Newsweek,* (June 2, 1997): 60-1.

Other

"Martina Hingis." Sanex WTA Tour. http://www.sanexwta.com (January 8, 2003)

Sketch by Kari Bethel

Elroy Hirsch
1923-

American football player

Elroy "Crazy Legs" Hirsch was one of the National Football League's early pass receiving standouts

Elroy "Crazy Legs" Hirsch

who helped glamorize that position, just as pro football offenses were opening up. "Start with those Crazy Legs, the long, muscular limbs that appeared to gyrate in six different directions when shifted into warp speed," the *Sporting News* wrote. "Elroy Hirsch walked like a duck but ran pass patterns like an awkward young gazelle trying to evade a hungry pursuer."

Defensive backs wore themselves out over 12 years trying to catch Hirsch, who starred for the Los Angeles Rams after three seasons with the Chicago Rockets of the All-America Football Conference. His best year was in 1951, when he caught 17 touchdown passes, nine of 44 yards or more, helping the Rams win the NFL championship. Hirsch, who was central to the Rams' revolutionary "three-end" offense in the 1950s, was inducted into the Pro Football Hall of Fame in 1968. Hirsch also starred in some movies before becoming a Rams executive. From 1969 through 1987, he was athletic director at the University of Wisconsin, where he helped the Badgers to one of their best seasons ever, in 1942.

Wolverine and Badger

Hirsch grew up in Wausau, Wisconsin. "His first challenge as a skinny high school running back in Wausau had been those crazy legs of his," it says on a Web site devoted to a road race named in his honor, the Crazylegs Classic. "One foot points out farther than the other, so he was the halfback who wobbled as he ran."

"Hirsch ran like a demented duck," Francis Powers wrote in the *Chicago Daily News* about Wisconsin's 13-7 win over Great Lakes Naval Station at Chicago's Soldier Field in 1942. "His crazy legs were gyrating in six different directions all at the same time during a 61-yard touchdown run that solidified the win."

At Wisconsin, Hirsch starred as a running back, teaming with Pat Harder to help the Badgers flourish in the grind-it-out Big Ten. In 1942, Wisconsin sported a 8-1-1 record, good for second place in the Big Ten and third nationally in the final Associated Press poll. It was, however, Hirsch's only season with the Badgers. The U.S. Marines sent Hirsch to training program at the University of Michigan the following year, where he also earned All-America honors. At Michigan, he became the only Wolverine athlete to letter in four sports (football, basketball, track, and baseball).

He was the most valuable player in the 1946 College All-Star Game at Chicago's Soldier Field as he led the All-Stars to a 16-0 upset victory over the Rams in a game that annually pitted the top rookies against the defending NFL champions. (The game was discontinued in 1976).

Launches Pro Career

Hirsch was a running back for three seasons for the Chicago's AAFC entry, which changed owners annually and went 1-13 in 1948. Hirsch suffered a fractured skull and missed most of the 1948 season. Hirsch joined the Rams in 1950 and found the environment far different With Hall of Famers Norm Van Brocklin and Bob Waterfield alternating at quarterback, Hirsch and fellow wideouts Tom Fears and Bob Boyd challenged defenders game after game. Van Brocklin threw for 554 yards in one afternoon. "He was quick, elusive and deceptively fast, a deep-threat receiver who terrorized defensive backs for 12 pro seasons," the *Sporting News* wrote. "When Crazy Legs turned on the burners, somebody usually got scorched."

Wide-Open Offense

Rule changes helped open up pro football during this period and helped creative offensives such as the Rams's

prosper. In 1950, the NFL restored unlimited free substitution, opening the way for two-platoon football and specialization. Hirsch changed his position from running back to wide receiver that year. The Rams, gaining in popularity in Los Angeles and perceived as one of the NFL's glamour teams, became the first NFL team to televise all its games, home and away.

Los Angeles competed in four NFL championship games within a seven-year span while Hirsch played, three against the Cleveland Browns. Ironically, the Rams's franchise originated in Cleveland (they are now in St. Louis). In 1951, with Hirsch averaging 22.7 yards during the regular season, the Rams atoned for a last-second 30-28 defeat in the previous year's NFL championship game in Cleveland by defeating the Browns 24-17 in Los Angeles. This was the first NFL game to be televised nationwide, and was the only championship in Los Angeles for the Rams, who had defeated the Chicago Bears 24-14 in a special Western Conference playoff game.

The Rams, who fell to the Philadelphia Eagles for the 1949 title game, also lost to the Browns in 1955. Hirsch retired in 1957, having hauled in 343 receptions over his nine NFL seasons. A movie, *Crazylegs,* was based on his life and career. Hirsch also starred in the 1955 movie *Unchained,* with Chester Morris and Todd Duncan, based on a true story about life on a Chino, California prison farm.

GM, Athletic Director

In 1960, Hirsch succeeded Alvin "Pete" Rozelle as Rams' general manager when the NFL named Rozelle commissioner following the death of **Bert Bell**. Hirsch named Waterfield head coach, but the team struggled on the field and fell to 1-12-1 in 1962. He eventually became special assistant to the president before leaving the organization, after 20 years, to succeed Ivy Williamson as University of Wisconsin athletic director.

He retired from Wisconsin in 1987 after serving the longest tenure ever for a Wisconsin AD. During that time, the men's ice hockey team won four of its five NCAA championships. Hirsch, however, drew fire for botching the search for a men's basketball coach in 1982. Several top candidates rejected Wisconsin, and according to the *Milwaukee Sentinel,* Hirsch was on a

Career Statistics

		Rushing				Receiving			
Yr	Team	Att	Yds	Avg	TD	Rec	Yds	Avg	TD
1946	CHR	87	226	2.6	1	27	347	12.9	3
1947	CHR	23	51	2.2	1	10	282	28.2	3
1948	CHR	23	93	4.0	0	7	101	14.1	1
1949	RAM	68	287	4.2	2	22	326	14.8	4
1950	RAM	2	19	9.5	0	42	687	16.4	7
1951	RAM	1	3	3.0	0	66	1495	22.7	17
1952	RAM	0	0	0.0	0	25	590	23.6	4
1953	RAM	1	6	6.0	0	61	941	15.4	4
1954	RAM	1	6	6.0	0	35	720	20.6	3
1955	RAM	0	0	0.0	0	25	460	18.4	2
1956	RAM	0	0	0.0	0	35	603	17.2	6
1957	RAM	1	8	8.0	0	32	477	14.9	6
TOTAL		207	693	3.3	4	387	7029	18.2	60

CHR: Chicago Rockets (All-America Football Conference); RAM: Los Angeles Rams (National Football League).

Caribbean cruise while appointee Ken Anderson was twice misidentified at a press conference. Days later, Anderson said he would stay at Wisconsin-Eau Claire.

Hirsch's Legacy

Elroy "Crazy Legs" Hirsch is retired and living in Madison, Wisconsin. In addition to his pro football enshrinement, he was inducted into the University of Wisconsin Hall of Fame in 1991. A road race in his honor, the Crazylegs Classic, is held annually in Madison, Wisconsin. He has also been named to the State of Wisconsin, National Football Foundation and the Madison Pen and Mike Club-Bowman Sports Foundation Halls of Fame. He is an ardent booster of Badger sports.

Hirsch, had he played today, would have been a "plays of the week" staple on sports highlight shows. But while he starred before television exposure of football because pervasive, the star appeal of Hirsch, and his Los Angeles Rams teammates of the 1950s, helped popularize the sport and usher in the TV era.

FURTHER INFORMATION

Other

Christl, Cliff. "Only Brewers, Bucks Find Some Success." *Milwaukee Journal Sentinel,* http://www.jsonline.com/sports/century/dec99, (December 4, 1999).

Football Reference.com, Elroy Hirsch statistics, http://www.football-reference.com.players/HirsE100.htm, (January 17, 2003).

Pro Football Hall of Fame, http://www.profootballhof.com/players/enshrinees/ehirsch.efm, (January 18, 2003).

RamsUSA, http://www.ramsusa.com, (January 17, 2003).

Sporting News, http://www.sportingnews.com/nfl/100/89/html, (January 17, 2003).

University of Wisconsin Web site, Elroy "Crazylegs" Hirsch profile, http://www.uwbasgers.com/history/hall_of_fame/1991/hirsch_elroy.aspx, (January 18, 2003).

Sketch by Paul Burton

Mat Hoffman
1972-

American BMX rider

Mat Hoffman, five years old, stood at the top of a home-made ramp in the family's backyard, perched on his BMX bike with only an older brother's grip to keep him from falling over the edge. He pleaded with his brother to hold on tight so, as older brothers will, he dropped him. Hoffman flew down the ramp, and took the jump while keeping his balance. After yelling at his brother for the breach in confidence, Hoffman demanded they do it again. And with that, an extreme athlete was born.

The World's Most Extreme Athlete

BMX's Vert competitions might be the most extreme of extreme sports. The events show off incredible but dangerous bike stunts, crafted by some of the most daring, and some would say deranged, athletes in recent memory. The point is to get as high in the air with your bike as possible so you can come down with the most tricks possible; all while riding within the confines of a

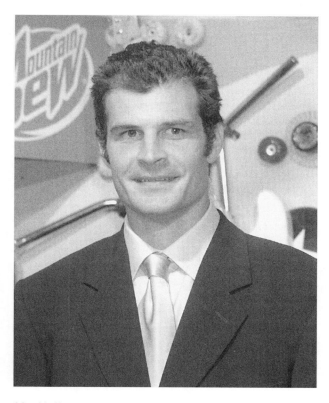

Mat Hoffman

Chronology	
1972	Born January 9 in Oklahoma City, Oklahoma
1985	Goes amateur in the Bicycle Freestyle circuit at the age of 13
1988	Goes pro at the age of 16, a sport record
1991	With BMX suffering, Hoffman starts his first business, Hoffman Promotions, meant to promote his own image as well as vert riding
1992	Starts Hoffman Bikes, a line of bikes designed by Hoffman.
1993	Starts Hoffman Manufacturing to keep up with demand for the Hoffman Bikes lineup

twelve-foot high and sixty foot wide half-pipe. But if BMX is the most extreme sport, then that would make Hoffman the most extreme athlete. Hoffman, considered the greatest Vert rider of all time, pioneered the sport, changing it from a hobby of a select few to a huge community of exceptional athletes and millions of fans.

Hoffman was born January 9th, 1972 in Oklahoma City, Oklahoma. He displayed his trademark eagerness for danger early on. At five, he leapt from two stories high with an open umbrella in his hands, inspired by television's *The Flying Nun*. Once he showed an interest in BMX bikes his father supported him by building bike ramps in the backyard. At first his mother, Joni, couldn't even watch him practice. But after Hoffman went amateur in the Bicycle Freestyle circuit at the age of thirteen, she knew he was good. She also knew he was hooked and when he got hooked there was no talking him out of it. Eventually, she became such a fan that she started bringing cameras to the competitions. Hoffman quickly climbed to the top of his amateur class and eventually became a pro at sixteen—his first record of many more to come.

He quickly established himself as an athlete unlike any other in his sport. He set record after record as he created new tricks on a weekly basis that captured the imagination of everyone who saw him perform. He believes his unique tricks may end up being his legacy "I just love creating new tricks," he told Ram Ganesan of

New Straits Times. "It's all about using your imagination, being part of a constant building process. I believe in challenging myself, in seeing whether I can master a certain move." He holds the world record for "highest air," floating five stories high over a sold out auditorium. One of his biggest stunts got him a lot of media attention when he rode off a 3,800-foot cliff. With a parachute, of course.

Pioneer on a Bicycle

While America's youth abandoned BMX in droves in the 1980s and early '90s Hoffman stuck with it and displayed an athleticism that drew millions of kids back into the fold. Primarily known for his incredible jumps and innovative stunts, Hoffman, also known as 'Condor,' likes to make a point that BMX isn't simply a sport, it's a lifestyle. His successful forays into promotion, design, manufacturing, and licensing back him up; his name has been on everything from an autobiography (*The Ride of My Life*) to best-selling video games (BMX Pro 1 and 2) to his own Hoffman-branded merchandise, like a recent action-figure lineup that sold 1.7 million figures.

But the notoriety came with a lot of pain. After fourteen operations, fifty broken bones and a three day coma, Hoffman's love for BMX has taken its toll on him. "I actually flat-lined once," he told ESPN's Dan Patrick. In 1993, after a stunt for MTV went bad, Hoffman's spleen burst. The doctors thought Hoffman had around twenty minutes to live due to excessive internal bleeding. They removed his spleen as a last-ditch effort and it ended up saving his life. "You can say I've challenged medical science on several occasions," he told Patrick. His attitude toward such risk? He told Sophia Hollander of the *New York Times,* "In order to experience all the pleasures and successes in life, you have to be willing to take all the pain and failures."

He founded Hoffman Promotions in 1991, a company designed to promote Hoffman's skyrocketing fame and, consequently, BMX in general. That same year he began to design and manufacture bikes under the Hoffman brand. Though he started small (the industry was in a serious slump) his company now churns out around

Awards and Accomplishments

1987	Wins first Vert World Championship
1989	Lands his first 900 - a double spin on the bike
1995-96	1st Place, X-Games, Bicycle Stunt, Vert
1997	3rd Place, X-Games, Bicycle Stunt, Vert
1999	1st Place, Freestyle Challenge, Bicycle Stunt, Vert
1999	1st Place, B3, Bicycle Stunt, Vert
2000	1st Place, X Games trial, Bicycle Stunt, Vert
2000	1st Place, X Games trial, Bicycle Stunt, Vert
2000	1st Place, World Championships, Bicycle Stunt, Vert
2000	1st Place, Soul Bowl, Bicycle Stunt, Vert
2000	1st Place, Freestyle World Championships, Bicycle Stunt, Vert
2000	1st Place, CFB, Bicycle Stunt, Vert
2000	1st Place, CFB, Bicycle Stunt, Vert
2000	1st Place, CFB, Overall Bicycle Stunt
2000	1st Place, Bicycle Stunt Series, Overall Bicycle Stunt
2000	1st Place, B3, Bicycle Stunt, Vert
2000	1st Place, Alp Challenge, Bicycle Stunt, Vert
2000	1st Place, Alp Challenge, Bicycle Stunt, High Air
2001	1st Place, CFB, Bicycle Stunt, Vert
2001	Launches 26½ feet off of a 24 foot ramp, achieving a world record 50 feet of air
2001	ESPN Action Sports and Music Awards honored Hoffman with a Lifetime Achievement Award

30,000 bikes a year. But his greatest contribution to the sport may be the Hoffman Sports Association (HSA), responsible for producing ESPN's successful *X Games*. The X-Games, a competition designed for extreme sports like BMX and skateboarding, has become a phenomenon after only a few short years. Cities around the world vie to host the games since they're reported to net tens of millions of dollars for local economies. HSA also developed the Crazy Freakin' Bikers Series (CFB), a competition that provides stunt bikers a forum to compete in. Over the years it has become a major stepping-stone to the Bicycle Stunt (BS) Series. In a true testament to his well-deserved pioneer reputation, Hoffman has earned Vert series titles for the CFB, the BS Series, and has been world champion ten times.

Athlete and Entrepreneur

Hoffman was injured so often that he got used to waking up from a bad stunt with no idea who he was. He would need someone there to remind him and fill him in on why he was hospitalized. But after surviving a frightening accident during big-ramp racing (where a motorcycle drags the bike full throttle to the top of the ramp and then releases it) his wife held their newborn baby up and played with her to remind him of what he'd miss if he kept going. He agreed to retire from the riskier stunts, but swears he'll keep going until he can't go any more. "When the day comes that I choose to not ride anymore it won't be because of injury," he wrote in his ESPN online journal. "It will be because the challenge of injury will have become more than what my will and determination can overcome." In the meantime, Hoffman continues to build his legacy by performing in select competitions and

even appearing in movies. His most recent appearances include *XXX* and *Jackass: The Movie*; as well as an IMAX film called *Ultimate X: The Movie*.

Because of Hoffman's tireless dedication to his sport, BMX and many other "extreme sports" have become commercially viable and respected, especially among the world's young people. He lives in the same town he grew up in, Oklahoma City, with his wife, Jaci, and their daughter, Giavanna.

CONTACT INFORMATION

Address: Mat Hoffman, Hoffman Bikes, 4307 N Walnut Avenue, Oklahoma City, OK, 73105.

FURTHER INFORMATION

Periodicals

Ganesan, Ram. "Promise of the Flying Condor." *News Straits Times—Management Times* (January 10, 2003).

Hollander, Sophia. "Taking Life to the Edge, And Spins and Jumps, Too." *New York Times* (October 8, 2002): D2.

Other

Patrick, Dan. "Outtakes with Mat Hoffman." ESPN. com.http://espn.go.com/talent/danpatrick/s/2001/ 0808/1236775.html (December 6, 2001).

Sketch by Ben Zackheim

Ben Hogan
1912-1997

American golfer

Ben Hogan was one of the greatest golfers of all time, but his greatness stemmed from his personality as much as from any innate skills at golf. Hogan was known for his icy concentration, for his marathon practice sessions, but most of all for battling back from a near-fatal 1949 car crash and returning to golf when the doctors said that he would never walk again.

Growing Up

Hogan was one of three children of rural Texas blacksmith Chester Hogan and his wife, Clara. The family moved to Fort Worth in 1921, and shortly thereafter, on Valentine's Day 1922, Chester Hogan shot himself, in the family home, with his wife and children in the house. After Chester Hogan's death, the Hogan family's life became financially precarious. Clara Hogan took a

Ben Hogan

Chronology

1912	Born August 13 in Stephensville, Texas
1921	Hogan family moves to Fort Worth
1922	Hogan's father commits suicide
1930	Turns professional in February
1935	Marries Valerie Fox April 14
1938	Wins first professional tournament, the Hershey Four-Ball
1943	Drafted into the U.S. Army Air Corps in March
1945	Discharged from the military in August
1948	Wins first major tournaments
1949	Involved in near-fatal car accident
1951	*Follow the Sun* is released
1954	Founds Hogan Company
1971	Retires from competitive golf
1989	Ben Hogan Tour for aspiring professionals launched
1990	Hogan Award, honoring the top U.S. college golfer, first awarded
1997	Dies at his Fort Worth home July 25
1999	Room dedicated to Hogan opens at the USGA Museum

job as a seamstress, and Hogan's fourteen-year-old brother, Royal, quit school and became a deliveryman. Hogan, then nine, sold newspapers at a nearby train station after school for a time, but a few years later he discovered that he could make much better money working as a caddie at the Glen Garden Country Club: fifty cents or more for each bag carried.

Boys were only allowed to caddie at Glen Garden until they were sixteen, so at that point Hogan was forced to broaden his horizons to the affordable public courses in the area. He, his brother Royal, and some other friends, sometimes including fellow former Glen Garden caddy and future fellow golfing star Byron Nelson, would often play together, although Hogan spent much time practicing alone as well. He had dropped out of high school during his senior year, so he had all day to work on his game. Soon his obsessive practicing began to pay off: Hogan placed second in the first amateur tournament he competed in, in the summer of 1928, and achieved another second place in the summer of 1929.

The Professional Tour

In February of 1930, after the Depression had dealt another blow to the already-struggling Hogan family, Hogan registered for the Texas Open as a professional. He had a poor beginning and quit after the first two rounds. He tried again a week later, at a tournament in Houston, and again quit after two rounds. Hogan went home and worked at odd jobs for a year while continu-

ing to practice whenever possible in preparation to give the tour another try in 1931.

The professional tour was not a place to get rich in the Depression years, even for the winners, and Hogan was not yet one of those. He finished in the money for the first time in Phoenix in the winter of 1931-32, but that win only provided $50. After a few more opens, with occasional but always small winnings, Hogan was broke. He returned to Texas and took a job as the club professional at the Nolan River Country Club, an hour south of Fort Worth. There, he continued to practice, but he also found some time to date a young woman named Valerie Fox, whom he had first met in Sunday school in Fort Worth several years before.

Hogan and Fox were married on April 14, 1935. Two years later, after buying a used Buick and saving up $1,400, they decided to give life on the professional tour one more try. By January of 1938, they were down to $86, but then, just before they went completely broke, Hogan won $285 at the Oakland, California Open. Within months, he was offered a $500 a year job as a club professional in White Plains, New York, and he was invited to play in his first Masters. That July, Hogan had his first ever tournament win, at the Hershey Four-Ball, which paid him $1,100. He finished in the money in all of the remaining tournaments of the year, for total winnings of $4,150.

Success

Hogan came into his own starting in 1940. He had a three-tournament winning streak in March of that year, and although he only won one more that year he was still the tour's leading money winner for 1940. He was on top again in 1941, with five tournament wins, and again in 1942. Also, in the spring of 1941, Hogan returned to Hershey as its club professional. At that club, Hogan had no responsibilities to give lessons or otherwise interact

Awards and Accomplishments

1940-42. 1946, 1948	Won Varden Trophy
1941, 1951	Ryder Cup (player)
1946	Professional Golfers' Association Tour
1947	Ryder Cup (player and captain)
1948	Professional Golfers' Association Championship
1948, 1950-51, 1953	U.S. Open
1948, 1950-51, 1953	Named Player of the Year
1949, 1967	Ryder Cup (captain)
1951, 1953	Masters
1953	British Open

Related Biography: Golfer Byron Nelson

Byron Nelson got his start in golf the same way that Ben Hogan did, working as a caddy at the Glen Garden Country Club. Nelson, born John Byron Nelson on February 4, 1912, was notable among the caddies for lacking their usual vices, most notably smoking, swearing, and fighting, and for his unusual level of skill at golf. Nelson just barely edged out Hogan in Glen Garden's caddy tournament in December of 1927. The next year, when the boys became too old to caddy, Nelson was honored with a junior membership in the club. This gave Nelson a competitive advantage over Hogan, since Nelson could enter the many members-only tournaments in which Hogan, who was relegated to public courses, could not compete.

After high school, Nelson originally took a job clerking for a railroad company, but when he was laid off because of the Depression he turned professional and tried to make a living at golf instead. For the next thirteen years, Nelson consistently out-golfed Hogan, although the two became close friends. Nelson's wife Louise and Valerie Hogan got along very well, often sitting together in the clubhouse while their husbands competed, and the Nelsons and the Hogans often caravanned together when touring.

Nelson took third in the first professional tournament he entered, in 1932, and was winning tournaments by 1935. His most spectacular season was 1945, when many but by no means all of the other top-level golfers were unable to compete because of the war. (Nelson, who had mild hemophilia, was considered medically unfit to serve.) That year Nelson won eleven straight PGA tour events, as well as seven others for a season total of eighteen. Both figures are records that still stand, as is Nelson's record of finishing in the money in 113 consecutive tournaments.

In 1946 Nelson retired from touring full-time and settled down back in Texas on the Fairway Ranch, which he bought with his winnings from the 1945 season and where he still makes his home.

with the fellow members: all he had to do was play in tournaments, provide publicity for the club, and play the course often enough that the members could observe him and attempt to learn from what they saw. For this, he received several thousand dollars per year.

The one thing lacking for Hogan was a win in a major tournament, and the entry of the United States into World War II and the accompanying decrease in the touring schedule deprived him of several chances from 1942 on. Hogan did win the Hale America Open in 1942, which was held in lieu of the U.S. Open, but this was not technically a major. At the Masters, the only official major to be held that year, Hogan tied with Nelson in the first three rounds, only to lose by one during a playoff round the next day.

The tour was officially suspended in 1943, and in March of that year Hogan was drafted. He trained to become a flight instructor, went to Officer Candidate School, and eventually became a captain. He continued to play golf as often as he could, including a weekly round with the commander of his base for a time, and in 1944 when professional golf resumed Hogan made it to a few tournaments. He was discharged in August of 1945 and rejoined the tour almost immediately.

Nelson had not been drafted because of a medical condition, so he had spent the war years working on his golf full-time, playing war-benefit exhibitions in 1943 when there was no tour. With so many other players off to war, Nelson had been the undisputed champion in 1944 and early 1945. Although Hogan had not been practicing with his usual ferocity for more than two years, he quickly challenged Nelson for the top spot. Although the major championships again eluded him, he won thirteen of the thirty-two tournaments he entered, becoming the Professional Golfers' Association of America champion and the top money-winner of 1946.

Disaster

Hogan went on to repeat his success in 1947 and 1948. "I've found the secret," he told one sportswriter in 1947, although he never told the sportswriter, or anyone else, what exactly that secret was. Hogan again lost at the majors in 1947, but in 1948 he won both the PGA Championship and the U.S. Open. On January 10, he was on the cover of *Time* magazine. Less than a month later, it looked as if his career was over.

Hogan and Valerie collided head-on with a Greyhound bus on bridge in rural Texas on February 2, 1949. Just before impact, Hogan threw himself across Valerie to try to protect her. It worked—Valerie suffered only scratches and bruises—and saved Hogan's life as well. The steering wheel of the Hogans' Cadillac shot into the passenger compartment and impaled the empty driver's seat, fracturing Hogan's left collarbone on the way, while the engine crushed Hogan's left leg, fractured his pelvis, and caused severe internal injuries. After two weeks in the hospital, he started developing life-threatening blood clots in his veins. Hogan was operated on by the best vascular surgeon in the country, who tied off the large vein that returns blood from the lower body. This prevented blood clots from reaching Hogan's lungs, where they were most dangerous, but it also hampered circulation to his legs, leading to problems walking that would last for the rest of his life.

Comeback

Hogan was discharged from the hospital two months later, and before the end of the year he was well enough to captain the United States' Ryder Cup team on its trip

Ben Hogan

to Britain. His left shoulder still caused him great pain, and his putting, never his strong suit, was hampered by a partial loss of sight in his left eye caused when the dashboard smashed into his face, but he was determined to make it back into competitive play. In January of 1950, less than a year after the accident, he did, losing the Los Angeles Open to Sam Snead in a playoff. Then he went on to win the U.S. Open that spring. The story of Hogan's comeback was so compelling that in March of 1951 a movie about it, *Follow the Sun,* was released.

The year 1951 was also a strong one for Hogan. Just weeks after the premiere of *Follow the Sun* he won his first Masters ever, and later in the season he won the U.S. Open for a second year in a row. 1953, though, was Hogan's best year ever. He won the U.S. Open for a fourth time and the Masters for a second, breaking the former tournament record for the Masters by five shots. He also traveled to Scotland to play in the British Open, the only time he would ever do so, and won.

The fanfare that accompanied Hogan's trip to the British Open in July of 1953 was intense. The Scots, who dubbed him "The Wee Ice Mon" (Hogan stood five-foot-eight and never weighed much over 130 pounds), turned out to give him the largest audience in the history of the Open. A train that ran by the first hole even made an unscheduled stop to watch him tee off for his first qualifying round. The Americans, for their part, gave him a ticker-tape parade on his return to New York City on July 21. "I've got a tough skin, but this kind of brings tears to my eyes," the notoriously composed Hogan said in a speech in New York that afternoon.

Later Years

Hogan never won another major tournament after the British Open, but he soon started on a new and profitable career: manufacturing golf equipment. Hogan had had an endorsement deal with MacGregor for about twenty years, but they had a very public falling-out around the time of the 1953 U.S. Open. Days after returning to the United States from Scotland, Hogan was hard at work setting up his own club and ball factory in Fort Worth. Once the Hogan Company was established, Hogan worked a two-hour day, from ten to noon, and then spent the afternoon playing golf. He continued to compete in tour events until 1971, winning his last tournament, the Colonial National Invitation, in 1959.

Marvin Leonard, a department store magnate whom Hogan had caddied for at Glen Garden and become friends with, built his own golf course in Fort Worth in the late 1950s. When the Shady Oaks Country Club opened its doors in 1959, it became Hogan's home course and would be for the rest of his life. He and Valerie even built a new home near the course. Hogan had a private, reserved table in a corner of the clubhouse, overlooking the eighteenth hole, where he ate lunch alone many days even after he stopped playing golf in the late 1980s. Hogan died in Fort Worth in 1997, after battling colon cancer and Alzheimer's disease.

Hogan's Legacy

Hogan's most lasting contribution to the sport of golf may be his 1957 guide *Five Lessons: The Modern Fundamentals of Golf,* which became a handbook for thousands of weekend golfers and aspiring professionals. "Never has there been a golfer who influenced the swing more than Ben Hogan," PGA Tour Hall of Fame inductee Johnny Miller told Jimmy Burch of the *Knight Ridder/Tribune News Service.* "I still study his book as if it's true scripture." Other golfers studied not just Hogan's writings, but his actual swing; **Lee Trevino** and **Jack Nicklaus** both changed their golfing styles after watching Hogan, and **Nick Faldo** and **Tiger Woods** have both admitted to spending hours studying old films of Hogan's playing. Presumably, knowing this would make Hogan very happy: "Hogan wanted the standards he left for the game to speak more eloquently than his words," Nelson wrote in *Sports Illustrated*, shortly after Hogan's death.

SELECTED WRITINGS BY HOGAN:

Power Golf, New York: Barnes, 1948.
The Complete Guide to Golf by Ben Hogan and Others, New York: Maco Magazine Corporation, 1955.
(With Herbert Warren Wind) *Five Lessons: The Modern Fundamentals of Golf*, New York: Barnes, 1957.

FURTHER INFORMATION

Books

Sampson, Curt. *Hogan*. Nashville: Rutledge Hill, 1996.

Periodicals

Alexander, Jules. "Hogan: One of a Kind." *Sports Illustrated* (fall, 1992): 42-51.

Arkush, Michael. "1940s: Byron Nelson." *Golf World* (December 17, 1999): 44.

Blount, Terry. "Golfing Legend Ben Hogan Dies." *Houston Chronicle* (July 26, 1997): 1.

Burch, Jimmy. "Ben Hogan's Impact on Golf Reached from One Era into Another." *Knight Ridder/Tribune News Service* (July 26, 1997): 726K3093.

Burch, Jimmy. "Hogan Award Receiving New Distinction, and Other Notes." *Knight Ridder/Tribune News Service* (July 25, 1997): 725K2859.

Burch, Jimmy, and Piller, Dan. "Legendary Golfer Ben Hogan Dies at Age 84." *Knight Ridder/Tribune News Service* (July 25, 1997): 725K2859.

Curtis, Gregory. "Golfer of the Century." *Texas Monthly* (December, 1999): 148.

Goodwin, Stephen. "Ben Hogan (1912-1997): He Changed the Game, and How We Play It, Forever." *Golf Magazine* (October, 1997): 68-70.

Hanna, Vincent. "Memories of a Morose Master of Golf." *Guardian* (London, England) (September 18, 1996): 24.

Heaster, Jerry. "Ben Hogan Stood for Everything His Fans Revered." *Knight Ridder/Tribune News Service* (July 31, 1997): 731K4267.

"Hogan Room Opens at USGA Museum." *Florida Times Union* (June 11, 1999): D-3.

Huggan, John. "Hogan's Command Performance." *Golf Digest* (July, 1999): 108.

Kindred, Dave. "Golf's Greatest Shotmaker." *Sporting News* (August 4, 1997): 8.

Maher, John. "Golf's Self-Made Master Passes On." *Austin American-Statesman* (July 26, 1997): A1.

Nelson, Byron. "The Mystique Lives On." *Sports Illustrated* (August 4, 1997): 26-29.

Rushin, Steve. "Hogan's Golfing Heroes: Ben Hogan's Company Has Funded a Tour for Pros Aiming at the Big Time." *Sports Illustrated* (May 7, 1990): 59-60.

Sirak, Ron. "1950s: Ben Hogan." *Golf World* (December 17, 1999): 48.

Skidmore, Roger. "Hogan the Hero Will Live in Carnoustie's Memory Forever as Open Prepares for New Champion." *Sunday Mercury* (Birmingham, England) (July 18, 1999): 92.

"Texas Classics." *Texas Monthly* (December, 2000): S32.

Verdi, Bob. "The Grillroom: Byron Nelson." *Golf Digest* (July, 2000): 228.

Sketch by Julia Bauder

Chamique Holdsclaw
1977-

American basketball player

Chamique Holdsclaw's story is one of courage. She struggled against imposing odds to escape the inner city of Queens, New York, becoming Women's National Basketball Association (WNBA) Rookie of the Year in 1999. Setting milestones all along the way, Holdsclaw set all-time scoring and rebound records in high school and college. In 1999 when *Sports Illustrated* listed the fifty greatest sports figures from New York, newcomer Holdsclaw appeared at number forty-seven, cited for her four high school championships for Christ the King High School, and for her four-time run as an All-American. Her high school team's four-year record of 106-4 was impressive. She was a member of championship teams for eight consecutive seasons, beginning with a junior national championship in junior high school, through four Class A state championships at Christ the King High School, and three successive National College Athletic Association (NCAA) titles for the Lady Vols of Tennessee.

Born Chamique (pronounced Sha-MEEK-Wah) Shaunta Holdsclaw on August 9, 1977, in Flushing, Queens, she lived with her unmarried parents, Bonita Holdsclaw and Willie Johnson until the age of eleven. Holdsclaw's mother, a data entry clerk, and her father, an auto mechanic, battled alcohol problems, leaving Holdsclaw and Davon, her younger brother, too frequently on their own. The children sometimes scrounged for meals, and were unsupervised overall, with Holdsclaw looking after her brother as best as a small girl might.

Holdsclaw was eleven when she and her brother were placed with their grandmother, June Holdsclaw, at Astoria House in Queens, a housing project well-known for depravity and crime. June Holdsclaw provided a stable, structured home life for the two children, and when

Chamique Holdsclaw

Chronology

1977	Born August 9 in Flushing, New York
1999	Goes to Washington Mystics as a forward, number one draft pick in the inaugural WNBA draft, and only college player taken in the first round; achieves season average of 16.9 points, 7.9 rebounds, and 2.4 assists per game after starting 31 of 32 games; ranks sixth in scoring, third in rebounding; named as Special Sports Correspondent for Nickelodeon Games and Sports (GAS) cable network on May 11; graduates with a degree in political science
2000	Ranks seventh in average scoring in WNBA at 17.5 and seventh in rebounds per game at 7.5 and third in minutes per game with 35.3
2001	Publishes a book during the off-season, *Chamique: On Family, Focus and Basketball*; releases her own shoe: BBMiqueShox

Holdsclaw skipped school the first time, there were no second chances. She was enrolled immediately at Queens Lutheran School where the teachers were more demanding and students were better supervised.

By junior high school Holdsclaw's innate effervescence overflowed onto the neighborhood basketball courts. Already as a child she had studied ballet and jazz and performed on stage at New York's Lincoln Center for the Performing Arts. Now, living just minutes from Madison Square Gardens, she dreamed of playing basketball there as an adult. She had learned some game technique from her Uncle Thurman and soon earned the nickname Flat-out for her flat-out refusals to miss a chance to shoot hoops with her friends.

At the Astoria House after school program she dominated the all-male playground field. She had hops and she had a game, giving new definition to "Playing like a girl!" As she readied for high school, Tyrone Green, her coach in the after school program, dropped the word to Christ the King High School coach Vincent Cannizzaro to come and take a look. Holdsclaw could toss the ball goal-to-goal, a skill that duly impressed Cannizzaro, as did her ability to dominate the all-male court.

Four straight championship seasons followed at Christ the King, and as the dust cleared, Holdsclaw graduated from high school, leaving behind two all-time school records. She accumulated 2,118 points and 1,532 rebounds over four years. Additionally Holdsclaw spent her secondary school summers traveling for the Amateur Athletic Union (AAU) with Cannizzaro. By her senior year she was posting stats of 24.8 points per game and averaging 15.9 rebounds.

While some high school athletes might peak early, Holdsclaw's court dominance was far from over. At her grandmother's urging she accepted a scholarship to the University of Tennessee in Knoxville where she impressed the women's coach, **Pat Summitt**, with a special sense of confidence and strong will to win. Harriet Barovick quoted Summitt in *Time*, "Coaching Holdsclaw was an opportunity to 'raise the intensity level of one of the most gifted high school players I'd seen....' [she] used to laugh away losses.... [but] hates to lose." Summitt put Holdsclaw on the varsity team, the Lady Vols (Volunteers), with little hesitation.

As a freshman starter, Holdsclaw was named Southeastern Conference Player of the Week in her first week. Also as a freshman Holdsclaw made All-American first team. ESPN named her College Basketball Player of the Week, and she was the first woman ever to get the nod. The Lady Vols won the NCAA championship that year, and in the end the fuss over the first-year starter proved to be much more than hype. The final stats showed that she led her team both in scoring and in rebounding for the season.

What amounted to a sophomore year slump for Holdsclaw and the Lady Vols during the 1996-97 season might have been the envy of a lesser team. Despite finishing the season with ten games in the loss column, the squad won an historic back-to-back NCAA championship—only the second on record with the NCAA. Holdsclaw led the team with 20.2 points per game that year.

Holdsclaw returned at full steam for a most impressive college season in 1997-98. She led the team to a 39-0 record and a third championship. In the conference finals against Louisiana Tech University, she scored twenty-five points, hooked ten rebounds, and recorded six assists and a steal, bringing Tennessee to a final

Career Statistics

Yr	Team	GP	FG%	3P%	FT%	RPG	APG	SPG	BPG	TO	PF
1999	WAS	31	.437	.172	.773	7.90	2.4	1.19	.87	3.48	2.20
2000	WAS	32	.465	.256	.680	7.50	2.5	1.47	.56	2.91	2.30
2001	WAS	29	.400	.239	.682	8.80	2.3	1.52	.48	3.24	1.70
2002	WAS	20	.452	.393	.830	11.60	2.3	1.00	.30	2.25	2.50
TOTAL		112	.438	.261	.737	8.70	2.4	1.32	.58	3.04	2.10

WAS: Washington Mystics.

Awards and Accomplishments

1995	Olympic Festival; Naismith award as best female high school player, Atlanta's Tip-Off Club; named to Street & Smith All-American; three-time *USA Today* All-American; named Player of the Year by New York City, Rawlings/Women's Basketball Coaches Association, and Touchdown Club (Columbus, Ohio); Southeastern Conference Player of the Week; won Kodak All-American Honors
1997	World Qualifying Tournament; USA Basketball Player of the Year Award; Honda-Broderick Cup from the National College Athletic Association
1997-98	Named most valuable player of the National College Athletic Association playoffs
1997-99	Naismith finalist; won James E. Sullivan award (first female recipient); named AP Women's Basketball Player of the Year
1998	Won Gold medal at the World Championships; honored as one of 12 female athletes selected as inspirational role models by *Women's Sports and Fitness;* Broderick Awards for Basketball Player of the Year and for Athlete of the Year
1998-99	Named female college player of the year; ESPY award for Women's Basketball Player of the Year
1999	Named Women's National Basketball Association Rookie of the Year ($5,000); Named to Kodak 25th Anniversary Team, *Women's Basketball Journal, Sports Illustrated,* and *Sporting News;* National Women's Player of the Year; ESPY award for Female Athlete of the Year; starter in the inaugural Women's National Basketball Association All-Star game
1999-2000	Selected to the USA Basketball team
2000	Selected as one of the Naismith College Basketball Players of the 20th Century on March 21; won a gold medal at the Olympic Games in Sydney; league All-Star game starter

Recipient of Conde Naste's Woman of the Year and *USA Today*'s "Shining Star in Basketball."

University of Tennessee male/female all-time leading scorer with 3,025 points, and leading rebounder (1,295).

One of only five NCAA females to achieve 3,000 points.

College jersey, number 23, was retired by University of Tennessee Lady Volunteers (only the fourth jersey ever retired).

Led Lady Volunteers to three Southeastern Conference titles.

Twice-named most valuable player of the Southeastern Conference play-offs.

Has a street named after her in Tennessee.

Named Miss Basketball of New York State on three occasions.

score of 93-75. Holdsclaw at that point boasted a track record of eight championships in eight years. She earned the most valuable player (MVP) title for the collegiate final four (NCAA finals). Two years behind Holdsclaw were freshmen Tamika Catchings and Semeka Randall, who rounded out a collegiate power player trio, which came to be called "The Meeks."

Tennessee lost the championship in 1999—Holdsclaw's senior year—having recorded only fourteen losses during the previous three-year period. Holdsclaw regardless was one of only twelve college athletes to be drafted that year, going to the Washington Mystics as the first pick in the first round. The recent demise of the American Basketball League (ABL) had created large pool of professional players from which to pick, and Holdsclaw was the only collegiate draftee to go in the first round. When she graduated with a B.A. in political science that year, she left behind an all-time school record of 3,025 points and 1,295 rebounds, more than any player ever in the history of the school—male or female.

Holdsclaw's pro rookie season was as remarkable as was her past. She started in thirty-one out of thirty-two games and was the only rookie to appear on the WNBA's inaugural All-Star team. With a year-end scoring average of 16.9 points per game she was named Rookie of the Year. Having spent her college summers traveling internationally with the U.S. National team, Holdsclaw was named to the gold-medal U.S. women's basketball team for the summer Olympics in Sydney, Australia, in 2000.

From her outstanding high school and college years, her participation on the Olympic Basketball team, and now as a star in professional basketball with the Washington Mystics, Chamique Holdsclaw has proven herself one of the greats in American basketball.

CONTACT INFORMATION

Address: c/o Washington Mystics, MCI Center, 601 F St. NW, Washington, DC, 20004-1605.

SELECTED WRITINGS BY HOLDSCLAW:

(With Jennifer Frey) *Chamique: On Family, Focus, and Basketball,* Scribner, 2000.

FURTHER INFORMATION

Periodicals

Business Wire (May 11, 1999).
Business Wire (May 13, 1999).
Jet (March 8, 1999).
Jet (May 24, 1999).
Jet (September 20, 1999).
Jet (February 19, 2001).
Sports Illustrated For Kids (December 1, 1998): 66.
Time (March 22, 1999): 95.

Other

"University of Tennessee Basketball." http://ath.utk.edu/womens/wbb/bios/catchings.htm (January 17, 2003)

Sketch by G. Cooksey

Mike Holmgren

Mike Holmgren
1948-

American football coach

Mike Holmgren has been a NFL head coach since 1992. During his time with the Green Bay Packers, he earned a reputation as one of the game's great strategists, leading the Packers to two Super Bowls, winning the big game in 1997. He is now the coach of the Seattle Seahawks, where he has been unable to repeat his winning performance in Green Bay.

A Teacher and Coach

As a teenager in San Francisco, Holmgren was a star athlete at Lincoln High School. He was an all-city quarterback, president of his class, and, during his senior year, the best football player in the state of California. Holmgren's father was a real-estate sales person and a former semipro football player.

Holmgren attended the University of Southern California from 1966 to 1970. At the school, he played football and dreamed of a career as a quarterback, but injuries prevented him from having more than a backup role with the Trojans. In 1970, he was an eighth-round draft pick of the St. Louis Cardinals, and then played briefly with the New York Jets. He quickly realized that he did not have a future as a player, so he became certified as a teacher and married his wife Kathy, whom he had known since he was 13 years old.

In 1971, Holmgren taught history and coached football at his alma mater, Lincoln High School, then taught and coached at Sacred Heart, a private high school in San Francisco, from 1972-75. He taught history, mechanical drawing, and economics, and coached the football team. Although Holmgren eventually moved entirely into coaching, he retained the belief that teaching was the foundation of all coaching, and even as an NFL coach, he continued to think of himself as a teacher who just happened to be a coach. Holmgren's history keeps him grounded. He remarked to Dan Daley of the *Washington Times,* "[Being a high school coach before becoming an NFL coach] teaches you to appreciate a little more the things that are available on this level. When you've had to count jocks or worry about some little freshman forgetting his mouthpiece, when you've had to ride on buses … it just makes you more grateful for what we have here in the NFL."

In 1975, Holmgren moved on to teach and coach at Oak Grove, a school in the San Diego area, before taking a leave of absence in 1980 to work as offensive co-ordinator/quarterbacks coach at San Francisco State University. His family of six was so poor that they lived in a one-room apartment. This poverty ended when Holmgren became quarterbacks coach at Brigham Young University from 1982 to 1985.

In 1986, Holmgren moved on to become quarterbacks coach of the San Francisco 49ers. Bill Walsh, who hired him, told Paul Attner in the *Sporting News* that he was aware that Holmgren's experience as a coach was limited. However, Walsh noted, "He had an outstanding football mind, he had excellent communication skills, he had a natural easy-going but assertive personality, and he proved to be a hands-on guy who was an excellent teacher. The consummate coach."

Holmgren was quarterbacks coach for the 49ers from 1986 to 1988, and offensive coordinator from 1989 to 1991. During his tenure, San Francisco won the Super Bowl in 1989 and 1990. In 1990, Holmgren received head coaching offers from both the New York Jets and the St. Louis Cardinals. He and his wife, who are both deeply religious, felt that these jobs were simply not right. "We were convinced God had a plan for our lives," Kathy Holmgren told Attner. They decided to wait and see what else came along.

Head Coach of Green Bay

When Holmgren was offered the position of head coach of the Green Bay Packers in 1992, he took it. The Packers, who had done poorly through the 1970s and 1980s, were still shadowed by the memory of their past great coach, **Vince Lombardi**, and it seemed that no one would ever bring them back to the level of greatness they had enjoyed under his guidance during the 1960s. Five coaches had come and gone since Lombardi; Holmgren was the sixth. When he arrived in Green Bay, he told the players that he would expect a lot from them, but if they worked as he told them, they would win. They had an 8-2 record during his first season and made the playoff in his second for the first time since 1982.

Under Holmgren, the Packers added some stellar players: outstanding quarterback **Brett Favre** and defensive end **Reggie White**. White, like Holmgren, was very religious, and said he was waiting for a sign from God to join the Packers; when Holmgren heard this, according to Attner, he left a message on White's answering machine, saying "Reggie, this is God. Go to Green Bay." White went.

In *The Sporting News*, Attner wrote that under Holmgren, "for the first time since the 1960s the Packers have a coach who has nudged aside, albeit just slightly, Vince

Lombardi's still-intense aura and carved out some turf of his own." Lombardi was noted for his tough, bullying manner; Holmgren treated his players with more respect. As Attner noted, "Holmgren disliked being called too nice to coach an NFL team, but he at least directs his cooperation using reasonable tough love."

Holmgren rose to the top of his profession in 1997, leading the Packers to a 35-21 victory over the New England Patriots in Super Bowl XXXI. Green Bay returned to the big game the next year, but lost to the Denver Broncos.

Head Coach and General Manager of Seattle Seahawks

In January of 1999, Holmgren, who had long wanted an opportunity to be both general manager and coach of a team, became the head coach and general manager of the Seattle Seahawks, with an eight-year, $32-million contract. The team had a 9-7 season in 1999 under Holmgren's leadership. However, by October of 2001, the Seahawks had lost 17 of 25 games, including losing in the first round of the 1999 playoffs and 10 of 16 games in 2000. It was the first losing season of Holmgren's 15-year career with the NFL, and according to Michael Silver in *Sports Illustrated,* Holmgren was unsure how to handle losing. "When that negativity permeates the locker room, it can become a cancer," Seahawks linebacker Chad Brown revealed to Silver. "Once certain guys decided he had crossed the line and had said some things they felt weren't appropriate, they sort of shut him off."

In 2001, Holmgren got rid of several veterans, replacing them with inexperienced players and older free agents. Derrick Mayes, who played for Holmgren both in Green Bay and in Seattle, told Silver, "He came to Seattle because he wanted to run the whole show. Well, be careful what you wish for, because you could be neck deep in responsibility."

The Seahawks had a 7-9 season in 2002, and late in December of 2002, Holmgren resigned from his position as general manager of the team, saying he would remain as head coach. In a press conference posted on the Seahawks' Web site, he said that this change would allow him to be freed "just a little bit from the nuts and bolts and daily grind of the general manager field and spend more time on coaching. I just care about doing the best we can and win[ning] some more games," he said.

Unlike many other coaches, Holmgren has a full life outside the stadium, spending time with his family. Holmgren, who is of Swedish descent, told Attner, "With Swedes, the dinner table is very important. Growing up with my parents and grandparents, we would use the dinner table to discuss world problems. Everyone said their piece. My four girls are very verbal. I have to raise my hand to get in a word." Holmgren insists on having Friday nights free to spend with his wife. He told Attner that when he began coaching, he decided that he would never let his job disrupt his marriage, and that he would never take himself too seriously. "I'd like to think I have done a good job with both," he said.

CONTACT INFORMATION

Address: c/o Seattle Seahawks, 11220 NE 53rd Street, Kirkland, WA 98033. Phone: 1-800-635-4257. Online: www.seahawks.com.

FURTHER INFORMATION

Periodicals

Attner, Paul. "Confronting the Lombardi Legend." *Sporting News,* January 27, 1997: 12.
Attner, Paul. "Supreme Seahawk." *Sporting News,* July 12, 1999, 50.
King, Peter. "Green Bay Blues." *Sports Illustrated,* February 16, 1998: 104.
King, Peter. "Homebody Holmgren." *Sports Illustrated,* March 24, 1997: 77.
King, Peter. "Warmed Up." *Sports Illustrated,* January 27, 1997, 70.
Pompei, Dan. "Don't Bet Against Holmgren in His Dual Role in Seattle." *Sporting News,* April 12, 1999: 77.
Silver, Michael. "No Forward Progress." *Sports Illustrated,* October 1, 2001: 38.

Other

"Mike Holmgren," Seahawks.com. http://www.seahawks.com/ (January 4, 2003).
"Mike Holmgren's Tuesday Media Session," Seahawks.com. December 31, 2002. http://www.seahawks.com/ (January 4, 2003).

Sketch by Kelly Winters

Evander Holyfield
1962-

American boxer

Evander Holyfield

Evander Holyfield is a three-time world heavyweight champion who consistently beat heavier opponents through determination and faith in himself. But for many, he will always be the man who got his ear bitten off by **Mike Tyson**. That event actually was a perfect illustration of the differences between Holyfield's calm, professional style and that of some other boxers: thuggish, menacing, angry, and violent beyond reason. In contrast Holyfield, a devout Christian, has always attributed his success in the ring to his faith in God, and while he has not always led an entirely exemplary personal life, he has steadfastly maintained an image of decency and self-control in the ring. He has also displayed considerable courage in the face of opponents who were often bigger and seemingly tougher than he.

"You Finish It Out"

Evander Holyfield was born in Atmore, Alabama, on October 19, 1962, the youngest in a family of eight headed by his mother Annie. When Evander was 5, Annie moved the family to Atlanta, Georgia, where Evander grew up. Nicknamed "Chubby" as a child, Evander was remembered as a rather quiet and unaggressive boy, who tended to avoid fights. But at the age of 8 he started taking boxing lessons at the nearby Warren Memorial Boys Club from Carter Morgan, the Center's boxing coach. According to Holyfield's brother, Bernard, "What initially lured Evander into the ring was the attention he received from Carter Morgan. In a way,

Chronology

1962	Born October 19 in Atmore, Alabama.
1967	Family moves to Atlanta, Georgia
1970	Begins boxing lessons at Warren Memorial Boys Club, trains with Carter Morgan
1978	Death of Carter Morgan, trainer and mentor
1980	Begins amateur boxing
1984	Birth of Evander's first son, Evander Jr., with fiancée Paulette Bowen
1984	Participates on Olympic Boxing Team, gets to finals
1984	Begins professional boxing, as a cruiserweight
1985	Marries Paulette Bowen, May 17
1988	Becomes undisputed World Cruiserweight Champion
1989	Begins boxing as heavyweight, undertakes "Project Omega" to bulk up
1990	Becomes undisputed World Heavyweight Champion
1990	Paulette files for divorce
1992	Loses heavyweight title to Riddick Bowe, October
1993	Regains WBA and IBF heavyweight title from Bowe, November 6
1994	Loses heavyweight title, to Michael Moorer
1996	Mother, Annie, dies after car accident
1996	Marries Dr. Janice Itson, October 3
1996	Defeats Mike Tyson, November 9
1997	In third round of rematch, Mike Tyson bites off part of Holyfield's ear
1997	November, retakes IBF heavyweight title, from Michael Moorer
1998	Settles paternity suit filed by Tamie Dewan Evans, who claims Holyfield is the father of her daughter; court records sealed
1999	March, controversial "draw" in fight with Lennox Lewis lets him keep title
1999	April, Janice files for divorce
1999	November, loses title to Lennox Lewis in rematch
2000	Divorce from Janice finalized, July 10
2000	Wins WBA title from John Ruiz

A Plethora of Titles

One of the more confusing aspects of boxing is the presence of three major organizations, each of which has a champion in 16 different weight classes (including the junior weight classes). These organizations are the World Boxing Association (WBA), the World Boxing Council (WBC), and the International Boxing Federation (IBF), and at any one time there may be a different champion in each organization. At other times, one man may hold the title in two of these, or the title might be vacant. To be undisputed champion in a weight class means that a fighter holds the title in all three organizations.

The Rise of a Boxer

With football proving a disappointment, despite his best efforts, Holyfield returned to boxing, which had the advantage of different weight divisions. He began training seriously with Coach Morgan, who pushed the youth to test his limits, and transcend them. At times, the coach seemed to be driving Holyfield too hard, but Morgan expressed such faith in his potential that Holyfield struggled to be worthy of that faith. Then came a major setback. When Holyfield was 16, Morgan died following a long illness. Again he contemplated quitting, feeling that without Morgan pushing him there was no reason to go on. "Then," recalled his brother Bernard, in *Holyfield: The Humble Warrior,* co-written with Evander, "with a jolt of clarity, Evander realized that their last few training sessions together must have been harder on the ailing coach than on himself. With the clear judgement of hindsight, Evander recognized that the old man's relentless goading had not been based on loss of patience but rather on loss of time." Suddenly it seemed that quitting would be an insult to Morgan's memory. Holyfield returned to the gym to train with Morgan's son, Ted.

Holyfield's next big inspiration occurred when the Olympic Trials came to Atlanta in 1980. Watching the competition closely, he began to see himself as a gold medal contender. It was a question of training and experience, and he knew how and where to get both. After graduating from high school, he worked two jobs, as a lifeguard and as a plane fueler. But mostly he trained, getting up at four in the morning to jog before work and training at the gym after work. He almost never missed a workout, and rested only on Sundays.

He also fought in the Golden Gloves amateur competitions. Between 1980 and 1984 he racked up an impressive record of 160 wins against 14 losses, with 75 knockout wins. He also won the national Golden Gloves amateur title in 1982 and the National Sports Festival boxing title in 1983. And in 1984, he qualified for the Olympic boxing team. Unfortunately, the 1984 Olympics proved somewhat disappointing. After knocking out three opponents, he was disqualified in the championship match after allegedly hitting an opponent a second after the referee had ordered the fighters to separate. This call remains highly controversial, and to this day, Holyfield says, people still ask him, "What

that crusty, freckle-faced coach was the father figure Chubby had always wanted." Before long he was participating in pee wee boxing tournaments in Atlanta, where he was undefeated for two years.

But while he enjoyed boxing, Holyfield's first love was football. He did quite well as a linebacker for the Warren Boys Club team, and dreamed of making the football team in high school. He did make the team as a sophomore at Fulton High School, but the results were frustrating for Holyfield. At five-foot-four inches and 115 pounds, Holyfield was just too small, and game after game he found himself warming the bench. It got so bad that he decided to quit before the end of the season, and told his mother of his decision. She ended the conversation with a simple declaration: "You finish it out."

Indeed, to this day, Holyfield attributes much of his later success to his mother's determination to foster this kind of character in her children. She instilled in him a strong work ethic, a refusal to quit in the face of adversity, and a deep Christian faith that has often carried him through difficult times. Even now, when he signs autographs, he often includes a citation for a Biblical verse. He also gives generously to churches in Atlanta and elsewhere.

Evander Holyfield, left

happened at the Olympics?" Holyfield did get a bronze medal, but after the controversial decision, it seemed more like a badge of shame.

Project Omega

After the Olympics, Holyfield decided to turn pro, as a cruiserweight (maximum 190 pounds). Shortly after turning pro, Holyfield married Paulette Bowen, who had already borne their first child, Evander Jr., and was pregnant with their second. On July 20, 1986, he became the first in his Olympic class to win a championship, after defeating Dwight Muhammad Qawi after a grueling fifteen rounds. This gave him the cruiserweight titles for the World Boxing Federation and the International Boxing Federation, but it would be another two years before he became undisputed champ by defeating Carlos DeLeon, the World Boxing Council's title holder. The win was sweet, but Holyfield soon realized that he'd have to enter the heavyweight division if he wanted to break into the big money and earn the fame of a "real" champ.

With the support of his trainers, a father-son team named Lou and Dan Duva, he announced that he would be fighting as a heavyweight, starting in 1989. Sportswriters were almost unanimous in declaring their disapproval. Holyfield, who usually weighed less than 215 pounds, would be going up against fighters weighing over 230 pounds. Holyfield was determined to overcome

the doubters, and he underwent a new training regime dubbed "Project Omega." For over a year, he ran, swam, lifted weights, and did aerobic exercises under a staff of trainers that included an orthopedic surgeon, an Olympic triathlete, and even a ballet instructor. With their help, he improved his strength, endurance, speed, and agility. The all-around training helped him reach the finals in television's *Superstars*, in which he competed against athletes from a multitude of different sports.

But the real test came in the ring, where Holyfield passed with flying colors. He beat his first six opponents as a heavyweight, opponents who were heavier and, they thought, stronger than he was. He began moving steadily up the ranks and, after he defeated Michael Dukes in March of 1989, he began to be seen as a potential challenger to heavyweight champ "Iron Mike" Tyson. In the midst of negotiations to have the two meet, the incredible happened. In a major upset, Tyson lost his title to James "Buster" Douglas. So Douglas agreed to fight Holyfield.

World Heavyweight Champion

On October 25, 1990, champion and challenger met. Douglas had almost 40 pounds on Holyfield, but it was 40 pounds of flab. And Holyfield was in top shape. Not that he was without problems. A car dealership he had been involved with failed a little before the fight, embarrassing him, and closer to home, his wife Paulette filed

Awards and Accomplishments

1982	Golden Gloves national title
1984	Bronze medal, Olympics, boxing
1986	WBA Cruiserweight champion (Defeats Dwight Qawi)
1987	IBF Cruiserweight champion (Defeats Rickey Parkey)
1988	Undisputed World Cruiserweight Champion (Defeats Carlos DeLeon)
1990	Undisputed World Heavyweight Champion (Defeats Buster Douglas)
1993	Retakes IBF/WBA Heavyweight titles (Defeats Riddick Bowe) (One of three heavyweight champions to regain title from the man who beat him)
2000	Retakes WBA Heavyweight title (Defeats John Ruiz)

for divorce just weeks before the big match. Holyfield's devoutness didn't always translate into strict fidelity to his marriage vows, and when women began throwing themselves at the rising boxing star, he sometimes gave in. Despite all this, Holyfield was primed and ready the night of the fight. In the third round, he felled Douglas with a right-hand punch, and Douglas made little effort to get back up. Holyfield became the undisputed world heavyweight champion. As Douglas Lyons summed it up in *Sports Illustrated,* "It took Evander Holyfield just seven minutes to win boxing's biggest crown." Many critics declared that Douglas had simply lacked heart. Holyfield was more generous in his autobiography: "Who can really judge the heart, or the lack thereof, of another man except God? It appeared to me that Douglas lacked a sense of consciousness."

In Holyfield, the world clearly had a different kind of champion. "A drop of golden sun to Mike Tyson's dark side of the moon, Holyfield is a fervently religious, gospel-singing man who seems to take no visceral pleasure in dismantling his opponents and never stoops to dissing them beforehand," wrote William Plummer in *People Weekly,* summing up the champ's appeal. But he still had to prove himself. The cry for a Tyson-Holyfield match went up almost immediately, but Holyfield settled on an easier fight with a 42-year-old **George Foreman**. Actually, Foreman had won 24 straight fights to get there, and this match proved considerably harder than expected. After twelve grueling rounds, Holyfield won a unanimous decision, but without the expected knockout.

That summer, negotiations began for the expected match with Tyson, but Tyson's rape charge, and subsequent conviction, put an end to them. Instead, he fought Bert Cooper in November 1991, before a hometown audience in Atlanta. Perhaps feeling cocky in his hometown, Holyfield got a little sloppy and Cooper knocked him down in the third round, the first such blow he'd suffered in his professional career. He came back to knock out Cooper in the seventh round, but observers noted the fall more than the victory. The following year, he went up against another aging former champ, Larry Holmes, and again he won by a decision after twelve rounds in-

stead of the expected knockout. Critics grumbled that the champ was looking less and less impressive.

On November 13, 1992, Holyfield found himself in a much harder match, against Riddick Bowe, a younger, heavier man who was as hungry for the title as he himself had been. The fight had been promoted as "Friday the 13th: Anything Can Happen." In fact, it was another grueling 12 rounder, but this time the decision went against Holyfield. Ironically, Holyfield earned back some respect in this losing match by proving he could go the distance against a more powerful opponent. Even Bowe told Holyfield, "You were always a class act."

The Hard Road Back

After the fight, Holyfield announced that he was retiring from boxing, but by January 1993 he'd changed his mind. In *Holyfield: The Humble Warrior,* his brother Bernard attributes this to a growing anger that the bout with Bowe had been much closer than the judges seemed to think and an anger at Bowe for "talking noise" about Evander's supposed deficiencies. Others thought it might be simple restlessness. Under a new trainer, Emanuel Steward, Holyfield threw himself into another grueling regimen, at the same time developing a more subtle kind of boxing than his previous style. On June 26, 1993, Holyfield was back in the ring, dispatching Alex Stewart in a unanimous decision after 12 rounds. Unimpressed, Rock Newman, Bowe's manager, told *Sports Illustrated,* "Holyfield won and eliminated himself. He's got no chance for a title fight now."

But despite Newman's comments, Holyfield had earned his rematch with Bowe, which took place on November 6, 1993. Holyfield weighed in at 217 pounds, Bowe at 250. Clearly this would not be an easy fight, and a stunt by a publicity seeker didn't make it easier. In the middle of the match, someone parachuted into the ring, causing 20 minutes of confusion before the fight resumed. Perhaps because his pregnant wife had fainted during the interruption, Bowe seemed more distracted in the second half of the fight, and Holyfield won on a 2-1 decision. Holyfield had performed a rare act in boxing, taking his title back from the man who'd taken it from him. Only **Floyd Patterson** and **Muhammad Ali** could say they had done the same.

But he did not hold the title for long. On May 6, 1994, he lost another 12-round decision, this time to Michael Moorer. Again, Holyfield announced his retirement, this time attributing it to a heart condition and his doctors' advice. He did leave the door open for a return in case his heart improved, and subsequent tests at Emory Clinic in Atlanta and the Mayo Clinic revealed that his symptoms had probably been due to dehydration and that his heart was fine. Holyfield himself attributed his "miraculous cure" to faith healer Benny Hinn.

In May 1995, he was back in a professional boxing match, when he beat Ray Mercer in a unanimous decision after a brutal fight. In November 1995, the last Bowe-Holyfield match took place in Las Vegas. This time, the younger ex-champ proved too much for the older one. In the 8th round Bowe sent Holyfield to the mat with a right hand and two chopping rights. Their long rivalry was over.

Going Up Against Iron Mike

But for Holyfield a new rivalry was beginning, one that would lead to one of the most bizarre incidents in boxing history. In November 1996, Evander Holyfield went up against Mike Tyson, fresh out of prison, for the World Boxing Association championship. The fight was highly controversial, and many felt that ex-con Tyson should be banned from boxing altogether. Others felt that Holyfield was risking serious injury going up against the man they still called Iron Mike. But Holyfield was confident, announcing calmly, "I will beat Mike Tyson. There is no way I cannot, if I trust in God." His faith was justified, and throughout their match Holyfield withstood the punishment of Mike Tyson's punch. And he gave as good as he got. He managed to knock Tyson senseless in the second round, and again in the sixth round. In the eleventh round, Tyson collapsed against the ropes. Holyfield had again entered exclusive company. Alone with Muhammad Ali, he had become a three-time heavyweight champion.

But the surprise of that upset was nothing compared to the pandemonium of the Tyson-Holyfield rematch in June 1997. Once again, Holyfield showed a determination to take the fight to Tyson, enraging the already frustrated ex-champ. In the third round, Tyson spit out his mouthpiece and bit down on Holyfield's right ear, drawing blood. Incredibly, the referee deducted two points and let the fight continue. Before the round was up, Tyson had latched onto Holyfield's left ear, this time biting off a piece. "There is no way to reconcile what was happening with human behavior, or even boxing," wrote *Sports Illustrated* reporter Richard Hoffer. This time, the referee finally called off the match and disqualified Tyson. Holyfield was actually quite calm in the hospital while getting his ear sewn up, telling reporters stoically: "It was told to me by the prophets that the fight was going to be short, but that there'd be some distractions."

Still Boxing

Evander Holyfield continues to box, and has even said he'd be willing to box Tyson again, "if time permits." In fact, Holyfield has been fairly busy. In November 1997, he stopped Michael Moorer in the eighth round, taking the IBF heavyweight championship and avenging his '94 title loss. In September 1998, he defeated Vaughn Bean in a lackluster 12-round decision. Then in March of 1999 he fought World Boxing Council champ **Lennox Lewis** in an attempt to consolidate his titles. The fight ended in a controversial draw that many observers thought should have gone to Lewis. Even Muhammad Ali weighed in with a protest against the decision. In an unusual show of unity, all three

world boxing organizations ordered a rematch within six months. Eight months later, on November 13, 1999, Holyfield lost his title in a unanimous decision for Lewis.

On August 12, 2000, Holyfield took the World Boxing Association title from John Ruiz, becoming the first heavyweight champion to win the title four times. Seven months later he lost it back to Ruiz. Holyfield calmly accepted the unanimous decision, saying, "I was four-time champion and now I'm going to have to become a five time champion." On December 15, 2001, in another controversial decision, judges declared a draw in his rematch with John Ruiz, although Holyfield had appeared to dominate the fight. Ruiz retained his title. A year later, he lost a unanimous decision to Chris Byrd as they were vying for the vacant IBF heavyweight title.

Holyfield continues to box, claiming that he made a promise to himself to regain the title of undisputed heavyweight champion of the world. Every year the goal looks more elusive, but Holyfield has come back before, and surprised the critics. Outside the ring, his personal life has seen its share of upheavals. In 1999, his second wife, Janice, filed for divorce, an event that turned ugly when Evander asked for a paternity test for their child and Janice's lawyers deposed Evander's minister on suspicion that he had been given millions of dollars improperly. Evander Holyfield admits to fathering a number of children out of wedlock, but claims that he is financially supporting them.

Regardless, the man who could forgive Mike Tyson for taking a bite out of him remains a symbol of grace in the ring, a boxer who has proved you don't have to be a killer to be a winner. "I don't believe you have to be mean to be successful," he once declared. "In boxing, two athletes compete against one another. When it's over, you hug." Throughout his long career, Holyfield has tried to live up to that image.

SELECTED WRITINGS BY HOLYFIELD:

(With Bernard Holyfield) *Holyfield: The Humble Warrior*, Atlanta: Thomas Nelson Publishers, 1996.

FURTHER INFORMATION

Books

Holyfield, Evander and Bernard Holyfield. *Holyfield: The Humble Warrior*. Atlanta: Thomas Nelson Publishers, 1996.

Suster, Gerald. *Champions of the Ring*. London: Robson Books, 1994.

Periodicals

"Boxing: Holy eyes high fives." *Europe Intelligence Wire* (October 20, 2002).

"Boxing: The king, the rock, and the white buffalo." *Africa News Service* (May 24, 2001).

"Boxing: Veterans in search of more ring glory." *Africa News Service* (March 1, 2001).

Daly, Dan. "Holyfield's ticket has looked punched before." *The Washington Times* (August 15, 2000): 1.

"Evander Holyfield loses WBA title, but says he won't quit boxing." *Jet* (March 19, 2001): 51.

"Foolish heart." *Sports Illustrated* (June 17, 1996): 31.

Hoffer, Richard. "Now it gets serious: after beating Seamus McDonough, Evander Holyfield may finally get his shot." *Sports Illustrated* (June 11, 1990): 34.

Hoffer, Richard. "Heart and soul." *Sports Illustrated* (May 29, 1995): 36.

Hoffer, Richard. "Feeding frenzy." *Sports Illustrated* (July 7, 1997): 32.

Hoffer, Richard. "This one didn't faint." *Sports Illustrated* (December 30, 1996): 90.

Hoffer, Richard. "Grisly requiem." *Sports Illustrated* (December 29, 1997): 88.

Hoffer, Richard. "Grand larceny." *Sports Illustrated* (March 22, 1999): 60.

"Holyfield forgives Tyson for biting his ears." *Jet* (January 26, 1998): 48.

"Holyfield hanging on for wrong reasons." *The Washington Times* (December 14, 2002): C01.

Loverro, Thom. "Indebted Holyfield still keeps the faith." *The Washington Times* (November 7, 1997): 1.

Loverro, Thom. "Keeping the faith: Holyfield refuses to believe his time as a heavyweight champion is up." *The Washington Times* (November 12, 1999): 1.

Loverro, Thom. "Is boxing on the ropes?" *Insight on the News* (January 24, 2000): 32.

Lyons, Douglas. "Evander Holyfield: Coping with sudden success." *Ebony* (January 1991): 48.

"Muhammad Ali calls Holyfield-Lewis fight decision 'a fix.'" *Jet* (April 12, 1999): 48.

Pearlman, Jeff. "Ragged night in Georgia." *Sports Illustrated* (September 28, 1998): 81.

Plummer, William. "Tough guys do dance." *People Weekly* (November 16, 1992): 69.

Putnam, Pat. "One angry man." *Sports Illustrated* (November 13, 1989): 38.

Putnam, Pat. "No joke: Evander Holyfield discovered that George Foreman was to be taken seriously." *Sports Illustrated* (April 29, 1991): 22.

Putnam, Pat. "Sluggards." *Sports Illustrated* (July 5, 1993): 18.

"To ear is human." *The Washington Times* (October 21, 1998): 16.

"Tyson and Holyfield should be banned." *The Washington Times* (July 6, 1997): 3.

Wulf, Steve. "The bible thumper." *Time* (November 25, 1996): 119.

Sketch by Robert Winters

Rogers Hornsby
1896-1963

American baseball player

Rogers Hornsby wanted to play baseball so badly that when he was sixteen he donned a wig, pretended to be a woman, and barnstormed through his native Texas with the Boston Bloomer Girls. As an adult, he cared for nothing except baseball. Often overlooked when baseball's greatest players are ranked, Hornsby was arguably the best right-handed batter in the game's history, retiring with the second-highest lifetime batting average, surpassed only by his contemporary, Detroit's **Ty Cobb**. With few other interests, the gruff, profane, outspoken Hornsby was an early model of an athlete completely dedicated to his sport.

Baseball Hungry

The Hornsby family came from Wales to colonial Virginia in the early 18th century, and about a century later moved to west Texas, to a settlement near Austin that became known as Hornsby's Bend. Ed Hornsby married Mary Dallas Rogers, from nearby Rogers Hill, in 1882. They had four children before moving to a homestead near Abilene. There, Rogers Hornsby—named after his mother—was born on April 27, 1896. His father died two years later of unknown causes. His mother took the children to live with her parents on a farm near Austin, then later moved to Fort Worth, a booming meatpacking town. In Fort Worth, Rogers began playing baseball in earnest, and by the time he was nine was the star of a local team. Mary Hornsby sewed his team's blue flannel uniforms, and the boys traveled to their games by trolley. By age ten, when he went to work after school and during the summer for the Swift and Company meatpacking plant, he substituted on teams of stockyard and packing plant workers.

Young Hornsby was slight, smooth on defense at any position, and cocky, but not much of a hitter. But he was determined to be a professional baseball player. At age fifteen, he was playing on the North Side Athletics in the Fort Worth adult league, and on other teams, including the semipro Granbury club, where he made two dollars per game plus room and board and rail fare. Granbury manager H.L. Warlick remembered praising Hornsby after one game for making all the plays at second base, and recalled Hornsby replying: "Yeah, and there are eight other positions I can play just as good," according to Charles Alexander's biography, *Rogers Hornsby*. The next summer, Hornsby and a friend took a train to Dallas, answering a newspaper ad looking for players under eighteen to play with the touring women's team, the Boston Bloomer Girls. Donning wigs and bloomers, Hornsby and his friend played as female impersonators.

In high school, Hornsby played football and baseball, but dropped out after two years to help support his mother

Rogers Hornsby

by working as an office boy at Swift and Company. In the spring of 1914, Hornsby had grown to his adult height of nearly six feet but still weighed only 135 pounds. His older brother Everett, who had played seven years in the Class B Texas League and one season at Class A with Kansas City, was on the Dallas Steers and got his little brother a tryout. He signed a contract but never played and was released after two weeks. He tried out with a new team in the Class D Texas-Oklahoma League, the lowest level of the minors. He made the team, located in the small town of Hugo, and played for $75 a month as the regular shortstop. But the franchise folded and Hornsby's contract was sold to Denison. There, he hit .232 and made forty-five errors in 113 games. "Won't somebody teach me how to hit?" he pleaded to teammate Herb Hunter, according to Alexander.

After another season at Denison, where he boosted his average to .277 but still made fifty-eight errors in 119 games, Hornsby was called up at the end of 1915 to St. Louis, a struggling National League club. Rosters in the major leagues had been severely depleted by players defecting to the upstart Federal League. Hornsby, whose record to that point hardly merited such a rapid promotion, arrived in St. Louis as a callow, wholesome young man, and he frequently got lost in the unfamiliar big city. He played in his first game on September 10, a week after joining the club, and was hitless in two at-bats. In all, he batted .246, appearing in eighteen games at shortstop and making many mistakes in the field.

After the season, when the manager told Hornsby he wanted to "farm him out for a year"—send him down to the minors for more seasoning—Hornsby misunderstood him and decided he would spend the off-season on his uncle's farm near Austin. He worked hard, ate steak and fried chicken, drank a lot of fresh milk, and slept twelve hours a night. He put on thirty-five pounds. A bulked-up Hornsby returned to spring training a much more impressive hitter. He stood far back in the box and away from home plate, used an open stance, and rifled line drives to all fields. Confident, hustling, and eager, Hornsby forced his way onto the team and into the regular lineup and played every infield position, finishing the season primarily as a third baseman and hitting .313. By the end of the season, several other National League clubs were trying to get Hornsby in a trade.

In 1917, Hornsby hit .327 and led the league with 253 total bases, a .484 slugging percentage and seventeen triples, in an era when triples were the prime measure of a power hitter. His defense was nothing to brag about, though. Playing the entire year at shortstop, he made fifty-two errors, third-highest in the league.

Hitting Machine

In 1918, injuries—including a groin pull, a spiked thumb, and a sore shoulder—hampered Hornsby, and he slumped to .281, the worst full-season performance of his major-league career. The season was cut short by

Awards and Accomplishments

1917, 1920-25, 1927-29	Led National League in slugging percentage
1920-25, 1928	Led National League in batting average
1920-25, 1927-28	Led National League in on-base percentage
1920-22, 1925	Led National League in runs batted in
1920-22, 1924	Led National League in hits
1920-22, 1924	Led National League in doubles
1921	Led National League in triples
1921-22, 1924, 1927, 1929	Led National League in runs scored
1922, 1925	Leads National League in home runs
1922, 1925	National League Triple Crown
1924, 1927-28	Led National League in walks
1925	National League Most Valuable Player
1926	Manager of World Series champion St. Louis Cardinals
1926, 1929	Played in World Series
1929	National League Most Valuable Player
1942	Inducted into National Baseball Hall of Fame

World War I, and Hornsby was drafted to go to Wilmington, Delaware, to work in the naval shipyards and play ball for military teams. There, he married Sarah Martin. The war ended, and over the winter Hornsby and his bride traveled around Texas and set up a string of automobile dealerships, capitalizing on his sudden fame. In 1919 Hornsby was groomed for second base but played all four infield positions and rebounded to hit .318, almost winning the batting championship.

The next year, Hornsby was installed at second base, the position that Cardinals management decided he was best suited to play. Settled there for the entire year, Hornsby had a breakout season, winning the batting championship with a robust .370 average and leading the league in hits, runs batted in, doubles, and slugging percentage.

In his prime, Hornsby piled up offensive numbers that have never been equaled. The 1920 season was the first of six consecutive seasons, and seven overall, in which Hornsby won the National League batting championship. His accomplishments over the next five-year stretch, 1921 through 1925, could hardly have been imagined a few years earlier, when he was a scrawny kid struggling to hit. It helped that baseball had instituted a new, livelier ball, but even in that context his achievements were astounding. No one before or since has averaged over .400 for a five-year period, even Cobb, but Hornsby hit .397, .401, .384, .424. and .403. He didn't just hit for average. He compiled high on-base percentages with many walks and increased his power output. In 1922, he won the Triple Crown (batting average,

home runs, and RBIs) and set a new National League record with forty-two home runs. He drove in 152 runs, and led the league with 250 hits, forty-six doubles, 141 runs scored, and a slugging mark of .722 along with a .459 on-base percentage. It was almost certainly the best offensive season in league history—at least until **Barry Bonds'** performances in 2001 and 2002—and was surpassed only by the top seasons of his American League contemporary **Babe Ruth.**

Everything seemed to have fallen in place for Hornsby. He was the proud father of a little boy, Rogers Jr., and the top player in the National League. But Hornsby's love of gambling soon led to some off-the-field troubles. One day in 1922, he met a married woman named Jeannette Pennington Hine at a dog track. After the 1922 season, both spouses found out about the affair. Hornsby's wife Sarah took their son and left him to live with her mother. In 1923, Hornsby had to overcome a serious knee injury, legal problems stemming from his extramarital affair including a costly divorce settlement, and his mother's illness. At the end of the season, he was fined and suspended for refusing to play. Still, he hit .384 and qualified for the batting title despite playing in only 107 games. In February 1924, with all legal matters settled, Hornsby married Pennington.

In 1924 Hornsby compiled the highest batting average by any player in the post-1900 era—.424. That year, he played in 143 games and hustled out every ball he hit, hitting safely in 119 games. Hornsby's batting feat won him national attention and for that year he even eclipsed the fame of Babe Ruth, America's most popular athlete. Hornsby led the league in hits, doubles, runs, and slugging percentage, and also in on-base percentage and walks. Incredibly, he failed to win the league's Most Valuable Player award, which was bestowed on Brooklyn Dodgers pitcher Dazzy Vance.

Swinging at Strikes

Hornsby had simple rules for hitting. The most important was never to swing at balls out of the strike zone. He didn't vary his stance, standing almost upright and rigid in the batters' box, left foot closer to the plate than right. He rarely pulled the ball down the left-field line, and always tried to hit the ball where it was pitched. He also placed paramount importance on a confident attitude, saying, as quoted in Alexander's biography, "Never get the idea that you can't hit a certain pitcher. ... You must believe in yourself." Other than that, he tried not to think too much or overanalyze the situation or the pitcher he faced. "The only emotion or thought I ever had for a pitcher," he said, "was to feel sorry for him."

Though Hornsby always hustled and had enough speed to beat out many infield hits, he never was much of a base-stealer. As a fielder, he was inconsistent. His fielding percentage of .958 lifetime is subpar. Even after settling at second base as a regular position, he contin-

Hall of Famer John McGraw is considered by many baseball experts to be the best manager in major league history. As a player with the Baltimore Orioles in the 1890s, McGraw was instrumental in perfecting an all-out style of play now known as "small ball" that focused on stealing bases, bunting, and hustling. He mixed these skills with an intimidating approach to opposing players and umpires. McGraw was constantly baiting and brawling and was frequently ejected from games.

As the manager of the New York Giants from 1902 through 1932, McGraw drove his players to 2,784 wins, second only to Connie Mack on the all-time list. His teams won nine pennants and three World Series and dominated the National League throughout most of his tenure. He was known as "The Little Napoleon" for his autocratic managing methods.

McGraw was constantly trying to get star players from other teams to help his club. From the very start of Rogers Hornsby's career, McGraw coveted him. He frequently urged Giants owners to propose trades to the St. Louis Cardinals. McGraw finally got his wish when Hornsby was traded to the Giants after the 1926 season. During the 1927 season, the only one they spent together, McGraw and Hornsby became close friends. They shared a love of betting on horse races and they shared a single-minded, ruthless approach to baseball. When McGraw battled illnesses during the season, Hornsby took over as manager and did so well that McGraw did not return at the season's end even though he had recovered.

After the 1927 season, Hornsby was traded to the Boston Braves after several run-ins with Giants owner Horace Stoneham. The deal was done while McGraw was spending the off-season in Havana, Cuba, and it was executed without McGraw's knowledge. He surely would not have consented to losing the player he had always wanted to get.

ued to play games at first base, third base, and the outfield. But he was excellent at turning the double play. With a runner on first base, he would play in on the edge of the infield dirt and "cheat" toward second base to get a jump on any potential double-play grounders. He was unmatched at taking throws from other infielders, making the difficult pivot with a runner sliding into him, and getting off quick, accurate throws to first base.

In an era when many players indulged in drinking and carousing and cared little for conditioning, Hornsby subordinated every other aspect of his life to baseball. He never drank or smoked. He went to bed before midnight and tried to sleep 12 hours a night. He took special care of his eyesight. He avoided reading, and preached that hitters shouldn't ruin their eyes by reading on trains or trolleys. He never went to the movies during baseball season, saying that motion pictures would harm his eyesight and lessen his batting abilities. His one vice was overeating. He ate lots of steaks, milk, and ice cream, and after his playing days ended, his weight ballooned.

In fact, baseball was about the only thing Hornsby really cared about. His only other hobby was gambling, and that got him into trouble. Despite organized baseball's well-publicized problems with gamblers in that era, Hornsby always defended his right to bet on horse (and dog) racing. He lost much of his salary in doing so. But the other interests shared by most ballplayers, such as golf, left him cold. It's once said that Cardinals owner **Branch Rickey** dragged Hornsby to a golf course during spring training in Florida in 1924, and Hornsby, who had never played golf, shot a 39 for nine holes, beating Rickey, an experienced golfer, by nine shots. But Hornsby never played golf again.

Hornsby was far from gregarious. He insisted on rooming alone, and was aloof from his teammates. He rarely talked with anyone about anything other than baseball, and he always spoke his mind—often too bluntly. His usual pastime on the road was to sit in hotel lobbies and watch people come and go, talking about baseball to anyone who approached him.

Management Problems

Hornsby and his second wife had a new son in 1925. In mid-season, he took over as manager of the Cardinals, displacing Branch Rickey, and bought one-eighth of the club's stock, as part of a three-way power struggle for control of the club that also involved owner Sam Breadon. As a manager, Hornsby drove his players hard. He told pitchers they should knock down a batter if the count was no balls and two strikes, and he fined them $50 if a batter hit a pitch on that count. Hitters were fined $50 if they took a called third strike with runners on second or third base. Battling minor injuries, Hornsby again won the Triple Crown, with a .403 average, 39 home runs and 143 RBIs. He was named Most Valuable Player, and local newspapers dubbed him "the Rajah."

In 1926, Hornsby pushed the Cardinals ever further. Relentlessly hectoring his teammates and charges, Hornsby made winning a championship his first priority. He battled a thigh infection and fell into a batting slump, sinking to a .317 average. He defied Breadon by refusing to send many of his key players to exhibition games that Breadon had scheduled in September in the middle of the pennant race. The championship was the first in the history of the Cardinals franchise.

In the 1926 World Series, St. Louis faced Ruth and the heavily favored New York Yankees. Ruth homered three times in the fourth game of the series, the first two times after Hornsby had told his pitcher to throw him something slow. As he had during the pennant drive, Hornsby kept calling on **Grover Cleveland Alexander**, an epileptic and heavy drinker. After Alexander started the sixth game, Hornsby brought him back in the seventh and deciding game in relief, and he struck out Tony Lazzeri with the bases loaded and saved the game by walking Ruth in the ninth inning; the series ended when Ruth was thrown out trying to steal second base.

Hornsby was now at the pinnacle of the baseball world—at thirty years old, he was the game's best hitter, and he had managed a World Series winner. Things went quickly downhill, however. Breadon and Hornsby had had a long-standing feud, exacerbated by Hornsby's refusal to quit gambling on horses. Commissioner Kenesaw Mountain Landis was trying to clean up baseball and backed Breadon. In a stunning trade, Breadon sent Hornsby to the New York Giants for second baseman Frankie

Rogers Hornsby

Frisch and pitcher Jimmy Ring. There was one problem: Hornsby still owned stock in the Cardinals, now his rival team in the same league. After long negotiations, pushed by Landis's insistence on cutting Hornsby's ties to his former team, Hornsby sold the stock for a handsome profit just before Opening Day of the 1927 season.

Hornsby fit perfectly with longtime Giants manager John McGraw, who had been trying to acquire him for ten years. Both men were demanding perfectionists on the diamond, and they shared a love for betting on the ponies. McGraw had health problems in 1927, and Hornsby took over as manager for thirty-three games near the end of the season. He led the league in runs and walks and hit .361. But Hornsby again made enemies in the front office and among his Giants teammates and had well-publicized legal problems involving gambling debts. Hornsby was traded again, this time to the lowly Boston Braves for two mediocre players, Jimmie Welsh and James Hogan.

Shuffling Around

In Boston, Hornsby again assumed the managerial reins during the season and won his final batting championship with a .387 average. He also led the league in walks and slugging percentage. But the Braves were inept and finished next to last. After the season, it was announced that Hornsby had signed a three-year contract to manage Boston, but then he was traded to the Chicago Cubs for five inconsequential players and $200,000.

In 1929, playing on his fourth National League team in four years, Hornsby didn't have to manage, and he played in every inning of every game. He won his second Most Valuable Player Award with another exceptional season—thirty-nine homers, a .679 slugging percentage, a .380 batting average, and a league-high 156 runs. The Cubs won the pennant but lost the World Series to the Philadelphia Athletics. During the season, Hornsby developed a calcified heel and played in pain. Shortly after the World Series ended, he lost many thousands of dollars in the great stock market crash of October 1929. He had off-season heel surgery and appeared healthy, but he injured his ankle in 1930 and his season ended early. Near the end of the 1930 season, he took over as manager. Although he continued to play himself on occasion, his regular playing days had ended because of age and injuries, and he concentrated on managing. The Cubs had winning records under Hornsby in 1931 and 1932, but he was released in August 1932. It came out that Hornsby owed money to several of his teammates; he had been borrowing from them to finance his gambling habit. Newspapers raised allegations that Hornsby had led a horse-race betting pool among Cubs players, but he denied it, and Landis refused to investigate the charges. Privately, Landis said, according to Alexander's book: "That fellow will never learn. His betting has got him in one scrape after another, cost him a fortune and several jobs, and still he hasn't enough sense to stop it."

In 1933, Hornsby hooked on for a last tour with the Cardinals, playing in forty-six games. He then served as player-manager for the American League's St. Louis Browns, where he stayed through 1937. The Browns were a perennial also-ran, and Hornsby used himself mainly as a pinch-hitter. His playing career ended when he hit .321 at age forty-one in twenty games. He finished with a career batting average of .358, second only to Cobb. Hornsby also ranks eighth in lifetime on-base percentage at .434, and his .577 lifetime slugging percentage is ninth among all retired players.

Because of his refusal to stop gambling and his prickly personality, Hornsby eventually became unwelcome in major league baseball. But baseball was everything to Hornsby, especially considering that his second marriage had also ended in divorce, and he continued to manage in the minor leagues, in Mexico and Texas. Umpire Len Roberts remembered Hornsby as "a true gentleman on the field—he never questioned a decision. I don't think there was a dishonest bone in his body," according to the *Baseball Research Journal*.

In 1942, when Hornsby was inducted into the Hall of Fame, he was managing in the low minors. He got a re-

Career Statistics

Yr	Team	Avg	GP	AB	R	H	HR	RBI	BB	SO	SB	E
1915	SLC	.246	18	57	5	14	0	4	2	6	0	8
1916	SLC	.313	139	495	63	155	6	65	40	63	17	45
1917	SLC	.327	145	523	86	171	8	66	45	34	17	52
1918	SLC	.281	115	416	51	117	5	60	40	43	8	46
1919	SLC	.318	138	512	68	163	8	71	48	41	17	34
1920	SLC	.370	149	589	96	218	9	94	60	50	12	34
1921	SLC	.397	154	592	131	235	21	126	60	48	13	27
1922	SLC	.401	154	623	141	250	42	152	65	50	17	30
1923	SLC	.384	107	424	89	163	17	83	55	29	3	21
1924	SLC	.424	143	536	121	227	25	94	89	32	5	30
1925	SLC	.403	138	504	133	203	39	143	83	39	5	34
1926	SLC	.317	134	527	96	167	11	93	61	39	3	27
1927	NYG	.361	155	568	133	205	26	125	86	38	9	25
1928	BOS	.387	140	486	99	188	21	94	107	41	5	21
1929	CHC	.380	156	602	156	229	39	149	87	65	2	23
1930	CHC	.308	42	104	15	32	2	18	12	12	0	11
1931	CHC	.331	100	357	64	118	16	90	56	23	1	22
1932	CHC	.224	19	58	10	13	1	7	10	4	0	4
1933	SLC/SLB	.326	57	92	11	30	3	23	14	7	1	2
1934	SLB	.304	24	23	2	7	1	11	7	4	0	0
1935	SLB	.208	10	24	1	5	0	3	3	6	0	0
1936	SLB	.400	2	5	1	2	0	2	1	0	0	0
1937	SLB	.321	20	56	7	18	1	11	7	5	0	4
TOTAL		.345	2259	8173	1579	2930	301	1584	1038	679	135	500

BOS: Boston Red Sox; CHC: Chicago Cubs; NYG: New York Giants; SLB: St. Louis Browns; SLC: St. Louis Cardinals.

prieve when the Browns hired him as manager in 1952, but he was fired in mid-season and took over in Cincinnati, where he lasted through most of the 1953 season before again getting dismissed. In his managerial career, he was traded or fired six times, and compiled a record of 701 wins and 812 losses. In the 1950s, Hornsby coached for the Chicago Cubs and in 1962 joined the New York Mets coaching staff. Late that year, he went to a Chicago hospital for eye surgery, but suffered a heart attack and died on January 5, 1963.

Hornsby will be remembered as a hitter of unequalled accomplishments and a player of exceptional drive and focus. Though not as reviled as Cobb, Hornsby was never a popular player among his teammates. But social skills don't win ball games, and Hornsby concentrated on winning. His discipline at the plate—swinging only at strikes, and not trying to overpower the ball—became a model for many future great hitters.

FURTHER INFORMATION

Books

Alexander, Charles C. *Rogers Hornsby: A Biography.* New York: Henry Holt, 1995.

The Baseball Encyclopedia. New York: Macmillan, 1997.

Burns, Ken, and Ward, Geoffrey C. *Baseball: An Illustrated History.* New York: Knopf, 1994.

Thorn, John, and Palmer, Pete. *Total Baseball.* New York: Warner Books, 1989.

Periodicals

"Hail to the Rajah: Before Ted Williams, there was Rogers Hornsby, the forgotten father of the father of hitting." *Sports Illustrated* (June 24, 2002): R14.

"Hornsby, in Death, Acclaimed for Great Hitting." *New York Times* (January 6, 1963).

"The Rajah at 100." *The Sporting News* (May 6, 1996): 55.

"A tale of two Hornsbys: a sweetheart back home." *Baseball Research Journal* (Annual, 2001).

Other

baseball-reference.com. http://www.baseball-reference. com (November 22, 2002).

"Hornsby cared only about results." *ESPN.com.* http:// espn.go.com/sportscentury/features/00014249.html (November 22, 2002).

"Hornsby, Rogers." *The Handbook of Texas Online.* http://www.tsha.utexas.edu/handbook/online/ articles/view/HH/fho61.html (November 22, 2002).

"Rogers Hornsby." *Baseball Library.com.* http://www. pubdim.net/baseballlibrary/ballplayers/H/Hornsby_ Rogers.stm (November 22, 2002).

"Rogers Hornsby." *National Baseball Hall of Fame.* http://www.baseballhalloffame.org/hofers_and_ honorees/hofer_bios/hornsby_rogers.htm (November 22, 2002.htm

Sketch by Michael Betzold

Paul Hornung

Paul Hornung
1935-

American football player

Star running back Paul Hornung led the great Green Bay Packer teams of the early 1960s to four National Football League (NFL) championships. One of the most versatile football players ever, in addition to being a tenacious rusher—especially within the ten-yard line—Hornung also kicked field goals and extra points for the Packers, he was a halfback who could pass, he could even quarterback for the team in a pinch. From 1959 through 1961, Hornung led the NFL in points scored. He scored an astounding 176 points in 1960. An achievement that helped win him the Most Valuable Player award, it is a record that still stands as the all-time NFL season high. Hornung was famed for his exploits off the gridiron as well. He cultivated and relished his reputation as a ladies' man. In 1963 he was banished from the NFL for a full season for gambling. He was nonetheless cherished by other Green Bay players and the team's fans. "Paul was always the star of our team," Jerry Kramer wrote of his former teammate in his book *Distant Replay*, "we all loved Paul."

Growing Up with a Football

Paul Vernon Hornung was born in 1935 in Louisville, Kentucky. His parents separated in 1939 while Paul was

Chronology	
1935	Born December 23 in Louisville, Kentucky
1953	Named Kentucky's Most Valuable High School Football Player
1953	Enters Notre Dame University
1955-56	College football All-American
1956	Wins Heisman Trophy
1956	Number One NFL draft pick
1956	Plays in Hula Bowl
1959-61	Leads the NFL in points scored
1960	Makes All-Pro
1961	Named NFL Most Valuable Player
1961	Called up as Army reservist
1963	Suspended for one year for gambling on football games
1965	Five touchdown game against the Baltimore Colts
1967	Selected by New Orleans in NFL expansion draft
1967	Retires from NFL
1967	Gets married for the first time
1975	Elected to Green Bay Packers Hall of Fame
1980	Marries second wife, Angela
1985	Elected to NFF College Football Hall of Fame
1986	Elected to the Pro Football Hall of Fame

still a young child and throughout his life he remained particularly close to his mother. Hornung fell in love with football as a boy, even ignoring the new bicycle he received one Christmas in favor of another present—a football. His mother would later recall how whenever football practice let out early enough, Hornung would race home on his bike to be able to play again in a neighborhood pick-up game. "He loved playing football twice a day," she told the *Los Angeles Times*.

Hornung was enthusiastic about most sports. At Louisville's Flaget High School, he pitched for the baseball team, was a twenty-point forward on the basketball team, and quarterbacked for the football team. He was the school's star athlete, indeed one of the best in all Kentucky, and it was assumed that he would go on to attend the University of Kentucky. However, when his football team won the state championship and Hornung was named the state's most valuable player, recruiters from colleges across the country began to knock on the Hornung family's door. Hornung's talent was great and the scholarship offers were just as extravagant. Besides full scholarships, schools offered Hornung cash bonuses, clothing and cars. One even promised a scholarship for his girlfriend too. Hornung was leaning toward U. of Kentucky, but when Notre Dame came calling, Mrs. Hornung, a devout Catholic, urged Paul to accept their scholarship. It was not a difficult decision. Hornung had already realized he liked playing on winning teams and figured he have a good chance of winning again with the Fighting Irish. He was also impressed by Notre Dame's coach, Frank Leahy.

Hornung began displaying his gridiron versatility at Notre Dame. When he arrived at the school, the team already possessed a fine quarterback in Ralph Guglielmi, and Hornung was put at halfback. Although he had never played the position before, before long he was

Career Statistics

Yr	Team	Receiving				Rushing				Kicking		
		REC	YDS	AVG	TD	ATT	YDS	AVG	TD	FGM	FGA	XPM
1957	GB	6	34	5.7	0	60	319	5.3	3	0	4	0
1958	GB	15	137	9.1	0	69	310	4.5	2	11	21	22
1959	GB	15	113	7.5	0	152	681	4.5	7	7	17	31
1960	GB	28	257	9.2	2	160	671	4.2	15	15	28	41
1961	GB	15	145	9.7	2	127	597	4.7	10	15	22	41
1962	GB	9	98	10.7	2	57	219	3.8	7	6	10	14
1964	GB	9	98	10.9	0	103	415	4.0	5	12	38	41
1965	GB	19	336	17.7	3	89	299	3.4	8	0	0	0
1966	GB	14	192	13.7	3	76	200	2.6	5	0	0	0
TOTAL		130	1480	11.4	12	893	3711	4.2	50	66	140	190

GB: Green Bay Packers.

starting there, and to such fanfare that a Louisville sports writer dubbed the strapping, six-foot blond Hornung, the "Golden Boy," a nickname that would stick with him throughout his career and into his retirement. Hornung finally became quarterback when he was a senior. The injury-laden team was only able to win two games all season. Hornung turned in a well-rounded performance—he ran, threw, tackled, kicked, and called plays. **Harold Red Grange** told the *New York Times* that Hornung was "the best running back I saw all year." At the end of the season Hornung won the Heisman trophy.

Goes to Green Bay Packers

Hornung was the top pick in the 1957 college draft, selected by the Green Bay Packers, the last place team in the NFL in 1956. His first two seasons were disappointing. Packer coach Lisle Blackbourn mistook Hornung's versatility for ineptness. After playing him at various positions, Blackbourn concluded that Hornung was too slow for halfback, couldn't pass well enough for quarterback, wasn't powerful enough for fullback. By the end of the 1958 season, Hornung was completely frustrated and wanted to be traded. His life changed when **Vince Lombardi** was brought in to replace Blackbourn as coach.

Lombardi, to the contrary, saw in Hornung a halfback who ran hard, could throw on the run and hence would open up a world of plays for the Packers. Lombardi also began using him to kick field goals and extra points. Hornung blossomed under Lombardi's mentorship. Abruptly he went from the player who couldn't do anything particularly well, to the NFL's leading scorer three years running, from 1959 to 1961. In 1960 Hornung led the Packers to their first-ever conference title. He threw two touchdown passes, ran for thirteen touchdowns, caught two touchdown passes, and kicked fifteen field goals and forty-one extra points for 176 points, a NFL record that no one since has come close to breaking. The following year he was almost as remarkable, scoring

146 points. He scored thirty-three of them in a single game against the Baltimore Colts.

Hornung might have challenged his 1960 record himself in 1961 except for the Cold War crisis in Berlin. A member of the Army Reserve, Hornung was called to active duty. Although he was able to play most games on weekend passes, he had to forego most workouts with the team and missed two entire games working as a truck driver and radio operator based in Fort Riley, Kansas. President John Kennedy himself arranged for a week's pass for Hornung so he could play against the New York Giants in the NFL title game. Just showing up for the game inspired the Packers. "When Paul got that leave from the Army and walked into that locker room, you could just feel the confidence grow in that room," recalled Packer Henry Jordan in Michael O'Brien's Lombardi biography *Vince*. Hornung's contribution to that game went much deeper than inspiration, though. He scored a touchdown in the second quarter that broke a scoreless tie, then kicked three field goals and four extra points, setting a record for championship play. The Packers whipped the Giants 37-0 and Hornung was the game MVP. After the game he told the *New York Times,* "This is the greatest day in my life." The paper asked him if the Heisman Trophy didn't hold that honor. "That was five years ago—this was today!" he answered.

Ladies Man and Gambler

By the spring of 1962, Paul Hornung was on the top of the world. He had been named the NFL's MVP for 1961. Their rival, the American Football League (AFL), was trying to lure him away from the Packers with $250,000 contract offers. He was being wooed by both parties to run for public office in Wisconsin. He had a roster of product endorsements he did regularly. His face was one of the most recognizable in the country. If that wasn't enough to make him the envy of most adult American males, Hornung also had a reputation as the country's most successful ladies' man.

The stories began to circulate while he was still in college when he returned to his dorm room late one evening and found a girl there waiting for him. On another occasion, not long after he joined the Packers, a woman approached him as he sat on the bench—during a game! She refused to leave until he had his picture taken with her. As she left the field, he told her to meet him outside the locker room after the game. Hornung played down the rumors, saying that if he had done half of what he was said to have done with women he would be in a bottle at the Smithsonian Institution. At the same time, he admitted frequently, "I like girls."

Hornung's rollicking, party-boy lifestyle occasionally got him into hot water with Green Bay's coach Vince Lombardi. Lombardi put few restrictions on his players but he was a stickler for the rules he had. He fined Hornung and Max McGee, both hard drinkers who liked to do the town together, $250 each for coming in five minutes after curfew. On another occasion Hornung was fined $500 when Lombardi caught him standing with his date at a hotel bar in Chicago, in violation of team rules. Lombardi later reduced the fine to $250 when he learned that Hornung had only been drinking ginger ale.

The greatest test of Hornung's relationship with the coach occurred in 1963 when Hornung was suspended by NFL commissioner **Pete Rozelle**. Hornung had befriended a pinball machine operator, Barney Shapiro, who took to calling Hornung for advice before placing bets on pro football games. Eventually Hornung started making bets himself, between $100 and $500 a game, on both college and pro football. Rozelle himself admitted that Hornung had never bet against the Packers. Rozelle opened an investigation into gambling in the NFL in 1962. When Rozelle's spotlight hit Hornung, he quickly admitted his guilt. Despite Hornung's immediate and evidently sincere repentance, in April 1963, Hornung and Detroit Lion Alex Karras were put on indefinite suspension for their gambling activities.

Lombardi was naturally dismayed to lose his star back. Making matters worse, Lombardi, aware of Rozelle's investigation, had asked Hornung about gambling before Hornung was confronted by the commissioner. Hornung had denied any complicity. More than the suspension, Lombardi was more disappointed that Hornung had lied to him. Rumors circulated regularly that if Hornung were allowed to return to the Pack, Lombardi would trade him. In the spring of 1964, however, when Rozelle lifted the suspensions, Lombardi welcomed the Golden Boy back, insisting only that he begin training two months before the rest of the team to get back into playing shape.

Lombardi appreciated Hornung too much as a player and leader to let him go so easily. In *The Great Running Backs,* George Sullivan quotes Lombardi's thoughts on Hornung: "You have to know what Hornung means to this team. I have heard and read that he is not a great runner or a great passer or a great field-goal kicker, but he led the league in scoring for three seasons. In the middle of the field he may be only slightly better than an average ballplayer, but inside the twenty-yard line he is one of the greatest I have ever seen. He smells that goal line." Ultimately Hornung's performance and dedication was what mattered most to Lombardi. Hornung also did things off the field that Lombardi valued, for example, befriending new players whom he often took along to his speaking engagements and split his fee with afterwards. In addition, Lombardi just liked Paul Hornung and was said to be closer to him than to any other Packer player.

Never the Same

Hornung was never the same again after his return from the suspension. He struggled particularly making his kicks. He had lost his timing and missed 26 of 38 field goal attempts in 1964. Lombardi replaced him with another kicker to allow Hornung to concentrate on his rushing. He suffered a string of injuries though that kept him on the bench, including a pinched nerve in his neck that would eventually end his career. He had one last brilliant flash of glory in 1965 against the Colts when he ran for sixty-one yards, caught two passes for 115 yards, and scored *five* touchdowns. The win put the Packers in a tie for first place with the Colts. Green Bay went all the way and won the NFL championship again.

He sat out much of the 1966 season, including Super Bowl I, because of his hurt neck. At the end of the season, Lombardi, thinking no team would want an injured player, put Hornung's name on the list of Green Bay players available for the expansion draft. He had figured wrong. The New Orleans Saints grabbed Hornung. Lombardi was mortified, but Hornung was prepared to go to New Orleans to play. Unfortunately, a medical examination revealed that the nerve injury in his neck was more serious than first thought. When doctors told him that continued play could result in paralysis, Hornung retired. As it was, the injury resulted in the loss of much of the use of Hornung's right arm.

After his retirement Paul Hornung became a sports broadcaster, in particular covering Notre Dame and other college games. He invested his football earnings well in a number of real estate ventures in Louisville. The man-about-town, who, when an angry Vince Lombardi demanded whether he wanted to be a football player or a playboy, answered "A playboy!" got married once in 1967, divorced, and married again in 1980.

An All-Pro and MVP, Paul Hornung rushed for 3,711 yards and fifty touchdowns in his nine seasons with the Packers. He had 130 pass receptions for 383 yards. As kicker, he hit 190 of 194 extra points and sixty-six of 140 field goals. Paul Hornung was the heart and soul of the Green Bay Packers in the early 1960s. He was voted into the Green Bay Packers Hall of Fame in 1975, to the NFF College Hall of Fame in 1985, and to the Pro Football Hall of Fame in 1986.

CONTACT INFORMATION

Address: Waterfront Plaza, Suite 1116, 325 West Main Street, Louisville, KY 40202. Email: autographs@paulhornung.com. Online: www.paulhornung.com.

SELECTED WRITINGS BY HORNUNG:

(With Tim Cohane) "How Winning Changed My Image." *Look* (November 20, 1962).

"The Girls and I." *Look* (July 27, 1965).

"Why I Gambled and What It Cost Me." *Look* (August 10, 1965).

(With Al Silverman) *Football and the Single Man*, Doubleday, 1965.

FURTHER INFORMATION

Books

Bengston, Phil, with Todd Hunt. *Packer Dynasty*. Garden City, NY: Doubleday, 1969

Hornung, Paul, and Al Silverman. *Football and the Single Man*. Garden City, NY: Doubleday, 1965.

Kramer, Jerry, with Dick Schaap. *Distant Replay*. New York: G.P. Putnam's Sons, 1985.

O'Brien, Michael. *Vince*. New York: William Morrow & Co, 1987.

Sullivan, George. *The Great Running Backs*. New York: G.P. Putnam's Sons, 1972.

Wiebusch, John, (ed.). *Lombardi*. Chicago: Follett Publishing Co., 1971.

Periodicals

"Confessions of a Legend." *Time* (October 29, 1965): 78.

Hornung, Paul. "The Girls and I." *Look* (July 27, 1965): 60.

Hornung, Paul, with Tim Cohane. "How Winning Changed My Image." *Look* (November 20, 1962): 124

Hornung, Paul. "Why I Gambled and What It Cost Me." *Look* (August 10, 1965): 61.

"The Indispensable Man." *Time* (October 27, 1961): 74.

Oates, Bob. "The Golden Boy." *Los Angeles Times* (February 24, 1986): C10.

"Packers' Golden Boy." *New York Times* (January 7, 1962): 16.

Wallace, William N. "Pro Football Ban on Hornung and Karras Lifted After 11 Months." *New York Times* (March 17, 1964): 41.

White, Gordon S., Jr. "Football Stars Banned for Bets." *New York Times* (April 18, 1963): 1.

Sketch by Gerald E. Brennan

Gordie Howe
1928-

Canadian hockey player

Often called "Mr. Hockey," Gordie Howe is acknowledged as one of the best-ever all-around players in the history of the sport. Fast and powerful on the ice, with the ability to shoot the puck left- or right-handed, Howe set records during his career with the National Hockey League's (NHL) Detroit Red Wings that included most goals scored during the regular season, most winning goals scored, most seasons played, and most regular-season games played. The right-wing offenseman also scored the most career points (goals plus assists) for any player in his position. Howe burnished his own legend by coming out of retirement to play in the World Hockey Association (WHA) in 1973 alongside his sons, Marty and Mark. During his six seasons in the WHA with the Houston Aeros and New England Whalers, Howe helped to popularize hockey in the growing sports markets of the

Gordie Howe

American Sunbelt. He returned for one last season in the NHL when the Whalers became the Hartford Whalers, and retired as a professional athlete in 1980. In the decades since then, he has continued to promote an array of philanthropic efforts and manage his own business interests with his wife, Colleen. In 2002 Howe cut back on his public appearances to care for his wife, who had been diagnosed with Pick's Disease, a form of dementia that causes memory loss and behavioral changes.

A Childhood on the Canadian Prairie

Born in the small farming town of Floral, Saskatchewan, Canada on March 31, 1928, Gordon Howe grew up in nearby Saskatoon with his eight brothers and sisters. His father, Albert Howe, had just given up a life of farming at the time of his son's birth and subsequently worked as a mechanic and construction worker, finally achieving the position of superintendent of maintenance for the City of Saskatoon. Money was tight in the Howe household during the Great Depression and his mother, Katherine Schultz Howe, could sometimes only feed the family oatmeal porridge for each meal. When he was five years old, Gordie Howe developed a health-threatening calcium deficiency in part caused by his family's poverty. In addition to taking vitamins to correct the problem, Howe began to exercise regularly to improve his bone and muscle strength. His dedication to a demanding physical regimen would later prove crucial in the longevity of his career, particularly after suffering some major injuries during his first years in the NHL.

Like most boys growing up on the Canadian Prairie, Howe played hockey with his friends during the long winters on any frozen surface. He got his first pair of skates after his mother gave a dollar-and-a-half to a neighbor whose husband was hospitalized; in exchange, Mrs. Howe got a sack filled with assorted odd items, including a pair of skates. Although they were far too large for him, Howe put on several pairs of socks and spent all day out on the ice. After he outgrew them, Howe sometimes had to strap blades onto his street shoes in lieu of proper skates. Although he was at times embarrassed by his lack of equipment, Howe increasingly turned to hockey as his refuge as he was growing up. After failing the third grade twice, he was often the target of teasing at school and developed into an introverted teenager.

Signs with the Red Wings

Howe's hockey team at King George Community School won its league championship in 1941, 1942, and 1944. Howe was also a member of the team at the King George Athletic Club, a sports center set up for the youth of Saskatoon's West End. The team made it all the way to the finals of Saskatechewan's bantam league in 1942, where it lost to Regina. Based on the teams' winning records, Howe attracted the attention of a New York Rangers scout in 1943 and he was invited to the team's training camp in Winnepeg that year. The experience overwhelmed the awkward fifteen-year-old, who quickly returned home. Within months, a scout from the Red Wings convinced Howe to attend his team's training

Career Statistics

Yr	Team	GP	G	A	Pts	+/-	PIM	SOG	SPCT
1946-47	DET	58	7	15	22	---	52	---	---
1947-48	DET	60	16	28	44	---	63	---	---
1948-49	DET	40	12	25	37	---	57	---	---
1949-50	DET	70	35	33	68	---	69	---	---
1950-51	DET	70	43	43	86	---	74	---	---
1951-52	DET	70	47	39	86	---	78	---	---
1952-53	DET	70	49	46	95	---	57	---	---
1953-54	DET	70	33	48	81	---	109	---	---
1954-55	DET	64	29	33	62	---	68	---	---
1955-56	DET	70	38	41	79	---	100	---	---
1956-57	DET	70	44	45	89	---	72	---	---
1957-58	DET	64	33	44	77	---	40	---	---
1958-59	DET	70	32	46	78	---	57	---	---
1959-60	DET	70	28	45	73	---	46	---	---
1960-61	DET	64	23	49	72	---	30	---	---
1961-62	DET	70	33	44	77	---	54	---	---
1962-63	DET	70	38	48	86	---	100	---	---
1963-64	DET	69	26	47	73	---	70	---	---
1964-65	DET	70	29	47	76	---	104	---	---
1965-66	DET	70	29	46	75	---	83	---	---
1966-67	DET	69	25	40	65	---	53	---	---
1967-68	DET	74	39	43	82	+12	53	311	13.0
1968-69	DET	76	44	59	103	+45	58	283	15.5
1969-70	DET	76	31	40	71	+23	58	268	11.6
1970-71	DET	63	23	29	52	-2	38	195	11.8
1973-74	HOU	70	31	69	100	---	46	---	---
1974-75	HOU	75	34	65	99	---	84	---	---
1975-76	HOU	78	32	70	102	---	76	---	---
1976-77	HOU	62	24	44	68	---	57	---	---
1977-78	WHAL	76	34	62	96	---	85	---	---
1978-79	WHAL	58	19	24	43	---	51	---	---
1979-80	WHAL	80	15	26	41	+9	42	94	16.0
TOTAL		1767	801	1049	1850	---	1685	---	---

DET: Detroit Red Wings (NHL); HOU: Houston Aeroes (WHA); WHAL: New England Whalers (WHA), then Hartford Whalers (NHL)

camp. With the promise that some of his friends from Saskatoon would also be attending, Howe agreed to give it a try. He immediately demonstrated his promise in the training camp and the Red Wings signed him to a contract. Although Howe was supposed to finish high school while playing for the Galt, Ontario Red Wings in the 1944-45 season, he decided to end his formal education and instead work at a local metal works. The next year he was sent to the Omaha Knights for the full season at a salary of $2,200; with twenty-two goals and twenty-six assists in fifty-one games, Howe was brought up to the Red Wings for the 1946-47 season. He was eighteen years old and made $5,000 in his debut season in the NHL.

Howe was not a breakout star in his first season with the Red Wings. Although he played fifty-eight games, he scored just seven times and had fifteen assists. Teamed with left wing Ted Lindsay and veteran center Sid Abel in 1947, Howe about doubled his numbers to sixteen goals and twenty-eight assists in sixty games. The three players became known as the "Production Line," one of the best offensive lineups in the history of the sport. The Red Wings made it to the finals of the NHL championships at the end of the 1947-48 and 1948-49 seasons, but the team was routed both times by the Toronto Maple Leafs, who swept both titles.

Four Stanley Cup Wins

The 1949-50 season was the first standout season of Howe's career. The Production Line of Lindsay, Abel, and Howe went one-two-three in that year's total points standings and the Red Wings made it to the championship against the New York Rangers. The finals produced a four-to-three games victory for the Wings, the team's first title in seven years. Unfortunately, Howe was not on the ice for the victory. In a playoff game against the Maple Leafs on March 28, 1950, Howe skidded into the boards while attempting to block an opponent; the freak mishap left him with a fractured nose and cheekbone, a lacerated eyeball, and a brain hemorrhage. After a surgeon drilled a hole through his skull to relieve the pressure from his brain, Howe's quick recovery astounded his doctors. Although his life had been in danger, the resilient Howe immediately announced that he would return to the Red Wings line up for the full 1951-52 season. Over the course of his career, the six-foot, two-hundred-eight pound hockey player would suffer

Related Biography: Wife Colleen Howe

Colleen Joffa was born in 1933 and spent part of her childhood in Sandusky, Michigan. After her parents' divorce, she moved with her mother and stepfather to Detroit, where she completed high school. She was working as a secretary at Bethlehem Steel when she first met Gordie Howe at the Lucky Strike bowling lanes on Grand River Avenue in Detroit in 1951. The couple dated for two years and married on April 15, 1953. They raised four children: future hockey players Marty and Mark, physician son Murray, and daughter, Cathy, who later worked for the family's business.

As the manager of her husband's business interests, Colleen Howe broke new ground in major-league sports. In addition to running Power Play International, Howe became an Amway distributor, sold life insurance, and even ran for U.S. Congress as a Republican candidate when the family lived in Connecticut. She was also a founder of the Detroit Junior Red Wings, the first junior-league hockey team in the United States. These accomplishments made her a pioneer in the sport of hockey, but sometimes brought her into conflict with the teams' owners and managers.

During her husband's retirement, Howe organized the couple's time around their philanthropic efforts, including the Howe Foundation. The first woman inducted into the U.S. Hockey Hall of Fame, Howe was also honored as Michigan's Sportswoman of the Year in 1973. In 2002 Gordie Howe announced that Colleen was suffering from Pick's Disease, which causes sudden and debilitating dementia in its victims.

Where Is He Now?

Enjoying his second retirement since 1980, Howe returned to play a game in 1997 with the Detroit Vipers of the International Hockey League. Although he played for less than a minute, Howe scored a goal and became the first hockey player to have played a game in each of six decades. Howe was sixty-nine years old at the time of his final professional hockey game.

From their home in the Detroit suburb of Bloomfield Hills, Howe and his wife, Colleen, conducted an extensive schedule of charity-raising appearances in the 1990s. In 2002 Howe disclosed that Colleen had been diagnosed with Pick's Disease, an incurable form of dementia that leads to behavioral changes and memory loss. "I've never had so many worries in my life," Howe admitted to the *Detroit News* in September 2002, "Sleepless nights. Every day is a constant reminder. What is, what was. Outside it's different, but inside . . . it eats you up."

from torn knee cartilage, a broken wrist, a dislocated shoulder, several concussions, numerous broken ribs and toes, and over three hundred stitches.

Howe began his run of four consecutive NHL scoring titles, symbolized by the Art Ross Trophy, in 1951; he won the title again in 1957. He added the Hart Trophy as the NHL's most valuable player to his collection in 1952, 1953, 1957, 1958, 1960, and 1963. Once again healthy for the 1952 Stanley Cup finals against Montreal, Howe helped the team to sweep the series in four games. The match was an early highlight of the legendary rivalry between the Red Wings and the Canadiens and between Howe and **Maurice Richard**, one of the most dynamic players of the day. Detroit would emerge as the winner in the 1954 and 1955 finals over Montreal, but the Canadiens took the Stanley Cup in 1956 over Detroit, the first of five consecutive championships for the team. Despite Howe's brilliance, the Red Wings would not win another Stanley Cup during his tenure with the team.

A series of poor trades by domineering Red Wings general manager Jack Adams sapped the team's strength from the mid-1950s onward. So too did his fury at the players for attempting to form a players' union. Ted Lindsay, who led such efforts in Detroit, was suddenly traded to the failing Chicago Blackhawks in 1957 in retribution. Howe, who was criticized for not speaking out in favor of the players' union at the time, later came to regret his unquestioning loyalty to Red Wings management. Although he earned about $20,000 in salary and up to $9,000 in bonuses in the late 1950s, it was only after the successful formation of the NHL Players' Association in 1967 that his salary climbed above $40,000. By that time Howe had assured himself of a place in the record books by breaking the all-time goal-scoring

record held by Maurice Richard. On November 10, 1963, Howe scored his 545th goal in a game against the Canadiens. He went on to score 801 goals in 1,767 NHL games over twenty-six seasons.

Comes Out of Retirement

At the end of the 1970-71 season, Howe announced that he was retiring from the Red Wings after twenty-five seasons. Honored with the Order of Canada by his homeland's government in 1971, he was inducted into the International Hockey Hall of Fame in 1972. Although Howe planned on entering the management ranks of the Red Wings, the arrangement turned out badly, in part because of tensions between the team's owner, Bruce Norris, and Colleen Howe, who took an increasingly active role in managing her husband's business affairs. After two unfulfilling years doing public relations work for the Red Wings, Howe laced up his skates again to play with the Houston Aeros in the upstart WHA. Alongside him were two of his sons, Marty and Mark, who were making their big-league debuts with the team. Howe played for the Aeros for four seasons before joining the New England Whalers for two more seasons. When the Whalers were incorporated into the NHL as the Hartford Whalers for the 1979-80 season, Howe racked up his twenty-sixth NHL season with eighty games, fifteen goals, and twenty-six assists. At the time of his second retirement as a professional athlete in 1980, Howe was fifty-two years old.

Philanthropic Efforts

Gordie and Colleen Howe had developed numerous business interests during his athletic career, but the couple was more often in the public eye for their philanthropic work. In honor of her husband's sixty-fifth birthday in 1993, Colleen Howe arranged a sixty-five city fundraising tour for a variety of charities, including the Howe Foundation and Howe Center for Youth Hockey Development. The recipient of numerous awards for her own philanthropic activities, Colleen Howe was named a Michiganian of the Year by the *Detroit News*

Gordie Howe

along with her husband in 2001. The following year, Gordie Howe revealed that his wife had been diagnosed with Pick's Disease, causing irreversible memory loss.

Sixth Decade of Hockey Playing

Although most of Howe's NHL records have been broken—most famously, his all-time points record fell to **Wayne Gretzky** in 1989—his status as one of the sport's best-ever players is unquestioned. Twenty years after his final retirement as a player, Howe also remains one of the most respected figures in any sport for his professionalism on the ice and his unassuming demeanor and dignity away from it. In October 1997 Howe returned to play one game with the Detroit Vipers of the International Hockey League, making him the first hockey player to participate in a professional game in each of six decades. He played for less than a minute, but still managed to score a goal "I've been blessed with a lot of great moments," Howe told Neil Stevens of the *Canadian Press* with characteristic modesty at the end of the game, "And this was one of them."

FURTHER INFORMATION

Books

Diamond, Dan, ed. *Total Hockey: The Official Encyclopedia of the National Hockey League.* Kansas City: Andrews McMeel Publishing, 1998.

Macskimming, Roy. *Gordie: A Hockey Legend.* Vancouver: GreyStone Books, 1994.

McFarlane, Brian. *The Red Wings.* Toronto: Stoddart Publishing, 1998.

Periodicals

Green, Jerry. "Gordie Talks for First Time About Colleen's Dementia." *Detroit News* (September 26, 2002).

Other

"Mr. Hockey Biography." Mr. Hockey Official Web site. http://www.mrhockey.com/history/mr_hockey_bio.shtml (November 1, 2002).

"Mrs. Hockey Biography." Mr. Hockey Official Web site. http://www.mrhockey.com/history/mrs_hockey_bio.shtml (November 3, 2002).

Stevens, Neil. "Howe Skates Again!" Canoe/Canadian Press Web site. http://www.canoe.ca/IHL/howe_oct3.html (October 3, 1997).

Sketch by Timothy Borden

Sarah Hughes
1985-

American figure skater

American figure skater Sarah Hughes is among the most consistent competitors in the sport, but no one expected her show at the 2003 Olympic Games in Salt Lake City, Utah. Hughes, just sixteen years old, upset both the favorite, **Michelle Kwan**, and other strong contenders to take the gold medal in women's figure skating.

Hughes was born on May 2, 1985 in Great Neck, New York. She is the fourth of six children of John, a lawyer and former hockey player, and Amy Hughes, an accountant. She began skating at age three in the backyard rink, following the lead of her two older brothers and sister. Her parents bought her hockey skates, but Hughes was incredibly competitive from an early age, and wanted to skate by herself. When she started taking classes, it was obvious that she had natural ability; she quickly mastered moves that challenged other skaters her age. She was a jumping whiz and began training with a coach, Patti Johnson, at age four. By the time she was five, Hughes knew she wanted to skate for the rest of her life.

As word traveled about the precocious young skater, Hughes was invited to skate in ice shows and exhibitions, performing in front of thousands of people. She loved being the center of attention, and thrived on the

Sarah Hughes

Chronology

1985	Born May 2 in Great Neck, New York
1988	Begins skating
1992	Skates in exhibitions and ice shows
1996	Enters first major competition
1997	Enters junior-level skating competition
1998	Enters senior-level competition
2002	Earns spot on 2003 Olympic skating team
2002	Wins Olympic gold

crowds. At age six she was part of a show that included **Kristi Yamaguchi**, whom she had just watched win the gold medal at the 1992 Olympic Games. She appeared on a Christmas special with Kathie Lee Gifford, and did a European tour with famous Russian coach Natalia Dubova and the world ice dance champions. She was friends with figure skating legends **Scott Hamilton**, JoJo Starbuck, and **Peggy Fleming** by the time she was eight years old. When Hughes was nine, choreographer Robin Wagner joined her team to help prepare her for competitions. Wagner would later become her coach. She entered her first major competition in 1996 at age ten, the North Atlantic Regional, and came in third place in the novice division. In 1997, she placed first.

When she was twelve, Hughes decided to compete in the junior category, the penultimate level in women's figure skating. While other skaters left home to skate with the best coaches, it was important to Hughes that she remain with her family in Great Neck. As Hughes began training for her first junior competitions, her mother was diagnosed with breast cancer, which made Hughes glad she chose to stay home. Her mother encouraged her to keep skating. After surgery and chemotherapy, Amy Hughes was too ill to travel, but managed to make it to Philadelphia to see her daughter win the gold medal at the 1998 Junior National Championships. She ultimately survived the cancer.

Hughes was invited to skate on the Junior Grand Prix circuit, a series of international competitions. Before she

graduated junior high school, she'd skated at the Hungarian Trophee in Budapest, the Mexico Cup in Mexico City, and the World Junior Figure Skating Championships in Zagreb, Croatia. When she had skated everything she could in Juniors, and decided to move on to the Senior level at age thirteen. There, she would compete against seasoned skaters like 1996 European champion Irina Slutskaya, 1999 world champion Maria Butyrskaya, and 1998 Olympic silver medallist Michelle Kwan.

Pubescent growth spurts have been the downfall of many a skater. They learn to maneuver their bodies on the ice as girls, but have trouble adapting when they start developing fuller bodies. Hughes's success in the Juniors did not guarantee her success later on. Luckily, Hughes' childhood gawkiness evolved into grace and poise. The ballet lessons Hughes took from the age of three to fourteen paid off. Hughes was second behind Kwan in the 1999 National Championships as they entered the long program, or free-skate competition. An extremely challenging program saved her from catastrophe after two falls, and she finished in a respectable fourth place. As a result, she was able to go on to the 1999 World Championships, where she finished in seventh place. The next year, as a rite of passage, Hughes had her girlhood ponytail lopped off in lieu of a more sophisticated short cut, and had her braces removed. She skated to fifth place in the 2000 World Championships.

While at Great Neck North High School, Hughes was skating two-and-a-half hours and conditioning two hours, six days a week. She got up at four or five in the morning to skate before school, and ultimately sought out tutors and worked with her teachers via e-mail when her competition schedule got too dense.

By 2001, Hughes was a regular figure on the podium at the senior level. She placed second behind Kwan in the Nationals and third behind Kwan and Irina Slutskaya at the Worlds. Four months before the 2002 Olympics, Hughes got a huge boost when she beat both Kwan and Slutskaya at the international competition Skate Canada. She entered the most important Nationals of her career—the one that would determine the Olympic team—with confidence and high expectations. On January 12, 2002, Hughes placed third behind Kwan and Sasha Cohen at the Nationals, which wasn't what she had hoped for, but

Awards and Accomplishments

1996	Third place, North Atlantic Regional, Novice
1997	First place, North Atlantic Regional, Novice
1998	First place, North Atlantic Regional, Junior, Eastern Sectional, Junior, and U.S. Junior Championships
1998	Second place, Hungarian Trophy and Mexico Cup
1999	First place, World Junior Team Selection
1999	Second place, World Junior Championships
1999	Fourth place, U.S. Championships
1999	Second place, ISU Junior Grand Prix
1999	Seventh place, World Championships
1999	Second place, Hershey's Kisses Challenge (team) and Keri Lotion Classic (team)
1999	First place, Vienna Classic
1999	Fourth place, Skate America
1999	Third place, Trophee Lalique
1999	First place, Keri Lotion USA vs. World (team)
2000	Third place, U.S. Figure Skating Championships
2000	Fifth place, World Championships
2000	Second place, International Figure Skating Challenge (team), Skate America, and Nations Cup
2000	Third place, Cup of Russia and Canadian Open
2000	First place, Hershey's Kisses Challenge (team)
2001	Second place, U.S. Championships
2001	Third place, Grand Prix Final, World Championships, and Great American Figure Skating Challenge (Team)
2002	Third place, U.S. Championships
2002	First place, Winter Olympic Games, Salt Lake City
2002	Third place, Grand Prix Final
2002	Second place, Hershey's Kisses Challenge (team)
2002	Third place, Campbell's Classic
2002	Second place, Crest Whitestrips Challenge
2003	Second place, U.S. Championships

was enough to land her on the Olympic team. She had less than one month to train for the event of her life.

Hughes went into the Olympics on a wave of media attention. Kwan was the favorite to win, after having lost the gold to fifteen-year-old **Tara Lipinski** in 1998. While *Newsweek* had put Kwan on its cover, and *Sport Illustrated* had chosen Slutskaya, Hughes was *Time* magazine's cover girl. She did her best to focus, and left the frenzy behind after the opening ceremonies to practice for six days in the low-pressure environment of Colorado Springs, Colorado.

Hughes was in fourth place after the short program, behind Kwan, Slutskaya, and Cohen. But Hughes skated like she had nothing to lose. Her long program was one of the most technically demanding ever attempted in an Olympic women's competition. She successfully landed two clean triple-triple combinations. Cohen fell during her program, which took her out of the running and guaranteed Hughes a medal. Kwan skated a lackluster program, but Slutskaya wowed the judges. The judges spent a grueling three minutes calculating Slutskaya's scores, which were impressive, but were only good enough for a silver medal. Hughes had won the gold. The crowd went wild. "What an upset!" commentator Scott Hamilton exclaimed to the TV audience.

An NBC cameraman informed Hughes she had won, and she and her coach, Robin Wagner, fell to the floor of a locker room, clutching each other, crying and screaming gleefully. When the gold medal was placed around her neck, Hughes became the fourth youngest Olympic women's figure skating champion of all time. Kwan looked on and wept from her third-place position on the Olympic podium.

Hughes immediately accepted invitations to appear on the *Today Show* with Katie Couric, *Saturday Night Live, The Tonight Show with Jay Leno, The Rosie O'Donnell Show,* and was a presenter on the Grammy Awards. A leg injury forced Hughes to withdraw from the 2002-03 Grand Prix of Figure Skating, but she came back in to finish second in the Crest Whitestrips Challenge in December 2002. Her first television special, *Sarah Hughes: A Life in Balance,* aired on NBC on December 22. She finished second behind Kwan at the 2003 Nationals. Hughes was accepted to Harvard University, and hopes to study medicine and become a doctor. She claims her greatest accomplishment is getting up in the morning.

CONTACT INFORMATION

Address: Sarah Hughes, U.S. Figure Skating Association, 20 First St., Colorado Springs, CO 80906-3624.

FURTHER INFORMATION

Books

Ashby, R.S. *Going for the Gold—Sarah Hughes: America's Sweetheart.* New York: Avon Books, 2002.
Sivorinovsky, Alina. *Sarah Hughes: Skating to the Stars.* New York: Berkley Books, 2001.

Other

"Person of the Week: Sarah Hughes." *Time* Online. http://www.time.com (January 15, 2003).
"Sarah Hughes." U.S. Figure Skating Online. http://www.usfsa.org (January 15, 2003).
"Sarah Hughes: Olympian fine-tunes her routine." U.S. Olympic Team Web site. http://www.olympic-usa.org (January 15, 2003).
"Sweet sixteen." CNN.com. http://www.cnn.com (January 15, 2003).

Sketch by Brenna Sanchez

Bobby Hull
1939-

Canadian hockey player

O ne of the most dynamic players in the National Hockey League (NHL) in the 1960s, Bobby Hull earned the nickname "The Golden Jet" for his quick moves and solid shooting ability on the ice and his colorful personality off the ice. Setting numerous scoring records during his fifteen seasons with the Chicago Blackhawks, Hull was the first player to win a contract paying him over $100,000 a year. He was also the first star player to be signed to the fledgling World Hockey Association (WHA) in 1972, another move that helped to shake up the staid management that characterized the sport at the time. Hull returned to a final season in the NHL in 1979-1980 but ended his career on a sour note as it coincided with some nasty headlines about his divorce from his wife of twenty years, Joanne McKay. The separation affected Hull's relationship with the couple's five children, one of whom, **Brett Hull**, would grow up to become a gifted NHL player in his own right. In his retirement Hull put most of energy into running his cattle ranching operations in Canada, but he remained an active commentator on the sport the made him famous and was frequently in the headlines for his blunt remarks.

Hockey Prodigy

Robert Marvin Hull, Jr. was born on January 3, 1939 in Point Anne, Ontario, Canada, where his father worked in a cement plant. The eldest son in a family of eleven children, Hull received a pair of ice skates as a Christmas present when he was three years old and took to the ice immediately. During his childhood he often cleared the ice so that he could skate on the frozen surface of the Bay of Quinte near his family's home. Before he had reached his teens Hull was playing alongside his father in a local amateur hockey league. His skills were so impressive that Bob Wilson, the head of scouting for the NHL's Chicago Blackhawks, signed the twelve-year-old to a contract committing him to the team. After playing for a juvenile-league team in Hesperer, Ontario in 1952, Hull joined the Blackhawks' junior-league affiliate in Woodstock, Ontario. He then spent the 1954-55 season playing for the Galt Black Hawks in the Ontario Hockey Association and the following two seasons with the St. Catherines Teepees in Ontario. He almost left the team after his coach, Rudy Pilous, told him to play left wing instead of center, which Hull perceived to be a demotion. After talking it over with his father, he decided to rejoin the team after missing four games over his protest.

At five feet, ten inches tall and weighing about 190 pounds, Hull was already an impressive figure on the ice as a teenager. Although he sported huge forearms and thighs and a barrel chest, Hull seemed to move faster on the ice than any of his opponents. His talent was on full display in 1956 when he was unexpectedly called to an exhibition game staged by the Blackhawks against the New York Islanders in St. Catherines. The high schooler scored two goals against the Islanders in the game. Desperate for new talent—the team had finished last in the league for the

Chronology	
1939	Born January 3 in Point Anne, Ontario, Canada
1951	Signs contract with Chicago Blackhawks
1957	Begins playing for Chicago Blackhawks
1960, 1962, 1966	Leads National Hockey League in scoring
1965	Wins Lady Byng Trophy for sportsmanship in NHL
1965, 1967	Wins Hart Trophy as NHL's Most Valuable Player
1967-69	Leads National Hockey League in goals
1972	Signs contract with World Hockey Association's (WHA) Winnepeg Jets
1973	Named Most Valuable Player in WHA
1975	Leads WHA in scoring
1975	Named Most Valuable Player in WHA
1979	Plays for Hartford Whalers in NHL
1981	Retires from professional hockey

past four seasons—the Blackhawks brought Hull to the NHL in 1957 and named Pilous head coach as well.

Top Scorer in NHL

The infusion of new talent into the Blackhawks' line up did not pay dividends at first. Hull had just thirteen goals in seventy games in his debut season in 1957-58. The next season he improved his record to eighteen goals in seventy games. The 1959-60 season proved to be the turning point in Hull's NHL career. Hull shared the goal-scoring title with thirty-nine goals and led the league in total points as his forty-two assists gave him an overall score of eighty-one points. Although Hull was plagued by a knee injury the following season, he managed to score thirty-one goals in sixty-seven games; more important, he helped the Blackhawks to win the NHL championship, symbolized by the Stanley Cup, in a four-to-two-game series over the Detroit Red Wings. It was the first such victory for the team since 1938; the team had not even made the finals since 1944. Now hailed as "The Golden Jet" for his rapid plays on the ice as well as for his blond good looks, the feat turned Hull into one of hockey's biggest stars.

1960 was also a pivotal year in Hull's personal life. After a short-lived marriage as a teenager, Hull wed the former Joanne McKay, who had performed as an ice skater. The couple eventually had five children before divorcing in 1980. The latter event made headlines across North America for the allegations of adultery and spousal abuse leveled at Hull, including one incident that occurred in Hawaii in 1966. According to his wife, Hull had beaten her with a steel-heeled shoe before hanging her over a balcony ledge. She left him in 1970 but they reconciled and stayed together for another ten years. Joanne McKay Hull moved to Vancouver with their children and eventually remarried. After several years of estrangement, Hull started to rebuild his relationship with his children, who included NHL player Brett Hull. In 1984 Hull married for a third time; his

Career Statistics

Yr	Team	GP	G	A	PTS	+/−	PIM	SOG	SPCT	PPG	SHG
1957-58	Black Hawks	70	13	34	47	—	62	—	—	—	—
1958-59	Black Hawks	70	18	32	50	—	50	—	—	—	—
1959-60	Black Hawks	70	39	42	81	—	68	—	—	—	—
1960-61	Black Hawks	67	31	25	56	—	43	—	—	—	—
1961-62	Black Hawks	70	50	34	84	—	35	—	—	—	—
1962-63	Black Hawks	65	31	31	62	—	27	—	—	—	—
1963-64	Black Hawks	70	43	44	87	—	50	—	—	—	—
1964-65	Black Hawks	61	39	32	71	—	32	—	—	—	—
1965-66	Black Hawks	65	54	43	97	—	70	—	—	—	—
1966-67	Black Hawks	66	52	28	80	—	52	—	—	—	—
1967-68	Black Hawks	71	44	31	75	14	39	364	12.1	8	2
1968-69	Black Hawks	74	58	49	107	−7	48	414	14.0	20	2
1969-70	Black Hawks	61	38	29	67	+20	8	289	13.1	10	2
1970-71	Black Hawks	78	44	52	96	+34	32	378	11.6	11	0
1971-72	Black Hawks	78	50	43	93	+54	24	336	14.9	8	3
1972-73	Jets	63	51	52	103	—	37	—	—	—	—
1973-74	Jets	75	53	42	95	—	38	—	—	—	—
1974-75	Jets	78	77	65	142	—	41	—	—	—	—
1975-76	Jets	80	53	70	123	—	30	—	—	—	—
1976-77	Jets	34	21	32	53	—	14	—	—	—	—
1977-78	Jets	77	46	71	117	—	23	—	—	—	—
1978-79	Jets	4	2	3	5	—	0	—	—	—	—
1979-80	Jets	18	4	6	10	7	0	25	16.0	1	0
	Whalers	9	2	5	7	−3	0	13	15.4	1	
NHL Totals		1063	610	560	1170	—	640	—	—	—	—
WHA Totals		411	303	335	638	—	183	—	—	—	—

Black Hawks: Chicago Black Hawks (NHL); Jets: Winnipeg Jets (WHA, later NHL); Whalers: Hartford Whalers (NHL).

marriage to Deborah Hull also made headlines when he was charged with assault and battery against his wife. The complaint was later withdrawn, but Hull pled guilty to a charge of assaulting a police officer who had come to make the initial arrest.

The NHL's Most Popular Player

Although the 1961 Stanley Cup was the only one the Blackhawks won during Hull's time with the team, his popularity eclipsed that of almost any other player in the NHL in the 1960s. His powerful slap shot—once clocked at 119 miles per hour—led to another title of the league's top scorer in 1962, when he racked up fifty goals and eighty-four total points. That year the Blackhawks lost the Stanley Cup to the Toronto Maple Leafs. The team returned to the finals again in 1965 and 1971, losing both times to the Montreal Canadiens.

Hull subsequently won the title of top goal scorer again in 1966 with fifty-four goals and ninety-seven total points. The achievement also shattered the record of total goals in a season, set by the Montreal Canadiens' **Maurice Richard** with fifty goals in 1945. Hull followed up an amazing season in 1966 with three more seasons when he led the league in goals, reaching a pinnacle with the fifty-eight goals of the 1968-69 season. A solid all-around player, Hull won the Hart Trophy as NHL's Most Valuable Player of the regular season in 1965 and 1966, as well as the Lady Byng Trophy for sportsmanship in NHL in 1965.

Signs with World Hockey Association

It seemed that Hull had almost single-handedly revived the Blackhawks' fortunes and his salary climbed to $100,000 for the 1968-69 season. Yet he faced a series of battles with the team's owners. After investors started up a rival hockey league, the World Hockey Association (WHA), in 1972 to compete with the NHL, Hull was one of the first players they approached about the venture. "Going to the WHA was not one bit about money," Hull recalled in an interview with *Sports Illustrated*'s Allen Abel in 1998, "I had been at war with the Blackhawks' management for years. We hated each other." Still, when the WHA made an offer of a quarter million dollars a year, plus a one-million-dollar signing bonus, Hull thought the offer was bogus. "I thought it was a joke," he told Abel, "I pretended to go along with it, just to scare Chicago. Then my agent, Harvey Weinberg, said, 'Bobby, these guys are serious.'" The total value of the final contract with the WHA's Winnepeg Jets came to $1.75 million, which ensured the WHA a huge amount of advance publicity for the new league.

After sitting out several games when Chicago sued to prevent his departure, Hull joined the lineup of the Jets, where he remained for the next seven years. He won most valuable player honors in the 1972-73 and 1974-75 seasons and was widely regarded as the WHA's biggest star. Even Hull's popularity could not

---

Awards and Accomplishments

1960, **1962**, **1966**	Art Ross Trophy as NHL's top scorer
1961	Stanley Cup as NHL champions (Chicago Blackhawks)
1965	Lady Byng Trophy for sportsmanship in NHL
1965-66	Hart Trophy as NHL's Most Valuable Player
1973, **1975**	Most Valuable Player in WHA
1983	Inducted into Hockey Hall of Fame

---

pull the entire WHA out of its management problems, however, and it folded in 1979. Four of its teams and dozens of its players were absorbed into the NHL, and Hull finished out his career playing for the league's Hartford Whalers in 1980. Now in his forties, Hull practiced with the New York Rangers in preparation for a comeback in 1981, but he did not make the team's final cut. In all he had played fifteen seasons with the NHL, seven seasons with the WHA, and one season split between the two leagues.

Controversy in Retirement

Hull completed his NHL career with 1,063 games, 610 goals, and 560 assists. His WHA statistics included 411 games, 303 goals, and 335 assists. As an offensive player with few peers, Hull was inducted into the Hockey Hall of Fame in 1983. That same year his son, Brett Hull, began playing for the Penticton Knights, the first step in a hockey career that would eventually take him to the Stanley Cup-winning Detroit Red Wings in 2002.

Retiring from his career as a professional athlete to manage his cattle ranching operations in Canada, Hull was often sought out for his comments as an elder statesman of hockey. The outspokenness that made him such a popular sports figure sometimes got him into trouble, however. While attending a hockey game in Moscow in 1998, the English-language *Moscow Times* printed an interview that quoted Hull as favorably evaluating the racial breeding practices of Adolf Hitler as well as making racist comments against African Americans. Hull insisted that he had not made the comments and that he had only been discussing his cattle ranching operations without any racist implications whatsoever. Whatever the truth of the event, it was widely reported in the North American press and tarnished Hull's image with some of his fans. Despite the controversy, Hull remained a sought-after figure on the fan circuit, where his autographed merchandise remained popular with generations of hockey followers.

A Pivotal Era in Hockey

Although contemporary NHL fans are more familiar with the impressive career of his son, Detroit Red Wings right wing Brett Hull, Bobby Hull retains his legendary status in the sport's history. Both on and off the ice, Hull

---

Related Biography: Team Owner Ben Hatskin

A native of Winnipeg, Manitoba, Canada, Ben Hatskin was born in 1918 to parents who had emigrated from Russia. A standout football player in high school, he became one of the first Canadian students to win an athletic scholarship to an American university. He played for the Sooners at the University of Oklahoma but returned to Winnipeg to play for the Blue Bombers before he graduated from college. During World War II he began raising racehorses and his wealth grew as the Hatskin family invested in everything from lumber companies to juke box distributorships.

In 1967 Hatskin attempted to win an NHL franchise during the league's expansion. His bid failed, which fueled his desire to participate in a new, rival league, the WHA, in 1972. Hatskin knew that the credibility of the WHA depended on getting established hockey stars to join its teams. He aggressively sought out the services of Bobby Hull for his team, the Winnipeg Jets, and eventually signed Hull to a contract estimated to be worth at least $1.75 million.

Although it was one of the more successful teams in the WHA, Hatskin had to ask for a public subsidy to keep the financially troubled Jets alive after 1974. The team was absorbed into the NHL in 1979 and was purchased by Barry Shenkarow. At the end of the 1995-96 season Shenkarow sold the team to a consortium of Minneapolis businessmen, who ended up moving the team to Phoenix, where it was renamed the Coyotes. A few years later, hockey legend Wayne Gretzky bought an interest in the team and started working as its general manager. In Winnipeg, Hatskin is still remembered as visionary who performed a near-miracle in bringing a major-league sports franchise to a medium-sized city on the Canadian prairie.

---

instigated some fundamental changes in the way hockey was played and managed. As a player Hull transformed the sport into a game that emphasized offensive maneuvers, quick action, and scoring, in contrast to its former emphasis on a defensive game plan. Hull's salary demands also led to significant increases in the value of contracts earned by NHL players, particularly after he bolted to the WHA in 1972. Hull's media presence and popularity with his fans also helped to increase interest in the sport at a time when it was still limited to six teams. Without Hull's presence at a crucial juncture in the sport's history, it is questionable whether the NHL would have expanded to include its teams north of the Canadian border. For each of these reasons, Bobby Hull ranks as one of the most important hockey players of his, or indeed any, era in the sport.

FURTHER INFORMATION

Books

Diamond, Dan. *Hockey Hall of Fame: The Official Registry of the Game's Honour Roll*. Toronto: Doubleday Canada, 1996.

Diamond, Dan, ed. *Total Hockey: The Official Encyclopedia of the National Hockey League*. Kansas City: Andrews McMeel Publishing, 1998.

Jacobs, Jeff. *Hockey Legends*. New York: MetroBooks, 1995.

Periodicals

Abel, Allen. "When Hell Froze Over." *Sports Illustrated* (April 6, 1998): 98.

Brett Hull

Davies, Tanya. "Was It Bigotry, or Animal Husbandry?" *Maclean's* (September 7, 1998): 48.

Friesen, Paul. "Hatskin Silenced Skeptics" *Winnipeg Sun* (December 30, 1999).

Jenish, D. "'Like Father, Like Son.'" *Maclean's* (March 18, 1991): 52.

Other

Schwartz, Larry. "Hull Helped WHA into Hockey Family." ESPN Classic Web site. http://espn.go.com/classic/biography/s/hull_bobby.html (October 24, 2002).

Sketch by Timothy Borden

Brett Hull
1964-

Canadian hockey player

Son of Hockey Legend

S on of hockey legend **Bobby Hull**, Brett Hull has carved out his own place in the sport's history books alongside his father. Although he was criticized early in his career for being a one-dimensional player who could score goals but do little else on the ice, Hull grew into an impressive all-around player who adapted his game to help his teams win. One of the ten leading all-time scorers in the National Hockey League (NHL), Hull played on the Stanley Cup-winning teams of the Dallas Stars in 1999 and the Detroit Red Wings in 2002. One of the more vibrant personalities in the NHL, Hull was also popular with hockey audiences for his outspoken comments on the sport. As he related to Jennifer Floyd of the *Hockey Digest* in 2001, "[The fans] are the most important part of the game. Without them, there is no game.... It's not like I [became a fan advocate] to be a pain in the [butt] to the league or to the organizations I played for. I did it because I loved the game."

Born in Belleville, Ontario, Canada on August 9, 1964, Brett Hull arrived at the height of his father's fame as an NHL player. Bobby Hull took the Chicago Blackhawks to the Stanley Cup finals in 1965, the same year that he won the first of his two consecutive Hart Trophies as the league's Most Valuable Player. Brett and his three brothers spent considerable time with their father at Blackhawks training sessions; when the Blackhawks banned the Hull boys from the ice, Bobby Hull briefly walked off the team in protest.

The stormy relationship of his parents—which ended in divorce in 1980 after allegations of spousal abuse by his mother—estranged Hull from his father during his adolescence. The family had been living in Winnipeg, where Bobby Hull had played with the Jets between 1972 and 1980, but relocated to Vancouver without the elder Hull after the divorce. Hull also gave up playing hockey around this time; at five foot, nine inches tall and 220 pounds, he was too out of shape to contemplate a career as a professional player. After his mother encouraged him to give the sport another try, Hull made the Penticton junior hockey team in 1983 and played well enough to earn a sports scholarship to the University of Minnesota-Duluth.

Signs with the Calgary Flames

Hull spent just two years in college, but it was a pivotal experience in his career. A finalist for the Hobey

Baker Award as the best college hockey player of the 1985-86 season, Hull was signed by the Calgary Flames, who had selected him in the 1984 draft. He immediately made his debut at the end of the 1986 season during the Flames' appearance in the Stanley Cup finals, which the team lost to the Montreal Canadiens. Sent to the Moncton Golden Flames, Calgary's American Hockey League affiliate, for most of the 1986-87 season, Hull returned to Calgary in 1987. His tenure with the team turned out to be short-lived. With a reputation as a "sniper," or a player who lurked around the net waiting for a chance to score a goal, the right wing's style of play differed from the team-oriented approach of Calgary's coaches.

Finishing the 1987-88 season with the St. Louis Blues, Hull returned with a respectable forty-one goals and forty-three assists the following year. Working with coach Brian Sutter to improve his all-around game and his physical endurance, Hull had an impressive 1989-90 season with seventy-two goals and forty-one assists. He was also honored in 1990 with the Lady Byng Trophy, given to the NHL player exhibiting the most gentlemanly style of play on the ice.

Builds Popularity of the St. Louis Blues

Hull signed a four-year, $8.3 million contract with the Blues in 1990 and immediately demonstrated his worth to the team. His eighty-six goals in the 1990-91 season fell just short of **Wayne Gretzky**'s all-time record; Gretzky also edged Hull as that season's scoring leader. Hull, however, walked away with the Hart Trophy as the league's Most Valuable Player. Despite Hull's impressive playing, the Blues failed to make the Stanley Cup's final round.

Although the Blues never made it to the finals during his eleven seasons in St. Louis, Hull became one of the city's most popular sports figures. His colorful personality generated excitement around the team's fortunes in St. Louis, which had not previously been known as a hockey-oriented town. Injuries hampered his playing during the 1994-95 season, but Hull remained the key to the team's offense. Many were surprised when St. Louis declined to

sign him again at the end of the 1997-98 season; instead, Hull joined the Dallas Stars. As in St. Louis, he quickly raised the profile of hockey in a city that had a small fan base for winter sports. He also worked to change his game to complement the more defensive style coached by the Stars' Ken Hitchcock. As Hull wrote in a column published in *Sports Illustrated* in 1999, "When I came to Dallas last summer as a free agent, that style of play was an adjustment for me. I had to alter my game. At first it was tough to remember to check here and check there and not worry about goals. When I was back in St. Louis, with the Blues, everyone said I was a one-dimensional guy who could score goals and do nothing else. . . . well, it's nice to prove everyone wrong. Really nice."

Scores Deciding Goal in 1999 Stanley Cup Finals

Hull once again energized his new team and the Stars made it to the Stanley Cup finals for the first time in the young franchise's history in 1999. It was also Hull's first appearance in the finals since his debut with the Calgary Flames. He finished the series against the Buffalo Sabres in dramatic fashion by scoring the game- and series-winning goal in a triple overtime period. Although the Sabres complained that Hull had his foot in the goalie's crease, rendering the goal invalid, the referees stood by their initial decision and the Stanley Cup went to the Stars.

When his contract with the Stars expired in 2001, Hull publicly expressed his willingness to take a pay cut from his then-$7 million yearly salary to stay in Dallas, where he was now raising three children with his wife, Alison. "They've got a big payroll here, but I'd be more than happy to help with that because like I was telling Ken Hitchcock, I don't think I'm worth the money I'm being paid," he told Jennifer Floyd of the *Hockey Digest* with typical candor in the summer of 2001. "I'm not the type of player that earns that type of money any more," he added, "So I'd be willing to take a little cut to get a couple of extra years." Given his flexibility on the issue, Hull was shocked when the Stars failed to offer him a contract.

Signs with Detroit Red Wings

Bouncing back from the rejection by the Stars, Hull signed with the Detroit Red Wings in 2001. The timing

Career Statistics

Yr	Team	GP	G	AST	PTS	+/−	PIM	SOG	SPCT	PPG	SHG
1985-86	Flames	0	—	—	—	—	—	—	—	—	—
1986-87	Flames	5	1	0	1	−1	0	5	20.0	0	0
1987-88	Flames	52	26	24	50	+10	12	153	17.0	4	0
	Blues	13	6	8	14	+4	4	58	10.3	2	0
1988-89	Blues	78	41	43	84	−17	33	305	13.4	16	0
1989-90	Blues	80	72	41	113	−1	24	385	18.7	27	0
1990-91	Blues	78	86	45	131	+23	22	389	22.1	29	0
1991-92	Blues	73	70	39	109	−2	48	408	17.2	20	5
1992-93	Blues	80	54	47	101	−27	41	390	13.8	29	0
1993-94	Blues	81	81	57	97	−3	38	392	14.5	25	3
1994-95	Blues	48	29	21	50	13	10	200	14.5	9	3
1995-96	Blues	70	43	40	83	+4	30	327	13.1	16	5
1996-97	Blues	77	42	40	82	−9	10	302	13.9	12	2
1997-98	Blues	66	27	45	72	−1	26	211	12.8	10	0
1998-99	Stars	60	32	26	58	—	30	—	—	—	—
1999-00	Stars	79	24	35	59	—	43	—	—	—	—
2000-01	Stars	79	39	40	79	—	18	—	—	—	—
2001-02	Red Wings	82	30	33	63	—	35	—	—	—	—
TOTAL		1101	679	567	1246	—	424	—	—	—	—

Blues: St. Louis Blues (NHL); Flames: Calgary Flames (NHL); Red Wings: Detroit Red Wings (NHL); Stars: Dallas Stars (NHL).

of his move proved fortuitous, as the team led the league all season and emerged as the winner of the Stanley Cup over the Carolina Hurricanes. A key player in the team's march to the championship, the victory vindicated Hull's talent and renewed his enthusiasm for the game. As he described his Stanley Cup experience to Dan Patrick in an interview for the ESPN Web site, "I enjoyed it. I was genuinely aware of what was happening and enjoyed looking at the people I won it with and how they enjoyed it. Before, I was just so excited that I won it that I didn't get to really enjoy the experience." Now ranked as one of the NHL's half-dozen all-time top goal scorers during the regular season and playoffs, Hull looked forward to another season with the Red Wings in 2002-03. He was also proud of his participation on the U.S. men's hockey team sent to the 2002 Winter Olympic Games in Salt Lake City; the team emerged with a Silver Medal, falling in the final game to Canada in one of the most-watched hockey games ever broadcast on North American television.

FURTHER INFORMATION

Books

Diamond, Dan, ed. *Total Hockey: The Official Encyclopedia of the National Hockey League.* Kansas City: Andrews McMeel Publishing, 1998.

Periodicals

Farber, Michael. "Sniper, Anyone?" *Sports Illustrated* (July 30, 2001).

Related Biography: Hockey Coach Ken Hitchcock

Ken Hitchcock was born in 1951 in Alberta, Canada. His rise through the coaching ranks began with a six-season stint with the Kamloops Blazers in Canada's Western Hockey League in 1984. He then jumped into the NHL as assistant coach of the Philadelphia Flyers. In 1993 he became the head coach of the International Hockey League's Kalamazoo Wings, and in 1996 he returned to the NHL as the head coach of the Dallas Stars.

Hitchcock's strategy emphasized the importance of teamwork, which clashed with the style of some players such as Brett Hull, who joined the Stars in 1998. Hull and Hitchcock sometimes clashed over their approaches to the game, but Hull admitted that Hitchcock forced him to become a better all-around player. Although the Stars won the Stanley Cup in 1999, the team declined to renew Hull's contract in 2001. Hull later signed with the Detroit Red Wings, who won the Stanley Cup in 2002.

For the 2002-2003 season, Hitchcock joined the Philadelphia Flyers as head coach. Hitchcock also served as the assistant coach on the Canadian men's hockey team at the 2002 Winter Olympic Games, where the squad won the Gold Medal.

Floyd, Jennifer. "'The Biggest Pain in the Neck Ever." *Hockey Digest* (summer, 2001).

Hull, Brett. "Wild, Wild West." *Sports Illustrated* (June 7, 1999).

Other

"Brett Hull: Girl's Death 'So Sad.'" Click on Detroit Web site. http://www.clickondetroit.com/det/sports/redwings/stories/redwings-131551920020321-100341.html (March 21, 2002).

"Brett Hull." Internet Hockey Database Web site. http://www.hockeydb.com/ihdb/stats/pdisplay.php3?pid=2410 (November 6, 2002).

"Ken Hitchcock." Philadelphia Flyers Web site. http://www.philadelphiaflyers.com/team/roster/Roster Detail.asp?PlayerID=59 (November 13, 2002).

"Outtakes with Brett Hull." ESPN Web site. http://espn.go.com/talent/danpatrick/s/2002/1001/1439731.html (November 6, 2002).

"Philadelphia Flyers: Ken Hitchcock." CBS SportsLine Web site. http://cbs.sportsline.com/nhl/teams/head-coach/PHI (November 13, 2002).

"Stars Win Stanley Cup!" CNN-Sports Illustrated Web site. http://sportsillustrated.cnn.com/hockey/nhl/1999/playoffs/ (November 7, 2002).

Sketch by Timothy Borden

Jim "Catfish" Hunter

Jim "Catfish" Hunter
1946-1999

American baseball player

Jim "Catfish" Hunter was a master hurler whose presence on the mound struck fear in his opponents. During his 15-year baseball career, Hunter took part in eight All-Star Games, won 20 or more games five seasons in a row (1971-1975), and pitched in six World Series, coming away a winner five times.

What endeared Hunter to the hearts of his fans, however, was his gentle demeanor. Though he threw a mean fastball on the field, Hunter's aggressiveness never followed him off the mound, and no matter how bad things got for him, he never lost his temper. He was known for his kindness and modesty. When Hunter pitched a perfect game on May 8, 1968, the humble hurler wouldn't let his teammates hoist him on their shoulders in celebration. Hunter never made a big deal of this accomplishment, though he was only the 10th pitcher in baseball history to toss a perfect game.

Even when Hunter was hot on the mound and clearly contributing to his team's victory, he always maintained that baseball was a game in which all nine players on the field were needed to win. According to the book *Catfish, The Three Million Dollar Pitcher,* once, when reporters tried to single out Hunter following a victory, he said, "I've said this before and I'll say it again. This is a team game and I'm only a part of our team."

Raised on a Farm

James Augustus Hunter was born on April 8, 1946, in Hertford, North Carolina, one of 10 children born to Abbott and Lillie Harrell Hunter, though two died at birth. The family lived in a farmhouse without plumbing and stoked a pot-bellied stove for heat. Hunter's father was a tenant farmer who worked long days to support the family, never grumbling, never taking a day off. Through his example, Hunter learned the merits of an uncompromising work ethic.

Growing up with seven siblings provided Hunter with plenty of opportunities to practice baseball. Day after day, Hunter pitched to his brothers and developed the extraordinary ball control that would later make him famous. Baseballs, however, were rare, but the Hunter children didn't mind batting corncobs or potatoes, any substitute for a ball. Hunter also spent many long days loading cantaloupe and melons. The heavy lifting helped Hunter earn enough money to buy baseballs and also helped him develop his upper-body strength.

Hunter began playing organized baseball in grammar school and became a local hero. Though he was quite young, townsfolk began bragging about his future. In his book *Catfish: My Life in Baseball,* Hunter explained that all this talk bothered his father. "Don't let what you do go to your head," his father warned him. "If you play good ball, people will certainly brag about it to your face. Just thank them. If you don't play good, they will certainly tell you." Hunter's father also reminded him that a pitcher couldn't win a game by himself. Those words stuck with Hunter, and during his entire career, he never took sole credit for a win.

Chronology

1946	Born April 8 in Hertford, North Carolina, to Abbott and Lillie Harrell Hunter
1960s	Becomes star of Perquiman High baseball team
1963	Injures foot in hunting accident
1964	Signs with Kansas City A's
1965	On May 13, pitches two innings in his major league baseball debut
1966	Marries high school sweetheart, Helen, on October 9
1968	On May 8, pitches a perfect game to beat the Minnesota Twins 4-0
1971	Compiles a 21-11 season to help the A's win the Western Division title
1972	Plays in first World Series, comes away a winner
1973	Helps team win the World Series
1974	Helps team win the World Series
1974	Wins contract dispute, becomes free agent, and signs a $3.75 million deal with New York Yankees, making him baseball's first multi-millionaire player
1975	Makes his debut in pinstripes as a New York Yankee
1976	Plays in fourth World Series, though team loses
1977	Has trouble with sore arm; plays and wins fifth World Series
1978	Spends most of season on the disabled list; makes comeback for the World Series, winning game six, the deciding game
1978	Diagnosed with diabetes
1979	Retires from baseball after 15 years
1979	Returns to Hertford, North Carolina
1987	Elected to the Baseball Hall of Fame
1988	Diagnosed with amyotrophic lateral sclerosis, or ALS
1999	Dies on September 9 of complications due to ALS

Awards and Accomplishments

1966	Selected for first All-Star Team
1967	Selected for All-Star Team
1970	Selected for All-Star Team
1972	Selected for All-Star Team
1972	Won first World Series ring
1973	Selected for All-Star Team
1973	Won second World Series ring
1974	Selected for All-Star Team
1974	Won third World Series ring
1974	Won the Cy Young Award
1974	Named *The Sporting News* Pitcher of the Year
1975	Pitched his fifth consecutive season with 20 or more wins
1975	Selected for All-Star Team
1976	Selected for All-Star Team
1987	Inducted into the Baseball Hall of Fame

At Perquiman High, Hunter became a hurling hero. In *Catfish, the Three Million Dollar Pitcher,* baseball scout Floyd "Dutch" Olafson described Hunter's high school days. "The first time I saw Jim pitch, I knew he'd make the major leagues. He throwed smoke then." Hunter came of age before there was a baseball draft, so he was eligible to sign with any team. Scouts flocked to Hertford to watch him play.

Hunter's future took a turn for the worse in November 1963, however, when his brother Pete accidentally blasted buckshot into Hunter's right foot—the foot he used to push off with when pitching. His foot ached, yet Hunter made a comeback his senior year, though his pitching form was awkward at first. Throughout the season, Hunter improved, pitching to a 14-1 record and helping his team win the state championship.

Signed with the Kansas City A's

Hunter, however, never recaptured the speed he had before the accident, and most scouts wanted nothing to do with him. The Kansas City A's, however, took a chance and signed Hunter, then sent him to a doctor, who removed more pellets from his foot.

When Hunter reported to the A's for duty, the team's owner, Charles Finley, decided that Hunter needed a nickname. Finley relied on nicknames to increase fan hype for his players. After speaking with Hunter's family, Finley came up with "Catfish" after finding out that

Hunter liked catfish as a child. Hunter didn't like the moniker, yet he didn't complain, and it stuck.

During 1965, Hunter's rookie season, he compiled a record of 8 wins and 8 losses. Following the close of the 1967 season, Hunter had amassed an iffy career record of 30 wins and 36 losses. The losing A's relocated to Oakland in 1968.

The move did something for Hunter. On May 8, 1968, Hunter had a magical night. Not only did he connect with the ball four times to drive in three runs, but Hunter's pitching was unhittable. When all was said and done, Hunter had pitched a "perfect" game, meaning he had not allowed any walks, hits, or runs, and the team made no errors. No American League pitcher had tossed a perfect game in regular season play since 1922.

Suddenly, Hunter became a hero. As he improved, so did the A's, who became unstoppable. Buoyed by Hunter, the team won three consecutive World Series titles, in 1972, 1973, and 1974.

Earned the Cy Young Award

For Hunter, 1974 was a dream year. He led the league in complete games (23), and ERA (2.49), had the most wins (25), and most shutouts (6). For his efforts, he won the **Cy Young** Award.

During the 1974 season, Hunter got embroiled in a contract dispute with the A's, and his contract was terminated. As a free agent, Hunter was courted by nearly every team in baseball. In the end, he signed a deal worth about $3.75 million with the New York Yankees. With the A's, Hunter had made about $100,000 a year. Thus, Hunter became baseball's first multi-million-dollar player.

In 1975, Hunter finished the season with 23 wins, giving him five seasons in a row with more than 20 wins. He was the third American League pitcher to accomplish that feat. In 1977, Hunter made his fifth World Series appearance. The Yankees had played in the 1976

Career Statistics

Yr	Team	W	L	ERA	GS	CG	SHO	IP	H	R	BB	SO
1965	KC	8	8	4.26	20	3	2	133	124	63	46	82
1966	KC	9	11	4.02	25	4	0	176.7	158	79	64	103
1967	KC	13	17	2.81	35	13	5	259.7	209	81	84	196
1968	Oak	13	13	3.35	34	11	2	234	210	87	69	172
1969	Oak	12	15	3.35	35	10	3	247	210	92	85	150
1970	Oak	18	14	3.81	40	9	1	262.3	253	111	74	178
1971	Oak	21	11	2.96	37	16	4	273.7	225	90	80	181
1972	Oak	21	7	2.04	37	16	5	295.3	200	67	70	191
1973	Oak	21	5	3.34	36	11	3	256.3	222	95	69	124
1974	Oak	25	12	2.49	41	23	6	318.3	268	88	46	143
1975	NYY	23	14	2.58	39	30	7	328	248	94	83	177
1976	NYY	17	15	3.53	36	21	2	298.7	268	117	68	173
1977	NYY	9	9	4.72	22	8	1	143.3	137	75	47	52
1978	NYY	12	6	3.58	20	5	1	118	98	47	35	56
1979	NYY	2	9	5.31	19	1	0	105	128	62	34	34
TOTAL		224	166	3.26	476	181	42	3449.3	2958	1248	954	2012

KC: Kansas City A's; NYY: New York Yankees; Oak: Oakland A's.

series but lost. With Hunter's pitching help, the Yankees won the 1977 series.

By the start of the 1978 season, Hunter's arm was constantly in pain. Not surprising, considering he'd pitched more than 3,000 innings in 13 years. Hunter spent most of the season on the disabled list, though he went 6-0 in August. Next came the World Series. When called to pitch in the sixth game of the series, Hunter came through, delivering a win that decided the title.

At the end of the 1979 season, the 33-year-old pitcher retired. Hunter returned to his hometown of Hertford where he raised hunting dogs and appeared in spots for Dodge trucks, Red Man Chewing Tobacco, and Purina Dog Food. In 1987, he was inducted into the Baseball Hall of Fame. A year later, Hunter was diagnosed with amyotrophic lateral sclerosis (ALS), a degenerative disease of the nerve cells that control movement. The disease is most often called **Lou Gehrig**'s disease, for the famed Yankee who died of it. Hunter succumbed to ALS on September 9, 1999, leaving behind his wife, Helen, and three children, Kim, Todd, and Paul.

While Hunter's feats on the mound have earned him a place in baseball history, he will also be remembered for what he did off the mound. Hunter was an ace pitcher, to be sure, but he was also an ace of a human being, whose down-home farm boy personality endeared him to the hearts of many. Years after his retirement, he remained a household name. After being diagnosed with ALS, Hunter struck back and founded the Jim "Catfish" Hunter ALS Foundation hoping to use his name as a baseball Hall of Famer to raise awareness about the disease and raise funds for research and for ALS patients. In this way, Hunter hoped to "strike out" the disease, just as he did so many batters. Even after he'd lost control of most of his body, Hunter continued in the fight to raise funds for his cause. His widow continues today.

Though Hunter is gone, his foundation and his feats on the mound live on.

SELECTED WRITINGS BY HUNTER:

(With Armen Keteyian) *Catfish: My Life in Baseball.* McGraw-Hill Book Co., 1988.

FURTHER INFORMATION

Books

Emert, P.R. *Sports Heroes: Great Pitchers.* New York: Tom Doherty Associates, Inc., 1990.

Hunter, Jim "Catfish," with Armen Keteyian. *Catfish: My Life in Baseball.* New York: McGraw-Hill Book Co., 1988.

Kuenster, John. *From Cobb to "Catfish."* New York: Rand McNally & Co., 1975.

Libby, Bill. *Catfish, The Three Million Dollar Pitcher.* New York: Coward, McCann & Geoghegan, Inc., 1976.

Reichler, Joseph L., ed. *The Baseball Encyclopedia.* New York: Macmillan Publishing Co., 1985.

Periodicals

"Catfish was a Credit to Baseball, and His Fans." *Asheville Citizen-Times* (September 12 ,1999): A8.

Gergen, Joe. "'Catfish' Hunter's Professional Example Lives On." *Seattle Times* (September 10, 1999): D1.

Roberts, Frank. "Catfish Hunter's Wife Searches for a Cure: She Strives to Raise Money for Lou Gehrig's Disease Research." *Virginian Pilot* (June 25, 2001): B1.

Other

"Catfish Hunter Statistics." Baseball-Reference.com. http://www.baseball-reference.com/h/hunteca01.shtml (October 8, 2002).

Sketch by Lisa Frick

Miguel Indurain
1964-

Spanish cyclist

Perhaps one of the most physically grueling of all sports, cycling requires incredible physical endurance and the ability to withstand searing pain for hours on end. Miguel Indurain has the ability to endure this pain, and then some. In the world of cycling his name rests alongside those of Eddie Merckx, Jacques Anquetil and, in recent years, **Lance Armstrong.** Indurain's unmatched feat of five consecutive Tour de France victories in the 1990s made him a hero in his native country of Spain, and it has made him a legend in the world of cycling.

Growing Up

Miguel Indurain-Larraya was born July 16, 1964, in the small village of Villava, Navarre province, Spain. He grew up on a farm with a brother and three sisters, and were it not for his natural aptitude for the bicycle, he may well have been very happy as a farmer (he has since retired to a modest house and a quiet life in his home village). Though he would give cycling a try when he was eleven, he was not yet ready for the dedication the sport takes, and instead followed his interests in soccer and track. Less than five years later, however, he would get back on the bike.

Indurain won the Spanish Amateur Road Championship in 1983, and began his training program with Eusebio Unzue, who coached the local racing team. Indurain was nineteen at the time, and the next year he won 14 races, enough to convince him that it was time to turn professional. He joined a team in Pamplona headed by the former Spanish national team coach. The training rides were grueling, and Indurain, as he prepared for the many races he would participate in, logged tens of thousands of miles to increase his endurance.

Though he would not make it into his first Tour until 1985, Indurain had the ability to become a competitor in the Tour, and his coach and teammates knew it as well. It

Miguel Indurain

would take time. The three weeks the Tour de France entails requires riders to sit on their bikes for five to seven hours a day nearly every day, often requiring years of cycling experience before a cyclist will even be able to complete his first race. Many riders drop out before the finish, and Miguel, in these early years, was no exception. In 1986 he pulled out of the race after the 12th stage.

A Matter of Time

But as the eighties progressed, so did Indurain's strength and endurance. As he moved into the 1990s, he was now a veteran in the world of cycling and had ridden in enough Tours to know how to compete. Indurain began his string of five consecutive Tour de France victories in the 1991 race, defeating defending champion Greg LeMond of America. He stood on the podium in Paris wearing the yellow jersey.

Chronology

1964	Born in Villava, Spain, on July 16
1975	Takes up cycling, but then quits to play soccer and track
1978	Having returned to cycling in his teens, Miguel receives his official card as a "cadet" in the Spanish Cycling Federation
1983	Wins the Spanish Amateur Road Championship at age 19
1984-89	Signs contract to ride for the Reynolds team
1986	Wins 1st place at Tour of Murcia; also takes first at Tour L'Avenir
1988, 1991-92	Winner of the Tour of Catalonia
1989	Wins first of two consecutive victories in Paris-Nice
1990	Signs contract with Banesto, the Spanish team with whom he will win 5 Tour de France victories
1990	Wins San Sebastian Classic
1991	Wins Tour of Valcluse
1991	Wins first of five consecutive Tour de France victories
1992	Wins the Spanish National Championships
1992-93	Wins the Tour of Italy
1993	Wins Castilla-Leon Trophy
1994	Wins Tour de L'Oise
1995	Wins Tour of Rioja, the Tour of Galicia and the World Time Trial Championship
1996	Wins Tour of Asturias and the Olympic Time Trial Championship
1997	Retires from the world of professional cycling in January

Awards and Accomplishments

1992	*Velo News* Cyclist of the Year
1994	World Hour Record (53.040 km)
2000	Voted Spain's Sportsperson of the Century

to be considered among the true greats of the sport." Indurain responded to this by saying, "I respect all opinions, but I cannot accept Guimard's. After all, what have the French racers managed to do in recent years?" Many believe his accomplishment speaks for itself.

Indurain chose to retire in 1997. Many fans were expecting the announcement, since two weeks prior the Spanish press had leaked the news. With the money he earned from cycling, Indurain still leads a relatively simple life, choosing to live with his wife Marisa and family in his homeland in the Spanish Basque region. Spain voted Miguel Indurain their Athlete of the Century in 2000.

CONTACT INFORMATION

Address: Home—Villava, Navarre Province, Spain.

FURTHER INFORMATION

Books

Abt, Sam. *Champion: Bicycle Racing in the Age of Indurain*. Bicycle Books, Inc., 1993.

"Miguel Indurain." *Newsmakers 1994*. Detroit: Gale Research, 1994.

Periodicals

Atlanta Journal-Constitution (August 4, 1996).

The Austin American-Statesman (TX) (January 3, 1997).

Bicycling (July 1992; September/October 1992; July 1993; November 1, 1996).

Crothers, Tim. "End of an Era." *Sports Illustrated* (July 29, 1996).

"Indurain Retires From Pro Racing." *International Herald Tribune* (January 3, 1997).

Los Angeles Times (August, 4, 1996).

Murphy, Austin. "A Test of Heart." *Sports Illustrated* (July 31, 1995).

"My Tour With Miguel." *Sports Illustrated* (August 1, 1994).

New York Times (July 20, 1994; July 25, 1994).

Nicholl, Robin. "Matchless but Modest Miguel." *The Independent* (London, England) (January 3, 1997).

Outside (July 1995).

Powell, David. "Indurain's winning cycle draws to a halt." *The Times* (London, England) (January 3, 1997).

Sports Illustrated (August 3, 1992; August 2, 1993).

Indurain's tall and thin body was well suited for two parts of the three main aspects of the Tour, and he used them to full advantage. He was an excellent climber when the Tour reached the mountains, and he also had tremendous speed, which helped him take many of the individual and team-time trials in the Tour (the one aspect he did not excel at, the sprints, is not a necessary requirement for being able to finish and win the Tour). In 1992, coming off a victory in the Giro d'Italia and the Spanish National Championship, Indurain repeated his Tour victory, as he would for the next three Tours. Each year he dominated the field. His fellow cyclists (and teammates) often hurt themselves as they tried to keep up with him in the mountains.

End of an Era

Though Indurain is not the only cyclist to have won five Tour de Frances, he is the first person to win five consecutive Tour victories. He slipped back in the 1996 Tour and many of his fans waited for a comeback that never happened. His feat, however, is still considered by many to be one of the major performances in sporting history.

Some of his detractors claim that Indurain, unlike Eddie Merckx or Jacques Anquetil, trained solely for the Tour and avoided the many other races in which Merckx and Anquetil consistently competed even as they amassed their five Tour victories. One of France's top coaches, Cyril Guimard, was quoted in the *Washington Post* as saying that Indurain "never really accomplished any great individual physical exploits, other than a lot of winning races. For that reason, I don't think he deserves

USA Today (August 4, 1996).
Washington Post (July 25, 1994).

Sketch by Eric Lagergren

Michael Irvin

Michael Irvin
1966-

American football player

During his twelve-year career as a wide receiver for the Dallas Cowboys, Michael Irvin was one of the National Football League's (NFL) most flamboyant players. Blessed with lightening speed and soft hands, he helped lead the Cowboys to three Super Bowl titles in a four-year span. Flashy both on and off the field, Irvin, often weighed down with diamonds and gold, led a free-for-all life of drugs and sex that resulted in his arrest on cocaine possession in 1996. His is a see-saw story of rising fame, falling from grace, and searching for redemption.

Always Hungry

Michael Irvin was born on March 5, 1966, in Fort Lauderdale, Florida, to Walter and Pearl Irvin. He was the fifteenth of seventeen children. His father brought two children from a previous marriage and his mother had six; together they added nine more. Irvin's house on 27th Avenue in Fort Lauderdale only had two bedrooms until his father converted the porch and the garage into extra living space. Still, Irvin never had his own bed until he went to college. Irvin's father was a hardworking roofer who worked long hours six days a week. Irvin's mother took care of the house full of children.

Irvin's family was poor, and he was often without shoes that fit, but his father refused to allow his children to complain. Irvin's main problem as a growing boy was getting enough to eat. With little food in the house, Irvin would scheme to fill his rumbling stomach. He would often wait until everyone went to sleep and then sneak into the kitchen to polish off a whole box of cereal, usually softened with tap water as milk was often not to be found in the refrigerator. When there was nothing else, he would eat mayonnaise or ketchup sandwiches.

Christmases often passed with no presents, and Irvin dreamed of an easier life. By the time he was a teenager, he was determined to make things better for both himself and his family. He began hanging out with a rough crowd and, by his own admission, made some poor choices. After he was suspended at the end of his sophomore year at Piper High School, his father decided his son needed a more positive environment and in 1982 enrolled him at St. Thomas Aquinas, a private Catholic school. Piper High, which didn't want to lose the school's star athlete, protested the transfer. A court ruling determined that Irvin could attend St. Thomas but would be required to sit out of athletics his junior year because Piper had refused to sign a waiver allowing him to participate.

The Playmaker

Irvin lettered in football and basketball at St. Thomas. His football team went undefeated and won the state championship when he was a senior. However, his senior year was marred by the death of his beloved father from cancer. Staying close to home, Irvin attended the University of Miami, playing for the Hurricanes under head coach Jimmy Johnson. As Irvin began receiving attention for his outstanding athletic abilities, he also began being noticed for his mouth and his ego. But Johnson and the Miami coaching staff gave Irvin a wide berth, knowing his background and correctly assuming that his ability and enthusiasm could lead the team to a national championship.

During his three years as a starting receiver for the University of Miami, Irvin, who had become known by the nickname "Playmaker," set Miami records for most career catches (143), receiving yards (2423), and touchdown receptions (26). He was selected as the eleventh overall pick in the 1988 NFL draft by the Dallas Cowboys. The Cow-

1994 Super Bowl XXVII by making two touchdowns on receptions in the span of just fifteen seconds, leading the Cowboys to a 52-17 romp of the Buffalo Bills. Following the team's second storybook season, owner Jerry Jones shocked the sports world by announcing the firing of Johnson. Irvin, who was personally close to his coach, was livid and demanded to be traded. Yet in the end, he decided to remain committed to his teammates and stay in Dallas.

Hopes for an unprecedented third straight Super Bowl ring following the 1994 season were dashed when the San Francisco 49ers beat the Cowboys, 38-28, in the National Football Conference championship. Irvin had outdone himself in the game, catching twelve passes for 192 yards, setting new championship game records, but the devastated wide receiver was crying on the sidelines at the end of the game. Despite his legendary showboating, winning, not personal glory, was his main objective.

Irvin posted the best statistics of his career in 1995, catching 111 passes for 1,603 yards and ten touchdowns. His eight straight 100-yard games and eleven 100-yard games overall tied the NFL records. Irvin's numbers take on added significance considering many teams tried to stop him, or at least slow him down, with double coverage. Although it wasn't a perfect season for the Cowboys, the team's 12-4 record carried them easily into the playoffs, where they won a record third Super Bowl in four years by beating the Pittsburgh Steelers, 27-17.

boys had been struggling, finishing the previous season just 3-13. Despite Irvin's reputation as an egomaniacal trash talker who was potentially trouble off the field, Dallas was desperate for an influx of fresh talent.

As a rookie Irvin became the team's starting wide receiver. He used his $1.8 million contract to buy his mother a four-bedroom house with a swimming pool in Fort Lauderdale and supplied her with the first credit card she had ever carried. In his second year, Irvin was reunited with his college coach when the Cowboys' new owner, Jerry Jones, fired long-time coach **Tom Landry** and hired Jimmy Johnson. Irvin, who tore an anterior cruciate ligament in his left knee in the sixth game of the 1989 season, missed the remainder of the season.

Returning to play in the fifth game of the 1990 season, Irvin led the team in yards-per-carry, but the Cowboys still finished with a losing record of 7-9. The following year the team started off 6-5 before winning the last five games of the season and earning a spot in the playoffs. The 1991 season proved to be Irvin's break-out year. In his fourth season in the league he caught ninety-three passes for 1,523 yards, compared to a combined total of seventy-eight receptions for 1,445 yards during his first three seasons. As the leading receiver in the nation in 1991, Irvin was invited to his first Pro Bowl and selected as the game's most valuable player. Typical of Irvin's demeanor and emotion, he ranted on the sidelines of the Pro Bowl, which is commonly a laidback affair, because he felt he should be getting more receptions. His Pro Bowl teammates shrugged their shoulders, and Irvin ended up with eight receptions for 125 yards.

The Cowboys' powerful offense, led by Irvin, quarterback **Troy Aikman**, and running back **Emmitt Smith**, rolled through the next two seasons, winning back-to-back Super Bowls. Irvin had seventy-eight receptions for 1,396 yards in 1992 and eighty-eight receptions for 1,330 yards in 1993. He thrilled Cowboy fans in the

Falls from Grace

At the top of his game in 1995, Irvin's world came crashing down in 1996. On March 3, 1996, two days before his thirtieth birthday, Irvin was arrested in a room at a Residence Inn in Irving, Texas, where cocaine and marijuana were found. Known for his heavy indulgence, Irvin was in the company of teammate Alfredo Roberts and two young women whose professions were noted as topless "models." Police found close to three ounces of marijuana and nearly four ounces of cocaine on two dinner plates, along with rolling papers, razors, other drug paraphernalia and sex toys. According to *Sports Illustrated*, when the police officers pulled out the handcuffs, Irvin rebuffed them saying, "Hey, can I tell you who I am?"

From that moment Irvin's life became a media circus, with Irvin himself adding fuel to the fire by showing up to court in a full-length black mink coat and dark sun-

Career Statistics

Yr	Team	GP	Receiving			
			REC	YDS	AVG	TD
1988	DAL	14	32	654	20.4	5
1989	DAL	6	26	378	14.5	2
1990	DAL	12	20	413	20.7	5
1991	DAL	16	93	1523	16.4	8
1992	DAL	16	78	1396	17.9	7
1993	DAL	16	88	1330	15.1	7
1994	DAL	16	79	1241	15.7	6
1995	DAL	16	111	1603	14.4	10
1996	DAL	11	64	962	15.0	2
1997	DAL	16	75	1180	15.7	9
1998	DAL	16	74	1057	14.3	1
1999	DAL	4	10	167	16.7	3
TOTAL		159	750	11904	15.9	65

DAL: Dallas Cowboys

Where Is He Now?

Following retirement, Irvin was working on a deal with Fox Sports as a pre-game analyst; however, in August of 2000, he was found with a woman in a North Dallas apartment raided by police, who discovered marijuana. Although Irvin insisted that he hadn't touched drugs since 1996, Fox Sports terminated the talks. Then in early 2001, with his wife by his side, Irvin went to a church and underwent a religious conversion experience. Taking to Jesus with the same compulsive enthusiasm that he took to the football field, Irvin has professed to be a new man, spending a good deal of his time in his church and in prayer.

Although Irvin continues to have detractors who doubt his sincerity, his spiritual rebirth has redeemed his image sufficiently for Fox Sports to find him a spot in front of the camera. After appearing as a regular panelist on Fox Sports' "Best Damn Sports Show," in June 2002 Irvin was given a permanent spot on the network's studio show, "The NFL Show."

glasses. The whole ordeal became even more unbelievable when a Dallas police officer was arrested for conspiring to murder Irvin. The officer's common law wife was called before the Grand Jury to testify because her name had appeared in the motel's log along with Irvin's on numerous occasions. Another topless model, the woman testified at length about Irvin's drug and sex habits. Irvin found out about the testimony and allegedly threatened the woman. The police officer in turn reportedly paid $3,000 down on $30,000 to put a hit on Irvin.

Irvin went to trial on drug-related charges, but before the decision was turned over to the jury, he agreed to a plea bargain, pleading guilty to cocaine possession, a second-degree felony, that cost him $10,000 and 800 hours of community service. On July 17, 1996, the day the trial ended, Irvin held a news conference and was, for the first time, contrite. His wife was at his side although she had never appeared with him in court, and Irvin publicly apologized to his family, fans, teammates, and the Dallas organization. Suspended for the first five games of the 1996 season, Irvin spent time in Florida trying to make amends with his family.

Irvin continued to make periodic headlines. In December of 1996 he and a teammate were falsely accused of rape, and in 1998 he was involved in a bizarre incident during training camp when he allegedly inflicted a two-inch cut in the neck of Dallas guard Everett McIver while some team members were getting haircuts. Whether it was assault or "horseplay," McIver did not press charges, and rumors swirled that Jones brokered a six-figure settlement with McIver to drop the matter.

Retires

Irvin suffered a serious neck injury early in the 1999 season and was advised by doctors that returning to the field could be risky. After playing just four games in 1999, Irvin announced his retirement. Over the course of his twelve-year career in a Dallas Cowboys' uniform, Irvin was the city's biggest hero and its biggest villain. When asked whether he thinks he will make it into the Pro Football Hall of Fame, according the Knight Ridder Newspapers, Irvin reflected, "I don't know. The things I experienced off the field could be held against me. But the things I accomplished on the field cannot be taken away. Say whatever, but when you fix your mouth to talk about me as a football player, you will say, 'He played football.'"

CONTACT INFORMATION

Address: Fox Sports, PO Box 900, Beverly Hills, CA 90213.

FURTHER INFORMATION

Books

Newsmakers, Issue 3. Detroit: Gale Group, 1996.

Sports Stars 1-4. Detroit: U•X•L, 1994-98.

Who's Who Among African Americans, 14th ed. Detroit: Gale Group, 2001.

Periodicals

Bamberger, Michael. "Dropping the Ball." *Sports Illustrated* (April 1, 1996): 36-37.

"Big D, Why Hast Thou Forsaken Me?" *Esquire* (September 1997): 66-71.

Dent, Jim. "Air Traffic Controller." *Sporting News* (September 1, 1997): 34.

Galloway, Randy. "Television Show Captures Irvin's Glory, Agony." Knight Ridder/Tribune News Service (August 31, 2002).

Hill, Clarence E., Jr. "The Transformation Isn't Complete, but Michael Irvin has Gone from Partying Hard to Praying Hard." Knight Ridder/Tribune News Service (November 30, 2001).

Hoffer, Richard. "The Party's Over." *Sports Illustrated* (July 8, 1996): 30.

Hollandsworth, Skip. "Michael Irvin." *Texas Monthly* (September 1996): 110-113.

Horn, Barry. "Irvin Back in Front of Camera." Knight Ridder/Tribune News Service (June 3, 2002).

Horn, Barry. "Irvin's Exposure Increasing." Knight Ridder/Tribune News Service (July 1, 2002).

Jenkins, Sally. "The Mouth That Roars." *Sports Illustrated* (October 25, 1993): 72.

Leland, John, and Ginny Carroll. "The Cop, the Cowboy, and the Topless Dancer." *Newsweek* (July 8, 1996): 61.

"Michael Scissorhands?" *Sports Illustrated* (August 17, 1998): 18-19.

Wagner, William. "A Warrior Departs." *Football Digest* (October 2000): 6.

Other

"Michael Irvin." National Football League. http://www.nfl.com/ (December 28, 2002)

Sketch by Kari Bethel

Allen Iverson

Allen Iverson
1975-

American basketball player

At six-feet, 160 pounds, Allen Iverson is one of the smallest players in the National Basketball Association (NBA). But opposing teams can't stop what they can't see, and by all accounts, Iverson is as fast as they come. His lightening speed, prolific scoring ability, and tough competitiveness took his Philadelphia 76ers to the 2001 NBA championship series. Yet Iverson's image as a hip-hop "bad boy" follows him around like a shadow. Covered in tattoos, dressed in baggy clothes, weighed down by diamonds and gold, and never seen with his hair out of its tightly braided rows, Iverson's unconventional and controversial style is unmatched in the NBA.

Tough Beginnings

Allen Iverson was born on June 7, 1975 in Hampton, Virginia. His mother, Ann Iverson, was fifteen years old when her son was born. Iverson's father, Allen Broughton, never had much contact with his son. Iverson's childhood was filled with constant hardship. As an infant he and his mother depended on his maternal grandmother, but soon after his birth she died from complications after surgery. Michael Freeman, who moved in with the family when Iverson was young, served as

Iverson's father and taught him the game of basketball. But Freeman moved in and out of jail after a work-related accident caused him to lose his job, and he turned to distributing illegal drugs.

Iverson and his two half-sisters lived with his mother in a poverty-stricken neighborhood of Hampton. When his mother couldn't afford to pay the bills, the family would go without water, lights, and heat. A ruptured sewer line under the house filled it with a noxious smell and would sometimes seep onto the floor. Iverson spent his childhood dreaming of making things better for his family, but everything around him pulled him back into the ghetto. During his youth eight of his friends were murdered, including his best friend.

Despite poor school attendance, frequent confrontations with teachers, and troubles at home, Iverson kept it together just enough to be eligible to participate in sports. Football was his first love. As quarterback at Bethel High School, Iverson, nicknamed Bubbachuck by his friends, led the team to the state Class AAA football title in 1992. Only after his mother encouraged him did Iverson agree to try basketball, and the game soon replaced football as his favorite sport. Early on Iverson believed that basketball would be his ticket out of the slums. He had what he called "the Plan," to make it through high school, get to college, and earn a place in the NBA. Most warned him of his slim chance for success, but Iverson was determined.

Chronology

1975	Born June 7 in Hampton, Virginia
1992	Star quarterback for Bethel High School; wins AAA Division title
1993	Arrested for assault; spends four months incarcerated
1994-96	Star point guard for the University of Georgetown Hoyas
1996	Drafted by the Philadelphia 76ers as first overall pick
1997	Arrested for marijuana and weapons charges after being pulled over for speeding
1999	Wins National Basketball Association (NBA) scoring title but conflicts on and off the court lead to trade rumors
2000	Release of single from debut rap album is criticized for treatment of women and gays
2001	Leads 76ers to NBA championship series; marries Tawanna Turner
2001-02	Earns NBA scoring title in back-to-back years
2002	Faces assault charges after an altercation with his wife; charges are later dropped

Southern Discomfort

Last Saturday 150 protesters marched through Hampton, chanting, "Free the Hampton Four" and "No justice, no peace," and singing, "Which Side Are You On?"... The moving force behind the demonstrations is a group called SWIS, an acronym for Simmons, Wynn, Iverson, and Stephens. To a large degree, the group is responsible for turning the case into a national cause celebre. Tom Brokaw, *USA Today, The Washington Post*—they've all gone down, as have the SCLC and the NAACP, which set up a local office to monitor the case. . . . Some SWIS supporters—and there are more than 3,000 throughout the country—describe the case as a "judicial lynching" of "uppity" blacks by the white establishment. "Let's be honest," says Joyce Hopson, the Hampton teacher who heads the SWIS, "if this weren't Allen Iverson, these kids don't go to jail. That's it."

Source: *Sports Illustrated* 79 (October 25, 1993): 46.

First Legal Troubles

It appeared that Iverson's promise to someday buy his mother a red Corvette would go unfulfilled after the seventeen-year-old was arrested on February 14, 1993 for being involved in a mob scene at a local bowling alley. Iverson was hanging out with friends when a confrontation quickly developed into a large brawl divided along racial lines. Accused of throwing a chair that hit a woman, knocking her unconscious, Iverson was charged and tried as an adult. Although he had no previous criminal record, he was sentenced to five years in prison and denied bail pending an appeal. Of approximately fifty people involved in the incident, only four arrests were made; all four were black, causing accusations of racism. Iverson, who denies any direct involvement in the incident, spent four months in prison before being granted conditional release by the governor of Virginia. Two years later the conviction was overturned in a state appeals court due to insufficient evidence, and the crime was stricken from Iverson's record.

Refusing to be detoured from his plans for the NBA, Iverson continued to hone his basketball skills and spent five days a week with a tutor to earn his high school diploma. After passing his final exams in 1994, Iverson accepted an athletic scholarship to Georgetown University. As a member of the Georgetown Hoyas, Iverson immediately became the team's star. During his freshman year he averaged twenty points, 4.7 assists, and 3.5 steals per game and was named the 1995 Big East Rookie of the Year and Big East Defensive Player of the Year. His performance was equally impressive during his sophomore year, and he was once again named Big East Defensive Player of the Year as well as named to the Associated Press's 1996 First Team All-American.

Rookie of the Year

Selected as the first overall pick of the 1996 NBA draft by the Philadelphia 76ers, Iverson quickly became the team's leader and one of the premiere point guards in the country. His $9.4-million contract was an instant ticket out of poverty for him and his family. During his rookie season, he led his team in per-game statistics, including points (23.5), assists (7.5), steals (2.1), and minutes played (40.1). During the final eight games of the season he averaged thirty-nine points per game, and on April 12, in a 125-118 loss to the Cleveland Cavaliers, he became the second youngest player in NBA history to score fifty points in a game. (Iverson was twenty-one years, 310 days; **Rick Barry** scored fifty-plus at the age of twenty-one years, 261 days). He was named Rookie of the Year. In his second season, Iverson moved from the point guard position to shooting guard, which provided him with even more opportunities to score. In his third year in the NBA, he clinched the NBA scoring title for the 1999 season with 26.8 points per game and was named to the All-NBA First Team.

Questions about "The Answer"

While Iverson, who became known as "The Answer," was developing a reputation for his lightening speed and cross-over drill that could break down most defenses, he was also receiving his share of negative attention. On the court Iverson was criticized for selfish play and poor decision-making that led to off-balanced shots and turnovers. Critics pointed to Iverson's poor shooting percentage and large number of turnovers. **Charles Barkley** ruefully called him Allen Me-Myself-and-Iverson. He also came under fire for a perceived lack of respect for the NBA's veteran players. His cockiness and trash talk on the floor only added fuel to the fire. During his first years in the NBA, Iverson was notorious for missing practices, showing up late, and leaving early. His choice of clothes—baggy pants, pounds of gold jewelry, and a 'do rag'—fueled the media's talk of Iverson's past and annoyed his coach Larry Brown, who was also concerned about the friends Iverson chose to hang out with off the court.

The public's reaction to his attire, braided hair, and twenty-one tattoos frustrated Iverson. He told *Sports*

Awards and Accomplishments

1995	Big East Rookie of the Year, Big East Defensive Player of the Year, and Big East All Rookie Team
1996	Big East Defensive Player of the Year, First Team All American, and First Team Big East; selected first overall in the National Basketball Association (NBA) draft by the Philadelphia 76ers
1997	NBA Rookie of the Year and All Rookie Team
1999	First Team All NBA and led the NBA in scoring with 26.8 points per game (ppg)
2000	Second Team All NBA
2000-02	Selected to the NBA All Star Team
2001	NBA Most Valuable Player and First Team All NBA; NBA leader in scoring with 31.1 ppg
2002	NBA leader in scoring (31.4 ppg), steals (2.80 per game), and minutes played (42.7 per game); named to Second Team All NBA

Illustrated, "I got rows, but that don't mean I'm no gangbanger. I ain't never been in a gang. Why do people want to judge me like that?" For Iverson his appearance is simply part of who he is, and serves as a reminder that he will not forget where he came from. While the NBA establishment shakes its collective head in disbelief, Iverson is a hero and an idol to youth around the nation who don the same oversized clothes and braid their hair into rows. His endorsement of Reebok products was highly successful, and Reebok's signature Iverson shoe was a hot seller in the mid-1990s.

Although he insists that he has often been unfairly judged, Iverson's arrest in 1997 on marijuana and firearms charges did little to enhance his image. Iverson was pulled over for speeding, and the trooper discovered a marijuana cigarette and a .45-caliber pistol in the car. Iverson insisted that the joint belonged to the two other men in the car, but admitted that he had used very poor judgment.

By the end of the 1997-98 season Brown was fed up with his young star's poor work ethic, increasing focus on off-court matters such as his Reebok responsibilities, and his aspirations as a rap artist. Rumors began to circulate that a trade was in the works. Eventually Iverson and Brown, both known for their stubborn, determined natures, developed a working, if sometimes volatile, relationship, and in January of 1999 Iverson re-signed with the 76ers for $70.9 million over six years. "When I first got him, I couldn't tell him anything," Brown told *Sports Illustrated.* "He went crazy on the court. Now he'll listen a little bit." After winning the 1999 NBA scoring title with 26.8 points per game, in October of 2000 Iverson was once again the center of controversy when he released a single of a rap album he cut under his artist name Jewelz. "40 Bars" came under fire for numerous derogatory references to women and gays. Eventually Iverson agreed not to release the full album.

New Focus

During the 2000-01 season Iverson showed a new sense of maturity. He arrived for practices on time, fulfilled team obligations, and began involving his teammates in the offense. He averaged 31.1 points and 4.6 assists per game. Because his teammates were also getting their shots, thanks to Iverson's decision to pass the ball sometimes rather than shoot every time it touched his hands, the 76ers began to see themselves as a team, a team with a shot at an NBA title. They made it into the 2001 NBA finals, but lost the title bid to the Los Angeles Lakers. Iverson was named the NBA Most Valuable Player. The following year he improved to 31.4 points and 5.5 assists per game, and for the second year in a row and the third time in his career, Iverson won the NBA scoring title.

In August of 2001 Iverson married long-time girlfriend Tawanna Turner, with whom he already had two children, a daughter Tiaura, born during Iverson's days at Georgetown, and a son, Allen II, born three years later. Once again Iverson made the news in July of 2002 when he faced arrest on criminal charges stemming from an altercation with his wife that allegedly resulted in Iverson carrying a handgun on a hunt to track down his wife, who had failed to return after Iverson kicked her out of their house. Charges were eventually dropped.

Iverson has more than proven himself as a basketball player, but how history writes the final chapters of his life in the NBA remains an uncertainty. Some view him a "bad boy" from the ghetto who could never leave trouble behind; others see a basically good person who occasionally makes bad decisions and has been unfairly vilified by the press. Iverson has, certainly, fulfilled his "Plan." He bought his mother a red Corvette, as well as a new house, and financially supports an extended family. Evidence of his ongoing impact on the American culture is Reebok's decision in 2002 to extend Iverson's $50 million, 10-year endorsement contract.

CONTACT INFORMATION

Address: Philadelphia 76ers, 1 Corestates Complex, Philadelphia, Pennsylvania 19148. Phone: (215) 339-7676.

FURTHER INFORMATION

Books

Contemporary Black Biography, Volume 24. Detroit: Gale Group, 2000.
Newsmakers Issue 4. Detroit: Gale Group, 2001.
Sports Stars. Series 1-4. Detroit: U•X•L, 1994-98.
Who's Who Among African Americans, 14th ed. Detroit: Gale Group, 2001.

Career Statistics

Yr	Team	GP	PTS	PPG	FG%	3P%	FT%	RPG	APG	SPG	TO
1997	PHIL	76	1787	23.5	.416	.341	.702	4.1	7.5	2.1	337
1998	PHIL	80	1758	22.0	.461	.298	.729	3.7	6.2	2.2	244
1999	PHIL	48	1284	26.8	.412	.291	.751	4.9	4.6	2.3	167
2000	PHIL	70	1989	28.4	.421	.341	.713	3.8	4.7	2.1	230
2001	PHIL	71	2207	31.1	.420	.320	.814	3.8	4.6	2.5	237
2002	PHIL	60	1883	31.4	.398	.291	.812	4.5	5.5	2.8	237
TOTAL		405	10908	26.9	.421	.318	.756	4.1	5.6	2.3	1452

PHIL: Philadelphia 76ers.

Periodicals

"Allen Iverson Clinches NBA Scoring Title." *Jet* (May 24, 1999): 48.

Ballantini, Brett. "Dr. Jekyll and Mr. Iverson." *Basketball Digest* (May 2001): 26.

"Basketball's Bad Boy." *Newsweek* (November 6, 2000): 58.

Bradley, Michael. "Can He Last?" *Sporting News* (April 2, 2001): 40.

D'Alessandro, Dave. "Iverson Hasn't Changed; He Has Changed Us." *Sporting News* (June 18, 2001): 26.

Edelson, Mark. "You Don't Know The Answer." *Sport* (April 2000): 28

Montville, Leigh. "Flash Point." *Sports Illustrated* (December 9, 1996): 58.

"NBA Rookie of the Year Arrested on Marijuana and Firearm Charges." *Jet* (August 18, 1997): 53.

Pearlman, Jeff. "It's About Time." *Sports Illustrated* (November 13, 2000): 44.

Reilly, Rick. "Counter Point." *Sports Illustrated* (March 9, 1998): 82.

Rushin, Steve. "No. 3 with a Bullet." *Sports Illustrated* October 23, 2000): 21.

Samuels, Allison. "Will Iverson Foul Out?" *Newsweek* (July 22, 2002): 32.

Smallwood, John, Jr. "Brotherly Love Like." *Basketball Digest* (March 2001): 46.

Smallwood, John, Jr. "The Right Answer." *Basketball Digest* (Summer 2001): 26.

Smith, Gary. "Mama's Boys." *Sports Illustrated* (April 23, 2001): 54.

Starr, Mark, and Allison Samuels. "Going Hard to the Hoop: Allen Iverson is Talent and Tumult: Which Will Win?" *Newsweek* (October 27, 1997): 52-53.

Taylor, Phil. "A Turn For the Better." *Sports Illustrated* (March 15, 1999): 42+.

Tyrangiel, Josh. "Little Big Man." *Time* (September 17, 2001): 65.

Zeman, Ned. "Southern Discomfort." *Sports Illustrated* (October 25, 1993): 46.

Other

"Allen Iverson." National Basketball Association. http://www.nba.com/ (December 11, 2002)

"Allen Iverson." Sports Stats.com. http://www.sportsstats.com/bball/national/players/1990/Allen_Iverson/ (December 10, 2002)

Sketch by Kari Bethel

Bo Jackson
1962-

American football and baseball player

Although not the first professional athlete to partici- pate in more than one sport, when Bo Jackson de- cided to play both professional baseball and football concurrently, he became the most recognized person ever to do so. In the late 1980s, all of America knew who Bo Jackson was. They knew him simply by his first name, "Bo," due to a hugely successful national advertising campaign with Nike, the "Bo Knows…" series that made his face and name common in living rooms across the country. Jackson's speed and power on both the baseball diamond and the football field were legendary, earning him awards as well awe and respect.

Growing Up

Bo Jackson was born November 30, 1962, in Besse- mer, Alabama. He was born Vincent Edward Jackson, the eighth child of Florence Jackson Bond's ten chil- dren. His mother was barely able to support her family with her job as a housekeeper, since Jackson's father, A.D. Adams, never wed Florence and in fact had a fami- ly of his own on the opposite side of town.

The name Vincent quickly disappeared as Jackson en- tered adolescence and gained a reputation as a trouble- maker. He seemed unable to stay out of trouble, breaking windows, stealing bicycles, and beating up the other kids in the neighborhood. As Jackson wrote in his autobiogra- phy, *Bo Knows Bo* (co-authored with sportswriter Dick Schaap), "I even hired kids to beat up other kids for me [because] I didn't have time to beat all of them up my- self." His brothers started calling him a "wild boar," be- cause it was the only animal they felt he compared to. They soon shortened the nickname to "Bo."

Jackson's life as a hoodlum was short-lived, however, when at thirteen he was caught throwing rocks at the Baptist minister's hogs. The boys had killed several of the pigs and the minister made them pay back the loss. Jackson had to take on odd jobs in order to earn his por- tion of the three thousand dollar loss. His mother, at her

Bo Jackson

wit's end and unsure of what to do, was encouraged by the preacher to send Jackson to reform school. Jackson realized that he needed to change his ways or be sent away. He decided to focus his attention on sports.

Athletics proved to be what Jackson needed to stay out of trouble. He proved a natural talent at baseball, but he also had an incredible work ethic that allowed him to surpass his peers. At thirteen years old, he had already moved up to the Industrial League in Bessemer, where he played against grown men.

A Father Figure Appears

Prior to entering high school, the neighboring com- munity's track coach, Dick Atchinson, asked Jackson to join their team. Atchinson would become Jackson's mentor at McArdory High School, serving as his coach in both track and football, and later becoming his guid-

Chronology

1962	Born November 30 in Bessemer, Alabama, to A.D. Adams and Florence Bond
1975	At age 13, faced with reform school, Jackson makes choice to clean up his act and focus energies into sports rather than getting into trouble
1982	Offered a contract with the New York Yankees. Turns it down to go to college
1982	Enters Auburn University, becomes standout in football and baseball
1983	Runs for 1213 yards his sophomore season and compared to Herschel Walker
1984	Sidelined from football with a severe shoulder separation
1985	Selected in the Major League Baseball (MLB) draft by the California Angels. Declines and returns to Auburn for his senior year
1986	Joins Auburn's baseball team in the spring. Dominates with his bat
1986	Overall first choice in NFL Draft
1986	Signs contract with the Kansas City Royals
1987	Drafted by the Los Angeles Raiders to play in the NFL after the baseball season
1987	Marries Linda Garrett. They will have three children together
1990	Pens autobiography, *Bo Knows Bo*
1991	Suffers debilitating hip injury while playing for the Raiders, ending his football career.
1991	The Chicago White Sox pick up Jackson's option from Kansas City
1992	Undergoes hip replacement surgery
1993	Dedicates season to his mother, who had recently died of cancer
1993	Helps White Sox capture the American League West Championship
1994	Deciding to dedicate more time to his family, he retires from baseball following the '94 season
1995	Completes his undergraduate degree and graduates from Auburn in December
1996	Studies acting, and gets bit parts in movies *The Chamber* and *The Sentinel*

Awards and Accomplishments

1982	*Football News* Freshman All-American
1983	Named Most Valuable Player in Sugar Bowl; consensus All-American
1984	Named Most Valuable Player in Liberty Bowl
1985	Won Heisman Trophy
1985	Named *Sporting News* and UPI College Player of the Year
1985	*Sporting News* College All-American
1985	College Baseball Coaches Association All-Region Team
1985	College Baseball Coaches Association All-District Team
1985	Wins the Tanqueray award for excellence in amateur sports
1986	Voted Most Valuable Player in the Cotton Bowl
1987	Bert Bell Trophy; earned NFL's Rookie of the Year Award
1989	Voted American League All-Star and All-Star Game's MVP
1990	Named among the 25 Most Intriguing People by *People* magazine
1990	Selected to the Pro Bowl
1992	Winner of Jim Thorpe Legacy Award
1992	Recipient of "Power to Overcome Award" by Easter Seals
1993	Named the *Sporting News* Comeback Player of the Year
1999	Inducted into College Football Hall of Fame

ance counselor. Here was the father figure Jackson lacked as a boy. In his autobiography, Jackson credits Atchinson as the person who made him the standout athlete he was. He writes that "I couldn't have become the human being I am without him."

At the end high school, the New York Yankees selected Jackson in the second round of the draft, but Jackson declined. His mother encouraged him to get a college degree, so in 1982 he entered Auburn University, where he went on to letter in baseball, football and track. He was the first athlete ever to do so.

After his junior year in school, Jackson was the ranked at the top of the list of eligible draftees for the Major League draft. Instead of entering, however, he chose instead to complete his final year of school. It would prove to be a wise decision. The next year in football he would earn All-Southeastern Conference running back honors (for the third straight year), be named an All-American, and would win the Heisman Memorial Trophy.

The Injury

In 1991, Jackson suffered a hip fracture in an NFL playoff game. It was severe and prognosis by the doctors had the Royals believing he would never return to pro-

fessional athletics. They let him out of his contract early and the Chicago White Sox picked up his option. Football was over for the season, but Jackson's love of baseball motivated his rehab, and in 1992 he was back on the field, helping the White Sox capture the 1993 American League West championship.

Retires From Sports Early

Jackson married his college sweetheart Linda Garrett in 1987. Together they had two sons, Garrett and Nicholas, followed by daughter Morgan. In 1994, Jackson left professional athletics for good. It was another of his surprising moves. He said he wanted to spend more time with his family. He had grown up poor, without a father, and with a mother who was too busy to spend much time with her children. Jackson had vowed not to let that happen to his family.

After leaving professional athletics, Jackson declined offers to coach or work with the administrative staffs of many teams that came to him. As he told ESPN reporter Bob Brown, he wants "no part of big-time sports." "Now I cherish my privacy," he says. "I've left professional sports. Believe it. I got a life."

Jackson now has many business ventures, all of which are centered in Alabama. He organizes his many businesses under N'Genuity. He has Bo Jackson Enterprises, based in Mobile, and this business is the coordinating hub of many of the other businesses he operates, from nutritional food products to suppliers of manpower nationwide.

Though he wasn't the first professional athlete to play more than one sport concurrently, Bo Jackson has become the most recognized person ever to do so. Jackson's speed and power on both the baseball diamond and the football field were legendary, earning him awards as well awe and respect. His decision to leave the world of professional sports in 1994 stunned people,

Career Statistics: Baseball

Yr	Team	AVG	GP	AB	R	H	HR	RBI	BB	SO	SB	E
1986	KC	.207	25	82	9	17	2	9	7	34	3	4
1987	KC	.235	116	396	46	93	22	53	30	158	10	9
1988	KC	.246	124	439	63	108	25	68	25	146	27	7
1989	KC	.256	135	515	86	132	32	105	39	172	26	8
1990	KC	.272	111	405	74	112	28	78	44	128	15	12
1991	CHW	.225	23	71	8	16	3	14	12	25	0	0
1993	CHW	.232	85	284	32	66	16	45	23	106	0	1
1994	CAL	.279	75	201	23	56	13	43	20	72	1	3
TOTAL		.250	694	2393	341	598	141	415	200	841	82	44

CAL: California Angels; CHW: Chicago White Sox; KC: Kansas City Royals.

Career Statistics: Football

Yr	Team	GP	Receiving				Rushing			
			REC	YDS	AVG	TD	ATT	YDS	AVG	TD
1987	LA	7	16	136	8.5	2	81	554	6.8	4
1988	LA	10	9	79	8.8	0	136	580	4.3	3
1989	LA	11	9	69	7.7	0	173	950	5.5	4
1990	LA	10	6	68	11.3	0	125	698	5.6	5
TOTAL		38	40	352	8.8	2	515	2782	5.4	16

LA: Los Angeles Raiders.

leaving many to wonder, were it not for injuries that plagued him throughout his career, how many records he might have broken.

CONTACT INFORMATION

Address: Bo Jackson, c/o Susann C. McKee, Bo Jackson Enterprises, 1765 Old Shell Rd., Mobile, AL, 36604.

SELECTED WRITINGS BY JACKSON:

(With Dick Schaap) *Bo Knows Bo: The Autobiography of a Ballplayer,* Doubleday, 1990.

FURTHER INFORMATION

Books

"Bo Jackson." *Contemporary Newsmakers.* Detroit: Gale Group, 1986.

Gutman, B. *Bo Jackson: A Biography.* New York: Pocket Books, 1991.

Hanks, Stephen. *Bo Jackson.* New York: St. Martin's Press, 1990.

Jackson, Bo, and Dick Schaap. *Bo Knows Bo: The Autobiography of a Ballplayer.* New York: Doubleday, 1990.

Rooney, Terrie M., ed. "Bo Jackson." *Contemporary Heroes and Heroines, Book III.* Detroit: Gale Group, 1998.

Periodicals

Associated Press (June 22, 1986).
Chicago (May 1997): 18.
Detroit Free Press (June 22, 1986).
Detroit Free Press (July 1, 1986).
Ebony (August 1993): 72-76.
Jet (April 19, 1993).
Jet (April 24, 1995).
Jet (January 8, 1996).
Los Angeles Times (June 22, 1986).
Newsweek (December 4, 1989): 80-81.
New York Times (December 29, 1984) .
New York Times (May 19, 1985).
New York Times (November 4, 1985).
New York Times (December 2, 1985).
New York Times (December 7, 1985).
New York Times (December 8, 1985).
New York Times (June 2, 1986).
New York Times (March 20, 1991).
The New York Times Book Review (December 9, 1990): 37.
People (December 2, 1985).
People (July 21, 1986).
Sporting News (January 9, 1984).
Sporting News (August 26, 1985).
Sporting News (December 16, 1985).
Sporting News (January 13, 1986).
Sporting News (February 10, 1986).
Sporting News (February 24, 1986).

Sporting News (June 30, 1986).
Sporting News (July 14, 1986).
Sporting News (October 27, 1986).
Sporting News (April 18, 1988).
Sporting News (December 24, 1990).
Sports Illustrated (October 3, 1983).
Sports Illustrated (September 5, 1984).
Sports Illustrated (May 13, 1985).
Sports Illustrated (December 2, 1985).
Sports Illustrated (March 31, 1986).
Sports Illustrated (July 14, 1986).
Sports Illustrated (May 4, 1987).
Time (September 29, 1986): 62.
United Press International (June 22, 1986).
USA Today (June 24, 1986).
Washington Post (June 22, 1986).
Washington Post (July 6, 1986).

Other

"Bo Jackson." http://www.pubdim.net/baseballlibrary/ (January 1, 2003).
"Bo Jackson." http://baseball-reference.com/ (January 1, 2003).
"Bo Jackson." http://www.pro-football-reference.com (January 1, 2003).
"Bo Knows the Heisman." *Sports Illustrated* http://sportsillustrated.cnn.com/football/college/heisman/news/2000/11/04/bo_jackson/ (January 1, 2003).
Brown, Bob. "Bo Jackson Means Business." *ESPN Outdoors*. http://espn.go.com/outdoors/general/s/g_tv_NAS_brown_bo.html (January 1, 2003).

Sketch by Eric Lagergren

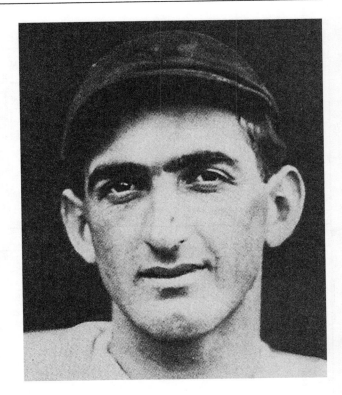

Shoeless Joe Jackson

Joseph "Shoeless Joe" Jackson
1888-1951

American baseball player

Joseph Jefferson "Shoeless Joe" Jackson was one of the most talented baseball players of all time. **Babe Ruth**, who acknowledged that Jackson "was the greatest hitter I'd ever seen," copied his style, and **Ty Cobb** once called Jackson "the greatest natural hitter I ever saw." In a still-contested decision, Jackson was barred forever from baseball by commissioner Kenesaw Mountain Landis over the "Black Sox" scandal of 1920, when Jackson and seven teammates from the **1919 Chicago White Sox** were accused of throwing the 1919 World Series to the Cincinnati Reds. Evidence that was to be presented to the grand jury in September 1920 mysteriously disappeared, and he was not prosecuted, but Jackson has never been honored by induction into the Baseball Hall of Fame because of the charge. However, sports figures and fans who believe him innocent, or at least not guilty enough to warrant the exclusion, continue to campaign to so honor Jackson.

Humble Beginnings

Jackson was born to a poor family, the eldest of eight children. He had no formal education and worked from a very young age, beginning with a job cleaning up in the textile mill where most of the members of his family were employed. He played for the mill's team, but when he broke the catcher's arm with his powerful throw he was re-assigned to the outfield. He next played for a semipro Greenville team, then the professional Greenville Spinners. During a game, he removed the new cleats that were giving him blisters, and a fan of the opposing team yelled out an insult to the shoeless runner as he rounded third base. The intended insult—"Shoeless Joe"—stuck even though Jackson had played without his spikes only one time.

Sportswriter Joe Williams, who knew Jackson, called him "pure country, a wide-eyed, gullible yokel. It would not have surprised me in those days to learn he had made a down payment on the Brooklyn Bridge. . . . He was a drinker and a heavy one. He carried his own tonic: triple-distilled corn. And on occasions he carried a parrot, a multicolored pest whose vocabulary was limited to screeching, 'You're out!'"

A Major League Player

Jackson's illiteracy haunted him for his entire career. When he first joined the Philadelphia Athletics, team

Chronology

1888	Born July 16 in Pickens County, South Carolina to George and Martha Jackson
1893	Moves to Brandon Mill, South Carolina, near Greenville
1894	Begins working in a textile mill at age six
1901	Becomes the pitcher for the Brandon Mill team
1906	Begins semipro career with Greenville Near Leaguers
1908	Marries Katherine Wynn
1908	Begins pro career with the Greenville Spinners in the Carolina Association
1908	Signed by the Philadelphia Athletics
1909	Traded to Cleveland Indians
1915	Traded to Chicago White Sox
1918	Accepts draft-exempt employment in a shipbuilding plant
1919	White Sox lose World Series to Cincinnati
1920	Charged with throwing 1919 World Series with seven other White Sox players and suspended
1921	Acquitted by Chicago jury but banned from baseball by Judge Kenesaw Mountain Landis, first commissioner of baseball
1922	Moves to Savannah, Georgia and opens dry cleaning business
1922	Plays baseball with a team in Bastrop, Louisiana
1923	Leaves the Bastrop team to play for the Americus, Georgia team, which wins the Georgia Little League Series in six games.
1924	Manages the Waycross team for two seasons, winning the Georgia State Championship in 1924
1929	Returns to Greenville when his mother becomes ill, then takes her to Savannah, Georgia, where she is cared for by his wife and sister Lula
1932	Returns to Greenville where he plays most of the season with the Greenville Spinners and finishes with a semipro team in Philadelphia, Pennsylvania
1933	Returns to Greenville with Katie to open first a barbecue restaurant then Joe Jackson's Liquor Store
1933	Plays ball for Poe Mills in Greenville
1934	Plays and manages the Winnsboro Mill Royal Cords
1937	Manages the Woodside Mill team
1951	Suffers a heart attack and dies at home on December 5

Awards and Accomplishments

1910	Bats .387 with 29 hits in 75 at bats
1911	First full major league season; bats .408, second only to Ty Cobb with .420 and highest ever by a rookie
1912	Bats .395 and sets season record in triples with 26
1913	Leads American League with 197 hits
1916	Sets White Sox season record in triples with 21
1917	Bats .307 as White Sox win American League pennant and the World Series over the New York Giants
1919	Member of pennant-winning White Sox team
1919	In World Series against the Cincinnati Reds, leads all hitters by batting .375 and ties World Series record with 12 hits
1951	Inducted into the Cleveland Sports Hall of Fame
1951	Receives award from the Baseball Writers Association of America
2002	Honored by statue erected in Greenville, South Carolina
2002	Inducted into the Baseball Reliquary's Shrine of the Eternals

members took him to an upscale restaurant and told him he could drink from the finger bowl, which he did. Humiliated upon learning of the trick, he jumped a train and ran away the next day. He left the team a second time in 1908, his first full season. Manager **Connie Mack** was sympathetic to Jackson's plight and the teasing he took from his mostly Northern teammates. Mack offered to hire a tutor for him, but Jackson was too embarrassed to accept.

Jackson was traded to the Cleveland Indians in 1910 and played with the team until 1915. During this period, he and his wife Katie, whom he had married in 1908, became more accustomed to life in the North. Although he still took a ribbing about going shoeless, with Katie's support and bolstered by a growing number of fans, he began to accumulate a number of records, and eventually achieved the third-highest lifetime batting average in history, at .356. (Cobb is first with .366, and **Rogers Hornsby** is second with .358.) Jackson invested carefully and earned extra income by making appearances on the vaudeville stage.

Black Sox Scandal

In 1915 the Indians traded Jackson to the Chicago White Sox for three players and $15,000. He was instru-

mental in the team's capture of the 1917 pennant, but there was unrest on the bench. White Sox owner Charles A. Comiskey was so cheap that he wouldn't even pay for the cleaning of the team's uniforms, thus leading the players to call themselves the Black Sox and wear their increasingly dirty uniforms for several weeks in protest in 1918. When Jackson avoided wartime service by taking a job in a shipbuilding factory, Comiskey criticized him for being unpatriotic.

During the first season following the war, the Sox again won the pennant. Jackson picked up where he had left off, and fans soon forgave his military exemption. However, Comiskey failed to pay the players the bonuses they were due, and Jackson, his star hitter, received a measly salary of $6,000 for the 1919 season. Most of the other team members were also underpaid, leaving many desperate to earn extra income.

First baseman Chick Gandil approached gambler Joseph "Sport" Sullivan and told him that he and his teammates were willing to throw the 1919 World Series for $100,000. He then brought the idea to pitchers Eddie Cicotte and Claude "Lefty" Williams, and both men agreed to go along with the scheme. The three met with outfielder Happy Felsch, infielders Swede Risberg and Buck Weaver, utility infielder Fred McMullin, and Jackson. Jackson later claimed that when Gandil offered him $10,000 to help throw the series, he initially turned it down, as well as a higher offer of $20,000. Gandil told Jackson he could take it or leave it, that the fix was going forward with or without him if the money could be raised. Jackson ultimately agreed.

In *Baseball: An Illustrated History,* the companion book to the PBS documentary film produced by Ken Burns and Geoffrey C. Ward, a writer noted that "someone did [raise the money], although the evidence is murky and contradictory as to just who it was. Several gamblers—including Sport Sullivan; Bill Maharg, a mysterious figure, whose real name may have been Graham ('Maharg' spelled backward); Abe Attell, the former

Shoeless Joe Jackson

featherweight boxing champion; and one-time White Sox pitcher 'Sleepy Bill' Burns—served as go-betweens. However, the cash seems to have been provided mostly by New York's most celebrated gambler, Arnold Rothstein, known as 'Mr. Bankroll' at the track, who was said to have been willing to bet on anything except the weather because there was no way he could fix that."

As the series began, there were rumours that something was wrong, and sportswriter Hugh Fullerton advised his readers not to bet on the games. The White Sox lost the first game, as planned, but the money that was supposed to be paid for this loss was out on bets, the players were told. They agreed to throw the second game, and did, but when it was over, Attell gave Gandil just $10,000 of the $40,000 owed the players at that point. The Sox won the third game when Dickie Kerr, a rookie who wasn't in on the fix, pitched a three-hit shutout to win 3-0. Attell lost a fortune on that game but finally agreed to pay $20,000 before the fourth game and an equal amount if the Sox lost. According to the *Baseball* historians, Jackson was upset that he was receiving only one fourth of his promised payoff; Weaver and McMullin never received a penny.

The Sox lost the fifth game, but the conspirators decided that since there was no more money forthcoming, they might as well play to win, considering that they all wanted their contracts to be renewed. They won games six and seven, due in part to Jackson's strong showing, and the series stood at 4-3 in favor of Cincinnati. Manager Kid

Gleason, who couldn't understand what had happened to his men during the early games, finally had hope.

Williams was the opening pitcher for the eighth game, but he had been visited by a thug who worked for Rothstein, who threatened the lives of Williams and his wife if he didn't throw it. Rothstein hadn't bet on the individual games, and his money was on Cincinnati to win the series. Fearful, Williams gave up three runs on four hits before he was pulled, but it was too late. Even with Jackson's and Gandil's hitting power, the Sox lost the series. Fullerton called attention to the scandal in baseball, but others defended the game and refused to believe the allegations.

According to *Baseball,* Comiskey "just wanted the whole business to go away. While he had himself feared the worst after the game, he had a big investment in protecting the reputation of the team he'd built. When Joe Jackson, apparently conscious stricken, had tried to see him right after the series, to ask what he should do with the $5,000 he'd been given, Comiskey refused to let him in his office. Jackson then sent Comiskey a letter—dictated by his wife, of course—suggesting that some series games had been rigged, but Comiskey did not answer it. Instead, he stoutly defended his men."

The matter became old news, but when the 1920 season opened, players from several teams realized the advantage of working with the gamblers, and when a grand jury investigated a three-game losing streak by the Cubs to the Phillies, the old suspicions were revisited, and the White Sox players were called to testify. Jackson was one of the players to confess, and he admitted to receiving $5,000 of the promised $20,000 that was to have been his share.

Rothstein, who was eventually gunned down by another gambler over a poker game, denied any part in the scheme. There was no Illinois law forbidding throwing or fixing a game, and so Attell, several other gamblers, and the eight ballplayers were indicted for conspiring to defraud the public and harm the business of Comiskey and the American League, but they were acquitted for lack of evidence when the transcripts of Jackson's and Cicotte's testimonies disappeared from court files.

The team owners had to do something to regain the peoples' trust, and so they replaced the three-man National Commission led by Ban Johnson with a new post and a new commissioner of baseball, a federal judge known for his self-promotion named Kenesaw Mountain Landis. On the day the eight players were found not guilty, Landis banned them from baseball for life. Even Buck Weaver, who had not taken any money and had played his best, was banned for not revealing the plot as it unfolded. Those team members who had received money would have made at least as much by winning the World Series. The only winners in the entire fiasco were the gamblers.

"New commissioner Kenesaw Landis wanted scapegoats," observed *Knight Ridder/Tribune News Service* writer Frank Fitzpatrick, "and Jackson was an easy one." Jackson biographer Harvey Frommer wrote that "Landis fancied himself an intellectual, and Jackson was easily a fall guy. He was from the South, and he was illiterate." There was reason to believe that Jackson—who accomplished the highest batting average of the series, an amazing .375, and had a perfect fielding average—ultimately made the decision to play his best in spite of his agreement to throw the series.

"The only man to ever say that Joe Jackson was present at any meetings between the gamblers and the players was Abe Attell," wrote Mike Nola, who maintains a web site on Jackson. "Abe told this story to Eliot Asinof when Asinof was doing research for his book *Eight Men Out*. The meeting between Attell and Asinof took place in **Jack Dempsey**'s restaurant in New York City. Dempsey was present that day in the restaurant and came over after Attell left and asked Asinof what he was doing talking to that scum. Dempsey said something to the effect that he would rather go twelve rounds with **Joe Louis** than be caught talking to that scum."

Going Home Again

At the end of the 1920 season, Jackson returned to the South, where he played semipro ball in order to survive, all the while hoping he would be reinstated. Ironically, he often made more money playing for unsanctioned teams than he had for the Sox. Jackson and his wife returned to Greenville and opened first a dry cleaning establishment, then a liquor store, which he ran until his death. They lived comfortably, and Jackson continued to deny that he had adjusted his play during the 1919 World Series.

Still a Hero to Many

On December 16, 1951, Jackson was to be honored by the Baseball Writers Association of America in a ceremony held on Ed Sullivan's *Toast of the Town* television program. His former Cleveland teammate, Tris Speaker, was to present him with a gold clock. But Jackson died on December 5. "No ruling could bar Shoeless Joe from his fans' hearts," said Peter Ames Carlin and Lorna Grisby in

a *People* article. "As recalled in biographies and embellished in movies such as *Field of Dreams* and *Eight Men Out*, Jackson's saga grew into a parable of the struggle between innocence and greed. Though not everyone agrees that Jackson played the series to win, as some supporters claim, many believe the time has come to enshrine him in baseball's Hall of Fame in Cooperstown, New York."

Jackson died of a heart attack in his small home, a short distance from Shoeless Joe Jackson Memorial Park, which was created in his honor on the site of the baseball diamond behind Brandon Mills. He is buried at Woodlawn Memorial Park, where visitors, many of whom first came to know him through the films that portrayed him, leave flowers and sometimes notes. Frommer said Jackson "has become an American icon, one of those figures who is both hero and antihero. Joe Jackson is an epic figure in our sports culture. His story is one of continuing fascination and interest."

In 2002, Joe Wade Anders, grandson of Joe Anders, one of Jackson's closest friends, unveiled the life-size statue of Jackson in Greenville's West End. The clay model was sculpted by Douglas R. Young, who worked on it in the lobby of Greenville City Hall. Visitors stopped each day to follow his progress—schoolchildren, workers on their lunch hour, and other visitors. Young allowed them to knead the clay for the statue, and Jackson's right shoe, more easily reachable than his left, is now permanently larger because of the many times it was touched by small hands before it was bronzed.

In 2002 members of the Baseball Reliquary in Monrovia, California inducted Jackson into their Shrine of Eternals, often referred to as the "West Coast Hall of Fame." He was honored with inductees Mark Fidrych of the Detroit Tigers and Minnie Minoso of the Chicago White Sox in a ceremony held at the Donald R. Wright Auditorium in the Pasadena Central Library, Pasadena, California, where Nola accepted the award on behalf of the family.

"The obstinacy of the baseball establishment seems only to have added to the fondness for Jackson in West Greenville," noted an *Economist* writer. "Local children have written letters on behalf of their hero. Another project is to set up a museum devoted to mill-league baseball teams. Reunions have been organized for mill-league players.... Jackson's characteristically modest grave is distinguished from its neighbours by the presence of several baseballs quietly left there by admirers."

Two of Jackson's most ardent supporters have been Hall of Famers Bob Feller and **Ted Williams** (the last man to hit .400 in the majors), and Williams died unsuccessful in his quest. Through the decades since the scandal, Jackson's induction has gained support, but not everyone feels that time can erase his guilt, if in fact he was guilty, something that may never be known for certain. Dick Heller noted in *Insight on the News* that even if he didn't participate, Jackson at least knew of the plot to throw the series and yet never told manager Kid Gleason or Comiskey.

Career Statistics

		AVG	GP	AB	R	H	HR	RBI	BB	SO	SB
1908	Phi	.130	5	23	0	3	0	3	0	0	0
1909	Phi	.294	5	17	3	5	0	3	1	0	0
1910	Cle	.387	20	75	15	29	1	11	8	0	4
1911	Cle	.408	147	571	126	233	7	83	56	0	41
1912	Cle	.395	152	572	121	226	3	90	54	0	35
1913	Cle	.373	148	528	109	197	7	71	80	26	26
1914	Cle	.338	122	453	61	153	3	53	41	34	22
1915	Cle	.331	82	299	42	99	3	45	28	11	10
1915	Chi	.265	46	162	21	43	2	36	24	12	6
1916	Chi	.341	155	592	91	202	3	78	46	25	24
1917	Chi	.301	146	538	91	162	5	75	57	25	13
1918	Chi	.354	17	65	9	23	1	20	8	1	3
1919	Chi	.351	139	516	79	181	7	96	60	10	9
1920	Chi	.382	146	570	105	218	12	121	56	14	9
TOTALS		.356	1330	4981	873	1774	54	785	519	158	202

Chi: Chicago White Sox; Cle: Cleveland Indians; Phi: Philadelphia Athletics.

"Some see the campaign to reinstate Jackson—the first step toward Cooperstown—in the same terms as **Pete Rose**'s ... application to have his ban lifted," wrote Heller. "Really, though, there are no similarities. Rose probably bet on baseball games—the circumstantial evidence is overwhelming—but there is no indication that he did less than his best as a player or manager."

"Jackson's rags to riches story and figurative return to his original condition has made him a legendary sports figure," wrote Lowell L. Blaisdell in *American National Biography*. "Sympathy for his humble origins, admiration of his great natural ability, and dismay at his eventual exclusion from baseball's Hall of Fame caused many sports fans to identify with his name and career."

"In a country that gives second chances to countless miscreants—Richard Nixon, **Marv Albert**, **Latrell Sprewell**—why not a salute to Shoeless Joe?" commented David A. Kaplan in *Newsweek*. "His part in The Fix will always be remembered. It must be. But should not this baseball immortal at long last be celebrated?"

FURTHER INFORMATION

Books

Asinof, Eliot. *Eight Men Out*. New York: Holt, Rinehardt and Winston, 1963.

Bildner, Phil, illustrated by C. F. Payne. *Shoeless Joe and Black Betsy*. New York: Simon & Schuster for Young Readers, 2002.

Fleitz, David L. *Shoeless: The Life and Times of Joe Jackson*. Jefferson, NC: MacFarland, 2001.

Frommer, Harvey. *Shoeless Joe and Ragtime Baseball*. Dallas: Taylor Publishing Co., 1992.

Garraty, John A. and Mark C. Carnes, editors. *American National Biography*. New York: Oxford University Press, 1999.

Gutman, Dan. *Shoeless Joe and Me: A Baseball Card Adventure*. New York: HarperCollins, 2002.

Hickok, Ralph. *A Who's Who of Sports Champions*. New York: Houghton Mifflin, 1995.

Kavanagh, Jack. *Shoeless Joe Jackson*. New York: Chelsea House, 1995.

Kinsella, W. P. *Shoeless Joe Jackson Comes to Iowa*. Ottawa: Oberon Press, 1980.

Kinsella, W. P. *Shoeless Joe*. Boston: Houghton Mifflin, 1982.

Vernoff, Edward, and Rima Shore. *The Penguin International Dictionary of Contemporary Biography from 1900 to the Present*. New York: Penguin Putnam, 2001.

Ward, Geoffrey C., and Ken Burns. *Baseball: An Illustrated History*, (companion book to PBS documentary). New York: Knopf, 1994.

Periodicals

Carlin, Peter Ames, and Lorna Grisby. "Extra Innings: Major League Baseball Reconsiders the Case of Exiled Legend 'Shoeless Joe' Jackson." *People* (July 3, 2000): 107.

Ebert, Roger. Review of *Eight Men Out*. *Chicago Sun Times* (September 2, 1988).

Ebert, Roger. Review of *Field of Dreams*. *Chicago Sun Times* (April 21, 1989).

Fitzpatrick, Frank. "Shoeless Joe Jackson still the subject of lore and curiosity." *Knight Ridder/Tribune News Service* (September 16, 1996).

Heller, Dick. "Ted and Bob go to bat for Shoeless Joe." *Insight on the News* (March 23, 1998): 40.

Kaplan, David A. "Infamy and Immortality: 'Shoeless Joe' Jackson was part of baseball's worst scandal. Should he still be let into the Hall of Fame?" *Newsweek* (August 2, 1999): 59.

"Shoeless Joe runs again." *Economist* (April 1, 2000): 31.

Other

Eight Men Out. Orion Pictures (1988).

Field of Dreams. Universal Pictures (1989).

Shoeless Joe Jackson's Virtual Hall of Fame. http://
www.blackbetsy.com (October 1, 2002).

Sketch by Sheila Velazquez

Phil Jackson
1945-

American basketball coach

Phil Jackson

Phil Jackson's preeminence as a National Basketball Association (NBA) coach is evidenced by his top-ranking winning percentage and nine championship rings. During the 1990s he coached the Chicago Bulls to six NBA titles. While star player **Michael Jordan** was given considerable credit for the Bulls' unprecedented pair of "three-peats," it is questionable whether he would have had such success under any other coach. Jackson, using the triangle offense, got the Bulls to play well as a team rather than just serve as a background to Jordan's solo act. He has since strengthened the Los Angeles Lakers, a team that had great talent in **Shaquille O'Neal** and **Kobe Bryant**, but could not prove that they were championship material. Under Jackson's eye, and again using the triangle offense, they quickly racked up three consecutive NBA titles. Since the days when he played for the New York Knicks, Jackson has been known as a non-conformist who is deeply interested in politics, philosophy, religion, and psychology. He touches on all of these subjects when he talks about basketball, but most analysts agree that amidst team meditations and recommended reading lists, it is Jackson's knowledge of the game and ability to work with star players that make him a highly effective coach.

Born in Deer Lodge, Montana, Jackson had an unusual childhood as the offspring of two fundamentalist ministers. His strict upbringing did not include dancing, rock music, movies, or television. However, he did participate in extracurricular activities at school, including basketball, football, and baseball. At six feet, eight inches tall and weighing 180 pounds, he was a great asset to his high school basketball team and went on to play at the University of North Dakota. Going to college, where he majored in religion, philosophy, and psychology, gave Jackson the freedom to question his beliefs and lifestyle. He also gained some forty pounds and drew attention from NBA scouts.

The New York Knicks selected Jackson in the second round of the 1967 NBA draft. He became a rookie along with teammates **Bill Bradley** and Walt Frazier. They would soon play under Red Holtzman, who influenced Jackson's later coaching style with his team-oriented approach. As a player, Jackson was not a star, but was especially good at setting picks, rebounding, and playing man-to-man defense. He was also popular, though not universally admired, for his off-court behavior. Many young fans liked the fact that he rode his bike to Madison Square Garden, supported liberal political causes, was a (temporary) vegetarian, and experimented with LSD and marijuana. In 1975 Jackson detailed some of these experiences in his autobiography *Maverick*.

Jackson played in the NBA until 1980, missing the Knicks' 1970 championship season because of a back injury, but contributing to the team's 1973 title. In 1978 he was traded to the New Jersey Nets, for whom he would serve as a player-assistant coach for two years. Although he has been described as the least likely player to turn coach, Jackson soon began a coaching career with the Albany Patroons, a Continental Basketball Association team. With the hope of reaching the NBA, he spent five seasons with the Patroons. When he resigned from this job in 1987, Jackson was discouraged and considered going back to school. That was when the Bulls asked him to interview for an assistant coaching position prior to the 1987-88 season. Jackson shaved his beard and adopted a more conventional style of dressing than he had used at an earlier, unsuccessful interview with the team. He got the job, assisting Doug Collins.

Chronology

1945	Born September 17 in Deer Lodge, Montana, to Charles and Elisabeth Jackson
1967	Drafted by the New York Knickerbockers
1969-70	Misses Knicks' championship season due to spinal fusion surgery
1978	Traded to the New Jersey Nets
1980	Ends NBA playing career
1982-87	Coaches Albany Patroons in CBA
1987	Hired as assistant coach by Chicago Bulls
1989	Named head coach of Chicago Bulls
1998	Retires from coaching, temporarily
1999	Signs five-year, $30 million contract with Los Angeles Lakers

Related Biography: Basketball Coach Tex Winter

Tex Winter learned basketball's triangle offense while playing at the University of Southern California in the 1930s, and he taught the complicated system better than anyone else. He was a key figure in grooming the Chicago Bulls and the Los Angeles Lakers for a total of nine NBA titles. Phil Jackson said of Winter in *Texas Monthly*, "Tex is officially the God of Basketball.... I find him, as a mentor or a teacher, a wonderful guy to have around."

From an assistant role at Kansas State, Winter went on to jobs at Marquette University, Northwestern University, Long Beach State College, and Louisiana State University. He had a fifteen-year stint as head coach for Kansas State, where he was honored with the national coach of the year award for 1959. Winter briefly worked as an NBA head coach for the San Diego Rockets during 1971-73.

When Jerry Krause became general manager of the Chicago Bulls he quickly hired Winter in 1985. He worked under coaches Stan Allbeck and Doug Collins, neither of whom used the triangle offense. Winter was thinking of retiring when Jackson replaced Collins and adopted the system. When he joined Jackson with the Los Angeles Lakers in 2000, Winter had been working longer than any other active coach.

One night in Milwaukee, the Bulls played exceptionally well under Jackson after Collins was ejected from the game. When Collins was later fired, his assistant became head coach for the 1989-90 season. Jackson proceeded to put a new emphasis on defense and to institute the triangle offense, as taught by his assistant Tex Winter, despite grumbling from a skeptical team. The triangle offense involves giving all five players on the floor opportunities to score by focusing on penetration, spacing, ball movement, offensive rebounds, and getting the ball to the open man. The move cut Jordan's scoring stats slightly, but drastically improved the team's performance as a whole. The Bulls were eliminated in the Eastern Conference finals that first year under Jackson, but went on to win the NBA championship in 1991, 1992, and 1993. Jordan retired after the 1993 season, troubled by his father's death and wanting to try his hand at professional baseball. But the Bulls' star returned to the team late in 1995 and was part of Chicago's championship teams of 1996, 1997, and 1998. A "repeat three-peat" was something that had never been done before in the NBA. This second string of titles was ended when Jordan retired again, **Scottie Pippen** was traded to Houston, and Jackson temporarily retired from coaching.

After a one-year hiatus, Jackson accepted a job offer from the Los Angeles Lakers and a five-year contract worth $30 million. The Lakers had some of the most highly-touted talent in the league, but they also had a reputation for disrespecting coaches, having huge egos, and fizzling in the playoffs. Since 1994, the team had performed disappointingly under **Magic Johnson** (briefly), Del Harris, and Kurt Rambis. It was a chance for Jackson to prove his skill with players and his knowledge of the game without the overshadowing presence of Michael Jordan.

In Los Angeles, Jackson did not hesitate to criticize his players. He warned that O'Neal was losing his role as a dominant figure in the NBA and that Bryant needed to stop showing off and shooting at will. He grumbled that his players had tiny attention spans. Yet another problem was bad feelings between O'Neal and Bryant.

At practice, Jackson took a more disciplined approach and taught the basics, then the complicated triangle offense. O'Neal was quick to voice his support of Jackson, even calling him "my white father." Bryant looked forward to using the new offense to advantage but was offended by Jackson's gift of the book *The White Boy Shuffle* about a black kid living amidst whites. As a whole, a team known for partying was trying to show Jackson that they were cleaning up their act.

Under Jackson's new regime, the Lakers finally put it all together on the court. The team proceeded to claim the NBA title in 2000, their first since 1988, and again in 2001 and 2002. Even before the last of these titles was won, Jackson had achieved the best-ever winning percentage among NBA coaches at .738. His 156-54 win-loss record in the playoffs was also the best. The team's prospects in subsequent seasons will depend on whether Jackson will stay beyond his five-year contract, which ends with the 2003-04 season. O'Neal has said that if his coach leaves Los Angeles, he will also. However, by 2002 Jackson had formed an unusual alliance that might strengthen his ties to the Lakers, a serious personal relationship with Jeanie Buss, daughter of Lakers' owner Jerry Buss and vice president of business operations for the team. Jackson was divorced from his wife June, who had not moved to Los Angeles with him.

The question of why Phil Jackson is so successful constitutes an ongoing debate. As Jackson himself has pointed out, neither he nor Winter originated the triangle offense. He has simply used it more successfully than other coaches. His unconventional behavior, such as assigning poetry, philosophy, and novels for his players to read, is sometimes dismissed as mind games or as a screen used to mystify his other methods. The result, however, is clear. Jackson gets his players to focus on a common goal and in this mode they play well consis-

Career Statistics

Yr	Team	GP	PTS	FG%	FT%
1967-68	NYK	75	463	40.0	58.9
1968-69	NYK	47	332	42.9	67.2
1970-71	NYK	71	331	44.9	71.4
1971-72	NYK	80	577	44.0	73.2
1972-73	NYK	80	644	44.3	79.0
1973-74	NYK	82	913	47.7	77.6
1974-75	NYK	78	841	45.5	76.3
1975-76	NYK	80	480	47.8	73.3
1976-77	NYK	76	255	44.0	71.8
1977-78	NYK	63	153	47.8	76.8
1978-79	NJN	59	374	47.5	81.9
1979-80	NJN	16	65	63.0	70.0
TOTAL		807	5428	45.3	73.6

NJN: New Jersey Nets; NYK: New York Knickerbockers.

Awards and Accomplishments

1973	Played on New York Knicks championship team
1985	Named CBA Coach of the Year
1991-93, 1996-98	Won NBA championship with the Chicago Bulls
1996	Named NBA Coach of the Year
2000-02	Won NBA championship with the Los Angeles Lakers
2001	Became first NBA coach to lead two different teams to multiple titles

tently. In an era when star players far outrank their coaches in salary and influence, he has proven that coaching is still essential to winning NBA titles. He has taken some of the NBA's finest individual players—Jordan, O'Neal, and Bryant—and made them integral parts of championship teams rather than independently functioning stars on teams that disappear in the playoffs.

CONTACT INFORMATION

Address: Los Angeles Lakers, 3900 W. Manchester Blvd., P.O. Box 10, Inglewood, CA 90306.

SELECTED WRITINGS BY JACKSON:

Maverick, Playboy Press, 1975.
(With Hugh Delehanty) *Sacred Hoops: Spiritual Lessons of a Hardwood Warrior,* Hyperion, 1995.
(With Charley Rosen) *More Than A Game,* Seven Stories Press, 2001.

FURTHER INFORMATION

Periodicals

Callahan, Tom. "The New Age of coaching." *U.S. News & World Report* (May 11, 1992): 61.
Deford, Frank. "Father Phil." *Sports Illustrated* (November 1, 1999): 82.
Deveney, Sean. "A close to perfect fit." *Sporting News* (June 26, 2000): 12.
Farley, Christopher John. "The Philospher Coach." *Time* (March, 20, 2000): 61.
Heisler, Mark. "Lost in the triangle." *Sporting News* (November 8, 1999): 36.
Jackson, Phil. "Phil Jackson Takes Off on His Sideline Offense." *Scholastic Coach & Athletic Director* (November, 2001): 4.

Reese, Joel. "Winter in L.A." *Texas Monthly* (June, 2000): 92.
Reilly, Rick. "He Dreams of Jeanie." *Sports Illustrated* (March 11, 2002): 80.
Samuels, Allison, and Mark Starr. "Doing it Without the Man." *Newsweek* (November 22, 1999): 85.
Samuels, Allison, and John Leland. "'My White Father.'" *Newsweek* (June 19, 2000): 56.

Other

"Phil Jackson Coach Info." NBA.com. http://www.nba.com/coachfile/phil_jackson/ (2002).
Sheridan, Chris. "Shaq says he won't play for anyone other than Jackson." Associated Press File (January 18, 2002).

Sketch by Paula Pyzik Scott

Reggie Jackson
1946-

American baseball player

In a career that spanned twenty-one seasons, with four different teams, Reggie Jackson, known as "Mr. October," for his outstanding play in the post-season, was known as an intelligent, outspoken, and often controversial figure. He was also a Hall of Fame player who became a drawing card wherever he played.

Growing Up

Reggie Jackson was born May 18, 1946, in Wyncote, Pennsylvania, to Martinez and Clara Jackson. He was the fourth of six kids and grew up in a mostly white Philadelphia suburb. His parents had a rocky marriage and divorced when he was six. Jackson went to live with his father, a self-employed tailor and dry cleaner. Martinez Jackson had played second base in the semi-pro

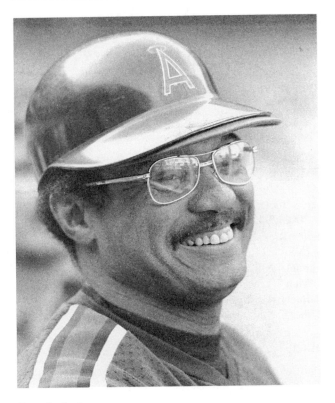

Reggie Jackson

Negro Leagues, and he passed along his love of the game to his son.

Jackson revered his father. "To this day," Jackson says in his autobiography, "My father is almost a mythical figure to me." His dad instilled in him the desire to settle for nothing less than excellence. Except for his relationship with his father, however, Reggie was mostly a loner. Early on he became self-reliant. He was very determined and questioned everything, always ready with an opinion on whatever subject was being discussed.

Whether it was his father's influence or the time he spent in solitude, Jackson decided early on to never settle for mediocrity. He was going to be the best at baseball, just like his idol **Willie Mays**. In 1960, Jackson enrolled in Cheltenham Township High School in Philadelphia, and the coaches there gave him the guidance and discipline he needed to succeed.

By the time he was thirteen, Jackson was considered the best ballplayer in town. Not only that, but he was the only black ballplayer on the Greater Glenside Youth Club, where he would experience racial prejudice and see for the first time that "being black," as he put it in his autobiography, "could be a problem." Yet it would not deter him; in fact, it made him work even harder.

Football or Baseball?

Reggie Jackson began his college career in 1964 at Arizona State University. He entered the school on a full football scholarship, but soon discovered he didn't like the football regimen and began hanging around with the baseball team. By the end of his sophomore year, he was ranked second in the pro baseball draft and football was merely an afterthought.

The Kansas City (later Oakland) Athletics chose Reggie in the 1967 amateur draft, taking him second overall, and he soon was making his mark in professional baseball. After a few quiet years, Jackson caught the nation's attention by hitting a home run over the roof of Tiger Stadium in the 1971 All-Star Game. He also was in the spotlight because he was on a red hot A's team that dominated the World Series from 1972 to 1974.

Reggie Jackson was fast becoming a household name. Though he sat out the '72 Series, he came back from his hamstring injury and in '73 and '74, began his reign over the fall classic. Free agency allowed Jackson to move to the New York Yankees after the 1974 season, and he was on his way to the media capital of the world. Thus, his rocky relationship with Yankee owner **George Steinbrenner** would become legendary.

The postseason would be Reggie's stage. In the 1977 World Series, Jackson became the first player to ever hit five home runs in one World Series. He hit three in sixth

Career Statistics

Yr	Team	AVG	GP	AB	R	H	HR	RBI	BB	SO	SB	E
1967	KCA	.178	35	118	13	21	1	6	10	46	1	4
1968	OAK	.250	154	553	82	138	29	74	50	171	14	12
1968	OAK	.275	152	549	123	151	47	118	114	142	13	11
1970	OAK	.237	149	426	57	101	23	66	75	135	26	12
1971	OAK	.277	150	567	87	157	32	80	63	161	16	7
1972	OAK	.265	135	499	72	132	25	75	59	125	9	9
1973	OAK	.293	151	539	99	158	32	117	76	111	22	9
1974	OAK	.289	148	506	90	146	29	93	86	105	25	10
1975	OAK	.253	157	593	91	150	36	104	67	133	17	12
1976	BAL	.277	134	498	84	138	27	91	54	108	28	11
1977	NYY	.286	146	525	93	150	32	110	74	129	17	13
1978	NYY	.274	139	511	82	140	27	97	58	133	14	3
1979	NYY	.297	131	465	78	138	29	89	65	107	9	4
1980	NYY	.300	143	514	94	154	41	111	83	122	1	7
1981	NYY	.237	94	334	33	79	15	54	46	82	0	3
1982	CAL	.275	153	530	92	146	39	101	85	156	4	6
1983	CAL	.194	116	397	43	77	14	49	52	140	0	1
1984	CAL	.223	143	525	67	117	25	81	55	141	8	0
1985	CAL	.252	143	460	64	116	27	85	78	138	1	7
1986	CAL	.241	132	419	65	101	18	58	92	115	1	1
1987	OAK	.220	115	336	42	74	15	43	33	97	2	0
TOTAL		.262	2820	9864	1551	2584	563	1702	1375	2597	228	142

BAL: Baltimore Orioles; CAL: California Angels; KCA: Kansas City Athletics; NYY: New York Yankees; OAK: Oakland Athletics.

game alone, setting yet another record by hitting those three off of three *consecutive* pitches, and off of three *different* Los Angeles Dodger pitchers. The feat has never been duplicated.

Jackson would earn Most Valuable Player (MVP) honors in the series and become The Big Apple's most popular man. He even had a candy bar, The *Reggie!* bar, named after him. A great story from the candy bar fiasco is how one day the Yankee promoters gave out a bar to the almost 45,000 fans at a 1978 early season home opener. When Jackson hit a home run in the game, the fans tossed their uneaten *Reggie!* bars to the field (the candy bars were reportedly not that tasty). White Sox manager Bob Lemon said, "People starving all over the world and 30 billion calories are laying on the field."

Jackson helped lead two teams to five World Championships in only seven years. Writer Mike Lupica, in an article that appeared in *Esquire*, called Jackson, "The most theatrical baseball player in the last quarter century."

Legacy

Jackson retired after his 1987 season with the California Angels. He was inducted into the Baseball Hall of Fame in 1993, becoming only the 216th inductee, and the only player inducted that year. His achievements run both sides of the spectrum, from success to infamous. He hit ten World Series home runs, has five World Championship rings, and eleven American League Championships with three different teams. But Jackson also holds the major league record for lifetime strikeouts, at 2597. In later years, Jackson would say that, "all

those pitches strung together, that's five years. For five years I never touched the ball." But when he did touch it, it often left the park. He belted 563 home runs, placing him sixth among all-time home run leaders at the time of his retirement.

In July of 2002, the Yankees honored Jackson with a plaque at Yankee Stadium. According to the *New York Daily News,* Jackson told reporters that he was "more nervous" on that day than he was during his first at bat with the Kansas City A's in 1967.

After he retired from baseball, Jackson became a prominent businessman. As recently as 1999, the *Los Angeles Times* reported that Jackson was interested in purchasing the Oakland Athletics, but it never came to fruition. Had he done so, he would have "become baseball's leading minority investor."

In 2002, Jackson purchased a NASCAR team, becoming a partner with the Herzog Motorsports Busch Series team. The main tasks Jackson oversees, according to the *Milwaukee Journal Sentinel*, is as a motivator and team builder.

Reggie Jackson thrived on attention and affection. He was an intelligent, outspoken, and often controversial figure who was highly recognizable, whether it be from his candy bar, his hot temper, or his famous left-handed swing. He hit hard, ran fast, and in a career that spanned twenty seasons, became a positive role model for black children. Jackson was an inspiration, demonstrating that that an athlete could be respected and successful without the use of drugs. Though people either loved him or

Awards and Accomplishments	
1966	College Player of the Year
1967	Southern League Player of the Year
1969, 1971-75, 1977-84	American League All-Star team
1969, 1973, 1975-76, 1980	Sporting News American League All-Star Team
1973	American League most valuable player; Sporting News Major League Player of the Year
1973, 1977	World Series most valuable player
1993	Inducted into National Baseball Hall of Fame

hated him, he brought drama and excitement to the game, especially in the World Series as "Mr. October." His ability to shine in post-season play made him legend.

CONTACT INFORMATION

Address: Reggie Jackson, c/o Matt Merola (agent), 185 E 85th Street, Apt 18G, New York, NY 10028-2146.

SELECTED WRITINGS BY JACKSON:

Reggie Jackson's Scrapbook, E. P. Dutton, 1978.
(With Mike Lupica) *Reggie: The Autobiography,* Villard Books, 1984.

FURTHER INFORMATION

Books

Allen, Maury. *Mr. October: The Reggie Jackson Story.* New York: Times Books, 1981.
Halter, Jon C. *Reggie Jackson: All Star in Right.* New York: GP Putnam's Sons, 1975.
Jackson, Reggie. *Reggie Jackson's Scrapbook.* New York: E. P. Dutton, 1978.
Jackson, Reggie, with Mike Lupica. *Reggie: The Autobiography.* New York: Villard Books, 1984.
Libby, Bill. *The Reggie Jackson Story.* New York: Lothrop, Lee & Shepard, 1975.
"Reggie Jackson." *Great Athletes,* volume 4. Hackensack, N.J.: Salem Press, Inc.

Periodicals

Boston Globe (January 6, 1993): 1.
Boston Globe (January 10, 1993):54.
Boston Globe (August 2, 1993): 37.
Deford, Frank. "Behind the Fence." *Sports Illustrated* (July 27, 1981): 50-64.
Dolson, Frank. "With flair for showmanship, Reggie Jackson was ahead of his time." Knight Ridder/Tribune News Service (July 31, 1993).

Esquire (June 1993): 69-71.
Garcia, Julian. "Reggie finds his place at Monument Park." Knight Ridder/Tribune News Service (July 6, 2002).
"How the Franchise Went West." *Time* (June 27, 1977): 49.
Jet (January 25, 1993): 45.
Jet (May 1993): 47.
Jet (August 16, 1993): 51.
Jet (September 6, 1993); 51.
Kallmann, Dave. "Reggie Jackson becomes NASCAR team owner," Knight Ridder/Tribune News Service (February 28, 2002).
Los Angeles Times (January 12, 1993; August 1, 1993; August 2, 1993; March 5, 1995).
Murray, Chass. "Compensation System Showing Flaws." *Sporting News* (February 6, 1984).
Newhan, Ross. "Baseball: Hall of Famer Jackson has met with Orange County billionaires trying to buy team from Disney." *Los Angeles Times* (September 24, 1999): 6.
New York (April 19, 1993): 158-160.
New Yorker (August 2, 1993): 40-41.
New York Times (July 4, 1979): 50-64.
Sports Illustrated (August 2, 1993): 58-64.
Ward, Robert. "Reggie Jackson in No-Man's Land." *Sport* (June, 1977): 89-96.

Other

"Reggie Jackson." http://www.baseball-reference.com/ (November 10, 2002).
"Reggie Jackson." http://www.pubdim.net/baseballlibrary/ (November 10, 2002).

Sketch by Eric Lagergren

Jaromir Jagr
1972-

Czech hockey player

Playing with the Pittsburgh Penguins, Czech Jaromir Jagr established himself as one of the greatest, most dynamic scorers in the National Hockey League (NHL) in the 1990s. Though he had a reputation for being temperamental and moody, and letting these aspects negatively affect his game, the right winger was still a star. He won two Stanley Cups with the Penguins his rookie and sophomore seasons, as well as a gold medal with the Czech Republic at the 1998 Winter Olympic Games. Jagr forced a trade to the Washington Capitals in 2001, where he did not play as well as he had in Pittsburgh.

Jagr was born on February 15, 1972, in Kladno, in what was then Czechoslovakia, the son of Jaromir (a coal mine administrator and farmer) and Anna Jagr. Both his grandparents and parents suffered under the Communist regime that ruled his country at the time. Both of his grandfathers were jailed for some time. When Jagr became a professional, he wore the number 68 in honor of the Prague Spring, the failed 1968 attempt of his countrymen to rid themselves of the Soviets.

Hockey was one way of getting a better way of life in the Communist country. Jagr began skating at the age of four, and soon became consumed by hockey. As a child, he played on three different teams, usually against older players to improve his skills. When he reached the age of eight, he was playing in multiple games on weekends after practicing for hours daily. His skills attracted much attention, and he was raised in the Czechoslovakia system that produced many future NHL players. One of Jagr's heroes as a teenager was future teammate and consummate goal scorer in his own right, **Mario Lemieux.**

Turned Professional

When Jagr was sixteen years old, he became a professional hockey player. He signed with Poldi Kladno, which played in the Czech Elite League, the best league in the country. In Jagr's first season, he scored only eighteen points in thirty-nine games. But in his second season, 1988-89, he played in fifty-one games, posting an impressive thirty goals and fifty-nine points. Jagr also got some international exposure. When he was seventeen, he played on the Czech national team at the 1990 World Championships. The Czech team beat Team Canada in at least one game. These numbers and this exposure got Jagr noticed by the National Hockey League.

Drafted by the Penguins

In 1990, Jagr was drafted by the Pittsburgh Penguins in the NHL's entry draft with the fifth pick in the first round. When he was drafted, he did not have to defect, marking the first time the Czechoslovakian government allowed a player to attend the draft. He signed a three-year deal worth $3.8 million, and joined the Penguins that fall, playing alongside boyhood hero Lemieux.

Jagr's rookie season was memorable for a number of reasons. On the ice, he scored twenty-seven goals and thirty assists—third among NHL rookies—and won the Stanley Cup with the Penguins. He used his size (6'2", 228 lbs.) to his advantage. His coach during part of his rookie season was **Scotty Bowman**. Bowman who told E. M. Swift of *Sports Illustrated,* "He's a different player than the league has seen in a long time. ... His skating style and strength make him almost impossible to stop one-on-one. A lot of big guys play with their sticks tight to their bodies and don't use that reach to their advantage like Jaromir does."

Off the ice, Jagr found the transition to life in the United States difficult. He did not yet speak the lan-

Jaromir Jagr

guage, though he was learning it from television. While the Penguins placed him with a Czech family in the city, he missed his own family and friends. During the season, the team traded for an elder Czech—Jiri Hrdina—to translate for him and help him make the transition as a player and away from the rink. But each summer in the 1990s, Jagr would return to his native country and train.

Improved as a Pro

As Jagr grew more comfortable and matured as a player, his numbers also grew. In his sophomore year, he had thirty-two goals and thirty-seven assists. The Penguins again won the Stanley Cup, his last with the Penguins, though the team would make the playoffs every year in the 1990s. Before his third year, Jagr wanted a renegotiated contract, because a player of similar age and stature, **Eric Lindros**, was making fifteen times more than him. (At the time, Jagr was only making $200,000 year in base salary.) He went to the media with his salary complaints.

Over the next two seasons, Jagr continued to improve. In 1992-93, he had thirty-four goals and sixty assists. In 1993-94 had thirty-two goals and sixty-seven assists. By the mid-1990s, Jagr had to step up as Lemieux, the acknowledged leader of the team, had injury and health issues, including bad back pain and cancer. Jagr, like Lemieux, had to fight the clutching and grabbing that was common in the NHL at this time.

Chronology

1972	Born December 15, in Kladno, Czechoslovakia
c. 1976	Begins playing hockey
1987	Turns professional, joining the Poldi Kladno in the Czech Elite League
1990	Drafted by the Pittsburgh Penguins; joins them for 1990-91 season; also plays for the Czech national team at the World Championships
1991	Wins Stanley Cup with the Penguins; named to the NHL All-Rookie team
1992	Wins Stanley Cup with the Penguins
1994	Plays for Czechoslovakia in the World Championships
1994-95	Briefly plays for Poldi Kladno in Czechoslovakia and a professional team in Italy during NHL strike
1995-96	Sets record for right wing and European player by scoring 62 goals and 87 assists in 82 games
1998	Wins the Art Ross Trophy; named captain of the Penguins; wins Gold Medal in the Winter Olympic games in Nagano, Japan; appears in the All-Star Game
2001	Traded to the Washington Capitals in the off-season
2002	Plays for the Czech Republic in the Winter Olympics

Awards and Accomplishments

1991	Won Stanley Cup with the Penguins; named to the NHL All-Rookie team
1992	Won Stanley Cup with the Penguins
1995, 1998-2001	Won the Art Ross Trophy as the league's leading scorer
1998	Gold Medal in the Winter Olympic games; appeared in the All-Star Game
1999	Lester B. Pearson Award

At the beginning of the 1994-95 season, the NHL players went on strike. During the strike, Jagr played for his old team in Czechoslovakia. Appearing in only eleven games, he posted twenty-two points. When the NHL season started, Jagr returned to score thirty-two goals and thirty-eight assists in the strike-shortened season. This gave him his first Art Ross Trophy as the league's leading scorer. This was a hint of his future scoring explosion. Jagr was finally becoming the star that many thought he could be.

Breakout Season

In 1995, Jagr signed a five-year deal worth $19.5 million. To continue his comfort zone in Pittsburgh, he moved his mother over to live with him during the season. His first season under his new contract was his breakout year. In eighty-two games, he had sixty-two goals and eighty-seven assists. This set a new record for a right wing as well as for a European-bred player.

Jagr could not match these numbers in 1996-97 because he was out part of the season with an injury. Though he appeared in sixty-three games, he did manage ninety-five points with a high shooting percentage of 20.09. When Lemieux retired in 1997, the Penguins became Jagr's team, further forcing his maturation process. He returned to form in 1997-98, when he again won the Art Ross Trophy.

In 1998, Jagr played for the Czech team in the 1998 Winter Olympic games in Nagano Japan. The team won the gold, with Jagr contributing one goal and six assists in the tournament. During the 1998-99 season, he became the Penguins' captain, and again won the Art Ross Trophy with forty-four goals and eighty-three assists. Despite a groin injury, Jagr played in the playoffs.

By 1999, Jagr was one of the most recognized players in the world. Relatively media shy, he became a little accommodating of the media as he posted impressive numbers. He also had a new contract that was the biggest in the league, $42 million over six years. Jagr did not let the off-ice distraction of the Penguins being in bankruptcy court throw him off his game. The team was saved by Lemieux who became part-owner.

In 1999-2000, Jagr was again dominant, especially at the beginning of the season. In his first thirty-nine games, he put up thirty-two goals. Jagr continued to make the players who played with him better, and again earned the scoring title. In 2000-01 season, Jagr had a Czech coach, Ivan Hlinka, but the pair did not get along during Hlinka's short-lived tenure. Jagr got to play with Lemieux again when he returned as a player in December, but Jagr twice asked to be traded. He still won the Art Ross Trophy, scoring fifty-two goals and sixty-nine assists, but was unhappy in Pittsburgh.

Traded to Washington

After the 2000-01 season ended, Jagr was traded from the Penguins, who could not afford him. He went to the Washington Capitals for three prospects and $4.9 million in cash. The Capitals hoped Jagr would increase their chances of winning the Stanley Cup. (The team last made it to the Cup finals in 1998 when they were swept by the Detroit Red Wings.)

Though Jagr got his wish and was traded, he was still unhappy. In his first two seasons, he did not play well. During the 2001-02 season, he had a knee injury, and while he played through it, he did not have the same scoring touch. After playing for the Czech Republic during the 2002 Winter Olympics, Jagr felt he fit in better when he returned to Washington. He signed a contract extension for seven years for $77 million.

During the 2002-03 season, Jagr was again plagued by trade rumors, but ultimately remained in Washington. The team hoped he would return to the kind of player he was in his heyday in Pittsburgh. One of his Penguin coaches, Ed Johnston, told Gerry Callahan of *Sports Illustrated,* "He knows the game better than anyone on the team. He's very smart out there. He knows the little

Career Statistics

Yr	Team	GP	G	A	PTS	+/−	PIM	SOG	SPCT	PPG	SHG
1990-91	Penguins	80	27	30	57	−4	42	136	19.9	7	0
1991-92	Penguins	70	32	37	69	12	34	194	16.5	4	0
1992-93	Penguins	81	34	60	94	30	61	242	14.0	10	1
1993-94	Penguins	80	32	67	99	15	61	298	10.7	9	0
1994-95	Penguins	48	32	38	70	23	37	192	16.7	8	3
1995-96	Penguins	82	62	87	149	31	96	403	15.4	20	1
1996-97	Penguins	63	47	48	95	22	40	234	20.1	11	2
1997-98	Penguins	77	35	67	102	17	64	262	13.4	7	0
1998-99	Penguins	81	44	83	127	17	66	12.8	12.8	10	1
1999-2000	Penguins	63	42	54	96	25	50	290	14.5	10	0
2000-01	Penguins	81	52	69	121	19	42	317	16.4	14	1
2001-02	Capitals	69	31	48	79	0	30	197	15.7	10	0
TOTAL		875	470	688	1158	207	623	3108	15.5	120	9

Capitals: Washington Capitals (NHL); Penguins: Pittsburgh Penguins (NHL).

things, things you can't teach. He knows how to play the angles and how to protect the puck."

CONTACT INFORMATION

Address: c/o Washington Capitals, Market Square North, 401 Ninth St. NW, Suite 750, Washington, D.C. 20004.

SELECTED WRITINGS BY JAGR:

(With Sam Staid) *Jagr: An Autobiography,* 68 Productions, Ltd., 1999.

FURTHER INFORMATION

Books

Macmillan Profiles: Athletes and Coaches of Winter. New York: Macmillan Reference USA, 2000.

Periodicals

Bechtel, Mark. "17 Pittsburgh Penguins." *Sports Illustrated* (October 16, 2000): 108.

Callahan, Gerry. "Looming Large." *Sports Illustrated* (March 13, 1995): 36.

Edelson, Mat. "Captaining Conundrum." *Sport* (March 1999): 44.

El-Bashier, Tarik. "Caps Add Two, Come Up Short." *Washington Post* (November 30, 2002): D1.

Farber, Michael. "Capital Punishment." *Sports Illustrated* (November 26, 2001): 44.

Farber, Michael. "Throwback." *Sports Illustrated* (January 17, 2000): 52.

Farber, Michael. "Trading Up." *Sports Illustrated* (July 23, 2001): 44.

Greenberg, Jay. "Czeching in." *Sports Illustrated* (February 25, 1991): 32.

Related Biography: Hockey Player Jiri Hrdina

One of the players who eased Jagr's transition into the NHL was fellow Czech Jiri Hrdina, who did not begin playing in the NHL himself until the age of 30. He began playing hockey growing up in Mlada Boleslav, Czechoslovakia. In the early 1980s, he was recruited to play for Sparta Praha, in Prague, and soon became an important player on the team as a center. He also played with his native country in several world championships and Olympics. After the 1988 Winter Olympics in Calgary, Hrdina signed with the NHL's Calgary Flames. He was traded to the Penguins to guide Jagr in the 1990-91 season, and won two Stanley Cups with the team in 1991 and 1992. Hrdina retired after the 1992 season, and later worked as a NHL scout.

"He's game to win—at all costs." *Maclean's* (May 17, 1999): 52.

Kennedy, Kostya. "5 Washington Capitals." *Sports Illustrated* (October 8, 2001): 81.

Kennedy, Kostya. "Reality Czech." *Sports Illustrated* (February 17, 2002): 10.

Kovacevic, Dejan. "Jagr, Lang Silence Small Crowd with Inspired Play for Capitals." *Pittsburgh Post-Gazette* (December 4, 2002): D6.

La Canfora, Jason. "Czech Mate Jagr Helps Lang Get Acquainted." *Washington Post* (October 24, 2002): D6.

La Canfora, Jason. "For Jagr, Familiarity Breeds Excitement." *Washington Post* (September 17, 2002): D2.

La Canfora, Jason. "Jagr Is a More Seasoned Capital." *Washington Post* (October 23, 2002): D1.

La Canfora, Jason. "Jagr Reflects on First Season." *Washington Post* (September 12, 2002): D2.

"Standing Tall." *Sports Illustrated* (April 12, 1999): 50.

Swift, E.M. "The kid from Kladno." *Sports Illustrated* (October 12, 1992): 40.

"10 Washington Capitals." *Sports Illustrated* (October 14, 2002): 92.

Other

"Jaromir Jagr." ESPN.com. http://sports.espn.go.com/nhl/players/statistics?statsId=35 (December 14, 2002).

"Jiri Hrdina." Legends of Hockey Web Site. http://www.legendsofhockey.net (December 16, 2002).

Sketch by A. Petruso

Dan Jansen
1965-

American speed skater

Dan Jansen

Dan Jansen was known as the world's best speed skater in the late 1980s and early 1990s, dominating the world in international competition. However, he is most known for what he didn't accomplish; he competed in three Olympiads before finally earning a gold medal in his final competition of the 1994 Olympic Games in Lillehammer, Norway.

The Skating Jansens

Jansen was born June 17, 1965, the youngest of nine children of Harry, a policeman, and Geraldine (Grajek) Jansen, a part-time nurse. The Jansens of West Allis, Wisconsin were a clean-cut, athletic, religious and close-knit family who defied the limits of economics on two meager salaries. Harry Jansen often worked a second, part-time job. Dan Jansen and his siblings followed his oldest sister Mary onto the ice when she was bitten by the skating bug after watching the North American Skating Championships at a local rink.

West Allis "may the best place in the country" to develop as a speed skater, Jansen recalled in his autobiography, *Full Circle*. The West Allis Speed Skating Club was founded in the 1930s, and the town was site to one of the two official 400-meter ovals in the United States. In most parts of Wisconsin, where winters are long and frozen lakes are plentiful, hockey is virtually the state pastime. But in West Allis, kids who are inclined to skate generally forgo clunky hockey skates for the long blades of speed skates. Jansen's three brothers and three of his sisters skated competitively.

Jansen was in contention for the 1977 national championship when he was just eleven years old. He slipped on a lane marker, losing the championship by one point, and cried all the way home. "You know, Dan, there's more to life than skating in a circle," he recalled his dad saying in *Full Circle*. Wise as his father may have been, for much of Jansen's life skating was his focus. He played high school football until, at age sixteen, he decided to dedicate himself fully to skating. He competed overseas for the first time when he was in tenth grade, setting a junior world record in the 500-meter event. He

took ninth place overall in 1983. His success in the shorter-distance events encouraged Jansen to concentrate on his talent for sprinting.

Overcame Physical Setbacks

Jansen gave up a social life to train and compete, but maintained good grades. As his friends went off to college in 1983, Jansen was preparing for the 1984 Olympics in Sarajevo, Yugoslavia. He qualified to compete in the 500- and 1,000-meter races there and, at age 18, was the youngest competitor. Jansen finished fourth in the 500-meter event in 1984, just 16-hundreths of a second behind the bronze-medal winner, and placed 16th in the 1,000. He was unfazed to be coming home without a medal, setting his sights on the 1988 Games.

Jansen recovered from hamstring injuries in both of his legs to win the silver medal in the 500-meter at the 1985 world sprints. In 1986, he won a medal in every event he raced and became the first American to skate the 500 in under thirty-seven seconds. He finished first in both the 500 and 1,000 at the World Cup in Inzell, West Germany. Jansen was riding high when he stepped on a glass and cut his foot open in West Germany, severing one tendon and seriously damaging another. After six weeks in a cast, Jansen returned to training. He faced another setback when, exhausted, feverish, and sick, he performed horribly in all of his events at the final World Cup meet of 1987. He returned home be diagnosed with mononucleosis. Healthy again, Jansen returned to win the world sprint title that season, and to qualify for the 1988 Olympics in Calgary, Canada.

No Good Time for Tragedy

Jane Jansen, Dan's older sister, was diagnosed with leukemia in 1987, which devastated the entire family. He had guilt feelings about continuing to train, travel, and compete while his sister was struggling for her life in the hospital, but Jane encouraged him keep it up. On February 14, 1988, the morning of his 500-meter race, Jane Jansen died, leaving behind three small daughters and an incredibly close family who loved her.

Geraldine Jansen encouraged her son to go ahead and skate his race. After an emotional day, Jansen recalls stepping onto the ice that night and feeling like he had not skated in six months. After a rare false start, Jansen skated poorly, much slower than usual. As he headed into a turn, he slipped and fell hard, taking Japan's Yasushi Kuroiwa down with him. All eyes were on Jansen that day, "But from that moment forward I was unofficially ordained Dan Jansen, The Guy Who Fell on the Day His Sister Died," he recalled wryly in *Full Circle*.

Hoping to be able to make something good come from the Games, Jansen dedicated his 1000-meter race to Jane. He got off the starting block confidently, and led the field for the first 600 meters, thinking to himself, "Do it for Jane." 200 meters short of the finish, he was down again. The Calgary Olympics had been a bust for Jansen, who now had to return home to bury his sister. He received more than seven thousand letters after the Games. Just three weeks after the Olympics, Jansen sprang back to win a World Cup 500-meter race in Savalen, Norway, and placed second in the 1,000. Afraid he couldn't maintain his stride until the next Olympics, Jansen took a few college courses. But in a turn, his skating actually improved in the four years between 1988 and the 1992 Games in Albertville, France.

Just as he had at Calgary, Jansen entered Albertville on a positive wave. Several weeks before the Games, he skated the best 500 of his life at the Olympic trials, and then beat his own time three weeks later at a World Cup meet in Davos, Switzerland. On the day of his first event, the 500, however, things took a turn. Warm temperatures and rain created poor ice conditions on the outdoor oval and, though he stayed upright, turned in an uncompetitive time, placing fourth. Jansen admits that he was unprepared, mentally or physically, to perform in the 1,000 three days later. He tired badly and finished in 26th place. His critics called him an Olympic choker. The fact that his next shot at an Olympics was only two years away was a small consolation.

Gold, Finally

By the time he arrived in Lillehammer, Norway for the Olympic Games, Jansen had won seven overall World Cup titles and set seven world records. He opted out of the opening ceremonies to prepare for his first event, the 500-meter race, set to take place just two days later. Jansen was remaining calm and quiet before the Games, leaving his expectations at a minimum. As he humbly pointed out in his autobiography, after missing the bronze in 1984 by 16-hundreths of a second, tragedy in 1988, and suffering slow ice and burnout in 1992, "The only thing left was for the Zamboni to run over me on the last turn, and we just didn't think that would happen."

Jansen was paired against Canadian Sean Ireland in the 500. After a false start by Ireland, Jansen was not skating his quickest, but was in the lead. Heading into the last turn, however, he slipped and his hand touched the ice, costing him valuable time. His parents, three eldest siblings, and wife and daughter were watching from the stands, and their hearts broke to see Jansen miss his chance yet again. His family did not weep for the missed medal, as the media misconstrued, but for Jansen and his run of Olympic disappointments. Jansen felt the "sadness of realization," he recalled in *Full Circle*. "I'm probably the best ever, but I am not going to win an Olympic medal in the 500 meters."

With one chance left to win an Olympic medal, Jansen set about practicing furiously for the 1,000-meter race, and psyching himself up to win it. He recalls feeling "off" the day of the 1,000, but knew he was ready when it was time to skate. He settled into a steady rhythm right away, and repeated in his mind, "I love the 1,000 ... I love the

1,000." He seemed to be in control of the race when, 300 meters from the finish, he slipped and put his left hand down toward the ice. Despite his Olympic history, Jansen is not a skater who falls often, but the crowd collectively gasped when it happened, likely thinking "Oh no, not again!" He regained his form, and pushed toward the finish, and the crowd saw his world-record time, 1:12.43, before he did. He carried his baby daughter Jane with him around the rink on his victory lap.

Jansen was chosen to carry the American flag in the closing ceremony of the Lillehammer Games. After a whirlwind three weeks, he headed to Heerenveen, the Netherlands, to skate the season's final World Cup meet. Though he was unprepared for the event, he took second in the 500 and first in the 1,000, seizing the overall World Cup championship. After a decade of ups and downs at the top of his sport, Jansen retired.

CONTACT INFORMATION

Address: Dan Jansen, Dan Jansen Foundation, 1832 Alta Vista Ave., Milwaukee, WI 53213.

SELECTED WRITINGS BY JANSEN:

(With Jack McCallum) *Full Circle: An Autobiography,* Villard Books, 1994.

FURTHER INFORMATION

Books

Jansen, Dan, with Jack McCallum. *Full Circle: An Autobiography.* New York: Villard Books, 1994.

Other

"Dan Jansen." U.S. Olympic Team Web site. http://www.usolympicteam.com/athlete_profiles/d_jansen.html (January 15, 2003.)

"Jansen wins fifth gold, most for an individual." *Washington Post* Online. http://www.washingtonpost.com/wp-srv/sports/longterm/olympics1998/history/1994/articles/94-tkjansen.htm (January 15, 2003.)

"Ten Burning Questions for Dan Jansen." ESPN.com. http://espn.go.com/page2/s/questions/danjansen.html (January 15, 2003.)

"Welcome to the Dan Jansen Foundation." Dan Jansen Foundation Web site. http://www.djfoundation.org (January 15, 2003.)

Sketch by Brenna Sanchez

Bruce Jenner
1949-

American decathlete

Bruce Jenner won a gold medal in the decathlon in the 1976 Olympic Games. He also set a new world record for the decathlon, with 8,176 points. After the Olympics, he used the fame he had won to develop a new career as an entrepreneur, product spokesperson, and motivational speaker.

Jenner was born and grew up in Mt. Kisco, New York, the second of four children of William Jenner, a tree surgeon, and Estelle Jenner. William Jenner had competed in the U.S. Army Olympics in Nuremberg, Germany, in 1945, and won a silver medal in the 100-yard dash. In addition, Jenner's grandfather had run in several Boston Marathons. Jenner inherited their athletic ability and high energy level. Despite his athletic talent, Jenner soon grew to hate school because he had a reading disability that caused him to fail second grade (a big embarrassment). He would do anything to get out of reading in front of the class, and focused his energy on sports instead.

When he was in fifth grade, Jenner's teacher had all the students run, timing them to see who was the best. Jenner was the fastest runner in the school. This success encouraged his interest in sports. According to Mike Downey in the *Los Angeles Times,* "On a field of play he would challenge anyone he knew to be a good student, just so he could clobber that kid and then say, `Read that.'" Jenner told Downey that because nothing came easily to him, he had to work harder, and that if everything had been easy for him, "I never would have realized the way you get ahead in life is hard work." Thus, he credited his learning disability for giving him his intense drive to work and succeed.

Jenner's family moved to Newtown, Connecticut before he began high school. While in high school, he was a pole vault and high jump champion. He also won the Eastern States water-skiing competition three times and was a member of his school's football and basketball teams.

Jenner wanted to go to college, mainly because the Vietnam War was raging, and college students were ex-

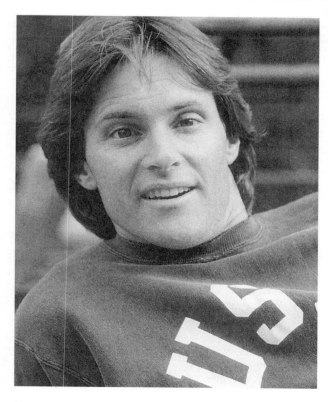

Bruce Jenner

empt from the military draft. He also wanted to play football. He won a football scholarship for $250 a year to Graceland College in Lamoni, Iowa, but during his freshman year he was sidelined by an injury. Bored, he turned to the decathlon. At his first meet, in 1970, he not only won but set a school record, earning 6,991 points. From that point on, he decided to devote all his energy to the decathlon.

The decathlon involves ten running, jumping, and throwing events, held over two days: on the first day, the events include the 100-meter run, long jump, shot put, high jump, and 400-meter run. On the second day, they include the 110-meter hurdles, discus, pole vault, javelin, and 1500-meter run. The events are scored and athletes accumulate points for each performance; the athlete with the highest total score after all the events are completed is the winner. Of the events, the most challenging is the 1,500 meter run; British gold-medal-winning decathlete Daley Thompson once described the decathlon as "nine Mickey Mouse events and the 1,500," according to Downey.

When Jenner went to the trials for the 1972 Olympics he was not expected to do well enough to make the team. Only the three top athletes would be allowed on the team, and by the end of the first day of the trials, Jenner was in 11th place. On the second day, with three events left, he was in tenth place, and still did not look like a good prospect for the team. However, he moved

up to seventh place after the pole vault, and to fifth place after his javelin throw. If he could beat the athlete who was currently in third place by 18 seconds in the 1500 meters, he would make the team. Jenner beat his competitor by 21 seconds. At the 1972 Olympic Games in Munich, Germany, Jenner finished in tenth place. His finish was disappointing to him, and he vowed to train harder and do better.

In December of 1972, Jenner married Chrystie Crownover, a minister's daughter whom he had met in college. For the next four years, he trained while she supported the couple by working as a flight attendant. Jenner also sold insurance part-time. In 1974 and 1976, Jenner won the Amateur Athletic Union decathlon. In 1975, he won the Pan-American Games decathlon. These wins made him a sure member of the U.S. Olympic team for 1976.

In preparation for the Olympics, Jenner trained eight hours a day. He was so intense about his training that he put a hurdle in his living room, and jumped over it more than 25 times each day. He told Downey, "It was not a well-rounded life. But it was [going to be] my last decathlon. I knew that I would have 60 or 70 years to recover."

At the 1976 Olympic Games in Montreal, Jenner was expected to win. He planned to stay within 200 points of the leader's score by the end of the first day. In fact, he ended the day with 4,298 points, only 35 points behind the leader. And by the eighth event on the second day, he was so far ahead that there was no way anyone else could catch up with him. He did so well in the first nine events that he only needed to place third in the 1,500 in order to win a gold medal for the entire event. He came in first, winning gold and setting a new world record for the decathlon, with 8,176 points. Jenner planned to retire after the 1976 Olympics, and he even left his vaulting poles behind in the Olympic stadium because he had already decided he would never compete again.

Jenner was named Associated Press Athlete of the Year for 1976, and also received the Sullivan Award for

Related Biography: Decathlete Daley Thompson

Daley Thompson is one of the best decathletes in history. Born Francis Ayodele Thompson in London, England in 1958, Thompson was interested in sports and highly competitive from early childhood. He entered his first meet at the age of 14, in 1973, and by 1976, was good enough to make the Olympic team. He came in eighteenth, but gold medal decathlete Bruce Jenner predicted that Thompson would one day win gold in the event.

Jenner was right. Thompson won the gold medal at the 1980 Olympics, held in Moscow, and was prevented from setting a new world record only by foul weather. He did set an Olympic record, with a point total of 8,798, which was not broken until 1996. Thompson won another gold medal at the 1984 Olympics, but his dream of winning three Olympic gold medals was crushed when he broke his pole during the pole vault, injuring his adductor muscle.

After retiring from competition, Thompson continued to work as a coach and trainer.

Awards and Accomplishments

1974	Wins Amateur Athletic Union decathlon
1975	Wins Pan-American Games decathlon
1976	Wins Amateur Athletic Union decathlon
1976	Wins gold medal in Montreal Olympic decathlon
1976	Sullivan Award; Associated Press Athlete of the Year
1980	Inducted into National Track and Field Hall of Fame
1986	Inducted into Olympic Hall of Fame

best amateur athlete in the United States in 1976. He was inducted into the National Track and Field Hall of Fame in 1980 and into the Olympic Hall of Fame in 1986.

After winning the decathlon, Jenner wanted to buy a house, but had no assets. At the time, he was making $9,000 a year by selling insurance. He put up his Olympic gold medal as collateral. He got the loan; perhaps the officer foresaw that Jenner would turn his performance into more gold, through personal appearances and endorsements, than any athlete had ever made before.

Jenner's success in the decathlon received intense publicity and was a source of great pride for Americans. It was the year of the Bicentennial, an occasion of patriotic pomp ad circumstance; and Jenner, an American, had beaten a Soviet athlete during a period of great tension between the Soviet Union and the United States. In addition, he had movie-star good looks and a great deal of personal charm. Jenner told Jason Swancey in the *Sarasota Herald Tribune,* "I happened to be the right guy in the right place at the right time."

Jenner's face promptly appeared on the Wheaties box as an example of athletic prowess and health, and he has made his living ever since by riding on his success as an Olympic athlete, promoting various products. He was one of the first athletes to do this, and told Swancey, "Sports marketing has become very big and I would like to think I was one of the guys who kind of got that started." Jenner also told Brian Cazeneuve in *Time,* "Nobody's worked one performance better than I have. I was in that stadium 48 hours and now you can't get rid of me."

Jenner's schedule soon became so demanding that he learned to fly in order to get to all his appearances on time. He bought a 1978 Beechcraft Bonanza airplane, learned to fly, and got his ratings as a pilot. But his hectic schedule hurt his family file. Jenner and Crownover divorced in 1980. In 1981, Jenner married Linda Thomp-

son, an actor, but they divorced in 1986. Thompson told a reporter for *People* that the reason was Jenner's frequent absences from home while he pursued his career as a product spokesperson, actor, and television commentator.

Jenner also rode his reputation into television and movie roles. Although he appeared in a movie, *Can't Stop the Music,* the film was a flop. Jenner jokingly told Jay Weiner in the Minneapolis *Star Tribune,* "What 'Can't Stop the Music' proved is that you can stop the music." According to Downey, Michael Sauter, author of the book *The Worst Films of All Time,* wrote that the film has scenes that "you find yourself wanting to see a second time, because you can't quite believe what you think you just saw." Jenner also appeared in a forgettable episode of the television drama "CHiPs." He was host of a celebrity sports program, "Star Games," and occasionally substituted for anchor David Hartman on the television program "Good Morning America."

Jenner told a reporter for *People* that the late 1980s were a difficult period for him. "I was drifting. I had worked really hard and didn't have much to show for it." He also told a reporter on the Longevity Network Web site that constantly being in the public eye was making him nervous. "I found myself thrown into a glass fishbowl as a celebrity and an American hero. What I was hiding was that I had the same mindset as the nervous schoolboy hiding from my teacher." He also said that his public life as a celebrity did not match the reality of his private life: "In 1990 you would have found me living in a one-bedroom Los Angeles bungalow, my sink piled high with dirty dishes and my living room decorated with a dried-out Christmas tree." He said that at his public appearances, he always wore his best suit: "an out-of-style 1976 tuxedo."

Jenner's life changed for the good when he met his third wife, Kris Kardashian, on a blind date in 1990. They were married five months later, in 1991. He and Kardashian had each had four children before marrying each other, and they eventually had two children together. During the 1990s, Jenner and Kris sold stairclimbing machines through a television infomercial, "SuperFit with Bruce Jenner," for which Kris was the driving force. In 1993 alone, according to an article in *American Fitness,* the infomercial was aired over 2,000 times each month in 17 countries. They also branched out into selling resis-

Bruce Jenner

tance exercise equipment. Jenner was also active in his support for various nonprofit organizations, including the Special Olympics, the Inner City Games, and the California Governor's Council on Physical Fitness and Sports.

Jenner told Dawson that his wife was a major influence on his life: "The reason today I am working as hard as I am is Kris. I got rid of all agents, all managers, all the outsiders who prey on you. She knows how to keep all the percentages everyone else is always taking from you, until there's nothing left for ol' Bruce. She remade me from head to toe."

On the SportsStarsUSA Web site, Jenner summed up his "Rule for Life": "I love life and I want to LIVE it! Activity, variety and the next challenge around the bend and my. . . kids—keep me excited and inspired. I wouldn't have it any other way."

CONTACT INFORMATION

Address: c/o Keppler Associates, 4350 North Fairfax Drive, Suite 700 Arlington, VA 22203. Fax: 703-516-4819. Phone: 703-516-4000. Online: www.bruce-jenner.com.

SELECTED WRITINGS BY JENNER:

(With Philip Finch) *Decathlon Challenge: Bruce Jenner's Story,* Prentice-Hall, 1977.
(With Chrystie Jenner and Ross Olney) *Bruce and Chrystie Jenner's Guide to Family Fitness,* Grosset, 1978.
(With Marc Abraham) *Bruce Jenner's Guide to the Olympics,* Andrews and McMeel, 1979.
(With R. Smith Kiliper) *The Olympics and Me,* Doubleday, 1980.
(With Bill Dobbins) *Bruce Jenner's The Athletic Body: A Complete Fitness Guide for Teenagers: Sports, Strength, Health, Agility,* Simon and Schuster, 1984.
(With Marc Abraham) *Bruce Jenner's Guide to the 1984 Summer Olympics,* Andrews, McMeel and Parker, 1984.
(With Priscilla Davis Dann) *Finding the Champion Within: A Step-By Step Plan for Reaching Your Full Potential,* Simon and Schuster, 1997.

FURTHER INFORMATION

Books

"Bruce Jenner," *Encyclopedia of World Biography Supplement,* Vol. 21, Gale Group, 2001.
"Daley Thompson," *Encyclopedia of World Biography Supplement,* Vol. 20, Gale Group, 2000.

Periodicals

"After Five Years, Bruce Jenner and Second Wife Linda Find Happiness Is Not Working Out," *People,* (February 10, 1986): 105.
"Bruce Jenner," *Christian Science Monitor,* (August 19, 1999): 23.
"Bruce Jenner: After Years of Turmoil The Champ Gets His Life Back in Gear," *People,* (July 15, 1996): 93.
Cazeneuve, Brian, "Bruce Jenner, Decathlete," *Sports Illustrated,* (December 16, 2002): 29.
Downey, Mike, "Twenty Years Later, 1976 Decathlon Champion Bruce Jenner is Better Than Ever," *Los Angeles Times,* (June 23, 1996): 3.

Jordan, Peg, *American Fitness,* (January-February, 1994): 16.

Swancey, Jason, "Jenner Upped Ante in '76," *Sarasota Herald Tribune,* (April 26, 1998): 1C.

Weiner, Jay, "Where Are They Now? Former Decathlon Star Jenner Has a Job That Fits Him to a T," *Star Tribune* (Minneapolis, MN), (July 31, 1996): 2S.

Other

"Bruce Jenner," SportsStarsUSA. http://www.sportsstarsusa.com/ (January 17, 2003).

Keppler Associates. http://www.kepplerassociates.com/ (January 17, 2003).

"Seeking Olympic Gold," Longevity Network. http://www.longevitynetwork.com/ (January 3, 2001).

Sketch by Kelly Winters

Ben Johnson
1961-

Canadian sprinter

Canadian sprinter Ben Johnson was once considered the fastest man on earth, and had an Olympic gold medal to prove it. However, when he was found to be using illegal performance-enhancing drugs, he was stripped of his honors and suspended from competition.

Shy and Quiet

Born in Falmouth, Jamaica, Johnson was the fifth of six children of Ben Johnson, Sr., a telephone repair worker who also had a small farm, and Gloria Johnson. Johnson grew up playing outside, swimming all day, and running whenever he could. As a child, he idolized Jamaican sprinter Donald Quarrie and Trinidadian sprinter Hasely Crawford. He also wanted to be like his older brother, Edward, who was a local running star. In school, Johnson was quiet and shy, perhaps as a result of a speech impediment; he frequently stuttered.

In 1972, Johnson's mother decided that she wanted her children to have a better life than they could have in Jamaica, and took Johnson and three of his siblings to Toronto, Canada, where she had found work as a cook. Although Johnson's father joined the family for a short time, he eventually returned to his job with the Jamaican telephone company, visiting the family on holidays and staying in touch over the phone.

Johnson's stutter had not improved, and combined with his Jamaican accent, made him self-conscious in school. Placed in remedial classes, he finally graduated from Yorkdale High School with basic reading and math

skills. He briefly attended Centennial College, a community college in the Toronto suburb of Scarborough, but quit to devote himself to track.

Trains with Charles Francis

In 1977 he and his brother Edward began training with coach Charles Francis at the Scarborough Optimist Track Club. Johnson was not promising when he first arrived: he could barely run one lap around the club track. However, under Francis's guidance, he gained weight and strength. In 1978, he came in fourth in the 50 meters at the Canadian National Indoor Track and Field Championships. In 1980, he came in second in the 100 meters in the Canadian men's championships.

In 1980, Johnson was beaten for the first time by American sprinter **Carl Lewis**. It would not be the last time Lewis beat Johnson, and Johnson became determined to beat Lewis. At the 1984 Olympics, however, Lewis won four gold medals, and Johnson had to settle for two bronze medals in the 100 meters and 400 meters.

The Fastest Man in the World

In 1985, Johnson finally beat Lewis at the World Championships in Canberra, Australia. For the next two years he was the top sprinter in the world, winning the 100 meters in the 1986 Goodwill Games in Moscow. In 1987 he set four indoor world records and won the outdoor World Championships in Rome with a world-record time of 9.83. In Rome, Johnson finished a meter ahead of Lewis, and was widely hailed as the fastest man on earth and a Canadian national hero.

Lewis told members of the press that some of the other athletes in the Rome competition must be using illegal performance-enhancing drugs. He didn't mention Johnson by name, but it was clear that he meant Johnson. Johnson, like the other athletes, was tested after his Rome victory and passed, making it seem that Lewis's charges were unfounded and based only on jealousy. In addition to Lewis's charges, Johnson struggled with a hamstring injury, numerous endorsement deals and business opportunities, and questions about his amateur status; he was making so much money from his endorsements that he hardly qualified as an amateur.

Stripped of His Gold Medal

Nevertheless, Johnson was expected to win gold in the 100 meters at the 1988 Olympics in Seoul, Korea. He did win, setting a new record with an amazing time of 9.79 seconds. But when he was tested for drugs authorities found traces of an anabolic steroid, stanozolol, in his urine. Johnson was stripped of his gold medal, which went to Lewis, who had come in second. In addition, he was suspended from competition for two years. Johnson denied having taken drugs for some time, until Francis testified in court that Johnson had been using them. Johnson finally admitted that he had been taking drugs since 1981, making all his previous achievements seem questionable.

Stripped of His World Records

Johnson lost all his endorsement contracts, and officials considered stripping him of his 1987 Rome victory. Francis testified in 1989 that Johnson had indeed taken steroids before setting his Rome world record. In 1989, the International Amateur Athletic Foundation passed a resolution stating that as of January 1, 1990, Johnson's previous world records would be declared invalid. As of that date, Carl Lewis held the record for the 100 meters with a time of 9.92, and lee McRae held the 60-meter record with a time of 6.50.

In 1990, Johnson was reinstated to Olympic competition. He began working with a new coach, Loren Seagrave, and planned to compete in the 1992 Olympics in Barcelona. He told Nancy Wood in *Maclean's*, "I'll win the gold medal for sure." However, when he went to the Olympics, he did not make it into the final competition in the 100 meters. In January of 1992, Johnson competed in a Montreal track meet, where he was tested for drugs and found to be using testosterone. As a result, the International Amateur Athletic Foundation slapped him with a lifetime ban from competition.

In *Maclean's*, Mary Nemeth quoted Carl Lewis's agent, Joe Douglas, who said of Johnson's career, "I think his entire life has been a make-believe world. He has talent, but his performances are chemical.... When you lose everything, I don't think anybody should be surprised that there's temptation." In 1999, Johnson appealed to be reinstated to competition, but his appeal was denied. Johnson told Charles P. Pierce in *Esquire*, "I cannot get my name back. Over the years, the media make me a monster, a villain. They make me a one-way figure on a two-way street."

FURTHER INFORMATION

Books

"Ben Johnson," *Contemporary Black Biography*, Vol. 1, Gale Research, 1992.

Periodicals

"Ban Again," *Sports Illustrated*, (March 15, 1993): 9.

Benjamin, Daniel, "Shame of the Game," *Time*, (October 10, 1998): 74.

"Denied," *Maclean's*, (August 30, 1999): 9.

Hersch, Hank, "The Erasing of Johnson," *Sports Illustrated*, (September 18, 1989): 17.

Moore, Kenny, "Clean and Slower," *Sports Illustrated*, (July 22, 1991): 26.

Moore, Kenny, "Rising From the Shadows," *Sports Illustrated*, (November 30, 1987): 94.

Nemeth, Mary, "Scandal: At 21, Ben Johnson Faces a Lifetime Ban from Track," *Maclean's*, (March 15, 1993): 18.

Noden, Merrell, "A Dirty Coach Comes Clean," *Sports Illustrated*, (March 13, 1989): 22.

O'Brien, Richard, "A New Start," *Sports Illustrated*, (January 21, 1991): 26.

Pierce, Charles P., "Ten Years Later, He Can Laugh About It," *Esquire*, (February, 1999): 50.

Wood, Chris, "Dash of Humility," *Maclean's*, (July 27, 1992): 50.

Wood, Nancy, "A Clean Break: Ben Johnson Gets Set to Compete Again," *Maclean's*, (August 20, 1990): 14.

Sketch by Kelly Winters

Jack Johnson
1878-1946

American boxer

Jack Johnson was the first African American to hold the title of world heavyweight champion, a distinction he earned by defeating Tommy Burns in a 1908 fight. During an era of blatant racism, Johnson was a flamboyant character who provoked a worldwide search for the "Great White Hope" who could defeat him. Johnson, both as a brilliant fighter and as a man who lived lavishly, was one of the most well-known sports figures of his day. Boxing historian Nat Fleischer wrote in 1949, "after years devoted to the study of heavyweight fight-

Jack Johnson

Chronology

1878	Born March 31 in Galveston, Texas
1897	First professional fight
1898	Marries Mary Austin
1902	Defeats George Gardiner, former light-heavyweight world champion
1903	Defeats Denver Ed Martin, becoming unofficial black world heavyweight champion
1903	First wife dies
1908	Defeats Tommy Burns, becoming world heavyweight champion and sparking controversy because of his race
1910	Defeats Jim Jeffries, retired world heavyweight champion, and defends his title; race riots break out, and the public cries out for the "Great White Hope"
1911	Marries Etta (Terry) Duryea, a white divorcee from Brooklyn, provoking public outrage
1912	Second wife commits suicide
1912	Marries Lucile Frances Cameron, his white bookkeeper at the cabaret
1913	Convicted of violating the Mann Act, sentenced to one year and one day in prison
1913	Flees to Europe
1915	Loses title to Jess Willard in Havana, Cuba; insists fight was fixed
1920	Returns to United States and serves prison term
1924	Divorces third wife
1925	Marries Marie Pineau, a white divorcee
1946	Dies in car crash in North Carolina

ers, I have no hesitation in naming Jack Johnson as the greatest of them all."

Early Training

Johnson was born into a large, poor family in Galveston, Texas. His father was a former slave from Tennessee, and worked as a janitor and porter. Johnson left school after the fifth grade and began working odd jobs. He worked on the docks as a longshoreman, and got some of his first experience as a fighter in that rough atmosphere. Johnson also worked in a carriage shop, where his boss— an ex-prize fighter—taught him to box. Even though boxing was still illegal in most of the country, Johnson began traveling around the United States, fighting in exhibition bouts for food or lodging. He also participated in the "Battle Royals," competitions staged for white audiences in which several black youths—some blindfolded or naked—fought until only one was left standing.

Success in the Ring

Between 1902 and 1908, Johnson fought fifty-seven official fights, predominantly against other black boxers. Johnson, whose fighting style was fast and nimble, with a strong defense and tremendous power in both fists, won fifty-four of those fights. He was also known for his flamboyant personal style: Johnson joked with the crowd, taunted his opponents, and would defiantly flash his "golden smile" (several teeth had been replaced with

gold). In 1902, Johnson defeated the former world light-heavyweight champion George Gardiner. He went on to defeat Denver Ed Martin in 1903, becoming the unofficial black world heavyweight champion. White boxers, including world heavyweight champion Jim Jeffries, refused to fight Johnson because of his race.

On December 26, 1908, Johnson finally was allowed his chance to fight the world heavyweight champion. The 6-foot, 200 pound Johnson faced 5 foot 7, 175 pound Tommy Burns, a white Canadian fighter, in a match in Sydney, Australia. Even though Johnson was forced to agree to allow Burns's manager to referee the match, he won easily in the fourteenth round when police stopped the match. Although he was the undisputed winner of the bout, Johnson received just $5,000 of the $40,000 purse and some boxing experts refused to acknowledge him as world champion because of his race.

Johnson was disliked and ridiculed not just for being black, but also for his unabashed flamboyance. When he wasn't boxing, Johnson performed in a vaudeville act, singing, dancing, playing the fiddle, and giving speeches. He had tastes for fast cars, stylish clothes, and loose women. His brashness outside the ring (and the outrage that a black man held the world title) led critics to call for another fight, this time with Jeffries, who had retired as the undefeated champion. Novelist Jack London wrote in the *New York Herald,* "Jim Jeffries must now emerge from his alfalfa farm and remove that golden smile from Jack Johnson's face. Jeff it's up to you. The White Man must be rescued."

Jeffries finally agreed to fight Johnson on July 4, 1910. The match was held in front of a crowd of 16,000 in Reno, Nevada, and was billed as "The Hope of the White Race vs. The Deliverer of the Negroes." Johnson entered the ring in an ivory satin robe, gold chains, and a turquoise feathered scarf. His confidence was warranted: he won the fight in a knockout in the fifteenth round. Johnson's victory sparked race riots around the country, and eleven people died in the violence. There followed a nationwide call for competitions to find the "Great White Hope" who could stop the champion Johnson.

Controversial Figure

Johnson's flamboyance was not only a problem for him in the ring. Not only did he openly enjoy his winnings by opening the cabaret Café de Champion in Chicago, he dared to publicly court white women. Johnson—who married three white women over his lifetime—was denounced on the floor of the United States Senate, and some states passed legislation outlawing interracial marriage based on his case. Reformers during the "white slavery" hysteria managed to have Johnson's liquor license revoked, and also had him charged under the Mann Act, which prohibits transporting women across state lines "for immoral purposes." Johnson had moved across state lines both with his wives and with white prostitutes, but before the Mann Act was enacted. Nevertheless, an all-white jury found him guilty of the offense in May 1913, and he was sentenced to a year and a day in prison.

Rather than serve his prison sentence, Johnson escaped to Europe with his then-current wife, Lucile. He boxed in exhibition matches and performed in vaudeville acts there and in Latin America for two years. In 1915, Johnson agreed to fight the "white hope" Jess Willard for the title. The bout was held in Havana, Cuba, since Johnson could not return to the United States. The boxers fought under a blazing sun for 26 rounds, until Willard knocked Johnson out. Johnson claimed afterward that he had thrown the fight in return for a pledge of amnesty from the United States, but none was forthcoming. He fled back to Europe and lived mostly in Spain, performing in exhibition fights and wrestling matches, acting in a film, and performing as a matador.

In 1920, Johnson returned to the United States and served his prison term in Leavenworth. He worked some odd jobs and spent most of the rest of his life working as a lecturer at Hubert's Museum, a sideshow and penny arcade, on 42nd Street in New York. On June 10, 1946, Johnson was speeding through Franklin, North Carolina, toward the **Joe Louis**-Billy Conn rematch when his car hit a light pole. He died hours later in a Raleigh hospital.

Legacy as a Boxer

Johnson was among the first boxers to be inducted into the Boxing Hall of Fame in 1954, and he was in-

---

Awards and Accomplishments	
1902-08	Wins 54 of 57 fights
1903	Becomes unofficial black world heavyweight champion
1908	Becomes world heavyweight champion
1910	Defends title against Jim Jeffries
1954	Included in Boxing Hall of Fame
1990	Inducted into the International Boxing Hall of Fame

---

cluded in the International Boxing Hall of Fame in 1990. In his obituary, the *New York Times* called Johnson "one of the craftiest boxers known to the ring, recognized by many as one of the five outstanding heavyweight champions of all time."

Jack Johnson's life was fictionalized by Howard Sackler in the play *The Great White Hope,* performed on Broadway in 1967. The play starred James Earl Jones and Jane Alexander, and helped launch their careers. The work focuses on the romance between a black boxer and his white lover, and on his prosecution under the Mann Act. Sackler's play won the Tony Award, the New York Drama Critics' Award, and the Pulitzer Prize. *The Great White Hope* was released as a film in 1970 starring the Broadway leads.

Johnson was a flamboyant and widely-despised figure, but also a tremendously talented boxer. He was the first African American athlete to raise such controversy and enjoy such success, and his story haunted the careers of later African American boxers like Joe Louis. Throughout his career, Louis worked to prove his modesty and his moral character; he was always combating the public's memories of Johnson's white wives, flashy suits, and golden smile. Louis, often called "a credit to his race," became the second black world heavyweight champion in 1937.

Later world champion **Muhammad Ali** was tremendously influenced not only by Johnson's boxing technique, but also by his relentless self-promotion and "trash talk." Ali would watch tapes of Johnson's bouts before his own fights, and was inspired by the African American boxing pioneer. Johnson's flamboyance presaged the later antics not just of Ali, but also of star athletes like **Dennis Rodman**. The controversy Johnson stirred up in the American public reflected the racism of the time, and gave other black sports heroes an idea of what they, too, would face.

SELECTED WRITINGS BY JOHNSON:

Jack Johnson In the Ring and Out. National Sports Publishing, 1927.

Jack Johnson Is a Dandy: An Autobiography. Chelsea House, 1969.

FURTHER INFORMATION

Books

Batchelor, Denzil. *Jack Johnson and His Times*. London: Phoenix Sports Books, 1956.

Farr, Finis. *Black Champion: The Life and Times of Jack Johnson*. New York: Scribner, 1964.

Hietala, Thomas R. *Fight of the Century: Jack Johnson, Joe Louis, and the Struggle for Racial Equality*. Armonk, NY: M.E. Sharpe, 2002.

Johnson, Jack. *Jack Johnson In the Ring and Out*. Chicago: National Sports Publishing, 1927.

Johnson, Jack. *Jack Johnson is a Dandy: An Autobiography*. New York: Chelsea House, 1969.

Periodicals

Ebony (April 1994): 86-98.

Foglio, James. "The First Black Heavyweight Champion." *American History* (August 2002): 18-19.

Obituary. *New York Times* (June 11, 1946): 1.

"The Original Natural." *Newsweek* (October 25, 1999): 49.

Sketch by Christine M. Kelley

Junior Johnson

Junior Johnson
1930-

American race car driver

Junior Johnson was among the pioneers of organized stock car racing and one its most successful practitioners as a driver, mechanic, and team owner. Johnson brought both notoriety and respect to a motorsport that had its beginnings in the hills and mountains of the American South, and grew into the multi-million dollar Winston Cup National Association of Stock Car Auto Racing (NASCAR). The notoriety derived from the fact that many of the sport's best drivers—of whom Johnson was the best known—learned and honed their talents by evading the law. These individuals not only mastered the art of evasive and fast driving on the hairpin turns and gouged roadways of the North Carolina countryside, they also became shade-tree mechanics of note. They fine-tuned their cars into professional race-worthy vehicles in order to run illegal, bootlegged liquor from the mountain stills where it was manufactured to the cities and saloons where it was sold.

After serving eleven months of a two-year prison term in 1956, Johnson devoted more of his time to professional racing than bootlegging, and proceeded to revolutionize the sport with an intimidating driving style. It included the first use of aerodynamic drafting—driving in the vacuum developed behind the bumper of a leading car to save fuel, which increases the speed of both vehicles in a push-pull dynamic-in the 1960 Daytona 500. He also pioneered the use of two-way radios between the driver and pit crew. Johnson garnered fifty NASCAR wins before retiring from driving in 1966, the year following publication of Tom Wolfe's essay, "The Last American Hero" in *Esquire* magazine, in which Johnson was portrayed as a savvy good 'ol boy who flummoxed both the law and Detroit's Big Three automakers with his mechanical savvy and hard-charging driving style. This characterization was reinforced when Jeff Bridges portrayed Johnson in the 1973 movie *The Last American Hero*. After retiring from driving, Johnson then turned his attention to running race operations with such drivers as Cale Yarborough, Bobby Allison, Bill Elliott, Darrell Waltrip, and Terry Labonte. In 1970, Johnson was already a pioneer in obtaining corporate sponsorship for his racing vehicles. He furthered these inroads when he became instrumental in the decision of R.J. Reynolds to underwrite the sponsorship for NASCAR, thus beginning the Winston Cup NASCAR series brand.

Son of a Moonshiner

Born Robert Glenn Johnson in 1930 in Ingle Hollow, Wilkes County, North Carolina, Junior Johnson learned

Chronology

1930	Born Robert Glenn Johnson, in Ingle Hollow, North Carolina
1953	Makes his NASCAR driving debut at Southern 500, Darlington
1956	Arrested for moonshining, and spends eleven months in prison
1958	Earns six victories in twenty-seven starts
1960	Wins Daytona 500 and discovers aerodynamic drafting in car owned by John Masoni
1962	Wins National 400
1963	Wins eight Grand National events, including National 400 and Dixie 400
1965	Wins thirteen races, including Rebel 300
1966	Announces his retirement from driving to run racing operation
1970	Introduces NASCAR's William French to R.J. Reynolds' Ralph Seagraves, which initiates the Winston Cup NASCAR series
1986	President Ronald Reagan grants Johnson a presidential pardon
1990	Inducted into International Motorsports Hall of Fame
1995	Sells team and retires from racing with more than 139 NASCAR victories, 128 pole positions, and six Winston Cup Championships as a team owner

Awards and Accomplishments

1960	Won Daytona 500
1962	Won National 400
1963	Won eight Grand National events, including National 400 and Dixie 400
1965	Won thirteen races, including Rebel 300
1973	Inducted into National Motorsports Press Association Hall of Fame
1986	Granted presidential pardon by President Ronald Reagan
1990	Inducted into International Motorsports Hall of Fame
1995	Sold team and retired from racing with more than 139 NASCAR victories, 128 pole positions, and six Winston Cup Championships as a team owner
1996	Inducted into Charlotte (North Carolina) Motor Speedway Court of Legends
1997	Inducted into Bristol (Tennessee) Motor Speedway Heroes of Bristol Hall of Fame
1998	Named greatest NASCAR driver of all time by *Sports Illustrated* magazine

how to drive when he was only eight or nine years old. By the time he was fourteen, he was making bootleg liquor deliveries in his father's pickup truck. His father, Robert Johnson, owned and operated what was considered the largest copper stills in North Carolina. "My dad was in the bootleg business and I was pretty much into it myself at that particular time," he told Andy Clendennen of *The Sporting News*. "I had two brothers and all three of us was [sic] helping him on the farm and helping him in the moonshine business.... Everybody we'd grown up with was doing the same thing we was and we didn't really think basically it was against the law as far as we was concerned, because everybody was doing it," he told Clendennen. While running illegal corn liquor across the mountain roads of North Carolina, Johnson often was chased by local law enforcement agents. His evasive driving abilities, however, became legendary, and he was never caught as long as he was behind the wheels of his souped-up Oldsmobiles and Chevrolets. It was during this spell that Johnson invented and perfected what became known as the "bootleg turn," a 180-degree turn implemented by dropping the vehicle into second gear and jarring the steering wheel to the left.

The family business resulted in other altercations with the law. In 1956, a federal raid of the Johnson home seized the largest inland cache of illegal whiskey in U.S. history. Johnson himself was foiled when legal officers arrested him at the site of his father's still. He was sentenced to two years in the federal reformatory at Chillicothe, Ohio, an experience that he recalled to Clendennen: "I learned a lot of discipline, and to listen to people and evaluate their ideas and stuff I didn't do that before I went there. I learned that you had to do what you was supposed to do when you was doing something for somebody else, and of course in there you was always doing something for the prison system. Obedience is a great thing if you take it and use it in the

right direction, and I learned a lot in that respect." He was released after eleven months, and turned the majority of his efforts toward stock car racing.

Professional Racer

Not all of the income for the Johnsons derived from bootlegging, however. Johnson worked the family farm with his brothers, and was plowing a field behind a mule one day in the late 1940s when his brother L.P. asked him to pilot his car at a race at North Wilkesboro Speedway. Believing a car race would be more fun than plowing a field, Johnson consented. He eventually placed second, casting the die for a long, distinguished career as NASCAR's bad boy, often adapting such tricks as the bootleg turn on corners of oval tracks.

In 1953, Johnson entered his first NASCAR race at the 1953 Southern 500 held in Darlington. He began to establish speed records and local race tracks until his arrest in 1956. Upon his release from prison, he proceeded to make his mark as one of NASCAR's most innovative and intimidating drivers. The world of stock car racing had changed significantly in the late 1950s; changes that included paved tracks, the organization of NASCAR, and the participation of marketing and gear heads from Detroit's Big Three automakers.

Fifty NASCAR Wins

From 1960 to 1965, Johnson was a dominant force in NASCAR racing. Beginning with a win at only the second year of the Daytona 500, Johnson refined and expanded his capabilities as a driver by discovering the competitive advantages of aerodynamic drafting during a practice race. Driving a 1959 Chevrolet, which was outgunned by the faster and more powerful Pontiacs, Johnson devised the strategy that has been a critical element of NASCAR racing ever since. "When we was out

---

The Last American Hero

In 1973, director Lamont Johnson released the filmed version of Tom Wolfe's 1965 essay "The Last American Hero." Alternately titled *Hard Driver*, the film starred Jeff Bridges as Johnson, as well as Gary Busey as Johnson's mechanic, and Valerie Perrine as Johnson's love interest. The film remains mostly true to Johnson's life story, emphasizing his background as a runner of bootlegged corn liquor, and garnered positive critical reviews for Bridges's performance.

---

practicing and a Pontiac would come by, I'd grab one, get as close to it as I could and hang onto it, and they couldn't get away from me," Johnson told Clendennen. "Cotton Owens and Jack Smith come over and told me we really had that Chevrolet flying. Well, little did they know that they was draggin' me around the race track, there was no way possible to keep up with them any other way." Johnson applied what he had learned on the day of the race, as he explained to Clendennen: "I just held on to every Pontiac I could get hold of."

Johnson added to his growing reputation by refusing to rely on help from the Chevrolet factory in Detroit, opting instead to remain independent. This decision added to his prestige when he repeatedly became the driver to beat, which caused fans and writers alike to consider him a David jousting a mighty Goliath. By the time he retired from driving after the 1965 season, Johnson was a 34-year-old motorsport legend. As a team owner, he fielded NASCAR Winston Cup teams to 139 wins and six Winston Cup Championships until 1995, when he retired to his beef farm and business interests in northern North Carolina. In 1998, he was named the greatest NASCAR driver of all time by *Sports Illustrated* magazine.

CONTACT INFORMATION

Address: 1950 Flintstone Drive, Statesville, NC 28677.
Address: c/o Penske Corporation Headquarters, 2555 Telegraph Rd., Bloomfield Hills, MI 48302-0954.
Phone: (248) 614-1122.

FURTHER INFORMATION

Books

"Junior Johnson." *A Who's Who of Sports Champions: Their Stories and Records*. Boston: Houghton Mifflin, 1965.

Other

Clenndennen, Andy. "Junior Johnson Is Still Running in Circles." *Sporting News* (February 15, 2001). http://www.sportingnews.com/features/where-arethey/johnson/ (October 24, 2002).

"Roger Penske." Motorsports Hall of Fame and Museum of America. http://www.mshf.com/index.htm?/hof/penske_roger.htm (January 18, 2003).

Vance, Bill. "Junior Johnson: Legend of Moonshine Running and Stock Car Racing." Canadian Driver. http://www.canadiandriver.com/articles/bv/junior.htm (January 18, 2003).

Sketch by Bruce Walker

Magic Johnson
1959-

American basketball player

Had Earvin Johnson's earliest nickname stuck with him, he would be known today as "June Bug" rather than "Magic." A reference to his childhood proclivity for bouncing from basketball court to basketball court in search of a game, Johnson's later nickname gained preference when, as a high school player, his superior skills began to earn him acclaim. Magic continued to dazzle through his days at Michigan State University and in twelve years with the championship Los Angeles Lakers of the National Basketball Association (NBA). With his friendly demeanor and infectious smile, he shone as much off-court as on, becoming one of the world's best-known, and most well-loved, sports figures. Personally and professionally, he seemed unstoppable. In 1991, however, came an overwhelming test of this belief. At a November 7, 1991 press conference Johnson announced that he had contracted the Human Immunodeficiency Virus (HIV), which leads to the incurable, fatal Acquired Immunodeficiency Syndrome, or AIDS. True to form, Johnson has faced this obstacle head-on and with optimism. While he retired from the NBA following his announcement (returning for a brief stint in 1996), he has focused the same unyielding drive and buoyant energy he displayed on the court into numerous business ventures aimed at revitalizing largely African American areas of the nation's cities. In addition, he has become an unofficial spokesperson for HIV and AIDS awareness, promoting disease prevention measures and railing against the stigmatization of those who are afflicted. Twelve years after his announcement, Johnson still shows no signs of AIDS himself, and remains as energetic and focused as ever.

From "June Bug" to "Magic"

Earvin Johnson Jr. was born on August 14, 1959 in Lansing, Michigan, the middle of seven children. His father, Earvin Sr. worked on an assembly line at Gen-

Earvin "Magic" Johnson

Chronology

1959	Born August 14 in Lansing, Michigan
1973	Begins freshman year at Lansing Everett High School; named starter on basketball team and given nickname "Magic"
1975	Leads team to Class A tournament quarterfinals, named to All-State Squad
1976	Leads team to Class A semifinals, again named All-State
1977	Leads team to Class A championship, named All-State for third time, enters Michigan State University on basketball scholarship
1978	Leads MSU Spartans to Big Ten championship
1979	Leads Spartan to NCAA championship, named tournament MVP, sets new school record for season assists, begins rivalry with Larry Bird
1979	Foregoes remainder of college career to turn pro, drafted by the Los Angeles Lakers in the first round
1980	Proves instrumental in Lakers' NBA tournament win, named championship series MVP
1981	Son Andre is born on February 20
1987	Named league MVP
1988	Leads Lakers to yet another NBA championship, the first time a team wins two in a row since the Boston Celtics in 1969
1991	Marries Earleatha "Cookie" Kelly in September
1991	On November 7, publicly announces that he has been diagnosed with HIV and will retire from the NBA
1991	Named to President Bush's National AIDS Commission on November 15
1992	Johnson's Number 32 is retired by the Los Angeles Lakers
1992	Wins Olympic gold medal as member of U.S. "Dream Team"
1992	Son Earvin III is born on June 4
1992	Resigns from National AIDS Commission, citing the government's lack of genuine interest in fighting the disease
1992	Joins NBA All-Star team despite his retirement and named game MVP
1992	Aborts NBA comeback after several players express fear of catching HIV from contact with Johnson
1993	Founds Johnson Development Corporation
1993-94	Becomes Lakers head coach for 15 games at end of season
1994	Becomes minority owner of Los Angeles Lakers
1995	Adopts daughter Elisa
1996	Announces on January 29 that he will return to play for the Lakers
1996	Retires on his "own terms" on May 14
1997	Founds Magic Johnson Entertainment
1998	Hosts talk show, which is canceled after two months
2002	Named to Basketball Hall of Fame

eral Motors and held a second job hauling garbage; his mother Christine worked as a janitor and cafeteria worker at a local school while taking primary responsibility for rearing the children. Johnson was expected to adopt the same tireless work ethic as his parents. "'You want five dollars Junior?'" his father would ask, as Johnson recalled in his autobiography. "'Here, take the lawn mower. There's a lot of grass in this town, and I bet you could earn that money real quick.'" When Earvin Sr. did relax, he often did so by watching basketball and critiquing the players' moves. Johnson took keen note and then hit all the courts in the neighborhood to try out what he learned. This is when his older neighbors began to call him "June Bug." All the practice paid off, and by the time he joined the team at Lansing Everett high school he was clearly destined for greatness. It was during his sensational freshman year where, in one game, he scored thirty-six points and grabbed eighteen rebounds, that Fred Stabley, Jr., a sportswriter for the *Lansing State Journal* decided the rising star needed a nickname. Reasoning that "Dr. J" and "Big E" were already taken, he opted for "Magic." Johnson recalls that, while the nickname gave opposing teams, and their fans, additional heckling fodder, this only fueled his drive. "The name became a challenge, and I love challenges," Johnson recalled. "The signs and the slogans only served to fire me up." Johnson was named an All-State player three times and, during his senior year, led his team to the state championship.

Taking Off

Johnson stayed in his hometown for college, attending Michigan State University. As a freshman, he led the team to a Big Ten championship. In Johnson's sophomore year, the Spartans advanced to the 1979 NCAA Championship finals. It was in this game, against Indiana State University, that he had his first well-publicized match-up with ISU star and later Boston Celtic **Larry Bird**, with whom he maintained a friendly rivalry throughout his career. The Spartans won the game 75-64 and it was Johnson who was named the tournament's Most Valuable Player. After this stunning victory, Johnson forfeited his remaining two years of college eligibility and turned pro. He was the first pick for the Los Angeles Lakers in 1979 and became the team's key to winning the NBA championship that season. With star **Kareem Abdul-Jabbar** in-

Awards and Accomplishments

1974-76	Michigan Class A All-State Team
1976	Michigan Class A Championship Team
1979	NCAA Championship Team
1980	NBA All-Rookie Team
1980, 1982-92	NBA All-Star Team
1980, 1982, 1985, 1987-88	NBA Championship Team
1980, 1982, 1987	MVP NBA Championship
1982	All-NBA second team
1982	Citizenship Award
1983-91	All-NBA first team
1984	Schick Pivotal Player award
1984	IBM All-Around Contributions to Team Success Award
1987	Player of the Year, *Sporting News*
1987, 1989-90	League MVP
1990, 1992	MVP NBA All-Star Game
1992	U.S. Olympic Gold Medal
2002	ROBIE Humanitarianism Award (Jackie Robinson Foundation)
2002	Named to Naismith Memorial Basketball Hall of Fame

Life After Death

November 7, 1991, was one of those seismic Where-were-you-when-you-heard? moments in American culture. Even if you didn't follow pro sports, you knew Magic—whose last name, like Michael's and Larry's, was superfluous—was part of the holy triumvirate that had saved pro basketball. There he was, telling us, with the imprecise language that was part of his charm, that he had "attained" the AIDS virus, as if it were another goal he'd reached in a storied career: five championship rings, three MVP awards, three Finals MVP awards, one deadly disease. From what information he gave us in succeeding days, it was in fact a form of attainment, the consequence of sexual encounters—heterosexual encounters, Magic emphasized as rumors about his sexual orientation swirled—in offices, in elevators, with multiple partners, the profane fruit of the Penthouse Forum fantasy life available to superstars. ...

Ten years. Michael has retired, unretired, retired and perhaps unretired again. Larry is just gone. The Lakers have fallen and risen. And Magic is still here. Millions of young people have never lived in a culture without AIDS. Almost all of us know someone who has died of the disease, but almost all of us know someone who is living with it, too. Ten years. We know everything about AIDS. We know nothing.

Source: McCallum, Jack. *Sports Illustrated* (August 20, 2001): 70+.

jured and unable to play in the sixth game of the finals, Johnson started at center. Scoring forty-two points and grabbing fifteen rebounds, he led his team to victory and was named tournament MVP.

Johnson's second year for the Lakers was not nearly so magical. In addition to suffering a knee injury that forced him to miss forty-six games that season, tension had begun to mount between the popular player and his teammates. When the Lakers lost to the Houston Rockets in the first round of the NBA Championship playoffs, Johnson was largely blamed for the defeat. The fact that he subsequently signed a $25 million contract to remain with the Lakers increased the animosity, and raised the ire of fans, as did his public criticism of Lakers coach Paul Westhead, who was fired the day after Johnson asked, via the media, to be traded. Following these events, Johnson was booed on many courts, both away and at home. Ever fickle, teammates and fans began to come around when Johnson, under new coach **Pat Riley**, led the team to a second NBA Championship in the 1981-82 season, for which he was again named MVP. Johnson also experienced a personal roller-coaster during this time: a high school friend with whom he had a brief casual relationship announced that she was pregnant. On February 20, 1981, Johnson's son Andre was born.

After losing the championship to the Philadelphia 76ers in 1983, the Lakers entered into one of the most enduring rivalries in all of professional basketball, alternating tournament wins with the Boston Celtics for the next five seasons. A second rivalry, between Johnson and Celtics star Bird, naturally built up over this time as well. While both Johnson and Bird initially lived up to the media portrayals of them as opponents off-court as

well as on, exchanging glares and refusing to shake hands, the pair eventually became close friends. So close, in fact, that Johnson imagined the pair retiring at the exact same moment: "It's the seventh game of the Finals, the Lakers against the Celtics. There's one minute left in the game and score is tied. And then, suddenly, it's time to leave. Larry and I just shake hands, walk off the court, and disappear." Prior to retirement, though, Johnson credited Bird with pushing him to play his best ball. "We feed off one another, that's why we go on," he told the *Los Angeles Times*.

The Celtics won the first of the five-year string of championship bouts, spurring the press to, for a time, refer to Johnson as "Tragic" and his team the "Los Angeles Fakers." Johnson and his teammates turned it around the following year, however, beating the Celtics four games to two. The Lakers didn't make the final round in 1985-86, and the Celtics went on to take the title from the Houston Rockets. But the Lakers came back with a vengeance the next season, again beating the Celtics in the finals four games to two. That year, Johnson averaged 21.8 points per game, led the league in assists with 12.2 per game, and led his team to an NBA-best 65 wins. For his efforts, he was awarded his first-ever league Most Valuable Player award. He was named MVP of the tournament again that year as well. It was the last time he and Bird met each other in the NBA finals.

In 1988, Johnson faced another close friend across the court as the season came to a close. Playing the Detroit Pistons for the title this year, Johnson's and Piston guard **Isiah Thomas**'s mutual respect and deep friendship was demonstrated when the pair kissed before the opening tip-off of Game One. Ultimately, Johnson went home with the trophy, as the Lakers bested the Pistons four games to three. By this time, the star of Hollywood celebrities' favorite team—Lakers fans included Jack Nicholson, Michael Douglas and Michael Jackson—had become a celebrity himself, and he found it necessary to travel with bodyguards and reside in a guarded estate due to his immense popularity. Johnson and Thomas faced each other again in the 1989 NBA Championship, but this time Thomas emerged the victor, with Johnson sitting out a portion of the final series due to an injured hamstring. Still, Johnson was awarded his second MVP award for his regular-season play. While his team did not progress to the finals the next season (although Johnson was again named league MVP), Johnson made one more championship trip in 1990, facing the Chicago Bulls. Again, he emerged disappointed, with the Bulls winning four games to one. While he did not know it at the time, this series marked the end of Johnson's NBA career.

Off-Court Battle

The fall of 1991 started out beautifully for Johnson. In September he married Earleatha "Cookie" Kelly, a longtime friend. But just a few weeks later, during a routine physical examination, the seemingly invincible ball player tested positive for HIV, the virus that leads to the incurable and fatal disease AIDS. The world as he knew it came crashing to a halt. Johnson revealed the news to the public on November 7, 1991, and announced he would be retiring from basketball. The sports world was stunned. "I didn't believe it," UCLA player Ed O'Bannon recalled in *Sports Illustrated* years later. "When I watched the press conference later that day, it broke my heart. It was one of the lowest moments of my life because he was my favorite player of all time. We all thought he was going to die." Both Cookie and their son, Earvin II., who was born on June 4, 1992, have repeatedly tested negative for the virus. The Johnsons adopted a daughter, Elisa in 1995. Defying many of the stereotypes—and medical realities—of living with HIV, Johnson has yet to manifest any signs of the disease. This does not mean, however, that he was immune to the prejudices often levied against those with HIV and AIDS. After he made the announcement, people jumped out of swimming pools when he jumped in, afraid they would contract the virus, he told *Jet* in 2002. Indeed, he abruptly aborted a 1992 NBA comeback after many players expressed fear of coming into contact with him. Johnson did, however, play on the 1992 NBA All-Star Team and was named the game's MVP.

Johnson also began channeling his still-unbridled energy into AIDS prevention and awareness efforts. Soon after he announced he was HIV-positive he established the Magic Johnson Foundation to promote HIV/AIDS prevention and awareness. He briefly served on President George Bush's National AIDS Commission, but resigned on September 25, 1992, citing the government's lack of genuine interest in fighting AIDS as his reason. He still continues many of the duties he took on as a committee member, such as speaking at various AIDS

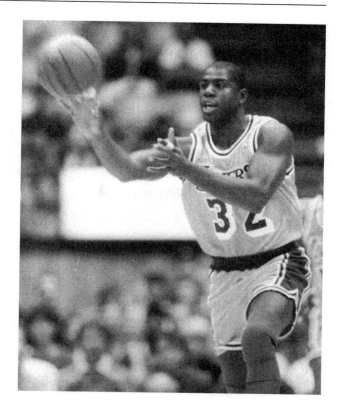

Earvin "Magic" Johnson

awareness events, helping to raise funds for research, and lending his words and well-recognized image to publications and public service announcements promoting precautionary measures. In one particularly bold move, Johnson has been candid about the way he contracted the disease, admitting that he often failed to practice safe sex and encouraging others to learn from his example. One byproduct of his efforts has been a growing realization that HIV and AIDS do not only affect homosexuals or people of certain races or classes. Johnson's current efforts focus on raising HIV and AIDS awareness in the Black and Latino communities

Building an Empire

Johnson has also been busy overseeing a number of business ventures, primarily aimed at revitalizing poor, largely African American urban areas and specifically targeting African American patrons. His $500 million Magic Johnson Enterprises includes shopping plazas in Las Vegas and Los Angeles; part-ownership of movie theaters in Atlanta, Cleveland, Houston, Los Angeles and New York City; and part ownership in twenty-six Starbucks stores, with commitments to build nineteen others. True to his "do what can't be done" ethos, Johnson is the only outsider to enter into a financial partnership with Starbucks. "We always said no," Starbucks Corporation CEO Howard Schultz told *Sports Illustrated*. "But Magic had a vision, an idea, a genuine commitment to

Career Statistics

Yr	Team	GP	Pts	FG%	3P%	FT%	Reb	Ast	STL	BLK	TO	PF
1979-80	LA	77	1387	.530	.226	.810	596	563	187	41	305	218
1980-81	LA	37	798	.532	.176	.760	320	317	127	27	143	100
1981-82	LA	78	1447	.537	.207	.760	751	743	208	34	286	223
1982-83	LA	79	1326	.548	.000	.800	683	829	176	47	301	200
1983-84	LA	67	1178	.565	.207	.810	491	875	150	49	306	169
1984-85	LA	77	1406	.561	.189	.843	476	968	113	25	305	155
1985-86	LA	72	1354	.526	.233	.871	426	907	113	16	273	133
1986-87	LA	80	1909	.522	.205	.848	504	977	138	36	300	168
1987-88	LA	72	1408	.492	.196	.853	449	858	114	13	269	147
1988-89	LA	77	1730	.509	.314	.911	607	988	138	22	312	172
1989-90	LA	79	1765	.480	.384	.890	522	907	130	34	289	167
1990-91	LA	79	1531	.477	.320	.906	551	989	102	17	314	150
1995-96	LA	32	468	.466	.379	.856	183	220	26	13	103	48
TOTAL		906	17707	.520	–	.848	6559	10141	1724	374	3506	2040

LA: Los Angeles Lakers.

create a business in an underserved community that was both profitable and benevolent." Johnson attributes his business success to the same driven personality that allowed him to dazzle on-court in the face of his high school basketball hecklers. "I got turned on when people said it was all over for me," he told *Sports Illustrated*. "I wanted to show them I wasn't going away." Johnson's short-lived 1998 talk show met with less success and was cancelled after two months.

Johnson has not left basketball completely. In addition to a brief return to the Lakers in 1996 and a glorious stint on the gold medal-winning U.S. Olympic "Dream Team" in 1992, he formed and coached a traveling exhibition team, "Magic Johnson All-Stars" and coached his old team, the Lakers, for fifteen games during the 1993-94 season, after which he decided to move up in the ranks and become an executive with and minority owner of the team. For all he contributed to the game, he was named to the Naismith Memorial Basketball Hall of Fame in 2002. A decade after his whole life took such an unforeseeable shift, Johnson reflected on all he had achieved, and all he still would like to, with the trademark optimism that has been key to both his on- and off-court success and popularity. "Everything is for a reason; I don't go back," he told *Sports Illustrated*. "HIV happened for a reason. I'm a person who moves forward, and I continue to do it."

CONTACT INFORMATION

Address: c/o Johnson Development Company, 9100 Wilshire Blvd., Suite 710 East, Beverly Hills, CA 90212.

SELECTED WRITINGS BY JOHNSON:

Magic, Viking Press, 1983.
(With William Novak) *My Life,* Random House, 1992.

FURTHER INFORMATION

Books

Johnson, Earvin. *Magic*. New York: Viking Press, 1983

Johnson, Earvin, and William Novak. *My Life*. New York: Random House, 1992

Sports Stars, Series 1-4, U•X•L, 1994-98.

Periodicals

"Jackie Robinson Foundation Honors Magic Johnson, Gordon Parks, Hank Greenberg." *Jet* (April 8, 2002): 49-50.

"Magic Johnson, Globetrotters Inducted into Basketball Hall of Fame." *Jet* (June 24, 2002): 48-49.

"Magic Johnson Retires Again Saying It's On His Own Terms This Time." *Jet* (June 3, 1996): 46.

"Magic Johnson Talks About Living 10 Years with AIDS Virus, Juggling Family and Business, the L.A. Lakers." *Jet* (January 7, 2002): 54.

McCallum, Jack. "Life After Death: Magic Johnson Has Pulled Off One of the Great Comebacks in Sports History, and It's Got Nothing to Do with Basketball." *Sports Illustrated* (August 20, 2001): 70.

Sketch by Kristin Palm

Michael Johnson
1967-

American track and field athlete

The first man ever to win both 200-meter and 400-meter dashes at the same world championship, Michael Johnson is considered by many the greatest combined 200/400 sprinter who ever lived. One of the most colorful competitors at the Summer Olympic Games of 1992, 1996, and 2000, Johnson captured a total of five gold medals in Olympic competition, as well as nine gold medals at International Association of Athletics Federations (IAAF) world championships. Before he retired from competition in September 2001, Johnson had been ranked number one in the 400-meter ten times and number one in the 200-meter five times by *Track & Field News*. In announcing his retirement after the 2001 Goodwill Games in Brisbane, Australia, Johnson told reporters: "I will miss the sport because it's been such a big part of my life. I am a little sad that this year is going to end because I have had a great time. But I'm looking forward to retirement."

Born in Dallas

He was born Michael Duane Johnson in Dallas, Texas, on September 13, 1967. The youngest child of Paul, a truck driver, and Ruby Johnson, an elementary school teacher, he grew up in a stable family environment in Dallas. Johnson, like his four older siblings, showed an early interest in sports, but he clearly leaned toward running and shunned such contact sports as football and basketball. Of his attraction to running, he later told *USA Today*: "I don't like depending on anyone for anything in life. In track, it's just you." Although sports played an important role in Johnson's childhood, he also devoted a good deal of time and energy to his academic studies, attending classes for gifted children. As a boy, he wore black, horn-rimmed glasses that brought taunts of "nerd" from some of his classmates. As much as he loved running, his boyhood goal was to become an architect.

He first began to compete in track as a teenager, and although he clearly enjoyed it, he was hardly an overnight star. As he told *Boy's Life,* "I first competed in track at Atwell Junior High in Dallas, and then just because it was something fun to do. I ran the 200 and the sprint relay, but I wasn't outstanding and had no big plans for high school track." In fact, Johnson, opting to concentrate on his studies, didn't compete at all during his first two years at Skyline High School. As a junior he tried out and landed a spot on the school's track team. He got some good advice from high school coach Joel Ezar, who urged Johnson to just relax and enjoy running. "Track is a big sport in Texas, but he [Ezar] didn't put pressure on me," Johnson told *Boy's Life.* "I ran the 200 and both relays [400 and 1,600]. I never went to a meet intent on running great times and trying to impress college coaches and get a scholarship. As a result, I never felt burned out." As a senior, Johnson won the district title in the 200-meter dash but lost at the state meet.

Michael Johnson

Runs Track for Baylor

Despite—or perhaps because of—his relaxed approach to competition, Johnson was recruited by coach Clyde Hart to run track for Baylor University in Waco, Texas. Hart was particularly taken by Johnson's stable upbringing, good grades, and solid maturity, qualities he felt would make the runner a natural leader on Baylor's relay teams. However, it was not long before he was able to see even greater potential in Johnson. In his very first 200-meter race at Baylor, Johnson broke the school record with a time of 20.41 seconds. By the time he graduated from Baylor with a bachelor's degree in accounting and marketing in 1990, Johnson had become the top-ranked runner in both the 200- and 400-meter sprints, the first man ever to hold a dual top ranking in both these events.

Johnson began running track professionally shortly after his graduation from Baylor. He quickly made a name for himself in track circles. In the 400-meter sprint, he was virtually unbeatable, and in the 200-meter he won the world championship in 1991, beating the field by a third of a second. Outside the Olympics, Americans pay only minimal attention to track and field events and the sport's leading competitors. As a result, Johnson first attained stardom among European and Asian fans of the sport. Back home he was far from being a household name. Discussing his low profile in America, Johnson told the *New York Times*: "When I'm in Europe and everybody knows who I am, and every-

Chronology

1967   Born September 13 in Dallas, Texas
1986   Graduates from Skyline High School in Dallas
1990   Receives bachelor's degree in accounting and marketing from Baylor University
1998   Marries Kerry Doyen on October 3
2000   Becomes a father with birth of a son, Sebastian, in May
2001   Announces retirement from competition

body wants an autograph and wants to shake your hand, you sometimes worry about going out. It's kind of relaxing to come home and not have to worry about that. But it's frustrating to know that I'm the best in the world in two events, and there are guys in other sports who are good but not the best, and they have $3 million contracts. It's kind of tough. But I look at the positive side. I've traveled, seen the world. I could be a great writer and not make $3 million in a lifetime."

Waylaid by Illness in 1992

Looking ahead to the 1992 Summer Olympic Games in Barcelona, Johnson planned to compete in both the 200- and 400-meter sprints. On the basis of Johnson's record during his first two years of professional competition, he looked like a likely winner in both events. Traveling to Spain in advance of the Olympics, he ate some tainted ham and developed a severe case of food poisoning. By the time his events rolled around, he had shaken off the symptoms of the illness but remained weakened. As a result, he failed to qualify for the finals in either event, although he did win a gold medal as a member of the U.S. 4x400 relay team that set a new world record time of two minutes, 55.74 seconds. Bitterly disappointed by the failure to qualify for his two main individual events, Johnson vowed to soldier on toward Atlanta.

As a short-range goal, Johnson set his sights on winning the 400-meter sprint at the 1993 IAAF World Championships in Stuttgart, Germany. In a series of qualifying races leading up to Stuttgart, he blew away the competition. At the USA/Mobil Track and Field Championships, Johnson, facing off against such keen competitors as world record holder Butch Reynolds and 1992 Olympic gold medalist Quincy Watts, won the race in a personal record time of 43.74 seconds. He followed up this win with victories at major competitions in Oslo, Gateshead, and Zurich. At Stuttgart, Johnson, the favorite, won the 400 sprint with a championship record time of 43.65 seconds. At the 1994 Goodwill Games in St. Petersburg, Russia, Johnson took the gold medal in the 400-meter sprint, and for the year as a whole he won all of his 400-meter events. In 1995, he became the first athlete in history to win both the 200- and 400-meter sprints at the U.S. National Championships. Not long thereafter, Johnson was the first man ever to win the world title in both events.

Wins Both Events at Atlanta

Johnson was primed and ready when the Atlanta Summer Olympic Games opened in July 1996. He raced to victory in the 400-meter sprint with a new Olympic record time of 43.49 seconds. Only three days later, he set a new world record time of 19.32 seconds in winning the 200-meter sprint. The victories were particularly sweet for Johnson, who four years earlier had been waylaid by illness on his race for gold in the same events at Barcelona. Never before had a man won gold in both events at the same Olympics. (The only woman to win gold in both the 200- and 400-meter sprints was **Valerie Brisco-Hooks**, who accomplished the feat at the 1984 Summer Games in Los Angeles.) Of his remarkable performance, Johnson told the *Olympian*: "I've always wanted to bring the two events together in a way that nobody else had ever done; this sums up what my career is about." In a bold display of confidence, Johnson ran both events in gold-colored running shoes and sported a thick gold chain around his neck.

Shortly after his impressive win at Atlanta, Johnson published a motivational book titled *Slaying the Dragon: How to Turn Your Small Steps to Great Feats,* and toured extensively in late 1996 to promote it. In recognition of Johnson's accomplishment in winning both the 200- and 400-meter sprints, the U.S. Olympic Committee named Johnson Sportsman of the Year for 1996, an honor he'd previously won in both 1993 and 1995. The IAAF named him Legend Athlete of the Year for 1996, and the Amateur Athletic Union gave him its 76th annual James E. Sullivan Memorial Award. Things also improved financially for Johnson when he was signed by Nike to a six-year, $12 million endorsement deal.

Michael Johnson

Pulls Up Lame in Race with Bailey

Something of a shadow was cast across Johnson's otherwise sterling reputation by his participation in a privately organized 150-meter race against Canadian sprinter **Donovan Bailey**. The race, held at Toronto's SkyDome in 1997, ostensibly was staged to find out who was the "world's fastest man." Favored three to one by bettors, Johnson shocked everyone when he pulled up lame halfway through the run as Bailey raced past him. Johnson grabbed his left thigh and walked to the finish line. Opponent Bailey later called Johnson a "coward," and the media flooded Johnson with questions about whether he had purposely thrown the race. The American sprinter explained that he'd suffered an intense cramp, forcing him to drop out of the race. An x-ray later confirmed that Johnson had torn his quadriceps muscle. This was just the beginning of a string of physical problems for Johnson, who also suffered problems with his left hamstring and other troubles associated with a skeletal imbalance that forced his spine into misalignment. Despite these leg problems, he continued to train.

In 1998 Johnson was a member of the gold-medal winning U.S. 4x400 relay team at the Goodwill Games in New York City. During his leg of the relay, he ran the fastest 400-meter sprint of the year at 43.30 seconds. The following year, at the IAAF World Track and Field Championships in Seville, Spain, Johnson won the 400-meter sprint with a new world record time of 43.18 seconds. At the 2000 U.S. Olympic Track and Field Trials in Sacramento, a hamstring cramp forced Johnson out of competition in the 200-meter sprint. He did, however, qualify for the 400-meter, his signature event. At Sydney, he successfully defended his Olympic title in the 400-meter sprint and also won gold as a member of the U.S. 400x4 relay team, bringing the total of his Olympic gold medals to five. In winning the individual 400-meter sprint at Sydney, Johnson became the first sprinter in history to win consecutive gold medals in the event.

Johnson wrapped up his brilliant running career with another gold medal as a member of the winning 4x400 relay team at the 2001 Goodwill Games in Brisbane, Australia. Although he had maintained a home in Texas for most of his professional career, Johnson in the fall of 2001 put his Dallas home on the market and moved to Mill Valley, California, a suburb of San Francisco in nearby Marin County. There he lives with wife Kerry and their son, Sebastian, born in May 2000. Interviewed in April 2002 by *Runners World Daily,* Johnson's longtime coach, Clyde Hart, was asked what the sprinter was doing now that he'd retired. "He's keeping busy and enjoying retirement," Hart replied. "I think he retired at the right time in his career." Asked if he thought there was any chance that Johnson might return to running, Hart said, "No, Michael is not going to do that. That decision was made and there's no looking back. That's the kind

Awards and Accomplishments

1989	NCCA 200-meter indoor championship
1990	Named Male Athlete of the Year by *Track & Field News*
1991	Gold medal in 200-meter sprint at IAAF world championships
1992	Gold medal as member of U.S. 4x400 relay team at Olympics in Barcelona
1993	Gold medal in 400-meter sprint at IAAF world championships
1993-94	U.S. Track Athlete of the Year
1995	Gold medals in 200- and 400-meter sprints at IAAF world championships
1996	Gold medals in 200- and 400-meter sprints at Olympics in Atlanta
1996	Named Get Smart Player of the Year by *Sport* magazine
1996	Named Legend Athlete of the Year by IAAF
1997	Gold medals in 400-meter sprint and 4x400 relay at IAAF world championships
1998	Gold medal in 4x400 relay at IAAF world championships
1999	Gold medals in 400-meter sprint and 4x400 relay at IAAF world championships
2000	Gold medals in 400-meter sprint and 4x400 relay at Olympics in Sydney

of guy he is." Although it seems unlikely Johnson will ever run competitively again, he has a glorious record to reflect upon for the rest of his life.

CONTACT INFORMATION

Address: Michael Johnson, c/o IMG Speakers, 825 7th Ave., New York, NY 10019.

SELECTED WRITINGS BY JOHNSON:

(With Jess Walter) *Slaying the Dragon: How to Turn Your Small Steps to Great Feats*, HarperCollins, 1996.

FURTHER INFORMATION

Books

"Michael Johnson." *Contemporary Black Biography*, Volume 13. Detroit: Gale Group, 1996.

"Michael Johnson." *Newsmakers 2000,* Issue 1. Detroit: Gale Group, 2000.

"Michael Johnson." *Sports Stars*, Series 1-4. U•X•L, 1994-1998.

"Michael Johnson." *St. James Encyclopedia of Popular Culture,* five volumes. Detroit: St. James Press, 2000.

Periodicals

"Champion and Family." *Jet* (September 24, 2001): 50.

Other

"Baylor Track and Field Coach Clyde Hart Honored." BaylorBears.com. http://baylorbears.ocsn.com/sports/c-track/spec-rel/112002aaa.html (January 29, 2003).

"Clyde Hart." *Runner's World.* http://www.runnersworld.com/home/0,1300,1-0-0-1954-1-0-P,00.html (January 29, 2003).

"Clyde Hart: Profile." BaylorBears.com. http://baylorbears.ocsn.com/sports/c-track/mtt/hart_clyde00.html (January 29, 2003).

"Johnson, Michael." Microsoft Encarta Online Encyclopedia 2002. http://encarta.msn.com/encnet/refpages/RefArticle.aspx?refid=761580521 (January 29, 2003).

"Michael Johnson." USA Track & Field. http://www.usatf.org/athletes/bios/oldBios/2001/Johnson_Michael.shtml (January 29, 2003).

"More Magic Might Await Michael Johnson." SLAM! Track. http://www.canoe.ca/TrackWorldChampionships/aug30_mor.html (January 29, 2003).

"Olympic Spirit: Michael Johnson." IMG Speakers. http://www.imgspeakers.com/speaker_detail.asp?SpeakerID=119 (January 29, 2003).

Sketch by Don Amerman

Rafer Johnson
1935-

American decathlete

Rafer Johnson's victory in the decathlon at the 1960 Summer Olympic Games in Rome, Italy, earned him the title of "world's greatest athlete," but the track star never competed in another Olympiad again. Johnson was one of the outstanding college athletes of his day, breaking several track and field records and winning *Sports Illustrated*'s "Sportsman of the Year" award while a student at the University of California at Los Angeles. At the opening ceremonies of the 1960 Rome Games, he carried the American flag at the front of the Olympic delegation, the first African American athlete ever chosen for the honor.

Standout Athlete

Johnson was born in 1935 in Texas's cotton country, and grew up in a house there that had neither indoor plumbing nor electricity. The family eventually resettled in small town in California's San Joaquin Valley, where they were one of the few black families in the area. Johnson's talents were apparent by his late teen years, and he was Kingsburg High School's star athlete in baseball, basketball, and track and field. One day, his track coach took him to watch another San Joaquin athlete, Bob Mathias, train for the 1952 Olympics, and Johnson decided that day to make the grueling decathlon his sport of choice.

Rafer Johnson

Offered a football scholarship to the University of California at Los Angeles (UCLA), Johnson declined it in order to concentrate on track and field, and eventually captained the UCLA team. He was also elected student-body president, and became the first black at the school to pledge a national fraternity. After qualifying for the 1956 Olympics in Melbourne, Australia, Johnson was hampered by injury and placed second in the decathlon. Its punishing series of ten events over two days caused its victors to earn the superlative "world's best athlete" designation, for they challenged both speed and strength in jumps, foot races, the discus throw and pole vault, among others. Between 1956 and 1960, Johnson won three U.S. national decathlon titles. In 1958, he competed against one of the decathlon's greatest names of the day, two-time Olympic bronze medallist Vasily Kuznetsov of the Soviet Union. They met in a showcase U.S.-Soviet track competition held at Moscow's Lenin Stadium, and Johnson bested his idol and set a world record that day.

Marched into Stadium

After qualifying for the 1960 U.S. Olympic track and field team, Johnson was designated captain of the entire American athletic contingent, and carried his country's flag during the opening ceremonies in Rome. He was slated to compete against C. K. Yang, a fellow track star at UCLA and a member of Taiwan's national Olympic team. On the first day of the decathlon, John-

son and Yang remained close in points; on the second day, Johnson lost points when he failed to clear one of the 110-meter hurdles, but did well with a pole vault of 13 feet, 5½ inches. The final event, the 1,500-meter race, was Johnson's least favorite, and he and Yang remained neck and neck for much of it; Johnson finished 1.2 seconds behind Yang, but his overall score of 8,392 points gave him the gold as well as the Olympic decathlon record. "At that moment, I gave it everything I could," he told *Los Angeles Times* writer Eric Sondheimer. "I couldn't have expended more energy than I did during those two days." Despite his gold-medal finish, Johnson felt bad for his friend. As elated as I was to win the gold medal," he told Sondheimer, "part of me was disappointed for C.K. because I know how hard he worked." Johnson and Yang have remained friends since the 1960 Olympic Games.

Johnson's dedication and drive helped him land a post-collegiate job as an international goodwill ambassador. He acted in Hollywood films, worked as a sports broadcaster, recruited Peace Corps trainees, and served as a personnel executive at a California telephone company. He also became involved in Democratic Party politics, and was a member of the security detail for 1968 U.S. presidential hopeful Robert F. Kennedy. When Kennedy exited through Los Angeles's Ambassador Hotel after his California primary victory speech, shots were fired, Kennedy fell, and Johnson pushed the candidate's pregnant wife Ethel out of the way; he and football player Rosey Grier, another bodyguard, then tackled the assailant, Sirhan Sirhan, and Johnson disarmed him.

Opening Ceremony Honoree Again

Devastated by the incident, Johnson recovered with the help of Kennedy's sister, **Eunice Kennedy Shriver**, who encouraged him to become involved in a project she had started, the Special Olympics, a competition for developmentally and physically disabled children and adults.

Awards and Accomplishments

1955	Won gold medal in decathlon at the Pan American Games
1956	Won silver medal in decathlon at the Melbourne Summer Olympic Games
1956, 1958, 1960	Named U.S. national decathlon champion
1958	Set world record in the decathlon at United States-Soviet track meet in Moscow
1958	Named Sportsman of the Year by *Sports Illustrated*
1960	Won gold medal in decathlon at the Rome Summer Olympic Games; named Sportsman of the Year by *Sport* magazine
1960	Named Athlete of the Year by the *Associated Press*
1960	Received James E. Sullivan Memorial Award from the Amateur Athletic Union of the United States
1974	Inducted into the National Track and Field Hall of Fame, Athletics Congress of the United States of America
1983	Inducted into the United States Olympic Hall of Fame
1990	Inducted into the National High School Hall of Fame

Johnson married in 1971, and kept both his silver and gold Olympic medals in a bank vault, rarely mentioning them to his children. "The house was for everybody, not just me and my things," Johnson told *Independent Sunday* journalist Ronald Atkin. "We put up the medals or citations the kids got but almost none of my stuff was up. We never talked much about that." Both youngsters were stunned one day in 1984 when they drove with their father to Los Angeles Coliseum, where he disappeared and then emerged to light the Olympic flame during the opening ceremonies. "I felt a part of all those great Olympians on the field.... I think the torch run may be the great legacy of these Olympic Games," *Sports Illustrated* writer Robert Sullivan quoted him as saying. "I think it tied us together and made it all warm—a feeling of binding us all together."

In 1998 Johnson wrote an autobiography, *The Best That I Can Be.* He has long been active in the California Special Olympics (CSO) organization, serving on the board of directors as president and, since 1992, chair of the CSO Board of Governors. He is credited with bringing hundreds of thousands of dollars in financial support to CSO coffers through his fundraising efforts. Both of Johnson's children, Jennifer and Josh, followed their father to UCLA and were standout athletes there; Josh nearly made it onto the 2000 Olympic team in javelin, and Jennifer went to Sydney as a member of the U.S. beach volleyball team. "I am a very proud father," Johnson said in the interview with Atkin for the *Independent Sunday.* "In terms of motivation and preparation and desire to be the best they can be, I'd put my children right up there with the best I've ever known. They give their all."

CONTACT INFORMATION

Address: c/o Santa Barbara Speakers Bureau, P.O. Box 30768, Santa Barbara, CA 93130-0768.

SELECTED WRITINGS BY JOHNSON:

Johnson, Rafer, and Philip Goldberg. *The Best That I Can Be.* Garden City: Doubleday, 1998.

FURTHER INFORMATION

Periodicals

Atkin, Ronald. "Olympic Games: Beach Volleyball." (London, England) *Independent Sunday* (September 17, 2000): 6.

Barnacle, Betty. "Rafer Johnson Recalls His Olympic Win." Knight-Ridder/Tribune News Service (November 6, 1997).

Cazeneuve, Brian. "Rafer Johnson, Olympic Hero: August 6, 1984." *Sports Illustrated* (September 11, 2000): 20.

Danzig, Allison. "Rafer Johnson Picked to Carry U.S. Flag in Olympic Ceremony." *New York Times* (August 23, 1960): 33.

Gustkey, Earl. "Johnson Set Record Straight in Decathlon." *Los Angeles Times* (July 28, 1999): 1.

Sondheimer, Eric. "Ex-Olympian Johnson Leads by Example." *Los Angeles Times* (November 5, 1997): 3.

Sullivan, Robert. "The Legacy of These Games." *Sports Illustrated* (August 20, 1984) 96.

"Torch Bearers." *People* (July 10, 2000): 149.

Other

"Rafer Johnson." Santa Barbara Speakers Bureau. http://www.sbweb.com/prospeakers/rjohnson.htm (January 21, 2003).

Sketch by Carol Brennan

Randy Johnson
1963-

American baseball player

Standing at least a head taller than most of his fellow players, Randy Johnson is one of the tallest players ever to play in Major League Baseball (MLB). At six feet, ten inches, Johnson's towering stature has earned him the nicknames "Big Unit" and "Big Bird." But it's not Johnson's height but his incredible pitching skills that have earned him the greatest fame. Johnson first won glory as baseball's "strikeout king." And he continues to hurl 100-mile-an-hour fastballs and sliders that confound batters, but he also boasts one of the best earned-run averages (ERAs) in MLB history. As compelling a force as

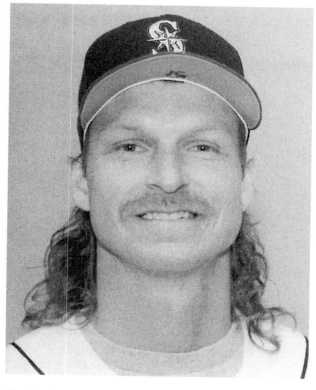

Randy Johnson

he is on the pitching mound, Johnson is surprisingly modest, avoiding the spotlight away from the game whenever possible. After nearly fifteen years in the game, Johnson was still going strong in the early years of the new millennium, driven by a quest for perfection. As he told AskMen.com, "The one thing that keeps me going is [that] I'm never content with anything. . . . If I was to retire today, I'd like to think this was my best year. But I'd like to think [that] with hard work and determination, I could get better in certain categories." A five-time winner of the **Cy Young** Award, Johnson trails only **Roger Clemens**, a six-time winner. Johnson won the award four years in a row (1999, 2000, 2001, and 2002).

Born in Walnut Creek, California

He was born Randall David Johnson in Walnut Creek, California, on September 10, 1963. The son of Bud and Carol Johnson, he boasted a strong throwing arm as a boy but lacked ball control. To improve control, Johnson and his dad marked out a strike zone on the family's garage door. The young Johnson would hurl tennis balls at the door and later check to see how many balls had left their mark within the zone. When he was old enough, Johnson signed up to play in his local Little League but got off to a shaky start when he showed up late for his first game. To make matters worse, he could not locate his team and returned home in tears.

Things looked up for Johnson during his years at Livermore High School, where he developed into a star in

two sports—baseball and basketball. In basketball he twice led the East Bay Athletic League in scoring. It was in baseball, however, that Johnson truly made his mark. As a starting pitcher for the Livermore nine, he concluded his high school baseball career in a blaze of glory, pitching a perfect game at the end of his senior year. After graduating from Livermore High in 1982, Johnson went to the University of Southern California on a combined baseball-basketball scholarship. He played both sports his freshman and sophomore years but decided to focus exclusively on baseball his third year at USC.

Drafted by Montreal Expos in 1985

Johnson entered the Major League Baseball (MLB) draft in 1985 and was selected by the Montreal Expos in the second round. For the next three years he pitched for a number of minor league teams in the Expos' farm system. Late in the 1988 season, the Expos called Johnson up to the majors, where he did well for the remainder of the regular season, going 3-0 with an earned-run average (ERA) of 2.42. Despite his auspicious debut in major league ball, the next season was anything but promising for Johnson. After a dismal start to his 1989 season (an ERA of 6.67), Johnson was sent back to the minors by Montreal. Once again his problem was ball control. He walked twenty-six batters in twenty-nine innings. In late May 1989, the Expos traded Johnson to the Seattle Mariners. Johnson did better in Seattle but still posted a losing 7-9 record with an ERA of 4.40 for the remainder of the 1989 season.

Johnson showed improvement in 1990, going 14-11 with an ERA of 3.65. The highlight of his season was a 2-0 no-hitter he pitched against the Detroit Tigers. He also was tapped for his first All-Star Game, although he never got an opportunity to pitch. Although he turned in fairly creditable pitching records during the seasons of 1991 and 1992 with ERAs of 3.98 and 3.77, respectively, Johnson continued to be plagued by problems of ball control. Although he led the majors in strikeouts in 1992 with 241, he also led the majors in walks for the third consecutive season. Personal tragedy struck on Christmas Day 1992. As Johnson was flying home to spend the holidays with his parents, his father suffered a massive heart attack and died before Johnson could reach the hospital. In the wake of his father's death, he seri-

Career Statistics

Yr	Team	W	L	ERA	GS	CG	SHO	IP	H	R	BB	SO
1988	MON	3	0	2.42	4	4	0	26.0	23	7	7	25
1989	MON	0	4	6.67	6	0	0	29.7	29	22	26	26
	SEA	7	9	4.40	22	2	0	131.0	70	64	70	104
1990	SEA	14	11	3.65	33	5	2	219.7	174	89	120	194
1991	SEA	13	10	3.98	33	2	1	201.3	151	89	152	228
1992	SEA	12	14	3.77	31	6	2	210.3	154	88	144	241
1993	SEA	19	8	3.24	34	10	3	255.3	185	92	99	308
1994	SEA	13	6	3.19	23	9	4	172.0	132	61	72	204
1995	SEA	18	2	2.48	30	6	3	214.3	159	59	65	294
1996	SEA	5	0	3.67	8	0	0	61.3	48	25	25	85
1997	SEA	20	4	2.28	29	5	2	213.0	147	54	77	291
1998	SEA	9	10	4.33	23	6	2	160.0	146	77	291	213
	HOU	10	1	1.28	11	4	4	84.3	57	12	26	116
1999	ARI	17	9	2.48	35	12	2	271.7	207	75	70	364
2000	ARI	19	7	2.64	35	8	3	248.7	202	73	76	347
2001	ARI	21	6	2.49	34	3	2	249.7	181	69	71	372
2002	ARI	24	5	2.32	35	8	4	260.0	197	67	71	334
TOTAL		224	106	3.06	426	87	34	3008.3	2310	1023	1231	3746

ARI: Arizona Diamondbacks; HOU: Houston Astros; MON: Montreal Expos; SEA: Seattle Mariners.

Awards and Accomplishments

1982	Pitched perfect game in his last outing for Livermore High School
1990	Pitched no-hitter against the Detroit Tigers
1992	Led the major leagues in strikeouts
1993	Struck out 18 batters in a single game
1993-94	Led the major leagues in strikeouts
1995, 1999-2002	Cy Young Award
2001	Named Co-MVP of World Series

Related Biography: Pitching Coach Tom House

In the struggle to overcome his problems with ball control, Johnson got some valuable tips from world-famous pitching authority Tom House during the early 1990s. At the time House was pitching coach for the Texas Rangers. To show his gratitude for House's help, Johnson later wrote the foreword to House's *Fit to Pitch*, published by Human Kinetics in 1996.

House, who holds a Ph.D. in psychology, pitched professionally for the Atlanta Braves, Boston Red Sox, and Seattle Mariners between 1967 and 1979. He began his career as a pitching coach in 1980 and has worked in that capacity for the Houston Astros, San Diego Padres, Texas Rangers, and Japan's Chiba Lotte Marines. House is also the founder of Absolute Performance Group, which integrates sports science and sports technology with the health and fitness needs of the everyday individual. He travels extensively and serves as the information and instruction coordinator for twelve baseball academies across the United States and Canada.

ously considered leaving baseball. As he told an interviewer for *Sport* magazine, "Baseball meant so little. I enjoyed the thrill of telling my dad how good I was on a given night. When he passed away, I realized I had no one to call. Part of me had died too."

Grief Strengthens His Game

Johnson's mother convinced him not to leave baseball. To remind him of his father, he drew a cross and the word "Dad" on the palm of his glove. When troubled by feelings of weakness on the pitcher's mound, he would glance at these symbols. "My heart got bigger," Johnson told *Sports Illustrated*. "After my dad died, I was convinced I could get through anything. I don't use the word 'pressure' anymore. That's for what he [his father] went through. Life or death. I use the word 'challenge.' And I'll never again say, 'I can't handle it.' I just dig down deeper."

Johnson got help in overcoming his control problem from ace pitcher **Nolan Ryan** and Tom House, the pitching coach of the Texas Rangers. As a young pitcher, Ryan had experienced similar problems, and he saw a lot of himself in Johnson. The help from Ryan and House worked won-

ders, and in 1993 Johnson enjoyed his best season ever, going 19-8 with an ERA of 3.24. He tied an American record for left-handed pitchers when he struck out eighteen batters in a single game. The following year Johnson compiled an enviable 13-6 record with an ERA of 3.19 before a players' strike ended the season in August.

Wins First Cy Young Award in 1995

In 1995 Johnson posted an 18-2 record with an ERA of 2.48, earning him his first Cy Young Award. Even more significantly, Johnson helped the Mariners make it to the playoffs where Seattle upset the New York Yankees in five games, largely on the strength of Johnson's brilliant relief performance in the fifth and deciding game. Sidelined by injury for most of 1996, Johnson bounced back in 1997 with a 20-4 record and an ERA of 2.28. After a mediocre start to his 1998 season with the Mariners, Johnson was traded by Seattle to the Houston Astros, where he posted an amazing record of 10-1 with an ERA of 1.28.

Despite Johnson's stunning success with the Astros, at season's end he became a free agent and signed to pitch for the Arizona Diamondbacks. It proved to be a marriage made in heaven. For the next four years, Johnson's incredible pitching earned him four consecutive Cy Young awards. His ERA for each of his first four years in Arizona never climbed higher than 2.64. In 2001 came what was for Johnson the brightest moment yet. Arizona made it into the playoffs, where Johnson compiled an astounding record of 5-1 with forty-seven strikeouts in forty-one innings. The Diamondbacks went on to win baseball's World Championship with a thrilling seventh-game victory over the New York Yankees in the World Series. Johnson and teammate **Curt Schilling** were named co-MVPs of the World Series.

When Johnson learned in early November 2002 that he'd earned his fourth consecutive Cy Young Award, he told the Associated Press: "I'm a very simple person. I work hard, and I push myself, and this is the reward. . . . If you remain consistent and have a good year, it's kind of a bonus. This has come from maintaining consistency, hard work, and dedication, and my teammates being very supportive offensively, defensively, and in the bullpen."

CONTACT INFORMATION

Address: Randy Johnson, c/o Arizona Diamondbacks, P.O. Box 2095, Phoenix, AZ 85001. Phone: (602)462-6500.

SELECTED WRITINGS BY JOHNSON:

(With Tom House) *Fit to Pitch,* Human Kinetics, 1996.

FURTHER INFORMATION

Books

"Randy Johnson." *Newsmakers,* Issue 2. Detroit: Gale Group, 1996.
"Randy Johnson." *Sports Stars,* Series 1-4. U•X•L, 1994-98.

Periodicals

Baum, Bob. "Johnson Wins 4th Straight Cy Young." Associated Press (November 6, 2002).
"Johnson Captures Fourth Straight Cy Young Award." Reuters (November 5, 2002).

Other

"APG: Living Younger Longer." Absolute Performance Group. http://www.absoluteperformancegroup.com/tomhouse.htm (December 26, 2002).
"Randy Johnson." AskMen.com. http://www.askmen.com/men/sports//44_randy_johnson.html (December 23, 2002).

"Randy Johnson." Baseball-Reference.com. http://www.baseball-reference.com/j/johnsonra05.shtml (December 22, 2002).

Sketch by Don Amerman

Bobby Jones
1902-1971

American golfer

Although he retired from competitive golf in 1930, at age twenty-eight, Bobby Jones is widely regarded as the greatest golfer of all time. While earning three college degrees Jones played golf as an amateur, winning thirteen of the twenty-one national championships he entered in the United States and Great Britain between 1923 and 1930. In 1930 he achieved the golfing "Grand Slam" by winning the U.S. Amateur, U.S. Open, British Amateur, and British Open Championships in the same year. He surprised the world by retiring from competition soon afterward. In retirement he wrote books and articles on golf and made a series of instructional films, while practicing law. In 1931 he helped to design and build the Augusta National Golf Club in Augusta, Georgia. The club's tournament soon came to be known as the Masters Tournament. The Masters is one of four tournaments known as the modern Grand Slam, along with the U.S. Open, the British Open, and the American Professional Golfers Association (PGA) Championship. Jones died in 1971 after suffering for twenty-three years with a rare central nervous system disease, syringomyelia. He received numerous awards and honors, including induction into the World Golf Hall of Fame in 1974.

Child Prodigy

Robert Tyre "Bobby" Jones, Jr., named for his grandfather, was born March 17, 1902, in the Grant Park neighborhood of Atlanta, Georgia. He was the second son of Robert Purmedus Jones, an attorney who had played baseball at the University of Georgia, and Clara Merrick Thomas Jones. At age five, he and a friend laid out a small golf course in the front yard, and Jones played with a set of clubs cut down to fit his size. Soon afterward, the family moved to the suburb of East Lake, where they lived next to the East Lake golf course. There, young Jones watched the head professional golfer, Stewart Maiden, and learned to play by imitating his swing. These were the only "lessons" Jones ever had. Maiden coached him informally as the talented young golfer began to win local tournaments.

Jones played in his first U.S. Open Championship in 1920, at the Inverness Club in Toledo, Ohio, where he

Bobby Jones

tied for eighth place. In 1921 he played his first British Amateur at Hoylake, England, where he was eliminated after the fourth round. From there he entered the British Open on the Old Course at St. Andrew's, Scotland, considered the birthplace of golf, but he withdrew in frustration after the eleventh hole after missing a putt.

Winning Streak

Jones did not win a national contest until 1923. At age twenty-one, he won the U.S. Open Championship on Long Island, New York, beating both amateurs and professionals. According to *Newsweek,* he later recalled moving through the congratulatory crowd and thinking, "I've won a championship. At last, I've won one." But this tournament was only the beginning of a successful period when Jones would win a total of thirteen major championships over the next seven years. By 1926 he became the first person to win both the U.S. and British Opens in the same year. On returning home he was treated to a ticker-tape parade down Broadway in New York City, the first of several he would receive. He won the U.S. Amateur in 1924, 1925, 1927, 1928, and 1930. He again won the U.S. Open in 1929 and 1930, disqualifying himself on a one-stroke technicality in 1925, adding to his reputation as a gentleman and sportsman. He also won the British Open in 1926, 1927, and 1930 and the British Amateur in 1930.

Winning all four major championships in 1930 gave him the golfing Grand Slam, an accomplishment that

Jones was the first to achieve. Jones also became the first man in history to break par in the U.S. Open, winning with a score of 287, one under par.

Jones and his two major rivals during the 1920s, Walter Hagen and Gene Sarazen, were known as the Three Musketeers because they took all the major titles in the United States and Great Britain. Jones also led his team to victory five times in the Walker Cup competition, inaugurated in 1921 as a tournament between amateur teams from the United States and Great Britain.

Even though golfing great **Jack Nicklaus** eventually broke Jones's record of thirteen major championships, no one has accomplished what Jones did within such a short period of time. In 1950 an Associated Press poll found Jones's Grand Slam to be "the Supreme Athletic Achievement of the Century."

Personal Style

Jones was an average-size man, standing 5'8" tall and weighing about 165 pounds at the height of his golfing career. He had a clean-cut, boyish manner that made him the favorite of golfing fans. He did not like to practice golf and played on average about eighty rounds a year.

Obviously gifted, Jones had superb timing and a long, powerful stroke. He wasted no time on the golf course and averaged about three seconds to address and strike the ball. He played with a set of clubs that were mismatched but chosen for their perfect feel. Jones named his favorite putter Calamity Jane.

Although his record-breaking scores indicated he could be a successful pro golfer, he remained an amateur, probably believing that his nervous temperament made him ill-suited to turning professional. In his youth, Jones had a fiery temper and was known to throw golf clubs when he was dissatisfied with a shot. It is said that he became extremely stressed before and during a competition, sometimes to the point of vomiting, and lost as much as eighteen pounds during a tournament.

Once Jones learned to control his temper, he always appeared calm and focused on the golf course. Considerate of opponents and spectators, he earned a reputation for being the consummate gentleman. He was also a very private person and extremely modest.

Contribution to the Game

During the years that Bobby Jones played amateur golf, the sport experienced a phenomenal increase in popularity. The number of weekend golfers doubled, and new golf courses were constructed throughout the United States. The middle class began to enjoy golf as spectators, a position once reserved for the wealthy.

After giving up his amateur status and retiring from competitive golf in 1930, at age twenty-eight, Jones was

Chronology

1902	Born March 17 in Atlanta, Georgia
1907	Begins playing golf
1911	Wins junior championship cup of Atlanta Athletic Club
1915	Wins East Lake Country Club and Druid Hills Country Club championships
1916	Wins Georgia State Amateur Championship; competes in U.S. Amateur at Merion Cricket Club, Philadelphia, Pennsylvania, as event's youngest competitor
1917	Wins Southern Amateur
1919	Is runner-up in both Canadian Open and U.S. Amateur
1921	Disqualifies himself during third round of British Open
1922	Receives degree in mechanical engineering from Georgia Institute of Technology
1923	Wins U.S. Open Championship
1924	Receives degree in English literature from Harvard University; marries Mary Rice Malone on June 17—they will have three children
1926	Wins U.S. and British Open Championships, first player to do so in same year
1927	Publishes first book, *Down the Fairway*; receives degree from Emory University Law School
1928	Is admitted to the Georgia bar and begins working in his father's law practice in Atlanta. Jones will continue to practice law after retirement from golf and will head the firm until his death.
1930	Wins Grand Slam: U.S. Open, U.S. Amateur, British Open, and British Amateur Championships; retires from competitive golf on November 18 and surrenders amateur status
1930-34	Makes a series of motion picture films demonstrating his golfing techniques
1931	With broker Clifford Roberts and golf architect Alister Mackenzie, purchases Fruitland Nurseries property in Augusta, Georgia, and begins design and construction of Augusta National Golf Club
1932	Designs first matched set of golf clubs for A. G. Spalding and Company
1933	Augusta National Golf Club opens
1934	First Augusta National Invitation Tournament is held; Jones plays four rounds
1938	Name of Augusta tournament is changed to Masters Tournament
1948	Plays in last Masters Tournament and plays final round of golf in Atlanta; has back surgery and begins to suffer pain and atrophy on his right side
1956	Ailment is diagnosed as syringomyelia
1958	Receives Freedom of the City and Royal Burgh of St. Andrews, Scotland
1968	Attends final Masters Tournament
1971	Dies December 17 in Atlanta; is buried in Oakland Cemetery
1972	Inducted into Southern Golf Hall of Fame; 10th hole at St. Andrews Old Course named in his honor
1974	Inducted into World Golf Hall of Fame
1989	Inducted into Georgia Hall of Fame
2002	Atlanta History Center hosts tribute to Jones on March 17, the 100th anniversary of his birth.sidebar text

in a position to earn money from his golfing career. He made a series of instructional films in which he taught actors how to play golf. He also designed the first matched set of iron golf clubs for Spalding and Company, in 1932. Jones had already published his first book on the subject, *Down the Fairway* in 1927. From 1939 to 1969 he published four more books on playing golf.

Augusta National Golf Club and Final Years

In 1931 Jones formed a partnership with Wall Street broker Clifford Roberts and announced plans to build the Augusta National Golf Club in Augusta, Georgia. With the help of architect Alister Mackenzie, Jones fulfilled his dream of designing a golf course. It opened in 1933, and Roberts suggested that Augusta host its own major tournament. He wanted to call it the Masters Tournament, but Jones thought the name too lofty. Instead, he called it the Augusta National Invitation Tournament. As the Augusta Invitation grew in reputation, by 1938 Jones agreed that it should be called the Masters. Jones played in the tournament until 1949, when his health had deteriorated to the point that he could no longer play. However, he continued to preside over the tournament, finally attending with the help of crutches and braces and enduring intense pain.

After two back surgeries, it was discovered in 1956 that Jones suffered from the rare central nervous system disease syringomyelia. His condition worsened year by year until he was confined to a wheelchair and could not even turn the pages of a book. In 1958, Jones received his greatest honor when the people of St. Andrew's,

Scotland, awarded him the Freedom of the City and the Royal Burgh of St. Andrew's awards in what has been called the most moving ceremony in the history of golf. Jones died of an aneurysm on December 18, 1971, at age 69. At his request, a small, private funeral was held.

Jones's Legacy

Golf historians and experts agree that Jones's sportsmanship is his greatest legacy. Winning the Masters Tournament has also become the most prestigious award in golf, and Jones's books and films have been reprinted and are still used as guides to playing the game. Although he rejected the idea of any monument being made to him—considering the Augusta Golf Club his memorial—a statue of Jones created after his death graced the lobby of a major hotel in Augusta until 2002, when it was moved to the Augusta Golf and Gardens as part of a centennial celebration of his birth. The statue is now the first to greet visitors to the gardens and joins sculptures of **Arnold Palmer**, Jack Nicklaus, Byron Nelson, Raymond Floyd, and **Ben Hogan**.

SELECTED WRITINGS BY JONES:

(With O. B. Keeler) *Down the Fairway: The Golf Life and Play of Robert T. Jones, Jr.,* Minton, Balch & Company, 1927.

(With Harold E. Lowe) *Group Instruction in Golf: A Handbook for Schools and Colleges,* American Sports Pub. Co., 1939.

St. James Encyclopedia of Popular Culture. "Bobby Jones." five volumes. Detroit: St. James Press, 2000.

Periodicals

"Golfer of the Golden Era." *Newsweek* (December 27, 1971): 48.

Other

American Decades CD-ROM. "Robert 'Bobby' Tyre Jones, Jr." Detroit: Gale Group, 1998.

Augusta Chronicle. "The Life of Bobby Jones." CNN/Sports Illustrated. http://sportsillustrated.cnn.com/ (October 21, 2002).

Boyette, John. *Augusta Chronicle.* "Golf's Gentleman." CNN/Sports Illustrated. http://sportsillustrated.cnn.com/ (October 21, 2002).

Boyette, John. *Augusta Chronicle.* "Golf World Pays Tribute to Legend." CNN/Sports Illustrated. http://sportsillustrated.cnn.com/ (October 21, 2002).

DISCovering Biography. "Bobby Jones." Detroit: Gale Group, 1997.

DISCovering U.S. History. "Golf in the 1920s." Detroit: Gale Group, 1997.

Golf Europe. "The Walker Cup." http://golfeurope.com/almanac/majors/walker_cup.htm (October 22, 2002).

Internet Movie Database. "Bobby Jones." http://us.imdb.com/ (October 24, 2002).

Smith, Jason. *Augusta Chronicle.* "Jones Statue Joins Golf Gardens." CNN/Sports Illustrated. http://sportsillustrated.cnn.com/ (October 21, 2002).

Sketch by Ann H. Shurgin

Awards and Accomplishments

Year	Accomplishment
1911	East Lake (Georgia) Junior Championship, at age 9
1916	Georgia State Amateur Championship; qualified in National Amateur Championship
1917	Southern Amateur Championship
1919	Runner-up, Southern Open Championship; runner-up, Canadian Open Championship; runner-up, National Amateur Championship
1920	Southern Amateur Championship; tied for eighth place in National Open; National Amateur Championship, medalist
1922	Southern Amateur Championship; tied for second place in National Open Championship
1923	Won National Open Championship after play-off; National Amateur Championship, medalist after play-off
1924	National Amateur Championship; National Open Championship, second place
1925	National Amateur Championship; National Open Championship, second place after play-off
1926	British Open Championship; U.S. Open Championship; U.S. Amateur Championship, medalist and runner-up
1927	British Open, won with new record score of 285; U.S. Amateur Championship, medalist and winner
1928	National Amateur Championship; U.S. Open Championship, second place after play-off
1929	Won National Open Championship in play-off; National Amateur Championship, co-medalist with Gene Homans
1930	Savannah Open Tournament, second place; won Southeastern Open; *Golf Illustrated* Gold Vase Tournament; British Amateur Championship; British Open Championship; U.S. Amateur Championship; U.S. Open Championship
1950	Associated Press poll judged Jones's Grand Slam "the Supreme Athletic Achievement of the Century"
1955	U.S. Golf Association's highest honor named the Bob Jones Award
1958	Received Freedom of the City and Royal Burgh of St. Andrews at St. Andrews, Scotland
1966	Named president in perpetuity of the Augusta National Golf Club
1972	Inducted into the Southern Golf Hall of Fame; 10th hole at Old Course, St. Andrews, Scotland, named in his honor.
1974	Inducted into World Golf Hall of Fame
1989	Inducted into Georgia Hall of Fame, Augusta

Winning all four major championships-the U.S. Open, U.S. Amateur, British Open, and British Amateur-was known as the Grand Slam. Today the Grand Slam consists of the Masters Tournament, the Professional Golfer's Association (PGA) Tournament, the U.S. Open Championship, and the British Open Championship.

St. Andrews, Scotland, is home of the Old Course, said to be the founding place of golf.

Golf Is My Game, Doubleday, 1960.

Bobby Jones on Golf, Doubleday, 1966. Reprint, Golf Digest/Tennis, Inc., 1986. Rev. ed., edited by Sidney L. Matthew, Sleeping Bear Press, 1997.

Bobby Jones on the Basic Golf Swing, Doubleday, 1969.

FURTHER INFORMATION

Books

Jebsen, Harry. "Robert Tyre Jones, Jr." *Dictionary of American Biography, Supplement 9: 1971-1975.* New York: Charles Scribner's Sons, 1994.

Rice, Grantland, from the writings of O. B. Keeler. *The Bobby Jones Story.* Atlanta: Tupper & Love, 1953.

Kevin Jones
1975-

American snowboarder

One of the most decorated snowboarders in the history of the sport, Kevin Jones has medaled in all but three of the X Games events he's ever entered, settling for fourth place in big air competition at the Summer X Games of 1999, fifth place in big air at the Winter X Games of 2001, and fourth in slopestyle at the 2002 Winter X Games. An avid skateboarder as a boy, he decided to give snowboarding a try after seeing a film in which ace skateboarders Noah Salaznek and John Cardiel showed their stuff on the snow. He competes in an average of only three contests each year—usually the Winter X Games, the Sims World Championships, and one Vans Triple Crown of Snowboarding event. A resident of Truckee, California, not far from Lake Tahoe,

Kevin Jones

Jones most often boards at Squaw Valley. Of himself and other pioneers in snowboarding, Jones says: "We didn't start snowboarding for the money, but now it's turned into the hunt for the almighty dollar. I think snowboarding should be called 'Jock Boarding'."

Born in Sacramento, California

He was born Kevin Christopher Jones in Sacramento, California, on January 23, 1975. As a boy he took up skateboarding and in his late teens became intrigued by snowboarding after seeing popular skateboarders John Cardiel and Noah Salaznek snowboarding in the film *Riders on the Storm*. Jones was seventeen when he first began snowboarding and a year later he entered his first competition. Almost from the start, he showed unusual talent for the sport, quickly developing into one of the young sport's emerging stars. To stay close to the slopes, he moved a hundred or so miles east of Sacramento to Truckee, not far from Squaw Valley where he began training.

Throughout the history of the X Games, which were launched in 1995 by the ESPN cable TV network, Jones has been a dominant force in the snowboard events, which consist of two main forms of competition—big air and slopestyle. Slopestyle events are judged competitions in which one rider at a time goes through a series of jumps and other obstacles, performing tricks along the way. In big air competition, boarders perform tricks, including flips and multiple rotations, while airborne. In the Summer X Games of 1997, Jones took the silver medal in big air

Chronology

1975	Born January 23 in Sacramento, California
1992	Begins snowboarding
1993	Enters first snowboarding competition
2001	Signs endorsement deal with Von Zipper eyewear

Awards and Accomplishments

1997	Silver medal in big air competition at Summer X Games
1998	Silver in slopestyle and bronze in big air at Winter X Games
1998	Gold medal in big air competition at Summer X Games
1999	Silver medal in slopestyle and bronze in big air at Winter X Games
1999	Placed fourth in big air competition at Summer X Games
2000	Gold medal in slopestyle and bronze in big air at Winter X Games
2001	Gold medal in slopestyle and placed fifth in big air at Winter X Games
2001	Named Best Freestyle Rider in TransWorld Rider's Poll Awards
2002	Placed fourth in slopestyle at Winter X Games

competition. At the 1998 Winter X Games he won silver in slopestyle and bronze in big air. Jones got the gold medal in big air competition at the Summer X Games of 1998.

In 1999, Jones took silver and bronze medals in slopestyle and big air, respectively, at the Winter X Games. In big air competition at the Summer X Games of 1999, Jones failed to medal, finishing in fourth place. He really performed brilliantly in slopestyle at the Winter X Games of both 2000 and 2001, taking home the gold medal in the event both years. In slopestyle, he went bronze at the 2000 Winter X Games and placed fifth at the 2001 event. For his impressive performance in 2001, Jones was named Best Freestyle Rider of the Year in the annual Transworld Rider's Poll, an honor that he again received the following year. At the Winter X Games of 2002, there was no big air competition, but Jones finished fourth in the slopestyle event. Jones has been linked romantically with gold medal-winning female boarder Tara Dakides.

Takes Care of Business

Not only is Jones one of the country's premier snowboarders, but he's a businessman as well. A co-owner (with Tara Dakides) of Jeenyus, a manufacturer of competition-class snowboard and other boarding gear, including boots, Jones also gets corporate support from Billabong, Go Ped, and Mountain Surf, all of which sponsor him in competition. Late in 2001 he signed an endorsement deal with Von Zipper, a big player in the sports eyewear market.

In addition to his competition stateside, Jones travels extensively around the globe, filming snowboarding action documentaries. In an interview with Dave Sypniewski of *TransWorld SNOWboarding,* Jones explained his fascination with film. "I like to film because I liked watching them when I was a tadpole. I would watch them over and over 'til they wouldn't work anymore." Film companies for which Jones has filmed include Standard Films, FLF, and Mack Dawg.

Jones is likely to continue to be a major player in professional snowboarding competition for some time to come. Between competition, his filming schedule, and tending to his business, he has little time for non-snowboarding activities, but when he can grab an hour or two, he loves to go fly fishing. In July 2002, he participated in the Great Outdoor Games Fly Fishing Tournament at Lake Placid, New York. Asked how he thought he'd do in the fishing competition, Jones told an interviewer, "I enjoy fly fishing, and I think it's great that I get to experience something that puts me outside of my element. I'm not expecting to win or anything; these guys are heavy hitters."

CONTACT INFORMATION

Address: Kevin Jones, c/o Jeenyus Snowboards, Truckee, CA.

FURTHER INFORMATION

Periodicals

"Snowboard Warrior Kevin Jones Joins Von Zipper Tribe." *TransWorld Snow Boarding* (December 13, 2001).
Sypniewski, Dave. "Kevin Jones Interview: The Golden Boy." *TransWorld Snow Boarding* (August 30, 2000).

Other

"Jones and Dakides Sweep Rider's Poll Awards Again." EXPN.com. http://expn.go.com/snb/s/riderspoll 2002.html (February 2, 2003).
"Kevin Jones." Snowlodge. http://www.angelfire.com/ ab4/snowlodge/kevin.html (February 1, 2003).
"Kevin Jones." EXPN.com. http://expn.go.com/athletes/ bios/JONES_KEVIN.html (February 1, 2003).
"Kevin Jones." Kevin Jones Fan Site. http://www. geocities.com/chung_girl/kevinjones.html (February 1, 2003).
"Kevin Jones." TransWorld Snow Boarding. http://www. transworldsnowboarding.com/snow/features/ article/0,13009,246375,00.html (February 1, 2003).
"Kevin Jones to Compete at Great Outdoor Games." EXPN.com. http://expn.go.com/snb/s/kjflyfsh.html (February 1, 2003).

Sketch by Don Amerman

Marion Jones
1975-

American track and field athlete

Marion Jones

Marion Jones is widely considered to be today's greatest female athlete and one of the greatest athletes of all time. She became the first woman to win five medals in a single Olympics when she won three gold and two bronze medals in the 2000 Summer Games in Sydney, Australia. Jones has also won scores of other medals and awards, including being the unanimous choice as *Track & Field News*'s Athlete of the Year in 1998. Jones played basketball for the Lady Tar Heels at the University of North Carolina at Chapel Hill and may consider a future career in professional basketball, but first she has her sights set on winning track-and-field gold at the 2004 Olympics.

"I Want To Be an Olympic Champion"

Marion Lois Jones was born October 12, 1975, in Los Angeles, California, the daughter of George and Marion Jones. Her mother, a medical and legal secretary, had immigrated to the United States from Belize. When Jones was an infant, her parents divorced, leaving her mother to raise her and her older half-brother, Albert Kelly, alone. In 1983, Mrs. Jones married Ira Toler, whose death four years later of a stroke was a devastating loss to young Marion and her brother.

Jones played T-ball and soccer and took ballet, gymnastics, and tap dancing lessons. By age seven she was participating in organized track events, and by the sixth grade she was playing basketball. In 1984, she was deeply

Chronology

1975	Born October 12 in Los Angeles, California
1976	Parents divorce
1983	Family moves to Palmdale, California; mother marries Ira Toler
1987	Ira Toler dies of a stroke, leaving wife to raise Marion and her brother alone
1988	After watching Seoul Olympics, Marion writes on her blackboard, "I want to be an Olympic champion."
1991	Sets national high school record in the 200-meter dash and receives invitation to appear on *Good Morning America*; mother moves the family to Thousand Oaks, California, so Marion can play basketball for Thousand Oaks High School; runs the year's fastest high school girls' 100-meter dash, at 11.14 seconds
1992	At state championship meet, Jones records long jump of 23', the second longest ever made by a high school girl; misses qualifying for the 1992 Olympics by only .07 second; declines offer to be an alternate on U.S. Olympic team
1993	Offered scholarship to the University of North Carolina at Chapel Hill to play basketball; mother moves to Chapel Hill
1994	Lady Tar Heels win National Collegiate Athletic Association (NCAA) championship, 60-59; earns All-American honors in four events at NCAA track-and-field championships
1995	Breaks metatarsal bone in left foot while practicing with U.S. basketball team at World University Games in August; misses entire basketball season; in December, breaks same bone again while working out on a trampoline
1996	Becomes engaged to shot putter C. J. Hunter; is unable to recover from foot injury in time for 1996 Olympic Trials; returns to play with Lady Tar Heels for 1996-97 season
1997	In March, announces she will not play with Lady Tar Heels during last year of athletic eligibility but will instead concentrate on track and field; begins training with Trevor Graham, a Jamaican track

	medalist in 1988 Olympics; graduates from University of North Carolina in May, wins two events at U.S. national championships, defeating Jackie Joyner-Kersee in long jump; signs a contract with Nike soon afterward
1998	Wins three gold medals at U.S.A. Outdoor Track & Field Championships, becoming first woman in fifty years to accomplish that feat; sets personal best time of 10.65 seconds in 100-meter at World Cup, fourth fastest time in history; marries Hunter on October 3
1999	Wins every 100-meter and 200-meter race she enters until world championships in August
2000	Sets much-publicized goal of winning five gold medals in 2000 Olympics at Sydney, Australia; Nike airs series of "Mysterious Mrs. Jones" television ads, in which Marion asks why women professional athletes earn less than men; wins her first Olympic gold medal, in 100-meter dash, with a margin of .37 seconds, second greatest margin in Olympic history; two days later, news breaks that husband C. J. Hunter failed tests for use of a steroid drug—Hunter denies it; Jones wins a total of three gold and two bronze medals at Sydney, the most by any woman in a single Olympiad
2001	Announces that she will file for divorce from Hunter, citing irreconcilable differences; loses the 100-meter for the first time in four years, to Zhanna Pintusevich-Block, of Ukraine, but reclaims her title in September at Goodwill Games in Brisbane, Australia; films public service announcements at the Olympic Sport and Immunization Festival in Accra, Ghana
2002	Records first undefeated season of her track-and-field career; debuts as CBS network television sports analyst; in December, announces she will leave coach Trevor Graham and work with Canadian Derek Hansensidebar text

impressed by track stars **Florence Griffith-Joyner**, **Jackie Joyner-Kersee**, **Evelyn Ashford**, and **Carl Lewis** as she watched the Olympic Games on television. She wrote on her blackboard at home, "I want to be an Olympic Champion." Jones later said, "I just always believed it was in my future to compete in the Olympics. I knew from about age five that someday I would do something special in life."

High School Star

In her sophomore year at Rio Mesa High School in Oxnard, California, Jones set a national high school record in the 200-meter, at 22.76, and was named *Track & Field News*'s Female High School Athlete of the Year. The following summer, she won five state titles and set a U.S. high school record in the 200 meters (22.58 seconds). Playing basketball for Thousand Oaks High School her junior and senior years, she also trained with Mike Powell, world-record holder in the long jump. During 1992, her first year to try the long jump, she leapt twenty-three feet, the second-longest jump ever made by a high school girl, at the state championships. In June 1992, at age sixteen, Jones tried out for the Olympics and missed making the U.S. team by only .07 second. Jones received the Gatorade Circle of Champions National High School Girls Track and Field Athlete of the Year Award in 1991, 1992, and 1993. She was the only athlete to win the award more than once and the first non-senior to win the award.

As a senior basketball player, Jones won the California Interscholastic Federation Division I Player of the Year award. Thousand Oaks had a 60-4 record the two years that Jones was on the team and won the state championship in 1992. Her success in both track and basketball won her an athletic scholarship to the University of North Carolina at Chapel Hill, where she would play both sports.

Tar Heels Point Guard

As a 5'11" point guard with the Lady Tar Heels at UNC, Jones developed a natural leadership role and earned the nickname "Flash" for her speed with the ball. The team won North Carolina's first national championship in 1993-94. Winning All-American honors in track the following season, Jones came back in the 1994-95 basketball season to help her team finish 30-5.

In August 1995, however, Jones broke the fifth metatarsal bone in her left foot while practicing basketball at the World University Games. Missing the 1995-96 season, she broke the bone again in December while training on a trampoline. The injury dashed her 1996 Olympic hopes. While recuperating, she began dating shot putter C. J. Hunter. Her family and friends disapproved of the relationship, but Jones and Hunter would marry in 1998.

Jones returned to play basketball with the Lady Tar Heels in the 1996-97 season. The team finished the season at 29-3.

Awards and Accomplishments

1991	Set national high school record of 22.76 in 200-meter dash at U.S. Senior Track and Field Championships
1991-93	Received Gatorade Circle of Champions National High School Girls Track and Field Athlete of the Year Award, only athlete to win award more than once
1993	Named California's Division I Player of the Year for basketball
1994	Named All-American in four events at National Collegiate Athletic Association (NCAA) Track and Field Championships
1997	Named Most Valuable Player in Atlantic Coast Conference as member of Lady Tar Heels basketball team at University of North Carolina; won 100-meter dash at U.S.A. Outdoor Track & Field (USATF) Championships and at World Track and Field Championships; ranked #1 in the world in 100-meter and 200-meter races and named Woman of the Year by *Track & Field News*; International Amateur Athletic Federation Athlete of the Year
1998	Won 100-meter and 200-meter dash and long jump at U.S.A. Outdoor Track & Field Championships, first woman to win all three since Stella Walsh in 1948; won World Cup in 100-meter and 200-meter; anchored Nike international team to a new American record at 4 x 200-meter relay at Penn Relays; gold medals, 100-meter and 200-meter dash at Goodwill Games; gold medal in Grand Prix Finals in Moscow; ranked #1 in the world in 100-meter, 200-meter, and long jump by *Track & Field News* and unanimously chosen Athlete of the Year; won USATF's Jesse Owens Award for Outstanding U.S. Female Track and Field Athlete; International Amateur Athletic Federation (IAAF) Athlete of the Year
1999	Won first place in 100-meter and 200-meter at U.S.A. Outdoor Track & Field Championships; won gold medal in 100-meter and bronze in long jump at World Championships
2000	At 2000 Summer Olympic Games in Sydney, Australia, won gold medals in 100-meter, 200-meter races and 4 x 400-meter relay and won bronze medals in long jump and 4 x 100-meter relay; won first place in 200-meter dash at U.S.A. Outdoor Track & Field Championships; named World Sportswoman of the Year at the first Laureus Sports Awards in Monaco; named Athlete of the Year by Associated Press, ESPN cable television network, Reuters News Service, and the IAAF
2001	Named Associated Press Female Athlete of the Year; won first place in 200-meter dash at U.S.A. Outdoor Track & Field Championships; finished first in 200-meter dash and second in 100-meter at World Championships; won 100-meter dash at Goodwill Games in Brisbane, Australia, with a time of 10.84 seconds, breaking her own record set in 1998
2002	Gold medal in 100-meter dash at World Cup; won fifth-straight national title in 200-meter dash and fourth-straight in 100-meter dash at U.S.A. Outdoor Track & Field Championships; undefeated season in track and field, first of her career; won ESPN's Excellence in Sports Performance Yearly (ESPY) Award as Best Female Track and Field Athlete

The Laureus Sports Awards, presented at the Sporting Club of Monaco for the first time in 2000, celebrate sporting excellence across all disciplines and all continents.

Full-Time Track

By the spring of 1997, Jones decided to devote herself solely to track and field. She began training with coach Trevor Graham, a Jamaican who was a silver medalist in the 1988 Summer Olympics. Jones won the 100-meter dash and defeated Joyner-Kersee in the long jump at the 1997 U.S.A. Outdoor Track & Field Championships. At the 1997 World Championships, she won gold in the 100 meters and as part of the 4 x 100-meter relay team.

In the 1998 U.S.A. Championships, Jones won the gold in the 100 meters, the 200 meters, and the long jump. It was the first time in fifty years that a woman had achieved these three wins in a single competition. Jones was undefeated in every competition she entered-a total of thirty-six-until the last one, the World Cup, where Heike Drechsler of Germany beat her in the long jump. She married Hunter in October. By the end of the year, Jones was the unanimous choice as *Track & Field News*'s Athlete of the Year. She was only the third athlete to be chosen unanimously, after Carl Lewis and the Polish athlete Irena Szewinska.

Olympics Bound

The 1999 season again brought Jones consistent victories in the 100-meter and 200-meter, until she was forced to withdraw from competition because of back spasms while running the 200-meter during the World Championships. Seeking four gold medals in that competition, she brought home only one gold and one bronze.

As the time neared for the 2000 Summer Games in Sydney, Jones announced to the press that she wanted to win five gold medals, one in each event she entered. The news made headlines around the world, because no woman had ever won five golds in a single Olympics. (American swimmer **Amy Van Dyken** became the first woman to win four gold medals, in the 1996 Games.) NBC promised to cover Jones's quest "like a miniseries."

"The Dream for Five Is Not Alive"

Jones got off to a blazing start at the Olympics in Sydney, winning a gold in the 100-meter final, with a time of 10.75 seconds, .37 second over silver medalist Ekaterini Thanou of Greece. Jones's winning margin was the second largest in Olympic 100-meter history. On winning her first gold, Jones sobbed, "It's been my dream for 19 years, and finally it's here." She went on to win the 200-meter final by the largest margin since **Wilma Rudolph** won it in 1960; Jones won the gold with a time of 21.84 seconds. She and her team also took gold in the 4 x 400-meter relay. However, Jones won a bronze medal in the long jump, after fouling four times, with a distance of 22'8.5". She and another team also took a bronze in the 4 x 100-meter relay, after missing some baton handoffs. Jones passed two runners on her leg of the relay, helping to win the bronze.

After her quest was over, Jones told reporters, "The dream for five is not alive." However, she had no regrets in going for the five gold medals and said she felt the Games were an overall success. She said the fans "are what I'm really going to remember."

Trouble at the Games

Only one event threatened to mar the 2000 Olympics for Jones. Two days after her 100-meter win, news broke that her husband had failed four tests over the preceding summer for use of the steroid nandrolone. Although he did not compete in the 2000 Olympics because of knee surgery, the news was unsettling for Jones. She gracefully fielded questions at a press conference, telling reporters that all those closest to her knew she was "a clean athlete." Hunter denied the accusations that he had used drugs to help him compete, and Jones supported him. However, by June 2001, Jones announced that she and Hunter were divorcing due to irreconcilable differences that had nothing to do with Hunter's two-year suspension due to the positive drug tests.

Looking to the Future

After the 2000 Olympics, Jones has continued to compete and win, although she lost the 100-meter to Ukrainian Zhanna Pintusevich-Block—Jones's first 100-meter loss in four years—as she was going through the separation from Hunter. She reclaimed her 100-meter title at the Goodwill Games and brought home her fourth 200-meter championship in the U.S.A. Outdoor in 2001. In 2002 she took the 100-meter and the 200-meter titles in that event and recorded the first undefeated season of her career. Awards and honors continued to pour in, and Jones made her debut as a television sports analyst with CBS in January 2002.

In December 2002, Jones made the disturbing announcement that she would no longer work with long-time coach Trevor Graham, switching to the tutelage of Canadian Derek Hansen. Hansen was rumored to be an associate of Charlie Francis, who damaged Olympic champion **Ben Johnson**'s career by putting him on a steroid program. A photo of Francis working with Jones later gave credibility to the rumors.

Marion Jones is one of the most gifted athletes, male or female, of the twentieth and twenty-first centuries. With her talent, leadership ability, and fresh good looks, she has become an inspiration to young women athletes the world over. They will be watching her in the 2004 Olympics, when Jones will be only twenty-eight and likely to win multiple gold medals. From there, who knows how far she will go.

CONTACT INFORMATION

Address: U.S.A. Track and Field, One Hoosier Dome, Suite 140, Indianapolis, IN 46225.

FURTHER INFORMATION

Books

Contemporary Black Biography, Volume 21. Edited by Shirelle Phelps. "Marion Jones." Detroit: Gale Group, 1999.

Newsmakers 1998, Issue 4. "Marion Jones." Detroit: Gale Group, 1998.

Sports Stars, Series 1-4. "Marion Jones." Detroit: U•X•L, 1994-98.

Periodicals

"10 Greatest Women Athletes." *Ebony* (March 2002): 74.

"Breaking the Tape: Track: Marion Jones's Dream Ended in the Long-Jump Pit, but Her Five Medals Secured Her Place as Fastest Woman Alive." *Newsweek* (October 9, 2000): 54.

Deitsch, Richard, et al. "Scorecard." *Sports Illustrated* (December 30, 2002): 25.

Deitsch, Richard. "Speedy Learner." *Sports Illustrated* (January 14, 2002): 28.

Layden, Tim. "Ever Greene: Outrunning Injury as Well as a Brilliant New Challenger, Maurice Greene Claimed a Third 100-meter World Title, While Marion Jones Lost for the First Time in Four Years." *Sports Illustrated* (August 13, 2001): 44.

"Marion Jones and Tiger Woods Named AP Athletes of the Year for 2000." *Jet* (January 15, 2001): 53.

"Marion Jones Invincible in 200 Meters; Blacks Win National Titles." *Jet* (July 8, 2002): 52.

"Marion Jones, Tiger Woods and Pele Feted at Laureus Sports Awards in Monaco." *Jet* (June 12, 2000): 51.

"More Victory for Jones." *Jet* (July 19, 1999): 50.

"Parting Ways." *Jet (June 25, 2001): 48.*

"Record-Breaking Race." *Jet* (September 24, 2001): 52.

Reifer, Susan. "'There Is Nothing Stopping Me…Except Me': Marion Jones, the fastest woman on earth, takes on her toughest competitor ever." *Sports Illustrated Women* (September 1, 2002): 90.

Starr, Mark. "Whatever Happened to…? After Sydney, Marion Jones Searches for the Limelight." *Newsweek* (August 6, 2001): 53.

Other

2002 ESPY Awards. http://www.espn.go.com/espy2002/ (July 11, 2002).

Ledbetter, D. Orlando. *Milwaukee Journal Sentinel* Online. http://www.jsonline.com/ (October 1, 2000).

"Marion Jones' Final Count: Three Golds, Two Bronzes." SportsLine.com Wire Reports. http://cbs.sportsline.com/ (October 1, 2000).

"Project Promotes Immunization, Right to Play, for Children; Dorothy Hamill, Marion Jones, Team Up With Olympic Aid and the Vaccine Fund." PR Newswire. http://galenet.galegroup.com/ (February 6, 2002).

Sports Illustrated Scrapbook. "Marion Jones." CNN Sports Illustrated. http://sportsillustrated.cnn.com/ (January 22, 2003).

U.S.A. Track & Field. "Marion Jones." http://www.usatf.org/athletes/ (January 23, 2003).

Sketch by Ann H. Shurgin

Michael Jordan

Michael Jordan
1963-

American basketball player

Michael Jordan is considered by many to be the greatest basketball player in the history of the game, even by some to be the greatest player of *any* sport. As Jerry Sloan, the coach of the Utah Jazz told the *Daily News* of Jordan, "I think everybody knows how he should be remembered, as the greatest player that has ever played." A two-time Olympic gold medal winner with the U.S. basketball team, Jordan distinguished himself in a 15-season career with the NBA by, among many other achievements, leading the league in scoring more seasons (10) than any other player in history, and by setting a record for the most consecutive games scoring more than nine points (842 games). He started his career with the NBA during the 1984-85 season, playing as a guard for the Chicago Bulls until 1993, when announced the first of three retirements. He went back to the Bulls in 1994-95, "retired" again in 1999, and went back to the game, this time with the Washington Wizards for the 2001-02 and 2002-03 seasons. In 2002, at the age of 39, he announced his intention to quit playing for good after the 2002-03 season.

Cut from His High School Team

Michael Jeffrey Jordan was born in Brooklyn, New York in 1963. He was the youngest of four boys born to James and Deloris Jordan. James Jordan was the son of a share cropper from rural North Carolina, and he was in Brooklyn to attend a school that trained employees of General Electric. Jordan's mother, Deloris, was a homemaker until her children were old enough to attend school, and then she became a bank clerk.

When Jordan was about seven years old, in 1970, his family moved to Wilmington, North Carolina, the town he would later consider to be his hometown. He began playing basketball at an early age, often with his older brother Larry. "When I was younger," Jordan said on his Web site, "my motivation came from wanting to beat my brother. This inspired my extremely competitive nature."

As a freshman in high school, Jordan joined his school basketball team. It was on his high school team that Jordan chose the jersey number he was later to make famous as a pro, number 23. When later asked why he chose that number, he replied to the Associated Press, "I wanted to wear No. 45 in high school, but my older brother (Larry) wore that number. So I decided to go with half of 45, which is actually 22½." Jordan at first had trouble standing out on the school team. In fact, only a year after joining the team, as a tenth grader, he was cut from the varsity team. But this only pushed him to work harder at perfecting his game. As he later said on his Web site, "I think that not making the Varsity team drove me to really work at my game, and also taught me that if you set goals, and work hard to achieve them—the hard work can pay off."

"That Boy Is Devastating"

Jordan began to distinguish himself on the junior varsity team, and was soon averaging more than 20 points a game. "I remember going to Laney High on a Friday night, Michael's junior year, and now he'd grown to, maybe 6 foot 1," Jordan's uncle Gene Jordan later recalled to Kevin Paul Dupont in the *Boston Globe*. "Before the game he's telling me, 'Watch me, I'm going to

Chronology

1963	Born in Brooklyn, NY
1970	Moves with his family to Wilmington, North Carolina
1979	Is cut from his high school varsity basketball team
1982	Scores game-winning basket in NCAA championship game for the University of North Carolina
1984	Plays on gold-medal-winning U.S. Olympic basketball team in Los Angeles
1984	Signs as a player with the Chicago Bulls
1984	Plays on the gold-medal-winning U.S. Olympic basketball team
1985	Named NBA Rookie of the Year
1987	Breaks Bulls record by scoring 58 points in a single game
1987	Breaks the record again by scoring 61 points in one game
1987	Breaks NBA record by scoring 23 points in a row
1990	Scores his career best of 69 points in a single game
1991	Scores his career best of 19 rebounds in one game
1992	Plays on gold-medal-winning U.S. Olympic basketball team in Barcelona
1993	Father James Jordan murdered
1993	Announces retirement from playing basketball, briefly plays baseball
1995	Returns to playing basketball
1996	Named one of the top 50 basketball players of time
1997	Called by *People* one of the Most Intriguing People of the Century
1998	Publishes autobiography, *For the Love of the Game*
1999	Named the 20th century's greatest athlete by ESPN
1999	Retires again
2000	Becomes part owner and director of basketball operations for the Washington Wizards
2001	Comes out of retirement to play for the Washington Wizards
2002	Again announces retirement

Related Biography: Father James Jordan

James Jordan was in the habit of driving long distances overnight, stopping only for brief naps in his car, rather than staying in hotels. "Oh, I know he's stopped in Lumberton before," his brother, Gene Jordan, told Kevin Paul Dupont in the *Boston Globe* after James's death. "I'm sure he's pulled over at that exact spot before. A hotel room? That wasn't James, uh-uh. After Michael's fame and everything, people used to ask him, 'Are you going to get a bodyguard?' He'd laugh at that. Stopping at the side of the road was nothing for my brother. He didn't think anything of it. He figured he didn't have an enemy in the world."

Not enemies, but thieves took James Jordan's life as he napped in his car on a Lumberton, North Carolina roadside in the early morning hours of July 23, 1993. James Jordan was on his way home from the funeral of a former coworker at the General Electric plant where he used to work. After the killing shot to the chest, the thieves took off in James Jordan's car, later stripping it, and then dumping Jordan's body in a nearby creek, where it was found a week and a half later. Jordan would have turned 57 less than two weeks after the day he died. "The world's lost a good man," Gene Jordan told Dupont.

James Raymond Jordan was born on July 31, 1936 in rural North Carolina, the first child born to sharecropper William Jordan and his wife Rosa Bell Jordan. He began a career at General Electric in 1967, moving up to become a parts department manager. He retired from GE in the late 1980s, at which time the Jordan family moved from Wilmington, North Carololina, where Michael Jordan grew up, to the suburbs of Charlotte, North Carolina.

Those who knew both James and Michael Jordan noted that Michael was very much like his father. Both had shaved heads, and both stuck their tongues out when concentrating on a difficult task—in Michael's case, when lining up a shot. Their handwriting was alike enough that many people couldn't tell them apart. Proud supporters of Michael Jordan's basketball playing from the beginning, James Jordan and his wife, Michael's mother Deloris, never missed a game Michael played in during his time at the University of North Carolina.

James Jordan was buried alongside his grandfather and parents in the graveyard of the Rockfish African Methodist Episcopal Church in Teachey, North Carolina. His tombstone reads simply, as reported by Dupont, "James Jordan, 1936-1993."

slam dunk three balls tonight. You'll see. I'm going to slam three.' And I'm there saying, 'Boy, who you kiddin'? You can't slam no ball.' Well, he didn't slam three, but he sure as hell slammed two. And I told my brother that night, 'Hey, that boy is devastating.'"

Even so, Jordan was not on the lists of most college basketball team recruiters. He was noticed by recruiters at the University of North Carolina, however, and there he went to college, playing guard on the school team under coach Dean Smith. True success touched Jordan for the first time at the NCAA tournament in which his team played against the Georgetown Hoyas. Jordan scored the three of the last five winning shots to bring North Carolina its first title in a quarter of a century. "I've never seen anybody pick up the game so fast," one of his former UNC teammates and later Lakers player told Filip Bondy in the *Daily News* years later. "Michael just doesn't repeat mistakes."

After his success at the NCAA championship, Jordan became nationally famous, and a celebrity in North Carolina. He even landed on the cover of the Chapel Hill telephone book. Next came his selection to the U.S. team in the Olympic Games, played in Los Angeles in 1984. Team U.S.A. took home the gold medal. Jordan graduated college in 1985 with a bachelor's degree in

cultural geography. After college, Jordan was picked up as the first choice in a draft lottery by the Chicago Bulls.

When Jordan signed on with the Bulls, he began a marketing relationship with Nike that was to last throughout his career; Nike released a sport shoe called Air Jordans. As for his performance as a player, he was soon unrivaled as an unstoppable force. As his coach, Kevin Loughery later said to Bondy in the *Daily News*, "If I put him with the starters, they win. If I put him with the second team, they win.... No matter what I do with Michael, his team wins."

Jordan was slowed at the beginning of 1985-86 season, when he suffered a stress fracture in his foot. Nevertheless, in 1986, he scored 63 points in a playoff game against the Celtics. In 1988, he was named NBA Defensive Player of the Year, leading the NBA in steals. He also earned MVP honors at the 1988 All-Star Game, held that year in Chicago. Another gold medal at the Olympics followed in 1992 when he again played on U.S. Olympic Team. By 1993, Jordan led the NBA in scoring, and been named the NBA's Most Valuable Player 3 times. He was

Awards and Accomplishments

1981	Breaks record at McDonald's All-American game by scoring 30 points
1982	Scores winning points in NCAA championship game
1984	Named college Player of the Year
1984	Wins Olympic gold medal with U.S. basketball team
1985	Named NBA Rookie of the Year
1986-87	Named to the All-NBA First Team
1987	Winner, Slam Dunk Contest
1987-88	Named NBA Most Valuable Player
1987-88	Named NBA Defensive Player of the Year
1987-88	Named to the NBA All-Defensive First Team
1987-88	Named to the All-NBA First Team
1988	Wins Slam Dunk Contest
1988	Named NBA Most Valuable Player
1988	Named NBA All-Star Games Most Valuable Player
1988-89	Named to the All-NBA First Team
1988-89	Named to the NBA All-Defensive First Team
1989-90	Named to the All-NBA First Team
1989-90	Named to the NBA All-Defensive First Team
1990-91	Named NBA Most Valuable Player
1990-91	Named to the All-NBA First Team
1990-91	Named to the NBA All-Defensive First Team
1991	Leads Chicago Bulls to their first NBA title
1991-92	Named NBA Most Valuable Player
1991-92	Named to the All-NBA First Team
1991-92	Named to the NBA All-Defensive First Team
1992	Wins Olympic gold medal with U.S. basketball team
1992-93	Named to the All-NBA First Team
1992-93	Named to the NBA All-Defensive First Team
1995-96	Named NBA Most Valuable Player
1995-96	Named to the All-NBA First Team
1995-96	Named to the NBA All-Defensive First Team
1996	Named one of the 50 Greatest Players in NBA History
1996	Named NBA All-Star Games Most Valuable Player
1996-97	Named to the All-NBA First Team
1996-97	Named to the NBA All-Defensive First Team
1997-98	Named NBA Most Valuable Player
1997-98	Named to the All-NBA First Team
1997-98	Named to the NBA All-Defensive First Team
1998	Named NBA All-Star Games Most Valuable Player

also earning $30 million a year, not including millions of dollars more he earned endorsing products.

Tragedy Strikes

In the summer of 1993, Jordan's high-flying career came to a crashing halt with an event that was to forever change his life. In the very early morning hours of July 23, 1993, Jordan's father, James Jordan, was making a long drive from the North Carolina coast, coming back from a friend's funeral, when he stopped on a roadside in Lumberton, North Carolina. There he hoped to grab a few minutes of rest before driving the last 130 miles home. But it was not to be. He was set upon by a pair of robbers, shot once in the chest, and killed. The 18-year-old murderers did not know who their victim was; they wanted nothing more than his car and whatever valuables it might contain. They stripped his car, and dumped his body in a creek near where they shot him, and there he was found 11 days later.

After the death of his father, the steam went out of Jordan's career. "When my father died," he explained to Bondy in the *Daily News* "there was a different emphasis on everything." Jordan no longer felt the same fire to play basketball. He announced his retirement, and then went into seclusion. "There's nothing left to prove," he told Filip Bondy in the *New York Daily News.*

Back in the Game

After a brief attempt to start a baseball career, Jordan roared back from retirement in 1995, again playing for the Bulls. His first season back, he was named the NBA's Most Valuable Player. In 1996, he was named one of the 50 Greatest Players in NBA History. He was named the NBA's Most Valuable Player again in 1997.

In 1999, he "retired" again at 36 years old but stayed in the game as an owner and executive when he became part owner of the Washington Wizards in 2000 and director of basketball operations for the team.

Jordan, however, found it impossible to stay off the court. He was 38 years old when he announced the end of his second retirement, saying that he would play for the Wizards. NBA rules required that he sell his ownership stake in the Wizards before playing for the team. He also had to give up his management position with the Wizards to avoid a conflict of interest created by being both a manager and a player.

Before Jordan could play again, he had to get back in shape, shedding 28 pounds, and undergoing a training regimen that included practicing with increasingly expe-

Michael Jordan, shooting for basket

Career Statistics

Yr	Team	GP	PTS	FG%	3P%	FT%	RPG	APG	SPG	BPG	TO	PF
1984-85	CHI	82	28.2	.515	.173	.845	6.50	5.9	2.39	.84	3.55	3.50
1985-86	CHI	18	22.7	.457	.167	.840	3.60	2.9	2.06	1.17	2.50	2.60
1986-87	CHI	82	37.1	.482	.182	.857	5.20	4.6	2.88	1.52	3.32	2.90
1987-88	CHI	82	35.0	.535	.137	.841	5.50	5.9	3.16	1.60	3.07	3.30
1988-89	CHI	81	32.5	.538	.276	.850	8.00	8.0	2.89	.80	3.58	3.00
1989-90	CHI	82	33.6	.526	.376	.848	6.90	6.3	2.77	.66	3.01	2.90
1990-91	CHI	82	31.5	.539	.312	.851	6.00	5.5	2.72	1.01	2.46	2.80
1991-92	CHI	80	30.1	.519	.270	.832	6.40	6.1	2.28	.94	2.50	2.50
1992-93	CHI	78	32.6	.495	.352	.837	6.70	5.5	2.83	.78	2.65	2.40
1994-95	CHI	17	26.9	.411	.500	.801	6.90	5.3	1.76	.76	2.06	2.80
1995-96	CHI	82	30.4	.495	.427	.834	6.60	4.3	2.20	.51	2.40	2.40
1996-97	CHI	82	29.6	.486	.374	.833	5.90	4.3	1.71	.54	2.02	1.90
1997-98	CHI	82	28.7	.465	.238	.784	5.80	3.5	1.72	.55	2.26	1.80
2001-02	WAS	60	22.9	.416	.189	.790	5.70	5.2	1.42	.43	2.70	2.00
2002-03	WAS	18	17.1	.454	.385	.733	4.30	2.8	1.67	.39	1.72	2.20
TOTAL		1008	30.7	.500	.328	.835	6.20	5.3	2.40	.85	2.76	2.60

CHI: Chicago Bulls; WAS: Washington Wizards.

rienced basketball players. As he said on his Web site: "It was definitely tougher to come back…than I had expected. After taking time off the sport, I had to work much harder to get my body back into shape. My body is also a lot older than it used to be…that that's ok. I came back for the love of the game.…"

Jordan stepped onto the court as a player once again in the 2001-02 season, but after a knee injury requiring surgery forced him to miss 20 games the following season, he again announced his retirement. "At the end of this season, I'm not looking to enter another contract," he told the *Washington Post*'s Steve Wyche in November, 2002. "Right now I want to finish this year out and hopefully fulfill my obligations and let this team take its own course." He also indicated that he would resume his managerial role with the Wizards, and other sources reported that he planned to repurchase the ownership stake in the team that he had given up in order to become a player.

Jordan is married to Juanita Jordan. They have two sons, Jeffrey Michael and Marcus James, and a daughter, Jasmine Mikail. His leisure pursuits include shopping. "I am a huge shopper," Jordan said on his Web site, "although it is hard for me to go to malls and stores since I am easily recognized. Therefore, I do a lot of my shopping through catalogues. I love shopping in New York City and some stores will even open on their off hours for me." Jordan also enjoys playing golf. In fact, he said on his Web site, "When I'm not on the court, you can probably find me on the golf course. However, I am a total hack! For the most part it is a great mental sport that allows me to relax and get away."

Jordan is also involved in many business ventures and charities not related to basketball. Among them, a chain of restaurants located in Chicago, New York, Chapel Hill, and in Connecticut. Among the charities he supports are Make-A-Wish, Ronald McDonald House, and the Boys & Girls Clubs. "It is very important for me to give back to others," he explains on his Web site. "My wife and I also give to many local charities which benefit children."

After finally retiring as a player, Jordan looked forward to spending more time with his family "as well as trying to live for the moment and enjoy each day as it comes," he said on his Web site. He also planned to play a lot of golf.

FURTHER INFORMATION

Periodicals

Bondy, Filip. "Out of This World: In Redefining Greatness, Michael Jordan Made a Lasting Impact on an Entire Generation." *Daily News* (January 13, 1999): Special, 2.

DeShazier, John. "Rare Air; Jordan Soared to Unforeseen Heights, Standing Head and shoulders Above the Rest in the NBA." *Times-Picayune* (October 31, 1999): C16.

Dupont, Kevin Paul. "Cold Blood in Carolina; Family, Friends and Townspeople Try to Make Sense out of a Senseless Killing." *Boston Globe* (August 29, 1993): Sports, 47.

"Jordan Stuns Students at his Prep Alma Mater." *Chicago Sun-Times* (November 16, 1993): Sports, 1.

Wyche, Steve. "Jordan Says This Will be Final Season." *Washington Post* (November 29, 2002): D1.

Wyche, Steve. "Jordan Will Return, Play for Wizards." *Washington Post* (September 24, 2001): D1.

Other

"Biography for Michael Jordan." Internet Movie Database. http://us.imdb.com/Bio?Jordan,%20Michael. (December 6, 2002).

"Michael Jordan—One on One." Michael Jordan Official Website. http://www.sportsline.com/u/jordan/2001/oneonone/index.htm. (December 6, 2002).

"Michael Jordan—The Player." Michael Jordan Official Website. http://www.sportsline.com/u/jordan/2001/player/index.htm. (December 6, 2002).

"Michael Jordan Player Info." NBA.com. http://www.nba.com/playerfile/michael_jordan/?nav=page. (December 6, 2002).

"Space Jam." Suntimes.com. http://www.suntimes.com/ebert/ebert_reviews/1996/11/111505.html. (December 6, 2002).

"Space Jam (1996)." RottenTomatoes.com. http://www.rottentomatoes.com/m/SpaceJam-1073294/about.php. (December 6, 2002).

Sketch by Michael Belfiore

Joan Joyce

Joan Joyce
1940-

American softball player

In August, 1961, a 21 year-old woman stood on a pitching mound facing recently retired baseball great **Ted Williams**, who positioned himself at the plate with the same competitiveness and determination as he did during his major league career. An over-capacity crowd at Municipal Stadium in Waterbury, Connecticut, cheered as young softball pitcher Joan Joyce hurled one unhittable softball after another past one of baseball's greatest hitters during the charity exhibition game. In a profile issued by the Waterbury Hall of Fame in 1997, Joyce recalled the incident this way: "I threw to him about 10 minutes. He fouled off one or two pitches, but that's all. He threw his bat down and walked away." Her triumphant face-off with "The Splendid Splinter," repeated in 1968, demonstrated her legendary pitching ability. It remains her best known and favorite achievement in a long and dazzling athletic career.

An Athletic Family

Joyce was born August 1, 1940, in Waterbury, Connecticut. Her father was a baseball player and coach for local teams, and Joyce and her brother tagged along to the ball fields. Naturally athletic, she showed an interest and aptitude for the game. With her family's encouragement, Joyce began practicing softball by throwing against a home-made target.

By the age of 16, she was good enough to join the powerhouse Raybestos Brakettes (now the Stratford Brakettes), an amateur fast pitch softball team based in Stratford, Connecticut. When the team's starting pitcher was injured during the 1958 National Championships, Joyce was moved from first base to the pitching mound. The 18-year-old pitched a no-hitter to win the championship game for her team. Her pitching career was launched.

Joyce developed an arsenal of pitches—drop, riser, curve, and change-up—all delivered from a slingshot motion. She may not have been the fastest pitcher, but her ball movement and stamina soon made her one of the best. Still, her pitches were said to reach up to 118 miles per hour, although they were never timed with a speed gun. She told Tom Yantz of *The Hartford Courant,* "They probably were in the 70s." They just looked much faster to the batter. And her approach to pitching was simple and effective. She explained to Yantz, "My pitching philosophy was to keep the umpires out of it. That meant pitch to the area where the batter didn't want to swing."

Softball's Brightest Star for Two Decades

Joyce interrupted her stretch with the Brakettes to attend Chapman College in Orange, California. During her three years there, she played softball for the Orange Lionettes, leading the team to a national title in 1965.

She compiled astounding records during her amateur years—507 pitching wins with just 33 losses, 123 no-hitters, 33 perfect games, and a 0.19 ERA (Earned Run Average). She led the Brakettes to the world championship title in 1974, the first time a team from the Unit-

Chronology

1940	Born August 1 in Waterbury, Connecticut
1956	Joins the Raybestos Brakettes
1958	Pitches a no-hitter for the National Fast Pitch Softball Championship
1962	Joins the Orange (California) Lionettes while attending Chapman College
1967	Re-joins the Raybestos Brakettes
1974	Leads Raybestos Brakettes to a world championship title, the first for a United States team
1975	Retires from the Raybestos Brakettes
1976	Co-founds the International Women's Professional Softball Association, which lasts four seasons
1977	Qualifies for the Ladies Professional Golf Association (LPGA)
1994	Becomes first women's softball coach at Florida Atlantic University
1996	Becomes women's golf coach and senior women's administrator at Florida Atlantic University

Awards and Accomplishments

1957	Selected as an Amateur Softball Association All-American, the first of 18 consecutive years
1974	First woman honored with a Gold Key from the Connecticut Sports Writers Alliance
1975	Named Bill Lee Male Athlete of the Year
1983	Inducted into the National Softball Hall of Fame
1989	Inducted into the International Women's Sports Hall of Fame
1991	Inducted into the Hank O'Donnell Sports Hall of Fame
1995	Named Atlantic Sun Conference Softball Coach of the Year, the first of five times
1995	Named Palm Beach County (Florida) Coach of the Year
1996	Inducted into the Palm Beach County (Florida) Sports Hall of Fame
1997	Inducted into the Waterbury (Connecticut) Hall of Fame
1997	Inducted into the Connecticut Sports Museum Hall of Fame
1998	Inducted into the Connecticut High School Coaches Association Hall of Fame
1999	Inducted into the New England Women's Sports Hall of Fame
1999	Inducted into the International Softball Federation Hall of Fame

ed States won. But she was not just a great pitcher. She also was a skilled fielder and batter, with a career batting average of .327, good enough to lead the Brakettes in batting six times. Joyce's success was well recognized—she won eight Most Valuable Player (MVP) Awards in the playoffs, the Brakettes won 12 national championships, and she was named an Amateur Softball Association All-American 18 times.

Her amateur success prompted an attempt at a professional career. In 1976, she co-founded the International Women's Professional Softball Association along with tennis star **Billie Jean King**, golfer Jane Blalock, and promoter Dennis Murphy. Joyce was the star player, manager, and part-owner of the Connecticut Falcons, as well as the league's commissioner. Nearing forty, she compiled a 101-15 pitching record, threw 34 no-hitters, and had eight perfect games. Only her .290 batting average hinted at her advancing age. The league folded after four seasons due to inadequate financing and marketing, but Joyce led the Falcons to the World Series title all four seasons.

Excelled at Other Sports

Joyce's achievements would be remarkable even if they were limited to softball. But she was a sports phenomenon at a time when few opportunities existed for women athletes. She was a star volleyball player at Crosby High School in Waterbury, and later played in amateur leagues and served as an official. As a teenager, she had a 180 bowling average and sought out the best competition she could find. She pursued basketball, another childhood love, at Chapman College, where she was a three-time Amateur Athletic Union (AAU) All-American. She took up golf while teaching at Waterbury Catholic High School after college. She joined the Ladies Professional Golf Tour (LPGA) at the age of 37 after playing in just three amateur tournaments. In almost 20 years of consistently good play on the LPGA

tour, her best finish was a sixth place. She also was a teaching pro at Deer Creek Country Club in Florida.

Joyce's multi-sport prowess earned comparisons to an earlier legendary athlete. Former Connecticut Falcons player Kathy Neal remarked to Tom Yantz of *The Hartford Courant*, "She really was the **Babe Didrikson Zaharias** of her era."

Asked what made her such a talented all-around athlete, Joyce told Lori Riley of *The Hartford Courant*, "Probably determination. I was basically a pretty good athlete from when I was real young. I had good teachers. And I worked real hard at what I did."

Joyce has successfully made the transition from player to coach. In 1994, she became the first women's head softball coach at Florida Atlantic University in Boca Raton. She has guided the Lady Owls to a number 10 national ranking, the highest softball ranking in the history of the Atlantic Sun Conference. She has been named the Conference's Coach of the Year five times in eight seasons. She continues to conduct softball clinics. In 1996, Joyce also was named head coach of Florida Atlantic University's women's golf team and the senior women's administrator.

A Softball Great

Rival pitcher Charlotte Graham, who played against Joyce in the professional league, told Joe Jares of *Sports Illustrated* in 1976, "She's a fantastic lady. She's my idol. I've watched her closely for 10 years. She's truly the best player women's softball has ever had." In *Great Women Athletes of the 20th Century*, writer Robert Condon agreed, calling her "the finest women's softball player of all time." Her dominating presence inspired awe and helped lay the foundation for the sport's future.

Joyce enjoyed great acclaim for more than 20 years of softball playing, but her well known match-ups with Ted Williams stay with her. Williams was quoted by Tom Yantz in *The Hartford Courant* as declaring, "Joan Joyce was a tremendous pitcher, as talented as anyone who ever played." Joyce is surprised about the lingering fame, telling Yantz in 1999, "It's amazing. I've been in airports, hotels all over the world. It doesn't matter where, but people will come up to me and say, `You struck out Ted Williams. I was there.'"

SELECTED WRITINGS BY JOYCE:

(With John Anquillare) *Winning Softball,* Henry Regnery Co., 1975.

FURTHER INFORMATION

Books

Condon, Robert J. *Great Women Athletes of the 20th Century.* Jefferson, NC: McFarland & Company, Inc., 1991.

Woolum, Janet. *Outstanding Women Athletes: Who They Are and How They Influenced Sports in America.* Phoenix, AZ: Oryx Press, 1998, 2nd ed.

Periodicals

Bohls, Kirk. "Joyce's Ability to Make Softball Dance Has Left All-Stars on Floor." *The Austin-American Statesman* (July 11, 1997):C1.

Jares, Joe. "She's Still Wonder Woman." *Sports Illustrated* (July 26, 1976):60.

Riley, Lori. "A Chance to Excel." *The Hartford Courant* (November 29, 1998).

Special to The Palm Beach Post. "Palm Beach Hall Inducts Five." *The Palm Beach Post* (March 11, 1996):3C.

White, Jr., Gordon S. "Joan Joyce Enjoys Moments of Glory." *The New York Times* (May 30, 1981):17.

Yantz, Tom. "The Missing Legend; Ted Couldn't Touch Joan." *The Hartford Courant* (December 30, 1999).

Young, Al. "Joyce Personified Softball League." *USA Today* (June 8, 1992):8C.

Other

"Bill Lee Male Athlete of the Year Award." Connecticut Sports Writers Alliance. www.ctsportswriters.org/honorroll.html (December 4, 2002).

"Brakettes All-Time Roster." http://www.brakettes.com/alltime_roster.html (December 26, 2002).

"Brakettes History." http://www.brakettes.com/history.htm (December 26, 2002).

"Hall of Fame." Women's Sports Foundation. http://www.womenssportsfoundation.org/cg.../iowa/about/awards/results.html?record=4 (December 4, 2002).

"Hall of Fame 1999." New England Women's Sports Hall of Fame. http://www.newfund.org/files/hallFame1999.htm (December 4, 2002).

"Joan Joyce." National Softball Hall of Fame. http://www.softball.org/hall_of_fame/pff_memberdetail.asp?mbrid=147 (December 4, 2002).

"Joan Joyce." Waterbury (CT) Hall of Fame. http://www.biblio.org/bronson/joan.htm (December 4, 2002).

"Joan Joyce Profile." The Official Site of Florida Atlantic University Athletics. http://fausports.ocsn.com/sports/w-softbl/mtt/joyce_joan00.html (December 4, 2002).

"Joyce, Joan." Encyclopedia of Women and Sport in America, by James Haskins. http://vweb.hwwilsonweb.com/cgi-bin/webspirs.cig (December 4, 2002).

"Myers, Joyce and Freel Named A-Sun Player, Coach and Freshman-of-the-Year; FAU Sweeps Atlantic Sun Softball Honors." Atlantic Sun Conference News Release. http://www.atlanticsun.org/news/may02/All%20Conf%20Sb%2002.htm (December 4, 2002).

"Softball — WPSL Team Information." The Official Site of National Pro Fastpitch. http://www.profastpitch.com/league/index.shtml (December 4, 2002).

Sketch by Carole Manny

Jackie Joyner-Kersee
1962-

American track and field athlete

Known as the greatest multi-event track and field athlete of all time, Jackie Joyner-Kersee is the winner of three Olympic gold medals, one silver medal, and two bronze medals, more than any other woman has ever won in the history of track and field. She competed in the 1984, 1988, 1992, and 1996 Olympics and is the first American woman to win over 7,000 points in the heptathlon. She set a new world record in the heptathlon in 1986, and was the first athlete in 64 years to win gold medal in both a multi-event and a single event in track and field. She is also the first American ever to win a gold medal in the long jump.

An Impoverished Beginning

Joyner-Kersee was born Jackie Joyner in 1962, the second child of two impoverished teenage parents, Alfred and Mary Joyner. Mary was 14 when her first child was born, and 16 when Joyner-Kersee was born. Alfred Joyner worked in construction and on the railroad, and Mary Joyner worked as a nurse's aid. According to the *Encyclopedia of World Biography,* Kenny Moore wrote in *Sports Illustrated,* "Their house was little more than

Jackie Joyner-Kersee

Chronology

1962	Born in East St. Louis, Illinois
1974	Wins first of four consecutive national junior pentathlon championships
1980-84	Attends University of California-Los Angeles
1984	Competes in Olympic, wins silver medals
1985	Sets world record in long jump
1986	Sets two world records, receives several awards
1986	Marries Bob Kersee
1988	Wins two Olympic gold medals
1992	Wins Olympic gold medal and bronze medal
1996	Wins Olympic bronze medal
1996	Briefly plays with Richmond Rage basketball team
1996-present	Works on behalf of a variety of philanthropic causes
1997	Announces creation of the Joyner-Kersee Boys and Girls Club
1998	Announces retirement from competition, but it is not official
2000	Does not qualify for U.S. Olympic team
2001	Officially retires from competition

wallpaper and sticks, with four tiny bedrooms. During the winters, when the hot-water pipes would freeze, they had to heat water for baths in kettles on the kitchen stove. Their great-grandmother … lived with them until she died on the plastic-covered sofa in the living room while Jackie was at the store buying milk."

Joyner-Kersee, who had been named Jackie by a grandmother who hoped she would grow up to be as influential as then-first-lady Jacqueline Kennedy Onassis, swore that she would make something of herself and improve her life. Mary Joyner, who knew the difficulty of life as a teenage mother, did not let Joyner-Kersee or her brother Al date until they were 18 years old. Instead, she encouraged them to become involved in other activities.

Joyner-Kersee and Al grew up in East St. Louis and became involved in sports at the Mayor Brown Community Center there. She began running track there and, when she saw the 1976 Olympics on television, was inspired to try and become an Olympian too. Al encouraged her, and became her first competitor—and the first person she beat in a race.

First Pentathlon Win

When she was 14, she won the first of four consecutive national junior pentathlon championships. During those years, she also played basketball and volleyball and was listed on the honor roll for her high grades. In 1980, Joyner-Kersee accepted a scholarship to the University of California in Los Angeles, where her main sport was basketball. During her freshman year, her mother became ill with meningitis, and died. Joyner-Kersee decided to devote herself even more wholeheartedly to athletics because of her mother's desire for her to succeed. After her mother's funeral, she returned to college with a new resolve.

She soon caught the eye of track coach Bob Kersee, who convinced her that multi-event track should be her sport. He was so convinced that she had hidden talent in this event that he told the university authorities that if they did not allow her to switch from basketball to the heptathlon, he would quit his job. They agreed. Joyner-Kersee was already a good long-jumper and 200-meter runner, so she learned to run the 100-meter hurdles and the 800 meters, do the high jump, throw the javelin, and toss the shot put. These seven events are combined in the heptathlon; an athlete's performance in each event is scored, and the athlete with the highest point total for all the events is the winner. In 1982, Joyner-Kersee qualified for the world championships, but she pulled a hamstring and did not compete in the event.

Competes in First Olympics

In 1984, the same year she graduated from college, Joyner-Kersee's Olympic dreams came true. Not only did she compete in the Olympics, but she won a silver medal in the heptathlon. Joyner-Kersee set a world record in the long jump in 1985, with a jump of 23 feet 9 inches. In 1986 she set a new world record in the heptathlon at the Goodwill Games in Moscow, accumulating 7,148 points. Three weeks later, running on a 100-degree day in Houston, Texas, she beat her own record. For these two world records, she was awarded the 1986 Sullivan Award for Best Amateur Athlete, as well as the **Jesse Owens** Award. On January 11, 1986, she married Bob Kersee, changing her name from Jackie Joyner to Jackie Joyner-Kersee.

Awards and Accomplishments

1974-78	Wins four consecutive national junior pentathlon championships
1984	Silver medal, Olympic heptathlon
1985	Sets U.S. record in long jump
1986	Sets two world records in heptathlon
1986	Sullivan Award for Best Amateur Athlete; Jesse Owens Award; *Track and Field* Athlete of the Year
1987	McDonald's Amateur Athlete of the Year
1988	Olympic gold medals in heptathlon and long jump
1989	Honorary doctorate, University of Missouri
1992	Olympic gold medal, heptathlon; Olympic bronze medal, long jump
1996	Olympic bronze medal, long jump
1998	Gold medal, heptathlon, Goodwill Games

Where Is She Now?

Joyner-Kersee continues to work to encourage young people to improve their lives, largely through her work with the Joyner-Kersee Boys and Girls Club. She told a reporter for *PR Newswire*, "I will be there as often as I can, hopefully every other day. I don't want the Center to just be my namesake, but to be a center that I am very active in. I want to be there for the kids."

Joyner-Kersee returned to the Olympics two years later to match her performance in her first Olympiad. At the 1988 Olympics, Joyner-Kersee won gold medals in the heptathlon and the long jump, setting yet another record in the heptathlon with 7,291 points. She won the gold medal in the heptathlon again at the Barcelona Olympics in 1992. She also won a bronze medal in the long jump.

Before the 1996 Olympics in Atlanta, some observers questioned whether or not Joyner-Kersee would be able to win a medal in the heptathlon. She was 34, and no athlete, male or female, had ever won a multievent at that age. According to *Great Women in Sports,* Joyner-Kersee told a reporter for *Women's Sports + Fitness,* "That's the ultimate challenge—to do something nobody has been able to do. I would love that." She also said that one secret of her longevity as an athlete is that she took good care of herself, and didn't compete very often: she only did two heptathlons a year, avoiding burnout.

At the Atlanta Olympics in 1996, Joyner-Kersee suffered a hamstring injury and had to withdraw from the heptathlon, but took a bronze medal in the long jump. She later said that because she was battling the injury, she was as proud of the bronze medal as if it were gold. After the Olympics, Joyner-Kersee signed a one-year contract to play basketball with the Richmond Rage, but did not play much. She left in the middle of the season because of injuries.

An Athlete Committed to Helping Others

Joyner-Kersee continued to compete in track and field, but also turned her attention to other projects. She had long been known not only as a star athlete, but as a generous and gracious person who was committed to helping others. She became involved in Nike's PLAY (Participate in the Lives of American Youth) program, raising funds for youth activity centers, and founded a scholarship fund, the Joyner-Kersee Community Foundation. She worked with children in her home town, East St. Louis. Although she spent some time trying to rebuild the old Mayor Brown Community Center where she had played as a

child, she announced in 1997 that the Joyner-Kersee Community Foundation would finance the construction of a new center, occupying 37 acres in downtown East St. Louis. The center would have facilities for basketball, baseball, indoor and outdoor track and field, but would also house a library, computer center, and other educational resources.

In 1998, Joyner-Kersee signed to become an agent with the National Football League Players Association, and created a sports management company to represent a variety of athletes. By the end of that year, she was representing three NFL players. In that same year, she won a gold medal in the heptathlon in the Goodwill Games. On August 1, 1998, she announced that she was retiring from competition, but she did not fill out the official forms that are required to certify such an announcement.

In 2000, Joyner-Kersee tried to qualify for the 2000 Olympic team, but did not make the cut. After this, she said that she would not compete again, even in Masters competitions for older athletes. In that same year, the Jackie Joyner-Kersee Boys and Girls Club was officially opened in East St. Louis.

Retires from Competition

On February 1, 2001, USA Track and Field announced that the paperwork regarding Joyner-Kersee's retirement was complete, and she was officially retired. In *Ebony,* Joyner-Kersee told a reporter that she wanted to pass on the support that people gave her when she was young. "I feel that in return I can do that for the next generation. I probably can't do much, but at least I hope I can inspire someone to take the right path and be successful."

CONTACT INFORMATION

Address: c/o Jackie Joyner-Kersee Boys and Girls Club, 101 Jackie Joyner-Kersee Circle, East St. Louis, IL 62204. Fax: 618-274-1868. Phone: 618-274-5437. Online: www.jjkbgc.org.

SELECTED WRITINGS BY JOYNER-KERSEE:

(With Sonja Steptoe) *A New Kind of Grace: The Autobiography of the World's Greatest Female Athlete,* Warner, 1997.

FURTHER INFORMATION

Books

"Jackie Joyner-Kersee," *Encyclopedia of World Biography Supplement, Vol. 19,* Detroit: Gale Group, 1999.

"Jackie Joyner-Kersee," *Great Women in Sports,* Detroit: Visible Ink Press, 1996.

"Jackie Joyner-Kersee," *Sports Stars, Series 1-4,* Detroit: U•X•L, 1994-1998.

Periodicals

"Can World's Greatest Woman Athlete Cash in on Olympic Gold?" *Ebony,* (April, 1989): 96.

Duckett, Joy, "The Jackie Nobody Knows," *Essence,* (August, 1989): 62.

"For the Love of New Horizons," *Interview,* (June, 1997): 82.

"Formally Retired," *Jet,* (March 5, 2001): 50.

"Olympic Gold Medalist Joyner-Kersee Accomplishes Her Dream With Opening of Youth Center in East St. Louis," *PR Newswire,* (April 7, 2000): 8973.

Sketch by Kelly Winters

Jackie Joyner-Kersee

Duke Kahanamoku
1890-1968

American surfer

Duke Kahanamoku achieved legendary status in two sports—swimming and surfing—and in the process became Hawaii's best-known citizen. More than a sports champion or media celebrity, however, Kahanamoku also represented a vital link with his native land's past. In popularizing surfing among new generations of athletes around the world, Kahanamoku helped to keep the ancient sport alive after it had almost perished along with other Hawaiian traditions in the nineteenth century. At the time of his death in 1968, Kahanamoku was celebrated not only as a superb athlete, but as a cultural icon as well.

A Hawaiian Childhood

Duke Paoa Kahinu Mokoe Hulikohola Kahanamoku was born on August 24, 1890 in the Kalia District of Honolulu to Duke Halapu and Julia Paakonia Lonokahikini Paoa Kahanamoku. His father, who worked as a police officer, was born during a visit by the Duke of Edinburgh to Hawaii in 1869, and had been given the first name Duke to commemorate the event. When his first-born son arrived, the elder Kahanamoku passed the name along. The Kahanamoku family eventually grew to include six sons and three daughters.

Kahanamoku grew up during one of the most turbulent periods in Hawaii's history, one that brought its people close to extinction. There is no written record of when Polynesian groups settled the islands, but the arrival of Captain James Cook in 1778 is well documented. After shooting some islanders, the British explorer was killed in February 1779—but not before he left an extensive written record of his travels in the South Pacific. European audiences were fascinated by his descriptions of native traditions, particularly the sport of surfing, in which men, women, and even children would sail out into the ocean on long, flat boards, to be carried back to shore by cresting waves.

Duke Kahanamoku

Cook's misadventure in Hawaii did not dissuade other explorers and missionaries from coming to the islands throughout the nineteenth century. Unfortunately, the effects of their settlements were far from benign on the Hawaiian people. Christian missionaries condemned many native traditions—including surfing—as uncivilized, and attempted to ban such practices. More threateningly, a slew of diseases cut the population of the islands from about 300,000 when Cook visited to just 40,000 in 1893. That year the islands were plunged into upheaval when pineapple grower Sanford Dole used American military forces to overthrow the governing Hawaiian monarchy under Queen Liliuokalani. Dole established a republic on the islands in 1894 and in 1900 all Hawaiians were made United States citizens.

As a son in a fairly privileged family, Kahanamoku's childhood was relatively untouched by the political con-

Chronology

1890	Born August 24 in Honolulu, Hawaii to Duke Halapu and Julia Paakonia Lonokahikini Paoa Kahanamoku
1912	Wins gold medal in 100-meter freestyle swimming event at Stockholm Olympic Games
1914	Popularizes surfing in Australia during an exhibition tour
1920	Wins gold medal in 100-meter freestyle swimming event in Antwerp Olympic Games
1924	Wins silver medal in 100-meter freestyle swimming event in Paris Olympic Games
1925	Saves several swimmers from drowning off the coast of Corona del Mar, California
1936	Elected sheriff of Honolulu
1940	Marries Nadine Alexander
1948	Appears in John Wayne movie *Wake of the Red Witch*
1952	Suffers heart attack
1962	Suffers from cerebral blood clot
1968	Dies in Honolulu on January 22
1990	Statue is dedicated to Kahanamoku on Waikiki Beach

Awards and Accomplishments

1911	Gold medal, Amateur Athletic Union, 100-yard freestyle swimming
1912	Olympic gold medal, 100-meter freestyle swimming; silver medal, freestyle relay swimming
1920	Olympic gold medal, 100-meter freestyle swimming; gold medal, 800-meter freestyle relay swimming
1924	Olympic silver medal, 100-meter freestyle swimming
1965	Inducted into International Swimming Hall of Fame
1966	Inducted into Surfing Hall of Fame
1984	Inducted into U.S. Olympic Committee Hall of Fame

troversies of the period. From his family's home near Waikiki Beach, he showed a talent for swimming and surfing from an early age. By the time he reached adulthood, Kahanamoku stood at six feet and weighed one-hundred-ninety pounds; his greatest asset in the water, however, was his size-thirteen feet, which he used as a propeller in the water in a flutter kick. Later in his career, the innovation would become known as the "Kahanamoku Kick," a variation of the Australian crawl that he used in freestyle swimming events.

After completing the eleventh grade, Kahanamoku devoted much of his time to a budding career as an athlete. Along with his surfing friends he founded the Hui Nalu Surf Club in 1911. The club often competed against the Outrigger Canoe and Surfboard Club in sailing regattas and the events proved to be a great tourist attraction. Kahanamoku also made headlines during his participation in the first Amateur Athletic Union (AAU) swimming event held in Hawaii, which took place in August 1911. The 100-yard freestyle event was held in between two piers in Honolulu Harbor on a temporary course set up just for the event. Consequently, when Kahanamoku won the race with a time of 55.4 seconds—the current record then stood at 60 seconds—AAU officials remeasured the course four times before declaring Kahanamoku the winner. In the 50-yard freestyle, Kahanamoku tied the world record of 24.2 seconds. The national AAU office refused to recognize his achievements, claiming that the course's irregularities must have helped Kahanamoku set the records.

Olympic Star

Kahanamoku was unfazed by the controversy over his record-breaking performances in the 1911 AAU event. Instead, he focused on making the U.S. Olympic Men's Swimming Team, set to compete in Stockholm for the 1912 Games. In a May 1912 qualifying meet in Philadel-phia for the 100-meter freestyle event, Kahanamoku swept the field with a time of 60 seconds. He also qualified for the U.S. 800-meter relay team at a trial held in New Jersey, where he set a record for his leg of the race with a 200-meter time of 2 minutes and 40 seconds. At the 1912 Olympic Games Kahanamoku became one of the event's most famous athletes. On July 6 he took the gold medal in the 100-meter freestyle event and set a new Olympic record in the process of 63.4 seconds. Kahanamoku also helped the U.S. 800-meter freestyle team take the silver medal in that event. Perhaps the only other American athlete to emerge with a higher profile from the 1912 Olympic Games was **Jim Thorpe**, who, like Kahanamoku, was of aboriginal descent.

The First World War led to the cancellation of the 1916 Olympic Games, where Kahanamoku was a favorite to win at least one more gold medal. Forced to wait until the 1920 Olympic Games in Antwerp, Belgium, Kahanamoku once again made the U.S. Team in the 100-meter freestyle and 800-meter freestyle relay. The first run of the finals for the 100-meter freestyle was nullified after some countries protested the outcome, which had thirty-year-old Kahanamoku setting another world-record of 61.4 seconds. In the rescheduled finals, he again proved his mastery of the event with an even better time of 60.4 seconds. This time, there was no protest and Kahanamoku was awarded the gold medal. He also helped to set a record as part of the 800-meter freestyle relay team, which took the gold medal with a record-setting time of 10 minutes and 4.4 seconds.

Kahanamoku's final Olympic medal came at the 1924 Games in Paris, where he placed second to **Johnny Weissmuller** in the 100-meter freestyle event. Kahanamoku did not make the swim team for the 1932 Olympics in Los Angeles, but he did attend the event as a member of the Los Angeles Athletic Club Water Polo Team, which failed to make it into the final competition. In all, Kahanamoku won three individual and two team medals in his Olympic career.

The Father of Surfing

After his appearance at the 1912 Olympics, Kahanamoku was an international celebrity. He toured the

United States giving swimming and surfing exhibitions and even went to Australia at the invitation of the Australia Swimming Association in late 1914. Although some Australians had tried to surf before, Kahanamoku's appearance at the Freshwater Beach near Sydney in February 1915 caused a sensation in the country. Kahanamoku spent two-and-a-half hours giving a demonstration of surfing on a board that he had made himself, and even took a young woman out on the board for a ride. Surfing eventually became one of the Australia's most popular past-times, and many credited Kahanamoku with being the "Father of Modern Surfing" for increasing interest in the sport at home and abroad.

By now the most famous resident of Hawaii, Kahanamoku was sought out by numerous celebrities during their visits to the islands. One of his most notable acquaintances was the Prince of Wales, whom he taught to surf in 1920. Kahanamoku also rubbed shoulders with some of Hollywood's most famous stars, a by-product of his own career as a character actor—usually playing tribal chiefs—that began in the 1920s. Kahanmoku's most memorable appearances came at the end of his acting career in the 1948 John Wayne movie *The Wake of the Red Witch* and the 1955 Jack Lemmon movie *Mister Roberts*.

Kahanamoku also earned praise for his heroism during a daring rescue of passengers from a capsized boat off the coast of Corona del Mar, California on June 14, 1925. Twenty-nine passengers on the pleasure boat the *Thelma* had been pitched into the Pacific Ocean after the craft had capsized. Upon hearing the news, Kahanamoku jumped onto his surfboard and paddled out to the scene. He managed to drag eight people out of the ocean and ferry them back to shore; only four others survived the wreck. As Leonard Leuras later quoted a story from the *Los Angeles Times* on Kahanamoku's life in his *Surfing: The Ultimate Pleasure*, "His role on the beach that day was more dramatic than the scores he played in four decades of intermittent bit-part acting in Hollywood films. For one thing, that day he was the star."

Hawaii's Official Greeter

In 1934 Kahanamoku gained office as Sheriff of Honolulu; he also owned and operated two gas stations in the city. In 1940 he married Nadine Alexander; the couple did not have any children. While serving as sheriff, a post he held until it was abolished in 1960, Kahanamoku continued to make film appearances and attended numerous international surfing events as the sport's elder statesman. In his retirement Kahanamoku was appointed Hawaii's official greeter, a ceremonial post that recognized his contribution to promoting the state's culture and traditions. In 1965 Kahanamoku was inducted into the International Swimming Hall of Fame; the following year, he was inducted into the Surfing Hall of Fame.

Although Kahanamoku still cut an impressive figure as he reached his seventies, a heart attack in 1955 and

---

The Beloved Duke of Waikiki

The newspapers called him "the Bronze Duke of Waikiki," and his biography was subtitled *Hawaii's Golden Man*. Twenty-two years after his death, Duke Kahanamoku remains Hawaii's greatest athlete. The state has just concluded a month long celebration of its native son that culminated in the unveiling of a statue on Waikiki Beach....

Kahanamoku "has been to [surfing and swimming] exactly what Babe Ruth was to baseball, Joe Louis to boxing, Bill Tilden to tennis, Red Grange to football, and Bobby Jones to golf," wrote Red McQueen in *The Honolulu Advertiser* shortly before Kahanamoku's death at the age of 77. "He has been Mister Surfer and Mister Swimming rolled into one incredible giant of a man."

Source: Gullo, Jim. *Sports Illustrated*, September 17, 1990.

---

cerebral blood clot in 1962 limited his physical activities. One of his last major appearances was as guest of honor at the U.S. Surfing Championships in Huntington Beach, California in September 1965. In December 1965 he attended the Duke Kahanamoku Invitational Surfing Championships in Hawaii; when the event was telecast the following year on CBS, it attracted the largest audience ever to watch a surfing competition, estimated at up to fifty million viewers. He also made headlines for showing the Queen Mother how to dance the hula during her visit to Hawaii in May 1966.

The Duke's Legacy

Duke Kahanamoku suffered a fatal heart attack at the Waikiki Yacht Club and died on January 22, 1968. His death marked the passing of a world-class athlete in swimming and surfing who also served as a vital link to Hawaii's past.

In 1984 Kahanamoku was posthumously inducted into the U.S. Olympic Committee Hall of Fame. In 1990 his widow led efforts to have a statue of Kahanamoku dedicated on Waikiki Beach. The figure showed a nine-foot Kahanamoku with a surfboard facing away from the ocean with his arms outstretched in a welcoming embrace. Nadine Alexander Kahanamoku also supported efforts to set up the Outrigger Duke Kahanamoku Foundation, a public trust devoted to funding youth athletic activities and traditional Hawaiian sports. These activities continue to promote the ideals expressed in Kahanamoku's life while preserving his culture's heritage for future generations.

Kahanamoku is still regarded a generation after his death as Hawaii's best-ever athletic champion. His five Olympic medals also rank Kahanamoku as one of the greatest athletes in the history of the modern Summer Olympic Games. If not for his efforts to promote surfing, it could well have become a cultural relic of Hawaii's past. Instead, Kahanamoku popularized the sport around the world and in doing so, helped to preserve a part of his culture's history.

FURTHER INFORMATION

Books

Kampion, Drew. *Stoked: A History of Surf Culture.* Los Angeles: General Publishing Group, 1997.

Lueras, Leonard. *Surfing: The Ultimate Pleasure.* New York: Workman Publishing, 1984.

Periodicals

"Duke Kahanamoku Dies at 77; Leading Swimmer of His Time." *New York Times* (January 23, 1968).

Gullo, Jim. "The Beloved Duke of Waikiki." *Sports Illustrated* (September 17, 1990).

Other

"Duke Kahanamoku." Internet Movie Database. http://www.imdb.com (September 19, 2002).

"Duke Kahanamoku." Surfside Sports. http://www.surf sidesports.com/The%20Duke.htm (August 28, 2001).

"Duke Kahanamoku." U.S. Olympic Committee Web Site. http://www.olympic-usa.org/about_us/programs/halloffame/1984detail.html (September 25, 2002).

"Kahanamoku Gallery." Hawaiian Swim Boat Web Site. http://www.hawaiianswimboat.com/galler.html (September 25, 2002).

"The Outrigger Duke Kahanamoku Foundation." Planet Hawaii. http://planet-hawaii.com/duke/ (August 28, 2001).

Sketch by Timothy Borden

Al Kaline

Al Kaline
1934-

American baseball player

Known as "Mr. Tiger," Albert William (Al) Kaline devoted his entire twenty-one year playing career (1953-1974) to the American League Detroit Tigers. Indeed, only Kaline and 1920s legend **Ty Cobb** played twenty or more seasons in a Detroit uniform. The Hall of Famer distinguished himself throughout his competitive years as a power hitter and gifted right-fielder. He appeared in fifteen All-Star games, won ten Gold Glove awards, and personified Tiger excellence during the 1968 World Series. On retirement, Kaline continued to serve as a television commentator for Tiger games.

Born in Baltimore to a sports-minded family, Kaline came by his baseball skills through his father and two uncles, who all played semi-pro ball. Though smaller than the typical player, the young Kaline overcame his physical shortcomings by practicing harder and longer than his teammates. His early ambition aimed Kaline not toward the plate, but the mound: "I guess all kids interested in baseball first want to be pitchers," he was quoted in a 1955 *Saturday Evening Post* interview. But the thin teen was not suited for hurling balls at the high-school level, and concentrated on his hitting game instead. At Baltimore's Southern High School, Kaline batted .333, .418, .469, and .488, and was named to the all-Maryland high-school team each of his academic years. Kaline's family supported his goals, driving him from league to league. Kaline grew to a slender six-foot-one; by the time he graduated from high school, the young hitter was the object of scrutiny from baseball scouts.

From the Sandlot to the Stadium

One scout, Ed Katalinas, signed the eighteen-year-old Kaline to a $35,000 bonus "right off the Baltimore sandlots," as a BaseballLibrary.com article put it, "and Al never played one inning in the minor leagues." Drafted by the Tigers, Kaline made his professional bow midseason, on June 25, 1953, in the game that also marked his debut as a right-fielder. Kaline was given the modest task of a pinch-runner that day, but the young man soon began to make his mark. In fewer than thirty trips to the plate that year, Kaline collected seven hits, including a home run. He even hit a single off the great pitcher **Satchel Paige**.

Kaline's first full rookie year of 1954 was characterized by a relatively low .276 batting average. A highlight

Chronology

1934	Born December 19, in Baltimore, Maryland
1949-53	Named to all-Maryland baseball team all four year of high school
1953	Signs with the Detroit Tigers
1953	Professional debut, June 24
1968	Hits game-winning single in World Series Game Five
1974	Makes 3,000th career hit
1974	Retires from play after twenty-one seasons

Awards and Accomplishments

1955	Youngest winner of American League Batting Championship
1955	First of fifteen All-Star Game appearances
1955	Runner-up, American League Most Valuable Player
1955, 1963	Named Player of the Year, *Sporting News*
1957	First of ten Gold Glove awards
1959	American League slugging champion
1963	Runner-up, American League Most Valuable Player
1968	Detroit Tigers clinch World Series championship
1968	Lou Gehrig Memorial Award
1980	Named to Baseball Hall of Fame

of that year was Kaline's first grand-slam home run, making him the second-youngest player to date to accomplish that feat. But by the 1955 season, Kaline had hit his stride, muscling up to 175 pounds and hitting .340. At age twenty, he was the youngest player to win an American League batting championship. But all the early acclaim didn't sit well with the soft-spoken hitter. "The worst thing that happened to me in the big leagues was the start I had," he was quoted by *Sports Illustrated* writer Jack Olsen in 1964. "Everybody said this guy's another Ty Cobb, another **Joe DiMaggio.** How much pressure can you take? What they didn't know is I'm not that good a hitter. . . . I have to work as hard if not harder than anybody in the league."

Kaline's early reticence regarding his celebrity led some newspapermen to label the ballplayer as standoffish. But in Kaline's view, "I was just quiet," as he told Olsen. "And the guys who didn't know me would say, 'Look at this stuck-up kid.' But it was just my way. I don't talk much." Instead, Kaline let his bat do the talking. Known for his consistency, the right-hander averaged 150 hits per season. By 1959 Kaline had clinched the American League slugging championship when he compiled a .530 slugging percentage in 511 times at bat. Overall, Kaline's batting average for the year was .327.

For all his talent, Kaline was no stranger to adversity, beginning in 1954 when he ran into a wall chasing a fly ball and spent five days in the hospital. Kaline fractured his cheekbone in 1959. He also fractured his right collarbone diving for a catch on May 26, 1962, and was benched for two months, returning to play with a game-winning single. Showing no further break in his momentum, Kaline finished that abbreviated season with twenty-nine home runs and ninety-four runs batted in. But injuries continued to plague Kaline throughout his career, sidelining the hitter for some 200 games over fifteen years. In June 1967, for instance, Kaline broke his hand after jamming his bat into a bat rack after striking out. He missed twenty-eight games that season.

The Tigers on a Tear

Indeed, Kaline had missed much of the 1968 season nursing a broken arm while the Tigers were roaring to the top of the American League standings. But he recov-

ered in time to take his place in the World Series, which pitted the Tigers against the National League St. Louis Cardinals. The "Cards" had taken the three of the first four games of the series, placing the Tigers in a precarious position. But in the seventh inning of Game Five, with the Cardinals leading three to two, the Tigers put men on all three bases. Kaline stepped to the plate and singled to center field, driving in two runs and earning the hitter a standing ovation. The single gave Detroit a five-to-three win. The Tigers rallied to take Game Six. The Detroit team went on to win the tiebreaking Game Seven, clinching the Tigers' first World Series victory in decades—and providing much-needed emotional lift for the city of Detroit following a year marked by racial strife and rioting.

Kaline's fielding skills in the outfield were unsurpassed. He "made playing right field into an art form," wrote a contributor to BaseballLibrary.com. "Never a wasted motion, never a wrong decision." Kaline once played 242 consecutive games without a single outfield error. In a 1994 wire article for the Knight-Ridder/Tribune News Service, George Puscas recalled the artistry of Kaline's glovework: "The best throw I ever saw was one Kaline made from the rightfield fence down the line to home plate, on the fly, to nail a Yankee runner.... Yankees poured from the dugout not to protest the call, but to applaud Kaline." Only Kaline and Joe DiMaggio, added Puscas, "are viewed as the near-equal of all the outfield greats who proceeded them."

But it was his batting that won Kaline the most acclaim. He celebrated his 2,500th hit in June, 1970. Four years later, on September 24, 1974, Kaline tallied his 3,000th hit in his hometown, Baltimore. By now a senior member of the Tigers organization, Kaline continued to play out the 1974 season. When it was over he retired, having logged 3,007 hits, 399 home runs, and a .297 lifetime average. He was also one of the highest-paid ballplayers of his day, earning $92,000 per year by 1970.

Could this soft-spoken slugger possibly have accomplished more? No less an authority than **Ted Williams** thought so. The legendary hitter included Kaline among the greats—like **Willie Mays** and **Mickey Mantle**—who

Career Statistics

Yr	Team	AVG	GP	AB	R	H	HR	RBI	BB	SO	SB
1953	DET	.250	30	28	9	7	1	2	1	5	1
1954	DET	.276	138	504	42	139	4	1	22	45	9
1955	DET	.340	152	588	121	200	27	43	82	57	6
1956	DET	.314	153	617	96	194	27	102	70	55	7
1957	DET	.295	149	577	83	170	23	128	43	38	11
1958	DET	.313	146	543	84	170	16	85	54	47	7
1959	DET	.327	136	511	86	167	27	94	72	42	10
1960	DET	.278	147	551	77	153	15	68	65	47	19
1961	DET	.324	153	586	116	190	19	82	66	42	14
1962	DET	.304	100	398	78	121	29	94	47	39	4
1963	DET	.312	145	551	89	172	27	101	54	48	6
1964	DET	.293	146	525	77	154	17	68	75	51	4
1965	DET	.281	125	399	72	112	18	72	72	49	6
1966	DET	.288	142	479	85	138	29	88	81	66	5
1967	DET	.308	131	458	94	141	25	78	83	47	8
1968	DET	.287	102	327	49	94	10	53	55	39	6
1969	DET	.272	131	456	74	124	21	69	54	61	1
1970	DET	.278	131	467	64	130	16	71	77	49	2
1971	DET	.294	133	405	69	119	15	54	82	57	4
1972	DET	.313	106	278	46	87	10	32	28	33	1
1973	DET	.255	91	310	40	79	10	45	29	28	4
1974	DET	.262	147	558	71	146	13	64	65	75	2
TOTAL		.297	2834	10116	1622	3007	399	1583	1277	1020	137

DET: Detroit Tigers.

Where Is He Now?

A longtime television commentator, Kaline has also parlayed his playing experience into other fields. He served as an instructor in Tigers spring-training camps and was a board member of the organization. In 2001, Kaline was named by owner Mike Ilitch to a special board established to improve the status of the struggling franchise. The 2002 season marked Kaline's fiftieth year as an employee of the Detroit Tigers. At the same time, Kaline found a new outlet for his competitive instincts. An avid golfer, he splits his time between courses in suburban Detroit and Lakeland, Florida. "This is my game now, and I love it," he told *Florida Golf Monthly*. "I love to play in competition. I get nervous, but it feels good to get nervous again, and I can handle it."

might have reached Williams's legendary batting average. "I used to think that Al Kaline could hit .400, or Mantle," wrote Williams in his autobiography. "But Mantle missed the ball too much … And time ran out on Kaline and Mays."

Staying close to his game, Kaline joined the Detroit Tigers broadcast team and served as a commentator, along with fellow teammate George Kell, for many years. In 1999 he once again donned his uniform to mark the end of an era—the last day of 90-year-old Tiger Stadium, which had been closed in favor of a new ballpark in Detroit. *Detroit Free Press* writer Steven Crowe attended the September ceremony and reported that Kaline's introduction sparked a 76-second standing ovation. Showing uncharacteristic emotion, the hitter "stepped back from the microphone, cleared his throat, took his hat off, lowered his head," noted Crowe. Then

"Mr. Tiger" recovered and "delivered a superbly fitting and brief farewell."

FURTHER INFORMATION

Books

Hirshberg, Al. *The Al Kaline Story.* New York: Julian Messner, Inc., 1964.

Nicholson, Lois. *From Maryland to Cooperstown: Seven Maryland Natives in Baseball's Hall of Fame.* Tidewater, 1999.

Williams, Ted. *My Turn at Bat.* New York: Fireside, 1988.

Periodicals

Butler, H. C. *Saturday Evening Post* (September 3, 1955).

Crowe, Steve. "Bringing down the House Again." *Detroit Free Press* (September 28, 1999).

Olsen, Jack. *Sports Illustrated* (May 11, 1964).

Puscas, George. "Al Kaline's Star Rose at 20, Kept Soaring." *Knight-Ridder/Tribune News Service* (April 3, 1994).

Other

"Al Kaline." BaseballLibrary.com. http://www.pubdim. net/baseball library/ (October 31, 2002).

"Al Kaline." National Baseball Hall of Fame. http:// www.baseballhalloffame/org/ (October 31, 2002).

Florida Golf Monthly. http://www.floridagolfing.com (November 7, 2002).

Sketch by Susan Salter

Alexander Karelin
1967-

Russian wrestler

Russia's Alexander Karelin is the most successful Greco-Roman wrestler of the modern era, having won twelve European Championships, nine World Championships, and three Olympic gold medals during his reign. Karelin's dominance is unparalleled: he won every match he entered for thirteen years and went ten years without giving up a single point. He also is an opera and ballet aficionado, a student of great literature, and a member of his country's parliament. Karelin is so loved in his homeland that Russia mourned his loss in the 2000 Olympic finals, his first and only defeat in international competition. It's even been suggested that the 6-foot, 4-inch, 286-pound Renaissance man could someday become Russia's president. "You consider this ancient sport and this monumental man who's had a perfect career," said NBC commentator Jeff Blatnick, himself an Olympic gold medalist who lost to Karelin in 1987, "and the only thing you come up with is that he is what Hercules was to the ancient Greeks."

Siberian childhood

Karelin was born in Novobirsk, Siberia, where his great-grandparents, progressive intellectuals, had been dispatched against their will. Temperatures there can reach -50 degrees farenheit. Nicholas Davidoff described the city this way in *Sports Illustrated*: "For months its snow-covered sidewalks are traversed by men and women swathed to anonymity in wools and furs. Days are short and grim. Gray buildings line streets that eventually give way to the endless pine forests that long ago gave this brooding part of the world its name: Siberia, the Sleeping Land. . . . Today, within some of those gray buildings are more than 100 universities and research centers, an opera house admired internationally for its architecture and its programs, a ballet company and a circus." Karelin's father was a truck driver and his mother an office worker. He weighed fifteen pounds at birth and, as a boy, hunted on skis and built his strength hauling logs through the snow. Victor Kusnetzov, the only coach Karelin would ever have, convinced the boy to take up wrestling at the relatively late age of thirteen. He trained by running through thigh-deep snow two hours at a stretch and rowed a boat

Alexander Karelin

on frigid lakes until his hands bled. He once carried a refrigerator, alone, up eight flights of stairs.

A terrifying maneuver

In 1986, Karelin lost only one match—to 6-foot, 5-inch, 280-pound world champion Igor Rostorotsky. The following year, Karelin became the world junior champion and a member of the Soviet national team. At the same time, he and Kusnetzov were refining a vicious wrestling maneuver that would make Karelin indomitable—the reverse body lift. The move was unprecedented for a heavyweight, because it requires the wrestler to lift his 280-pound opponent—a feat that was unthinkable until Karelin came along. "To execute it, Karelin locks his arms around the waist of an opponent," John Greenwald explained in *Time* magazine, "then lifts the wrestler like a sack of potatoes and, arching his back, heaves the hapless fellow, feet first, over his head." Following the severe impact, Karelin would descend upon his opponent. Top heavyweights so feared the move that they would roll over and allow themselves to be pinned rather than being subjected to it. "When it happened to me, every hair on the back of my neck raised up," Blatnick told *Sports Illustrated*. "I was doing everything humanly possible to prevent him from lifting me off the mat. I weighed 265 pounds. I was in good shape. I was scared—intense fear. I don't like flying through the air like that. I kept thinking, 'Don't get hurt. Don't get hurt.' With him, it's almost a victory if you don't get thrown."

Chronology

1967	Born September 19 in Novobirsk, Siberia
1980	Takes up wrestling at age 13
1988	Wins Olympic gold medal in Seoul, South Korea; also wins European Championship
1989-91, 1993-95, 1998-99	Wins European and World Championships
1992	Wins Olympic gold medal in Barcelona, Spain; also wins European Championship
1996	Wins Olympic gold medal in Atlanta, Georgia; also wins European Championship
1997	Wins World Championship
1999	Elected to the State Duma, the lower house of the Russian parliament
2000	Wins European Championship
2000	Wins Olympic silver medal in Sydney, Australia; also wins European Championship
2000	Retires from wrestling

Awards and Accomplishments

1985	Wins Espoir World Championship
1987	Wins World Cup Championship
1988	Wins European Championship
1988, 1992, 1996	Olympic gold medals
1989-91, 1993-95, 1998-99	Wins European and World Championships
1997	Wins World Championship
2000	Wins Olympic silver medal
2000	Wins European Championship
2003	One of the first 10 inductees into the new International Wrestling Hall of Fame

Soon, Karelin was defeating Rostorotsky regularly. In 1988, he won the European Championship and earned a super-heavyweight berth on the wrestling team Russia would send to the Summer Olympics in Seoul, South Korea. It was the beginning of an unprecedented thirteen-year winning streak that would elevate Karelin to the top of the wrestling world and to folk hero status in his native Russia. He won the Olympic gold in Seoul in 1988 and again in Barcelona in 1992 and Atlanta in 1996. He won the European Championship for nine consecutive years, from 1988-96, and again in 1998, 1999 and 2000. And he won the World Championship from 1989-91, 1993-95, and 1997-99. "You can't beat him until you score on him," said Mitch Hull, national teams director for U.S. wrestling. "And Karelin's . . . not allowing anyone to score. Guys just can't get any position to move him."

A political career

In 1999, Russian President Vladimir Putin's Unity Party selected Karelin to run for a seat representing his hometown in the parliament. Karelin was elected in December 1999, although he disliked campaigning: "They told me to grow hair instead of having my favorite short haircuts. They told me I should not drive sport-utility vehicles—but I don't fit in a regular car. Finally I said, 'Maybe you want me to pierce my ears and nose, paint my cheeks, use lipstick and makeup? Look, the people who vote for me see me every day as I am. I don't have to pretend to make them like me.'"

Karelin loves the opera, theater and ballet, voraciously reads Russian history and literature, and writes poetry. "This is a highly talented man," said Larisa Mason, a graduate of Leningrad State University who has served as an interpreter for Karelin. "His knowledge and his feeling for poetry, literature and music are incredible. He is witty, full of puns and constantly embellishing his language with passages from books and music. And he is a big teddy bear, too."

A brilliant career ends

Finally, the impossible happened. Alexander Karelin lost a match. In one of the biggest upsets in Olympic history, American Rulon Gardner, a relative unknown, defeated Karelin 1-0 in the super-heavyweight finals at the 2000 Summer Olympics in Sydney, Australia. In overtime, Gardner was able to wiggle free of Karelin's grasp, avoiding the dreaded reverse body lift and scoring the first point against the Russian in a decade. It was enough for the gold medal. Karelin earned silver; Russia was devastated. "Karelin lost," the country's main sports newspaper said in a front-page column. "The great and unbeatable champion, who had never stood on the second step of the medals podium, ascended to it yesterday as to a gallows."

Alexander Karelin retired from wrestling in 2000 to devote himself full-time to his legislative responsibilities. He lives with his wife and three children in a mansion in Novobirsk, Siberia, his hometown. "Greco-Roman is an original Olympic sport," he once said. "I like the idea of being a classical man, of belonging to a classical tradition."

FURTHER INFORMATION

Periodicals

"Alexander Karelin: Russian Greco-Roman Wrestling." *Time International* (September 18, 2000).

Clark, Kim. "Wrestling with Demons." *U.S. News & World Report* (October 9, 2000).

Davidoff, Nicholas. "A Bruiser and a Thinker: Soviet Greco-Roman Wrestler Alexander Karelin is a Rare Combination of Massive Physique and Imposing Intellect." *Sports Illustrated* (May 13, 1991).

Dolgov, Anna. "Russia Laments Losses at Sydney Games." Associated Press (September 28, 2000).

"Famous Wrestler Alexander Karelin Goes in for Politics." *Pravda* (English language version) (April 25, 2001).

Greenwald, John. "Alexander Karelin." *Time* (September 11, 2000).

"International Hall Planned for Stillwater." Associated Press (January 13, 2003).

McCallum, Jack. "Bumper Crop: By Beating the Unbeatable Karelin, U.S. Farm Boy Rulon Gardner Reaped a Stunning Golden Harvest." *Sports Illustrated* (October 9, 2000).

"Russian Wrestler Karelin Says He Won't Compete in Another Olympics." Associated Press (October 13, 2000).

Stein, Joel. "Rulon Gardner." *Time* (October 9, 2000).

Tresniowski, Alex. "Giant Killer." *People* (October 16, 2000).

Sketch by David Wilkins

Paul Kariya

Paul Kariya
1974-

Canadian hockey player

Paul Kariya, the talented young left wing who is the captain of the Anaheim Mighty Ducks, may be best known for his courteous behavior on the ice. However, the two-time winner of the Lady Byng trophy, given to the most gentlemanly player in the National Hockey League (NHL), is also a prodigious scorer and gifted play-maker. Although a serious concussion, a contract dispute, and the Mighty Ducks' in troubles fielding other skilled players have at times hampered Kariya's career, he continues to be a rising star within the NHL.

Ambassador for the Game

Kariya was born and raised in Vancouver, British Columbia, where he learned to play not only hockey but also lacrosse, rugby, tennis, golf, and basketball. As an amateur, he played for the University of Maine, leading them to a National Collegiate Athletic Association (NCAA) championship in 1993 and becoming the first freshman ever to win the Hobey Baker award. Although drafted by the Anaheim Mighty Ducks in 1993, Kariya won a silver medal at the 1994 Winter Olympics and a gold at the 1994 world championships with Team Canada before beginning to play with the Mighty Ducks in the 1994-95 season.

One of Kariya's claims to fame that first season with the Mighty Ducks was his G-rated life off of the ice. Despite having a $6.5 million contract, rather than getting his own place to live he rented a room from a family in Orange County, California. "I've never cooked," Kariya told *Sports Illustrated* writer Leigh Montville. "I don't own any furniture. It's my first year in the National Hockey League, and there are going to be things I have to learn every night. I just decided I didn't have time to go looking for a condominium or a house, to go through all that and then have to learn all of those other things on the ice. Living with a family seemed to be the right thing for me."

Kariya's good image, on and off the ice, has prompted many to suggest that he should become an ambassador for the game of hockey, which, with its recent expansion into unfamiliar southern and western territory, particularly needs a media-friendly face to introduce potential new fans to the game. Kariya is aware of this suggestion, but is not necessarily enthusiastic about the role. "I'm going to try to be the best Paul Kariya that can be, wherever that leads. Trying to promote the game is part of it, but if you're not performing on the ice, they won't want to talk to you, so I have to take care of that part first. I don't get caught up in it, but I understand my responsibility," he said to *Sporting News*'s Sherry Ross.

Injuries and Other Problems

Kariya's and the Mighty Ducks' best season may have been 1996-97. In that year, with the dynamic duo of Kariya on left wing and his good friend **Teemu Selanne** on right wing, as well as the inspiring coaching of Ron Wilson, the Mighty Ducks made it to the playoffs for the first time in the club's history. Selanne and

Kariya were the second and third highest scorers, respectively, in the NHL that season, and although the team was knocked out in the second round of the playoffs, the future looked bright. "I've played with a lot of great players, guys like **Eric Lindros**, and we've had good chemistry," Kariya told *Sports Illustrated* reporter Austin Murphy at the time, "but not the kind of chemistry Teemu and I have. It's so much fun playing the game when you know exactly what the other person's going to do."

However, Kariya's career did not go smoothly after that. In 1997, he missed the first thirty-two games of the season because of a contract dispute. Then he suffered a major concussion on February 1, 1998, when Chicago Blackhawks player Gary Suter cross-checked him on the jaw. Kariya spent months recovering, missing the last twenty-eight games of the NHL season that year as well as the Nagano Olympics. For a while it looked as if Kariya's career might be over, but he was finally cleared to begin practicing again that August.

The Mighty Ducks, who performed miserably after losing their leading scorer, signed enforcer Stu Grimson, known as the "Grim Reaper," and assigned him with making opposing players think twice about taking cheap shots at Kariya. Kariya himself, painfully aware of how close he had been to losing his career after that concussion, said that he would be less hesitant to assert himself in on-ice conflicts. However, the rest of the Mighty Ducks lineup was coming apart. Coach Ron Wilson went to the Washington Capitals after the 1997 playoffs, and Selanne was traded to San Jose during the 2000-01 season. By the 2001-02 season, Kariya's $10 million per year contract was almost thirty percent of the Mighty Ducks' $35 million total payroll, and opposing teams had discovered that all they needed to do to beat the Mighty Ducks was to prevent Kariya from scoring.

"The Best Job I Can Possibly Do"

Although Kariya's statistics in recent years have not been as spectacular as those at the beginning of his career, he is still working hard to improve himself and the team he captains. During the 2000-2001 season, Kariya explained his philosophy of the game to *Hockey Digest* interviewer Ashley Jude Collie: "I try to make myself a better player each time I go out on the ice. Each game presents situations and plays from which you can learn and make yourself a better hockey player. I focus on what I have to work on every night and just have a goal in mind for that game.... I want to do the best job I can possibly do. That's just he way I was brought up and the way that I feel that I can achieve the most success and the most enjoyment in life."

CONTACT INFORMATION

Address: c/o Mighty Ducks of Anaheim, 2695 Katella Avenue, Anaheim, CA 92806.

FURTHER INFORMATION

Periodicals

Betchel, Mark. "18: Anaheim Mighty Ducks." *Sports Illustrated* (October 16, 2000): 108.

Betchel, Mark. "19: Anaheim Mighty Ducks." *Sports Illustrated* (October 14, 2002): 102.

Bisheff, Steve. "The Mighty Duck." *Sporting News* (February 24, 1997): 27.

Collie, Ashley Jude. "Getting Better All the Time." *Hockey Digest* (February, 2001): 18.

Farber, Michael. "Goal Oriented." *Sports Illustrated* (December 22, 1997): 80-82.

Farber, Michael. "Stuck Duck." *Sports Illustrated* (December 3, 2001): 58.

Farber, Michael. "Two Different Worlds." *Sports Illustrated* (January 26, 1998): 66-69.

Farber, Michael. "A Welcome Sight." *Sports Illustrated* (October 19, 1998): 58.

Guss, Greg. "Kariya Town." *Sport* (April, 1998): 96-99.

McManus, John. "Nice on Ice." *Boys' Life* (November, 1997): 38-40.

Montville, Leigh. "A Duck's Tale." *Sports Illustrated* (February 13, 1995): 62-65.

Murphy, Austin. "Heating Up." *Sports Illustrated*. (April 28, 1997): 38-41.

Ross, Sherry. "Back in the Driver's Seat." *The Sporting News* (November 16, 1998): 62.

Career Statistics

Yr	Team	GP	G	A	PTS	+/−	PIM
1994-95	AMD	47	18	21	39	−17	4
1995-96	AMD	82	50	58	108	8	20
1996-97	AMD	69	44	55	99	36	6
1997-98	AMD	22	17	14	31	12	23
1998-99	AMD	82	39	62	101	17	40
1999-00	AMD	74	42	44	86	22	24
2000-01	AMD	66	33	34	67	−9	20
2001-02	AMD	82	32	25	57	−15	28
TOTAL		593	283	320	603	52	179

AMD: Anaheim Mighty Ducks.

Wigge, Larry. "Kariya's Talent Never Wavers." *The Sporting News* (February 11, 2002): 43.

Other

Hobey Baker Award. http://www.hobeybaker.com/ (November 13, 2002).

Mighty Ducks Web site. http://www.mightyducks.com/ (November 13, 2002).

Sketch by Julia Bauder

Bela Karolyi

Bela Karolyi
1942-

Romanian gymnastics coach

Visionary Romanian-born coach, Bela Karolyi, revitalized the field of elite women's gymnastics competition during the 1970s and 1980s. The sport, which was traditionally dominated by women in their late twenties, became a bastion of underage ingenues under Karolyi's watchful eye. By introducing very young girls to the sport and providing them with intensive training he introduced new displays of power and athletic movement to the traditional spins and aesthetic twists that were normally seen in competition and that were limited by the larger size and limited flexibility of older competitors. Karolyi added new leaps, flips, and contortions consistent with the lithe lightness of younger gymnasts.

Early Life in Romania

Karolyi was born on September 13, 1942, in Cluj, Romania. His father, Nandor, was a civil engineer. Iren, his mother was an accountant and homemaker. Karolyi was the youngest of two siblings; his sister, Maria, became a civil engineer like her father, while Karolyi turned to athletic pursuits. As a teen he set national records in the hammer throw, learned to box, and was competitive in track and field. After winning the National Boxing Championship, he quit his day job at a local slaughterhouse and in 1959 enrolled at Cluj Technical College. There he played rugby and competed on the school's world championship handball squad. Also in college he became friends with a classmate, Marta Eross, whom he eventually married. Eross would figure prominently in Karolyi's future career as a gymnastics coach.

As a young man Karolyi was large and muscular, weighing 286 pounds in college. While earning his degree in physical education he confronted one of his biggest challenges: attempting to pass a gymnastics proficiency test, which was a requirement for the curriculum. For two years he persisted, determined to earn a spot on the school's gymnastics team. Although he succeeded in his junior year, soon afterward he broke his arm, thus ending his career in competition. After that he turned his sights to coaching.

Karolyi graduated second in his class in 1963; Eross graduated first. Karolyi then served a mandatory three-month tour in the Romanian national army. They were married on November 28, 1963, and went to live in the Vulcan mining region of Romania where Karolyi's own grandfather had once made a home and had served the townspeople as a community impresario. It was Karolyi's desire to serve the community too—by providing physical fitness training to area youth.

Chronology

1942	Born in Cluj, Romania, on September 13
1963	Graduates from Cluj Technical College; marries Marta Eross on November 28; establishes a physical fitness facility for miners' families in Vulcan region
1968	Establishes national institute for the training of gymnasts in Onesti
1971	Brings Romanian team to the United States for a state-sponsored exhibition tour
1973-74	Dominates Friendship Cup competition
1974	Brings Romanian team to Paris for exhibition tour
1977	Closes Onesti facility; reopens facility in Vulcan
1980	Resigns from national post in protest of Moscow Olympic gymnastics judging, but resignation is rejected
1981	Brings Romanian team to the United States on tour; remains in the United States and requests political asylum; moves to California and then to Oklahoma; secures backing for a gymnastics facility in Houston
1982	Buys out his backers in the Houston gymnastics facility; secures a $500,000 loan for expansion
1986	Publishes *Mary Lou: Creating an Olympic Champion* with John Powers and Mary Lou Retton
1989	Opens a gymnastics summer camp at Texas ranch
1990	Adopts American citizenship in May 1
1992	Retires from Olympic coaching
1994	Publishes *Feel No Fear* with Nancy Ann Richardson

Awards and Accomplishments

1972	Coaches team to a silver medal and coaches Comaneci to the individual gold, at the Eastern Bloc Friendship Cup in Sofia
1976	Brings Nadia Comaneci to the Montreal Olympics where she wins the individual gold medal; coaches Romanian team to first Olympic medals since 1960; wins Romanian Labor Union Medal
1977	Wins the Romanian national championships
1978	Wins the Friendship Cup
1979	Sweeps the European championships and the world championships
1984	Brings Mary Lou Retton to the Los Angeles Olympics where she wins the individual gold medal; coaches the United States team to first Olympic team medal since 1948
1996	Coaches the United States team to Olympic gold medal
1997	Inducted into the International Gymnastics Hall of Fame

Karolyi at first offered youth programs in soccer, and in track and field. His methods generated controversy almost immediately because he encouraged the young athletes to dress in loose, comfortable clothing like t-shirts and shorts. While he patiently overcame the objections of conservative parents, the young boys began to wear appropriate attire, and eventually the girls were wearing more comfortable outfits too.

Recognition in Competition

In an unconventional move, the Karolyis provided the most agile of the young girls between the ages seven and eleven with training in gymnastics. Although training in women's gymnastics at that time was reserved for older girls in their mid-teens, Karolyi's students made rapid strides in part because of their youthful bravado. The pre-adolescent girls took easily to learning to perform somersaults and back flips in mid air. Because of their tiny frames, they performed these gyrations easily, even between the parallel bars. Because of their small lithe body types they experienced relatively few injuries from falls and other mishaps. Karolyi called them flying squirrels because of their graceful airborne movements.

Within three years he had assembled six gymnastics teams of pre-adolescent girls. He took the squads to competitions where they prevailed over much older contestants—many as old as 15 to 17 years old. Gymnastics officials, taking notice of the new and younger gymnasts from Vulcan, labeled Karolyi's teams as experimental. A new, junior competition division was defined to accommodate these youngsters, and by the late

1960s junior gymnastic teams were forming nationally throughout Romania.

In August of 1968 the national Education Ministerium recruited Karolyi to start a national institute for the training of gymnasts. He abandoned the gym at Vulcan and established a facility at a decade-old chemical-factory town called Onesti. The mayor of Onesti donated a school building and a dormitory, and provided funding to Karolyi to build a gymnasium in the town. After scouting throughout the region, he recruited his first class of six- and seven-year olds for the new institute. Among them was a young street tumbler named **Nadia Comaneci** and her schoolmate Viorica Dumitru. Comaneci was destined to become an Olympic champion, while Dumitru developed into a premiere ballerina.

After a state-sponsored exhibition tour to the United States in 1971, Karolyi took his team to the Eastern Block Friendship Cup competition in Sofia in 1972. With the budding Olympian Comaneci on the squad, Karolyi's girls upset the competition, beating both East Germany and the Soviet Union for the silver medal. Comaneci took the gold medal in the all-around individual competition.

Under Karolyi the Romanians dominated the competition in 1973 and again in 1974, but they were barred that year by the Romanian government from competing at the global level before age 15. Karolyi's squad performed instead in a Paris exposition after the world championships. One year later, at the European championship of 1975, Comaneci bested a 23-year-old Russian, Lyudmila Turishcheva, who had dominated Russian women's gymnastics in the late 1960s and the women's all-around competition since 1972.

Olympians

At the Montreal Olympics in 1976, working with premiere choreographer Geza Pozsar, Karolyi brought 14-year-old Nadia Comaneci into the competition, where she stole the show with an uncanny series of performances. Karolyi's girls made history when they took

Bela Karolyi, bottom

a silver medal in the team competition for the first time in Romanian history. Overall it was Romania's first Olympic medal since 1960.

Comaneci herself received an unprecedented perfect score of 10 in seven events. She was the first gymnast to receive a perfect 10 ever in the history of the Olympics. Her seven perfect scores, therefore, were extraordinary. She returned home with three gold medals, plus one silver, and one bronze.

Encouraged by the exceptional Olympic showing in Montreal, the Romanian government removed the athletes from Karolyi's care and relocated the national team. They were taken from Onesti to train in Bucharest instead.

Dissatisfaction

Karolyi was neither consulted nor advised of the team's movement in advance. Highly offended and upset at losing his best students, he shut down the school at Onesti and returned to the Vulcan region where he established a new facility at Deva in early 1977.

Karolyi's new students won the Romanian championships in October of 1977, and in 1978 they beat the Russians again at the Friendship Cup in Cuba that year. The girls from Deva took the top six places in the final standings of the national championships of 1978. Under pressure, soon afterward Karolyi accepted an eleventh-hour assignment to coach the Romanian national team. With only five weeks to train for the world championships, he brought the team to nothing less than a second place finish. His team swept both the European championships and the world championships in 1979.

When Comaneci received unjustified low scores and failed to win a gold medal at the Olympic competition in Moscow in 1980, Karolyi lodged a protest, causing a temporary disruption of the games. Upon his return to Romania he received a reprimand from the national gov-

ernment. Although Karolyi resigned in protest, the government refused to recognize his resignation.

Defection

In 1981 the Karolyis along with Pozsar, their choreographer of seven years, were dispatched with the national team to tour the United States in an exhibition that was guaranteed to raise a minimum of $180,000 for the Romanian Gymnastics Federation. When the exposition drew to a close, a midday flight departed from New York City on March 30, returning with the gymnasts to Romania. Karolyi was not on board. He had decided—along with his wife and Pozsar—to remain in the United States and request political asylum.

After filing appropriate immigration paperwork he migrated to Southern California at the urging of the vice president of the U.S. Gymnastics Federation. In California Karolyi picked up an odd job as a janitor and addressed the task of adding English to his six-language repertoire that included Hungarian, Russian, Romanian, German, French, and Italian.

Before long an opportunity at the University of Oklahoma sent the Karolyis packing to accept a summertime position at a gymnastics camp in Norman. A long-term post with the physical education department at the university was also in the offing for the following fall. With help from then-Texas Congressman Bill Archer, Karolyi sent for his seven-year-old daughter, Andrea, who had not attended the Romanian gymnastics exhibition and

Where Is He Now?

Unable to resist the lure of Olympic competition, Karolyi returned to coach the U.S. women's team that won Olympic gold in Atlanta in 1996. As the team competition came to a dramatic conclusion that summer, he swept an injured gymnast, Kerri Strug, from the floor as she completed her final vault despite a seriously sprained ankle. The gesture by the coach left onlookers with a lasting impression of his warmth and concern for his young gymnasts.

Despite intermittent controversy over his aggressive coaching style with such very young athletes, Karolyi's innovative contributions to the sport of women's gymnastics endure into the twenty-first century. On September 12, 2001, he accepted an appointment as the national coordinator for the U.S. women's gymnastics team, in preparation for the 2004 Olympics.

was in Deva on the day that her parents defected. She arrived in the United States some months later, after the diplomatic channels were cleared.

By the fall of 1981, plans were in progress for Karolyi to open a gymnasium in Houston, Texas. With $40,000 in backing from a small group of investors, Karolyi opened the Sundance Gym in Houston in the early months of 1982. He brought his first American team to competition soon afterward, winning the Texas Class I title. By September of the year Karolyi successfully bought out his partners, thus owning the facility outright. With 86 students in October of that year, he nearly doubled the enrolment to 168 by January of 1983. Additionally he secured one-half million dollars in loan funding from Texas Commercial Bank, to purchase the entire grounds and building of the facility. He expanded the gymnasium and purchased new equipment.

By 1983 Karolyi had purchased 1,200 acres near Huntsville, just north of Houston; and in 1989 the Houston gymnastics facility overflowed onto the rural acreage. That year the Karolyis established a summer camp, with log cabin residences for the gymnasts. In addition to athletes, the ranch housed chickens, turkeys, and swans along with such exotic livestock as camels, emus, ostriches, and llamas. Local wildlife—including deer and antelope—graced the grounds as well. By the early 2000s the camp accommodated more than 2,000 gymnasts annually.

Success in the U.S.

Just prior to his September 1982 buyout of the Houston gymnasium, Karolyi met a young gymnast named **Mary Lou Retton** at the Junior Nationals in Salt Lake City, Utah. He invited her to come to Houston to train at his gym. She departed from her home in Fairmont, West Virginia, and arrived at Karolyi's on New Year's Day.

Less than three months later—in March 1983—Retton competed in and won the McDonald's American Cup competition in New York City. In December Karolyi brought her to Japan where she won the Chunichi Cup. In all, from the spring of 1983 until the time of the summer Olympics in Los Angeles in 1984, she collected 14

consecutive all-around titles, including a successful defense of the American Cup title early in 1984. She was one of two of Karolyi's trainees to make the Olympic team that year, the other being Julianne McNamara.

The Olympic gymnastic competition that year was held at the Pauley Pavilion at the University of California. Ironically, the entire Communist Bloc of nations participated in a boycott of the Los Angeles Olympics—with the exception of Romania. Karolyi, although not a member of the official coaching staff, managed to secure a spot as an equipment mover on the Olympic competition floor.

At the finals McNamara scored a 10 on the parallel bars; it was the first time an American woman recorded a perfect score in any gymnastics event in the history of the Olympics. What is more, the team won a bronze medal that year. It was the first U.S. medal for women's gymnastics since 1948. In the all-around competition Retton scored a perfect 10 on the floor exercise and another 10 on the vault event. She emerged with a gold medal in the individual competition, after a neck-and-neck rivalry against Ecaterina (Kathy) Szabo, one of Karolyi's former students from Romania.

Back in Houston after the Olympics, the enrollment at Karolyi's gym skyrocketed to 1,400 students in the shadow of the impressive outcome. Then-16-year-old Retton continued her domination of women's gymnastics by taking the American Cup for an unprecedented third time in 1985.

Karolyi adopted U.S. citizenship on May 1, 1990. He accompanied the U.S. women's gymnastics team to the Olympic games in Barcelona, Spain in 1992, to a disappointing outcome. Although he retired from Olympic coaching after Barcelona he continued to operate his Houston gym and the summer camp in New Waverly. He remained one of the premiere gymnastic coaches worldwide.

Having published *Mary Lou: Creating an Olympic Champion,* with John Powers and Mary Lou Retton in 1984, Karolyi in his retirement wrote a personal memoir. The book, *Feel No Fear: the Power, Passion, and Politics of a Life in Gymnastics* with Nancy Ann Richardson, was published by Hyperion in 1994. In both volumes he presents his philosophies of aggressive coaching. He praises further the personal fortitude of the many gymnasts who have displayed the presence of character to follow his regimen and reap the rewards.

CONTACT INFORMATION

Address: Office: RR 12 Box 140, Huntsville, TX, 77320-9812.

SELECTED WRITINGS BY KAROLYI:

(With John Powers and Mary Lou Retton) *Mary Lou: Creating an Olympic Champion,* New York: McGraw-Hill, 1986.

(With Nancy Ann Richardson) *Feel No Fear: The Power, Passion, and Politics of a Life in Gymnastics,* New York: Hyperion, 1994.

FURTHER INFORMATION

Books

Jackson, Kenneth T. and Arnold Markoe, *The Scribner Encyclopedia of American Lives: Sports Figures,* New York: Charles Scribner's Sons, 2002.
Karolyi, Bela, John Powers, and Mary Lou Retton, *Mary Lou: Creating an Olympic Champion,* New York: McGraw-Hill, 1986.

Periodicals

Newsweek, August 5, 1996, p. 40.
Publishers Weekly, March 28, 1994, p. 76.
Sports Illustrated, April 3, 2000, p. 88.

Sketch by G. Cooksey

Ekaterina Karsten

Ekaterina Karsten
1972-

Belarussian rower

Ekaterina Karsten is a champion rower who has won three World Championship medals and three Olympic medals. A native of Belarus, Karsten started competing professionally for the Soviet Union. However, in 1996 she became the first athlete to win an Olympic medal, particularly a gold medal, for the newly independent state of Belarus. Her success in rowing has made her a national hero. Karsten repeated her Olympic gold medal performance in 2000, winning the single sculls competition by only one tenth of a second.

Ekaterina Karsten was born Ekaterina Khodotovich on June 2, 1972 in Osetcheno, Belarus, which then was a republic of the Soviet Union. Osetcheno is a rural community about fifty miles from Minsk, the capital of Belarus. Karsten, popularly known as Katya, was the youngest of seven children who grew up on a farm. She was not especially interested in sports as a young child. When she was fifteen years old, she was approached by her gym coach to consider taking up rowing. The school had received a letter from the Minsk School of Rowing to scout "tall, healthy girls" for the republic's rowing team. Karsten was six feet tall and weighted 172 pounds, so she caught the attention of her gym teacher. Her gym teacher spoke with her parents about the opportunity to become a state-sponsored athlete and they agreed to let Karsten move to Minsk.

Quickly Became a National Champion

It only took two years for Karsten to become a national champion. In 1989, at the age of seventeen, Karsten won a gold medal at the Belarussian Junior Championships. A year later she won first place for single sculls at the All Soviet Union Championships and the Junior World Championships. In 1991 she won a bronze medal for double sculls at the World Championships. This was the last year she competed for the Soviet Union because the union of nations broke up after the fall of communism in Europe in the early 1990s.

Karsten made her Olympic debut in 1992 in Barcelona, Spain. She competed as a member of the Unified Team of Soviet States and she won a bronze medal in the quad scull. Karsten continued to compete after the 1992 Olympics, but she did not win any championships. In 1993 she placed seventh in the double sculls at the World Championships, and the following year she finished fifth in the same event. In 1995 Karsten finished seventh in the single sculls at the World Championships.

First Olympic Hero for Belarus

Karsten was prepared for her next Olympic appearance in Atlanta, Georgia in 1996. At the age of twenty-four she took first place in the single sculls competition. This time she was competing for the independent nation of Belarus and she won the first gold medal for the new country. In the final she defeated Silken Laumann, who was the fa-

Chronology

1972	Born on June 2 in Osetcheno, Belarus
1987	Begins training at the Minsk School of Rowing
1989	Wins Belarussian Junior Championships
1990	Wins Junior World Championships
1992	Wins bronze medal in Olympics as member of the Unified Team of Soviet States
1996	Wins gold medal in Olympics as member of Belarussian team
1997	Wins World Championship in single sculls
1998	Marries Wilfred Karsten
1998	Gives birth to Alexandra
1999	Wins World Championship in single sculls
2000	Wins gold medal in Olympics in single sculls
2002	Wins silver medal in World Championships in single sculls

Awards and Accomplishments

1989	Gold medal, Belarussian Junior Championship
1990	Gold medal, single sculls, All Soviet Union Championships
1990	Gold medal, single sculls, Junior World Championships
1991	Bronze medal, double sculls, World Championships
1992	Bronze medal, quad sculls, Olympic Games
1993	Finished seventh, double sculls, World Championships
1994	Finished fifth, double sculls, World Championships
1995	Finished seventh, single sculls, World Championships
1996	Gold medal, single sculls, Olympic Games
1997	Overall champion, single sculls, Rowing World Cup
1997	Gold medal, single sculls, World Championships
1999	Gold medal, single sculls, World Championships
1999	Gold medal, single sculls, Rowing World Cup, Lucerne, Switzerland
2000	Gold medal, single sculls, Olympic Games
2000	Gold medal, single sculls, Rowing World Cup, Munich, Germany
2000	Gold medal, single sculls, Rowing World Cup, Lucerne, Switzerland
2001	First place, single sprint, Head of the Charles Regatta
2001	Gold medal, single sculls, Rowing World Cup, Seville, Spain
2001	Gold medal, single sculls, Rowing World Cup, Vienna, Austria
2001	Gold medal, single sculls, Rowing World Cup, Munich, Germany
2001	Silver medal, double sculls, Rowing World Cup, Munich, Germany
2001	Bronze medal, single sculls, World Championships
2001	Bronze medal, double sculls, World Championships
2002	Gold medal, single sculls, Rowing World Cup
2002	Silver medal, single sculls, World Championships
2002	Bronze medal, quad sculls, World Championships

vorite from Canada. Karsten returned to her home country as a national hero. She was welcomed not only with public recognition, but also with rewards, such as assistance buying an apartment, which was a luxury at that time.

Karsten's celebration was cut short when only six months later her father, her biggest supporter, was killed in a car crash. However, Karsten was able to overcome her grief and continue training for her best year yet. In 1997 Karsten won a gold medal in the single sculls at the World Championships. She also won World Cup regattas at Lucerne, Paris, and Munich, which led to her victory as overall champion in the single sculls at the World Cup.

Karsten took a break from rowing in 1998 to marry Wilfred Karsten of Potsdam, Germany. On May 12, 1998 she gave birth to her daughter, Alexandra. By December of 1998 Karsten returned to training. She and her family now lived in Potsdam, but she split her training time between Minsk and Potsdam. She retained her Belarussian coach, Anatoliy Kviatkovskiy, who traveled twelve hours from Minsk to Potsdam once a month to check up on Karsten. Karsten found it difficult to maintain her training regiment after having a baby and she considered retiring from rowing. However, she did not give up and she won yet another World Championship in single sculls in 1999. She also set a world-best time of seven minutes and 11.68 seconds.

Close Finish

In 2000 Karsten made her third Olympic appearance in Sydney, Australia at the age of 28. The reigning World Champion was favored to win the single scull competition, but Bulgarian Rumyana Neykova did not make it easy for her to win. Neykova led the final race until the final 300 meters when Karsten made a strong dash for the finish. The two rowers were tied with only 150 meters left in the race and they seemed to finish at the same time. The race judges had to review tapes and photos of the finish to determine the winner. "Two women waged war for just under 7½ gut-wrenching minutes yesterday, but it took three times as long to separate the victor from the vanquished," wrote Michael

Horan of the *Sunday Mail* on September 24, 2000. After twenty-three minutes of deliberation, the judges announced that Karsten had won by only one tenth of one second. With this victory Karsten won her second consecutive Olympic gold medal for Belarus.

Karsten continued to compete internationally after the 2000 Olympics. In 2001 she won the single sculls World Cup races in Seville, Vienna, and Munich. She finished third in the single sculls World Championships in 2001 and second in 2002, where she was defeated by Neykova, her rival from the Olympics. Karsten is expected to compete in her fourth Olympic Games in Athens, Greece in 2004.

CONTACT INFORMATION

Address: FISA Headquarters, Av. de Cour 135, Case Postale 18, 1000 Lausanne 3, Switzerland. Phone: (41) 21-617-8373.

FURTHER INFORMATION

Periodicals

Chamberlain, Tony. "Party's Over for Olympic Champ." *Boston Globe* (October 19, 2000): E1.

Guinness, Rupert. "Like Water for Chocoladovitch." *Weekend Australian* (August 5, 2000): S14.

Horan, Michael. "0.01 The Margin." *Sunday Mail* (South Africa) (September 24, 2000): L14.

Other

2001 Head of the Charles Regatta. http://www.boston. com/sports/head_of_the_charles/news/2001/102201_ us_men.htm (January 20, 2003).

Biography Resource Center Online. http://www.galenet. com (January 20, 2003).

CNNSI.com - Olympic Sports. http://sportsillustrated. cnn.com/olympics/news/2000/03/28/olympic_bio_ khodotovich (January 20, 2003).

FISA - The Official World Rowing Web Site. http:// www.worldrowing.com (January 31, 2003).

International Olympic Committee. http://www.olympic. org (January 20, 2003).

Sydney Games. http://www.olympics.smh.com/au/ rowing/2000/09/23/FFXBVZOCGDC.html (January 31, 2003).

Thames World Sculling Challenge. http://www.twsc. rowing.org.uk/karsten.html (January 20, 2003).

Sketch by Janet P. Stamatel

Jim Kelly

Jim Kelly
1960-

American football player

Although Jim Kelly led his team, the Buffalo Bills, to a record-setting four consecutive Super Bowls, he never won the NFL's championship game. Kelly's standing in the eyes of his colleagues and fans, however, was never affected by his failure to win the big game. His record on the field and off was nearly universally respected. Born outside Pittsburgh in an area known for producing legendary quarterbacks, **Joe Namath** and **Johnny Unitas** were among the many, greatness was Kelly's dream from the beginning.

Born James Edward Kelly on February 14, 1960, in East Brady, Pennsylvania, he was the fourth of six sons. His father, a machinist, often held multiple jobs in order to provide for his family. Although money was tight, Kelly learned the value of hard work and soon began contributing with the money he earned cutting grass and shoveling snow. Typical young boys, the Kelly's played sports year round and eventually five of the six would go on to play college football.

Early Excellence

Kelly excelled almost immediately. At the age of ten he nearly won the national Punt, Pass and Kick competi-tion. In high school, he was a star on both the basketball and football teams. He led the football team at East Brady High to two state championships and had his jersey retired after graduation. Although he was recruited by Penn State's legendary coach **Joe Paterno**, Kelly chose the University of Miami where he would be able to play quarterback rather than linebacker, which Paterno had suggested.

Once at Miami, it didn't take very long for Kelly to assert himself. Ironically, his first start, in the eighth game of his first season, came against his hometown favorite Penn State. After leading his team to a 26-10 upset, Kelly was made starting quarterback the following year. Kelly led his team successfully and in his senior season was in the running for the Heisman Trophy.

The Class of 1983

Selected fourteenth in the first round of the famed 1983 National Football League (NFL) draft, Kelly was not pleased with the prospect of playing in Buffalo. He instead chose to play for the Houston Gamblers of the United States Football League (USFL), a new spring football league competing with the NFL. In Houston, Kelly benefited from a pass-oriented offense and went on to win the USFL's Most Valuable Player (MVP) award in 1984. When the USFL went out of business in 1986, Kelly reluctantly signed with the Bills after being offered the biggest contract in the NFL.

Kelly received a warm welcome in Buffalo but despite his performance on the field the team endured an-

Career Statistics

				Passing				
Yr	Team	Att	Com	Yds	COM%	TD	INT	RAT
1986	BUF	480	285	3593	59.4	22	17	83.3
1987	BUF	419	250	2798	59.7	19	11	83.8
1988	BUF	452	269	3380	59.5	15	17	78.2
1989	BUF	391	228	3130	58.3	25	18	86.2
1990	BUF	346	219	2829	63.3	24	9	101.2
1991	BUF	474	304	3844	64.1	33	17	97.6
1992	BUF	462	269	3457	58.2	23	19	81.2
1993	BUF	470	288	3382	61.3	18	18	79.9
1994	BUF	448	285	3114	63.6	22	17	84.6
1995	BUF	458	255	3130	55.7	22	13	81.1
1996	BUF	379	222	2810	58.6	14	19	73.2
TOTAL		4779	2874	35467	60.1	237	175	84.4

BUF: Buffalo Bills.

Chronology

1960	Born February 14 in East Brady, Pennsylvania
1979	Starts in his eighth game at the University of Miami
1980	Leads team to Peach Bowl appearance
1983	Drafted by the Buffalo Bills, but signs with Houston Gamblers of USFL
1984	Named USFL's Most Valuable Player
1986	Signs with the Buffalo Bills
1987	Named All-Pro
1988	Leads team to AFC East division title
1990	Leads Buffalo to first ever Super Bowl
1991	Makes second Super Bowl appearance
1992	Leads team to third Super Bowl
1993	Leads Buffalo to record setting fourth consecutive Super Bowl
1996	Retires after disappointing season
1997	Son is born with rare Krabbe's Disease
2002	Inducted into Pro Football Hall of Fame

Awards and Accomplishments

1983	Selected in first round of NFL draft
1984	Named USFL Most Valuable Player
1988-89, 1991-93	Selected to Pro Bowl
1990-93	Wins AFC Championship
1990-93	Played in Super Bowl
2002	Inducted Pro Football Hall of Fame

other losing season. After hiring Marv Levy to coach both the Bills and Kelly would improve and begin to contend. In 1988, the Bills went 12-4 and won the AFC East division title. Kelly's performance that season wasn't his best but he led his team to the American Football Conference (AFC) championship before losing to the Cincinnati Bengals. The following season was riddled by mediocrity and injury for the Bills and Kelly. Buffalo's fans became frustrated with Kelly and the team was in disarray. The trouble of the 1989 season subsided in 1990 when the Bills had their best season ever and their first trip to the Super Bowl. Kelly's Super Bowl dreams were dashed when Bills' kicker Scott Norwood missed a 47-yard field goal with four seconds left and the Bills lost to the New York Giants, 20-19.

So Close, So Far

The Bills' would go on a record setting streak of four consecutive Super Bowl appearances in the early 1990's. In his second Super Bowl appearance, Kelly threw four interceptions and the Bills lost to the Washington Redskins, 37-24. The following year, the Bills weren't as dominant but an improbable playoff run led them back to the Super Bowl. An injury sidelined Kelly but he returned to play in the AFC championship game and then the Super Bowl where the Dallas Cowboys handed the Bills a humiliating loss, 52-17. In 1993, the Bills made history becoming the first team in major professional sports to lose four straight years in a championship game. The game also made history for being the first Super Bowl rematch. The defending Dallas Cowboys soundly defeated Buffalo, 30-13. Despite leading the league in completion percentage the next year, the Bills failed to make the playoffs. The final two years of his career were riddled by injury and disappointment. Kelly retired a Buffalo Bill in 1996.

Retirement and Beyond

He worked the 1997 season as a broadcaster for NBC. He also had his first child in 1997. His son, Hunter James Kelly, was born with Krabbe's Disease, a rare disorder that affects the brain and usually leads to an early death. Kelly redirected his focus and formed an organization to raise money for research for the disease. He and his wife Kelly also have a daughter, Erin.

Kelly briefly considered returning to the NFL in 1998 with the Baltimore Ravens, a decision influenced by a desire to raise money for Hunter's Hope, his research foundation. He remained retired, however, and close to his family. Kelly was inducted into the Pro Football Hall of Fame in 2002.

Although Kelly never became a Super Bowl champion his performance on and off the field earned him the respect of his fans and colleagues. A hard-nosed player who had to endure his share of criticism and failure, Kelly never succumbed to the pressures of the NFL. He led a floundering franchise to the promise land and kept them there for many years.

FURTHER INFORMATION

Books

Newsmakers. Detroit: Gale Group, 1991.

Periodicals

"A New Namath, but with Knees." *Sports Illustrated* (September 15, 1986): 40.

"Back in the Fast Lane." *Sports Illustrated* (November 18, 1996): 86.

"Bills' Kelly to Announce his Retirement on Friday." *New York Daily News* (January 29, 1997).

"Even Today, You Can't Dismiss the Class of '83." *Sporting News* (April 29, 1996): 14.

"Frozen Buffalo Warms Up to Jim Kelly." Knight Ridder/Tribune News Service (January 21, 1994).

"Hall of a Day for 2002 Inductees." *Akron Beacon Journal* (August 3, 2002).

"He Won't Let it Buffalo Him." *Sports Illustrated* (September 7, 1992): 88.

"Jim Kelly." *Sport* (January 1992): 22.

"Jim Kelly Likes Arm, Bills." *New York Daily News* (June 27, 1996).

"Jim Kelly Offers Words of Inspiration at Hall of Fame Induction." *Akron Beacon Journal* (August 3,2002).

"Jim Kelly was the show on Hall of Fame Day." *Miami Herald* (August 3, 2002).

"Life with Lord Jim." *Sports Illustrated* (July 21, 1986): 58.

"Nice Month, Jim." *Sports Illustrated* (October 7, 1991): 86.

"The Class of '83." *Sports Illustrated* (February 10, 1999): 14.

Sketch by Aric Karpinski

Shawn Kemp
1969-

American basketball player

Shawn Kemp

When Shawn Kemp was drafted by the Seattle Supersonics in 1989, he became the fifth player to go directly to the NBA from high school. His exceptional talent and fierce presence on the court drew comparisons to **Michael Jordan**, but Kemp's youth was seen as a serious obstacle to his ever reaching superstar status. In a few years the young forward proved that he was indeed All-Star material. His screaming slam dunks and dramatic blocks were loved by fans. But the pressure of being in the media spotlight also increased. Personal problems have haunted Kemp and his level of play has been inconsistent. In 1997 he was traded to the Cleveland Cavaliers, where he had limited playing time and gained some twenty-five pounds by the end of his three-season stay. Kemp became a Portland Trailblazer in 2000, after which he voluntarily entered a drug rehabilitation program. In 2002 Kemp gave up $20 million to start for the Orlando Magic.

Kemp learned early on that talent and fame are not antidotes to adversity. Growing up in Elkhart, Indiana, he was raised by his mother Barbara and became determined to excel at basketball. As a high school star at Concord High, NBA scouts started coming to his games when he was in the tenth grade. However, Kemp was not preparing himself for the academic demands of college life. He was given a scholarship to the University of Kentucky, but his low score on the SAT exam made him ineligible to play as a freshman. He left the school before he had a chance to play, after getting caught but not

Career Statistics

Yr	Team	GP	PTS	FG%	3P%	FT%	RPG	APG	SPG	BPG	TO	PF
1989-90	SEA	81	525	.479	.167	.736	4.3	0.3	0.6	0.9	107	204
1990-91	SEA	81	1214	.508	.167	.661	8.4	1.8	1.0	1.5	202	319
1991-92	SEA	64	994	.504	.000	.748	10.4	1.3	1.1	1.9	156	261
1992-93	SEA	78	1388	.492	.000	.712	10.7	2.0	1.5	1.9	217	327
1993-94	SEA	79	1431	.538	.250	.741	10.8	2.6	1.8	2.1	259	312
1994-95	SEA	82	1530	.547	.286	.749	10.9	1.8	1.2	1.5	259	337
1995-96	SEA	79	1550	.561	.417	.742	11.4	2.2	1.2	1.6	315	299
1996-97	SEA	81	1516	.510	.364	.742	10.0	1.9	1.5	1.0	280	320
1997-98	CLE	80	1442	.445	.250	.727	9.3	2.5	1.4	1.1	271	310
1998-99	CLE	42	862	.482	.500	.789	9.2	2.4	1.1	1.1	127	159
1999-00	CLE	82	1463	.417	.333	.776	8.8	1.7	1.2	1.2	291	371
2000-01	POR	68	441	.407	.364	.771	3.8	1.0	0.7	0.3	99	184
2001-02	POR	75	454	.430	.000	.794	3.8	0.7	0.6	0.4	81	184
TOTAL		972	14810	.491	.280	.741	8.6	1.7	1.2	1.3	2664	3587

CLE: Cleveland Cavaliers; POR: Portland Trailblazers; SEA: Seattle SuperSonics.

charged for selling stolen jewelry that belonged to the coach's son.

Kemp briefly attended Trinity Valley Community College in Athens, Texas before he entered the 1989 NBA draft. As a first round pick for the Seattle SuperSonics, he became a professional basketball player at age nineteen. The young forward was considered well suited to the NBA's style of play, but he faced the daunting prospect of learning the game in front of a vast, critical audience. He needed to do more than his trademark dunks. Kemp worked exceptionally hard as a rookie and was rewarded in 1990, when the Sonics traded Xavier McDaniel and gave him the position of starting power forward. He flourished in this role, and during the 1992-93 season was named an All-Star for the first time. That year he averaged almost eighteen points and eleven rebounds per game.

Soon Kemp was being compared to Michael Jordan, someone who has routinely been described as the greatest basketball player of all time. In a 1992 article for *Sport,* Mike Kahn remarked, "The natural strength, quickness and jumping, plus the daunting expressions after a particularly impressive move, all bear a striking resemblance to Michael Jordan." Jordan himself saw the resemblance, and agreed that Kemp showed a remarkable talent and creative sense. Amidst such heady comments, Kemp escaped injury twice and was made to realize that he had nothing to fall back on if he didn't succeed in basketball.

Kemp became an extremely popular player in Seattle. However, after the team lost to the Denver Nuggets in the first round of the 1993-94 season playoffs, he was almost traded to the Chicago Bulls. The discovery hurt Kemp's relationship with the Sonics. He also was unhappy that he was still branded a bad character because of his behavior at Kentucky. He complained that the press ignored more positive aspects of his life, such as the basketball camps he ran in Elkhart. In 1996 the Sonics lost to

Chicago in the NBA finals. Following this disappointment, Kemp's next season was punctuated with reports that he was always late and had problems with alcohol.

In 1997 Kemp was traded to the Cleveland Cavaliers, signing a contract worth $107 million over seven years. During his second season with the Cavs, Kemp accumulated a career-high average of 20.5 points per game. In 1999 he led his team in scoring and blocked shots. At the same time, however, negative reports about Kemp's personal life continued to appear. A 1999 *Sports Illustrated* story asserted that Kemp had fathered seven children with six women. Other coverage that year speculated that the forward, who had recently been listed as weighing 256 pounds, had ballooned to some 300 pounds. The most damaging concern, however, was the issue of drug use. After being traded to the Portland Trailblazers in 2000, Kemp ended his season ahead of schedule in order to check into a drug rehabilitation program for cocaine abuse. Less than a year later, he would be suspended for five games for not complying with his aftercare agreement.

In 2002 Kemp hoped to find more playing time with the Orlando Magic and gave up some $20 million to leave Portland, where he played behind Rasheed Wallace. He signed a $1.03 million, one-year deal with the Magic, accepting the league minimum for a player with ten years of experience. The move gave Kemp a chance to straighten out his career while, at age thirty-two, he denied being interested in retirement. Orlando desperately needed a strong inside player, making it a critical partnership for both the team and Kemp. The team, however, was making only a brief commitment to Kemp, while his career was on the line.

Kemp has proven that he is one of the most talented players to star in the NBA. Initially criticized for not having a game beyond slam dunks, he developed into a scoring and rebounding leader. As his coach with the

SuperSonics, George Carl judged that he was among the top five players in the league. Others compared his playing style to that of Michael Jordan. But Kemp began his NBA career under the shadow of his SAT failure and alleged theft involvement and has yet to shake the image of being a problem player. Anger and resentment are said to be some of the great motivating factors in his career. In Orlando he is faced with the multiple challenge of staying away from drugs and surviving media scrutiny of the process. Once again Shawn Kemp is being asked if he has what it takes to make it in the NBA.

CONTACT INFORMATION

Address: Orlando Magic, Orlando Arena, 1 Magic Place, Orlando, FL 32801. Online: www.reignman.com.

FURTHER INFORMATION

Books

Newsmakers 1995, Issue 4. Detroit: Gale Group, 1995.

Periodicals

Ballard, Chris. "10 Orlando Magic: Thinner in the wallet but still hefty in the waistline, Shawn Kemp seems ill-equipped to carry this center-starved franchise." *Sports Illustrated* (October 28, 2002): 114.

"Father of 7 Children by 6 Women, Shawn Kemp Admits 'Wrong.'" *Jet* (February 22, 1999): 37.

Kahn, Mike. "Super Sonic: In his third season in the NBA, 22-year-old Shawn Kemp has proven he belongs." *Sport* (March 1992): 88.

Keown, Tim. "Reign man." *Sports Illustrated* (February 19, 1996): 70.

Kiersh, Edward. "Sonic Boom: Seattle's Shawn Kemp has thundered onto the NBA scene." *Sport* (June 1994): 48.

MacMullan, Jackie. "Turning the page." *Sports Illustrated* (April 20, 1998): 86.

Scanlon, Dick. "Money's No Object." *The Ledger (Lakeland, FL)* (September 10, 2002): C1.

Taylor, Phil. "The late show." *Sports Illustrated* (April 14, 1997): 34.

Other

"Kemp's signing is low risk, high upside for Magic." Associated Press State & Local Wire (September 6, 2002).

Shawn Kemp Player Info. NBA.com. http://www.nba.com/playerfile/shawn_kemp/ (December 7, 2002).

Sketch by Paula Pyzik Scott

Nancy Kerrigan
1969-

American figure skater

Nancy Kerrigan was born on October 13, 1969 in Stoneham, Massachusetts, where she was raised along with her two older brothers by her parents, Dan and Brenda Kerrigan. When she was one year old, her mother was struck by a rare illness that left her almost completely blind. Kerrigan began skating when she was six years old, taking group lessons at a nearby ice rink. The instructor quickly assessed Kerrigan's exceptional talent and suggested to her parents that they consider private lessons for her.

Early Years on Ice

To afford the expensive private skating lessons, Kerrigan's father, a welder at a local food plant, took on an extra job as a maintenance man in the evening. Due to his wife's physical limitations, he also managed many of the household and family affairs. Eventually he would take out substantial loans to keep his daughter's skating career afloat. Never pressured by her parents to skate, Kerrigan enjoyed the support of a large extended family that lived nearby and also helped with lessons and transportation.

Kerrigan's day started at four o'clock in the morning, roused out of bed by her mother who would always eat breakfast with her. Her father drove her to her five o'clock early morning lessons, often staying to drive

<table>
<tr><td>

Chronology

1969	Born in Massachusetts
1974	Begins skating
1994	Attacked during practice for the national championships, planned by Tonya Harding's former husband; turns pro after Olympics
1995	Marries her agent, Jerry Soloman
1996	Gives birth to son, Matthew
1998	Appears on Fox television show with Harding

</td></tr>
</table>

the Zamboni to prepare the ice. Kerrigan, who was drawn to the more athletic skating performances of the male skaters she watched on television, thrived on the physical dimensions of skating. After her instructors taught her how to skate without leaning over like her hockey-playing brothers, Kerrigan focused on speed and strength in her routines.

Kerrigan entered her first competition when she was eight years old. Because of her constant training schedule during her youth, she missed out on many social activities and found it difficult to develop close friendships simply because she spent so much time on the ice. Yet Kerrigan loved to skate, and her determination and commitment soon began to pay off. She landed her first triple-triple (two consecutive triple toe loops) in practice when she was 14 years old, successfully completing the jump for the first time in competition the following year. Having mastered the difficult combination not attempted by other women skaters at the time, Kerrigan began to realize that she could become an exceptional skater.

Winning Ways

In 1985 Kerrigan finished second at the Eastern Junior Regionals, and in 1987 she placed fourth at the National Junior Championships. After graduating from Stoneham High School, she enrolled at nearby Emmanuel College, from which she received an associate's degree. In 1988 19-year-old Kerrigan won the National Collegiate Championships, as well as three other competitions. In the same year she finished twelfth in her first appearance at the U.S. Figure Skating Championships. In 1989 she took first place in the New England and the Eastern Regionals, and finished fifth at the U.S. Championships. Winning a bronze medal at the 1989 U.S. Olympic Festival, Kerrigan returned to take the gold in 1990.

Continuing her ascent up the rankings, Kerrigan finished fourth, third, and second at the U.S. Championships in 1990, 1991, and 1992, respectively. Her second-place finish in 1992 earned her a place on the U.S. Olympic team, along with winner **Kristi Yamaguchi** and third-place winner **Tonya Harding**. The 1992 Olympics, held in Albertville, France, was billed as a showdown between Yamaguchi and Japan's Midori Ito. Nonetheless, Kerrigan

made her presence known by finishing the short program in second, behind Yamaguchi. Both Yamaguchi and Kerrigan made mistakes in their long programs, but Yamaguchi held on to win the gold medal, with Ito second, and Kerrigan taking the bronze medal.

When Yamaguchi announced that she was turning professional, Kerrigan became the top-ranked skater in the nation and proved her standing by winning the U.S. Championships in 1993. Attracting national attention, she was named by *People* magazine as one of the fifty most beautiful celebrities, and she was beginning to garner endorsement contracts that would finally make her skating pay off financially. However, feeling the pressure of her standing and her new role as a media darling, Kerrigan began to falter. In 1993 at the World Championships in Prague, Kerrigan, favored to win, was in first place after the short program, but she fell apart in the long program. Missing her first jump, she lost concentration and turned two triple jumps into unimpressive singles. She finished ninth in the long program and fifth overall. It was a devastating loss for Kerrigan, who sobbed in defeat after the competition.

Attacked

Determined to return to form, Kerrigan recommitted herself to long, arduous practices. She was soon back in form, winning two major competitions before the end of the year (the Piruetten in Norway and the AT&T Pro Am in the United States). Stepping onto the ice at the U.S. Championships, Kerrigan was overwhelmingly favored to defend her title. Her closest competition was Harding, who skated a very physically challenging routine but lacked Kerrigan's artistic elegance and routinely finished behind her more polished opponent.

What played out at the 1994 U.S. Championships, held in Detroit, Michigan, was one of the most bizarre sporting dramas of all time. Two days prior to the competition, Kerrigan was leaving the practice arena, Cobo Hall, around 2:30 p.m. She walked behind a blue curtain that separated the rink from a hallway leading to the locker rooms. When she stopped to talk briefly to a reporter, a man ran by, crouched down, hit Kerrigan on the knee with a lead pipe, and kept running. Kerrigan fell to the floor in pain and was quickly taken to the hospital. Although she had no broken bones, the damage to her knee cap and quadriceps tendon was severe enough to cause her to withdraw from the U.S. Championships.

In the ensuing investigation, police linked the crime to Harding's former husband, Jeff Gillooly, who had hired two buddies to carry out the attack, supposedly to remove Harding's main competition. (All three served time in jail.) As it turned out, Harding won the championship and was named to the Olympic team. Because Kerrigan did not skate in the nationals, she did not qualify for the Olympics, but the U.S. Figure Skating Association, acknowledging that Kerrigan was the country's best shot at bringing home a gold medal, named her to the team anyway. Kerrigan had six weeks between the championships and the Olympics to rehabilitate her injured knee.

The events surrounding Kerrigan's attack played out in the media headlines for months. Harding denied any direct involvement, and the police could not link her to the crime. As a result she was allowed to remain on the Olympic team, much to the dismay of Kerrigan and her supporters. However, distracted by the overwhelming media attention in the aftermath of the attack, she performed well below her best and was never a challenge to Kerrigan's medal hopes. Later Harding admitted that she learned of the attack shortly after it occurred. She was subsequently banned from the 1994 World Championships and charged with hindering an investigation, for which she received three years of probation.

Silver Medalist

Kerrigan's main competition at the 1994 Olympics was 17-year-old Oksana Baiul from the Ukraine, who had won the 1993 World Championships. Kerrigan, who was continuously surrounded by multiple security guards during the Olympics, won the short program, and although she made a small mistake near the beginning of her free skate, she completed a near-perfect routine. Baiul also made a minor mistake but also otherwise skated flawlessly. In the end, four judges voted for Kerrigan and five voted for Baiul. Kerrigan took the silver medal, missing the gold by a mere one-tenth of a percentage point.

Following the Olympics Kerrigan turned professional and became one of the most successfully marketed athletes ever. Despite never winning an Olympic gold, she was incredibly popular for her gritty determination to return to the ice alongside Harding to take the silver. Kerrigan turned that popularity into millions in endorsements and ice show appearances. She competed for her last medal at the 2000 Goodwill Games, where she took the bronze.

On September 9, 1995, Kerrigan married her agent, Jerry Soloman. She continued to skate, including tours with "Champions on Ice," "Grease on Ice," "Footloose on Ice," and "Halloween on Ice." She recorded a song, "The Distance," which she used during her routine at **Brian Boitano**'s Skating Spectacular in January 2003. In the same year she published an instructional book entitled *Artistry on Ice*. She has also hosted several skating events, including an international competition produced by Lifetime television in 2002. In December 1996 Kerrigan gave birth to a son, Matthew. When he was an infant, he traveled often with his mother, but Kerrigan expects as he ages that she will cut back on her travels to stay home. Kerrigan and Solomon live close to Kerrigan's family in Massachusetts.

Awards and Accomplishments	
1988	Gold medalist, National Collegiate Championships
1989	Gold medalist, New England Senior and Eastern Senior; bronze medalist, World University Games and U.S. Olympic Festival
1990	Gold medalist, U.S. Olympic Festival
1991	Bronze medalist, U.S. Championships, World Championships
1992	Silver medalist, U.S. Championships and World Championships; bronze medalist, Olympics
1993	Gold medalist, U.S. Championships
1994	Silver medalist, Olympics
2000	Bronze medalist, Goodwill Games

In spite of her many attempts to move past the saga of her attack, she is still questioned about it often. In 1998 she agreed to appear for an interview on the Fox network with Harding. The segment was, in itself, bizarre as the two had their first encounter since the Olympics. Kerrigan, who remains convinced that Harding had prior knowledge of the attack, did not receive an apology from Harding. Nonetheless, she has done her best to move on. "Sometimes I think, 'Why do I always have to be linked to something like that?'" she told *The Boston Globe*. "It all seems so bizarre, weird. I don't think about it much, really, until some totally bizarre incident happens and it's in the news all the time and I think, 'I was part of something like that?' It doesn't even seem real to me."

CONTACT INFORMATION

Address: c/o ProServe, 1101 Wilson Boulevard, Suite 1800, Arlington, Virginia 22209. Online: http://www.nancyfans.com.

SELECTED WRITINGS BY KERRIGAN:

(With Steve Woodward) *Nancy Kerrigan: In My Own Words*. New York: Hyperion Paperbacks for Children, 1996.

(With Mary Spencer) *Artistry on Ice: Figure Skating Skills and Style*. Champagne, IL: Human Kinetics, 2003.

FURTHER INFORMATION

Books

Edelson, Paula. *A to Z of American Women in Sports*. New York: Facts on File, Inc., 2002.

Great Women in Sports. Detroit: Visible Ink Press, 1996.

Newsmakers 1994, Issue 4. Detroit: Gale Research, 1994.

St. James Encyclopedia of Popular Culture. 5 vols. Detroit: St. James Press, 2000.

Sports Stars. Series 1-4. Detroit: U•X•L, 1994-98.

Periodicals

Brennan, Christine. "Skater Attacked at Olympic Trials." *The Washington Post,* (January 7, 1994): A1.

Dupont, Kevin Paul. "Fame and Shame." *The Boston Globe,* (January 28, 1998): F1.

"Figure Skater Nancy Kerrigan Glides into Song on New CD." *The Associated Press,* (October 14, 1999).

"Ice Follies." *Entertainment Weekly,* (January 8, 1999): 76.

Knisley, Michael. "In This Sport, Everything Figures." *The Sporting News,* (March 7, 1994): 13-15.

Lane, Randall. "Nancy's Gold." *Forbes,* (March 28, 1994): 20.

"Melting the Ice." *People Weekly,* (January 13, 2003): 125+.

"Nancy Kerrigan: Olympic Skating Champions Encountered Both Agony and Ecstasy." *People Weekly,* (March 15, 1999): 274.

Olympic Medallist Nancy Kerrigan Hosts Lifetime's Coverage of the 2002 ISU Grand Prix of Figure Skating in November and December." *PR Newswire,* (October 30, 2002).

Rosellini, Lynn. "Fighting the Ghosts Within: Nancy Kerrigan's Handlers Wager that Keeping the Olympian in a Cocoon Will Help her Cope." *U.S. News and World Report,* (February 14, 1994): 51-52.

Other

"Nancy Kerrigan." The Official Nancy Kerrigan Fan Site. http://www.nancyfans.com (January 30, 2003).

Sketch by Kari Bethel

Jason Kidd
1973-

American basketball player

W hen Jason Kidd was traded from the powerhouse Phoenix Suns to the woebegone New Jersey Nets in June 2001, many seasoned basketball observers predicted the move would be the beginning of the end for Kidd's career on the court. Kidd proved them all wrong, when he reinvigorated the Nets, powering the team's march to the NBA championship game in 2002. Quite a feat for a team that had enjoyed only three winning seasons since 1984-1985. Making Kidd's accomplishment all the more impressive was the fact that he did it under a cloud of bad publicity related to his January 2001 arrest on charges of punching his wife in the face during a domestic dispute. Kidd came back even stronger in 2002-2003. As of December 31, 2002, the Nets stood at the top of the Atlantic

Jason Kidd

Division of the National Basketball Association's (NBA) Eastern Conference, with a record of 23-9. The Nets led the division by 3½ games over its closest rival, the Boston Celtics. At the same point in the season, Kidd was averaging about twenty-one points per game (PPG), up sharply from 14.7 PPG the previous season.

Born in San Francisco

He was born Jason Fredrick Kidd in San Francisco, California, on March 23, 1973. The product of an interracial marriage, Kidd is the son of Steve, an African American who worked his way up through the ranks at TWA from baggage handler to ticket counter supervisor, and Anne Kidd, a white computer programmer for the Bank of America. Although his parents later divorced, they remained on amicable terms until Steve's death in 1999. Kidd grew up in Alameda, a solidly middle-class suburb of Oakland. While still quite young, he became interested in soccer but by the time he entered third grade he had switched his allegiances to basketball and spent most of his free time playing the game with older boys. It was during this period that Kidd developed his strong passing skills. To ensure that he was invited back to play, he made sure to get the ball to his older teammates for easy scores.

Kidd had developed into a local scoring sensation by the time he entered high school at St. Joseph's of Notre Dame in Alameda. During his high school basketball career, he averaged twenty-five points, ten assists, seven

Chronology

1973	Born March 23 in San Francisco, California
1992-94	Attends University of California, Berkeley
1994	Picked by Dallas Mavericks in NBA draft
1996	Traded by Mavericks to Phoenix Suns
1997	Marries Joumana Samaha
2001	Arrested in January on charges of punching his wife in the face
2001	Traded by Suns to New Jersey Nets

Awards and Accomplishments

1991-92	Naismith Award as nation's top high school player
1991-92	Named High School Player of the Year by *USA Today* and *Parade*
1992-93	All-Pac-10 team
1993-94	Pac-10 Player of the Year
1994-95	NBA Co-rookie of the Year (with Grant Hill)
1996, 1998, **2000-02**	NBA All-Star
1997-98	Topped 700 assists and 500 rebounds in a single season
1998-99	Led NBA in assists
1999-00	Led NBA in assists
2000	Gold medal at Olympic Games in Sydney
2000-01	Led NBA in assists

rebounds, and seven steals per game and led his team to back-to-back California Division I championships. As a senior he was named High School Player of the Year by both *USA Today* and *Parade* magazine. After graduating from high school, Kidd enrolled at the University of California in nearby Berkeley. As a freshman he averaged thirteen points, 7.7 assists, and 4.9 rebounds per game, good enough to earn him a berth on the All-Pac-10 team. In his sophomore year, Kidd averaged 16.7 points, 6.9 rebounds, and 9.1 assists per game and was named Pac-10 Player of the Year, becoming the first sophomore ever to win this honor.

Drafted by the Dallas Mavericks

In the wake of his strong performance as a college sophomore, Kidd declared himself eligible for the 1994 NBA draft. The hapless Dallas Mavericks, a lackluster team for much of its history, were looking for a strong point guard prospect and selected Kidd second overall in the draft. It proved an inspired choice for the Mavericks, as Kidd, working with Jamal Mashburn at forward and Jimmy Jackson at shooting guard, quickly turned around the team's fortunes. However, an injury sidelining Jackson for the second half of the season put an end to the team's hopes for a playoff berth. For his first season in the NBA, Kidd averaged 11.7 points, 5.4 rebounds, and 7.7 assists and was named NBA Rookie of the Year.

Kidd came back even stronger for his second season with the Mavs, averaging 16.6 points, 6.8 rebounds, and 9.7 assists per game. But he also began to earn a reputation as a disruptive influence, refusing to speak to teammate Jimmy Jackson for six weeks after the two had an argument. Kidd also feuded with new Mavericks coach Jim Cleamons. He played only the first twenty-two games of the 1996-1997 season with Dallas before being traded to the Phoenix Suns. It was Kidd's inability to get along with new Mavericks coach Jim Cleamons that triggered the decision by Dallas management to trade Kidd to the Phoenix Suns. When the team's new owners fired former coach Dick Motta and replaced him with Cleamons, Kidd complained that he should have been consulted about the coaching change. Not long after Cleamons arrived in Dallas, he and Kidd had an argument, following which Kidd refused to speak to the coach for two months.

An injury in his very first game with the Suns sidelined him for the next twenty-one games, but he came back strong in the final thirty-two games of the season to lead Phoenix into the playoffs, where the team lost to the Seattle Supersonics. Averaging 11.6 points, 6.2 rebounds, and 9.1 assists per game, Kidd helped the Suns to reach the playoffs once again in 1997-1998.

Leads NBA in Assists

Kidd became the first Phoenix player ever to lead the NBA in assists during the 1998-1999 season, averaging 10.8 per game. His performance powered another Suns' trip to the finals. He once again topped the NBA in assists per game in the 1999-2000 season, averaging 10.1. Although he suffered an ankle injury late in the season, he returned in time to help his team beat the San Antonio Spurs in the first round of the playoffs. The Suns, however, lost to the Los Angeles Lakers in the Western Conference semifinals.

During the 2000-2001 season, Kidd led the NBA in assists for the third consecutive season, averaging 9.8 per game, and earning for the Suns another berth in the playoffs. But it was Kidd's personal life that earned him the most publicity during this period. In January 2001 he was arrested on charges of striking his wife, Joumana, in the face. Kidd and his wife quickly reconciled, but the after-effects of the case had a major impact on Kidd's career. It was a key factor in the Suns' decision to trade Kidd to the Nets, a move that many believed would sound the death knell for his career.

Vows to Take Nets to Playoffs

Determined to make the best of his trade to the Nets, Kidd boldly vowed to take the down-on-their-luck Nets to the playoffs in 2001-2002. Most of his teammates on the Nets, as well as the team's fans, were doubtful, but Kidd delivered, leading his new team to the NBA finals. Even though they were roundly defeated by the Lakers in the finals, it was a stellar achievement for a team that had only once made it past the first round of the playoffs.

Career Statistics

Yr	Team	GP	PTS	FG%	3P%	FT%	RPG	APG	SPG	BPG
1994-95	DAL	79	11.7	38.5	27.2	69.8	5.4	7.7	1.9	.30
1995-96	DAL	81	16.6	38.1	33.6	69.2	6.8	9.7	2.2	.32
1996-97	DAL	22	9.9	36.9	32.3	66.7	4.1	9.1	2.1	.36
1996-97	PHO	33	11.6	42.3	40.0	68.8	4.8	9.0	2.4	.36
1997-98	PHO	82	11.6	41.6	31.3	79.9	6.2	9.1	1.9	.32
1998-99	PHO	50	16.9	44.4	36.6	75.7	6.8	10.8	2.3	.38
1999-00	PHO	67	14.3	40.9	33.7	82.9	7.2	10.1	2.0	.42
2000-01	PHO	77	16.9	41.1	29.7	81.4	6.4	9.8	2.2	.30
2001-02	NJN	82	14.7	39.1	32.1	81.4	7.3	9.9	2.1	.24
TOTAL		573	13.8	40.3	32.9	75.1	6.1	9.5	2.1	.33

DAL: Dallas Mavericks; NJN: New Jersey Nets; PHO: Phoenix Suns.

With Kidd firmly established as the Nets' leader, the team seemed almost certain to make it into the playoffs again in 2002-2003. However, whatever the outcome for the season may be, Kidd has made it clear that he's far from washed up in basketball. Barring injury, he's likely to remain a major force in pro ball for years to come.

CONTACT INFORMATION

Address: Jason Kidd, c/o New Jersey Nets, 390 Murray Hill Pkwy., East Rutherford, NJ 07073.

FURTHER INFORMATION

Books

"James Mitchell Cleamons." *Who's Who Among African Americans,* 14th ed. Detroit: Gale Group, 2001.

"Jason Kidd." *Sports Stars,* Series 1-4. Detroit: U•X•L, 1994-1998.

Periodicals

Iannazzone, Al. "No Kidding—Jason Getting Even Better." *Record* (Bergen County, NJ) (December 21, 2002): SO1.

Tejada, Justin. "Point Man Jason Kidd Helped Turn the Woeful New Jersey Nets into a Topflight Team. But He Had to Get His Own Act Together First." *Sports Illustrated for Kids* (November 1, 2002): 27.

Other

"#5, Jason Kidd." ESPN.com. http://sports.espn.go.com/nba/players/statistics?statsId=2625 (January 1, 2003).

"Jason Kidd, #5." NBA.com. http://test.nba.com/playerfile/jason_kidd/ (January 1, 2003).

"Jason Kidd: Bio." JockBio.com. http://www.jockbio.com/Bios/Kidd/Kidd_bio.html (January 1, 2003).

"Jason Kidd: Facts." JockBio.com. http://www.jockbio.com/Bios/Kidd/Kidd_numbers.html (January 1, 2003).

"Jason Kidd: What Others Say." JockBio.com. http://www.jockbio.com/Bios/Kidd/Kidd_quotes.html (January 1, 2003).

"Player Profile: Jason Kidd." NBA.com. http://www.chicagobulls.com/playerfile/jason_kidd/printable_player_files.html (January 1, 2003).

Sketch by Don Amerman

Harmon Killebrew
1936-

American baseball player

Harmon Killebrew ranks seventh on baseball's all-time home run list, having hit 573 homers in his twenty-two-year career. Killebrew homered once every 14.2 at-bats. He played all but one season with the Washington Senators/Minnesota Twins franchise, playing his final year with the Kansas City Royals in 1975. Killebrew, an eleven-time all-star, won or tied for the American League home run title six times, led the league in runs batted in three times and earned the league's Most Valuable Player award in 1969. He also played in the 1965 World Series.

His nickname, "Killer," belied Killebrew's gentlemanly reputation. He didn't drink and was never ejected from a game. He has established events such as golf tournaments to benefit charities. Killebrew himself had a brush with death in the early 1990s, when he was hospitalized for about three months and developed complications from medicine given for his knees. He also overcame financial problems after his playing career ended.

From Idaho to Stardom

Killebrew, born in Payette, Idaho, signed with the Washington Senators as a second baseman in 1954, a

Harmon Killebrew

week before his 18th birthday under the "bonus baby" rules in effect at the time. He made his major league debut that June, but did not crack the Senators' starting lineup for good until 1959, when he replaced the injured Pete Runnels. He tied Rocky Colavito of the Cleveland Indians for the American League in home runs that year with forty-two.

In 1961, owner Calvin Griffith moved the Washington franchise to Minnesota and renamed it the Twins. Killebrew took advantage of dimensions in suburban Bloomington's Metropolitan Stadium that were amenable to right-handed power hitters and belted 188 homers in his first four seasons in the Twin Cities. He won the AL home-run titles in 1962, 1963 and 1964.

Killebrew's power, however, was feared everywhere. In 1962, he hit a ball completely over the left-field roof at Detroit's Tiger Stadium, a ballpark tough on right-handed, pull hitters. In 1967, he shattered two seats in the sixth row of the upper deck of Metropolitan Stadium with a homer estimated at 530 feet. One day later, another Killebrew home run nearly reached the same spot, hitting the upper-deck facing. "Killebrew can knock the ball out of any park, including Yellowstone," Baltimore Orioles manager Paul Richards said in the early 1960s.

Killebrew was moved to several positions during his career, playing primarily at third base and left field. "But Killer never groused and his lack of a permanent defensive spot never seemed to affect his power," according to the Web site BaseballLibrary.com.

Chronology

1936	Born June 29 in Payette, Idaho
1954	Signed by Washington Senators as a "bonus baby," one week before 18th birthday. Makes major league debut on June 23.
1959	Becomes regular in Washington starting lineup
1961	Washington Senators relocate to Minneapolis-St. Paul—renamed Minnesota Twins.
1965	Bats .286 in seven games, hitting one home run as Twins lose World Series to Los Angeles Dodgers, 4 games to 3.
1969-70	Plays in American League Championship Series as Twins lose each year in three straight to the Baltimore Orioles.
1974	Released by Twins
1975	Plays final season for Kansas City Royals; ends career with 573 homers
1977	Helps found Danny Thompson Memorial Golf Tournament in honor of teammate who died of leukemia
1998	Founds Harmon Killebrew Foundation, Ltd., with his wife, Nita

Pennant in 1965

The Twins, meanwhile, built a formidable lineup around Killebrew. The middle of the batting order featured Killebrew with the likes of batting champion Tony Oliva and power hitters Bob Allison and Don Mincher. Shortstop and leadoff hitter Zoilo Versalles often gave Minnesota a needed jump-start. In 1965, with the New York Yankees declining after having won fourteen of the previous sixteen American League pennants, the Twins stepped into the breach and won the AL championship by seven games with a 102-60 record. In the World Series, Minnesota won the first two games against the favored National League champion Dodgers, but Los Angeles won the Series in a full seven games. Killebrew batted .286 and homered in Game 4 in Los Angeles, off Hall of Fame pitcher Don Drysdale. In the 1965 All-Star game, also in Minnesota, Killebrew hit a two-run homer.

"The team without Killebrew is like dressing up for a formal affair with a white tie and tails and then wearing muddy shoes," catcher Earl Battey once said.

MVP Season

Killebrew tied Carl Yastrzemski of the Boston Red Sox for the American League home run title in 1967, but the Twins lost the pennant the final weekend when they dropped the final two games in Boston. Two years later, Killebrew, rebounding from a hamstring pull suffered in the 1968 All-Star game, had a career season. He belted forty-nine homers, drove in 140 runs and was voted Most Valuable Player as the Twins, in baseball's new divisional realignment system, won the AL West title. Minnesota, however, lost the AL Championship Series in three straight to Baltimore in both 1969 and 1970. Killebrew homered twice in those six games.

After the 1970 season, Killebrew's career began a gradual decline, and the Twins released him after the 1974 season. Press reports cited fiction between Killebrew and Griffith, which Killebrew denied. Killebrew played his

Career Statistics

Yr	Team	AVG	GP	AB	R	H	HR	RBI	BB	SO	SB	E
1954	WSH	.308	9	13	1	4	0	3	2	3	0	0
1955	WSH	.200	38	80	12	16	4	7	9	31	0	5
1956	WSH	.222	44	99	10	22	5	13	10	39	0	4
1957	WSH	.290	9	31	4	9	2	5	2	8	0	1
1958	WSH	.194	13	31	2	6	0	2	0	12	0	0
1959	WSH	.242	153	546	98	132	42	105	90	116	3	30
1960	WSH	.276	124	442	84	122	31	80	71	106	1	17
1961	MIN	.288	150	541	94	156	46	122	107	109	1	23
1962	MIN	.243	155	552	85	134	48	126	106	142	1	9
1963	MIN	.258	142	515	88	133	45	96	72	105	0	3
1964	MIN	.270	158	577	95	156	49	111	93	135	0	7
1965	MIN	.269	113	401	78	108	25	75	72	69	0	12
1966	MIN	.281	162	569	89	160	39	110	103	98	0	18
1967	MIN	.269	163	547	105	147	44	113	131	111	1	12
1968	MIN	.210	100	295	40	62	17	40	70	70	0	7
1969	MIN	.276	162	555	106	153	49	140	145	84	8	22
1970	MIN	.271	157	527	96	143	41	113	128	84	0	20
1971	MIN	.254	47	500	61	127	28	119	114	96	3	13
1972	MIN	.231	139	433	53	100	26	74	94	91	0	9
1973	MIN	.242	69	248	29	60	5	32	41	59	0	1
1974	MIN	.222	122	333	28	74	13	54	45	61	0	2
1975	KCR	.199	106	312	25	62	14	44	54	70	1	0
TOTAL		.256	2435	8147	1283	2086	573	1584	1559	1699	19	215

KCR: Kansas City Royals; MIN: Minnesota Twins; WSH: Washington Senators.

final season with the Kansas City Royals before retiring. He worked as a Twins broadcaster for a few years and was elected to the Baseball Hall of Fame in 1984.

Personal Struggles, Charity Endeavors

Killebrew struggled financially when a golf-course investment in the 1980s soured. According to *The Desert Sun* of Palm Springs, California, Killebrew and former Idaho congressman Ralph Harding were among those defrauded in the "RM-Eighteen" golf course and condominium project near Rancho Mirage, California. News accounts portrayed Killebrew sympathetically. Hall of Famer **Reggie Jackson**, who had loaned Killebrew money, was said to have relaxed repayment terms.

Killebrew was hospitalized for thirteen weeks in the early 1990s and nearly died of complications from medicine administered to benefit knee pain. It "caused a lot of damage to my insides," he said years later. Over several years, Killebrew battled ulcers, a perforated stomach, a collapsed lung and "a tumor the size of a small football located behind his lung," according to the *San Angelo Standard-Times*. At one point his doctor sent him home, essentially to die in comfort, in the care of his wife, Nita, and a home-health nurse. "When I went back to see the doctor, he said, 'I didn't expect to see you in here,'" Killebrew said.

Following his near-death experience, Harmon Killebrew, who lives in Scottsdale, Arizona with his wife, Nita, has since become a national spokesman for the VistaCare Hospice Foundation, which the *Arizona Re-public* described as "sort of the adult version of the Make-a-Wish Foundation."

Said Killebrew during a Thanksgiving Day visit to a terminally ill patient in November, 2002: "If you haven't been touched by hospice care yet, you will be. Every family will be." He recalled an admonition from his mother, Katie: "We're here to help each other. What other reason could there be? So get with it, son."

Killebrew also visits his former Minnesota Twins team, helping during spring training, visiting their minor-league affiliates and making promotional appearances. He spoke to the Minnesota crowd on Opening Day in 2002 at the Hubert H. Humphrey Metrodome in downtown Minneapolis. Killebrew Drive was named in his honor near the site of Metropolitan Stadium in Bloomington, now the Mall of America shopping and entertainment complex.

Touched by the leukemia death of teammate Danny Thompson at age 29 in 1976, Killebrew a year later helped found the Danny Thompson Memorial Golf Tournament in Sun Valley, Idaho, to raise money for leukemia research. In 1996, he started the Harmon Killebrew Signature Classic Golf Tournament to benefit the American Red Cross and two years later established, with his wife, the Harmon Killebrew Foundation, a fund-raising charity.

Killebrew's Legacy

Killebrew was an intimidating home-run hitter, but teammates and opponents alike remember him for his

<table>
<tr><td colspan="2">**Awards and Accomplishments**</td></tr>
<tr><td>1955</td><td>Hit first major league homer June 24, against Billy Hoeft of the Detroit Tigers</td></tr>
<tr><td>1959</td><td>Tied Cleveland's Rocky Colavito for American League lead in home runs with 42.</td></tr>
<tr><td>1959, 1961, 1963-71</td><td>All-Star Team</td></tr>
<tr><td>1962-64</td><td>Led American League in home runs with 48, 45 and 49, respectively</td></tr>
<tr><td>1967</td><td>Tied Boston's Carl Yastrzemski for American League lead in home runs with 44.</td></tr>
<tr><td>1969</td><td>Voted American League Most Valuable Player after leading league in home runs (49) and runs batted in (140).</td></tr>
<tr><td>1971</td><td>Hit 500th home run, off Mike Cuellar of Baltimore Orioles</td></tr>
<tr><td>1974</td><td>Twins retire his uniform number (3)</td></tr>
<tr><td>1984</td><td>Elected to Baseball Hall of Fame</td></tr>
</table>

softspokenness and community outreach. "I didn't have evil intentions, but I guess I did have power," he once said. Killebrew still visits baseball parks and autograph shows across the country while promoting hospice care and typically gives short shrift to his baseball accomplishments. "People get all excited about players who hit home runs," he said at one minor league ballpark. "I actually always felt runs batted in were more important than home runs."

The Twins' unexpected appearance in the 2002 American League playoffs—Minnesota won the AL Central and upset Oakland in the first round before losing to eventual World Series champion Anaheim—brought back memories of the Killebrew days in Minnesota, and reminded out-of-towners what "Killer" meant to one of baseball's smaller markets. Eric Slater of the *Los Angeles Times* described the Twins as one of "history's great smaller-town teams, a club that lost more often than it won but came through just frequently enough—with the help of Hall of Famers such as Harmon Killebrew—to allow major league baseball to survive even in a place where the number crunchers said it couldn't."

FURTHER INFORMATION

Other

"A Troubled Financial Past: Timeline of Franks' Legal Problems." *The Desert Sun.* http://www.thedesertsun.com/news/stories/breaking (October 22, 2002).

"Hall-of-Famer Killebrew Spreads the Wealth." *Athens Daily News.* http://www.onlineathens.com/1998/ (October 22, 1998)

"Harmon Killebrew." BaseballLibrary.com. http://www.pubdim.net/baseballlibrary/ballplayers/K/Killebrew_Harmon.stm (December 4, 2002)

"Harmon Killebrew Foundation: Making the Difference." Harmon Killebrew Home Page. http://www.harmonkillebrew.org/sys-tmpl/door/ (December 4, 2002).

Harmon Killebrew Lifetime Statistics. http://www.baseball-reference.com/ (December 4, 2002).

"Hospice Has Big Surprise for a Dying Baseball Fan." *Arizona Republic.* http://www.arizonarepublic.com (November 29, 2002).

"Killebrew to Throw First Pitch at Colts Home Opener." *San Angelo Standard-Times.* http://www.texaswest.com/archive/00 (May 13, 2000).

"Puckett's Role with Twins to Change." *Minneapolis Star Tribune.* http://www.startribune.com (December 4, 2002).

"Team May Strike Out if Players Walk." *Los Angeles Times.* http://www.latimes.com (August 29, 2002).

"The Killer on a Killer: Harmon Killebrew Signs on to Cypress Systems' Prostate Cancer Awareness Campaign." Cypress Systems Inc. press release. http://www.cypsystems.com/ (January 21, 2000).

"Twins History: Harmon Killebrew." http://minnesota.twins.mlb.com/ (December 4, 2002).

Sketch by Paul Burton

Jean-Claude Killy
1943-

French skier

Downhill ski racer Jean-Claude Killy won the first World Cup overall title in 1967, and took gold medals in all three alpine races at the 1968 Olympic Games. He was instrumental in organizing the 1982 Olympic Games in Albertville, France, and is a member of the International Olympic Committee. He also founded a successful ski apparel company.

"I Was Always Called by the Outdoors"

Killy's father, Robert Killy, was a Spitfire pilot for the Free French during World War II. At the close of the war, he and his wife Madeleine, along with their four-year-old daughter, France, and their two-year-old son, Jean-Claude, moved to the village of Val d'Isere, France, and opened a small ski shop. The village, historically a pocket of deep poverty, had been revived in the 1930s when a skier named Charles Diebold opened a ski school there.

Killy grew up in Val d'Isere, where skiing was a local pastime. He told Sebastian Coe in the London *Daily Telegraph* that he began skiing at the age of three, as did everyone else in Val d'Isere. "If you didn't ski they thought you were strange. There was nothing else to do, no swimming pools, no television. I knew nothing about the outside world. . . . I had no plans; life was simply going to school, eating and skiing."

Jean-Claude Killy

According to William Oscar Johnson in *Sports Illustrated,* Killy often sped down a mountain, "pursued by a priest on skis, robes flapping, because he had cut catechism class." Killy told Coe that this priest "was probably the best skier I came across for several years, but he never caught me."

Killy's younger brother, Mic, was born in 1950. Shortly afterward their mother, Madeleine, left the family and moved to the southern Alps, where she had a relationship with another man. Killy told Johnson, "I have no explanation for what happened. We never really established a relationship after she left. It was very painful to find yourself at seven or eight, a little boy by himself." Although Killy's father tried to make up for the loss, he was unable to handle the three children, and Killy was sent to a boarding school in Chambery, eighty miles away. Used to the freedom of the mountains, he hated being enclosed in the school and felt like he was suffocating in the classrooms there. "I was always called by the outdoors," he told Johnson. He skipped classes often, hitchhiking back to Val d'Isere to ski.

In 1957, Robert Killy remarried; his new wife, Renee, developed a warm relationship with Killy. However, he still refused to attend school, and when he was fifteen, his father allowed him to drop out.

When Killy was fourteen he broke his leg at a downhill ski competition in Cortina, Italy, but by the time he was sixteen, in 1960, he was chosen for the French national ski team. That was the same year he heard about the Olympics; when he saw newsreels of the Squaw Valley Olympics, he realized that he too could become a world-class ski racer.

In the 1960-1961 season, Killy won the slalom, giant slalom, downhill, and combined gold medals in the French junior championships. His joy over these wins was tempered by sadness later in 1961, when he was driving a borrowed car, skidded, and overturned it on an icy road in Morzine, France. His best friend, who was sitting in the passenger seat, was crushed and killed. At the time, Killy did not even have a license to drive.

Even at a young age, Killy had a notably businesslike attitude toward skiing. He told Johnson, "I always believed that skiing was serious, that it was a way of living, a whole life." He noted that one of his friends was a better skier than he was, but did not believe that skiing could form the backbone of one's life. "He went down in the valley somewhere and began driving a truck," Killy told Johnson.

Despite his pragmatic approach to skiing, Killy was also reckless. His coach, Honore Bonnet, told Johnson that Killy was often in the lead during a race, but lost control and fell in the final seconds. "I reminded him that . . . if he wished ever to win he would have to arrange to also finish. But at the time I believed this young man had everything. Eventually I was proved right."

Killy won his first international race in 1961, after being ranked 39th; it was a giant slalom, held on his home mountain of Val d'Isere. Although Bonnet chose Killy to compete in the giant slalom at the 1962 world championships, Killy broke his leg in a fall three weeks before the competition began.

In 1962, Killy had also spent a summer doing compulsory service with the French army in Algeria, and he had contracted amebic dysentery and hepatitis. Although he competed in the 1962 Olympics, these ailments weakened him, and he did not place in any of the events he entered—the downhill, the special slalom, or the giant slalom.

Killy won the downhill and the combined at the world championships in 1966. During 1966-1967, he won twenty-three of thirty races, including all five World Cup downhill races; this was the first World Cup overall title.

After this great year, Killy considered retiring from the sport while he was still at the top of his form, but he kept skiing, with his eye on the 1968 Olympics. The 1967-1968 season was a bad one for Killy, who won only one of the six World Cup races before the Olympics.

Three Gold Medals

At the 1968 Olympics, held in Grenoble, France, Killy lost all the wax on his skis during a warmup run for the downhill, and felt that he was sure to lose. Nevertheless, he leaped out of the start and took every possible risk to make his descent faster. He also knew that if he cut a sharp line near the finish, he could gain a couple of meters, but he had never practiced this move because he didn't want any of the other skiers to learn about it. As he sped down the mountain, his intervals became slower as the few remaining bits of wax on his skis wore off. His shortcut saved him, giving him a .08 of a second lead over the second-place winner, Guy Perillat of France.

Killy followed his gold medal in the downhill with gold medals in the giant slalom and the slalom. The slalom course was obscured by a dense fog, and Killy's win was somewhat controversial: two other skiers had a faster time, but it turned out that in the fog, they had both missed gates on the course. Arguments ensued, but in the end, Killy had the gold. He was only the second skier ever to win gold medals in all three events; the only other person who had accomplished this was Austrian Toni Sailer, in the 1956 Olympics.

After Killy's wins, he wanted to go home to Val d'Isere, and he asked the mayor there if he could have a job as a representative of the local office of tourism. The mayor said that the salary Killy wanted, $1,000 a month, was too high and there was no room for him. "Then," Killy told Johnson, "my life took care of itself."

Killy signed a contract with agent Mark McCormack of the International Management Group (IMG). Before signing, he warned McCormack that he hated traveling and meeting strangers at cocktail parties. By 1990, he told Johnson, he had visited 55 countries on hundreds of trips, and had met almost as many strangers as someone campaigning for the American presidency.

In addition to trying his skill as a car racer, Killy made commercials, became a professional ski racer in the United States, and made two television series. One, *The Killy Style*, was a thirteen-week series that showcased various ski resorts, and the other, *The Killy Challenge*, featured him racing against celebrities, who were all given handicaps. He was also sponsored by a champagne company, Moet Chandon, which paid him to be seen with a bottle of their champagne on his table everywhere he went.

In 1972, Killy made a movie, *Snow Job*, which Johnson described as "a stinker." Johnson also noted that a *Time* reviewer wrote, "Waxing romantic or working out plans for an elaborate robbery, Jean-Claude always manages to sound as if he were making a half-hearted pitch for Chap Stick." Killy, perhaps realizing that his acting talent was not equal to his skiing ability, stayed out of the movies from then on.

However, Killy did reap one benefit from his film experience: his costar, Daniele Gaubert, became his wife on November 2, 1973, in a private ceremony in Archamps, France. Killy adopted Gaubert's two children from an earlier marriage, Maria-Daniele and Rhadames, and the couple later had a daughter, Emilie.

Killy told Johnson, "She was the love of my life, the girl of my life for 20 years. I was going to retire with my

Jean-Claude Killy

wife and live forever, well organized and with enough money, forever."

Killy left McCormack in 1977 and began a ski apparel company, Veleda S.A., in Paris. By 1987 it was making $35 million. With his father and brother, he also owned three ski shops in Val d'Isere.

Olympic Work Behind the Scenes

In 1981, Killy became involved with the campaign to bring the Olympic Games to the small town of Albertville, France, which had no ski area and no particular attractions. This project, called Le Comite d'Organisation des Jeux Olympiques (COJO), would occupy him for more than a decade, as it involved such huge tasks as improving the infrastructure and building new roads and rail lines in the region, which historically had been one of the most disorganized in France. Working with local politician Michel Barnier, Killy and other supporters traveled worldwide to promote the idea, visiting every member of the International Olympic Committee at least once. Killy told Johnson that at the beginning of this venture, he was so inexperienced that he thought lobbying "meant hanging around hotel lobbies and leaping out from behind the potted palms to talk to people." Killy's fame as a skier from the Albertville region proved to be helpful in con-

vincing people that it was a plausible site for the Olympics.

In 1984, the Albertville backers were dismayed to hear that Paris was launching a bid to host the 1992 Summer Olympics. This would be disastrous, because the Winter and Summer Olympics in any one year were never held in the same country. The Paris campaign, led by French prime minister Jacques Chirac, was a powerful opponent to Killy and his team. However, the president of the International Olympic Committee, **Juan Antonio Samaranch** of Spain, was an even more powerful opponent of the Paris bid, and it soon became clear that the Summer Olympics would be held in Barcelona, Spain. Chirac then endorsed the Albertville bid, and in 1986, Albertville won the position of host for the 1992 Olympics.

In January of 1987, Killy immediately became the center of a controversy when he announced a plan to cut costs for the Olympics, moving events from one venue to another, leaving some villages with no events. Killy, who was under a great deal of stress because his wife had been diagnosed with cancer, became furious at the arguments that ensued, and resigned from his position as co-president of COJO with Barnier on January 29, 1987.

Killy's dream of a long and happy life with his beloved wife was tragically cut short when Gaubert died of cancer later in 1987, on November 3. It was one day after their fourteenth wedding anniversary. Her death impressed Killy with the idea that life is short and one should live fully, in every moment.

Both Chirac and Samaranch convinced Killy to return to COJO, and he returned as co-president on March 11, 1988. In the meantime, many of the old arguments against him had died off. Killy signed a contract with IMG to promote the Olympics, and by 1990 COJO had $100 million in its treasury.

At the 1992 Albertville Olympics, most of the men's alpine events were held at Val d'Isere, where the mountainside was renamed "l'Espace Killy," or "Killy's area," in honor of its most famous skier. Killy, as co-president of the Albertville venture, had to resort to flying a helicopter to survey this huge domain, spread out over many different villages.

In 1995, Killy became a member of the International Olympic Committee, which oversees the Olympic Games. He was also president of the Tour de France bicycle race and the Paris-to-Dakar auto rally.

Summing up his philosophy of life, Killy told John Fry in *Ski,* "Win some, lose some. The object is to win more than you lose, but never give up. . . . Every young kid who worked with me, I told him to find the answer, not to complain, just find the answer, please. There is one, always."

CONTACT INFORMATION

Address: 13 Chemin Bellefontaine, 1223 Cologny, Geneva, Switzerland.

SELECTED WRITINGS BY KILLY:

One Hundred Thirty-Three Skiing Lessons, DBI Books, 1975.
Jean-Claude Killy's Guide to Skiing, Barron's, 1981.

FURTHER INFORMATION

Periodicals

Coe, Sebastian. "Killy Too Much His Own Man to Step Into Samaranch's Shoes: Monday Interview." *Daily Telegraph* (London, England) (April 16, 2001).

Johnson, William Oscar. "A Man and His Kingdom." *Sports Illustrated* (February 12, 1990): 206.

"Killy Completes Ski Triple After Protest Refused." *Washington Post* (February 18, 1966): C1.

Other

Fry, John. "In His View: Jean-Claude Killy." *Ski* (November, 2001). http://www.skimag.com/ (November 15, 2002).

Fry, John. "Killy's Kingdom." *Ski* (October, 2002). http://www.skimag.com/ (November 26, 2002).

IAAF World Championships in Athletics, Paris 2003 St-Denis. http://www.paris2003saintdenis.org/ (November 26, 2002).

Mojon, Jean-Marc. "Olympic Skier Jean-Claude Killy." *Christian Science Monitor* (November 4, 1999), http://www.csmonitor.com/ (November 26, 2002).

Sketch by Kelly Winters

Billie Jean King
1943-

American tennis player

Billie Jean King, more than anyone, revolutionized women's tennis. One of the greatest players ever, King was in the Top Ten five times between 1966 and 1972, and has won 20 Wimbledon championships. She founded charitable organizations as well as the Women's Tennis Association and the Women's Sports Foundation, which she established to ensure that females have equal access to participation and leadership opportunities in sports and fitness. King, involved with

Billie Jean King

the sport for more than five decades, has been most effective in addressing matters of financial equity and respect for women's tennis. *Life* magazine in 1990 named King one of the "100 Most Important Americans of the Twentieth Century," and *Sports Illustrated* in 1994 ranked her No. 5 in its list of top 40 athletes who have elevated their sport. King, honored frequently for athleticism and public service, is a member of the International Tennis Hall of Fame and the National Women's Hall of Fame.

Against All Odds

Billie Jean Moffitt was only a teenager when she took the international spotlight by winning, with Karen Hantze, the women's doubles tournament at Wimbledon in 1961. Her journey to the first of an amazing run of victories there began on the public tennis courts at Long Beach, California.

The daughter of Betty Jerman Moffitt, who sold Avon and Tupperware products, and fireman Willis "Bill" Moffitt, King grew up in a working-class family with brother Randy, five years her junior. She was named after her father, though the family often called her the more affectionate "Sister" or "Sissy." She was "a little angel," her mother recalled in a 1975 interview with journalist Joe Hyams. Like their father, the young Moffitts were baseball fans, and Billie Jean, who played softball as a youngster, became an excellent hitter. (Randy earned 96 saves in 12 years as a major league relief pitcher, mostly for the San Francisco Giants.) Real-

Chronology

1943	Born November 22 in Long Beach, California
1954	First formal tennis lessons
1958	Works with coach Alice Marble
1964	Travels to Australia to work with coach Mervyn Rose; wins U.S. doubles
1965	Marries Larry W. King
1970	Helps organize the first all-women's pro tennis tournament
1974	Founds Women's Sports Foundation
1975	With husband, helps launch women's professional softball team
1980	President of Women's Tennis Association, which she co-founds
1983	Retires from singles competition
1983-84	Played World Team Tennis for Chicago Fire
1987	King and husband Larry divorce
1995-96, 1998	Captain of Federation Cup team
1996, 2000	Captain of U.S. Olympic tennis team

Billie Jean King

izing at age 11 that "there was no place for an American girl to go in the national pastime," she wrote in *Billie Jean,* the young athlete sought an alternate sport.

Afraid to swim and bored by golf, she was left with tennis—"what else could a little girl do if she wasn't afraid to sweat?" she wrote in her 1982 autobiography. Her parents signed her up for instruction with the Long Beach city recreation program, where she borrowed a racquet and received free lessons. At the time, however, tennis was mostly an activity for the elite, and the adolescent felt out of place among her teammates. For one thing, King wore eyeglasses to correct her 20-40 vision. In addition, at 5 feet, 4½ inches, she struggled with weight problems. Her knee problems would require many surgeries. And as if those obstacles weren't enough, her family could not afford the traditional tennis whites, leaving her to play in a blouse and shorts her mother had made. Though fiercely competitive and gifted, King had to sit out the photo session of her peers in the Southern California Junior Championships because of her homespun outfit. Not yet a teen, she had already felt the stings of exclusion.

Career of Firsts

Playing with the cheaper nylon instead of gut strings and enduring the snobbery of players groomed at elite country clubs, she won her first junior championship at age 14. She told her family of her intention to one day win Wimbledon, the world's most prestigious tourney.

A year following her first big win, King received a coaching offer from tennis legend Alice Marble, the lone voice to stand up to the United States Lawn Tennis Association (USLTA) in 1950 and insist the organization rescind its policy of segregation. Throughout the late 1950s, King spent weekends with Marble, whose biggest challenge was getting King off the court to at-

tend to her schoolwork. With additional coaching by Frank Brennan, she qualified for women's play at Wimbledon in 1961. She was only 18.

Though she suffered the first bout of what would become chronic sinus trouble in England, she was clearly at home at Wimbledon. King and Hantze, also 18, became the youngest team to win women's doubles there. They repeated as champions in 1962.

Returning from Europe, she graduated from Los Angeles State College of Applied Arts and Sciences, which she financed with her job as a playground instructor. She was playing at the highest amateur level and was generating ample media attention, but at the time, athletic scholarships for women were practically unheard of. In 1965 she married Larry W. King, a pre-law student at the College of Applied Arts and Sciences and a year behind her. The two had been dating for about two years, with periods of interruptions, including a three-month break when she went to Australia on an all-expenses-paid trip to study with coach Mervyn Rose, former Davis Cup player for Australia. Rose changed King's forehand and service.

Awards and Accomplishments

1958	Southern California Junior champion
1961	Wimbledon doubles champion with Karen Hantze; enrolls in Los Angeles State College of Applied Arts and Sciences
1961-67	Wightman Cup
1966	Wimbledon singles, U.S. indoor singles, and U.S. hard-court and indoor doubles tournaments (with Rosemary Casals) champion
1967	U.S. singles champion; Wimbledon singles champion and doubles champion (with Casals), U.S. Open, and South Africa champion; French mixed doubles champion; awarded Woman Athlete of the Year by the Associated Press
1968	U.S. singles champion; Wimbledon singles and doubles champion (with Casals); Australian singles and mixed doubles champion; U.S. indoor doubles champion
1970	Wimbledon doubles champion (with Casals); French mixed doubles champion; Italian singles and doubles champion; Wightman Cup
1971	U.S. singles and mixed doubles champion; Wimbledon doubles and mixed doubles champion
1971	First female athlete to earn $100,000 in prize money
1972	Named first Sportswoman of the Year by *Sports Illustrated*; "Tennis Player of the Year" by *Sports* magazine; U.S. doubles champion; Wimbledon singles and doubles champion (with Betty Stove); French singles and doubles champion
1973	Wins Battle of the Sexes against Bobby Riggs; U.S. mixed doubles champion; Wimbledon singles, doubles (with Casals), and mixed doubles champion
1973-75, 1980-81	President, Women's Tennis Association, which she co-founds
1974	U.S. singles and doubles champion; Wimbledon mixed doubles champion; plays World Team Tennis for Philadelphia Freedoms; first woman to coach a professional team (Philadelphia Freedoms)
1975	Wimbledon singles champion; announces partial retirement
1975-78	Plays World Team Tennis for New York Sets/Apples
1976	U.S. mixed doubles champion; captain of Federation Cup team; named Woman of the Year by *Time* magazine
1977	Wightman Cup
1978	U.S. doubles champion
1979	Wimbledon doubles champion with Martina Navratilova, breaking the record for most career wins at Wimbledon; Wightman Cup
1980	U.S. doubles champion
1981	Plays World Team Tennis for Oakland Breakers; is sued by Marlyn Barnett, leading to publicity about her sexuality
1982	Plays World Team Tennis for Los Angeles Strings
1984	First woman commissioner (World Team Tennis) in professional sports history
1987	Inducted into the International Tennis Hall of Fame
1990	Listed as one of the "100 Most Important Americans of the 20th Century" by *Life* magazine; inducted into the National Women's Hall of Fame
1994	Ranked No. 5 in *Sports Illustrated*'s "Top 40 Athletes" for significantly altering/elevating sports the last four decades
1997	Named one of the "Ten Most Powerful Women in America" by *Harper's Bazaar* magazine; named one of the "Twenty-five Most Influential Women in America" by *World Almanac*
1998	First athlete to receive the Elizabeth Blackwell Award, given by Hobart and William Smith College to a woman whose life exemplifies outstanding service to humanity
1999	Wins the Arthur Ashe Award for Courage for her fight to bring equality to women's sports
2002	Receives the Radcliffe Medal, awarded annually to a person whose life and work has significantly improved society

---

During the first six months of their marriage, King stayed home in an attempt to be "a good wife," as was the expectation at the time. But she was miserable. With her husband's full support, she started hitting a few balls around again and soon completely dedicated herself to tennis. A year later, she won her first Wimbledon singles. (The prize: a self-confidence boost and a gift certificate for tennis wear.) In 1966 she and doubles partner **Rosemary Casals** won the U.S. hard-court and indoor tournaments. In 1967 Casals and King took the doubles title at Wimbledon, the U.S. Open, and the South African championship. King and Casals dominated women's doubles for years, becoming the only doubles team to have won American titles on grass, clay, indoor, and hard surfaces.

King even played a tournament while suffering from typhus. The Associated Press named her Woman Athlete of the Year in 1967 for defending her Wimbledon singles title, which she would repeat again in 1968. Other wins of the decade included U.S. Open, French Open, and Australian Open titles. With such recognition and nine Wimbledon titles under her belt, King felt confident enough to approach the USLTA with champion **Rod Laver** and insist on prize money for tournament winners. Laver and King felt they should be fairly compensated; otherwise, the sport would remain available only to wealthy players. She referred to "shamateurism" as the USLTA's practice of paying top players under the table to guarantee their entry into association-sponsored tournaments.

Though the USLTA finally gave in to their demands—the "Open Era" began in 1968—the prize money it offered women was consistently, and steeply, far less than male players. When she won the Italian Open in 1970 she received $600; her male counterpart, Ilie Nastase, won $3,500. The men's purse in the Pacific Southwest Championships that year was $12,500 to the women's $1,500. Nonetheless, King in 1971 became the first female athlete to earn $100,000 in prize money in a season of competition. That year she won again at Wimbledon (mixed doubles), and the U.S. Open (singles, mixed doubles).

Champions Women's Rights

King took a stand on the red-hot issue of abortion, when in 1971 she admitted to having had one. Despite the highly personal revelation, she felt defensive about publicity regarding hers and her husband's private life.

In 1972 she won the French Open and Wimbledon singles, ending a three-year drought in the latter. She also won her third U.S. Open singles title, which awarded her $10,000. Nastase, the men's singles champion, won $25,000. King was irate. It was hardly the first time she recognized prize-money disparity, but it was the last time she would remain quiet about it. When she complained

---

Related Biography: Tennis Promoter Gladys Heldman

Tennis promoter Gladys Medalie Heldman grew up as an non-athletic, intellectual young woman. A 1942 Phi Beta Kappa graduate of Stanford University, Heldman received her M.A. in medieval studies the following year from the University of California, Berkeley.

Born May 13, 1922 in New York, Heldman took up tennis late, after her marriage in 1947 to Julius Heldman, the 1936 left-handed U.S. Junior champion. She quickly adapted, playing in the U.S. Championships from 1949 to 1953, and at Wimbledon in 1954. Both her daughters, Trixie and Julie, held national junior rankings. Julie won the Italian Open in 1969 and ranked fifth in the world that year and again in 1974. Heldman achieved USTA rankings in the top ten in women's 35 doubles, women's 45 doubles, and mother-daughter events.

In 1953, she founded *World Tennis* magazine, which she edited until 1972. Heldman aligned herself and her magazine with the female players, most notably Billie Jean King and Rosemary Casals, King's doubles partner, who rebelled against the male tennis establishment. Heldman and the "Houston Nine" (King, Casals, Peaches Bartkowicz, Kerry Melville, Valerie Ziegenfuss, Nancy Richey, Kristy Pigeon and Judy Tegart Dalton) departed from the traditional, mixed-sex tournaments and in 1970 set up a women's-only tour, which, with backing from friend Joe Cullman, chairman of Philip Morris, became the hugely successful Virginia Slims Championships.

Shortly thereafter, Heldman brought the first women's pro tour to Europe in 1971 and Japan in 1972. She has received numerous awards, including the U.S. Tennis Writers award in 1965, World Championship Tennis award in 1980, and the Women's Sports Foundation award in 1982. In 1979 she was inducted into the International Tennis Hall of Fame. She wrote three books on tennis and one novel, *The Harmonetics Investigation* (Crown, 1979). She lives with her husband in Santa Fe, New Mexico.

---

to the U.S. tennis establishment, she was told that men were paid more because few people watch women's tennis. But King insisted women's tennis enjoyed many enthusiastic fans. In fact, when Hyams interviewed King in 1975 in a hotel coffee shop, he says they were interrupted half a dozen times by autograph seekers, mostly men.

King continued to sweep up Grand Slam titles and break ground for her sport. Fed up with the tennis establishment's attitude and lack of financial commitment to women's tennis, she took action. After she and a small group of other players refused to play a tournament where the women's prize money was one eighth of the men's, King organized the first women's-only professional tennis tournament. When the nine defectors were threatened with suspension by the U.S. Tennis Association (USTA), King, with the help of *World Tennis* magazine founder Gladys Heldman, put together their own prize money. The nine players all agreed to accept a $1 contract from Heldman, who secured sponsorship from Philip Morris Company just as it was to target a new cigarette, Virginia Slims, to women. Thus the Virginia Slims Championships were launched in Houston. By 1973 the tour covered 22 cities and had $775,000 in prize money. After its 1994 season, the Slims became the Women's International Tennis Association Tour Championship.

In 1973 King was elected first president of the Women's Tennis Association (WTA), a players' union. She also created "team tennis," America's only professional co-ed team sport, and became the first woman to coach a professional co-ed team when she signed on with the Philadelphia Freedoms. But she cemented her status as a heroine of the women's movement with her match against Bobby Riggs, a self-proclaimed "male chauvinist pig," who claimed even a mediocre male player, such as the 55-year-old Riggs himself, could beat the best female player, regardless of age.

Riggs, who won Wimbledon (1939) and the U.S. national championships (1939, 1941), had beaten Australian **Margaret Smith Court** in May 1973. So when King took up his challenge in September, in an exhibition that became known as the Battle of the Sexes, the stakes were higher. King says she was sick to her stomach before the match, which was unusual for her. "Sissy Bug will murder this Riggs," her father told *Sports Illustrated* writer Curry Kirkpatrick. "I hope Sissy shuts him up good. ... Sissy will kill him, bet you five."

Bill Moffitt was right. His daughter ruled the court that night. Before 30,472 fans (a record crowd for one tennis match) in the Houston Astrodome, and 40 million television viewers, King beat Riggs in straight sets, 6-4, 6-3, 6-3, and became a potent symbol of the women's movement. King went home with the $100,000 purse, the largest amount of prize money ever paid for a single match. "Billie Jean King didn't just raise consciousness, which was the feminist mantra then," Frank Deford wrote in *Sports Illustrated*. "No, she absolutely changed consciousness." In 2001, the TV movie *When Billie Beat Bobby* dramatized this event, with Holly Hunter playing King, Ron Silver as Riggs.

A Safer Place

Between 1961 and 1979, King collected six singles, ten doubles, and four mixed doubles championships at Wimbledon, and reached 27 final events. King, the only woman to win U.S. singles titles on all surfaces (grass, clay, indoor, hard), holds a singles title in every Grand Slam event. Even upon her 1983 retirement, King was still ranked 13th in the world. King and Rosemary Casals virtually dominated women's doubles. King took numerous late-career wins, including the 1979 Wimbledon doubles and 1980 U.S. Open doubles, both with **Martina Navratilova**. She helped the U.S. to seven Federation Cup victories. During the 2000 Olympics in Sydney, King coached the American women's team, which included **Lindsay Davenport**, **Monica Seles**, and **Venus Williams** and **Serena Williams**. The team came home with two golds (Venus Willams in singles, Venus and Serena Williams in doubles) and a bronze (Monica Seles in singles).

In 1999, King urged Wimbledon officials to set the prize money for women ($651,000) equal to that of men ($724,000). "Treating women as less valuable than men generates ill-will that is disproportionate to the amount of money you are saving," she urged in her statement.

Always outspoken on women's rights, King was initially reticent about gay rights. Then, former lover Marilyn Barnett, a Beverly Hills hairdresser, "outed" her in

1981. King has long been openly gay, though the attention has cost her about $1.5 million in endorsements. She lost sponsorship of the women's tour after publicly acknowledging her homosexuality. King, never fully comfortable living her life in public, is more an effective organizer and strategist. She told Michele Kort of *The Advocate* magazine she was trying to work within corporations to get them to set up domestic-partner benefits. "I think it's better if you do those things internally, rather than talking about them publicly," she said.

Clearly wounded by Barnett's palimony suit, King remained silent about her sexuality for quite a while, much to the criticism of gay activists. She said she feared a backlash. "It's really tough if I hurt the business [team tennis]," she told Kort, "because it ends up hurting others, not just me." Still, King said gay young athletes being open about their sexuality "will help set them free." She added, "Each person's circumstances are unique, so I think it's impossible to judge whether another person should come out. You just hope they will on their own time and their own terms. And, hopefully, we'll make the world a safer place so young people will feel safe to deal with their sexuality and whatever else."

King has supported various initiatives on behalf of tennis, sports, health, education, women, minorities, gays and lesbians, children, and families. Today she remains an activist for health, fitness, education, and social change. She sits on the board of directors for the WTA, the Elton John AIDS Foundation, and the National AIDS Fund. She is also the national ambassador for AIM, which assists handicapped children, and is a member of the Gay, Lesbian and Straight Education Network. King has regularly worked as a sports commentator for numerous networks and cable stations. Most recently, King was captain of the U.S. Federation Cup team for the USTA. Her status as a catalyst has resonated beyond the tennis courts. Her outspokenness boosted measures such as the 1972 enactment of Title IX, which helped assure gender equity in sports funding and participation among female students. As for women's tennis itself, the changes are so immense there will be no going back.

CONTACT INFORMATION

Address: c/o Diane Stone, 960 Harlem Ave., Suite 983, Glenview, Ill 60025. Fax: 847-904-7362. Email: dstone @wtt.com.

SELECTED WRITINGS BY KING:

(With Kim Chapin) *Tennis to Win*. New York: Harper, 1970.
(With Joe Hyams) *Billie Jean King's Secrets of Winning Tennis*. New York: Holt, 1974.
(With Kim Chapin) *Billie Jean*. New York: Harper, 1974.
(With Greg Hoffman) *Tennis Love: A Parents' Guide to the Sport*. New York: Macmillan, 1978.
How to Play Mixed Doubles. New York: Simon & Schuster, 1980.
(With Reginald Brace) *Play Better Tennis*, New York: Smithmark, 1981.
(With Frank Deford) *Billie Jean*. New York: Grenada, 1982.
(With Cynthia Starr) *We've Come a Long Way: The Story of Women's Tennis*. New York: McGraw-Hill, 1988.

FURTHER INFORMATION

Books

American Decades CD-ROM. Detroit: Gale Research, 1998.
The Bodywise Woman: Reliable Information about Physical Activity and Health (with a foreward by Billie Jean King). Champaign, IL: Human Kinetics Publishers, 1993.
Contemporary Authors Online. Detroit: Gale Group, 2001.
Contemporary Heroes and Heroines, Book III. Detroit: Gale Research, 1998.
Encyclopedia of World Biography. Detroit: Gale Research, 1998.
Gay and Lesbian Biography. Detroit: St. James Press, 1997.
Great Women in Sports, Detroit: Visible Ink Press, 1996.
Reader's Companion to American History. Boston: Houghton Mifflin, 1991.
St. James Encyclopedia of Popular Culture. Detroit: St. James Press, 2000.

Periodicals

"American Diabetes Association and Billie Jean King Foundation Present the Fourth Annual 2001 Donnelly Award Winners."*PR Newswire* (August 7, 2001).

"Billie Jean King: A Candid Conversation with the Contentious Superstar of Women's Tennis."*Playboy* (March 1975).

Braley, Sarah J. F. "Legends of the Court." *Meetings and Conventions* (August 1997): 19.

Kort, Michele. *The Advocate.* (August 18, 1998): 40.

Kort, Michele. *The Advocate.* (September 26, 2000): 34.

Richmond, Ray. "When Billie Beat Bobby,"*Hollywood Reporter.* (April 16, 2001): 10.

"Williams Sisters to Play for USA Olympic Team in Sydney, Australia." *Jet.* (August 21, 2000): 46.

Other

Barnard College. www.barnard.columbia.edu/ (December 22, 2002; December 23, 2002; December 26, 2002; December 29, 2002).

Baseball Library.com. Randy Moffitt Statistics, www.pubdim.net/ (December 22, 2002).

Billie Jean King Foundation. vpr2.admin.arizona.edu/ (December 22, 2002).

Daily Celebrations. www.dailycelebrations.com/ (December 22, 2002).

Delaware Smash World Team Tennis. www.delaware smash.ck/king.htm (December 23, 2002).

Gale Free Resources. www.gale.com/ (December 27, 2002).

Infoplease.com, Bobby Riggs Profile. www.infoplease.com/ (December 26, 2002).

International Tennis Hall of Fame, Billie Jean King, Gladys Heldman and Mervyn Rose Profiles. www.tennisfame.org/ (December 23, 2002).

"Radcliffe Medalist 2002—Billie Jean King." Radcliffe College, www.radcliffe.edu/ (December 23, 2002).

Tennis Corner, Billie Jean King Career Highlights. www.tenniscorner.net/ (December 23, 2002).

"There She Is, Ms. America." CNN/SI, sportsillustrated.cnn.com/ (December 27, 2002).

William and Mary College. www.wm.edu/ (December 27, 2002).

Wimbledon Championships. www.wimbledon.org/ (December 26, 2002).

Women's Sports Legends Online. www.wslegends.com/ (December 23, 2002; December 30, 2002).

World Team Tennis. www.worldteamtennis.com/ (December 23, 2002).

Sketch by Jane Summer

Don King

Don King
1931-

American boxing promoter

With his trademark "gravity-defying" hair, the image of Don King has hovered over professional boxing since he helped put together the "Rumble in the Jungle" in 1974, in which **Muhammad Ali** regained his championship title from **George Foreman**. All the elements that have marked King's career came together in his first big match: brilliant showmanship, the ability to massage outsized egos, and shady financing that left a number of people—though not Don King—unpaid and unsure where the money went. Since then, King's legend has grown to the point where his own fame, with a few exceptions, eclipses the various heavyweight champions and challengers he's promoted.

Early Years

Donald King was born in Cleveland, Ohio, on August 20, 1931, in a Depression-era ghetto. On December 7, 1941, King's father was killed in an explosion at the steel factory where he worked. With the small insurance settlement, Don King's mother Hattie relocated the family to a middle-class neighborhood. When the money ran out, Hattie began to bake pies, which her sons sold along with bags of roasted peanuts. As a sales gimmick, Don and his brothers began to slip a "lucky number" into each bag, a habit that soon made them very popular with the local gamblers and numbers runners.

As a high school student, he began to take an interest in boxing, entering Golden Gloves tournaments as "The Kid." After being knocked cold in a few early bouts, The

Chronology

1931	Born August 20 in Cleveland, Ohio
1950-67	Numbers runner in Cleveland
1954	On December 12, shoots and kills Hillary Brown, who is attempting to rob one of King's gambling houses. The shooting is ruled a "justifiable homicide."
1967	On April 20, beats Sam Garrett to death. Convicted of second degree murder, but sentenced on a reduced manslaughter charge, to Marion Correctional Institute, in Ohio.
1971	Paroled on September 30
1972	Brings Muhammad Ali to Cleveland to fight in exhibition match on behalf of a local black hospital
1973	Becomes co-manager of Larry Holmes with Don Butler, by 1975 Butler has been eased out (he later sues King)
1974	Promotes "Rumble in the Jungle" between Muhammad Ali and George Foreman
1975	Promotes "Thrilla in Manilla" between Ali and Joe Frazier, often considered the greatest boxing match ever
1977	Investigated by FBI for doctoring fighters' records; no charges filed, but ABC cancels contract with King for several fights
Early 1980s	Again investigated by FBI as part of larger probe in boxing; no charges filed
1983	Granted full pardon for earlier murder conviction by Governor of Ohio
1984	Indicted on insurance fraud charges, with secretary Constance Harper
1984	Promotes Michael Jackson's reunion "Victory Tour" with Jackson brothers
1984	Indicted on insurance fraudcharges, with secretary Constance Harper
1985	Acquitted of insurance fraud (Harper found guilty)
1985	Found not guilty of insurance fraud (Harper found guilty)
1988	Sued by Larry Holmes for $300,000 (settles for $100,000)
1988	Signs Mike Tyson
1995	Tried on wire fraud charges stemming from the insurance fraud investigation; case ends in a mistrial
1998	Acquitted in second trial for wire fraud
1998	Sued by Mike Tyson for $100 million
2002	Sues longtime rival Bob Arum for "stealing" heavyweight Julio Cesar Chavez

Awards and Accomplishments

1974	Promotes "Rumble in the Jungle" between Muhammad Ali and George Foreman
1975	Promotes "Thrilla in Manilla" between Ali and Joe Frazier, often considered the greatest boxing match ever
1975	Man of the Year, National Black Hall of Fame
1976	Urban Justice Award, Antioch School of Law
1976	Heritage Award, Edwin Gould Society for Children
1976	Man of the Year, NAACP
1980	Citation for Outstanding Support and Service, U.S. Olympic Committee
1981	George Herbert Walker Bush Award, President's Inaugural Committee
1981	Award of the Year, National Black Caucus
1983	Promoter of the Year, North American Boxing Federation
1984	Humanitarian Award, World Boxing Council
1986	Merit Award, Black Entertainment and Sports Lawyers Association
1987	Dr. Martin Luther King Jr. Humanitarian Award, Jamaica America Society and U.S. Information Service
1997	Inducted in Boxing Hall of Fame
1998	Honorary Doctorate in Humane Letters, Shaw University, Raleigh, NC

Kid decided that boxing was not the way to go, at least not inside the ring. Instead, he began to focus on the numbers rackets that he had encountered as a boy selling peanuts. After being accepted to Kent State University, he decided to spend his summer after high school working for a numbers runner, to raise the tuition money. Unfortunately, after hustling all summer, he lost a winning betting slip and had to make up for it out of his own pocket, putting his college plans on hold. While he did eventually take a few classes at Case Western University, he decided that college was an unnecessary diversion.

Instead he set himself up in the numbers business, and by the time he turned 20, he was a well-established and successful numbers runner. He soon began to show the panache that would mark his career, buying fancy clothes and driving around town in shiny new cars. At the same time he began to reveal the talents that would make him more than a flash in the pan. He used an insider's tips to rig a popular numbers game based on stock market results, reducing his risk to 200:1 odds while collecting at 500:1 odds. This complex system worked well enough to make Don King the most successful "numbers banker" in Cleveland by the time he was 30. And King had also emerged as a man to be feared. In December of 1954, he shot to death a man named Hillary Brown who was trying to rob one of King's gambling houses. The killing was ruled a "justifiable homicide."

A Prison Education

King's next brush with the law would be much more serious, and would very nearly cost him everything. On April 20, 1966, Don King walked into the Manhattan Tap Room and spotted a man by the name of Sam Garrett—a former employee in King's racket who owed him $600 on a bet. Sickly, small, and drug-addicted, Garrett was no match for King. But King was in no mood for forgiveness. Their argument very quickly turned into a brawl, and then a beating in the street outside the bar, a beating that ultimately left Garrett dead from his injuries. King claimed self-defense, and witness accounts vary, but for the first officer on the scene, the beating was a brutal, almost demonic assault. In an interview with sportswriter Jack Newfield, Officer Bob Tonne said he saw "a man's head bouncing off the asphalt pavement like a rubber ball. Then he saw another man standing over him with a gun in his right hand, applying another kick to the head." Even after he was subdued and the fight was over, "King got in one last vicious kick that Tonne would never forget."

Despite reports of witness intimidation and attempted bribery, King was convicted of second-degree murder. Normally, this would have meant a life sentence with eligibility for parole after eight and a half years. Oddly, the presiding judge—in a highly controversial decision reached in the privacy of his chambers—set aside the execution of the sentence, in effect changing the convic-

---

Only in America

The world got a good sample of Don King's audacious tactical imagination and deal-making in February 1978 when he stole not a fighter but the heavyweight championship of the world.

On Februay 15, Leon Spinks upset the aging Muhammad Ali and won the title. Bob Arum promoted this fight and he had a contract giving him options on the fist three defenses by Neon Leon. This was not good for King....

Spinks revered Ali ... and he promised Ali a rematch in September. King saw this honorable gesture as an opportunity to play boxing politics.

King called Jose Sulaiman, the president of the World Boxing Council (WBC), one of the comic regulating authorities, based in Mexico City, and convinced him to strip Spinks of his title for the crime of giving Ali an immediate rematch, instead of fighting the Number 1 contender, Ken Norton.

By stripping Spinks without due process or a fair hearing, Sulaiman created a second version of the heavyweight title, a great advantage to King, who had all the other contenders under contract.

Source: Newfield, Jack. *Only in America,* New York: Knopf, 1993, pp. 139-140.

---

tion to manslaughter, which allowed King to emerge from prison in less than four years.

There is no question that Don King used his years in prison to great advantage. He read widely in literature and philosophy, getting the education he had bypassed before. As he put it himself: "I didn't serve time. I made time serve me." He also managed to purchase from a Cleveland city councilor a 40-acre farm for a mere $1,000, a decidedly small sum for such a property. Interestingly, the farm was occupied by a woman named Hattie Renwick, a widow who eventually married Don King.

The Promoter

On September 30, 1971, Don King emerged from prison considerably wiser and wealthier and with more faithful friends than the typical ex-con. One friend in particular would set him on the path to fame and fortune. Lloyd Price was a very successful singer-songwriter who had been performing benefits and concerts at a tavern owned by Don King since 1959. The two had become fast friends, and the day after King's parole, Price flew to Cleveland to offer his support and advice. It took a little while, but in June of 1972, Don King came up with an idea that would require Lloyd Price's assistance.

A local black hospital had fallen on hard times, and King came up with the idea of holding a charitable event to rescue it. The centerpiece would be a couple of exhibition matches with Price's good friend Muhammad Ali—that is, if Ali could be persuaded to do the event for a man who had never promoted a boxing match in his life. Price made the necessary introductions, and King's unstoppable flow of words did the rest. Ali agreed to participate, and the match was a success, although there is some question as to how much money the hospital ultimately received.

Don King had found his calling—and very soon, the world would know it. The fledgling boxing promoter convinced Ali and his Nation of Islam managers that they were morally obligated to do business with a black promoter. As if to cinch the deal, about this time King claimed to have received a sign from God, when his natural Afro uncurled itself into the shock of hair that the world would soon recognize as his trademark. Over the years, the story would grow more elaborate, to the point where he claimed his hair could not be cut or combed, and electric shocks would fly from it when barbers got too close with shears or scissors.

Rumble in the Jungle

In 1974, King put together a title fight between the champion, George Foreman, and challenger Muhammad Ali. To add a note of black pride, he decided to hold the event in Africa, in Zaire, and coined it the "Rumble in the Jungle." He promised each of the contenders $5 million, twice what any previous fighter had earned, and despite the suspicions of both Ali's managers and George Foreman, the corruption of Zaire's megalomaniac ruler Mobutu, and a five-week delay that threatened to torpedo the whole project, King pulled off a match that was a huge financial success for all concerned. Or nearly all. Lloyd Price, one of numerous singers who had flown in to perform on the night of the big fight, never received payment.

With Ali's title regained, and Don King firmly in his camp, the two began to plan his next big match. The result was the "Thrilla in Manilla," which put Ali up against former heavyweight champion **Joe Frazier**. Many consider this the greatest title fight in boxing history, adding a note of quality to King's reputation for mounting lucrative spectacles.

King's growing influence soon attracted the attention of the federal government, notably the FBI and IRS. After numerous investigations, the FBI concluded that the chaotic structure of modern boxing meant that King probably was not criminally liable for his shady deals, although it continued to watch him. He has also survived IRS investigations for tax evasion and a 1995 federal charge for insurance fraud, which ended in a hung jury. In fact, the jury convicted King's secretary, Constance Harper, while letting King himself off. A grateful King sprung for first-class plane tickets and ringside seats for the jurors. In addition, King has fended off a number of lawsuits from his own clients, but these have generally been settled out of court. As former heavyweight Larry Holmes, who settled for $100,000 after suing for $300,000, once put it: King "looks black, lives white, and thinks green."

As Muhammad Ali entered his declining years, especially after losing his title to Larry Holmes, Don King emerged more and more as the face of modern boxing. In fact, for a time in the 1980s, everyone who contended for the heavyweight championship was promoted or managed by Don King. As a *Sports Illustrated* reporter put it in 1990, "Boxing is run out of King's right-hand drawer." And it wasn't just his business savvy. Heavyweight champions like Michael Dokes, Mike Weaver, and Trevor Berbick did not resonate with the public the way Don King did. Only one recent boxer, **Mike Tyson**, has eclipsed Don King's fame—or notoriety. When Tyson lost his title and then went to jail on a rape conviction, it seemed to some that King had lost his last big meal ticket.

But Don King has gone ever on. Promotions (including a brief detour into the music industry when he promoted the Jacksons's Victory Tour in the late 1980s), law suits, grand schemes for reviving the sagging fortunes of heavyweight boxing, intense rivalries with other promoters, all continue to fill the busy life of Don King. Even Mike Tyson returned to the fold after his prison term, earning more money for the promoter, although he has since sued King for $100 million. Undoubtedly, many boxers and promoters wish Don King had never entered boxing, but they might consider two of his legacies. First, he dramatically increased the prize money for fighters. Second, and rather more importantly, he brought a charisma and undeniable showmanship to a sport that has always depended on such fireworks to attract the public's interest, and the money that flows from that interest. As King himself once put it: "I never cease to amaze myself. I say this humbly."

FURTHER INFORMATION

Books

Newfield, Jack. *Only in America: The Life and Crimes of Don King*. New York: Knopf, 1993.

Periodicals

"Don King Trying to Resurrect the Heavies." *Washington Times* (September 14, 2002): C1.

Hauser, Thomas. "Corner Man." *Nation* (August 28, 1995): 189.

"The King's Reign." *Sports Illustrated* (July 14, 1997): 15.

Kirshenbaum, Jerry. "They Said It." *Sports Illustrated* (October 15, 1984): 26.

Llosa, Luis Fernando. "Inside Boxing." *Sports Illustrated* (May 21, 2001): 74.

"Main Event: Tyson-King." *Sports Illustrated* (March 16, 1998): 16.

Raab, Scott. "The Last Boxing Story." *Esquire* (August 1998): 94.

Reilly, Rick. "Your Hair-raising Gall: Nice Try, Don King, but You Can't Steal Buster Douglas's Title." *Sports Illustrated* (February 19, 1990): 90.

Steptoe, Sonja. "Tyson's Trials." *Sports Illustrated* (May 18, 1992): 13.

Wulf, Steve. "A Win by Split Decision: Thanks to a Hung Jury, Boxing Promoter Don King Ducks Under Federal Charges of Insurance Fraud." *Time* (November 27, 1995): 83.

Ziegel, Vic. "The King of Boxing: How Did Don King Get to Promote Michael Jackson? You'll See." *Rolling Stone* (January 19, 1984): 13.

Sketch by Robert Winters

Karch Kiraly
1960-

American volleyball player

The only volleyball player in Olympic history to win three gold medals, Karch Kiraly pushed his career earnings past the $3 million mark with a third-place finish in the Association of Volleyball Professionals (AVP) last tournament of the 2002 season. He became the winningest beach volleyball player of all time when he and Adam Johnson captured the 1999 Chicago Open, Kiraly's 140th career win. And he is not ready to call it quits yet. In an interview with CBS SportsLine.com in October 2002, Kiraly was asked how much longer he thought he would compete as a pro. He replied: "Until it's not fun, or until we can't contend to win tournaments, or both." As well as Kiraly's been playing in recent years, it seems unlikely he ll turn his back on the game anytime soon.

Born in Jackson, Michigan

The son of Laszlo and Toni (Iffland) Kiraly, he was born in Jackson, Michigan, on November 3, 1960. Shortly after his birth, the family moved to San Clemente, California, where Kiraly grew up. When he was 6 years old, he began to play volleyball with his father, who had played the game for a junior national team in Hungary before immigrating to the United States. Asked by an interviewer for CBS SportsLine.com if he was any good at first, Kiraly replied that "all I wanted to do at first was keep the ball going back and forth 10 times, 20, 50, and so on. So no, I was not any good when I first started, but improvement seemed to come steadily, and it was a big advantage starting so much younger than almost any other player." Kiraly entered his first beach volleyball tournament when he was 11. He played on the volleyball team at Santa Barbara High School and in 1978 was named the most valuable player (MVP) in California high schools. During his senior year, Kiraly's team was undefeated winning 83 matches. Kiraly has credited his high school coach, Rick Olmstead, with teaching him the value of hard work and

Karch Kiraly

dedication, lessons that have served him well throughout his amateur and professional careers.

After graduating from high school, Kiraly enrolled at the University of California, Los Angeles (UCLA) to study biochemistry. Playing on his college volleyball team as a setter and a hitter, he led the team to first place in its conference three out of four years. In his first year in the Pacific Rim Tournament, Kiraly was named MVP. His team played a total of 125 matches during Kiraly's four years at UCLA. A year after receiving his bachelor's degree from UCLA, he played in the Olympics, leading his team to the gold medal. At 23, Kiraly was the youngest player on the U.S. team, but he nevertheless played in all 19 games of Olympic competition, more than any of his teammates. During the Olympic Games, he connected on 74 out of 158 spike attempts, in recognition of which he was awarded the FIVB (Federation Internationale de Volleyball) Sportsmanship Award. For Kiraly, it signaled the beginning of an outstanding career in professional volleyball.

Leads US Team to 5 Gold Medals

Over the next three years, Kiraly led the U.S.A. National Team to a total of five gold medals and one silver medal. During the World Championship in 1986, he was named "world's best volleyball player" by FIVB President Ruben Acosta. In December of 1986, Kiraly married Janna Miller, with whom he has two sons, Kristian and Kory. In 1988 he again led the U.S. team

to Olympic gold. With 137 kills, 16 block stuffs, 15 block assists, and a kill percentage of 60 percent, Kiraly was voted MVP of the 1988 Olympics volleyball competition.

While leading the U.S.A. National Team to glory throughout much of the 1980s, Kiraly was also involved in beach volleyball, having gone professional in 1983. However, it was not until the 1990s that he truly began to shine in beach competition. In 1991 Kiraly compiled six open wins, a number he almost tripled the following year when he put together a total of 16 open wins, scoring 13 of those wins consecutively. His partner for much of the 1990s was Kent Steffes. The two first played together in 1991 and continued as partners off and on through 1996, compiling a total of 76 titles together. In 1993 Kiraly and Steffes won 18 of 20 tournaments, including three Jose Cuervo tourneys, the Manhattan Open, and the U.S. Championship. The two also won the Miller Lite Grand Prix.

Wins 17 of 22 Tourneys in 1994

Again partnered with Steffes in 1994, Kiraly won 17 of 22 tournaments, including all three Jose Cuervos and the U.S. Championship. He was forced to skip the Manhattan Open because of an injury. For the year, Kiraly's earnings totaled $430,636, and he was voted the AVP's Best Offensive Player of 1994. he piled up 12 open wins in 1995, four of them with Steffes and eight with Scott Ayakatubby, on his way to total winnings of $392,610 for the year. Playing with Steffes, he also won the 1995 FIVB exhibition in Curacao. In winning the 1995 Miller Lite Cup, Kiraly became the first beach volleyball player to reach $2 million in career earnings. For the fifth time, he was voted MVP by the AVP, and he also was given the AVP Sportsman of the Year Award, an honor voted by his peers.

Paired once again with longtime partner Steffes, Kiraly won gold in the inaugural beach volleyball competition at the 1996 Olympic Games in Atlanta, Georgia. In all, he compiled 11 open wins with Steffes in 1996. Kept out of competition for much of 1997 by shoulder surgery, Kiraly came back to the game late in the season, winning a total of four tournaments. He once again was named AVP Sportsman of the Year and also received the AVP's Comeback Player Award. Paired with Adam Johnson in 1998, Kiraly won four tournaments and came in second at the 1998 Goodwill Games.

Wins Inaugural Oldsmobile Beach Series

On May 16, 1999, in Huntington Beach, California, Kiraly, paired with Johnson, won the inaugural Oldsmobile Beach Volleyball Series, an event sanctioned by USA Volleyball. He's also won the King of the Beach Invitational four times (1991, 1992, 1993, 1996). For all of 1999, Kiraly won a total of five tournaments, four in AVP-sanctioned events and one at a USA Volleyball-sanctioned event. The following year Kiraly won only one AVP-sanctioned tournament. In 2001 Kiraly suffered leg and shoulder injuries and competed in only two domestic tournaments. For the first time since 1986, he won no tournaments at all in 2001. Bouncing back from his injuries in 2002, Kiraly pushed his career earnings past the $3 million mark at the final AVP tournament of the season in Las Vegas, becoming the first player to do so.

Interviewed by *Sports Illustrated* in September 2002, Kiraly was asked if it was important to him to be known as the greatest volleyball player of all time. The modest Kiraly responded: "No. There have been a lot of great players. I was lucky to play in a period when we had more tournaments every summer than the guys before me, so I accumulated a lot more victories." Just how many more wins Kiraly will accumulate, no one can say, but it's certain that he's made an impression on volleyball that will linger long after he's left the game forever.

CONTACT INFORMATION

Address: Karch Kiraly, c/o Association of Volleyball Professionals, 330 Washington Blvd., Ste. 600, Marina del Rey, CA 90292-5147.

Awards and Accomplishments

1978	Named California High School MVP
1979	Named MVP after winning Pacific Rim Tournament
1981-82	Leads UCLA to NCAA Championship
1982	Named MVP at U.S. Volleyball Association Tournament
1984	Leads U.S. National Team to gold medal victory at Olympics
1985	Leads U.S. National Team to World Cup victory as team captain
1986	Leads U.S. National Team to World Championship
1988	Captains U.S. National Team to gold medal victory at Olympics
1991	Scores win in six beach volleyball tournaments
1992	Wins 16 of 19 beach volleyball tournaments
1993	Teams with Kent Steffes to win 18 of 20 beach tourneys
1994	Teams with Steffes to win 17 of 22 beach tournaments
1995	Compiles 12 tournaments wins with two different partners
1996	Teams with Steffes to win inaugural beach volleyball competition at Olympics
1997	Named AVP Comeback Player of the Year
2002	Passes $3 million mark in career winnings

SELECTED WRITINGS BY KIRALY:

(With Jon Hastings) *Karch Kiraly's Championship Volleyball,* Fireside, 1996.

(With Byron Shewman) *Beach Volleyball,* Human Kinetics, 1999.

(With Byron Shewman) *The Sand Man: An Autobiography,* Renaissance Books, 1999.

FURTHER INFORMATION

Books

"Karch Kiraly." *Almanac of Famous People,* 6th ed. Detroit: Gale Research, 1998.

"Karch Kiraly." *The Complete Marquis Who's Who.* New York: Marquis Who's Who, 2001.

"Karch Kiraly." *Contemporary Newsmakers 1987,* Issue Cumulation. Detroit: Gale Research, 1988.

"Kent Steffes." *The Complete Marquis Who's Who.* Marquis Who's Who, 2001.

Periodicals

Deitsch, Richard. "Q&A: Karch Kiraly." *Sports Illustrated,* (September 16, 2002): 32.

Moore, David Leon. "Volleyball Star Kiraly Still Has Some Spike Left." *USA Today,* (August 23, 2002): 3C.

Other

"Karch Kiraly." Jack's World of Volleyball. http://207.28.11.252/eblue/hsone/volleyball/karchkiraly.html (January 12, 2003).

"Karch Kiraly Professional Volleyball Player." CBA. SportsLine.com. http://ww1.sportsline.com/u/rewards/qa/0902kiraly.htm (January 12, 2003).

"Karch Kiraly, Three-Time Olympic Gold Medalist, Professional Volleyball Player." Volleyball World Wide. http://www.volleyball.org/people/karch_kiraly.html (January 12, 2003).

"Karch Kiraly: United States." Beach Volleyball Database. http://www.bvbinfo.com/Player.asp?ID=69 (January 12, 2003).

"Kent Steffes." Volleyball World Wide. http://www.volleyball.org/people/kent_steffes.html (January 12, 2003).

"The King Lives." Association of Volleyball Professionals. http://www.avp.com/content.asp?articleid=1503 (January 12, 2003).

"Resolution of Commendation and Appreciation." USA Volleyball. www.usavolleyball.org/natoff/karch.pdf (January 12, 2003).

Sketch by Don Amerman

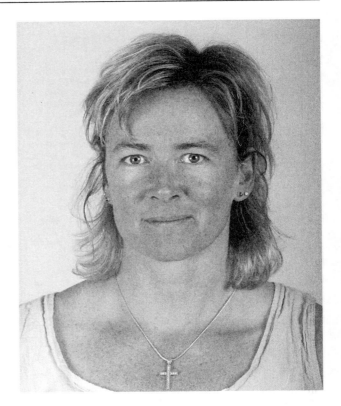

Karolyn Kirby

Karolyn Kirby
1961-

American beach volleyball player

During her 16-year career as a professional beach volleyball player, Kirby, who stands five-feet, eleven inches tall, had a record 67 tournament wins (61 domestic; 6 international) and career total earnings of $681,471 ($488,146 domestic; $193,325 international). Partnered with Liz Masakayan from 1993 to 1995, the pair formed the winningest team in the history of the game, posting a tournament record of 26-8, including a 55-match win streak and an overall match record of 183-20.

All-American Player

Karolyn Kirby was born on June 30, 1961 in Brookline, Massachusetts, the hometown of one-time governor and presidential candidate Mike Dukakis and newscaster Mike Wallace and an unlikely hometown for one of the nation's best beach volleyball players. Kirby didn't play volleyball until she was a freshman in high school. Previously a competitive swimmer, she was burned out and looking for something new. Kirby and a group of friends decided to give volleyball a try. She never looked back.

Kirby took to the sport quickly and became especially known for her setting abilities. As a freshman with no previous experience, she made the varsity squad, and by the summer after her sophomore year she was good enough to be invited to join the junior Olympic team. During her senior year in high school she sent off tapes of her play to several universities. Rutgers offered her a partial scholarship, but Utah State University, home of the National Collegiate Athletic Association volleyball champions, offered her a full ride. Kirby was both thrilled and worried by the invitation to play at Utah State, where she would join one of the best college teams in the nation. "When I was in high school, [my father] and I would sit around and talk about playing volleyball and going to the Olympics," Kirby later recalled to *The Boston Globe*. "I was so nervous, I didn't know if I wanted to go to Utah State. But [my father] encouraged me to do it. He had the vision I lacked." A month before she left for Utah State, Kirby's father passed away.

While at Utah State, Kirby was named an All-American in 1981. When her coaches left to take over the University of Kentucky volleyball team, Kirby transferred to the school, where she finished out her college play. In 1983, her final year in college, she was once again named an All-American and was also named as the Southeast Conference's Most Valuable Player. In the same year Kirby was named to the Olympic training team, and in 1984, she served as an alternate on the Olympic team.

Introduced to Beach Volleyball

Being from the northeast, where the weather can be unpleasant, and attending college in the nation's interior, Kirby did not come into contact with beach volleyball until 1984. As the captain of the U.S. national volleyball team, she was taking a break from tournament action, walking on a California beach with teammate Angela Rock. The two came upon an open beach volleyball tournament and decided to give it a shot, figuring they could easily beat the local competition. The experience was a humbling one; the two volleyball superstars failed to win a single game. What Kirby quickly discovered is that beach volleyball is a serious sport for serious athletes. The court, ball, and net are all the same as indoor volleyball, but with only two on a team, each member must cover an incredible amount of the court as well as compete with the wind, sun, hot temperatures, and shifting sand under foot.

The experience on the sand court stayed with Kirby. During 1986-87 Kirby played for the New York Liberties in Major League Volleyball. She also traveled Europe playing in tournaments. In 1987 she decided to give beach volleyball a try at the professional level during her summers and joined the Women's Professional Volleyball Association (WVPA). Teaming up with Sandy Aughinbaugh-Fahey for two events in 1987 and with Jo Ellen Vrazel for five events in 1988, Kirby posted a record of 11-14.

Gaining skills and experience, Kirby stepped up the competition in 1989 with her new partner, Dale Hall. She entered 13 tournaments, posted a positive record of 40-24, and took home more than $10,000 in prize money. Her best finish was third place. Kirby won her first tournament in 1990, the year she began her five-year domination of the tour, playing with partners Patty Dodd and Jackie Silva. In 16 tournament appearances, Kirby posted eight wins and finished in the money six other times. She earned over $41,000 on the beach in 1990 and was named the Women Professional Volleyball Association's (WPVA) Most Valuable Player as well as the tour's top offensive player.

Dominates the Tour

Teamed with Rock in 1991, Kirby won 12 of 17 tournaments (and finished in the top four in the other five events) with a record of 98-14. Kirby finished the season with 548 points, putting her first in the WPVA standings, a position she would hold for four consecutive years. She was once again named the tour's Most Valuable Player. Kirby led the tour in earnings with $67,815. In 1992 she and Rock partnered for the first 11 events of the season, winning five. Their record of 17 wins in 26 team appearances broke the previous record of 15. Kirby won three out of the final five tour events with Nancy Reno as her partner. For the second year Kirby led the tour in points and earnings, with $65,488.

In 1993 Kirby began a tremendously successful partnership with Liz Masakayan. The two became the top team on the beach, winning a record-tying 12 of 13 WPVA tour events during the year and earning co-MVP honors. Kirby once again finished the season first in points and earnings, with $65,025. She teamed with Masakayan again in 1994, and again the two dominated

<table>
<tr><td colspan="2">**Chronology**</td></tr>
<tr><td>1961</td><td>Born in Brookline, Massachusetts</td></tr>
<tr><td>1975</td><td>Begins playing volleyball as a freshman in high school</td></tr>
<tr><td>1977</td><td>Plays on the junior Olympic team</td></tr>
<tr><td>1979</td><td>Attends Utah State University on a volleyball scholarship</td></tr>
<tr><td>1983</td><td>Transfers to University of Kentucky; named to the Olympic volleyball training team</td></tr>
<tr><td>1984</td><td>Named as an Olympic alternate</td></tr>
<tr><td>1987</td><td>Joins the Women's Professional Volleyball Association (WPVA) to play beach volleyball professionally</td></tr>
<tr><td>1993-95</td><td>Dominates the WPVA tour with partner Liz Masakayan</td></tr>
<tr><td>1996</td><td>Fails to make first official Olympic beach volleyball team after Masakayan sustains a knee injury</td></tr>
<tr><td>2000</td><td>Last season on tour</td></tr>
<tr><td>2001</td><td>Begins coaching</td></tr>
</table>

the sand courts. They won 11 of 13 events, with an astonishing record of 72-3. From 1993 through 1994 they won a record 13 straight WPVA tournaments. Also, between 1992 and 1994 Kirby won five of eight Federation Internationale de Volleyball sponsored-tournaments. For the fourth consecutive year she was ranked first in the standing and in earnings, with her best career take-home of $83,010. She was named MVP for the fourth time of her career. Kirby and Masakayan also played together in the 1994 Goodwill Games, taking the gold medal.

Olympic Disappointment

With Masakayan struggling with a knee surgery in 1995, by July Kirby was looking for a new partner. She finished the year fifth in the standings, with only three tournament wins and $32,120 in earnings. The following year proved to be even more of a disappointment for Kirby as her inability to find a good replacement for Masakayan robbed her of her longtime dream to compete in the Olympics, as the 1996 Games in Atlanta, Georgia, was the first time that beach volleyball was recognized as a medal sport. With experienced top-rated players already committed to teams, Kirby competed unsuccessfully at the Olympic trials with Lisa Arce in their first partnership. "It was a dream of mine and I felt like I failed myself, failed on my dream," she explained to Vancouver's *Columbian,* then added, "But, I'm stronger for it. I'm really beginning to realize how fortunate I am. I enjoy and appreciate more than ever my career."

Kirby managed three tournament wins in both 1996 and 1997, spending most of the latter year teamed with Reno. She was rejoined by Masakayan for the 1998 Goodwill Games, but the defending gold medalists finished sixth, out of the medals. By the end of the 1990s, Kirby was winding down her career. She played in several international tournaments and numerous events sponsored by the Association of Volleyball Professionals and USA Volleyball. Following the 2000 season, in which her best finish was fifth place, Kirby, who lives in San Diego, California, turned to coaching. She is on staff with Masakayan, who continued to play competitively into the 2000s.

Awards and Accomplishments

1981	Named collegiate All-American
1983	Named collegiate All-American
1990	Named Women's Professional Volleyball Association's (WPVA) Most Valuable Player and Best Offensive Player
1991	Named WPVA Best Setter and Most Valuable Player
1992	Federation Internationale de Volleyball (FIVB) Tour Champion (with Nancy Reno); named WPVA Best Hitter
1993	FIVB Tour Champion (with Liz Masakayan)
1993-94	Named WPVA Most Valuable Player
1993-97	Named WPVA Best Setter for six consecutive years
1994	Gold medalist, Goodwill Games (with Masakayan)

Kirby won 13 of 30 grand slam events during her career and a record 67 tournaments. For complete career results, see http://www.volleyball.org.

FURTHER INFORMATION

Books

Great Women in Sports. Detroit: Visible Ink Press, 1996.

Markel, Robert, ed. *The Women's Sports Encyclopedia.* New York: Henry Holt and Company, 1997.

Periodicals

Goldberg, Karen. "Seriously, Folks: Beach Volleyball is Ready to Kick Sand in the Faces of its Skeptics." *The Washington Times,* (January 26, 1996): B5.

Hardie, Ann. "Olympic Weekly: 133 Days." *The Atlanta Journal and Constitution,* (March 8, 1996): 1F.

"Karolyn Kirby and Liz Masakayan May be the Best-ever Volleyball Tandem in Coors Light Women's Tour History." *Business Wire,* (July 1, 1993).

"Kirby and Masakayan Share MVP Award." *Business Wire,* (August 23, 1993).

"Kirby / Masakayan Tie Mark." *Business Wire,* (June 6, 1994).

Vondersmith, Jason. "Bittersweet Times." *The Columbian,* Vancouver, Wash. (September 1, 1996): C9.

Other

"Karolyn Kirby." Beach Volleyball Database. http://www.bvbinfo.com/player.asp?ID=1207 (January 30, 2003).

"Karolyn Kirby." Volleyball World Wide. http://www.volleyball.org (January 30, 2003).

Sketch by Kari Bethel

Harri Kirvesniemi
1958-

Finnish cross-country skier

Harri Kirvesniemi

Harri Kirvesniemi and his wife, Marja-Liisa Hämäläinen, were the best cross-country skiers in Finland for many years. Hämäläinen was the more successful of the pair in terms of first-place finishes, but both consistently finished in the top five in international events for about twenty years. Hämäläinen retired in the mid-1990s, still a Finnish hero, but the end of Kirvesniemi's career was marred when he was caught up in a doping scandal involving several members of the Finnish national team in 2001.

King and Queen of Finnish Skiing

Kirvesniemi and Hämäläinen met at a ski camp in 1978. He had only graduated from high school the year before. Hämäläinen, three years older than Kirvesniemi (she was born September 10, 1955), had already been skiing for the Finnish team for several years and had even competed in the 1976 Winter Olympics, where she placed twenty-second in the ten kilometer. Kirvesniemi, who grew up in central Finland as the son of a policeman and a schoolteacher, had been skiing competitively since he was four, while competitive skiing ran in Hämäläinen's family: her father, Kalevi, won a gold medal in the fifty kilometer freestyle at the 1960 Winter Olympics.

Both Kirvesniemi and Hämäläinen hovered around third place in the Finnish national standings for several years, but Hämäläinen broke through first. In 1983 she won the World Cup title, and at the Olympics in Saraje-

Chronology

1958	Born May 10 in Mikkeli, Finland
1977	Graduates from high school
1977-78	Spends eleven months in the Finnish army
1978	Meets future wife, Marja-Liisa Hämäläinen, at a ski camp
1980	Begins studying for a Master of Sport degree at the University of Yveskyla
1983	Hämäläinen wins World Cup championship
1984	Hämäläinen wins three Olympic gold skiing medals
1985	First daughter, Elisa, born
1994	Hämäläinen becomes only woman to have competed in six Winter Olympics
2001	Implicated in Finnish ski team doping scandal
2001	Retires from competitive skiing

Awards and Accomplishments

1998	Sets a record for number of Olympic bronze medals won in a lifetime by winning sixth bronze in the 4 x 10 kilometer relay

vo, Yugoslavia, the next year she took home three gold medals, winning the five, ten, and twenty kilometer events. She also won a bronze medal with the Finnish four-by-five kilometer relay team. Hämäläinen would never have another Olympics like that, but she did collect three more bronzes in her career, one with the relay team in 1988 and one each in the five kilometer classical and thirty kilometer classical in 1994. The latter two bronzes earned Hämäläinen (who was by then married and competing as Marja-Liisa Kirvesniemi) a place in the record books as the oldest female Winter Olympian ever to earn a medal in an individual event.

Kirvesniemi never won an Olympic gold medal, but he did set a record of his own: he is one of only two athletes to have won six Olympic bronze medals in his lifetime. Five of those six came with the Finnish national four-by-ten kilometer relay team, which placed third in the relay at five of the six Olympics held between 1980 and 1998. (The exception was 1988, when they finished eighth.) In 1984 Kirvesniemi also earned a bronze in the fifteen kilometer. This third-place pattern was set early in his career. As he told *Sports Illustrated* reporter Kenny Moore shortly before the 1988 Olympics, "I've got six bronze medals in Olympic and world championship races, and in the World Cup point totals I've been third twice. My place has always been third."

The Doping Scandal

The Finnish national team had an excellent year at the 2001 world championships, which were held in Lahti, Finland from February 15-25. But almost from the beginning their victories were tainted with suspicion. Rumors that Jari Isometsae, fourth-place finisher in the fifteen kilometer classic (held February 15) and silver medalist in the pursuit (held February 17), had had a positive test for banned drugs were circulating by the evening of the seventeenth. On the eighteenth Isometsae told reporters assembled at a press conference that he had been taking Hemohes (HEH), a newly banned plasma expander.

The men's four-by-ten kilometer relay team, composed of Kirvesniemi, Janne Immonen, Sami Repo, and Mika Myllylae, won the gold medal in that event on February 22. Immonen and Myllylae were already under suspicion: Myllylae had withdrawn from the pursuit race on the seventeenth due to feeling ill and Immonen had (apparently intentionally) broken one of his poles during the same race, and some thought that they had done these things so that they would not have to take any drug tests that day. On February 22, after the relay team's win, the World Anti-Doping Agency (WADA) performed a surprise test on the entire Finnish team. Immonen tested positive, and as a result the entire relay team was stripped of their golds.

The scandal continued to grow. By February 28 it was known that four more skiers, among them Kirvesniemi and Myllylae, had tested positive for HEH. That day the team's coach, Kari-Pekka Kyro, admitted that most members of the team were using banned substances and that this was common knowledge. As Kyro explained, he had thought that the drug tests would only be able to detect HEH for a brief period of time after the athletes used it. After Myllylae's involvement became known he fled the country, while Kirvesniemi begged his fans for their forgiveness while fighting back tears.

Kirvesniemi was banned from competitive skiing for two years after he was proved guilty of using banned substances, and rather than try to return to competition when he would be nearly forty-five, he simply retired. Kirvesniemi then became the head of the racing department at Karhu, a ski manufacturing company that had long been among his sponsors.

The End of a Great Career

Kirvesniemi had long been considered the "grand old man of Finnish cross-country skiing," as one Web site put it, and the revelation that he had been involved in doping stunned the Finnish public. His twenty years of training and his numerous hard-fought races were immediately discounted in millions of eyes. Plus, if even someone as respected as Kirvesniemi could cheat, "[m]any people wonder if there are any clean athletes left in our sport," Jay Tegeder wrote on Adelsman's Cross-Country Ski Page. "[T]here are no winners when our heroes have been found to be fallible."

CONTACT INFORMATION

Address: Suksitie 50, FIN-56800 Simpele, Finland.

FURTHER INFORMATION

Periodicals

Moore, Kenny. "Show on Snow." *Sports Illustrated,* (January 27, 1988): 212-215.

"Sporting Digest: Drugs in Sport." *Independent,* (London, England) (March 7, 2001): 26.

Other

"Four More Skiers Exposed in WADA Tests." Helsingin Sanomat (international edition). http://www.helsinki-hs.net/news.asp?id=20010228IE9 (January 28, 2001).

"Harri Kirvesniemi." Great Olympians. http://users.skynet.be/hermandw/olymp/bioki.htm (January 21, 2003).

"Manuela Bosco." International Association of Athletics Federations. http://www2.iaaf.org/wjc00/Athletes/Bosco.html (January 22, 2003).

"Marja-Liisa Hämäläinen." Great Olympians. http://users.skynet.be/hermandw/olymp/bioh.htm (January 21, 2003).

"Marja-Liisa Hämäläinen." International Olympic Committee. http://www.olympic.org/uk/athletes/heroes/bio_uk.asp?heros=78514 (January 21, 2003).

Stange, Erik. "Ski Equipment Companies Take Stance on Doping." FasterSkier.com. http://www.fasterskier.com/news/021001SkiCompanies.html (January 21, 2003).

Tegeder, Jay. "Nordic Worlds Erupt in Scandal! Adelsman's Cross-Country Ski Page." http://www.skinnyski.com/racing/articles/intlracing1.html (March 1, 2001).

"2001 World Championships: Lahti Finland, February 15-25." Australian Cross Country Skiing Website. http://www.hoppet.com.au/xc/xcfiles/reports/r_0001_doping.htm (March 1, 2001).

Sketch by Julia Bauder

Chris Klug
1972-

American snowboarder

Extreme athletes like snowboard slalom champion Chris Klug brought a new look and a new rhythm to the Olympics with the introduction of (e)Xtreme sports at Nagano, Japan, in 1998. Without altering the Olympic ideals, the personas of the heroes of the Games were redefined. For Klug, who took the Olympic bronze in 2002, the win was an anticlimax to a life-saving surgery that preceded the Olympic competition by six months.

Chris Klug

By the time he arrived at the competition in Salt Lake City, he was no stranger to victory, having scored and survived a liver transplant in July of 2002.

Born on November 18, 1972 in Vail, Colorado, the son of Kathy and Warren Klug, Chris Klug has an older brother, Jim, a younger sister, Hillary, and a foster brother, Jason. With the a backdrop of Vail in his early life it is easily understood how he evolved into an Olympic snowboarding medallist.

At age two, according to Klug, he toyed with his first downhill sport by taking to the slopes and learning to ski. The family relocated to Bend, Oregon, in 1976, where his father bought a hotel called the Inn of the Seventh Mountain, located at the foot of Mt. Bachelor. Bend, at the base of the Cascade Mountains is located at an altitude of 3,628 feet and is conducive to developing a proficiency in winter sports. Mt. Bachelor is a snowboard heaven, with many popular snowboard competitions and training grounds available in the region, so the move changed little for Klug and his love affair with winter sports.

Klug received his first snowboard at age eleven, and according to his own recollection he spent long hours building his skill on Mt. Bachelor. He entered amateur competitions at the junior level, and won the Mt. Baker Banked Slalom three times as a junior amateur. He won his first tour victory in 1988 as a sophomore in high school and went on to win back-to-back overall championships in the North West Race Series.

Chronology

1972	Born on November 18 in Vail, Colorado
1976	Moves with parents to Bend, Oregon
1991	Goes professional; participates in 25-30 events as a rookie; finishes in eighth place in first World Cup slalom event (Garmish, Germany)
1993	Receives a diagnosis of PSC
2000	Grand Prix Overall Alpine Champion; receives a new liver on July 28; returns to competition in November
2001	Wins first World Cup event after transplant

Awards and Accomplishments

1988	Won Professional Snowboard Tour ($4,000)
1989	Slalom National Amateur Championship
1997	U.S. Open Slalom championship
1998	Named as the top pick on the first-ever U.S. Olympic snowboarding team
2000	Grand Prix Overall Alpine Champion
2001	U.S. National Champion
2002	Bronze medal, Winter Olympics

Klug won back-to-back Northwest Series Overall Championships.

Klug is a three-time junior amateur Mt. Baker Banked Slalom Champion.

As Klug continued to grow, he attained an adult height of 6-feet-3-inches and a comfortable body weight of 210 pounds. An all-state quarterback at Mountain View high school, he faced a moment of truth when confronted by recruiters from Oregon State University—and other schools—with offers of football scholarships. Klug weighed his options and elected to forego college in favor of a career as a professional snowboarder. He entered competitions and won the overall National Amateur Championship Slalom in 1989. In 1991 he tied into the professional circuit, racing in over two dozen events as a rookie.

After undergoing bone surgery to his ankle in 1995, he missed the entire winter sport season that year. The surgery, to repair an errant bone beneath his Achilles tendon, was a precarious operation for an athlete. Hoping against the odds for a complete recovery, he remained active and attended classes at Aspen's Colorado Mountain College with an eye on a career in international snowboarding promotions. He applied and was accepted to Middlebury College in Vermont, but never acted on the acceptance. After winning the 1997 U.S. Open Slalom, he distinguished himself in 1998 as the first-ranked qualifier for the first-ever U.S. Olympic snowboarding team headed for the winter games in Nagano.

The Business of Boarding

According to a report in the *Patriot-News,* the debut of Olympic snowboarding generated more than a tidbit of controversy sparked by antagonistic snowboarders who view their sport as (e)Xtreme, and above all, nonconformist. The potential confinement of these athletes, within the regulated agenda of Olympic competition, rankled many who sensed a threat to their own individuality. Others were outright compromised, and for some the notion of wearing Olympic uniforms incited ire.

Not all snowboarders were opposed, however. The inaugural event attracted teams from fifteen countries, totaling more than fifty athletes. "There's a fine line between selling out and buying in," the *Patriot-News* quoted half-pipe contender and Olympic proponent Todd Richards. Likewise Klug told J. Lieber in *USA Today,* "This is an exciting time for snowboarding. The Olympics … [will] put us all on the map." Klug, in fact, advertises "professional snowboarder" on his business card and totes a portable office in his backpack. He carries quantities of his resume, stat sheet, and press biography, all ready for distribution to media personnel and to agents at snowboard meets.

Klug arrived in Nagano as a frontrunner in the giant slalom competition. On the day of the event, a thick shroud of fog cloaked the venue at Mount Yakebitai. It was in fact, the debilitating fog that caused a ten-minute delay in the race and ultimately spelled disaster for Klug. At the outset of the second round mere seconds separated him from first place, and he tied for second with a time of 59.38. In the second round, with visibility impaired he narrowly missed taking a fall. After leading through the first half of the course, he let his arm catch a banner as he sped toward a 290-meter vertical drop that comprised the remainder of the run. The interference hampered his time, and he ended with a final combined time of 2:5:05 for a sixth-place finish, less than three seconds behind the gold medallist.

First Olympic Transplantee

Five years prior to the Nagano Olympics, in 1993 at age twenty, Klug had confronted an unnerving medical diagnosis when he was found ailing with Primary Sclerosing Cholangitis (PSC). Doctors stabilized his condition with semi-annual liver treatments until 2000 when the treatments lost their effectiveness.

During the Grand Prix Overall Alpine Championships that year his strength waned. The following spring, he awoke one morning, feeling severe pain in his side, caused by a blockage in his bile ducts. The need for a transplant was then critical; Klug's health deteriorated. His weight dropped to 190 pounds, and he developed anemia, but met the challenge of a pending organ transplant with rare fortitude. He occupied himself with maintaining his fitness in order to minimize his recuperation time.

A compatible organ became available on July 28, 2000, and Klug was admitted to the University of Colorado Hospital in Denver. There he underwent the exhaustive transplant surgery, which lasted more than six

Chris Klug

hours. To the general amazement of all, he was out of bed and riding an exercise bike within two days of the surgery. He returned home in four days.

Barely seven weeks passed before Klug was preparing to re-board his board. In November he resumed competition, winning first place in a parallel slalom. He nailed a victory in a World Cup event by January of 2001.

February of 2002 brought the Winter Olympic Games to Salt Lake City and with it the second-ever Olympic snowboarding competition in history. For the giant slalom event at Park City Mountain Resort, Klug qualified as number eleven of sixteen competitors. In snowboarding's giant slalom, boarders compete in pairs, making timed runs on parallel courses. The competitors switch courses for a second run, and their time on the second run is added to their time from the first run, to calculate a combined final score. Klug made successful runs and advanced into the semifinals where he lost to Swiss boarder Philipp Schoch in the wake of a disappointing crash. The crash carried a steep penalty that day of 1.78 seconds, based on the trial times of the athletes. In the end Schoch took it all—winning the gold for Switzerland.

Although he crashed out of the finals, Klug was encouraged, knowing that a medal remained within his grasp. With gold and silver out of reach, he faced a pair of runs versus Nicolas Huet of France in a race for the bronze medal. In the first run Klug bested Huet but took little time to gloat when confronted by a potentially disastrous setback of a broken boot buckle. He jury-rigged a temporary fastener with duct tape, hoped for the best, and went into the final run with a 0.15 second advantage. Klug ended the run with a plump margin of 1.2 seconds, to win the bronze decisively, with a total margin of 1.36.

Klug returned to Aspen a hero, and the city threw a parade in his honor, despite frigid temperatures. The victory was celebrated nationwide; Klug was invited—and accepted the invitation—to the New York Stock Exchange, to ring the opening bell. Similarly the Detroit Tigers invited Klug to throw out the first pitch at a game. At the Transplant Games in Orlando, Florida, Klug was given the honor of lighting the torch. Television talk shows, and morning news shows hosted Klug and encouraged him to share his story with the viewing public.

Klug remained unmarried in 2003. He splits his time between a residence in Sisters, Oregon, and a family home in Aspen. Fly-fishing, golf, mountain biking, and water skiing fill his time when he is not snowboarding. In 2001 he established the Burton/Klug snowboard camp for youth at Aspen, where attendance tripled to 100 during the second season of operation.

Klug's interest in snowboarding was aroused at age eleven, when manufactured snowboards were relatively new on the market. With nowhere to turn for advice, his early technique on the board was largely self-taught. Before winning the North American Junior Championship in 1987 he turned to a Bend area ski instructor, Bob Roy, for guidance. Roy accepted the challenge, however skeptically, and went on to head an international team. It is said that Sherman Poppen invented the snowboard, but if the sport had its pioneers, then Klug's name must appear on the list. The first-ever athlete named to the U.S. Olympic team on snowboard, he was also the first athlete ever to win an Olympic medal after undergoing transplant surgery.

CONTACT INFORMATION

Address: c/o Burton/Klug Aspen Snowboard Camp, Buttermilk Mountain, Aspen, Colorado. Email: chris@ chrisklug.com. Online: www.chrisklug.com/.

FURTHER INFORMATION

Periodicals

People (December 3, 2001): 141.
Sports Illustrated (February 4, 2002: 148; February 14, 2002: 10).
Sunday Patriot-News (February 8, 1998): A1.
USA Today (February 3, 1998): 6C; February 15, 2002, p. 10D; February 16, 2002 (bonus section).

Sketch by G. Cooksey

Bobby Knight

Bobby Knight
1940-

American college basketball coach

Pete Axthelm of *Newsweek* has called Bobby Knight a "boiling blend of brilliance and loyalty, fanaticism and temper." And in fact, there isn't a college coach who can incite more debate and who can get the blood of fans boiling more (both his fans and those of opposing teams). Knight is one of those people about whom the phrase "either you love him or you hate him" seems to ring true. But regardless of what you think of Knight's actions and the way he handles his job, there is no denying that the coaching he has done for four decades now is anything short of amazing. Though his methods are, at times (indeed, often times) suspect, he gets results. He has led his teams to 25 NCAA tournament appearances, three NCAA Tournament Championships, and five Final Four appearances. He has also been one of only three coaches to win the Pan American Games gold and an Olympic gold medal.

Growing Up

Robert Montgomery Knight was born on October 25, 1940, in the small Ohio town of Orrville. His father was a railroad man (who died when Bobby was 29) and his mother taught elementary school across the street from his boyhood home. It was a small railroad town, but not isolated, with little more than 5,000 people. Knight grew up closest to his maternal grandmother, who lived with the family. She paid attention to him and, since his parents did not care about basketball, his grandmother was the one who listened and the one for whom he developed a great fondness.

In high school Knight was not a standout on the court or on the field, but nonetheless, he still participated in basketball, football and baseball. It has been said that he never would have become the winning coach he became if he had been a stellar athlete; he would have concentrated on his technique rather than focusing on improving the basketball games of others.

Knight had always wanted to coach. According to Frank DeFord of *Sports Illustrated* (and DeFord, it might be noted, has been an admirer of Bobby Knight for years), Knight "officially" expressed his desire to coach "in an autobiography he wrote when he was in junior high school." He soon developed a close relationship with his high school basketball coach, Bill Shunkwiler. "When other kids were hanging out [and] chasing girls," DeFord writes, "Bobby would come by Shunkwiler's house, and the two of them would sit and have milk and cookies and talk coach talk."

Knight graduated from high school and decided to attend Ohio State University, where he participated in the team's 1960 National Championship victory. Knight, however, was the 6th man on the team, and started only two games in his three years on the team. "He didn't amount to a hill of beans as a player," DeFord writes. But in spite of Knight's inability to perform on the court, he still hassled the coach Fred Taylor, for playing time. Taylor in turn labeled Knight "the Brat from Orrville."

Chronology

1940	Born October 25 in Massillon, Ohio
1958	Graduated from Orrville (OH) High School
1958	Enters Ohio State, where he'll play basketball for three years
1960	Wins NCAA Championship as member of Ohio State basketball team
1962	Graduates from Ohio State with a B.S. in History and Government
1962	Becomes assistant basketball coach at Cuyahoga Falls High School (in Ohio)
1963	Takes position as assistant basketball coach at U.S. Military Academy at West Point
1965	Becomes head basketball coach at U.S. Military Academy at West Point (youngest varsity coach in major college history)
1971	Decides to leave Army coaching job with a record of 102-50
1971	Begins tenure as head coach at Indiana University
1973	Leads Indiana to its first Big 10 conference title (they will win 11 titles under Knight)
1973	Indiana plays in first Final Four (by the time he is fired he will have coached Indiana in five Final Fours)
1976	Upset over a few turnovers, grabs sophomore Jim Wisman by jersey and jerks him into his seat
1976	Records 200th career coaching victory
1976	Leads Indiana to an undefeated season and wins first of three NCAA Championships
1979	Leads Hoosiers to victory in NIT Tournament Championship
1979	Coaches Pan-Am Team to Gold Medal
1979	Tried and convicted (in absentia) for hitting a Puerto Rican policeman at Pan Am practice. Sentenced to six months in jail, which he does not serve because he has already left country
1980	Earns 300th career win
1981	Wins second NCAA Championship at Indiana
1981	While at Final Four in Philadelphia, shoves an LSU fan into a garbage can
1983	Stands at midcourt and swears at Big Ten commissioner Wayne Duke over what Knight calls "the worst officiating I have seen in 12 years"
1984	Coaches U.S. Olympic team to gold medal
1984	Becomes one of three coaches in history to win "Triple Crown" of coaching (NCAA, NIT and Olympic Gold Medal)
1985	Allows reporter John Feinstein access to Indiana's program for '85-'86 season. Feinstein would write about what he saw in *A Season on the Brink*
1986	Recieves technical foul in a game against Illinois, then kicks a megaphone and yells at Indiana cheerleaders for disrupting a free throw attempt by Steve Alford
1987	Puerto Rico drops charges on Knight and ceases attempts to extradite him
1987	Wins third NCAA Championship at Indiana
1988	In interview with Connie Chung, Knight says, "If rape is inevitable, relax and enjoy it." Knight claims that the quote was taken out of context
1989	Gets 500th win in a victory over Northwestern in January
1989	Becomes winningest coach in Big 10 history
1991	Had asked not to be considered for his induction into Naismith Basketball Hall of Fame, calling his rejection in 1987 "a slap in the face"
1992	Gives a mock whipping to Hoosier Calbert Cheaney. Claims it wasn't racially motivated and apoligizes; this same year he bars a female AP reporter from the Indiana locker room
1993	Wins 600th career game; wins 11th Big Ten regular season title. Ties for first among all Big Ten coaches
1994	Head-butts a player while screaming at him on the bench. Claims it was unintentional
1995	Fined $30,000 for an outburst at a post-game news conference
1997	Earns 700th victory on March 5
1999	Accidentally shoots hunting partner in the back and is cited for failing to report incident
2000	Accused of grabbing freshman Indiana student by the arm in fall of '99. Knight yelled at him for "disrespecting him." The student had said, "What's up, Knight."
2000	Fired from Indiana University in September
2001	Named head coach at Texas Tech University on March 23
2001	Compiles a 23-10 record at Texas Tech in his first season as coach

Youngest College Coach

Upon graduating from Ohio State in 1962, Knight immediately had two high school coaching offers to deal with. Though at one school he could have made more money coaching football as well as basketball, Knight chose instead to take the lesser of the two positions, wanting to focus his energies on the basketball program. He later told *Sports Illustrated,* "I thought, if I'm going to be a basketball coach, I can't be diverted. I wanted vertical concentration." Soon he was offered an assistant coaching position at the United States Military Academy, and by the time he was 24, Knight was the head coach at the Academy, becoming the youngest head coach in major college history.

Knight remained at the Military Academy for six years (he had to enlist in the Army to get the position). He was already compiling winning numbers that would follow him, for the most part, for the rest of his career. Army was never much of a basketball school, but in his six seasons there, Coach Knight took the team to four NIT playoffs, and ended his career at the school with a record of 102-50.

In 1971, Knight took a position with Indiana University, fulfilling his childhood dream of coaching at a Big Ten school. They took their basketball very seriously in Indiana (see the film *Hoosiers*), and in Coach Knight they got a man who took the definition of serious to a completely different realm.

The Hoosier Era

Under Knight the Indiana program took off, and within ten years the Hoosiers had won six Big Ten titles, as well as an NIT and two NCAA championships. He took his team to yet another victory in the NCAA championships in 1987, wearing his trademark Bobby Knight red sweater and white collar—and he also brought along his verbal tirades and technical fouls.

During his tenure with Indiana, which ended after the 2000 basketball season, Knight had one of the most impressive coaching careers, on paper, in the record books. He led the Hoosiers to 24 NCAA tournament appearances and, although they won the championship three times, they appeared in the Final Four five times. In almost thirty years, Knight won eleven Big Ten

Awards and Accomplishments

1973	Big Ten Coach of the Year
1975	National Coach of the Year (unanimous choice); Big Ten Coach of the Year
1976	National Coach of the Year honors by AP, UPI and *Basketball Weekly*; Big Ten Coach of the Year
1980	Big Ten Coach of the Year
1981	Big Ten Coach of the Year
1987	Named Naismith Coach of the Year
1989	National Coach of the Year
1991	Enshrined in the Naismith Memorial Basketball Hall of Fame

Championships, coached 11 Big Ten Most Valuable Players, 13 All-Americans, and he was named the national Coach of the Year four times (in 1975, 1976, 1987, and 1989).

Knight, who coached the 1984 U.S. Olympic team to a gold medal, was honored by being named into the National Basketball Hall of Fame in 1991, in spite of his request that they disregard his name on the ballot (he was irritated that he had been passed over in 1987). Additionally, Knight was one of only two coaches to win NCAA championships—as a player and coach. When he was fired from Indiana in September of 2000, Bobby Knight had amassed a career record of 763 wins and 290 losses. And he is still adding to it by compiling wins at Texas Tech, where he is currently head coach.

Knight the Enigma

Knight's reputation was rather indifferent at the beginning of his career. While he was coaching for the Military Academy, the main pressure on him was that which he put on himself. When he made it to Indiana in 1971, however, he was for all intents and purposes where he wanted to be—in the hotbed of college basketball. It was where he planned to stay for quite some time. But with the responsibility of a Big Ten team and the expectations of Indiana's fans, combined with Knight's perfectionism and his tendency to speak and act before he thought about the ramifications of his actions, Knight's brand of fame—or infamy—soon became the stuff of legend.

Beginning in 1976, Knight captured the eyes of America when he pulled guard Jim Wisman off the court by his jersey, much as an angry father would jerk aside a misbehaving son. As the nation watched, increased attention was bestowed upon Knight (also known as "The General"). Most parents, trusting that their kids were in good hands with their various sports after school, wondered how this man got away with it. Knight, in his defense, told *Sport* magazine, "When I grabbed Jimmy by the shirt on national t.v., the first person who said anything about it was Jimmy Wisman's mother. She said, 'If I had been there, I would have grabbed him too.'"

Bobby Knight

Pan Am Mishap

In spite of the great academic successes he had at Indiana (and nearly all of his players graduated, far above the national average) the press preferred to highlight the dramatic—and occasionally violent—interactions between Knight on one hand and everyone else on the other. In 1979 at the Pan American Games, Knight, in a confrontation with a Puerto Rican police officer, punched the cop after Knight was ejected from a game on a technical foul. The Puerto Rican government then put out a warrant for Knight's arrest, but he could not be extradited from the U.S. In the late 1980s Puerto Rico recalled the warrant. Knight, quoted in *Sports Illustrated* at the time, said of the Puerto Ricans, "F— 'em, f— 'em all.... The only thing they know how to do is grow bananas."

Indeed, Knight's list of notable mishaps seemed to get longer and longer, and as his team seemed to make earlier exits, the severity of actions grew in correlation with his team's failure to win in the NCAA tournament. He stuffed a fan from an opposing team (LSU) into a trash can. He told Connie Chung during an interview, "I think that if rape is inevitable, relax and enjoy it," though he later said that Chung took the quotation completely out of context. He has told women, in general, "There's only two things you people are good for: having babies and frying bacon." He pretended to bullwhip his star player, who happened to be black. He tossed a chair across the court during a game, kicked his own son (a player for him at the time) in the leg,

---

A Season on the Brink

Bobby Knight's 1985-86 NCAA season at Indiana is dramatized in this two-hour made-for-ESPN movie that first aired in the spring of 2002. In fact, it aired the night men's college basketball's "Selection Sunday" took place (when teams find out who will play in the tournament). Based on John Feinstein's in-depth and well-written book of the same name, *A Season on the Brink* is an adaptation that leaves much to be desired. Brian Dennehy stars as the red-sweatered Knight—and though Dennehy is a pillar of stage and screen, and though his performance as Knight enraged at his players, or the media (or whoever else crossed his path) is far from hackneyed—the material with which cast and crew had to work turned Feinstien's book into a farce. "It is cartoonlike, more shriek than Shrek, more avalanche than Snow White," writes Stan Hochman in his review for Knight-Ridder Newspapers.

---

and head-butted a player on the sidelines in a game, later claiming that he slipped as he was approaching the bench.

In 1986 Knight, in an attempt to show the country that he was not as bad as he was made out to be, allowed reporter John Feinstein total access to the Hoosier locker room and practices. This was unprecedented for Knight, who typically closed his practices to the press and the public. When John Feinstein's tell-all book, *A Season on the Brink,* came out in 1987, Knight claimed Fienstein distorted the facts.

As the nineties drew to a close, Knight's position at Indiana grew tenuous in spite of his nearly three decades of success at the school. Though many people would have weathered any turbulence with The General at the helm (and many Indiana fans still remain loyal to Bobby Knight, regardless of the fact that he coaches a thousand miles away in Texas), his questionable actions seemed to grow in intensity. In 1999 he was accused of choking Indiana basketball player Neil Ried in a 1997 practice (the act was caught on videotape). The school investigated and issued Knight a warning, suspended him for three games, and fined him $30,000.

He was also issued what the University referred to as its "zero-tolerance" policy in the spring of 2000. In the media storm that erupted in the fall of that year, it seemed that the reign of Coach Knight would come to an end. But just how it would end, no one knew.

On September 7, 2000, Knight allegedly grabbed Indiana freshman Kent Harvey and screamed profanities at him. Harvey claimed that he'd only said, "Hey, what's up, Knight?" and then Knight proceeded to berate him for disrespecting his elders. The picture gets blurry, however, and the true story of what happened—whether Knight used force or whether he merely held Harvey by the arm as he berated him—are not known. Knight would not apologize, however.

Indiana University claimed this was the type of incident their zero-tolerance policy was meant to prevent. University officials declared Knight's behavior unacceptable, and fired their coach on September 10, 2000. The

president of Indiana University, Miles Brand, said that no one incident broke the policy; rather, Knight's continued display of bad behavior was the cause of his dismissal.

In 2001, after six months away from college coaching (the first time he had been away from coaching in nearly four decades), Knight accepted the head coaching position with the Texas Tech Red Raiders, members of the Big 12 conference. In only two seasons he began turning around a program that was sinking and put the Knight pedigree on Texas basketball. Located in Lubbock—a good distance from Indiana—Knight still wears red (the Raiders colors), and his office happens to be on Indiana lane. It seems that he cannot escape his past.

In November of 2002 Knight filed a lawsuit against Indiana, claiming that the University owes him more than $2 million in lost income since they fired him. He still maintains that he was fired without just cause and that he never got a chance to defend himself properly.

CONTACT INFORMATION

Address: Coach Bob Knight, Texas Tech University, United Spirit Arena, Men's Basketball Office, 1701 Indiana Avenue, Lubbock, Texas 79409.

SELECTED WRITINGS BY KNIGHT:

(With Bob Hammel) *Knight: My Story.* Thomas Dunne Books, 2002.

FURTHER INFORMATION

Books

Alford, Steve and John Garrity. *Playing for Knight: My Six Seasons With Coach Knight.* New York: Simon & Schuster, 1991.

Berger, Phil. *Knight Fall: Bobby Knight, The Truth Behind America's Most Controversial Coach.* Kensington Publishing Corporation, 2000.

"Bobby Knight." *Contemporary Newsmakers 1985,* (Issue Cumulation). Detroit, MI: Gale Research, 1986.

Carpenter, Monte and Mike Towle. *Quotable General.* Towlehouse Publishers, 2001.

Feinstein, John. *A Season on the Brink: A Year With Bobby Knight and the Indiana Hoosiers.* New York: Pocket Books, 1987.

Hammel, Bob. *Beyond the Brink With Indiana: 1987 NCAA Champions.* Bloomington, IN: Indiana University Press, 1987.

Isenhour, Jack. *Same Knight, Different Channel: Basketball Legend Bob Knight at West Point and Today.* Brassey's, 2003.

Knight, Bobby and Bob Hammel. *Knight: My Story.* Thomas Dunne Books, 2002.

Mellon, Joan. *Bob Knight: His Own Man.* Donald I.
    Fine, 1988.
Sulek, Robert Paul. *Hoosier Honor: Bob Knight and
    Academic Success at Indiana University.* Praeger
    Publishers, 1990.

Periodicals

Deitsch, Richard. "TV Talk." *Sports Illustrated* (March
    18, 2002).
Hewitt, B. "Bobby Knight: Interview." *Sport* (February
    1982).
Knight Ridder/Tribune News Service (March 5, 2002).
"The Rabbit Hunter." *Sports Illustrated* (January 10, 1994).

Other

"Bobby Knight Sues Indiana University." CNN. http://
    www.cnn.com/2002/US/Midwest/11/12/knigh.
    lawsuit.ap (January 23, 2003).
Boehlert, Eric. "Why Bob Knight Should Bag It."
    Salon. http://www.salon.com (January 23, 2003).
Knight, Bobby. "Bobby Knight Basketball Clinic #1."
    Video. Katz Sports, 1983.
Shields, David. "Bob Knight, c'est moi." Salon. http://
    www.salon.com (January 23, 2003).

Sketch by Eric Lagergren

Bill Koch

Bill Koch
1955-

American cross-country skier

Cross-country skier Bill Koch is the only American ever to medal in cross-country skiing at the Olympic Games. He won a silver medal in the 30-km freestyle race at the 1976 Olympics, and also competed in the 1980, 1984, and 1992 Olympics. He was first in World Cup standings in 1982, the first American ever to reach this position, and third in 1983.

"A Future Fantasy"

Koch was born in Brattleboro, Vermont, a state noted for its downhill skiers, and he originally chose to compete in the Nordic combined event, which features cross-country skiing and ski jumping. He told Ron Bergin in *Cross Country Skier,* "As a kid I grew up with Olympic stars in my eyes—I always had it in mind as a future fantasy."

When he was sixteen he tried out for the U.S. Olympic Nordic Combined team as well as the Olympic cross country team, and during the midpoint of both trials, was asked by ski authorities to choose between them. He chose Nordic Combined, but in his final qualifying event, he fell, broke a ski, and came in sixth, not high enough to make the team.

Partly as a result of this experience, Koch decided to concentrate on cross-country skiing from then on. Two years later, at the age of eighteen, he became the first American to win a medal in international competition when he came in third in the 15-km race at the European junior championships.

Koch made the 1976 Olympic team in Nordic skiing, and in competition in Innsbruck, Austria, became the first American to win an Olympic medal in Nordic skiing, finishing second in the 30-km (18.6 mile) race. His time was 1 hour, 31 minutes, and 59.57 seconds. The winner, Sergei Savaliev of the Soviet Union, finished in 1:30:29.35. Koch told Leonard Shapiro in the *Washington Post,* "It makes me feel very excited and I hope the American people are very excited, too." In 2002, looking back on his Olympic wins, he told Ron Bergin in *Cross Country Skier,* "It was a wonderful gift in my life—those performances. I feel so privileged and enriched to have them in my past. At the same time I don't dwell on them at all. I think that they are best viewed as a feather in the cap."

As an Olympic athlete, Koch was deeply influenced by skier Bob Grey, who had skied on several Olympic teams. Another mentor was Mike Gallagher, a fellow skier who later became Koch's coach.

Chronology

1955	Born June 7, in Brattleboro, Vermont
1976	Wins silver medal in Olympic 30-km race
1980	Comes in 15th in Olympic 50-km race
1982	Becomes first American to medal in world championship Nordic competition: wins bronze medal in 30-km race in Oslo, Norway
1982	Wins overall Nordic World Cup title
1983	Wins 30-km and 50-km, comes in second in 15-km at U.S. National Championships
1983	Ranked third in overall World Cup championship
1984	Competes in Olympics, but does not medal
1986	World Cup officials allow Koch's skating technique in races
1987	Says he is retiring from competition
1992	Returns to competition in the Olympics, but does not medal.
1994	Competes in U.S. Olympic trials, but does not make the team
1997	Moves to Hawaii and begins developing the sport of sand skiing

Awards and Accomplishments

1976	Silver medal, Olympic 30-km race
1982	Bronze medal, World Championship 30-km race
1982	Winner, overall Nordic World Cup title
1983	Gold medals, 30-km and 50-km, silver medal, 15-km, U.S. National Championships
1983	Bronze medal, overall World Cup championship

For the next few seasons, Koch struggled with exercise-induced asthma, but at the 1980 Winter Olympic Games, held at Lake Placid, New York, he came in 15th in the 50-km race.

After the 1980 Olympics, Koch began working on his endurance, training at longer distances. He also used a technique borrowed from speed skaters, holding his skis at an angle with the tips outward, and pushing off the inside of the ski edge. The new technique made his times faster by 10 percent, and aroused controversy among ski officials; some tried to ban its use, and others simply added so much vertical climb to courses that the technique was unusable.

Wins Nordic World Cup

In 1982, Koch became the first American to win a medal in a world championship Nordic competition; he finished third in the 30-km race in Oslo, Norway. In the same year, based on that season's results, he won the overall Nordic World Cup title.

In 1983, Koch won the 30-km and 50-km events and came in second in the 15-km race at the U.S. National Championships. He also led the World Cup rankings until the last three races of that season, and placed third overall in the World Cup championship. Koch went to the Olympics, held in Sarajevo, Yugoslavia, in 1984, where he competed in four events. He did not earn any medals at these Games.

In 1986, Koch's fight to introduce a new skiing style was victorious. The World Cup officials decided to allow his skating technique, but hold separate races for skiers who used the new skating stride and those who used the traditional diagonal stride.

Also in 1986, Koch came up with the idea of inventing a single layer of fabric that would be suitable for ski clothing, which traditionally has used multiple layers. Although the right fabric was finally invented in 1992, the same year Koch licensed his line of clothing to a company called SportHill, its manufacturing process was subsequently changed, eliminating the fabric's resistance to wind. Because of this, Koch's clothing line was dropped.

Koch retired temporarily in 1987, but came back to competition for the U.S. at the 1992 Olympics in Albertville, France. He did not medal at those Olympics, but he was chosen to carry the U.S. flag during the opening ceremonies. Koch told Bergin, "That was a very great honor to have been chosen by my peers to do that."

Although Koch competed in the 1994 Olympic trials, he did not make the final team.

Koch believes that his international wins can be repeated by other American skiers. In an interview in *Ski*, he told Andrew Bigford, "I don't think I'm that special. There's plenty of talent out there. What I did is repeatable." He founded the Bill Koch Ski League, a national cross-country ski program for children aged seven to thirteen, to encourage kids to ski and develop their talent. Koch told Bigford that he believed the sport was hampered by the fact that good snow for the sport is not always available, since most people don't live in snowy areas and for those who do, the weather and snow conditions are so variable. "If you could count on snow, I think cross-country would flourish."

Sand Skiing

Koch became interested in traditional Hawaiian spirituality in the early 1990s, but soon became interested in another feature of the islands: the sand. He brought his skis, tried skiing on the sand, and found that it offered a surprisingly fast surface. In the past, Koch had skied through gravel pits and over pine-needle-covered forest floor, so skiing on sand was no surprise to him. He noticed that sand, like snow, varied according to the season, location, and weather conditions. He had been interested in sand skiing since the early 1980s, but could never find any really fast sand that was conducive to his workouts.

In 1997, Koch moved to Hawaii so he could sand-ski year-round, and created a Web site, www.sandskiing.com, about the sport.

In an article in *USA Today,* Koch told Sharon Raboin that when he skis on Hawaiian beaches, the sunbathers "almost can't believe their eyes. One in 10 are amazed enough to get off their towel and take your picture. I never complete a workout without being stopped a couple of times." Koch doesn't mind, since he wants to publicize this new twist on the sport; his mission is to get more people out on cross-country skis, and if the sport can move to sand, so much the better.

Koch told Raboin that sand skiing had one notable feature: "This won't work with just any sand. It must be coarse, yet firm." He explained to Bigford, "Finding the right sand is kind of elusive. Like snow, it changes every day, seasonally and according to conditions." But when the sand is good, he told Raboin, "This is the best way to train."

U.S. biathlon manager told Lyle Nelson told Raboin, "When Bill says this [sand skiing] is better, you can't discount it. He's the most creative person I've ever met. He always comes at things at a different angle. That's why he was world champion in a sport that's not popular in the U.S."

In recent years, Koch has become concerned about the use of illegal, performance-enhancing drugs by athletes. "It seems that everybody is convinced that drugs are very, very important to winning," he told Bergin. "This is a false notion that has to be dispelled." He said that although he knew that other athletes were using banned substances during the years he was competing, he decided that competing with them would simply be a greater challenge, and he was able to beat them. Koch also noted that young skiers "need to be guided to focus on learning how to tap into their own personal powers, which always have more potential than any drug."

Koch told Raboin that he believes more people should try cross-country skiing: "I love the sport so much. I truly believe it's a therapeutic, healing endeavor. I believe if more people cross-country skied, the world would be a better place." And, he told Bergin, "I certainly plan to ski all the days of the rest of my life."

CONTACT INFORMATION

Address: c/o Sports Unlimited, 1991 NW Upshur, Suite B, Portland, OR 97209. Fax: 503-227-4383. Phone: 503-227-3449. Email: Sandski2000@cs.com. Online: www.sportsu.com; www.sandskiing.com.

SELECTED WRITINGS BY KOCH:

*Bill Koch on Cross-Country Skiing,*Collier, 1993.

FURTHER INFORMATION

Periodicals

Auran, John Henry. "Coming on Strong in an Off-Year." *Skiing* (September, 1983): 64.

Bergin, Ron. "Bill Koch: America's Cross-Country Skier." *Cross-Country Skier* (January-February, 2002): 30.

Shapiro, Leonard. "Koch Stuns Nordic Skiers; Klammer Wins Downhill." *Washington Post* (February 6, 1976): D1.

Other

Bigford, Andrew. "Last Run: Bill Koch," *Ski Magazine*. http://www/skimag.com/ (November 11, 2002).

"Bill Koch." *Sports Unlimited*. http://www.sportsu.com/feat-koch.htm (November 11, 2002).

Sand Skiing with Bill Koch. http://www.sandskiing.com/ (November 18, 2002).

Sketch by Kelly Winters

Olga Korbut
1955-

Belarussian gymnast

Olga Korbut brought qualities to Olympic gymnastics that few had seen before. She brought innovation—her backwards flips from the balance beam and the uneven bars became a staple of the sport's repertoire. She brought youth—Korbut and her American peer **Cathy Rigby** were the standard-bearers of gymnastics' new breed of teenage prodigies. And she brought a smile—Korbut freely expressed the joy and pain behind her craft, countering the image of Soviet athletes as stoic and inaccessible. As *Sports Illustrated* writer Leigh Montville put it, "she was 85 pounds of pigtailed détente, flipping her way into the American consciousness."

Talent Shows Early

Korbut was born in 1955 (some sources say 1956) in Grodno, on the Niemen River in the country of Belarussia, then part of the Union of Soviet Socialist Republics (U.S.S.R.). Now called Belarus, the nation was a training ground for the Soviet gymnastics system, which had produced such stars as Yelena Volchetskaya, Larissa

Olga Korbut

Petrik, and Tamara Lazakovich. The youngest daughter of an engineer and a cook, Korbut was small for her age. But "she more than made up for it, in the opinion of her physical education instructor," noted *Soviet Life* reporter Vladimir Golubev in 1973. "Olga was good at exercises, [and] ran faster than the tall girls and many of the boys."

At age eleven the young girl qualified to enter the Soviet sports-school system (following her older sister, Ludmilla, also a master gymnast). The government-run program provides extracurricular athletic training to children who show high aptitude. Within a year Korbut was training under Renald Knysh, a top coach. It was Knysh who worked with his young charge to develop some of the groundbreaking moves that would amaze spectators years later. He recognized Korbut's strength and daring, and rehearsed her on the heretofore untried backward somersault on the balance beam. Korbut demonstrated the move at the U.S.S.R. championship meet, at which she placed fifth. Korbut's outstanding performance, however, was not without its critics, who said that her "tricks" were too dangerous to be emulated by any other gymnast.

A year after that, the rising gymnast took home a gold medal in the vault at a national meet and went on to attend her first international championship, where reserve-athlete Korbut gave a gymnastic demonstration that impressed a panel of referees. Adolescent angst caught up with Korbut briefly: "The praise went to her head, she began to put on airs, ignored her teammates and, in gen-

eral, made herself objectionable," wrote Golubev. "But that was a passing phase." Injury and illness sidelined Korbut for several months, but she recovered in time to place third overall in the 1972 Soviet national championships, qualifying her for the Olympics that year.

In an interview posted on the Public Broadcasting System (PBS) Web site, Korbut revealed that as early as age thirteen she felt ready to compete with world-class gymnasts. "I was ready for the [1968] Olympic Games," she said, "but I was fourteen years old, thirteen even and you couldn't compete [before age sixteen]." Korbut arrived in Munich as part of a team that included Ludmilla Turischeva, acknowledged to be the best female gymnast in the world; Tamara Kazakovich, and Antonina Koshel.

Raising the Bar in Gymnastics

The sight of the petite, pigtailed seventeen-year-old was duly noted by the audience, who were accustomed to not just more sober, but much older, Soviet gymnasts. (As recently as 1964, the gold medal winner from Russia was a 29-year-old mother.) In the past, gymnastics had been likened to a heightened form of ballet. By 1968, Cathy Rigby helped pioneer the athletic bent the sport would soon embrace; competing in her second summer games in 1972, Rigby was considered a favorite for an all-around gold medal. As the underdog, Korbut took the opportunity to show the judges her now-signature moves: the balance-beam backflip, and the Korbut Flip, a soaring backward leap from the higher to the lower section of the uneven parallel bars.

Nobody had seen anything like it. "I don't believe it!" exclaimed ABC commentator Gordon Maddux on seeing the four-foot-eleven gymnast fly around the bars. "Give her an 11!" Korbut's performance helped the Soviets secure the team gold medal. Her work on the balance beam and the floor exercise earned Korbut two additional golds in the all-around team competition. She set her sights on winning the uneven bars, but fate got in the way: During a maneuver, Korbut stubbed her toe and fell to the floor. As a worldwide audience watched, she dried her tears, rallied, and finished the routine. Later, she returned to the bars in the individual event and finished with a silver medal, bringing her Munich total to four.

In the eyes of Americans who harbored negative impressions of Soviet athletes, the sight of Korbut, smiling, waving, even crying when things went poorly, touched a common nerve. "Americans who didn't know a thing about gymnastics when the Munich Olympics began were arguing at the end whether or not Korbut deserved a perfect 10 for her work on the beam," wrote Montville. "Through television, the American public saw a fascinating, delicate creature, the little girl down the street, who seemed as removed as possible from the unemotional, cold Communist stereotype perpetuated by her teammates," Paul Attner stated in a *Washington Post* piece.

Chronology

1955	Born May 16, in Grodno, Belarussia (now Belarus)
1963	Begins gymnastics training
1967	Enters Belarussian junior championship
1969	Competes in first Soviet national championship
1972	Represents Soviet Union at Olympic summer games, Munich, Germany
1976	Represents Soviet Union at Olympic summer games, Montreal, Quebec, Canada
1977	Retires from competition
1978	Marries Leonid Bortkevich (divorced, 2000)
1979	Gives birth to son, Richard
1986	Becomes active in relief efforts following Chernobyl nuclear accident
1991	Relocates to U.S.
1993	Becomes gymnastics coach
2001	Marries Alex Voinich; becomes gymnastics instructor in Dunwoody, Georgia
2002	Arrested for shoplifting and investigated for counterfeiting

Awards and Accomplishments

1968	Gold medal, Spartakiade championship
1969	Introduced Korbut Flip, Soviet national gymnastics championships
1970	Reserve competitor, world championships
1971	Placed fourth, Soviet national championships
1972	Team gold, individual gold (2) and individual silver, Olympic summer games
1972	Named "Athlete of the Year," ABC *Wide World of Sports*
1972	Youngest person named Honored Master of Sport, Soviet Union
1973	Named "Athlete of the Year," Associated Press
1974	Won five medals at world championships
1975	Named "Woman of the Year," United Nations
1976	Team gold and individual silver, Olympic summer games
1988	First inductee, Gymnastics Hall of Fame
1994	Named one of the top athletes of past 40 years, *Sports Illustrated*
1996	Official attaché of Belarus, Olympic summer games
1999	Named among the best sportswomen of the twentieth century, by Italian news agency ACHA

Indeed, the memory of Korbut's charm helped offset the trauma engendered by the worst terrorist attack ever to strike an Olympic games. On September 5, days after the women's gymnastic competition ended, a faction of the Palestinian Liberation Army known as Black September kidnapped and murdered the entire Israeli Olympic contingent: nine athletes and two coaches. The games stopped cold during the crisis, and controversy arose when it was decided to resume immediately afterward.

A Worldwide Favorite

For gymnastics' newest star, life would not be the same. She toured the United States and Europe, meeting everyone from the British Prime Minister to Mickey Mouse. In one notable encounter, Korbut met a stranger who greeted her by saying, "You're so tiny." "You're so big," she replied to President Richard Nixon. At the same time, Korbut felt the pressure of compliance with the Soviet government, who put the teenager into exhibition after exhibition to feed their financial coffers and to show the world, as she told the PBS interviewer, that the "former Soviet Union is the best." From 1972 to 1976, she added, "I wasn't at home. I was always being somewhere in different countries." She knew, as Korbut told same interviewer, that the Soviet secret service, the KGB, trailed her during those years.

"Athlete of the Year" honors came Korbut's way, and she continued to compete. In 1973 she was second all-around to Turischeva at the European Championships; she won the all-around title at the World University Games in Moscow. Over the next two years she continued to pursue Turischeva in national and international meets, but finished second all-around.

In 1976 Korbut again represented the Soviet Union at the Olympic summer games in Montreal, Quebec. Now twenty-one, Korbut saw firsthand the legacy of her Mu-

nich triumph in the form of young, bold, highly athletic competitors. Chief among them was Romania's **Nadia Comaneci**, who would go on to make history as Korbut had four years earlier. Plagued by uncharacteristic poor performance, Korbut won just one medal in the competition, a silver for the balance beam. Though her smile never faded, Korbut was eclipsed in the public eye by Comaneci, a fourteen-year-old phenom who posted gymnastics' first perfect "tens."

Athlete Turns Activist

Montreal represented Korbut's farewell to competition; she returned to the Soviet Union, married in 1978, and gave birth to her son, Richard, a year later. But the world had not heard the last of Olga Korbut. In 1986, the nuclear reactor in Chernobyl exploded. Some 180 miles away at her home in Minsk, Korbut could see the cloud of radiation. "But the government never even told us to stay indoors," she was quoted in a *Sports Illustrated* article by Hank Hersch. When some of her friends and relatives began falling ill, Korbut went into action. She became personally involved in Chernobyl relief projects, traveling to the U.S. to raise consciousness and money on behalf of the victims of radiation poisoning. Working with the Fred Hutchinson Cancer Research Center, Korbut helped collect $70,000 for medical supplies.

The United States became Korbut's adopted home. After sending her son, Richard, to live with friends New Jersey to keep him out of harm's way following Chernobyl, the former gymnast and her family settled in Atlanta. She established a new life and career—gymnastics coaching—but the damage had been done. Korbut revealed in 1991 that she was suffering from thyroid problems, which she attributed to radiation poisoning. Talking to *People* correspondent Bill Shaw, Korbut recalled the frightening atmosphere in the wake of a nuclear leak: "When people began hearing bits of

Where Is She Now?

Having survived the Communist regime and Chernobyl radiation, Olga Korbut moved to the United States to begin a new life. All would not go smoothly, however. In January 2002, Korbut was arrested, charged with shoplifting $19 worth of food from a Publix supermarket in Norcross, Georgia. The gymnast's representative, Kay Weatherford, told the *Atlanta Journal-Constitution* that it was a misunderstanding. Korbut, she explained, had mistakenly walked out of the store with the items to retrieve her wallet, left in the car. A more serious charge came shortly after that incident, when it was revealed that authorities had found $30,000 in counterfeit $100 bills in the Korbut home during eviction proceedings. The home had been most recently occupied by the athlete's grown son. The investigation was continued by the Secret Service.

Korbut's denied any involvement with this federal offense. Still, her attorney Howard Weintraub told Beth Warren in the *Atlanta Journal-Constitution,* "it must be absolutely devastating to have millions of people the world over now look at you in a light differently . . . for something you didn't do." In a 1992 *Sports Illustrated* piece, Korbut revealed a philosophy that may have well served her during these hard times. "I try not to focus on annoying things in my past," she said. "It's like the Russian proverb says: `If I always watch who steps on my feet, I wouldn't walk.'"

information, they felt panicky. They were afraid to drink the water, breathe the air, afraid of everything. We were all outdoors, because it was close to the [May Day] celebration, and we were planting gardens and enjoying the spring. If they had told us Chernobyl had exploded, we would have stayed inside and maybe avoided those early heavy doses of radiation." Cancer, she added, was rampant: "There are some people who were perfectly healthy and all of a sudden came down with severe illnesses we hadn't heard of." Worse, conditions in the impoverished region hampered treatment: "There are no machines for chemotherapy or drug therapy.... We can't find produce or meat or anything you need for a normal existence." As Korbut told Shaw, "I have never seen in my entire life such a lack of everything."

Subsequent to her move to the United States, Korbut faced challenging personal crises. In 1999 she went public with a claim that, as young as fifteen, the gymnast was coerced into sex by one of her coaches. The man told her to comply or risk being thrown off the Soviet team, she said. "Many of my teammates were forced to become sexual slaves ... and I was one of them," she was quoted in a Moscow-based article printed in the *Globe and Mail.* Her marriage to Bortkevich broke up in 2000; she remarried a year later. But her image as a representative of her sport stayed with Korbut; during the 1996 Olympic summer games in Atlanta, she was an official attaché for Belarus.

Olga Korbut changed the face of gymnastics and made possible the goals of small girls to reach great heights in sport. She "flew across the screens as if she were drawn by a cartoonist's pen," Montville remarked. "No boundaries existed, no laws of nature.... She was

pixie, elf, amazing Soviet sylph. Her smile was the definition of innocence. She made an entire world fall in love." But in her later years, the former teenage star spoke up for the older athlete. "I always thought there should be a separate classification for older gymnasts," she said to Montville in a 1989 *Sports Illustrated* article. "There should be different expectations for someone in a mature stage of womanhood than for a young girl. The audiences should not cheer only out of fear. There should be an appreciation of the beauty of gymnastics. That is what should be shown. A gymnast should be able to stay in the sport for a long time."

CONTACT INFORMATION

Online: http://www.olgakorbut.com.

FURTHER INFORMATION

Books

Great Women in Sports. Detroit: Visible Ink Press, 1996.

Periodicals

Attner, Paul. *Washington Post* (March 18, 1973).

Calkins, Laurel Brubaker. "10 Again." *People* (July 15, 1996).

Golubev, Vladimir. *Soviet Life* (February, 1983).

Hersch, Hank. "Beaming Again." *Sports Illustrated Classic* (fall, 1992).

"Korbut Says Coach Forced Her to Have Sex." *Globe and Mail* (June 24, 1999).

Montville, Leigh. "Return of the Pixies." *Sports Illustrated* (November 27, 1989).

Montville, Leigh. "Forty for the Ages." *Sports Illustrated* (September 19, 1994).

"Olga's Midlife Crisis." *Life* (November, 1988).

Shaw, Bill. "Olga Korbut's Deadly Foe." *People* (March 4, 1991).

Torpy, Bill. "Life Turns Sour for Olympic Sweetheart Korbut." *Atlanta Journal-Constitution* (February 10, 2002).

Warren, Beth. "Olga Korbut Denies Any Link to Counterfeit Money at Former House." *Atlanta Journal-Constitution* (February 7, 2002).

Other

International Gymnast. http://www.intlgymnast.com/legends/korbut.html (January 14, 2003).

Olga Korbut Web Site. http://www.olgakorbut.com (January 14, 2003).

Red Files. http://www.pbs.org/redfiles/sports/deep/interv/s_int_olga_korbut.htm (January 14, 2003).

Olga Korbut

Sketch by Susan Salter

Janica Kostelic

Janica Kostelic
1982-

Croatian skier

With a tenacious spirit forged in her war-torn homeland, Janica Kostelic of Croatia became the only Alpine skier ever to win four medals in one Winter Olympics at the 2002 games in Salt Lake City, Utah. She also is Croatia's first Winter Olympic medalist since the country declared independence from the former Yugoslavia in 1991. Kostelic, a national hero in a land with little skiing tradition, is widely considered the world's best slalom skier. The "Croatian Sensation," as she's called in the media, is the only woman and one of only three Alpine skiers in history to win three gold medals in one Olympiad. The others are **Jean-Claude Killy** of France and Toni Sailer of Austria. And by all appearances, Kostelic isn't done yet. "History is not something I think about," she told the *New York Times* during her record-setting run in Salt Lake City. "Who has time to think of history right now? I'm too busy skiing."

Relentless

Ante Kostelic, who, with his wife Marica, had been a top national handball player in the former Yugoslavia, established a demanding skiing regimen for his children when they were small. If others trained four hours a day, Janica and brother Ivica worked eight. If a typical practice consisted of skiing through 400 gates, Janica skied through 1,200. When war ripped their country in the early 1990s, the Kostelics fled their home in Zagreb and sought out training sites in Central and Eastern Europe. They had little money. When Janica and Ivica began skiing competitively, the family drove from race to race, camping in tents along the way. When the weather turned cold, they slept in the car. They often ate sandwiches for every meal. Once, they took shelter in a cave for a week because they feared air strikes. "For 10 to 12 years we never stopped," Ante Kostelic told the *New York Times.* "Maybe we did not know better. We did what we thought was right."

Janica entered twenty-two junior races during the 1996-97 season. She won them all. "Despite that impressive record," *Time International* reported, "in her first World Cup season, 1998-99, her third place in a slalom event at Park City, Utah, took officials by surprise. They couldn't find a Croatian flag for the award ceremony and Janica had to dig one out of her ski bag."

Ups and downs

At age sixteen, Kostelic competed in five events at the 1998 Winter Olympics in Nagano, Japan. Her eighth-place finish in the combined was the best ever by a Croatian in the Winter Games. The following year, she earned her first World Cup victory—and its $50,000 purse—but then missed most of the season after tearing four ligaments in her right knee while training in St. Moritz. "The extra work required to get fit again, including long-distance running, cycling, gymnastics and even free diving, made her stronger," Kate Noble reported in *Sports Illustrated.* Kostelic returned for the 2000-01 World Cup season and dominated the field. At one point, she won eight straight slalom races. She finished the season as the overall World Cup champion—the fourth-youngest woman ever to do so.

Kostelic was the overwhelming favorite to win gold at the 2001 World Championships, but a fall cost her the combined event and she finished fifth in the slalom. She was devastated; Ante Kostelic was quoted saying his daughter was quitting the sport. At the same time, Janica was coping with chronic knee problems, which some observers contended were the result of the demanding training she had endured since early childhood. (Ivica has similar knee problems.) Surgeons operated on her left knee twice, in the spring and summer of 2001, but the pain lingered. During a third operation doctors discovered and removed a piece of floating cartilage. Janica was back in training in October and returned to the World Cup circuit in November.

Olympic uncertainty

Kostelic arrived in Salt Lake City for the Winter Olympics in February 2002 with a cloud of uncertainty hanging over her. She had undergone three operations in the past year. She was ranked 17th overall. Her World Cup season had been abbreviated and unnoteworthy. She had been avoiding the downhill event and rarely trained at high speed due to concern for her reconstructed knees. She passed up the last pre-Olympic World Cup races to spend time resting and doing dryland training. Could she possibly compete for an Olympic medal? The 20-year-old skier with the solid 5-foot 8-inch, 166-pound frame did not take long to answer that question.

In the first women's Alpine event, the combined, Kostelic led the field by more than a full second after the two slalom runs. Her success was not altogether surprising; the slalom was her specialty. She was expected to falter, however, on the demanding downhill leg of the event. "But skiing last among the leaders, Kostelic sped along the downhill course in a low, seamless tuck, her hands and arms rarely rising as she negotiated the turns," Bill Pennington wrote in the *New York Times.* "If the 70-mile-an-hour speeds bothered her state of mind or her knees, she did not show it." Her combined time of 2 minutes 43.28 seconds was nearly 1.5 seconds faster than the second-place finisher. Kostelic and Croatia had their first gold medal. "This is a family medal," she told Pennington. "Everything was always me, my brother and my father. My mother was always there on the side, too, and she's the boss. This is great, the family's dream come true."

Three to go

Kostelic had to tackle the super-G before moving onto her best events—the slalom and giant slalom. A few weeks earlier, she had finished fourth in the super-G during a World Cup competition in Cortina, Italy. The Olympics brought out the competitive quality, however, last evident in Kostelic's championship 2000-01 season. She missed Olympic gold in the super-G by eight-hundredths of a second, finishing behind Italy's Daniela Ceccarelli. Medal No. 2 was silver.

The women's slalom was run in a steady snowstorm on a treacherous course. Poor visibility obscured holes and ruts. Thirty skiers failed to finish one of their first two runs. Once again, Janica Kostelic overcame the obstacles to win. It was her second gold medal and third medal overall.

She faced difficult course conditions again as she sought her record-breaking fourth medal in the giant slalom. "Because she is not ranked among the top competitors worldwide in the giant slalom," Pennington explained in the *Times,* "Janica Kostelic began her pursuit of Olympic history as the 19th skier from the starting gate today. That meant she skied about a half-hour after the first of the favorites, enough time for the snow on the race course to develop ruts like foxholes. But it takes more than ruts to hinder Kostelic." After the first run, Kostelic led the field by nearly a half-second, a sizeable margin. She was the 15th skier—the last of the leaders—to tackle the second run. She beat the field again and captured her fourth medal in nine days. Pennington likened her astonishing achievement to a runner winning both a 400-meter and a one-mile race. "Kostelic, as healthy as she has been in two years, is crossing over from category to category and beating the speed specialists in the speed events, like the super-G, and defeating the technicians in a technical event like the slalom," he wrote. "In these Olympics, there is no other skier—male or female—in Kostelic's class. In any single Olympics, there has been no other skier in Kostelic's category: four-time medal winner."

A hero's welcome

On Feb. 22, 2002, Janica Kostelic became the first Alpine skier ever to win four medals in a single Olympic games and joined Jean-Claude Killy and Toni Sailer as the only skiers to win three gold medals in one Olympics. Even her toughest competitors acknowledged that she was unbeatable. "She's proved that mentally she's the best," said Swedish medalist Anja Paerson. "Right now, she's incredible. After all she's been through, I'm really happy for her." Switzerland's Sonja Nef, another medal winner, agreed: "She is too strong in the head. She was too good in these days." A few days later, thousands of Croats packed Zagreb's main square to give her a hero's welcome. She and her family, after their arduous journey, are icons in their homeland.

CONTACT INFORMATION

Email: janica@croski.hr.

FURTHER INFORMATION

Periodicals

"Brother and Sister Win on Same Day." *New York Times* (January 6, 2003).

Habib, Hal. "In the Danger Zone Thrills and Spills: Athletes Learn to Harness Their Fear." *Palm Beach Post* (February 19, 2002).

Layden, Tim. "Scorecard." *Sports Illustrated* (February 17, 2002).

Layden, Tim. "Golden Gates: Having Overcome Injury, Smiling Janica Kostelic Gave Croatia Something to Grin About With Her Dominating Four-Medal Skiing Performance." *Sports Illustrated* (March 4, 2002).

"Miller Finishes Fourth Overall." *New York Times* (March 11, 2002).

Noble, Kate. "Croatian Contenders: Two for the Snow: For the talented Kostelics, Janica and Ivica, winning races is a family affair." *Time International* (February 11, 2002).

Noble, Kate. "The Croatian Sensation's Comeback." *Time International* (March 4, 2002).

Pennington, Bill. "First Croatian Medalist Wins Gold for Her Family." *New York Times* (February 15, 2002).

Pennington, Bill. "Letting Go, an Italian Stuns the Super-G Final." *New York Times* (February 18, 2002).

Pennington, Bill. "Third Medal in Hand, Kostelic Focuses on Fourth." *New York Times* (February 21, 2002).

Pennington, Bill. "Kostelic Smooths Rough Road With 3rd Gold." *New York Times* (February 23, 2002).

Sketch by David Wilkins

Sandy Koufax
1935-

American baseball player

During his prime, Sandy Koufax dominated major league baseball with his powerful, yet fatally fragile left arm. From 1962 to 1966, Koufax pitched four no-hitters (including a perfect game) and struck out more than 1,400 batters, winning 111 games and losing only 34. What makes Koufax's story so marvelous, however, is his transformation. During his early years, Koufax struggled at times to get the ball near the plate. Yet in the end, Koufax tamed his fastball, prompting Pittsburgh's Willie Stargell to remark that hitting Koufax was like "trying to drink coffee with a fork." What Koufax is most remembered for, however, occurred off the pitcher's mound. Koufax became a hero for refusing to pitch in the opening game of the 1965 World Series because it fell on the Jewish holiday Yom Kippur. Koufax's dedication to his religion helped generations of American Jews take pride in their heritage. As quickly as Koufax's arm brought him into the spotlight, it also took him out. In the end, Koufax's arm proved to be as delicate as it was powerful. Arm pain forced Koufax into retirement in 1966 when he was only 30 years old and still at the top of his game.

Preferred Basketball as Youngster

Sandy Koufax was born Sanford Braun on December 30, 1935, in Brooklyn, New York, to Jack and Evelyn Braun, though his parents soon divorced. As a youngster, Koufax stayed with his Jewish grandparents, Max and Dora Lichtenstein, while his mother, an accountant, worked. When Koufax was nine, his mother married a lawyer named Irving Koufax. Young Sandy took his stepfather's last name and pretty much severed ties with his birthfather.

Growing up, Koufax's true love was basketball. At Brooklyn's Lafayette High School, the 6-foot-2 Koufax dominated the league. With his Herculean arm, Koufax could launch a basketball the length of the court to a teammate waiting under the basket.

Koufax was a shy kid who preferred staying out of the spotlight, yet his muscles continually drew him in.

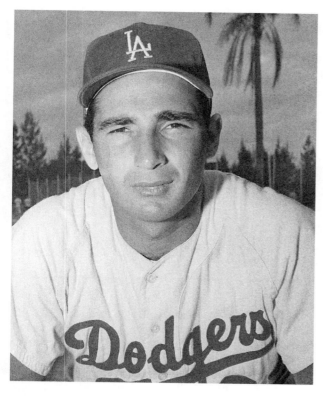

Sandy Koufax

Chronology

1935	Born on December 30 in Brooklyn, New York
1939	Parents divorce
1945	Mother remarries
1953	Enters college at the University of Cincinnati; makes basketball team
1954	Pitches only season of college baseball
1954	Signs with the Brooklyn Dodgers
1955	Makes major league debut on June 24 against the Milwaukee Braves
1959	Appears in World Series
1960	Nearly quits baseball due to poor record
1965	Arthritic arm plagues him during the season
1966	Appears in World Series
1966	Wins last major league game on October 2
1966	Announces retirement from baseball on November 18
1969	Marries Anne Heath Widmark on January 1
1972	Watches Dodgers retire his uniform number (32)
1979	Begins working as a pitching instructor for the Dodgers
1980s	Divorces wife in the early part of the decade
1990	Retires from work as Dodgers pitching instructor
1990s	Divorces second wife, Kim Koufax, in latter part of the decade
1990s	Appears in charity golf tournaments
2002	Continues to help coach various struggling pitchers

In *Sandy Koufax: A Lefty's Legacy,* author Jane Leavy recalled that a childhood friend noted that strangers at the beach gawked at the teenage Koufax's build, calling him "a Greek god."

Though Koufax loved basketball, he dabbled in baseball and played in a sandlot league. Legend has it that when Koufax pitched, his teammates sat down because they didn't expect any hits: Koufax either walked the batters with his wild pitches, or struck them out with his fastball.

Following high school, Koufax headed to the University of Cincinnati in 1953, hoping to study architecture. He made the basketball team and earned a partial scholarship from coach Ed Jucker. Jucker also coached the baseball team and by the spring of 1954, Koufax was on the roster. That season, Koufax had 51 strikeouts in 32 innings, coupled with 30 walks. Despite his wildness, the Brooklyn Dodgers saw potential and signed Koufax in 1954. Because Koufax received a large signing bonus, the Dodgers had to place Koufax on their roster. The rule was supposed to keep wealthy clubs from signing all the best prospects. Unfortunately for Koufax, who had pitched only one season of college ball, skipping the minor leagues proved disastrous.

Overcame Ball-Control Problem

The inexperienced pitcher struggled in the majors. At the end of the 1960 season, Koufax was a career-losing pitcher with a record of 36 and 40. His mediocrity gnawed at him; Koufax considered quitting, yet had a change of heart and reported to spring training in 1961 determined to take responsibility for his career. He began to sacrifice speed for accuracy. Slowly, Koufax gained control of his unruly fastball.

Koufax explained his transformation in John Grabowski's book, *Sandy Koufax,* saying that he became a good pitcher when he stopped trying to make batters miss the ball and started trying to make them hit it.

Koufax ended the 1961 season 18-13 and made his first All-Star appearance. He also fanned 269 batters to break a National League strikeout record.

In 1962, Koufax pitched his first of four no-hitters, and by 1963 he was at the top of his game, ending the season 25-5, with 11 shutouts. At 1.88, his earned-run average (ERA) was the lowest posted in the National League in 20 years. Koufax also led his team to a 1963 World Series victory over the New York Yankees by winning two games in the series. Koufax's stellar pitching earned him his first of three **Cy Young** Awards, presented to the best pitcher in baseball. He was also named the World Series MVP and won the Hickok Belt, awarded to the top professional athlete.

Plagued with Sore Arm

The strain of throwing 90-mph fastballs, however, soon caught up with Koufax. His arm muscles tore and his elbow cartilage broke down causing inflammation. Koufax sat out part of the 1964 season, though he still pitched to a 19-5 record.

Career Statistics

Yr	Team	W	L	ERA	GS	CG	SHO	IP	H	R	BB	SO
1955	Bk. D	2	2	3.02	5	2	2	41.2	33	15	28	30
1956	Bk. D	2	4	4.91	10	0	0	58.2	66	37	29	30
1957	Bk. D	5	4	3.88	13	2	0	104.1	83	49	51	122
1958	LA D	11	11	4.48	26	5	0	158.2	132	89	105	131
1959	LA D	8	6	4.05	23	6	1	153.1	136	74	92	173
1960	LA D	8	13	3.91	26	7	2	175	133	83	100	197
1961	LA D	18	13	3.52	35	15	2	255.2	212	117	96	269
1962	LA D	14	7	2.54	26	11	2	184.1	134	61	57	216
1963	LA D	25	5	1.88	40	20	11	311	214	68	58	306
1964	LA D	19	5	1.74	28	15	7	223	154	49	53	223
1965	LA D	26	8	2.04	41	27	8	335.2	216	90	71	382
1966	LA D	27	9	1.73	41	27	5	323	241	74	77	317
TOTAL		165	87	2.76	314	137	40	2,324.1	1,754	806	817	2,396

Bk. D: Brooklyn Dodgers; LA D: Los Angles Dodgers (the team relocated from Brooklyn to Los Angeles in 1958).
Pitched in four World Series (1959, 1963, 1965, 1966) for a total of four wins (two of them shutouts) and three losses.

Koufax's arm continued to pester him during the 1965 season. To ease the painful swelling, Koufax marinated his body with a skin-searing ointment called Capsolin. He gobbled codeine along with an anti-inflammatory medicine used to treat thoroughbred horses. The medicines sickened Koufax and slowed his reaction time.

Koufax's 1965 stats obscured his pain. His record stood at 26-8 at the start of the World Series, when the Dodgers faced the Minnesota Twins. The first game was held on Yom Kippur, and Koufax refused to pitch, becoming a hero to legions of American Jews. In the end, he won two games in the series, helping the Dodgers secure the championship.

In 1966, Koufax pitched to a 27-9 record and shocked the world by announcing his retirement because he faced the prospect of losing the use of his arm if he kept pitching. Unfortunately, Koufax lived before laparoscopic surgery could have fixed his arm and kept him pitching for years to come.

Remembered as True Champion

Following his retirement, Koufax worked as a sports commentator for NBC, although that position didn't fit the reserved pitcher very well. On January 1, 1969, Koufax married Anne Heath Widmark; they divorced in the early 1980s. Koufax later married Kim Koufax, though they divorced in the late 1990s. He never had any children.

In 1972, when Koufax was 36, he was inducted into the Baseball Hall of Fame in Cooperstown, New York, the youngest player to receive such honors. In 1979, Koufax began working as a coach for the Dodgers, quitting in February 1990.

After leaving baseball, Koufax lived a reclusive, quiet life, making his home in Vero Beach, Florida, the off-season home of the Los Angeles Dodgers. He refused to cash in on his fame, appearing rarely in public. Koufax is a modest man who has tried to be forgotten. He tells authors not to write about him. But the very fact that authors are still calling and fans are still clamoring to know him is a testament to the impact he made. Though more than three decades have passed since he hurled his last game, Koufax still enjoys working out at the Dodgers clubhouse, where he has a key.

Though Koufax quit as a Dodgers pitching instructor in 1990, he still coaches players intermittently from time to time. In February 2002, during spring training, Koufax tutored then-Dodger Terry Mulholland on his curveball. Likewise, Koufax has worked wonders with Texas Rangers hurler Chan Ho Park and New York Mets pitcher Al Leiter.

Perhaps former teammate Don Sutton said it best when he told *Sports Illustrated*, "He was a star who didn't feel he was a star. That's a gift not many people have."

SELECTED WRITINGS BY KOUFAX:

(With Ed Linn) *Koufax*. New York: Viking Press, 1966.

FURTHER INFORMATION

Books

Grabowski, John. *Sandy Koufax*. New York: Chelsea House Publishers, 1992.

Gruver, Edward. *Koufax*. Dallas: Taylor Publishing Co., 2000.

Leavy, Jane. *Sandy Koufax: A Lefty's Legacy*. New York: HarperCollins Publishers, Inc., 2002.

Sanford, William R. and Carl R. Green. *Sandy Koufax*. New York: Macmillan Publishing Co., 1993.

Awards and Accomplishments

1961-66	Selected for National League All-Star game
1962	Pitched no-hitter against the New York Mets on June 30
1963	Pitched no-hitter against the San Francisco Giants on May 11
1963	Struck out 15 Yankees on October 2, setting a new World Series strikeout record
1963	Won two games in the World Series against the New York Yankees to help team clinch the championship
1963	Named National League Most Valuable Player (MVP), World Series MVP, Associated Press Male Athlete of the Year, United Press International Player of the Year, *Sporting News* Player of the Year, Fraternal Order of Eagle Man of the Year, and Southern California Athlete of the Year; also earned Cy Young Award and the Hickok Belt
1963, 1965	Won World Series ring
1964	Pitched a no-hitter against the Philadelphia Phillies on June 4
1965	Pitched in National League All-Star game on July 13, coming away the winning pitcher
1965	Pitched a perfect game against the Chicago Cubs on September 9
1965	Ended season with 382 strikeouts, a new National League season record
1965	Won two games, including a shutout, in the World Series against the Minnesota Twins to help his team clinch the championship
1965	Named World Series MVP, *Sporting News* Player of the Year, Associated Press Male Athlete of the Year, and *Sports Illustrated* Sportsman of the Year; also won Cy Young Award and the Hickok Belt
1966	Won a record fifth consecutive ERA title and received third Cy Young Award
1972	Inducted into the National Baseball Hall of Fame
1999	Named *Sports Illustrated* Athlete of the Century
1999	Named to the ESPN Top 50 Athletes of the Century
1999	Named to the Major League Baseball Team of the Century

Koufax retired in 1966 with 165 wins to 87 losses.

Periodicals

"The Left Arm of God." *Sports Illustrated* (July 12, 1999): 82.

Other

"Sandy Koufax's Career Pitching Statistics." Baseball Hall of Fame. http://www.baseballhalloffame.org/ hofers%5Fand%5Fhonorees/hofer_stats/Pitching/ koufax_sandy.htm (November 1, 2002).

Sketch by Lisa Frick

Anna Kournikova
1981-

Russian tennis player

Anna Kournikova is arguably the most marketable woman in sports, despite having won no WTA Tour

Anna Kournikova

singles tournaments. "Anna Kournikova is sex with a tennis racket attached," Bud Collins, longtime expert in the sport, said on ESPN Classic's *SportsCentury* series. Kournikova has only once reached the semifinals of a Grand Slam event, yet Web sites related to the attractive young Russian woman annually receive among the most "hits" worldwide. ESPN televised the filming of her skin-revealing 2003 calendar five times during Christmas week, 2002. It drew a 1.1 rating, considered high for an ESPN non-event telecast.

"Kournikova is of the post-feminist generation, one more likely to take its cues from MTV, Madonna and Camille Paglia than *Ms.*," Peter Bodo wrote on the *ESPN.com* Web site. "She also is of a realistic generation, and in a world in which sex sells—no matter what anyone has said or done so far—she has what the market wants. Having grown up relatively poor in a confused and desolate place (post-Soviet Russia), she is more than glad to exploit her natural gifts for personal gain." In 2000, she was one of five female tennis players named to *Forbes* magazine's Power 100 in Fame and Fortune list at No. 58.

Kournikova, beset by injuries in 2001 and 2002, does have two Grand Slam women's doubles titles. She and **Martina Hingis** teamed together to capture the Australian Open in 1999 and 2002 (they no longer play together). She was ranked as high as eighth among singles in May, 2001, before injuring her ankle. As 2002 ended, Kournikova was playing **Monica Seles** in exhibition matches. In tune-ups for the January, 2003 Australian Open, she was 35th in the Women's Tennis Association rankings. As the year 2003 began, Kournikova's pro singles career tournament drought stood at 115.

Bollettieri Protege

Born an only child in Moscow, Kournikova first swung a tennis racquet at age 5. She came from an athletic family; her father, Sergei, was a Greco-Roman wrestler and her mother, Alla, ran the 400 meters. At age seven, Kournikova was accepted as a junior member in Moscow's renowned Spartak Athletic Club, but the city's climate limited outdoor play to four months, and indoor courts were cost prohibitive.

The family moved to Florida in the early 1990s, enabling Kournikova to enroll at Nick Bollettieri's tennis academy, which launched the likes of Seles, **Andre Agassi** and **Pete Sampras** to stardom. Kournikova spoke no English when she arrived. "But Anna knew who she was, and wanted everyone to know who she was, too," Bollettieri recalled. "She thought she was Queen Tut."

She turned pro at 14, making her WTA Tour debut at Moscow as a qualifier, defeating Marketa Kochta before losing to Sabine Appelmans. A year later, she surged 224 spots to a No. 57 ranking and, in her first Grand Slam, reached the fourth round before losing top-ranked **Steffi Graf**. She also represented Russia in the 1996 Summer Olympic Games in Atlanta.

Wimbledon Semifinalist

In 1997, at age 16, Kournikova toppled No. 5 Iva Majoli and No. 10 Anke Huber at Wimbledon and reached the semifinals before losing 6-3, 6-2 to Hingis. She was the second woman in the open era, after **Chris Evert**, to reach the Wimbledon semifinals in her debut. Kournikova, who admitted to soreness in her left hip, said she saw her run as a learning experience. "It's unbelievable, I got to the semi-finals," she said. "I was dreaming about this.

I'm definitely going to take a lot with me from this tournament, and from this experience."

Early the next year, she rose to No. 16 by reaching her first final, in Key Biscayne, Florida. She knocked off four straight top-10 players (Seles, Conchita Martinez, **Lindsay Davenport** and **Arantxa Sanchez Vicario**) before losing the title match to **Venus Williams** in a full three sets. She also defeated Graf at Eastbourne. Kournikova missed Wimbledon that year, however, because of a thumb injury. In her other noteworthy Grand Slam singles performance, she reached the 2001 Australian Open quarterfinals, where Davenport proved too much, 6-4, 6-2.

Off-Court Headlines

Kournikova ended 1999 with a number one in doubles. A year later she finished number eight, her first top 10 singles ranking. Her beauty and success were magnets for sponsors. She pitched brokerages and dot-com companies on television. By then, her personal life had also made big headlines. She was romantically linked to Russian-born hockey stars **Sergei Federov** and Pavel Bure. She was also linked to musician Enrique Iglesias, with whom she made a video. Some observers say her off-court distractions hurt her game, although an injured left foot has also troubled her. Her record in singles matches in 2002 was only 28-24.

"I do think someday she will hate herself for not giving tennis her best shot," *ESPN.com*'s Chris McKendry wrote. "I don't think Kournikova is a fraud or the product of PR packaging. I do think she's a lucky winner of the 'birth lottery'—born beautiful and athletic—and that's not her fault. But she is to blame for underachieving." McKendry added: "So when exactly did Kournikova become less of a tennis player and more of a pop icon?

In 2001, Kournikova reached the quarterfinals of the Australian Open. Then came the stress fracture and, although she withdrew from the year's other major tournaments, she did not withdraw from public life. That decision has proven to be costly. Fair or not, it looked as though she did not care to be on the court. She attracted flashbulbs everywhere she went, making headlines with her latest beaus, and making a music video with one steady, Enrique Iglesias. "Smooching and rolling around with the singer in his 'Escape' video sent Kournikova's negative public image—and the media—over the top. This season, back from injury, Kournikova's life, not her tennis, became topic No. 1 ... and only."

Seles Defends Her

After an exhibition match in December, 2002, in St. Paul, Minnesota, Seles quickly denied reports about resentment toward Kournikova by other WTA tour players. "I don't think there's animosity. My gosh, that's a strong word to use," Seles said after beating Kournikova in the Minnesota Tennis Challenge. "She's dedicated her life to this sport. She's one of the hardest workers on tour. She's a gorgeous girl. What can she do about that? She can't just hide her face."

Bodo admires Kournikova's work ethic. "Consider this: In the spring of 2000, Kournikova badly tore ligaments in her left ankle in Berlin, just 19 days before the French Open," he wrote. "Doctors advised that Kournikova rest the ankle for a month, but two days before Roland Garros began, she booked a practice court and hit balls fed right to her racket because she could not yet run properly. Ignoring all advice, she entered the French Open and won a round before a loss to Sylvia Plischke left her open to charges that by now constitute a ceaseless refrain: Kournikova is all glitz and no substance, she's overrated, she can't handle Grand Slam-level pressure."

Looking Ahead

Kournikova's one wish for 2003, she said, was "to stay healthy, go back and try to play a full season this time." Her latest coach is former men's star Harold Solomon, a no-nonsense type credited with saving **Jennifer Capriati**'s career. Off the court, meanwhile, she sued *Penthouse* magazine, which published photos in 2002 purporting to be Kournikova frolicking on a topless beach. The magazine apologized for a misidentification and settled out of court.

McKendry feels Kournikova's best chance for a Grand Slam title may have eluded her, given the dominance of the Williams sisters. "Both (Hingis and Kournikova) are missing what the Williams sisters, Jennifer Capriati, Lindsay Davenport and even Monica Seles have—incredible strength and a powerful serve," she wrote. "It has been too long since Kournikova's play justified her popularity. But don't call her a nontalent. Nobody, not even Anna, can fake their way to even the No. 36 ranking in the world. Fact is, somewhere under the piles of publicity is a good tennis player. And the only way for her to prove her critics wrong is to prove that ... again."

While leveling her share of criticisms at Kournikova, McKendry still feels there's more to like than not to like. "As for young girls looking up to her, all I can say is this: Kournikova is an athletic 5-foot-8, 125-pound beauty," she writes. "Who's a better role model—Anna or some skinny heroin chic model?"

SELECTED WRITINGS BY KOURNIKOVA:

(With Greg Brown) *Make Your Point,* Dallas: Taylor, 2001.

FURTHER INFORMATION

Books

Berman, Connie. *Anna Kournikova*. Philadelphia: Chelsea House, 2001.

Other

"Anna Kournikova Career Highlights." ESPN.com, http://espn.go.com/tennis/s/wta/profiles/kournikova. html, (December 30, 2002).

"Anna Kournikova Press Conference Interviews Archive." http://quickfound.net/sports/kournikova_ interviews_archive_index.html, (December 30, 2002).

Bodo, Peter. "Kournikova's Got Game, Fame." ESPN. com, http://espn.go.com/classic/biography/s/ Kournikova_Anna.html, (December 28, 2002).

Hamilton, Brian. "Model or Tennis Player? You Glow, Girl." *St. Paul Pioneer Press,* http://www.twincities. com/mld/twincities/sports/4736736.htm, (December 14, 2002).

Harris, Elliott. "Contemplating Anna and Other Moot Points." *Chicago Sun-Times,* http://www.suntimes. com, (December 30, 2002).

McKendry, Chris. "Not Just Another Pretty Face." ESPN.com, http://espn.go.com/page2/s/mckendry/ 021010.html, (October 10, 2002).

Mushnick, Phil. "Fran's the Man in Booth." *New York Post.* http://www.nypost.com/sports/66178.htm, (January 5, 2003).

"The Official Anna Kournikova Website." http://www. kournikova.com, (December 30, 2002).

Schatz, Aaron. "Lycos 50: Anna on Top Again in 2002." Fox Sports, http://foxsports.lycos.com/content, (December 3, 2002).

"Seles: No Kournikova Hatred." Sky Sports, http://msn.skysports.com, (December 18, 2002).

"Tennis Men Joining the Fashion Parade." The Star Online, http://thestar.com.my/news, (December 17, 2002).

Sketch by Paul Burton

Petra Kronberger

Petra Kronberger
1969-

Austrian downhill skier

Petra Kronberger dominated women's alpine skiing for a few brief years between 1988 and 1992. Although she skied on the World Cup circuit for fewer than six full seasons, in that time Kronberger won three World Cup overall titles and two Olympic gold medals. Yet her personality was as famous and appreciated in Austria as her winning record. Kronberger prayed when she was nervous, always spoke kindly of her fellow athletes, and never gave off even a whiff of scandal. Even after she became rich and famous, she still rode her bicycle around her tiny hometown, Pfarrwerfen, Austria (population 2,100). For a time Kronberger was even a spokeswoman for a brand of European cocoa drink called Ovomaltine, which is noted for only using modest, down-to-earth, outdoorsy-type people in its advertisements.

First Mountains

Kronberger grew up on a farm in the Alps near Salzburg, Austria. The farm belonged to her maternal grandparents, but her parents were still living there while they saved up the money necessary to build their own house. Her father, Heinrich, drove cement trucks, and her mother, Waltraud, did cleaning and dishwashing. The family also included Kronberger's brother, Robert, who was a year younger than she, but he died of the flu when he was thirteen months old.

Kronberger's father first taught her to ski when she was two. She soon stood out as a champion skier, winning her first trophy in a race at age six. When Kronberger was ten, a development coach noticed her and suggested to her parents that she start training more seriously. This entailed enrolling in a residential school in Bad Gastein, Austria, that combined ski training and academics. Although the Kronbergers had finally built their dream house, with their own hands, money was still tight and the $100 monthly tuition was difficult for them. Yet, as Kron-

berger's mother later explained to *Sports Illustrated* reporter Anita Verschoth, "We didn't want to be sorry later."

It All Clicked into Place

Kronberger did not disappoint them, although it took her many years to bloom into a world-class skier. She battled homesickness, the challenges of puberty, and a serious injury to her ankle while making excellent grades throughout her years at the school in Bad Gastein and later at Schladming, where she transferred to another skiing school at age fourteen.

When Kronberger graduated, it did not look as if she was going to be able to make a living as a skier, so she took a job as a bank teller at the large Raiffeinsenbank. (Throughout her career, Kronberger continued to work there when she had the time.) But she continued to race, and finally, shortly before her eighteenth birthday, she won her first race on the Europa Cup circuit, one step below the World Cup. Kronberger went on to win three titles in the Austrian juniors division in quick succession. "For two years I had been thinking, I am no good," she recalled to Verschoth. "I'll never be good; I have chosen the wrong profession. Then, suddenly, it all clicked into place."

Three Championship Seasons

Kronberger joined the World Cup circuit in the 1987-88 season. Although she did not win any races that year,

Chronology

1969	Born February 21 in Pfarwerfen, Austria
1988	Competes in Olympics for the first time
1989	Wins first World Cup event, a downhill race in Panorama
1990	Wins four World Cup races in the month of December
1991	Pulls out of world championships after second event after suffering a knee injury during the Super-G
1992	Quits competitive skiing early in the 1992-93 season

Awards and Accomplishments

1990	World Cup, overall
1991	World Championships, downhill
1991	World Cup, overall
1992	Olympics, slalom
1992	Olympics, combined
1992	World Cup, overall

Won a total of sixteen World Cup events between 1989 and 1991.

she did finish in the top three on occasion, and she was expected to be a contender at the 1988 Calgary Winter Olympics. In the end she did not win any medals in Calgary, but she did give a good performance for an athlete still in her teen years: she finished sixth in the downhill and eleventh in the combined.

Kronberger only won her first World Cup events, two downhill races, in December of 1989, but by the end of that season she had captured the World Cup overall title. This made her an instant hero in Austria: ever since that country's skiing star of the 1970s, Annemarie Pröll (later Moser-Pröll) had retired, the Swiss team had almost completely dominated the alpine world, which had long rankled the Austrian fans.

Kronberger's skiing only improved in the next two seasons, in which she successfully defended her World Cup overall champion title twice. Over the course of thirty-eight days in December, 1990, and January, 1991, Kronberger became the first skier in the modern era to win one race in each of the five alpine events in one season. Four of those wins in all but the combined came in the month of December alone, another notable feat.

Kronberger won a gold medal in her first event, the downhill, at the 1991 world championships, and many observers were expecting her to go on to win as many as four more. However, she fell in her second event, the Super-G, and injured her right knee, forcing her to miss the rest of the races. (Despite her fall, she still finished sixth in that event.) Her performances at the Olympics the next year in Albertville, France, were equally solid. She went home with two gold medals, one in the slalom and one in the combined, and she finished a respectable fourth in the Super-G and fifth in the slalom.

Retiring a Hero

By the beginning of the 1992-93 season, the pressures of being the star of the long-overshadowed Austrian team were beginning to wear on Kronberger. She had lost her motivation to compete, she said, and her weak results in the first few events of that season showed it. Only a few months into the season, she quit the Austrian national team and went back to Pfarwerfen. Still, the Swiss national team's decade-long dominance of the skiing world had been broken, and Kronberger's Austrian compatriots will long remember her for that.

FURTHER INFORMATION

Periodicals

Verschoth, Anita. "A Pair of Queens." *Sports Illustrated,* (January 27, 1992): 50-53.

Other

"Petra Kronberger." The History of the Ski World Cup. http://ski-db.com/db/profiles/wkrnpe.asp (January 22, 2003).

"Petra Kronberger: Alpine Come From Behind." International Olympic Committee. http://www.olympic.org/uk/athletes/heroes/bio_uk.asp?PAR_I_ID=471 (January 22, 2003).

"Petra Krongerger: Overview." SKI-DB. http://ski-db.com/db/profiles/wkrnpe.asp (January 22, 2003).

Sketch by Julia Bauder

Julie Krone
1963-

American jockey

The winningest woman jockey in thoroughbred racing history, Julie Krone has shattered records throughout her two-decade career, including having the distinction of being the first woman to ride to the winner's circle in a Triple Crown race. But records were not the only things shattered in the course of Krone's streak. She has suffered career-threatening injuries, most notably a smashed ankle in a 1993 on-track spill that could have ended her riding or even taken her life.

Like Mother, Like Daughter

Though countless little girls dream of glory on horseback, Krone had the single-mindedness, the physical attributes, and the emotional toughness to make her dream come true. Julieanne Louise Krone was born in 1963 near Benton Harbor, Michigan. Her first trainer, champion, and sometimes adversary, was her mother, Judi

Julie Krone

Krone, a woman who lived and breathed horses. It was Judi, a former high-school equestrian champion, who put her diapered two-year-old on the back of a palomino and sent the animal trotting off to show a prospective buyer how gentle the horse could be with children. Julie instinctively sat the trot, then took up the reins and guided the horse back to Judi. It was Julie who began living her mother's dream: "Every time she looked out and saw her baby girl gliding bareback across the field, wearing nothing but a pair of shorts, holding nothing but a handful of mane, [Judi] would feel tears filling her eyes," wrote Gary Smith in a lengthy profile of Julie Krone for *Sports Illustrated*. "Tears of love, tears of jealousy. Her little girl's childhood was the childhood she had read about in all those books, the childhood she should have had, she would have had, if only she hadn't been a girl in a three-story apartment house in Chicago."

Indeed, horses both bonded and divided the Krone family. In one corner was Judi, who let dishes pile up and clothes clutter the house while she spent hours training the family's horses, dreaming of a career in the saddle she herself would never realize. In the other corner was husband Don Krone, a photography and art instructor, who lost himself in his darkroom night after night. "There was love in a house like that, but sometimes you had to cock your head in a different way to see it," as Smith wrote. "No dinners together around a table, no Easter baskets."

Julie Krone grew up fierce and fearless, a riding daredevil who never stopped to consider the consequences.

Chronology

1963	Born July 24, in Benton Harbor, Michigan
1979	Goes to work at Churchill Downs
1980	Becomes apprentice jockey
1981	Makes professional debut, February 12
1992	Rides in Kentucky Derby, finishing fourteenth
1993	Rides in Belmont Stakes, finishing first
1993	Suffers serious injury, August 30
1994	Returns to racing
1995	Marries Matthew Muzikar
1995	Rides in Kentucky Derby
1999	Announces retirement from racing
2002	Marries second husband, Jay Hovdey
2002	Announces return to racing

She never cried, even when thrashed by the tempestuous Judi as punishment for fighting. At the same time, Julie's mother painstakingly trained her, corrected her, and encouraged her. At age five, Krone won the Berrien County Youth Fair Horse Show in the under-18 division, besting competitors three times her age. But even then, "Judi would snap at the girl for letting her elbows bounce during the ride, then wait until she was gone and say to Julie's friend.... 'Wasn't she great?'," noted Smith.

A Love of Speed

For all her precocious dedication, Krone was also possessed of the body of a perpetual child. She topped out at four-foot-ten, petite even by jockey standards. Her high-pitched voice got the girl ridiculed in high school; she took comfort in her animals and her poetry. She nearly ran off to join a circus after impressing the owner with her stunts on horseback, then backed out when she decided she didn't trust the man. But Krone's heart belonged to racing. She hung a racetrack picture on her bedroom ceiling, studying the turns as she fell asleep clutching a riding crop.

Time could barely catch up with Krone's ambition. Too young at fifteen to work at Churchill Downs, home of the Kentucky Derby, the would-be jockey had her mother rectify the problem by forging a birth certificate. Krone began her professional career as a "hot-walker," cooling off the thoroughbreds after their workouts and races.

But Krone wanted more—much more. She became an exercise rider and by 1980 had advanced to apprentice jockey. On February 17, 1981, Krone won her first race on a horse called Lord Farkle, in Tampa, Florida. But the ride to the winner's circle was never an easy one, and could be particularly tough for a woman. Thoroughbred racing had a longstanding men-only culture; the first professional female jockeys, including **Barbara Jo Rubin**, faced bias, suffered numerous indignities, and even endured the threat of physical violence. As for Krone, her own idiosyncrasies, including a penchant for brawling and a conviction of marijuana possession, threatened to

Awards and Accomplishments

1981	Won first race in Tampa, Florida
1982	Leading jockey at Atlantic City, New Jersey, 1982-83
1987	First woman to win four races in one day
1987	First woman named top rider at a major racetrack
1988	Meadowlands champion, 1988-90
1988	Named all-time winningest female jockey
1991	Rode in first of two Kentucky Derby races
1991	First woman to ride in Belmont Stakes
1992	Ninth-ranked jockey in the nation
1993	First woman jockey to win a Triple Crown race
1993	ESPY award, Outstanding Female Athlete; Women's Sports Foundation Sportswoman of the Year; *Glamour* Top 10 Women of the Year; CBS News top five Women of the Year
1994	Made comeback from serious injury
1995	Published autobiography, *Riding for My Life*
1999	Retired with record $81 million in career winnings
1999	Julie Krone Classic race named in her honor, Lone Star Park
2000	First female jockey inducted to Thoroughbred Racing Hall of Fame

Where Is She Now?

Julie Krone, the winningest woman jockey in the world, hung up her tack in April, 1999, after establishing her place in sports history. Two traumatic injuries, in 1993 and 1995, had sapped from Krone the love of speed she had nurtured since she was a child. But in October, 2000, Krone made an appearance in Lexington, Kentucky, piloting the harness racer Moni Maker to a new world-record finish in a race for trotters-under-saddle. And in October, 2002, the Hall of Fame inductee announced her return to thoroughbred racing. After three and a half years of retirement, Krone rode Justly Royal at Santa Anita Park on November 1, 2002.

undercut her budding career. In one notable example, Krone angered another jockey, Miguel Rujano, who took his whip to Krone's face. She retaliated by delivering a roundhouse punch, which escalated into a shoving, chair-throwing melee. "Both were fined $100," noted *People* writer Jack Freidman, "but Krone had scored some points by giving the lie to that old canard that women aren't tough enough to ride with the men."

Still, there was no denying Krone's gift for working with thoroughbreds. She was known as a rider of unusual patience, able to settle down on a galloping horse and let him run relaxed until the moment he needed her guidance to take the lead. The wins and titles piled up through the 1980s. Years of riding anonymous animals at small tracks prepared Krone to move to quality thoroughbreds at sites like Pimlico, Saratoga, and Churchill Downs. It was at the latter location that Krone rode her first Kentucky Derby, in 1991. That same year, she became the first woman to ride in the Belmont Stakes, the second jewel of the Triple Crown.

History at Belmont

Though she did not win either Triple Crown race in 1991, Krone returned for the Belmont Stakes, held in Elmont, New York, in 1993. She was assigned the long-shot Colonial Affair. "Let's go out and make some history," she reportedly said to her horse as they made their way to the track. And history was made that June 5, as Krone became the first woman to drive home a Triple Crown winner, riding a race characterized by *Sports Illustrated* writer William Nack as dominated by "patience, intelligence and tactical savvy." The Belmont win highlighted Krone in many fans' eyes as one of the best jockeys of her time, regardless of gender. That summer a writer for England's *Economist* sang her praises: "In an industry in which so many are obsessed by

money—owners, trainers, and the midget millionaires who flog horses down the track—Ms Krone is a refreshing exception. She talks about few things other than her [horses], and she does this as an indulgent young schoolmarm would speak of her well-bred girls."

If the Belmont victory represented a career high, fate soon came crashing down. On August 30, 1993, riding in a race in Saratoga, New York, Krone was piloting Seattle Way down the homestretch when a horse to her inside, Bejilla Lass, cut in front of her. Standing in the stirrups, Krone screamed, "No, no!" But the warning came too late. The foreleg of Seattle Way clipped a hind leg of Bejilla Lass, and Krone's mount catapulted onto the hard turf. It was not Krone's first fall, but this crash was devastating, shattering the jockey's ankle. The damage was compounded when a passing horse caught Krone in the chest with a thrusting hind kick.

In Nack's article, the crash was recounted as "a kind of eerie free fall through spinning shadows, turning light to dark to light again." The injuries were instantly, horribly apparent: an right elbow bone protruding through the skin; a mutilated right ankle. "I've had bones that were broken clean in two," Krone told Nack, "but this was beyond that.... Normally you can say things to separate yourself from the pain: 'O.K., breathe. Do yoga. Don't lose control.' But with this, there was no control. My neck hurt and I couldn't breathe. I had no faculties. I was in outer space. I tried to pass out, but I couldn't. I swear, if I'd had the choice then, I would have contemplated suicide because it hurt so bad."

The Long Road Back

Krone underwent two operations in nine days to repair the broken fibula and shattered tibia. A three-week hospital stay and an eight-month recovery followed. But Krone was lucky: had she not been wearing an equestrian safety vest that day, her doctor reported, the blow to her chest from the horse's hoof would likely have killed her. During Julie's recovery, Judi Krone rallied to her daughter's side.

But even as her body began to heal, Krone faced a new adversary: fear. The child who grew up on the back of a galloping horse for the first time gained a sense of the danger inherent in her sport. Nightmares, insomnia, depression, and pain plagued her; "there was even a time when Krone wondered whether she would ever make it back," wrote Nack. But the thirty-year-old was determined to return to the saddle. "Getting used to living with the pain. That's been the hardest thing so far," Krone told Dean Chang in a *Knight-Ridder/Tribune News Service* wire story. "It only hurts when I walk. And sleep. And skip and run. But not when I'm riding."

Krone made her comeback in 1994 and on May 26 that year rode her first post-accident winner. But in January 1995, just days after the pins in her still-healing ankle were removed, she fell again during a race at Florida's Gulfstream Park, this time breaking both hands. This crash, though physically less devastating than the Saratoga incident, seemed to be the final straw for Krone. "That was too much," she was quoted by Mark Beech in a *Sports Illustrated* article. "I had always been like, 'I can't wait!' But I just didn't want to ride anymore. It was miserable." Krone did stay in the sport for four more years, even riding another Kentucky Derby. She announced her retirement in April, 1999.

The racing community was quick to recognize Krone's contribution to the sport. In 2000, a year after Judi Krone's death from cancer, Julie was elected to the Thoroughbred Racing Hall of Fame in Saratoga Springs, New York, the first woman jockey to be so named. Married twice, Krone has admitted her intentions on starting a family; she also became a spokesperson on behalf of Post-Traumatic Stress Disorder (PTSD), an illness that affects one in thirteen Americans.

Krone realizes that the numbers attached to her name—20,000 mounts, 3,500 winners, and $81 million in purses—are the stuff of record books. What matters more, Krone said in a *Knight-Ridder/Tribune New Service* wire story by Gil LeBreton, is the fact that she was able to provide an example. "Athletes tend to be known for their success," she said. "But I would rather have some little girl say, 'Oh, Julie Krone fell down but she came back. She wasn't afraid.'"

SELECTED WRITINGS BY KRONE:

(With Nancy Ann Richardson) *Riding for My Life*. Little, Brown, 1995.

FURTHER INFORMATION

Books

Great Women in Sports. Visible Ink Press, 1996.
Krone, Julie, and Nancy Ann Richardson. *Riding for My Life*. Little, Brown, 1995.

Periodicals

Beech, Mark. "Julie Krone, Star Jockey." *Sports Illustrated*. (May 21, 2001).

Chang, Dean. "Julie Krone Making Her Comeback in a Very Public Way." *Knight-Ridder/Tribune News Service*. (May 8, 1994).

Friedman, Jack. "Julie Krone Rides Headlong into Racing's Record Books as the Winningest Woman Jockey." *People*. (May 2, 1988).

"Julie Krone Inducted into Hall of Fame." *Knight-Ridder/Tribune News Service*. (August 7, 2000).

"Julie Krone Sets Record in Her Return." *Knight-Ridder/Tribune News Service*. (October 6, 2000).

Kindred, Dave. "Living to Ride." *Sporting News*. (May 15, 1995).

LeBreton, Gil. "The Princess Rides off Like a Queen." *Knight-Ridder/Tribune News Service*. (April 19, 1999).

Maranto, Gina. "A Woman of Substance." *Sports Illustrated*. (August 24, 1987).

Nack, William. "Bittersweet Victory."*Sports Illustrated*. (June 14, 1993).

Nack, William. "The Ride of Her Life."*Sports Illustrated*. (June 13, 1994).

Smith, Gary. "She Who Laughs Last." *Sports Illustrated*. (May 22, 1989).

"The Woman's Touch." *Economist*. (August 14, 1993).

Sketch by Susan Salter

Gustavo Kuerten
1976-

Brazilian tennis player

Gustavo Kuerten took the tennis world by storm in 1997 when the virtually unknown player won the French Open championship, the clay court Grand Slam event. Kuerten has won the championship three times. He has also won a total of sixteen singles titles and eight doubles titles since turning professional in 1995. Kuerten reached the number one ranking in the world by the end of 2000 and held that position for much of 2001. Aside from being a great clay court player, Kuerten is known as being a friendly, laid back, and humble person.

Coached by Surrogate Father

Gustavo Kuerten, popularly known as "Guga," was born on September 10, 1976 in Florianopolis, Brazil. Florianopolis is a city of 270,000 people on the island of Santa Catarina off of the Brazilian coast. He is the second of three sons born to Aldo Amadeu and Alice Kuerten. His father owned an aluminum siding business and his mother was a social worker. Both parents en-

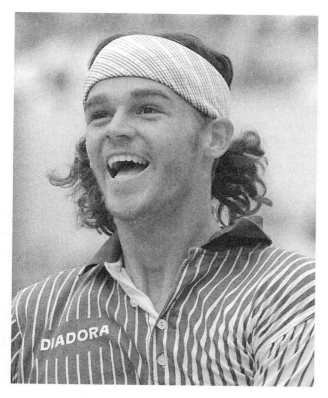

Gustavo Kuerten

joyed playing tennis and encouraged their sons to do the same. Aldo Kuerten was also an avid basketball player.

Aldo Kuerten taught his young sons to play tennis. Guga started playing when he was only six years old. Two years later his father tried to get former Brazilian tennis player Larri Passos to coach his son. According to John Gustafson of the *Chicago Sun-Times,* Passos told Kuerten, "One day, but not now. He's too young. He has to enjoy his life, play football and other sports." Just one year later, when Guga was nine years old, his father was umpiring a juniors tennis match and died suddenly of a heart-attack at only forty-one years old. The eldest son, Rafael, had to quit playing tennis so that he could help support the family.

In 1989 when Guga was thirteen, Passos kept his promise to Aldo Kuerten and began to coach his son. He liked Guga's carefree spirit, but he helped him improve his concentration on the court. He also made him change his two-handed backhand to a smoother one-handed shot. Passos also frequently traveled to Europe with Kuerten to expose him to international competition. Passos became a surrogate father to Kuerten and he is credited not only with Kuerten's success as a tennis player, but also with his good-natured disposition and healthy perspective on life.

Clay Court Champion

Kuerten turned professional in 1995 when he was nineteen. Within a year he broke into the top 100 rank-ings of male tennis players worldwide and he became the number one player in Brazil. In 1996 he won his first doubles title with Fernando Meligeni at the Tour de Santiago. Only one year later Kuerten won his first singles title, which also happened to be a Grand Slam championship. Kuerten won the French Open championship at Roland Garros by defeating two-time champion Sergi Bruguera. This was quite a feat since Kuerten was virtually unknown on the tennis scene and ranked only number sixty-six in the world before the tournament. This victory moved Kuerten to number fourteen in the world rankings and he became an overnight star in his home country.

Kuerten won two more clay court singles titles in 1998 at Stuttgart and Mallorca. However, he was unable to successfully defend his French Open title. In fact, Kuerten did not make it past the second round of any of the four Grand Slam tournaments that year and his ranking fell to number twenty-three. In 1999 Kuerten achieved more consistency in his play. He won two more singles titles at Monte Carlo and Rome. He also reached the quarter finals of three Grand Slam tournaments, including Wimbledon, which is his least favorite surface.

Kuerten continued his success in 2000. Although he did not do well at three of the Grand Slam events that year, he did manage to repeat his French Open victory, defeating Yevgeny Kafelnifov, Juan Carlos Ferrero, and Magnus Norman to reach his second Grand Slam title. He also won singles titles at Santiago, Hamburg, Indianapolis, and the Master's Cup in Lisbon. In his victory at Lisbon, Kuerten defeated such top players as the number one tennis player at that time **Pete Sampras**, as well as **Andre Agassi**, Yevgeny Kafelnikov, and Magnus Norman. He was the only player that decade to beat both Sampras and Agassi back-to-back. He finished the year with the number one ranking, becoming the first South American to hold this position.

In 2001 Kuerten dominated the clay court season, winning five of seven clay court titles. He repeated his victory

Awards and Accomplishments

Year	Accomplishment
1996	Doubles title at Santiago with Fernando Meligeni
1997	Doubles title at Estoril with Fernando Meligeni
1997	Doubles title at Bologna with Fernando Meligeni
1997	Doubles title at Stuttgart with Fernando Meligeni
1997	Finished year ranked number 14 in the world
1997, 2000-01	French Open singles title
1997, 2000-01	Named Brazil's Sportsman of the Year
1998	Doubles title at Gestaad with Fernando Meligeni
1998	Singles title at Mallorca
1998, 2001	Singles title at Stuttgart
1999	Doubles title at Adelaide with Nicolas Lapentti
1999	Singles title at Rome
1999, 2001	Singles title at Monte Carlo
2000	Doubles title at Santiago with Antonio Prieto
2000	Singles title at Santiago
2000	Singles title at Hamburg
2000	Singles title at Indianapolis
2000	Masters Cup singles title at Lisbon
2000	Named Association of Tennis Players Player of the Year
2000	Finished year ranked number one in the world
2001	Doubles title at Acapulco with Donald Johnson
2001	Singles title at Buenos Aires
2001	Singles title at Acapulco
2001	Singles title at Cincinnati
2001	Finished year ranked number two in the world

at the French Open, capturing his third Grand Slam title. His other singles titles were won at Cincinnati, Stuttgart, Monte Carlo, Acapulco, and Buenos Aires. His win in Cincinnati was his first hard court title. Kuerten also reached the finals of the U.S. Open that year. Kuerten spent most of the year ranked the number one male tennis player in the world, although he slipped to number two by the end of the year. "I think I was the happiest number one player in the history of tennis and I really enjoyed the year," Kuerten explained on his official Web site.

"Stayed the Same Person"

Kuerten missed most of the 2002 tennis season because he was recovering from hip surgery. He is expected to return to the circuit once he is physically able to play a regular schedule. For Kuerten to return to the number one position in the world tennis rankings, he will probably have to become a more versatile player and win more tournaments on surfaces other than clay. "For me [that] would be the next stage for my career, maybe [to] win a [grand] slam on another surface. I think each year I'm getting closer," Kuerten told John Barrett of the *London Financial Times* in November of 2001.

Regardless of whether Kuerten wins another Grand Slam, he is already a hero in Brazil. Kuerten is now the most famous athlete in Brazil, surpassing soccer star **Pele**. Despite his success, Kuerten remains very humble and grounded. When he is home, he enjoys the same friends and activities that he did before he was famous. Surfing is his favorite pastime. "My life has changed, but I've stayed the same person," Kuerten told the *Hindu* newspaper in March of 2001. "I have the same friends, the same people working with me, my family by my side all the time. I have a simple life." Kuerten is very close to his family. His older brother, Rafael, works as his manager. Kuerten also sends all of his trophies to his younger brother, Guilherme, who has cerebral palsy. Throughout his career Kuerten has donated a portion of his earnings to the Parents and Friends of the Handicapped Association. In 2000 he founded the Institute Guga Kuerten to raise awareness and money for the handicapped and his mother serves as the institute's director.

CONTACT INFORMATION

Address: ATP Tour International Headquarters, 201 ATP Tour Boulevard, Ponte Vedra Beach, FL 32082.

FURTHER INFORMATION

Periodicals

Barrett, John. "Surfing or the Net for World Number One." *Financial Times* (London, England) (November 10, 2001): 22.

Bellos, Alex. "Tennis: Brazil Goes Gaga Over Guga." *The Guardian* (London, England) (January 13, 2001): 12.

"Getting to Know Gustavo Kuerten." *Hindu* (March 10, 2001).

Gustafson, John. "Guga!" *Chicago Sun-Times* (August 27, 2000): 132.

"Gustavo Kuerten Enters Final." *Hindu* (June 9, 2001).

Margolis, Mac. "Going Gaga Over Guga." *Newsweek* (June 26, 2000): 33.

Price, S.L. "French Farce." *Sports Illustrated* (June 16, 1997): 50-53.

Other

ATP Tennis Players Profiles - Gustavo Kuerten. http://www.cliffrichardtennis.org/player_profiles/gustavo_kuerten.html (January 24, 2003).

Biography Resource Center Online. http://www.infotrac.com (January 24, 2003).

CNNSI.com - Tennis - Gustavo Kuerten 2001 Win-Loss Record. http://sportsillustrated.conn.com/tennis/news/2001/kuerten01 (January 24, 2003).

ESPN.com: Gustavo Kuerten. http://espn.go.com/tennis/s/atp/profiles/kuerten.html (January 24, 2003).

Guga. http://www.guga.com.br/en/01_site_root/atleta_perfil.htm (January 24, 2003).

Sketch by Janet P. Stamatel

Michelle Kwan

Michelle Kwan
1980-

American figure skater

The most decorated American figure skater in the sport's history, Michelle Kwan became one of the most respected and admired athletes of her generation for her grace on and off the ice. First making headlines in 1994 when she was named an alternate to the American team at the Lillehammer Olympics during the **Tonya Harding** scandal, Kwan was a national silver medalist at the age of thirteen. At fifteen, she claimed her first U.S. and World Championship titles and at the 1998 National Championship delivered performances in the short and long programs that received the highest-ever marks in the modern history of the sport. Already something of a legend when she competed at the 1998 Nagano Winter Olympic Games, Kwan finished second in a surprising upset to **Tara Lipinski**, who performed two triple-jump combinations to take the gold medal. Ironically, the loss served to increase Kwan's popularity for her gracious comments and philosophical outlook after the event. Reigning as U.S. Champion from 1998 to 2002, Kwan also picked up gold medals at the World Championship in 1998, 2000, and 2001. As in 1998, Kwan was disappointed at the 2002 Salt Lake City Olympic Games, where she finished third after a fall in the free skate. Once again Kwan won the public's sympathy

Chronology

1980	Born July 7 to Danny and Estella Kwan in Los Angeles, California
1985	Begins taking figure skating lessons
1988	Begins taking private figure skating lessons with coach Derek James
1992	Begins association with coach Frank Carroll
1992	Places ninth at United States Figure Skating Association (USFSA) National Junior Championship
1993	Places sixth at USFSA National Championship
1993	Advances to senior USFSA ranks against the advice of her coach
1993	First appearance at senior level of USFSA National Championship
1994	Places eighth at International Skating Union (ISU) World Championship
1994	Becomes alternate for U.S. delegation to Lillehammer Winter Olympic Games
1995	Places fourth at ISU World Championship
2001	Ends association with coach Frank Carroll

and respect through her disappointment, which did little to diminish her impact on the sport and her status as one of the most popular athletes in North America.

Started Skating with Sister

The third and youngest child of Danny and Estella (Wing) Kwan, Michelle Kwan was born on July 7, 1980 in Los Angeles, California. Her father had been born in China and grew up in Hong Kong, where he met her mother when they attended the same grade school. The two met again at a school reunion and after marrying moved to Los Angeles in the early 1970s. Danny Kwan worked for the phone company while Estella Kwan helped her family run the Golden Pheasant restaurant in suburban Torrance. It was son Ron, the oldest of the three Kwan children, who first took up ice skating as a hockey player. Younger sister Karen, who would one day rank among the country's top skaters, then asked for skating lessons, which Michelle begged to join. Her parents finally gave in and the girls took lessons at a shopping mall in Rancho Palos Verdes, where the family lived, when Kwan was five years old.

After winning some local competitions, Kwan and her sister began taking private lessons with coach Derek James in 1988. With the financial burden of daily lessons for their two daughters, the Kwans sold their home in Rancho Palos Verdes to pay for their training and moved into a house in Torrance owned by Danny Kwan's parents. After Kwan won a gold medal in the United States Figure Skating Association's (USFSA) Southwest Pacific Junior Championship in 1991 and a bronze medal the following year in the Pacific Coast Junior Championship, she won a scholarship to study at the Ice Castle, an elite training facility in Lake Arrowhead, California. Karen Kwan was also accepted into the program; accompanied by their father, the girls moved to the facility, about one

Awards and Accomplishments

1991	Won gold medal, USFSA Southwest Pacific Junior Championship
1992	Won bronze medal, USFSA Pacific Coast Junior Championship
1993	Won gold medal, U.S. Olympic Festival
1994	Won gold medal, ISU World Junior Championship
1994	Won silver medal, Goodwill Games
1994-95, 1997	Won silver medal, USFSA National Championship
1996, 1998-2003	Won gold medal, USFSA National Championship
1996, 1998, 2000-01	Won gold medal, ISU World Championship
1996, 1998-2000	Named U.S. Olympic Committee Athlete of the Year, Figure Skating
1997, 1999, 2002	Won silver medal, ISU World Championship
1998	Won silver medal, Nagano Winter Olympic Games
1998	Won gold medal, Goodwill Games
1998	Won gold medal, World Professional Championship
2002	Won bronze medal, Salt Lake City Winter Olympic Games
2002	Awarded James E. Sullivan Award, Outstanding Amateur Athlete, Amateur Athletic Union

Related Biography: Skating Coach Frank Carroll

Until their partnership ended in 2001, Michelle Kwan and coach Frank Carroll had one of the most productive relationships in figure skating. Born in Massachusetts in the late 1930s, Carroll grew up skating at a Worcester rink and in the 1950s trained with former U.S. Champion Maribel Vinson Owen. Although he became one of the top U.S. skaters of the late 1950s, Carroll put aside his amateur career after failing to make the 1960 Olympic team. He instead completed a degree in education at Holy Cross and spent four years in the Ice Follies, a popular figure skating review that toured the country.

Carroll took bit parts in several low-budget movies in the mid-1960s but was drawn into coaching after giving a few informal lessons to skaters around Los Angeles. With the death of Owen and several other of the country's top coaches in a 1961 plane crash en route to the World Championship—an accident that devastated the USFSA's ranks—the demand for skilled coaches was high. By the mid-1970s Carroll had coached several outstanding skaters, including 1977-1980 U.S. and 1977 and 1979 World Champion Linda Fratianne, who won the silver medal at the 1980 Olympics. Carroll had a less harmonious relationship with 1989 and 1992 U.S. Champion Christopher Bowman, who was eventually sidelined with drug and alcohol problems.

Although he considered retiring from coaching at various points in his career, Carroll began working with Michelle Kwan at the Ice Castle in Lake Arrowhead, California in 1992. The two developed into one of the strongest teams in figure skating and seemed so close that Kwan's announcement in October 2001 that she had left Carroll to compete without a coach came as a surprise. "I think maybe she's feeling like a woman now," Carroll told David Davis of the *Los Angeles Magazine* in a January 2002 profile, "She's twenty-one, she's wealthy, she has a boyfriend. She's probably feeling she should take charge of her life. She's feeling her oats." Carroll remained one of the most respected coaches in figure skating with pupils that included 2002 Olympic bronze medalist Timothy Goebel and former U.S. bronze medalist Angela Nikodinov.

hundred miles away from Los Angeles, and started working with coach Frank Carroll in 1992.

Although the relationship between Kwan and Carroll eventually resulted in one of the most productive teams in figure skating, Kwan's first year with her new coach got off to a rocky start. She finished a disappointing ninth place at her first appearance at a national USFSA event, the Junior Championship, in 1992. Kwan also raised Carroll's ire by taking the USFSA test to advance to the senior ranks in 1993. Carroll had hoped that Kwan would make a strong showing at the 1993 Junior Nationals as a springboard to entering senior competitions. Motivated by a desire to earn a place on the 1994 U.S. Olympic team, Kwan ignored his advice and took the test while Carroll was out of town. It was days before Carroll would even speak to his driven pupil after he found out what she had done.

Unexpected Trip to 1994 Olympics

Kwan was not perfect in her first USFSA National Championship appearance in 1993, but her performance was good enough to land her in sixth place. She had a much better showing at that year's U.S. Olympic Festival, where she won the gold medal. Already earning predictions of future greatness based on her jumping ability, Kwan was slowly incorporating the artistry into her program that would later become her trademark. Yet she was unprepared for the unprecedented attention focused on women's figure skating at the 1994 Nationals, which she entered as a still relatively unknown skater. Leaving the practice session ice at the Cobo Arena in Detroit, the site of the event, Kwan was just a few feet away when Shane Stant clubbed reigning U.S. Champion **Nancy Kerrigan** in the knee. Stant had carried out the attack in a plot coordi-

nated by rival skater **Tonya Harding**'s husband, Jeff Gillooly, in the hope of forcing Kerrigan out of Olympic contention. With Kerrigan sidelined by the injury, Harding won the championship, with Kwan placing second. Kerrigan and Harding were named to the Olympic team, but with the investigation around the attack centering on Harding's entourage, Kwan's nomination as an alternate to the team made her a featured attraction of the media circus that surrounded the Lillehammer Games.

U.S. and World Champion in 1996

Kerrigan recovered in time to compete at the 1994 Olympics, where she took the silver medal. Harding delivered two disastrous performances at the Games and was later banned for life from the amateur ranks by the USFSA for her knowledge of the plot against Kerrigan. Kwan went on the represent the U.S. at the 1994 International Skating Union's (ISU) World Championship, where she placed eighth. The following year, skating to Camille Saint-Saens' "Rondo Capriccioso," she earned another silver medal at the U.S. National Championship. At the World Championship, Kwan skated two perfect performances. The low marks she received from the

Michelle Kwan

judges for her short program, however, had placed her in fifth going into the free skate. Despite having the best technical content in her long program, with seven triple jumps, Kwan placed fourth overall at the end of the event. Many observers, Carroll included, could not recall when a skater had performed so well without receiving a medal.

Looking forward to the 1996 season, Carroll and Kwan decided that her youthful appearance had dissuaded the judges from giving her the marks she had deserved. Kwan had previously appeared with her hair in a simple ponytail and without makeup, but her look for the 1996 season changed dramatically. In her long program, Kwan portrayed Salome, the Biblical woman who had asked for the head of John the Baptist after mesmerizing an audience with her dancing. Kwan's artistry on the ice matched her more mature appearance, and she swept the U.S. Nationals, even with minor mistakes on two of her jumps.

At the 1996 World Championship, however, Kwan faced an almost insurmountable challenge. China's Lu Chen had skated a beautiful long program and received two perfect marks of 6.0 for her presentation. Taking the ice, Kwan knew that she had to skate perfectly and hit all of her seven planned triple jumps. After doubling one of the triple toe jumps she performed in combination, Kwan made a last-second change at the end of her program, throwing in another triple toe jump instead of a simpler double axel. The technical edge—along with two perfect presentation scores she received—gave Kwan the victory, with six of the nine judges putting her ahead of Chen. It was one of the closest competitions in the history of the event, and it made Kwan into the leading figure skater of the day.

Astounding Performance at 1998 Nationals

Kwan's reign as U.S. and World Champion lasted just one year. Hampered by new skates and a lack of self-confidence, Kwan stumbled badly in her free skate at the Nationals and finished second to **Tara Lipinski**. With another mistake in the short program at the 1997 World Championship, Kwan placed second to Lipinski again, even though her free skate was the best at the competi-

tion. With a stress fracture in her left foot, Kwan was unable to go through full run-throughs of her programs and did not enter the 1998 Nationals as the favorite. After Lipinski unexpectedly fell on her triple flip jump in the short program, however, Kwan took the ice in her program, skating to selections from Sergei Rachmaninoff. After completing a stunning program, Kwan made history as the first women to receive a perfect score for her short program at the Nationals; in fact, she received seven 6.0 marks from the nine judges for her presentation. Her long program, skated to "Lyrica Angelica" by composer William Alwyn, was even better: Kwan received eight out of nine possible perfect scores for her presentation. The performances were immediately rated as the best short and long programs ever seen at the Nationals, and they made Kwan the heavy favorite going into the 1998 Winter Olympic Games in Nagano, Japan.

Olympic Disappointment

In first place after her short program at the Nagano Games, Kwan seemed to be fulfilling the expectations that had grown out of her astounding victory at the 1998 Nationals. Despite the pressure, Kwan delivered another clean program in her free skate, although some of her moves were a bit slower than they had been in her prior competitions. Kwan was also at a disadvantage by skating first in the final group in the long program; even though her artistry was again impressive, she had to settle for a string of 5.9 marks for her presentation. Lipinski, skating later in the event, again did not match Kwan's aesthetic quality on the ice; she more than made up for that, however, in her technical content with a triple-loop, triple-loop combination jump midway through her program and a triple salchow-half loop-triple toe jumping pass to conclude it. It was technically the most difficult program of the evening, and it earned Lipinski the gold medal over Kwan.

A model of graciousness in her defeat, Kwan earned praise for the way she handled her disappointment at the Olympics. She won her second world title at the 1998 Championship a few weeks later, a victory that took place without the presence of Lipinski, who had immediately retired from amateur ranks after the Olympics. For her part, Kwan announced that she was looking forward to competing at the 2002 Olympics, to be held in Salt Lake City.

Continued Success at U.S. and World Competitions

In the meantime, Kwan racked up a string of medal-winning performances. Repeating as National Champion in 1999, Kwan struggled with a bad cold at that year' World Championship and placed second. She won the 2000 national title and made a surprising comeback in the World Championship to claim another gold medal with a program skated to haunting music from the soundtrack to *The Red Violin*. With a triple toe-triple toe combination jump and intricate and sophisticated chore-ography, Kwan had reached another athletic and artistic pinnacle with the program.

Kwan chose another unusual piece of music for her 2001 season, "The Black Swan," by Brazilian composer Heitor Villa-Lobos. Although her performance at the U.S. Nationals did not include a triple-triple jump, Kwan still managed to win the event. Her performance at the World Championship, however, was perfect; in addition to her triple-triple combination, Kwan completed five other triple jumps. With another gold medal, Kwan reigned for a second consecutive year as the U.S. and World Champion.

Most-Decorated Skater in U.S. History

Many observers were stunned when Kwan announced that she was leaving her longtime coach in October 2001. She had no plans to hire another coach and intended to train and compete on her own, a move that few other skaters had ever attempted. After a stunning performance in the long program at the 2002 U.S. Nationals to Nikolai Rimsky-Korsakov's "Sheherazade," however, Kwan entered the Salt Lake City Olympics once again as the fa-vorite. In first place after her short program, Kwan took the ice midway through the final group of competitors in the free skate. American teammate **Sarah Hughes** had al-ready completed an astounding program that included two triple-triple jump combinations. Indeed, Hughes's performance contained the highest degree of technical difficulty ever accomplished in the women's free skate. Although her artistry remained intact, a fall on a triple flip jump midway through her program once again dashed Kwan's hope for a gold medal. With Hughes in first place and Russian Irina Slutskaya in second, Kwan had to settle for the bronze medal.

Kwan again gained the public's respect with her grace, dignity, and good humor after her second Olympic loss. She also gained a lucrative contract with the Disney Corporation as a spokesperson and performer. Still in the amateur ranks, Kwan announced in 2002 that she would return to the U.S. Nationals in 2003 and perhaps to the World Championship as well. "I've been very fortunate," Kwan told Sharon Ginn of the *Boston Globe* in Novem-ber 2002 about her decision to keep competing, "I've never felt stronger or better. I haven't reached that point yet, so until that time I guess I'll keep competing until I know when to stop. When do you actually know [when to give it up]? The worst thing I can do is regret." Off the ice, Kwan decided to take time away from her studies at the University of California-Los Angeles to fulfill her en-dorsement contracts and to spend more time with her boyfriend, Brad Ference, who played with the National Hockey League's Florida Panthers.

The most decorated American figure skater ever, Kwan entered the 2002-2003 season as a six-time Nation-al Champion, four-time World Champion, and two-time

Olympic medalist. At the 2003 USFSA National Champi-onship in Dallas, Texas, Kwan took a gold medal, her sev-enth gold medal at a National Championship.

Although the Olympic gold medal still eludes her, Kwan did not rule out making a bid for the 2006 U.S. Olympic team for the Turin Winter Games. Such drive and dedication are typical of Kwan's outlook and have in-deed made her into one of the most respected and ad-mired athletes of her generation. In overcoming her losses at the Olympics and emerging as an even more popular personality, Kwan has seemed to transcend her sport. Em-bodying the ideals not just of figure skating but of athleti-cism and good sportsmanship in general, Kwan was honored with the James E. Sullivan Award as Outstanding Amateur Athlete by the Amateur Athletic Union in 2002.

SELECTED WRITINGS BY KWAN:

(With Laura James) *Heart of a Champion: An Autobiog-raphy.* New York: Scholastic, 1997.

FURTHER INFORMATION

Books

Brennan, Christine. *Edge of Glory: The Inside Story of the Quest for Figure Skating's Olympic Gold Medals.* New York: Scribner, 1998.

Brennan, Christine. *Inside Edge: A Revealing Journey into the Secret World of Figure Skating.* New York: Scribner, 1996.

Kwan, Michelle, with Laura James. *Heart of a Champi-on: An Autobiography.* New York: Scholastic, 1997.

U.S. Figure Skating Association. *The Official Book of Figure Skating.* New York: Simon & Schuster Edi-tions, 1998.

Periodicals

Brennan, Christine. "Kwan's Skating Had Even Judges in Tears." *USA Today* (February 19, 1998).

Davis, David. "Lord of the Rink: Frank Carroll Lost His Star Pupil, Michelle Kwan, But Not His Hopes for Olympic Gold." *Los Angeles Magazine* (January 2002): 30.

Ginn, Sharon. "Her Turn in Turin?" *Boston Globe* (No-vember 27, 2002): C7.

Smith, Russell Scott. "Whither the Queen?" *Sports Il-lustrated Women* (February 1, 2002).

Starr, Mark. "Kwan Song." *Newsweek* (February 18, 2002).

Other

"Kwan in Seventh Heaven with Dazzling Performance." United States Figure Skating Association. http://www.usfsa.org/uschamp03/index.htm (January 20, 2003).

"Michelle Kwan." United States Figure Skating Association. http://www.usfsa.org/team/ladies/kwanmich. htm (December 12, 2002).

Sketch by Timothy Borden

Marion Ladewig
1914-

American bowler

Marion Ladewig was known as the "Queen of Bowling." Many people consider her the greatest female bowler who ever lived. She set the pace in the opening days of women's professional bowling. Not only did she lead the nation in high average for a woman four times between 1949 and 1963 but, in 1951 she outscored the men.

Born Marion Margaret Van Oosten on October 30, 1914 in Grand Rapids, Michigan, Ladewig was a policeman's daughter who grew up a tomboy. She was a high school sprinter and played first base on her brother's baseball team. By age twenty-two she was a softball player of some distinction in local women's leagues. By her own estimation she was a good shortstop, slick fielder, and hard-hitting batter. When it came to pitching, however, Ladewig described herself as a "batting practice pitcher for other teams" because her balls brought easy hits.

It was her softball skill that led to her career in bowling. Local businessman, William T. Morrissey, Sr., saw the makings of a bowler in her strong throwing arm. In 1937 he invited her to roll some balls at his alley but it took a group of girlfriends to lure Ladewig onto the lanes. After just one game, she was hooked on the sport.

Career Begins In Local Alley

Morrissey offered Ladewig a job in his establishment, The Fanatorium. She honed her skills in the tan building at 40 Jefferson Ave SE, decorated with green awnings, vaulted striped ceilings and checkered floors. Affectionately known as "the Fan," the bowling alley became a Grand Rapids institution. In later years locals called it "the house that Marion built."

Ladewig credits Morrissey for her success. He offered her career direction and recruited outstanding local male bowlers as impromptu coaches. Although Ladewig was on the lanes in league play three nights a week,

Marion Ladewig

Morrissey insisted that she practice daily. As a result, she said she bowled every day from 1940 through 1962.

In her first bowling attempts Ladewig barely tallied an 80 score in ten frames and ended her first season with a 149 average. Three years later her average was 182. Ladewig's first competitive triumph came at the Western Michigan Gold Pin Classic where she and a partner won the doubles crown for the 1940-41 season.

One winter night, while filling in for an absent pin-boy, Ladewig saw the means for improving her game. From the vantage point of the pit behind the set pins she observed how balls approached their target. She saw two styles of play—speed and spin—and noted that the spin was more successful. By dropping her backswing to shoulder height and focusing on spin rather than speed, she soon added ten points to her average score. For the

1944-1945 season she recorded the women's high average in the nation. She repeated that feat three times (1948-49, 1951-52, 1954-55).

Wins First All-Star

In 1949 Ladewig won the first Women's All-Star Tournament, sponsored by the Bowling Proprietors Association of America (BPAA), and successfully defended that title in five succeeding tournaments. In the 1950-51 season she became the only bowler in history to win the All-Events title at the city, state and national levels in the same year. All-Events tallied a bowlers points in singles, doubles and team events. She knocked down 1,796 pins to win the Women's International Bowling Congress (WIBC) All-Events category. Her WIBC success included winning the team championship as a member of the hometown Fanatorium Majors.

During the 1951-52 season Ladewig won both the Women's All Star and the WIBC tournaments, plus every Michigan competition she entered. She completed the All-Star with a 211.46 average for thirty-two games of match play, setting a tournament record unmatched for the next twenty-two years. She was named Michigan Woman Athlete of the Year in 1953.

Ladewig repeated her WIBC All-Events win in 1954-55 with a 1,980 pin count. With partner Wyllis Ryskamp, she also captured the WIBC doubles title. Teaming with LaVerne Carter, wife of men's champion **Don Carter**, Ladewig captured the women's doubles title again in both 1958 and 1959. The first year they won by four pins. The 1959 championship was decided by Ladewig's "Brooklyn Strike" (a right hander into the 1-2 pocket) for a two-point victory.

Ladewig and Don Carter dominated bowling's heyday in the 1950's and 1960's. The pair won more All Star and World Invitational tournaments than any other bowlers and appeared together on television commercials and demonstration tours. Men and women tuned in at 5:00 pm on Saturday evenings to watch Ladewig control the lanes on the "Women's Major League Bowling" show introduced by the National Broadcasting Company in 1958.

Personal Struggles

Easily unnerved by the stress of competition, Ladewig struggled to maintain her control. She later ad-

mitted that Morrissey often berated her severely in his attempts to revive her fighting spirit. After Ladewig discovered that chewing gum relieved her stress she was never without a supply. Sportswriters dubbed her "The Chiclet-Chewing Lady" for her noticeable gum chomping during competition.

Success came at a price. Ladewig was on the road often for competitions and promotions. She filmed bowling commercials with Don Carter and presented exhibitions with male star Buddy Bomar on alleys laid over two flatbed trucks. And there was always the practice to maintain competitive form. The toll on Ladewig and her family prompted her to announce that the 1955 All-Star tournament would be her last. Rather than going out on top, she came in third. Looking like a youthful bobby soxer in stylish skirt and sweater sets, forty year old Ladewig graciously accepted her defeat as *Life Magazine* captured the event in photos for a feature titled "An Ordeal On the Alleys." The winner, Sylvia Wene Martin, had trailed Ladewig as runner-up in the event for the previous three years.

Ladewig's retirement was short lived. She returned to capture the All-Star title in 1956 and again in 1959. She tossed her fifteen pound eight ounce ball down the lanes at seventeen miles per hour delivering 507 foot pounds of energy to her ten pin target to win the first of five World Invitational titles (1960, 1962-1964).

Back in top form in 1960 Ladewig won the first Women's Professional Bowling Association (WPBA) tournament over a field of 100 women at the North Miami Beach Pinerama Lanes. She was a contender for the 1961 Associated Press Female Athlete of the Year. Olympic gold medal track star **Wilma Rudolph** was chosen but Ladewig's fourth place standing was the highest ever for a female bowler. She again won the two most important individual bowling tourneys—the All-Star and the World Invitational—in 1963 when she was a near-fifty grandmother. The following year she retired from professional competition and was inducted into the WIBC Hall of Fame.

Off the lanes Ladewig was a charmer. In competition she was cool, known for her closed mouth and intense concentration. "None of us got much talk out of her while we were on the lanes," commented Marge Merrick, who defeated Ladewig for the 1961 WIBC crown. "It just wasn't her idea to pass the time of day out there. She was only out to win and she's certainly done enough of that to prove the worth of keeping quiet."

Ladewig described her delivery as an angle ball with a slight hook. Observers swore the hook was invisible and described her consistent delivery as machine-like. Accuracy was her greatest asset. Ladewig said the game never became easy for her and that fact kept her working hard. No one could match her in taking down spares. "I spared 'em to death," she liked to say.

Honors In Retirement

Honors continued to mount for Ladewig. In 1973 she was voted the Greatest Woman Bowler of All Time by the Bowling Writers Association of America (BWAA). She was named to the Women's Sports Foundation Hall of Fame in 1984. Her Ladies Pro Bowlers Tour (LPBT) trading card was issued in 1991. She was inducted into the International Bowling Museum Hall of Fame in 1991 and became one of ten charter members of the Women's Professional Bowling Hall of Fame in 1995. Ladewig was the only bowler named to the Sports Illustrated top 100 sports women of the century.

Marion Ladewig loved the game and continued to bowl after her professional career ended. She served on Brunswick Corporation's Advisory Staff of Champions and wrote syndicated columns offering bowling tips. At age 81 she carried a respectable 160 average but complained, "Sometimes I get tired." In the summer of 1999, at age 85, she rolled her last balls on her familiar home alley. "The Fan" closed its doors in 2000.

Marion Ladewig was voted Woman Bowler of the Year nine times by the Bowling Writers Association of American, more than any other person, male or female. The *Detroit News* sportswriter Jo Falls compared her to baseball legend, **Babe Ruth,** and hockey stand-out, **Gordie Howe.** Her media accolades drew unprecedented national

---

Related Biography: Bowler Sylvia Wene Martin

Sylvia Wene Martin was the first woman to roll three perfect 300 games in sanctioned competition. She marked her first perfect game in 1951 and repeated the feat in 1959 in the World Invitational Match Game Tournament. This was also the first perfect game by a woman in match play. Her third perfect score came in the 1960 qualifying rounds of the BPAA All-Star Tournament. She won the All-Star in both 1955 and 1960.

Born in 1928, Martin called Philadelphia, Pennsylvania home. In addition to three perfect scores, she held records for all-time high league average of 206 and for fourteen career three-game 700 series, the most for a woman bowler.

Martin was named Woman Bowler of the Year in 1955 and 1960 by the Bowling Writers Association of America. She was elected to the WIBC Hall of Fame in 1966 and to the International Jewish Sports Hall of Fame and the Philadelphia Jewish Sports Hall of Fame.

---

attention to the sport of women's bowling. The five time World Invitational title holder and eight time All-Star champion left her mark on the sport and truly earned the title "Queen of Bowling."

FURTHER INFORMATION

Books

David, Mac. *The Giant Book of Sports*. New York: Grosset & Dunlap, 1967.

Weiskopf, Herman. *The Perfect Game*. New York: Rutledge, 1978.

Periodicals

"Detroit's Legends of Bowling." *The Detroit News* (May 12, 2001).

"Final Frame." *The Grand Rapids Press* (April 21, 2000).

"Mrs. Ladewig and Mrs. Carter Retain Bowling Doubles Crown." *New York Times* (May 11, 1959): 38.

"An Ordeal On The Alleys." *Life* (February 7, 1955): 134-136.

"Silence Is Golden." *New York Times* (December 26, 1961): 31.

"A Tale of the Gauge." *New York Times* (July 28, 1959): 31.

Other

"Marion Ladewig, Bowling." http://womensportsonline. com/ladewig.shtml (October 25, 2002).

"Marion Ladewig." LPBT Card Collection. http://www. leggnet.com/pbacard/lpbt/911pbtcard2.html (October 18, 2002).

"94. Marion Ladewig, Bowler." *Sports Illustrated Women*. http://sportsillustrated.cnn.com/siforwomen/ top_100/94/ (October 25, 2002).

Sketch by Cynthia Becker

Guy Lafleur

Guy Lafleur
1951-

Canadian hockey player

Right wing/center Guy Lafleur was one of the best scorers of his generation. Winning three Art Ross Trophies as the National Hockey League's (NHL) leading scorer, Lafleur scored with power and grace. He was an all-around player, with strong skating, puck handling, and passing skills, an accurate shot, and the strength to handle defenders. Lafleur also won several Stanley Cups, a Conn Smythe Trophy as play-off most valuable player, and a Hart Trophy as the league's most valuable player.

Lafleur was born on September 20, 1951 in Thurso, Quebec, Canada, the only son of five children born to Rejean (a welder) and Pierette Lafleur. Lafleur learned to skate on a local outdoor rink that his father and their neighbors built. The young Lafleur loved hockey from an early age, to the point that he would sleep in his equipment.

When Lafleur was fifteen-years-old, he began playing junior hockey first for the Quebec Aces from 1966-69, then for the Quebec Remparts in 1969-71. He had an amazing season in 1970-71. In sixty-two games, Lafleur scored 209 points.

Chronology

1951	Born in Thurso, Quebec, Canada, on September 20
1966-69	Plays junior hockey for the Quebec Aces
1969-71	Plays junior hockey for the Quebec Remparts
1970-71	In 62 games for the Remparts, scores 209 points
1971	Drafted in first round of the Amateur Draft; begins professional playing career with the Montreal Canadiens
1984	Retires from hockey with the Canadiens; briefly works for the team
1988	Makes return to professional hockey with the New York Rangers
1989	Signs with the Quebec Nordiques
1991	Retires from professional hockey
1992	Works as director of corporate affairs for the Quebec Nordiques
1993	Leaves the Nordiques to be vice president of Titrex
1999	Earns helicopter pilot license

Drafted by the Canadiens

In the 1971 Amateur Draft, Lafleur was selected in the first round by the Montreal Canadiens. When he was drafted, it was with high expectations. He was to save the struggling franchise. Though he scored at least fifty points in each of his first three seasons, he did not post brilliant numbers until the mid-1970s.

When Lafleur's contract with the Canadiens expired in 1974, he had an offer to join the World Hockey League's Quebec Nordiques. Though he did not take the offer, it would have removed him from the pressure of expectations of the Canadiens. Instead he plowed through, refusing to be intimated by those who played tough defense on him. Lafleur continued to develop his own strong defensive skills to complement his artistic offensive skills.

Became Leading Scorer

The 1974-75 season was Lafleur's best offensive year to date, with fifty-three goals and sixty-six assists in the regular season. In eleven playoff games, he had twelve goals and seven assists. This was the first of six consecutive seasons in which he scored fifty plus goals.

By 1975-76, Lafleur had hit his stride, winning the Art Ross Trophy as the league's leading scorer in 1976 and the Lester B. Pearson Award. He had fifty-six goals and sixty-nine assists. He also won the Stanley Cup against Philadelphia in four games. Lafleur contributed two game winning goals.

Lafleur continued to dominate in the 1976-77 and 1977-78 seasons, winning the Ross Trophy, Hart Trophy, Lester B. Pearson Award, and the Stanley Cup again in both seasons. In 1977, he also won the Conn Smythe Trophy as most valuable player in the playoffs. In both playoffs, Lafleur scored ten goals and eleven assists.

By this time, Lafleur was recognized as a great hockey player. He told Robert Fachet of the *Washington Post*,

Career Statistics

Yr	Team	GP	G	A	PTS	+/−	PIM
1971-72	Canadiens	73	29	35	64	+27	48
1972-73	Canadiens	69	28	27	55	+16	51
1973-74	Canadiens	73	21	35	56	+10	29
1974-75	Canadiens	70	53	66	119	+52	37
1975-76	Canadiens	80	56	69	125	+68	36
1976-77	Canadiens	80	56	80	136	+89	20
1977-78	Canadiens	78	60	72	132	+73	26
1978-79	Canadiens	80	52	77	129	+56	28
1979-80	Canadiens	74	50	75	125	+40	12
1980-81	Canadiens	51	27	43	70	+24	29
1981-82	Canadiens	66	27	57	84	+33	24
1982-83	Canadiens	68	27	49	76	+6	12
1983-84	Canadiens	80	30	40	70	−14	19
1984-85	Canadiens	19	2	3	5	−3	10
1988-89	Rangers	67	18	27	45	+1	12
1989-90	Nordiques	39	12	22	34	−15	4
1990-91	Nordiques	59	12	16	28	−10	2
TOTAL		1126	560	793	1353	+453	399

Canadiens: Montreal Canadiens (NHL); Nordiques: Quebec Nordiques (NHL); Rangers: New York Rangers (NHL).

"It is more difficult playing for the Canadiens. There is lots more pressure on you. But I'm sure most guys on our team would not want to go to a team that's not winning. You never get tired of winning." He capitalized on his fame by doing many commercials in the late 1970s. He won his last Stanley Cup in 1979.

Though Lafleur continued to post high numbers in the late 1970s, he could not match them in the first half of the 1980s. Though he had eighty-four points in the 1981-82 season, he feuded with coaches, including Jacques Lemaire, who put a defense-first system on the ice. Lafleur also had tax and injury problems, which affected his game.

Short-Lived Retirement

Lafleur only played in nineteen games in the 1984-85 season. His speed and skating skills had diminished, and he was played on the third or fourth line. Lafleur was frustrated by his lack of playing time and burned out by his dealings with management. He felt his coach destroyed his confidence by not using him in big goal situations. Scoring only two goals and three assists in the nineteen games, Lafleur retired from hockey in November 1984 because management would not change.

After retiring, Lafleur was hired to work for the Canadiens in public relations, but this was short-lived. He continued playing hockey in a recreational league. The lure of playing professionally was too great. After he was elected to the Hall of Fame in 1988, Lafleur decided to unretire a few days later. He began to train in earnest as soon as he was mentally ready. As Stan Fischler quoted him as saying in *The All-New Hockey's 100,* "Hockey is like a drug for me. I am hooked. I can't do anything about it."

Returned to Professional Hockey

After being turned down by several teams, Lafleur went to training camp in 1988 with the New York Rangers. He played well enough to earn a spot on the team. Though Lafleur was not the same player he was at the height of his career, he made contributions. He scored eighteen goals and twenty-seven assists in sixty-seven games, and gave the team stability in the face of front office turmoil.

In 1989, Lafleur signed with the Quebec Nordiques when the Rangers did not match their offer. Thus he was traded to Quebec for $100,000 and a draft choice. Lafleur played for two more seasons before finally retiring in 1991.

After spending a year working in the front office of the Quebec Nordiques as director of corporate affairs, Lafleur went to Titrex as a vice president of public relations in 1993. But hockey still had its lure for him. He played in a number of old timers games, including the Oldtimer's Hockey Challenge Tour, which benefited the Ontario Special Olympics. He also worked for the Montreal Canadiens as a Special Ambassador, making special appearances for the team. In recognition of his impact on hockey, the Quebec Major Junior Hockey League named their most valuable player in the playoffs trophy after him. Off the ice, in 1999, Lafleur earned his helicopter pilot license and considered starting a related transport business.

Over the course of his career, Lafleur played in 1028 regular season games, with 509 goals and 793 assists. In 128 playoff games, he had fifty-eight goals and seventy-six assists. Known as "the Flower" (the literal meaning of his last name), his legacy was his undying love for the

Awards and Accomplishments

1970-71	Quebec Junior Hockey League All-Star (first team)
1975	All-Star (first team)
1976	Won Art Ross Trophy; won the Stanley Cup; All-Star (first team); won Lester B. Pearson Award
1977	Won Art Ross Trophy; won Hart Trophy; won Conn Smythe Trophy; won Stanley Cup; All-Star (first team); won Lester B. Pearson Award
1978	Won Art Ross Trophy; won Hart Trophy; won Stanley Cup; All-Star (first team); won Lester B. Pearson Award
1979	Won Stanley Cup; All-Star (first team)
1980	All-Star (first team)
1988	Elected to the Hall of Fame

game and his scoring expertise. As sportswriter Bill Libby was quoted as saying on LegendsofHockey.net, "He is an artist on skates, creating scoring plays the way a painter puts a vivid scene on a canvas with a brush. ... He is a spectacular athlete in a spectacular sport and it is wonderful watching him work."

CONTACT INFORMATION

Address: 14 Place du Moulin, L'ile-Bizard, Quebec H9E 1N2 Canada.

FURTHER INFORMATION

Books

Diamond, Dan, and Joseph Romain. *Hockey Hall of Fame: The Official History of the Game and Its Greatest Stars*. New York: Doubleday, 1988.

Fischler, Stan. *The All-New Hockey's 100: A Personal Ranking of the Best Players in Hockey History*. Toronto: McGraw-Hill Ryerson Ltd., 1988.

Hickok, Ralph. *A Who's Who of Sports Champions: Their Stories and Records*. Boston: Houghton Mifflin Company, 1995.

Kariher, Harry C. *Who's Who in Hockey*. New Rochelle: Arlington House, 1973.

McGovern, Mike. *The Encyclopedia of Twentieth-Century Athletes*. New York: Facts on File, Inc., 2001.

Periodicals

"Canadiens' Lafleur Retires as Player." *New York Times* (November 27, 1984): B12.

Dupont, Kevin. "Lafleur Wilts in Reverse Role." *New York Times* (May 4, 1984): A25.

Fachet, Robert. "It's All Coming Back to a Hustling Ranger; Hall of Famer Lafleur Gathering Speed." *Washington Post* (October 19, 1988): C1.

Fachet, Robert. "Lafleur Still Tingles Before Canadien Games; Lafleur as an Artist: the Young Rafael." *Washington Post* (May 16, 1978): E1.

Finn, Robin. "Lafleur Impressing Rangers." *New York Times* (September 29, 1988): B19.

Finn, Robin. "Lafleur, 37, Returns to Prove a Point." *New York Times* (October 17, 1988): C13.

Lapointe, Joe. "Lafleur's Next Goal a Historical One." *New York Times* (November 23, 1989): B21.

McEntegart, Pete. "Catching Up With ...: Guy Lafleur, Canadiens Hall of Famer." *Sports Illustrated* (February 7, 1977): 12.

McGraw, Bill. "Lafleur, in an Encore, Bids Fans Adieu." *New York Times* (April 1, 1991): C8.

McRae, Earl. "Lafleur Still Creating Little Bits of Heaven for Adoring Fans." *Ottawa Sun* (April 15, 2001): 5.

Murphy, Austin. "The late-blooming flower; out of the game four years, Guy Lafleur attempts a comeback." *Sports Illustrated* (September 26, 1988): 88.

Richman, Alan. "Guy Lafleur, hockey's faded flower, blooms anew in New York." *People Weekly* (February 6, 1989): 57.

Sexton, Joe. "Lafleur Gets a Shot with the Rangers." *New York Times* (August 20, 1988): section 1, p. 47.

Sexton, Joe. "Rangers Send Lafleur Back Home in Deal with Nordiques." *New York Times* (July 15, 1989): section 1, p. 45.

Yannis, Alex. "Lafleur Dispelling Doubts." *New York Times* (September 13, 1988): B7.

Other

"Guy Lafleur." http://www.hockeysandwich.com/lafleur.html (November 2, 2002).

"The Legends: Players: Guy Lafleur: Biography." Legends of Hockey. http://www.legendsofhockey.net:8080/LegendsOfHockey/jsp/Legen... (November 2, 2002).

"The Legends: Players: Guy Lafleur: Statistics." Legends of Hockey. http://www.legendsofhockey.net:8080/LegendsOfHockey/jsp/Legen... (November 2, 2002).

Sketch by A. Petruso

Alexi Lalas
1970-

American soccer player

One of the most recognized American soccer players because of his red hair and trademark goatee, Alexi Lalas contributed to the popularity of the sport in the United States in the 1990s. A defender, Lalas played on the U.S. national team, and professionally for MLS (Major League Soccer) and in Europe for Italy's Serie A, one of

Alexi Lalas

Chronology

1970	Born on June 1, in Birmingham, Michigan
1988-91	Attends Rutgers University
1990	Makes several appearances with U.S. national team
1991	Joins U.S. National Team
1992	Plays for the United States at the Summer Olympics
1994	Plays for the United States at World Cup, playing every minute of every game
1994-95	Plays with Padua in Serie A (Italy)
1996	Plays for the United States at the Summer Olympics
1996-97	Plays for the New England Revolution (MLS)
1997	Plays for club in Ecuador in MLS off-season
1998	Plays for New York/New Jersey MetroStars; records *Ginger* which was released on CMC Intl.; reserve for U.S. in World Cup competition
1999	Plays for the Kansas City Wizards (MLS); retires from professional soccer; begins broadcasting career
2000	Commentator for MLS season, Nickelodeon Games and Sports programming, and Olympic coverage of soccer; shaves his trademark goatee
2001	Signed by Los Angeles Galaxy (MLS)

the best leagues in the world. He was also a singer and guitar player who recorded and performed with bands.

Lalas was born on June 1, 1970, in Birmingham, Michigan, the son of Dimitrious Lalas and his wife Anne Woodworth. His father was a professor who later became the director of Greece's national observatory, while his mother was a writer and poet. Lalas did not begin to play soccer until he was 10 or 11 years old, but by his senior year of high school at Cranbrook Kingswood, he was Michigan's prep soccer player of the year. Soccer was not his only sport. Lalas was also a star hockey player, and his team won the state's high school hockey championship.

Plays College Soccer

When Lalas entered Rutgers in 1988, he joined the soccer team playing sweeper after a try-out. He grew tremendously as a player. Lalas was named captain in 1989, and by 1991 was selected as the national player of the year. Rutgers went to the semifinals of the NCAA tournament in 1989 and the finals in 1990. Coach Bob Reasso told Alex Yannis of the *New York Times,* "He's the most dominant player we've had at Rutgers on and off the field. His intensity, his fire and passion for the game is like no one I've ever seen."

Lalas left Rutgers before completing his degree in English, having already been selected to play for the

United States in international competition several times. In 1989, he was captain of the West Team that won the gold medal at the U.S. Olympic Festival. In 1990, he played for the U.S. national team several times, but not in World Cup competition. Two years later, he was a member of the U.S. Olympic soccer team that did not make it past the first round.

High Profile Player at World Cup

Lalas garnered the national spotlight when he was a key member of the 1994 U.S. national team that played at the World Cup competition held in the United States. A defender, Lalas played every minute of every game. Both his play and appearance drew attention. Not a finesse player, Lalas played his role as defender with determination, heart, and hard work. Sometimes opponents accused him of playing too much like a hockey player with his propensity for checking.

Played in Italy

After the World Cup, Lalas was offered a contract with Padua, a Serie A team in Italy, as well as with teams in England and Germany. He took the Padua contract, becoming the first American to play in this league, often considered the best in the world. For both the team and Lalas, this was a gamble because Lalas had never played professionally. He played well, becoming a star on the team. Lalas scored three goals on the season, and played with Padua through 1995.

Played for MLS Team

After again playing for a disappointing U.S. team at the Summer Olympics in 1996, Lalas was asked to leave Padua to become one of the faces for the MLS in its first season. This was the first professional soccer league in

Awards and Accomplishments	
1987	Named Michigan's soccer player of the year
1989	Led Rutgers to NCAA Final Four appearance; captain of West team that wins gold medal at U.S. Olympic Festival
1990	Led Rutgers to NCAA championship game appearance
1991	Wins Hermann Trophy and Missouri Athletic Club award as national college player of the year
1994	Named U.S. representative to All-Tournament team for World Cup
1995	Wins U.S. Soccer Athlete of the Year Award
1996	Named to Eastern Conference All-Star team (MLS)
1998	Inducted in the Rutgers University Olympic Sports Hall of Fame
1998-99	Selected for MLS All-Star Game
2000	Won F.C. Champions Cup with Los Angeles Galaxy (MLS)
2002	Won MLS Cup and Supporters Shield with the Los Angeles Galaxy

America in a number of years, and having a high profile player like Lalas would bring attention to the young league. He agreed, and was assigned to the New England Revolution. Lalas explained to Rob Hughes of the *International Herald Tribune*, "I wanted to do something for football back home. I didn't want to have the feeling later that I had sat back and done nothing."

While Lalas had a decent season on a poor Revolution team in 1996, the 1997 and 1998 seasons were even worse for both his professional and U.S. national team play. In 1997, he was benched on the U.S. team. Lalas continued to struggle in 1998 when he was traded to the New York/New Jersey MetroStars. Though this team made the playoffs, it was the first time Lalas did not register an assist in the season. He was also on the U.S. national team in World Cup competition that year, but only as a reserve and never played in the tournament, in which the American team faired poorly.

Briefly Retires

After turning down a chance to play for Bruce Arena when he took over the U.S. national team in late 1998, Lalas was again traded in 1999, this time to the Kansas City Wizards. Though he played decently on a poor team, he decided to retire after the season ended.

During his hiatus from soccer, Lalas began a career in broadcasting, covering soccer for ABC, ESPN, and Fox Sports Net, the Olympics for NBC, and other sports programming. He also continued to work on his musical career. This physical and mental break served Lalas well. He emerged at the end of the 2000 MLS season signing with the Los Angles Galaxy for the playoffs. The team won the Football Confederation Champions Cup.

Lalas opted to re-sign with the Galaxy, and played for them during the 2001 and 2002 seasons. In 2002, he had a career high four goals and four assists, playing center back. The team won both the MLS Cup and Sup-

porters Shield that season. No matter what he chose to do, Lalas remained true to himself. He told the *Tampa Tribune*, "I made my bed with who I am and the way I look. It's honest and I believe in it from an individual standpoint and from a soccer standpoint. If I ever felt I was being manipulated against my will, where I was becoming this cartoon or something, I would get out of it."

CONTACT INFORMATION

Address: c/o Los Angeles Galaxy, 1001 Rose Bowl Dr., Pasadena, CA 91103.

SELECTED WRITINGS BY LALAS:

(With Thomas Lee Wright) *Kickin Balls: The Alexi Lalas Story*. Simon & Schuster, 1996.

FURTHER INFORMATION

Periodicals

Dell Apa, Frank. "Red-Hot: Soccer May Need Lalas' Fiery Image." *The News & Record,* (April 28, 1996): C8.

DeSimone, Bonnie. "Lalas Kicks Back With His Guitar." *Seattle Times,* (January 31, 2000): D10.

Dure, Beau. "Major League Soccer—So What's Up with Alexi Lalas." *Seattle Times,* (October 17, 1999): C3.

French, Scott. "Galaxy Preview: Lalas Finds Himself in New Surroundings." *Daily News,* (March 28, 1998): S2.

Haydon, John. "Lalas Challenges U.S. Team to Develop Better Chemistry." *Washington Times,* (May 16, 1998): 8.

Hersch, Hank. "Alexi Lalas." *Sports Illustrated,* (January 31, 1994): 68.

Hughes, Rob. "Soccer Returns to U.S. On a Stronger Footing." *International Herald Tribune,* (April 3, 1996): 21.

Jones, Grahame L. "Career Makeover." *Los Angeles Times,* (December 22, 2000): D1.

Jones, Grahame L. "Lalas Goals Puts Galaxy in Final." *Los Angeles Times,* (August 23, 2001): D3.

Jones, Grahame L. "Lalas to Join Galaxy for Season." *Los Angeles Times,* (January 12, 2001): D5.

Jones, Grahame L. "Start of MLS Season Can't Come Soon Enough for Lalas." *Los Angeles Times,* (April 7, 2001): D2.

Kuhns, Ike. "Lalas Coming Home to MetroStars." *Star-Ledger,* (February 5, 1998): 55.

"Lalas Refuses to Let Fame Go to Trademark Red Head." *Tampa Tribune,* (May 3, 1998): 7.

Leonard, Tim. "Lalas Returns Home." *The Record,* (February 7, 1998): S3.

Leonard, Tim. "Metros Trade of Lalas Blindsided Defender." *The Record,* (June 20, 1999): S4.

Longman, Jere. "Carrot-Top Defender of the U.S." *New York Times,* (June 26, 1994): section 8, p. 1.

Lopez, John P. "MLS Takes Show on Road to Try to Gain Acceptance." *Houston Chronicle,* (November 6, 2002): 1.

Mcintyre, Jason. "Lalas is Always the Entertainer." *The Record,* (June 15, 2002): S5.

Montville, Leigh. "Uncharted Waters." *Sports Illustrated,* (September 26, 1994): 50.

Murphy, Mark. "Rolling with the Punches." *Boston Herald,* (May 31, 1998): B20.

Robledo, Fred J. Older, "Better Lalas Path Leads to MLS Cup." *Daily News,* (October 16, 2002): S11.

"Soccer Gypsy Glad to be Back Home." *The Star-Ledger,* (March 17, 1996): 21.

Starr, Mark, and Niccolo Vivarelli. "Good Enough for Majors." *Newsweek,* (October 10, 1994): 64.

Stephenson, Colin. "Lalas Hopes to Find That Lost Step Somewhere in France During the Cup." *Star-Ledger,* (June 10, 1998): 5.

Trusdell, Brian. "Unlikely Celebrity." *Denver Rocky Mountain News,* (August 10, 1997): 26C.

Yannis, Alex. "Rutgers Lalas Named Top Collegian." *New York Times,* (December 18, 1991): B14.

Other

"Coaching Staff: Sigi Schmid." Los Angeles Galaxy. http://www.lagalaxy.com/coaching.html (January 25, 2003).

"MLS—Alexi Lalas Player Profile." Yahoo! Sports. http://sports.yahoo.com/mls/players/3/34/ (January 13, 2003).

"Player Bio—Alexi Lalas." MLSnet.com. http://www.mlsnet.com/bios/alexi_lalas.html (January 13, 2003).

"Profile: Sigi Schmid." SoccerTimes.com. http://www.soccertimes.com/usteams/roster/u-20men/schmid.htm (January 25, 2003).

"Win or lose, Sigi a success." ESPN.com. http://espn.go.com/soccer/s/2002/1019/1448218.html (January 25, 2003).

Sketch by A. Petruso

Earl Lambeau
1898-1965

American football coach

E arl "Curly" Lambeau was the founder and first coach of the Green Bay Packers football team. He led the team to six world titles in the 1930s and 1940s, and had a

Earl Lambeau

winning percentage of .657. The Packers' stadium in Green Bay, Lambeau Field, is named in his honor.

Founds Green Bay Packers

In 1898, when Lambeau was born, Green Bay, Wisconsin was a busy commercial center, populated largely by northern European immigrants, and was noted for its breweries, cheese factories, and paper mills. Although it only had 30,000 residents, the town also had a symphony orchestra, street lamps, and trolley cars. What it did not have was a football team. Lambeau, who was a hero on his high school football team as well as during his freshman year at Notre Dame University, returned to Green Bay after a year at Notre Dame and took a job at a local meat company, the Indian Packing Company, but he never lost his desire to play football.

Each morning before going to work, Lambeau stopped at the home of his high school sweetheart, Marguerite Van Kessel and threw a pebble against her window; then they talked until his ride to work showed up. Van Kessel urged Lambeau to go back to school at Notre Dame, but he wanted to stay in Green Bay and marry her. In 1919, he did.

In that same year Lambeau and several friends decided that Green Bay needed an official football team. Lambeau convinced his employer to buy the team jerseys and equipment and let the team use the company's athletic field for practice, and in exchange, they named the team after the company.

Career Statistics

Yr	Team	Passing					Rushing			Receiving		
		ATT	COM	YDS	TD	INT	ATT	YDS	TD	REC	YDS	TD
1921	GB	58	18	361	1	8	29	96	2	0	0	0
1922	GB	55	26	469	2	4	60	203	3	0	0	0
1923	GB	118	43	752	3	17	133	416	1	13	217	2
1924	GB	179	75	1094	8	29	132	457	0	7	112	1
1925	GB	121	47	711	5	7	74	224	0	5	39	0
1926	GB	80	30	504	3	5	44	112	0	5	86	0
1927	GB	54	26	417	1	4	64	231	2	6	121	0
1928	GB	30	11	149	1	3	10	14	0	4	48	0
1929	GB	5	2	36	0	1	3	9	0	0	0	0
TOTAL		700	278	4493	24	78	549	1762	8	40	623	3

GB: Green Bay Packers.

Lambeau, who had played under famed coach **Knute Rockne** at Notre Dame, ran three practice sessions each week and taught the players what Rockne had taught him. In addition to being the team's coach, he was also its star player. Newspaperman George Calhoun was the team's business manager and publicist.

For their first season, the Packers played eleven other small-town Wisconsin and Michigan teams. They won the first ten games, then lost 6-0 to the Beloit Fairies; the Packers later claimed the game was rigged. For pay, the players passed a hat among the spectators at halftime, and split the proceeds. In that first season, they made $16.75 each. From this money, or their own funds, they had to pay any doctor bills resulting from injuries on the field.

During the team's second season, Lambeau introduced a new play: throwing the ball to other players instead of running with it and crashing through a line of opponents. Opposing teams hated this move, saying passing was for sissies, and when the Packers played a passing game against a team of miners in Michigan's Upper Peninsula, Lambeau "had to run for his life," according to Jim Doherty in *Smithsonian*. Lambeau later remarked, "Those miners were tough."

Joins the NFL

In 1921 the Packers joined the new National Football League, a move that cost $50. Lambeau got into trouble by playing college students under assumed names, and the team's franchise was revoked. However, when Lambeau apologized and paid $250, it was returned.

Financially, the team struggled just to stay afloat, and throughout the 1920s, the team made enough to scrape by through holding dances at the Green Bay Elks Club and raffles at the local American Legion post. During this period, Lambeau realized that he could not simply rely on local talent, and began scouting for players, convincing them that despite its harsh winters, Green Bay was a great place to play and live. He acquired several superstar players, including Verne Llewellen, Lavvie Dilweg, and Red Dunn. When the team played the young Giants in New York, they won, 7-0.

In 1929, 1930, and 1931, Lambeau led the team to championship victories. In the next thirteen years, they won four division titles and three more NFL championships. Green Bay celebrated with parades, torchlight parties, and near-worship of Lambeau. But although fans loved Lambeau, the players had a difficult relationship with him. When he won, he would buy drinks for everyone; when he lost, he had seething tantrums.

Despite their success, the Packers went through bouts of financial trouble and were only bailed out by the efforts of their fans, who held benefits and raised enough to keep the team barely afloat.

During these hard times, Lambeau began to slip out of favor with fans and players alike. Local fans believed he was too extravagant, arrogant, and flashy; they questioned his management methods, and argued about the merits of his coaching. Committees were set up to oversee Lambeau's work.

Lambeau had also alienated himself from his wife, and on May 23, 1934, he and Van Kessel divorced. He moved to California, bought a house and a ranch, married twice more, and divorced both times. He was married to his second wife, Sue, from 1935 until their divorce in 1940; his third marriage, to Grace Nichols, lasted from 1945 to 1955.

After World War II, many of Lambeau's players were ex-servicemen who would not put up with his attitude. His relations with players and fans came to a final showdown when he tried to arrange a takeover of the team, and it failed. He left the team in 1949.

In the early 1950s, Lambeau coached for the Chicago Cardinals and Washington Redskins; his coaching career ended in 1954. In 1963, Lambeau was inducted into the

"Lambeau's Ex-Wife Dies." *Capital Times* (Madison, WI) (July 5, 2001): 2C.

Sullivan, Paul. "Green Bay's Affair with Pack Dates to '19." *Boston Herald* (January 15, 1997): 6.

Other

"Earl L. (Curly) Lambeau," *Packers.com*, http://www.packers.com/ (November 8, 2002).

Sketch by Kelly Winters

Pro Football Hall of Fame. Lambeau died from a heart attack on June 1, 1965, in Sturgeon Bay, Wisconsin.

Lambeau's Legacy

Lambeau's legacy, the Packers football team, is still going strong. Lambeau took the team from playing in front of crowds of 4,000 to 5,000 in its early days to playing for almost 25,000 fans in the mid-1930s; today, because of television, millions of fans watch every game.

The team is famed not only for winning division championships and Super Bowls, but also for the intense loyalty of its fans. The Packers are completely owned by their fans and by the Green Bay community, and the team is run as a nonprofit venture. Team bylaws, beloved and supported by fans, prevent the team from being moved to any other town. Season tickets are passed on through families as cherished legacies, and all home games are sold out. And when the outdoor stadium at Lambeau Field, known as "The Frozen Tundra," fills up with snow after winter storms, an army of fans arrives to cheerfully shovel it out.

FURTHER INFORMATION

Periodicals

Berghaus, Bob. "The Coach of the Century." *Green Bay Press-Gazette* (December 31, 1999): MP9.

Christl, Cliff. "Lambeau: More Than a Name." *UW-Green Bay Voyageur* (Winter-Spring, 2001): 10.

Doherty, Jim. "In Chilly Green Bay, Curly's Old Team is Still Packing Them In." *Smithsonian* (August, 1991): 80.

"Hall of Fame Members." *Gazette* (Colorado Springs, CO) (February 3, 2002): SP15.

Jake LaMotta
1921-

American boxer

Jake LaMotta grew up a street kid whose skills with his fists earned him the amateur light heavyweight championship's Diamond Belt. At nineteen, he began a pro career that would include eighty-three wins (including thirty by knockouts), nineteen losses, and four draws. After retiring from boxing, he developed a comedy routine that drew on his fighting experiences and his failed relationships.

The "Bronx Bull"

Jake LaMotta was born Giacobe LaMotta on July 10, 1921 on the Lower East Side of New York, and was first encouraged to fight at a very young age by his father, who collected the coins thrown into the street by enthusiastic onlookers to help pay the family's bills. LaMotta spent time in reform school after a failed jewelry store robbery and had an estimated 1,000 street fights before beginning his pro boxing career at age nineteen, a career most remembered for his six fights with **Sugar Ray Robinson**.

LaMotta first fought Robinson in New York in 1942 in a fight that Robinson won on a decision. In 1943 they met twice in Detroit in fights that were held twenty-one days apart. In the initial fight, Robinson experienced his first career loss in forty-one professional fights, then took a decision in the second match. Robinson won in a

Jake LaMotta

ten-round decision in 1945 in New York, but LaMotta was beating other top fighters from the welterweight to light heavyweight divisions. They included Fritzie Zivic, Tommy Bell, George Kochan, Bert Lytell, Jose Basora, Holman Williams, Bob Satterfield, and Tony Janiro. "He was not a special talent," wrote Steve Bunce in *Scotland on Sunday,* "just a 'tough, young punk,' as he was once referred to by the former heavyweight champion **Jack Dempsey**, whose restaurant on 51st and Broadway was the last resort for the fight fraternity in New York. His initial nickname, before the Bronx Bull stuck, was 'One-man Gang.' That is exactly how he fought."

Middleweight Champ

LaMotta refused to become a pawn of the mob and for years was prevented from getting the matches that could lead to a title. He finally won the middleweight championship from Frenchman Marcel Cerdan on June 16, 1949, with a technical knockout. Cerdan, who had beaten the legendary Tony Zale to win the title, was killed in an airplane crash while flying back to the United States for a rematch. LaMotta later admitted to the Kefauver Committee, a panel investigating corruption in boxing, that he had thrown a 1947 fight with Billy Fox to get that title shot. Earlier in 1947, LaMotta had been offered $100,000 to throw a different fight, an offer he refused. He accepted only that part of the deal for throwing the Fox fight that guaranteed him a chance to win the title and refused the money that went with it.

In beating Tiberio Mitri, LaMotta retained his title, and again successfully defended it in a fight against Laurent Dauthuille which ended with a knockout in the fifteenth round. The judges who scored the fight round by round had given it to Dauthuille, and if the fight were played by today's rules, which limit a fight to twelve rounds, LaMotta would have lost. And he did lose his next defense of his title to Robinson the following year. In the famous "St. Valentine's Day Massacre" of 1951, he lost the crown to Robinson. LaMotta, who himself had brutalized so many opponents, was being beaten so badly that the referee stopped the match in the thirteenth round.

A Fall from Grace

LaMotta had one more fight in 1951 and six in 1952. He had no matches in 1953 and fought his final three in 1954. By then he bore the scars of his career, including a nose that had been broken six times. LaMotta then quit the ring and settled in Miami, Florida where he opened a club and dated a string of movie stars, including Jayne Mansfield, Ginger Rogers, Jane Russell, and Hedi Lamar. He fell from grace with the sportswriters and most of his friends because of his violent behavior. He drank too much, pursued the wives of his friends and admitted to raping the wife of one. He was arrested and served time on a chain gang for acting as the pimp of an underage girl, although he has maintained that he was innocent.

Bunce, who wrote of meeting LaMotta, said that "there are so many tales of LaMotta groping a friend's wife or girlfriend at social events that it would be impossible to start listing them. It seems that retaliation was left to the women, presumably the men were too scared, and LaMotta was variously hit with full ice buckets or else doused with cocktails."

LaMotta's earlier loss to Bill Fox had been suspect since the event, and in 1960, he confessed to the Kefau-

---

Raging Bull

Robert DeNiro received an Oscar for his stark portrayal of LaMotta in the film directed by Martin Scorsese. To portray LaMotta, DeNiro learned the sport from the champ. The film was true in its depiction of LaMotta's ruthlessness, and DeNiro was applauded for his performance. The black and white film received seven other nominations, and it is considered by many to be the best film of the 1980s. It showed how LaMotta's jealousy and passions fueled his intensity in the ring. He once beat an opponent to a pulp because his teenaged wife Vicki (Cathy Moriarity) called him "good looking."

Nominations went to Joe Pesci, who plays LaMotta's brother, for supporting actor, and editor Thelma Schoonmaker. The brutality of the fight scenes is emphasized by the sound and visual effects. Tubes containing simulated sweat and blood were hidden in the boxers' hair, realistically releasing the fluids when blows were landed. Scorsese slowed the speed in filming scenes in which LaMotta became angry or paranoid, and the scene most remembered is when DeNiro/LaMotta, sitting before a dressing room mirror, repeats Marlon Brando's line from *On the Waterfront*, "I coulda been a contender." LaMotta's autobiography was adapted for film by Mardik Martin and Paul Schrader.

Awards and Accomplishments

1949	Wins world middleweight title from French champion Marcel Cerdan
1990	Elected to the Boxing Hall of Fame

---

ver Committee that he had thrown that fight. His honesty degraded his reputation even further, and when Robinson quit boxing, LaMotta was barred from attending his farewell dinner.

Washington Times writer Thom Loverro, who caught LaMotta's comedy act at Café Milano in Georgetown, wrote that his one-liners "would have made Henny Youngman proud: 'I'm in great shape, every artery in my body is as hard as a rock. . . . We're going to talk about the art of self-defense tonight. In order to defend yourself you need two things, a good lawyer and a good alibi. . . . My doctor told me once if I didn't stop drinking I'd lose my hearing. I told the doctor so what, the stuff I'm drinking is better than the stuff I'm hearing.'" The line that LaMotta is famous for is his, "I fought Sugar Ray so many times, it's a wonder I don't have diabetes."

Always a storyteller, LaMotta performed his comedy routine for many years, and his minor celebrity received a boost when the movie *Raging Bull* was released. Married seven times, his marriage to his second wife, Vickie, is an integral component of the film based on his autobiography. LaMotta regularly abused Vickie, the mother of his sons, Jack and Joe, and one of his four daughters. Robert DeNiro won an Oscar for his portrayal of LaMotta in *Raging Bull,* a Martin Scorsese film that pulls no punches in depicting the life of one of the toughest boxers ever to step into the ring.

Roger Ebert reviewed *Raging Bull* in the *Los Angeles Times,* saying that the film "is the most painful and heartrending portrait of jealousy in the cinema—an *Othello* for our times. It's the best film I've seen about the low self-esteem, sexual inadequacy, and fear that lead some men to abuse women. Boxing is the arena, not the subject. LaMotta was famous for refusing to be knocked down in the ring. There are scenes where he stands passively, his hands at his side, allowing himself to be ham-

mered. We sense why he didn't go down. He hurt too much to allow the pain to stop."

Personal Tragedy and the Later Years

Jack LaMotta, who had managed his father, died of cancer in February 1998. LaMotta's other son, Joe, had been convicted of trafficking in cocaine and served half of a five-year sentence. When he was paroled, he did his best to take his brother's place in helping his father. S. L. Price noted in *Sports Illustrated* that "it wasn't until the final months of his life that Joe began to shine. He traveled with Jake to autograph shows and cooked up the concept of LaMotta's Tomato Sauce. In July 1998, Joe and Jake went to Geneva to gauge prospects for the sauce in Europe, where Jake is popular. Joe was gaining confidence. 'He had always been in the shadow of his father,' says [Joseph] Fell, Jake's lawyer and Joe's best friend, 'but now he was psyched. If the sauce had done well, he would've moved to Geneva. He was already asking me to find somebody to manage his dad. I think he just wanted to start living his own life.'" On September 2, 1998, Joe died in the explosion of Swissair Flight 111, which had departed from Kennedy Airport and was bound for Geneva. LaMotta, who claims that he never earned more than a million dollars in his lifetime, filed a lawsuit against the airlines and Boeing for $125 million because of the death of his son. He was the first relative of a victim to file.

After the death of his sons, LaMotta retired to his Manhattan apartment and returned to managing his own life. "You know what people do now?" he said to Price. "They think I'm the godfather. They kiss my hand, women and men! Men come over and kiss me on the forehead. When my son died? More people were stopping me in the street. They hugged me, women, men."

Stephanie, daughter of LaMotta and his fourth wife, Dimitria, is a fighter like her father. An actress and boxing and fitness instructor, since 1979 she has also battled multiple sclerosis (MS), the disease of the central nervous system for which there is no known cure. In spite of bouts of paralysis and near blindness, Stephanie trained dozens of clients, including celebrities, at the Los Angeles Youth Athletic Center gym and created a video, *Stephanie LaMotta's Boxersize Workout,* before MS confined her to a wheelchair. She developed boxing workouts for women during the 1980s, but she was ahead of her time. Gym owners couldn't envision women hitting the bag, jumping rope, and shadow boxing, programs that are now enjoyed by women who have found that these routines are not only enjoyable but an excellent way to stay in shape.

Stephanie LaMotta was able to manage her symptoms until she was involved in an automobile accident that collapsed one of her lungs. In an interview with Earl Gustkey for the *Los Angeles Times,* she said, "I have a heavy bag in my garage and I punch it as part of my therapy." Speaking of her MS, Stephanie said, "I'm fighting this with all my heart. I'm like my dad in that way—we're both fighters. We talk about once a month and he inspires me."

LaMotta has been an inspiration to young boxers who have, like him, risen from poverty to grab championship with both hands. Sadly, LaMotta's admission that he threw a fight in order to achieve that chance has tarnished his image, but his refusal, except for that once, to cooperate with the mob bosses who controlled the game must be viewed as an act of extreme bravery. Boxing was a different game when LaMotta fought—dirty around the edges and taking a tremendous toll on young men who fought hundreds of fights without ever getting their big chance. That the Bronx Bull survived all this and can still laugh about it, is truly a story of courage and survival.

SELECTED WRITINGS BY LAMOTTA:

(With Joseph Carter and Peter Savage) *Raging Bull: My Story,* Prentice-Hall, 1970.
(With Chris Anderson and Sharon McGehee) *Raging Bull II,* Lyle Stuart, 1986.

FURTHER INFORMATION

Books

Hickok, Ralph. *A Who's Who of Sports Champions: Their Stories and Records.* New York: Houghton Mifflin, 1995.
LaMotta, Jake, Joseph Carter, and Peter Savage. *Raging Bull.* Englewood Cliffs, NJ: Prentice-Hall, 1970.
LaMotta, Jake, Chris Anderson, and Sharon McGehee. *Raging Bull II.* Secaucus, NJ: Lyle Stuart, 1986.
Markoe, Arnold, editor. *The Scribner Encyclopedia of American Lives, Sports Figures,* (two volumes). New York: Charles Scribner's Sons, 2002.
Roberts, James, and Alexander G. Skutt. *The Boxing Register.* Ithaca, NY: McBooks Press, 1997, 1999.

Periodicals

Bunce, Steve. "*Raging Bull* was released twenty years ago this month." *Scotland on Sunday* (Edinburgh, Scotland) (November 25, 2002): 33.
Gustkey, Earl. "Body Blow." *Los Angeles Times* (July 14, 2001): D1.

Loverro, Thom. "Rageless Bull." *Washington Times* (February 12, 1997): 1.
Price, S. L. "After the Fall." *Sports Illustrated,* (September 6, 1999): R24.

Other

Ebert, Roger. Review of *Raging Bull. Chicago Sun Times.* http:www.suntimes.com/ (January, 1999).
Raging Bull. United Artists (1981).

Sketch by Sheila Velazquez

Tom Landry
1924-2000
American football coach

Every football Sunday for twenty-nine years, Tom Landry stood expressionless on the sidelines as coach of the Dallas Cowboys in the National Football League (NFL). Whether winning or losing, Landry, in his suit and trademark fedora, always remained calm. His stoic demeanor and aura of control demanded respect from both his opponents and his players. He possessed a superior football mind and was recognized for his innovations even as a young man. As a player-coach with the New York Giants, Landry created the 4-3 defense, a staple of pro football, featuring four linemen and three linebackers. In Dallas, he was the first to use computers for scouting and game preparation. Landry's continuing influence on the game is carried forward by former staff members and players still active in the league.

The Early Years

Born Thomas Wade Landry on September 11, 1924 in Mission, Texas, he was the son Ron Landry, an auto mechanic. As a child, he shared an attic bedroom with his two older siblings and was nearly killed when he was struck in a car accident. Somewhat shy, he was an A student, class president and football standout in high school. During Landry's senior year his team went undefeated and he was offered a football scholarship to the University of Texas. After just one semester, Landry left to serve in the Army Air Corps during World War II, flying 30 missions as a B-17 pilot and surviving a crash landing in the French countryside.

As an All-Pro halfback for the New York Giants, Landry was an extremely emotional player. In 1954, Landry intercepted three passes against Philadelphia and was voted All-Pro for the first time. The following year

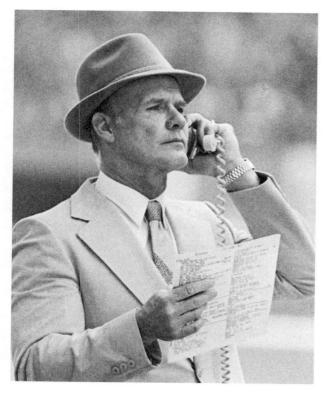

Tom Landry

he went to the Pro-Bowl. It was 1956, when Landry became a defensive assistant, after two years as a player-coach for the Giants. His coaching career had officially started and Landry wasted no time bringing his ideas to the table. In addition to creating the 4-3 defense, he was the first coach to call defensive audibles with signals from the sidelines. Although Landry always insisted he had no interest in coaching after his playing career was over, his knowledge of the game and innovative ideas would keep him at the helm for years to come. The head coach of the Giants, Jim Lee Howell, called Landry "the greatest football coach in the game today."

It was an offer from the expansion Dallas football franchise, awarded in 1960, that convinced Landry to continue his coaching career. A native Texan, who ran an insurance business in Dallas during the off-season, Landry accepted the offer to become the team's first head coach. Although the expansion Cowboys didn't win a game in their inaugural season and didn't show much improvement during the following two seasons, Cowboys owner Clint Murchison Jr. signed Landry to a ten year contract as a show of support. Landry's original plan, to coach for a few seasons and then go into business full-time, had changed once and for all.

While Landry enjoyed the respect and admiration of his players and colleagues later in his career, during the first six years in Dallas he lacked patience and his players lacked faith. Players privately referred to him as Pope Landry I or Ol' Stone Face. It wasn't until 1966 that the Dallas Cowboys had their first winning season. Few could have predicted that it would be twenty more seasons before the Dallas Cowboys would have another losing season.

The Innovator

The list of Landry's innovations is long and impressive and what he considered most important to his legacy. In Dallas, he created the umbrella-like flex defense, began using computers, reintroduced the shotgun formation and popularized situational substitutions. His command of the X's and O's of the game was matched only by his ability to keep a cool distance from his players. Landry's philosophy was that a coach shouldn't get too close to his players because then he would no longer be able to command the respect and authority needed to be successful. As a result, his players regarded him as something like a father figure and tried hard not to disappoint him. His need for control was so overwhelming that he refused to stay off the field one particular Monday night, when told there was a gunman in the stands that had threatened his life.

America's Team

Landry's Cowboys' rise to the top culminated in their first trip to the Super Bowl in 1971. With their loss to the Baltimore Colts, the fans didn't take long to place

Awards and Accomplishments	
1954	Named All-Pro
1955	Played in first Pro Bowl
1966	Won first conference title
1966	Named NFL coach of the year
1971	Won first NFC title
1972	Won first Super Bowl
1973	Won 100th game
1977	Won second Super Bowl
1982	Won 200th game
1990	Inducted into Pro Football Hall of Fame
1993	Inducted into Dallas Cowboys' Ring of Honor

Landry retired with a career coaching record of 270 wins, 178 losses, and 6 ties.

A Chapter Closed

The great stone face flinched and the flinty blue eyes went glassy when Tom Landry heard the verdict: He had been summarily removed as coach of the Dallas Cowboys, after 29 years. There was no appeal, no recourse, no room for negotiation. Landry, 64, gazed in shock at the two men who had brought him the terrible news. He said in disbelief, "You've taken my team away from me." ...

Thus it was that America's Team came up with a new owner (only its third in 29 years), a new coach (only its second), a new high in the gross price paid for a U.S. sports enterprise (next best: the reported $110 million paid for the New England Patriots and their stadium in 1988) and a new low in insulting a living legend ....

Source: William Oscar Johnson. *Sports Illustrated,* March 6, 1989, p. 22.

blame squarely on Landry. Noting his lack of emotion on the sidelines and the Cowboy's recent record of coming up short in big games, the fans lashed out at Landry for his apparent inability to win. Dallas returned to the Super Bowl the following year, and after beating Miami, the memories of previous disappointments vanished. It was a rare occasion when Landry let his happiness show as he was carried off the field by his victorious team with a smile on his face

Landry's teams during the 1970s seemed to be perennial winners and that, along with his growing celebrity, resulted in the tag, "America's Team." After losing the Super Bowl in 1975, the Cowboys were back again in 1977 beating Denver 27-10. They returned once more the following year but lost to the Pittsburgh Steelers. The Cowboys then spent the next three seasons knocking on the door but falling one game short of the Super Bowl.

Awards and Retirement

Landry's status as icon and legend never changed, but the NFL did and in 1989, after three consecutive losing seasons, he was unceremoniously fired by Dallas' new owner, Jerry Jones. Although most onlookers felt it was the wrong choice at the time, Landry never expressed public bitterness. In 1990, he entered the Pro Football Hall of Fame alongside five of his former players. He made a rare appearance at Texas Stadium, in 1993, to be inducted into the Dallas Cowboys' Ring of Honor.

In retirement, Landry remained active in business with his son and various Christian organizations. He indulged his love of flying and became a successful motivational speaker. His death from Leukemia at the age of 75 was marked by many tributes and the unveiling of a statue of his likeness, fedora and all, in Texas Stadium.

Landry's Legacy

Tom Landry's influence on the game and the city of Dallas is difficult to measure. His coaching statistics are surpassed by few and his loyalty to one team is a NFL record. As years go by, the memory of his iconic figure pacing the sidelines may fade but his influence on the game will remain. Many of Landry's former assistants have gone on to successful coaching careers of their own, including **Mike Ditka** and Dan Reeves, and it is in their teaching that Landry's influence will ultimately be measured.

FURTHER INFORMATION

Periodicals

Sports Illustrated (March 6, 1989).

Other

New York Times. http://www.nytimes.com/ (October 23, 2002).

Sporting News. http://www.sportingnews.com/ (October 23, 2002).

Sports Illustrated/CNN. http://www.sportsillustrated.cnn.com/ (October 23, 2002).

Tom Landry 1924-2000. *Dallas News.* http://www.dallasnews.com/ (October 23, 2002).

Sketch by Aric Karpinski

Steve Largent
1954-

American football player

Although his fourteen seasons with the Seattle Seahawks did not result in any National Football League (NFL) championships, Steve Largent retired as the holder of NFL records in receptions, yards, and

Steve Largent

touchdowns. Often underestimated by his opponents, who thought that Largent was too small and slow to be an offensive threat, the wide receiver eventually gained recognition as a Pro Football Hall of Fame inductee. After retiring as a professional athlete in 1989, Largent returned to his native Oklahoma and opened an advertising agency while cultivating his contacts with the state's Republican Party leadership. In 1994 he won election to the U.S. Congress as the Representative of the First District of Oklahoma, a feat that made him one of just five former NFL players ever to have served in Congress. Reelected in 1996, 1998, and 2000, Largent resigned from office in late 2001 in order to enter Oklahoma's gubernatorial race in 2002. Although he held a wide lead in the polls throughout most of the race, Largent lost the election and said that he would return to the private sector.

Sooner Childhood

Steven Michael Largent was born on September 28, 1954 in Tulsa, Oklahoma to Jim and Sue (Stewart) Largent. The couple separated when their son was about six years old and Sue Largent subsequently remarried. Largent's step-father, John Cargill, was an abusive alcoholic who sometimes became physically violent against his stepson. As Largent later told the *New York Times* in an interview included in a *Campaigns and Elections* profile, "I can remember crying myself to sleep many times, saying, 'My family will never be like this.'"

Largent took refuge from his turbulent home life in sports, particularly baseball and football. He lettered in both sports at Oklahoma City's Putnam City High School, where he graduated in 1972. Later that year he entered the University of Tulsa on a football scholarship. Even though Largent was somewhat smaller than the other players, at five-feet, eleven inches tall and about 190 pounds, he overcame the handicap and emerged as one of the school's best-ever football players. As a wide receiver he held the national records in touchdown receptions at the end of the 1974 and 1975 seasons, and in a 1974 game against Drake University Largent scored five touchdowns, tying his school's record for most touchdowns in a single game. Despite these accomplishments, Largent was not selected in the 1976 NFL draft until the fourth round, when he was chosen by the Houston Oilers. In a major setback to his NFL dreams, the Oilers dropped Largent after he had played in just four preseason games.

Seahawks Star

Largent was immediately picked up by the Seattle Seahawks, a new franchise with an assistant coach, Jerry Rhome, who had previously coached Largent at the University of Tulsa. Rhome helped to instill confidence in Largent, who made his NFL debut in a 1976 game against the St. Louis Cardinals with five receptions. Largent ended up being the Seahawks' most reliable receiver in his fourteen years with the team. Although his opponents typically dismissed him as slow and slight of stature, Largent ended up exceeding 1,000 yards in receptions in eight seasons between 1978 and 1986. Unfortunately, the Seahawks never claimed an NFL championship during Largent's years with the team, which ended in 1989.

Perhaps Largent's finest moment came in a December 10, 1989 game against the Cincinnati Bengals, when he broke the existing record for touchdown receptions. Largent ended his career at the end of that season as the

Career Statistics

		Receiving				Rushing				
Yr	Team	REC	YDS	AVG	TD	ATT	YDS	AVG	TD	FUM
1976	SS	54	705	13.1	4	4	−14	−3.5	0	2
1977	SS	33	643	19.5	10	0	0	0.0	0	0
1978	SS	71	1168	16.5	8	0	0	0.0	0	0
1979	SS	66	1237	18.7	9	0	0	0.0	0	0
1980	SS	66	1064	16.1	6	1	2	2.0	0	1
1981	SS	75	1224	16.3	9	6	47	7.8	1	2
1982	SS	34	493	14.5	3	1	8	8.0	0	0
1983	SS	72	1074	14.9	11	0	0	0.0	0	3
1984	SS	74	1164	15.7	12	2	10	5.0	0	1
1985	SS	79	1287	16.3	6	0	0	0.0	0	0
1986	SS	70	1070	15.3	9	0	0	0.0	0	3
1987	SS	58	912	15.7	8	2	33	16.5	0	2
1988	SS	39	645	16.5	2	1	−3	−3.0	0	3
1989	SS	28	403	14.4	3	0	0	0.0	0	0
TOTAL		819	13089	16.0	100	17	83	4.9	1	17

SS: Seattle Seahawks.

holder of the NFL records for most receptions (819), yards (13,089), and touchdowns (100). He also held the record for receptions in the most consecutive games (177) during his career, a title that was later claimed by **Jerry Rice**.

After retiring as a professional athlete, Largent moved back to Tulsa with his wife, the former Terry Bullock, whom he had married in January 1975. The Largents had four children—a daughter, Casie Lee, and three sons, Kyle, Kelly, and Kramer. Largent opened an advertising and marketing consulting firm in Tulsa after returning to the city, but he remained a popular sports personality in Seattle, where he often appeared at political fundraisers for Republican candidates. Largent also cultivated ties to the Republican Party in Oklahoma and in 1994 opened up his own campaign for the U.S. House seat from the First District. Running as a conservative in a heavily Republican state, Largent took the election with sixty-three percent of the vote.

Serves in Congress

Largent was reelected in 1996, 1998, and 2000. During his four terms in Congress, Largent followed a staunchly conservative platform against abortion rights and equal rights for homosexuals and in support of allowing prayer in public schools and granting government subsidies to private, religious schools. An advocate of the business community, Largent rarely voted for legislation endorsed by organized labor groups. In 1999 Largent attempted to ban same-sex couples from adopting children in the District of Columbia, a measure that was narrowly defeated. In 2000 he provoked criticism for suggesting that a Roman Catholic priest should not serve as the Congressional chaplin because it might make some members of Con-gress uncomfortable. Largent rejected the criticism as politically motivated.

In October 2001 Largent announced his resignation from his fourth term in Congress in order to run for the Oklahoma Governor's office in 2002. Although polls put Largent far ahead of his opponents, Democrat Brad Henry and independent Gary Richardson, a series of missteps plagued his campaign. A leading beneficiary of campaign contributions from Enron and Arthur Andersen, Largent became linked with the scandals that had rocked those companies. His critics noted that Largent had failed to author any major pieces of legislation and had failed to implement several measures that would have brought millions of dollars in federal money to Oklahoma, actions that suggested Largent was preoccupied with the national spotlight instead of serving his constituents. Largent's conservative image was also tarnished by the six-count indictment in December 2001 of his daughter, a university student, on charges that included underage drinking, possession of false identification, and various traffic violations.

In the final weeks of the race, when questioned about his ineffectual legislative record in Congress in a television interview, Largent responded with an expletive that shocked many viewers. It was the turning point in the campaign and Largent ended up losing the election by just 6,000 votes to Henry. Largent told *USA Today*, "The underdog won. That happens in life, that happens in athletics, and that happened in politics last night." Rejecting Governor-elect Henry's offer of a position with his administration, Largent announced that he would resume his career in business and did not foresee any future runs for public office.

FURTHER INFORMATION

Periodicals

Babson, Jennifer, and Bob Benenson. "Steve Largent." *Congressional Quarterly Weekly Report* (January 7, 1995).

Benedetto, Richard. "State Senator Defeats Former Star of NFL." *USA Today* (November 7, 2002).

"Career Paths: How They Got Where They Are." *Campaigns and Elections* (October 2001).

Deitsch, Richard, and Kostya Kennedy. "Q&A: Steve Largent." *Sports Illustrated* (October 7, 2002).

"House Narrowly Approves Homosexual Adoption in D.C." *Human Events* (August 13, 1999).

Largent, Steve, and Jennifer Dunn. "U.S. Representatives Steve Largent and Jennifer Dunn Deliver Republican Response." *FDCH Political Transcripts* (January 19, 1999).

Ota, Alan K., and Stephen Gettinger. "Stephen Largent Seeks Return to Limelight." *CQ Weekly* (November 8, 1998).

Other

"Enron and Andersen: Contributions to Congressional Committees." Open Secrets Web site. http://www. opensecrets.org/news/enron/enron_hene.asp (December 3, 2002).

"State of Oklahoma v. Casie Lee Largent." Oklahoma State Courts Network Web site. http://www.oscn.net (December 3, 2002).

"Steve Largent." Football Reference Web site. http:// www.football-reference.com/players/LargSt00.htm (December 4, 2002).

"Steve Largent." Seattle Seahawks Web site. http:// www.seahawks.com/ardisplay.aspx?ID=1402 (December 2, 2002).

"Steve Largent Biography." Pro Football Hall of Fame Web site. http://www.profootballhof.com/players/ mainpage.cfm?cont_id=99969 (December 4, 2002).

"Steve Largent: Top Contributors." Open Secrets Web site. http://www.opensecrets.org/1998os/contrib/ N00005597.htm (December 3, 2002).

Van Viema, David. "Catholic Bashing?" CNN Web site. http://www.cnn.com/ALLPOLITICS/time/2000/02/ 28/catholic.html (February 28, 2000).

Sketch by Timothy Borden

Tommy Lasorda
1927-

American baseball manager

Tommy Lasorda has been called one of the most successful managers in baseball history. In 20 years as a manager of the Los Angeles Dodgers, he led his team to a total of eight division titles. Also on his watch, the Dodgers went to the World Series four times, winning it twice (in 1981, and again in 1988). He retired as Dodger manager in 1996, and became a Dodgers vice president. In 1999, with a total of 50 years with the Dodgers under his belt, he managed the United States Olympic baseball team, leading it to its first-ever Olympic gold medal at the 2000 Olympic games in Sydney.

Born for Baseball

Thomas Charles Lasorda was born in 1927 in Norristown, Pennsylvania, one of five sons of immigrants from Italy. Growing up, Lasorda's passion was baseball. In particular, he was inspired by the great players of the day. "They were my heroes," he told Woody Woodburn of the *Denver Rocky Mountain News* many years later. "I knew them all by their names, their middle names, their batting averages." Lasorda's greatest dream was to become a major league pitcher. A dream which he would later realize, albeit briefly. "My father used to say to me," he told Woodburn, "If you studied in school as hard as you do those batting averages you'd be a professor at Yale one day."

After serving in the U. S. Army for a year, from 1946 to 1947, Lasorda began his career in baseball as a minor league pitcher. In 1948, he set a Canadian-American League record for number of strikeouts in a single game; while pitching for the Schenectady Blue Jays in a 15-inning game against the Amsterdam Rugmakers, he struck out 25 batters. To top it off, during that same game, he hit the winning runner home. Around this time, Lasorda also married his wife, Jo.

Starts a Half-Century with the Dodgers

Lasorda's pitching record attracted the attention of scouts for the Brooklyn Dodgers, and he was signed to that organization's Montreal team—the Dodgers' top farm team. He played for the Dodgers from 1950 to 1955, and again from 1958 to 1960. During his tenure with the Dodgers' Montreal team, he helped the team win five International League championships.

Lasorda played briefly for the major leagues as a pitcher, playing a total of only 26 games—for the Dodgers in 1954 and 1956, and for the Kansas City Athletics in 1956. "I always wanted to be a major leaguer," Lasorda later told Woodburn. "When I was growing up all I ever wanted to do was be a major league baseball player. That was the goal of my life. And by golly I reached that goal. I was in the major leagues as a player.

Tommy Lasorda

Chronology	
1927	Born on September 22 in Norristown, Pennsylvania
1946	Serves in the U.S. Army
1948	Becomes a professional baseball player in the minor leagues
1940s	Marries wife Jo
1954	Makes major league debut as a pitcher for the Brooklyn Dodgers
1956	Plays in the major leagues a final season, pitching for the Kansas City Athletics
1961	Becomes a talent scout for the Los Angeles Dodgers
1965	Becomes a manager in the minor leagues
1977	Becomes manager of the Dodgers
1996	Retires from managing the Dodgers, becomes Dodgers vice president
2000	Selected to manage the U. S. Olympic baseball team

Not very long, not very successful, but I reached the level of the top."

In 1961, Lasorda retired from playing baseball, and became a talent scout for the Dodgers. It was during this time that he resolved to become a major league manager. "I was at the 1963 World Series between the Dodgers and the Yankees," he later told the *St. Petersburg Times,* "and I was sitting with the scouts up behind home plate. I was up so high I could give the guy in the blimp a high-five. And I said to my wife, 'You want to know something, Jo. One day I'm going to be in that dugout managing the Dodgers to a World Series.'"

An Outstanding Manager

In 1965, Lasorda became a manager in the minor leagues, winning five pennants. In 1977, Lasorda became manager of the Los Angeles Dodgers, a post he would hold for about the next 20 years, until his retirement in 1996. In Lasorda's very first season, 1977, he took the Dodgers to the World Series, a feat he repeated the following season. Unfortunately the Dodgers lost each time to the Yankees. The Dodgers came back, though, in 1981, beating the Yankees at the World Series.

In June, 1996, Lasorda, then 68 years old, suffered a mild heart attack that required him to step away from his managerial duties. Less than two months later, his doctors cleared him to return to work, but the time away had forced him to examine the high-stress lifestyle that had

brought on the attack. With great reluctance, he decided to step down as manager of the Dodgers.

Lasorda officially retired as Dodgers manager in July, 1996. The Dodgers organization had left open the option for him to return, but, as he said in a press conference quoted by the *St. Petersburg Times,* "even though the doctors gave me a clean bill of health, for me to put on a uniform again, as excitable as I am, I could not go down there and not be the way I've always been." Lasorda said he felt his resignation was "best" for himself and for the Dodgers organization. Struggling to compose himself, Lasorda spoke through tears of his enthusiasm for managing, but noted the importance of his family and his desire to spend time with them.

Lasorda did remain with the Dodgers, however, as a vice president. As he explained his appointment to the new job to the *Daily News*'s Bill Madden, "[Dodgers owner Peter O'Malley] supplied the answer [Jo and I] needed to hear after I made my decision to give up managing. He said: 'You did the right thing and now you'll be vice president helping us in many different directions. We need you.'"

Olympic Gold

In May, 2000, four years into his new job as a vice president for the Dodgers, Lasorda was called on to manage the U.S. Olympic baseball team at the Olympic games in Sydney, Australia. "Being selected to manage the U. S. Olympic team is a great privilege and honor; it's bigger than the World Series," he told *USA Today*'s Mike Dodd on the occasion. "It's bigger than the Dodgers, bigger than Major League Baseball, because it's the United States of America. It's your country."

Chosen from among minor league players from around the United States, the members of the U. S. Olympic team would not even be brought together as a team until just a month before they played. "Wish it was like it used to be," Lasorda told Dodd, "here you went around the country playing some games. I want to show the country, let them see these guys. I want to show my team off."

Career Statistics

Yr	Team	W	L	ERA	GS	CG	SHO	IP	H	R	BB	SO
1954	BRK	0	0	5.00	0	0	0	9	8	5	5	5
1955	BRK	0	0	13.50	1	0	0	4	5	6	6	4
1956	KC	0	4	6.15	5	0	0	45.1	40	31	45	28

BRK: Brooklyn Dodgers; KC: Kansas City Athletics.

Awards and Accomplishments

1981, 1988	As manager, led Los Angeles Dodgers to victory in World Series
1988	Named National League Manager of the Year honors (with Jim Leyland)
1997	Inducted into the National Baseball Hall of Fame
2000	As manager, led U.S. Olympic baseball team to gold medal victory

Instead, Lasorda told Dodd, "September the first, I will meet with the players and that'll be the first time I've seen these guys in person. September the second, we board a plane for Brisbane.... I'm only going to have eight or nine (exhibition) games to know what they can do. It's not going to be easy."

Nevertheless, the American baseball team took home the gold in 2000 in a stunning 4-0 defeat of the favored Cuban team. Lasorda described his reaction to the victory to Bill Conlin in the *Sunday Mail:* " bawled like a baby. I was just so thrilled for these young men and what they accomplished. I told my wife before I left home, 'Fifty years from now, I'm gonna be a trivia question. The question will be: Name the only man in history to manage both a World Series team and an Olympic gold medal winner. I'm gonna be the answer to that question.'"

It was a fitting finish to a long and illustrious managing career for Lasorda. As for what the future might bring for him, he gave this hint to Woodburn: "I'll do everything I can to make baseball better. I love to go around this great country of ours, and around the world, and spread the word of baseball." Lasorda spoke with pride of his 46-year association with the Dodgers organization, and of his 45-year marriage to wife, Jo.

FURTHER INFORMATION

Periodicals

Brunt, Cliff. "Lasorda's Message: Love and Respect." *Omaha World-Herald* (June 14, 2002): 6C.

Conlin, Bill. "Against All Odds; US No-Names Steal Cuba's Gold." *Sunday Mail* (October 1, 2000): L21.

Dodd, Mike. "Patriot for the Games Lasorda All Wrapped Up in Olympic Excitement." *USA Today* (July 3, 2002): 1C.

Where Is He Now?

After leading his team to a gold medal at the 2000 Olympic games in Sydney, Australia, Lasorda returned to his duties as vice president at the Los Angeles Dodgers. He manages the team's public relations efforts and scouting activities, and helps to develop the organization's minor league teams.

Lasorda also acts as something of an ambassador for the sport. The close of 2002 saw him in Japan for the ninth time to scout for players and help Japanese players play the game right. "I'm a consultant, scout, general manager and a teacher all rolled into one," he said to Bill Gallo of the *Daily News* about his activities in Japan.

At home in the United States, Lasorda also spends time seeking to motivate young people to realize their full potential, not just in the area of sports, but in every aspect of their lives. "If you make up your mind what you want to be, you can be it," he told a group of youths in Omaha in the spring of 2002, wrote Cliff Brunt in the *Omaha World-Herald*. "All you have to do is pay the price. Nobody's going to hand it to you."

Gallo, Bill. "These Skippers Mean World to Tommy." *Daily News* (October 20, 2002): 75.

Madden, Bill. "Pastime Always His Time: Preachin' Dodger Gospel Is Still Essence of Lasorda." *Daily News* (September 8, 1996): 92.

"Sadly, Lasorda Hangs Up His Dodger Blues." *St. Petersburg Times* (July 30, 1996): 5C.

Woodburn, Woody. "Lasorda Returning to the Game He Loves." *Denver Rocky Mountain News* (October 15, 1995): 30B.

Other

"Tommy Lasorda." Baseballlibrary.com. http://www.pubdim.net/baseballlibrary/ballplayers/L/Lasorda_Tommy.stm (November 13, 2002).

"Tommy Lasorda." Infoplease.com. http://www.infoplease.com/ipsa/A0109380.html (November 13, 2002).

"Tommy Lasorda." National Baseball Hall of Fame. http://www.baseballhalloffame.org/hofers_and_honorees/hofer_bios/lasorda_tommy.htm (November 13, 2002).

"Tommy Lasorda Statistics." *Baseball Almanac*. http://www.baseball-almanac.com/players/player.php?p=lasorto01 (November 13, 2002).

Sketch by Michael Belfiore

Larisa Latynina
1934-

Soviet gymnast

Gymnast Larisa Latynina won 18 medals in Olympic competition, and is the most decorated Olympian to date in any sport. She competed in the 1956, 1960, and 1964 Olympics, as well as at the world championships in 1954, 1958, 1962, and 1966. She is the only gymnast to have won medals in every event on the program in two different Olympics.

An Orphan Seeking Beauty

Born in Kherson, Ukraine in 1934, Latynina, who began her gymnastic career under her maiden name, Dirii, initially dreamed of becoming a ballet dancer, but her childhood was difficult. Deeply affected by years of poverty, World War II, and its aftermath, Latynina was also an orphan. She dreamed of making a better, more beautiful life, and as part of this dream, she began studying ballet when she was eleven years old.

Like many other schools in the Soviet Union at the time, Latynina's incorporated exercises with hoops and balls performed to music, and her teachers soon steered her into gymnastics. By the time she was sixteen, she was the national gymnastics champion of the schools division.

She was a dedicated student, and graduated from high school with honors in 1953. In school, she had also studied gymnastics, and her devotion to the sport paid off at the 1954 World Championships, when she placed 14th all-around.

Latynina studied at the Physical Training College in Kiev; at the school, she met and married Ivan Latynin, a ship's engineer.

Becomes a Gymnastics Superstar

At the 1956 Olympics in Melbourne, Australia, Latynina won gold medals in the all-around and on vault, and tied for gold on floor exercises. Her team won silver medals on bars and bronze medals in the team drill event. Their wins were part of a notable shift in the sport of gymnastics: "away from strength, power, and sustained movements," according to an article on the *Women in Gymnastics* Web site, and toward "beauty, grace and choreography." Latynina made such an impression at Melbourne that she became the first internationally acclaimed superstar in the sport of gymnastics. She was twenty-one years old.

Interestingly, Latynina noted that her routines were not particularly difficult or innovative; instead, she tried to perform each move perfectly and with elegance.

In 1957 and 1958, Latynina won every event at the European championships, and in 1958, at the World

Larisa Latynina

Championships, she almost duplicated this feat, winning gold medals in every event except the vault, in which she won a silver medal. Her winning sweep was made even more remarkable by the fact that while competing in these events, she was pregnant with her daughter, Tanya. Tanya was born ten days before Latynina's twenty-fourth birthday.

In a 1964 article in *USSR Soviet Life Today,* Latynina told Alexandr Maryamov that her daughter deserved half of the credit for her win at the World Championships. Latynina knew that she was five months pregnant during the tournament, but had kept her condition a secret from her doctors, since she knew that they would make her withdraw from competition.

Latynina skipped the 1959 European Championships because of her pregnancy, but after giving birth to her daughter, Latynina returned to competition. At the 1960 Olympics, Latynina won a medal in every event she competed in: a gold medal in all-around, floor exercises, and in team competition; silver medal on uneven bars and balance beam; and a bronze medal in the vault.

In competition at the 1961 European championships, Latynina won gold in floor and all-around, and silver on uneven bars and balance beam. She repeated her gold wins in floor and all-around at the 1962 world championships, and also won silver in the vault and balance beam.

In 1963, Latynina began graduate study at the Kiev Physical Training Institute. She was also a member of a

Chronology

1934	Born December 27, in Kherson, Ukraine, Soviet Union
1953	Graduates from high school with honors
1954	Comes in 14th at World Championships
1956	Wins four gold medals and one silver at Olympic games in Melbourne, Australia
1957	Wins European Championship gold medals in all-around, vault, uneven bars, beam, and floor exercises
1957	Receives Order of Lenin
1958	Wins World Championship gold medals in team competition, all-around, floor exercises, uneven bars, and beam; wins silver in vault
1958	Gives birth to her daughter, Tanya
1959	Graduates from Kiev Institute of Physical Culture
1960	Wins two gold medals, two silver medals, and a bronze medal in Olympic games
1960	Receives Soviet Badge of Honor
1961	Wins European Championship gold medals in all-around and floor exercises; silver medals in uneven bars and beam; comes in fourth in vault
1962	Wins World Championship gold medals in team, all-around, and floor exercises; wins silver in vault and beam; wins bronze in uneven bars
1963	Begins graduate study at the Kiev Physical Training Institute
1964	Wins two gold medals, two silver medals, and two bronze medals at Olympic games in Tokyo, Japan
1964	At USSR Championships, wins silver medal in all-around
1965	At European Championships, wins silver medals in all-around, uneven bars, beam, and floor exercises; bronze medal in vault
1966	At USSR cup, comes in fifth in all-around
1966	At USSR World Trials, comes in sixth in all-around
1966	At World Championships, wins silver in team competition; comes in eleventh in all-around
1966-77	Coaches USSR international women's team
1972	Becomes honorary coach of the USSR
1977	Member of Organizational Committee, 1980 Olympics
1998	Inducted into International Gymnastics Hall of Fame
2002	Receives Ukrainian Star Award

Awards and Accomplishments

1956	Olympic gold medals in team competition, all-around, vault, floor exercises; silver medal in uneven bars
1957	European Championship gold medals in all-around, vault, uneven bars, beam, and floor exercises
1957	Order of Lenin
1958	World Championship gold medals in team competition, all-around, floor exercises, uneven bars, and beam; silver in vault
1960	Olympic gold medals in team competition and all-around; silver in uneven bars and beam; wins bronze in vault
1960	Soviet Badge of Honor
1961	European Championship gold medals in all-around and floor exercises; silver medals in uneven bars and beam
1961	USA-USSR meet gold medal in team and all-around
1962	World Championship gold medals in team, all-around, and floor exercises; silver in vault and beam; bronze in uneven bars
1964	Olympic gold medal in team competition and floor exercises; silver medal in all-around and vault; bronze medal in uneven bars and beam
1964	Sweden-USSR meet gold medal in team competition
1964	USSR Championships silver medal in all-around
1965	European Championships silver medals in all-around, uneven bars, beam, and floor exercises; bronze medal in vault
1966	World Championships silver in team competition
1998	International Gymnastics Hall of Fame
2002	Ukrainian Star Award

committee that judged movies made by the Kiev Film Studios. As a celebrity, she met other Soviet heroes, such as cosmonaut Gherman Titov and his family.

1964 Olympics

At the 1964 Olympics in Tokyo, Latynina won gold medals in floor exercises and team competition; silver medals in all-around and vault; and bronze medals in uneven bars and beam. In an article in the London *Times,* a reporter commented that because Latynina was twenty-nine at the time, her career might be winding to a close, and "we may never see her like again. . . . But at such moments as she gave us this evening, hope springs eternal."

At the European championships in 1965, Latynina won four silver medals, in all-around, uneven bars, beam, and floor exercises, and a bronze medal in vault.

Latynina's daughter Tanya expressed no interest in following in her mother's footsteps. Tanya's father, Ivan Latynin, told Maryamov that he was grateful for this: "One gymnast in the family is quite enough! I'm a nervous wreck every time Larisa competes." He said that

when she competed on beam, he had to either close his eyes or leave the venue.

Latynina's coach, Alexander Mishakov, told Maryamov, "It's a pleasure to work with Latynina because she demands so much of herself." He noted that Latynina filled every moment she had with activities. At the time, she was doing graduate work at the Kiev Physical Training Institute, and had been elected to the Kiev City Soviet for five years in a row. In addition to these duties and her intense gymnastics training routine, she found time for the theater, movies, fishing, dancing, getting together with friends, and spending time with her husband and daughter. Part of her intense activity was a result of the Soviet system of training athletes: athletes received many privileges in the Soviet system, but they were then obligated to serve their government by giving lectures and undertaking public service. Latynina's stint in the Kiev City government was part of this obligatory service.

Maryamov asked Latynina if she had a favorite medal, and Latynina replied, "The small gold medal I was awarded in 1953 for graduating from school with honors." Latynina also noted that in addition to gymnastics, she enjoyed reading poetry, listening to classical music and jazz, and watching theater and ballet. She told Maryamov, "I'd say they all help in my gymnastics work. I suspect that without them I'd be less of a gymnast."

Knowing that she could not continue competing forever, Latynina began planning a career shift, from competing to coaching. By 1964, her first protégé, Tanya

Palamarchuk, had already won a Master of Sports rating. In addition to coaching, Latynina often spoke, hoping to popularize the sport among young people. "It's the sport closest to the arts that we have," she told Maryamov.

At the 1966 World Championships, she placed 11th all-around. She retired from competition after this event.

From 1966 to 1977, Latynina was a Soviet national team coach, and from 1977 on, coached a local team in Moscow. She was director of gymnastics for the 1980 Moscow Olympics, and was honored with the Olympic Order from the International Olympic Committee in 1989.

Latynina has been married three times. She lives with her current husband, Yuri Israilevich Feldman, a former cycling champion, in Kolyanino, near Moscow. She is still revered as a national sports hero in the former Soviet Union, particularly in Ukraine, and often attends gymnastics competitions in Moscow. In 2002 she was honored with a Ukrainian Star Award.

In 1998, Latynina was named to the International Gymnastics Hall of Fame. She was also honored in 2000, when a path in the Sydney Olympic Village was named "Larisa Latynina Way" in her honor.

SELECTED WRITINGS BY LATYNINA:

Ravnovesie, Moscow, 1975.
Gimnastika K=Skvoz' Gody, Moscow, 1977.

FURTHER INFORMATION

Books

Riordan, James. *Soviet Sports Background to the Olympics.* New York: New York University Press, 1980.
Schultz, Heinrich, and Stephen S. Taylor. *Who's Who in the USSR 1961-62.* Metuchen, NJ: Scarecrow Press, 1962.

Periodicals

"Mrs. Latynina Falls from Power." *Times* (London, England) (October 22, 1964): 4.

Other

"Larisa Latynina (USSR)." *Gymn Forum,* http://www.gymn-forum.com/bios/latynina_1.html (November 19, 2002).
"Larisa Latynina," *International Gymnastics Hall of Fame.* http://www.ighof.com/honorees_latynina.html (November 19, 2002).
"Larisa Latynina." *International Gymnast.* http://www.intlgymnast.com/legends/latynina.html (November 19, 2002).
"Larisa Latynina: The First International Superstar." *Women in Gymnastics.* http://historypages.org/gymnastics/latynina.html (November 19, 2002).

Maryamov, Alexandr. "Grace and Charm." reprinted from *Soviet Life Today,* September, 1964, in *Gymn Forum.* http://www.gymn-forum.com/Articles/SL-Latyn.html (November 19, 2002).
Ostrovsky, Ihor. "Ukrainian Stars Isolated." *Day* (Kiev, Ukraine) (June 4, 2002). http://www.day.kiev.ua/ (November 19, 2002).

Sketch by Kelly Winters

Rod Laver
1938-

Australian tennis player

Rod "Rocket" Laver has been called the greatest tennis player of the twentieth century, and for good reason. He is the only player in the history of tennis to win two Grand Slams—taking the singles titles of the Australian Open, French Open, Wimbledon, and the U.S. Open in a single year. His first Grand Slam came in 1962, while he was still an amateur, but when later that year he turned professional, he was no longer eligible to play those tournaments. With the advent of the Open era in 1968, however, pros like Laver were once again allowed to compete in the Grand Slam tournaments, and the Australian wonder once again scored the Royal Flush of tennis, winning his second Grand Slam in 1969. Tennis historians contend that, had Laver been able to play in those intervening years, he may have won as many as nine Wimbledons in a row and no telling how many Grand Slams.

A small man, Laver is credited with bringing power to the game, turning his left-handed topspin into an offensive weapon, and influencing future generations from **John McEnroe** to **Pete Sampras**. His blend of aggressive play and rapid movement makes him one of the first truly modern players in the sport, and his record of 11 major titles held for many years into the Open era. Laver was the first tennis millionaire, earning almost $300,000 in tournaments in 1971, an unheard of amount up to that time. When he retired in 1978, he had earned over $1.5 million on the courts, thus paving the way for other tennis professionals to make a living from the sport from winnings, sponsorships, and endorsements. In both his style of play and his earnings as a professional, Laver thus became a model for later players and helped pave the way for modern tennis.

An Aussie Upbringing

Rodney George Laver was the product of a tennis family. The third of four children, Laver was born on August 9, 1938, in Rockhampton, Queensland, Australia. His father,

Rod Laver

Roy, a cattle rancher, was one of 13 children, all tennis players. When Roy went looking for a wife, he found Melba Roffey, another tennis player, at a tournament in the Queensland town of Dingo. Married, the couple had a tennis court next to every house they ever lived in, and it was not untypical for the father to cook dinner while his wife was outside playing tennis with the kids. Melba and Roy played singles and mixed doubles in every tournament they could in and around Rockhampton, winning them all, and soon their four children were following in their footsteps, winning in a variety of age categories. Rod Laver began challenging his older brothers when he was six, using a hand-me-down racquet with a sawed-down handle to fit him. When he was thirteen, Laver, small for his age, took on his brother Bob in the junior final of the Central Queensland championship. As the match was an all-Laver event, it was held on the Laver's court, and Rod—barely able to see over the net—narrowly lost to his older brother.

Shortly thereafter, Laver was selected for inclusion at a tennis camp sponsored by a Brisbane newspaper. At the camp his play won the attention of the legendary Harry Hopman, "and the lid was nailed on his future," as Rex Lardner wrote in a *Sports Illustrated* profile of Laver. Hopman, captain of Australia's Davis Cup team for many years and an influential player/coach who developed a number of Australian players, took the young Laver under his wing and began refining his left-handed game. It was Hopman who dubbed Laver "Rocket," and not because of his speed but because of the youngster's grit, determination, and work ethic. It was soon apparent to this genius of Australian tennis that the teenager he was working with had more talent than all the other Australian players of his day. At 15, Laver, suffering from jaundice, missed two months of school and feeling left behind in his studies decided to stop his formal education and work at his tennis. His father agreed with the decision, and with Hopman's help the boy got a job with a sporting goods firm in Brisbane, "the kind of job that pays a tennis player whether he is there to punch a time clock or not," remarked Lardner. Three years later, Laver stormed onto the American tennis scene when he won the United States junior championship.

Amateur Years

After serving a year in the Australian Army in 1957, Laver was again back in the amateur rankings, and in

June of 1958 surprised one of America's top-seeded players, Barry MacKay, knocking him out of the second round of London's Queen's Club Tournament, 6-3, 6-3. This victory was an announcement to the tennis world: Laver was at the gates. At the time of his victory over MacKay, Laver was ranked only eighth in Australia, demonstrating the depth of tennis talent Down Under. In 1959 Laver, who had to wait his turn until older players either retired or turned pro, was finally selected for his country's Davis Cup team, along with Neale Fraser and Roy Emerson. The Australians defeated the Americans that year, and though Laver lost twice—one of the losses in 66 games to Alex Olmedo—his performance did not go unnoticed. Arthur Dale of the *New York Times* noted that "Laver's performance in defeat made the victory of The Chief [Olmedo] all the more noteworthy. The twenty-one year old left-hander [Laver] made chalk shots that would have discouraged anyone less hardy." Already Laver was developing his reputation for risky play and line shots that sent the chalk spitting. Laver lost again to Olmedo at Forest Hills, going all the way to the finals.

Lead Up to First Grand Slam

The year 1960 was pivotal for Laver. In the first major tournament of the year, the Australian National championships, he faced his Davis Cup teammate Fraser in the finals. Down two sets, Laver came back to win his first major title, 5-7, 3-6, 6-3, 8-6, 8-6. Laver did not

have a perfect tennis body. Relatively short, at only 5'8" and weighing about 155 pounds, his speed and agility on court made up for his lack of height. In his playing years, Laver was compact, and his left forearm had developed, after hitting thousands of tennis balls, into Popeye dimensions, as big as that of **Rocky Marciano**, boxing's heavyweight champion. In addition to his wristy, topspin forehand, Laver combined strength of will and determination on the court. He had no weaknesses for his opponents to attack. Though his serve was not huge, he could disguise it well and place it in the corners of the service box. He also was good at net, learning an aggressive game from Hopman, but particularly excelled from the backcourt. Hopman had also schooled Laver in behavior on and off the court. A true sportsman, he played a generally quiet game, and was an intensely private individual, giving few interviews.

That same year, 1960, Fraser avenged his defeat at the Australian singles by beating Laver in the finals at Wimbledon and at Forest Hills, though Laver was able to take home a trophy from the United States championships that year, in mixed doubles. From rivals, Laver and Fraser returned to being teammates to beat Italy in the Davis Cup finals in December of 1960. Laver failed to defend his Australian championship in 1961, losing in the finals, as he did at Forest Hills, as well. But he was more successful at Wimbledon, defeating his American opponent, Chuck McKinley, in a mere 55 minutes. Following the matches at Forest Hills that year, the former player and now organizer of professional tennis, Jack Kramer, offered Laver $33,600 to come on his pro tour, but the Aussie refused. He had his sights still set on the Grand Slam tournaments to which he would be barred if he turned pro.

Laver began the tennis year of 1962 with a bang, beating Roy Emerson in the finals of the Australian championship. He beat Emerson again consecutively in Paris and Rome, though his was two sets down in the French championships, and then at Wimbledon he demolished his fellow countryman Martin Mulligan in less than 52 minutes, 6-2, 6-2, 6-1. With three of the four majors under his belt coming into the U.S. championships, Laver was all the buzz at the 1962 Forest Hills tournament. As Lardner noted of that year's tournament, "this hawk-nosed, freckle-faced, bowlegged Australian is a prime product of the almost unbeatable Australian system of spotting, nurturing and financing its best tennis players from the cradle." The world's press, fans, and other tennis players were wondering if Laver would be able to repeat **Don Budge**'s accomplishment of winning all four majors in one year. Laver tore through the early rounds of the tournament, and then faced one of his usual Australian rivals, Emerson, in the finals. Laver hit "wildly spinning, hard, shoe-top-high shots almost impossible to volley," wrote Lardner of the match. "Very often he hit the ball so fast that Emerson could merely watch as it skimmed by." Laver won in four sets and after tossing his racquet in the air, finally cracked a smile, his first of the tournament.

Later that same year, Laver teamed up with Emerson in Davis Cup to defeat Mexico, bringing the Cup home for their country for the eleventh time in 13 years. It would be his last Davis Cup competition for over a decade.

Turns Pro

Laver announced in late December of 1962 that he was joining the International Professional Tennis Players Association, whose members had chipped in to guarantee him $110,000 for the next three-year period. In the early days of pro tennis, such a contract was very lucrative, indeed. In his first pro match, Laver lost to fellow Australian Lew Hoad, and went on to lose his next three professional matches, as well, until settling into the pro ranks. A long and vigorous rivalry began between Laver and Australian Kenny Rosewall, another of Hopman's students. Rosewall beat Laver in the 1963 U.S. Pro singles, but in 1964, Laver turned around to beat Rosewall and **Pancho Gonzalez** to win the first of five of those titles. Life in the pros was, however, far from romantic or even illustrious. In those days it meant long drives in a station wagon from one gym to another across the country, playing exhibition matches in front of a few hundred spectators at best. Once the evenings double match was finally concluded, perhaps as late as one in the morning, the players piled into their cars and drove a few hours in the darkness toward their next destination, then stayed at some roadside motel, got up in the late morning, and continued on their way to the next venue. The 1964 final, in which he beat Gonzalez, was indicative of the difficulties of the early pro tour. Laver and Gonzalez played in a raging storm that turned Boston's grass courts into a swamp, but the show had to go on and Laver managed to pull off some amazing shots to win the title, even under such inclement conditions.

Disappointingly, Laver's decision to turn pro eliminated him from competition in the world's major titles, still amateur affairs. Thus he missed the years 1963-1967 at any of the Grand Slams. Only when open tennis began in 1968 could he attempt to reproduce his former greatness at those events. That year at Roland Garros, Laver again lost to Rosewall in the finals, 6-3, 6-1, 2-6, 6-2. Returning to Wimbledon for the first time in five championships, he took the tournament, defeating Tony Roche in under an hour. The advent of open tennis also increased prize money available to the players. Whereas in 1968, there were only two prize-money tournaments in the U.S., with combined winnings of $130,000, by 1969 the U.S. Open alone offered a larger purse, and all the U.S. tournaments combined were worth $440,000. Worldwide, prize money had grown to $1.3 million, and Laver garnered $124,000 of that, becoming the top money winner. But Laver was after an even bigger prize than money in the 1969 season.

Wins Second and Historic Grand Slam

Laver's first strong competition in his run for a second Grand Slam came early in the year at the Australian

---

Awards and Accomplishments

1959	Australian doubles; Wimbledon mixed doubles
1960	Australian singles; Australian doubles; Wimbledon mixed doubles
1961	Wimbledon singles; Australian doubles; French doubles; French mixed doubles
1962	Australian singles; French singles; Wimbledon singles; U.S. singles
1968	Wimbledon singles
1969	Australian Open singles; French Open singles; Wimbledon singles; U.S. Open singles; Australian Open doubles
1971	Wimbledon doubles

Davis Cup: 1959-62, 1973; 16-4 in singles and 4-0 in doubles.

Retired in 1978, Laver won 47 titles and was runner-up 21 times in his 23-year career both in amateur and pro tennis, and was in the World Top Ten for 13 years between 1959 and 1975, ranked number 1 in 1961, 1962, 1968, and 1969.

Open when he and Roche played 80 games over four hours under the melting Brisbane sun in the semifinals. The second set alone was a 22-20 marathon lasting longer than many full matches. Both players resorted to the old Australian trick of sticking cabbage leaves in their hats to avoid sunstroke. Surviving that, partly as the result of a questionable line call against Roche, Laver had a relatively easy final, defeating Andres Gimeno in straight sets. There was another scare at the French open when another Australian, Dick Crealy, took a couple sets off him in the second round, but Laver came back to win that one and ultimately beat Rosewall in straight sets in the finals. Laver was again challenged at Wimbledon, two sets down in the second round, but went on to win that match and subsequent rounds against Stan Smith, **Arthur Ashe**, and John Newcombe to take Wimbledon for the fourth time.

Laver moved on to the U.S. Open, still played on grass in 1969, ready for a repeat of his 1962 amateur Grand Slam. Record crowds greeted this first hyped U.S. Open, until the rains set in. Still Laver prevailed, cruising through opponents, and ultimately having to wear spikes on the slippery court in the final against Roche, which he won in four sets. The prize money presented him that day—a check for $16,000—took second place to Laver's elation at his second slam. This one, also, was sweeter than his first, for in 1962 some of the best players in the world had already turned pro and thus had not been allowed to play. In 1969, Laver met the best in the world, amateur or pro, and bested them all.

Sets the Pro Example

For Laver, 1970 was a letdown after the glory of 1969. Not only was he unable to retain any of his Grand Slam titles, but he also lost the U.S. Pro title for the first time since 1966. One consolation, however, was the fact that he became the first player to exceed $200,000 in annual earnings in the pro ranks, winning more prize money than

Rod Laver

golf's leading money earner that year, **Lee Trevino**. The following year, though failing to win any major tournaments but the Italian Open, Laver was victorious in six of 25 smaller tournaments, winning 78 of 86 matches. His prize earnings for that year escalated to $292,717, making him the first career millionaire in professional tennis. The World Championship of Tennis was held in 1972, in Dallas, Texas, with Rosewall and Laver once again doing battle in what some observers have called the greatest match of the century, a five-set battle that has been "credited with establishing tennis as a sport worth televising," according to Mike Lupica in an *Esquire* article.

In 1973, pros were allowed to compete in Davis Cup for the first time, and Laver teamed up with John Newcombe to end the United States' five-year stranglehold on the cup. Laver also played a big part in Australia's victories in the 1972, 1974, and 1975 World Cups, a team competition which has since been discontinued. Laver continued to play on the pro circuit until 1978. As late as 1976, at 38 years of age, he signed with San Diego in World Team Tennis. When he finally decided to call it quits in 1978, he left behind an illustrious career including two Grand Slams, 11 major titles, 47 pro titles, and 13 years in the World Top Ten. Additionally, he had earned over $1.5 million in his career, making him the all-time money winner of his day.

Laver's Legacy

In Laver's 23-year career, he won four Wimbledon titles, three Australian, two French, and two U.S. singles, and led Australia to five Davis Cup victories. It is doubt-

ful that his record of two Grand Slams will be matched, especially with the heightened level of play in the competitive Open era. "Laver is widely rated as the best tennis player the world has seen, both for his 1962 and 1969 Grand Slams and the powerful style that won them," wrote Lisa Clausen in a *Time* magazine retrospective of the 100 sports greats of the twentieth century. "He was master of a left-handed topspin that overwhelmed his opponents, who also struggled to counter his tremendous speed around the court."

But it is not simply his play for which Laver will be remembered. He was truly one of the last gentlemen in the game as tennis spun out of the amateur ranks and into its professional stage. However, Laver was also realist enough to know that you could not be too much of a gentleman on court. "Sportsmanship is the essence of the game," he wrote in *The Education of a Tennis Player*, "and yet you do not want to be too good a sport. Or what I call a false sportsman." This middle ground was characteristic of the understated Laver style. Somewhat unassuming and quiet on court, Laver yet brought a love and intensity to the game of tennis that attracted and inspired a new generation of players, from McEnroe to Sampras. Through his personal model he showed players that an honorable living could be made in professional tennis, and in his career, spanning both amateur and open tennis, he became the epitome of the modern player-turned-businessman.

CONTACT INFORMATION

Address: Rancho Mirage, CA.

SELECTED WRITINGS BY LAVER:

(With Jack Pollard) *How to Play Winning Tennis,* Mayflower, 1970.
(With Bud Collins) *The Education of a Tennis Player,* Simon & Schuster, 1971.
(With Bud Collins, editors) *Rod Laver's Tennis Digest,* Follett, 1973.
(With Roy Emerson and Barry Tarshis) *Tennis for the Bloody Fun of It,* Quadrangle, 1976.
228 Tennis Tips, DBI Books, 1977.

FURTHER INFORMATION

Books

Baltzell, E. Digby. *Sporting Gentlemen: Men's Tennis from the Age of Honor to the Cult of the Superstar.* New York: Free Press, 1995.
Bartlett, Michael and Bob Gillen, editors. *The Tennis Book.* New York: Arbor House, 1981.
Christopher, Andre. *Top Ten Men's Tennis Players.* Hillside, NJ: Enslow, 1998.
Collins, Bud and Zander Hollander, editors. *Bud Collins' Modern Encyclopedia of Tennis.* Detroit: Gale, 1994.

Where Is He Now?

Following his 1978 retirement, Laver remained involved in tennis, playing on the senior tour. However, retirement from tennis did not mean an end to work for the Australian. For many years he worked for Nabisco Brands, acting as an ambassador for Nabisco's involvement in various worldwide sporting events. As such he ran tennis clinics, gave speeches, and shook a lot of hands. Three years after retirement from tennis, Laver was inducted into the International Tennis Hall of Fame.

Real retirement came later for Laver when he moved to Rancho Mirage, California, a suburb of Palm Springs, and took to playing golf as much as he did tennis. In 1999, during an interview, he suffered a stroke. Luckily the interviewer recognized the signs, and Laver was rushed to nearby UCLA Medical Center, getting immediate care. The stroke destroyed the sensory receptors on his right side. Laver, one of the greatest tennis players of all time, had to relearn how to play the game he loves. Tennis became, in fact, part of his therapy. Working with speech and physical therapists, Laver slowly recovered his speech and movement. "I still have a little way to go," Laver told a reporter for *Sports Illustrated*, "but I'm very happy with my performance. I feel I'm going to get all the way back." In 2000, Laver was honored by his native Australia when its tennis federation named center court at Melbourne Park, home of the Australian Open, after him. On hand for the naming ceremony, Laver said, "I am delighted to accept this wonderful honor. This is a crowning achievement to my tennis career."

Danzig, Allison and Peter Schwed, editors. *The Fireside Book of Tennis.* New York: Simon & Schuster, 1972.

Flink, Steve. *The Greatest Tennis Matches of the Twentieth Century.* Danbury, CT: Rutledge Books, 1999.

Laver, Rod and Bud Collins. *The Education of a Tennis Player.* New York: Simon & Schuster, 1971.

Lorimer, Larry. *The Tennis Book: A Complete A-to-Z Encyclopedia of Tennis.* New York: Random House, 1980.

Phillips, Caryl, editor. *The Right Set: A Tennis Anthology.* New York: Vintage Books, 1999.

St. James Encyclopedia of Popular Culture. Detroit: St. James Press, 2000.

Vecchione, Joseph J. *The New York Times Book of Sports Legends.* New York: Times Books, 1991.

Periodicals

Berry, Elliot and E. H. Wallop. "Love-50." *Forbes* (May 9, 1954).

Daley, Arthur. *New York Times* (August 31, 1959).

Dillman, Lisa and Larry Stewart. "Laver Suffers Stroke, Taken to UCLA Medical Center." *Los Angeles Times* (July 28, 1998): 3.

Lardner, Rex, "Rod Rockets into Orbit." *Sports Illustrated* (September 17, 1962): 51.

Lupica, Mike. "The Conscience of the Court." *Esquire* (January, 1988): 37-39.

Mravic, Mark and Richard O'Brien. "Rocket Refit." *Sports Illustrated* (April 5, 1999): 36.

"The Rocket's Slam." *Time* (September 21, 1962): 57.

Shmerler, Cindy. "The Road Back." *Tennis* (September, 1999): 94-98.

Stambler, Lyndon. "A Tennis Great, Felled by a Stroke, Makes a Stirring Return from the Brink." *People* (October 26, 1998): 153.

Other

Clausen, Lisa. "Time 100 Sports Stars: Rod Laver." *Time.com* http://www.time.com/ (October 25, 1999).

Contemporary Authors Online. http://galenet.galegroup.com/ (July 4, 2002).

"Crowning Achievement: Australian Open Honors Rod Laver." *Sports Illustrated/CNN* http://sports illustrated.cnn.com/ (January 14, 2000).

"Harry Hopman, Class of 1978. International Tennis Hall of Fame. http://www.tennis.fame.org/ (September 26, 2002).

Hyundai/Hopman Cup. http://www.hopmancup.com/ (September 26, 2002).

Muscatel, Cyndy. "Rod Laver Triumphs Again." World Tennis Ratings. http://www.worldtennisratings.com/ (September 18, 2002).

"Rod Laver." BBC Sport. http://news.bbc.co.uk/ (September 18, 2002).

"Rod Laver, Class of 1981." International Tennis Hall of Fame. http://www.tennisfame.org/ (September 22, 2002).

Sketch by J. Sydney Jones

Mario Lemieux
1965-

Canadian hockey player

One of the most admired figures in professional sports, Mario Lemieux has enjoyed a lengthy career filled with dramatic moments. A member of two Stanley-Cup winning squads with the Pittsburgh Penguins, Lemieux was sidelined after a diagnosis of Hodgkin's Disease, a form of cancer, in 1993. After completing radiation therapy and missing the 1994-95 season, he returned to the Penguins the following year and scored sixty-nine goals on his way to winning the Hart Trophy as the National Hockey League's (NHL) Most Valuable Player. Citing the indifferent refereeing that plagued the NHL in the mid-1990s, Lemieux went into retirement in 1997. When the Penguins franchise encountered financial difficulties, Lemieux stepped in to negotiate a part-ownership of the team that helped it recover from bankruptcy. Even more surprising, Lemieux came out of retirement to rejoin the Penguins as an active player in 2000, an event that immediately revived the team's fortunes. Although he was criticized for taking time away from the team to prepare for the 2002 Salt Lake City Winter Olympic Games as a member of the Canadian men's hockey team, Lemieux retained his popularity in his adopted hometown of Pittsburgh for his

Mario Lemieux

Chronology

1965	Born October 5 in Montreal, Quebec, Canada to Jean-Guy and Pierette Lemieux
1984	Selected as first choice in draft by Pittsburgh Penguins
1991-92	Pittsburgh Penguins win two consecutive Stanley Cup championships
1993	Marries Nathalie Asselin on June 26
1993	Diagnosed with Hodgkin's Disease
1997	Announces retirement as professional athlete
1999	Becomes part-owner of Pittsburgh Penguins
2000	Returns to lineup of Pittsburgh Penguins
2002	Member of Canadian men's hockey team at Salt Lake City Olympic Games

Awards and Accomplishments

1985	Calder Memorial Trophy as NHL Rookie of the Year
1986, 1988, 1993, 1996	Lester B. Pearson Award as Player of the Year, National Hockey League Players Association
1988-89	Art Ross Trophy as NHL's top scorer
1988, 1993, 1996	Hart Trophy as NHL's Most Valuable Player
1991-92	Conn Smythe Trophy as Most Valuable Player in Playoffs
1993	Bill Masterton Trophy for NHL player who best exemplifies the qualities of perseverance, sportsmanship, and dedication to hockey
1997	Induction into Hockey Hall of Fame
2002	Olympic Gold Medal, hockey, Salt Lake City Winter Games (Canadian men's hockey team)

philanthropic work as well as his continued top-notch excellence on the ice.

Drafted by Pittsburgh Penguins

The third of Jean-Guy and Pierette Lemieux's three sons, Mario Lemieux was born on October 5, 1965 in the working-class Ville Emard neighborhood of Montreal, Quebec, Canada. He first began to skate and play hockey on a rink at the family's local church and his father, a construction worker, sometimes packed snow in the family's front hallway so that his sons, Richard, Alain, and Mario, could get in more practice time. Lemieux was already a standout player by the time he reached his teens and joined the Laval Voisins in the Quebec Major Junior Hockey League at age fifteen. In order to concentrate completely on his budding career as a hockey player, Lemieux left school after the tenth grade. Lemieux's three years with the Voisins culminated in a league record of 282 scoring points in the 1983-84 season. Recognized as one of the strongest up-and-coming players in North America, Lemieux was the first pick in the first round of the 1984 draft. He was selected by the Pittsburgh Penguins.

One of the teams added in the expansion of the NHL beyond its original six teams in 1967, the Penguins had never made it to the Stanley Cup finals. The squad also suffered from unfavorable comparisons with its cross-state rival, the Philadelphia Flyers, who won back-to-back victories in 1974 and 1975 and remained viable contenders for the Cup throughout the 1980s. Lemieux was an unlikely savior for the Penguins. Although the teenage center was an impressive figure on the ice, at six feet, four inches tall and about 220 pounds, he was shy and awkward off the ice. A native French speaker, Lemieux gradually learned English, which helped him adapt to life in Pittsburgh. His excellent performance also helped him become a favorite with Penguins fans; in his debut appearance with the team, Lemieux scored a goal on his very first attempt. By the end of the season, he had racked up 100 scoring points and earned the Calder Memorial Trophy as NHL Rookie of the Year.

Two Consecutive Stanley Cup Wins

Lemieux's initial success ranked alongside **Wayne Gretzky**'s astounding entry into the NHL in 1979. In 1986 and 1988 Lemieux won the Lester B. Pearson Award as Player of the Year, chosen by his follow NHL players. He added the Art Ross Trophy as NHL's top scorer in 1988 and 1989 and the Hart Trophy as NHL's Most Valuable Player in 1988. Yet it took a couple of years for the Penguins to build a solid team around their standout center; it was 1991 before the team made it to the Stanley Cup finals.

Injured with a herniated disk for much of the 1990-91 season, Lemieux played just twenty-six games that

Mario Lemieux

year. His return in time for the finals, however, proved crucial to the team's success as Lemieux amassed forty-four points in the playoffs, leading to the Penguins' eventual victory in the championships over the Minnesota North Stars. He was recognized for his contribution by winning the Conn Smythe Trophy at the end of the season as the playoff's Most Valuable Player.

Healthy for the 1991-92 season, Lemieux emerged with his third Art Ross Trophy with 131 total scoring points. The Penguins made it to the championship finals for the second straight year and defended their title, this time in a four-game sweep over the Chicago Blackhawks. The victory was especially meaningful for the team as it made it to the finals with an interim coach, **Scotty Bowman**, who stepped in after coach Bob Johnson was diagnosed with the brain cancer that took his life in November 1991. In addition to his second Stanley Cup ring, Lemieux received the Conn Smythe Trophy for the second year in a row.

Diagnosed with Hodgkin's Disease

Although the Penguins failed to make the finals in 1993, Lemieux had another great season. His 160 scoring points earned him another Art Ross Trophy and he received the Hart Trophy as league MVP and Pearson Award as Player of the Year from the Players' Association as well. His personal life was also filled with good news. On June 26, 1993, Lemieux married Nathalie Asselin; the couple eventually had four children.

While going in for a routine medical checkup related to his recurring back problems in 1993, Lemieux pointed out a growth on his neck to his doctor. A biopsy showed that cancer had invaded the node and Lemieux received a diagnosis of nodular lymphocytic Hodgkin's Disease. He immediately began radiation treatment to fight the illness and was eventually declared cancer-free; however, the treatment left him too lethargic to return to his ice for the 1994-95 season. In his year off the ice, Lemieux created the Mario Lemieux Foundation to fund grants on cancer research and to establish a patient-care center at the University of Pittsburgh Medical Center, which opened in 2001. After his son, Austin, was born three months prematurely in March 1996, Lemieux also raised money to inaugurate a neonatal research project at the Magee-Womens Hospital in Pittsburgh. These efforts, as well as the time he took to talk with other cancer patients and survivors, made Lemieux into one of the most beloved athletes of his generation. A sign of this esteem was the Bill Masterton Trophy, awarded to the NHL player who best exemplifies the qualities of perseverance, sportsmanship, and dedication to hockey, which Lemieux received in 1993.

Upon his return to the Penguins in 1995, Lemieux completed one of his best-ever seasons in the NHL with 161 points in seventy games, a total that included sixty-nine goals. Once again the winner of the Hart and Art Ross Trophies, Lemieux's comeback was an unqualified success. He added a sixth Art Ross Trophy in 1997. **Jaromir Jagr**, a Penguins player who had looked up to Lemieux as an early role model, was the Ross Trophy winner in 1995 and 1998. Despite these achievements, the Penguins did not return to the Stanley Cup finals after their 1992 win.

Career Statistic

Yr	Team	GP	G	A	PTS	+/−	PIM	SOG	SPCT	PPG	SHG
1984-85	Penguins	73	43	57	100	−35	54	209	20.6	11	0
1985-86	Penguins	79	48	93	141	−6	43	276	17.4	17	0
1986-87	Penguins	63	54	53	107	+13	57	267	20.2	19	0
1987-88	Penguins	77	70	98	168	+23	92	382	18.3	22	10
1988-89	Penguins	76	85	114	199	+41	100	313	27.2	31	13
1989-90	Penguins	59	45	78	123	−18	78	226	19.9	14	3
1990-91	Penguins	26	19	26	45	+8	30	89	21.3	6	1
1991-92	Penguins	64	44	87	131	+27	94	249	17.7	12	4
1992-93	Penguins	60	69	91	160	+55	38	286	24.1	16	6
1993-94	Penguins	22	17	20	37	−2	32	92	18.5	7	0
1995-96	Penguins	70	69	92	161	+10	54	338	20.4	31	8
1996-97	Penguins	76	50	72	122	+27	65	327	15.3	15	3
2000-01	Penguins	43	35	41	76	—	18	—	—	—	—
2001-02	Penguins	24	6	25	31	—	14	—	—	—	—
TOTAL		812	654	947	1601	—	769	—	—	—	—

Penguins: Pittsburgh Penguins (NHL).

Retires and Becomes Part-Owner of Penguins

In April 1997 Lemieux surprised the sports world by announcing his retirement from professional hockey. He had long been disenchanted with the sloppy refereeing in the NHL, which allowed many cheap shots on the ice to go unnoticed by officials. "It's to the point where it's not hockey anymore. It's like football on skates," *Sports Illustrated* quoted him in 1997. "The best teams win in basketball because the players can run up the court without carrying two guys on their backs. Not so in hockey. That's why there are so many teams with mediocre records. . . . It's the worst I've seen since I've been in the league." Lemieux was also crippled by constant back pain, which was not relieved despite two major operations. Thus, when the Penguins were knocked out of that year's playoffs on April 11, 1997, Lemieux retired from hockey. "I'll miss the guys," he told *Sports Illustrated*, "What I won't miss is the way the game's being played." Lemieux was inducted into the International Hockey Hall of Fame in 1997.

Lemieux's criticism added a sour note to the end of one of the most storied careers in hockey. Even more worrisome to Penguins fans was the news in 1999 that the team was now facing bankruptcy. If the financial problems—including a $16 million loss for the 1998-99 season—could not be resolved, it seemed certain that the franchise would be sold and moved to Portland, Oregon. With his ties to the team still strong, Lemieux stepped forward with an offer to buy a thirty-five percent stake in the Penguins with $5 million in cash and $20 million in deferred past salary payments owed to him. When it was completed, the deal made Lemieux into a hero in the opinion of many Pittsburghers, as he had saved the team from moving away. With Lemieux as the principal owner of the team, ticket sales increased and the team showed a modest profit in following season.

Comes Out of Retirement in 2000

Even more impressive than the Penguins' comeback from financial ruin was Lemieux's own return as an NHL player on December 27, 2000 in a game against the Toronto Maple Leafs. In doing so, Lemieux became the only player-owner in the NHL. Showing that the time away from the ice had not dimmed his skills, Lemieux scored one goal and had two assists in the game. He ended up playing in forty-three games in the 2000-2001 season and had thirty-five goals and forty-one assists. Lemieux also rediscovered his love for the sport, in part because the changes that he had long advocated had been implemented. "[The style of play] was certainly a big part of my decision to leave the game," he told Darren Pang of the ESPN Network in January 2001, adding, "I like the way the game is going right now, and I like the direction it's heading in and that's why I came back and would like to be part of it."

A hip injury bothered him throughout the 2001-2002 season and Lemieux's time on the ice with the Penguins was further curtailed by his decision to join Canada's men's hockey team at the 2002 Salt Lake City Winter Olympic Games. Despite the accusations that his decision would hurt his team's chances to make the playoffs, Lemieux was thrilled to represent his country at the event. In one of the most exciting international matches in the history of the sport, Canada triumphed in the final over the United States; it was the country's first Gold Medal in the event in fifty years.

Although he is often ranked second to his contemporary Wayne Gretzky in discussions of the greatest hockey players of the last generation, Lemieux's ability to come back not once, but twice, to the sport has earned him special distinction in the sport's history. Hailed as a prodigy in his youth, Lemieux fulfilled his early promise in his first years in the NHL when he won nu-

---

Owner Operator

After a sabbatical of forty-four months, Lemieux—father, team owner, and player again at age thirty-five—stepped into the NHL void, reinvigorating a league of faceless players and system-mad teams. On his first night back he needed only thirty-three seconds to set up a goal against the Toronto Maple Leafs. Later that evening he scored and then assisted on a third goal. The 17,148 fans and twenty stunned Maple Leafs (who played more like unindicted coconspirators than opponents) witnessed perfection. Lemieux's nearly twenty-one minute performance was so impeccable, his accomplishment so pure, that it had to be reduced to fit our shrunken frame of reference. . . .

Source: Michael Farber, *Sports Illustrated*, January 8, 2001.

---

merous awards and led his team to two consecutive Stanley Cups. His ability to rebound from a potentially life-threatening disease and return to a level of play that surpassed almost any other player, however, was a testament to his own perseverance and determination. Returning once again to help his team regain its financial footing and league standing, Lemieux added another compelling chapter to an already storied career.

FURTHER INFORMATION

Books

Diamond, Dan, ed. *Total Hockey: The Official Encyclopedia of the National Hockey League.* Kansas City: Andrews McMeel Publishing, 1998.

Periodicals

Allen, Kevin. "Lemieux Takes Long-Overdue Olympic Trip with Canada." *USA Today* (February 1, 2002).

Brehm, Mike. "Lemieux Feels Too Good to Take Extra Day Off." *USA Today* (October 25, 2002).

Charland, Bill. "Multifaceted Mario Re-Steels Pittsburgh." *Christian Science Monitor* (February 9, 2001).

Farber, Michael. "Owner Operator." *Sports Illustrated* (January 8, 2001).

Kostya, Kennedy and Michael Farber. "A Different Goal." *Sports Illustrated* (February 25, 2002).

Kostya, Kennedy. "Super, Mario." *Sports Illustrated* (December 18, 2000).

Molinari, Dave. "Mario's Costly Hip Check." *Sporting News* (March 11, 2002).

Swift, E.M. "No Regrets." *Sports Illustrated* (April 14, 1997).

Wigge, Larry. "The Good Guys: Mario Lemieux." *Sporting News* (July 16, 2001).

Other

"Foundation History." Mario Lemieux Foundation Web site. http://www.mariolemieux.org/foundation/history.htm (November 7, 2002).

"Jagr Reaping Benefits, Happiness with Lemieux." ESPN Web site. http://espn.go.com/nhl/s/2000/1231/985819.html (December 31, 2000).

"Lemieux: 'I think I made the right decision.'" ESPN Web site. http://espn.go.com/nhl/s/lemieuxpang2.html (January 8, 2001).

"Lemieux Biography." Mario Lemieux Official Web site. http://www.mariolemieux.com/bio.asp (November 7, 2002).

"Mario Lemieux." Internet Hockey Database Web site. http://www.hockeydb.com/ihdb/stats/pdisplay.php3?pid=3105 (November 7, 2002).

"Robert 'Bob' Johnson.'" U.S. Hockey Hall of Fame Website. http://www.ushockeyhall.com/Enshrinees/Robert%20Johnson.htm (November 13, 2002).

Sketch by Timothy Borden

Meadowlark Lemon
1932-

American basketball player

Like a crazed captain at the helm of a ship, Meadowlark Lemon could take over a court and steer a crowd into the throes of laughter. During his 23 seasons with the Harlem Globetrotters, Lemon proved he was more than just a basketball player. Full of wisecracks and wise moves, Lemon became the "Clown Prince of Basketball," and night after night, year after year, he used his laughter-coaxing charisma to charm fans around the globe. In his career with the Globetrotters, Lemon played in more than 7,500 consecutive games and logged more than four million miles, charming audiences in more than 100 countries, from Algeria to Zimbabwe.

Los Angeles Times sportswriter Jim Murray once called Lemon "an American institution whose uniform should hang alongside the Spirit of St. Louis and the Gemini Space Capsule in the halls of the Smithsonian Institute."

Though more than 20 years have passed since Lemon was a staple in the Globetrotters' lineup, he remains the team's most well-known name and is better known than even the team's current stars.

Inspired by Globetrotters as Child

Meadow George Lemon III was born April 25, 1932, in Wilmington, North Carolina. When his parents separated a few years later, Lemon's mom moved to New York City. His father, Meadow George "Peanut" Lemon II, worked for the Wilmington Waste Paper & Recycling Co. and gambled to help make ends meet. Needless to

Meadowlark Lemon

Chronology

1932	Born on April 25 in Wilmington, North Carolina
1952	Drafted into the U.S. Army
1954	Leaves Army
1954	Joins Kansas City All-Stars
1955	Joins the Harlem Globetrotters
1970	Stars on television cartoon "The Harlem Globetrotters Show"
1971	Becomes player/coach for the Globetrotters
1978	Leaves Globetrotters
1979	Embarks on career in show business
1986	Becomes an ordained minister
1980s-present	Works as traveling evangelist
1993	Has 50-game "comeback" season with the Globetrotters
2002	Embarks on tour with the Meadowlark Lemon Harlem All-Stars

say, young Lemon spent a great deal of his childhood living with his aunt and uncle and cousins.

As a youngster, Lemon and his friends played football and spent their weekends at the Ritz movie theater, where they could watch a whole day's worth of shows for 25 cents.

When Lemon was 11, he went to the Ritz and saw a news clip that irrevocably changed the course of his life. The clip featured the Harlem Globetrotters, strutting their stuff to their theme song, "Sweet Georgia Brown."

"They flew up and down the court, passing, dribbling, shooting, rebounding," Lemon recalled in his autobiography, *Meadowlark*. "My heart raced. My head nearly ached. I couldn't believe what I was seeing."

It wasn't just the athletic prowess that captivated young Lemon. "It was the joy, the teamwork, the sense of family," Lemon recalled. "It was the most wonderful thing I had ever seen in my life."

Lemon bolted from the theater before the feature even started, leaving his buddies behind. Lemon's mind was made up: he would do whatever it took to become a Globetrotter. At the time, Lemon had never even touched a basketball—the neighborhood kids said the sport was for sissies. Undaunted, Lemon went home and crafted a basketball hoop from a clothes hanger and an onion bag. In place of a ball, he used an empty evaporated milk can and started shooting.

A year later, when Lemon was in the seventh grade, a Boys' Club opened in his neighborhood. Lemon finally got his hands on a genuine basketball, limp and flat as it was. He spent his free time at the Boys' Club, dedicating hours and hours to dribbling and ball-handling. In time, a man named Earl Jackson took an interest in Lemon. He showed the youngster how to shoot a right-handed hook shot. Lemon worked endlessly on the shot, until the motion felt fluid, instinctive. That's when Jackson showed him the left-handed hook shot, and he began all over again. It was a shot Lemon would become famous for as a Globetrotter.

During eighth grade, Lemon spent nearly every afternoon and every Saturday at the Boys' Club. Months and months had passed since he first began practicing, yet Lemon didn't feel as though he'd made any progress. The other boys seemed to possess a natural ability for the sport. Lemon yearned to float around the court instinctually, to find the rhythm of the game.

Lemon was good enough to make the Boys' Club basketball team—as a benchwarmer. Over the course of the season, however, Lemon worked his way off the bench and into the game. Finally, the game began to click. Lemon floated around the court gracefully, knowing when to gather speed, when to slow down, all the while pivoting, passing, and shooting.

Excelled at Football, Basketball

At Williston Industrial High School, Wilmington's all-black school, Lemon excelled at both football and basketball. He also found a friend and father figure in coach E. A. "Spike" Corbin. Throughout high school, Lemon spent many weekends at Corbin's house perfecting his game or just hanging out. At Williston, Lemon averaged 20 points per game his sophomore year and close to 30 his senior year.

As an All-State in both football and basketball, Lemon was courted by colleges across the United States. But he didn't want to go. All Lemon wanted to do was become a Globetrotter. Lemon spent the summer after high school graduation working with his father at the recycling com-

Awards and Accomplishments

1974	Received Presidential Citation from then-President Gerald Ford as part of Globetrotter team
1975	Inducted into the North Carolina Sports Hall of Fame
2000	Received the International Clown Hall of Fame's Lifetime of Laughter Award
2000	Received the Basketball Hall of Fame's John Bunn Award

pany. Then one day, Lemon's father packed his suitcase and put him on a train to Tallahassee, Florida, saying he'd accepted a scholarship for Lemon to Florida A & M. College life didn't agree with Lemon, and he grew uneasy waiting for basketball season to begin. When his draft notice came, Lemon left college, although he could have received an education deferral and stayed. The United States was deep into the Korean War, and Lemon figured serving his country wasn't such a bad idea.

Tries Out for Globetrotters

Before leaving for basic training, Lemon returned to Wilmington and learned that the Globetrotters were coming to nearby Raleigh, North Carolina. He'd never seen them in person. Because the game was sold out, Lemon had his high school coach call Globetrotter promoter Abe Saperstein to get tickets. Coach Corbin and Saperstein were acquaintances.

Saperstein invited Lemon to the game. Because Saperstein wasn't able to attend the game, he told Globetrotter Marques Haynes to meet with Lemon and look him over. Just as the game was about to begin, Haynes tossed Lemon a uniform and told him to suit up because there wouldn't be time for a tryout later.

Lemon recalled the moment in his autobiography, "Just getting to see the Trotters would have been more than enough. I'd have paid. To meet Marques Haynes, that was bonus.... To wear a uniform stunned me. To play, unreal. I thought I was going to throw up."

Stunned, Lemon drifted around the court in a haze. He finally came to his senses, realizing he had to make the most of this opportunity. Lemon stepped up his game and soon, he was faking out the other team, driving toward the basket, and showing off with his reverse lay-up. The applause energized Lemon, and he pulled off an impressive performance.

Lemon was on a high when he shipped off to basic training at Fort Jackson, South Carolina. He spent two years in the military (1952-54), stationed in Salzburg, Austria. There, he sharpened his game while playing on an army base team, averaging 55 points per game. Combined, his teammates averaged just 13.

Becomes 'Clown Prince' of Basketball

Lemon left the Army after two years and was invited to join the Kansas City All-Stars, one of the opposition

A History of the Harlem Globetrotters

The Harlem Globetrotters came into being in the 1920s thanks to a young entrepreneur named Abe Saperstein, who had grown up watching black boys play basketball in the streets of Chicago. Their pure talent impressed Saperstein, and he envisioned a pro team for black players. At the time, they weren't allowed to play on the all-white professional teams. Though only five-foot-three, Saperstein had been a basketball star himself. In 1926, he pulled together a team called the Savoy Big Five because they played their games in Chicago's Savoy Ballroom.

In the early days of basketball, the professional teams didn't have home courts. They just traveled around, or "barnstormed." In 1927, Saperstein took his team on the road, too. He called them the Harlem Globetrotters: Harlem to let people know they were black; globetrotters so they would think the team had traveled the world.

The Globetrotters played their first game in January 1927 in Hinckley, Illinois. The team spent the season traveling around in a Model T Ford, just five players and coach Saperstein. They barely made enough money to eat and spent many nights in the car. Playing night after night, the five players got tired; they had no substitutes. The ball-handling routines that made the Globetrotters famous grew out of a need to rest players. If one player showed off with the ball, the others could rest. The team also relied on showmanship to keep the scores down and the crowds from growing bored. In 1940, the team beat the Chicago Bruins at the World Tournament, winning the national pro title.

In 1950, Saperstein booked a tour to Western Europe and North Africa, making the team live up to its name. They garnered rave reviews and in 1952 played for the pope. Back home in the United States, they faced racial discrimination. While on the road in the South, restaurants refused to serve them. In many cities, they had to play two games in a day—one for the white crowd, and one for the black. Despite the hardships, the Globetrotters endured.

More than 75 years have passed since the Globetrotters first set out in their Model T. To this day, they continue to travel around the world lighting up the hearts of the young and old alike.

teams that toured with the Globetrotters. Within time, Lemon worked his way to the other side, and by 1955, was a bona fide Globetrotter.

With his zany, on-court persona, the six-foot-three Lemon soon established himself as the Globetrotters' most prolific court jester, earning the title "Clown Prince of Basketball." By the 1958-59 season, Lemon was the lead clown and held that position for the next 20 years. The team's lead clown oversees the game by managing the pace, along with the comedy routines.

Lemon's injury act was one of the crowd's favorites. The act began with Lemon dropping to the floor "in pain" after just the slightest contact with an opponent. When **Wilt Chamberlain** was on the team, he'd seize Lemon like a rag doll and cart him off the court, ball in hand. That's when Lemon would substitute a new ball-one with an elastic string. Lemon would step to the free-throw line and build the suspense by bouncing the ball. Naturally, when he shot the ball, it would soar upward, then snap back like a boomerang. Lemon would try to get rid of the ball by tossing it at the referee, but of course, it came right back. When the referee told Lemon to get rid of the ball, he'd return with a weighted ball that wobbled around. Or he'd hand the referee a ball so

Meadowlark Lemon

full of holes it would deflate almost immediately. Lemon was a born actor, and the court became his stage. Game after game, year after year, the crowds laughed over this routine.

Over the years, Lemon refined his skills along with his comedy. Once, when the opposing team guarded Lemon so heavily he couldn't shoot, he shot the ball underhanded through the opponent's legs to score. The move garnered immediate laughs and was added to the routine. Another trademark of Lemon's was his non-stop yakking. Throughout the game, he talked in a high-pitched voice that had even the fans in the upper seats laughing.

While his antics held a crowd's attention, Lemon's skills awed them. Game after game, Lemon amazed crowds with his uncanny ability to sink hook shots. He'd walk away from the basket, not even looking, and flip the ball over his head for two points. In his autobiography, *A View from Above,* Wilt Chamberlain writes that he would be happy to make that shot just once. "You can't practice those things," he wrote. "How do you practice a once-in-a-lifetime shot, even though you're asked to make it every night? It's like practicing drowning."

Besides his antics and ball-handling skills, Lemon's other secret weapon was his wide smile. The more he smiled, the more the crowd laughed, and the laughter sustained him. "I couldn't believe the applause, the laughter. It was almost physical, lifting me, inspiring

me, warming me," Lemon noted in his autobiography. "I couldn't get enough of it. Every night I could hardly wait to charge from the locker room into the gym to get another fix of crowd reaction."

Lemon's antics made him so popular that a 1978 nationwide poll named him the fourth most popular personality in the United States, behind John Wayne, Alan Alda, and Bob Hope.

"Globe-Trotting" Affected Family Life

Just after he left the Army, Lemon had married childhood friend Willye Maultsby. However, as Lemon's fame on the court advanced, his home life deteriorated. Lemon traveled ten months a year, playing more than 300 games, leaving his wife home with their five children.

Lemon was absent so often that his daughter Beverly wrote a school paper describing her father as a dishwasher because that's what she saw him do when he was home. Another daughter, Robin, told her teacher that her father lived at the airport.

Lemon and his wife began to argue, so he stayed away more and more. During the off-season, he jumped at the chance to do promotions for the team so he wouldn't have to go home. In time, Lemon was hitting the clubs with the other guys, picking up women. In his autobiography, Lemon said that he rationalized the behavior at the time. After all, he'd grown up in Wilmington watching other men do the same. He figured other women were just a part of married life. Needless to say, they divorced around 1977.

Moved from the Court to the Pulpit

In 1971, Lemon became both a coach and player for the Globetrotters, and his relationship with teammates began to slowly unravel. Playing both roles proved problematic, as petty jealousies and contract disputes popped up. Things turned so sour he quit in 1978.

Following his retirement from the Globetrotters, Lemon received offers from Hollywood, and in 1979 appeared in *The Fish that Saved Pittsburgh.* In the film, he starred as a basketball-playing reverend alongside Philadelphia 76ers star **Julius Erving**. He also landed a spot on the TV sitcom "Hello, Larry" (1979 and 1980), where he played an aging athlete.

Sometime around 1979, Lemon formed his own basketball comedy act, called the Bucketeers. Former teammate Wilt Chamberlain joined the Bucketeers from time to time, although they still struggled financially and folded around 1982.

By the mid-1980s, Lemon had a new career as a jetsetting evangelist. As an ordained minister of a Christian non-denominational church, Lemon began traveling around the country talking about God. He also took a brief break from the ministry in 1993 for a 50-game "comeback" season with the Globetrotters. He also remarried and has ten children, three of them adopted.

Remembered for Bringing Laughter to World

Though Lemon has been out of the Globetrotter limelight for more than two decades, he has yet to fade from memory. In 2000, Lemon was awarded the Basketball Hall of Fame's John Bunn Award, given for outstanding contributions to basketball. He also received an award from the International Clown Hall of Fame.

To this day, Lemon is remembered as a basketball phenomenon, whose antics transcended race and culture. He was loved by the world around. The Globetrotters, along with Lemon, were so appreciated that former President Gerald Ford awarded the team a special 1974 Presidential Citation. He thanked the Globetrotters—and Lemon—for giving millions of people "the priceless gifts of love and laughter." Truly, that's what Lemon's life has been about, and no one has done it better.

CONTACT INFORMATION

Address: (care of Meadowlark Lemon Ministries)13610 N. Scottsdale Road, Ste. 10267, Scottsdale, AZ 85254. Phone: (480) 951-0030. Email: info@meadowlarklemon foundation.org. Online: http://www.meadowlarklemon. org.

SELECTED WRITINGS BY LEMON:

(With Jerry B. Jenkins) *Meadowlark*. Nashville: Thomas Nelson Publishers, 1987.

FURTHER INFORMATION

Books

Chamberlain, Wilt. *A View From Above*. New York: Villard Books, 1991.
Lemon, Meadowlark and Jerry B. Jenkins. *Meadowlark*. Nashville: Thomas Nelson Publishers, 1987.
Wilker, Josh. *The Harlem Globetrotters*. Philadelphia: Chelsea House Publishers, 1997.

Periodicals

Betowt, Yvonne. "Ex-Globetrotter Ministers to Kids Through Basketball." *(Minneapolis) Star Tribune* (April 6, 2002): 8B.
Derrick, Mel. "A Globetrotting Preacher; Meadowlark Trades in Basketball for Bible." (Montreal) *Gazette* (March 3, 1996): D7.
"Hall of Fame Honors Globetrotters' Lemon." *Milwaukee Journal Sentinel* (August 9, 2000): 2C.
Kugiya, Hugo. "'I'm A Better Father Now.'" *Seattle Times* (June 18, 1993): C1.

Other

"Basketball Hall of Fame Announces Prestigious John Bunn Award." Basketball Hall of Fame. http://www. hoophall.com/news/bunn_award080800.htm (November 24, 2002).
"Ernie Harwell, Sportscaster." Radio Hall of Fame. http://www.radiohof.org/sportscasters/ernieharwell. html (November 21, 2002).
The Harlem Globetrotters. Troy, Michigan: Anchor Bay Entertainment, Inc., 1996.
"International Clown Hall of Fame." Meadowlark Lemon.com. http://www.meadowlarklemon. com/news_intclownoffame.html (July 31, 2000).

Sketch by Lisa Frick

Sugar Ray Leonard
1956-

American boxer

Olympic gold medallist Sugar Ray Leonard generated broad interest in the sport of boxing during the 1970s and into the 1980s. In 1981 he beat Thomas Hearns for the unification of the WBC and WBA world welterweight titles, winning a prize purse of more than $10 million. It was an unprecedented sum for a welterweight bout, in a sport where the spoils of fame rested traditionally with heavyweight fighters, to the exclusion of most others.

Sugar Ray Leonard was born Ray Charles Leonard in Wilmington, North Carolina, on May 17, 1956. The fifth of seven children of Cicero and Getha Leonard, he was named for singer Ray Charles. In Wilmington, Leonard's father worked in a soda pop plant, and his mother was a nursing assistant. When Leonard was four the family

Sugar Ray Leonard

moved to Washington, D.C., where they rented an apartment on Avenue L. Seven years later they moved to Seat Pleasant, Maryland, and in 1968 Leonard's parents purchased a home on Barlowe Road in nearby Palmer Park. Ray, the youngest of the five Leonard boys, was also the least aggressive. He seemed shy by nature, a fact that was perhaps aggravated by the family's frequent moves during his formative years.

When in 1970 the community of Palmer Park built a youth recreation center, Leonard frequented the new facility after school. There, under the guidance of a volunteer coach, David Jacobs, Leonard and other neighborhood boys learned the fine points of *pugilism* (boxing). Although the program lacked funding, Jacobs marked off an imaginary boxing ring with colored tape in the middle of the gymnasium at the recreation center. He assembled his would-be amateur boxing squad at five a.m. daily for a conditioning run, and worked with the boys in the imaginary boxing ring after school.

Leonard overall had little interest in athletics or in any other pursuit prior to joining Jacobs's boxing group. Aside from a brief foray with the wrestling squad at his junior high school, he had participated minimally in cross-country and in track and field. By the time his voice dropped at age fourteen, Leonard had

abandoned even his participation in the church choir. To the surprise of many who knew the shy boy, he had a natural flair for boxing. After becoming involved with Jacobs, Leonard focused squarely on boxing to the exclusion of all else during his four years at Parkdale High School in Palmer Park.

With guidance from Jacobs, Leonard participated in amateur boxing matches sponsored by the U.S. Amateur Athletic Union (AAU). He gained twenty-five pounds during his first year of competition. After winning a bout against the top amateur boxer in his region, Leonard entered competition at the national level, winning the Golden Gloves lightweight title at age sixteen in 1972. He appeared in the AAU national quarterfinals that year, and competed internationally with that group.

Olympic Glory

In 1973 a boxing promoter noticed Leonard's natural talent and offered him $5,000 to fight in a commercial bout. Leonard dismissed the offer because he wanted to qualify for the 1976 Olympics—and qualify he did. Leonard earned a spot on the 1976 U.S. team, which included future heavyweight champions **Michael Spinks** and his brother Leon.

After spring training in Burlington, Vermont, the team headed for the Olympic Village in Montreal, Quebec, where Leonard performed superbly in the three-round Olympic bouts. He won his first match against Ulf Carlson of Sweden and a second match against left-hander Valery Limasov of the former Soviet Union. After taking England's Clinton McKenzie in the third match, Leonard entered the quarterfinals where he beat Ulrich Beyer of Germany.

Leonard up to that point in his amateur career had lost only five fights, among them a contested bout in 1974 against Kazimier Szczerba of Poland. In a subtle irony, Leonard faced Szczerba in the Olympic semifinals and defeated the Pole with a resounding knockout.

It was a fine day for Leonard and the United States when in the Olympic finals Leonard brought the Cuban fighter Andres Aldama to his knees with a left hook to the chin. Twice during the final bout, the referee had required Aldama to take a standing eight-count to prove that he was able to continue the fight. Although Aldama persisted in the match, Leonard emerged the victor and won the gold medal for the United States. It was Leonard's one hundred and forty-fifth victory as an amateur boxer.

Even as he basked in the glory of the moment, Leonard was quick to assure interviewers that he would never turn to boxing as a profession. He returned home to the United States, bent on majoring in communications in college. With his handsome features and photogenic smile, it was Leonard's intention to become a television sports journalist. Upon his return to the United States, however, financial concerns soon took precedence over his educational plans, causing him to rethink his decision about professional boxing. Both of his parents had be-

come seriously ill around the time of the Olympics. What was more, his high school sweetheart, Juanita Wilkinson, filed a paternity suit against him, for money to support their child, Ray Jr., born on November 22, 1973.

With assistance from a group of supporters, Leonard secured front money totaling approximately $24,000 in loans and used the funds to assemble a professional boxing team. To lead the entourage he hired **Muhammad Ali**'s popular cornerman, Angelo Dundee, as a trainer and ringside coach. Leonard's long-time coach and friend, David Jacobs remained with Leonard and his team, to serve as head coach for the young champion.

Leonard's professional debut, against Luis "the Bull" Vega of Pennsylvania, was a six-round bout at the Baltimore Civic Center in February of 1977. A victory for Leonard, the bout netted him enough money to repay his start-up loans. Following his next match in April—also a victory—against Willie Rodriguez, Leonard signed a lucrative contract giving ABC Sports the rights to televise future fights. There followed a technical knockout (TKO) of Vinnie De Barros on June 19 in Hartford, Connecticut, and a series of bouts in such small East Coast venues as Springfield, Massachusetts, and Portland, Maine. Within a year of his debut, Leonard was regularly scheduled for ten-round bouts with his opponents. He went on to defeat Javier Muniz on March 19, 1978, by a knockout (KO), just two minutes and forty-five seconds into the fight. The next month in Landover, Maryland, on April 13 he knocked out Bobby Haymon in three. One month later in Utica, New York, he toppled Randy Milton in eight.

Despite the limited audience for welterweight boxing, Leonard's appeal grew. ABC renewed his contract, and the fighter did not disappoint. In March 1979 he defeated Daniel Gonzalez with a KO after two minutes and three seconds. In April in Las Vegas, Leonard won a decision against Adolfo Viruet. In another decision on May 20 in Baton Rouge, Louisiana, Leonard beat Marcos Geraldo. Leonard finished off Pete Ranzany and Tony

Chiaverini with TKOs and in September downed Andy Price in the first round of their bout.

When Leonard went against world welterweight champion Wilfredo Benitez on November 30, 1979, the purse—which guaranteed each fighter more than $1 million—was the first seven-figure purse in welterweight history. The fight went only six seconds shy of the full 15 rounds before the referee stopped the fight. In the end Leonard, at age twenty-three, won the World Boxing Council (WBC) welterweight championship. Both fighters earned their pay that day, and spectators got their money's worth on the cost of admission.

Amid the lingering glow of Leonard's championship win, he and Wilkinson were married on January 19, 1980, in Landover, Maryland. It was a marriage that was long overdue—their courtship had lasted since high school, and their son, Ray Jr., was by then seven years old and served as a ring bearer for his parents.

Ringside Politics

Because of the existence of two prominent worldwide boxing organizations, a subsequent bout between Leonard and another world welterweight champion, Pipino Cuevo, was anticipated. Cuevo at that time was the sanctioned champion of the World Boxing Association (WBA), and representatives for the two fighters went into negotiations almost immediately. As talks convened to schedule a two-way championship fight, WBA officials inexplicably refused to sanction the bout whatsoever—even the notion of a non-title bout between the two title holders was diffused, for reasons never stated.

When negotiations for the Cuevo fight stalled, an interim bout was scheduled, pitting Leonard against Davey "Boy" Green of Britain. The fight nearly ended in tragedy when Leonard in the fourth round dealt a KO punch that

dropped Green onto the mat where he remained motionless for many seconds. Green regained consciousness after some minutes and left the ring with assistance.

As an alternative to the Cuevo fight, a contest was set for June 20, 1980, in Montreal, between Leonard and a prominent Panamanian fighter, Roberto Duran. Duran's reputation as a vicious street fighter was well founded. He had boxed in amateur matches since the age of ten and had entered professional competition at age seventeen. Originally classified as a lightweight, Duran lacked the self-discipline to maintain the weight requirement and was forced to fight against men much larger than him in stature. Duran was notorious for his wild, aggressive, and animal-like boxing style by which he cornered his opponents into serious jeopardy, forcing them against the ropes with no chance for escape.

In preparation for the bout with Duran, Leonard went into training at his personal facility in New Carrolton, Maryland. Bookmakers set odds at 9-5 in favor of Leonard, but fate was to side with the underdog. Duran pummeled Leonard, winning the fight by a unanimous decision and taking the world welterweight title in the process. The loss was the first of Leonard's professional career.

The Leonard camp pressed Duran representatives for a rematch, and a second meeting was set for the New Orleans Superdome on November 25. Bookmakers were more cautious for the second encounter, laying odds at 3-2, albeit still in Leonard's favor.

Leonard appeared for the rematch dressed in black trunks and shoes, in a stark and pointed contrast from the signature white outfits that he habitually wore. As the match got underway, Leonard assumed a menacing posture. It was a rare attitude for Leonard—he mimicked Duran's own aggressive boxing style and used it against him, besting Duran at his own game. In a surprise conclusion, Duran threw in the towel. Ceding the fight in the eighth round, he begged, "No more," and Leonard was proclaimed welterweight champion for the second time.

Duran returned to his native Panama in disgrace, with no explanation for his apparent cowardice. The fight was Duran's final appearance in the ring. He was ordered by the WBC to pay a $7,500 fine for failing to perform in compliance with council standards. No further explanation was ever given for the curious fight.

Growing and Gaining

Still growing taller, at age twenty-five Leonard considered a move into the junior middleweight class, where the weight limits ranged over 147 pounds. After a bout with Harry Bonds of Denver in Syracuse, New York, in March 1981 Leonard went against Ajub Kalube, who at 154 pounds was the WBA junior middleweight champion. On June 21 Kalube lost his title to Leonard by a TKO in the ninth round at the Houston Astrodome.

Sugar Ray Leonard, left

Leonard's next fight was a two-way title bout against Thomas Hearns. The contenders—Leonard and Hearns—were long-time rivals, with Hearns holding claim to the WBA welterweight title and Leonard wearing the WBC belt. Leonard was rated the favorite, with 8-5 odds when the contract was signed. At age twenty-two, however, Hearns was three inches taller and three years younger than the 5-foot-10-inch Leonard. By fight night, Hearns went into the arena as a 7-5 favorite.

Before a capacity crowd of 25,000 at Caesar's Palace in Las Vegas, on September 16, 1981, the two boxers battled through thirteen full rounds. Leonard went into the fight with one sore eye, only to have it throttled by Hearns until it was swollen shut. Miraculously, Leonard summoned an untapped reserve in the final rounds. Fourteen seconds into the fourteenth round, he wore down Hearns and won the fight in a TKO. In accomplishing the defeat, Leonard successfully unified the welterweight championship belts and earned a prize purse of more than $10 million. Indeed, the loser's share alone topped more than $5 million, which combined with Leonard's take totaled the richest purse in prize-fight history at that time.

Retirement and Return

In 1982 Leonard was diagnosed with a detached retina and underwent surgery to repair the injury. He announced his retirement from boxing at that time, turning his attention to broadcast journalism. After some years as a commentator for the Home Box Office cable network, he returned to the ring with aspirations of fighting **Marvin Hagler** for the middleweight championship.

A much-publicized contest came about in 1987, when Leonard issued a challenge to Hagler, whose hold on the middleweight title was by then entering its seventh year—since September 27, 1980. Twelve times Hagler had fought in defense of his title, and twelve times he had won. With the challenge accepted, Leonard returned to the ring in April 1987 at Caesar's Palace in Las Vegas, to fight what would be the fight of the year, according to *Ring* magazine.

Leonard took the middleweight title from the aging Hagler by TKO in the ninth round and used the surge of momentum to issue another challenge. He returned to training and defeated double-title holder Donny Lalonde, for the WBC super middleweight and light heavyweight championships in November 1988. After the victory Leonard retired holding both world titles.

CONTACT INFORMATION

Address: c/o IMG New York, 825 7th Avenue, New York, NY 10019. Fax: (310) 471-1410. Phone: (310) 471-3100. Email: Ray@SRLBoxing.com. Online: sugar-rayleonard.com.

FURTHER INFORMATION

Books

Goldstein, Alan. *Fistful of Sugar: The Sugar Ray Leonard Story.* New York: Coward, McCann & Geoghegan, 1981.

Haskins, James. *Sugar Ray Leonard.* New York: Lothrop, Lee & Shepard Books, 1982.

Markoe, Arnold, and Kenneth T. Jackson. *Scribner Encyclopedia of American Lives: Sports Figures.* New York: Charles Scribner's Sons, 2002.

Periodicals

Sports Illustrated (April 20, 1987): 50.

Sketch by G. Cooksey

Lisa Leslie

Lisa Leslie
1972-

American basketball player

Hard as it may be to believe, there was a time when Los Angeles Sparks star and WNBA pioneer member Lisa Leslie renounced basketball. Standing six feet tall in the seventh grade, Leslie was asked constantly if she played the game. Rather than spurring her interest, though, the repeated inquisitions turned her against the sport. "I hated it," she has admitted. At a friend's prodding, however, she eventually tried out for her middle school team, and her entire mindset changed. "I just changed my whole attitude," she noted in *People*. "I guess it was my destiny, but I never knew it."

Hard Work All Around

Once Leslie gained an interest in basketball, she worked hard to excel in the sport. With the encouragement of a cousin, she embarked on a self-directed training regimen, which included sit-ups, push-ups, drills and shooting baskets, as well as taking on male players after whom she then modeled her own style of play.

Hard work and perseverance were familiar to Leslie, whose father left the family when she was four years old. Raised by her mother Christine, Leslie learned about hard work and struggle watching her mother work as a cross-country truck driver to earn money to support her three daughters. During the school year, Leslie was often cared for by a babysitter or an aunt. Her mother's absence forced her to mature and gain self-reliance early. In the summers, she and a sister accompanied their mother, sleeping on a bunk in the back of the rig. Despite her mother's long absences, Leslie credits Christine with imparting numerous life lessons. Christine, who stands 6'3", taught her daughter to be proud of her stature. "She raised me to be confident and hold my head up," Leslie told *People* magazine.

High School Standout

Leslie entered Morningside High School in Inglewood, California in 1987. By her junior year she was receiving national attention for her on-court prowess. Averaging 21.7 points, 12.8 rebounds and 6.2 block shots per game that year, *USA Today* named her a first-team high school All-American.

The following season, Leslie achieved an almost unfathomable feat, scoring 101 points in the first half of a game against South Torrance High. She set a national

Chronology

1972	Born July 7
1987	Enters Morningside High School in Inglewood, California and joins the basketball team
1989	Named to *USA Today*'s high school All-American first team
1989	Competes with U.S. women's Junior World Championship team
1990	Scores 101 points in the first half of game against South Torrance High; denied national record for points in one game when South Torrance forfeits
1990	Leads Morningside to state title
1990	Awarded Naismith and Dial awards
1990	Becomes last player cut from U.S. women's National Team
1991	Enters University of Southern California as most highly recruited female basketball player since Cheryl Miller in 1983
1991	Earns National and Pac-10 Freshman of the Year honors
1991	Becomes first freshman named to Pac-10 first team
1991	Leads U.S. to gold at the World University Games
1992	Attends Olympic trials as youngest player trying out for U.S. women's team
1993	Named Female Athlete of the Year by USA Basketball
1994	Earns second Naismith Award
1994	Qualifies for U.S. women's national team and leads team to gold in Goodwill Games
1994	Travels to Italy to play professionally
1996	Named to U.S. women's Summer Olympics "Dream Team" and leads team to gold medal
1996	Assigned to Los Angeles Sparks of newly formed Women's National Basketball Association
2001	Leads L.A. to first WNBA title and named tournament MVP
2002	On July 30 becomes first woman to slam dunk in a professional game
2002	Leads L.A. to second WNBA title and named tournament MVP
2002	Named regular season, All-Star and tournament MVP, becoming first WNBA player to win all three MVP trophies in one season

Awards and Accomplishments

1989	Named to *USA Today*'s high school All-American first team
1989	Competes with U.S. women's Junior World Championship team
1990	Awarded Naismith and Dial awards
1991	National and Pac-10 Freshman of the Year honors
1991-94	Named to All-Pac-10 first team
1992-94	Named All-American
1993	Named Female Athlete of the Year by USA Basketball
1994	Qualifies for U.S. women's national team
1994	Wins gold medal at Goodwill Games and bronze at World Women's Basketball Championships
1996	Qualifies for U.S. Olympic team and leads team to gold medal
2001	Leads L.A. to first WNBA title and named tournament MVP
2002	Leads L.A. to second WNBA title
2002	Named regular season, All-Star and tournament MVP

high school record with thirty-one free throws and added thirty-seven field goals as well. With Leslie having scored all but one of her team's 102 points and her school leading 102-24 at the half, South Torrance forfeited, much to Leslie's dismay. Continuance of the game wold have allowed her to best the women's national high school record for points in a single game, held by basketball legend Cheryl Miller. Leslie begged the South Torrance coach to reconsider, but to no avail. Miller's record still stands today.

While that personal triumph was denied, Leslie and her team recognized a collective victory when they captured the California state title later that year. Leslie averaged 26.9 points, fifteen rebounds and 6.9 blocked shots per game that season and scored thirty-five points, grabbed twelve rebounds and blocked seven shots in the championship game against Berkeley High School, despite suffering from chicken pox. Her efforts yielded her a prestigious Naismith Award and a Dial Award for the nation's top high school student-athlete. Leslie graduated with a new state record for rebounding (1705). She held varsity letters in volleyball and track, as well as basketball. She also served as class president for three years.

Colleges, Nation Take Notice

Leslie became the most recruited female basketball player since Miller in 1983, and she elected to stay near home and play for Miller's alma matter, University of Southern California (USC). Leslie shone at USC, and was named national and Pac-10 Freshman of the Year. She also became the first-ever freshman to be named to the Pac-10 first team, to which she would be named every year of her college career. She led USC to four NCAA tournaments, advancing to the "Great Eight" in both 1992 and 1994. After her senior season, in which she averaged 21.9 points and 12.3 rebounds per game, she was awarded her second Naismith Award. She was named an All-American in 1992, 1993 and 1994 and USA Basketball named her Female Athlete of the Year in 1993.

In the off-season, Leslie experienced international competition. She played with the U.S. women's Junior World Championship team in 1989 and averaged a team-high 13.3 points and 11.7 rebounds per game. A year later she was the last player cut from the U.S. women's national team and a year after that, she led the U.S. women's team to a gold medal at the World University Games. Leslie was the youngest player to try out for the U.S. Olympic Team in 1992. She did not make the cut, but two years later she made the U.S. women's national team, which captured a gold medal at the Goodwill Games.

Goes Pro, Makes 'Dream Team'

Leslie traveled to Sicilgesso, Italy to play professionally in 1994, as there were at the time no U.S. outlets for female players. The lack of opportunities at home frustrated Leslie. "I think we are cheated as a gender," she told *Entertainment Weekly* "No one knows what happens to all the great people in our game. It seems like we're written off."

Leslie returned home in 1996 to play with the U.S. Olympic "Dream Team." The team earned a gold medal and Leslie led the team in scoring with 19.5 points per

Career Statistics

Yr	Team	GP	Pts	FG%	3P%	FT%	RPG	APG	SPG	BPG	TO	PF
1997	LAS	28	445	.431	.261	.598	9.50	2.6	1.39	2.11	3.89	3.50
1998	LAS	28	549	.478	.391	.768	10.20	2.5	1.50	2.14	3.64	4.30
1999	LAS	32	500	.468	.423	.731	7.80	1.8	1.13	1.53	2.94	4.30
2000	LAS	32	570	.458	.219	.824	9.60	1.9	.97	2.31	3.22	4.20
2001	LAS	31	606	.473	.367	.736	9.60	2.4	1.10	2.29	3.16	4.30
2002	LAS	31	523	.466	.324	.727	10.40	2.7	1.48	2.90	3.48	4.00
TOTAL		182	3193	.463	.336	.732	9.50	2.3	1.25	2.21	3.37	4.10

LAS: Los Angeles Sparks.

Related Biography: Basketball Coach Michael Cooper

Before he became coach of the Los Angeles Sparks, Michael Cooper made his mark as a player with the powerhouse Los Angeles Lakers. Playing in the 1980s alongside such talents as Magic Johnson and Kareem Abdul-Jabbar, "Coop" and the Lakers won five NBA titles and made it to the finals eight times in that decade. He retired as a player for the team in 1990, but he became an assistant coach in 1994. Although his grandfather, a player in the Negro Baseball League, encouraged Cooper to try baseball, Cooper started out as a football player. After sustaining an injury in his first game, he turned to basketball, and stuck with it, playing for Pasadena High School, Pasadena City College and the University of New Mexico. It was at PCC where he began wearing his trademark knee-high athletic socks. He later explained that he opted for the look so his grandmother, who had cataracts, could distinguish him from the other players when she watched his games. Cooper was drafted by the Lakers in 1978 and he was named NBA Defensive Player of the Year in 1987. His full story is recounted in the 1987 autobiography *No Slack.*

game. She also broke the women's Olympic record with thirty-five points in a semifinal game against Japan. After the Olympics, Leslie was offered an opportunity to play professionally at home, in the newly formed Women's National Basketball Association (WNBA). While initially unsure if she wished to continue playing after the Olympics, she eventually signed on with her hometown team, the Los Angeles Sparks.

Again, Leslie emerged as the star of the team. Coach Michael Cooper, who played for the L.A. Lakers, likened her to one of his former teammates. "Lisa is smooth like **Kareem [Abdul-Jabbar]**," he once told *Sports Illustrated.* Leslie led the Sparks to two WNBA championships, in 2001 and 2002, and was named MVP of the finals both times. In the summer of 2002, she scored one giant leap for womankind when, on July 30, she became the first woman to slam dunk in a professional game.

Shines Off-Court

Leslie has not limited her professional interests to basketball. Prior to the Olympics, she signed a contract with the prestigious Wilhelmina Models agency and has been featured in *Vogue.* She has also been a guest actor on several sitcoms, including *Moesha* and *Sister, Sister.*

In addition, after her mother experienced a breast cancer scare, Leslie became a spokesperson for breast cancer awareness and prevention. "Having that scare so close to home, I had to become more educated about it," she told *Ebony.* "I used to wear the pink ribbons but I did not really understand breast cancer." Now, she travels the country to speak on the topic, sometimes accompanied by her mother, and her public service announcements are shown on television and at sports arenas. "I've had a wonderful opportunity to reach a lot of people in inner-city communities and just around the world," Leslie told *Ebony.* "A lot of people come up to me and say 'Thank you. I saw your public service announcement and I got checked and they found a lump. It was benign.' People have told me so many different stories about how they used to be afraid of [the exam]."

Whether its on the basketball court, on television or during public service activities, Leslie maintains a pioneering spirit wherever she ventures. The days when she swore she'd never see a basketball court are clearly behind her. Today, it is impossible to talk of the strides women have made in the sport without mentioning Leslie's name.

CONTACT INFORMATION

Address: c/o Los Angeles Sparks, 555 N. Nash Street, El Segundo, CA 90245.

FURTHER INFORMATION

Books

Sports Stars, Series 1-4. U•X•L, 1994-98

Periodicals

Anderson, Kellie. "That Old L.A. Magic." *Sports Illustrated* (September 9, 2002): 56.

". . . But White Men Still Can't Jump." *Newsweek* (August 12, 2002): 11.

Collier, Aldore. "Lisa Leslie's Crusade." *Ebony* (October 2001): 60.

McCollum, Jack. "Life After Death: Magic Johnson Has Pulled Off One of the Great Comebacks in Sports History, and It's Got Nothing to Do with Basketball." *Sports Illustrated* (August 20, 2001): 70.

"WNBA 2001: L.A. Sparks Take First Title, Three MVPs for Lisa Leslie." *World Almanac and Book of Facts* (Annual, 2002): 1026.

Sketch by Kristin Palm

Carl Lewis
1961-

American track and field athlete

C arl Lewis, the greatest track and field star of the 20th century, attracted intense attention to his sport in the United States in the 1980s. His early successes as a sprinter and long-jumper inspired writers to compare him to **Jesse Owens**, even before he equaled Owens' feat of winning four gold medals in a single Olympics. Negative publicity about his flashy style, his financial ambitions, and what many considered his arrogance made him a controversial figure. But he went on to surpass even Owens' feats by winning gold medals in three more Olympics, and questions about his personality have given way to respect for his unequaled accomplishments.

Growing up

Lewis was born in Birmingham, Alabama in 1961 to Bill and Evelyn Lewis, both teachers and gifted athletes. Evelyn was herself an accomplished track and field athlete who competed in the 80-meter hurdles at the Pan American Games while in college. Bill played football at the Tuskegee Institute, where the couple met. They worked as teachers and marched in civil-rights protests, and Martin Luther King, Jr. baptized Carl's brothers.

The Lewis family moved to New Jersey in 1963. There, Carl and his younger sister Carol picked up their parents' passion for sports. They built a homemade long-jump pit in their back yard and invited friends over for neighborhood track meets. At first, Carl didn't show much athletic talent. "I was small for my age, the runt of the family, the nonathlete," he wrote in his autobiography, *Inside Track*. But when he heard about Bob Beamon's world record long jump of 29 feet 2½ inches at the Olympics in Mexico City in 1968, Lewis marked off the distance in his front yard.

As a kid, Lewis participated in track meets named for Jesse Owens, and he met Owens at two of the meets. He had a growth spurt while a sophomore in high school, and

Carl Lewis

soon became a track and field standout. He put the number 25 on his jacket to show he wanted to jump 25 feet before he graduated. By his senior year, he was meeting his goal regularly. The day of his senior prom, he beat his aging sprinting idol, Steve Williams, in a race.

Several colleges tried to recruit him. In his autobiography, Lewis named the coaches and shoe companies who offered him money and gifts in violation of NCAA rules. He accepted shoes and equipment from Puma and Adidas while still in high school, and signed a six-figure contract with Nike while in college. He chose to go to college at the University of Houston in 1979, though no one there offered him money or a shoe deal, he wrote, so he could compete under well-regarded coach Tom Tellez—who became his personal coach after graduation.

The "next Jesse Owens"

Since long-jumping was causing soreness in Lewis's knees, Tellez convinced him to change his long-jump style from a "hang" jump to a "double-hitch kick," in which the jumper pumps his arms and legs, as if running through the air. Soon he was jumping 27 feet with the double-hitch kick. In 1980, Lewis beat the world's top-rated sprinter in a 100-meter race. Writers began comparing him to Jesse Owens because he was so good at both the long jump and sprinting. He and his sister Carol both qualified for the U.S. Olympic team in 1980, although the U.S. boycotted the Olympics in Moscow to protest the Soviet Union's invasion of Afghanistan.

Chronology

1961	Born July 1 in Birmingham, Alabama
1980	Wins NCAA long-jump titles
1980	Named to U.S. Olympic team (but U.S. boycotts Olympics)
1981	Breaks indoor long-jump world record
1984	Wins four gold medals at Olympics in Los Angeles
1985	Releases album, *The Feeling That I Feel*
1987	Declares that several top athletes are using steroids
1988	Wins two gold medals and one silver at Olympics in Seoul, including gold in 100-meter dash after Ben Johnson tests positive for steroids
1989	Testifies about steroids in sports before Congress
1990	Publishes autobiography, *Inside Track*
1991	Breaks 100-meter world record, but loses long jump when Mike Powell sets new world record at Tokyo World Track Championships
1992	Wins third long-jump gold medal at Olympics in Barcelona
1996	Wins fourth long-jump gold medal at Olympics in Atlanta
1997	Retires

Awards and Accomplishments

1979	New Jersey long jumper of the year
1980	Indoor and outdoor NCAA long-jump titles
1981	Sullivan Award for nation's top amateur athlete
1983	Won three events at national track championships
1983	Associated Press Male Athlete of the Year
1984	Four gold medals at Olympics
1984	Associated Press Male Athlete of the Year
1985	Jesse Owens Award
1988	Two gold medals and one silver medal at Olympics
1991	World record of 9.86 seconds in 100-meter dash
1992	Two gold medals at Olympics
1996	Fourth Olympic long-jump gold medal
1999	Named greatest U.S. Olympian of the 20th century by *Sports Illustrated*
2001	Inducted into National Track and Field Hall of Fame

In summer 1980, Lewis competed on the European track circuit for the first time. He was one of several college athletes who were paid money for running abroad, in violation of NCAA rules. "Any college athlete who had been to Europe and been exposed to the opportunities for track athletes would be crazy not to think about the money," he wrote in his autobiography—whose subtitle, "My Professional Life in Amateur Track and Field," was meant to show that the "amateur" status of his sport had become a facade.

In 1981, Lewis set a world record for an indoor long jump: 27 feet, 10¼ inches, beating a previous record set by Larry Myricks, who had been favored to win the gold medal at the 1980 Olympics. The two developed a bitter rivalry. At the U.S. national championships in 1981, Lewis beat Myricks by making the second-longest jump unaided by wind of all time: 28 feet, 3½ inches. He also won the 100-meter run. In 1982, at a meet in Indianapolis, he made a jump that some say spanned 30 feet. But in a much-disputed ruling, an official nullified the jump, claiming Lewis had stepped past the board at the end of the runway, so the jump was never measured.

That same year, Lewis joined the Lay Witnesses for Christ, a group of Christian athletes, after meeting some of its members at a meet. In 1983, a musician friend introduced Lewis to Sri Chinmoy, an Indian guru who assured Lewis that his teachings about inner peace and meditation didn't conflict with the teachings of Jesus. Lewis came to regard both Chinmoy and the Lay Witnesses as spiritual advisers.

By 1983, Lewis was the most famous athlete in track and field. At the national championships in Indianapolis, he became the first person in decades to win the 100- and 200-meter dashes and the long jump the same year. At the World Track Championships in Helsinki, he led an American sweep of the 100-meter dash, won the long jump, and led the U.S. relay team to a world-record victory.

But as the 1984 Olympics approached, Lewis was developing a reputation for arrogance. A profile in *Sports Illustrated* painted him as self-absorbed. Competitors thought his habit of raising his arms in victory as he reached the finish line was disrespectful to them. Some of them also resented the isolating limos and hotel suites meet promoters gave him.

The 1984 Olympics

Lewis won four gold medals in the Olympics in Los Angeles, matching Owens' performance in Berlin in 1936. He won the 100-meter race in 9.99 seconds, jumped 28 feet ¼ inch to win the long jump, led a U.S. sweep of the 200-meter, and anchored the U.S. team that set a new world record with its win in the 4 x 100 relay.

But a backlash against Lewis's personality detracted from his feats. He was attacked as greedy when his personal manager declared that he wanted Lewis to make as much money as singer Michael Jackson. Lewis decided to stay at a friend's house, not the Olympic village, during the games, leading some to call him a prima donna. He ran his victory lap after the 100-meter race with a large U.S. flag a fan handed him. Some news reports claimed Lewis had planted the fan there to give him the flag—though he hadn't. When Lewis chose not to take all his jumps in the long-jump competition, spectators who hoped to see him break the world record booed—even though he was following good track-meet strategy, saving his strength for his other events. After the controversies, product-endorsement deals Lewis expected didn't come through, and he became bitter toward the press for a while.

After the games, Lewis took acting lessons, played a bit part in a movie, and recorded an album, *The Feeling That I Feel,* and some singles. The album "wasn't bad. It just wasn't good," Lewis later admitted. Still, his single "Break It Up" went gold in Sweden. He recorded with Quincy Jones and sang the national anthem at a few meets.

The Best Ever

Being the world's fastest human and longest jumper wasn't enough for Carl Lewis. ... But in the end there was one thing he couldn't escape: his own talent. One by one, all the trappings that were supposed to make him unique fell away like leaves, leaving only this rare, bare-trunk truth: Excelling at the simplest things — running and jumping — for the longest time is what has made Carl Lewis unlike any athlete who ever lived.

Source: Smith, Gary. *Sports Illustrated* (August 17, 1992): 40.

Related Biography: Track and Field Athlete Carol Lewis

Carol Lewis, Olympic track and field athlete, bobsledder, television sports commentator, and younger sister of track legend Carl Lewis, was born in 1963. As a child, Carol and Carl built a long-jump pit in their back yard and raced against each other. At thirteen, she competed in her first pentathlon, and broke the national record for 13-year-old girls. At fourteen, she came in first in the long jump at the junior nationals in Indianapolis.

In 1980, she earned a place on the U.S. women's Olympic long jump team, which boycotted the Olympics in Moscow. In college, she competed for the University of Houston track and field team, and was an NCAA long-jump champion twice. In 1983, she won both the indoor and outdoor titles. She competed in the 1984 and 1988 Summer Olympics, finishing ninth in the long jump in 1984.

Lewis is also a member of the U.S. bobsled team and a track and field commentator for NBC sports.

In 1987, Lewis's father died. He left his coveted 100-meter gold medal in his father's coffin and pledged to win another one.

Lewis and Ben Johnson

As the 1988 Olympics approached, Canadian sprinter **Ben Johnson** emerged as Lewis's top sprinting rival. At the 1987 World Track Championships in Rome, Johnson beat Lewis and set a new world record of 9.83 seconds in the 100-meter, while Lewis ran a 9.93. While in Rome, Johnson's coach was overheard making a comment that implied Johnson was taking steroids to enhance his performance. Word got back to Lewis. "A lot of people have come from nowhere and are running unbelievably," Lewis told a reporter. "There are gold medalists at this meet already that are on drugs," he added, but didn't reveal any names. In 1988, Lewis beat Johnson at a meet in Zurich, where he heard another allegation that Johnson was using performance-enhancing drugs.

At the Olympics in Seoul, South Korea, just before Lewis and Johnson raced in the 100-meter dash, the two shook hands. "As I looked at him," Lewis recalled in *Inside Track,* "I noticed that his eyes were very yellow. A sign of steroid use." Johnson took first in the race with a record-breaking 9.79 seconds, while Lewis took second with 9.92. Lewis thought he'd failed in his goal to win another gold medal in the 100-meter for his father. But before the games were over, Johnson tested positive for steroid use and was stripped of the record and the medal. Lewis was awarded the gold instead. He also won the gold for the long jump with a jump of 28 feet, 7½ inches, and won a silver medal in the 200-meter (his friend Joe DeLoach took the gold).

Lewis continued to speak out against steroid use. He testified before a U.S. congressional committee on the subject, and he called for an independent drug-testing agency to monitor each sport. Once, speaking to a group of college students, he implied that he thought fellow U.S. Olympic athlete **Florence Griffith-Joyner** used steroids —but the charges were never proved, and Lewis backed down from his statement.

The 1992 and 1996 Olympics

As Lewis turned 30, other athletes challenged his dominance of track and field. Leroy Burrell, Lewis's teammate in the Santa Monica Track Club, edged him out in the 100-meter dash at the 1990 Goodwill Games and the 1991 national championships. At the World Track Championships in Tokyo in 1991, Lewis set a new world record in the 100-meter, 9.86 seconds, beating Burrell by .02 seconds. But at the same meet, long jump rival **Mike Powell** broke Lewis's ten-year undefeated long jump streak. Lewis surpassed 29 feet three times, including a personal best of 29 feet, 11½ inches—but Powell broke the world record with a jump of 29 feet, 4½ inches.

The next year, Lewis had a sinus infection during the Olympic trials, and he only qualified for the long-jump team and as a relay team alternate. But at the Olympics in Barcelona, Lewis beat Powell with a jump of 28 feet 5½ inches to win his third long-jump gold. He led the relay team to a new world record, just as he had in Los Angeles. "This was my best Olympics," he said—two gold medals, no controversy.

Ever since 1979, when a young Lewis beat his aging idol Williams, he vowed to stop running once he was past his prime. By 1996, it looked like the time might have come for him to take his own advice. That March, he finished last in a 60-meter semi-final heat at one meet. But he was determined to make the Olympic team once more. In the Olympic trials, he almost failed to qualify as a long-jumper, but pulled it out with a 27-foot, 2½-inch jump. At the Olympics in Atlanta, at age thirty-five, with gray peppering his hair, he stunned the crowd and himself with a 27-foot, 10 ¾-inch jump, winning his fourth long-jump gold medal. It was "better than all the others," he told a *People* reporter. "All the others, I was expected to win. This time I was a competitor. Before I was an icon."

Lewis retired from track and field in 1997 at a ceremony during halftime of a football game at his old alma mater, the University of Houston. His nine Olympic gold medals leave him tied with 1920s Finnish runner Paavo Nurmi for the most ever. In 1999, *Sports Illustrated* named him the best American Olympic athlete of the 20th century.

Today, Carl Lewis lives in Los Angeles. Since retiring from sports, he has been co-owner of a Houston restaurant and created his own line of sportswear, named SMTC after his old Santa Monica Track Club. In 1999, *Texas Monthly* reported that he was still running twice a week, as well as lifting weights and cycling.

Lewis is pursuing an acting career. He played a security guard in the 2002 made-for-TV movie *Atomic Twister,* and he will appear in the science-fiction movie *Alien Hunter,* scheduled for release in 2003.

CONTACT INFORMATION

Address: CLEG, Inc., 3350 Wilshire Blvd., Suite 675, Los Angeles, CA 90010.

SELECTED WRITINGS BY LEWIS:

(With Jeffrey Marx) *Inside Track: My Professional Life in Amateur Track and Field,* Simon & Schuster, 1990.
(With Jeffrey Marx) *One More Victory Lap: My Personal Diary of an Olympic Year,* Aum Publications, 1996.

FURTHER INFORMATION

Books

Klots, Steve. *Carl Lewis.* New York: Chelsea House, 1995.
Lewis, Carl, with Jeffrey Marx. *Inside Track: My Professional Life in Amateur Track and Field.* New York: Simon & Schuster, 1990.

Periodicals

"Ali, Jordan, Lewis and Brown named among century's greatest athletes." *Jet* (December 20, 1999): 51.
"Between halves of a football game, Carl Lewis's storied career comes to a close." *Sports Illustrated* (September 22, 1997): 26.
"Hall of Honor add six former Cougars." *Daily Cougar* (University of Houston student newspaper) (April 23, 2002).
Hollandsworth, Skip. "Athlete of the Century: Carl Lewis." *Texas Monthly* (December 1999): 146.
"Just like gold times." *People* (August 12, 1996): 92.
Layden, Tim. "A fleeting glimpse of the past." *Sports Illustrated* (April 15, 1996): 84.
"Olympians inducted into National Track and Field Hall of Fame." *Capper's* (December 11, 2001): 12.
Reilly, Rick. "Leap to glory." *Sports Illustrated* (August 5, 1996): 54.

Other

Carl Lewis Web Site. http://www.carllewis.com

Sketch by Erick Trickey

Lennox Lewis
1965-

British boxer

In the late 1990s and early 2000s, Lennox Lewis was the boxing heavyweight champion of the world. He was Great Britain's first heavyweight champion since 1897 when he became the World Boxing Council heavyweight champion in 1993. After not posting a loss in his 109 amateur bouts, Lewis had a professional record of 40-2-1 through 2002. While Lewis had a great right, he often played it safe in fights, which drew criticism from observers who believed that he never unleashed his full potential as a boxer.

Lewis was born on September 2, 1965 in the East End of London, the son of Violet Lewis and her then boyfriend Carlton Brooks. Both were natives of Jamaica. Lewis's father worked in an auto plant, but was not involved in the upbringing of Lewis or his older brother Dennis. Lewis was raised in tough, working class neighborhoods.

When he was nine years old, Lewis moved with his mother to Canada. After a year or so, he went back to England to live with an aunt. In the two years he spent in England, he began getting in trouble, picking fights, among other problems. His mother brought him back to Canada when he was twelve years old, where he spent the rest of his youth.

Introduced to Boxing

While Lewis's mother worked in a Styrofoam factory, he attended schools in Kitchener, Ontario. A hyperactive child, he began getting into fights in Canada as well. Lewis told Pat Putnam of *Sports Illustrated,* "That's when I became a fighter. All the kids made fun of my accent, and I punched out the lot. After my third strapping with the belt, my teacher advised I take my aggressions out in sport."

In 1978, Lewis had his first amateur bout. He calmed down, and learned to love boxing. He told William Nack of *Sports Illustrated,* "I liked it. It was ego against ego. Both looking at each other all the time. A chess game. The one-on-one is what appealed to me about boxing." Lewis was growing so large that he boxed against boys older than him.

In high school, however, Lewis did not just box. While attending Cameron Heights Collegiate High, he played fullback on football team, power forward on basketball team, and did track as a shot-putter. But boxing was his focus after a while, and Lewis was a big fan of **Muhammad Ali.**

Success as Amateur Boxer

Throughout his successful amateur career, Lewis was coached by Arnie Boehm and Adrian Teodorescu.

Lennox Lewis

Boehm was particularly influential in Lewis's development as a boxer and a man. By the early 1980s, Lewis was gaining a reputation as an impressive boxer. In 1983, he won gold medals at both the Canada Winter Games and the World Junior Championships. That led to Lewis being named athlete of the year in Canada in 1983.

Lewis won a number of major tournaments. He captured gold at the National Senior Championships in 1984, 1985, 1986 and 1987, and at the Commonwealth Games in 1986 and the Pan Am games in 1987. He was the Canadian Super Heavyweight champion every year from 1984 to 1988. In 1988, Lewis represented Canada at the Summer Olympic Games in Seoul, Korea, as a super heavyweight. He won the gold medal by defeating Riddick Bowe in the second round by knockout. At the end of his amateur career, Lewis had won all 109 of his bouts.

Turned Professional as a Boxer

In 1989, Lewis turned professional, but instead of remaining in Canada, he returned to Great Britain. He did this, in part, because a group of British backers, including manager Frank Maloney, gave him big signing bonus. There were also accusations that he was being used in Canada and his boxing career was not moving forward. Lewis also picked up a new trainer, American John Davenport, who emphasized the athleticism of the 6'5", 230 lbs boxer.

Lewis's first professional fight was against Al Malcolm on June 27, 1989, in London. Lewis won in the second round. He soon dominated the competition in Europe. In 1990, he became European heavyweight champion by defeating Jean Chanet. In 1991, he defeated Gary Mason by TKO to become British heavyweight champion. The fight ended Mason's career, though it was not much of a bout.

Many of Lewis's early fights were not unlike the Mason fight. Most of his first sixteen fights were with unworthy competition, like 39-year-old former WBA (World Boxing Association) champion Mike Weaver, whom Lewis knocked out in the sixth round. These fights brought Lewis little respect in the boxing community, but his handlers wanted to start him slowly.

Lewis had undeniable talent. He was not just a fighter, but a great boxer and great puncher. While his knockout punch was his right, he also had a strong jab. Though his competition had not been strong, Lewis had attracted enough attention to get a two-fight deal with HBO and three-fight pay per view deal with Time Warner in 1991.

In February 1992, Lewis was pushed to the full ten rounds in a fight against Levi Billups. This led to a change in trainers, as Lewis felt he had become a very mechanical fighter. He hired **Sugar Ray Leonard**'s trainer Pepe Correa. Correa was in Lewis's corner as Lewis was inching near to contending for a world heavyweight title.

Won First Professional Title

In 1992, Lewis defeated Donovan Ruddock, making him the best challenger for a world heavyweight champion. Lewis had been an underdog in the fight, but Lewis knocked Ruddock down once in the first round and twice in round two. While Lewis did become a champion, he did not have to fight for it.

In December 1992, World Boxing Council (WBC) heavyweight champion Riddick Bowe (who defeated **Evander Holyfield** to win the belt) refused to fight Lewis, except for what the Lewis camp considered an absurdly low amount of money, and had the WBC belt taken from him—Bowe did retain the WBA and IBF (International

Related Biography: Trainer Arnie Boehm

Arnie Boehm was Lennox Lewis's trainer during the whole of his amateur career. Boehm guided Lewis from childhood to his Olympic gold medal to the end of his amateur career, acting as a father figure to the young boxer. Boehm himself had been a boxer and trained with Jerome "Hook" McComb, a police officer who founded the Waterloo Regional Boxing Academy in Kitchener, Ontario, Canada. Boehm also learned how to train boxers from McComb, and later ran the Waterloo Academy himself after 1981. In addition to guiding his boxers in the ring, he also encouraged them to lead productive lives. Lewis was arguably the best fighter trained by Boehm, though he did train three other Olympians and twenty-four national champions. He died of a heart attack at his gym in October 2002.

Boxing Federation) titles. Bowe literally threw the belt in the trash in a media spectacle. Though Lewis obtained the championship in an unconventional matter, he became a national hero in Great Britain. The last British heavyweight champion was Ruby Robert Fitzsimmons in 1897. Lewis then signed a four-fight deal with Time Warner Sports.

In May 1993, Lewis had his first fight in defense of his WBC tile. He defeated Tony Tucker by unanimous decision after knocking him down twice in twelve rounds. Later that year he also knocked out fellow Brit Frank Bruno in the seventh round in another defense of his title. In 1994, Lewis defeated Phil Jackson by technical knockout in the eighth round. Despite these victories, Lewis still did not have much professional respect among fighters, especially in the United States, and he found it hard to get Americans to fight him.

Lost WBC Title

Lewis's reputation as a boxer took a big hit in 1994 when he lost his WBC title to Oliver McCall in an upset. Lewis wanted the fight, but lost by technical knockout. McCall was the underdog, and a former sparring partner of heavyweight champion **Mike Tyson**. McCall got Lewis with his use of a quick overhand right.

For his next fights, Lewis looked to put himself in a position to be eligible at another shot at a heavyweight title and perhaps at a fight with Tyson. He again switched trainers, hiring the legendary Emanuel Steward, who trained a number of winning boxers, in 1995. Steward added more punches to Lewis's repertoire including a left hook, uppercuts, and the jab, but could not give Lewis the aggression many fight experts believed Lewis lacked.

To be eligible for a chance at the title, Lewis fought Ray Mercer in 1996. Though Lewis won by split decision, many who saw the fight did not believe that he deserved the victory. One judge scored it as a draw, while the other two gave it to Lewis by a small margin.

Lewis's next goal was WBC heavyweight champion Tyson. A deal could not be reached between the boxers, and Tyson gave up the belt rather than fight Lewis. Lewis

sued him to force a fight, but it did not happen. Lewis then regained the WBC title by defeating McCall in 1996.

In 1997, Lewis defended his WBC title by defeating Andrew Golota. Lewis only took thirty-six punches in the first round to win. He knocked Golota down twice before knocking him out. This was one of his best fights, showing Lewis's power. Richard Hoffer wrote in *Sports Illustrated*, "Lewis's swarming knockout of challenger Golota was so swift and conclusive that it was impossible not to be encouraged by his emergence as a force in the sport." This fight gave Lewis the test that he needed and his British handlers had avoided. He also defended his WBC title by defeating Shannon Briggs and Zelijko Mavrovic in 1998.

Controversial Fight with Holyfield

In early 1999, Lewis faced the biggest challenge of his career to that point when he fought IBF and WBA titleholder Evander Holyfield in a title unification bout. Their March fight was extremely controversial. The judges ruled the twelve rounds a draw, though most observers believed that Lewis defeated Holyfield easily and cleanly with Lewis connecting on 348 punches while Holyfield only managed 130. The crowd at the Madison Square Garden match booed the decision, and the sanctioning bodies ordered a rematch within six months.

Won Unified Titles

Lewis fought Holyfield again in November 1999, and this time, he won the fight to become the undisputed heavyweight champion. Lewis won by decision over twelve rounds, and while many believed that he outfought Holyfield, there was some division among ringside observers. Lewis used his tactical abilities to win, instead of fighting, and was criticized for not knocking Holyfield out. As Hoffer wrote in *Sports Illustrated*, "Lewis seems to be a guy who, above all, doesn't want to get knocked out. He's not a coward, or else he wouldn't have achieved what he has, and he has fought bravely when he has had to. He's just too particular, too fastidious to give into any unnecessary abandon."

Lewis defended his unified title a number of times, defeating Michael Grant, Francois Botha, and David Tua in 2000. Defeating Grant was a significant victory. It was the first time Lewis beat someone taller than himself, with Grant at 6'7". Lewis beat him by knockout in second round, after dropping him in three times in first round. The fight showed Lewis's greatness and ability to dominate, and improved his reputation as a boxer. Though over thirty-four, he had finally found his way.

Lost Unified Titles

Lewis suffered the second defeat of his professional career when he had a title defense fight against Hasam Rahman in South Africa in April 2001. Rahman was a 20-1 underdog in his second title fight ever. Lewis es-

Lennox Lewis, right

sentially did not take the fight seriously enough. Lewis did not train that hard and came to the bout at his highest fighting weight ever. Rahman knocked out Lewis in the fifth round. This was a bad loss for Lewis, and negatively affected his reputation.

The rematch between Rahman and Lewis came seven months later, and Lewis had something to prove. He used his devastating right after a combination in the fourth round to knockout Rahman. Though he won, even his trainer Steward believed Lewis did not live up to his potential in this fight. Hoffer wrote in *Sports Illustrated,* "He is not a man who seems inclined to realize his immense potential, but past disappointments—his often overly cautious style in victories has been ever more damning than his knockout defeats—will dim in the reflection of this powerful win."

Defeated Tyson

Lewis again showed his power as a fighter when he finally got the chance to fight Tyson in June 2002. Lewis had wanted this fight for years, but Tyson had avoided him. The pair even got into a scuffle at the press conference announcing the fight in February 2002. Tyson charged Lewis and bit him in the leg. The fight took place at the Pyramid in Memphis, Tennessee, because Tyson had problems getting a license elsewhere. Lewis dominated the fight, the first in which Tyson was an underdog. He knocked Tyson out in the eighth round, though he could have done it earlier in the fight.

After the victory, Lewis was left with a problem. He was arguably the best heavyweight fighter but had no real competition except to fight Tyson again and was an enigma who did not draw many boxing fans. He was forced to give up his IBF belt in September 2002 because the challenger they picked, Chris Byrd, would not be challenging. Lewis was scheduled to fight Vitali Klitschko, a Ukrainian, in the United States in April 2003, then Klitschko's brother, Wladimir, and perhaps Tyson again, then retire. After the Tyson fight in 2002, Hoffer wrote in *Sports Illustrated,* "He avenged those defeats [McCall and Rahman], his attention restored, and now with this fight he must be recognized as a pretty powerful performer. If Lewis retired now—and that's possible, as he seems at long last to have cleaned out the division—he need not apologize for his departure."

CONTACT INFORMATION

Address: c/o Office of Lennox Lewis, Gainsborough House, 81 Oxford St., London W1D 2EU England. Online: www.lennox-lewis.com.

FURTHER INFORMATION

Books

Page, James. *Black Olympian Medalists*. Englewood, CO: 1991.

Parry, Melanie, ed. *Chambers Biographical Dictionary*. Chambers, 1997.

Periodicals

Associated Press (October 10, 2002).

"Boxing: IBF Axed by Lewis." *Birmingham Evening Mail* (September 6, 2002): 83.

"Boxing: Lewis Lines Up Title Defence in US Vitali Klitschko." *Birmingham Evening Mail* (December 21, 2002): 45.

"Boxing: Lewis Plans Next Attack After Tyson." *Birmingham Evening Mail* (December 24, 2002): 50.

Dettmer, Jamie. "Fighting Expectations." *Insight on the News* (June 3, 1996): 37.

"The Doctor is a Champ." *Jet* (December 27, 1999): 50.

Eskenazi, Gerald. "Lennox Lewis Is a Man on a Mission." *New York Times* (May 6, 1994): B14.

Friend, Tom. "No One Knows Him, Except Her Majesty." *New York Times* (May 8, 1993): section 1, p. 31.

Gildea, William. "Boxers and History Collide in New York." *Washington Post* (March 12, 1999): D3.

Gildea, William. "In Vegas, No Laying a Globe on Lewis." *Washington Post* (May 6, 1993): B1.

"Heavyweight champion Lewis hints at retirement." Associated Press (August 4, 2002).

Hoffer, Richard. "Bad Hair Day." *Sports Illustrated* (November 20, 2000): 48.

Hoffer, Richard. "Drawn and Cornered." *Sports Illustrated* (October 13, 1997): 68.

Hoffer, Richard. "Grand Larceny." *Sports Illustrated* (March 22, 1999): 60.

Hoffer, Richard. "Hard Rocked." *Sports Illustrated* (April 30, 2001): 36.

Hoffer, Richard. "Hitting It Big." *Sports Illustrated* (May 8, 2000): 44.

Hoffer, Richard. "It Takes Tua to Tango." *Sports Illustrated* (November 13, 2000): 48.

Hoffer, Richard. "Lights Out." *Sports Illustrated* (June 17, 2002): 50.

Hoffer, Richard. "Payback." *Sports Illustrated* (November 26, 2001): 40.

Hoffer, Richard. "Redefining Moment." *Sports Illustrated* (November 15, 1999): 54.

Hoffer, Richard. "Triumph of Timidity." *Sports Illustrated* (November 22, 1999): 60.

"Holyfield-Lewis Heavyweight Championship Bout Ends in Controversial Draw." *Jet* (March 29, 1999): 51.

"Lennox Lewis Cements His Legacy After Beating Mike Tyson for Heavyweight Championships." *Jet* (June 24, 2002): 52.

"Lennox Lewis regains titles in 4th-round KO of Rahman in Vegas." *Jet* (December 10, 2001): 46.

"Lewis defends WBC crown." *Jet* (May 23, 1994): 51.

"Lewis Stops Botha in Second Round." *Jet* (August 7, 2000): 48.

Nack, William. "The great Brit hope." *Sports Illustrated* (February 1, 1993): 38.

"Pre-fight brawl." *Jet* (February 11, 2002): 50.

Putnam, Pat. "Bloody poor show." *Sports Illustrated* (October 11, 1993): 36.

Putnam, Pat. "The champ who fights chumps." *Sports Illustrated* (October 28, 1991): 102.

Putnam, Pat. "Good show!." *Sports Illustrated* (November 9, 1992): 102.

Putnam, Pat. "Lennox Lewis." *Sports Illustrated* (May 17, 1993): 58.

Remnick, David. "The MORalist." *New Yorker* (July 1, 2002).

"Tyson gives up WBC crown." *Jet* (October 14, 1996): 46.

Williams, David et al. "Lewis: It's Rematch or Retirement." *Commercial Appeal* (July 13, 2002): D1.

Other

"Arnie Boehm." theloxx.com. http://theloxx.com/Arnie Boehm/default.htm (January 5, 2003).

"Boxing legend Arnie Boehm dies." TheRecord.com. http://www.therecord.com/cgi-bin/PFP.cgi?doc=news/obituaries (January 5, 2003).

Sketch by A. Petruso

Nancy Lieberman
1958-

American basketball player

One of the greatest women's basketball players of all time, Nancy Lieberman had a lengthy, decorated career and logged a number of "firsts." At age 18 she was the youngest basketball player to win an Olympic medal as part of the 1976 U.S. team. Ten years later she became the first woman to play in a men's professional

Nancy Lieberman

league, the United States Basketball League. Lieberman was also the first woman to earn a million dollars as a basketball player. Inducted into the Basketball Hall of Fame in 1996, "Lady Magic" came out of retirement less than a year later to play one season in the new Women's National Basketball Association (WNBA); at 38 she was the league's oldest player. Lieberman remains a presence in the sport as a television commentator and as an outspoken promoter of women's athletics.

Lieberman, born in Brooklyn, New York, grew up in a Jewish family in Far Rockaway, Queens. As a 10-year-old tomboy, she spent her free time playing basketball with boys in the schoolyard. She scoffed when her mother said playing sports wasn't "ladylike." Lieberman, according to the *Richmond Times Dispatch,* recalled at her Hall of Fame induction: "I remember getting up and standing there with my hands on my hips and saying [to my mother], 'Yeah, well, I'll tell you something: That's how I'm going to make history one of these days'—and then turning around and walking out of the kitchen."

She quickly established herself as a star at Far Rockaway High School. As a 14-year-old All-American athlete, she would take the subway to Harlem to shoot hoops with the best players. There, she developed an aggressive, street-smart style new to women's basketball. By 1974, when Lieberman was a high school sophomore, she was invited to try out for the American Basketball Association's national team, which would train to compete in the 1975 Pan American Games and the 1976 Olympics. She became one of the 12 women selected for the USA Team.

Dubbed "Lady Magic"

Lieberman helped lead her club to gold medals at the 1975 Pan American Games and the World Championships. The following year, the team participated in the inaugural women's Olympic basketball team competition. Lieberman was 17 when she started playing at the 1976 Olympics in Montreal; she had just turned 18 when the team won silver, making her the youngest basketball player to win an Olympic medal.

Lieberman's Olympic glory caught the attention of universities around the country. Thanks to a new law, Title IX, that barred discrimination at federally funded schools, colleges were starting to offer scholarships to female athletes. Lieberman received more than 100 scholarship offers. She chose Old Dominion University in Norfolk, Virginia. "I always wanted to go to a place nobody had heard of because I thought of myself as an underdog, and I wanted to help build something," she said in the *Omaha World Herald.*

As a 5-foot-10 point guard, Lieberman helped lead Old Dominion to national titles in 1979 and 1980. During her collegiate career, she scored 2,430 points, grabbed 1,167 rebounds, and dealt 961 assists. Three times an All-American, she was the only two-time winner of the Wade Trophy, which recognizes the National Player of the Year in women's college basketball. Lieberman became known as "Lady Magic," deeming her the female equivalent of Los Angeles Lakers star **Magic Johnson**.

Played in Men's League

Drafted in 1980 by the Dallas Diamonds of the Women's Professional Basketball League (WBL), Lieberman left college before completing her degree.

Where Is She Now?

Lieberman lives in Dallas, her hometown of more than 20 years. She is chief executive officer of Nancy Lieberman Enterprises, a business launched in the 1980s to run Nancy Lieberman basketball camps for girls. She is also a basketball analyst for ESPN, calling WNBA games and men's and women's college games for the television network. An active public speaker at Fortune 500 companies and high school banquets, Lieberman promotes the benefits of sports for young women. "Research shows that girls who are involved in sports have fewer unwanted pregnancies, are less likely to drop out of school, and have higher self-esteem," she told Brian D. Sweany of *Texas Monthly*. Lieberman, in February, 2003, expressed interest in the coaching job for the WNBA's Connecticut Sun (the former Orlando Miracle).

She could not compete in the 1980 Olympics because of President Carter's boycott over the Soviet Union's invasion of Afghanistan. Instead, she helped guide the Diamonds to the 1981 championship series, where they lost to the Nebraska Wranglers. After leaving basketball briefly to serve as a personal trainer to tennis star **Martina Navratilova**, Lieberman in 1984 returned to the Diamonds, now part of the new Women's American Basketball Association (WABA). Averaging 27 points per game and voted the league's Most Valuable Player, Lieberman helped lead the Diamonds to a 1984 WABA championship. Both the WBL and the WABA eventually folded, however.

Lieberman made history in 1986 when she became the first woman to play in a men's professional league. Drafted by the Springfield Fame of the United States Basketball League (USBL), she took her place in her first men's team. In 1987 she switched to the USBL's Long Island Knights, and in 1988 she joined the Washington Generals, where she met her future husband, teammate Tim Cline. The couple's career with the Generals included a world tour with the Harlem Globetrotters. Regarding her USBL experience, Lieberman said at her Hall of Fame induction: "They should put the bench I sat on in the Hall of Fame because I saw more time there."

Lieberman retired from basketball in the early 1990s after two disappointments. For the first time in her career, she was cut from a team, failing to qualify for the 1990 Goodwill Games. Nor did she qualify for the 1992 Olympics. Yet Lieberman had begun a new career as a sports commentator and writer. At the 1988 and 1992 Olympics in Seoul, South Korea and Barcelona, Spain, respectively, she served as an NBC-TV women's basketball commentator. She had also completed her autobiography, *Lady Magic*.

In 1993 Lieberman became the first woman ever inducted into the New York City Basketball Hall of Fame. The following year she gave birth to her son, Timothy Joseph, Jr., or "T.J." On May 6, 1996, she was inducted into the Naismith Memorial Basketball Hall of Fame in Springfield, Massachusetts.

Made Brief Comeback

Just a few months after her Hall of Fame induction, word spread that Lieberman was considering coming out of retirement to play in the WNBA. American sports fans, it seemed, were beginning to take women's basketball seriously; the WNBA, with its partnership with the deep-pocketed NBA, seemed poised for growth. Lieberman started training seriously and in February, 1997, the 38-year-old player was the next-to-last draft pick of the Phoenix Mercury. "I feel like I'm a cat that has nine lives," she told Tom Flaherty of the *Milwaukee Journal Sentinel*. "I mean, how many chances do you get to do what you love at this level?"

Lieberman played with the Mercury for one year. Turning 39 during the season, she was the oldest player on the WNBA. Phoenix led the league in attendance and won the Western Conference title before losing to the New York Liberty in the playoff semifinals.

From 1998 to 2000, Lieberman was general manager and coach of the WNBA's Detroit Shock. In her first year, while leading the Shock to a 17-13 winning record and a WNBA playoff; players regarded her as highly critical. According to the Associated Press, player Korie Hlede was "abusive and manipulative, playing mind games." Lieberman, who traded Hlede to Utah, downplayed any controversy. "Korie had a very good rookie season, and she really did a lot to jump-start our program," she said. "Korie, her self-esteem was tied to her minutes and starting, and that's why I'm not mad at Korie because I went through that as a young player, too."

Before she left coaching in 2000, Lieberman received her degree from Old Dominion, having gone back to school to complete a marketing degree. Also during her coaching tenure, Lieberman served as president of the Women's Sports Foundation, an advocacy organization

Career Statistics

Yr	Team	GP	Pts	FG%	FT%	RPG	APG	SPG	BPG
1976-77	ODU	27	563	.473	.709	10.1	7.9	–	–
1977-78	ODU	34	681	.432	.730	9.6	5.9	–	–
1978-79	ODU	36	625	.478	.790	7.7	7.1	4.0	0.4
1979-80	ODU	37	561	.533	.779	7.9	8.0	3.8	0.6
1997	PHO	2	8	.273	–	3.0	2.5	–	–

ODU: Old Dominion University; PHO: Phoenix Mercury.

founded by tennis legend **Billie Jean King**, from 1999 through 2000.

Retired from playing but still highly visible in basketball as an ESPN commentator and columnist on its Web site, Lieberman, as a pioneer of the game, remains a source of inspiration to female athletes of all ages.

"I think I've always played with sort of a chip on my shoulder," she said at her Hall of Fame induction ceremonies. "It seems like there has always been someone there at every step of the way to say, 'You can't,' or 'You shouldn't,' or 'You won't.' I've always felt driven to prove those people wrong. If you tell me I can't, my reaction is: 'Yes, I can-watch, and I'll prove it.'"

SELECTED WRITINGS BY LIEBERMAN:

(With Myrna Frommer and Harvey Frommer) *Basketball My Way.* New York: Scriber, 1982.

(With Debby Jennings) *The Autobiography of Nancy Lieberman-Cline.* Champaign, IL: Sagamore, 1992.

(With Nancy, Robin Roberts and Kevin Warneke) *Basketball for Women: Becoming a Complete Player.* Champaign, IL: Human Kinetics, 1996.

FURTHER INFORMATION

Books

Greenberg, Doreen, and Michael Greenberg. *A Drive to Win: The Story of Nancy Lieberman-Cline.* Terre Haute, IN: Cardinal, 2000.

Periodicals

Dorr, Vic, Jr. "Lieberman's Induction Proves She Did Know Best." *Richmond Times Dispatch* (May 7, 1996): E1.

Flaherty, Tom. "Ready, Set, Go: Lieberman Is Prepared for Another Run at History." *Milwaukee Journal Sentinel* (June 21, 1997): Sports, 1.

Greenberg, Mel. "Love of Game Led to Fame." *Omaha World Herald* (May 11, 1996): 52.

"Lieberman a Taskmaster as Shock Coach." Associated Press (May 31, 2000).

Sweany, Brian D. "Where Are They Now?" *Texas Monthly* (September 2001): Sports, 109.

Ziegel, Vic. "Nancy, 1st Lady of Women's Hoops." *Daily News* (New York; February 28, 1997): 78.

Other

Altavilla, John. "Coaching List Grows." Hartford Courant, http://www.ctnow.com/sports/ (February 5, 2003).

Nancy Lieberman Official Web Site. http://www.ladymagic.com (January 22, 2003).

"Nancy Lieberman." Naismith Memorial Basketball Hall of Fame. http://www.hoophall.com/hall offamers/nancy_lieberman.htm (January 22, 2003).

Sketch by Wendy Kagan

Eric Lindros
1973-

Canadian hockey player

Though considered one of the most talented players to ever play in the National Hockey League (NHL), Eric Lindros has had a controversial career from his days in junior hockey. Some believe that he has never fully realized his potential as a player. A power forward in the truest sense, Lindros has size (6'5"; 220 lbs), strong skating ability, a scorer's touch, and is a master of physical play. However, he has also had numerous injuries, including a series of concussions, that affected his abilities. In addition, Lindros had public run-ins with the management of the team that drafted him (Quebec Nordiques) and the team he spent much of his career with (Philadelphia Flyers), that left his public image tainted.

Lindros was born on February 28, 1973, in London, Ontario, Canada to Carl and Bonnie Lindros. He had a

Eric Lindros

younger brother, Brett (who also became a professional hockey player, though his career was cut short because of concussions), and younger sister, Robin. Lindros's father was an accountant who had played minor league hockey in the Chicago Blackhawk system as well as college football at Western Ontario University. His mother was a nurse who had been a track athlete in high school.

When Lindros was seven years old, he began playing hockey in a youth league in London. It soon became evident that he had outstanding abilities, and he was motivated to play from an early age. He was better than most players his age. But hockey was not the focus of Lindros's life. His parents ensured that he had outside interests, including playing the trumpet, and that he took summers off from hockey. The family moved to Toronto when Lindros was ten, and it was there that he played Junior B hockey for St. Michael's College in Toronto.

Refused to Play for Greyhounds

When he was fifteen, Lindros was drafted number one by the Junior A Ontario Hockey League. He was selected by the Sault Ste. Marie Greyhounds, for which **Wayne Gretzky** had played. Lindros was not allowed to play for them because his parents did not want him to go there. They believed the travel involved in playing for

Chronology

1973	Born on February 28, in London, Ontario, Canada
1988	Drafted by the Sault Ste. Marie Greyhounds (OHL), but refuses to play
1988-90	Plays junior hockey for Detroit Compuware (NAHL)
1990-92	Plays junior hockey for Oshawa Generals
1991	Drafted by the Quebec Nordiques in the first round. Because he refuses to play for them, does not play in the 1991-92 season
1992	Plays on the Canadian Olympic team, winning silver medal; the rights to Lindros are traded to Flyers, who sign him; plays on the Canada Cup team
1996	Plays on World Cup team for Canada
1997	Plays in Stanley Cup Finals but loses in four straight games to Detroit
1998	Plays in the Olympics for Team Canada, serving as captain
1999	Suffers collapsed lung and chest injury after game in Nashville on April 1
2000	Plays in the NHL All-Star Game
2000-01	Sits out regular season in contract dispute with Flyers
2001	Rights traded to the New York Rangers; on December 28, suffers his seventh known concussion
2002	Plays for Team Canada in the Olympics, winning gold medal

such a remotely located team would negatively affect his education.

Instead, Lindros chose to play for the less prestigious North American Junior Hockey League. He played for the Detroit Compuware team based in Farmington, Michigan, and attended a local high school. Though he was playing against lesser talent, he was already regarded as one of the best young players in hockey. His future general manager, Bobby Clarke of the Philadelphia Flyers, told Jay Greenberg of *Sports Illustrated,* "He's the best 16-year-old player I've ever seen. He could play in the NHL right now."

After graduating from Farmington High School in January 1990, Lindros was left with several options because of his talent. He had a scholarship offer to play for the University of Michigan. Instead, Lindros was allowed to play Junior A hockey for the Oshawa Generals near his Toronto home, after the Greyhounds traded his rights (for three players, two draft picks and cash) to Oshawa because of a rule created just to service him.

Lindros spent the second half of the 1989-90 season with the Generals. In twenty-five games, scored nine goals and had nineteen assists. But his refusal to play for the Greyhounds still had repercussions: he was derided about the situation. He also had to deal with much physical play because he was so much bigger than the other players. He was often challenged and had to defend himself. Lindros stuck it out and played well. In the full 1990-91 season, Lindros had seventy-one goals and seventy-eight assists. In addition to hockey, Lindros also attended York University on a part-time basis.

Drafted by Quebec

By the time of the 1991 NHL draft, the first Lindros was eligible for, he was the clear cut best player avail-

Awards and Accomplishments

1992	Silver medal as part of the Canadian hockey team at the Winter Olympics
1994	Voted the Flyers MVP by his teammates for the 1993-94 season
1995	Hart Memorial Trophy as the NHL's MVP and Lester B. Pearson Award; All-Star, first team; *Sporting News* and *The Hockey News* player of the year
2002	Gold medal as part of the Canadian hockey team at the Winter Olympics

Related Biography: President and General Manager Bobby Clarke

One of Eric Lindros's early champions who later became one of his biggest adversaries was Philadelphia Flyer general manager and president Bobby Clarke. Through Clarke and Lindros had a solid relationship when Clarke came to the Flyers as general manager and president in 1994, their relationship disintegrated in the late 1990s. He made Lindros sit out a year as Clarke waited for the right deal to trade his rights. Clarke had been with the Flyers in some capacity for over thirty years.

Clarke began playing hockey as a child and put up impressive numbers as a junior player for the Flin Flon Bombers of the Western Canada Junior Hockey League. Because he suffered from diabetes, NHL teams shied away from him. Still, he was drafted by the Philadelphia Flyers in 1969, and played his way on to the team at that fall's training camp. By the early 1970s, he became a prolific scorer and was named captain of the Flyers. As one of the notorious "Broad Street Bullies," as the tough Philadelphia team was known, Clarke won three Hart Trophies, one Selke Trophy, and two Stanley Cups, among other honors.

After retiring as a player in 1984, Clarke was named the Flyers general manager, a position he held until 1990. He then took the same position for two years with the Minnesota North Stars (1990-92), returned to the Flyers as senior vice president (1992-93), then joined the expansion Florida Panthers as vice president and general manager (1993-94). But the Flyers remained Clarke's primary team. He again returned to the Flyers' front office in 1994, when he was named president and general manager. Clarke was not afraid to take chances as a general manger during his second stint with the Flyers, firing a number of coaches and waiting for the right deal to come along before trading Lindros. Though he received some public criticism, Clarke stuck to philosophy of doing what was best for the Flyers. He was elected to the Hall of Fame for his playing accomplishments in 1987.

able. As Joe Lapointe of the *New York Time* wrote, "The scouts and press clippings say Lindros has the size of **Mario Lemieux**, the earning potential of Wayne Gretzky, the potential impact of **Bobby Orr** and the mean streak of **Gordie Howe**." The first pick of the draft was held by the Quebec Nordiques, a team Lindros publicly stated he would not play for for a number of reasons. It was a last-place, small market team, there were ethnic and political tensions in the French-Canadian city, and he would have to pay high taxes.

Despite Lindros's stance, Quebec selected him with the first pick. As he stated before the draft, Lindros refused to sign with them. He had some leverage as he already had endorsement deals, and had the option of not turning professional for several years, letting Quebec's hold on him run out. Lindros sat out the 1991-92 season, returning to the Oshawa Generals. In 1992, he also played for Team Canada at the Winter Olympics and in Canada Cup play. In the former, Lindros contributed five goals and six assists to silver medal victory for Canada.

Rights Traded to Flyers

At the end of the 1991-92 season, Quebec gave in to Lindros's demand and began negotiating a trade for his rights. A number of teams were interested, but when the trade was finally made, there was again controversy. The Nordiques traded his rights to two teams, the New York Rangers and the Philadelphia Flyers, at about the same time in a confusing timeline. This created a mess that had to be settled by an independent arbitrator. The Flyers came away with the rights to Lindros, giving up $15 million, five players (Ron Hextall, Mike Ricci, Steve Duchesne, Kerry Huffman, Peter Forsberg), and other considerations. This fiasco changed some procedures in the NHL concerning trades. The Flyers signed Lindros to a six-year $21 million deal, at the time the biggest in the NHL.

In his first two seasons with Philadelphia, Lindros played well but not to his full, huge potential. He was still a teenager with many expectations on him. He had injury issues (sprained knee first year and torn ligament in his right knee in his second) and missed forty-two games over both seasons. Lindros did set a rookie record for the Flyers by scoring forty-one goals in his first sea-

son, and was second place in NHL's rookie of the year voting. Though Lindros did not play the full 1993-94 season and the Flyers missed the playoffs, he still managed to score ninety-seven points. While it took time for him to adjust, Lindros was not intimated and had fun. Bruce Wallace wrote of his style of play in *Maclean's,* "On the ice, he is a menacing presence to opponents: a marauding, extremely physical player with spectacular scoring skills and a locomotive drive to win at all costs."

Breakout Season

The next season was shortened by strike. Lindros began the season by taking classes at the University of Western Ontario, where he practiced with the university's hockey team. After the strike was settled, Lindros had his best year as a professional. He had the most points in the NHL with seventy (tied with **Jaromir Jagr**). He was also named captain of the team. With teammates John LeClair and Mikael Renberg, he played on the Legion of Doom line. In the playoffs, the Flyers made it to the Eastern Conference finals where they lost to New Jersey Devils—who eventually won the Stanley Cup. Lindros won the Hart Memorial Trophy as the league's most valuable player, and almost won the scoring title.

By this time, Lindros was regarded as a great player with a long career ahead of him. Teammate Shawn Antoski told Michael Farber of *Sports Illustrated,* "There's no one else in the league who's capable of scoring 50

Career Statistics

Yr	Team	GP	G	A	PTS	+/−	PIM	SOG	SPCT	PPG	SHG
1992-93	Flyers	61	41	34	75	28	147	180	22.8	8	1
1993-94	Flyers	65	44	53	97	16	103	197	22.3	13	2
1994-95	Flyers	46	29	41	70	27	60	144	20.1	7	0
1995-96	Flyers	73	47	68	115	26	163	294	16.0	15	0
1996-97	Flyers	52	32	47	79	31	136	198	16.2	9	0
1997-98	Flyers	63	30	41	71	14	134	202	14.9	10	1
1998-99	Flyers	71	40	53	93	35	120	242	16.5	10	1
1999-2000	Flyers	55	27	32	59	11	83	187	14.4	10	1
2001-02	Rangers	72	37	36	73	19	138	196	18.9	12	1
TOTAL		558	327	405	732	197	1084	1840	18.0	94	7

Flyers: Philadelphia Flyers (NHL); Rangers: New York Rangers (NHL).

goals and using you as a speed bump." Lindros was seen as having a mean streak and a chip on his shoulder, qualities which appealed to the Flyer fans who had the Broad Street Bullies in the 1970s.

Played in Stanley Cup Finals

During the 1996-97 season, Lindros had seventy-nine points in fifty-two games, another career high. Though he did not get along with his coach, Terry Murray, Lindros and the Flyers made it to the Stanley Cup finals. Philadelphia struggled defensively. The team was swept in four games by the Detroit Red Wings, and Lindros did not play as well again. Murray was fired, and Lindros shouldered some of the blame.

Lindros was also accused of not playing well at the World Cup games, where Canada lost to the United States in 1996. While he was captain of the 1998 Canadian Olympic team, one favored to win the gold, the Canadians did not medal at all. Again, Lindros was accused of not being the leader he could be. The 1997-98 NHL season was also a struggle for Lindros. He missed eighteen games because of a concussion, and only had seventy-one points. In the 1998 playoffs, the Flyers were eliminated in the first round by the Buffalo Sabres in five games. Lindros only scored one goal and two assists in the series.

While Lindros took the blame for the playoffs, the Flyers struggles were not all because of Lindros. Yet his injuries and high profile leadership position put a strain on his relationship with Flyers GM Bobby Clarke. As a restricted free agent, Lindros further enraged the team by spurning the team's offer of a five-year $42 million deal, and only taking a one-year contract extension that took him through 1999-2000. Beginning in the 1998-99 season, Lindros and Clarke traded shots in the press.

Lindros began the 1998-99 season by playing well, and very physical. Yet he played a cleaner game with fewer retaliatory penalties. He did have a major concussion in January, 1999, which knocked him out. While the Flyers were pushing for a playoff spot, Lindros struggled as a player before suffering a bizarre injury. During a game against the Nashville Predators on April 1, 1999, Lindros suffered a collapsed lung, and nearly died from blood seeping into his chest cavity. Because of his injury, he was unavailable for the playoffs and the team again lost in the first round. This was again seen as Lindros's fault, and there was talk of trading him.

Concussion Problems

Despite the public feuding with Clarke and growing number of concussions, there were still high expectations that Lindros would win a Stanley Cup with Philadelphia. He continued to put points on the board (scoring 600 points in 429 games), but the team was in turmoil. Coach Roger Neilson had to leave the team for cancer treatment, and was replaced by Craig Ramsay. Neilson was later fired and not allowed to return as promised to coach in the playoffs. Before the end of the regular season, Lindros was stripped of his captaincy and had another major concussion. He publicly criticized the team's medical staff for allegedly mishandling his injury, his fourth concussion in two years and his fifth known head injury. While Lindros did return for playoffs, he suffered another concussion on May 26, 2000, when Scott Stevens of the New Jersey Devils leveled a massive open ice hit on him in the Eastern Conference Finals. This was Lindros's sixth concussion in twenty-seven months. He never played for the Flyers again.

Because of his concussion problems, Lindros could not even think about playing before November 2000. He was a restricted free agent whose rights were held by the Flyers. Lindros demanded a trade, and publicly stated that he would only play for the Toronto Maple Leafs. The Flyers and Clarke would not trade his rights. Lindros kept fit at home, but sat out the entire 2000-01 season.

Rights Traded to Rangers

Spurned by the Maple Leafs, the rights to Lindros were traded, with his approval, to the New York Rangers.

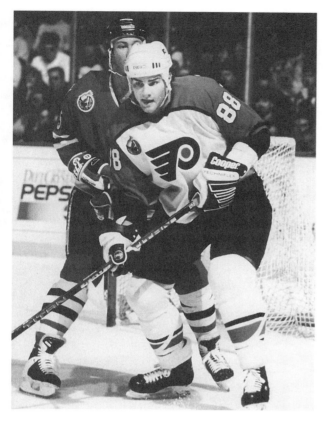

Eric Lindros

He received a four-year deal worth $38 million. Though Lindros wanted to play for a contender, which the Rangers were not, he was happy to play with **Mark Messier**, his childhood idol and captain of the Rangers. Lindros himself was named an alternate captain.

When Lindros began playing at the beginning of the 2001-02 season, he was very rusty and did not play as hard as he had in Philadelphia. He would not use his size to open up the middle as much and gave up big hits. While he showed flashes of his brilliance, he still retained his bad habit of carrying the puck with his head down, leaving him vulnerable to big hits. He suffered another concussion in December 2001. Until then, the Rangers and Lindros were playing well, but after, Lindros was content to play on the perimeter. Though the Rangers did not make the playoffs, Lindros did play for Team Canada in the 2002 Olympics. He was a key player and contributed to Canada winning the gold medal.

In 2002-03 season, Lindros still had moments where his skills showed, but it was tempered by his other problems. He was benched early in the season by new coach **Bryan Trottier** for taking bad penalties. He was suspended for one game for illegal use of his stick. He also had a long scoring drought, a problem on a team that was struggling to win games despite its many talented players. When Lindros did score, he showed he had the touch, despite all the issues surrounding his career. Of a

goal against the Phoenix Coyotes, Messier told Jason Diamos of the *New York Times,* "That was a typical Lindros goal. Hard forecheck. Beat somebody out of the corner. Carry somebody on your back. Then score a goal."

CONTACT INFORMATION

Address: c/o New York Rangers, 2 Pennsylvania Plaza, New York, NY 10121.

SELECTED WRITINGS BY LINDROS:

(With Randy Starkan) *Fire on Ice,* HarperCollins, 1991.
(With Greg Brown) *Pursue Your Goals,* Taylor Publishing, 1999.
(With Tom Worgo) "One last shot?" *Sport* (February 2000): 52.

FURTHER INFORMATION

Books

Macmillan Profiles: Athletes and Coaches of Winter. New York: Macmillan Reference, 2000.

Periodicals

Alexander, Rachel. "Lindros: Healing, Waiting." *Washington Post* (April 30, 1999): D5.
"Big and tough and turbocharged, Eric Lindros, 17, ices the competition as hockey's next superstar." *People* (February 4, 1991): 60.
Bloom, Barry M. "Flying high." *Sport* (February 1996): 69.
Bloom, Barry M. "The next one?" *Sport* (November 1997): 64.
Bondy, Filip. "Hockey; Lindros Moves to Broad Street, Not Broadway." *New York Times* (July 1, 1992): B7.
Brady, Erik. "Lindros dreams of gold, silver." *USA Today* (February 13, 2002): 1C.
Callahan, Gerry. "The complete package." *Sports Illustrated* (June 2, 1997): 62.
Deacon, James. "Coming into his own." *Maclean's* (May 8, 1995): 64.
Diamos, Jason. "Hockey: For Lindros, Frustrations Continue to Increase." *New York Times* (November 11, 2002): D10.
Diamos, Jason. "Hockey: Lindros Tries to Adjust with a Restrained Style." *New York Times* (January 14, 2002): D8.
Diamos, Jason. "Hockey: The Rangers Already Have Cause for Concern." *New York Times* (October 13, 2002): section 8, p. 10.
Diamos, Jason. "Hockey: Rangers Win, and Bure and Lindros Aren't Strangers." *New York Times* (November 20, 2002): D4

Diamos, Jason. "Hockey: Scoring Slump Continues as the Rangers Lose." *New York Times* (November 17, 2002): section 8, p. 8.

Diamos, Jason. "Hockey: Things Look Up for Rangers, Until Penalty Shot." *New York Times* (December 6, 2002): D10.

"Dropping the gloves over Eric." *Maclean's* (March 5, 2001): 27.

Farber, Michael. "Heads Up." *Sports Illustrated* (October 15, 2001): 60.

Farber, Michael. "Looming large." *Sports Illustrated* (October 9, 1995): 78.

Farber, Michael. "Team Turmoil." *Sports Illustrated* (April 10, 2000): 62.

Fisher, Red. "Lindros a sad situation for all." *Gazette* (January 5, 2002): F3.

Fleming, David. "Over and out?." *Sports Illustrated* (May 11, 1998): 106.

Grange, Michael. "With Hockey in Limbo, Lindros Goes Back to College." *New York Times* (December 4, 1994): section 8, p. 9.

Greenberg, Jay. "The face of the future." *Sports Illustrated* (December 11, 1989): 86.

Gulitti, Tom. "Lindros Injects Life into Rangers." *Record* (Bergen County, NJ) (March 31, 2002): S8.

Kilgannon, Corey. "Hockey: Trottier Enlists Lindros in Bid to Revive Rangers." *New York Times* (November 5, 2002): D4.

Lapointe, Joe. "Be It Canadian or U.S., It's Money to Lindros." *New York Times* (June 22, 1991): section 1, p. 31.

Lapointe, Joe. "Grasping Stardom at Age 17." *New York Times* (March 19, 1990): C1.

Lapointe, Joe. "Hockey: In a Dispute with Trottier, Lindros Is Benched." *New York Times* (November 4 2002): D2.

Lapointe, Joe. "Hockey: On Ice with the Big Boys, Lindros Does Little Wrong." *New York Times* (August 20, 1991): B11.

Lapointe, Joe. "Hockey; N.H.L. Guard Changes Amid Lindros Uproar." *New York Times* (June 23, 1992): B14.

Lapointe, Joe. "Hockey: Rangers Push to the Front of the Line in Bid for Lindros." *New York Times* (June 20, 1992): section 1, p. 31.

Lapointe, Joe. "Nagano '98: Wearing C, for Canada." *New York Times* (February 1, 1998): section 8A, p. 5.

Montville, Leigh. "Young gun." *Sports Illustrated* (September 23, 1991): 44.

O'Brien. "On ice: for now, the career of junior hockey star Eric Lindros." *Sports Illustrated* (March 23, 1992): 90.

"Put Up or Shut Up." *Sports Illustrated* (December 28, 1998): 46.

Scher, Jon. "Pass the pacifier." *Sports Illustrated* (October 26, 1992): 50.

Sell, Dave. "Lindros Wields a Big Stick at Early Age." *Washington Post* (September 29, 1992): E1.

Stein, Joel. "Lindros: The Best of Canada." *Time International* (January 31, 2000): 42.

Thomas, Robert McG., Jr. "Hockey; Eric's in Orange: Lindros Signs a $22 Million Pact with Flyers." *New York Times* (July 15, 1992): B9.

Wallace, Bruce. "Lucky Lindros." *Maclean's* (September 9, 1991): 34.

Yannis, Alex. "Hockey; Lindros Called Good for Business." *New York Times* (July 1, 1992): B11.

Other

"Bobby Clarke, President and General Manager." Philadelphia Flyers Web Site. www.philadelphiaflyers.com (December 14, 2002).

"Eric Lindros." ESPN.com. http://sports.espn.go.com/nhl/players/statistics?statsId=88 (December 14, 2002).

Foreman, Chris. "Bobby Clarke." LCS Hockey. www.lcshockey.com/archive/greats/clarke.asp (December 14, 2002).

Sketch by A. Petruso

Tara Lipinski
1982-

American figure skater

Although her competitive career in the amateur ranks of figure skating was brief, Tara Lipinski filled the record books with her accomplishments. As a thirteen-year-old, Lipinski claimed her first national medal with a third-place finish at the 1996 United States Figure Skating Association (USFSA) National Championship in San Jose, California. The following year, in just her second appearance at the nationals, Lipinski took the gold medal and started a rivalry with former champion **Michelle Kwan** as the country's top figure skater. Lipinski beat Kwan again at the International Skating Union (ISU) World Championship in Lausanne, Switzerland in 1997; in fact, she triumphed over the entire field and won the gold medal, becoming the youngest women's World Champion in the sport's history. After losing her title to Kwan at the 1998 nationals, the two skaters became the most talked-about athletes entering that year's Winter Olympic Games in Nagano, Japan. Although Kwan entered the final stage of the competition as the favorite, Lipinski skated a program that included the highest level of technical difficulty that had ever been accomplished by a female skater. Winning a decisive victory over Kwan, Lipinski retired as an amateur and started a new career as a professional skater. She also struggled to recover from a series of health problems that had been triggered by her intensive training schedule.

Tara Lipinski

Figure Skating Prodigy

Born on June 10, 1982 to Jack and Patricia (Brozyniak) Lipinski in Philadelphia, Pennsylvania, Tara Kristen Lipinski grew up in Sewell, New Jersey in a close-knit, Polish-American family. She started taking roller skating lessons at the age of three and demonstrated enough talent and dedication that she started private lessons the following year. Lipinski enjoyed the sport so much that her twice-a-week lessons soon turned into daily practice sessions; she even joined a roller hockey team as the squad's only female member. Eventually, Lipinski won over fifty medals in various roller skating competitions, including a gold medal in the Roller Skating National Championship in the primary division when she was nine years old.

Despite her precocious talent on roller skates, Lipinski did not try figure skating until she was six years old. "I was a mess," Lipinski described her debut on the ice in her memoir *Triumph on Ice: An Autobiography,* "My ankles bent in. My elbows pointed out. And I kept ending up on my backside. My parents were a little surprised I was so awful. After all, I was a natural on roller skates." After forty-five minutes on the ice, however, the young skater was no longer falling down and even performed a few jumps. A week later Lipinski started figure skating lessons at the University of Delaware, which sponsored one of the country's best skating programs.

Chronology

1982	Born June 10 to Jack and Patricia (Brozyniak) Lipinski in Philadelphia, Pennsylvania
1989	Begins taking figure skating lessons
1991	Moves to Sugarland, Texas
1993	Moves to Delaware with mother to continue figure-skating training
1995	Begins working with coach Richard Callaghan at Detroit Figure Skating Club
1995	Places fourth at International Skating Union (ISU) World Junior Championship
1996	Places fifth at ISU World Junior Championship
1996	Places fifteenth at ISU World Championship
1998	Retires from amateur ranks; begins professional skating career

Her persistence and hard work in transferring her roller skating skills to the ice soon paid off with a second-place finish in a local meet.

Endured Family Separations

Although she continued to pursue both roller and figure skating for the next couple of years, ice skating became the focus of Lipinski's life after her family moved to the Houston, Texas suburb of Sugarland in 1991. By now taking three skating lessons a day, Lipinski woke up at three o'clock each morning in order to get her time on the ice before school. After a year in Texas, Lipinski and her mother decided to move back to Delaware so that she could train full time. Her father, an oil company executive, remained in Texas and visited his family on weekends. The Lipinskis planned on a one- or two-year separation, but after coach Richard Callaghan of the Detroit Figure Skating Club had an opening for a new student in 1995, Lipinski and her mother moved again, this time to Bloomfield Hills, Michigan. Looking back on the sacrifices of living apart for so long, Patricia Lipinski recalled in an interview with Nancy Kruh of the *Dallas Morning News* in 1999, "It was a disaster for us. The stress on the family—you will never know stress like this."

Part of the tension over Lipinski's career came from the intense media scrutiny that the young skater encountered almost from the start. By the time she won a silver medal at the USFSA National Novice Championship in 1994, Lipinski had already been featured in several national publications and network television programs. The tone of the media coverage typically focused not only on her considerable talent, but also on the question of whether her parents should have allowed her to pursue an amateur figure-skating career at such a young age. Her parents insisted that their daughter's motivation was entirely self-derived and that they carefully watched over her well being to prevent her from becoming burned out.

Won National and World Titles

Lipinski's first major victory occurred at the 1994 U.S. Olympic Festival, where she earned a gold medal.

Awards and Accomplishments

1991	Won gold medal, Roller Skating National Championship, primary division
1994	Won gold medal, United States Figure Skating Association (USFSA) Midwestern Novice Championship
1994	Won gold medal, USFSA Southwestern Novice Championship
1994	Won silver medal, USFSA National Novice Championship
1994	Won gold medal, U.S. Olympic Festival
1995	Won silver medal, USFSA National Juniors Championship
1996	Won gold medal, USFSA South Atlantic Juniors Championship
1996	Won bronze medal, USFSA National Championship
1997	Won gold medal, USFSA National Championship
1997	Won gold medal, ISU World Championship
1997	Named U.S. Olympic Committee Sports Woman of the Year
1998	Won silver medal, USFSA National Championship
1998	Won gold medal, women's figure skating, Nagano Winter Olympic Games
1999	Won gold medal, World Professional Championship

Her Olympic Triumph Now a Memory, Tara Lipinski's Skating in New Directions

The question in inevitable, and Tara knows she'll probably hear it the rest of her life. This summer, as she's been going around the country teaching children's skating clinics, it comes up at practically every question-and-answer session.

How did it feel to win the Olympic gold medal?

"I can't put it into words," she tells a group of about 100 children at a recent clinic in Plano. "It's a memory I can look back on ... that moment when you skated the best you could. It's a feeling you can't describe. I can't explain it."

Ah, well. She's a skater, not a poet. But hey, cut the kid some slack. She doesn't have to explain it. If you saw her perform her long program the night of Feb. 20, 1998, you could tell how she felt. Every square inch of her fleet-footed, 4-foot-11 frame seemed to radiate the fact that she was having the skate of her life.

Source: Nancy Kruh, *Knight Ridder/Tribune News Service,* August 3, 1999, p. K6313.

Moving into the junior ranks, she took the silver medal at the 1995 USFSA Junior Championship. Already hailed as a potential figure-skating star for her jumping ability, Lipinski made an impressive debut in the senior-level ranks with a third-place finish at the 1996 USFSA National Championship in San Jose. Although Michelle Kwan garnered most of the headlines at the event with her stunning "Salome" program, Lipinski's bronze medal was good enough to earn her a spot on that year's U.S. delegation to the International Skating Union's (ISU) World Championship.

Although her rise had been nothing short of spectacular up to that point, Lipinski encountered her first major setback at the 1996 World Championship. Her performance in the short (or technical) program left her in twenty-third place and had almost disqualified her from the final free skate, in which only the top twenty-four competitors skated. Although she was shaken by the experience, Lipinski rebounded with a free skate that was nearly perfect, and she ended up in fifteenth place overall.

At the 1997 U.S. National Championship in Nashville, Tennessee, fourteen-year-old Lipinski stunned the figure skating community with a victory over heavily favored Michelle Kwan, who stumbled badly in the free skate. Lipinski's most surprising move was the triple-loop, triple-loop jump, which she had mastered only at the beginning of the season. Although her artistry and presence on the ice were sometimes criticized as too youthful in comparison to the other skaters, Lipinski's sheer jumping and spinning abilities were indeed the best of any skater in the competition. Despite her victory—which made her the youngest-ever U.S. champion—Lipinski did not go to the World Championship as the favorite, as most observers expected Kwan or Russia's Irina Slutskaya to take the gold medal. After Kwan and Slutskaya both made mistakes in the short program, Lipinski entered the free skate in first place. Again performing a perfect program, Lipinski placed second to Kwan in the free skate but emerged as the first-place skater overall. The feat made her into the youngest-ever World Champion in women's figure skating.

Few athletes in the sport's history had made such a sudden rise to the top of the American and world ranks in figure skating, and Lipinski's achievements came at the price of intense scrutiny. To some critics, Lipinski's victories proved that jumping ability had surpassed artistic development in importance to the judges; some also feared the impact of forcing young athletes to perform technically difficult moves before their bodies had fully matured. Yet as the most technically brilliant skater among her contemporaries, Lipinski also received praise for her single-minded dedication to the sport. An intense competitor, Lipinski did not give her rivals—especially Michelle Kwan—a chance to rest on their laurels.

Olympic Gold Medalist

At the 1998 U.S. National Championship in Philadelphia, Lipinski made a rare mistake when she failed to land her triple flip jump in the short program, which put her into fourth place. Although she responded with a clean long program in the free skate, Michelle Kwan took the national title with a performance that ranked as one of the best in the history of the sport. Given Kwan's amazing performance at the event, she was immediately considered the favorite going into the 1998 Winter Olympic Games in Nagano, Japan. For her part, Lipinski was glad to enter the event as an underdog, which motivated her to deliver a performance in the long program at the Games that ranked as the most impressive jumping display ever seen in a women's free skate to that time. In addition to her triple-loop, triple-loop combination jump, Lipinski ended with a triple-salchow, half-loop, triple toe loop combination. Out of nine judges, six ranked Lipins-

Tara Lipinski

ki ahead of Kwan; in winning the gold medal, Lipinski became the youngest-ever Olympic champion in the event, a distinction previously held by **Sonia Henie**. Although most figure skating commentators had predicted that Kwan would win if she skated a clean program, as indeed she did, their predictions did not hold true in light of Lipinski's inspired performance.

With the USFSA setting minimum age requirements for competition in the senior ranks, Lipinski's place in figure skating history as the youngest-ever American and Olympic champion would remain in the record books forever. Indeed, Lipinski's very success at such a young age fueled the drive to change USFSA rules. Although she was universally praised for her jumping ability, some critics argued that Lipinski was pushing the sport away from its artistic side in favor of putting on mere technical displays of triple jumps. Even with the rule changes, however, the trend favoring teenaged skaters with impressive triple jumps continued. In the 2002 Winter Olympic Games in Salt Lake City, sixteen-year-old **Sarah Hughes** won the gold medal by performing two triple-jump combinations, a feat the surpassed even Lipinski's performance four years before.

Joined Professional Ranks

In need of surgery on her hip, Lipinski withdrew from amateur ranks in April 1998. She joined the tour of *Stars on Ice* and resumed competing at events such as the 1999 World Professional Championship, where she won the gold medal. Lipinski also pursued an acting career with appearances on *Touched by an Angel, The Young and the Restless,* and the television movie *Ice Angel.* Her commercial endorsements included deals to promote Snapple beverages, the DKNY children's clothing line, and awareness of deep-vein thrombosis, a malady that Lipinski herself had faced after her hip surgeries.

Although she was criticized by some commentators for abandoning her amateur career—which had lasted little more than two years at the senior level—Lipinski's accomplishments during that period included national, world, and Olympic titles. Indeed, the teenager proved capable of becoming not just a superb technical skater, but an artistic one as well. The most outstanding jumper of her day, Lipinski's command of the ice allowed her to make the transition to a professional skating career at the age of fifteen. "I feel that I accomplished everything I wanted to, and now I can look back with such happiness while I pursue a pro career and keep expanding my horizons," Lipinski told David Barron of the *Houston Chronicle* in December 2001, "It makes skating as a whole so special to me."

SELECTED WRITINGS BY LIPINSKI:

(With Emily Costello) *Triumph on Ice: An Autobiography.* New York: Bantam Books, 1997.

FURTHER INFORMATION

Books

Brennan, Christine. *Edge of Glory: The Inside Story of the Quest for Figure Skating's Olympic Gold Medals.* New York: Scribner, 1998.

Brennan, Christine. *Inside Edge: A Revealing Journey into the Secret World of Figure Skating.* New York: Scribner, 1996.

Lipinski, Tara, with Emily Costello. *Triumph on Ice: An Autobiography.* New York: Bantam Books, 1997.

U.S. Figure Skating Association. *The Official Book of Figure Skating.* New York: Simon & Schuster Editions, 1998.

Periodicals

Barron, David. "Lipinski Says Her Gold Won't Lose Gleam when Title Passed On." *Houston Chronicle* (December 10, 2001).

Sketch by Timothy Borden

Sonny Liston

Sonny Liston
1932-1970

American boxer

When Sonny Liston became the world heavyweight boxing champ by knocking out **Floyd Patterson** in 1962, he hoped his criminal past and unsavory reputation could be put behind him. It was too late. At a time of growing racial unrest, he was cast in the public imagination as the angry, dangerous black man. Even the NAACP had asked "good guy" Floyd Patterson not to fight him. There was no ticker tape parade when he returned to his hometown of Philadelphia after the fight, just petty police harassment that ultimately drove him out of town. Still, nobody disputed his power in the ring, and virtually everyone expected him to easily dispatch a young upstart named Cassius Clay, soon to be renamed **Muhammad Ali**, who challenged him for the title in February 1964. Instead, after six rounds of pummeling, it was Liston who refused to leave his corner, ceding the championship to Cassius Clay and raising questions about whether the fight was fixed. Even more controversial was the rematch a year later, when Ali knocked out Liston with a "phantom punch" so fast that many thought Liston had taken a dive. Liston began a comeback in 1966, but he never got another shot at the title, and for the last months of his life he was jobless and nearly broke. He was found dead in his home on January 5, 1971, officially from heart failure, but reportedly from a heroin overdose.

Born to an Arkansas tenant farmer named Tobe Liston and his second wife, Helen, Charles L. Liston was one of twenty-five children. Other than that, little is definite about his birth, but he seems to have been born in a shack on the cotton plantation where his parents worked, a little outside Forrest City, in Arkansas, which did not at that time require birth certificates for those born at home. In later years, he gave his birth date as May 8, 1932, saying those who challenged this were calling his mother a liar. But she herself at various times gave January 8th or January 18th as his birthday, and many thought he was years older than he claimed. Even his name is a mystery. According to his mother, he was given the name by the midwife, and nobody remembered what the "L." stood for.

Birth of a Prison Boxer

What is fairly certain is that he had a difficult upbringing. Lost among his dozens of siblings, young Charles Liston worked beside them as soon as he was old enough, rarely attending school and never learning to read and write. Never close to his father, he once said, in a rare commentary on his childhood, "The only thing my old man ever gave me was a beating." Eventually, he was sent to live with a stepbrother, and after his father's death, in 1946, he followed his mother to St. Louis.

Actually, young Charles simply showed up in St. Louis one night, thinking it was like the small towns he was used to, where anybody he met would be able to point him to the home of Helen Liston. A couple of policemen found him wandering around and took him to an all-night café where a friend of Helen's told him where she lived. The cops agreed to drive him there. It would be Liston's last friendly contact with the police. With his huge hands and menacing attitude, Charles Liston soon fell in with St. Louis' youth gangs, beginning with petty crimes and moving on to harder stuff. On January 15, 1950, he was sentenced to the Missouri State Penitentiary in Jefferson City on two counts of armed robbery and two counts of larceny. It was there he found his calling.

The big man with the bad attitude soon caught the attention of Father Edward Schlattmann, the Catholic chaplain who doubled as the prison's athletic director. As he did with other prison brawlers, Fr. Schlattmann convinced Liston, who had somehow acquired the nickname "Sonny," to work out his aggression in the prison's boxing ring. After a few weeks, other inmates refused to get into the ring with Liston. Father Schlattmann's successor, Father Alois Stevens, told a *Sport Illustrated* reporter that Liston "was the most perfect specimen of manhood I had ever seen. Powerful arms, big shoulders. Pretty soon he was knocking out everybody in the gym. His hands were so large! I couldn't believe it. They always had trouble with his gloves, trouble getting them on when his hands were wrapped." Sonny's fists were some fifteen inches around, in sharp contrast to the foot or less claimed by the vast majority of heavyweight boxers.

From the Big House to the Big Time

With the help of Father Stevens, Liston came to the attention of boxing promoter Frank Mitchell and trainer Monroe Harrison, who secured his parole on October 30, 1952. In February 1953, they entered him in the open-and-novice heavyweight division of the amateur Golden Gloves tournament sponsored by the *St. Louis Globe-Democrat*. Liston swept the competition, going on to win the Midwestern Golden Gloves title, beating an Olympic heavyweight champion, and then the national title, becoming the Golden Gloves heavyweight champion in March. In June of that year, he defeated West German Herman Schreibauer to become the Golden Gloves world heavyweight champion. In five months, Sonny Liston had gone from unknown ex-con to amateur champion. Clearly, it was time to turn pro.

On September 2nd, he fought and won his first professional boxing match, knocking out Don Smith in thirty-three seconds, with the first punch of the first round. It was a spectacular beginning to a career that would take him to the top. Over the next few years, his menacing scowl and quick knockouts of his opponents would become legendary. By the end of 1961, with thirty-four wins in thirty-five fights, twenty-three of them by knockouts, Sonny Liston had established an unassailable reputation in the ring. Even his one loss, against Marty

Chronology

1932	Born May 8 in Forrest City, Arkansas (birth date according to one official document signed by Liston; other dates and birthplaces given variously by Liston, his mother, and other sources)
1946	Leaves his father to go live with his mother in St. Louis
1950	Sentenced to Missouri State Penitentiary, Jefferson City, for armed robbery and larceny; begins boxing in prison under tutelage of athletic director Father Edward Schlattmann
1952	Paroled from prison
1953	Enters professional boxing, knocking out Don Smith in first round
1957	Sentenced to nine months in St. Louis workhouse for assaulting a police officer; released August 1957
1957	Marries Geraldine Clark
1958	Signs contract with Joseph "Pep" Barone, associate of alleged mobsters Frankie Carbo and "Blinky" Palermo
1962	Defeats Floyd Patterson to win heavyweight title
1964	Loses heavyweight title to Cassius Clay
1965	Loses rematch to Muhammad Ali (formerly Cassius Clay) after so-called "Phantom Punch"
1966	Defeats Gerhard Zach in Stockholm, Sweden, as start of comeback
1967	With Geraldine, adopts three-year-old son, Daniel
1970	Wins technical knockout in his last fight, against Chuck Wepner
1971	Discovered dead on January 5 by Geraldine and Daniel in their Las Vegas home. Official date of death put as December 30. Lung congestion and heart failure ruled as official cause of death

Marshall on September 7, 1953, showed the man's power and determination. Marshall caught Liston unawares in the fourth round with a punch that broke his jaw, but Sonny fought on, losing in a close decision after eight full rounds. Before long, the crowds were clamoring to give him a shot at taking the World Heavyweight Title from Floyd Patterson. Some were even calling him the uncrowned heavyweight champion.

But Liston was also cementing another reputation. His troubles with the police continued unabated. Between 1953 and 1958, when he left St. Louis for good, he was arrested fourteen times. To escape the constant harassment, he relocated to Philadelphia. By that time, Liston was being secretly managed by Frankie Carbo and Blinky Palermo, two notorious mobsters who controlled big time boxing throughout the 1950s and 1960s. Both California and Pennsylvania suspended Liston's boxing license, and Liston himself had to appear before a Senate subcommittee investing organized crime's influence in professional boxing. For Floyd Patterson's manager, Cus D'Amato, who had spent years trying to clean up boxing's image and get the mob out, all this made him completely unacceptable as a challenger. But on December 4, 1961, Liston fought in the opening match in a pay-per-view double-header featuring Floyd Patterson in the main event. In less than two minutes, Liston had knocked out West German Albert Westphal, who remained unconscious longer than the fight had lasted. There was no denying it. Patterson was the only fighter left for Liston, and Liston was the only chal-

Awards and Accomplishments

1953	Golden Gloves world heavyweight champion
1953	In his first professional boxing match, knocks out Dan Smith in first round
1953-61	Wins 34 of 35 matches, 23 by knockouts
1954	Defeats Michigan state heavyweight champion John Summerlin
1962-64	World Heavyweight Boxing Champion
1966	Defeats Gerhard Zech in first match of comeback attempt
1968-69	Wins 12 of 13 matches
1970	Defeats Chuck Wepner in final boxing match of his career

lenger left for Patterson. In March of 1962, Floyd Patterson overrode all the objections and signed a contract to fight Sonny Liston.

The Champ Nobody Wanted

A grand debate on the morality of letting Liston vie for the championship erupted in the media. Sportswriters emphasized his criminal background as much as his brutal reputation in the ring. *New York Herald-Tribune* columnist Red Smith asked simply, "Should a man with a record of violent crime be given a chance to become a champion of the world?" Many felt boxing's reputation was on the line. Others worried about the reputation of black America. NAACP president Percy Sutton said that erudite, soft-spoken Floyd Patterson "represents us better than Liston ever could or would." Years later, in *"In This Corner…!" 42 World Champions Tell Their Stories*, Patterson described the terrible pressure he was under, when civil rights leaders, including President Kennedy himself, made it clear to Patterson that they needed him to win, as if a loss would doom the civil rights movement itself.

But in the ring none of that mattered. On September 25, 1962, Sonny Liston knocked out Floyd Patterson in two minutes, six seconds. For the first time in history, a world heavyweight champion had been knocked out in the first round. Heavyweight belt in hand, Sonny Liston thought that at last his turn would come for a little respect, or even affection. He hoped for a ticker tape parade when he flew back to his adopted hometown of Philadelphia. Instead, when he stepped off the plane, all he found were his usual tormentors, a few reporters, a few cops. As his friend Jack McKinney told *Sports Illustrated* reporter William Nack, "What happened in Philadelphia that day was a turning point in his life. He was still the bad guy. He was the personification of evil. And that's the way it was going to remain. He was devastated." Soon after, he moved to Denver.

On July 22 the following year, Liston beat Patterson again, this time in two minutes, twenty-three seconds. The new champ seemed invincible, and a few days later *Los Angeles Times* columnist Jim Murray wrote, "The

central fact . . . is that the world of sport now realizes it has gotten Charles (Sonny) Liston to keep. It is like finding a live bat on a string under your Christmas tree." But that night there was already a hint of the champ's coming fall. In the confusion after the knockout, while the crowd actually booed the triumphant Liston, a young boxer named Cassius Clay rushed the stage, making a beeline for the microphone and launching into his "I am the greatest" speech and daring Liston to take him on.

The Fall and Decline

In February 1964, Liston finally gave the loud-mouthed young boxer a shot at the title. When Cassius Clay stepped into the ring, he was counted out by virtually everyone. Instead, after six rounds, the two boxers stood even in points. Then Sonny Liston refused to leave his corner for the seventh round, claiming a shoulder injury. The champ had conceded defeat to the upstart, and many people wanted to know why. Liston's manager, Jack Nilon, said the injury had occurred during training before the fight, but nobody had heard anything about it before. Liston himself claimed the injury occurred in the first round of the fight. A few days later, speculation deepened when it came out that Inter-Continental Promotions, in which Nilon and Liston had a major stake, had signed a $50,000 contract in October 1963 securing the rights to promote Cassius Clay's next fight after the Liston-Clay fight, a contract that had just become much more valuable. Suspicious officials even withheld the fight purse until a doctor confirmed that Liston's left shoulder had indeed been injured.

Still, questions remained, but they were nothing compared to the storm that would erupt after the rematch on May 25, 1965, held in the Central Maine Youth Center in Lewiston, Maine, after other venues rejected the idea of hosting the tarnished ex-champ. Even as the challenger, Liston was favored 8-5 against the champion, now renamed Muhammad Ali. But what happened defied all the odds. Liston went down in the first round, after Ali threw an overhand right that seemed to barely graze his head. The punch would go down in boxing lore as the "Phantom Punch."

A Mysterious Death

Sonny Liston never again got a shot at the title, but he never quite retired from the ring either. He won eleven straight fights by knockout, mostly in Europe, through 1968. In his last fight, against Chuck Wepner in June of 1970, he won a 10th round technical knockout. At the time of this last fight, Liston claimed to be 38, but many think he was closer to 50.

As in birth, mystery surrounds Sonny Liston's death. On January 5, 1971, Geraldine Liston returned from a trip to St. Louis to find her husband dead in their Las Vegas home. The coroner's report was inconclusive, but strongly implied heart failure, although traces of heroin were

---

A "Phantom Punch"

When Sonny Liston went down in the first round of his rematch with Muhammad Ali, fans were amazed—and angry. In *The Devil and Sonny Liston* Nick Tosches wrote: "One thing is certain: in that rematch . . . when Sonny lay down in the first, he showed less acting ability than in the episode of *Love American Style* in which he later bizarrely appeared. That fight was not merely a fix . . . it was a flaunted fix." Tosches suggested the Mob was tired of its tarnished champ and saw more lucrative possibilities with Ali. Others suggested that Nation of Islam figures threatened Liston's life if he didn't throw the fight. But not all saw a fix. *Sports Illustrated* ran a frame-by-frame analysis of the fight on June 7, 1965, concluding that Ali had in fact knocked out Liston. *Los Angeles Times* columnist Jim Murray wrote: "What happened? I'll tell you what happened. Sonny Liston got the hell beat out of him is what happened . . . an old man groping his way into a speedy, insolent, reckless kid." Decades later, sportswriter Allen Barra agreed, concluding in *The New York Times* that "Murray's shot seems right on target, but it's hard to knock out a myth."

---

found in his blood. Some thought the ex-champ, jobless and nearly broke, had killed himself. Others thought an accidental overdose had carried him off. Still others, of course, concluded that the mob had decided it was time for Sonny Liston to take another dive, permanently.

Sonny Liston's death, at an indeterminate age, of an undetermined cause, may seem a fitting end for a controversial fighter with such shadowy connections. Even more fitting may be a comment he once made to an interviewer: "Ever since I was born, I've been fighting for my life." Sonny Liston lived and died a fighter, and in the words of the simple epitaph over his grave: "A Man."

FURTHER INFORMATION

Books

Tosches, Nick. *The Devil and Sonny Liston*. Boston: Little, Brown and Company, 2000.

Periodicals

Barra, Allen. "Sonny Liston: He Never Knew What Hit Him." *New York Times* (May 21, 2000)

Hochman, Stan. "Few Come Away Unscarred in New Book on Sonny Liston." *Knight Ridder/Tribune New Service* (May 26, 2000): K3039.

Hoffer, Richard. "A Lot More Than Lip Service . . ." *Sports Illustrated* (November 29, 1999): 86.

Lehmann-Haupt, Christopher. "A Hazy Start, a Dark End, a Champion in Between." *New York Times* (April 10, 2000): B6.

Lipsyte, Robert. "Decades Pass, and What's New Under the Sun?" *New York Times* (February 25, 1994): B10.

Nack, William. "O Unlucky Man: Fortune never smiled on Sonny Liston, even when he was champ."*Sports Illustrated* (February 4, 1991): 66.

"This Week in Black History." *Jet* (September 27, 1999): 19.

Sketch by Robert Winters

Earl Lloyd
1928-

American basketball player

Earl Lloyd was one of a handful of black basketball players who broke the racial barrier and helped integrate the National Basketball Association (NBA). In 1950, with the Washington Capitols, he became the first African American to play in an NBA game. The top defensive player later joined the Syracuse Nationals and became the first black player to win an NBA championship. Later with the Detroit Pistons, he was the first African American to be named an assistant coach and the first to be named a bench coach. Lloyd was enshrined in the Virginia Sports Hall of Fame, was nominated to the Basketball Hall of Fame, and saw February 9, 2001, named Earl Lloyd Day by Virginia's governor.

Virginia Native Makes History

A native of Alexandria, Virginia, Earl Lloyd began playing basketball at Parker Gray High School. In 1947 he attended West Virginia State College and played for the Yellow Jackets where he quickly became known for his defense and guard for the team's best offensive players. The team went to two Central Intercollegiate Athletic Association (CIAA) Conference and Tournament Championships in 1948 and 1949 where they finished in second place. Lloyd was named All-Conference for three years, from 1948 to 1950, and named All-American by the *Pittsburgh Courier* for 1949 and 1950. During his senior year, he averaged 14 points and 8 rebounds per game.

Racial tensions may have been strong in 1950, but in sports, barriers were being broken. A triumvirate of black basketball players went down into history when they were named to NBA teams. Chuck Cooper was the first African American drafted by an NBA team. Nat "Sweetwater" Clifton of the Harlem Globetrotters was known as the first black to sign an NBA contract when he signed with the New York Knicks.

Rounding out the trio, Earl Lloyd, after he left West Virginia State and was drafted in the ninth round to the Washington Capitols, was the first black to play in an NBA game. On October 31, 1950, Lloyd played in that historic game against the Rochester Royals. Although the Royals defeated the Capitols 78-70, Lloyd scored 6 points and began the inevitable acceptance of African Americans in the NBA.

Although making history, Lloyd spent only seven games with the Capitols before leaving for a two-year stint in the army. In 1952 he returned to the NBA to play for the Syracuse Nationals.

Nicknamed "Big Cat," Lloyd achieved the best performance of his career in the 1954-55 season when he

Earl Lloyd

scored 731 points and helped the Nationals to the Eastern Division Championship. This shored up Lloyd as the first African American to win an NBA title. His average that year was 10.2 points and 7.7 rebounds per game. In 1956 Lloyd was named CIAA Player of the Decade for the years 1947 through 1956.

In 1958 Lloyd was traded to the Detroit Pistons where he remained until his retirement from professional basketball in 1960 at the age of 32. He ended his career with averages of 8.4 points and 6.4 rebounds. Lloyd's other achievements include being named to the CIAA Silver Anniversary Team and to the National Association of Intercollegiate Athletics Golden Anniversary Team.

After retirement, Lloyd remained with the Pistons as a scout, and is credited with discovering basketball talents Willis Reed, Earl Monroe, Ray Scott, and Wally Jones.

No Jackie Robinson

Quick to play down the significance of his achievement, Lloyd in later years refused to compare his experience with that of **Jackie Robinson**, who was the first African American to play major league baseball when he signed with the Brooklyn Dodgers in 1945. In an Associated Press article, "Lloyd Says He's No Jackie Robinson," Lloyd noted that his first game caused little controversy because it was played in a city that had already embraced integration.

Chronology	
1947	Plays for West Virginia State
1950	One of three blacks drafted by NBA teams
1950	Joins the army for two years
1952	Plays with Syracuse Nationals from 1952 to 1958
1958	Traded to Detroit Pistons
1960	Retires from professional basketball
1968	Becomes assistant coach of Detroit Pistons
1971	Becomes head coach for Pistons
1972	Is fired as coach for Pistons
2000	Honored at 50th anniversary of black players in NBA

According to the article, Lloyd experienced a relatively easy transition from college to the NBA because of the acceptance of his white teammates during training camp, where he proved he could play at their level. Lloyd commented, "So you get to training camp with these guys from Southern Cal and Ohio State and UCLA and Georgetown and N.C. State, you kind of ask yourself: Do I belong? For a young black man from Virginia to compete at that level and learn that he belongs there, it was a true defining moment."

Lloyd has contended that Jackie Robinson faced a much more hostile environment in the late 1940s in baseball, often from his own teammates. Unlike Robinson who was the sole black in baseball, Lloyd had the solace of fellow black colleagues, Clifton and Cooper, in the NBA. Lloyd said, "In basketball, folks were used to seeing integrated teams at the college level. There was a different mentality."

First Black Coach

In 1968 Lloyd broke another color barrier when he was named the first African American assistant coach in the league, signing on with the Detroit Pistons. Three years later he became the second black to be named a head coach, and the Pistons' first black coach. Lloyd was the first African American to serve as bench coach. During his short tenure, he coached future Hall of Famers Dave Bing and Bob Lanier.

Unfortunately, the Pistons went just 20-52 under Lloyd in the 1971-72 season, and Lloyd was fired after only seven games into the next season. Pistons owner Fred Zollner replaced Lloyd with Ray Scott, the first time in the NBA that a black coach succeeded a black coach. Nevertheless, Lloyd should be commended for his dedicated service to the Detroit Pistons, having served as the team's assistant coach, scout, and head coach, and as a television analyst as well.

Recognized for his contributions to basketball, he was enshrined in the Virginia Sports Hall of Fame in 1993. In 1998 Lloyd was voted one of the CIAA's 50 Greatest Players and named to the CIAA Hall of Fame.

Career Statistics

Yr	Team	GP	PTS	FG%	FT%	RPG	APG	PF
1950	WSC	7	43	.457	.846	6.7	1.6	3.7
1952	SYR	64	472	.344	.693	6.9	1.0	3.8
1953	SYR	72	654	.374	.746	7.3	1.6	4.2
1954	SYR	72	731	.365	.750	7.7	2.1	3.9
1955	SYR	72	612	.335	.772	6.8	1.6	3.7
1956	SYR	72	646	.373	.749	6.0	1.6	3.9
1957	DET	61	317	.331	.745	4.7	1.0	2.9
1958	DET	72	605	.349	.753	6.9	1.3	4.0
1959	DET	68	602	.356	.800	4.7	1.3	3.3
TOTAL		560	4682	.356	.750	6.4	1.4	3.7

DET: Detroit Pistons; SYR: Syracuse Nationals; WSC: Washington Capitols.

Awards and Accomplishments

1948-49	Leads West Virginia State to two CIAA Conference and Tournament Championships
1948-50	Named All-Conference for three consecutive years
1949-50	Named All-American
1950	First African American to play in an NBA game, on October 31
1954	Career best of 731 points
1955	First black player to win an NBA title
1956	Named CIAA Player of the Decade, 1947-56
1968	First black assistant coach in NBA
1971	First black bench coach
1993	Enshrined in Virginia Sports Hall of Fame
1998	Voted to CIAA's 50 Greatest Players, and CIAA Hall of Fame
2001	February 9, 2001, named Earl Lloyd Day throughout Virginia
2002	Finalist for induction into Basketball Hall of Fame

Where Is He Now?

To commemorate the 50th anniversary of African Americans joining the NBA, the league in 2000 honored Earl Lloyd, Chuck Cooper, and Nat Clifton with special events during the season. Lloyd was joined in pregame introductions by Clifton's daughter Anita Brown and Cooper's wife Irva and son Chuck Jr., along with 78-year-old Hank DeZonie, a former member of the New York Rens who played in 1950. Lloyd tossed up the opening tip in the season-opener between the Philadelphia 76ers and the New York Knicks.

In Lloyd's hometown of Alexandria, Virginia, the board of directors of Kids In Trouble, Inc. recognized Lloyd in 2001 by coordinating a youth basketball clinic at the Charles Houston Community Center. That same year, the mayor of Alexandria and the governor of Virginia declared February 9, 2001, as Earl Lloyd Day.

As recently as 2002, Lloyd was still receiving accolades. He was speaker for the CIAA's Men's Tip-Off Banquet held in Raleigh, North Carolina, and was named as a finalist for enshrinement into the Naismith Memorial Basketball Hall of Fame. Selected from 37 candidates, Lloyd had previously been a finalist once before.

He outlived his other two black NBA history makers; Cooper died in 1984 and Clifton died in 1990.

Lloyd also found success after leaving professional basketball. He worked in the field of job placement for Detroit Board of Education for more than ten years. More recently Lloyd was employed in the community relations department of Dave Bing, Inc., a steel and automobile-parts company owned by the former Piston whom Lloyd had briefly coached. Lloyd has lived in Detroit and in Fairfield, Tennessee, with his wife Charlita. Though Lloyd was "never one to blow my own horn," his groundbreaking role in basketball assures his place in history.

FURTHER INFORMATION

Books

"Earl Lloyd." *Contemporary Black Biography,* Volume 26. Detroit, MI: Gale Group, 2000.

Other

Basketball Hall of Fame, http://www.hoophall.com/news/veteran_nominees_041802.htm (December 15, 2002).

Black Athlete Sports Network. http://www.blackathlete. net/basketball/index.shtml (December 15, 2002).

Black Web Portal. http://www.blackwebportal.com/wire (December 15, 2002).

NBA. http://www.nba.com/history/true_trailblazers_ moments.html (December 15, 2002).

Online Athens. http://www.onlineathens.com/stories/ 103100/spo_1031000042.shtml (December 15, 2002).

Sketch by Lorraine Savage

Rebecca Lobo
1973-

American basketball player

Defeat is not a common word in Rebecca Lobo's vocabulary. During her senior year playing basketball

Rebecca Lobo

for the University of Connecticut, her team did not lose a single game. The following year she joined USA Basketball's Women's National Team, which won fifty-two straight games on its way to the Olympics, and continued on to win a gold medal. Off-court, too, Lobo has come out a winner, remaining strong while her mother battled—and survived—breast cancer. Today, Lobo is one of the most recognized faces in women's professional basketball, and her popularity is credited as one of the factors that spurred creation of the Women's National Basketball Association (WNBA).

Sporting Family

The 6'4" Lobo comes from a sports-oriented—and tall—family. Her dad and mom, both school administrators, stand 6'5" and 5'11", respectively. Her 6'10" brother, Jason, played basketball at Dartmouth and her sister, Rachel, is an assistant basketball coach at Massachusetts' Salem State. Lobo learned the sport of basketball in her backyard and expressed an early interest in going pro, writing to Boston Celtics president **Arnold 'Red' Auerbach** when she was in third grade to announce she would be the first girl on his team. The following year, when plans for a girls' community basketball team in Lobo's hometown of Granby, Connecticut (her family later moved to Massachusetts) fell through, Lobo joined the boys' team and earned a spot as a starter with the traveling unit.

At Massachusetts' Southwick-Tolland Regional High School, Lobo excelled in track, softball and field hock-

Chronology

1973	Born October 6 in Connecticut
1987	Enters Massachusetts' Southwick-Tolland Regional High School as starter for varsity basketball team
1991	Graduates from Southwick Tolland as salutatorian and top scorer in Massachusetts history
1991	Enters University of Connecticut
1992	Named Big East Rookie of the Year
1994	Becomes only Big East player to win Player of the Year and Scholar-Athlete honors
1994-95	Leads UConn through undefeated season and NCAA tournament championship
1995	Captures second Big East Player of the Year and Scholar-Athlete awards
1995	Earns Naismith National Player of the Year award and Final Four MVP award
1995	Jogs with President Clinton and appears on David Letterman
1996	Tours with USA basketball Women's National Team
1996	Becomes youngest member of gold-medal winning U.S. Olympic team
1997	Assigned to New York Liberty in newly formed Women's National Basketball Association
1997	Achieves All-WNBA second-team honors
1997	Signs on as sports commentator with ESPN
2002	Traded to Houston Comets

ey, in addition to basketball. She made the varsity basketball team as a freshman and scored thirty-two points in her first game. She went on to score a total of 2,710 points over her high school career, the most ever scored by a player, male or female, in state history. Lobo shone off-court as well, graduating as class salutatorian.

Strength on- and off-court

Lobo's college career at the University of Connecticut began inauspiciously. While she performed well personally—her average of 14.3 points and 7.9 rebounds per game earned her Big East Rookie of the Year honors— the Huskies were eliminated from the NCAA tournament in the second round. The team's performance was even more lackluster the following year. During Lobo's junior year, however, the team began to turn around, making it to the "Great Eight" of the NCAA tournament. Crisis struck on the homefront, however, when Lobo's mother, RuthAnn learned that she had breast cancer. An ardent supporter of her daughter, RuthAnn arranged her chemotherapy treatments around Rebecca's games. But Lobo told *People* that basketball took a back seat to her mother's concerns. "Scoring points means nothing compared to what she went through," Lobo remarked.

By Lobo's senior year, her mother's cancer was in remission. It was during this season that Lobo and the Huskies accomplished a rare and amazing feat—not only did they enter the NCAA tournament with an unbelievable 33-0 record, they captured the championship, making them undefeated for the entire season. For her role in this amazing season, Lobo received the Naismith National Player of the Year Award and the Wade Trophy.

Career Statistics

Yr	Team	GP	Pts	FG%	3P%	FT%	RPG	APG	SPG	BPG
1997	NYL	28	348	.376	.286	.610	7.30	1.9	.93	1.82
1998	NYL	30	350	.484	.308	.710	6.90	1.5	.57	1.10
1999	NYL	1	0	.000	.000	.000	1.00	.0	.00	.00
2001	NYL	16	17	.318	.500	.500	.90	.1	.13	.00
2002	HOU	21	34	.469	.429	.250	1.10	.6	.05	.24
TOTAL		96	749	.422	.306	.646	4.70	1.1	.48	.93

HOU: Houston Comets; NYL: New York Liberty.

Awards and Accomplishments

1990	Becomes top scorer in Massachusetts high school history with 2,710 points
1992	Big East Rookie of the Year
1994	Kodak All-American
1994-95	Big East Player of the Year
1994-95	Big East Scholar-Athlete
1994-95	Big East tournament MVP
1994-95	Academic All-American
1995	Naismith National Player of the Year
1995	NCAA Final Four MVP
1995	Wade Trophy
1995	Named Sportwoman of the Year by Women's Sports Foundation
1996	Named to UA Basketball Women's National Team and U.S. Olympic team

In addition, she was named Final Four MVP and Women's Sports Foundation's Sportswoman of the Year, among numerous other honors.

During Lobo's tenure at UConn, the popularity of women's basketball grew significantly, with Lobo's team drawing record crowds and young girls donning their hero's trademark French braid. At the time, Lobo's coach, Geno Auriemma, summed up Lobo's allure. "What is she great at?" he asked *Sports Illustrated*. "I can't say any one thing. But the sum of the parts is unreal."

Remains in Limelight

Lobo remained in the limelight following graduation from UConn. In 1996 she became the youngest member of the USA Basketball Women's National Team, which won all fifty-two of its games leading up to the Olympics and went on to capture the gold. That same year, Lobo and her mother released a co-autobiography, *The Home Team: Of Mothers, Daughters, and American Champions.*

Following the Olympics Lobo signed on to the newly formed Women's National Basketball Association, playing for the New York Liberty, and became the main focus of the league's marketing campaign. In 1997 Lobo was named to the all-WNBA second team and in 1999 she made the first-ever WNBA Eastern Conference All-Star team. A knee injury forced her to sit out the Madison Square Gardens game, however. She tore her anterior cruciate ligament in the first minute of the Liberty's first game that season. After almost six months of rehabilitation she returned to the Liberty, only to re-injure herself. She was back on the court in 2001 and in 2002 the Liberty traded her to the Houston Comets.

In 1997 Lobo also began to explore a career she had considered before going pro: sports broadcasting. In the off-season she began providing sports commentary for ESPN.

Today, Lobo remains one of the most popular personalities in the WNBA. She is continually sought after for endorsements and has even had a shoe, the Reebok "Lobo" named after her. She keeps fans close, no matter what team she's playing for, through numerous public appearances and her Web site, www.wnba.com/rebeccalobo.

CONTACT INFORMATION

Address: c/o Houston Comets, 2 Greenway Plaza, Suite 400, Houston, TX 77046. Online: www.wnba.com/rebeccalobo.

SELECTED WRITINGS BY LOBO:

(With RuthAnn Lobo) *The Home Team: Of Mothers, Daughters and American Champions*, Kodansha International, 1996.

FURTHER INFORMATION

Books

Contemporary Heroes and Heroines, Book IV. Detroit: Gale Group, 2000.

(With RuthAnn Lobo) *The Home Team: Of Mothers, Daughters and American Champions.* New York: Kodansha International, 1996.

Sports Stars, Series 1-4. U•X•L, 1994-98.

Periodicals

Abrahams, Andrew. "The Enforcer." *People* (March 20, 1995): 61-62.

Telander, Rick. "The Post with the Most." *Sports Illustrated* (March 20, 1995): 98.

Sketch by Kristin Palm

Vince Lombardi
1913-1970

American football coach

Vince Lombardi

More than three decades after Vince Lombardi's death, books about this legendary and inspiring football coach are still making the best seller list. These books cover not only the details of his life and career but also his philosophy and practical approach to winning, which remains relevant today. His reputation as one of the most consistently successful coaches in professional football, with victories that include the first two Super Bowl games, makes Lombardi a subject of interest on and off the football field. Lombardi was famous for his locker room speeches, which provided his players with enough motivation to win games in spite of the odds stacked against them. As he gained championships, business people took notice of Lombardi's tactics, and often invited him to speak, realizing that the same winning principles could be used in their companies.

The Early Years

Vince Lombardi was born on June 11, 1913, to second-generation Italian immigrant parents. His father, Harry, was known as a big-hearted man, who wanted to give his children everything that he had had to do without in his childhood. They lived in comfortable homes and enjoyed all the necessities of life. Harry and his wife Matilda encouraged their children to seek the education that had alluded them, resulting in all three of their sons eventually receiving a college educations. One of the lessons that Harry passed onto his sons was the virtue of hard work. Thus Lombardi, from a young age, helped his father in the family butcher shop. He quickly learned how to heave enormously heavy sides of meat around the store and how to cut up the carcasses, a job he was not fond of. However, the weightlifting helped to shape his body, an asset that would later come to his aid in his athletic endeavors.

As a teenager, Lombardi fell in love with sports and would drag his friends to Yankee and Dodger baseball games and to the football stadium to watch the Giants.

He also often played sandlot football games, most of which he organized and then dictated the rules, insisting that they be followed correctly. His father encouraged his son's football interests, although his mother did not. She feared that he would be hurt.

When it was time to enter high school, Lombardi decided upon Cathedral College of the Immaculate Conception Preparatory Seminary, a school not unlike other local Catholic high schools—except for the fact that the main focus of the school was to turn its scholars into priests, a role that at one time Lombardi thought he wanted to pursue. Lombardi became the center on the school's basketball team, a position in which he flourished. On the baseball team, he played outfielder and catcher. As a baseball player, he was not as adept, but his coach admired his courage. After three years at Cathedral, Lombardi decided against a religious profession and came up with a new plan. He decided to transfer to another high school and play football his senior year with the intention of winning a college scholarship. The plan worked better than he expected.

Lombardi first won a scholarship to St. Francis Prep High School in Brooklyn where he played guard on defense and halfback on offense and was described as aggressive and powerful. He also reportedly played every minute of every game. He was well liked by his teammates and his classmates and earned the respect of his teachers and coaches, who eventually helped him win a football scholarship to Fordham University. On the col-

Chronology

1913	Born June 11 in the Sheepshead Bay section of Brooklyn, New York, to Harry and Matilda Izzo Lombardi
1929	Enrolls as high school freshman at Cathedral College of the Immaculate Conception Preparatory Seminary to study to become a priest, where he plays on both the basketball and baseball teams
1937	Plays guard for the semiprofessional team, the Wilmington Clippers, from Delaware
1938	Plays for the Brooklyn Eagles, a semiprofessional team affiliated with the American Football Association. Later this year, he enrolls at Fordham's Law School
1939-47	Works as teacher and coach of basketball, baseball, and football at St. Cecilia High School in Englewood, New Jersey
1940	Marries Marie Planitz
1942	Vincent, Jr. is born on April 27
1947	Susan, Lombardi's daughter, is born on February 18. Lombardi accepts the assistant football coach position at Fordham
1949-53	Works as assistant football coach at the U.S. Military Academy at West Point
1954-58	Coaches the offensive team for the New York Giants
1959-68	Is head coach and general manager of the Green Bay Packers
1969-70	Head coach, business manager, and part owner of the Washington Redskins
1970	Dies on September 3

Awards and Accomplishments

1956	Helped coach the New York Giants to NFL Championship
1958	Assisted in taking the New York Giants to another NFL Championship game
1960	Took Green Bay Packers to league Championship
1961-62, 1965	Coached Packers to victories in league Championships
1967	Led Green Bay Packers to victory in first Super Bowl game.
1968	Won Super Bowl II.
1970	Inducted as a charter member to the Fordham University Hall of Fame. Also has the Super Bowl trophy renamed in his honor. Rotary Club dedicates an annual Lombardi Award to outstanding football linesmen. The NFL named Lombardi their 1960s Man of the Year
1971	Inducted into the Pro Football Hall of Fame
1975	Inducted into the Green Bay Packer Hall of Fame. Lombardi's overall professional coaching record was 105-35-6.

lege level, Lombardi continued to play both offense and defense positions. In his senior year, after a particularly hard fought battle against Pittsburgh, the *New York Post* ran a feature story about him, referring to him as a New York hero.

First Coaching Position

After graduating from college, Lombardi floundered a bit as he tried to figure out what he wanted to do with the rest of his life. He had a degree in business, so he first tried his hand at that but was soon discouraged. Next, he thought he would try to obtain a law degree, but after one semester, he knew that was not what he wanted. Then he worked as a chemist for one year, but that also was not something that inspired him. He liked being around young people and thought about teaching and coaching. Then in 1939, Lombardi received a phone call from a former college classmate who asked him if he would accept a teaching job at St. Cecilia High School in Englewood, New Jersey. The teaching position would also offer Lombardi a chance to coach. Lombardi accepted, and this job would mark the beginning of his long, successful career in coaching.

The job at St. Cecilia's was a difficult one. Lombardi had to teach physics, chemistry, Latin, and physical education on top of coaching basketball and assisting with football. But Lombardi later claimed that his eight years at that high school were some of the best years of his life. As a coach, Lombardi was a strict disciplinarian. He studied each sport intensely, breaking it down into systematic and logical portions. Then he taught regimented plays and expected his players to follow his rules com-

pletely. A few complained that he held tight reins on his players, but most appreciated his system and enjoyed playing for him. Others noted that he frequently lost his temper whenever a player repeated a mistake. Lombardi was also known for throwing things or kicking when he got angry. However, he was a winning coach, so the dramatics were usually tolerated. When Lombardi later announced his resignation from St. Cecilia and his acceptance to become an assistant football coach at Fordham, the community gave him a farewell dinner.

College Football

Lombardi honed his coaching skills for six years on the campuses of Fordham University and the U.S. Military Academy at West Point. The prospects at Fordham were not very encouraging when Lombardi arrived there in 1947. At that time, the university's football record was so depressing that Lombardi believed that his St. Cecelia's varsity squad could have defeated the college team. He accepted the job, hoping that the head coach position might soon be available to him. Many people at Fordham held the same thought and tried unsuccessfully to oust the head coach, Ed Danowski. Popular sentiment for Danowski made the plan backfire, however, and Lombardi's reputation suffered in the aftermath. The atmosphere at Fordham was ruined for him, however, and after one year he left to take a job at West Point.

Colonel Earl Blaik, the head coach at West Point, was famous for his excellent training of assistant coaches. He was so good that almost every year he had to replace his assistants because they moved on to head coaching positions at other colleges. Blaik's military discipline and natural inclination toward perfectionism matched Lombardi's personality.

After winning the Eastern championship in 1952, officials at West Point decided to downplay football. About this same time, the executives of the New York Giants had offered Blaik a chance to take on the head coach po-

Vince Lombardi, center

sition, but Blaik turned them down. Then the Giants, who also needed to fill an assistant coach slot, asked Blaik if they could offer that job to Lombardi; Blaik gave his approval. So in 1954, Lombardi said good-bye to West Point and headed back to his hometown with his first assignment in the professional leagues.

Moving up with the Giants

Lombardi turned forty-one during his first year with the Giants, approaching middle age in professional football. But he still had a lot to prove, and so did the Giants. Steve Owen had been the head coach for the Giants for twenty-three years. His glory days, such as in the 1934 Championship game against the Chicago Bears in a freezing rain, were behind him. Owen had one of his worst seasons in 1953, winning only three games. So the Giants offered Owen a front office job and brought Lombardi in as offensive coordinator, with Jim Lee Howell as head coach, and as defensive coach, **Tom Landry**, who later led the Dallas Cowboys to several championship games. Lombardi and Landry were as opposite as two people could be, except that they both had strong minds and huge imaginations that served the Giants well. They were very competitive and their respective squads got caught up in the contest to outdo one another.

The Giants reached a turning point in the mid-fifties and went all out, recruiting some of the top college players, including All-American **Frank Gifford**, whom Lombardi quickly recognized as one of the key players for the Giants' offense. Gifford had almost quit the team the year before and he was not sure Lombardi's arrival would make much difference. However Gifford quickly became his star, helping to take the Giants to first place in the Eastern Conference three years in a row, winning the right to play in the NFL Championship Games in 1956, 1957, and 1958.

If the Giants experienced a turning point upon Lombardi's arrival, Lombardi himself experienced one after successfully completing his fourth year with the New York team. In 1958, Earl Blaik decided to resign as head coach at West Point and most people thought that Lombardi would be Army's first choice to replace him. However, the academy decided to stick with tradition and to hire a West Point graduate. When Lombardi heard the news that he was no longer in contention for the position, he turned his attention to Wisconsin's Green Bay Packers, a team with a long winning history that had suffered through several losing seasons. The 1958 season ended with Green Bay eking out only one victory. Although the executives at Green Bay knew very little about Lombardi, Blaik and **Paul Brown**, head coach of the Chicago

Bears, highly recommended him, and on January 28, Lombardi signed a five-year contract with the team in the dual role of head coach and general manager.

Legendary Years with the Packers

By the time that Lombardi arrived in Green Bay, his knowledge of football was as strong as the best professional coaches in the league. His task in those first few months was to get to know the players. The New York Giants and the Packers were in different conferences, so Lombardi had had little opportunity to see them play. He had been right to choose Gifford as his key player for the Giants, and he needed to find someone similar for the Packers. His intuitions told him that player might be **Paul Hornung**, a Heisman Trophy winner from Notre Dame. Like **Bart Starr**, an equally talented young Packers player, Hornung considered quitting the team after suffering through a first miserable year with the Packers. However, something about Lombardi made both players want to give football one more chance. Hornung became Lombardi's left halfback and Starr his quarterback. Both proved to be wise choices.

Lombardi's genius was demonstrated in many ways, but the one that his players appreciated the most was the way he reduced each play down to its basic elements. Lombardi threw out much of the repetitive jargon that many coaches forced their players to memorize. Instead of a code system, Lombardi used one number to designate each play. The playbook that each player had to memorize was one-third the size of other coaches' playbooks. He also relieved some of the pressure on the quarterback by having offensive linemen call their own blocking patterns. He was a tough disciplinarian, but he knew the game, and the players admired his knowledge and the way he taught. Having had experience in the classroom, Lombardi knew that he had to make each and every player understand his system of football. Although repetitive, his method of teaching was rarely dull, for he had a way of making everything that he and his players did seem of utmost importance.

Lombardi also drilled into their heads that his players represented the Packers on and off the field. This meant that on trips, they were required to wear their blazers and ties at all times while in public. He also enforced strict curfews and rules of social conduct that they were required to follow. Right before their first practice, as quoted in Michael O'Brien's book, *Vince: A Personal Biography of Vince Lombardi,* Lombardi told his new team, "I've never been a losing coach, and I don't intend to start here.... I'm going to find thirty-six men who have the pride to make any sacrifice to win." He then added that if any of them sitting in front of him were not capable or not willing to do so, he would find someone to replace them. Later, he confided to one of the veteran players, Max McGee, that he had been concerned that they might all stand up and leave town at the end of his speech.

For the nine years that Lombardi worked with the Packers he never saw a losing season. In those nine years, the Packers played six League Championship games, winning five of them. They also won the first and second Super Bowl games. With Lombardi at the helm, the Packers seemed unstoppable. However the wear and tear, both physical and emotional, on Lombardi began to show, and after winning Super Bowl II, he announced his retirement.

The Last Years

It did not take long for Lombardi to realize that retirement was not for him. He had tried to keep himself busy promoting products for several commercial companies as well as maintaining his responsibilities as general manager of the Packers. As the NFL Players' Association gained strength and threatened to strike, Lombardi became involved in the negotiations. However, this was not enough to satisfy him. So when the owners of the Washington Redskins made him an offer in February of 1969, it did not take long for Lombardi to accept it. He was made head coach, general manager, and part-owner of the team.

Like the Packers, the Redskins were an old franchise that had seen its glory years. Lombardi turned them around, making their 1969 season one of the best in their history. Sonny Jurgensen, the beloved quarterback for the Skins—an excellent passer who had suffered many years with poorly coached defensive teams—became what Frank Gifford and Paul Hornung had been before him. Had Lombardi lived longer, the Redskins may have enjoyed a longer winning streak, but that was not in the plans. On June 24, 1970, Lombardi entered Georgetown University Hospital in Washington, DC, for tests. The results determined that he had colon cancer. Although Lombardi fought his disease with his usual pattern of strict discipline and prayer, he succumbed to the disease on September 3.

A story in the *Green Bay Press-Gazette* on September 8, 1970, stated that at a dinner party at the White House, President Nixon, upon hearing of Lombardi's death, proclaimed that Lombardi was a "man who in a time when the moral fabric of the country seems to be coming apart, he was a man who was deeply devoted to his family ... at a time when permissiveness is the order of the day.... he was a man who insisted on discipline ... and strength." A few days before he died, Lombardi received a large bouquet of flowers in his hospital room. As reported in David Maraniss's book, *When Pride Still Mattered*, the card attached to the flowers read: "You are a great coach and a great individual to all of us." The card was signed by the National Football League Players Association.

SELECTED WRITINGS BY LOMBARDI:

(With W. C. Heinz) *Run to Daylight,* Fireside, 1963.

Vince Lombardi's Pro Football Guide, edited by Ray Stergener, Aurora Publishers, 1970.

Lombardi: Winning Is the Only Thing, edited by Jerry Kramer, World Publishing Company, 1970.

Vince Lombardi on Football, edited by George L. Flynn, New York Graphic Society, 1973.

Coaching for Teamwork: Winning Concepts for Business in the Twenty-First Century, Reinforcement Press, 1995.

Seeing the Win: Why I Believe Vision-Coaching Is Vital to Winning Business Teams in the Twenty-First Century, Dartnell Corporation, 1997.

Winning Is a Habit: Vince Lombardi on Winning, Success, and the Pursuit of Excellence, edited by Gary R. George, HaperCollins, 1997.

(With Jennifer Briggs) *Strive to Excel: The Will and Wisdom of Vince Lombardi,* Rutledge Hill Press, 1997.

FURTHER INFORMATION

Books

Dowling, Tom, *Coach: A Season with Lombardi.* W. W. Norton, 1970.

Etter, Les, and Herman B. Vestal, *Vince Lombardi: Football Legend.* Garrard Publishing Company, 1975.

Fage, John Norwood, *Vince Lombardi.* Pendulum Press, 1979.

Flynn, George, *Vince Lombardi on Football.* Van Nostrand Reinhold, 1981.

Klein, David, *The Vince Lombardi Story.* Lion Books, 1971.

Kramer, Jerry, and Dick Schaap, *Coach Vince Lombardi's Power to Motivate.* Listen U.S.A., 1987.

Kramer, Jerry, *Lombardi: Winning Is the Only Thing.* Ty Crowell Company, 1976.

Lombardi, Vince, Jr., and John Q. Baucom *Baby Steps to Success.* Starburst Publishers, 1997.

Lombardi, Vince, Jr., *The Essential Vince Lombardi: Words and Wisdom to Motivate, Inspire, and Win.* McGraw-Hill, 2002.

Lombardi, Vince, Jr., *What It Takes to be Number 1: Vince Lombardi on Leadership.* McGraw-Hill, 2000.

Maraniss, David, *When Pride Still Mattered: A Life of Vince Lombardi.* Touchstone Books, 2000.

May, Julian, *Vince Lombardi: The Immortal Coach.* Crestwood House, 1975.

Myers, Hortense, *Vince Lombardi, Young Football Coach.* MacMillan Publishing Company, 1971.

O'Brien, Michael, *Vince: A Personal Biography of Vince Lombardi.* Quill, 1989.

Roensch, Greg, *Vince Lombardi (Football Hall of Famers).* Rosen Publishing Group, 2002.

Schoor, Gene, *Football's Greatest Coach, Vince Lombardi.* Doubleday, 1974.

Wells, Robert W., *Vince Lombardi: His Life and Times.* Prairie Oak Press, 1997.

Towle, Mike, ed., *I Remember Vince Lombardi: Personal Memoirs of and Testimonials to Football's First Super Bowl Championship Coach as Told by the People and the Players.* Cumberland House, 2001.

Zalewski, Ted, *Vince Lombardi—He is Still with Us.* Children's Press, 1974.

Other

Green Bay Packers. Green Bay Packers History. http://www.jt-sw.com/football/pro/teams.nsf/histories/packers/ (September 28, 2002).

Real Men/Vince Lombardi. Manlyweb. http://www.manlyweb.com/realmen/vincelombardi.html/ (September 18, 2002).

Vince Lombardi. The official website of the greatest coach of all time. http://www.vincelombardi.com/ (September 28, 2002).

Sketch by Joyce Hart

Nancy Lopez
1957-

American golfer

When Nancy Lopez burst onto the scene of the Ladies Professional Golf Association (LPGA) Tour during her rookie year in 1978 by winning a record five consecutive tournaments, she gave new life to the women's tour. Then-LPGA's director of publicity, Chip Campbell, told *Golf World*, "Thank the dear Lord, along came Nancy Lopez. She was a savior. What did Winston Churchill say, Comes the moment, comes the man? Well, comes the moment, comes the woman." With good distance off the tee and excellent putting skills, Lopez was an exceptional golfer. Also known on tour for her warmth and kindness, she embraced the fans who returned her affection tenfold.

Nancy Lopez

Nationally Ranked Amateur

Nancy Lopez was born on January 6, 1957, in Torrance, California, but was raised, along with her older sister, in Roswell, New Mexico, by her parents, Domingo and Marina Lopez. Of Mexican descent, Lopez grew up in a traditional Catholic household. Her father owned an auto repair business, and her mother tended the house and the children.

Lopez began to play golf with her family in 1964 at the age of eight, using old clubs with shortened shafts. Her natural ability was quickly apparent to her father, who began coaching her. Lopez won her first tournament when she was nine years old, finishing 110 strokes better than her nearest opponent. By the age of eleven Lopez was beating both her parents on the course, and her father became committed to developing his daughter's game. The family skimped and sacrificed to afford to finance Lopez's golf.

Lopez won the first of her three New Mexico Women's Amateur Championships when she was just twelve years old, but the pressure of competition was taking its toll. "I was so scared I always threw up," she admitted to *Sports Illustrated*. "I carried a trash can with me. My dad told me, 'If you're going to play golf, you've got to get over being sick.' I didn't want to quit so I decided to get over it." She did and kept winning.

A nationally ranked amateur during high school, Lopez led her otherwise all-male high school golf team

to a state championship. She won the U.S. Girls Junior championship in both 1972 and 1974. Lopez had her first brush with fame the following year as a high school senior when, as an amateur, she finished second at the 1975 U.S. Women's Open. Lopez enrolled at the University of Tulsa in 1975 on a golf scholarship. As a freshman she won the Association of Intercollegiate Athletics for Women golf championship and was named the University of Tulsa's Female Athlete of the Year. In need of new challenges, Lopez turned professional after her sophomore year.

Sensational Rookie Year

Although she joined the LPGA during 1977, Lopez's first full season, and official rookie year, was 1978. "When I first came out, I pretty much felt like I was the worst player on the tour," she later explained to *Golf World*. "I felt like you're supposed to start at the bottom of the barrel and work your way to the top. I'd watch the other players and think, 'Gosh, my game's not even close to theirs.' My goal was to hopefully win one tournament that first year." Lopez would quickly surpass her conservative expectations to help transform women's golf into a nationally recognized spectator sport.

In February 1978, Lopez won her first professional tournament by sinking a 15-foot birdie putt on the seventeen hole to claim the lead at the Bent Tree Classic in Sarasota, Florida. She dedicated her first title to her mother, who had passed away the previous fall. A week later Lopez won the Sunstar Classic in California. Then, in April she began an unbroken record of five straight tournament wins that nearly single-handedly raised the LPGA into its highest realms of popularity and profitability. Lopez won in Baltimore, Maryland, and then twice in New York, took a week off, and won her first major, the LPGA Championship in Kings Island, Ohio, in front of a national television audience. The phenomenon of her unprecedented success provoked NBC to cut into its baseball broadcast the following week to cover her fifth consecutive win at the Bankers Trust Classic in Rochester, New York.

Related Biography: Baseball Player Ray Knight

Ray Knight was born and raised in Albany, Georgia, in a close-knit family. His father, who supervised the recreational facilities for the parks department, began playing baseball with him when he was just two years old. Knight joined the Cincinnati Reds farm system after attending Albany Junior College. Replacing Pete Rose at third base in 1979, he was named the team's most valuable player.

Traded to the Houston Astros in 1983, Knight struggled with injuries. While playing in the minor leagues he had been hit by pitches twice. One pitch broke his cheek bone; the other hit him in the temple and he spent four days in intensive care. By 1986 Knight had undergone five surgeries and had suffered kidney stones, a variety of pulled muscles, and bone chips in his throwing arm. To top it all off, in 1984 he began suffering bouts of vertigo. Benched then traded to the New York Mets in late 1984, Knight struggled through 1985. In 1986 a change in his stance at the plate revived his bat, and he earned comeback player of the year honors. He was also named the most valuable player of the 1986 World Series, in which he batted .371 with one homerun and five runs-batted-in.

Knight played in Baltimore in 1987 and in Detroit in 1988 before retiring. He served as the manager, albeit with little success, of the Reds for two seasons, 1996 and 1997. After his retirement he spent more time on tour with Lopez and served as her caddy for a time.

The week following her record five straight wins, Lopez played in the Lady Keystone Open in Hershey, Pennsylvania, traditionally a smaller LPGA event, but made into an all-out media affair by Lopez's presence. Overwhelmed by press interviews, television appearances, and sponsor-backed events, she played terribly, shooting over par all three rounds. Yet Lopez, who had developed a wonderfully friendly relationship with the media, also had a special rapport with the fans. As she walked to the eighteenth green she was fifteen strokes behind eventual winner Pat Brady, but still the gallery roared. Cynthia Anzolut, who ran the Lady Keystone Open, told *Golf World,* "I think they still thought she could win it. She walked on water as far as they were concerned.... The people just loved her."

Exhaustion wasn't the only thing distracting Lopez in Pennsylvania. One of her hundreds of interviews during the week was with a young sportscaster named Tim Melton. By the third round, Lopez was deeply in love, and the two were married six months later. Lopez was on the top of the world. "I couldn't think ahead," she recalled in *Sports Illustrated.* "I was just so excited. I was being interviewed by so many people, and all of a sudden I was making so much money. I was in awe, and I was enjoying it all so much." After ending her five-tournament winning streak, Lopez followed with seven top ten finishes, winning two more tournaments before the season's end. In all, during 1979 she won nine tournaments and took home over $200,000, setting a record for LPGA earnings.

She was named as both the LPGA Rookie of the Year and the LPGA Player of the Year and, with a per-round average of 71.76, won the Vare Trophy, given annually to the player with the lowest scoring average. She was also named the Associated Press Female Athlete of the Year.

Lopez continued her storybook career into her second year on the tour, winning a remarkable eight of nineteen tournaments. She was once again named the LPGA Player of the Year and again won the Vare Trophy.

Slumps Then Rebounds

By 1981 Lopez's life, namely her marriage, was crumbling around her. Her relationship with Melton was not withstanding the demands of travel and her celebrity status. She gained weight, and at just five-feet, four-inches, she ended up at over 160 pounds. After three years of marriage, Lopez and Melton divorced in 1983. During these difficult times, she found a friend in her future husband, baseball player Ray Knight.

Lopez first met Knight while on tour in Japan at the same time that Knight was playing in a goodwill exhibition game. Later, after Melton took a job in Cincinnati, he and Knight, who then played for the Cincinnati Reds, became friends. In an odd coincidence, Melton was hired by a station in Houston about the same time that Knight was traded to the Houston Astros. Eventually Lopez and Knight, who was working through his own painful divorce, became close companions. "We started talking about my problems with my marriage, and we realized that we were alike," Lopez explained to *People Weekly.* "He had been devastated. So was I. I was playing poorly, and Ray could relate to that because he went into a hitting slump when he got his divorce. I really needed somebody because my family wasn't there. The only thing I could rely on was Ray as my friend, helping me through tough times." Friendship eventually turned to romance, and the two were married in October 1983.

Although she won a dozen tournaments between 1980 and 1984, Lopez's megastar status faded. Her naturally smooth swing abandoned her, and suddenly her game was not coming easy. Lopez's unhappiness prior to her divorce was being played out every weekend on the golf course. The tides turned for Lopez after her marriage to Knight and the birth of their first daughter in 1984. In 1985, she won five tournaments including the LPGA Championship and won Player of the Year honors as well as the Vare Trophy for the third time in her career. Sitting out all but four tournaments in 1986 to have her second child, Lopez returned to the tour full-time in 1987.

In 1987, Lopez earned her thirty-fifth tournament title at the Sarasota Classic, where she had her first career win in 1978, qualifying her for the LPGA Tour Hall of Fame. She was inducted as the Hall's eleventh member on July 20, 1987. The following year Lopez won three tournaments and was, for the fourth time in her career, named Player of the Year. She also topped $2 million in earnings, only the fourth LPGA player to do so. In 1989 she again won three tournaments and in 1990 became only the second player in LPGA history to earn more than $3 million. Sitting out most of 1991 to have her third child, Lopez returned in 1992 to win two tournaments.

Great Women in Sports. Detroit: Visible Ink Press, 1996.

St. James Encyclopedia of Popular Culture. 5 vols. New York: St. James Press, 2000.

Sports Stars. Series 1-4. Detroit: U•X•L, 1994-98.

Periodicals

Deford, Frank. "Hello Again to the Group." *Sports Illustrated*, (August 5, 1985): 58.

Diaz, Jaime. "Time for the Pat and Nancy Show." *Sports Illustrated*, (February 9, 1987): 84-5.

Lemon, Richard. "On the Beach No More, Nancy Lopez and Ray Knight Score a Tie for Golf and Baseball." *People Weekly*, (April 25, 1983): 85-88.

Moriarty, Jim. "Nancy's Last Dance." *Golf World*, (July 12, 2002): 54.

Newman, Bruce. "The Very Model of a Modern Marriage." *Sports Illustrated*, (August 4, 1986): 34.

Shipnuck, Alan. "Open and Shut." *Sports Illustrated*, (July 21, 1997): 44.

Stachura, Mike. "The Class of '78." *Golf World*, (November 24, 2000): 30.

Voepel, Mechelle. "Lopez Always a Winner to Fans Despite Having No Open Trophy." Knight Ridder/Tribune News Service, (July 3, 2002).

Voepel, Mechelle. "Lopez's Great Run Began 20 Years Ago." Knight Ridder/Tribune News Service, (May 13, 1998).

Other

"Nancy Lopez." *American Decades CD-ROM*. Detroit, Mich.: Gale Research, 1998. Reproduced in *Biography Resource Center*. Detroit, Mich.: The Gale Group, 2003. http://www.galenet.com/servlet/BioR (January 8, 2003).

Sketch by Kari Bethel

Awards and Accomplishments

Year	
1976	Named All-American and University of Tulsa's Female Athlete of the Year
1978	Wins LPGA Championship; named LPGA Rookie of the Year
1978-79	Named LPGA Player of the Year; awarded Vare Trophy
1985	Wins LPGA Championship; named LPGA Player of the Year; awarded the Vare Trophy
1987	Inducted into the LPGA Hall of Fame
1989	Wins LPGA Championship; inducted into the Professional Golf Association (PGA) World Golf Hall of Fame
1997	Receives the Hispanic Heritage Award
2002	Receives PGA of America's PGA First Lady of Golf Award

Moves Toward Retirement

As Lopez moved through the 1990s, age, injuries, and shifting responsibilities began impacting her game. After winning one tournament in 1993, Lopez did not finish first again until 1997, when she posted her forty-eighth, and last, career win at the Chick-fil-A Charity Championships. One of the most celebrated women in golf, Lopez never won a U.S. Open championship, although she finished second four times in her twenty-one appearances. In 1997 she missed a fifteen-foot birdie putt on the eighteenth green in the final round and lost by one stroke to Alison Nicholas, despite being the only woman to break 70 in all four rounds, posting scores of 69-68-69-69.

Lopez underwent knee surgery in 1999 and gall bladder surgery in 2000, which limited her play through the next several years. During 2002 she failed to make a single cut. With nagging knee problems and three growing daughters at home, Lopez retired after the 2002 season. She ended her career as a perennial fan favorite, with forty-eight tournament wins and over $5 million in earnings. Lopez has been credited for the increased popularity of the LPGA, which has resulted in an astonishing increase in purses. In 1978 Lopez was awarded $22,500 for her LPGA Championship victory. Twenty years later, first place netted $195,000—approximately what Lopez made during her entire nine-win rookie year. Lopez and her family live in Albany, Georgia, her husband's hometown.

SELECTED WRITINGS BY LOPEZ:

(With Peter Schwed) *The Education of the Woman Golfer*. New York: Simon and Schuster, 1979.

(With Don Wade) *Nancy Lopez's The Complete Golfer*. Chicago: Contemporary Books, 1987.

The Complete Golfer. New York: Galahad Books, 2000.

FURTHER INFORMATION

Books

The Complete Marquis Who's Who. 54th ed. New York: Marquis Who's Who, 2001.

Tegla Loroupe
1973-

Kenyan marathon runner

In 1998 Kenyan runner Tegla Loroupe became the first African woman to win a major marathon when she came in first at the New York City Marathon in 1994. She then set a women's world record on the 26.2-mile marathon course at the 1998 Rotterdam Marathon, a record she broke in 1999 in Berlin, Germany. Loroupe has continued to show herself as one of the world's top female athletes. At four feet 11 inches and 88 pounds, she has also become one of the most recognizable women marathoners to fans of distance running.

Tegla Loroupe

Chronology

1973	Born in rural Kenya
1980	Gets her first pair of running shoes
1993	Finishes 4th in first major 10K run
1994	Wins first major marathon in New York City
1995	Wins 2nd New York City Marathon days after death of sister Albina
1995	Wins bronze medal for 10K at World Track and Field Championships
1998	Sets world record for women's marathon at Rotterdam
1999	Sets new world record for women's marathon at Berlin Marathon
2000	Qualifies to compete in Olympics in 10K and marathon

A Way to Get Around

Born and raised on a farm in rural Kapenguria, Kenya, near the Ugandan border in 1973, Loroupe first began running because it was the quickest way to get where she wanted to go. She began her day with a six-mile sprint to school, burdened by her heavy backpack, the hills that stood between her and the schoolhouse, and the oxygen-poor air that starved her lungs as she ran in such high elevation. But Loroupe ran, nonetheless, knowing that late students were punished with a beating. Twice weekly after school, she put in another dozen miles while herding cattle for her parents. No matter what the terrain, Laroupe ran barefoot; shoes were a luxury. While most of her friends ran equally as much as Loroupe, school races showed her by age nine that she had a natural talent for running. Excelling at all but the 800-meter sprint indicated that Loroupe was a distance runner; it also indicated a path by which she could avoid the traditional future of a girl of her tribe: marriage, children, and housekeeping. Fortunately for Loroupe her father also saw her potential and he agreed to let her attend a private boarding school and run as long as she kept up her grades.

From the beginning, Loroupe's ambition to be a professional runner came as much from her love of running as it did from her desire to escape the life of most Kenyan women. Her enthusiasm for her sport has been obvious to any who meet her, and her energy and optimism remain contagious. Eschewing rigid training programs and stringent nutrition and sleep schedules, she runs frequently because it is what she wants to do. Working with coach Volker Werner from her training base in Detmold, Germany, four months out of the year, Loroupe developed a flexible schedule that includes runs of between seven and nine miles twice daily along with weekly interval training at the track as a way to build the muscles needed for speed and sprinting. Enjoying covering long distances, Loroupe especially welcomed the weekly long runs required for marathon training, and her enjoyment paid off: in her first high-profile attempt at racing the 10,000 meters (10K) at the 1993 World Track and Field Championships, she finished fourth in a crowded field.

In November of 1994 the 21-year-old Loroupe ran her first major race: the New York City Marathon. Winning the race in 2 hours, 27 minutes and 37 seconds, she became the first African woman to win a major marathon, the youngest winner, and the first black women ever to win in New York. While Loroupe received accolades from the media, her parents back in Kenya were also honored; Kenyan President Daniel Arap Moi presented her father and mother with enough livestock to make the family wealthy within the Pokot tribe. Loroupe's success also inspired others in her tribe to begin running, and with her winnings she provided track shoes to promising young female Pokot athletes.

In early 1995, confident after her performance in New York the previous November, the young Kenyan decided to tackle the most historic marathon of them all: April's Boston Marathon. Loroupe met her match in the challenging and hilly course and came in ninth in a field of women led by German long-distance phenomenon Uta Pippig, who had set the Boston course record of 2:21:45 only the year before. Undaunted by her performance at Boston, she continued racing and won the bronze medal for a 31:17 10K run at the World Track and Field Championships in Goteborg, Sweden.

In November of 1995 she returned to New York and repeated her previous performance, clocking a winning time in her 26.2-mile tour through the city's five boroughs. Loroupe's win was particularly inspiring considering the personal tragedy she was coping with: she ran the marathon only 14 days after the untimely death of her older and much-loved sister, Albina. Shortly after crossing the finish line, Loroupe collapsed to the ground, sobbing.

Her winning performance in New York in 1995 qualified Loroupe for the 1996 Olympic Games to be held in Atlanta, Georgia, the following year. Placing in the top three during the Olympic trials, she qualified for the team but placed a disappointing sixth in the 10K, her time only 31:23. Unruffled by her performance, Loroupe had another go at the Boston Marathon in April of 1996, this time finishing in second place behind Belgian runner L. Siegers. She returned to New York for her third attempt at the November marathon, confident that her training would propel her to a third win in 1996.

With two appearances in the Big Apple behind her, Loroupe was by now a favorite of New York crowds, and she showed her fans a confident start at the gun. However, she soon slowed, hampered by pain that was later diagnosed as the result of stress fractures in her spine. Finishing a lackluster seventh with 2:32:07, Loroupe followed her physician's orders and stopped running and donned a back brace for three weeks, curing the fractures but interrupting her rigorous training regime.

During 1997 her racing was sporadic: that April she took first place in the women's division at the Rotterdam, Netherlands Marathon, but placed seventh in New York seven months later and put in a sluggish 2:30:26 in the Osaka, Japan marathon in January of 1998. Fortunately, things turned around later that year. In the fall of 1998 she came in third in New York only months after setting a new world record of 2:20:47 for the women's marathon at Rotterdam; she went on to break her record by four seconds in Berlin, Germany the following September. As Laroupe told Peter Gambaccini of *Runner's World,* her ultimate goal was to break the magic time of 2:20. "I have the courage to go for it," she said. "In the beginning of my career, I didn't have the confidence that I could run so fast. But last year, when I ran 2:22:07 at Rotterdam, I thought it was possible"

Loroupe's 10K-win during Kenya's National Track and Field Championships in 2000 qualified her for that year's Summer Games, scheduled for Sydney, Australia. She ran in both the 10K and the marathon at the Olympics, placing 13th in the marathon and fifth in the shorter run. Far less disappointing to the runner was her first-place victory at the London Marathon the same

Awards and Accomplishments	
1994	Becomes first African woman to win the New York City Marathon.
1995	First woman finisher at New York City Marathon.
1995	Places third in women's 10K at World Track and Field Championships.
1996	Places second among women at Boston Marathon.
1997	First woman finisher at Rotterdam Marathon.
1998	Places first in women's 10K at Goodwill Games.
1998	Clocks world best time of 2:20:47 as first woman at Rotterdam Marathon.
1999	First woman finisher at Rotterdam Marathon.
1999	Places third in women's 10K at World Track and Field Championships.
1999	Beats 13-year record to clock world's best time of 2:20:43 as first woman at Berlin Marathon.
1999	First woman finisher at World Half-Marathon Championships.
2000	First woman finisher at London Marathon.
2000	First woman finisher at Rome Marathon.
2000	Places first in women's 10K at Kenyan National Track and Field Championships.
2000	Golden Shoe Award from Association of International Marathons and Road Races

year. In 2002 she competed in the all-women Avon Running Championship circuit, taking fourth place in the 10K race with a finishing time of 33:55.

Continuing to make her home in Detmold, Germany, where she trains, Loroupe returns often to Kenya, visiting family and friends in her village and spending time with young people interested in running. Her sport has provided her with an income that has made her one of the highest-paid women in her country, and she owns homes in the towns of Nakuru and Kapsait. However, much of her new-found wealth has found its way back to the region were she first trained, taking the form of boarding school tuition, medical care and supplies, food, and clothing for friends, neighbors, family, and others living there who are in need.

Recognizing her position as a role model for women runners around the world, Loroupe is quick to explain where her motivation comes from. "I don't run for myself, I run for others," she once told an interviewer for *Runner's World Daily* online. Among those "others" are those women who, unlike Loroupe, have been unable to break with tradition and follow their dreams. "When I ran in school, the men in my tribe said, 'Tegla, you're wasting your time,'" she once explained to *Olympics.com.* "They didn't want me to do sports. But God has given me a plan. Man cannot close my door."

FURTHER INFORMATION

Periodicals

Daily Telegraph, April 21, 2001.
Detroit Free Press, February 27, 1999.

Essence, September, 1999.
New York Times, November 13, 1995; October 30, 1996; November 3, 1998; June 11, 2000; August 13, 2000.
Runner's World, February, 1996; July, 1998; December, 2000.
Sports Illustrated, November 2, 1998.

Other

Olympics.com, http://www.olympics.com (September 18, 2000).
Runner's World Daily, http://www.runnersworld.com/dailynew/archive/1998/July/980717.html (October 6, 2000).
Yukonweb, http://www.yukonweb.com/community/athletics/ (January 15, 2003).

Sketch by Pamela L. Shelton

Greg Louganis

Greg Louganis
1960-

American diver

Two-time Olympic gold medal winner Greg Louganis is generally considered by sportswriters and fans the best diver in the history of the sport. For years he was simply unbeatable in diving competitions. At the same time, his personal struggles as a closeted gay man often left him feeling alone and worthless. This combination of public adulation and private torment created a complex pattern in Louganis' life, alternating between highly disciplined athletic prowess in the pool and self-destructive impulses in his private life. Louganis explored these themes in his cathartic autobiography *Breaking the Surface.*

Talents and Trials

Gregory Louganis was born on January 29, 1960, to two fifteen-year-olds, one Samoan and the other Northern European, who gave him up for adoption. Interestingly, his adoptive parents, Peter and Frances Louganis, were specifically looking for a darker child, in contrast to their own fair-haired, light-skinned community. Louganis' Samoan ancestry fit the bill, and he grew up looking and feeling different from most of his classmates. His dyslexia, misdiagnosed as a learning disability, did not help, and he was often taunted by other schoolchildren. His small stature also left him victimized by bullies, further undermining his self-esteem.

At the same time, Louganis was discovering special talents that would offset all the isolation and the taunt-

ing, and would ultimately carry him to Olympic glory. From the age of 18 months, he had been taking dancing and acrobatics lessons with his sister Despina. Louganis proved a natural, and with his partner Eleanor, he won a number of dance competitions. He developed a comfort on stage that he lacked at home and at school, but perhaps the most important aspect was the method his dance instructor used. She insisted that the children visualize their dance routines before performing them. These visualization techniques would help Louganis master highly technical routines in the sport that would ultimately capture his interest: diving.

When Louganis began doing acrobatic routines off the diving board at a nearby pool, his worried mother signed him up for diving lessons. Greg took to the sport immediately, and soon showed a rare ability, even more than with dancing. Before long, he dropped dancing altogether to focus on his diving. While his father had never shown any interest in his dancing, he showed an intense interest in Greg's diving. It was a sign that some things were okay for boys, and others were not.

The Young Olympian

Louganis was soon performing in amateur diving contests, and at the age of 11, he found himself at the 1971 AAU Junior Olympics. The event would prove a turning point, for there two-time Olympic gold medallist Sammy Lee discovered the young prodigy. Spotting the boy's talent, he decided to take him on and coach him to the Olympics. He was the first to suggest to Louganis that he could go that far—but he still needed work. As Louganis recalled in his autobiography: "Dr. Lee told me that I didn't have a killer instinct, that it wasn't in my nature to fight.... Part of his training was to toughen me up, which I needed. He taught me to dive in all kinds of weather and to dive whether I felt like it or not." Lee also emphasized that the future Olympic champion would have to become a proper role model.

This meant losing some bad habits that Louganis had already picked up, like drinking, sneaking cigarettes, and doing drugs. He was going through a painful adolescence, fighting with his parents, getting into legal troubles, and even attempting a half-hearted suicide attempt. In diving, Louganis found the necessary incentive to pull himself together and focus on a larger goal. Under Lee's training that goal became the Olympics, and in 1976 he got his first shot at the gold. In fact, that year he qualified for both the spring board and platform events.

Despite his thrill at being at the Montreal Olympics, at age 16, the games actually proved a rough time for Louganis. His mates on the U.S. team proved less supportive and more competitive than he had hoped, and because Lee was actually not the official team coach, he had trouble gaining entry to help train Louganis at poolside. Nervous and distracted, Louganis came in sixth in the spring board competition, but in the platform competition he seemed to regain his focus. In dive after dive he came close to matching two-time gold medallist Klaus Dibiasi, and in the end he came within 24 points of beating him, earning the silver medal. Surprised at the close score, Dibiasi told Louganis, "Next time, I watch you."

Getting the Gold

Despite being a 16-year-old silver medallist, Louganis actually found the next few years hard. He felt confused by his newfound celebrity status, having been largely invisible to his classmates just months before, and he continued to drink and smoke far too much. In addition, he injured his back at a practice session, and there were days when the pain was so bad he simply could not dive at all. And he was still wrestling with his sexuality. He actually began seeing an older man at this point, but the encounters were furtive, and he felt just as isolated as before.

Once again, diving was the only thing that gave him confidence. About this time he began working with Ron O'Brien, a coach who would also prove to be a great friend. At first, Louganis alternated between coaches, working with O'Brien when Dr. Lee was unavailable, but shortly after graduating from high school, he decided it was time to choose. He chose O'Brien. He was grateful to Lee, but he decided O'Brien's more encouraging coaching style was better for him.

O'Brien was gentle, but he was certainly no pushover. He continued to push Louganis to learn ever more difficult dives. In 1978, Louganis won the World

---

Chronology

1960	Born January 29, in San Diego, California. Adopted by Peter and Frances Louganis, of El Cajon, California.
1962	Begins taking dancing lessons; begins entering dancing and gymnastics competitions
1969	Begins taking diving lessons (USFSA) competition
1971	Spotted at AAU Junior Olympics by Dr. Sammy Lee, former gold medallist diver. Begins training under Dr. Lee
1976	Takes Silver Medal in Platform Diving at XXI Olympics
1978	Wins platform and springboard competitions at World Aquatic Championships
1978	Enters University of Miami
1981	Transfers to University of California at Irvine to continue training under coach Ron O'Brien
1982	Wins springboard and platform titles at World Championships
1984	Wins Gold Medals in platform and springboard competitions at XXIII Olympics (becomes first diver to break 700-point score, in platform)
1984	Moves in with "business manager" and lover, "Tom." Begins to let Tom handle most of his finances
1986	Participates in Circus of the Stars
1988	Diagnosed HIV-positive
1988	Again, takes gold medals in springboard and platform at XXIV Olympics (first diver to win two gold medals in two successive Olympics)
1988	Retires from diving, breaks off relationship with "Tom"
1994	Appears at Gay Games IV, official announcer at diving competition
1994	Plays himself in *D2: The Mighty Ducks*
1995	Appeared in Off Broadway one man show, *The Only Thing Worse You Could Have Told Me*; also appeared as Darius in *Jeffrey*

Aquatic Platform Championship and the U.S. Diving 1-meter and 10-meter titles. That same year he entered the University of Miami on a scholarship. Being in the NCAA, which had no platform competitions, forced him to concentrate on his weaker sport, springboard diving. This actually proved a boon later on.

In 1980, Louganis took the gold medals in both springboard and platform competitions at the Pan American Games. Most observers expected him to do the same at the Olympics, but that year the Soviet Union invaded Afghanistan and President Carter boycotted the Moscow Olympics in retaliation. Four years could mean the difference between peak performance and the second tier, but Louganis continued to push himself hard. In 1981, he transferred to the University of California at Irvine to train with Ron O'Brien at the world-famous Mission Viejo Nadadores Driving Club. In 1982, he took the springboard and platform titles at the World Championship, becoming the first diver to win the scores of a perfect 10 from seven judges, and the highest score ever for a single dive: 92.07.

Clearly, Greg Louganis was on his way to the 1984 Olympics, to be held in Los Angeles, and expectations were high. As one *Sports Illustrated* reporter put it in July of that year, "Louganis is as close to perfection in his sport as it's possible to be, and among all U.S. Olympic athletes, no one is a surer bet to win a gold medal in Los Angeles." Oddly, that would prove slightly

Awards and Accomplishments

1976	Silver Medal, 10-meter Platform, Montreal Olympics,
1978	First place, World Championships
1978	First place, platform and 1-meter springboard, U.S. Indoor and Outdoor National Championships
1979	Gold medal, Pan American Games, 3-meter springboard and platform
1979	First place, Phillips 66 Indoor and Outdoor National Championships, 1-meter springboard
1980	First place, Phillips 66 Indoor National Championships, 1-meter and 3-meter springboard; Outdoor National Championships, 1-meter and 3-meter springboards and platform
1981	First place, Phillips 66 Indoor and Outdoor National Championships, 1-meter and 3-meter springboard; National Sports Festival, first place, platform
1982	First Place, National Sports Festival, 3-meter springboard and platform; First Place, Phillips 66 Indoor National Championships, 1-meter and 3-meter springboard; Outdoor National Championships, 1-meter and 3-meter springboard
1982	First place, World Championships, springboard and platform
1983	First place, National Sports Festival, 3-meter springboard and platform; First place, Phillips 66 Outdoor National Championships, 3-meter springboard and platform
1983	Gold medal, Pan American Games, 3-meter springboard and platform
1984	First place, National Sports Festival, 1-meter and 3-meter springboard; First place, Phillips 66 Indoor National Championships, 1-meter and 3-meter springboard and platform,

	Outdoor National Championships, 1-meter and 3-meter springboard and platform
1984	Gold medal, XXIII Olympic Games, springboard and platform
1984	James A. Sullivan Award for outstanding achievements, AAU
1985	First place, National Sports Festival, 3-meter springboard and platform; First place, Phillips 66 Indoor National Championships, 1-meter and 3-meter springboard and platform, Outdoor National Championships, 1-meter and 3-meter springboard and platform
1985	Inducted in Olympics Hall of Fame
1986	First place, U.S. Olympic Festival, 3-meter springboard and platform; First place, Phillips 66 Indoor National Championships, 1-meter and 3-meter springboard and platform; Outdoor National Championships, 1-meter and 3-meter springboard and platform
1987	First place, U.S. Olympic Festival, 3-meter springboard and platform; First place, Phillips 66 Outdoor National Championships, 3-meter springboard and platform
1987	Gold medal, Pan American Games, 3-meter springboard and platform
1987	Jesse Owens Award
1988	First place, U.S. Olympic Festival, 3-meter springboard and platform; First place, Phillips 66 Indoor National Championships, platform; Outdoor National Championships, 1-meter and 3-meter springboard and platform
1988	Gold medal, XXIII Olympic Games, springboard and platform
1988	Olympic Spirt Award, U.S. Olympic Committee
1993	Inducted in International Swimming Hall of Fame
1994	Eighth place, Lillehammer Winter Olympics
1994	Robert J. Kane Award, U.S. Olympic Committee

pessimistic. For that year he won gold medals in both the platform and springboard competitions, the first male diver to do so since 1928. He also became the first diver to break the 700-point barrier, scoring 710.91 in the platform competition. But the scores were only part of the magic. As a *Time* reporter wrote, "The most ignorant of spectators sees Louganis go off a springboard and thinks, 'Oh, that's what it's all about.' The experts are awed."

Four years later, Greg Louganis went to his third Olympics, this time in Seoul, South Korea. By this time, he'd won five world championships, 47 national diving titles, a record ten Pan American gold medals, and two Olympic golds. He was widely hailed as the greatest diver ever, and was clearly the man to beat. Still, at 28, age was beginning to take its toll on Louganis. And something more ominous was weighing on his mind. Earlier that year, he'd been diagnosed HIV-positive. He was also involved in the last stages of an abusive relationship with a man, identified as "Tom" in his autobiography, who also acted as Louganis' manager. Tom was also HIV-positive, which added to Louganis' worries.

Given all this, it is surprising that Louganis was able to compete at all in the Seoul Olympics. As Louganis wrote in his autobiography, "In the past, it had always been a struggle to keep the turmoil of my daily life and the ups and downs of my own emotions from getting in the way of what I did on the diving board. In Seoul, it was almost impossible." Then in the preliminaries leading up to the event, Louganis cracked his head on the springboard on a

reverse dive with a two and a half somersault. It was a shock to spectators and a deeply traumatic event for Louganis, who worried that the blood in the water could infect other divers, and who was too afraid to tell even the doctor who treated him that he was HIV-positive.

Amazingly, Greg Louganis pulled in two more gold medals, in springboard and platform diving, becoming the only diver to win two medals in two successive Olympics. Just as satisfying, he was given the Olympic Spirit Award, meaning that he was considered the most inspiring athlete of that year's 9600 Olympic competitors. It was a deeply satisfying result for someone whose personal life was in such upheaval. And it meant for a triumphant farewell, for Louganis had already decided that this would be his last Olympics.

After Diving—and After Tom

Retired from diving competitions, Louganis had time to focus on his relationship with "Tom," and what he found was very disturbing. Among other things, he had only $2,000 to his name. Everything else was either in Tom's name or in both of their names. He also suspected that Tom was cheating on him, sometimes with gay youths who wrote him fan letters. Louganis hired a private investigator, who discovered that Tom had been charged with theft, insurance fraud, and even prostitution. After some prolonged negotiations, they agreed to go their separate ways. In fact, Louganis agreed to pro-

---

Breaking the Surface

The Ryan White story was impossible to miss, and it really caught my attention. I first saw Ryan on CNN. I was really impressed by this kid who had gone to court to go to school.... Ryan was sick, but instead of people having compassion for him, they were terrified that he'd spread AIDS by going to school. I thought if I showed I wasn't afraid of Ryan, then maybe others would follow my example.

As oblivious as I was in those days, I knew of course that most of the people who suffered from HIV and AIDS discrimination were gay men. There was no other way I felt I could get involved in the issue of AIDS without risking some reporter asking questions about my life. Helping Ryan was a way of lending my name and stature to the AIDS cause without having anyone get suspicious. And then I met Ryan and my life changed....

Despite his maturity, Ryan was still a teenager. Later, when we did press interviews together, he'd keep me in stitches by making faces at me from behind the reporter's back. But he never failed to impress me with his intelligence and his perseverance.... I was amazed at how he handled himself, whether it was one-on-one or on national television. He was—and is—an inspiration.

Source: Greg Louganis and Eric Marcus, *Breaking the Surface,* New York: Rand House, 1995, pp. 170-171.

---

vide for Tom for the rest of his life, a rather generous settlement given their recent history together.

Free of his "business manager" and retired from diving, Greg Louganis felt somewhat at loose ends. But about this time he rediscovered an old interest of his: acting. He had graduated from the University of California at Irvine with a degree in drama, and now he began to take acting and voice lessons. Already he was doing appearances and commercials for sponsors such as Speedo, but now he began to perform in musicals and in plays such as an off-Broadway production of *Jeffrey,* about a young man dealing with AIDS. He also got some television roles and movies such as *The Mighty Ducks.*

At the same time, he decided to come clean about being gay and HIV-positive, which he did in an autobiography, entitled *Breaking the Surface.* He also appeared at the Gay Games, in June of 1994, where he announced, "It's great to be out and proud." Shortly thereafter he was instrumental in getting the 1996 Olympic volleyball preliminaries moved from Cobb County, Georgia, where county commissioners had recently passed an anti-gay resolution.

SELECTED WRITINGS BY LOUGANIS:

(With Eric Marcus) *Breaking the Surface,* New York: Random House, 1995.

FURTHER INFORMATION

Books

Louganis, Greg, and Eric Marcus. *Breaking the Surface.* New York: Random House, 1995.

Where Is He Now?

Currently, Greg Louganis is focused on acting, speaking engagements, and a relatively new vocation, training dogs. One of his dogs, a Harlequin Great Dane, appeared in the movie *Beethoven II.* He has also continued his work as an AIDS activist, making speeches throughout the country. He remains healthy, and continues to work out, including a yoga regimen. In contrast, he has largely abandoned diving. In July of 2002 he told a Knight-Ridder reporter that "he hasn't performed a dive in eight or nine years." Still, he remains the man who set the standard for future divers. To date, none have matched his combination of grace and power on the diving board.

Periodicals

Callahan, Tom. "Star-spangled Home Team: U.S. Olympians Are Certain to Give the Nation Something to Shout About." *Time* (July 30, 1984): 60.

Gietschier, Steve. "Review of *Breaking the Surface.*" *The Sporting News* (May 1, 1995): 9.

"Greg Louganis: An Olympic Hopeful." *Co-Ed* (August-September 1983): 102.

"Greg Louganis: Freed from His Secrets, the Superstar Diver Plunges into AIDS Activism." *People* 49 (July 15, 1996): 74.

Harasta, Cathy. "Olympic Diving Legend Pursuing Artistry in Arenas Outside Pool." *Knight Ridder/Tribune News Service* (July 28, 2002): K4980.

"Leaps and Laps for L.A."*Life* 147 (June 1983): 62.

Leifer, Neil. "Getting Ready: With Six Weeks to Go, America's Athletes Pump Up for Their Moment in Seoul." *Times* (August 15, 1988): 48.

Neff, Craig. "A Double Victory with a New Twist." *Sports Illustrated* (May 9, 1983): 60.

Neff, Craig. "The Best is Getting Better." *Sports Illustrated* (August 29, 1983): 11.

Neff, Craig. "It's a Bird, It's a Plane, It's Supergreg!" *Sports Illustrated* (August 20, 1984): 80.

Neff, Craig. "Flying Over Troubled Waters: Greg Louganis Starred Again at the Olympic Trials, Which Were Touched by Controversy." *Sports Illustrated* (August 29, 1988): 28.

Neff, Craig. "High Flyers." *Sports Illustrated* (September 14, 1988): 85.

Neff, Craig. "Good and Tough: After Hitting His Head on the Springboard, Greg Louganis Won the Gold—Again." *Sports Illustrated* (October 3, 1988): 58.

"A New Leash on Life: Retired from Diving, a Healthy Greg Louganis Now Spends His Time Coaching Canines." *People Weekly* (June 25, 2001): 113.

Plummer, William. "Diver Greg Louganis Returns to Dancing, His First Love, Before the Eyes of His Pal Ryan White." *People Weekly* (November 9, 1987): 44.

Putnam, Pat. "Gaining at Last on the Top Guy." *Sports Illustrated* (April 27, 1987): 40.

Reed, Susan. "Primed and Pumped for Seoul." *People Weekly* (September 19, 1988): 48.

Skow, John. "A Soaring, Majestic Slowness That Describes Greg Louganis, the Class of a Classy Field." *Time* (August 20, 1984): 62.

Skow, John. "Splashes of Class and Acts of Heroism." *Time* (October 3, 1988): 58.

Stathoplos. "No One Does It Better." *Sports Illustrated* (July 18, 1984): 480.

Sketch by Robert Winters

Joe Louis

Joe Louis
1914-1981

American boxer

In his day, heavyweight champion Joe Louis was the most famous black man in America, virtually the only one who regularly appeared in the white newspapers. By breaking the color barrier that had been imposed on boxing after black heavyweight **Jack Johnson** outraged white sensibilities, Joe Louis began a process that would eventually open all of big-league sports to black athletes. Throughout his unprecedented twelve-year reign as world heavyweight champion, Louis projected a power inside the ring and a quiet dignity outside of it that would transform him from a black hero, obsessively identified in the white media with his race and alleged "savagery," into a national hero, and ultimately a sports icon. His later years were difficult, marked by financial worries and bouts with mental illness, but when he died, millions mourned his passing. As **Muhammad Ali** put it, "Everybody cried."

Growing Up

Part of Joe Louis' appeal lay in his rags to riches story. The seventh of eight children born to Alabama tenant farmers Munroe and Lillie Barrow, Joe lost his father early on. Two years after Joe's birth, Munroe Barrow was confined to the Searcy State Hospital for the Colored Insane, and Lillie was soon informed that he had died. In fact, Munroe lived on for another twenty years, an invisible man oblivious to his son's growing reputation. Believing herself a widow, Lillie Barrow soon married Pat Brooks, a widower with five children of his own. For a while Joe and the other children helped their parents work the cotton fields, but in 1926 the Brooks/Barrow family joined the growing swell of black migration northward.

The family resettled in Detroit, where twelve-year-old Joe found himself woefully unprepared for school. To his embarrassment, he was placed in classes with younger, smaller children, and eventually the school system shunted him off to the Bronson Vocational School. Fortunately for him, he discovered a vocation that would take him far beyond the precincts of the Detroit school system. When the Depression threw his stepfather out of work, Joe began doing odd jobs around town and hanging around with a rough crowd. To keep him off the streets, his mother scraped together 50 cents a week for violin lessons, but Joe used the money to join the Brewster Recreation Center, where he took up boxing.

Fearing that his mother would discover where the "violin money" was going, Joe dropped the Barrow from his name and began boxing neighborhood kids as Joe Louis. While he showed great promise, an exhausting, full-time job pushing truck bodies at an auto-body plant left him little time or energy for training. In late 1932, he entered his first amateur match against Johnny Miller, a member of that year's Olympic boxing team. Louis' lack of training showed, and Miller knocked him down seven times in the first two rounds. Mortified, Joe Louis gave up boxing altogether, taking his stepfather's advice to concentrate on his job instead. Interestingly, it was his mother who encouraged him to get back into the ring, seeing in boxing a chance for him to make something of himself doing what he enjoyed.

The Amateur Years

This time, Joe Louis quit his job and focused on his training. He returned to the amateur circuit, winning fifty of fifty-four matches over the next year, forty-three by knockouts. This impressive record soon brought him to the attention of John Roxborough, known throughout Detroit's black ghetto as the king of the numbers racket. Roxborough's other career was as a civic leader, sponsoring a number of charitable causes and helping local youngsters fulfill their dreams. He decided to take Joe Louis under his wing, even moving him into his house, putting him on a proper diet, and getting him some decent training equipment.

In June of 1934, on the verge of going pro, Joe Louis asked Roxborough to become his manager. To help fund Louis' career, Roxborough brought in Chicago numbers runner Julian Black, a longtime business associate. Together, they brought Louis to Chicago to train under Jack Blackburn, who had already taken two boxers to world championships. Those boxers, however, were white. The fact was that black boxers had very little chance of getting a shot at the title, particularly in the heavyweight division. Racism and segregation were endemic to American society, but in boxing there was a special reason that blacks were virtually ruled out as heavyweight contenders. That reason was Jack Johnson, who had held the heavyweight championship from 1908-1915.

Johnson was the first black heavyweight champion, and he reveled in the distinction, flouting white conventions by gloating over defeated white opponents, consorting openly with white prostitutes, and marrying white women. For seven years he defended his title against a series of "great white hopes," but in 1915 he finally lost to one of them, Jess Willard, in a match that may have been fixed. The white press openly rejoiced, and white boxing promoters and fighters vowed never to give another black man a shot at the title.

Given this history, Blackburn was reluctant to take on a black boxer, but he needed a job and Roxborough and Black promised him a "world beater." Blackburn put Louis on a strict training regimen, including running six miles a day, and trained him in a style that combined balanced footwork, a strong left jab, and rapid fire combination punches. At the same time, his management team carefully nurtured an image designed to draw a sharp contrast between Joe Louis and Jack Johnson. Louis was to be gracious before and after a fight, conform to an image of God-fearing, clean-living decency, and above all avoid outraging white opinion by dating white women. Together, training and image building would propel Joe Louis to a shot at the title.

Turning Pro

Joe Louis' first pro boxing match took place on July 4, 1934, when he knocked out Jack Kracken in the first round. By October 30th of that year, when he knocked out Jack O'Dowd in the second round, he had won nine straight matches, seven of them by knockouts. Along with his reputation, his payments were growing, from $59, to

Chronology	
1914	Born May 13 in LaFayette, Alabama
1926	Moves to Detroit, Michigan
1932	Fights first amateur boxing bout
1934	Moves in with John Roxborough, asks Roxborough to become his manager
1934	First professional boxing match, July 4
1935	Defeats Italian Primo Carnera, June 25, and becomes media sensation
1935	Marries Marva Trotter, September 24
1935	Defeats Max Baer to become top heavyweight contender, September 24
1936	Loses to German Max Schmeling, June 11
1937	Becomes World Heavyweight Champion, defeating James Braddock on June 22
1938	Defeats Max Schmeling in rematch, June 22, becoming national hero
1942	Enlists in U.S. Army
1945	Enlistment ends in October
1945	Divorces Marva Trotter
1946	Remarries Marva
1949	Divorces Marva
1949	Retires as undefeated World Heavyweight Champion
1950	Loses comeback attempt against new heavyweight champion Ezzard Charles, September 27
1951	Last professional boxing match, loses to Rocky Marciano, October 26
1955	Marries Rose Morgan, a successful beauty shop operator, on December 25
1958	Divorces Rose
1959	Marries attorney Martha Malone Jefferson
1967	Louises adopt a baby boy, naming him Joseph. Apparently, this the child of Joe Louis and a New York City prostitute, identified as "Marie" in Louis' autobiography. Martha would go on to adopt three more of Marie's children, of unknown paternity.
1970	Committed temporarily to Colorado state mental institution
1970	Takes position as greeter at Caesars Palace, Las Vegas, Nevada
1981	Dies of massive heart attack on April 12

$62, $101, $250, $450, in the midst of the Depression when most of his old neighborhood was struggling on relief and occasional work. Louis was conscientiously sending money home to support his family, but he also began to develop spending habits that would plague him in later years, buying expensive suits and a shiny black Buick he would use to cruise for girls on visits home.

It was soon clear that Louis had outgrown these carefully chosen opponents designed to nurture his early career. Louis' managers began to look around for tougher competition, and soon settled on Charlie Massera, ranked eighth in *Ring* magazine's survey of top heavyweight contenders. On November 30, 1934, Louis met Massera, knocking him out in the third round. Two weeks later, he went up against Lee Ramage, another up-and-coming heavyweight, and a real challenge for Louis. Ramage was quick on his feet and accomplished in defense. For the first few rounds he managed to fend off Louis' powerful jabs, and between rounds Blackburn advised Louis to start hitting Ramage's arms, if he couldn't reach anything else. Eventually, Ramage was

Awards and Accomplishments

1933	Won 50 of 54 amateur boxing matches, 43 by knockouts
1935	Won 20 of 20 professional boxing wins, including defeats of former world heavyweight champions Primo Carnera and Max Baer
1935	Associated Press "Athlete of the Year" award
1936, 1938-39, 1941	*Ring* magazine's "Boxer of the Year"
1937-49	World Heavyweight Champion, longest reign in boxing history
1941	Edward Neil Memorial Plaque (for man who contributed the most to boxing)
1993	First boxer honored on a U.S. postage stamp

too tired to lift his arms, and Louis got him against the ropes, knocking him out in the eighth round.

Roxborough decided Louis was ready for the big time, and that meant New York's Madison Square Garden, which had controlled big-league boxing since the 1920s, when it sewed up contracts with all the major heavyweight contenders. And that presented a major difficulty. Jimmy Johnston, the flamboyant manager of Madison Square Garden, said he could help Louis, but Roxborough had to understand a few things. As a Negro, Joe Louis wouldn't make the same as the white fighters, and more ominously, he "can't win every time he goes in the ring." In effect, he was telling Roxborough that Louis would be expected to throw a few fights. That went against one of Roxborough's commandments: no fixed fights, and he hung up on Johnston. Fortunately for them, Johnston's monopoly was getting a little shaky.

A man by the name of Mike Jacobs would prove their salvation. Passed over for leadership of the Madison Square Garden Corporation, Jacobs had been looking for a way to break the Garden's monopoly, and in a bizarre series of maneuvers surrounding a New York charity, he found it. Traditionally, Madison Square Garden had hosted a few boxing competitions for Mrs. William Randolph Hearst's Milk Fund for Babies. The Fund got a cut of the profits, and Garden boxing got good publicity from Hearst's powerful papers. When the Garden decided to raise the rent on Milk Fund events, some enterprising Hearst sportswriters, including Damon Runyan, decided to form their own corporation to stage boxing matches in competition with the Garden, with a share of the proceeds to go to the Fund. They could provide the publicity, but they needed an experienced promoter, so they brought in Jacobs, forming the 20th Century Club. Officially, Jacobs held all the stock, as the sportswriters didn't want to be publicly identified with matches they'd be covering.

In the meantime, Joe Louis' winning streak continued. On January 4, 1935, he defeated sixth-ranked Patsy Perroni, and a week later he beat Hans Birkie. Mike Jacobs needed a serious contender to get his Club off the ground, and before long the name of Joe Louis came to

his attention. He went to Los Angeles to witness a rematch between Louis and Ramage, and this time Louis knocked Ramage out in the second round. Impressed, Jacobs invited Louis to fight for the 20th Century Club, assuring his managers that "He can win every fight he has, knock 'em out in the first round if possible."

The Brown Bomber

Jacobs promoted a few "tune-up" fights for Joe Louis out of town, while his secret partners in the Club began to churn out the publicity that would eventually make Louis a household name. Scouting around for an opponent for a big New York match, Jacobs hit upon Italian Primo Carnera, a former heavyweight champion. The match was scheduled for June 25, 1935—and the timing couldn't have been better. Throughout the summer, Mussolini had been threatening to invade Ethiopia, one of the very few independent black countries. Feelings ran high throughout the international community, and particularly among black Americans. In the prematch publicity, Jacobs sold Louis as a kind of ambassador for his race, and by the time of the fight, black as well as white were deeply curious about this heavyweight contender crossing the color line.

More than 60,000 fans, and 400 sportswriters, poured into Yankee Stadium that night to see six-foot, one-inch Joe Louis, weighing in at 197 pounds, take on the six-foot, six-inch, 260-pound Italian giant Carnera. After a few lackluster rounds, they saw something amazing. Starting in the fifth round, Joe Louis came out swinging, nailing Carnera with a right that bounced him off the ropes, then a left, and another right. Only hanging onto Louis kept Carnera from going down. In the sixth round, Louis knocked him down twice for a count of four, but each time Carnera staggered to his feet. Finally, Carnera had had enough, collapsing against the ropes. The referee called the fight.

Overnight, Joe Louis became a media sensation, and Americans awoke to a rare phenomenon: a black man in the headlines. Naturally, commentators focused overwhelmingly on his race, hauling out a seemingly limitless supply of alliterative nicknames to characterize the newly prominent contender: "mahogany mauler," "chocolate chopper," "coffee-colored KO king," "saffra sandman," and one that stuck, "The Brown Bomber." Sportswriters played up and exaggerated Louis' Alabama accent and limited education to convey an impression of an ignorant, lazy "darkie" incapable of anything but eating, sleeping, and fighting.

At the same time, many sportswriters peppered their columns with dehumanizing savage references. For Davis Walsh, "Something sly and sinister and perhaps not quite human came out of the African jungle last night to strike down and utterly demolish Primo Carnera." Grantland Rice wrote in the *Baltimore Sun,* "His blinding speed, the speed of the jungle, and instinctive speed of the wild, was more than Carnera could face . . . Louis stalked Primo as the black panther of the jungle stalks his prey." Even *New York Daily News* sports editor Paul Gallico, widely viewed as a cultured liberal often sympathetic to black athletes, seemed overwhelmed and a little unhinged by Joe Louis. After watching a training session, he wrote: "I had the feeling that I was in the room with a wild animal. . . . He lives like an animal, fights like an animal, has all the cruelty and ferocity of a wild thing. . . . I see in this colored man something so cold, so hard, so cruel that I wonder as to his bravery. Courage in the animal is desperation."

Getting a Shot at the Top

Cruelty and laziness had nothing to do with the real Joe Louis, as his management team well knew, but it would take more than the truth to change the image. A combination of skillful public relations and external factors would be needed to transform the Brown Bomber into a national hero embraced by all segments of society. Fortunately for Louis, the public relations aspects were in the hands of skilled management team that had been successfully crafting Louis' image from the beginning. With his sudden rise to fame, they went so far as to release to the press a series of "seven commandments" that Joe Louis had lived by, rules that many newspapers would use in shaping their own coverage.

Other factors were out of Joe Louis' control, but worked to his advantage. Among these was the sorry state of boxing. Riddled by scandal and lackluster champions, professional boxing had been losing fans since the retirement of **Jack Dempsey** in 1929. Boxing was hungry for an exciting champion, and Louis' undeniable power in the ring and his willingness to fight any serious contender fit the bill.

And far beyond boxing's precincts, world events were undermining America's racial worldview. In Germany, Nazism's aggressive trumpeting of Aryan superiority was beginning to irritate many Americans, who started to ask themselves hard questions about what exactly they found offensive in the doctrine. Together, these factors began to soften the rigid color line that had prevailed in heavyweight title competitions for twenty years.

Another twist of fate would put Louis in sight of the championship, and dissolve that color line. Just weeks before Louis beat Carnera, James Braddock had defeated reigning heavyweight champ Max Baer in one of boxing's biggest upsets. Assuming a Baer victory against a challenger who'd lost twenty-six fights in his career, the Garden's Jimmy Johnston had made a fatal contractual error. He had signed Baer to the standard contract, obligating him to fight his next match in the Garden only if he won. Mike Jacobs went to work on Max Baer, eventually signing him up to fight Lewis on September 24, 1935.

But Louis had personal business to attend to first. That day he married Marva Trotter, a 19-year-old secre-

---

The "Seven Commandments" for Joe Louis

1. He was never to have his picture taken with a white woman.
2. He was never to go to a nightclub alone.
3. There would be no soft fights.
4. There would be no fixed fights.
5. He was never to gloat over a fallen opponent
6. He was to keep a "dead pan" in front of the cameras.
7. He was to live and fight clean.

---

tary at a newspaper, beautiful, intelligent, well-spoken, and perhaps most important to his managers, black. As Louis put it in his autobiography, "No Jack Johnson problem here." The new Mrs. Louis had a ringside seat when Max Baer was counted out in the fourth round when he refused to stand up from one knee. Later Baer told a reporter, "I could have struggled up once more, but when I get executed, people are going to have to pay more than twenty-five dollars a seat to witness it."

The Schmeling/Louis Matches

With his victory over Baer, Joe Louis was widely seen as the best fighter, and his drawing power eclipsed that of the hapless James Braddock. But there was another white hope on the horizon. Former heavyweight champion **Max Schmeling**, a German, was looking for an American comeback after years of successfully boxing in Europe. Naturally, he wanted a shot at the title, but the boxing commission informed him he'd have to fight Louis first. Unfortunately, Joe Louis was too busy enjoying his newfound wealth and fame to train seriously for the Schmeling match. On June 11, 1936, Joe Louis lost his first professional boxing match, in a twelfth-round knockout by Max Schmeling.

Louis and his fans were devastated, but not for long. The next year, it was Louis, not Schmeling, who got a shot at the championship. Partly this was due to events in Schmeling's homeland. Many Americans had been disgusted by Hitler's attempt to use sporting events, such as the 1936 Berlin Olympics, as a showcase for Nazism and Aryan superiority.

Everyone knew a Schmeling rematch was the next order of business if Louis' title was to be seen as fully legitimate. A year later, on June 22, 1938, it came. The buildup to the match was incredible, even by the standards of the most famous black man in America. The world was on the verge of war with Nazism, and Max Schmeling was seen as an Aryan poster boy. For the first time, white and black America were united behind Joe Louis, proof that America's best could defeat Germany's. Louis had a simple strategy for the fight: unrelenting attack. From the beginning Louis came out swinging, landing an overhead right that stunned Schmeling, breaking two of his verterbrae with a roundhouse right, and knocking him down three times in rapid

Joe Louis, right

succession. Two minutes and four seconds into the match, Schmeling's trainer threw in the towel. Seventy-thousand fans hailed Joe Louis as an American hero.

A National Hero

Between the Schmeling match and the outbreak of World War II, Joe Louis would defend his title fifteen times against opponents who were so clearly outmatched they were nicknamed the "Bums of the Month." Only light-heavyweight champion Billy Conn seemed to offer any kind of challenge, taking Louis thirteen rounds to defeat on June 18, 1941. Before the match, Joe Louis introduced a memorable phrase into the American lexicon by declaring of Conn, "He can run, but he can't hide."

Shortly after Pearl Harbor, Joe Louis enlisted in the U.S. Army, cementing his reputation in white America. The army sent him on a series of exhibition matches for the troops, as well as speaking engagements. Twice he donated the proceeds from title fights to the Navy Relief Fund. At the same time, he worked quietly to desegregate the armed forces, often participating in interracial events.

When Joe Louis left the service in 1945, he was at the peak of his popularity. He was finally accepted as an

all-American hero, and in press coverage, words like "integrity" and "dignity" took the place of the old savage stereotypes. He successfully defended his championship against all comers, earning huge purses and retiring undefeated in 1949 after the longest reign of any boxing champion in history. His legendary generosity to his family, old neighborhood friends, and virtually any worthy black cause, endeared him to the public.

But below the surface, things were not always so good. His constant womanizing, carefully shielded from the press, had taken its toll on his marriage. In 1945, he and Marva divorced. They remarried a year later, but finally called it quits in 1949. His generosity also took a toll, and throughout the war he'd actually had to borrow significant sums from his managers. Even more alarming, he owed hundreds of thousands of dollars in back taxes. A year after his retirement, financial considerations forced him back into the ring. He went up against the new heavyweight champion, Ezzard Charles, on September 27, 1950, losing in a fifteen-round decision. On October 26, 1951, he made one last comeback attempt, losing to future champion **Rocky Marciano** in an eighth-round knockout.

Declining Years

For the rest of his life, Joe Louis would struggle with financial difficulties. Money came from personal appearances, exhibition matches, and even a mercifully brief stint in professional wrestling. From 1955 to 1958, he was married to Rose Morgan, a successful beautician with her own business who could foot most of the bills. In 1959, he married attorney Martha Malone Jefferson, moving into her home in Los Angeles. Under political pressure, the IRS settled with Louis for payments of $20,000 a year on taxes owed, but even that sum remained out of reach.

In the 1960s, Louis' life began to unravel. He took up with a prostitute, identified as "Marie" in his autobiography, who presented him with a son in December of 1967. The Louises adopted the boy, naming him Joseph. At the same time, Louis began to get involved with drugs, including cocaine, and began to show signs of mental illness, warning his friends and family of plots against his life. For a few months, he was committed to a mental institution in Colorado. Martha stuck by him, and with her help and encouragement, he quit cocaine. Unfortunately, his paranoid delusions continued intermittently, though much of the time he was his old, genial self.

In 1970, Caesar's Palace, in Las Vegas, hired him as a greeter, a job which involved signing autographs, betting with house money when the action seemed a little slow, and playing golf with special guests. The job suited him, and the casino even provided him housing, as well as $50,000 a year. Joe Louis lived and worked at the Palace until a massive heart attack felled him on April 12, 1981.

Champion: Joe Louis

Journalists repeatedly wrote that Louis slept and ate a lot, read the comics, rooted for the Detroit Tigers, and liked to play baseball and golf. Coupled with the habit of quoting Louis in Uncle Remus dialect, these stories began to shape an image of Louis as a typical "darkie."

There was no truth to any of these generalizations. Even in the ring, much less outside it, Louis did not exhibit cruelty. He did not foul or eagerly attack his opponents when they were hurt or show pleasure at their pain. Nor was he indolent; Louis trained hard, and any writer who covered his training camps knew it. As far as his mind went, Louis was no intellectual, but what boxer was? All this imagery arose from one thing and one thing only: Louis' race.

Source: Mead, Chris. *Champion: Joe Louis, Black Hero in White America*. London: Robson Books, 1986.

Joe Louis' funeral became a huge media event. A nation that had almost forgotten him suddenly remembered everything he had meant, hailing him anew as a great boxer who had restored class and integrity to professional boxing. Three thousand mourners gathered to hear tributes from speakers like Jesse Jackson, who saluted Joe Louis for "snatching down the cotton curtain" and opening up the world of big-league sporting to black athletes. Perhaps the greatest tribute came from Muhammad Ali, who told a reporter: "From black folks to red-neck Mississippi crackers, they loved him. They're all crying. That shows you. Howard Hughes dies, with all his billions, not a tear. Joe Louis, everybody cried."

SELECTED WRITINGS BY LOUIS:

(With Edna and Art Rust, Jr.) *Joe Louis: My Life,* Harcourt Brace Jovanovich, 1978.

FURTHER INFORMATION

Books

Mead, Chris. *Champion: Joe Louis, Black Hero in White America*. London: Robson Books, 1986.

Periodicals

Cox, James A. "The Day Joe Louis Fired Shots Heard 'Round the World." *St. Louis Journalism Review* (October 1995): 11.

Deardorff, Don. "Joe Louis Became Both a Black Hero and a National Symbol to Whites after Overcoming Racism in the Media." *St. Louis Journalism Review* (October 1995): 11.

Gersten, Seymour P. "Ringside." *American Heritage* (July 1999): 27.

Hochman, Stan. "Bud Greenspan's 'King of the Ring' Documentary Full of Lessons." *Knight Ridder/Tribune News Service* (December 30, 1999): K5619.

Horn, Robert. "Two Champions and Enemies: Bad Blood Existed between Jack Johnson and Joe Louis." *Sports Illustrated* (May 14, 1990): 109.

"Joe Louis Becomes First Boxer Honored on U.S. Postage Stamp." *Jet* (June 28, 1993): 48.

McCormick, Bill. "Joe Louis-World Champion." *Washington Post* (June 23, 1999): C17.

McGowen, Deane. "Joe Louis, 66, Heavyweight King Who Reigned 12 Years, Is Dead." *New York Times* (April 13, 1981): A1.

Smith, Red. "Joe Louis: A Sense of Dignity." *New York Times* (April 13, 1981): C1.

Sketch by Robert Winters